January 11–13, 2015
Rehovot, Israel

I0047474

**Association for
Computing Machinery**

Advancing Computing as a Science & Profession

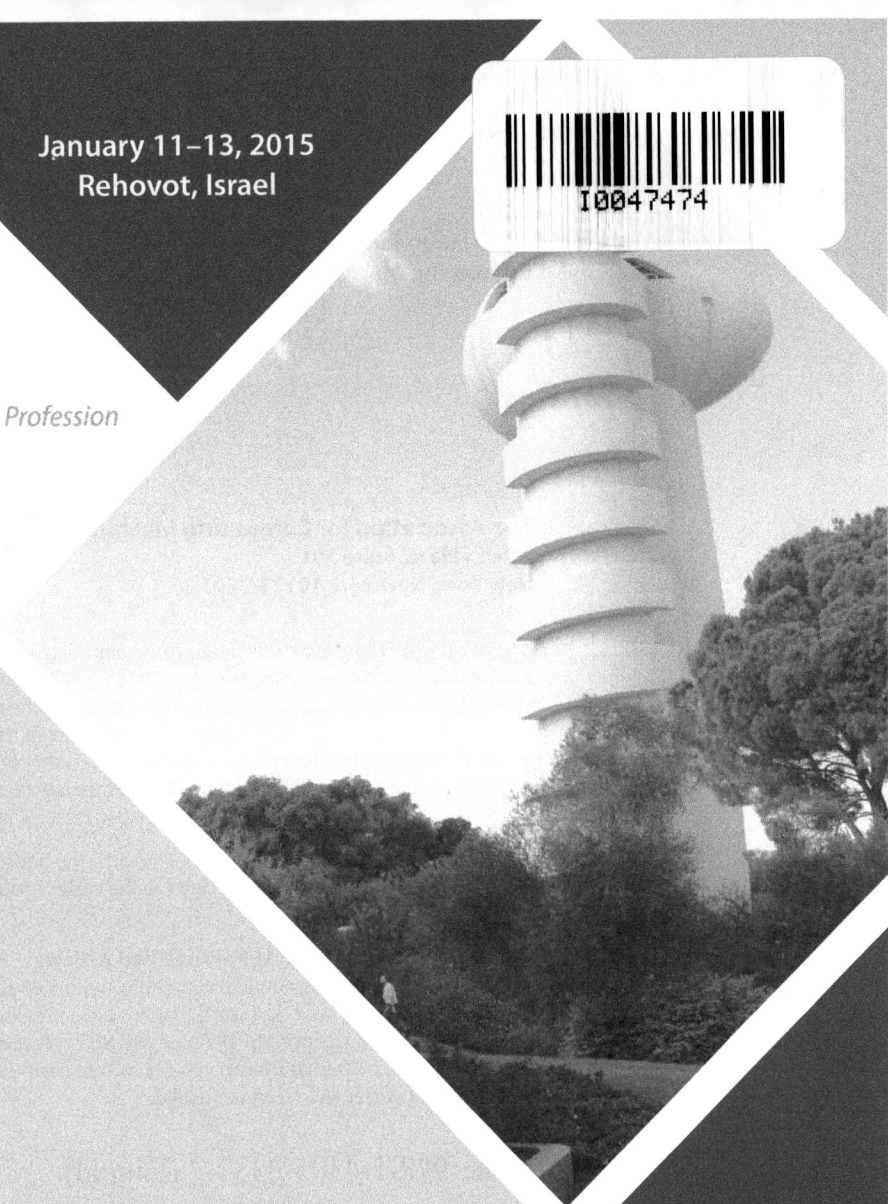

ITCS'15

Proceedings of the 6th
Innovations in Theoretical
Computer Science

Sponsored by:
ACM SIGACT

**Association for
Computing Machinery**

Advancing Computing as a Science & Profession

The Association for Computing Machinery
2 Penn Plaza, Suite 701
New York, New York 10121-0701

Notice to Past Authors of ACM-Published Articles
ACM intends to create a complete electronic archive of all articles and/or other material previously published by ACM. If you have written a work that has been previously published by ACM in any journal or conference proceedings prior to 1978, or any SIG Newsletter at any time, and you do NOT want this work to appear in the ACM Digital Library, please inform permissions@acm.org, stating the title of the work, the author(s), and where and when published.

ISBN: 978-1-4503-3333-7 (Digital)

ISBN: 978-1-4503-3506-5 (Print)

Additional copies may be ordered prepaid from:

ACM Order Department
PO Box 30777
New York, NY 10087-0777, USA

Phone: 1-800-342-6626 (USA and Canada)
+1-212-626-0500 (Global)
Fax: +1-212-944-1318
E-mail: acmhelp@acm.org
Hours of Operation: 8:30 am – 4:30 pm ET

Printed in the USA

Preface

The papers in this volume were presented at the 6th Innovations in Theoretical Computer Science (ITCS 2015) conference, sponsored by the ACM Special Interest Group on Algorithms and Computation Theory (SIGACT). The conference was held at the Weizmann Institute of Science in Rehovot, Israel, January 11–13, 2015. ITCS (previously known as ICS) seeks to promote research that carries a strong conceptual message, for instance, introducing a new concept or model, opening a new line of inquiry within traditional or cross-interdisciplinary areas, introducing new techniques, or making novel connections between existing areas and ideas. The conference format is single-session with ample time for discussion, to promote the exchange of ideas between different areas of theoretical computer science and with other disciplines.

The call for papers welcomed all submissions, whether aligned with current theory of computation research directions or deviating from them. 159 submissions were received. Of these, the program committee selected 45 papers. The accepted papers cover a wide range of topics in theoretical computer science, including algorithms, complexity, cryptography, learning, data privacy, quantum, physical and biological computing, and relations between computing and economics and the social sciences. In addition to the selected papers the committee invited Dr. Craig Gentry of IBM Research to give a keynote talk and we are grateful for his acceptance.

The program committee consisted of 24 members (plus the chair): Benny Applebaum (Tel Aviv University), Avrim Blum (Carnegie Mellon University), Costis Daskalakis (MIT), Uriel Feige (Weizmann Institute), Vitaly Feldman (IBM Research - Almaden), Parikshit Gopalan (Microsoft Research), Bernhard Haeupler (Carnegie Mellon University and Microsoft Research), Stefano Leonardi (University of Rome La Sapienza), Tal Malkin (Columbia University), Nicole Megow (Technische Universitat Berlin), Michael Mitzenmacher (Harvard University), Noam Nisan (Hebrew University and Microsoft Research), Ryan O'Donnell (Carnegie Mellon University), Rafael Pass (Cornell and Cornell NYC Tech), Dana Ron (Tel Aviv University), Guy Rothblum (Microsoft Research), Michael Saks (Rutgers University), Leonard Schulman (Caltech) C. Seshadhri (Sandia National Laboratories), Jonathan Ullman (Harvard University), Paul Valiant (Brown University), Thomas Vidick (Caltech), Nisheeth Vishnoi (Microsoft Research), and Mihalis Yannakakis (Columbia University). I wish to express my admiration for their hard work of reading, evaluating and debating the merits of the submissions. The many subreviewers who assisted the reviewing process deserve acknowledgment as well.

The organizing committee consisted of Weizmann Institute of Science professors Irit Dinur, Shafi Goldwasser (also of MIT), and Moni Naor. They, as well as the sponsor (SIGACT) and supporters (I-CORE and the Weizmann Institute of Science) deserve big thanks. I also thank Robert Kleinberg and Moni Naor (Program Chairs of ITCS 2013 and 2014) and Shafi Goldwasser (Steering Committee Chair) for all their help and advice. Above all, I thank the authors for contributing their outstanding research to ITCS 2015 --- it is their work that makes ITCS a unique conference in the theoretical computer science landscape.

Tim Roughgarden
ITCS 2015 Program Chair
Stanford University
Stanford, CA USA

Table of Contents

Session 5

Session 6

Session 8

Session 9

ITCS 2015 Conference Organization

Program Chair: Tim Roughgarden *(Stanford University)*

Organization Committee: Irit Dinur *(Weizmann Institute of Science)*
Shafi Goldwasser *(MIT and Weizmann Institute of Science)*
Moni Naor *(Weizmann Institute of Science)*

Steering Committee Chair: Shafi Goldwasser *(MIT and Weizmann Institute of Science)*

Steering Committee: Sanjeev Arora *(Princeton University)*
Manuel Blum *(Carnegie Mellon University)*
Bernard Chazelle *(Princeton University)*
Oded Goldreich *(Weizmann Institute of Science)*
Richard Karp *(University of California, Berkeley)*
Sanjeev Khanna *(University of Pennsylvania)*
Ueli Maurer *(ETH Zürich)*
Silvio Micali *(MIT)*
Peter Bro Miltersen *(Aarhus University)*
Christos Papadimitriou *(University of California, Berkeley)*
Michael Rabin *(Harvard University)*
Madhu Sudan *(Microsoft Research)*
Leslie Valiant *(Harvard University)*
Umesh Vazirani *(University of California, Berkeley)*
Avi Wigderson *(Princeton University)*
Andy Yao *(Tsinghua University)*

Program Committee: Benny Applebaum *(Tel Aviv University)*
Avrim Blum *(Carnegie Mellon University)*
Costis Daskalakis *(MIT)*
Uriel Feige *(Weizmann Institute of Science)*
Vitaly Feldman *(IBM Research - Almaden)*
Parikshit Gopalan *(Microsoft Research)*
Bernhard Haeupler *(Carnegie Mellon University)*
Stefano Leonardi *(University of Rome La Sapienza)*
Tal Malkin *(Columbia University)*
Nicole Megow *(Technische Universitat Berlin)*
Michael Mitzenmacher *(Harvard University)*
Noam Nisan *(Hebrew University of Jerusalem and Microsoft Research)*
Ryan O'Donnell *(Carnegie Mellon University)*
Rafael Pass *(Cornell and Cornell NYC Tech)*

Program Committee
(continued):   Dana Ron *(Tel Aviv University)*
Guy Rothblum *(Microsoft Research)*
Michael Saks *(Rutgers University)*
Leonard Schulman *(Caltech)*
C. Seshadhri *(Sandia National Laboratories)*
Jonathan Ullman *(Harvard University)*
Paul Valiant *(Brown University)*
Thomas Vidick *(Caltech)*
Nisheeth Vishnoi *(Microsoft Research)*
Mihalis Yannakakis *(Columbia University)*

Additional reviewers:

Jayadev Acharya	Naveen Garg
Marek Adamczyk	Dmitry Gavinsky
Dorit Aharonov	Sudipto Guha
Alexander Andoni	Alan Guo
Antonios Antoniadis	Guillaume Haeringer
Ery Arias-Castro	Moritz Hardt
Yossi Azar	Hamed Hassani
Nikhil Bansal	William Hoza
Luca Becchetti	Radu Jurca
Eli Ben-Sasson	Gautam Kamath
Umang Bhaskar	Daniel Kane
Liad Blumrosen	Haim Kaplan
Vincenzo Bonifaci	Iordanis Kerenidis
Elette Boyle	Swastik Kopparty
Mark Braverman	Ravishankar Krishnaswamy
Vladimir Braverman	Raghav Kulkarni
Jop Briet	Amit Kumar
Clement Canonne	Yin-Tat Lee
Timothy Chan	Francois Le Gall
Erick Chastain	Kevin Lewi
Shiri Chechick	Yingyu Liang
Shahar Chen	Huijia Lin
Andrew Childs	Edward Lui
Anindya De	Andrew McGregor
Bart de Keijzer	Ruta Mehta
Ronald de Wolf	Or Meir
Ilias Diakonikolas	Raghu Meka
Zeev Dvir	Dieter van Melkebeek
Klim Efremenko	Ashley Montanaro
Esther Ezra	Yoram Moses
Diodato Ferraioli	S. Muthukrishnan
Pierre Fraignaud	Assaf Nachmias

Additional reviewers (continued):

Seffi Naor
Rong Ge
Moshen Ghaffari
Paul Goldberg
Jelani Nelson
Valeria Nikolaenko
Igor Carboni Oliveira
Rasmus Pagh
Christos Papadimitriou
Periklis Papakonstantinou
Boaz Patt-Shamir
Chris Peikert
Anupam Prakash
Eric Price
Kirk Pruhs
Prasad Raghavendra
Mariana Raykova
Leonid Reyzin
Sebastian Roch
Liam Roditty
Aaron Roth
Rishi Saket
Grant Schoenebeck
Lior Seeman
Rocco Servedio
Karn Seth
Ronen Shaltiel
Or Sheffet
Amir Shpilka

Ali Kemal Sinop
Martin Skutella
Rob van Stee
Jukka Suomela
Vasilis Syrgkanis
Li-Yang Tan
Amnon Ta-Shama
Sidharth Telang
Justin Thaler
Gilad Tsur
Christos Tzamos
Rita Vald
Ameya Velingker
Carmine Ventre
Jose Verschae
Aravindan Vijayaraghavan
Jan Vondrak
Magnus Wahlstrom
Carol Wang
Hoeteck Wee
Andreas Wiese
Gerhard Woeginger
David Xiao
Jonathan Yaniv
Amir Yehudayoff
Sergey Yekahnin
Morteza Zadimoghaddam
Manolis Zampetakis
Mark Zhandry

ITCS 2015 Sponsor & Supporters

Sponsor:

Supporters:

I-CORE Program of the Planning and Budgeting Committee (ISF grant No. 4/11)

מכון ויצמן למדע
WEIZMANN INSTITUTE OF SCIENCE

WIS-CSP Foundation of the Weizmann Institute

Interactive Coding for Multiparty Protocols

Abhishek Jain
Boston University and MIT
Boston, MA
abhishek@csail.mit.edu

Yael Tauman Kalai
Microsoft Research
Cambridge, MA
yael@microsoft.com

Allison Bishop Lewko
Columbia University
New York, NY
alewko@cs.columbia.edu

ABSTRACT

The problem of constructing error-resilient interactive protocols was introduced in the seminal works of Schulman (FOCS 1992, STOC 1993). These works show how to convert any *two-party* interactive protocol into one that is resilient to constant-fraction of adversarial error, while blowing up the communication by only a constant factor.

In this work we extend the work of Schulman to the *multiparty* setting. We show how to convert any (non-adaptive) n-party protocol into one that is resilient to $\Theta(\frac{1}{n})$-fraction of adversarial error, while blowing up the communication by only a constant factor.

One might hope to get resilience to constant-fraction of errors, by restricting the adversary's error distribution, and allowing him to make at most a constant-fraction of errors *per party*. We present a black-box lower bound, showing that we cannot be resilient to such adversarial errors, even if we increase the communication by an arbitrary polynomial factor, assuming the error-resilient protocol has a fixed (non-adaptive) speaking order.

1. INTRODUCTION

Starting from the seminal work of Shannon [Sha48], the fundamental problem of error-resilient communication has been extensively studied. Today we know "good" error-correcting codes – ones that achieve constant information rate as well as constant error rate. In a sequence of innovative works, Schulman [Sch92, Sch93] started the study of error-resilience in the context of *interactive protocols*. Specifically, he considered the setting where two parties are interacting via a protocol over a noisy channel, where the noise could be stochastic or adversarial.

At first it may seem tempting to simply apply standard error correcting codes in the interactive setting. However, this would yield poor parameters. In particular, if the noise is adversarial, then all the errors may be concentrated a over a single message, and for protocols which consist of many rounds of interaction this would yield a poor error rate.

Moreover, even for stochastic noise, each message may be one bit long, and thus applying a standard error-correcting code to each message separately would yield either a poor information rate or a poor error rate.

Nevertheless, Schulman established a remarkable result, showing how to convert an arbitrary two-party interactive protocol into one that is resilient to a constant fraction of errors (anywhere in the protocol) with only a constant factor of overhead in the total communication complexity. (We subsequently refer to a process that converts an arbitrary protocol to an error-resilient version as a *compiler*.) This result is essentially the interactive analog of the existence of good error-correcting codes.

The Multiparty Setting. A common theme underlying all these results is that they only consider *two-party* protocols. Yet, many real-life applications require *multi-party* protocols, involving more than two parties. This is typical, for example, in distributed computing. As we discuss below, it is not clear how to extend existing solutions for error-resilient two-party interactive communication to the multi-party setting. Indeed, somewhat surprisingly, despite all the remarkable progress in the area of interactive coding, the multi-party setting has gone largely unnoticed, with only a few works studying it explicitly.

Rajgopalan and Schulman [RS94] initiated the study of interactive coding for multi-party protocols. They considered synchronous protocols that proceed in *rounds*, where in every round, *each* party P_i sends a message to all of its neighbors. (Thus, $\Omega(n^2)$ bits are transmitted per round on a fully connected network.) The main result in [RS94] establishes that any such (synchronous) protocol can be simulated in the presence of constant rate *stochastic* errors with a $(\Theta(\log n))$-factor overhead in the number of rounds. The compiler of [RS94] was inefficient and a subsequent work of Gelles, Moitra and Sahai [GMS11] provides an *efficient* compiler for the same setting of synchronous protocols and stochastic errors, achieving the same parameters.

We observe two drawbacks of these works that we address: their compilers are designed only for synchronous protocols and stochastic errors. They do not provide any guarantees in the more conservative setting of *adversarial* errors.[1] For general (not synchronous) protocols, their compilers incur an overhead of $\Omega(n^2 \log n)$ in the communication complexity.

---

[1] We emphasize that we do not necessarily believe that in reality there is an adversary that tries to insert worst-case errors. However, we do not want to make any assumptions on the error distribution, and thus dealing with adversarial error gives us the most robust guarantees.

This Work. We study error-resilience for *general* (not necessarily synchronous) multiparty protocols in the most general error-model: namely, we consider *adversarial* errors constrained only by a total rate, potentially occurring at any time on any communication link on a network connecting n parties. Our main result is a general compiler that converts any (non-adaptive) n-party protocol into one that is resilient to $\Theta(\frac{1}{n})$-fraction of adversarial errors, while incurring only a constant overhead in communication. We assume that there is at least one party that shares a communication link with all the other parties in the network. We call a network that has only n links connecting each party to this central party a "star network."

THEOREM 1 (INFORMAL). *There exists a deterministic compiler* Comp *and constants* $c > 1$ *and* $\epsilon \in (0,1)$ *s.t. for any (non-adaptive) n-party protocol π with and at least one party P_i that shares a communication link with all other parties $\{P_j\}_{j \neq i}$,* Comp *compiles π into a new protocol $\tilde{\pi}$ such that:*

1. *$CC(\tilde{\pi}) = c \cdot CC(\pi)$.*

2. *Protocol $\tilde{\pi}$ is resilient to $\frac{\epsilon}{n}$-fraction of (adversarial) errors in the total communication.*

We note that similarly to the compiler of Schulman [Sch93], our compiler is inefficient and incurs an exponential (in CC) blow-up in the running time of the parties.

Two remarks about our result are in place:

1. *On the adaptivity of the underlying protocol.* In Theorem 1, we require the underlying protocol to be non-adaptive, i.e., with an a priori fixed speaking order. We note that our result is actually stronger and generalizes to the case of "semi-adaptive" protocols, where the speaking order at any point in the protocol may depend adaptively on the communication transcript so far, but is otherwise independent of the inputs of the parties. We stress that our compiler also yields semi-adaptive (error-resilient) protocols.

   In the most general case of fully adaptive protocols, our compiler incurs an overhead of $\mathcal{O}(\log n)$ in the communication complexity.

2. *On the error rate.* At first glance, it seems that one cannot hope to withstand an adversarial error rate beyond $\Theta(\frac{1}{n})$ in the n-party setting, since an error rate of this order is sufficient to corrupt *all* communication from the least communicative party, hence destroying any hope of a correct simulation. We stress that this is true even for *adaptive* compilers [GHS14, AGS13] where the speaking pattern in the error-resilient protocol may depend on the adversarial behavior. To see this, let P_i be the least communicative party in the compiled protocol when there are no errors.[2] Consider an adversary that simply replaces all the outgoing messages of P_i with honestly generated messages corresponding to party P_i with an adversarially chosen input x_i^*. Note that this adversarial strategy is undetectable and therefore, simulation will fail even if the compiler is adaptive.

However, it was observed by William Hoza [Hoz14] that having additional links connecting parties can be used to tolerate an arbitrarily high error-rate. This observation is perhaps simplest to describe in the two-party setting. Suppose that Alice and Bob wish to communicate despite adversarial errors, and they are connected by two channels. If the adversary cannot insert or delete messages but can only alter their contents, then Alice can send a bit reliably by Bob by simply using channel 1 when she wants to send "0" and then using channel 2 when she wants to send "1". If we assume that Bob always knows which channel a message arrives through, then he can decode perfectly without even looking at the contents. This works similarly in a multi-party setting as long as any pair of parties are connected by multiple paths of channels.

This clever approach does not appear to apply to a network where there is only one path between each pair of parties, nor does it appear to be robust against an adversary that can insert and delete messages. We suspect that our techniques can be extended to be robust against an adversary that inserts and deletes packets as well, both in the two-party and multi-party setting, though we leave this as a topic for future work.

A Lower Bound for "Per-Party" Adversarial Error. We also consider *per party* adversarial errors. More specifically, we consider adversarial errors that are constrained to occur at a constant rate $\epsilon < 1$ for the transmissions emanating from each individual party. Note that this prevents the adversary from silencing a single party.

In this setting, we prove a severe lower bound for black-box compilers. Namely, we show that one cannot convert a multi-party protocol in a black-box manner to an error-resilient protocol with static speaking order that tolerates constant-rate per-party adversarial error, even while incurring a polynomial overhead in communication complexity. Thus, we not only rule out compilers with a constant overhead in communication, but rather compilers with *any polynomial* overhead in communication. We stress that our impossibility result is for "black-box" compilers, i.e., we assume that the error-resilient protocol makes black-box use of the next message functions of the parties in the underlying protocol. This is a very natural and far-reaching model of compilation, as all previous interactive coding results are black-box in this sense. We also assume that we are in a sufficiently limited network that routing paths of messages cannot be used to transmit information (like a star network).

THEOREM 2 (INFORMAL). *There exists a multiparty protocol π that cannot be black-box simulated by any error-resilient protocol with arbitrary polynomial communication complexity and static speaking order in the presence of constant rate per-party adversarial errors.*

Communication model for multiparty protocols. We model multiparty protocols as a chain of messages sent sequentially from one party to another. We note that one can convert any multiparty protocol into a sequential one with only a constant overhead in the communication complexity. However, converting an arbitrary multiparty protocol into a sequential one may incur a large blowup in the *round complexity*. For example, consider fully synchronous protocols where in each round, every party sends a bit to every other

---

[2]If the compiler is randomized, then the adversary can choose the party that is the least communicative on average.

party. The sequential analogue of such a protocol incurs n^2 blowup in round complexity. Towards that end, we note that our compiler can be in fact be adapted to avoid this blowup in round complexity. Due to space constraints, we defer this discussion to the full version of the paper.

1.1 Related Work

In addition to the seminal papers of Schulman [Sch92, Sch93] there have been several other works that consider interactive coding in the *two-party* setting.

The work of Braverman and Rao [BR11] obtains vast improvements in the constant fraction of adversarial errors that can be tolerated. While Schulman's original protocol only allows an error fraction of 1/240, [BR11] allow $\frac{1}{4} - \epsilon$ with a constant alphabet or $\frac{1}{8} - \epsilon$ for a binary alphabet. Very recently, the works [AGS13, GHS14] leverage adaptivity to achieve error-rates beyond $\frac{1}{4}$.

We note that Schulman's compiler [Sch93] for correcting adversarial errors, as well as the compiler in the followup work of [BR11], use *tree-codes* which are a beautiful combinatorial object. Unfortunately, we do not know how to construct or decode tree-codes efficiently, and as a result both compilers are inefficient. The recent works of Braverman [Bra12], and Moore and Schulman [MS13], make some progress towards efficient constructions of tree codes.

The work of Gelles, Moitra, and Sahai [GMS11] observes that a weaker notion of tree codes (called potent tree codes) suffices for resisting stochastic errors. They leverage this to improve on [Sch92, Sch93] in terms of efficiency in the stochastic errors case. They also leverage this to improve on [RS94] in terms of efficiency in the stochastic errors case.

The work of Brakerski and Kalai [BK12], constructs an efficient version of Schulman's compiler that is resilient to adversarial error. The subsequent work of [BN13] improves upon the computation complexity. Very recently, [GH14] show how to achieve optimal error and communication rates efficiently. Unfortunately, it is not immediately clear how to extend these ideas to the multi-party setting, and we leave this as an important open problem.

Finally, we mention the works of [GH14, BE14] which consider list-decoding for interactive communication and the works of [KR13, Hae14] that study the channel capacity for interactive communication.

2. OVERVIEW OF OUR TECHNIQUES

Recall that our goal is to construct a compiler that transforms any n-party protocol into one that is resilient to $\Theta(\frac{1}{n})$-fraction of adversarial errors (anywhere in the protocol), while incurring only a constant overhead in communication.

A First Approach. Since we have a solution for this problem for the special case of $n = 2$, a natural direction towards achieving our goal is the following: given an n-party protocol π, denote by $\pi_{i,j}$ the "sub-protocol" consisting of all the messages exchanged between parties P_i and P_j in π. Then, simply apply a standard two-party interactive coding scheme on every $\pi_{i,j}$ to make it error-resilient, thereby making π error-resilient as well.

There are two fundamental problems that arise with this approach. First, note that on a complete network, there are $\Omega(n^2)$ links, and therefore an overall error rate of $\Omega(\frac{1}{n^2})$ would be sufficient for an adversary to corrupt the "weakest" link and defeat this simple approach. Second, in the multi-party setting, each outgoing message of a party is a *dynamic* function of what it receives from *all* of the other parties. However, existing two-party interactive coding schemes were designed and analyzed for the more restrictive case of *static* inputs. This leads to the following important dilemma: how do we "synchronize" between these two-party sub-protocols $\pi_{i,j}$?

We note that known two-party interactive coding schemes (such as [Sch93]), when applied to $\pi_{i,j}$, would require the parties P_i and P_j to sometimes "rewind" to a previous state (say) s and then re-execute $\pi_{i,j}$ from that state. When this happens in the n-party setting, we may require *all* the parties in π to rewind at this point since any communication that happened between parties P_k and $P_{k'}$ after state s is rendered useless. In other words, every "local rewind" in $\pi_{i,j}$, in fact, corresponds to a "global rewind" in π that must be signaled to the other parties, without creating inconsistencies across the states of the n parties. However, note that none of the parties in π may have a global view of the entire protocol (this may happen, for example, when π is designed over an incomplete network). Therefore, it is not immediately clear how to achieve these goals, while minimizing the communication overhead.

A Coordination-based Approach. To address both of the above problems, we designate a single party to serve as a "coordinator" of the computation. More concretely, we assume that there exists at least one party (among the n parties), denoted as P^*, that shares a communication link with every other party. Then, as a first step, we transform π to operate over a star network design, with P^* being the central (i.e., star) node. This is achieved by simply requiring that each party P_i send *all* its outgoing messages in π to P^*, who will then deliver them to the intended recipients[3]. Thus, all of the communication is now routed via P^* who can keep a *global view* of the computation. Of course, if the original network contains more than a star, different approaches could be used to take advantage of these additional links instead of ignoring them, as we do. However, we stress that our approach applies to the case where the original network is only a star and has no other links.

Intuitively, centralizing the protocol through a single coordinator results in a scenario where there are only n (as opposed to n^2) communication channels to protect – those between P^* and every other party P_i. For convenience, throughout this paper, we think of P^* as a separate party.

At a high level, we will protect each of these channels using a two-party interactive coding scheme. That is, let π_i denote the two-party sub-protocol between P^* and P_i. Then, we will apply a two-party interactive coding scheme on π_i to make it error-resilient. However, as pointed out earlier, we cannot make black-box use of such schemes because we have to adapt to the dynamic nature of P^*'s "input" in its pairwise interactions, which it is continually learning and updating as

---

[3]We note that this coordinator-based approach restricts the adaptivity of the underlying protocol. In particular, we assume that P^* knows the intended recipient of each message. In other words, we require that the underlying protocol is "semi-adaptive", i.e., the identity of the recipient is either fixed a priori or only a function of the transcript so far, which is known to P^*. In general, if the underlying protocol is adaptive, then the parties must append the recipient's identity to their messages, which incurs a blowup of $\mathcal{O}(\log n)$.

a function of what it perceives to be happening on the other links. Thus, we adapt the underlying two-party interactive-coding scheme [Sch93], to allow for the level of indecision and inconsistency that will be exhibited by P^* as a consequence of errors on the *other* channels.

Detecting Errors on a Timely Basis. A natural approach for P^* is to try to simulate an error-free execution by communicating with other parties in the same order as in the original protocol while no errors are detected. Whenever P^* detects an error on a channel (either on his own or through correspondence with P_i), it rewinds to the point of confusion to re-execute the protocol from thereon. Note that P^* can signal such a rewind to every party. This approach indeed seems promising in terms of preserving the original communication complexity (up to constants), as long as the back-tracking is not too frequent or too long on average.

However, problems may arise when a party speaks with P^* briefly and then is left silent for a long period of time (this may happen if P_i speaks rather infrequently in π). In particular, at certain moments during an error-riddled execution, there may be only a *single party* who "knows" that an error has occurred (in the sense that the progress of the simulated computation is not consistent with his input). P^* can only detect and correct such an error in a timely fashion if he speaks to all parties on a frequent basis. Indeed, if the (sole) party who "knows" that an error has occurred gets a chance to report this only after (say) $\Theta(n^2)$ bits of total communication has elapsed, then fixing this error would require the parties to re-execute the entire $\Theta(n^2)$-bits sized transcript from the point of error to the present state. This is clearly much more than what we can afford.

An alternative strategy for P^* could be to simply proceed in a rigid, cyclic order, exchanging (say) X bits with P_1, then X bits with P_2, and so on, until exchanging X bits with P_n and then starting the cycle over. We note, however, that such a strategy, in general, may blow up the communication complexity by a factor of n.

Eliminating "Silent" Parties. Our key observation towards solving this problem, is that we can allow every party P_i to exchange at least one bit with P^* during the course of *every* "chunk" of $\Theta(n)$ bits (in the error-resilient protocol) without imposing a fixed speaking order all of the time. We achieve this in the following manner: we divide a chunk of $\Theta(n)$ bits (in the error-resilient protocol) into two phases of *equal* size – in the first phase, the parties exchange the regular protocol messages in an order that is chosen adaptively by P^* (based on errors that he detects on the different two-party channels). In the second phase, referred to as the "polling phase", P^* asks each party P_i to report its current state.

This strategy ensures that each party P_i gets a chance to report an error to P^* after *at most* $\Theta(n)$ bits, irrespective of how (in)frequently it speaks in the underlying protocol π. As a consequence, an adversary must spend one unit of its error budget every time in order to prevent an error from being detected after $\Theta(n)$ bits of communication. Since the adversary has a budget of $\Theta(\frac{1}{n})$, we can afford to repeat n bits of communication for every error. Finally, note that the above strategy also ensures that the total communication overhead is kept to a constant factor (as long as we use a two-party interactive coding scheme with constant overhead).

Overview of our Lower Bound.

We prove a black-box impossibility result for achieving error-resilience against constant rate *per-party* adversarial error via compilers that impose a static speaking order, meaning that the designation of who sends and receives the ith bit of the protocol is independent of the parties' inputs and the transcript "so far". Like our positive result on the star network, it is assumed here in our lower bound that information cannot be implicitly conveyed from one party to another by the path that messages can take - the only information transmitted is in the content of the messages themselves.

The intuition is as follows: suppose for contradiction that there is such a compiler allowing error rate $\frac{1}{10}$ (for example) on the transmissions emanating from each individual party. We consider an n-party variant of the "ping-pong" protocol protocol considered in [CPT13]. The protocol proceeds in several rounds, where in every round, the communication follows in a ring, with party P_1 speaking to P_2 then party P_2 speaking to P_3, and so on. Now, suppose that n is much larger than 20, and we divide the resulting error-resilient version of the protocol into 20 segments of equal bit length. Then in each segment, there must be some party P_i who sends $< 1/10$ of their total bits in the segment, and hence can be corrupted for the entirety of the segment. If we adjust the parameters and argue a bit more carefully, it can be shown that we can actually define segments in a way that allow us to corrupt a *distinct* party in each segment. When a party is corrupted for every transmission it sends in the course of a segment, the adversary can prevent the uncorrupted parties from learning anything new about the corrupted party's input, hence stalling progress in the simulation of the underlying protocol.

Remark. When the speaking order is static, it does not matter what the adversary forces the corrupted party to say, as long as it is independent of the party's input. However, we can imagine the adversary "impersonates" the corrupted party by sending messages that are consistent with uncorrupted messages for some other input. We suspect that carefully chosen impersonation patterns may help extend our lower bound techniques to compilers allowing adaptive speaking order, as the other parties will be prevented from detecting where the errors are, presumably limiting the power of adaptivity. This is an intriguing open direction.

3. PRELIMINARIES

In this section, we establish some notation and definitions that will be used throughout the paper. We start by describing syntax for multiparty protocols (Section 3.1). Next, we define tree codes (Section 3.2). Next, we give a brief description of the interactive coding scheme of Schulman [Sch93] along with some definitions that we will use in this paper (Section 3.3).

3.1 Noiseless Protocol π

Semantics of n-party Protocols. We start by describing the semantics of a noiseless protocol π for n parties $P_1, \ldots, P_n$. For simplicity of exposition, we make the following assumptions about π:

- *Sequential transmission of messages:* Protocol messages in π are sent in a *sequential* manner. More specifically, we assume that a party P_i is "activated" only upon receiving a message, (say) m, from some party P_j. Upon receiving m, party P_i sends a new message m' (as per the protocol specification) to P_k, which activates P_k, and so on. Finally, we assume that the party that sends the first message of π is activated via a dummy message.

We note that the above is without loss of generality when measuring total communication complexity up to constant factors, since one can simulate *simultaneous* messages by a sequence of messages with only a constant blowup in the total communication of the protocol. For example, consider the case where a party P_i wishes to send a message m to multiple parties $P_{\ell_1}, \ldots, P_{\ell_k}$ simultaneously. Note that this can be simulated by $2k$ sequential messages, where the odd numbered messages correspond to P_i sending m to some other party, and the even numbered messages correspond to some party simply sending an acknowledgement to P_i. The scenario where more than one party sends a message simultaneously can be simulated in an analogous manner.

- *Single bit messages:* Each message in protocol π consists of a single bit. Indeed, this is the "hardest" case when dealing with transmission errors.

  Again, we note that a party can always send a long message in a bit-by-bit manner, where the receiving party, after receiving each bit, re-activates the sending party by sending it an acknowledgement bit. This blows up the communication complexity by only a factor of 2.

Semi-adaptive protocols. We make the assumption that the communication pattern in π is *semi-adaptive*, i.e., the party that sends (or receives) the i'th message of the protocol is either fixed a priori or only depends on the (partial) protocol transcript before the i'th message, and is otherwise independent of the inputs of the parties. We leave open the problem of constructing interactive coding schemes for multiparty protocols where the speaking order is adaptive.

Let $x_1, \ldots, x_n$ denote the inputs of $P_1, \ldots, P_n$ respectively. For convenience, we will sometimes use the shorthand $X = x_1, \ldots, x_n$. Let $B_{\ell-1} = b_1, \ldots, b_{\ell-1}$ denote the first $\ell - 1$ messages of π. Then the ℓ'th message is defined as $b_\ell = \pi(X; B_{\ell-1})$. Note that if party P_i is the sender of message b_ℓ (as fixed by π), then formally, b_ℓ is computed as $b_\ell = \mathsf{NM}_i(x_i; \mathsf{trans}_i)$ where NM_i is the *next-message function* of P_i as specified by π and trans_i is the partial protocol transcript (which is a subset of $B_{\ell-1}$) observed by P_i.

(Noiseless) Protocol Tree. Let L denote the total communication complexity of protocol π. Then, the transcript of π on a set of inputs for $P_1, \ldots, P_n$, is described by a path from the root to a leaf in a binary tree of depth L, denoted by $\mathcal{T}$. Each node of $\mathcal{T}$ is labeled by the identity of a party P_i, and each arc is labeled by either 0 or 1. Then, an arc labeled with b from a parent node labeled P_i at level ℓ to a child node labeled P_j at level $\ell + 1$ refers to the fact that in π, the ℓ'th message is the bit b sent from party P_i to P_j. (Thus, the root node is at level 1.)

The execution of π on an input $X = x_1, \ldots, x_n$ specifies a path from the root to a leaf in $\mathcal{T}$, namely a sequence of arcs $b_1, \ldots, b_L$, at the end of which the outcome of π is determined. On a noiseless channel, this path is simply extended

by one arc each time a message is sent in π. Intuitively, in the noisy channel setting, the goal is to construct the correct protocol execution path on $\mathcal{T}$ without spending too much time on "incorrect" branches.

3.2 Tree Codes

A d-ary *tree code* over an alphabet Σ is a d-regular tree of arbitrary depth N whose arcs are labeled with elements of Σ. A d-ary tree code $\mathcal{TC}$ defines an encoding for any string $\tau = (\tau_1, \ldots, \tau_{\leq N})$, where every $\tau_i \in [d]$. This encoding, denoted by $\mathcal{TC}(\tau) = (\sigma_1, \ldots, \sigma_{|\tau|})$, where $\sigma_i \in \Sigma$, is defined by concatenating the labels along the path defined by τ, i.e., the path that begins at the root and whose i'th node is the τ_i'th child of the $(i-1)$'th node.

For any $k \leq N$ and any two strings $\tau, \tau' \in [d]^k$, let ℓ be the longest common prefix of τ and τ'. Denote by $\mathsf{div}(\tau, \tau') = k - \ell$ the distance from the k-th level to the least common ancestor of the paths τ and τ' in $\mathcal{TC}$.

DEFINITION 3. *We say that $\mathcal{TC}$ has distance α if for any $k \in [N]$ and any $\tau, \tau' \in [d]^k$, the Hamming distance $\Delta(\mathcal{TC}(\tau), \mathcal{TC}(\tau'))$ is at least $\alpha \cdot \mathsf{div}(\tau, \tau')$.*

Known Constructions of Tree Codes. Schulman proved an existential result for tree codes of arbitrary depth. We recall his result below:

THEOREM 4 ([SCH93]). *For any d and $\alpha < 1$, there exists a d-ary tree code of unbounded depth N and distance α over an alphabet Σ of size at most $|\Sigma| = 2\lfloor (4d)^{O(\frac{1}{1-\alpha})} \rfloor - 1$.*

Given such a tree code, the decoding operation takes time exponential in the depth N. Recently, Braverman [Bra12] gave the first deterministic construction of a tree code in time sub-exponential in depth N. However, till date, no efficient constructions of tree codes are known. Recently, Gelles, Moitra and Sahai [GMS11] gave an efficient construction of *potent* tree code, which is a relaxation of tree codes, and suffices in many applications. In this work, however, we will work with the standard notion of tree codes as defined above.

3.3 Two-Party Interactive Coding

In this section, we recall the interactive coding scheme of Schulman [Sch93] for two-party protocols. Specifically, we describe how tree codes can be used to compile a two-party protocol into one that tolerates a constant fraction of errors, with only a constant blowup in communication. Along the way, we establish some notation and syntax that we shall use in the rest of the paper.

We will follow the basic strategy of Schulman (as described in [Sch96]), but depart somewhat in the implementation details, in order to be consistent with our n-party error-resilient protocol. More specifically, recall that Schulman assumes that all parties *simultaneously* transmit a message in *every* round of the protocol. Note that such an assumption is problematic for n-party protocols because it incurs a multiplicative blowup of n in the communication complexity of the protocol. Since our main goal is to design error-resilient multiparty protocols with *minimal* communication overhead, we would like to avoid such a blowup. Therefore, in contrast to Schulman, as discussed earlier in Section 3.1, we assume that the parties speak in a *sequential* manner. That is, first a party P_i sends a message to P_j, then P_j

sends a new message, and so on. While the focus of this subsection is only on two-party protocols (as opposed to n-party protocols), we will use the same protocol semantics as we use in our n-party protocol, so as to remain consistent with our main compiler presented in Section 4.2. As such, the error-resilient protocol we present below slightly deviates from [Sch96].

Pebble Moves and History Tree. Let $\pi = \langle P_1, P_2 \rangle$ be a two-party protocol. Let $\mathcal{T}$ denote the protocol tree for π. In the error-resilient protocol, at every point, each party is equipped with a pebble (that points to a node) in the underlying protocol tree $\mathcal{T}$, which it moves about to keep track of the progress of the protocol π. Any move of the pebble is described by one of the four possibilities: 0 ("move down on left child"), 1 ("move down on right child"), H ("hold") and B ("move back", i.e., towards the root). Pebble move B by a party P_i denotes that it is going back one step in $\mathcal{T}$, whereas pebble move H by P_i denotes that it is staying at its current position. This gives rise to what we call a *history tree*, as defined below.

Let $\mathcal{HT}$ denote a 4-ary tree of arbitrary depth N where each arc is labeled by $\tau \in \{0, 1, B, H\}$. We will refer to $\mathcal{HT}$ as the *history tree*. A path from the root node to an internal node in $\mathcal{HT}$, represented as a sequence of arcs $\tau_1, \ldots, \tau_\ell$, denotes a possible sequence of pebble moves made by a party P_i.

Computing Pebble Position in Protocol Tree. We now describe two functions for computing pebble positions in a protocol tree $\mathcal{T}$. These functions are used by the parties for error-resilient communication, as described below.

The first function $\mathsf{SetPebble}_{\mathcal{T}}(\cdot, \cdot)$ takes as input the current pebble position α (that denotes a node in the protocol tree $\mathcal{T}$) and the next pebble move τ of a party P_i. It updates α to P_i's *next* pebble position, as determined by τ. More concretely, the function $\mathsf{SetPebble}_{\mathcal{T}}(\cdot, \cdot)$, on input α and τ, works as follows:

$\mathsf{SetPebble}_{\mathcal{T}}(\alpha, \tau)$:

- If $\tau = 0$, then set α to be its left child node in $\mathcal{T}$.
- Else, if $\tau = 1$, then set α to be its right child node in $\mathcal{T}$.
- Else, if $\tau = B$, then set α to be its parent node in $\mathcal{T}$.
- Output α.

The second function $\mathsf{GetPebble}_{\mathcal{T}}(\cdot)$ takes as input the history $\mathsf{hist} \in \{0, 1, H, B\}^*$ of pebble moves by a party P_i (from the start of communication) and computes P_i's *current* pebble position α. More concretely, the function $\mathsf{GetPebble}_{\mathcal{T}}(\cdot)$, on input $\mathsf{hist} = \tau_1, \ldots, \tau_{|\mathsf{hist}|}$, works as follows:

$\mathsf{GetPebble}_{\mathcal{T}}(\mathsf{hist})$:

1. Initialize α to the root of $\mathcal{T}$.
2. For $i = 1$ to $|\mathsf{hist}|$, do the following:
   - Set $\alpha = \mathsf{SetPebble}_{\mathcal{T}}(\alpha, \tau_i)$.
3. Output α.

In the sequel, we will omit $\mathcal{T}$ from the subscript whenever the protocol tree $\mathcal{T}$ is clear from the context.

A Variant of Schulman's Compiler. We now describe a variant of Schulman's compiler that converts any two-party protocol into an error-resilient version. To this end, fix any two-party protocol $\pi = \langle P_1, P_2 \rangle$. We show how to construct an error-resilient version of π. Since our aim is to only convey the main ideas, for simplicity of exposition, we omit the concrete parameters of the tree code from this description.

Before the start of the error-resilient protocol, parties P_1 and P_2 share a 4-ary tree code $\mathcal{TC}$ of (appropriate) depth N over an alphabet Σ of constant size c. The parties will use $\mathcal{TC}$ to encode paths in the 4-ary history tree $\mathcal{HT}$. Each party P_i is equipped with a pebble α_i that is positioned at the root node of the protocol tree $\mathcal{T}$. We now describe the strategy of party P_1 upon receiving a symbol from P_2 in the error-resilient protocol. Since the protocol is symmetric, the strategy of P_2 is defined analogously.

1. **Guess P_2's pebble:** Let $\vec{\sigma}$ be the sequence of symbols received so far from P_2. Party P_1 first guesses the entire history $\widetilde{\mathsf{hist}_2}$ of pebble moves of P_2 that minimizes the hamming distance $\Delta(\mathcal{TC}(\widetilde{\mathsf{hist}_2}), \vec{\sigma})$. Then P_1 uses $\widetilde{\mathsf{hist}_2}$ to compute a guess $\widetilde{\alpha_2} = \mathsf{GetPebble}(\widetilde{\mathsf{hist}_2})$ for P_2's pebble position in $\mathcal{T}$.

2. **Next pebble move:** The next step is to determine the next pebble move. Let α_1 be the position of P_1's pebble in $\mathcal{T}$. Party P_1 computes its next pebble move $\tau \in \{0, 1, B, H\}$ in the following manner:

   (a) If $\alpha_1 = \widetilde{\alpha_2}$, i.e., (in P_1's view) both P_1 and P_2 are at the same position in $\mathcal{T}$, then P_1 considers the following two cases:

      - If P_1 is the label of node α_1 in $\mathcal{T}$, then this means that it is P_1's turn to send the next message in π. Thus, P_1 computes its pebble move $\tau = \mathsf{NM}_1(x_1; \mathsf{trans})$, where NM_1 is the next-message function of party P_1 in the underlying protocol π, x_1 denotes the input on P_1, and trans is the "uncorrupted" transcript of π. Namely, trans is simply the concatenation of the labels of the arcs along the path from the root node to α_1 in $\mathcal{T}$.

      - Otherwise, if P_2 is the label of α_1, then this means that it is in fact P_2's turn to send the next message in π. Thus, P_1 simply sets its next pebble move $\tau = H$ to indicate that it is waiting to receive the next message from P_2.

   (b) Else, if α_1 is the parent of $\widetilde{\alpha_2}$ and P_2 is the label of node α_1 in $\mathcal{T}$, then this means that P_1 already received the last message in π from P_2 and should now simply move down an arc in the protocol tree $\mathcal{T}$ following P_2. Thus, P_1 sets its next pebble move τ to be 0 (resp., 1) if $\widetilde{\alpha_2}$ is the left (resp., right) child of α_1.

   (c) Else, if α_1 is an ancestor of $\widetilde{\alpha_2}$, then this indicates that P_2 may have moved down the wrong path in $\mathcal{T}$ due to communication errors. Since in P_1's view, P_2 is *strictly below* P_1 in the tree, P_1 decides to wait for P_2 to move back, and therefore sets its next pebble move $\tau = H$.

(d) Else, if the least common ancestor (say) A of α_1 and $\widetilde{\alpha_2}$ is a strict ancestor of α_1 in $\mathcal{T}$, then this means that P_1 and P_2 have followed different paths, diverging at A. Thus, P_1 decides to move back towards A, and sets its next pebble move to $\tau = B$.

Having determined its next pebble move τ, P_1 now sets its pebble at the node $\mathsf{SetPebble}(\alpha_1, \tau)$.

3. **Send next symbol to P_2:** Let hist_1 denote the entire history of pebble moves made by P_1 (including the last pebble move τ). P_1 now computes $\vec{\sigma} = \mathcal{TC}(\mathsf{hist}_1)$, where $\vec{\sigma} = \sigma_1, \ldots, \sigma_{|\mathsf{hist}_1|}$. Finally, P_1 sends the tree code symbol $\sigma_{|\mathsf{hist}_1|}$ to indicate its last pebble move to P_2.

4. OUR POSITIVE RESULT

In this section, we show how to convert any semi-adaptive[4] n-party protocol π into one that is resilient to $\frac{\epsilon}{n}$-fraction of adversarial errors with only constant blowup in communication complexity.

THEOREM 5. *There exists a compiler* Comp *and constants* $c > 1$ *and* $\epsilon \in (0, 1)$ *s.t. for any (semi-adaptive) n-party protocol* $\pi = \langle P_1, \ldots, P_n \rangle$, *with at least one party P_i that shares a communication link with all parties* $\{P_j\}_{j \neq i}$, Comp *compiles π into a new protocol $\tilde{\pi}$ such that:*

1. *$CC(\tilde{\pi}) = c \cdot CC(\pi)$.*

2. *$\tilde{\pi}$ is resilient to $\left(\frac{\epsilon}{n}\right)$-fraction of (adversarial) errors in the total communication.*

3. *The runtime of each party P_i in $\tilde{\pi}$ is at most $2^{\mathcal{O}(n \cdot C_{\max})}$, where $C_{\max}$ is the maximum numbers of bits sent and received by any party P_j in the underlying protocol π.*

We prove the above theorem by constructing such a compiler Comp. We stress that our compiler also yields semi-adaptive (error-resilient) protocols. In the most general case of fully adaptive protocols, our compiler incurs an overhead of $\mathcal{O}(\log n)$ in the communication complexity.

4.1 Overview of Comp

Our compiler works in two main steps. In the first step, Comp designates a single party to serve as the coordinator of the computation. Concretely, Comp first transforms π into a protocol π^* over a star network design with a single party, denoted P^* (that shares a communication link with every other party P_j), designated to be the "star node". This is achieved by simply requiring each party P_j to send each of its outgoing messages to P^* who forwards it to the designated recipient. (Note that this blows up the communication complexity of π by only a factor of two.) The star protocol π^* is then "decomposed" into n two-party protocols $\pi_1, \ldots, \pi_n$, where π_j denotes the two party sub-protocol between P^* and P_j. Intuitively, the party P^* now plays the role of a "central authority" that is aware of the global state of the n-party protocol π. Then, looking ahead, the main role of P^*

is to detect errors on any of the n communication links and whenever necessary, signal a "rewind" to all relevant parties so as to ensure that all the parties are "in sync". The main challenge here is to ensure that the rewinds are bounded; in particular, the number of rewinds should not cause a super constant blowup in communication complexity.

The second step, at a high level, involves the application of a two-party interactive coding scheme on every sub-protocol π_i to make π_i error-resilient. Note, however, that the inputs of P^* in π_i are decided *adaptively*, depending upon the other sub-protocols $\pi_{j \neq i}$. Indeed, existing two-party interactive codings are not analyzed for such a setting. Towards this end, we make a non-black-box use of (a variant of) Schulman's interactive coding scheme [Sch93].

The simulation of π is performed in the following manner. At the beginning, P^* shares a tree code with each party P_i. This tree code (of sufficient depth) is used by P^* and P_i to simulate a transcript of π_i. We think of the simulation of π as proceedings in "chunks", each consisting of $\Theta(n)$ tree code symbols in total. Each of these chunks is divided into two-parts: in the *first* part, referred to as the protocol phase, each party P_i simply follows the simulation strategy as prescribed by the two-party interactive coding scheme (applied on π_i) and determines its outgoing messages accordingly. On receiving a message (in the form of a tree code symbol) from P_i, P^* determines the "global consistency point" in the protocol tree for π, which, intuitively speaking, is the point (in π) where the first error occurred (in the view of P^*), resulting in incorrect simulation of π_i's. (If there were no errors, then this point would be the "current" point of execution.) If this point is "higher" in the protocol tree than the current point of execution, then P^* signals a rewind. Specifically, P^* determines the identity of the party P_j who was the recipient of the message (say m^*) where the error occurred, and then rewinds that party by sending a "back" instruction an appropriate number of times. Once P_j is rewound to the point of confusion, P^* re-sends m^* to P_j. Based on P_j's response, P^* now identifies the next party that needs to be brought in sync, in the same manner as described above. Otherwise, if there is no error to be rewound, P^* follows the same strategy as prescribed by the two-party interactive coding scheme and delivers the message of P_i to the designated recipient P_j.

The *second* part of a chunk, referred to as the polling phase, consists of P^* sending a tree code symbol to each party P_i. On receiving this message, every P_i follows its local protocol tries to indicate its current position in the protocol tree of π_i by sending a tree code symbol. The purpose of this phase is to allow the parties to report errors to P^* on a timely basis. Indeed, note that protocol π may be such that a party, say P_ℓ, is instructed to send messages much less frequently than the other parties. Now, if the adversary creates an error in the sub-protocol π_ℓ which goes undetected by P^*, then the only way to recover from this error, *without causing a super-constant communication blowup*, is for P_ℓ to report this error to P^* on a timely basis. This effect is achieved by the polling phase.

Note that the size of each chunk is chosen carefully to ensure that the polling phase (which is necessarily of size $\Theta(n)$ since *every* party reports its position to P^*) does not cause a blowup in the communication complexity, while still occurring at a sufficient frequency. Indeed, we cannot afford to perform polling after every message since it would incur

---

[4]In a semi-adaptive protocol, the speaking order at any point in the protocol may depend adaptively on the communication transcript so far, but is otherwise independent of the inputs of the parties.

an overhead of $\Theta(n)$. On the other hand, we cannot afford to do it any later than $\Theta(n)$ number of protocol phase symbols have been exchanged since then a single error caused by an adversary may require re-executing an $\omega(n)$-sized portion of π, which would lead to a super-constant blowup.

4.2 Our Compiler

Here we present a formal description of our compiler Comp to prove Theorem 5. Our compiler operates in two main steps, described below.

Step 1: Decomposing π into two-party protocols. Comp first transforms π into a protocol π^* that operates over a star network design. Let P_i be a party that shares a communication link with every other party P_j in π. For convenience, we will denote P_i by P^*. Protocol $\tilde{\pi}$, referred to as the star protocol, is the same as π, except that every message in π from a party P_i to another party P_j is routed via P^* in $\tilde{\pi}$. In other words, suppose that a party P_i wishes to send a message b to P_j in π. Then, in $\tilde{\pi}$, P_i first sends b to P^* and then P^* sends the same message b to P_j in the next protocol step.

For simplicity of exposition, in the sequel, we will treat party P^* as a separate (additional) party that does not have its own inputs and simply does the job of routing messages between parties $P_1, \ldots, P_n$.

Next, Comp "decomposes" π into n two-party sub-protocols $\pi_1, \ldots, \pi_n$. Protocol π_i is simply the sub-protocol of π that consists only of all the messages in π exchanged between P^* and P_i. Intuitively, π_i can be viewed as a protocol between P_i and the rest of the parties $P_{j \neq i}$ (viewed as a single party P^*) where all communication between any two parties P_j and P_k $(j, k \neq i)$ is "internal" to P^*, and the only "external" communication corresponds to the messages sent and received by P_i in π.

Step 2: Simulating π. Given protocol π, let $\pi_1, \ldots, \pi_n$ denote the n two-party protocols obtained by "decomposing" π, in the manner as described above. Let $\mathcal{T}$ denote the protocol tree for π, and for every $i \in [n]$, let $\mathcal{T}_i$ denote the protocol tree for π_i.

Initialization: Before the start of the protocol, each pair (P_i, P^*) shares a 4-ary tree code $\mathcal{TC}_i$ of depth $N = 6L$, where $L = CC(\pi)$, and distance $\alpha = \frac{1}{2}$ over an alphabet Σ of size $|\Sigma| = 512$ (as fixed by Theorem 4). Further, for every $i \in [n]$, players P_i and P^* are equipped with pebbles α_i and α_i^*, respectively, that are positioned at the root node of $\mathcal{T}_i$. Finally, P^* is additionally equipped with three variables: a flag flag initialized to FALSE, a counter count initialized to 1 and another counter Tcount initialized to 0.

We now describe the strategies of P_i and P^*, respectively, upon activation by a received symbol in the error-resilient protocol. We remark that the simulation is terminated by P^* and the simulated transcript is set to be the final output of P^*.

I. P_i receives a symbol from P^*: Upon receiving a symbol $\sigma \in \Sigma$ from P^*, party P_i follows the same strategy as that described in Section 3.3 for two-party protocols. We describe the steps below:

1. **Guess P^*'s pebble position:** Let $\vec{\sigma}$ be the sequence of symbols received so far from P^*. Guess the entire history $\widetilde{\text{hist}}^*$ of pebble moves of P^* that minimizes the

Hamming distance $\Delta(\mathcal{TC}_i(\widetilde{\text{hist}}^*), \vec{\sigma})$. Compute a guess for P^*'s pebble position $\widetilde{\alpha}_i^* = \text{GetPebble}(\widetilde{\text{hist}}^*)$ from $\widetilde{\text{hist}}^*$.

2. **Next pebble move:** Let α_i be the position of P_i's pebble in $\mathcal{T}_i$. Compute the next pebble move $\tau \in \{0, 1, B, H\}$:

   (a) If $\alpha_i = \widetilde{\alpha}_i^*$, then do the following:

   - If P_i is the label of node α_i in $\mathcal{T}_i$, then set $\tau = \text{NM}_i(x_i; \text{trans}_i)$, where NM_i is the next-message function of P_i in π, x_i is the input of P_i, and trans_i is the "uncorrupted" transcript of π_i observed by P_i. Namely, trans_i is simply the concatenation of the labels of the arcs along the path from the root node to α_i in $\mathcal{T}_i$.
   - Else, if P^* is the label of α_i, then set $\tau = H$.

   (b) Else, if α_i is the parent of $\widetilde{\alpha}_i^*$ and P^* is the label of node α_i in $\mathcal{T}_i$, then set τ to be 0 (resp., 1) if $\widetilde{\alpha}_i^*$ is the left (resp., right) child of α_i.

   (c) Else, if α_i is an ancestor of $\widetilde{\alpha}_i^*$, set $\tau = H$.

   (d) Else, if the least common ancestor of α_i and $\widetilde{\alpha}_i^*$ is a strict ancestor of α_i in $\mathcal{T}_i$, then set $\tau = B$.

   Move own pebble to the node $\text{SetPebble}(\alpha_i, \tau)$.

3. **Send next symbol to P^*:** Let hist_i denote the entire history of pebbles moves made by P_i (including the last pebble move τ). Compute $\vec{\sigma} = \mathcal{TC}_i(\text{hist}_i)$. Let $\vec{\sigma} = \sigma_1, \ldots, \sigma_{|\text{hist}_i|}$. Send the tree code symbol $\sigma_{|\text{hist}_i|}$ to P^*.

II. P^* receives a symbol from P_i: We now describe the strategy of P^*. Upon receiving a symbol from P_i, P^* first computes the next pebble move $\tau \in \{0, 1, B, H\}$ and a recipient P_j in the following manner:

1. PROTOCOL PHASE: If flag = FALSE then perform the following steps:

   (a) **Determine global consistency point:** Compute the *global consistency point* β in the n-party protocol tree $\mathcal{T}$ and the local consistency points γ_k on every tree $\mathcal{T}_k$ in the following manner:

   - For every $k \in [n]$, do the following:
     - Let $\vec{\sigma}_k$ be the sequence of symbol received so far from P_k. Guess the current history $\widetilde{\text{hist}}_k$ of pebble moves of P_k that minimizes $\Delta(\mathcal{TC}_k(\widetilde{\text{hist}}_k), \vec{\sigma}_k)$.
     - Compute a corresponding guess $\widetilde{\alpha}_k = \text{GetPebble}(\widetilde{\text{hist}}_k)$ for P_k's current pebble position in $\mathcal{T}_k$.
     - Compute the least common ancestor A_k of $\widetilde{\alpha}_k$ and α_k^*, where α_k^* is the pebble position of P^* in $\mathcal{T}_k$.
   - Compute $(\beta, \{\gamma_k\}) = \text{GCP}(\{A_k\})$, where function GCP is defined in Figure 1.

   (b) **Determine recipient P_j:** Set $j = j'$ such that $P_{j'}$ is the label of node β in $\mathcal{T}$.

   (c) **Determine next pebble move:** Perform the following steps to determine the next pebble move τ:

- If $\gamma_j < \alpha_j^*$, then set $\tau = B$.
- Else, if $\gamma_j = A_j$ and $A_j = \alpha_j^* = \widetilde{\alpha}_j$, then do the following:
  - If P^* is the label of node α_j^* in $\mathcal{T}_j$, then set τ to be 0 (resp., 1), depending upon whether β is the left (resp., right) child of its parent node in $\mathcal{T}$.
  - Else, if P_j is the label of node α_j^*, then set $\tau = H$.
- Else, set $\tau = H$.

2. POLLING PHASE: If flag = TRUE, then set $j = \text{count}$, and determine the next pebble move τ as follows:

   (a) Compute a guess $\widetilde{\alpha}_j$ for P_j's current pebble position, as above.

   (b) Compute the least common ancestor A_j of $\widetilde{\alpha}_j$ and α_j^*.

   (c) Compute the global consistency point $(\beta, \{\gamma_k\})$, as above.

   (d) If $\gamma_j < \alpha_j^*$, then set $\tau = B$, and set $\tau = H$ otherwise.

3. Having computed τ and j as above, P^* performs the following steps:

   (a) **Move pebble:** Move own pebble in $\mathcal{T}_j$ to the node $\mathsf{SetPebble}(\alpha_j^*, \tau)$.

   (b) **Send next symbol:** Let hist_j^* denote the entire history of pebbles moves made by P^* (including the last pebble move τ) in its interaction with P_j. Compute $\vec{\sigma} = \mathcal{TC}_j(\mathsf{hist}_j^*)$. Let $\vec{\sigma} = \sigma_1, \dots, \sigma_{|\mathsf{hist}_j^*|}$. Send the tree code symbol $\sigma_{|\mathsf{hist}_j^*|}$ to P_j.

   (c) **Update variables:** Perform the following steps:
   - If count = n, set flag = $\overline{\mathsf{flag}}$ and reset count = 1. Else, set count = count + 1.
   - **Termination Check:** If Tcount = N, then output $(\mathsf{trans}_1, \dots, \mathsf{trans}_n)$ and stop. Else, set Tcount = Tcount + 2.

This completes the description of our compiler.

5. A LOWER BOUND FOR PER-PARTY ADVERSARIAL ERROR

Here we investigate the setting where the adversarial errors are restricted in their distribution. Specifically, we consider the case where the adversarial error rate *per party* is a constant. That is, for a protocol $\pi = (P_1, \dots, P_n)$, the adversary is allowed to corrupt a constant fraction of messages sent out by a party P_i (for every $i \in [n]$). In contrast, recall that our positive result presented above concerns the case where the total adversarial error-rate is $\Theta(\frac{1}{n})$. We note that when the adversary is constrained to only a constant fraction of errors in the portion of the communication emanating from each individual party, the adversary cannot trivially silence any single party. On the other hand, constant error rate per-party gives the adversary a *total* error rate of up to a constant, which is much more than what is handled by our positive result.

We prove a (black-box) negative result in this setting, ruling out a large class of error-resilient protocols. Namely, we

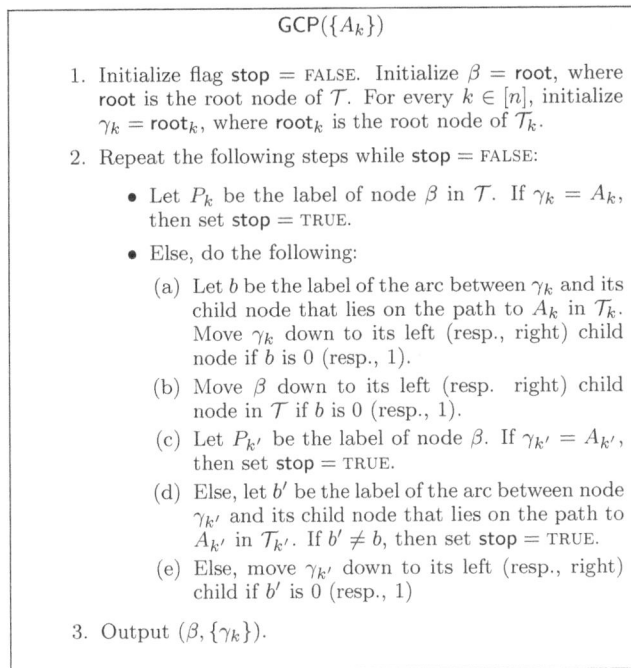

GCP($\{A_k\}$)

1. Initialize flag stop = FALSE. Initialize $\beta = \mathsf{root}$, where root is the root node of $\mathcal{T}$. For every $k \in [n]$, initialize $\gamma_k = \mathsf{root}_k$, where root_k is the root node of $\mathcal{T}_k$.

2. Repeat the following steps while stop = FALSE:
   - Let P_k be the label of node β in $\mathcal{T}$. If $\gamma_k = A_k$, then set stop = TRUE.
   - Else, do the following:
     (a) Let b be the label of the arc between γ_k and its child node that lies on the path to A_k in $\mathcal{T}_k$. Move γ_k down to its left (resp., right) child node if b is 0 (resp., 1).
     (b) Move β down to its left (resp. right) child node in $\mathcal{T}$ if b is 0 (resp., 1).
     (c) Let $P_{k'}$ be the label of node β. If $\gamma_{k'} = A_{k'}$, then set stop = TRUE.
     (d) Else, let b' be the label of the arc between node $\gamma_{k'}$ and its child node that lies on the path to $A_{k'}$ in $\mathcal{T}_{k'}$. If $b' \neq b$, then set stop = TRUE.
     (e) Else, move $\gamma_{k'}$ down to its left (resp., right) child if b' is 0 (resp., 1)

3. Output $(\beta, \{\gamma_k\})$.

Figure 1: Global Consistency Point

show that there does not exist a (black-box) error-resilient multi-party protocol compiler with a *static* speaking order and a *poly*(n) communication overhead that tolerates constant rate per-party adversarial error. Thus, not only do we rule out error-resilience compilers that incur a constant overhead in communication, but rather compilers with any polynomial overhead in communication. Naturally, this raises the question of what can be achieved by protocols allowing adaptive speaking orders, like our protocol in Section 4.2, where who speaks next can be a function of the content of the transmissions so far. Extending our lower bound to such protocols or obtaining a contrasting positive result is an intriguing open question for future work. We note that a similar gap in understanding between adaptive and nonadaptive protocols arises in the analysis of the achievable constant error rate in the two party setting in the work of Braverman and Rao [BR11]. This was recently resolved in the works of [GHS14, AGS13].

In what follows, we consider *black-box* simulation of protocols. That is, we assume that the error-resilient protocols makes black-box use of the next message functions of each party in the underlying protocol. See [CPT13] for further discussion on this. Informally stated, we will establish the following:

THEOREM 6. *There exists an n-party protocol π that cannot be black-box simulated by any error-resilient protocol with arbitrary polynomial communication complexity and static speaking order in the presence of constant rate per-party adversarial errors.*

5.1 The protocol π

This is an n-party variant of the ping-pong protocol considered in [CPT13]. The input of each party P_i is an index x_i specifying a hash function $H_{x_i} : \{0,1\}^* \to \{0,1\}^\ell$.

The Protocol..

Protocol π consists of m rounds, where in every round, each party P_i will transmit ℓ bits to party $P_{(i+1) \bmod n}$. Concretely, in the first round, party P_1 sends $a_{1,1} := H_{x_1}(\emptyset)$ to party P_2, which is followed by P_2 sending $a_{1,2} := H_{x_2}(a_{1,1})$ to party P_3, and so on. More generally, in round r, each party P_i sends $a_{r,i} := H_{x_i}(a_{1,i-1}, a_{2,i-1}, \ldots, a_{r,i-1})$ to party $P_{(i+1) \bmod n}$.

At the end of m rounds, each party will output the portion of the transcript corresponding to their own sent and received messages.

5.2 Impossibility of Simulating π

THEOREM 7. *Let κ be the security parameter, and let $\epsilon > 0$ and $k \in \mathbb{N}$ be constants. Let Comp be any black-box compiler that simulates an arbitrary $n = \mathsf{poly}(\kappa)$-party protocol in the presence of per-party adversarial error-rate of ϵ with a communication overhead of n^k. Then, for $m = \omega(1)$ and $\ell = \omega(\log \kappa)$, Comp fails to simulate π, except with probability negligible in κ.*

Towards proving Theorem 7, suppose for contradiction that there exists a black-box compiler Comp that simulates protocol π (as described above) for the parameters as stated above. Let $\tilde{\pi}$ denote an error-resilient version of π generated by Comp that makes black-box use of π (i.e., $\tilde{\pi}$ has oracle access to the next-message function of the parties in π). We let $T := CC(\pi) = \ell n m$ and $\tilde{T} := CC(\tilde{\pi})$. We suppose that $\tilde{T} = \mathcal{O}(n^k T)$ for some fixed constant k, and that $\tilde{\pi}$ is resilient to a constant error rate of $\epsilon > 0$ per party. We further assume that every execution of $\tilde{\pi}$ contains exactly $\tilde{T}$ bits and that $\tilde{\pi}$ has a *static* speaking order that is independent of the inputs of the parties (and the actual messages of $\tilde{\pi}$). For each i, we let $\tilde{T}_i$ denote the number of bits transmitted by P_i during $\tilde{\pi}$.

Intuition. Our strategy is as follows. First, we prove that for every $i \in [n]$, $\tilde{T}_i = \Omega(T_i)$ (up to low probability events). Second, we note that the n values $\{\tilde{T}_i\}$ only differ from each other by a $\mathsf{poly}(n)$ ratio. This follows from the fact that there is a polynomial (n^k) overall communication blowup. We will use this to define a subset B containing a suitable constant number of parties whose corresponding $\tilde{T}_i$ values are very close to each other (within a constant multiplicative factor close to 1). We will then divide an execution of $\tilde{\pi}$ into a (smaller) constant number of segments that each contain the same number of transmissions emanating from these parties in B. We will argue that in such segment, there are many parties in B that the adversary could potentially corrupt for the entire segment without violating its error constraints. This will allow the adversary to corrupt a distinct party in B in each segment. We finally show that such an adversary can obstruct progress of the simulation of the transcript of π. Intuitively, if some party is effectively impersonated during a segment, then no new oracle queries will be made corresponding to the true input of that party during that segment, and this will obstruct progress.

6. REFERENCES

[AGS13] Shweta Agrawal, Ran Gelles, and Amit Sahai. Adaptive protocols for interactive communication. *CoRR*, abs/1312.4182, 2013.

[BE14] Mark Braverman and Klim Efremenko. List and unique coding for interactive communication in the presence of adversarial noise. In *FOCS*, 2014.

[BK12] Zvika Brakerski and Yael Tauman Kalai. Efficient interactive coding against adversarial noise. In *FOCS*, pages 160–166, 2012.

[BN13] Zvika Brakerski and Moni Naor. Fast algorithms for interactive coding. In *SODA*, pages 443–456, 2013.

[BR11] Mark Braverman and Anup Rao. Towards coding for maximum errors in interactive communication. In *STOC*, pages 159–166, 2011.

[Bra12] Mark Braverman. Towards deterministic tree code constructions. In *ITCS*, pages 161–167, 2012.

[CPT13] Kai-Min Chung, Rafael Pass, and Siddartha Telang. Knowledge-preserving interactive coding. In *FOCS*, 2013.

[GH14] Mohsen Ghaffari and Bernhard Haeupler. Optimal error rates for interactive coding ii: Efficiency and list decoding. In *FOCS*, 2014.

[GHS14] Mohsen Ghaffari, Bernhard Haeupler, and Madhu Sudan. Optimal error rates for interactive coding i: Adaptivity and other settings. In *STOC*, 2014.

[GMS11] Ran Gelles, Ankur Moitra, and Amit Sahai. Efficient and explicit coding for interactive communication. In *FOCS*, pages 768–777, 2011.

[Hae14] Bernhard Haeupler. Interactive channel capacity revisited. In *FOCS*, 2014.

[Hoz14] William Hoza. personal communication, 2014.

[KR13] Gillat Kol and Ran Raz. Interactive channel capacity. In *STOC*, pages 715–724, 2013.

[MS13] Cristopher Moore and Leonard J. Schulman. Tree codes and a conjecture on exponential sums. *CoRR*, abs/1308.6007, 2013.

[RS94] Sridhar Rajagopalan and Leonard J. Schulman. A coding theorem for distributed computation. In *STOC*, pages 790–799, 1994.

[Sch92] Leonard J. Schulman. Communication on noisy channels: A coding theorem for computation. In *FOCS*, pages 724–733, 1992.

[Sch93] Leonard J. Schulman. Deterministic coding for interactive communication. In *STOC*, pages 747–756, 1993.

[Sch96] Leonard J. Schulman. Coding for interactive communication. *IEEE Transactions on Information Theory*, 42(6):1745–1756, 1996.

[Sha48] Claude E. Shannon. A mathematical theory of communication. *The Bell System Technical Journal*, 27:379–423, 623–656, 1948.

Maximal Noise in Interactive Communication over Erasure Channels and Channels with Feedback

Klim Efremenko
UC Berkeley*
klimefrem@gmail.com

Ran Gelles
Princeton University†
rgelles@cs.princeton.edu

Bernhard Haeupler
Carnegie Mellon University
haeupler@cs.cmu.edu

ABSTRACT

We provide tight upper and lower bounds on the noise resilience of interactive communication over noisy channels with *feedback*. In this setting, we show that the maximal fraction of noise that any robust protocol can resist is $1/3$. Additionally, we provide a simple and efficient robust protocol that succeeds as long as the fraction of noise is at most $1/3 - \varepsilon$. Surprisingly, both bounds hold regardless of whether the parties send bits or symbols from an arbitrarily large alphabet.

We also consider interactive communication over *erasure* channels. We provide a protocol that matches the optimal tolerable erasure rate of $1/2 - \varepsilon$ of previous protocols (Franklin et al., CRYPTO '13) but operates in a much simpler and more efficient way. Our protocol works with an alphabet of size 4, in contrast to prior protocols in which the alphabet size grows as $\varepsilon \to 0$. Building on the above algorithm with a *fixed* alphabet size, we are able to devise a protocol for *binary* erasure channels that tolerates erasure rates of up to $1/3 - \varepsilon$.

Categories and Subject Descriptors

E.4 [**Data**]: Coding and Information Theory; F.1.2 [**Theory of Computation**]: Modes of Computation—*Interactive and reactive computation*

General Terms

Algorithms, Theory

Keywords

Interactive communication; coding; adversarial noise; channels with feedback; erasure channels

---

*Work done while at Univ. of Chicago.
†Work done while a student at UCLA.

1. INTRODUCTION

In the interactive communication setting, Alice and Bob are given inputs x and y respectively, and are required to compute and output some function $f(x, y)$ of their joint inputs. To this end, they exchange messages over a channel that may be noisy: up to an ε-fraction of the transmitted bits may get flipped during the communication. Due to the noise, there is a need for error correction and sophisticated coding schemes that will allow the parties to successfully conduct the computation, yet keep the communication complexity small, ideally at most linear in the communication complexity of computing the same function over a noiseless channel (hereinafter, we say that such a scheme has a *constant rate*).

Coding schemes for interactive communication have been extensively explored, starting with the pioneering work of Schulman [Sch92, Sch93, Sch96] who gave the first constant rate scheme to resist up to a $1/240$-fraction of bit flips. Almost two decades later, Braverman and Rao [BR11] showed a constant rate coding scheme that successfully computes any function, as long as the fraction of corrupted transmissions is at most $1/4 - \varepsilon$. Furthermore, they show that it is impossible to resist noise of $1/4$ or more, for a large and natural class of *robust* protocols. In robust protocols both parties are guaranteed to agree whose turn it is to speak at each round, regardless of the noise, e.g., when their order of speaking is a fixed function of the round number (see definition in Section 2 below). It should be noted that the above result of $1/4 - \varepsilon$ applies only when the parties send symbols from a large alphabet, whose size is growing as ε goes to zero. When the parties are restricted to sending bits, the coding scheme of Braverman and Rao [BR11] tolerates up to a $(1/8 - \varepsilon)$-fraction of bit flips. The question of determining the maximal tolerable noise for binary channels is still open.

In this paper we examine different types of communication channels and noise. Specifically, we consider *channels with feedback* and *erasure channels*. In the former it is assumed that after each transmission, the sender learns the (possibly corrupted) symbol received by the other side, i.e., there is a noiseless feedback. In the erasure channel case, the noise can turn any symbol into an "erasure" (denoted $\perp$), but it cannot alter the transmission into a different valid symbol. Both erasure channels and channels with feedback have been studied in the classical one-way setting [Sha48, Ber64] albeit typically more from a perspective of optimizing communication rates.

For each of these channels we examine the maximal tolerable noise for interactive communication, both when the parties are restricted to sending bits and in the general case of a larger alphabet.

1.1 Our Results

Interactive communication over channels with feedback. We completely solve the question of the maximal tolerable noise for robust interactive protocols over channels with feedback, both for the binary alphabet and the large alphabet case. We note that while in the standard noisy model the parties in a robust protocol must have a fixed order of speaking which depends only on the round of the protocol [BR11], this is not the case for noisy channels with feedback. Indeed, due to the feedback both parties know the symbols received at the other side and may determine the next party to speak according to their joint view. While this decision may depend on the noise, the parties maintain a consensus regarding the next party to speak. We can therefore refine the class of robust protocols into ones in which the order of speaking is fixed (i.e., a function of the round number) and ones in which the order is arbitrary (i.e., possibly dependent on the noise). We stress that these two subsets of protocols are still robust, and refer the reader to [GHS14, AGS13] for a discussion on *adaptive* (non-robust) protocols.

As a helpful warm-up we first consider protocols with a fixed order of speaking. When the parties are allowed to send symbols from a large alphabet, we show for any $\varepsilon > 0$ an efficient coding scheme with a constant rate that resists a noise rate of up to $1/4 - \varepsilon$. Although the same bounds were already given by [BR11, GH14] for standard noisy channels, our protocol is considerably simpler while also being computationally efficient. Moreover, while in other schemes the size of the alphabet increases as $\varepsilon \to 0$, in our protocol a *ternary* alphabet suffices. The main idea is the following: the parties exchange messages as in the noiseless protocol, and use the feedback to verify that the messages were received intact. In case of a corrupted transmission, the parties transmit a special symbol '$\leftarrow$' that instructs both parties to rewind the protocol to the step before the corrupted transmission. Building on the above coding scheme we provide for any $\varepsilon > 0$ a simple and efficient *binary* protocol that resists up to a $(1/6 - \varepsilon)$-fraction of bit flips.

THEOREM 1.1. *For any $\varepsilon > 0$ and any function $f(x,y)$ there exists an efficient robust coding scheme with a fixed order of speaking and a constant rate that correctly computes $f(x,y)$ for each of the following settings: (i) over a channel with feedback with ternary alphabet, assuming at most a $(1/4 - \varepsilon)$-fraction of the symbols are corrupted, (ii) over a binary channel with feedback, assuming at most a $(1/6 - \varepsilon)$-fraction of the bits are corrupted*

Additionally, we prove that the above bounds of 1/4 and 1/6 are tight for the general feedback channel, and the binary feedback channel, respectively. The impossibility result for the binary case has a particular interesting implication: since feedback channels are more powerful than standard noisy channels, this impossibility applies also to robust protocols over standard binary noisy channels (i.e., without a feedback), narrowing the maximal tolerable noise for this setting to the region $[1/8, 1/6]$.

THEOREM 1.2. *There exists a function $f(x,y)$, such that any robust binary interactive protocol, succeeds in computing $f(x,y)$ with probability at most 1/2 assuming a 1/6-fraction of bit-flips.*

Next, we consider robust protocols with arbitrary (noise-dependent) order of speaking. In this case the simple idea

presented above immediately gives a higher noise-resilience of 1/3. The reason for this discrepancy in the bounds when we allow the order of speaking to be arbitrary stems from the following issue. When a transmission is corrupted, the *sender* is aware of this event and it sends a rewind symbol '$\leftarrow$' on the next time it has the right to speaks. However, when the order of speaking is fixed (say, alternating), the parties "lose" one slot: while we would like the sender to repeat the transmission that was corrupted, the *receiver* is the next party to speak after the round where the '$\leftarrow$' symbol is sent. If we allow the order of speaking to be arbitrary, we can avoid this excessive round and thus improve the noise resilience.

Translating the above idea to the binary case gives a protocol that resists a noise rate of $1/5 - \varepsilon$. However we can do better—we devise a protocol that resists noise rates up to $1/3 - \varepsilon$. Here the parties send messages of varying length, consisting of the original information followed by a varying amount of *confirmation bits*. The confirmation bits indicate whether or not the information was corrupted by the adversary. This practically forces the adversary to spend more of its corruption budget per message, or otherwise the receiving party learns about the corruption and simply ignores the message.

THEOREM 1.3. *For any $\varepsilon > 0$ and any function $f(x,y)$ there exists an efficient robust coding scheme with constant rate that correctly computes $f(x,y)$ over a binary channel with feedback assuming at most a $(1/3 - \varepsilon)$-fraction of the bits are corrupted.*

It is interesting to mention that in contrast to all the previous settings and in contrast to the case of standard (unidirectional) error correction, the size of the alphabet (binary or large) makes no difference to the noise resilience of this setting. We conclude this part by providing a matching impossibility bound of 1/3 that applies to any alphabet size, and in particular to the binary case.

THEOREM 1.4. *There exists a function $f(x,y)$, such that any robust interactive protocol over a channel with feedback (with any alphabet) that computes $f(x,y)$, succeeds with probability at most 1/2 if a 1/3-fraction of the transmissions are corrupted.*

Interactive communication over erasure channels. In [FGOS13] it was shown that the maximal noise over erasure channels when a large alphabet can be used is $1/2 - \varepsilon$. This is trivially tight for protocols with a fixed order by completely erasing all the symbols sent by the party that speaks less. [In fact, this applies to any *robust* protocol—we show that robust protocols over erasure channels must have a fixed order of speaking!] When the parties are restricted to using a binary alphabet, it is possible to resist an erasure rate of $1/4 - \varepsilon$ [FGOS13, BR11]. The main drawback of these coding schemes is that they are not computationally efficient for the case of adversarial noise, and can take exponential time to complete in the worst case.

Here we suggest a coding scheme with a constant rate that can tolerate an erasure rate of up to $1/2 - \varepsilon$, yet it is computationally efficient and very simple to implement. Moreover, our "large" alphabet is of size 6, regardless of ε.

THEOREM 1.5. *For any $\varepsilon > 0$ and any function $f(x,y)$ there exists an efficient, robust coding scheme with constant rate that correctly computes $f(x,y)$ over an erasure channel*

channel type	alphabet	order of speaking	lower bound	upper bound
feedback	ternary & large	fixed	1/4	1/4
feedback	binary	fixed	1/6	1/6
feedback	binary & large	arbitrary	1/3	1/3
erasure	4-ary & large	fixed	1/2	1/2
erasure	binary	fixed	1/3	??

Table 1: A summary of the lower (achievability) and upper (impossibility) bounds for the maximum tolerable error rate for all settings considered in this paper.

with a 6-ary alphabet, assuming at most a $(1/2 - \varepsilon)$-fraction of the bits are corrupted.

Interestingly, the small and fixed alphabet size serves as a stepping stone in devising a protocol that works for *binary* erasure channels. Encoding each symbol of the 6-ary alphabet into a binary string yields a protocol that resists erasures fraction of up to $3/10 - \varepsilon$. Yet, we are able to optimize the above simulation and reduce the size of the alphabet to only 4 symbols. This allows us to encode each symbol in the alphabet using a binary code with a very high relative distance, and obtain a protocol that tolerates a noise rate of $1/3 - \varepsilon$. This improves over the more natural and previously best known bound of $1/4 - \varepsilon$.

THEOREM 1.6. *For any $\varepsilon > 0$ and any function $f(x, y)$ there exists an efficient, robust coding scheme with constant rate that correctly computes $f(x, y)$ over a binary erasure channel, assuming at most a $(1/3 - \varepsilon)$-fraction of the bits are corrupted.*

The only impossibility bound we are aware of is again the trivial bound of 1/2 [FGOS13, GH14] which applies even to larger alphabets. We leave determining the optimal erasure rate for coding schemes over binary erasure channels as an interesting open question.

We summarize our results in Table 1.

1.2 Other Related Work

Maximal noise in interactive communication. As mentioned above, the question of interactive communication over a noisy channel was initiated by Schulman [Sch92, Sch93, Sch96] who mainly focused on the case of random bit flips, but also showed that his scheme resists an adversarial noise rate of up to 1/240. Braverman and Rao [BR11] proved that 1/4 is a tight bound on the noise (for large alphabets), and Braverman and Efremenko [BE14] gave a refinement of this bound, looking at the noise rate separately at each direction of the channel (i.e., from Alice to Bob and from Bob to Alice). For each pair of noise rates, they determine whether or not a coding scheme with a constant rate exists. Another line of work improved the efficiency of coding schemes for the interactive setting, either for random noise [GMS11, GMS14], or for adversarial noise [BK12, BN13, GH14].

Protocols in the above works are all robust. The discussion about non-robust or *adaptive* protocols was initiated by Ghaffari, Haeupler and Sudan [GHS14, GH14] and concurrently by Agrawal, Gelles and Sahai [AGS13], giving various notions of adaptive protocols and analyzing their noise resilience. Both the adaptive notion of [GHS14, GH14] and of [AGS13] are capable of resisting a higher amount of noise

than the maximal 1/4 allowed for robust protocols. Specifically, a tight bound of 2/7 was shown in [GHS14, GH14] for protocols of fixed length; when the length of the protocol may adaptively change as well, a coding scheme that achieves a noise rate of 1/3 is given in [AGS13], yet that scheme does not have a constant rate.

Interactive communication over channels with feedback and erasure channels. To the best of our knowledge, no prior work considers the maximal noise of interactive communication over channels with feedback. Yet, within this setting, the maximal *rate* of coding schemes, i.e., the minimal communication complexity as a function of the error rate, was considered by [Pan13, GH15] (the rate of coding schemes in the standard noisy channel setting was considered by [KR13, Hae14]).

For erasure channels, a tight bound of 1/2 on the erasure rate of robust protocols was given in [FGOS13]. For the case of adaptive protocols, [AGS13] provided a coding scheme with a constant rate that resists a relative erasure rate of up to $1 - \varepsilon$ in a setting that allows parties to remain silent in an adaptive way.

2. PRELIMINARIES

We begin by setting some notations and definitions we use throughout. We sometimes refer to a bitstring $a \in \{0, 1\}^n$ as an array $a[0], \ldots, a[n-1]$. $a \circ b$ denotes the concatenation of the strings a and b. $\mathsf{prefix}_k(a)$ denotes the first k characters in a string a, and $\mathsf{suffix}_k(a)$ denotes the last k characters in a. For two strings a, b of the same length n, their Hamming distance $d(a, b)$ is the number of indices $0 \le i \le n-1$ for which $a[i] \ne b[i]$.

DEFINITION 2.1. *A feedback channel is a channel $\mathsf{CH} : \Sigma \to \Sigma$ in which at any instantiation noise can alter any input symbol $\sigma \in \Sigma$ into any output $\sigma' \in \Sigma$. The sender is assumed to learn the (possibly corrupt) output σ' via a noiseless feedback channel.*

An erasure channel is a channel $\mathsf{CH} : \Sigma \to \Sigma \cup \{\bot\}$ in which the channel's noise is restricted into changing the input symbol into an erasure symbol $\bot$.

For both types of channels, the noise rate is defined as the fraction of corrupted transmissions out of all the channel instantiations.

An interactive protocol π over a channel CH, is a pair of algorithm π_{Alice}, π_{Bob} that determine the next message to be communicated, given the input and the transcript so far. The communicated message is assumed to be a single symbol from the channel's alphabet Σ. In all our protocols, $|\Sigma| = O(1)$. The protocol runs for $|\pi|$ rounds after which each party computes an output as a function of its input and the transcript that party sees. The Protocol is said to compute a function $f(x,y)$ if for any pair of inputs x, y, both parties output $f(x,y)$. A coding scheme Π is said to *simulate* π if for any pair of inputs x, y, the parties output $\pi(x,y)$—the transcript of running π on input (x,y) over a noiseless channel

We further assume that at every given round only one party sends a message. Protocols in which the identity of the sender of each round is well defined and agreed upon both parties are called robust.

DEFINITION 2.2. *We say that an interactive protocol π is* robust ([BR11]) *if,*
(1) for all inputs, the protocol runs for n rounds; (2) at any round, and given any possible noise, the parties are in agreement regarding the next party to speak.

A fixed order *protocol is one in which condition (2) above is replaced with the following*
(2') there exist some function $g : \mathbb{N} \to \{Alice, Bob\}$ such that at any round i, the party that speaks is determined by $g(i)$, specifically, it is independent of the noise.

Note that any fixed-order protocol is robust, but it is possible that a robust protocol will not have a fixed order. In that case we say that the robust protocol has an *arbitrary* or *noise dependent* order of speaking.

In the following we show how to take any binary alternating (noiseless) protocol, and simulate it over a noisy channel. Note that for any function f there exists a binary alternating (noiseless) protocol π, such that the communication of π is linear in the communication complexity of f, that is, $\mathrm{CC}(\pi) = O(\mathrm{CC}(f))$. Hence, simulating the above π with communication $O(\mathrm{CC}(\pi))$ has a constant rate, since its communication is linear in $\mathrm{CC}(f)$.

3. FEEDBACK CHANNELS WITH A LARGE ALPHABET: UPPER AND LOWER BOUNDS

3.1 Protocols with a fixed order of speaking

Let us consider simulation protocols in which the order of speaking is fixed and independent of the inputs the parties hold, and the noise injected by the adversarial channel. We show that $1/4$ is a tight bound on the tolerable noise in this case. The bound is the same as in the case of standard noisy channels (without feedback) [BR11]. We begin with the upper bound, by showing a protocol that correctly simulates π assuming noise level of $1/4-\varepsilon$. It is interesting to note that the alphabet used by the simulation protocol is independent of ε (cf. [BR11, FGOS13, GH14, BE14]); specifically, we use a *ternary alphabet*. In addition the simulation is deterministic and (computationally) efficient, given black-box access to π.

THEOREM 3.1. *For any alternating noiseless binary protocol π of length n, and for any $\varepsilon > 0$, there exists an efficient, deterministic, robust simulation of π over a feedback channel using an alphabet of size 3 and a fixed order of speaking, that takes $O_\varepsilon(n)$ rounds and succeeds assuming a maximal noise rate of $1/4 - \varepsilon$.*

PROOF. We use a ternary alphabet $\Sigma = \{0, 1, \leftarrow\}$. The simulation works in alternating rounds where the parties run π, and verify via the feedback that any transmitted bit is correctly received at the other side. Specifically, if the received symbol is either a 0 or a 1 the party considers

this transmission as the next message of π, and extends the simulated transcript T accordingly. If the received symbol is $\leftarrow$, the party rewinds three rounds of π, that is, the party deletes the last four undeleted symbols of T.[1] Each party, using the feedback, is capable of seeing whether the transcript T held by the other side contains any errors, and if so, it sends multiple $\leftarrow$ symbols until the corrupted suffix is removed. The above is repeated $N = n/4\varepsilon$ times (where $n = |\pi|$), and at the end the parties output T. The protocol is formalized in Algorithm 1.

Algorithm 1 A fixed-order simulation for channels with feedback

Input: a binary alternating protocol π of length n, a noise parameter $\varepsilon > 0$, an input value x.

Assume a fixed alternating order of speaking: Alice is the sender on odd i's, and Bob is the sender on even i's.

1: Set $N = \lceil n/4\varepsilon \rceil$, initialize $T \leftarrow \emptyset$; $T^F \leftarrow \emptyset$.
    ▷ T is the simulated transcript as viewed by the party. We can split T into two substrings corresponding to alternating indices: T^S are the sent characters, and T^R the received characters. Let T^F be the characters received by the other side (as learned via the feedback channel).

2: **for** $i = 1$ to N **do**
3:    **if** $T^F = T^S$ **then**
         ▷ run one step of π, given the transcript so far is T
4:      $T \leftarrow T \circ \pi(x \mid T)$
5:      $T^F \leftarrow T^F \circ \langle$symbol recorded at the other side$\rangle$
6:    **else**
7:      if sender:
8:        send a '$\leftarrow$' symbol
9:        $T \leftarrow T \circ$ '$\leftarrow$'
10:       $T^F \leftarrow T^F \circ \langle$symbol recorded at the other side$\rangle$.
11:      if receiver:
12:        extend T according to incoming symbol.

13:    **if** $\mathsf{suffix}_1(T^R) =$ '$\leftarrow$' or $\mathsf{suffix}_1(T^F) =$ '$\leftarrow$' **then**
14:      $T \leftarrow \mathsf{prefix}_{|T|-4}(T)$
         (also delete the corresponding transmissions in T^F)
15: Output T

Note that due to the alternating nature of the simulation, each corruption causes four rounds in which T doesn't extend: (1) the corrupted slot; (2) the other party talks; (3) sending a $\leftarrow$ symbol; (4) the other party talks. After step (4) the simulated transcript T is exactly the same as it was before (1). Also note that consecutive errors (targeting the same party[2]) simply increase the amount of $\leftarrow$ symbols the sender should send, so that each additional corruption extends the recovery process by at most another four rounds. Also note that corrupting a bit into a $\leftarrow$ has a similar effect: after four rounds, T is back to what it was before the corruption: (1) the corrupted slot; (2-4) re-simulating π after three bits of T were deleted.

Therefore, with $1/4-\varepsilon$ noise, we have at most $4 \cdot (1/4 - \varepsilon)N = N(1 - 4\varepsilon)$ rounds that are used to recover from errors and do not advance T. Yet, during the rest $4\varepsilon N = n$ rounds T extends correctly and the simulation succeeds to output the entire transcript of π. $\square$

---

[1] The four symbols removed from T are the received '$\leftarrow$' symbol plus three simulated rounds of π.
[2] consecutive corruptions targeting the other party will be corrected without causing any further delay.

Next we prove it is impossible to tolerate noise rates above 1/4.

THEOREM 3.2. *Any protocol with a fixed order of speaking that computes the identity function $f(x,y) = (x,y)$, succeeds with probability at most $1/2$ over a feedback channel assuming $1/4$ of the transmission are corrupted.*

PROOF. The proof is similar to the case of interactive communication over of a standard noisy channel (without feedback) [BR11]. Assume that Alice speaks for R rounds and without loss of generality assume $R \leq N/2$ (note that since the protocol has a fixed order of speaking, the party that speaks in less than half the rounds is independent of the input and noise, and is well defined at the beginning of the simulation). Define EXP0 to be an instance in which Alice holds the input $x = 0$, and we corrupt the first $R/2$ rounds in which Alice talks so that they are the same as what Alice would have sent had she held the input $x = 1$. Define EXP1 to be an instance in which Alice holds the input $x = 1$, and we corrupt the last $R/2$ rounds in which Alice talks so that they are the same as what Alice sends during the same rounds in EXP0.

Note that from Bob's point of view (including his feedback) EXP0 and EXP1 are indistinguishable, thus Bob cannot output the correct x with probability higher than $1/2$. In each experiment we corrupt only half of Alice's slots, thus the total noise is at most $R/2 \leq N/4$. $\square$

3.2 Protocols with an arbitrary order

It is rather clear that the protocol of Theorem 3.1 "wastes" one round (per corruption) only due to the fixed-order of speaking: when a corruption is noticed and a $\leftarrow$ symbol is sent, the parties would have liked to rewind only *two* rounds of π, exactly back to beginning of the round that was corrupted. However, this will change the order of speaking, since that round belongs to the same party that sends the $\leftarrow$ symbol. This suggests that if we lift the requirement of a fixed-order simulation, and allow the protocol to adapt the order of speaking, the simulation will resist up to a fraction $1/3$ of noise. In the following we prove that $1/3$ is a tight bound on the noise for this case.

We remark that although the protocol is adaptive in the sense that the order of speaking may change due to the noise, both parties are always in consensus regarding who is the next party to speak. Indeed, using the feedback channel, both parties learn the symbols *received* at both sides. Such a joint view can uniquely determine the next party to speak, thus, the protocol is robust (Definition 2.2).

THEOREM 3.3. *For any alternating noiseless binary protocol π of length n, and for any $\varepsilon > 0$, there exists an efficient, deterministic, robust simulation of π over a feedback channel using an alphabet of size 3, that takes $O_\varepsilon(n)$ rounds and succeeds assuming a maximal noise rate of $1/3 - \varepsilon$.*

PROOF. We use a ternary alphabet $\Sigma = \{0, 1, \leftarrow\}$. The simulation protocol is similar to Algorithm 1: each party maintains a simulated transcript T, and uses the feedback to verify that the other party holds a correct simulated transcript. As long as there is no noise in the simulated transcript, the parties continue to simulate the next step of π given that the transcript so far is T. Otherwise, the party that notices a corruption sends a $\leftarrow$ symbol at the next round assigned to that party. When a $\leftarrow$ symbol is received,

the party rewinds π by *two* rounds, that is, the party deletes the last three symbols of T.[3] The next party to speak is determined by $\pi(x \mid T^R, T^F)$; note that $(T^F, T^R)_{\text{Alice}} = (T^R, T^F)_{\text{Bob}}$, thus the parties progress according to the same view and are in-synch at all times. The above is repeated $N = n/3\varepsilon$ times (where $n = |\pi|$), and at the end the parties output T.

It is easy to verify that each corruption causes at most three recovery rounds, after which T is restored to its state prior to the corruption: (1) the corrupted slot; (2) the other party talks; (3) sending a $\leftarrow$ symbol; After step (3) the simulated transcript T is exactly the same as it was before (1), and the party that spoke at (1) has the right to speak again. Again, note that consecutive errors simply increase the amount of $\leftarrow$ symbols the sender should send, so that each additional corruption extends the recovery process by at most another three rounds. Also note that corrupting a bit into a $\leftarrow$ has a similar effect: after three rounds, T is back to what it was before the corruption: (1) the corrupted slot; (2–3) re-simulating the two bits of T that were deleted.

When the noise level is bounded by $1/3 - \varepsilon$, we have at most $3 \cdot (1/3 - \varepsilon)N = N(1 - 3\varepsilon)$ rounds that are used to recover from errors and do not advance T; yet, during the rest $3\varepsilon N = n$ rounds T extends correctly. Therefore, at the end of the simulation the parties output a transcript of π with a correct prefix of length at least n, thus they successfully simulate π. $\square$

THEOREM 3.4. *Any robust protocol that computes the identity function $f(x,y) = (x,y)$ over a feedback channel with an error rate of $1/3$, succeeds with probability at most $1/2$.*

PROOF. The proof is based on ideas from [GHS14] for proving a lower bound on the noise tolerable by adaptive protocols over a standard noisy channel (without feedback).

Consider a protocol of length N, and suppose that on inputs $x = y = 0$, Bob is the party that speaks less during the first $2N/3$ rounds of the protocol. Recall that due to the feedback, we can assume the parties are always in consensus regarding the party to speak on the next round, so that at every round only a single party talks; thus Bob talks at most $N/3$ times during the first $2N/3$ rounds. Consider the following experiment EXP1 in which $x = 0, y = 1$ however we corrupt Bob's messages during the first $2N/3$ rounds so that they are the same as Bob's messages given $y = 0$. From Alice's point of view, the case where Bob holds $y = 0$ and the case where $y = 1$ but all his messages are corrupted to be as if he had $y = 0$, are equivalent. Therefore, with the consensus assumption, in both cases Bob's talking slots are exactly the same, and this strategy corrupts at most $N/3$ messages.

Now consider the following experiment EXP0 in which $x = y = 0$, however, during the last $N/3$ rounds of the protocol we corrupt all Bob's messages to be the same as what he sends in EXP1 during the same rounds. Note that due to the adaptiveness of the order of speaking in the protocol, it may be that Bob talks in *all* these $N/3$ rounds, but corrupting all of them is still within the corruption budget.

Finally, in both EXP0 and EXP1 Alice's view (messages sent, received and feedback) is the same, implying she cannot output the correct answer with probability higher than $1/2$. $\square$

---

[3] The three symbols removed from T are the received '$\leftarrow$' symbol plus two rounds of π.

4. FEEDBACK CHANNELS WITH A BINARY ALPHABET: UPPER AND LOWER BOUNDS

We now turn to examine the case of feedback channels with a binary alphabet. We begin (Section 4.1) with the case that the robust simulation has a fixed order of speaking, and show a tight bound of 1/6 on the noise. We then relax the fixed-order requirement (Section 4.2) and show that 1/3 is a tight bound on the noise in this case. It is rather surprising that simulations with binary alphabet reach the same noise tolerance of 1/3 as simulations with large alphabet.

4.1 Protocols with a fixed order of speaking

THEOREM 4.1. *For any alternating noiseless binary protocol π of length n, and for any $\varepsilon > 0$, there exists an efficient, deterministic, robust simulation of π over a feedback channel with a binary alphabet and a fixed order of speaking, that takes $O_\varepsilon(n)$ rounds and succeeds assuming a maximal noise rate of $1/6 - \varepsilon$.*

PROOF. In Algorithm 1 we used a special symbol $\leftarrow$ to signal that a transmission was corrupted and instruct the simulation to rewind. When the alphabet is binary such a symbol can not be used directly, but we can code it into a binary string, e.g., "00". To this end, we first need to make sure that the simulation does not communicate 00 unless a transmission got corrupted. However, recall that while no corruption is detected, Algorithm 1 simply communicates the transcript of the protocol π it simulates. We therefore we need to preprocess π so that no party sends two consecutive zeros (cf. [GH15]). This can easily be done by padding each two consecutive rounds in π by two void rounds where each party sends a '1' (two rounds are needed to keep the padded protocol alternating). Denote with π' the preprocessed protocol, and note that $|\pi'| = 2|\pi|$.

We now simulate π' in a manner similar to Algorithm 1. The parties communicate in alternating rounds where at each round they send the next bit defined by π' according to the current simulated transcript T. In case that a corruption is detected via the feedback, the sender sends the string 00 to indicate a rewind request. Due the alternating nature of the simulation, it takes three rounds to complete communicating the rewind request. Whenever a party receives a 00 rewind command, both parties delete the last 6 bits of T (recall that both parties know the received symbols: one directly and the other via the feedback). Observe that we must remove an even number of bits so that the alternating order of speaking is maintained. Thus, although the erroneous bit is only 5 rounds prior to receiving the $\leftarrow$ command, we rewind six rounds, see Figure 1. The simulation is performed for $N = |\pi'|/6\varepsilon = O(|\pi|)$ rounds at the end of which both parties output T.

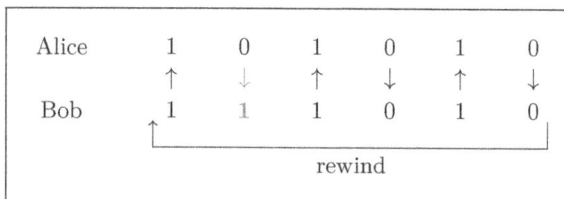

Figure 1: Illustration of rewinding the protocol after the first bit sent by Alice is corrupted.

The analysis is similar to the proof of Theorem 3.1, and we thus omit here the full details. The only difference is that each corruption takes at most six rounds to recover. This implies a maximal tolerable noise level of $1/6 - \varepsilon$. □

Even more interesting is the fact that the above protocol is the best possible, in terms of the maximal tolerable noise. Indeed, we show that in this setting, it is impossible to tolerate noise levels of 1/6 or higher.

THEOREM 4.2. *Any binary protocol with a fixed order of speaking that computes the identity function $f(x, y) = (x, y)$ over a feedback channel, succeeds with probability at most 1/2 assuming an error rate of 1/6.*

PROOF. Assume a binary robust protocol π that computes the identity function $f(x, y) = (x, y)$ where x, y belong to some domain of size at least 3; assume $|\pi| = N$, and without loss of generality let Alice be the party that speaks at most $T \leq N/2$ times in the protocol. We show an adversarial strategy that corrupts at most 1/3 of Alice's messages and makes Bob's view look the same for two different inputs of Alice. A similar approach appears in [Ber64, Ch. 4].

Assume Alice holds one of three inputs, x_0, x_1, x_2. For a given instance of the protocol, define $x_0[i], x_1[i], x_2[i]$ to be the i-th bit sent by Alice for the respective inputs. Note that the i-th transmission may depend on the transcript so far. If we fix a transcript up to the round where Alice sends her i-th bit, and look at her next transmission, $x_0[i], x_1[i], x_2[i]$, we observe that either the bit value is the same for all x_0, x_1, x_2, or it is the same for two of these inputs, and different for the third one. For every $i \leq T$, let $\mathsf{maj}(i) = \mathrm{majority}(x_0[i], x_1[i], x_2[i])$, given that previous transmissions are consistent with the adversarial strategy described below, and let $w[1, \ldots, T] = \mathsf{maj}(0) \cdots \mathsf{maj}(T)$.

The adversarial strategy only corrupts Alice, so we should describe what is being sent at each one of the T rounds in which Alice has the right of speak. The attack consists of two parts: the first R transmissions of Alice, and the last $T - R$ transmissions, for a number R we set shortly. For the first part, i.e., any transmission $i \leq R$, we corrupt the transmission so it equals $\mathsf{maj}(i)$ (i.e., if Alice sends $\mathsf{maj}(i)$ we leave the transmission intact and otherwise we flip the bit). The number R is set to be the minimal round such that for at least one of x_0, x_1, x_2, the above strategy corrupts exactly $R - 2T/3$ bits up to round R (included). It is easy to verify we can always find a round $2T/3 \leq R \leq T$ that satisfies the above: for every x_j the quantity $d(w[1, \ldots, R], x_j[1, \ldots, R])$ starts at 0, never decreases, and increases at most by one in every round. Furthermore since in the first part at most T corruptions happen over all rounds and all three inputs, at least for one input x_j the quantity $d(w[1, \ldots, R], x_j[1, \ldots, R])$ will grows from 0 to at most $T/3$. On the other hand, the quantity $R - 2T/3$ increases exactly by one in every round and thus goes from $-2T/3$ to $T/3$. Therefore, there exists a round R in which $R - 2T/3$ catches up with $d(w[1, \ldots, R], x_j[1, \ldots, R])$ for some input x_j.

Let x_0 be the input for which the number of corruptions up to round R is $R - 2T/3$; note that x_0 minimizes $d(w[1, \ldots, R], x_j[1, \ldots, R])$, or otherwise one of the other inputs would have satisfied $d(w[1, \ldots, R'], x_j[1, \ldots, R']) = R' - 2T/3$ for some earlier round $R' < R$. We can therefore assume without loss of generality that,

$$d(w[1,\ldots,R], x_0[1,\ldots,R])$$
$$\leq d(w[1,\ldots,R], x_1[1,\ldots,R])$$
$$\leq d(w[1,\ldots,R], x_2[1,\ldots,R]). \quad (1)$$

In the second part (the last $T - R$ of Alice's slots), we corrupt the i-th transmission so it equals $x_1[i]$. That is, if Alice holds x_1 we do nothing and if she holds x_0 we flip the bits as needed to correspond to what Alice would have sent on input x_1. We do not care about x_2 in this second part.

First note that from Bob's point of view, the transcripts he sees given that Alice holds x_0 or x_1 is exactly the same. Next, we claim that for both these inputs, the total amount of corruptions is at most $T/3 \leq N/6$. If Alice holds the input x_0, then the total amount of corruptions is at most

$$d(w[1,\ldots,R], x_0[1,\ldots,R]) + (T - R)$$
$$\leq (R - 2T/3) + (T - R) = T/3 \leq N/6.$$

If Alice holds x_1 then we do not make any corruption during the last $(T - R)$ rounds, and the total amount of corruptions is at most $d(w[1,\ldots,R], x_1[1,\ldots,R])$. Since w is the majority, at each round i, there exists at most a single input x_j, for which $d(w[i], x_j[i]) = 1$, while for both other inputs $x_{j'}$, the i-th transmitted bit is the same as their majority, $d(w[i], x_{j'}[i]) = 0$. It follows that

$$\sum_{j=1}^{3} d(w[1,\ldots,R], x_j[1,\ldots,R]) \leq R,$$

thus with Eq. (1) and the fact that $d(w[1,\ldots,R], x_0[1,\ldots,R]) = R - 2T/3$, we have

$$R - 2T/3 + 2d(w[1,\ldots,R], x_1[1,\ldots,R]) \leq R$$
$$d(w[1,\ldots,R], x_1[1,\ldots,R]) \leq T/3 \leq N/6.$$

□

As a corollary of the above, we note that the same impossibility bound of 1/6 holds also for the case of standard noisy channel (i.e., without feedback). Clearly, adding the resource of noiseless-feedback can only improve the noise resilience. This simple observation immediately leads to Theorem 1.2.

4.2 Protocols with an arbitrary order

When the order of speaking needs not be fixed, we can improve the noise resilience of the simulation. A simple observation is that we can take the protocol of Theorem 4.1 and change it so after receiving a 00 rewind command, the parties rewind only 5 rounds of π instead of six. This immediately yields a protocol that resists noise levels up to 1/5. However, we can do even better. We devise a protocol in which the parties adaptively change the length of the messages they send and force the adversary to make more corruptions in order to cause the parties to accept a corrupted message. In case the adversary does not corrupt a substantial part of the message, the parties detect the corruption and discard the message. Similar ideas appear in [AGS13].

We show a binary protocol that tolerates noise levels of up to 1/3, similar to the simulations over feedback channels over large-alphabet. The bound of 1/3 is tight due to the impossibility of Theorem 3.4 that applies to binary channels as well.

THEOREM 4.3. *For any alternating noiseless binary protocol π of length n, and for any $\varepsilon > 0$, there exists an efficient, deterministic, robust simulation of π over a feedback channel with a binary alphabet that takes $O_\varepsilon(n)$ rounds and succeeds assuming a maximal noise rate of $1/3 - \varepsilon$.*

The idea of the simulation is the following. The parties exchange messages of varying lengths. Each message consists of three parts: (a) 1 control bit (a *rewind* bit) — if set, this is an indication that the previous message was corrupted and the protocol should be rewound to the beginning of that message; (b) 1 bit of information — the next bit of π, in case no rewind is due; and (c) $t \geq 1$ confirmation bits, set according to how parts (a) and (b) are received at the other side (according to the feedback): if the information and rewind bits are received intact, the confirmation bits will be '1', or otherwise they will be '0'. The sender keeps sending confirmation bits, and checking via the feedback what the other side has received, until one of the following happens:

1. the number of *received* 0-confirmation bits is at least 1/3 of the length of the current message — in this case the message is *unconfirmed* and the protocol rewinds to the beginning of that message (so that the sender has the right of speak again to send the same message).

2. the number of received 1-confirmation bits minus the number of received 0-confirmation bits is larger than $1/\varepsilon$ — in this case the message is *confirmed* and the parties either rewind the protocol to the previous message of the sender (if the rewind bit is on), or the next simulated bit is the information bit.

The parties perform the above until a total number of n/ε^2 bits are communicated altogether. We formulate the simulation protocol in Algorithm 2. We now continue to prove Theorem 4.3.

PROOF. Consider a run of the protocol that did not compute the correct output, we will show that the noise must have been $\geq 1/3 - O(\varepsilon)$. Let N be the amount of times the protocol executed the for-loop, and for $i = 1,\ldots,N$ let m_i be the entire transmission communicated during the i-th instance of the loop (i.e., $|m_i| = sentLength$ when reaching line 18). We know that $\sum_i |m_i| = n/\varepsilon^2$.

Each message m_i can be confirmed or unconfirmed as explained above. If some message m_i is confirmed it can either be *correct* or *incorrect* according to whether or not any of its first two bits, msg, was flipped. Divide the messages $m_1,\ldots,m_N$ into three disjoint sets:

– $U = \{i \leq N \mid m_i \text{ is unconfirmed}\}$
– $C = \{i \leq N \mid m_i \text{ is confirmed and correct}\}$
– $W = \{i \leq N \mid m_i \text{ is confirmed and incorrect}\}$

It is easy to see that an unconfirmed message has no effect on the simulated transcript as any such message is just ignored. If a message is confirmed, it can either be interpreted as an information bit or as a rewind request, and the simulation is similar to the algorithm of Theorem 3.3 where each one of the symbols $\{0, 1, \leftarrow\}$ is encoded into a longer message. Specifically, similar to Theorem 3.3, after a single incorrect message the simulation takes two correct messages in order to recover from the error, i.e., in order to revert to the state before the corruption. Also here, multiple erroneous messages just linearly accumulate, hence,

---

Algorithm 2 Simulation for channels with feedback with a binary alphabet

---

Input: an alternating binary protocol π of length n, a noise parameter $\varepsilon > 0$, an input value x.

Initialize $T \leftarrow \emptyset$. $\triangleright$ $T = (T^S, T^R, T^F)$ is the simulated transcript, separated to sent, received and feedback bits

1: **for** $i = 1, 2, \ldots$ **do**
2:     **if** $\pi(x \mid T^F, T^R)$ is your turn to speak **then**
3:        $sentLength \leftarrow 2$
4:        $conf_0 \leftarrow 0, conf_1 \leftarrow 0$
5:        **if** $T^S = T^F$ **then** $\triangleright$ No corruptions are known
6:           $rewind = 0$
7:        **else** $\triangleright$ The transcript at the other side is corrupt
8:           $rewind = 1$

9:        $msg \leftarrow \pi(x \mid T^F, T^R) \circ rewind$
10:        send msg
11:        **while** $(conf_0 < sentLength/3)$ and $(conf_1 - conf_0 < 1/\varepsilon)$ **do**
12:           **if** msg received correctly **then** $\triangleright$ verify via the feedback
13:              send 1
14:           **else**
15:              send 0
16:           $sentLength \leftarrow sentLength + 1$
17:           $conf_b \leftarrow conf_b + 1$ $\triangleright$ b is the bit received at the other side (learned via the feedback)

18:        **if** $conf_0 \geq sentLength/3$ **then** $\triangleright$ message is not confirmed
19:           **continue** (next for loop instance)
20:        **else if** $conf_1 - conf_0 \geq 1/\varepsilon$ **then** $\triangleright$ message is confirmed: rewind or advance T
                                                           according to info/rewind received at other side
21:           **if** $\langle$rewind bit recorded at the other side$\rangle = 0$ **then**
22:              $T^S \leftarrow T^S \circ \pi(x \mid T^S, T^R)$
23:              $T^F \leftarrow T^F \circ \langle$info bit recorded at the other side$\rangle$
24:           **else if** $\langle$rewind bit recorded at the other side$\rangle = 1$ **then**
                                             $\triangleright$ Remove from T the last two simulated rounds
25:              $T^R \leftarrow \mathsf{prefix}_{|T^R|-1}(T^R)$
26:              $T^S \leftarrow \mathsf{prefix}_{|T^S|-1}(T^S)$
27:              $T^F \leftarrow \mathsf{prefix}_{|T^F|-1}(T^F)$

28:     **else** $\triangleright$ The other party is the speaker at this round
29:        Record msg, and confirmation bits according to the conditions of the while loop on line 11.
30:        If msg unconfirmed (line 18), ignore msg and **continue**.
31:        If msg confirmed (line 20):
          either extend T^R (if $rewind = 0$) or delete the suffix bit of T^R, T^S, T^F (if $rewind = 1$).

32:     If more than n/ε^2 bits were communicated, terminate and output T

CLAIM 4.4. *The simulation of a protocol π of length n succeeds as long as*

$$|C| - 2|W| \geq n.$$

Next, we bound the length and noise rate of a message. To avoid edge cases caused by rounding, let us assume without loss of generality that $1/\varepsilon$ is an integer (alternatively, replace ε with ε' for some $0 < \varepsilon' < \varepsilon$ with an integral reciprocal)

CLAIM 4.5. *For any i, $|m_i|$ is bounded by $2 + 3/\varepsilon$.*

PROOF. Assume a message reaches length $2 + 3/\varepsilon$, and consider its $3/\varepsilon$ confirmation bits: If $1 + 1/\varepsilon$ of these bits are zeros, then the message is unconfirmed since $(1 + 1/\varepsilon)/(2 + 3/\varepsilon) > 1/3$. Otherwise, there are at most $1/\varepsilon$ zeros and at least $3/\varepsilon - 1/\varepsilon \geq 2/\varepsilon$ ones, thus the difference between confirmation zeros and ones is at least $1/\varepsilon$ and the message is confirmed. $\square$

Note that for a confirmed message, $2 + 1/\varepsilon \leq |m_i| \leq 2 + 3/\varepsilon$, and for an unconfirmed message $3 \leq |m_i| \leq 2 + 3/\varepsilon$. Since

the total amount of bits the protocol communicates is n/ε^2, we have

$$|C| + |W| < \frac{n}{\varepsilon}. \tag{2}$$

The specific length of a message relates to the amount of corruption the adversary must make during that message.

— If $i \in C$ then the first two bits of m_i were received correctly, and the possible noise can only be flipping some of the one-confirmation bits, i.e., the amount of corrupted bits is exactly $conf_0$. Since the message was eventually confirmed, it holds that $conf_1 - conf_0 = 1/\varepsilon$, and thus $conf_0 = (|m_i| - 2 - 1/\varepsilon)/2$.

— For unconfirmed messages, $i \in U$, the message gets unconfirmed as soon as $conf_0 \geq |m_i|/3$. There are two cases: (i) if the information/control bits are correct, then the noise is any 0-confirmation bit, thus $conf_0 \geq |m_i|/3$; (ii) the information/control bits are corrupt, and then the noise is the corruption of the information/control plus any 1-confirmation bit. We have $3conf_0 \geq |m_i| = (2 + conf_0 + conf_1)$ thus $conf_1 \geq \frac{2|m_i|}{3} - 1 \geq \frac{|m_i|}{3}$.

- For $i \in W$, the corruption consists of at least one of the information/control bits and any $conf_1$ received. We have $conf_1 - conf_0 \geq 1/\varepsilon$ thus $conf_1 \geq conf_0 + 1/\varepsilon$ or equivalently $conf_1 \geq (|m_i| - 2 + 1/\varepsilon)/2$.

Therefore, the global noise rate in any given simulation is lower bounded by

$$\geq \frac{\sum_{i \in C} \frac{1}{2}(|m_i| - 2 - \frac{1}{\varepsilon}) + \sum_{i \in U} \frac{|m_i|}{3} + \sum_{i \in W} \frac{1}{2}(|m_i| + \frac{1}{\varepsilon})}{\sum_{i \in C} |m_i| + \sum_{i \in U} |m_i| + \sum_{i \in W} |m_i|}.$$

We can rewrite the noise rate as

$$\geq \frac{\frac{1}{2}\sum_{i \in C} |m_i| - \frac{1}{2}|C|(2 + \frac{1}{\varepsilon}) + \frac{1}{3}\sum_{i \in U} |m_i| + \frac{1}{2}\sum_{i \in W} |m_i| + \frac{1}{2}W \cdot \frac{1}{\varepsilon}}{n/\varepsilon^2}$$

$$\geq \frac{1}{3} + \frac{\frac{1}{6}\sum_{i \in C} |m_i| - \frac{1}{2}|C|(2 + \frac{1}{\varepsilon}) + \frac{1}{6}\sum_{i \in W} |m_i| + \frac{1}{2}W \cdot \frac{1}{\varepsilon}}{n/\varepsilon^2}$$

$$\geq \frac{1}{3} + \frac{\frac{1}{6}\sum_{i \in C} |m_i| - \frac{1}{2\varepsilon}|C| + \frac{1}{6}\sum_{i \in W} |m_i| + \frac{1}{2\varepsilon}|W|}{n/\varepsilon^2} - O(\varepsilon).$$

We now use the fact that the simulation instance we consider failed to simulate π correctly. Using Claim 4.4 we have that $|C| - 2|W| < n$, or equivalently, $|W| > \frac{1}{2}(|C| - n)$. If $|C| < n$ it is trivial that the error rate is $\geq 1/3 - O(\varepsilon)$. Otherwise, the error rate increases as we increase the length of messages in C and W. Since such messages are confirmed, they are of length $\geq 1/\varepsilon$. Then,

$$\geq \frac{1}{3} + \frac{\frac{1}{6\varepsilon}|C| - \frac{1}{2\varepsilon}|C| + \frac{1}{12\varepsilon}(|C| - n) + \frac{1}{4\varepsilon}(|C| - n)}{n/\varepsilon^2} - O(\varepsilon)$$

$$\geq \frac{1}{3} - O(\varepsilon). \quad \square$$

5. CODING FOR ERASURE CHANNELS

In this section we move to discuss *erasure channels* in which the noise may turn any symbol into an erasure mark $\perp$. No feedback is assumed in this setting, so the sender is unaware of erased transmissions. As in the above sections we seek after the maximal erasure rates that robust protocols can deal with. In this setting the parties have no longer joint view, and reaching consensus (e.g., regarding who is the next to speak) is not a trivial task. In fact, similar to the case of standard noisy channels [BR11], any robust protocol must have a fixed (predetermined) order of speaking.

THEOREM 5.1. *Any robust protocol over an erasure channel has a fixed order of speaking*

We defer the proof to the full version of this paper.

It is already known that $1/2$ is a tight bound on the erasure rate robust interactive protocols can tolerate over erasure channels [FGOS13]. Specifically, [FGOS13] shows that no protocol can resist an erasure level of $1/2$, due to the trivial attack that completely erases one party. Furthermore, they show that for any $\varepsilon > 0$, the coding scheme of [BR11] can tolerate an erasure level of $1/2 - \varepsilon$. However, that coding scheme has several drawbacks. First, it takes exponential time due assuming *tree codes*, a data structure whose efficient construction is still unknown (see [Sch96, GMS11, Bra12, MS14]). Furthermore, as $\varepsilon \to 0$ and the erasure level approaches $1/2$, the tree code needs to be more powerful, which implies the increase of the alphabet size (as a function of ε).

In the following subsection 5.1 we provide a simple, computationally efficient coding scheme for interactive communication over erasure channels in which the alphabet is small

(namely, 6-ary), and yet it tolerates erasure rates up to $1/2 - \varepsilon$. Then, in subsection 5.2 we transform this protocol to obtain the best known protocol for binary erasure channels, resisting an erasure level of up to $1/3 - \varepsilon$. It is there where having a fixed, relatively small, alphabet leads to an improved noise tolerance.

5.1 Erasure channels with a "large" alphabet

THEOREM 5.2. *For any alternating noiseless binary protocol π of length n, and for any $\varepsilon > 0$, there exists an efficient, deterministic, robust simulation of π over an erasure channel with a 6-ary alphabet, that takes $O_\varepsilon(n)$ rounds and succeeds assuming a maximal erasure rate of $1/2 - \varepsilon$.*

The main idea is the following. The parties talk in alternating rounds, in each of which they send a symbol $m \in \mathsf{Info} \times \mathsf{Parity}$ where $\mathsf{Info} = \{0, 1\}$ is the next information bit according to π (given the accepted simulated transcript so far) and $\mathsf{Parity} = \{0, 1, 2\}$ is the parity of the round in π being simulated, modulus 3.

Assume T is the transcript recorded so far, and let $p = |T| \bmod 3$. If a received m has parity $p + 1$, the receiving party accepts this message and extends T by one bit according to the Info part. Otherwise, or in the case m is erased, the party ignores the message, and resends its last sent message.

Since messages might get erased, the parties might get *out-of-sync*, e.g. when one party extends its accepted T while the other party does not. However, this discrepancy is limited to a single bit, that is, the length of Alice's T differs from Bob's by at most ± 1. Sending a parity—the length of the current T modulus 3—gives full information on the status of the other side, and allows the parties to regain synchronization. We formalize the above as Algorithm 3.

Algorithm 3 Simulation for erasure channels

Input: an alternating binary protocol π of length n, s noise parameter $\varepsilon > 0$, an input value x.

Assume a fixed alternating order of speaking: Alice is the sender on odd i's, and Bob is the sender on even i's.

1: Initialize: $T \leftarrow \emptyset$, $p \leftarrow 0$, and $m \leftarrow (0, 0)$. Set $N = \lceil n/\varepsilon \rceil$.

2: **for** $i = 1$ to N **do**

3:     **if** Sender **then**
4:         **if** your turn to speak according to $\pi(\cdot \mid T)$ **then**
5:             $t_{send} \leftarrow \pi(x \mid T)$
6:             $m \leftarrow (t_{send}, (p + 1) \bmod 3)$
7:             $T \leftarrow T \circ t_{send}$
8:             $p \leftarrow |T| \bmod 3$
9:             send m
10:         **else**
11:             send the m stored in memory

12:     **if** Receiver **then**
13:         record $m' = (t_{rec}, p')$
14:         **if** m' contains no erasures and $p' \equiv p + 1 \bmod 3$ **then**
15:             $T \leftarrow T \circ t_{rec}$

16: Output T

We defer the analysis of Algorithm 3 (and the proof of Theorem 5.2) to the full version of this paper.

5.2 Erasure channels with a binary alphabet

By encoding each symbol from our 6-ary alphabet using a binary code containing at least six codewords with maximal relative distance δ_6 we can immediately get a binary scheme that resists erasure rates of up to $\delta_6/2 - \varepsilon$. To our knowledge the maximal achievable distance δ_6 is $6/10$ (see [BBM+78]). This leads to the following corollary:

COROLLARY 5.3. *For any alternating noiseless binary protocol π of length n, and for any $\varepsilon > 0$, there exists an efficient, deterministic, robust simulation of π over a binary erasure channel, that takes $O_\varepsilon(n)$ rounds and succeeds assuming a maximal noise rate of at most $3/10 - \varepsilon$.*

Finally, we use the above ideas to devise a binary protocol that resists an adversarial erasure rate of up to $1/3 - \varepsilon$. The idea is to reduce the number of different messages used by the underlying simulation: since Algorithm 3 assumes a 6-ary alphabet, the best code has maximal distance $\delta_6 = 6/10$ which, as mentioned, leads to a maximal resilience of $\delta_6/2 - \varepsilon = 3/10 - \varepsilon$. However, were the alphabet in use smaller, say 4-ary, then we could have used better codes with a higher relative distance $\delta_4 = 2/3$ and achieve a maximal resilience of $\delta_4/2 - \varepsilon = 1/3 - \varepsilon$. In the following we adapt Algorithm 3 to use an alphabet size of at most 4, and obtain the following.

THEOREM 5.4. *For any alternating noiseless binary protocol π of length n, and for any $\varepsilon > 0$, there exists an efficient, deterministic, robust simulation of π over a binary erasure channel, that takes $O_\varepsilon(n)$ rounds and succeeds assuming a maximal noise rate of at most $1/3 - \varepsilon$.*

PROOF. Each message in Algorithm 3 consists of two parts: an information bit, and a parity modulus three. In order to reduce the number of possible messages we introduce a simple preprocessing step that takes an alternating protocol π of length n and converts it into a protocol π' of length $3n$ by padding each two consecutive transmutations of π with two vacuous transmissions (say, of the value 1). That is, if the communication in π is the bitstring $a_1, b_1, a_2, b_2 \ldots$, then in π' the parties communicate $a_1, 1, 1, b_1, 1, 1, a_2, 1, 1, \ldots$ (recall that the protocol is alternating, thus Alice sends the odd bits, and Bob the even ones).

In the preprocessed π', both parties know that a bit of information lies only in transmissions whose parity is 0 (mod 3). Thus, for the other parities there is no need to send the information bit — it is always 1! This reduces the size of the alphabet in use, specifically, the parties send messages out of the following message space[4] $\mathcal{M}$

$$\{0 \times (\bmod\ 0)\,,\ 1 \times (\bmod\ 0)\,,\ 1 \times (\bmod\ 1)\,,\ 1 \times (\bmod\ 2)\}\,.$$

Now that the message space is of size 4 we can encode each message using a binary code of relative distance $\delta_4 = 2/3$. For instance, we can use the code $\{000, 011, 110, 101\}$ (cf. [BBM+78]). Similar to Algorithm 3, the obtained simulation is deterministic, efficient and takes $O_\varepsilon(n)$ rounds. As for its noise resilience, for any $\varepsilon > 0$ the underlying Algorithm 3 can be set to resist up to $1/2 - \frac{3}{2}\varepsilon$ erased messages (Theorem 5.2). Since each message is coded into a binary string, in order to erase a codeword, $2/3$ of its bits must be erased. Therefore, in the concatenated algorithm we can resist a maximal erasure rate of $2/3 \cdot (1/2 - \frac{3}{2}\varepsilon) = 1/3 - \varepsilon$. $\square$

---

[4]In Algorithm 3 the first information bit will actually have parity 1 rather than 0; we can alter $\mathcal{M}$ to have the information bit on parity 1, and the rest remains the same.

6. REFERENCES

[AGS13] S. Agrawal, R. Gelles, and A. Sahai. Adaptive protocols for interactive communication. Manuscript, arXiv:1312.4182 (cs.DS), 2013.

[Ber64] E. R. Berlekamp. *Block coding with noiseless feedback.* Ph.D. thesis, Massachusetts Institute of Technology, 1964.

[BBM+78] M. Best, A. Brouwer, F. J. MacWilliams, A. M. Odlyzko, and N. J. Sloane. Bounds for binary codes of length less than 25. *IEEE Transactions on Information Theory*, 24(1):81–93, 1978.

[BK12] Z. Brakerski and Y. T. Kalai. Efficient interactive coding against adversarial noise. FOCS' 12, pp. 160–166, 2012.

[BN13] Z. Brakerski and M. Naor. Fast algorithms for interactive coding. SODA '13, pp. 443–456. 2013.

[Bra12] M. Braverman. Towards deterministic tree code constructions. ITCS '12, pp. 161–167. 2012.

[BE14] M. Braverman and K. Efremenko. List and unique coding for interactive communication in the presence of adversarial noise. FOCS '14, pp. 236–245. 2014.

[BR11] M. Braverman and A. Rao. Towards coding for maximum errors in interactive communication. STOC '11, pp. 159–166. 2011.

[FGOS13] M. Franklin, R. Gelles, R. Ostrovsky, and L. J. Schulman. Optimal coding for streaming authentication and interactive communication. CRYPTO 13, *LNCS*, vol. 8043, pp. 258–276. 2013.

[GH15] R. Gelles and B. Haeupler. Capacity of interactive communication over erasure channels and channels with feedback. SODA '15. 2015.

[GMS11] R. Gelles, A. Moitra, and A. Sahai. Efficient and explicit coding for interactive communication. FOCS '11, pp. 768–777. 2011.

[GMS14] R. Gelles, A. Moitra, and A. Sahai. Efficient coding for interactive communication. *Information Theory, IEEE Transactions on*, 60(3):1899–1913, 2014.

[GH14] M. Ghaffari and B. Haeupler. Optimal Error Rates for Interactive Coding II: Efficiency and List Decoding. FOCS '14, pp. 394–403. 2014.

[GHS14] M. Ghaffari, B. Haeupler, and M. Sudan. Optimal error rates for interactive coding I: Adaptivity and other settings. STOC '14, pp. 794–803. 2014.

[Hae14] B. Haeupler. Interactive channel capacity revisited. FOCS '14, pp. 226–235. 2014.

[KR13] G. Kol and R. Raz. Interactive channel capacity. STOC '13, pp. 715–724. 2013.

[MS14] C. Moore and L. J. Schulman. Tree codes and a conjecture on exponential sums. ITCS '14, pp. 145–154. 2014.

[Pan13] D. Pankratov. On the power of feedback in interactive channels. [Online:] http://people.cs.uchicago.edu/~pankratov/papers/feedback.pdf, 2013.

[Sch92] L. J. Schulman. Communication on noisy channels: a coding theorem for computation. *Foundations of Computer Science, Annual IEEE Symposium on*, pp. 724–733, 1992.

[Sch93] L. J. Schulman. Deterministic coding for interactive communication. STOC '93, pp. 747–756. 1993.

[Sch96] L. J. Schulman. Coding for interactive communication. *IEEE Transactions on Information Theory*, 42(6):1745–1756, 1996.

[Sha48] C. E. Shannon. A mathematical theory of communication. *ACM SIGMOBILE Mobile Computing and Communications Review*, 5(1):3–55, 2001. Originally appeared in *Bell System Tech. J.* 27:379–423, 623–656, 1948.

Simulating Noisy Channel Interaction

[Extended Abstract] *

Mark Braverman [†]
Department of Computer Science, Princeton
University
mbraverm@cs.princeton.edu

Jieming Mao
Department of Computer Science, Princeton
University
jiemingm@princeton.edu

ABSTRACT

We show that T rounds of interaction over the binary symmetric channel $BSC_{1/2-\epsilon}$ with feedback can be simulated with $O(\epsilon^2 T)$ rounds of interaction over a noiseless channel. We also introduce a more general "energy cost" model of interaction over a noisy channel. We show energy cost to be equivalent to external information complexity, which implies that our simulation results are unlikely to carry over to energy complexity. Our main technical innovation is a self-reduction from simulating a noisy channel to simulating a slightly-less-noisy channel, which may have other applications in the area of interactive compression.

Categories and Subject Descriptors

F.2.0 [**Theory of Computation**]: Analysis of algorithms and problem complexity—*General*

General Terms

Theory

Keywords

Communication Complexity; Information Complexity; Noisy Channel

1. INTRODUCTION

Much of modern coding theory revolves around the following question: "Given an imperfect (noisy) channel C, what is the best way of utilizing it to simulate noiseless communication?" A key objective of Shannon's classical information theory [Sha48, CT06] was to answer this question. It turns

---

*The full version of this paper can be found at ECCC.

[†]Research supported in part by an NSF CAREER award (CCF-1149888), a Turing Centenary Fellowship, a Packard Fellowship in Science and Engineering, and the Simons Collaboration on Algorithms and Geometry.

out that for memoryless channels, the number of utilizations of C needed to transmit n bits of information scales as $n/\text{cap}(C)$, where $\text{cap}(C)$ is the *channel capacity* of C.

In this paper we consider the converse problem:

Problem 1.1. *Can a noiseless channel be **effectively** utilized to simulate communication over a noisy channel C?*

We will focus entirely on binary channels with feedback — i.e. channels transmitting bits $\in \{0,1\}$, where the transmitting party gets to observe the (possibly corrupted) received bit — although the techniques can likely be generalized to a broader class of channels. Note that as our discussion is about simulating a noisy channel with a noiseless one, the fact that the channel has feedback only makes such simulation more difficult. Most of our discussion will focus on the *binary symmetric channel* $C = BSC_a$, for noise $0 \le a < 1/2$. A bit b transmitted over BSC_a is received as $b \oplus b_{err}$, where $b_{err} \sim B_a$ is a Bernoulli random variable that causes the received bit to be flipped. It is well known that $\text{cap}(BSC_a) = 1 - H(a) := 1 + a \log a + (1-a) \log(1-a)$. A particularly interesting regime in our context is when the noise level is very high: $a = 1/2 - \epsilon$. In this case $1 - H(a) = \Theta(\epsilon^2)$.

Of course, communication over a noisy channel can always be simulated by communication over a noiseless channel: the sender can simply apply the noise before transmitting her bit to the receiver. However, one would like to simulate the communication *effectively*, only paying $O(\text{cap}(C) \cdot n)$ bits of communication to simulate n utilizations of C.

We will consider the problem in a general interactive setting, where C is being used to conduct a general interactive protocol. In the non-interactive setting, classical results from information theory show that up to factor $(1+\delta)$, with $\delta \to 0$ as $n \to \infty$, n utilizations of C can be simulated by $\sim \text{cap}(C) \cdot n$ utilizations of C, and vice-versa. What can one say about the interactive case?

Coding for interactive communication, i.e. encoding a noiseless protocol over a noisy channel (the converse problem to the one we are trying to solve) has received a substantial amount of attention recently. An early result by Schulman [Sch96] showed that good (constant-rate, constant-fraction-of-errors) codes exist in the interactive setting even when the noise on the channel is adversarial. This work has since been recently improved in several directions, including error-tolerance and the code's computational efficiency [BR11b, BK12, GHS13, GH13, BE14]. Most relevant to our work is a result by Kol and Raz [KR13] showing a gap between interactive channel capacity and one-way channel capacity (interactive channel capacity is lower), once again giving an example of interactive coding theory being much more complicated than its one-way transmission counterpart.

Problem 1.1 can also be cast as a problem of *compressing interactive communication*. The general problem of compressing interactive communication arises in the context of information complexity and direct sum problems for randomized communication complexity [CSWY01, BYJKS04, BBCR10, BR11a]. The (internal) information cost of a two-party protocol π is the amount of information executing π reveals to the parties about each other's inputs. The formal definition of information cost of a protocol can be found in the preliminaries. In its full generality, interactive compression asks to simulate an information cost-I protocol with $O(I)$ communication, and is equivalent to the strong direct sum problem in communication complexity [BR11a]. Unfortunately, such strong interactive compression has recently been shown to be impossible [GKR14]. A less ambitious goal is to compress π to its external information cost $I^{ext} \geq I$. There are reasons to believe that compression to $O(I^{ext})$ communication is also impossible. For example, [Bra13] gives a specific problem that is conjectured to provide such a separation.

Communication over a noisy channel $BSC_{1/2-\epsilon}$ inherently reveals only $1 - H(1/2 - \epsilon) = \Theta(\epsilon^2)$ information to the observer in each round. Thus, a protocol π that runs for T rounds over such a channel has (both internal and external) information cost $O(\epsilon^2 T)$, although the *way* in which this information is limited round-by-round is highly structured. In this case, our first main result shows that compression with $O(1)$ multiplicative loss is possible:

Theorem 1.2. (Theorem 3.1, rephrased) *Any protocol π running for T rounds over $BSC_{1/2-\epsilon}$ with feedback can be perfectly simulated by a public-randomness protocol π' running for $O(\epsilon^2 T)$ rounds in expectation over the noiseless channel BSC_0.*

Remark. Here public randomness is necessary for a result of this nature, because for example π might be a protocol where Alice sends Bob a random string, and since they have feedback they now have a shared random string of length T. To achieve such functionality, you need either public randomness or at least T bits of communication even over a noiseless channel.

Theorem 1.2 provides a new result on the cusp between information complexity theory and interactive coding theory. It shows that (up to a constant) interaction over a noisy channel can be simulated by interaction over noiseless channel, giving an affirmative action to Problem 1.1 in this case.

The compression proof of Theorem 1.2 relies crucially on the fact that errors on the channel remain the same throughout the communication. We consider the following strengthening of the error model: in each round, the party transmitting the next bit *chooses* the error rate $1/2 - \epsilon$ of the next bit, while paying *energy cost EC* of $\Theta(\epsilon^2)$. This model corresponds to a scenario where the party gets to modulate its transmission power in a way that affects the noise level (and thus the channel capacity) of the transmission. While we chose ϵ^2 because it captures the channel capacity for the selected ϵ, this expression is known to capture actual energy-capacity tradeoffs in high-noise wireless scenarios (see e.g. [TV05]). We show that thus defined energy complexity is actually equivalent to the external information complexity:

Theorem 1.3. (Theorems 4.1 and 4.2, rephrased) *For any protocol π over a variable-noise BSC with feedback and any distribution μ over inputs, there is a protocol ϕ over a noiseless channel, such that the external information cost of ϕ is $O(EC_\mu(\pi))$ and ϕ simulates π. Conversely, any ϕ with external information cost I^{ext} can be simulated by a π over a variable-noise BSC with feedback with $EC_\mu(\pi) = O(I^{ext} + \epsilon)$ for any $\epsilon > 0$.*

Theorem 1.3 implies that the analogue of Theorem 1.2 is unlikely to hold for the more general variable-error model, since it is conjectured that one cannot compress a general interactive protocol π to $O(IC^{ext}(\pi))$. We note that the strongest known compression result is of the form $O(IC^{ext}(\pi) \cdot (\log |\pi|)^{O(1)})$ [BBCR10], where $|\pi|$ is the number of bits communicated by π. The ϵ in the theorem is caused by the technical reason of the proof, and we can make ϵ arbitrarily small.

We believe that techniques involved in proving Theorem 1.2 (discussed below) have the potential to be helpful in compressing interactive communication. While we know by [GKR14] that compressing π all the way down to $IC(\pi)$ is impossible, one can hope to beat the currently best compression scheme of $\tilde{O}(\sqrt{IC(\pi) \cdot |\pi|})$ of [BBCR10]. Specifically, to the best of our knowledge, the recursive approach we describe below has not appeared in past works in either the Information Theory or the Theoretical Computer Science literature.

1.1 Techniques and proof overview of Theorem 1.2

In this section we briefly discuss the technical contributions of this paper. We will mainly focus on the techniques in the proof of Theorem 1.2: while the proof of Theorem 1.3 requires care and work, it does build on existing techniques from past works in the area, such as [BGPW13].

Recall that to prove Theorem 1.2 we need to take a protocol π that runs for T steps over $BSC_{1/2-\epsilon}$, and simulate it using a protocol ϕ that runs for $O(\epsilon^2 T)$ steps over the noiseless channel BSC_0. A natural approach is to break π into "chunks" of $\Theta(1/\epsilon^2)$ communication each, and to try and simulate each chunk using $O(1)$ communication. Let π' denote a sub-protocol of π of $\gamma = 1/\epsilon^2$ rounds we are trying to simulate. There is a natural way to identify transcripts of π' with leafs of a binary tree $\mathcal{T}$ of depth γ. Each leaf ℓ corresponds to a transcript that contains $0 \leq m \leq \gamma$ mistakes. The goal of the parties (Alice and Bob) is to sample each ℓ with its correct probability $p_\ell := (1/2 - \epsilon)^m (1/2 + \epsilon)^{\gamma - m}$. Note that for a given ℓ, Alice and Bob do not know m. Rather, since each of them only knows what part of his or her messages were corrupted, Alice and Bob know two numbers m_x and m_y, respectively, such that $m = m_x + m_y$.

Following past works, Alice and Bob can try to first jointly sample a leaf ℓ and then use rejection sampling to make sure that each ℓ is selected with probability proportional to p_ℓ. Since the joint sampling happens without any communication, we select each leaf with probability $2^{-\gamma}$. Note that under such a procedure no leaf ever gets selected with probability $> 2^{-\gamma}$, thus if we want to accommodate leafs with $p_\ell > 2^{-\gamma}$ we should select each leaf with probability p_ℓ / M for a constant $M > 1$. Note that this means that each round will succeed with probability $\sim 1/M$, and thus we can only afford $M = O(1)$ a large constant. This will allow Alice and Bob to sample *most* but not *all* leafs correctly. Note that the probability of the most likely leaf in $\mathcal{T}$ is $2^{-\gamma} \cdot (1 + 2\epsilon)^{\gamma} \sim 2^{-\gamma} \cdot e^{2/\epsilon} \gg 2^{-\gamma}$, and our rejection sampling approach is bound to fail here by badly under-sampling this leaf.

A (partial) solution to the problem above is to choose γ slightly smaller than $1/\epsilon^2$ (e.g. $1/(\epsilon^2 \log |\pi|)$), and just ignore leafs for which the ratio exceeds M. This is the approach employed in [BBCR10] to compress to external information cost. One can show that at each round we add small (e.g. $< 1/|\pi|^2$) statistical error, and thus the simulation (mostly) works. This approach is unsuitable for us here for two reasons. Firstly, we would like to have a perfect simulation that does not incur any error. Secondly, in order to get a $O(1)$-bit simulation of π' we cannot afford the depth of $\mathcal{T}$ to be $o(1/\epsilon^2)$.

Instead, we adopt a recursive approach. We begin the simulation of π' by tossing (a properly biased) coin, and deciding whether we will be looking for a "high-error" or a "low-error" leaf, where the threshold distinguishing "high" and "low" is chosen appropriately (note that the "low-error" leafs are the ones getting under-counted by the rejection sampling protocol). If we are looking for "high-error" nodes, then rejection sampling with an appropriate constant $M > 1$ as described above will work well. What should we do about a "low-error" leaf? We would like to sample such a leaf ℓ with probability exceeding p_ℓ, since we are only trying to sample it conditioned on entering the "low-error" regime. To get such a sampling for the low error regime we just simulate π', but over $BSC_{1/2-2\epsilon}$ instead of $BSC_{1/2-\epsilon}$! We use induction to claim such a sampling is possible (note that when $\epsilon = \Theta(1)$ simulation is trivial since $|\pi'| = 1/\epsilon^2 = O(1)$). Simulating π' over a lower noise channel $BSC_{1/2-2\epsilon}$ has the effect of "punishing" high-error leafs (we don't care about those since they get sampled in the high error regime), and "rewarding" low-error leafs, which are the ones we would like to focus on. For example, the most likely no-errors leafs is approximately $e^{2/\epsilon}$ times more likely under $BSC_{1/2-2\epsilon}$ than under $BSC_{1/2-\epsilon}$. Of course, simulating π' over $BSC_{1/2-2\epsilon}$ is more expensive than over $BSC_{1/2-\epsilon}$ — ≈ 4 times more expensive as $(1/\epsilon)^2 \cdot (2\epsilon)^2 = 4$ — but as long as the low-error regime is invoked $< 1/4$ of the time, the total communication converges and remains $O(1)$ in expectation.

As the problem of sampling "low-error" nodes is the main difficulty in the general compression of interactive communication, we hope that the strategy above will be helpful in addressing this more general problem.

1.2 Techniques and proof overview of Theorem 1.3

In this section we give a proof overview of Theorem 1.3. Theorem 1.3 has two parts. We will discuss them separately.

Recall that the first part of Theorem 1.3 shows that for any protocol π over a variable-noise BSC with feedback and any distribution μ over inputs, we can construct a protocol ϕ over a noiseless channel, such that the external information cost of ϕ is $O(EC_\mu(\pi))$ and ϕ simulates π. The proof idea of this part of Theorem 1.3 is straightforward. The construction is simple: for each bit b transmitted over BSC_p in protocol π, the transmitter sends $b \oplus B_p$ to the receiver over a noiseless channel in ϕ. The analysis of external information cost of ϕ follows the standard information-theoretic argument which first converts the information cost into the

Table 1: Divergence lower bound

Cases	Lower bounds of $D(p\|q)$
$0 \le p \le 2q$	$\Omega\left(\frac{(p-q)^2}{q}\right)$
$2q < p < 0.02,\ q < 0.01$	$\Omega\left(p \log \frac{p}{q}\right)$
$2q < p,\ q \ge 0.01$	$\Omega(1)$
$p \ge 0.02,\ q < 0.01$	$\Omega\left(\log \frac{1}{q}\right)$

sum of the divergence between the true probability and the prior information and then bounds the divergence by the energy cost.

The second part of Theorem 1.3 shows that for any protocol ϕ over a noiseless channel, we can construct a protocol π over a variable-noise BSC with feedback, such that $EC_\mu(\pi) = O(IC^{ext}(\phi) + \epsilon)$ for any $\epsilon > 0$. The proof considers protocol ϕ bit by bit. For each transmitted bit in ϕ, let's assume the transmitter wants to send this bit as B_p and both the transmitter and the receiver have prior information that the distribution of this transmitted bit to be B_q. Then the external information cost of this bit is $D(p\|q)$. This divergence is the budget for the energy cost of the corresponding part in π.

The general protocol we used in the proof to send B_p with prior B_q and energy cost $D(p\|q)$ does a biased random walk on points $0, \frac{1}{2n}, ..., \frac{2n-1}{2n}, 1$. Here n is some previously fixed integer. For this biased random walk, the transmitter and the receiver start at the point closest to q based on the prior information. The transmitter starts to send bits over some binary symmetric channels with chosen crossover probability and they move left or right according to received bits. They stop this biased random walk when they reach either 0 or 1, and they pick the sampled bit as the stop position. The main technique used in this biased random walk is Lemma 4.3. This lemma shows that if the transmitter and the receiver do biased random walk on points $0, 1, ...a-1, a, a+1, ...a+b-1, a+b$, starting at point a and $a \ge b$, then the transmitter only needs to spend constant energy cost to always end at point $a + b$. Directly from this lemma, the transmitter can go from point q to point $q \cdot 2^t$ with energy cost $O(t)$.

Unfortunately, under this biased random walk framework, it is difficult to design an integral protocol for all kinds of p and q. So for different values of p and q, our approach uses different lower bounds of $D(p\|q)$ as the budget for energy cost. In each case, the transmitter will use Lemma 4.3 differently to meet the lower bounds of $D(p\|q)$. Table 1 shows the lower bounds of $D(p\|q)$ used in different cases.

The ϵ in the energy cost comes from the fact that q might not be a point where we do random walk (i.e. $\frac{i}{2n}$). So we will start with a point closest to q, and this approximation will make the energy cost increase by $O(\epsilon)$. In fact, this ϵ equals to $\frac{1}{2n}$. As increasing n will not make the energy cost increase, we can make this ϵ arbitrarily small.

2. PRELIMINARIES

2.1 Communication Complexity

In the two-party communication model, Alice and Bob want to jointly compute a function $f : \mathcal{X} \times \mathcal{Y} \to \mathcal{Z}$. Alice is only given input $x \in \mathcal{X}$ and Bob is only given input $y \in \mathcal{Y}$. In this paper, we consider the public coin model, which means that Alice and Bob have access to the shared randomness.

In order to compute function f, they have to communicate with each other following a protocol π which specifies when the communication is over, who sends the next bit if the communication is not over, and the function of each transmitted bit given the history, the input of the person who sends this bit and the shared randomness. The transcript of a protocol is a concatenation of all bits exchanged.

Definition 2.1. The *communication complexity* of a public coin protocol π, denoted by $CC(\pi)$, is defined as the maximum number of bits exchanged on the worst input.

Definition 2.2. The *randomized communication complexity with zero error* of a public coin protocol π, denoted by $R_0(\pi)$, is defined as the maximum expected number of bits exchanged over the randomness of the protocol on the worst input.

Definition 2.3. We will say that a protocol ϕ over a noiseless channel *simulates* a protocol π over a noisy channel if there is a deterministic function g such that $g(\Phi(x, y, R^\phi, R_A^\phi, R_B^\phi))$ is equal in distribution to $\Pi(x, y, R^\pi, R_A^\pi, R_B^\pi, R^c)$ for all x and y. Here R^ϕ and R^π are the public randomness used in protocol ϕ and π. R_A^ϕ, R_B^ϕ, R_A^π, R_B^π are the private randomness used in protocol ϕ and π. R^c is the randomness for the noisy channel. Π and Φ are random variables for transcripts of protocols π and ϕ.

Definition 2.4. We will say that a protocol π over a noisy channel *simulates* a protocol ϕ over a noiseless channel if there is a deterministic function g such that $g(\Pi(x, y, R^\pi, R_A^\pi, R_B^\pi, R^c))$ is equal in distribution to $\Phi(x, y, R^\phi, R_A^\phi, R_B^\phi)$ for all x and y. Here R^ϕ and R^π are the public randomness used in protocol ϕ and π. R_A^ϕ, R_B^ϕ, R_A^π, R_B^π are the private randomness used in protocol ϕ and π. R^c is the randomness for the noisy channel. Π and Φ are random variables for transcripts of protocols π and ϕ.

Additional definitions and results in basic communication complexity can be found in [KN97].

2.2 Binary Symmetric Channel and Energy Cost

Definition 2.5. The *binary symmetric channel* with crossover probability p $(0 \leq p \leq \frac{1}{2})$, denoted by BSC_p, is defined as a communication channel such that each bit sent by the transmitter is flipped with probability p when received by the receiver.

Definition 2.6. The BSC_p with *feedback* (noise-free feedback) is defined as the BSC_p such that the transmitter also gets the (potentially flipped) bit which the receiver receives.

In this paper, we consider two kinds of two-party communication protocols over binary symmetric channels. One is that the crossover probability of the channel is fixed during the whole protocol. The other is that the transmitter can choose the crossover probability of the binary symmetric channel for each transmitted bit and the receiver does not know the crossover probability. For protocols in these two models, we can still define the communication complexity as the maximum number of bits exchanged. However, the following definition of energy cost is more close to the sense of information exchanged in the protocol.

Definition 2.7. If the transmitter sends one bit over BSC_p with feedback, the *energy cost* of this bit is defined as $4(p - \frac{1}{2})^2$. The *energy cost* of a protocol π over binary symmetric channels (may have different crossover probabilities) with feedback, denoted by $EC(\pi)$, is defined as the maximum expected sum of *energy cost* of each transmitted bit of π over the randomness of the protocol on the worst input.

Definition 2.8. Given a distribution μ on inputs X, Y, the *distributional energy cost*, denoted by $EC_\mu(\pi)$, is defined as the expected sum of energy cost of each transmitted bit of π over input distribution μ and the randomness of the protocol.

2.3 Information Theory and Information Cost

More definitions and results from basic information theory can be found in [CT06]. All the logarithms in this paper are base 2.

Definition 2.9. The *entropy* of a random variable X, denoted by $H(X)$, is defined as $H(X) = \sum_x Pr[X = x] \log(1/Pr[X = x])$.

If X is drawn from Bernoulli distributions B_p, we use $h(p) = -(p \log p + (1 - p)(\log(1 - p))$ to denote $H(X)$.

Definition 2.10. The *conditional entropy* of random variable X conditioned on random variable Y is defined as $H(X|Y) = \mathbb{E}_y[H(X|Y = y)]$.

Fact 2.11. $H(XY) = H(X) + H(Y|X)$.

Definition 2.12. The *mutual information* between two random variables X and Y is defined as $I(X;Y) = H(X) - H(X|Y) = H(Y) - H(Y|X)$.

Definition 2.13. The *conditional mutual information* between X and Y given Z is defined as $I(X;Y|Z) = H(X|Z) - H(X|YZ) = H(Y|Z) - H(Y|XZ)$.

Fact 2.14. Let X_1, X_2, Y, Z be random variables, we have $I(X_1 X_2; Y|Z) = I(X_1; Y|Z) + I(X_2; Y|X_1 Z)$.

Definition 2.15. The *Kullback-Leibler divergence* between two random variables X and Y is defined as $D(X\|Y) = \sum_x Pr[X = x] \log(Pr[X = x]/Pr[Y = x])$.

If X and Y are drawn from Bernoulli distribution B_p and B_q, we use $D(p\|q)$ as an abbreviation of $D(X\|Y)$.

Fact 2.16. Let X, Y, Z be random variables, we have $I(X;Y|Z) = \mathbb{E}_{x,z}[D((Y|X = x, Z = z)\|(Y|Z = z))]$.

Fact 2.17. Let X, Y be random variables,

$$\sum_x \frac{|Pr[X = x] - Pr[Y = x]|^2}{2 \max\{Pr[X = x], Pr[Y = x]\}} \leq \ln(2) \cdot D(X\|Y)$$
$$\leq \sum_x \frac{|Pr[X = x] - Pr[Y = x]|^2}{Pr[Y = x]}.$$

Finally, we define the external and internal information cost of a protocol.

Definition 2.18. Given a distribution μ on inputs X, Y, and a public coin protocol π, the *external information cost* is defined as $IC_\mu^{ext}(\pi) = I(XY; \Pi)$, where $\Pi = \Pi(X, Y, R)$ is the random variable denoting the transcript and public randomness of the protocol and R is the public randomness.

Definition 2.19. Given a distribution μ on inputs X, Y, and a public coin protocol π, the *internal information cost* is defined as $IC_\mu^{int}(\pi) = I(X; \Pi|Y) + I(Y; \Pi|X)$, where $\Pi = \Pi(X, Y, R)$ is the random variable denoting the transcript and public randomness of the protocol and R is the public randomness.

3. SIMULATING THE NOISE CHANNEL USING THE NOISELESS CHANNEL

Theorem 3.1. *For every deterministic protocol π over $BSC_{1/2-\epsilon}$ with feedback, there exists a public coin protocol ϕ over noiseless channel such that ϕ simulates π and*

$$R_0(\phi) \leq \alpha \cdot \lceil \epsilon^2 \cdot 2CC(\pi) \rceil.$$

Here α is a constant and equals to $\max\{\frac{1}{\beta^2}, 50t^2 + 10\}$ where $t = e^6$ and β is a constant to be determined in the proof.

Proof overview..

The proof follows the intuition outlined in Section 1.1. In the language of the overview, protocol $\phi_{v,\gamma,1/2-\epsilon}$, which is the main protocol simulating γ layers starting from node v in the protocol tree, decides whether to call $\phi^0_{v,\gamma,1/2-\epsilon}$ or $\phi^1_{v,\gamma,1/2-\epsilon}$. $\phi^1_{v,\gamma,1/2-\epsilon}$ takes care of the "high-error" regime case, and is executed using rejection sampling. $\phi^0_{v,\gamma,1/2-\epsilon}$ takes care of the "low-error" regime case, and uses a recursive call to the execution of π' over $BSC_{1/2-2\epsilon}$, followed by rejection sampling to make probabilities align perfectly.

One technical detail which we omitted from the the intuitive description but that plays an important role in the protocols is the $threshold_{\theta,v,w,D}$ function. In order to be able to perform rejection sampling starting from a node v, we need to know whether a given node w located γ layers below v has more errors than the "high-error" threshold θ or less. This depends on whether the number of mistakes $m_x + m_y$ along the path from v to w exceeds θ or not. Unfortunately, only Alice knows m_x and only Bob knows m_y, and exchanging these values is prohibitively expensive: it would cost $\Theta(\log \gamma)$ bits of communication, whereas we can only afford $O(1)$ communication to perform this operation. Luckily, for nodes sampled from D, if the distribution of (m_x, m_y) is a product distribution (it is in our case), we are able to give an expected $O(1)$ protocol for the problem. In addition to answering whether $m_x + m_y > \theta$, the protocol $threshold_{\theta,v,w,D}$ outputs a pair of "witnesses" (θ_x, θ_y) such that $\theta_x + \theta_y = \theta$ that work as follows: if $m_x + m_y \leq \theta$, then $m_x \leq \theta_x$ and $m_y \leq \theta_y$; if $m_x + m_y > \theta$, then $m_x \geq \theta_x$ and $m_y \geq \theta_y$. These witnesses are then used by Alice and Bob when performing rejection sampling.

Proof. First we change π to be the protocol that Alice and Bob send messages alternatively. This modification will increase $CC(\pi)$ by at most a multiplicative factor of 2.

Now we consider the easy case when $\epsilon \geq \beta$. In this case, we just make ϕ to be the direct simulation of π. That is, if in protocol π Alice has to send a bit b, then in protocol ϕ, Alice sends the same bit b, and both Alice and Bob use public randomness to generate $b' \sim B_{1/2-\epsilon}$ and pretends the receiving bit to be $b \oplus b'$. In this way, the bit Bob receives in ϕ will have the same distribution as the bit Bob receives in π. When Bob sends a message in π, we do the same modification in ϕ. Therefore ϕ simulates π and $R_0(\phi) \leq 2CC(\pi) \leq \frac{1}{\beta^2} \cdot \epsilon^2 \cdot 2CC(\pi) \leq \alpha \cdot \epsilon^2 \cdot 2CC(\pi)$.

Now we prove this theorem by induction on the crossover probability for the case when $\epsilon < \beta$, showing that the theorem for 2ϵ implies it for ϵ. We construct ϕ by compressing $\gamma = \frac{1}{\epsilon^2}$ communication bits of π over $BSC_{1/2-\epsilon}$ into a protocol over a noiseless channel with constant number

of communication bits. For each step of the compression, we consider γ bits of π as a protocol tree with root node v and depth γ. In order to simulate this protocol tree, we only have to sample the leaf nodes with the same probabilities sampled from the protocol tree. The following protocols show how to do this. The main protocol is protocol $\phi_{v,\gamma,1/2-\epsilon}$. For notation convenience, we define $m_x(v,w)$ to be the number of errors Alice makes from node v to node w on the protocol tree of π, $m_y(v,w)$ to be the number of errors Bob from node v to node w on the protocol tree of π, and $m(v,w) = m_x(v,w) + m_y(v,w)$.

---

1. Let $\theta = \gamma \cdot (1/2 - 3\epsilon)$. Both players use public randomness to sample a bit b from Bernoulli distribution B_{1-p}, where $p = \sum_{i=0}^{i \leq \theta} (1/2 - \epsilon)^i (1/2 + \epsilon)^{\gamma-i} \binom{\gamma}{i}$.

2. Run $\phi^b_{v,\gamma,1/2-\epsilon}$.

Protocol 1: Protocol $\phi_{v,\gamma,1/2-\epsilon}$

---

1. Alice and Bob pretend the crossover probability of the protocol tree is $1/2 - 2\epsilon$ and run $\phi_{v,\gamma,1/2-2\epsilon}$ to sample a leaf node w.

2. Alice and Bob run $threshold_{\theta,v,w,D}$. Here D is the distribution from which w is sampled, which satisfies $Pr_{w \sim D}[w] = (1/2 - 2\epsilon)^{m(v,w)}(1/2 + 2\epsilon)^{\gamma - m(v,w)}$. If the result if 1, they repeat this protocol.

3. Alice samples a bit b_x which is 1 with probability
$$\frac{(1/2 - \epsilon)^{m_x(v,w)-\theta_x}(1/2 + \epsilon)^{-m_x(v,w)+\theta_x}}{(1/2 - 2\epsilon)^{m_x(v,w)-\theta_x}(1/2 + 2\epsilon)^{-m_x(v,w)+\theta_x}},$$
and sends this bit to Bob. Here θ_x gets its value from the previous run of $threshold_{\theta,v,w,D}$.

4. Bob samples a bit b_y which is 1 with probability
$$\frac{(1/2 - \epsilon)^{m_y(v,w)-\theta_y}(1/2 + \epsilon)^{-m_y(v,w)+\theta_y}}{(1/2 - 2\epsilon)^{m_y(v,w)-\theta_y}(1/2 + 2\epsilon)^{-m_y(v,w)+\theta_y}},$$
and sends this bit to Alice. Here θ_y gets its value from the previous run of $threshold_{\theta,v,w,D}$.

5. If both b_x and b_y are 1, they accept w. Otherwise they repeat this protocol.

Protocol 2: Protocol $\phi^0_{v,\gamma,1/2-\epsilon}$

Now let's intuitively understand how this set of protocols works. The set of protocols first divide the leaf nodes into two sets: $\{u|m(v,u) \leq \theta\}$ and $\{u|m(v,u) > \theta\}$. Since for each leaf node u, the probability that u is sampled is $(1/2 - \epsilon)^{m(v,u)}(1/2 + \epsilon)^{\gamma-m(v,u)}$, the probability that nodes in the first set are sampled is exactly p. Then the protocol uses $\phi^0_{v,\gamma,1/2-\epsilon}$ to sample a node in the first set and $\phi^1_{v,\gamma,1/2-\epsilon}$ to sample a node in the second set. $\phi^0_{v,\gamma,1/2-\epsilon}$ uses the induction result of sampling a node with smaller crossover probability and $\phi^1_{v,\gamma,1/2-\epsilon}$ uses rejection sampling to sample a node in the second set. Both of these two protocols use protocol $threshold$ to determine whether the sampled node w has $m(v,w)$ greater than θ or not.

Now let's analyze these protocols.

Analysis of $threshold_{\theta,v,w,D}$: This protocol's goal is to decide whether $m_x(v,w) + m_y(v,w) \leq \theta$ or not using only constant number of communication bits in expectation. This protocol will also make Alice and Bob get θ_x and θ_y which satisfy the following conditions:

- $\theta_x + \theta_y = \theta$.

- If $m_x(v,w) + m_y(v,w) \leq \theta$, then $m_x(v,w) \leq \theta_x$ and $m_y(v,w) \leq \theta_y$.

- If $m_x(v,w) + m_y(v,w) > \theta$, then $m_x(v,w) \geq \theta_x$ and $m_y(v,w) \geq \theta_y$.

The input distribution D is the distribution where w is sampled. This protocol only works for product distributions. More precisely, the product distribution here means that when w is drawn from distribution D, $m_x(v,w)$ has the same distribution as $m_x(v,w)$ given $m_y(v,w)$ to be any value and $m_y(v,w)$ has the same distribution as $m_y(v,w)$ given $m_x(v,w)$ to be any value. This product property is used for analyzing the probability that this protocol ends in each round. To analyze this protocol, we first have to make sure that in the first step of this protocol, the integer ξ exists. Consider the following two conditions:

- $Pr[m_x(v,w) \leq \zeta] \leq Pr[m_y(v,w) \leq \theta - \zeta - 1]$.

- $Pr[m_x(v,w) \leq \zeta] \geq Pr[m_y(v,w) \leq \theta - \zeta - 1]$.

For any integer ζ, at least one of these two conditions will be satisfied. Also, we know that when $\zeta = -1$, the first condition is satisfied and when $\zeta = \theta$, the second condition

is satisfied. So if when $\zeta = -1$, the second condition is also satisfied, we just have to pick $\xi = -1$. Otherwise, we can find some ζ between -1 and θ such that it violates the second condition and $\zeta + 1$ satisfies the second condition. Then we just have to pick $\xi = \zeta + 1$.

Finally let's analyze the communication cost of this protocol. Let $p_1 = Pr_{u \sim D}[m_x(v,u) \leq \xi - 1]$, $p_2 = Pr_{u \sim D}[m_x(v,u) \leq \xi]$, $q_1 = Pr_{u \sim D}[m_y(v,u) \leq \theta - \xi]$ and $q_2 = Pr_{u \sim D}[m_y(v,u) \leq \theta - \xi - 1]$. As distribution D satisfies the product property, the probability that this protocol recursively calls itself at step 9 is $(1 - p_2)q_2 \leq (1 - p_2)p_2 \leq \frac{1}{4}$. The probability that this protocol recursively calls itself at step 10 is $p_1(1 - q_1) \leq q_1(1 - q_1) \leq \frac{1}{4}$. Therefore, the probability that this protocol ends in one round is at least $\frac{1}{2}$. In expectation, Alice and Bob will communicate $4 \times 2 = 8$ bits running this protocol. In addition, if D is a product distribution as defined above, the distribution that this protocol recursively runs on is still a product distribution.

Analysis of $\phi^0_{v,\gamma,1/2-\epsilon}$: First we should make sure that the probabilities we use to sample b_x and b_y are no greater than 1. When Alice and Bob proceed to sample b_x and b_y, we know that $threshold_{\theta,v,w,D}$ returns 0. Therefore $m_x(v,w) \leq$

θ_x and $m_y(v,w) \leq \theta_y$. So

$$\frac{(1/2-\epsilon)^{m_x(v,w)-\theta_x}(1/2+\epsilon)^{-m_x(v,w)+\theta_x}}{(1/2-2\epsilon)^{m_x(v,w)-\theta_x}(1/2+2\epsilon)^{-m_x(v,w)+\theta_x}}$$

$$= \left(\frac{1/2-\epsilon}{1/2-2\epsilon}\right)^{m_x(v,w)-\theta_x}\left(\frac{1/2+\epsilon}{1/2+2\epsilon}\right)^{\theta_x-m_x(v,w)}$$

$$= \left(\frac{1/4-\epsilon/2-2\epsilon^2}{1/4+\epsilon/2-2\epsilon^2}\right)^{\theta_x-m_x(v,w)} \leq 1.$$

Similarly, we have

$$\frac{(1/2-\epsilon)^{m_y(v,w)-\theta_y}(1/2+\epsilon)^{-m_y(v,w)+\theta_y}}{(1/2-2\epsilon)^{m_y(v,w)-\theta_y}(1/2+2\epsilon)^{-m_y(v,w)+\theta_y}} \leq 1.$$

The probability that the protocol accepts some w in each round is:

$$\sum_{w,m(v,w)\leq\theta}(1/2-2\epsilon)^{m(v,w)}(1/2+2\epsilon)^{\gamma-m(v,w)}$$

$$\times\frac{(1/2-\epsilon)^{m_x(v,w)-\theta_x}(1/2+\epsilon)^{-m_x(v,w)+\theta_x}}{(1/2-2\epsilon)^{m_x(v,w)-\theta_x}(1/2+2\epsilon)^{-m_x(v,w)+\theta_x}}$$

$$\times\frac{(1/2-\epsilon)^{m_y(v,w)-\theta_y}(1/2+\epsilon)^{-m_y(v,w)+\theta_y}}{(1/2-2\epsilon)^{m_y(v,w)-\theta_y}(1/2+2\epsilon)^{-m_y(v,w)+\theta_y}}$$

$$= \sum_{w,m(v,w)\leq\theta}(1/2-2\epsilon)^{m(v,w)}(1/2+2\epsilon)^{\gamma-m(v,w)}$$

$$\times\frac{(1/2-\epsilon)^{m(v,w)-\theta}(1/2+\epsilon)^{-m(v,w)+\theta}}{(1/2-2\epsilon)^{m(v,w)-\theta}(1/2+2\epsilon)^{-m(v,w)+\theta}}$$

$$= \sum_{w,m(v,w)\leq\theta}(1/2-\epsilon)^{m(v,w)}(1/2+\epsilon)^{\gamma-m(v,w)}$$

$$\times\frac{(1/2-2\epsilon)^{\theta}(1/2+2\epsilon)^{\gamma-\theta}}{(1/2-\epsilon)^{\theta}(1/2+\epsilon)^{\gamma-\theta}}$$

$$= p\cdot\frac{(1/2-2\epsilon)^{\theta}(1/2+2\epsilon)^{\gamma-\theta}}{(1/2-\epsilon)^{\theta}(1/2+\epsilon)^{\gamma-\theta}}$$

$$= p\cdot\frac{(1/2-2\epsilon)^{(1/\epsilon^2)(1/2-3\epsilon)}(1/2+2\epsilon)^{(1/\epsilon^2)(1/2+3\epsilon)}}{(1/2-\epsilon)^{(1/\epsilon^2)(1/2-3\epsilon)}(1/2+\epsilon)^{(1/\epsilon^2)(1/2+3\epsilon)}}$$

$$\geq 5p.$$

The last inequality comes from the following argument:

$$\lim_{\epsilon\to0}\frac{(1/2-2\epsilon)^{(1/\epsilon^2)(1/2-3\epsilon)}(1/2+2\epsilon)^{(1/\epsilon^2)(1/2+3\epsilon)}}{(1/2-\epsilon)^{(1/\epsilon^2)(1/2-3\epsilon)}(1/2+\epsilon)^{(1/\epsilon^2)(1/2+3\epsilon)}}$$

$$= \lim_{\epsilon\to0}\left(1-\frac{12\epsilon^2}{1-4\epsilon^2}\right)^{\frac{1}{2\epsilon^2}-\frac{3}{\epsilon}}\left(1+\frac{2\epsilon}{1+2\epsilon}\right)^{\frac{6}{\epsilon}}$$

$$= \lim_{\epsilon\to0}\exp\left(-\frac{12\epsilon^2}{1-4\epsilon^2}\cdot\left(\frac{1}{2\epsilon^2}-\frac{3}{\epsilon}\right)+\frac{2\epsilon}{1+2\epsilon}\cdot\frac{6}{\epsilon}\right)$$

$$= e^6.$$

So there exists a constant β such that, when $0 < \epsilon < \beta$,

$$\frac{(1/2-2\epsilon)^{(1/\epsilon^2)(1/2-3\epsilon)}(1/2+2\epsilon)^{(1/\epsilon^2)(1/2+3\epsilon)}}{(1/2-\epsilon)^{(1/\epsilon^2)(1/2-3\epsilon)}(1/2+\epsilon)^{(1/\epsilon^2)(1/2+3\epsilon)}} \geq 5.$$

Therefore the expected number of rounds is at most $\frac{1}{5p}$. By induction, each call of $\phi_{v,\gamma,1/2-2\epsilon}$ uses at most $\alpha\cdot(2\epsilon)^2\cdot\gamma$ bits of communication in expectation. Thus the expected

number of bits communicated in $\phi^0_{v,\gamma,1/2-\epsilon}$ is

$$\frac{1}{5p}(\alpha\cdot(2\epsilon)^2\cdot\gamma+2+8) = \frac{4\alpha}{5p}+\frac{2}{p}.$$

From the above analysis, we can also see that for a specific node w with $m(v,w)\leq\theta$, the probability that w is sampled and accepted in each round of this protocol is

$$(1/2-\epsilon)^{m(v,w)}(1/2+\epsilon)^{\gamma-m(v,w)}\cdot\frac{(1/2-2\epsilon)^{\theta}(1/2+2\epsilon)^{\gamma-\theta}}{(1/2-\epsilon)^{\theta}(1/2+\epsilon)^{\gamma-\theta}}.$$

Then since the probability that the protocol ends in each round is

$$p\cdot\frac{(1/2-2\epsilon)^{\theta}(1/2+2\epsilon)^{\gamma-\theta}}{(1/2-\epsilon)^{\theta}(1/2+\epsilon)^{\gamma-\theta}},$$

the probability that w with $m(v,w)\leq\theta$ is sampled in this protocol is

$$\frac{(1/2-\epsilon)^{m(v,w)}(1/2+\epsilon)^{\gamma-m(v,w)}\cdot\frac{(1/2-2\epsilon)^{\theta}(1/2+2\epsilon)^{\gamma-\theta}}{(1/2-\epsilon)^{\theta}(1/2+\epsilon)^{\gamma-\theta}}}{p\cdot\frac{(1/2-2\epsilon)^{\theta}(1/2+2\epsilon)^{\gamma-\theta}}{(1/2-\epsilon)^{\theta}(1/2+\epsilon)^{\gamma-\theta}}}$$

$$= \frac{(1/2-\epsilon)^{m(v,w)}(1/2+\epsilon)^{\gamma-m(v,w)}}{p}.$$

Analysis of $\phi^1_{v,\gamma,1/2-\epsilon}$: First we should make sure that the probabilities we use to sample b_x and b_y are no greater than 1. Recall that $t = e^6$. When Alice and Bob proceed to sample b_x and b_y, we know that $threshold_{\theta,v,w,D}$ returns 1. Therefore $m_x(v,w)\geq\theta_x$ and $m_y(v,w)\geq\theta_y$. So

$$\frac{(1/2-\epsilon)^{m_x(v,w)}(1/2+\epsilon)^{\gamma/2-m_x(v,w)}}{t\cdot(\frac{1/2-\epsilon}{1/2+\epsilon})^{\theta_x-\theta/2}\cdot2^{-\gamma/2}}$$

$$\leq \frac{(1/2-\epsilon)^{\theta/2}(1/2+\epsilon)^{\gamma/2-\theta/2}}{t\cdot2^{-\gamma/2}}$$

$$= \frac{(1-4\epsilon^2)^{\theta/2}(1+2\epsilon)^{\gamma/2-\theta}}{e^6}$$

$$\leq \frac{(1+2\epsilon)^{3/\epsilon}}{e^6} \leq 1.$$

Similarly, we have

$$\frac{(1/2-\epsilon)^{m_y(v,w)}(1/2+\epsilon)^{\gamma/2-m_y(v,w)}}{t\cdot(\frac{1/2-\epsilon}{1/2+\epsilon})^{\theta_y-\theta/2}\cdot2^{-\gamma/2}} \leq 1.$$

The probability that the protocol accepts some w in each round is:

$$\sum_{w,m(v,w)>\theta}(2^{-\gamma}\cdot\frac{(1/2-\epsilon)^{m_x(v,w)}(1/2+\epsilon)^{\gamma/2-m_x(v,w)}}{t\cdot(\frac{1/2-\epsilon}{1/2+\epsilon})^{\theta_x-\theta/2}\cdot2^{-\gamma/2}}$$

$$\cdot\frac{(1/2-\epsilon)^{m_y(v,w)}(1/2+\epsilon)^{\gamma/2-m_y(v,w)}}{t\cdot(\frac{1/2-\epsilon}{1/2+\epsilon})^{\theta_y-\theta/2}\cdot2^{-\gamma/2}})$$

$$= \sum_{w,m(v,w)>\theta}(1/2-\epsilon)^{m(v,w)}(1/2+\epsilon)^{\gamma-m(v,w)}\cdot\frac{1}{t^2}$$

$$= \frac{1-p}{t^2}.$$

Therefore the expected number of bits communicated in $\phi^1_{v,\gamma,1/2-\epsilon}$ is at most

$$\frac{t^2}{1-p}(2+8) = \frac{10t^2}{1-p}.$$

From the above analysis, we can also see that for a specific node w with $m(v,w) > \theta$, the probability that w is sampled and accepted in each round is

$$(1/2-\epsilon)^{m(v,w)}(1/2+\epsilon)^{\gamma-m(v,w)} \cdot \frac{1}{t^2}.$$

Then since the probability that the protocol ends each round is $\frac{1-p}{t^2}$, the probability that w with $m(v,w) \leq \theta$ is sampled in this protocol is

$$\frac{(1/2-\epsilon)^{m(v,w)}(1/2+\epsilon)^{\gamma-m(v,w)}\cdot\frac{1}{t^2}}{\frac{1-p}{t^2}}$$
$$= \frac{(1/2-\epsilon)^{m(v,w)}(1/2+\epsilon)^{\gamma-m(v,w)}}{1-p}.$$

Analysis of $\phi_{v,\gamma,1/2-\epsilon}$: Combining the analysis of $\phi^0_{v,\gamma,1/2-\epsilon}$ and $\phi^1_{v,\gamma,1/2-\epsilon}$, the expected number of bits communicated in $\phi_{v,\gamma,1/2-\epsilon}$ is at most

$$p\cdot(\frac{4\alpha\epsilon^2\gamma}{5p}+\frac{2}{p})+(1-p)\cdot\frac{10t^2}{1-p} = \frac{4\alpha}{5}+2+10t^2 \leq \frac{4\alpha}{5}+\frac{\alpha}{5} = \alpha.$$

For node w with $m(v,w) > \theta$, the probability that w is sampled is

$$\frac{(1/2-\epsilon)^{m(v,w)}(1/2+\epsilon)^{\gamma-m(v,w)}}{p} \cdot p$$
$$= (1/2-\epsilon)^{m(v,w)}(1/2+\epsilon)^{\gamma-m(v,w)}.$$

For node w with $m(v,w) \leq \theta$, the probability that w is sampled is

$$\frac{(1/2-\epsilon)^{m(v,w)}(1/2+\epsilon)^{\gamma-m(v,w)}}{1-p} \cdot (1-p)$$
$$= (1/2-\epsilon)^{m(v,w)}(1/2+\epsilon)^{\gamma-m(v,w)}.$$

So all the nodes are sampled according to the correct probability distribution. $\square$

4. DISTRIBUTIONAL ENERGY COST IS EQUAL TO EXTERNAL INFORMATION COST

Theorem 4.1. *For any protocol π over a variable-error binary symmetric channel with feedback and any distribution μ over inputs, there is a private coin protocol ϕ over the noiseless binary channel, such that $IC^{ext}_\mu(\phi) \leq \frac{1}{\ln(2)}EC_\mu(\pi)$ and ϕ simulates π.*

The proof of Theorem 4.1 can be found in the full version of this paper.

Theorem 4.2. *For any protocol π over a noiseless channel, any distribution μ over inputs and any $\epsilon = \frac{1}{2n}, n \in \mathbb{Z}, n > 0$, there is a protocol ϕ over a variable-error binary symmetric channel with feedback, such that $EC_\mu(\phi) = O(IC^{ext}_\mu(\pi)+\epsilon)$ and ϕ simulates π.*

Proof. Similarly to the proof of Theorem 4.1, we first express the external information cost of π as the sum of the divergence between the true probability and the prior probability. Let $p_{x,y,i,\pi_i} = Pr[(\Pi_i|X = x, Y = y, \Pi_{<i} = \pi_{<i}) = 1]$

and $q_{i,\pi_i} = Pr[(\Pi_i|\Pi_{<i} = \pi_{<i}) = 1]$. Then we have

$$IC^{ext}_\mu(\pi) = \sum_{i=1}^{CC(\pi)} \mathbb{E}_{x,y,\pi_{<i}}[D(p_{x,y,i,\pi}\|q_{i,\pi_i})].$$

We are going to construct ϕ by simulating π's communication bit by bit. For the ith transmitted bit, given inputs x, y and the previous transcript $\pi_{<i}$, it is sufficient to prove that the corresponding simulation in ϕ uses energy cost at most $O(D(p_{x,y,i,\pi_{<i}}\|q_{i,\pi_{<i}})+\frac{\epsilon}{2^i})$ in expectation, and the receiver can sample a bit from Bernoulli distribution $B_{p_{x,y,i,\pi_{<i}}}$ given prior $q_{i,\pi_{<i}}$.

Now, we construct the simulation of the ith transmitted bit given inputs x, y and the previous transcript $\pi_{<i}$. Since we fix $i, x, y, \pi_{<i}$ here, we will abbreviate $p_{x,y,i,\pi_{<i}}$ and $q_{i,\pi_{<i}}$ as p and q. The main framework of the construction has following steps: Let $n_i = n \cdot 2^i$ and $\epsilon_i = \frac{1}{2n_i}$. Alice and Bob do biased random walk on points $0, \frac{1}{2n_i}, \frac{2}{2n_i}, \cdots, \frac{2n_i-1}{2n_i}, 1$, starting at a point closest to q. For each step, the transmitter sends one bit over some binary symmetric channel with some chosen crossover probability. They move right for one step if the received bit is 1, and they move left for one step if the the received bit is 0. They stop this random walk whenever they reach 0 or 1, and take the value on the point as the corresponding sampled bit. As $\sum_{i=1}^{CC(\pi)} \epsilon_i \leq \epsilon$, it is sufficient to prove that the energy cost of this communication of $O(D(p\|q)+\epsilon_i)$ and after random walk they reach 1 with probability p. Note that setting ϵ_i in this way is for the case when π has finite external information cost but a potentially unbounded communication complexity. Otherwise we can pick $\epsilon_i = \frac{\epsilon}{CC(\pi)}$.

We need the following lemma as the main technique of our construction.

Lemma 4.3. *Suppose Alice and Bob do biased random walk on points $0, 1, \ldots, a+b$ via communication over binary symmetric channels, and they start at point a. If $a \geq b$, the transmitter only has to send messages with energy cost at most 48 to make them always end at $a+b$.*

Proof. We prove this lemma by induction on $(a+b)^2 + b$, showing that the lemma for smaller $(a+b)^2 + b$ implies it for larger $(a+b)^2 + b$. The basis of this induction proof is the case when $b \leq 12$. If $b \leq 12$, the transmitter only has to send 1 over BSC_0 (noiseless channel) for b times. This will take at most $12 < 48$ energy cost and they will end at $a+b$.

If $b > 12$. Let $c = \lfloor \frac{a}{2} \rfloor$. The protocol is as follows:
Let's analyze this protocol. First we calculate the probability that they reach point $a - c$ after the first part of the protocol. This probability is no more than the probability of reaching $a-c$ if we change the stop condition of the first part to stopping only when reaching either $a-c$ or $a+b$. We can calculate the second probability by recursion. For $(\frac{1}{2}+\frac{3}{c})$-biased random walk on points $a-c, ..., a+b$ with start point t, define u_t to be the probability of reaching $a+b$. Then we have $u_{a-c} = 0$, $u_{a+b} = 1$ and $u_t = (\frac{1}{2}+\frac{3}{c})u_{t+1}+(\frac{1}{2}-\frac{3}{c})u_{t-1}$ for $a-c < t < a+b$. Let $\beta = \frac{\frac{1}{2}-\frac{3}{c}}{\frac{1}{2}+\frac{3}{c}}$, we have

$$u_t = \frac{1+\cdots+\beta^{t-(a-c)-1}}{1+\cdots+\beta^{b+c-1}}.$$

Protocol 5: Biased Random Walk

Since $c + 1 = \lfloor \frac{a}{2} \rfloor + 1 \geq b/2$ and $b > 12$, we know $3c \geq b$. Then we have

$$u_a = \frac{1 + \cdots + \beta^{c-1}}{1 + \cdots + \beta^{b+c-1}} \geq \frac{1}{1 + \beta^c + \beta^{2c} + \beta^{3c}} > \frac{1}{1 + 3\beta^c}.$$

We also have

$$\beta^c = \left(1 - \frac{\frac{6}{c}}{\frac{1}{2} + \frac{3}{c}}\right)^c \leq \left(1 - \frac{6}{c}\right)^c < e^{-6}.$$

So

$$u_a > \frac{1}{1 + 3\beta^c} > \frac{1}{1 + 3e^{-6}}.$$

Therefore, for the first part of the protocol, the probability of reaching $a - c$ is at most $1 - \frac{1}{1+3e^{-6}}$.

Now let's calculate the probability of stopping at point between $a - c$ and $a + b$ after c^2 steps of $(\frac{1}{2} + \frac{3}{c})$-biased random walk . For each step, with probability $\frac{1}{2} + \frac{3}{c}$, the coordinate will increase 1, and with probability $\frac{1}{2} - \frac{3}{c}$ the coordinate will decrease 1. If $a - c < d < a + b$, the sum of these values will be less than b. By Chernoff bound, the probability that the sum of these values is less than b is no more than

$$e^{-\frac{2(6c-b)^2}{4c^2}} < e^{-\frac{2(3c)^2}{4c^2}} = e^{-4.5}.$$

So the probability that $a - c < d < a + b$ is at most $e^{-4.5}$.

Now we can calculate the expected energy cost of this protocol. Let's assume the expected energy cost of this protocol is v. For the first part of the protocol, it takes $4(\frac{1}{2} - \frac{3}{c} - \frac{1}{2})^2 \cdot c^2 = 36$ energy cost. If $a - c \leq d < a$, the protocol will spend at most $v + 48$ energy cost after the first part. If $d = a$, the protocol will spend at most v after the first part. If $a < d < a + b$, the protocol will spend at most 48 energy. So if $d \neq a + b$, the protocol will spend at most $v + 48$ energy cost after the first part. Using the probability we calculate before, we have

$$
\begin{aligned}
v &\leq (e^{-4.5} + 1 - \frac{1}{1+3e^{-6}})(v+48) + 36 \\
&\leq (\frac{1}{16} + \frac{1}{16})(v+48) + 36 = \frac{v}{8} + 42.
\end{aligned}
$$

Therefore $v \leq 48$ as desired. $\qquad\square$

Directly from this lemma, the transmitter can go from point q to point $2^t \cdot q$ with energy cost $O(t)$ by applying the protocol in this lemma t times.

Let's start the construction. Without loss of generality, let's assume $0 < q \leq \frac{1}{2}$. Notice that we ignore the case when $q = 0$. Because if $q = 0$, p must be 0 and the receiver can sample one bit from B_p without any communication. Now we assume $2n_i q$ is an integer and we will consider the case that $2n_i q$ is not an integer later in the proof. The general protocol of sampling one bit from Bernoulli distribution B_p given prior q is as Protocol 6.

Protocol 6: General Protocol

The energy cost we are going to use when $2qn_i$ is an integer is $O(D(p\|q))$. We use different lower bounds of $D(p\|q)$ for different values of p and q. In all the cases, Alice and Bob will follow the general protocol. The only difference is that for different cases, the transmitter will choose different biases for biased random walk. The detailed differences are shown in Protocol 7.

Protocol 7: Detailed Protocols in cases

To analyze these protocols, we need the following simple lemma:

Lemma 4.4. *Suppose Alice and Bob do unbiased random walk on points $0, 1, ..., a+b$ via communication over $BSC_{\frac{1}{2}}$, and they start at point a. Then the probability that they end at $a+b$ is $\frac{a}{a+b}$.*

Proof. For unbiased random walk on points $0, ..., a+b$ with start point t, define u_t to be the probability of reaching $a+b$. Then we have $u_0 = 0$, $u_{a+b} = 1$ and $u_t = \frac{1}{2}(u_{t-1} + u_{t+1})$ for $0 < t < a+b$. Solve this we get $u_t = \frac{t}{a+b}$ and thus $u_a = \frac{a}{a+b}$. $\qquad\square$

Now we are going to show in cases that the detailed protocols sample a bit from Bernoulli distribution B_p and use energy cost $O(D(p\|q))$ in expectation. Notice that although the last 2 cases use the same protocol, as we use different lower bounds of $D(p\|q)$ in these 2 cases, we have to analyze them separately. Here we just list the 4 cases, and the detailed proof can be found in the full version of the paper.

1. $0 \le p \le 2q$

2. $2q < p < 0.02$, $q < 0.01$

3. $p > 2q$ and $q \ge 0.01$

4. $p \ge 0.02, q < 0.01$

After analyzing these cases, we know that when $2n_i q$ is an integer, our protocol can make the receiver sample a bit from Bernoulli distribution B_p and spends energy cost $O(D(p\|q))$. For the case when $2n_i q$ is not an integer, we can pick $q' = \frac{\lceil 2n_i q \rceil}{2n_i}$ and run the above protocol with prior q'. Then the receiver can still sample from Bernoulli distribution B_p, and the protocol has cost $O(D(p\|q'))$. Since we have

$$
\begin{aligned}
D(p\|q') - D(p\|q) &= p \log \frac{q}{q'} + (1-p) \log \frac{1-q}{1-q'} \\
&\le (1-p) \log\left(1 + \frac{q'-q}{1-q'}\right) \\
&\le (1-p) \cdot \frac{q-q'}{1-q'} \le 1 \cdot \frac{\epsilon_i}{0.5} = 2\epsilon_i,
\end{aligned}
$$

the energy cost is at most

$$
O(D(p\|q')) = O(D(p\|q) + \epsilon_i)
$$

as desired. $\qquad\square$

5. REFERENCES

[BBCR10] Boaz Barak, Mark Braverman, Xi Chen, and Anup Rao. How to compress interactive communication. In *Proceedings of the 2010 ACM International Symposium on Theory of Computing*, pages 67–76, 2010.

[BE14] Mark Braverman and Klim Efremenko. List and unique coding for interactive communication in the presence of adversarial noise. In *Electronic Colloquium on Computational Complexity (ECCC)*, volume 21, page 7, 2014.

[BGPW13] Mark Braverman, Ankit Garg, Denis Pankratov, and Omri Weinstein. From information to exact communication. In *Proceedings of the forty-fifth annual ACM symposium on Theory of computing*, pages 151–160. ACM, 2013.

[BK12] Zvika Brakerski and Yael Tauman Kalai. Efficient interactive coding against adversarial noise. In *Foundations of Computer Science (FOCS), 2012 IEEE 53rd Annual Symposium on*, pages 160–166. IEEE, 2012.

[BR11a] Mark Braverman and Anup Rao. Information equals amortized communication. In Rafail Ostrovsky, editor, *FOCS*, pages 748–757. IEEE, 2011.

[BR11b] Mark Braverman and Anup Rao. Towards coding for maximum errors in interactive communication. In *Proceedings of the 43rd annual ACM symposium on Theory of computing*, pages 159–166. ACM, 2011.

[Bra13] Mark Braverman. A hard-to-compress interactive task? In *51st annual Allerton Conference on Communication, Control, and Computing*, 2013.

[BYJKS04] Ziv Bar-Yossef, T. S. Jayram, Ravi Kumar, and D. Sivakumar. An information statistics approach to data stream and communication complexity. *Journal of Computer and System Sciences*, 68(4):702–732, 2004.

[CSWY01] Amit Chakrabarti, Yaoyun Shi, Anthony Wirth, and Andrew Yao. Informational complexity and the direct sum problem for simultaneous message complexity. In *Proceedings of the 42nd Annual IEEE Symposium on Foundations of Computer Science*, pages 270–278, 2001.

[CT06] Thomas M Cover and Joy A Thomas. *Elements of information theory 2nd edition*. Wiley-interscience, 2006.

[GH13] Mohsen Ghaffari and Bernhard Haeupler. Optimal error rates for interactive coding ii: Efficiency and list decoding. *arXiv preprint arXiv:1312.1763*, 2013.

[GHS13] Mohsen Ghaffari, Bernhard Haeupler, and Madhu Sudan. Optimal error rates for interactive coding i: Adaptivity and other settings. *arXiv preprint arXiv:1312.1764*, 2013.

[GKR14] Anat Ganor, Gillat Kol, and Ran Raz. Exponential separation of information and communication. In *Electronic Colloquium on Computational Complexity (ECCC)*, volume 21, page 49, 2014.

[KN97] Eyal Kushilevitz and Noam Nisan. *Communication complexity*. Cambridge University Press, Cambridge, 1997.

[KR13] Gillat Kol and Ran Raz. Interactive channel capacity. In *Proceedings of the 45th annual ACM symposium on Symposium on theory of computing*, pages 715–724. ACM, 2013.

[Sch96] Leonard J. Schulman. Coding for interactive communication. *IEEE Transactions on Information Theory*, 42(6):1745–1756, 1996.

[Sha48] Claude E. Shannon. A mathematical theory of communication. *Bell System Technical Journal*, 27, 1948. Monograph B-1598.

[TV05] David Tse and Pramod Viswanath. *Fundamentals of wireless communication*. Cambridge university press, 2005.

Deterministic Rateless Codes for BSC

[Extended Abstract] [*]

Benny Applebaum [†]
School of Electrical
Engineering
Tel-Aviv University
bennyap@post.tau.ac.il

Liron David [‡]
School of Electrical
Engineering
Tel-Aviv University
lirondav@post.tau.ac.il

Guy Even
School of Electrical
Engineering
Tel-Aviv University
guy@eng.tau.ac.il

ABSTRACT

A rateless code encodes a finite length information word into an infinitely long codeword such that longer prefixes of the codeword can tolerate a larger fraction of errors. A rateless code achieves capacity for a family of channels if, for every channel in the family, reliable communication is obtained by a prefix of the code whose rate is arbitrarily close to the channel's capacity. As a result, a universal encoder can communicate over all channels in the family while simultaneously achieving optimal communication overhead.

In this paper, we construct the first *deterministic* rateless code for the binary symmetric channel. Our code can be encoded and decoded in $O(\beta)$ time per bit and in almost logarithmic parallel time of $O(\beta \log n)$, where β is any (arbitrarily slow) super-constant function. Furthermore, the error probability of our code is almost exponentially small $\exp(-\Omega(n/\beta))$. Previous rateless codes are probabilistic (i.e., based on code ensembles), require polynomial time per bit for decoding, and have inferior asymptotic error probabilities.

Our main technical contribution is a constructive proof for the existence of an infinite generating matrix that each of its prefixes induce a weight distribution that approximates the expected weight distribution of a random linear code.

Keywords

rateless codes; binary symmetric channel; capacity achieving error correcting code

[*]A full version of this paper is available at http://arxiv.org/abs/1406.0157

[†]Supported by ISF grant 1155/11, Israel Ministry of Science and Technology (grant 3-9094), and GIF grant 1152/2011.

[‡]Supported by ISF grant 1155/11, Israel Ministry of Science and Technology (grant 3-9094), and GIF grant 1152/2011.

1. INTRODUCTION

Consider a single transmitter T who wishes to broadcast an information word $m \in \{0,1\}^k$ to multiple receivers $B_1, \ldots, B_t$ over a Binary Symmetric Channel (BSC) with crossover probability p. By Shannon's theorem, using error correcting codes it is possible to solve this problem with asymptotically optimal communication of $k \cdot \frac{1}{C(p)-\delta}$ bits where $C(p)$ is the capacity of the channel and $\delta > 0$ is an arbitrarily small constant. Furthermore, there are explicit capacity-achieving codes in which decoding and encoding can be performed efficiently in polynomial or even linear time, e.g. [4, 5, 6].

The task of noisy broadcast becomes more challenging when each receiver B_i experiences a different level of noise p_i (e.g., due to a different distance from the transmitter). Naively, one would use a code which is tailored to the noisiest channel with parameter $p_{\max}$. However, this will add an unnecessary communication overhead for receivers with lower noise level. To make things worse, the transmitter may be unaware of the noise parameters, and, in some cases, may not even have a non-trivial upper-bound on the noise level. Under these circumstances, the naive solution is not only wasteful but simply not applicable.

This problem (also studied in [7, 29]) can be solved by a *rateless code*. Such a code allows the transmitter to map the information word $m \in \{0,1\}^k$ into an infinitely long sequence of bits $\{c_i\}_{i \in \mathbb{N}}$ such that the longer the prefix of the codeword, the higher level of noise can be corrected. Ideally, we would like to simultaneously achieve the optimal rate with respect to all the noise parameters p_i. That is, for every value of p_i, a prefix of length $k \cdot \frac{1}{C(p_i)-\delta}$ should guarantee reliable communication.

Rateless codes were extensively studied under various names, [18, 16, 9, 14, 7, 29, 24, 8, 13, 25, 15, 22, 23]. Information-theoretically, the problem of rateless transmission is well understood [27], and, for many noise models, random codes provide an excellent (inefficient) solution. The task of constructing efficient rateless codes, which provide polynomial-time encoding and decoding, is much more challenging. Currently, only a few examples of efficient capacity-achieving rateless codes are known for several important cases such as erasure channels, Gaussian channels, and binary symmetric channels [17, 26, 10, 20]. Interestingly, all known constructions are probabilistic. Namely, the encoding algorithm employs some public randomness, which is shared by the transmitter and all the receivers. (Equivalently, these constructions can be viewed as *ensembles* of rateless codes.)

This raises the natural question of whether randomness is inherently needed for rateless codes.[1]

1.1 Our Results

In this paper, we answer the question to the affirmative by constructing deterministic efficient rateless codes which achieve the capacity over the binary symmetric channel. Letting $C(p)$ denote the capacity of the BSC with crossover probability p, we prove the following theorem.

THEOREM 1.1 (MAIN THEOREM). *Fix some super-constant function $\beta(k) = \omega(1)$. There exists a deterministic rateless encoding algorithm Enc and a deterministic rateless decoding algorithm Dec with the following properties:*

- *(Capacity achieving) For every information word $m \in \{0,1\}^k$, noise parameter $p \in (0, \frac{1}{2})$, and prefix length $n = k \cdot \frac{1}{C(p)-\delta}$ where $0 < \delta < C(p)$ is an arbitrary constant, we have that*

$$\Pr_{noise \xleftarrow{R} BSC(p)} [\mathsf{Dec}(\mathsf{Enc}(m,[1:n])+noise) \neq m] \leq 2^{-\Omega(k/\beta)},$$

where $\mathsf{Enc}(m,[1:n])$ denotes the n-bit prefix of the codeword $\mathsf{Enc}(m)$, and the constants in the big Omega notation depend on δ and p.

- *(Efficiency) The n-long prefix of Enc can be computed in time $n \cdot \beta$, and decoding is performed in time $n \cdot \beta$. Both algorithms can be implemented in parallel by circuits of depth $O(\beta + \log n)$.*

Letting β be a slowly increasing function, (e.g, $\log^*(k)$) we obtain an "almost" exponential error and "almost" linear time encoding and decoding.

One may also consider a weaker form of capacity achieving rateless codes in which the encoding is allowed to depend on the gap to capacity δ. (This effectively puts an a-priori upper-bound on the noise probability which makes things easier.) In this setting we can obtain an asymptotically optimal construction with linear time encoding and decoding and exponentially small error.

THEOREM 1.2. *For every $\delta > 0$, there exists a deterministic encoding algorithm Enc_δ and a deterministic decoding algorithm Dec_δ with the following properties:*

- *(Weak capacity achieving) For every information word $m \in \{0,1\}^k$, noise parameter $p \in (0, \frac{1}{2})$ such that $C(p) > \delta$, and prefix length $n = k \cdot \frac{1}{C(p)-\delta}$ we have that*

$$\Pr_{noise \xleftarrow{R} BSC(p)} [\mathsf{Dec}_\delta(\mathsf{Enc}_\delta(m,[1:n])+noise) \neq m] \leq 2^{-\Omega(k)}.$$

- *(Efficiency) The n-long prefix of the code can be encoded and decoded in linear time $O(n)$ and in parallel by circuits of logarithmic depth $O(\log(n))$.*

(The constants in the asymptotic notations depend on δ.)

---

[1]As we will see in Section 1.2, the question is non-trivial even for computationally unbounded encoders as a rateless code is an infinite object.

Comparison to Spinal codes.

Prior to our work, *Spinal codes* [19, 20, 1] were the only known efficient (randomized) rateless codes for the BSC. Apart from being deterministic, our construction has several important theoretical advantages over spinal codes. The upper bound on the decoding error of spinal codes is only inverse polynomial in k, and these codes only weakly achieve the capacity (i.e., the encoding depends on the gap δ to capacity). Moreover, the decoding complexity is polynomial (as opposed to linear or quasilinear in our codes), and both encoding and decoding are highly sequential as they require $\Omega(k)$ sequential steps. It should be mentioned however that, while Spinal codes were reported to be highly practical, we currently do not know whether our codes perform well in practice.

1.2 Overview of our construction

Our starting point is a simple (yet inefficient and randomized) construction based on a random linear code. Assume that both the encoder and decoder have an access to an infinite sequence of random k-bit row vectors $\{R_i\}_{i \in \mathbb{N}}$. To encode the message $m \in \{0,1\}^k$, viewed as a k-bit column vector, the encoder sends the sequence $\{R_i \cdot m\}_{i \in \mathbb{N}}$ of inner products over the binary field. To decode a noisy n-bit prefix of the codeword, we will employ the maximum-likelihood decoder (ML) for the code generated by the $n \times k$ matrix $R = (R_1, \ldots, R_n)$. A classical result in coding theory asserts that such a code achieves the capacity of the BSC. Namely, as long as the gap from capacity $\delta = C(p) - k/n$ is positive, the decoding error probability

$$\Pr_{noise \xleftarrow{R} BSC(p), R \xleftarrow{R} \{0,1\}^{n \times k}} [\mathsf{ML}_R(R \cdot m + noise) \neq m] \quad (1)$$

decreases exponentially fast as a function of k.

This construction has two important drawbacks: It is probabilistic and it does not support efficient decoding. For now, let us ignore computational limitations, and attempt to de-randomize the construction.

1.2.1 Derandomization

We would like to deterministically generate an infinite number of rows $\{R_i\}_{i \in \mathbb{N}}$ such that every n-row prefix matrix $R[1:n] = (R_1, \ldots, R_n)$ has a low ML-decoding error of, say, 0.01, for every p for which $C(p) - k/n$ is larger than, say, 0.01.[2]

Although we know that, for every n, almost all $n \times k$ matrices satisfy this condition, it is not a-priori clear that every such low-error matrix can be extended to a larger matrix while preserving low error.

To solve this problem, we identify a property of *good* matrices which, on one hand, guarantees low decoding error, and, on the other hand, is *extendible* in the sense that every good matrix can be augmented by some row while preserving its goodness. We will base our notion of goodness on the *weight distribution* of the matrix R.

Let $W_{i,n}$ denote the set of information words which are mapped by the matrix $R[1:n]$ to codewords of Hamming weight i, and let $w_{i,n}$ denote the size of this set. The sets $(W_{1,n}, \ldots, W_{n,n})$ form a partition of $\{0,1\}^k$, and the vector $(w_{i,n})_{i=1,\ldots,n}$ is called the weight distribution of the code.

---

[2]We use small constants to simplify the presentation, the discussion remains valid when the constants are replaced with a function that decreases with k.

When a row R_{n+1} is added, the weight of all information words which are orthogonal to R_{n+1} remains the same, while the weight of non-orthogonal words grows by 1. Thus R_{n+1} splits $W_{i,n}$ to two parts: the orthogonal vectors which "remain" in $W_{i,n+1}$, and the non-orthogonal vectors which are "elevated" to $W_{i+1,n+1}$. A random row R_{n+1} is therefore expected to split $W_{i,n}$ into two *equal* parts.

If in each step we could choose such an "ideal" row which simultaneously halves all $W_{i,n}$'s, we would get an "ideal" weight distribution in which $w_i^*(n,k) = \binom{n}{i} \cdot 2^{k-n}$, as expected in a random linear code. Such an ideal weight distribution guarantees a low ML decoding error over $\mathsf{BSC}(p)$ when $C(p) < k/n$ (cf. [21, 28, 3]).

While we do not know how to choose such an ideal row (in fact it is not clear that such a row exists), a probabilistic argument shows that we can always find a row R_{n+1} which approximately splits every sufficiently large $W_{i,n}$ simultaneously. Furthermore, by keeping track of the small sets and choosing R_{n+1} which elevates a constant fraction of the lightest vectors, we make sure that the distance of the code is not too small, e.g., $W_{i,n}$ is empty for all $i < \Omega((n-k)/\log n)$. Using these properties we show that the resulting code has low ML decoding error. (See Section 3.)

1.2.2 *Making the code efficient*

The above approach gives rise to a deterministic rateless code which achieves the capacity of the BSC with a subexponential error of $\varepsilon = 2^{-\Omega(\beta/\log\beta)}$ where β is the length of the information word. However, the time complexity of encoding/decoding the n-bit prefix of a codeword is $n \cdot 2^{O(\beta)}$. We solve this problem by noting that Forney's concatenation technique [11] naturally extends to the rateless setting. We sketch the construction below. (Full details appear in Section 4.)

The construction uses the inefficient rateless code as an "inner code" $C_{\mathsf{in}} : \{0,1\}^\beta \to \{0,1\}^*$, and, in addition, employs a standard efficient outer code $C_{\mathsf{out}} : B^{k_{\mathsf{out}}} \to B^{n_{\mathsf{out}}}$ where $B \triangleq \{0,1\}^\beta$ and $k_{\mathsf{out}} \triangleq k/\beta$.

To encode a message $m \in \{0,1\}^k$, we parse it as $M \in B^{k_{\mathsf{out}}}$, apply the outer code to obtain a codeword $C \triangleq (C_1, \ldots, C_{n_{\mathsf{out}}})$ and then apply the inner code to each of the symbols of C in parallel. Namely, each symbol C_i is encoded by the code C_{in} to an infinitely-long column vector. The $n_{\mathsf{in}} \cdot n_{\mathsf{out}}$ prefix of the concatenated encoding is obtained by collecting the binary vectors $(X_1, \ldots, X_{n_{\mathsf{out}}})$ where X_i denotes the prefix of length n_{in} of the inner codeword that corresponds to C_i.

Decoding proceeds in the natural way. Let $Y = (Y_1, \ldots, Y_{n_{\mathsf{out}}})$ denote the noisy $n_{\mathsf{in}} \cdot n_{\mathsf{out}}$ prefix of the encoding of the message m. First, maximum likelihood decoding is employed to decode each of the inner codewords Y_i into $\hat{X}_i$. Next, the decoder of the outer code recovers an information word M from the noisy codeword $(\hat{X}_1, \ldots, \hat{X}_{n_{\mathsf{out}}})$.

In order to prove Theorem 1.1, we need a somewhat non-standard setting of the parameters. To avoid having to fix the gap to the channel's capacity ahead of time, we use an outer code whose rate tends to 1 (i.e., $n_{\mathsf{out}} = k_{\mathsf{out}}(1 + o(1))$). Set $\beta = \omega(1)$. For concreteness, take an outer code $C_{\mathsf{out}} : B^{k_{\mathsf{out}}} \to B^{n_{\mathsf{out}}}$ with $n_{\mathsf{out}} = k_{\mathsf{out}} + k_{\mathsf{out}}/\mathrm{poly}(\beta)$, and assume that the code can be decoded from a fraction of $\varepsilon' = \Omega(1/\mathrm{poly}(\beta))$ errors in time $n_{\mathsf{out}} \cdot \mathrm{poly}(\beta)$ and can be

encoded with similar complexity.[3] A standard application of Chernoff's bound shows that the decoding error of p-noisy codeword of length $n \geq k \cdot \frac{1}{C(p)-\delta}$, is $2^{-\Omega(n_{\mathsf{out}}(\varepsilon'-\varepsilon)^2)}$, which, under our choice of parameters, simplifies to $2^{-\Omega(k/\mathrm{poly}(\beta))}$. For a slowly increasing $\beta = \omega(1)$, we derive an almost-exponential error, and an almost linear encoding/decoding time complexity of $n_{\mathsf{out}} \cdot \beta + n \cdot 2^{O(\beta)}$.

Theorem 1.2 is obtained by using a (large) constant β which depends on the gap to capacity δ. As a result the rate of the outer code is bounded away from 1, but the error becomes exponentially small and both encoding and decoding can be performed in linear time.

1.3 Discussion

One of the main conceptual contributions of this work is a formalization of rateless codes from an algorithmic point of view (see Section 2). This formulation raises a more general research problem:

> Is it possible to gradually generate an infinite combinatorial object $\mathcal{O} = \{\mathcal{O}_i\}_{i=1}^\infty$ via a deterministic algorithm?

Note that the question may be interesting even for inefficient algorithms as it may be infeasible, in general, to decide whether a finite sequence $\mathcal{O}_1, \ldots, \mathcal{O}_n$ is a prefix of some good infinite sequence $\mathcal{O}$. (This is very different than the standard finite setting, where inefficient derandomization is trivially achievable by exhaustive search.) It will be interesting to further explore other instances of this question (e.g., for some families of graphs).

The formulation of a deterministic construction of a rateless code can be formulated as follows. Refer to a generating matrix as "pseudo-random-weight" if the weight distribution of the code it generates is "close" to the expected weight distribution of random linear codes. Our main technical contribution is a deterministic construction of an infinite generating matrix, every finite prefix of which is "pseudo-random-weight".

An interesting open problem is to obtain stronger approximations for the "ideal" weight distribution. Specifically, it should be possible to improve the code's distance from sublinear ($\Omega((n-k)/\log n)$) to linear ($\Omega((n-k))$) in the redundancy. More ambitiously, is it possible to construct a rateless code which, for every restriction to n consecutive bits, achieves the capacity of the BSC? Getting back to our motivating story of noisy multicast, such a rateless code would allow the receivers to dynamically join the multicast.

2. RATELESS CODES

In this section we formalize the notion of rateless codes. We begin with some standard notation.

Notation.

The Hamming distance between two binary vectors x, x' of equal length is denoted by $\mathsf{dist}(x, x')$. Let μ denote a probability distribution and X denote a random variable.

---

[3]Such a code can be obtained based on expander graphs, e.g., [30, 31, 12]. In fact, we will employ the code of [12] which achieves a smaller alphabet of absolute size β. This is not a real issue as we can increase the alphabet to 2^β by parsing $\beta/\log\beta$ symbols as a single symbol without affecting the properties of the code. See Section 4.

We denote that X is distributed according to μ by $x \overset{R}{\leftarrow} \mu$. Let $\mathsf{BSC}(p)$ denote the binary symmetric channel with crossover probability $p \in (0, \frac{1}{2})$. We abuse notation and write $\mathsf{noise} \overset{R}{\leftarrow} \mathsf{BSC}(p)$ to denote that noise is a binary vector whose coordinates are random independent Bernoulli trials chosen to be 1 with probability p and a 0 with probability $1 - p$. (The vector's length will be clear from the context.) Recall that the capacity of the binary symmetric channel is $1 - H(p)$ where $H(p) \triangleq -p \log p - (1-p) \log p$ is the entropy function. (By default, the base of all logarithms is 2.)

We begin with a syntactic definition of a rateless code.

DEFINITION 2.1 (RATELESS CODE). *A rateless code is a pair of algorithms* $(\mathsf{Enc}, \mathsf{Dec})$.

1. *The encoder* $\mathsf{Enc} : \{0,1\}^* \times \mathbb{N} \to \{0,1\}$ *takes an information word* $m \in \{0,1\}^*$ *and an index* $i \in \mathbb{N}$, *and outputs the i-th bit of the encoding of m. (Equivalently, the encoding of m is an infinite sequence of bits* $(\mathsf{Enc}(m, i))_{i \in \mathbb{N}}$.)

2. *The decoder* $\mathsf{Dec} : \{0,1\}^* \times \mathbb{N} \to \{0,1\}^*$ *maps a noisy codeword* $y \in \{0,1\}^*$ *and an integer k (which corresponds to the length of the information word) to an information word* $m' \in \{0,1\}^k$.

Note that in our definition, both the encoder and the decoder are assumed to be *deterministic*. One can relax the definition and consider a probabilistic rateless code in which the encoder and the decoder depend on some shared randomness. This corresponds to an ensemble of codes from which a code is randomly chosen.

Conventions.

We let $\mathsf{Enc}(m, [1 : n])$ denote the first n bits of the codeword that corresponds to $m \in \{0,1\}^*$. Namely, $\mathsf{Enc}(m, [1 : n])$ is the binary string $c = (c_1, \ldots, c_n)$, where $c_i = \mathsf{Enc}(m, i)$. A rateless code defines (n, k) codes for every n and k via

$$C_{n,k} \triangleq \{\mathsf{Enc}(m, [1 : n]) \mid m \in \{0,1\}^k\}.$$

We measure the complexity of encoding (resp. decoding) of a rateless code as the time $T(k, n)$ that takes to encode (resp., decode) the code $C_{n,k}$. The encoder and the decoder are defined for every information block length k. We often consider a specific k and then abbreviate $\mathsf{Dec}(y, k)$ by $\mathsf{Dec}(y)$.

REMARK 2.2 (ADDITIONAL FEATURES). *In some scenarios it is beneficial to have a rateless code with the following additional features.*

- *(Linearity) A rateless code is* linear *if Enc is a linear function. Namely, for $m \in \mathrm{GF}(2)^k$, we have*

  $$\mathsf{Enc}(m, i) = R_i \cdot m,$$

  where $\{R_i\}_{i=1}^{\infty}$, is an infinite sequence of row vectors $R_i \in \mathrm{GF}(2)^k$. We refer to the infinite matrix $G = \{R_i\}_{i=1}^{\infty}$ as the generator *matrix of the code.*

- *(Systematic) An encoding is* systematic *if, for every $m \in \{0,1\}^k$, we have $\mathsf{Enc}(m, [1:k]) = m$.*

We define the *error function* of a rateless code $(\mathsf{Enc}, \mathsf{Dec})$ over the binary symmetric channel $\mathsf{BSC}(p)$ as a function of k, n and $p \in (0, 1/2)$.

DEFINITION 2.3 (THE ERROR FUNCTION).

$$\mathsf{err}(p, k, n) \triangleq \max_{m \in \{0,1\}^k}$$
$$\Pr_{\mathsf{noise} \overset{R}{\leftarrow} \mathsf{BSC}(p)} [\mathsf{Dec}(\mathsf{Enc}(m, [1 : n]) + \mathsf{noise}) \neq m].$$

Equivalently, this is the maximum error probability, over the $\mathsf{BSC}(p)$, of the code $C_{n,k}$ that is obtained by restricting the rateless code to a prefix of length n.

DEFINITION 2.4. (CAPACITY ACHIEVING RATELESS CODE FOR BSC) *A rateless code* $(\mathsf{Enc}, \mathsf{Dec})$ *achieves capacity with respect to the binary symmetric channel if, for every $p \in (0, 1/2)$ and every $\delta \in (0, 1 - H(p))$, if $n(k) \triangleq \frac{k}{1-H(p)-\delta}$, then*

$$\lim_{k \to \infty} \mathsf{err}(p, k, n(k)) = 0. \qquad (2)$$

Naturally, it is desirable to bound (2) by a quickly decaying function of k.

Motivated by the analysis of finite codes, one may be interested also in proving that, for a fixed k, increasing redundancy over the same channel also increases the probability of successful decoding, namely

$$\forall \, k \qquad \lim_{n \to \infty} \mathsf{err}(p, k, n) = 0.$$

Such a property implies that the minimum distance increases as a function of n and that the decoding algorithm benefits from this increase.

3. AN INEFFICIENT DETERMINISTIC RATE-LESS CODE

In this section we present an (inefficient) deterministic construction of a rateless code that achieves capacity with respect to binary symmetric channels. In fact, when all other parameters are fixed, the error function decreases almost exponentially as a function of n. This code will be later used as the inner code of our final construction. Formally, we prove the following theorem.

THEOREM 3.1. *There exists a deterministic, rateless, linear, systematic code $(\mathsf{Enc}, \mathsf{Dec})$ with the following properties:*

Capacity achieving: *For every $p \in (0, \frac{1}{2})$ and $\delta \in (0, 1 - H(p))$, if $n \geq k/(1 - H(p) - \delta)$, then the error function satisfies*[4]

$$\mathsf{err}(p, k, n) = e^{-\Omega(n/\log n)}.$$

Complexity: *Encoding and decoding of k-bit information words and n-bit codewords can be done in time $O(nk \cdot 2^{2k})$.*

The decoder is simply maximum likelihood decoding. The encoder multiplies the information word by the generating matrix. Each row of the generating matrix can be computed in time $O(k \cdot 2^{2k})$. Hence, the generating matrix of $C_{n,k}$ can

---

[4] Note that if $n = k/(1 - H(p) - \delta)$, then the theorem simply states that the error function is $e^{-O(k/\log k)}$. However, the bound also holds for rates far below the capacity. For example, if k is constant and n tends to infinity, then the error function is $e^{-\Omega(n/\log n)}$.

be computed in time $O(nk \cdot 2^{2k})$. Both the encoder and decoder require the generating matrix. Once the generating matrix of $C_{n,k}$ is computed, the running times of the encoding and the decoding are as follows:

- The encoding of $\mathsf{Enc}(m, [n:1])$ of $m \in \{0,1\}^k$ can be computed in time $O(n \cdot k)$.

- Computing $\mathsf{Dec}(y, k)$ for $y \in \{0,1\}^n$ can be done in $O(n \cdot k \cdot 2^k)$.

In the following sections we describe the construction of the generating matrix of the code and analyze the error of the maximum likelihood decoder.

3.1 Computing the generating matrix

Our goal is to construct an infinite generating matrix G with k columns. Let $R_i \in \{0,1\}^k$ denote the ith row of the generating matrix. Let G_n denote the $k \times n$ matrix, the rows of which are $(R_i)_{i=1...n}$. Let $C_{n,k}$ denote the code generated by G_n. The generating matrix G begins with the $k \times k$ identity matrix, and hence each code $C_{n,k}$ is systematic. Subsequent rows R_i (for $i > k$) of the generating matrix are constructed one by one. Let $W_{i,n} \triangleq \{x \in \{0,1\}^k : \mathsf{wt}(G_n \cdot x) = i\}$ denote the ith weight class of $C_{n,k}$. The rows are chosen so that the weight distribution $(|W_{1,n}|, \ldots, |W_{n,n}|)$ of $C_{n,k}$ is close to that of a random $[n,k]$-linear code $C^*_{n,k}$. Note that when a row vector R_{n+1} is added, if $x \in \{0,1\}^k$ is orthogonal to R_{n+1}, then $\mathsf{wt}(G_{n+1} \cdot x) = \mathsf{wt}(G_n \cdot x)$; otherwise, $\mathsf{wt}(G_{n+1} \cdot x) = \mathsf{wt}(G_n \cdot x) + 1$. Thus R_{n+1} splits each weight class $W_{i,n}$ to two parts: the orthogonal vectors which "remain" in $W_{i,n+1}$, and the non-orthogonal vectors which are "elevated" to $W_{i+1,n+1}$.

DEFINITION 3.2. *A vector $R \in \mathrm{GF}(2)^k$ ε-splits a set $S \subseteq \mathrm{GF}(2)^k$ if*

$$\left(\frac{1}{2} - \varepsilon\right) \cdot |S| \leq |\{s \in S \mid s \cdot R = 1\}| \leq \left(\frac{1}{2} + \varepsilon\right) \cdot |S|.$$

A vector $R \in \mathrm{GF}(2)^k$ ε-elevates a set $S \subseteq \mathrm{GF}(2)^k$ if

$$|\{s \in S \mid s \cdot R = 1\}| \geq \varepsilon \cdot |S|.$$

Ideally, we would like to find a row R_{n+1} that ε-splits every weight class $W_{i,n}$. Since we cannot achieve this, we compromise on splitting only part of the weight classes, as follows. By a probabilistic argument, there exists a single vector which ε-splits all weight classes that are large (where a weight class $W_{i,n}$ is large if $|W_{i,n}| \geq 2n^2$). However, we cannot find vector that also ϵ-splits every weight class that is small.

The algorithm for computing the rows R_i of G for $i > k$ is listed as Algorithm 1. The algorithm employs a marking strategy to deal with small weight classes $W_{i,n}$. Initially, all the nonzero information words are unmarked. Once an information word becomes a member of a small weight class, it is marked, and remains marked forever (even if it later belongs to a weight class $W_{i',n'}$ which is large). The unmarked vectors in $W_{i,n}$ are denoted by $\widehat{W}_{i,n}$. By definition, the set $\widehat{W}_{i,n}$ is either empty or large, and so there exists a vector R_{n+1} which ε-splits $\widehat{W}_{i,n}$. In addition, R_{n+1} is required to elevate the set of nonzero codewords of minimum weight. As we will later see, the distance of the resulting code grows

---

Algorithm 1 Compute-Generating-Matrix - An algorithm for computing rows R_n of the generating matrix of the rateless code for $n > k$.

1. Let $(R_1, \ldots, R_k)$ be the rows of the $k \times k$ identity matrix.

2. Initialize the set of marked information words $M \leftarrow \emptyset$.

3. For $n = k$ to ∞ do

   (a) For $1 \leq i \leq n$, let $W_{i,n}$ be the set of information words that are encoded by a codeword of weight i.

   (b) Let $d > 0$ be the minimal positive integer for which $W_{d,n}$ is non-empty.

   (c) For every i, if $|W_{i,n} \setminus M| < 2n^2$, then mark all the information words in $W_{i,n}$ by setting $M \leftarrow M \cup W_{i,n}$. Let $\widehat{W}_{i,n} \triangleq (W_{i,n} \setminus M)$ denote the unmarked vectors in $W_{i,n}$.

   (d) Let R_{n+1} be the lexicographically first vector in $\mathrm{GF}(2)^k$ that simultaneously $\frac{1}{2\sqrt{n}}$-splits every unmarked weight class $\widehat{W}_{i,n}$ and $1/8$-elevates $W_{d,n}$.

---

sufficiently fast as a function of n, and its weight distribution is sufficiently close to the expected weight distribution of a random linear code.

We remark that (according to the analysis) the $1/8$-elevation of $W_{d,n}$ can be skipped if $\widehat{W}_{d,n} \neq \emptyset$ (namely, the elevation is required only if every vector in $W_{d,n}$ is marked). It is not hard to verify that Algorithm 1 can compute the first n rows in time $O(nk \cdot 2^{2k})$. The following lemma states that Algorithm 1 succeeds in finding a row R_n for every $n > k$.

LEMMA 3.3. *The algorithm always finds a suitable vector R_{n+1} in Line 3d.*

The lemma is proven via a simple probabilistic argument (proof in full version).

3.2 Weight Distribution

In this section we analyze the weight distribution of the linear code $C_{n,k}$. We let $w_{i,n}$ be the size of $W_{i,n}$, the set of information words whose encoding under $C_{n,k}$ has Hamming weight i. We will show that $w_{i,n}$ is not far from the expected weight distribution $w_i^*(n,k) \triangleq \binom{n}{i} \cdot 2^{k-n}$ of a random $[n,k]$ linear code.

OBSERVATION 3.4. *After n iterations, the number of marked information words is less than $2n^4$.*

PROOF. For every $i, n' \leq n$ the set $W_{i,n'}$ contributes less than $2n^2$ information words to the set M of marked words. Hence there are most $2n^4$ marked vectors after the R_n is chosen. $\square$

CLAIM 3.5. *For every n and i, we have that $w_{i,n} \leq 2n^4 + w_i^*(n,k) \cdot \Pi_{k,n}$ where*

$$\Pi_{k,n} \triangleq \prod_{j=k+1}^{n-1} \left(1 + \frac{1}{\sqrt{j}}\right) \leq e^{2(\sqrt{n} - \sqrt{k})}.$$

PROOF. By Observation 3.4, it suffices to bound the unmarked vectors by

$$|\widehat{W}_{i,n}| \leq w_i^*(n,k) \cdot \Pi_{k,n} . \tag{3}$$

Indeed, $|\widehat{W}_{i,n}|$ and $w_i^*(n,k)$ satisfy the following recurrences:

$$w_i^*(n,k) = \frac{1}{2} \cdot (w_{i-1,n-1}^* + w_{i,n-1}^*)$$

$$|\widehat{W}_{i,n}| \leq \left(1 + \frac{1}{\sqrt{n-1}}\right) \cdot \frac{1}{2} \cdot \left(|\widehat{W}_{i-1,n-1}| + |\widehat{W}_{i,n-1}|\right) .$$

We can now prove Eq. 3 by induction on $n \geq k$. Indeed, $w_{i,k} = w_{i,k}^*$, and

$$\begin{aligned}
|\widehat{W}_{i,n}| &\leq \left(1 + \frac{1}{\sqrt{n-1}}\right) \cdot \frac{1}{2} \cdot \left(w_{i-1,n-1}^* \Pi_{k,n-1} + w_{i,n-1}^* \Pi_{k,n-1}\right) \\
&= \frac{1}{2} \left(w_{i-1,n-1}^* + w_{i,n-1}^*\right) \Pi_{k,n} \\
&= w_i^*(n,k) \Pi_{k,n}.
\end{aligned}$$

The claim follows. □

We will also need to prove that the distance of $C_{n,k}$ is sufficiently large.

CLAIM 3.6. *For every $n > k$, the minimum distance of the code $C_{n,k}$ is greater than $\frac{n-k}{55 \cdot \log n}$.*

PROOF. It is easier to view the evolution of the weight distribution of $C_{n,k}$ as a process of shifting balls in n bins. A ball represents a nonzero information word, and a bin corresponds to a weight class. We assume that $bin(1)$ is positioned on the left, and $bin(n)$ is positioned on the right. Moving (or shifting) a ball one bin to the right means that the augmentation of the generating matrix by a new row increases the weight of the encoding of the information word by one. Note that, as the generating matrix is augmented by a new row, a ball either stays in the same bin or is shifted by one bin to the right.

Step t of the process corresponds to the weight distribution of $C_{n',k}$ for $n' = t + k$. Let $bin_t(i)$ denote the set of balls in $bin(i)$ after step t. By Algorithm 1, the process treats marked balls and unmarked balls differently.

Let $t \triangleq (n-k)/2$ denote half the redundancy. Let $\alpha \triangleq \frac{2}{\log_2(8/7)} < 11$. Let $\Delta \triangleq \frac{n-k}{\alpha \log(2n^4)}$. In these terms, We prove a slightly stronger minimum distance, namely,

$$bin_{2t}(i) = \emptyset, \qquad \forall i \leq \Delta. \tag{4}$$

The proof is divided into two parts. First we consider the unmarked balls, and then we consider the marked balls. We begin by proving that

$$bin_t(i) \setminus M = \emptyset, \qquad \forall i \leq \Delta. \tag{5}$$

Namely, after t iterations of Algorithm 1, $bin(1), \ldots, bin(\Delta)$ may contain only marked balls. Note that if $bin_t(i) = \emptyset$ for every $i \leq \Delta$, then $bin_{2t}(i) = \emptyset$ for every $i \leq \Delta$.

The proof of Equation 5 is based on a claim proved in the full version that states the following:

$$|bin_t(i)| \leq \left(\frac{2}{3}\right)^t \cdot \binom{k+t}{i} \leq \left(\frac{2}{3}\right)^t \cdot (k+t)^i. \tag{6}$$

The intuition is as follows. Initially, $bin_0(i)$ contains at most $\binom{k}{i}$ vectors. After step $t+1$, $bin_{t+1}(i)$ contains roughly half the balls of $bin_t(i-1)$ (i.e. the elevated balls) and roughly

half the balls of $bin_t(i)$ (i.e. the non-elevated balls). A recursive analysis shows that after t steps we get the above expression (for simplicity the bound assumes only 1/3-elevation).

For $t = (n-k)/2$ and $i \leq \Delta$, the RHS of Eq. 6 is smaller than 1, and so Eq. 5 follows.

To prove that $bin_{2t}(i) \cap M = \emptyset$ for every $i \leq \Delta$, let $t(i) \triangleq t + i \cdot \log_{8/7}(2n^4)$. Note that $t(\Delta) = 2t$. We wish to prove, by induction on i, that the leftmost bin with a marked ball after $t(i)$ iterations is $bin(i+1)$. After $\log_{8/7}(2n^4)$ additional iterations, also $bin(i+1)$ lacks marked balls. In this manner, after $2t$ iterations all the marked balls are pushed to the right of $bin(\Delta)$. Formally, we claim that

$$bin_{t(i)}(j) \cap M = \emptyset, \qquad \forall j \leq i. \tag{7}$$

Equation 7 suffices because $t(\Delta) = 2t$, and hence it implies that $bin_{2t}(j) = \emptyset$ for every $j \leq \Delta$, as required. The proof of Eq. 7 is by induction on i. For $i = 0$ the claim is trivial (because every nonzero information word is encoded to a nonzero word). The induction step for $i > 0$ is as follows. For every $t(i-1) < t \leq t(i)$, if $bin_t(i)$ contains a marked ball, then, by the induction hypothesis, it is the leftmost bin that contains a marked ball. Hence, each new row R_{t+1} of the generator matrix 1/8-elevates $bin_t(i)$. Since $bin_t(i)$ consists only of marked balls, by Obs. 3.4, it follows that $|bin_{t(i-1)}(i)| < 2n^4$. Hence, after $\log_{8/7}(2n^4)$ steps, the bin is emptied, namely, $bin_{t(i)}(i) = \emptyset$, as required.

We proved that $bin_{2t}(i)$ is empty if $i \leq \Delta$, and the claim follows. □

Overall Claims 3.6 and 3.5 imply that $C_{n,k}$ is close to an "average" code in the following sense. Let $\alpha \triangleq \frac{2}{\log_2(8/7)} < 11$.

LEMMA 3.7. *The weight distribution of the constructed code $C_{n,k}$ satisfies the following bound:*

$$w_{i,n} \leq \begin{cases} 0 & \text{if } 0 < i \leq \frac{n-k}{\alpha \log(2n^4)} \\ 2n^4 + w_i^*(n,k) \cdot \Pi_{k,n} & \text{if } i > \frac{n-k}{\alpha \log(2n^4)}. \end{cases} \tag{8}$$

3.3 Analysis of the ML Decoding Error

In this section we complete the proof of Theorem 3.1. Let Dec be the maximum-likelihood (ML) decoder which, given a noisy codeword $y \in \{0,1\}^n$ and k, finds a closest codeword $\hat{y} \in C_{n,k}$ and outputs the message $m \in \{0,1\}^k$ for which $G_n \cdot m = \hat{y}$.

LEMMA 3.8. *For every p and $\delta \in (0, 1 - H(p))$. If $n \geq \frac{k}{1 - H(p) - \delta}$, then the error function of the maximum likelihood decoder satisfies*

$$\text{err}(p,k,n) = e^{-\Omega(n/\log n)} .$$

PROOF. Fix p and δ, and consider n and k such that $n \geq \frac{k}{1 - H(p) - \delta}$. Let δ_{GV} be the root $\delta \in (0, 1/2)$ of the equation $H(\delta) = 1 - \frac{k}{n}$. Since the code is linear, we may assume without loss of generality that the all zero codeword was transmitted. Our goal is to upper-bound the event that $\hat{y}$, the codeword computed by the ML-decoder, is non-zero. We divide the analysis into two cases based on the Hamming weight of $\hat{y}$.

Case 1: $\hat{y}$ is of weight smaller than $\delta_{\text{GV}} \cdot n$.

For a fixed codeword y of weight $i > 0$, erroneous decoding to y corresponds to the event that the BSC(p) flipped at least $i/2$ bits in the support of y. (The support of y is the set $\{j : y_j = 1\}$.) This event happens with probability

$$P_i \triangleq \sum_{j=\lceil i/2 \rceil}^{i} \binom{i}{j} \cdot p^j \cdot (1-p)^{i-j}.$$

By a union-bound, we can upper-bound the probability of the event that $0 < \mathsf{wt}(\hat{y}) < \delta_{\mathrm{GV}} \cdot n$ by

$$\sum_{i=1}^{\delta_{GV} \cdot n - 1} w_{i,n} \cdot P_i \leq \sum_{i=(n-k)/(55 \log n)}^{\delta_{GV} \cdot n - 1} (2n^4 + e^{2\sqrt{n}}) \cdot P_i, \quad (9)$$

where the upper-bound $w_{i,n} \leq (2n^4 + e^{2\sqrt{n}})$ follows from Lemma 3.7 and from the fact that $w_i^*(n,k) < 1$ if $i/n < \delta_{\mathrm{GV}}$. Below, we show that

$$P_i \leq 2^{-\beta \cdot i} \quad (10)$$

where $\beta \triangleq -\frac{1}{2} \cdot \log_2(4p(1-p))$ is positive since $p \in (0, \frac{1}{2})$. It follows that the error probability (9) is upper-bounded by

$$(2n^4 + e^{2\sqrt{n}}) \cdot \sum_{i=(n-k)/(55 \log n)}^{\delta_{GV} \cdot n} 2^{-\beta \cdot i} \leq e^{-\Omega(n/\log n)}.$$

It is left to prove Eq. (10). Indeed, by definition, P_i satisfies

$$P_i \triangleq \sum_{j=\lceil i/2 \rceil}^{i} \binom{i}{j} \cdot p^j \cdot (1-p)^{i-j}$$

$$\leq p^{i/2} \cdot (1-p)^{i/2} \cdot \sum_{j=\lceil i/2 \rceil}^{i} \binom{i}{j}$$

$$\leq p^{i/2} \cdot (1-p)^{i/2} \cdot 2^i,$$

which can be written as $(4p(1-p))^{i/2}$. Because $p < 1/2$, it follows that $\beta > 0$, and $P_i \leq 2^{-\beta \cdot i}$, as required.

Case 2: $\hat{y}$ is of weight larger than $\delta_{\mathrm{GV}} \cdot n$.

In this regime, the spectrum of our code is sufficiently close to that of a random linear code, and so the error of the ML-decoding can be analyzed via (an extension of) Poltyrev's bound [21] (see also [28]). The extension bounds the probability of the event that ML-decoding returns a "heavy" word. Note that no assumption is made on the minimum distance of the code. The proof is based on an analysis in [2].

THEOREM 3.9 (EXTENSION OF THM. 1 OF [21]). *Let $p \in (0, \frac{1}{2})$ be a constant, $\delta > 0$ be a constant such that $\frac{k}{n} < 1 - H(p) - \delta$, and $\tau \in [0,1]$ be a threshold parameter. There exists a constant $\alpha > 0$ for which the following holds. If C is an $[n,k]$ linear code whose weight distribution $\{w_i(C_n)\}_i$ satisfies*

$$w_i \leq 2^{(\delta/3)n} \cdot w_i^*(n,k) \quad \text{for every } i \geq \tau n.$$

Then, the probability over $\mathsf{BSC}(p)$ that the all zero word is ML-decoded to a codeword of weight at least τn is $2^{-\alpha n}$.

Since the weight distribution of our code satisfies the Poltyrev's criteria for codewords of weight at least $\delta_{\mathrm{GV}} \cdot n$, we conclude that the decoding error in case (2) is $2^{-\Omega(n)}$.

By combining the two cases, we conclude that the error-probability is at most $2^{-\Omega(n/\log n)}$, as required. $\square$

4. EFFICIENT RATELESS CODES

In this section we will prove our main theorems and construct an efficient rateless code $(\mathsf{Enc}, \mathsf{Dec})$ that achieves the capacity of the binary symmetric channel. We define $(\mathsf{Enc}, \mathsf{Dec})$ via its restriction $C_{n,k}$ to information words of length k and codewords of length n. Following the outline sketched in Section 1.2.2, we let $C_{n,k}$ be the concatenation of an $[n_{\mathsf{out}}, k_{\mathsf{out}}]$ outer code C_{out} and an $[n_{\mathsf{in}}, k_{\mathsf{in}}]$ inner code C_{in} defined as follows.

Inner Code.

The inner code C_{in} is the inefficient rateless code described in Section 3 restricted to input length k_{in} and output length n_{in}. Recall that this is an $[n_{\mathsf{in}}, k_{\mathsf{in}}]$ linear systematic code over $\{0,1\}$ which can be encoded in time $O(n_{\mathsf{in}} k_{\mathsf{in}} \cdot 2^{2k_{\mathsf{in}}})$. Maximum likelihood decoding requires $O(n_{\mathsf{in}} k_{\mathsf{in}} \cdot 2^{k_{\mathsf{in}}})$ time and achieves an error of $\mathsf{err}(p, k_{\mathsf{in}}, n_{\mathsf{in}}) = e^{-\Omega(n_{\mathsf{in}}/\log n_{\mathsf{in}})}$ over $\mathsf{BSC}(p)$ as long as $n_{\mathsf{in}} \geq k_{\mathsf{in}} \cdot (1 - H(p) - \delta)^{-1}$ for some $\delta \in (0, 1 - H(p))$. Both encoding and decoding can be implemented in parallel time of $O(k_{\mathsf{in}})$.

Outer Code.

The outer code C_{out} is taken from [12, Lemma 1]. It is an $[n_{\mathsf{out}}, k_{\mathsf{out}}]$ linear systematic code over an alphabet Σ_{out} with $n_{\mathsf{out}} = k_{\mathsf{out}} \cdot (1 + |\Sigma_{\mathsf{out}}|^{-1/2})$. Hence, the rate of the outer code tends to one as the alphabet Σ_{out} increases. The outer code can be encoded in time $O(n_{\mathsf{out}} \cdot |\Sigma_{\mathsf{out}}|^{1/2})$. Decoding in time $O(n_{\mathsf{out}} \cdot |\Sigma_{\mathsf{out}}|)$ is successful as long as the fraction of errors is bounded by $\varepsilon_{\mathsf{out}} = \Theta(|\Sigma_{\mathsf{out}}|^{-1})$. Furthermore, the code can be encoded and decoded in parallel time of $O(\log(n_{\mathsf{out}} \cdot |\Sigma_{\mathsf{out}}|))$.

CONSTRUCTION 4.1 (THE CONCATENATED CODE $C_{n,k}^{\beta}$). *For lengths k and n, and a parameter β let*

$$|\Sigma_{\mathsf{out}}| = k_{\mathsf{in}} = \beta,$$
$$k_{\mathsf{out}} = k/\log_2 |\Sigma_{\mathsf{out}}|,$$
$$L_{\mathsf{in}} = (n_{\mathsf{out}} \cdot \log_2 |\Sigma_{\mathsf{out}}|)/k_{\mathsf{in}},$$
$$n_{\mathsf{in}} = n/L_{\mathsf{in}}.$$

- *The encoder of the concatenated code $C_{n,k}^{\beta}$ maps k-bit information word to n-bit codeword as follows (see Figure 1).*

$$F_2^k \xhookrightarrow{1} \Sigma_{\mathsf{out}}^{k_{\mathsf{out}}} \xrightarrow{2} \Sigma_{\mathsf{out}}^{n_{\mathsf{out}}} \xhookrightarrow{3} (F_2^{k_{\mathsf{in}}})^{L_{\mathsf{in}}} \xrightarrow{4} (F_2^{n_{\mathsf{in}}})^{L_{\mathsf{in}}}.$$

The four steps of the encoder are: (1) A message $m \in \{0,1\}^k$ is parsed as the message $m_{\mathsf{out}} \in (\Sigma_{\mathsf{out}})^{k_{\mathsf{out}}}$. Namely, $\Sigma_{\mathsf{out}} = \{0,1\}^{\log \beta}$, and the message m is broken into k_{out} blocks of length $\log_2 |\Sigma_{\mathsf{out}}|$. (2) The encoder of the outer code maps m_{out} to a codeword $c_{\mathsf{out}} \in (\Sigma_{\mathsf{out}})^{n_{\mathsf{out}}}$. (3) The outer codeword c_{out} is parsed as L_{in} messages $(m_{\mathsf{in}}^1, \ldots, m_{\mathsf{in}}^{L_{\mathsf{in}}})$ each over $\{0,1\}^{k_{\mathsf{in}}}$. (4) The encoder of the inner code maps each message m_{in}^j to an inner codeword $c_{\mathsf{in}}^j \in \{0,1\}^{n_{\mathsf{in}}}$.

- *The decoder of the concatenated code $C_{n,k}^{\beta}$ maps n-bit codeword word to k-bit information as follows (see Figure 2).*

$$(F_2^{n_{\mathsf{in}}})^{L_{\mathsf{in}}} \xrightarrow{4} (F_2^{k_{\mathsf{in}}})^{L_{\mathsf{in}}} \xhookrightarrow{3} \Sigma_{\mathsf{out}}^{n_{\mathsf{out}}} \xrightarrow{2} \Sigma_{\mathsf{out}}^{k_{\mathsf{out}}} \xhookrightarrow{1} F_2^k.$$

The four steps of the decoder correspond to the encoding steps in reversed order: (4) The decoder of the in-

ner code applies maximum likelihood decoding to each inner noisy codeword $\hat{c}_{in}^j \in \{0,1\}^{n_{in}}$. We denote the ML-decoding of $\hat{c}_{in}^j \in \{0,1\}^{n_{in}}$ by $\hat{m}_{in}^j$. (3) The L_{in} (inner) information words $(\hat{m}_{in}^1, \ldots, \hat{m}_{in}^{L_{in}})$ each over $\{0,1\}^{k_{in}}$ are parsed as a noisy codeword $\hat{c}_{out} \in (\Sigma_{out})^{n_{out}}$ of the outer code. (2) The decoder of the outer code maps the noisy codeword $\ddot{c}_{out} \in (\Sigma_{out})^{n_{out}}$ to a message $\hat{m}_{out} \in (\Sigma_{out})^{k_{out}}$. (1) The message $\hat{m}_{out}$ is parsed as a message $\hat{m} \in \{0,1\}^k$.

The encoder of the rateless code (when n is not predetermined) outputs the encoding of $m_{in}^1, \ldots, m_{in}^{L_{in}}$ "row by row". Namely, after the i'th bit of the encodings is output, the encoder outputs bit $i+1$ of each inner-codeword. Hence, the code $C_{n,k}^\beta$ is a prefix of the code $C_{n',k}^\beta$ for $n < n'$ and so the code defines a rateless code. Also note that the code is systematic and the complexity of encoding is $O(n_{out} \cdot |\Sigma_{out}|^{1/2} + L_{in} \cdot n_{in} \cdot k_{in} \cdot 2^{2k_{in}}) = O(n \cdot \beta \cdot 2^{2\beta})$ and the complexity of decoding is $O(n_{out} \cdot |\Sigma_{out}| + L_{in} \cdot n_{in} \cdot k_{in} \cdot 2^{2k_{in}}) = O(n \cdot \beta \cdot 2^{2\beta})$. (We assume that the encoder and the decoder need to compute the generating matrix.) Furthermore, both operations can be performed in parallel-time of $O(k_{in} + \log(n_{out} \cdot |\Sigma_{out}|)) = O(\beta + \log n)$. The performance over $\mathsf{BSC}(p)$ is analyzed by the following claim.

In the following claim we bound the decoding error of the concatenated code $C_{n,k}$ over $\mathsf{BSC}(p)$. We consider two settings. In the first setting, the rate of the inner code is $(1 - H(p) - \delta)$, and we prove that the probability of erroneous decoding tends to zero almost exponentially in k. In the second setting, the outer code is fixed (hence k, β, k_{out}, and n_{out} are fixed), and the rate of the inner code tends to zero. In the second setting we prove that the probability of erroneous decoding tends exponentially to zero as a function of n. This implies that the decoder benefits from the increase in the minimum distance of the code as n increases.

CLAIM 4.2. For every $p \in (0, \frac{1}{2})$ and $\delta > 0$, if $n_{in} \geq k_{in} \cdot \frac{1}{1-H(p)-\delta}$, then the decoding error $\mathsf{err}(p,k,n)$ of the concatenated code $C_{n,k}$ over $\mathsf{BSC}(p)$ is $2^{-\Omega(\frac{k}{\beta^3})}$. Moreover, if p, k, and the outer code are fixed, then $\mathsf{err}(p,k,n) = 2^{-\Omega(n/\log n)}$.

PROOF. Let $\hat{c}_{in} = (\hat{c}_{in}^1, \ldots, \hat{c}_{in}^{L_{in}})$ denote the noisy prefix of length $n = n_{in} \cdot L_{in}$ of the encoding of the message m. Let $\hat{e}$ denote the fraction of the inner-code information words that are incorrectly decoded by the ML-decoder. The decoder of the outer-code is successful as long as $\hat{e} < \varepsilon_{out}$. (Note that each decoded inner information word is parsed into $k_{in}/\log_2 |\Sigma_{out}|$ symbols of the outer code. Hence, the fraction of erroneous symbols is bounded by $\hat{e}$.) When k tends to infinity, we bound the probability of the event that $\hat{e} \geq \varepsilon_{out}$ using an additive Chernoff bound. Let ε_{in} denote the probability of erroneous decoding of a noisy inner codeword $\hat{c}_{in}^j$. As the ML-decoding errors are L_{in} independent random events, we conclude that $\Pr[\hat{e} \geq \varepsilon_{out}] \leq 2^{-2L_{in}(\varepsilon_{out} - \varepsilon_{in})^2}$.

By Lemma 3.8, $\varepsilon_{in} = e^{-\Omega(n_{in}/\log n_{in})} = e^{-\Omega(\beta/\log \beta)}$. Under our choice of parameters $\varepsilon_{out} - \varepsilon_{in} = \Omega(1/\beta)$ and $L_{in} = (n_{out} \cdot \log \beta)/\beta > (k_{out} \cdot \log \beta)/\beta = k/\beta$, and so the the bound on the error probability simplifies to $2^{-\Omega(k/\beta^3)}$.

In the second setting, when the outer code is fixed, we bound the probability of the event that $\hat{e} \geq \varepsilon_{out}$ by a union bound over all ε_{out}-fractions of L_{in}. Namely, $\Pr(\hat{e} \geq \varepsilon_{out}) \leq \binom{L_{in}}{\varepsilon_{out} \cdot L_{in}} \cdot \varepsilon_{in}^{\varepsilon_{out} \cdot L_{in}}$ which is bounded by $2^{H(\varepsilon_{out}) \cdot L_{in}} \cdot \varepsilon_{in}^{\varepsilon_{out} \cdot L_{in}}$.

By Lemma 3.8, $\varepsilon_{in} = e^{-\Omega(n_{in}/\log n_{in})}$. Because ε_{out} and L_{in} are fixed, the probability of the event is bounded by $e^{-\Omega(n/\log n)}$, as required. $\square$

Letting β be an (arbitrary slowly) growing function of k we derive the following corollary, which in turn, directly implies Theorem 1.1.

COROLLARY 4.3 (THM. 1.1 REFINED). Let $\beta = \omega(1)$, the rateless code defined by $C_{n,k}^\beta$ is a linear systematic rateless code that can be encoded and decoded in time $O(n \cdot \beta \cdot 2^{2\beta})$ and parallel time of $O(\log n + \beta)$. Furthermore, for fixed $\delta > 0$ and crossover probability p for which $n \geq k \cdot \frac{1}{1-H(p)-\delta}$, the decoding error is $2^{-\Omega(\frac{k}{\beta^3})}$.

PROOF. Since $\beta = \omega(1)$ the rate of the outer code is $1 - o(1)$ and so for n, p and δ which satisfy $\frac{n}{k} \geq \frac{1}{1-H(p)-\delta}$, we have that

$$\frac{n_{in}}{k_{in}} = \frac{n}{k(1+\frac{1}{\sqrt{\beta}})} \geq \frac{1}{1-H(p)-\delta'}$$

for $\delta' = \delta - o(1)$. We can therefore apply Claim 4.2 and derive the corollary. $\square$

The proof of Theorem 1.2 is similar, except that now, when we are given the gap to capacity δ ahead of time, we can set β to be a sufficiently large constant.

COROLLARY 4.4 (THM. 1.2 RESTATED). Let $\delta > 0$ be a constant. Then there exists a constant β for which the rateless code defined by $C_{n,k}^\beta$ is a linear systematic rateless code that can be encoded and decoded in time $O(n)$ and parallel time of $O(\log n)$. Furthermore, for crossover probability p for which $n \geq k \cdot \frac{1}{1-H(p)-\delta}$, the decoding error is $2^{-\Omega(k)}$.

PROOF. Choose β for which the rate of the outer code $R_{out} = k_{out}/n_{out} = 1/(1 + \delta/2)$. As a result, an n-bit prefix of the concatenated code of rate $R = k/n \leq 1 - H(p) - \delta$ implies that the rate of the inner code k_{in}/n_{in} is at most $1 - H(p) - \delta/2$, and so by Claim 4.2, the decoding error $\mathsf{err}(p,k,n) \leq 2^{-\Omega(k/\beta^3)} = 2^{-\Omega(k)}$. By construction, encoding and decoding can be performed in linear-time and logarithmic parallel-time. $\square$

Acknowledgments.
We thank Uri Erez, Meir Feder, Simon Litsyn, Ronny Roth, and Rami Zamir for useful conversations.

5. REFERENCES

[1] H. Balakrishnan, P. Iannucci, J. Perry, and D. Shah. De-randomizing shannon: The design and analysis of a capacity-achieving rateless code. *CoRR*, abs/1206.0418, 2012.

[2] A. Barg. Lecture notes ENEE 739C: Advanced topics in signal processing: Coding theory (lecture 4), 2003. http://www.ece.umd.edu/ abarg/ENEE739C-03/lecture4.pdf.

[3] A. Barg and G. D. Forney Jr. Random codes: Minimum distances and error exponents. *Information Theory, IEEE Transactions on*, 48(9):2568–2573, 2002.

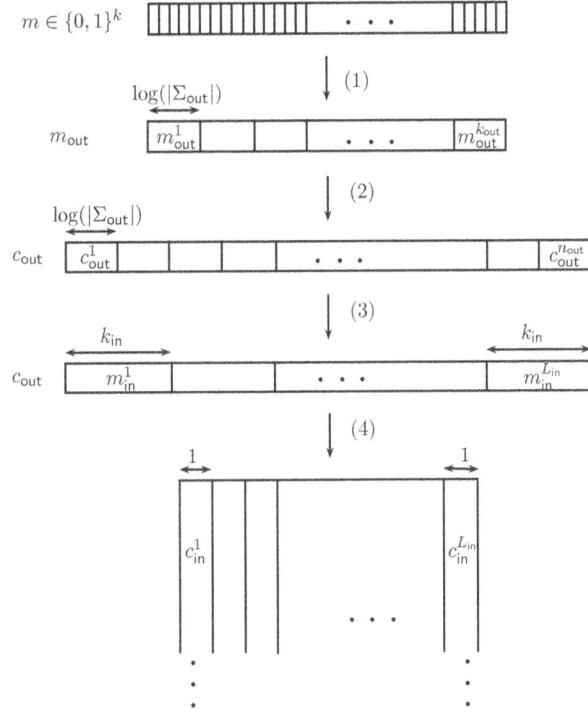

Figure 1: Encoder: concatenation of the outer code and the inner code

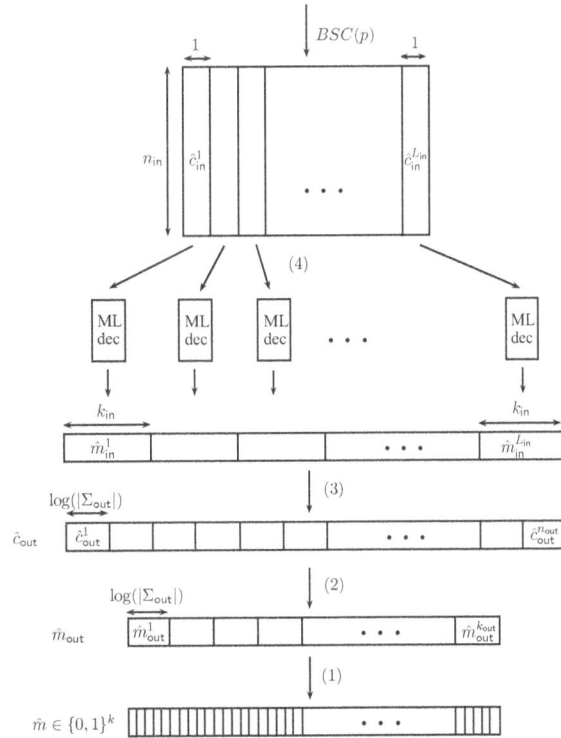

Figure 2: Decoder of the concatenated code uses ML-decoding for the inner code and the decoder of the outer code

[4] A. Barg and G. Zemor. Linear-time decodable, capacity achieving binary codes with exponentially falling error probability. *IEEE Transactions on Information Theory*, 2000.

[5] A. Barg and G. Zemor. Error exponents of expander codes. *Information Theory, IEEE Transactions on*, 48(6):1725–1729, Jun 2002.

[6] A. Barg and G. Zemor. Error exponents of expander codes under linear-complexity decoding. *SIAM Journal on Discrete Mathematics*, 17(3):426–445, 2004.

[7] J. W. Byers, M. Luby, M. Mitzenmacher, and A. Rege. A digital fountain approach to reliable distribution of bulk data. In *SIGCOMM*, pages 56–67, 1998.

[8] G. Caire and D. Tuninetti. The throughput of hybrid-ARQ protocols for the gaussian collision channel. *Information Theory, IEEE Transactions on*, 47(5):1971–1988, 2001.

[9] D. Chase. Code combining–a maximum-likelihood decoding approach for combining an arbitrary number of noisy packets. *Communications, IEEE Transactions on*, 33(5):385–393, 1985.

[10] U. Erez, M. D. Trott, and G. W. Wornell. Rateless coding for Gaussian channels. *Information Theory, IEEE Transactions on*, 58(2):530–547, 2012.

[11] G. D. Forney, Jr. *Concatenated Codes*. M.I.T. Press, Cambridge, MA, USA, 1966.

[12] V. Guruswami and P. Indyk. Linear-time encodable/decodable codes with near-optimal rate. *Information Theory, IEEE Transactions on*, 51(10):3393–3400, 2005.

[13] J. Ha, J. Kim, and S. W. McLaughlin. Rate-compatible puncturing of low-density parity-check codes. *Information Theory, IEEE Transactions on*, 50(11):2824–2836, 2004.

[14] J. Hagenauer. Rate-compatible punctured convolutional codes (RCPC codes) and their applications. *Communications, IEEE Transactions on*, 36(4):389–400, 1988.

[15] T. Ji and W. Stark. Rate-adaptive transmission over correlated fading channels. *Communications, IEEE Transactions on*, 53(10):1663–1670, 2005.

[16] S. Lin, D. Costello, and M. Miller. Automatic-repeat-request error-control schemes. *Communications Magazine, IEEE*, 22(12):5–17, 1984.

[17] M. Luby. LT codes. In *Annual Symposium on Foundations of Computer Science*, pages 271–280, 2002.

[18] D. Mandelbaum. An adaptive-feedback coding scheme using incremental redundancy (corresp.). *Information Theory, IEEE Transactions on*, 20(3):388–389, 1974.

[19] J. Perry, H. Balakrishnan, and D. Shah. Rateless Spinal Codes. In *HotNets-X*, Cambridge, MA, November 2011.

[20] J. Perry, P. A. Iannucci, K. E. Fleming, H. Balakrishnan, and D. Shah. Spinal codes. In *Proceedings of the ACM SIGCOMM 2012 conference on Applications, technologies, architectures, and protocols for computer communication*, pages 49–60. ACM, 2012.

[21] G. Poltyrev. Bounds on the decoding error probability of binary linear codes via their spectra. *Information Theory, IEEE Transactions on*, 40(4):1284–1292, 1994.

[22] D. Rajwan. Method of encoding and transmitting data over a communication medium through division and segmentation, Dec. 4 2007. US Patent 7,304,990.

[23] D. Rajwan, E. Lubetzky, and J. Y. Azar. Data streaming, Feb. 5 2008. US Patent 7,327,761.

[24] D. N. Rowitch and L. B. Milstein. On the performance of hybrid FEC/ARQ systems using rate compatible punctured turbo (RCPT) codes. *Communications, IEEE Transactions on*, 48(6):948–959, 2000.

[25] S. Sesia, G. Caire, and G. Vivier. Incremental redundancy hybrid ARQ schemes based on low-density parity-check codes. *Communications, IEEE Transactions on*, 52(8):1311–1321, 2004.

[26] A. Shokrollahi. Raptor codes. *Information Theory, IEEE Transactions on*, 52(6):2551–2567, 2006.

[27] N. Shulman. *Communication over an unknown channel via common broadcasting*. PhD thesis, Tel Aviv University, 2003.

[28] N. Shulman and M. Feder. Random coding techniques for nonrandom codes. *Information Theory, IEEE Transactions on*, 45(6):2101–2104, 1999.

[29] N. Shulman and M. Feder. Static broadcasting. In *Information Theory, 2000. Proceedings. IEEE International Symposium on*, page 23. IEEE, 2000.

[30] Spielman. Linear-time encodable and decodable error-correcting codes. *IEEETIT: IEEE Transactions on Information Theory*, 42, 1996.

[31] D. Spielman. *Computationally efficient error-correcting codes and holographic proofs*. PhD thesis, 1996.

Homophily and the Glass Ceiling Effect in Social Networks

Chen Avin *†
Ben Gurion University of the
Negev, Israel
avin@cse.bgu.ac.il

Barbara Keller ‡
ETH Zurich, Switzerland
barbara.keller@tik.ee.ethz.ch

Zvi Lotker *
Ben Gurion University of the
Negev, Israel
zvilo@cse.bgu.ac.il

Claire Mathieu
CNRS, École Normale
Supérieure, France
clairemmathieu@gmail.com

David Peleg *
Weizmann Institute, Israel
david.peleg@weizmann.ac.il

Yvonne-Anne Pignolet
ABB Corporate, Switzerland
yvonne-
anne.pignolet@ch.abb.com

ABSTRACT

The glass ceiling effect has been defined in a recent US Federal Commission report as "the unseen, yet unbreakable barrier that keeps minorities and women from rising to the upper rungs of the corporate ladder, regardless of their qualifications or achievements". It is well documented that many societies and organizations exhibit a glass ceiling. In this paper we formally define and study the glass ceiling effect in social networks and propose a natural mathematical model, called the *biased preferential attachment* model, that partially explains the causes of the glass ceiling effect. This model consists of a network composed of two types of vertices, representing two sub-populations, and accommodates three well known social phenomena: (i) the "rich get richer" mechanism, (ii) a minority-majority partition, and (iii) homophily. We prove that our model exhibits a strong moment glass ceiling effect and that all three conditions are necessary, i.e., removing any one of them will prevent the appearance of a glass ceiling effect. Additionally, we present empirical evidence taken from a mentor-student network of researchers (derived from the DBLP database) that exhibits both a glass ceiling effect and the above three phenomena.

Categories and Subject Descriptors

G.2.2 [**Mathematics of Computing**]: DISCRETE MATHEMATICS—*Graph Theory*; J.4 [**Computer Applications**]: SOCIAL AND BEHAVIORAL SCIENCES

Keywords

social networks; homophily; glass ceiling

*Supported in part by the Israel Science Foundation (grant 1549/13).
†Part of this work was done while the author was a long term visitor at ICERM, Brown university.
‡Part of this work was done while the author was a visiting student at the Weizmann Institute.

ITCS'15, January 11–13, 2015, Rehovot, Israel.
Copyright © 2015 ACM 978-1-4503-3333-7/15/01 ...$15.00.
http://dx.doi.org/10.1145/2688073.2688097.

1. INTRODUCTION

Attaining *equality of opportunity* is a fundamental value in democratic societies, therefore existing inequalities present us with a major concern. A particularly sore example is that many highly-qualified women and members of minority groups are unable to realize their full potential in society (and specifically in the workforce) due to a phenomenon commonly referred to as the *glass ceiling*, a powerful visual image for an invisible barrier blocking women and minorities from advancing past middle management levels [20]. This concern was raised in a recent US Federal commission report [18]:

> The "glass ceiling"... is the unseen, yet unbreakable barrier that keeps minorities and women from rising to the upper rungs of the corporate ladder, regardless of their qualifications or achievements.

The existence of the glass ceiling effect is well documented [8, 16, 30]. In academia, for example, gender disparities have been observed in the number of professors [34], earnings [13, 34, 40] funding [29] and patents [10]. A recent study [26] analyzed gender differences in research output, research impact and collaborations based on Thomson Reuters Web of Science databases. When prominent author positions were analyzed by sole authorship, first-authorship and last-authorship, it was discovered that papers with women in those leading roles were less frequently cited. The question we focus on in this article concerns the causes of this phenomenon. What are the invisible mechanisms that combine to create the glass ceiling effect, and in particular, what is the role of the social network in creating this effect? Many papers discuss possible causes of the glass ceiling effect and potential solutions to it, e.g., [9, 15, 24], but to the best of our knowledge, the present work is the first attempt to study it in the context of the social network structure and to propose a *mathematical model* capturing this phenomenon.

The paper's main contributions are the following. (1) We propose a model for bi-populated social networks extending the classical preferential attachment model [2], and augment it by including two additional basic phenomena, namely, a minority-majority partition, and homophily. (2) We propose a formal definition for the glass ceiling effect *in social networks*. (3) We rigorously analyze this extended model and establish its suitability as a possible mechanism for the emergence of a glass ceiling effect. We also show that omitting any one of the three ingredients of our model prevents the occurrence of a glass ceiling effect. (4) We present empirical evidence for a network exhibiting preferential attachment, minority-majority partition, homophily, and a glass ceiling effect.

In order to talk about the glass ceiling effect we have to agree on a measure of success in a social network. Following the traditional approach that sees network edges as the "social capital" of the network, we define successful members of a social network to be high degree vertices, namely, vertices that maintain a large number of connections, corresponding to high influence. We base our model on a bi-populated network augmented by three well-accepted observations on human behavior, namely (i) the "rich get richer" mechanism, (ii) minority-majority partition (with a slower growth rate of the minority group in the network), and (iii) homophily (affinity towards those similar to oneself). The main result of the paper is that under these three simple and standard assumptions the glass ceiling effect naturally arises in social networks. Let us first briefly describe these three social phenomena.

The "rich get richer" mechanism. This mechanism describes and explains the process of wealth concentration. It follows the basic idea that newly created wealth is distributed among members of society in proportion to the amount they have already amassed. In our setting, where the degree of the vertex captures its level of social wealth, this mechanism predicts that people may try to connect more often to people who already have many connections, either in order to profit from their social wealth or because they are more visible in the network.

Minority-majority partition. Many social groups exhibit unequal proportions of men and women. Certain occupations, such as construction, law enforcement, politics and computer science, tend to have a higher proportion of men. For example, the ratio of women taking up studies in the computing discipline varies per year and region between 10% and 35% [3, 21, 38, 44]. Other professions, such as elementary school teaching, nursing, and office administration, are occupied by a higher proportion of women. In fact, it is difficult to find an occupation with a balanced ratio of genders (this also holds for many other social partitions, e.g., ones based on ethnicity or family background). This imbalance is the second phenomenon underlying our model.

Homophily. It is a well established social phenomenon that people tend to associate with others who are similar to themselves. Characteristics such as gender, ethnicity, age, class background and education influence the relationships among human beings [27] and similarities make communication and relationship formation easier.

In summary, our model is obtained by applying the classical preferential attachment model (see Barabasi and Albert [2]) to a bi-populated minority-majority network augmented with homophily. The resulting model is hereafter referred to as the *Biased Preferential Attachment* Model.

Roadmap. The rest of the paper is organized as follows. In the next section we review related work, then in Section 3 we introduce the model and the formal definitions of the involved properties: glass ceiling, power inequality and homophily tests. In Section 4 we state our two main theorems, and in Section 5 we provide empirical evidence for the existence of all our necessary ingredients and for the glass ceiling effect in a student-mentor network of researchers in computer science. We conclude with a discussion.

2. RELATED WORK

Homophily in social networks. Different characteristics, such as gender, ethnicities, age, class background and education, influence the relationships human beings form with each other [27]. McPherson et al. [32] survey a variety of properties and how they lead to particular patterns in bonding. Gender-based homophily can already be observed in play patterns among children at school [31, 41]. Eder and Hallinan [12] discovered that young girls are more likely to resolve intransitivity by deleting friendship choices, while young boys are more likely to add them. Overall, children are significantly more likely to resolve intransitivity by deleting a cross-sex friendship than by adding another cross-sex friendship [45]. These results show that gender influences the formation of cliques and larger evolving network structures. These trends, displaying homophily and gender differences in resolving problems in the structure of relationships, mean that boys and girls gravitate towards different social circles. As adults, homophilic behavior persists, and men still tend to have networks that are more homophilic than women do. This behavior is even more pronounced in areas where they form the majority and in relationships exchanging advice and based on respect, e.g., mentoring [5, 22, 23, 39]. A homophilic network evolution model was studied in [4]. In this model new nodes connect to other nodes in two phases. First, they choose their neighbors with a bias towards their own type (the model allows a positive as well as a negative bias). In a second phase they make an unbiased choice of neighbors from among the neighbors of their biased neighbors. The authors show that the second phase overcomes the bias in the first phase and if the second phase is unbiased, then the network ends up in an integrated state. They illustrate their model with data on citations in physics journals.

Gender disparity in science and technology. Gender disparities have been observed in the number of professors [13, 34], earnings [40], funding [29] and patenting [10]. A related aspect is the "productivity puzzle": men are more successful when it comes to number of publications and name position in the author list [46], for reasons yet unclear. Some conjectures raised involve (unknown) biased perceptions related to pregnancy/child care [6]. E.g., it was observed in [34] that science faculty members of both sexes exhibit unconscious biases against women. Gender differences in research output, research impact and collaborations was analyzed in a study based on Thomson Reuters Web of Science databases [26]. It was not only revealed that papers with women in prominent author positions (sole authorship, first-authorship and last-authorship) were cited less frequently but the authors also found that age plays an important role in collaborations, authorship position and citations. Thus many of the trends observed therein might be explained by the under-representation of women among the elders of science. In other words, fixing the "leaky pipeline" [43] is key for a more equal gender distribution in science.

Minority of women in Computer Science. In the computing discipline, the ratio of women taking up studies varies by year and region between 10% and 35% [3, 21, 38, 44] (except in Malaysia, where women form a narrow majority [35]). This under-representation has been investigated [19, 42, 47] and remedial strategies have been proposed [17, 37]. There is a positive feedback loop [25]: the lack of women leads to a strong male stereotype which

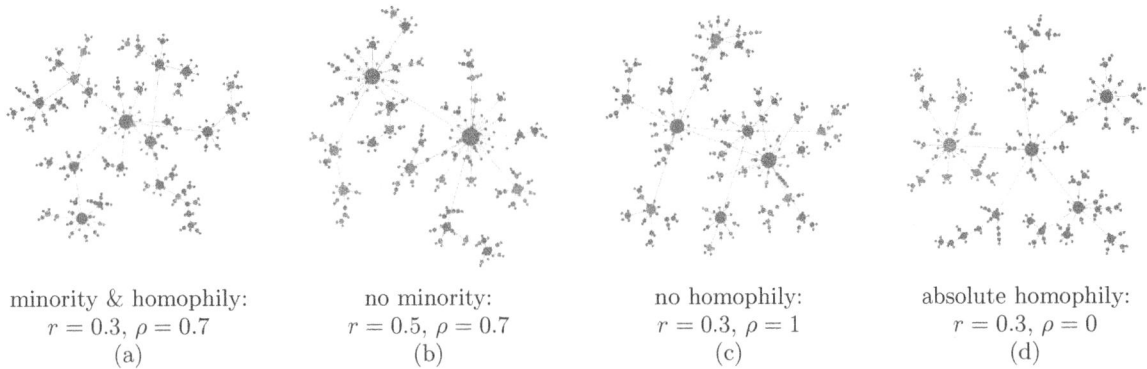

minority & homophily:
$r = 0.3$, $\rho = 0.7$
(a)

no minority:
$r = 0.5$, $\rho = 0.7$
(b)

no homophily:
$r = 0.3$, $\rho = 1$
(c)

absolute homophily:
$r = 0.3$, $\rho = 0$
(d)

Figure 1: Examples of the Biased Preferential Attachment (BPA) model with various parameter settings. All examples depict a 300-vertex bi-populated network generated by our BPA model starting from a single edge connecting a blue and a red vertex (with vertex size proportional to its degree).

drives away even more women. It's been explained that the increase of the relative number of women in computer science was the best of the investigated remedial strategies, up to a "critical mass" of women. However, as pointed out by Etzkowitz [14], even achieving a representation of 15% women might not guarantee that the effects of a critical mass come into play.

3. MODEL AND DEFINITIONS

3.1 Biased preferential attachment model

Our first contribution is in proposing a simple bi-populated preferential attachment model. In a gist, our model is obtained by applying the classical preferential attachment model [2] to a bi-populated minority-majority network augmented with homophily. The resulting model is hereafter referred to as the *Biased Preferential Attachment* Model. Formally, for $r \leq 1/2$ and $0 \leq \rho \leq 1$ let $G(n, r, \rho)$ be a variant of the preferential attachment model in which the vertices are red or blue, n is the total number of nodes, and r represents the relative arrival rate of the red vertices (and hence the expected fraction of red vertices in the network converges to r as well, as the relative size of the initial population becomes smaller over time), and ρ represents the level to which homophily (incorporated by using rejection sampling) is expressed in the system: for $\rho = 1$ the system is uniform and exhibits no homophily, whereas for $\rho = 0$ the system is fully segregated, and all added edges connect vertex pairs of the same color.

Let us describe the model in more detail. Denote the social network at time t by $G_t = (V_t, E_t)$, where V_t and E_t, respectively, are the sets of vertices and edges in the network at time t, and let $\delta_t(v)$ denote the degree of vertex v at time t (we may omit the parameter t when it is clear from the context). The process starts with an arbitrary initial (connected) network G_0 in which each vertex has an arbitrary color, red or blue. (For simplicity we require that a minimal initial network consists of one blue and one red vertex connected by an edge, but this requirement can be removed if $\rho > 0$). This initial network evolves in time as follows. In every time step t a new vertex v enters the network. This vertex is red with probability r and blue with probability $1 - r$. On arrival, the vertex v chooses an existing vertex

$u \in V_t$ to attach to according to preferential attachment, i.e., with probability p proportional to u's degree at time t, i.e., $\mathbb{P}[u \text{ is chosen}] = \delta_t(u) / \sum_{w \in V_t} \delta_t(w)$. Next, if u's color is the same as v's color, then an edge is inserted between v and u; if the colors differ, then the edge is inserted with probability ρ, and with probability $1 - \rho$ the selection is *rejected*, and the process of choosing a neighbor for v is restarted. This process is repeated until some edge $\{v, u\}$ has been inserted. Thus in each time step, one new vertex and one new edge are added to the existing graph.

Figure 1 presents four examples of parameter settings for our model on a 300-vertex bi-populated social network. First, Figure 1(a) provides an example for the *minority & homophily* case with $r = 0.3$ and $\rho = 0.7$ so the red vertices are a strict minority in the network and there is some homophily in the edge selection. The next three sub-figures present special cases. Figure 1(b) illustrates the *no minority* case (equal-size populations, i.e., $r = 0.5$) with homophily ($\rho = 0.7$). Figure 1(c) considers the *no homophily* case ($\rho = 1$) with minority ($r = 0.3$). The last extreme case, shown in Figure 1(d), is *absolute homophily*, where $\rho = 0$, but the red vertices are still in the minority ($r = 0.3$). This case results in *fully segregated* societies, namely, societies where members connect *only* to members of their own color. In this extreme case, the society in effect splits into two separate networks, one for each of the two populations (except for the single edge connecting the initial red and blue vertices).

Consider as an example for our model the social network of mentor-student relationships in academia. With time, new PhD students arrive, but for some fields female students arrive at a lower rate than male students. Upon arrival, each student needs to select exactly one mentor, where the selection process is governed by the mechanisms of preferential attachment and homophily. Namely, initially the student selects the mentor according to the rules of preferential attachment and then homophily takes its role, rejecting the selection with some probability if their gender is different and forcing a re-selection. Over time, graduated students may become mentors and some mentors become more successful than others (in terms of the number of students they advise). A glass ceiling effect can be observed in this network if, after a long enough time interval, the fraction of females among the most successful mentors tends to zero.

We would like to emphasize that the homophily effect that we look at is quite minor and "seemingly harmless", in two ways. First, it is "symmetric", i.e., it applies both to male students with respect to female mentors and to female students with respect to male mentors. Second, it does not adversely affect the student, in the sense that the student always gets admitted in our model. The only tiny (but ominous) sign for the potential dangers of this homophilic effect is that it does affect the professor: a male professor who rejects (or is rejected by) some fraction of the female candidates risks little, whereas a female professor who rejects (or is rejected by) some fraction of the male candidates will eventually have fewer students overall, since most of the applicants are male. In fact, as we show later on, this homophily-based consequence will only impact her if her future potential students use preferential attachment to select their mentors.

3.2 Power inequality and glass ceiling

Our second contribution is to propose formal definitions of the glass ceiling effect in social networks. Consider a *bi-populated* network $G(n)$ consisting of m edges and n nodes of two types, the groups R and B of red and blue nodes. We assume that the network size n tends to infinity with time. Let $n(\text{R})$ and $n(\text{B})$ denote the number of red and blue nodes, respectively, where $n(\text{R}) + n(\text{B}) = n$. The red nodes are assumed to be a minority in the social network, i.e., denoting the percentage of red nodes in the network by r, we assume $0 \leq r < \frac{1}{2}$. Let $d(\text{R})$ and $d(\text{B})$ denote the sum of degrees of the red and blue nodes, respectively, where $d(\text{R}) + d(\text{B}) = 2m$. Let $\text{top}_k(\text{R})$ (respectively, $\text{top}_k(\text{B})$) denote the number of red (resp., blue) nodes that have degree *at least* k in G. When $G(n)$ is a random graph, we replace variables by their expectations in the definitions below, e.g., we use $\mathbb{E}[n(\text{R})]$, $\mathbb{E}[d(\text{R})]$, and $\mathbb{E}[\text{top}_k(\text{R})]$. Next we provide formal definitions for the social phenomena discussed in the introduction. *Power inequality* for the minority is defined in the following way.

DEFINITION 1 (POWER INEQUALITY). *A graph sequence $G(n)$ exhibits a* power inequality *effect for the red nodes if the average power of a red node is lower than that of a blue (or a random) node, i.e., there exists a constant $c < 1$ such that*

$$\lim_{n \to \infty} \frac{\frac{1}{n(\text{R})} \sum_{v \in \text{R}} \delta(v)}{\frac{1}{n(\text{B})} \sum_{v \in \text{B}} \delta(v)} = \frac{d(\text{R})/n(\text{R})}{d(\text{B})/n(\text{B})} \leq c \ . \quad (1)$$

The definition of the glass ceiling effect is more complex. We interpret the most powerful positions as those held by the highest degree nodes, and offer two alternative definitions. The first tries to capture the informal, "dictionary" definition, which describes a decreasing fraction of women among higher degree nodes, i.e., in the *tail* of the graph degree sequence. Formally:

DEFINITION 2 (TAIL GLASS CEILING). *A graph sequence $G(n)$ exhibits a* tail glass ceiling *effect for the red nodes if there exists an increasing function $k(n)$ (for short k) such that $\lim_{n \to \infty} \text{top}_k(\text{B}) = \infty$ and*

$$\lim_{n \to \infty} \frac{\text{top}_k(\text{R})}{\text{top}_k(\text{B})} = 0 \ .$$

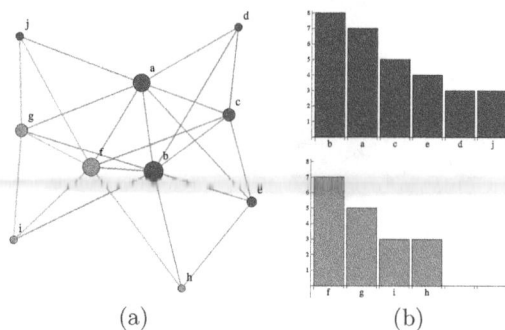

(a) (b)

Figure 2: (a) An example bi-populated social network with blue and red populations of 6 and 4 vertices respectively. (b) The degree sequences of both populations (i.e., the sequence specifying for each vertex its degree in the network). Considering the *tail glass ceiling* definition, there are four blue vertices of degree greater or equal to 4, but only two such red vertices so $\text{top}_4(\text{R})/\text{top}_4(\text{B}) = 1/2$. For the *moment glass ceiling* definition, the second moment for the blue vertices is $\frac{1}{6}(8^2 + 7^2 + 5^2 + 4^2 + 3^2 + 3^2) = 28.6$, while for the red vertices it is $\frac{1}{4}(7^2 + 5^2 + 3^2 + 3^2) = 23$ and the ratio is **23/28.6**. To exhibit a glass ceiling, these ratios should converge to zero as the network size increases. Regarding homophily, in a random network with the same population, i.e., 60% blue vertices and 40% red vertices, one expects to find 36% blue-blue edges, 16% red-red edges and 48% mixed edge. If we take the degree sequences into account we would expect to see 46.8% mixed edge. In the above example network we observe only about 33% mixed edges, which indicates the effect of homophily.

The second definition considers a more traditional, distribution-oriented measure, the second moment of the two degree sequences. Formally:

DEFINITION 3 (MOMENT GLASS CEILING). *A graph sequence $G(n)$ exhibits a* moment glass ceiling g *for the red nodes where*

$$g = \lim_{n \to \infty} \frac{\frac{1}{n(\text{R})} \sum_{v \in \text{R}} \delta(v)^2}{\frac{1}{n(\text{B})} \sum_{v \in \text{B}} \delta(v)^2} \ .$$

When $g = 0$, we say that $G(n)$ has a *strong* glass ceiling effect. The intuition behind this definition is that a larger second moment (and assuming a similar average degree, i.e., no power inequality) will result in a larger variance and therefore a significantly larger number of high degree nodes. As we show in the full version of the paper, the above two definitions for the glass ceiling are independent, in the sense that neither of the effects implies the other.

Testing for *homophily* in a bi-populated network is based on checking whether the number of *mixed* (i.e., red-blue) edges is significantly lower than to be expected if neighbors were to be picked randomly and independently of their color. Formally:

DEFINITION 4 (HOMOPHILY TEST). *[11] A bi-populated social network exhibits homophily if the fraction of mixed edges is significantly less than $2r(1-r)$.*

The above definition implicitly assumes that there is power equality between the colors and therefore is not always accurate. A more careful test should take the average degree of each gender into account.

DEFINITION 5 (NORMALIZED HOMOPHILY TEST). *A bi-populated social network exhibits homophily if the fraction of mixed edges is significantly less than* $2\frac{d(\mathrm{R})}{2m}\left(1 - \frac{d(\mathrm{R})}{2m}\right)$.

An illustration of these definitions can be found in Figure 2.

4. THEORETICAL RESULTS

4.1 Power inequality and glass ceiling

Our main theoretical result (Thm. 4.1) is that in the biased preferential attachment model, $G(n, r, \rho)$, the glass ceiling effect emerges naturally. Additionally, this process generates a *power inequality*, an independent property that is weaker than the glass ceiling effect. Power inequality describes the situation where the average degree of the minority is lower than that of the majority (although their members possess the same qualifications). Moreover, we also show (Thm. 4.2) that all three ingredients (unequal entry rate, homophily, preferential attachment) are necessary to generate what we call a *strong* glass ceiling effect, i.e., removing any one of them will prevent the appearance of a glass ceiling effect. One may suspect that the glass ceiling effect is in fact a byproduct of power inequality or unequal qualifications; we show in the full paper that this is not the case. Minorities can have a smaller average degree without suffering from a glass ceiling effect. We also note that our results are independent of the starting condition. Even if the network initially consisted entirely of vertices of one color, if a majority of the vertices being added are of the opposite color, then eventually the vertices that rise to the highest positions will be of the new color.

THEOREM 4.1. *Let* $0 < r < \frac{1}{2}$ *and* $0 < \rho < 1$. *For* $G(n, r, \rho)$ *produced by the Biased Preferential Attachment Model the following holds:*

1. *$G(n, r, \rho)$ exhibits power inequality, and*

2. *$G(n, r, \rho)$ exhibits both a tail and a strong glass ceiling effects.*

Moreover, all three ingredients are necessary to generate a *strong* glass ceiling effect.

THEOREM 4.2. *1. $G(n, r, \rho)$ will not exhibit a glass ceiling effect in the following cases:*

(a) *If the rate $r = \frac{1}{2}$ (no minority).*

(b) *If $\rho = 1$ (no homophily)*

(c) *If $\rho = 0$ (no heterophily).*

2. *$G(n, r, \rho)$ will not exhibit a strong glass ceiling effect if attachment is uniform rather than preferential, i.e., a new vertex at time t selects an existing vertex to attach to uniformly at random from all vertices present at time $t-1$ (and for any value of r and ρ).*

Let us graphically illustrate the above results. Figure 3 presents the degree distributions of both the red and blue populations (as well as of the entire population) for four 1,000,000-vertex networks with parameters identical to the examples in Figure 1. The plots clearly show (and we prove this formally) that in all cases the degree distribution of both populations follows a power-law. (A subset W of vertices in a given network obeys a power-law degree distribution if the fraction $P(k)$ of vertices of degree k in W behaves for large values of k as $P(k) \sim k^{-\beta}$ for parameter β.) All figures present (in log-log scale) the cumulative degree distributions, so a power-law corresponds to a straight line (we present the samples together with the best-fit line). Theorem 4.1 corresponds to Figure 3(a) with the *minority & homophily* settings of $0 < r < \frac{1}{2}$ and $0 < \rho < 1$. In this case (and only in this case), the power-law exponents of the red and blue populations, $\beta(\mathrm{R})$ and $\beta(\mathrm{B})$ respectively, are *different*, where $\beta(\mathrm{R}) > \beta(\mathrm{B})$; we prove that this will eventually lead to both tail and strong glass ceiling effect for the red vertices. Theorem 4.2 corresponds to Figures 3(b) and 3(c). The figures show that in the case of *no minority* (i.e., $r = 0.5$) or *no homophily* (i.e., $\rho = 1$), both $\beta(\mathrm{R})$ and $\beta(\mathrm{B})$ are the same (in particular they are equal to 3 as in the classical Preferential Attachment model), and therefore there will be no glass ceiling effect. Figure 3(d) considers the last extreme case of *absolute homophily*. Perhaps surprisingly, in this case a glass ceiling effect also does not occur, as each sub-population forms an absolute majority in its own network (see again Figure 1(d)). The case of no preferential attachment (which does not lead to a glass ceiling) is more delicate and presented in the full version of the paper.

Proof Overview of Theorem 4.1. The basic idea behind the proof of Theorem 4.1 is to show that both populations in $G(n, r, \rho)$ have a power law degree distribution but with different exponents. Once this is established, it is simple to derive the glass ceiling effect for the population with a higher exponent in the degree distribution. To study the degree distribution of the red (and similarly the blue) population, we first define α_t to be the random variable that is equal to the ratio of the total degree of the red nodes (i.e., the sum of degrees of all red nodes) divided by the total degree (i.e., twice the number of edges). We show that the expected value of α_t converges to a fixed ratio independently of how the network started. The proof of this part is based on tools from dynamic systems. Basically, we show that there is only one fixed point for our system. However, determining the expectation of α_t is not sufficient for analyzing the degree distribution, and it is also necessary to bound the rate of convergence and the concentration of α_t around its expectation. We used Doob martingales for this part. Using the high concentration of the total degree, we were able to adapt standard techniques to prove the power law degree distribution. Next we give an overview of the proofs and the helping lemmas, but due to space limitations we defer the details to the full version of this paper.

4.2 Proof sketch of Theorem 4.1 Part 1

An urn process. The biased preferential attachment model $G(n, r, \rho)$ process can also be interpreted as a Polya's urn process, where each edge in the graph corresponds to two balls, one for each endpoint, and the balls are colored by the color of the corresponding vertices. When a new (red or blue) ball y arrives, we choose an existing ball c from the urn uniformly at random; if c is of the same color as y, then we add to the urn both y and another ball of the same

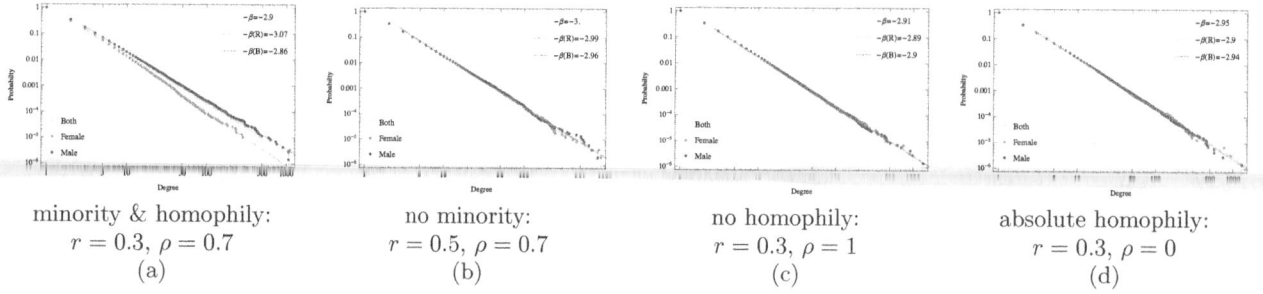

minority & homophily:	no minority:	no homophily:	absolute homophily:
$r = 0.3, \rho = 0.7$	$r = 0.5, \rho = 0.7$	$r = 0.3, \rho = 1$	$r = 0.3, \rho = 0$
(a)	(b)	(c)	(d)

Figure 3: Graphical illustrations of our formal claims concerning the glass ceiling effect in the Biased Preferential Attachment model. Each figure presents the degree distribution (on a log-log scale) of the red and blue populations from a 1,000,000-vertex network generated by the BPA model with the same parameters as the corresponding figure in Figure 1. In all cases both populations exhibit a power-law degree distribution but only in case (a) they with different exponents.

color as c; otherwise (i.e., if c is of a different color), with probability ρ we still add to the urn both y and another ball of the same color as c, and with probability $1 - \rho$ we reject the choice of c and repeat choosing an existing ball c' from the urn uniformly at random. To analyze power inequality, there is no need to keep track of the degrees of individual vertices; the sum of the degrees of all vertices of R is exactly the number of red balls in the urn.

Denote by $d_t(\mathtt{R})$ (respectively, $d_t(\mathtt{B})$) the number of red (resp., blue) balls present in the system at time $t \geq 0$. Altogether, the number of balls at time t is $d_t = d_t(\mathtt{R}) + d_t(\mathtt{B})$. Initially, the system contains d_o balls. Noting that exactly two balls join the system in each time step, we have $d_t = d_o + 2t$. Note that while $d_t(\mathtt{R})$ and $d_t(\mathtt{B})$ are random variables, d_t is not. Recall that balls represent degrees so $d_t = \sum_{w \in V_t} \delta_t(w)$.

Denote by α_t the random variable equal to $d_t(\mathtt{R})/d_t$, the fraction of red balls in the system at time t.

Convergence of expectations. We first claim that the process of biased preferential attachment converges to a ratio of α red balls in the system. More formally, we claim that regardless of the starting condition, there exists a limit

$$\alpha = \lim_{t \to \infty} \mathbb{E}[\alpha_t].$$

LEMMA 4.3. $\mathbb{E}[\alpha_{t+1}|\alpha_t] = \alpha_t + \dfrac{F(\alpha_t) - \alpha_t}{t+1}$, where

$$F(x) = \left(1 - (1-r)\frac{(1-x)}{1 - x(1-\rho)} + r\frac{x}{1 - (1-x)(1-\rho)}\right)/2.$$

LEMMA 4.4. 1. F is monotonically increasing.

2. F has exactly one fixed point, denoted α^*, in $[0, 1]$.

3. The image of the unit interval by F is contained in the unit interval: $F([0, 1]) = \left[\frac{r}{2}, \frac{1+r}{2}\right] \subset [0, 1]$

4. If $x < \alpha^*$ then $x < F(x) < \alpha^*$ and if $x > \alpha^*$ then $x > F(x) > \alpha^*$.

5. $\alpha^* < r$.

Now assume $\alpha_t < \alpha^*$. By Lemma 4.4, $\alpha_t < F(\alpha_t) < \alpha^*$, so by Lemma 4.3 we obtain $\alpha_t < \mathbb{E}[\alpha_{t+1}|\alpha_t] < \alpha^*$.

Moreover we can bound the rate of convergence and show:

LEMMA 4.5. $|\alpha^* - \mathbb{E}[\alpha_t]| = O(1/\sqrt[3]{t})$.

THEOREM 4.6. *For any initial configuration, as t goes to infinity, the expected fraction of red balls in the urn, $\mathbb{E}(\alpha_t)$, converges to the unique α^* in $[0, 1]$ satisfying the equation*

$$2\alpha^* = 1 - (1-r)\frac{(1-\alpha^*)}{1 - \alpha^*(1-\rho)} + r\frac{\alpha^*}{1 - (1-\alpha^*)(1-\rho)}. \quad (2)$$

Hence the limit α^* is the solution of the cubic equation Eq. (3).

$$(4\rho - 2\rho^2 - 2)\alpha^3 + (2 + 3\rho^2 - 5\rho + 2r - 2r\rho)\alpha^2 \quad (3)$$
$$+ (2\rho - 2r + 2r\rho - \rho^2)\alpha - r\rho = 0$$

Note that this limit is independent of the initial values d_o and α_0 of the system.

We know that the expected degree of a random vertex is 2 and since the expected degree of a red vertex tends to $2\alpha^*/r$, which is strictly less than 2 (because of Lemma 4.4 Part 5), we can claim:

COROLLARY 4.7. *Let $0 < \rho < 1$, $0 < r < 1/2$. Then $G(n, r, \rho)$ has a power inequality effect.*

4.3 Proof sketch of Theorem 4.1 Part 2

Concentration. To prove the glass ceiling effect we first bound the degree distribution. To do this we need to bound the rate by which $d_t(\mathtt{R})$ converge to $\alpha \cdot t$. Let $X_i \in \{0, 1, 2\}$ be the number of new red balls in the system at time i. Note that $d_t(\mathtt{R}) = \sum_0^t X_i$. Let

$$\Psi_i = \mathbb{E}_{X_{i+1}, X_{i+2}, \ldots, X_t}\left[\sum_{j=0}^t X_j | X_1, X_2, \ldots, X_i\right].$$

Observe that $(\Psi_i)_i$ is a Doob Martingale [33], and note that $\Psi_0 = \mathbb{E}\left[\sum_{i=0}^t X_i\right] = \mathbb{E}\left[d_t(\mathtt{R})\right]$.

THEOREM 4.8 (AZUMA'S INEQUALITY [1]). *Let Ψ_t be a martingale such that for all i, almost surely $|\Psi_i - \Psi_{i-1}| < c_i$. Then for all positive t and all positive reals x,*

$$\Pr(\Psi_t - \Psi_0 \geq x) \leq \exp\left(\frac{-x^2}{2\sum_i c_i^2}\right).$$

LEMMA 4.9. *Let $C_i = |\Psi_i - \Psi_{i-1}|$. Then $C_i = O(\sqrt{t/i})$.*

For simplicity of the description, let us assume hereafter that $d_o = 0$, hence $\alpha_t = d_t(\mathrm{R})/(2t)$. By Theorem 4.8 and Lemma 4.9 we have

LEMMA 4.10. $\Pr\left[|d_t(\mathrm{R}) - 2t\mathbb{E}(\alpha_t)| > O(2\sqrt{t}\log t)\right] \leq \frac{1}{t^4}$.

Combining Lemmas 4.5 and 4.10 yields:

COROLLARY 4.11.
$$\Pr\left[|\alpha^* - \alpha_t| > \max\left\{\frac{2\log t}{\sqrt{t}}, \frac{1}{\sqrt[3]{t}}\right\}\right] < \frac{1}{t^4}.$$

Degree distribution. We investigate the degree distribution of the red and blue vertices in a graph generated by the above described process, following the analysis outline of [7] for the basic preferential attachment model.

Let $m_{k,t}(\mathrm{B})$ (resp., $m_{k,t}(\mathrm{R})$) denote the number of blue (resp., red) vertices of degree k at time t. For $\mathbf{x} \in \{\mathrm{R}, \mathrm{B}\}$, define

$$M_k(\mathbf{x}) = \lim_{t \to \infty} \frac{\mathbb{E}(m_{k,t}(\mathbf{x}))}{t} . \tag{4}$$

THEOREM 4.12. *The expected degree distributions of the blue and red vertices follow a power law, namely, $M_k(\mathrm{B}) \propto k^{-\beta(\mathrm{B})}$ and $M_k(\mathrm{R}) \propto k^{-\beta(\mathrm{R})}$. If $0 < r < 1/2$ and $0 < \rho < 1$ then $\beta(\mathrm{R}) > 3 > \beta(\mathrm{B})$.*

Equipped with Theorem 4.12, Part 2 of Theorem 4.1 follows easily. Indeed, for the *tail glass ceiling* effect, let $k(n) = n^{\frac{1}{\beta(\mathrm{R})}}$. Then

$$\mathbb{E}[\mathrm{top}_k(\mathrm{R})] = n(\mathrm{R})\sum_{k' \geq k} M_{k'}(\mathrm{R}),$$

$$\mathbb{E}[\mathrm{top}_k(\mathrm{B})] = n(\mathrm{B})\sum_{k' \geq k} M_{k'}(\mathrm{B}).$$

For $k' = n^{\frac{1}{\beta(\mathrm{R})}}$ we have $nM_{k'}(\mathrm{R}) = O(n \cdot n^{-\frac{\beta(\mathrm{R})}{\beta(\mathrm{R})}}) = O(1)$ while $nM_{k'}(\mathrm{B}) = \Omega\left(n \cdot n^{-\frac{\beta(\mathrm{B})}{\beta(\mathrm{R})}}\right) = \Omega(n^{1-\frac{\beta(\mathrm{B})}{\beta(\mathrm{R})}}) = \Omega(n^\epsilon)$ for $\epsilon > 0$. The result then follows since $n(\mathrm{R}) < n(\mathrm{B})$ and $M_{k'}(\mathrm{R}) < M_{k'}(\mathrm{B})$ for $k' > k$.

For the *moment glass ceiling* effect we can show similarly:

$$g = \lim_{n \to \infty} \frac{\sum k^2 M_k(\mathrm{R})}{\sum k^2 M_k(\mathrm{B})} = \lim_{n \to \infty} \frac{O(n^{3-\beta(\mathrm{R})})}{\Omega(n^{3-\beta(\mathrm{B})})}$$
$$= \lim_{n \to \infty} O\left(\frac{1}{n^{\epsilon'}}\right) = 0$$

for some $\epsilon' > 0$.

The rest of this section sketches a proof of Theorem 4.12. Note that $m_{0,0}(\mathrm{B}) = d_o(\mathrm{B})$. We derive a recurrence for $\mathbb{E}(m_{k,t}(\mathrm{B}))$. A blue vertex of degree k at time t could have arisen from three scenarios: (s1) at time $t-1$ it was already a blue vertex of degree k and no edge was added to it at time t. (s2) at time $t-1$ it was a blue vertex of degree $k-1$ and an edge was added to it at time t. (s3) in the special case where $k=1$, at time $t-1$ it did not exist yet and it has arrived as a new blue vertex at time t. Thus letting $\mathcal{F}_t$ be the history of the process up to time t, for any $k > 1$, the expectation of $m_{k,t+1}(\mathrm{B})$ conditioned on $\mathcal{F}_t$ satisfies

$$\mathbb{E}(m_{k,t+1}(\mathrm{B})|\mathcal{F}_t) = $$
$$m_{k,t}(\mathrm{B})\left(1 - \frac{rd_t(\mathrm{B})\rho\frac{k}{d_t(\mathrm{B})}}{d_t(\mathrm{R})+d_t(\mathrm{B})\rho} - \frac{(1-r)d_t(\mathrm{B})\frac{k}{d_t(\mathrm{B})}}{d_t(\mathrm{R})+d_t(\mathrm{B})}\right)$$
$$+ m_{k-1,t}(\mathrm{B})\left(\frac{rd_t(\mathrm{B})\rho\frac{k-1}{d_t(\mathrm{B})}}{d_t(\mathrm{R})+d_t(\mathrm{B})\rho} + \frac{(1-r)d_t(\mathrm{B})\frac{k-1}{d_t(\mathrm{B})}}{d_t(\mathrm{R})+d_t(\mathrm{B})}\right).$$

For $k = 1$ we similarly have

$$\mathbb{E}(m_{1,t+1}(\mathrm{B})|\mathcal{F}_t) = $$
$$m_{1,t}(\mathrm{B})\left(1 - \frac{\rho r}{d_t(\mathrm{R})+d_t(\mathrm{B})\rho} - \frac{1-r}{d_t(\mathrm{R})\rho+d_t(\mathrm{B})}\right) + (1-r).$$

Recalling again that $\alpha_t = d_t(\mathrm{R})/(2t)$, the above can be rewritten as

$$\mathbb{E}(m_{k,t+1}(\mathrm{B})|\mathcal{F}_t) = $$
$$m_{k,t}(\mathrm{B})\left(1 - \frac{r\rho k}{2t(\alpha_t+(1-\alpha_t)\rho)} - \frac{(1-r)k}{2t(\alpha_t\rho+(1-\alpha_t))}\right)$$
$$+ m_{k-1,t}(\mathrm{B})\left(\frac{r\rho(k-1)}{2t(\alpha_t+(1-\alpha_t)\rho)} + \frac{(1-r)(k-1)}{2t(\alpha_t\rho+(1-\alpha_t))}\right)$$

and for $k = 1$,

$$\mathbb{E}(m_{1,t+1}(\mathrm{B})|\mathcal{F}_t) = $$
$$m_{1,t}(\mathrm{B})\left(1 - \frac{\rho r}{2t(\alpha_t+(1-\alpha_t)\rho)} - \frac{1-r}{2t(\alpha_t\rho+(1-\alpha_t))}\right) + (1-r).$$

This can be expressed as

$$\mathbb{E}(m_{k,t+1}(\mathrm{B})|\mathcal{F}_t) = m_{k,t}(\mathrm{B})\left(1 - A_t\frac{k}{t}\right) \tag{5}$$
$$+ m_{k-1,t}(\mathrm{B})A_t\frac{k-1}{t},$$

$$\mathbb{E}(m_{1,t+1}(\mathrm{B})|\mathcal{F}_t) = m_{1,t}(\mathrm{B})\left(1 - \frac{A_t}{t}\right) + (1-r), \tag{6}$$

using the notation

$$A_t = \frac{r\rho}{2\alpha_t + 2(1-\alpha_t)\rho} + \frac{(1-r)}{2\alpha_t\rho + 2(1-\alpha_t)} .$$

Note that A_t is a random variable so we next bound its divergence. Let

$$C_\mathrm{B} = \frac{r\rho}{2\alpha + 2(1-\alpha)\rho} + \frac{(1-r)}{2\alpha\rho + 2(1-\alpha)}$$
$$C_\mathrm{R} = \frac{(1-r)\rho}{2(\alpha\rho+1-\alpha)} + \frac{r}{2(\alpha+(1-\alpha)\rho)}.$$

We have

LEMMA 4.13. $\Pr\left[|A_t - C_\mathrm{B}| > \max\left\{\frac{2\log t}{\sqrt{t}}, \frac{1}{\sqrt[3]{t}}\right\}\right] < \frac{1}{t^4}$.

A similar claim can be made for C_R. This enables us to establish the following.

LEMMA 4.14.

- $M_1(\mathrm{B})$ *exists and equals* $(1-r)/(1+C_\mathrm{B})$,

- *For $k \geq 2$, $M_k(\mathrm{B})$ exists and equals* $M_{k-1}(\mathrm{B}) \cdot (k-1)C_\mathrm{B}/(1+kC_\mathrm{B})$,

- $M_1(\mathrm{R})$ *exists and equals* $r/(1+C_\mathrm{R})$*, and*

- *For $k \geq 2$, $M_k(\mathrm{R})$ exists and equals* $M_{k-1}(\mathrm{R}) \cdot (k-1)C_\mathrm{R}/(1+kC_\mathrm{R})$,

It is possible to show the following about C_B and C_R:

LEMMA 4.15.

- *If $0 < r < 1/2$ and $0 < \rho < 1$ then $C_\mathrm{R} < \frac{1}{2} < C_\mathrm{B}$*

- *If $r = 1/2$ then $C_\mathrm{R} = C_\mathrm{B} = 1/2$.*

- *If $\rho = 0$ or $\rho = 1$ then $C_\mathrm{R} = C_\mathrm{B} = 1/2$.*

To show that the degree distributions of both the red and the blue vertices follow power laws we recall that a power law distribution has the following property: $M_k \propto k^{-\beta}$ for large k, where β is independent of k. If $M_k \propto k^{-\beta}$, then

$$\frac{M_k}{M_{k-1}} = \frac{k^{-\beta}}{(k-1)^{-\beta}} = \left(1 - \frac{1}{k}\right)^{\beta} = 1 - \frac{\beta}{k} + O\left(\frac{1}{k^2}\right).$$

Solving for the blue vertices, $M_k(\mathtt{B})$ and the blue exponent $\beta(\mathtt{B})$, and using Lemma 4.14, we get:

$$\frac{M_k(\mathtt{B})}{M_{k-1}(\mathtt{B})} = \frac{(k-1) \cdot C_{\mathtt{B}}}{1 + k \cdot C_{\mathtt{B}}} = 1 - \frac{C_{\mathtt{B}} + 1}{k \cdot C_{\mathtt{B}} + 1}$$

$$= 1 - \frac{1 + \frac{1}{C_{\mathtt{B}}}}{k} + O\left(\frac{1}{k^2}\right)$$

hence $\beta(\mathtt{B}) = 1 + 1/C_{\mathtt{B}}$. Similarly, for red vertices of degree k, $M_k(\mathtt{R})$ decays according to a power law with exponent $\beta(\mathtt{R}) = 1 + 1/C_{\mathtt{R}}$. Note that when $C_{\mathtt{R}} < \frac{1}{2} < C_{\mathtt{B}}$ we have $\beta(\mathtt{R}) > 3 > \beta(\mathtt{B})$ thus proving Theorem 4.12.

5. EMPIRICAL OBSERVATIONS

To provide empirical evidence illustrating the results of our analysis in real-life, we studied a *mentor-student network* of researchers in computer science, extracted from DBLP [28], a dataset recording most of the publications in computer science. A filtering process, described in detail in the full version of this paper, creates a list of edges connecting students to mentors. For each edge we determined the gender of the student and the mentor and the year in which the connection was established. The resulting network spans over 30 years and has 434232 authors and 389296 edges. As may be expected based on previously reported studies, our mentor-student network exhibits a minority-majority partition (namely, a low proportion of 21% females), homophily, power law distribution and a glass ceiling effect.

Figure 4(a) reveals that over time, the fraction of females in the network ($n(\mathtt{R})/n$, the shaded red area) has increased, but it is still below 21%. Also the average degree for females vertices is lower (1.48 vs 1.87). Figure 4(b) presents an indication for homophily in the mentoring selection process. This is done by the *homophily test* of [11], which compares the expected number of "mixed" (female-male) edges to the observed one (see also Section 3.2).

Figure 5 presents indications for the glass ceiling effect. Figure 5(a) shows that the fraction of females among the vertices of degree k or higher, namely, $\text{top}_k(\mathtt{R})/\text{top}_k(\mathtt{B})$, decreases continuously as k increases. The first major decrease occurs when moving from the group of "students" (i.e., degree 1 vertices) to the group of researchers of degree 2 or higher: the fraction of females drops from $\text{top}_1(\mathtt{R}) \approx 21\%$ to $\text{top}_2(\mathtt{R}) < 15\%$. It is important to note that the data indicates that even at the high end of the graph, a few female researchers with very high degrees are still present; however, our definitions for the glass ceiling ignore this extremal effect, which is caused by a few individuals, and concentrate on the averages over large samples. Indeed, when the sample size is large enough, the fraction of the female researchers decreases. Figure 5(b) shows a strong indication that the degree distribution of the vertices (females, males and combined) follows a power law. This in turn is associated with a preferential attachment mechanism that is known to result in a power law degree distribution. Note that the power-law exponent β for the graph of the female

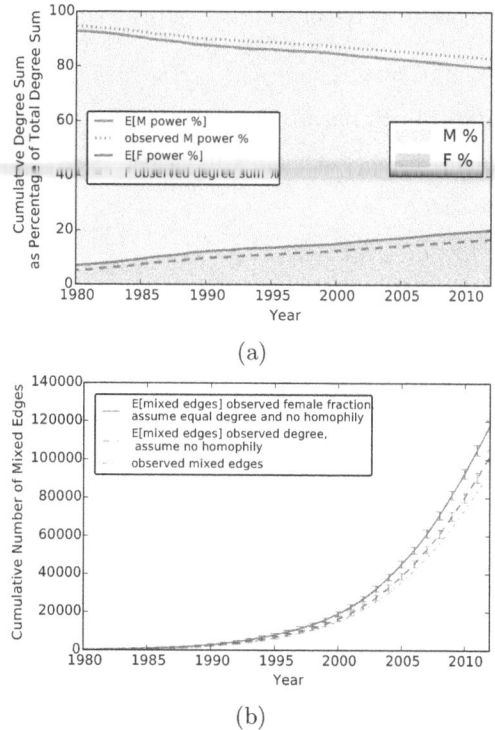

(a)

(b)

Figure 4: Female power and homophily in the computer science mentor graph. (a) The rate (i.e., percentage in the population) of females over time, compared with their normalized power, defined as $d(\mathtt{R})/(2m)$. Males have more power than expected by their rate, while females have less power than expected by their rate. (b) Evidence for homophily: a comparison of the observed number of "mixed" edges to the expected value assuming there is no homophily. We consider two cases: (i) the expected number of mixed edges ignoring the difference between the male and female average degree (expected: 127963.09 std: 293.08) and (ii) the expected number of mixed edges while considering the different degree sequences for males and females (expected: 110777.11 std: 281.52). In both cases the observed value (101607 edges) significantly deviates from the expectation (the error bars indicate the expected value ± 10 times the standard deviation) with extremely low p-values.

researchers is $\beta = 2.91$ (in the best fit), which is higher than the corresponding exponent in the graph for the male researchers, $\beta = 2.58$. Our analysis (presented in 4.2 and 4.3) establishes that if the degree distribution of both sub-populations follow a power law and the exponent for the minority sub-population is higher than that of the majority sub-population, then a strong moment glass ceiling effect will appear.

6. DISCUSSION

One obvious limitation of our model is that it is somewhat simplistic and captures only one possible mechanism for generating a glass ceiling effect. It ignores many impor-

(a)

(b)

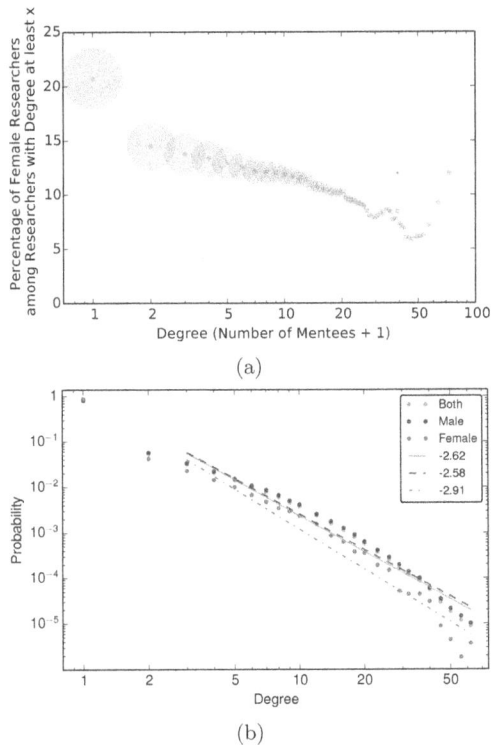

Figure 5: Glass ceiling effect in mentor graph: (a) percentage of females in the mentor population of degree at least k. Female start with 21% in the population and drop to below 15% when considering degree at least 2 (faculty members). It continues to decrease (ignoring small samples at the end, see text). Vertex size and darker color represent larger sample space. (b) The power-law-like degree distribution for both females and males. The exponent β for females is higher than for males, demonstrating the glass ceiling effect.

tant aspects of real life (such as sexual tension, fear, family responsibilities and jealousy, to name a few) and alternative (co-existing) mechanisms that contribute to the effect. For instance, our model cannot be used to explain the occurrence of a glass ceiling effect in contexts where pairwise individual interactions play a less dominant role than in academia. To account for the glass ceiling effect in such contexts as well as others, one may consider alternative explanations. In particular, a common possible explanation is the "leaky pipeline" phenomenon, namely, the phenomenon that women tend to quit or slow down their careers in order to invest more time in their families. This phenomenon can be modeled mathematically in several different ways. One such way is by introducing vertex departures in addition to vertex arrivals, with a bias in the form of increased departure rate of the minority group. But in fact, such a dynamic "leaky pipeline" model allows several reasonable sub-models that will not generate a glass ceiling effect, as well as some other sub-models that do. Moreover, the cause and effect relationships between glass ceiling and leaky pipeline are not necessarily one-directional; while the glass ceiling effect may indeed be the outcome of the "leaky pipeline" phenomenon

in certain settings, there are other settings where it may be its (partial) cause. An interesting direction for future work would be to describe a more complete model, most likely combining a number of different mechanisms contributing jointly to the glass ceiling effect. In any case, we find it remarkable that the simple mathematical mechanism presented here (based on homophily) is sufficient to explain (at least parts of) the glass ceiling effect, despite the fact that it does not utilize the "leaky pipeline".

Our Findings may suggest ways to deal with the glass ceiling phenomenon. By better understanding the roots of the glass ceiling effect, one can address each of the elements and attempt to mitigate them or deal with those elements that are easier to manage. Our research indicates that for certain mechanisms involved in the formation of a glass ceiling, removing one element may eliminate the glass ceiling effect. Hence, while it might be difficult to modify the human tendencies of homophily and preferential attachment one could attempt to balance the proportions of minorities within the population or impose a proportional representation of successful women at the top level. Both of these options may be classified as variants of affirmative action, but the latter, even if more common, seems to avoid the roots of the problem. In particular, a more equally represented society could be created by encouraging minorities to enter the system, as our findings indicate that increasing the ratio of minorities at the entry stage may mitigate the glass ceiling effect at least partially. This conclusion is in line with a common view [36, 43], which states that fixing the "leaky pipeline" is key for a more equal gender distribution in science. By determining and examining the causes of the glass ceiling effect, we can work on alleviating the glass ceiling effect, resulting in a richer and more diverse community.

Acknowledgements

The authors thank Eli Upfal for suggesting the use of a Doob Martingale and the anonymous reviewers of this paper for their helpful comments.

7. REFERENCES

[1] N. Alon and J. H. Spencer. *The probabilistic method.* John Wiley & Sons, 2004.

[2] A.-L. Barabási and R. Albert. Emergence of scaling in random networks. *Science*, 286(5439):509–512, 1999.

[3] S. J. Bock, L. J. Taylor, Z. E. Phillips, and W. Sun. Women and minorities in computer science majors: Results on barriers from interviews and a survey. *WOMEN*, 14(1):143–152, 2013.

[4] Y. Bramoulle, S. Currarini, M. O. Jackson, P. Pin, and B. W. Rogers. Homophily and long-run integration in social networks. *J. Economic Theory*, 147(5):1754–1786, 2012.

[5] D. J. Brass. Men's and women's networks: A study of interaction patterns and influence in an organization. *Academy of Management J.*, 28(2):327–343, 1985.

[6] S. J. Ceci and W. M. Williams. Understanding current causes of women's underrepresentation in science. *Proc. Nat. Acad. Sci.*, 108(8):3157–3162, 2011.

[7] F. R. K. Chung and L. Lu. *Complex graphs and networks*, volume 107 of *CBMS Regional Conf. Series in Mathematics*. AMS Bookstore, 2006.

[8] D. A. Cotter, J. M. Hermsen, S. Ovadia, and R. Vanneman. The glass ceiling effect. *Social forces*, 80(2):655–681, 2001.

[9] S. A. Davies-Netzley. Women above the glass ceiling perceptions on corporate mobility and strategies for success. *Gender & Society*, 12(3):339–355, 1998.

[10] W. W. Ding, F. Murray, and T. E. Stuart. Gender differences in patenting in the academic life sciences. *Science*, 313(5787):665–667, 2006.

[11] D. Easley and J. Kleinberg. Networks, crowds, and markets. *Cambridge Univ Press*, 6(1):6–1, 2010.

[12] D. Eder and M. T. Hallinan. Sex differences in children's friendships. *American Sociological Review*, pages 237–250, 1978.

[13] Education at a Glance. Organisation for economic co-operation and development. *OECD*, 2012.

[14] H. Etzkowitz, C. Kemelgor, M. Neuschatz, B. Uzzi, and J. Alonzo. The paradox of critical mass for women in science. *Science*, 266:51–54, 1994.

[15] A. Eyring and B. A. Stead. Shattering the glass ceiling: Some successful corporate practices. *J. Business Ethics*, 17(3):245–251, 1998.

[16] E. Falk and E. Grizard. The glass ceiling persists: The 3rd annual appc report on women leaders in communication companies. *The Annenberg Public Policy Center, University of Pennsylvania. Retrieved March*, 4:2005, 2003.

[17] W. Faulkner and M. Lie. Gender in the information society strategies of inclusion. *Gender, Technology and Development*, 11(2):157–177, 2007.

[18] Federal Glass Ceiling Commission. Solid investments: Making full use of the nation's human capital. US Government, Dept. of Labor. Washington DC, 1995.

[19] A. Fisher, J. Margolis, and F. Miller. Undergraduate women in computer science: Experience, motivation and culture. In *Proc 28th SIGCSE Technical Symp. on Computer Sci. Edu.*, pages 106–110. ACM, 1997.

[20] N. Frenkiel. The up and comers: Bryant takes aim at the settlers-in. *Adweek, March*, 1984.

[21] C. Hill, C. Corbett, and A. St Rose. *Why So Few? Women in Science, Technology, Engineering, and Mathematics*. ERIC, 2010.

[22] H. Ibarra. Homophily and differential returns: Sex differences in network structure and access in an advertising firm. *Administrative science quarterly*, pages 422–447, 1992.

[23] H. Ibarra. Paving an alternative route: Gender differences in managerial networks. *Social Psychology Quarterly*, pages 91–102, 1997.

[24] A. P. Kottis. Women in management: The "glass ceiling" and how to break it. *Women in Management Review*, 8(4), 1993.

[25] V. A. Lagesen. The strength of numbers: Strategies to include women into computer science. *Social Studies of Science*, 37(1):67–92, 2007.

[26] V. Lariviere, C. Ni, Y. Gingras, B. Cronin, and C. R. Sugimoto. Bibliometrics: Global gender disparities in science. *Nature*, 504:211–213, 2013.

[27] P. F. Lazarsfeld, R. K. Merton, et al. Friendship as a social process: A substantive and methodological analysis. *Freedom and control in modern society*, 18(1):18–66, 1954.

[28] M. Ley. Dblp: some lessons learned. *Proc. VLDB Endowment*, 2, 2009.

[29] T. J. Ley and B. H. Hamilton. The gender gap in NIH grant applications. *Science*, 322(5907):1472–1474, 2008.

[30] P. Longo and C. J. Straehley. Whack! i've hit the glass ceiling! women's efforts to gain status in surgery. *Gender medicine*, 5(1):88–100, 2008.

[31] E. E. Maccoby. *The two sexes: Growing up apart, coming together*. Harvard University Press, 1998.

[32] M. McPherson, L. Smith-Lovin, and J. M. Cook. Birds of a feather: Homophily in social networks. *Annual review of sociology*, pages 415–444, 2001.

[33] M. Mitzenmacher and E. Upfal. *Probability and computing: Randomized algorithms and probabilistic analysis*. Cambridge University Press, 2005.

[34] C. A. Moss-Racusin, J. F. Dovidio, V. L. Brescoll, M. J. Graham, and J. Handelsman. Science facultyís subtle gender biases favor male students. *Proc. Nat. Acad. Sci.*, 109(41):16474–16479, 2012.

[35] M. Othman and R. Latih. Women in computer science: No shortage here! *Commun. ACM*, 49(3):111–114, Mar. 2006.

[36] A. N. Pell. Fixing the leaky pipeline: women scientists in academia. *J. Animal Sci.*, 74(11):2843–2848, 1996.

[37] E. S. Roberts, M. Kassianidou, and L. Irani. Encouraging women in computer science. *SIGCSE Bull.*, pages 84–88, 2002.

[38] S. Sassler, J. Glass, Y. Levitte, and K. Michelmore. The missing women in stem? accounting for gender differences in entrance into stem occupations. In *Annual meeting of the Population Association of America Presentation*, 2011.

[39] J. M. Sheltzer and J. C. Smith. Elite male faculty in the life sciences employ fewer women. *Proc. Nat. Acad. Sci.*, 2014.

[40] H. Shen. Mind the gender gap. *Nature*, 2013.

[41] L. Smith-Lovin and J. M. McPherson. You are who you know: A network approach to gender. *Theory on gender/feminism on theory*, pages 223–51, 1993.

[42] E. Spertus. Why are there so few female computer scientists? Technical report, Cambridge, MA, 1991.

[43] P. E. Stephan and S. G. Levin. Leaving careers in IT: gender differences in retention. *J. Technology Transfer*, 30(4):383–396, 2005.

[44] R. Stross. What has driven women out of computer science? *New York Times*, 15, 2008.

[45] N. B. Tuma and M. T. Hallinan. The effects of sex, race, and achievement on schoolchildren's friendships. *Social Forces*, 57(4):1265–1285, 1979.

[46] J. D. West, J. Jacquet, M. M. King, S. J. Correll, and C. T. Bergstrom. The role of gender in scholarly authorship. *PloS one*, 8(7):e66212, 2013.

[47] M. A. Whitecraft and W. M. Williams. *Why Aren't More Women in Computer Science? In Making Software: What Really Works, and Why We Believe*. 2011.

Dynamic Models of Reputation and Competition in Job-Market Matching *

Jon Kleinberg[†]
Cornell University, Ithaca, NY.
kleinber@cs.cornell.edu

Sigal Oren[‡]
Hebrew University Microsoft Research, Israel.
sigalo@cs.huji.ac.il

ABSTRACT

A fundamental decision faced by a firm hiring employees — and a familiar one to anyone who has dealt with the academic job market, for example — is deciding what caliber of candidates to pursue. Should the firm try to increase its reputation by making offers to higher-quality candidates, despite the risk that the candidates might reject the offers and leave the firm empty-handed? Or is it better to play it safe and go for weaker candidates who are more likely to accept the offer? The question acquires an added level of complexity once we take into account the effect one hiring cycle has on the next: hiring better employees in the current cycle increases the firm's reputation, which in turn increases its attractiveness for higher-quality candidates in the next hiring cycle. These considerations introduce an interesting temporal dynamic aspect to the rich line of research on matching models for job markets, in which long-range planning and evolving reputational effects enter into the strategic decisions made by competing firms.

The full set of ingredients in such recruiting decisions is complex, and this has made it difficult to model the fundamental strategic tension at the core of the problem. Here we develop a model based on two competing firms to try capturing as cleanly as possible the elements that we believe constitute this strategic tension: the trade-off between short-term recruiting success and long-range reputation-building; the inefficiency that results from underemployment of people who are not ranked highest; and the influence of earlier accidental outcomes on long-term reputations.

Our model exhibits all these phenomena in a stylized setting, governed by a parameter q that captures the difference in strength between the top candidate in each hiring cycle and the next best. Building on an economic model of competition between parties of unequal strength, we show that when q is relatively low, the efficiency of the job market is improved by long-range reputational effects, but when q is relatively high, taking future reputations into account can sometimes reduce the efficiency. While this trade-off arises naturally in the model, the multi-period nature of the strategic reasoning it induces adds new sources of complexity, and our analysis reveals interesting connections between competition with evolving reputations and the the dynamics of urn processes.

1. INTRODUCTION

Markets for employment have been the subject of several large bodies of research, including the long and celebrated line of work on bipartite matching of employers to job applicants [25], sociological and economic approaches to the process of finding a job [12, 19, 24], and many other frameworks. Recent work in theoretical computer science has modeled issues such as the competition among employers for applicants [15, 16] and hiring policies that take a firm's reputation into account [5].

Despite this history of research, there remain a number of fundamental issues in job-market matching that have gone largely unmodeled. One of these, familiar to anyone who has dealt with job markets in academia or related professions, is the feedback loop over multiple hiring cycles between the job candidates that a firm (or academic department) pursues and the evolution of its overall reputation.

There is of course a very broad set of ingredients that go into the competition for job candidates over multiple hiring cycles. This makes it challenging to abstract the basic issues into a model for this type of multi-period competition. In the present paper we pare down this complexity to try formulating a model that captures, as cleanly as possible, what we view to be the basic sources of strategic tension in the process.

We develop a model based on two firms that compete for candidates over multiple periods, with a pool of candidates that has the same structure in each period; the outcome of the competition for a given candidate is determined probabilistically, based on the relative reputations of the two firms at the time they compete. This is a highly reduced and stylized model, but it produces a complex set of behaviors that we believe should be components of any of a range of richer extensions of the model as well. In particular, the process of

*A full version of this paper is available from the authors' websites.

[†]Supported in part by a Simons Investigator Award, a Google Research Grant, an ARO MURI grant, and NSF grants IIS-0910664, CCF-0910940, and IIS-1016099.

[‡]Supported in part by NSF grant CCF-0910940, a Microsoft Research Fellowship and an I-CORE ALGO fellowship.

job-market competition in our model exhibits the following fundamental trade-offs:

(i) Successfully recruiting higher-quality candidates can raise a firm's reputation, which in turn can make it more attractive to candidates in future hiring cycles.

(ii) On the other hand, competing for these higher-quality candidates comes with a greater risk of emerging from a given hiring cycle empty-handed.

(iii) The incentive to compete for top-ranked candidates can lead to underemployment of lower-ranked candidates, as they are at risk of receiving no offers while firms instead compete for their higher-ranked counterparts.

(iv) The trajectory of the process can be heavily influenced by a small number of "accidental" recruiting outcomes in the early stages, as reputations are first being established.

The trade-off between (i) and (ii) above arises from the equilibrium in the dynamic matching game played by the two firms with respect to the pool of available candidates. We find that in equilibrium, there is an initial period of competition, which can end when one firm decides it is so far behind the other that it is no longer worth competing for the top-ranked candidates. For certain natural ranges of parameters, there is in fact an interesting bifurcation — depending on the random outcomes of the initial stages, there is a positive probability one firm will "give up" on competing for the best candidates, but also a positive probability that the two firms will compete for the best candidates forever.

The issue in point (iii) is a question of efficiency: if a firm's utility is the total quality of all the candidates it hires, then our measure of social welfare — the sum of the firms' utilities — is simply the total quality of all candidates hired by either of them. We can then consider the natural performance guarantee question in this model: how does the social welfare under multi-period strategic behavior compare to the maximum social welfare attainable, where the maximum corresponds to a central authority that is able to impose a matching of candidates to firms? We obtain a tight bound of $\frac{2}{1+\sqrt{1.5}} \approx 0.898$ on the ratio of the social welfare under the canonical Nash equilibrium to the optimal social welfare in this model, as the number of periods goes to infinity. The exact numerical bound here will of course be a property of our modeling decisions, but the trade-off that leads to it seems inherent in the structure of the multi-period competition. Moreover, studying this *performance ratio*[1] as a function of the number of periods, we find that for some settings of the parameters, the performance ratio is worse for instances with a "medium" number of periods, rather than those with very few (where long-range planning does not have enough force to favor competition over star candidates) or those with very many (where the weaker firm is likely to stop competing, leading to a higher level of overall employment).

---

[1] We use the neutral term "performance ratio" rather than *price of anarchy* or *price of stability* because — as we will see — our game has a natural equilibrium, and we are interested in the relative performance of this natural equilibrium, rather than necessarily focusing on the best or worst equilibrium.

Finally, the issue in point (iv) — the "accidental" effects of early competition outcomes — turns out to be analyzable in our model via a concrete connection to Polya urn processes [22]. We show how the evolution of the two firms' reputations can be tracked through an analysis that is closely related to the evolving composition of a Polya urn; however, the analysis is made more complicated by the fact that the steps in the process are under the control of strategic agents who are calculating their actions inductively with respect to the expected outcomes in future periods.

This particular combination of phenomena (i)-(iv) appears to be new from an analytical perspective using formal models, despite its familiarity from everyday experience, and its connections with strands of more empirical and ethnographic work in economics [29] and sociology [7, 23]. We thus view the reduced-form model developed here as correspondingly shedding light on the interplay between the inherent strategic and probabilistic considerations as the process unfolds — including the emergence from the model of qualitative principles such as the transition between long-running competition and a decision by one firm to "give up" and accept a lower rank. Moreover, the use of a model with two firms is consistent with the long-standing style of analysis in terms of duopolies for multi-period game-theoretic models (see e.g. [2, 3, 17, 21]); two-firm competition is often the initial place where one looks for principles in establishing such models.

As a last point, we note that while our model is expressed in terms of job-market recruiting, there are many settings in which firms compete over multiple time periods, making decisions that have effects on their reputations and hence their relative performance in the future. As such, the type of probabilistic analysis we carry out here for the underlying dynamic multi-period process may be useful in thinking about the strategic management of evolving reputations more generally — thought still of course in the highly reduced form in which we have expressed it. For example, it would be interesting to see whether our framework can be adapted to settings where related issues have been explored, including the study of product compatibility [6]. The issue of whether a weaker firm decides to directly compete with a stronger one, or to avoid direct competition, is also implicit in studies of the branding and advertising decisions firms make — including whether to explicitly acknowledge a second-place status, such as the example (discussed in [20]) of the Avis car rental company's "We Try Harder" campaign.

Formulating the model

We now describe the model and its underlying parameters in more detail. Again, we stress that our model is designed to produce the essential phenomena in this multi-period competition as cleanly as possible, and hence is built on two firms that compete in a repeating structure over multiple periods. At the same time, the model is set up in such a way that it can be directly generalized to include larger numbers of firms and more variability between different time periods. We discuss some possible extensions briefly in the conclusions section (Section 5).

We set up the model as a game with two players over k rounds. We can think of each player as representing an academic department that is able to try hiring one new faculty candidate in each of the next k hiring seasons. In each round $t \in \{1, 2, \ldots, k\}$, the players are presented with a set of job candidates with fixed numerical *qualities*. Since we have only two firms in our model, we will assume that the firms' hiring will only involve considering the two strongest candidates; we therefore assume that there are only two candidates available. Normalizing the quality of the stronger candidate, we define the qualities of the two candidates to be 1 and $q < 1$ respectively.

We want to be able to talk separately about a department's *utility* — the total quality of all candidates it has hired — and its *reputation* — its ability to attract new candidates based on the quality of the people it has hired. A number of studies of academic rankings have emphasized that departments are judged in large part by their strongest members; intuitively, this is why a smaller department with several "star" members can easily rank higher than a much larger department, and ranking schemas often include measures that focus on this distinction.

Given this, a natural way to define reputation in our model is to say that the reputation of firm i in round t, denoted $x_i(t)$, is equal to the number of higher-quality candidates (i.e. those of quality 1 rather than q) that it has hired so far. This is distinct from the utility of firm i in round t, denoted $u_i(t)$, which is simply the sum of the qualities of all the candidates it has hired.

We assume that a firm is seeking to maximize its utility over the full k rounds; *however*, note that since this is a multi-period game, and reputation determines success in future rounds of hiring, a firm's equilibrium strategy will in fact involve actions that are effectively seeking to increase reputation even at the expense of short-term sacrifices to expected utility. This, indeed, is exactly the type of behavior we hope to see in a model of recruiting.

Building on this discussion, we therefore structure the game as follows.

- Each player i has a numerical *reputation* $x_i(t)$ and *utility* $u_i(t)$ in round t. We will focus mainly on the case in which the two players each start with reputation equal to 1, though in places we will consider variations on this initial condition.

- In each round $t \in \{1, 2, \ldots, k\}$, player i chooses one of the candidates j to try recruiting; this choice of j constitutes the player's *strategy* in round t.

- If player i is the only one to try recruiting j, then j accepts the offer. If both players compete for the same candidate j, then j accepts player i's offer with probability proportional to player i's reputation. This follows the *Tullock contest function* that is standard in economic theory for modeling competition [27, 28], thus we have : player 1 hires j with probability $\frac{x_1(t)}{x_1(t) + x_2(t)}$ and player 2 hires j with probability $\frac{x_2(t)}{x_1(t) + x_2(t)}$. The player who loses this competition for candidate j hires no one in this round.

- Finally, each player receives a payoff in round t equal to the quality of the candidate hired in the round (if any). The player's utility is increased by the quality of the candidate it has hired; the player's reputation is increased by 1 if it has hired the stronger candidate in round t, and remains the same otherwise.

Thus the model captures the basic trade-off inherent in recruiting over multiple rounds — by competing for a stronger candidate, a player has the opportunity to increase its reputation by a larger amount, but it also risks hiring no one. The model is designed to arrive at this trade-off using very few underlying parameters; but we believe that the techniques developed for the analysis suggest approaches to more complex variants, and we discuss some of these in the conclusions section (Section 5).

The maximum possible social welfare is achieved if the two players hire the top two candidates respectively in each round, achieving a social welfare of $k(1 + q)$. The key question we consider here is what social welfare can be achieved in equilibrium for this k-round game, and how it compares to the welfare of the social optimum. In effect, how much does the struggle for reputation leave candidates unemployed?

The subgame perfect equilibria in this multi-round game are determined by backward induction — essentially, in a given round t, a player evaluates the possible values its utility and reputation can take in round $t + 1$, after the (potentially probabilistic) outcome of its recruiting in round t. There are multiple equilibria, but there is a single natural class of *canonical equilibria* for the model, in which the higher-reputation player always goes after the stronger candidate, and — predicated on the equilibrium having this form in future rounds — the lower-reputation player makes an optimal decision to either compete for the stronger candidate or make an offer to the weaker candidate. (When the lower-reputation player is indifferent between these two options, we break the symmetry using the assumption that the lower player hires the weaker candidate.) The canonical equilibrium can be also viewed as the result of a best response order in which at every round the higher-reputation gets the advantage of making the first choice. Proving that this structure in fact produces an equilibrium is non-trivial; in part this is because reasoning about subgame perfect equilibria always involves some complexity due to the underlying tree of possibilities, but the present model adds to this complexity because the randomization involved in the outcome causes the possible trajectories of the game to "explore" most of this tree.

We study the behavior of this canonical equilibrium, and we define the *performance ratio* of an instance to be the ratio of total welfare between the canonical equilibrium and the social optimum.

Overview of Results

We first consider the performance ratio as a function of the number of rounds k. As an initial question, which choice of k yields the worst performance ratio? When $q < \frac{1}{2}$, the answer is simple: for $k = 1$, the players necessarily compete in the one round they have available, and this yields a performance ratio of $1/(1+q)$ — as small as possible. When $q > \frac{1}{2}$, however, the situation becomes more subtle. For $k = 1$, the players do not compete in the canonical equilibrium, and so the performance ratio for $k = 1$ is 1. At the other end of the spectrum, when $q \geq \frac{1}{2}$, the two players will eventually stop competing with probability 1 and the performance ratio converges up to 1 when k becomes large. But in between, the performance ratio can be larger than at both extremes; in particular, when the quantity $\frac{q}{1-q}$ approaches an integer value k from below, we show that the performance ratio is maximized when the number of rounds takes this intermediate value k. These results show how the time scale over which the players take reputational effects into account can have a subtle (and in this case non-monotonic) effect on the efficiency of the job market.

We then turn to the main result of the paper, which is to analyze the performance ratio in the limit as the number of rounds k goes to infinity. When $q \geq \frac{1}{2}$, as just noted, we show that the two players will eventually stop competing with probability 1 and the performance ratio converges to 1. But when $q < \frac{1}{2}$, something more complex happens: there is a positive probability, strictly between 0 and 1, that the players compete forever. This has a natural interpretation — as reputations evolve, the two players can settle into relative levels of reputation under which it is worthwhile for the lower player to compete for the stronger candidate; but it may also happen that after a finite number of rounds, one player decides that it is too weak to continue competing for the stronger candidate, and it begins to act on its second-tier status. What is interesting is that each of these outcomes has a positive probability of occurring.

The possibility of indefinite competition leads to a nontrivial performance ratio; we show that the worst case occurs when $q = \sqrt{1.5} - 1 \approx .2247$, with a performance ratio of $\frac{2}{1+\sqrt{1.5}} \approx 0.898$. We also show that the performance ratio converges to 1 as q goes either to 0 or to 1. Our analysis proceeds by defining an urn process that tracks the evolution of the players' reputations; this is a natural connection to develop, since urn processes are based on models in which probabilities of outcomes in a given step — the result of draws from an urn — are affected by the realized outcomes of draws in earlier steps. We provide more background about urn processes in the next section. Informally speaking, the fact that a player might compete for a while and then permanently give up in favor of an alternative option is also reminiscent of strategies in the multi-armed bandit problem, where an agent may experiment with a risky option for a while before permanently giving up and using a safer option; later in the paper, we make this analogy more precise as well. To make use of these connections, we study a sequence of games that begins with players who are constrained to follow a set sequence of decisions for a long prefix of rounds, and we then successively relax this constraint until we end up with the original game in which players are allowed to make strategic decisions from the very beginning.

In the full version of the paper, we also consider variants of the model in which one changes the function used for the success probabilities in the competition between the two players for a candidate. Note that the way in which competition is handled is an implicit reflection of the way candidates form preferences over firms based on their reputations, and hence varying this aspect of the model allows us to explore different ways in which candidates can behave in this dimension. In particular, we consider a variation on the model in which — when the two players compete for a candidate — the lower-reputation player succeeds with a fixed probability $p < \frac{1}{2}$ and the higher-reputation player succeeds with probability $1 - p$. This model thus captures the long-range competition to become the higher-reputation player using an extremely simple model of competition within each round. The main result here is that for all $p < q$, the performance ratio converges to 1; the analysis makes use of biased random walks in place of urn processes to analyze the long-term competition between the players.

Further Related Work

As noted above, there has been recent theoretical work studying the effect of reputation and competition in job markets. Broder et al. consider hiring strategies designed to increase the average quality of a firm's employees [5]. Our focus here is different, due to the feedback effects from future rounds that our model of competition generates: a few weak initial hires can make it very difficult for a player to raise its quality later, while a few strong initial hires can make the process correspondingly much easier. Immorlica et al. consider competition between employers, though in a quite different model where candidates are presented one at a time as in the *secretary problem* [15, 16], and each player's goal is to hire a candidate that is stronger than the competitor's. They do not incorporate the spillover of this competition into future rounds.

Our work can also be viewed as developing techniques for analyzing the performance ratio and/or price of anarchy in settings that involve dynamic matchings — when nodes on one side of a bipartite graph must make strategic decisions about matchings to nodes that arrive dynamically to the other side of the graph. In the context of job matching, Shimer and Smith consider a dynamic matching model of a labor market in which the central constraint is the cost of searching for potential partners [26]. Haeringer and Wooders apply dynamic matching to the problem of sequential job offers over time [13], but in a setting that considers the sequencing of offers in a single hiring cycle; this leads to different questions, since the consequence for reputation in future hiring cycles is not in the scope of their investigation. Dynamic matchings have also been appearing in a number of other recent application contexts (e.g. [8, 30]), and there are clearly many unresolved questions here about the cost of strategic behavior.

2. THE CANONICAL EQUILIBRIUM AND ITS PROPERTIES

An instance of the recruiting game, as described in the introduction, is defined by the initial reputations x_1 and x_2 of the two players; the relative quality q of the weaker candidate compared to the stronger one; and the number of rounds k. Accordingly, we denote an instance of the game by $G_{k,q}(x_1, x_2)$. Generally q will be clear from context, and so we will also refer to this game as simply $G_k(x_1, x_2)$. We will refer to the player of higher reputation as the *higher player*, and the player of lower reputation as the *lower player*. In case the players have the same reputation we will refer to player 1 as the higher player.

The game as defined is an extensive-form game, and as such it can admit many subgame perfect equilibria. For example, it is easy to construct a single-round game in which it is an equilibrium for the lower player to try to recruit the stronger candidate and for the higher player to go after the weaker candidate. This equilibrium clearly has a less natural structure than one in which the higher player goes after the stronger option; to avoid such pathologies, as noted in the introduction, we will study multi-round strategies $s_k(x_1, x_2)$ that are defined as follows:

DEFINITION 2.1. *Denote by $s_k(x_1, x_2)$ the following strategies for the players over the k rounds: in every round the higher player goes for the stronger candidate and the lower player best-responds by choosing the candidate that maximizes its utility, taking into account the current round and all later rounds by induction.*

For $s_k(x_1, x_2)$ to be well-defined we make the following two assumptions: (1) If the lower player is indifferent between going for the stronger candidate and the weaker candidate we assume it chooses to go for the weaker candidate. (2) If the two players have the same reputations we break ties in favor of player 1.

The strategies $s_k(x_1, x_2)$ can be summarized essentially by saying that in every round of the game, first the higher player gets to make an offer to its preferred candidate, and given this decision the lower player makes the choice maximizing its utility. To show that the strategies $s_k(x_1, x_2)$ form a sub-game perfect equilibrium we will show inductively that in every round it is in the higher player's best interest to make an offer to the stronger candidate. More formally we denote the strategy of making an offer to the stronger candidate in some round by $+$ and to the weaker candidate by $-$. We define $f(s_k(x_1, x_2))$ to be the pair of strategies that the players use in the first round of $s_k(x_1, x_2)$.

We denote player i's utility when the two players play the strategies prescribed by $s_k(x_1, x_2)$ by $u_i(s_k(x_1, x_2))$. We now formally write down the utility of the players in $s_k(x_1, x_2)$ based on the value of $f(s_k(x_1, x_2))$:

- If $f(s_k(x_1, x_2)) = \langle +, + \rangle$ then

$$u_1(s_k(x_1, x_2)) = \frac{x_1}{x_1 + x_2}(1 + u_1(s_{k-1}(x_1 + 1, x_2)))$$
$$+ \frac{x_2}{x_1 + x_2} u_1(s_{k-1}(x_1, x_2 + 1))$$
$$u_2(s_k(x_1, x_2)) = \frac{x_1}{x_1 + x_2} u_2(s_{k-1}(x_1 + 1, x_2))$$
$$+ \frac{x_2}{x_1 + x_2}(1 + u_2(s_{k-1}(x_1, x_2 + 1))).$$

- If $f(s_k(x_1, x_2)) = \langle +, - \rangle$ then

$$u_1(s_k(x_1, x_2)) = 1 + u_1(s_{k-1}(x_1 + 1, x_2))$$
$$u_2(s_k(x_1, x_2)) = q + u_2(s_{k-1}(x_1 + 1, x_2))$$

- If $f(s_k(x_1, x_2)) = \langle -, + \rangle$ then

$$u_1(s_k(x_1, x_2) = q + u_1(s_{k-1}(x_1, x_2 + 1))$$
$$u_2(s_k(x_1, x_2)) = 1 + u_2(s_{k-1}(x_1, x_2 + 1))$$

We denote the social welfare of playing the strategies $s_k(x_1, x_2)$ by

$$u(s_k(x_1, x_2)) = u_1(s_k(x_1, x_2)) + u_2(s_k(x_1, x_2)).$$

Even though it is natural to suspect that the strategies $s_k(x_1, x_2)$ are indeed a sub-game perfect equilibrium, proving that this is the case is not such a simple task. The first step in showing that the strategies $s_k(x_1, x_2)$ are a sub-game perfect equilibrium, and a useful fact by itself, is the monotonicity of the players' utilities $u_i(s_k(x_1, x_2))$. More formally, in the full version of the paper we show that:

CLAIM 2.2. *For any x_1, x_2, and $\epsilon > 0$:*

1. $u_1(s_k(x_1 + \epsilon, x_2)) \geq u_1(s_k(x_1, x_2)) \geq u_1(s_k(x_1, x_2 + \epsilon))$.

2. $u_2(s_k(x_1, x_2 + \epsilon)) \geq u_2(s_k(x_1, x_2)) \geq u_2(s_k(x_1 + \epsilon, x_2))$.

Next, we prove that the three following statements hold.

PROPOSITION 2.3. *For any integers x_1, x_2 and k the following holds for the strategies $s_k(x_1, x_2)$.*

1. $s_k(x_1, x_2)$ is a sub-game perfect equilibrium in the game $G_k(x_1, x_2)$.

2. If a player does not compete in the first round of the game $G_k(x_1, x_2)$, then it does not compete in all subsequent rounds.

3. The utility of the higher player in the game $G_k(x_1, x_2)$ is at least as large as the utility of the lower player.

Essentially, we prove all three properties simultaneously by induction on the number of rounds of the game. Let us mention two more claims that will be useful later on (all proofs are available in the full version of the paper):

CLAIM 2.4. *If $u_i(s_k(x_1, x_2)) = kq$, for some player i, then player i never competes in the game $G_k(x_1, x_2)$.*

CLAIM 2.5. *If player i competes in the first round of the game $G_k(x_1, x_2)$ and wins, then in the next round of the game it also makes an offer to the stronger candidate.*

Connections to Urn Processes

Note that since each player's reputation is equal to the number of stronger candidates it has hired, the reputations are always integers (assuming they start from integer values). These integer values evolve while the players are competing; and once they stop competing, we know by statement (2) of Proposition 2.3 the exact outcome of the game since the players will behave exactly the same as in the game that this is its first round. This brings us to the close resemblance between our recruiting game and a Polya Urn process [22].

First, let us define what the Polya Urn process is:

DEFINITION 2.6 (POLYA URN PROCESS). *Consider an urn containing b blue balls and r red balls. The process is defined over discrete rounds. In each round a ball is sampled uniformly at random from the urn; hence the probability of drawing a blue ball is $\frac{b}{b+r}$ and the probability of drawing a red ball is $\frac{r}{b+r}$. Then, the ball together with another ball of the same color are returned to the urn.*

There is a clear resemblance between our recruiting game and the urn model. As long as the players compete, their reputations evolve in the same way as the number of blue and red balls in the urn, since the probabilistic rule for a candidate to select which firm to join is the same as the rule for choosing which color to add to the urn, and by assumption the reputation of the winning player is increased by the stronger candidate's quality, which is 1.

A striking fact about urn models is that the fraction of the blue (or red) balls converges in distribution as the number of rounds goes to infinity. More specifically, if initially the urn contains a single red ball and a single blue ball then the fraction of blue balls converges to a uniform distribution on $[0, 1]$ as the number of rounds goes to infinity. More generally, the fraction of blue balls converges to the β distribution $\beta(b, r)$. Understanding urn processes is useful for understanding our proofs; however we should stress that our model and its analysis have added complexity due to the fact that players stop competing at a point in time that is strategically determined.

Connections to Bandit Problems

It is interesting to note that as long as the lower player stays lower our equilibrium selection rule makes this effectively a one-player game. In a sense, the lower player's strategy in this phase resembles the optimal strategy in a mulit-armed bandit problem [11], and more specifically in a one-armed bandit problem [4]. In a one-armed bandit a single player is repeatedly faced with two options (known as "arms" following the terminology of slot machines): the player can pull arm 1, which gives a reward sampled from some *unknown* distribution, or pull arm 2 which gives him a reward from a *known* distribution. Informally speaking, by pulling arm 1 the player gets both a reward and some information about the distribution from which the reward is drawn. The player's goal is to maximize its expected reward possibly under some discounting of future rounds. A celebrated result establishes that for some types of discounting (for example geometric) one can compute a number called the *Gittins index* for each arm (based on one's observations and the prior) and the strategy maximizing the player's expected reward is to pull the arm with the highest Gittins index in each round [11]. Since by definition the Gittins index of the fixed arm is fixed, this implies that once the Gittins index of the unknown arm drops below the one of the known arm, the player should only pull the known arm. This also means that the player stops collecting information on the distribution of the unknown arm and hence from this round onwards it always chooses the fixed arm.

There are analogies as well as differences between our game and the one-armed bandit problem. In our game, the lower player is also faced with a choice between a risky option (competing) and a safe option (going for the weaker candidate). On the other hand, an important difference between our model and the one-armed bandit problem is that our game is in fact a two-player game and at any point the lower-reputation player can become the higher-reputation one; this property contributes additional sources of complexity to the analysis of our game. Moreover, it is important to note that for many distributions and discount sequences (including the ones most similar to our game) a closed-form expression of the Gittins index is unknown.

3. ANALYZING THE GAME WITH A FIXED NUMBER OF ROUNDS

We begin by analyzing the game played over a fixed number of rounds k and study the dependence of the performance ratio on k. In the next section, we turn to the main result of the paper, which is to analyze the limit of the performance ratio as the number of rounds k goes to infinity.

Our first result is a simple but powerful bound of $\frac{2q}{1+q}$ on the performance ratio, which holds for all k. This is done by relating the performance ratio to players' decision whether to compete in the first round. The argument underlying this relationship is quite robust, in that it is essentially based only on the reasoning that the players can always decide to stop competing and go for the weaker candidate. This bound also implies that as q goes to 1 the performance ratio also goes to 1.

CLAIM 3.1. *The performance ratio of any game $G_{k,q}(x_1, x_2)$ is at least $\frac{2q}{1+q}$.*

PROOF. We begin with the simple observation that the expected social welfare equals the sum of the expected utilities of the two players in the beginning of the game. To get a lower bound on the performance ratio it is enough to compute an upper bound on the expected social welfare. This is done by observing that $u_i(s_k(x_1, x_2)) \geq kq$, since a player can always secure a utility of kq by always making an offer to the weaker candidate. Hence, the following is a bound on the performance ratio: $\dfrac{u_1(s_k(x_1, x_2)) + u_2(s_k(x_1, x_2))}{k(1+q)} \geq$

$$\frac{2kq}{k(1+q)} = \frac{2q}{1+q}. \quad \square$$

COROLLARY 3.2. *The performance ratio of any game $G_{k,q}(x_1, x_2)$ is at least 2/3.*

The previous corollary holds for $q > 1/2$ since $\dfrac{2q}{1+q} > 2/3$ and for $q \leq 1/2$ since the performance ratio is trivially lower-bounded by $1/(1+q) \geq 2/3$.

Next, we ask what is the length of a game for which the worst performance ratio is achieved. For $q < 1/2$, this is simply a single-round game. However, for $q > 1/2$ the answer is not so simple. We show that when $\frac{q}{1-q} + \epsilon$ is an integer for an arbitrarily small $\epsilon > 0$, a game of $k_q = \frac{q}{1-q} + \epsilon$ rounds exhibits a performance ratio arbitrarily close to $\frac{2q}{1+q}$. It is interesting that the players' strategies in the games achieving this maximum performance ratio have a very specific structure – the players compete just for the first round and then the player who lost goes for the weaker candidate for the rest of the game.

PROPOSITION 3.3. *Let $\epsilon = \lceil \frac{q}{1-q} \rceil - \frac{q}{1-q}$ and $k_q = \frac{q}{1-q} + \epsilon$. Then, as ϵ approaches 0 from above (remaining strictly positive), the performance ratio of the game $G_{k_q, q}(x, x)$ converges to $\frac{2q}{1+q}$.*

PROOF. Observe that by Claim 3.4 below the players in the game $G_{k_q, q}(x, x)$ compete for the first round (since $\epsilon > 0$) and then completely stop competing. Thus the expected social welfare of the canonical equilibrium is $k + (k-1)q$ and its performance ratio is:

$$\frac{1 + (k-1)(1+q)}{k(1+q)} = \frac{1 + ((\frac{q}{1-q} + \epsilon) - 1)(1+q)}{(\frac{q}{1-q} + \epsilon)(1+q)}$$

$$= \frac{2q^2 + \epsilon - \epsilon q^2}{q + q^2 + \epsilon - \epsilon q^2}.$$

It is not hard to see now that as ϵ approaches 0 the performance ratio approaches $\frac{2q}{1+q}$. $\quad \square$

We now prove for the k_q's discussed in the previous proposition the players indeed compete only for the first round and then stop competing. More formally we prove:

CLAIM 3.4. *In the game $G_{k,q}(x, x)$ for $\frac{q}{1-q} < k \leq \frac{1}{1-q}$ the players compete in the first round and then completely stop competing.*

PROOF. Player 2 (which is the lower player in the game) competes in the game $G_{k,q}(x, x)$ if:

$$\frac{1}{2}(1 + u_2(s_{k-1}(x, x+1))) + \frac{1}{2} u_2(s_{k-1}(x+1, x))$$
$$> q + u_2(s_{k-1}(x+1, x)).$$

After some rearranging we get that this implies that player 2 competes if:

$$1 + u_2(s_{k-1}(x, x+1)) > 2q + u_2(s_{k-1}(x+1, x)).$$

Note that $k \leq \frac{1}{1-q} \implies q \geq \frac{k-1}{k}$. Thus, by Claim 3.5 below we have that for any x_1, x_2 the players in the game $G_{k-1,q}(x_1, x_2)$ do not compete. This implies that $u_2(s_{k-1}(x, x+1)) = k-1$ and $u_2(s_{k-1}(x+1, x)) = (k-1)q$. Thus, the players in the game $G_{k,q}(x, x)$ compete if $k > (k+1)q$ implying $\frac{q}{1-q} < k$ as required. $\square$

Finally we prove:

CLAIM 3.5. *If $q \geq \frac{k}{k+1}$ then the players in the game $G_{k,q}(x_1, x_2)$ never compete.*

PROOF. Let $x_2 \leq x_1$. Player 2 competes in the game $G_{k,q}(x_1, x_2)$ if:

$$\frac{x_2}{x_1 + x_2}(1 + u_2(s_{k-1}(x_1, x_2 + 1)))$$
$$+ \frac{x_1}{x_1 + x_2}u_2(s_{k-1}(x_1 + 1, x_2))$$
$$> q + u_2(s_{k-1}(x_1 + 1, x_2)).$$

After some rearranging we get that player 2 competes if:

$$1 + u_2(s_{k-1}(x_1, x_2 + 1)) > \frac{x_1 + x_2}{x_2}q + u_2(s_{k-1}(x_1 + 1, x_2)).$$

Observe that $u_2(s_{k-1}(x_1, x_2 + 1)) \leq k - 1$ as this is the maximum utility a player can get in a $(k-1)$-round game. Also observe that $u_2(s_{k-1}(x_1 + 1, x_2)) \geq (k-1)q$ and that by assumption $\frac{x_1 + x_2}{x_2} \geq 2$. Thus, we have that a necessary condition for player 2 to compete is that $k > (k+1)q$. This implies that for $q \geq \frac{k}{k+1}$ player 2 does not compete in the first round of the game $G_{k,q}(x_1, x_2)$. By part (2) of Proposition 2.3 we have that if a player does not compete in the first round of the game it also does not compete in all subsequent rounds which completes the proof. A very similar proof works for the case that player 1 is the lower player. $\square$

4. ANALYZING THE LONG-GAME LIMIT

We now turn to the main question in the paper, which is the behavior of the performance ratio in the limit as the number of rounds goes to infinity.

Our main result here is that as k goes to infinity the performance ratio of the game $G_k(1, 1)$ goes to $\frac{1 + 2qr}{1 + q}$, where $r = \min\{q, \frac{1}{2}\}$. In particular for $q < 1/2$ this implies that as k goes to infinity the performance ratio goes to $\frac{1 + 2q^2}{1 + q}$. This function attains its minimum when $q = \sqrt{1.5} - 1 \approx .2247$ and at this point it has a value of $\frac{2}{1 + \sqrt{1.5}} \approx 0.898$. For $q \geq 1/2$, on the other hand, this simply implies that as k goes to infinity the performance ratio of the game $G_k(1, 1)$ goes to 1. Defining $r = \min\{q, \frac{1}{2}\}$ helps us to present a single unified proof both for $q < 1/2$ and for $q \geq 1/2$.

The proof of this theorem becomes somewhat involved even though its main idea is quite natural. Intuitively speaking, we know that as long as the players compete, our game proceeds the way an urn process does. This means that the probability that player 2, for example, is the one to hire the stronger candidate converges to a uniform distribution as the number of rounds k the players compete goes to infinity.

Henceforth, we will also refer to this probability as player's 2 *relative reputation*. We show that if the relative reputation of one of the players converges to a number smaller than r, then after a fairly small number of rounds – specifically $\theta(\ln(k))$ – the players stop competing. The probability that the relative reputation of one of the players converges to something less than r is simply $2r$. Therefore, the expected social welfare of our canonical equilibrium converges to $k + 2qr(k - \theta(\ln(k)))$ and the performance ratio converges to $\frac{1 + 2qr}{1 + q}$.

We divide the proof to four subsections. In Subsection 4.1 we introduce *t-binding games*, which give us a formal way to study games in which the two players compete for at least the first t rounds. By showing that the utilities of the players in our game are at least as large as their utilities in the t-binding game we reduce our problem to showing that the expected utility in a t-binding game is "large enough". This is done in Subsection 4.3. The proof relies on Subsection 4.2 which, loosely speaking, shows that if after t rounds of competition the relative reputation of the lower player is non-trivially smaller than r then the lower player stops competing. Finally, in Subsection 4.4 we state the formal theorem and wrap up the proof.

4.1 t-Binding Games

A recruiting game is *t-binding* if in the first t rounds the two players are required to compete for the stronger candidate. We denote a t-binding game by $G_k^t(x_1, x_2)$. We also denote by $s_k^t(x_1, x_2)$ the canonical equilibrium of the game $G_k^t(x_1, x_2)$ in which the players compete for the first t rounds and then follow the strategies $s_{k-t}(x_1', x_2')$ in the resulting game.

Denote by $u(s_k^t(x_1, x_2))$ the expected social welfare of the canonical equilibrium in the game $G_k^t(x_1, x_2)$. It is intuitive to suspect that making the players compete for the first t rounds can only decrease their utility. In the next lemma we prove that this intuition is indeed correct:

LEMMA 4.1. *The expected social welfare of the game $G_k(1, 1)$ is greater than or equal to the expected social welfare of the game $G_k^t(1, 1)$; that is, $u(s_k(1, 1)) \geq u(s_k^t(1, 1))$.*

PROOF. We prove the lemma by proving a stronger claim:

CLAIM 4.2. *The expected utility of each of the players in the game $G_k^t(1, 1)$ for $0 \leq t < k$ is greater than or equal to their expected utility in the game $G_k^{t+1}(1, 1)$.*

PROOF. For simplicity we prove the claim for player 2; however the claim holds for both players. By definition, in the game $G_k^t(1, 1)$ the players compete for at least the first t rounds. During this phase of competition, the two players' reputations evolve according to the update rule for a standard Polya urn process, as described in Section 2. A standard result on that process implies that at the end of these t rounds with probability $\frac{1}{t+1}$ player 1 has a reputation of $1 + t - i$ and player 2 has a reputation of $1 + i$ for $0 \leq i \leq t$. Thus, we have that:

$$u_2(s_k^t(1, 1)) = \frac{1}{t+1} \sum_{i=0}^{t} u_2(s_{k-t}(1 + t - i, 1 + i))$$

Let $I_\delta = \{i | f(s_{k-t}(1 + t - i, 1 + i)) = \delta\}$ for $\delta \in \{\langle +, + \rangle, \langle +, - \rangle, \langle -, + \rangle\}$. For example, $I_{\langle +, + \rangle}$ is the set of all indices i for which the players compete in the first round of the game $G_{k-t}(1 + t - i, 1 + i)$.

We can now write the sum, usefully, as

$$u_2(s_k^t(1,1)) = \frac{1}{t+1} \sum_{i \in I_{\langle +,+ \rangle}} u_2(s_{k-t}(1+t-i, 1+i))$$
$$+ \frac{1}{t+1} \sum_{i \in I_{\langle +,- \rangle}} u_2(s_{k-t}(1+t-i, 1+i))$$
$$+ \frac{1}{t+1} \sum_{i \in I_{\langle -,+ \rangle}} u_2(s_{k-t}(1+t-i, 1+i))$$

By this partition:

- For $i \in I_{\langle +,+ \rangle}$, we have $u_2(s_{k-t}(1+t-i, 1+i)) = u_2(s_{k-t}^1(1+t-i, 1+i))$ – since in both of these games the two players compete in the first round.

- For $i \in I_{\langle +,- \rangle}$, we have $u_2(s_{k-t}(1+t-i, 1+i)) \geq u_2(s_{k-t}^1(1+t-i, 1+i))$ – since $u_2(s_{k-t}^{\langle +,- \rangle}(1+t-i, 1+i)) \geq u_2(s_{k-t}^{\langle +,+ \rangle}(1+t-i, 1+i))$. (in the first round of the game player 2 prefers going after the weaker candidate over competing).

- For $i \in I_{\langle -,+ \rangle}$, we have $u_2(s_{k-t}(1+t-i, 1+i)) > u_2(s_{k-t}^1(1+t-i, 1+i))$ – since $u_2(s_{k-t}^{\langle -,+ \rangle}(1+t-i, 1+i)) = 1 + u_2(s_{k-t-1}(1+t-i+q, 1+i+1)) > u_2(s_{k-t}^{\langle +,+ \rangle}(1+t-i, 1+i))$ by monotonicity.

Thus, we have $u_2(s_k^t(1,1)) \geq \frac{1}{t+1} \sum_{i=0}^{t} u_2(s_{k-t}^1(1+t-i, 1+i)) = u_2(s_k^{t+1}(1,1))$.

$\square$

4.2 When does the lower player stop competing?

This next phase of our analysis is composed of two parts: in the first part we show that the utility of the lower player in a k-round game is upper bounded by $\max\{b_q(k,t,x), kq\}$ for some function $b_q(\cdot)$ to be later defined. In the second part we compute the conditions under which $b_q(k,t,x) < kq$ which implies that under the same conditions the lower player in the game stops competing.

For this subsection we denote player 1's reputation after t rounds by $t-x$ and player 2's reputation by x. Both statements below also hold for player 1 and the game $G_k(x, t-x)$.

The following notation will be useful for our proofs:

- $f_q(i, t) = \binom{t}{i} q^i (1-q)^{t-i}$ – probability mass function for the binomial distribution with t trials.

- $F_q(x, t) = \sum_{i=0}^{x} \binom{t}{i} q^i (1-q)^{t-i}$ – cumulative distribution function for an integer x.

The function that we use to upper bound the player's utility is:

$$b_q(k,t,x) = \frac{x}{t} + 3F_r(x,t)k + (1 - 3F_r(x,t))(k-1)q$$
$$= \frac{x}{t} + (k-1)q + 3F_r(x,t) \cdot ((k-1)(1-q) + 1)$$

To understand the intuition behind the upper bound function $b_q(k,t,x)$ it is useful to look at an alternative description of the urn process. Under this description, we have a coin whose bias is sampled from a uniform distribution on $[0,1]$;

then in each round the coin is tossed. If the coin turns up heads a blue ball is added to the urn; otherwise a red ball is added to the urn. Under this alternative description we can think of our lower player as trying to toss this coin (i.e. competing) in the hope that its bias is greater than r (recall that $r = \min\{q, \frac{1}{2}\}$). We refer to the event in which the bias of the coin is greater than r as a good event, and the event it is not a bad event. To upper-bound the player's utility we assume that if the good event happens the player wins the stronger candidate for all subsequent rounds and hence its utility is k. If the bad event happens then the player completely stops competing and thus its utility is $(k-1)q$.

We show that $\max\{b_q(k,t,x), kq\}$ is indeed an upper bound on the players' utility as the previous intuition suggests.

LEMMA 4.3. *For any k, x and $t > \frac{4\ln(1/12)}{\ln(1-r)}$, we have $u_2(s_k(t-x, x)) \leq \max\{b_q(k,t,x), kq\}$.*

PROOF. We divide the proof into two cases. When, $r \leq \frac{x+1}{t+1}$ the bound we need to prove is very loose and hence we can prove it directly. However, for $r > \frac{x+1}{t+1}$ proving this bound is more tricky and for this we use an induction that some times relies on the first case. The proofs of these two cases are included in the full version. $\square$

We can now use the previous bound to compute the conditions under which the lower player prefers to stop competing.

THEOREM 4.4. *In the game $G_k(t-p \cdot t, p \cdot t)$ for $p = r - \epsilon$, $\epsilon > 0$ and $t = \max\{\frac{4\ln(1/12)}{\ln(1-r)}, \frac{3\ln(k)-\ln(q-p)}{(r-p)^2}\}$ player 2 does not compete at all.*

PROOF. By Lemma 4.3 we have that $u_2(s_k(t-p \cdot t, p \cdot t)) \leq \max\{b_q(k,t,p\cdot t), kq\}$ for $t > \frac{4\ln(1/12)}{\ln(1-r)}$. Since we have that $u_2(s_k(t-p \cdot t, p \cdot t)) \geq kq$, if we show that $b_q(k,t,p \cdot t) \leq kq$, then we will have $u_2(s_k(t-p \cdot t, p \cdot t)) = kq$. It will then follow from Claim 2.4 that the lower player (player 2) does not compete at all. The theorem will thus follow if we show that for $t = \max\{\frac{4\ln(1/12)}{\ln(1-r)}, \frac{3\ln(k)-\ln(q-p)}{(r-p)^2}\}$, we have $b_q(k,t,p \cdot t) \leq kq$.

By Hoeffding's inequality with $\epsilon = r - p$, we get that $F_r(p \cdot t, t) \leq e^{-2t(r-p)^2}$. Now, to compute the value of t for which $u_2(s_k(t-p \cdot t, p \cdot t)) = kq$, we simply find the value of t for which the following inequality holds:

$$p + (k-1)q + 3e^{-2t(r-p)^2}((k-1)(1-q)+1) \leq kq$$

After some rearranging we get that:

$$3e^{-2t(r-p)^2}((k-1)(1-q)+1) \leq q - p$$
$$3(k-1)(1-q) + 1 \leq e^{2t(r-p)^2}(q-p)$$

Taking natural logarithms we get:

$$\ln(3(k-1)(1-q)+1) \leq 2t(r-p)^2 + \ln(q-p)$$
$$\frac{\ln(3(k-1)(1-q)+1) - \ln(q-p)}{2(r-p)^2} \leq t$$

In particular this implies that the claim holds for $t \geq \frac{3\ln(k)-\ln(q-p)}{(r-p)^2}$. $\square$

4.3 The Expected Social Welfare of a t-Binding Game

We show that for large enough k the social welfare of the t-binding game $G_k^t(1,1)$ is relatively high. This is done by showing that there exists some t, such that after competing for t rounds, with probability $2(r-\epsilon) - \frac{4}{t+1}$ the players reach a game in which the lower player (either player 1 or player 2) does not want to compete any more.

LEMMA 4.5. *For every $\epsilon > 0$ and $k \geq e^{\frac{8(r-\epsilon)}{\epsilon^3}} + e^{\frac{4\ln(1/12)}{\ln(1-r)}}$, there exists t such that the expected social welfare of the t-binding game $G_k^t(1,1)$ is at least $k \cdot \left(1 + 2q(r - 3\epsilon - \epsilon^2)\right)$.*

PROOF. By the assumption that the game is t-binding we have that both players compete over the stronger candidate for the first t rounds. This implies that at the end of these t rounds with probability $\frac{1}{t+1}$ player 1 has a reputation of $1 + t - i$ and player 2 has a reputation of $1 + i$ for $0 \leq i \leq t$. Or, in other words, the relative reputation of player 2 is $\frac{1+i}{t+2}$ with probability $\frac{1}{t+1}$.

Notice that for any $0 \leq i \leq \lfloor (r-\epsilon)(t+2) \rfloor - 2$ it holds that $\frac{1+i}{t+2} < r - \epsilon$. Thus, the probability that the relative reputation of player 2 is smaller than $(r-\epsilon)$ is

$$\frac{1}{t+1} \cdot (\lfloor (r-\epsilon)(t+2) \rfloor - 2 + 1) \geq \frac{1}{t+1} \cdot ((r-\epsilon)(t+2) - 2)$$

$$\geq (r-\epsilon) - \frac{2}{t+1}$$

This implies that with probability of at least $(r-\epsilon) - \frac{2}{t+1}$ after t rounds the current game is $G_{k-t}((t+2)(1-p), p \cdot (t+2))$ for $p < r - \epsilon$. Notice that by symmetry the same holds for player 1. By choosing t that obeys the requirements of Theorem 4.4 we get that the lower player in this game does not compete. Therefore, the probability that one of the players stops competing after t rounds is at least $2(r-\epsilon) - \frac{4}{t+1}$. To bound the expected social welfare we make the conservative assumption that with probability $1 - (2(r-\epsilon) - \frac{4}{t+1})$ the players compete till the end of the game and get that:

$$u(s_k^t(1,1)) \geq k + 2q\left((r-\epsilon) - \frac{2}{t+1}\right)(k-t)$$

$$\geq k + 2q(r-\epsilon)k - 2q(r-\epsilon)t - \frac{4kq}{t}$$

Next, we show that for $k \geq e^{\frac{8(r-\epsilon)}{\epsilon^3}} + e^{\frac{4\ln(1/12)}{\ln(1-r)}}$ and $t = \frac{4\ln(k) - \ln(\epsilon)}{\epsilon^2}$ the conditions for both Theorem 4.4 and this Lemma hold. Indeed, if Theorem 4.4 holds, we have that for every $0 < p < r - \epsilon$ the players in the game $G_{k-t}((t+2)(1-p), p \cdot (t+2))$ for $p < r - \epsilon$ do not compete, as required. Recall that Theorem 4.4 requires $t + 2$ to be at least $\max\{\frac{4\ln(1/12)}{\ln(1-r)}, \frac{3\ln(k) - \ln(q-p)}{(r-p)^2}\}$. Observe that $\frac{4\ln(k) - \ln(\epsilon)}{\epsilon^2} \geq \frac{3\ln(k) - \ln(q-p)}{(r-p)^2}$ as by definition $q-p \geq r-p > \epsilon$; and that since $\ln(k) > \frac{4\ln(1/12)}{\ln(1-r)}$ we also have that $t \geq \frac{4\ln(1/12)}{\ln(1-r)}$.

Next, we show that $u(s_k^t(1,1)) \geq k \cdot \left(1 + 2q(r - 3\epsilon - \epsilon^2)\right)$. We begin by plugging in $t = \frac{4\ln(k) - \ln(\epsilon)}{\epsilon^2}$: $u(s_k^t(1,1)) \geq$

$$k + 2kq(r-\epsilon) - 2q(r-\epsilon) \cdot \frac{4\ln(k) - \ln(\epsilon)}{\epsilon^2} - \frac{4kq}{\frac{4\ln(k) - \ln(\epsilon)}{\epsilon^2}}$$

$$> k + 2kq(r-\epsilon) - 2q(r-\epsilon) \cdot \frac{4\ln(k) - \ln(\epsilon)}{\epsilon^2} - \frac{kq\epsilon^2}{\ln(k)}$$

$$\geq k + 2kq(r - \epsilon - \epsilon^2) - 2q(r-\epsilon) \cdot \frac{4\ln(k)}{\epsilon^2} + 2q(r-\epsilon)\frac{\ln(\epsilon)}{\epsilon^2}$$

To prove the Lemma we show that for $k \geq e^{\frac{8(r-\epsilon)}{\epsilon^3}} + e^{\frac{4\ln(1/12)}{\ln(1-r)}}$ the following two inequalities hold:

1. $(r-\epsilon) \cdot \frac{8\ln(k)}{k\epsilon^2} < \epsilon$: For this we do a variable substitution and denote $\ln(k) = z$, so that $k = e^z$. Now we find z such that $4(r-\epsilon)z < \epsilon^3 \cdot e^z$. By Taylor expansion we have that $e^z > \frac{z^2}{2}$. Thus, we can instead compute when $4(r-\epsilon)z < \epsilon^3 \cdot \frac{z^2}{2}$ and get that the inequality holds for $z > \frac{8(r-\epsilon)}{\epsilon^3}$. This implies that the inequality holds for $k > e^{\frac{8(r-\epsilon)}{\epsilon^3}}$.

2. $|(r-\epsilon)\frac{\ln(\epsilon)}{k\epsilon^2}| < \epsilon$: This condition also holds for $k > e^{\frac{8(r-\epsilon)}{\epsilon^3}}$ since if $k > e^{\frac{8(r-\epsilon)}{\epsilon^3}}$ by Taylor expansion we have that $k > ((\frac{8(r-\epsilon)}{\epsilon^3})^2)/2 = \frac{16(r-\epsilon)^2}{\epsilon^6} > \frac{r-\epsilon}{\epsilon^3} \cdot |\ln(\epsilon)|$ and therefore $|(r-\epsilon)\frac{\ln(\epsilon)}{k\epsilon^2}| < \epsilon$.

Thus, for $k \geq e^{\frac{8(r-\epsilon)}{\epsilon^3}} + e^{\frac{4\ln(1/12)}{\ln(1-r)}}$ and $t = \frac{4\ln(k) - \ln(\epsilon)}{\epsilon^2}$ we have that $u(s_k^t(1,1)) \geq k \cdot \left(1 + 2q(r - 3\epsilon - \epsilon^2)\right)$ as required. □

4.4 Wrapping up the Proof

THEOREM 4.6. *For $\epsilon > 0$ and $k \geq e^{\frac{8(r-\epsilon)}{\epsilon^3}} + e^{\frac{4\ln(1/12)}{\ln(1-r)}}$, the performance ratio of the game $G_k(1,1)$ is at least $\frac{1+2q(r-3\epsilon-\epsilon^2)}{1+q}$.*

PROOF. By Lemma 4.1 we have that for any t, $u(s_k(1,1)) \geq u(s_k^t(1,1))$. By Lemma 4.5 we have that there exists a t such that $u(s_k^t(1,1)) \geq k\left(1 + 2q(r - 3\epsilon - \epsilon^2)\right)$. By combining the two we get that $u(s_k(1,1)) \geq k\left(1 + 2q(r - 3\epsilon - \epsilon^2)\right)$. This means that the performance ratio of the game $G_k(1,1)$ is at least $\frac{k\left(1+2q(r-3\epsilon-\epsilon^2)\right)}{k(1+q)} = \frac{1+2q(r-3\epsilon-\epsilon^2)}{1+q}$. □

COROLLARY 4.7. *As k goes to infinity, the performance ratio of the game $G_k(1,1,)$ goes to $\frac{1+2rq}{1+q}$.*

5. CONCLUSIONS

When firms compete for job applicants over many hiring cycles, there is a basic strategic tension inherent in the process: trying to recruit highly sought-after job candidates can build up a firm's reputation, but it comes with the risk that firm will fail to hire anyone at all. In this paper, we have shown how this tension can arise in a simple dynamic model of job-market matching. Although our model is highly stylized, it contains a number of interesting effects that we analyze, including the way in which competition can lead to inefficiency through underemployment (quantified in our analysis of the performance ratio at equilibrium) and the possibility of different modes of behavior, in which a weaker firm may end up competing forever, or it may give up at some point and accept its second-place status.

The model and analysis also suggest a number of directions for further investigation. One direction is to vary the *competition function* that determines the outcome of a competition between the two firms when they make offers to the same candidate. As noted above, this can be viewed as varying the way in which candidates make decisions between firms based on their reputations. In the full version of the paper, we explore this issue by considering an alternate rule for competition in which the lower-reputation player wins with a fixed probability $p < \frac{1}{2}$ (independent of the difference in reputation) and the higher-reputation player wins with probability $1 - p$.

This fixed-probability competition function is simpler in structure than the Tullock function, and it is illuminating in that it cleanly separates two different aspects of the strategic decision being made about future rounds. With the Tullock function, when the lower player competes, it has the potential for a short-term gain in its success probability even in the next round (since the ratio of reputations will change), and it also has the potential for a long-term gain by becoming the higher player. With the fixed-probability competition function, the short-term aspect is effectively eliminated, since as long as a player remains the lower party, it has the same probability of success; we are thus able to study strategic behavior about competing when the only upside is the long-range prospect of becoming the higher player. We show that the performance is generally much better with this fixed-probability rule than with the Tullock function, providing us with further insight into the specific way in which competition leads to inefficiency through a reduced performance ratio.

Other directions that lead quickly to interesting questions are to consider the case of more than two firms, and to consider models in which the candidates have different characteristics in different time periods. For both of these general directions, our initial investigations suggest that the techniques developed here will be useful for shedding light on the properties of more complex models that take these issues into account.

Acknowledgments

We thank Itai Ashlagi, Larry Blume, Shahar Dobzinski, Bobby Kleinberg, and Lionel Levine for very useful suggestions and references.

6. REFERENCES

[1] R. Albert and A.-L. Barabási. Statistical mechanics of complex networks. *Rev. Modern Physics*, 74(2002).

[2] A. Beggs and P. Klemperer. Multi-period competition with switching costs. *Econometrica* 60:3(1992), 651-666.

[3] J. P. Benoit and V. Krishna. Dynamic Duopoly: Prices and Quantities. *Review of Economic Studies*, 54(1987).

[4] D. Berry, B. Fristedt. Bernoulli one-armed bandits: arbitrary discount sequences. *Ann. Stat.*, 7(1979).

[5] A. Broder, A. Kirsch, R. Kumar, M. Mitzenmacher, E. Upfal, S. Vassilvitskii. The hiring problem and lake wobegon strategies. *SIAM J. Comp.*, 39(2009).

[6] J. Chen, U. Doraszelski, J. Harrington. Avoiding market dominance: product compatibility in markets with network effects. *RAND J. Econ.*, 40(2009).

[7] J. S. Coleman. Matching processes in the labor market. *Acta Sociologica* 34(1991).

[8] J. Dickerson, A. Procaccia, T. Sandholm. Dynamic matching via weighted myopia with application to kidney exchange. *Proc. 26th AAAI Conf.*, 2012.

[9] E. Drinea, A. Frieze, M. Mitzenmacher. Balls and bins models with feedback. *Proc. ACM-SIAM SODA*, 2002.

[10] W. Feller. *An Introduction to Probability Theory and Its Applications*, volume 1. Wiley, 1968.

[11] J. Gittins, D. Jones. A dynamic allocation index for the sequential design of experiments. In J. Gani, editor, *Progress in Statistics*, North-Holland, 1974.

[12] M. Granovetter. *Getting a Job: A Study of Contacts and Careers*. University of Chicago Press, 1974.

[13] G. Haeringer and M. Wooders. Decentralized job matching. *Intl. J. Game Theory*, 40(2011).

[14] K. Hazma. The smallest uniform upper bound on the distance between the mean and median of the binomial and Poisson distributions. *Stat. Prob. Let.*, 23(1995).

[15] N. Immorlica, A. Kalai, B. Lucier, A. Moitra, A. Postlewaite, M. Tennenholtz. Dueling algorithms. *ACM STOC*, 2011.

[16] N. Immorlica, R. Kleinberg, M. Mahdian. Secretary problems with competing employers. *WINE*, 2006.

[17] B. Jun and X. Vives. Strategic incentives in dynamic duopoly. *Journal of Economic Theory.* 116(2004).

[18] M. Mitzenmacher. A brief history of generative models for power law and lognormal distributions. *Internet Math.*, 2004.

[19] D. Mortensen and C. Pissarides. New developments in models of search in the labor market. In *Handbook of Labor Economics*, 1999.

[20] S. Mullainathan, J. Schwartzstein, A. Shleifer. Coarse thinking and persuasion. *Q. J. Econ.*, 123(2008).

[21] A. J. Padilla. Revisiting Dynamic Duopoly with Consumer Switching Costs. *Journal of Economic Theory.* 67(1995), Pages 520âĂŞ530.

[22] R. Pemantle. A survey of random processes with reinforcement. *Probability Surveys*, 4:1–79, 2007.

[23] Lauren A. Rivera. Hiring as Cultural Matching: The Case of Elite Professional Service Firms. *American Sociological Review* 77(6) 999âĂŞ1022.

[24] R. Rogerson, R. Shimer, R. Wright. Search-theoretic models of the labor market. *J. Econ. Lit.*, 43(2005).

[25] A. Roth, M. Sotomayor. *Two-sided matching: A study in game-theoretic modeling and analysis*. Cambridge University Press, 1990.

[26] R. Shimer and L. Smith. Assortative matching and search. *Econometrica*, 68(2):343–369, Mar. 2000.

[27] S. Skaperdas. Contest success functions. *Econ. Th.*, 7(1996).

[28] G. Tullock. Efficient rent seeking. In *Towards a theory of the rent-seeking society*, 1980.

[29] D. Turban and D. Cable. Firm reputation and applicant pool characteristics. *J. Organiz. Behav.* 24, 733âĂŞ751 (2003).

[30] J. Zou, S. Gujar, and D. Parkes. Tolerable manipulability in dynamic assignment without money. *Proc. 24th AAAI*, 2010.

Voting with Coarse Beliefs

[Extended Abstract][*]

Samantha Leung[†]
Cornell University
Ithaca, NY, USA
samlyy@cs.cornell.edu

Edward Lui
Cornell University
Ithaca, NY, USA
luied@cs.cornell.edu

Rafael Pass[‡]
Cornell University
Ithaca, NY, USA
rafael@cs.cornell.edu

ABSTRACT

The classic Gibbard-Satterthwaite theorem [1, 5] says that every strategy-proof voting rule with at least three possible candidates must be dictatorial—that is, there exists a fixed voter whose top choice is always chosen as the winner. Similar impossibility results hold even if we consider a weaker notion of strategy-proofness where voters believe that the other voters' preferences are i.i.d. (independent and identically distributed). In particular, McLennan [2] shows that if an anonymous voting rule (with at least 3 candidates) is strategy-proof w.r.t. *all* i.i.d. beliefs and is also Pareto efficient, then the voting rule must be a random dictatorship—that is, a uniformly random voter's top choice is chosen as the winner. Our first theorem strengthens McLennan's result by showing that relaxing Pareto efficiency to ϵ-Pareto efficiency (where Pareto efficiency can be violated with probability ϵ) does not help, even for rather large values of ϵ, and even for a significantly weaker notion of ϵ-Pareto efficiency. Thus, even for an extremely weak notion of what it means to be a "reasonable" voting rule, strategy-proofness w.r.t. all i.i.d. beliefs cannot be achieved.

In this paper, we take a bounded-rationality approach to this problem and consider a setting where voters have "coarse" beliefs (a notion that has gained popularity in the behavioral economics literature; e.g., see [3, 4]). A belief is said to be α-*coarse* if the probabilities in the belief are restricted to lie on a uniform discretization of $[0, 1]$ with "mesh size" at least α. We consider strategy-proofness w.r.t. coarse i.i.d. beliefs, and we focus on "large-scale" voting where the number of voters n is sufficiently large but is still polynomially-related to $1/\alpha$, where α is the coarseness parameter. A voting rule is said to be *large-scale strategy-proof w.r.t. coarse i.i.d. beliefs* if there exists a polynomial $p(\cdot)$ such that for every coarseness parameter $\alpha > 0$, and every $n \geq p(1/\alpha)$, no voter having an α-coarse i.i.d. belief can improve her expected utility by lying about her preferences.

We construct good voting rules that are large-scale strategy-proof w.r.t. coarse i.i.d. beliefs, thus circumventing the above impossibility results. In particular, we construct anonymous ϵ-Pareto efficient voting rules that are large-scale strategy-proof w.r.t. coarse i.i.d. beliefs, where ϵ is exponentially small in the number of voters. One of our voting rules is a variant of the well-known *instant-runoff* voting rule, which is used in many elections throughout the world.

Categories and Subject Descriptors

J.4 [**Computer Applications**]: Social and Behavioral Sciences—*Economics*

General Terms

Economics, Theory

Keywords

Voting; Gibbard-Satterthwaite

[*]A full version of this paper is available at http://arxiv.org/abs/1405.5827

[†]Leung was supported in part by NSF grants IIS-0911036 and CCF-1214844, AFOSR grant FA9550-08-1-0438, ARO grant W911NF-14-1-0017, and by the DoD Multidisciplinary University Research Initiative (MURI) program administered by AFOSR under grant FA9550-12-1-0040.

[‡]Pass is supported in part by an Alfred P. Sloan Fellowship, Microsoft New Faculty Fellowship, NSF CAREER Award CCF-0746990, NSF Award CCF-1214844, NSF Award CNS-1217821, AFOSR YIP Award FA9550-10-1-0093, and DARPA and AFRL under contract FA8750-11-2-0211.

ITCS'15, January 11–13, 2015, Rehovot, Israel.
ACM 978-1-4503-3333-7/15/01.
http://dx.doi.org/10.1145/2688073.2688089.

1. REFERENCES

[1] A. Gibbard. Manipulation of voting schemes: A general result. *Econometrica*, 41(4):pp. 587–601, 1973.

[2] A. McLennan. Manipulation in elections with uncertain preferences. *Journal of Mathematical Economics*, 47(3):370–375, 2011.

[3] S. Mullainathan. Thinking through categories. *NBER working paper*, 2002.

[4] S. Mullainathan, J. Schwartzstein, and A. Shleifer. Coarse thinking and persuasion. *The Quarterly Journal of Economics*, 123(2):577–619, 2008.

[5] M. A. Satterthwaite. Strategy-proofness and arrow's conditions: Existence and correspondence theorems for voting procedures and social welfare functions. *Journal of Economic Theory*, 10(2):187–217, April 1975.

Complex Contagions in Kleinberg's Small World Model

Roozbeh Ebrahimi*
Stony Brook University
Stony Brook, NY 11794
rebrahimi@cs.stonybrook.edu

Jie Gao
Stony Brook University
Stony Brook, NY 11794
jgao@cs.stonybrook.edu

Golnaz Ghasemiesfeh
Stony Brook University
Stony Brook, NY 11794
gghasemiesfe@cs.stonybrook.edu

Grant Schoenebeck†
University of Michigan
Ann Arbor, MI 48109
schoeneb@umich.edu

ABSTRACT

Complex contagions describe diffusion of behaviors in a social network in settings where spreading requires influence by two or more neighbors. In a k-complex contagion, a cluster of nodes are initially infected, and additional nodes become infected in the next round if they have at least k already infected neighbors. It has been argued that complex contagions better model behavioral changes such as adoption of new beliefs, fashion trends or expensive technology innovations. This has motivated rigorous understanding of spreading of complex contagions in social networks. Despite simple contagions ($k = 1$) that spread fast in all small world graphs, how complex contagions spread is much less understood. Previous work [11] analyzes complex contagions in Kleinberg's small world model [14] where edges are randomly added according to a spatial distribution (with exponent γ) on top of a two dimensional grid structure. It has been shown in [11] that the speed of complex contagions differs exponentially when $\gamma = 0$ compared to when $\gamma = 2$.

In this paper, we fully characterize the entire parameter space of γ except at one point, and provide upper and lower bounds for the speed of k-complex contagions. We study two subtly different variants of Kleinberg's small world model and show that, with respect to complex contagions, they behave differently. For each model and each $k \geq 2$, we show that there is an intermediate range of values, such that when γ takes any of these values, a k-complex contagion spreads quickly on the corresponding graph, in a polylogarithmic number of rounds. However, if γ is outside this range, then a k-complex contagion requires a polynomial number of rounds to spread to the entire network.

*The first three authors wish to acknowledge support from NSF through DMS-1221339, DMS-1418255, CNS-1217823, CCF-1114809, CCF-1217708, IIS-1247726, IIS-1251137, CNS-1408695, CCF-1439084, and from AFOSR through FA9550-14-1-0193.

†The last author wishes to acknowledge support from Google through a Google faculty award, and Facebook through a Facebook faculty award.

Categories and Subject Descriptors

J.4 [**Social and Behavioral Sciences**]: Sociology—*social networks, social contagion*; G.2.2 [**Discrete Mathematics**]: Graph Theory—*random network models*

Keywords

Social Networks; Complex Contagion; Kleinberg's Small World Model

1. INTRODUCTION

Social acts are influenced by the behavior of others while at same time influencing them. New social behaviors may emerge and spread in a social network like a contagion. Some of these contagions are beneficial (e.g., adopting healthy lifestyle) or profitable (e.g., viral marketing), while some others are destructive and undesirable (such as teenager smoking, alcohol abuse, or vandalism). To effectively promote desirable contagions and discourage undesirable ones, the first step is to understand how these contagions spread in networks and what are the important parameters that lead to fast spreading.

Social contagions can be categorized by the way they spread in networks. Our focus in this paper is on contagions that are *complex*, contagions that require social reaffirmation from multiple neighbors, as opposed to *simple* ones, which can spread through a single contact. Simple contagions are adequate models for many spreading phenomena such as rumors, disease, etc. But, when a spreading contagion is concerned with individual's actions and behavioral changes, it has been argued in sociology literature that complex contagions represent most of the realistic settings. This model of contagion makes an important distinction between the *acquisition* of information and the decision to *act* on the information. While it takes only a single tie for people to hear about a new belief, technology, fad or fashion, "it is when they see people they know getting involved, that they become most susceptible to recruitment", as Centola and Macy [7] explain.

Many examples of complex contagions have been reported in social studies, including buying pricey technological innovations, changes in social behaviors, the decision to migrate, etc. [9, 6]. Studies of large scale data sets from online social networks, like Facebook and Twitter, have confirmed the existence of the complex contagion phenomenon as well [21, 20].

The speed of simple contagions is inherently linked to the diameter of the network. As such, almost all generative social network models support fast (polylogarithmic) spreading of simple contagions, because they have a small diameter (reflecting the small world property of real world social networks) [14, 18]. But much less is known about the network properties that enable fast spreading of complex contagions. Complex contagions do not adhere to sub-modularity and sub-additivity upon which many analyses depend. Also, the super-additive character of complex contagions means that they are integrally related to community structure, as complex contagions intuitively spread better in dense regions of a network– an observation concurred by real world experiments [6].

There have been only a few results on formal analysis of the spreading characteristics of complex contagions. All of them use the model of a k-complex contagion, in which time is divided into rounds and a node becomes infected (e.g., adopting the new behavior) in the next round if at least k of its neighbors are infected in the current round. Immediate questions to answer include whether a complex contagion spreads to the entire graph, and if so, how many rounds it will take. Despite the simplicity of this model, it sufficiently captures the qualitative difference of single versus cumulative exposure in social influences and already embraces a fair amount of technical challenges. This is also the model we adopt in this paper.

Prior Work. Centola and Macy [7] studied complex contagions in the Watts-Strogatz model [22]. The Watts-Strogatz model has nodes on a ring where nodes nearby on the ring are connected by edges and a small fraction of the edges are uniformly randomly 're-wired'. The network diameter before random rewiring is large (linear in the number of nodes) but with even a small number of randomly rewired edges the diameter quickly shrinks. The strong community structure helps a complex contagion to spread but unfortunately the spreading is slow and cannot exploit the random edges that help to spread simple contagions. On the contrary, the random rewiring starts to erode the capability to support complex contagions as the community structure starts to break apart.

Ghasemiesfeh et. at [11] made this observation of the importance of the distribution of these random edges more rigorous, under the more general small world model proposed by Kleinberg [14]. In the 2D version of this model, nodes stay on an underlying 2D grid. Nodes that are within a constant Manhattan distance of each other are connected, these edges are denoted as *strong ties*, which model community structures. In addition, each node on the grid issues a constant number of random edges following the distribution that p chooses to connect to q with probability proportional to $1/|pq|^{\gamma}$, where $|pq|$ is the Manhattan distance between p, q, and γ is a nonnegative parameter. These randomly chosen edges are labeled as *weak ties* and help create the small world property and support fast spreading of simple contagions. When the initial seeds are chosen to be a cluster of nearby nodes in the underlying metric, it is proved in [11], that for $\gamma = 2$, a 2-complex contagion spreads in at most $O(\log^{3.5} n)$ rounds in a network of n nodes, but for $\gamma = 0$ the contagion needs $\Omega(\text{poly}(n))$ time to cover the entire network (this setting corresponds to a 2-dimensional Newman-Watts model [18]).

1.1 Our Results

We substantially improve upon the prior work [11] by characterizing k-complex contagions in the Kleinberg's small world model for *all* values of k and an almost complete range of the clustering coefficient γ, the exponent of the spatial distribution upon which random edges are created.

In addition, we also show that a subtle difference in the multiplicity of edges in Kleinberg's small world model implies large differences in which parameter regimes quickly spreads k-complex contagions. In the model analyzed by [11], it was implicitly assumed that the k random edges placed by the same node are sampled *without replacement*, thus disallowing multi-edges. In this

case, to spread the contagion, we need at least k initially infected nodes. In a slight variation, if the k edges are chosen independently of each other, i.e., *with replacement*, the generated graph may have multi-edges. Thus, a single node by itself may start a complex contagion. Both variations have real world interpretations. In the former variation, we need to have different infected neighbors to generate enough influence. In the latter, we count the number of repeated exposures to the new idea/belief, even if the exposure is from the same friend/entity. Analytically, however, this minor difference generates different behaviors. We show below that the parameter range for γ to allow fast spreading of a complex contagion in each of these variations differs.

Let $\alpha_k = \frac{2(k^2+k+2)}{k(k+1)}$ and $\beta_k = \frac{2(k+1)}{k}$. We show that k-complex contagions in the Kleinberg's small world model without multi-edges spread in $O(\text{polylog}(n))$ rounds if $\gamma \in [2, \alpha_k)$, and in $\Omega(\text{poly}(n))$ rounds otherwise (except for $\gamma = \alpha_k$ for which we do not know). We refer to polylogarithmic and polynomial speeds as *fast* and *slow* respectively. For k-complex contagions in the model allowing multi-edges, the fast spreading parameter range for γ changes to $[2, \beta_k)$ instead, outside of which the contagion spreads slowly, again, except for $\gamma = \beta_k$ for which we do not know. This is summarized in Figure 1. We note that the results for $\gamma = 2$ and $\gamma = 0$ were already known by previous work [11].

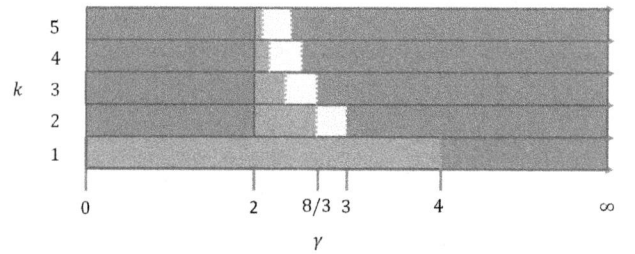

Figure 1: Speed for a k-complex contagion for Kleinberg's small world model with parameter γ. Green indicates polylogarithmic spreading in both models; red indicates that the contagions require polynomial number of rounds to spread in both models; and yellow indicates polylogarithmic spreading in the model with multi-edges and polynomial spreading in the model without multi-edges.

We note that as γ approaches 2 from the right, it successfully spreads k-complex contagions for a greater range of k, however, if $\gamma > 2$, this range is always bounded. Additionally, Figure 1 illustrates the results of $k = 1$ (the diameter), which were proven in a series of work [14, 15, 19]. Our results naturally reprove these results for $\gamma > 2$, however, we note that in contrast to the simple contagions, complex contagions do not spread fast for any parameter in the range $[0, 2)$.

We give a conceptual view of our results next. Note that complex contagions require a *wide bridge* to jump from the infected nodes to the uninfected ones. Such wide bridges are already supplied by the strong ties, allowing the complex contagion to spread along the underlying metric of the model. But such spreading is slow. To boost the speed, the weak ties must also form wide bridges. The ability to form such wide bridges is significantly affected by the changes in the parameter γ. In particular, when γ is in the sweet spot interval, the weak ties form wide bridges in a variety of different length scales. This triggers recursive cascading and allows the contagion to grow in size by an exponential rate and thus, the speed of complex contagions becomes fast (polylogarithmic). This intuition bears some similarity to the analyses of Kleinberg's myopic routing algorithm [14] and the diameter of Kleinberg's model [15, 19]. In those analyses, if γ is in a range where random edges are prevalent in all distance ranges, myopic routing is fast and the diameter is small (both polylogarithmic).

Our lower bound proofs, on the other hand, require a careful dissection of the spreading pattern of complex contagions in the graph. When γ is smaller than the sweet spot interval, the weak ties do not form wide bridges (Theorem 7). And when γ is larger than the sweet spot interval, the wide bridges formed by the weak ties are too short, and unable to reach far away regions of the network (Theorems 8 and 9). In both cases, it takes a polynomial number of rounds for the contagion to spread to the entire graph.

The results in this paper substantially enrich previous observations on how community structures are relevant to the spreading of complex contagions [6]. While many dense community structures could spread complex contagions, certain edge distributions could make the spreading exponentially faster than others. The analysis in this paper shows the delicacy and richness of the complex contagion phenomenon.

Organization of This Paper. In Section 2, we present the models and definitions. Section 3 discusses the polylogarithmic upper bounds. Section 4 shows polynomial lower bounds. Finally, in Section 5, we outline some of the related works to our paper. Some of the computational proofs are presented in the appendices.

2. PRELIMINARIES

We formally define a k-complex contagion process in a graph. We assume k is a small constant.

DEFINITION 1. *A **k-complex contagion** $CC(G, k, \mathcal{I})$ is a contagion that initially infects vertices of $\mathcal{I}$ and spreads over graph G. The contagion proceeds in rounds. At each round, each vertex with at least k infected neighbors becomes infected. The vertices of $\mathcal{I}$ are called the **initial seeds**.*

In the Kleinberg's small world model [14], n nodes are embedded on a $\sqrt{n} \times \sqrt{n}$ grid[1]. We connect each node u to nodes within grid Manhattan distance $\lceil \sqrt{m} \rceil$, where m is a constant. These edges are referred to as **strong ties**. In addition, each node generates m random outgoing edges, termed **weak ties**. The probability that node p connects to node q via a random edge is equal to $\lambda / |pq|^{\gamma}$, in which $|pq|$ is the Manhattan distance of p, q and λ is a normalization factor.

- When $\gamma > 2$, $\lambda = \Theta(\gamma - 2) = \Theta(1)$. That is, the probability that node p chooses node q as a neighbor through a weak tie is $\lambda / |pq|^{\gamma} = \Theta(1 / |pq|^{\gamma})$.

- When $0 \leq \gamma < 2$, $\lambda = \Theta(n^{\gamma/2-1})$. The probability that node p chooses node q as a neighbor through a weak tie is $\lambda / |pq|^{\gamma} = \Theta(n^{\gamma/2-1} / |pq|^{\gamma})$.

We consider the directed graph model where the weak ties issued by a node u has u as the tail and strong ties are bidirectional. A k-complex contagion spreads in the inverse direction of an edge: a node becomes infected if it follows at least k infected neighbors.

We consider two variations of the Kleinberg's small world model. First, the $K^W_{m,\gamma}(n)$ model, where the weak ties are chosen without replacement, that is, we do not permit multiple edges. Second,

---

[1] In order to eliminate the boundary effect, we wrap up the grid into a torus – i.e., the top boundary is identified with the bottom boundary and the left boundary is identified with the right boundary.

the $K^I_{m,\gamma}(n)$ model, where the weak ties are distributed *independently* (with replacements). We will see that these two models behave very differently with respect to complex contagions. We will use the notation $K^*_{m,\gamma}(n)$ to refer to both $K^W_{m,\gamma}(n)$ and $K^I_{m,\gamma}(n)$ simultaneously.

We say that two nodes u, v are a **seed pair** if they are adjacent on the grid structure of $K^*_{m,\gamma}(n)$. We will say that k nodes $u_1, \cdots, u_k$ are a **k-seed cluster** if they form a connected subgraph via *only* the grid structure.

3. UPPER BOUNDS

In this section, we prove two upper bound theorems. Let $\alpha_k = \frac{2(k^2+k+2)}{k(k+1)}$ and $\beta_k = \frac{2(k+1)}{k}$. We consider k-complex contagions on graphs $K^*_{m,\gamma}(n)$, where $2 \leq k \leq m = O(1)$. We first prove that a k-complex contagion spreads in polylogarithmic number of rounds on $K^W_{m,\gamma}(n)$ when $\gamma \in (2, \alpha_k)$. Using a similar technique, we prove a polylogarithmic upper bound on the speed of k-complex contagions in $K^I_{m,\gamma}(n)$ when $\gamma \in (2, \beta_k)$. The case of $\gamma = 2$ is handled for both of the models together (Theorem 6). We note that the subtle difference in how the networks are defined, makes a rather large difference in how complex contagions spread.

Both of the upper bound proofs are obtained by establishing the following recurrence relation:

$$T(n) = k + 2T(n^{1-\delta}),$$

where $T(n)$ is the time it takes to infect a square of n nodes in $K^*_{m,\gamma}(n)$. The idea behind the recursion is to start with a square, S, of n nodes. Divide S into n^{δ} many smaller squares for $0 < \delta < 1$. Fix a particular small square A where the initial seeds are located. We then show that when A is fully infected, there will be a new seed in each of the other $n^{\delta} - 1$ small squares and thus they will be infected in parallel. The main difference for allowing versus disallowing multi-edges is that when multi-edges are allowed it is often enough to infect a single node u to obtain a new seed. This means that new seeds appear more often compared to the case where multi-edges are not allowed. This is because, with constant probability, $k-1$ of u's local neighbors will have k redundant edges to this vertex, thus allowing the k-complex contagion to spread thereafter.

THEOREM 1. *Let $2 \leq k \leq m = O(1)$. Consider a Kleinberg's small world model $K^W_{m,\gamma}(n)$ of n vertices where $2 < \gamma < \alpha_k$. Let $0 < \delta < 1 - \frac{\gamma}{\alpha_k}$, $c \geq \frac{1-\delta}{((\binom{k+1}{2}+1)(1-\delta)+\binom{k+1}{2}\gamma/2)}$, $d > 2$, and $\alpha = \frac{c}{2} + \log_{\frac{1}{1-\delta}} 2$ be constants. If we start a k-complex contagion from a k-seed cluster $\mathcal{I}$, it takes at most $O(\log^{\alpha} n)$ rounds for the contagion to spread to the whole network with probability at least $1 - n^{-(d-2)}$.*

We first provide a definition.

DEFINITION 2. *Fix constants δ, c, k and $d > 2$. Let λ be the normalization factor of $K^*_{m,\gamma}(n)$ and let $r = (\frac{6d}{\lambda})^c$. We say that a $K^*_{m,\gamma}(n)$ model is (δ, c, d, k)-**recursively spreading** if whenever*

1. *S is an ℓ-sized square ($\sqrt{\ell} \times \sqrt{\ell}$) of vertices in $K^*_{m,\gamma}(n)$ where $\ell > (r \log^c n)^{(\frac{1}{1-\delta})}$;*

2. *A and B are any two disjoint $\ell^{1-\delta}$-sized subsquares of S; and*

3. *A is fully infected, then with probability at least $1 - \frac{\ell^{2(1-\delta)}}{n^d}$, there is a new k-seed cluster in B that is infected in $\leq k$ rounds.*

The probability is over the coin flips of the $K_{m,\gamma}^*(n)$ model.

We next state two lemmas. Theorem 1 follows directly from these lemmas.

LEMMA 2. *Fix constants $\delta, c, k,$ and $d > 2$. If Kleinberg's small world model $K_{m,\gamma}^*(n)$ is (δ, c, d, k)-recursively spreading. Then if we start a k-complex contagion from a k-seed cluster, it takes at most $O\left(\log^\alpha n\right)$ rounds for the contagion to spread to the whole network with probability at least $1 - n^{-(d-2)}$, where $\alpha = \frac{c}{2} + \log_{\frac{1}{1-\delta}} 2$, and the probability is over the coin flips of the $K_{m,\gamma}^*(n)$ model.*

LEMMA 3. *Fix constants $2 < \gamma < \alpha_k$, $0 < \delta < 1 - \alpha_k\gamma$, $c \geq \frac{1-\delta}{\left(\binom{k+1}{2}+1\right)(1-\delta)+\binom{k+1}{2}\gamma/2}$, and $d > 2$. Then the $K_{m,\gamma}^W(n)$ model is (δ, c, d, k)-recursively spreading.*

PROOF OF LEMMA 2. Let $T(\ell)$ be the time it takes to infect all vertices on an $\sqrt{\ell} \times \sqrt{\ell}$ square in a $K_{m,\gamma}^*(n)$ graph starting from a k-seed cluster with probability at least $1 - \ell^2/n^d$. Let $r = \left(\frac{6d}{\lambda^3}\right)^c$ where λ is the normalization factor (a constant) of the $K_{m,\gamma}^*(n)$ model. We establish the following recurrence relation for $T(\ell)$:

$$T(\ell) \leq \begin{cases} k + 2T(\ell^{1-\delta}) & \text{if } \ell > (r\log^c n)^{\left(\frac{1}{1-\delta}\right)} \\ 2\sqrt{\ell} & \text{o.w.} \end{cases} \quad (1)$$

The second case of the recurrence follows immediately because a complex contagion using only strong ties can cover a cell of size $\sqrt{\ell} \times \sqrt{\ell}$ in $2\sqrt{\ell}$ rounds. Next, we explain the first case in the recurrence.

Start with a square S of $\ell > (r\log^c n)^{\left(\frac{1}{1-\delta}\right)}$ nodes. Divide S into ℓ^δ many smaller squares, each with size $\ell^{1-\delta}$. Fix a particular small square A where the initial seeds are located. By the definition of $T(\ell^{1-\delta})$, with probability at least $1 - \ell^{2(1-\delta)}/n^d$, subsquare A will be infected in time $T(\ell^{1-\delta})$. By assumption of (δ, c, d, k)-recursively spreading, after k additional time steps, with probability at least $1 - (\ell^\delta-1)\ell^{2(1-\delta)}/n^d$ each of the other $(\ell^\delta-1)$ sub-squares will have a k-seed cluster (applying the union bound). And so with probability at least $1 - (\ell^\delta - 1)\ell^{2(1-\delta)}/n^d$ they will all be infected in time $T(\ell^{1-\delta})$. At this point every node of S is infected. By a union bound, the probability of failure is at most

$$\ell^\delta\left(2\frac{\ell^{2(1-\delta)}}{n^d}\right) = 2\frac{\ell^{2-\delta}}{n^d} < \frac{\ell^2}{n^d}$$

The last inequality follows because $2 \leq \ell^\delta$. Observe that $\ell \leq n$, so the probability of failure at the root is at most $n^{-(d-2)}$.

We use the recurrence to upper bound $T(\ell)$. The height h of the recurrence tree is such that

$$(r\log^c(n))^{\left(\frac{1}{1-\delta}\right)^h} > n.$$

Rearranging, we can see that $h \geq \frac{\log\log n - \log c\log\log(r\log n)}{-\log(1-\delta)}$ and taking $h = \frac{\log\log n}{-\log(1-\delta)} = \log_{1/1-\delta}\log n \approx (1/\delta)\log\log n$ suffices. The cost of the recurrence is dominated by the sum of the running times of the leaf cases. The branching factor of the tree is 2 and thus the number of leaves is at most $2^h = 2^{\log_{1/1-\delta}\log n} = (\log n)^{\log_{1/1-\delta} 2}$. Therefore,

$$T(n) = O\left(\log^{c/2} n\right) \cdot O\left((\log n)^{\log\frac{1}{1-\delta} 2}\right)$$
$$= O\left((\log n)^{\frac{c}{2}+\log\frac{1}{1-\delta} 2}\right).$$

□

We present the proof of Lemma 3 for $k = 2$ here, because the presentation is easier and gives more insight into the nature of the lemma. The essence of the argument for $k \geq 3$ is the same and its proof is presented in Appendix A.

PROOF OF LEMMA 3 WHEN $k = 2$. We take $2 < \gamma < 8/3$, $0 < \delta < \frac{8-3\gamma}{8}$, $\frac{2-2\delta}{8-3\gamma-8\delta} \leq c$, and $2 < d$. Then we argue that $K_{2,\gamma}^W(n)$ is $(\delta, c, d, 2)$-recursively spreading.

Fix $\ell > (r\log^c n)^{\left(\frac{1}{1-\delta}\right)}$, and ℓ-sized square S and two disjoint $\ell^{(1-\delta)}$-sized subsquares A and B, and partition B into $\ell^{(1-\delta)}/2$ disjoint pairs of (grid) neighbor nodes u, v. Assume that $a \in A$. Let $d(u, a)$ be the Manhattan distance of u and a.

i) $P_1(\ell) = \Pr\{u \text{ has a weak tie to } a \in A, \text{ via a particular edge}\}$

ii) $P_2(\ell) = \Pr\{u \text{ has a weak tie to } A, \text{ via a particular edge}\} \geq |A| \times P_1(\ell)$

iii) $P_3(\ell) = \Pr\{u \text{ is connected to } A, \text{ via 2 distinct weak ties}\}$

iv) $P_4(\ell) = \Pr\{u, v \text{ form a } new \ seed \text{ in } B\}$

v) $P_5(\ell) = \Pr\{\text{a new seed forms in } B\}$

$$P_1(\ell) \geq \frac{\lambda}{(d(u,a))^\gamma} = \frac{\lambda}{\sqrt{\ell^\gamma}};$$
$$P_2(\ell) \geq |A| \times P_1(\ell) = \lambda\ell^{1-\delta-\gamma/2};$$
$$P_3(\ell) \geq |\{(a,b)|a,b \in A\}|$$
$$\times \Pr\{u \text{ has a weak tie to } a \text{ and a weak tie to } b\}$$
$$\geq \binom{|A|}{2}P_1(\ell)^2 \geq \frac{\lambda^2\ell^{2-2\delta-\gamma}}{3};$$
$$P_4(\ell) \geq P_2(\ell) \times P_3(\ell) = \frac{\lambda^3\ell^{3-3\delta-3\gamma/2}}{3};$$
$$P_5(\ell) \geq 1 - (1 - P_4(\ell))^{|B|/2} \geq 1 - e^{-P_4(\ell)|B|/2}$$
$$\geq 1 - e^{-\frac{\lambda^3}{6}\ell^{4-4\delta-3\gamma/2}}$$

We want $P_5(\ell)$ to be very close to 1 and that means that we want the power of $\ell > 0$, which gives us:

$$4 - 4\delta - 3\gamma/2 > 0 \Rightarrow \gamma < 8/3, \ \delta < \frac{8-3\gamma}{8}.$$

Also, note that P_5 is increasing in ℓ. Therefore, the smallest probability happens when then size of ℓ is the smallest; that is $\ell^{1-\delta} = r\log^c n$ and $\ell = (r\log^c n)^{1/(1-\delta)}$. We want $1 - P_5(\ell)$ to be polynomially small even when ℓ takes on its smallest value. This requires that the power of $\log n$ be ≥ 1:

$$4c - \frac{3c\gamma}{2-2\delta} \geq 1 \Rightarrow c \geq \frac{2-2\delta}{8-3\gamma-8\delta};$$

and by replacing $r = (6d/\lambda^3)^c$, we get that

$$P_5(\ell) \geq 1 - e^{-\frac{\lambda^3}{6}\left((r\log^c n)^{1/(1-\delta)}\right)^{4-4\delta-3\gamma/2}}$$
$$\geq 1 - e^{-d\log n} \geq 1 - n^{-d}.$$

Finally, notice that this bound is stronger than required in the statement of the Lemma. □

Now, we prove a polylogarithmic upper bound for the speed of a k-complex contagion on $K_{k,\gamma}^I(n)$ when $2 < \gamma < \beta_k$ where $\beta_k = \frac{2(k+1)}{k}$. We note that the subtle difference in how the networks are defined, makes a rather large difference in how complex contagions spread.

Consider the case of $k = 2$. The main difference with Theorem 1 is that new configurations of nodes/edges can act as *new seeds* in $K_{2,\gamma}^I(n)$ compared to $K_{2,\gamma}^W(n)$. In $K_{2,\gamma}^I(n)$, a new seed appears in the graph if two grid neighbor nodes u, v have a total of 3 randomly created edges (weak ties) to the infected parts of the network. One of them, say u becomes infected first using its two weak ties and v becomes infected using one weak tie and one grid edge. However, in $K_{2,\gamma}^I(n)$, if a node u' has by itself 2 randomly created edges (weak ties) to the infected part, and a grid neighbor of u', called v', has one randomly created edge to u' besides the grid edge to u', then u', v' can constitute a new seed together.

THEOREM 4. *Let $k \leq m = O(1)$. Consider a Kleinberg's small world model $K_{m,\gamma}^I(n)$ of n vertices where $2 < \gamma < \beta_k$. Let $0 < \delta < 1 - \frac{\gamma}{\beta_k}$, $c \geq \frac{1-\delta}{(k+1)(1-\delta)-k\gamma/2}$, $d > 2$, and $\alpha = \frac{c}{2} + \log_{\frac{1}{1-\delta}} 2$ be constants. If we start a k-complex contagion from a k-seed cluster $\mathcal{I}$, it takes at most $O(\log^\alpha n)$ rounds for the contagion to spread to the whole network with probability at least $1 - n^{-(d-2)}$.*

Proof of Theorem 4 follows immediately from Lemma 2 and Lemma 5 (proved in Appendix A). The difference is that the bounds on values of γ, δ, c, r in Lemma 5 vary from those in Lemma 3.

LEMMA 5. *Fix constants $2 < \gamma < \beta_k$, $0 < \delta < 1 - \frac{\gamma}{\beta_k}$, $d > 2$, and $c \geq \frac{1-\delta}{(k+1)(1-\delta)-k\gamma/2}$. Then the $K_{m,\gamma}^I(n)$ model is (δ, c, d, k)-recursively spreading.*

3.1 When $\gamma = 2$

When $\gamma = 2$, an upper bound of $O(\log^{3.5} n)$ was proven in [11] for a 2-complex contagion in the Kleinberg's small world model $K_{m,2}^W(n)$. This bound can be slightly improved since we observe that for a new seed pair to be generated, we only need a total of three edges to the infected nodes, rather than four edges assumed in [11]. Thus, the upper bound can be improved to be $O(\log^3 n)$.

In [11] the result has also been extended to k-complex contagions ($k > 2$) on $K_{m,2}^W(n)$ and an upper bound of $O(\log^{k^2/2+1.5})$ can be obtained (there was a small typo in [11]). Again, we can slightly improve this upper bound: in order to get a new k-seed cluster $(u_1, ..., u_k)$, we do not need all u_i's, $1 \leq i \leq k$, to have k edges to the infected nodes. Since $(u_1, ..., u_k)$ is a clique, it is sufficient for u_1 to have k random edges to the infected nodes, u_2 to have $k - 1$ random edges to the infected nodes, etc. Thus, the total number of random edges needed from $(u_1, ..., u_k)$ to the infected nodes would be equal to $k + (k-1) + ... + 1 = k(k+1)/2$. The idea of the proof works for obtaining an upper bound on the speed of a k-complex contagion in the other Kleinberg's small world model variation $K_{m,2}^I(n)$ as well. Thus, we get the following theorem:

THEOREM 6. *Let $k \leq m = O(1)$. Consider a Kleinberg's small world model of n vertices where $\gamma = 2$, $K_{m,2}^*(n)$, (e.g. $K_{m,2}^I(n)$ or $K_{m,2}^W(n)$). If we start a k-complex contagion from a k-seed cluster, it takes at most $O\left(\log^{k(k+1)/4+1.5} n\right)$ rounds for the contagion to spread to the whole network with probability $1 - O(1/n)$.*

3.2 When $\gamma = \alpha_k, \beta_k$

The only points of parameter γ that we are not able to classify are α_k in the $K_{m,\gamma}^W(n)$ model and β_k in the $K_{m,\gamma}^I(n)$ model. We note that in both Theorems 1 and 4, the exponent of the logarithm in the upperbound on the speed of contagion, grows towards infinity. We conjecture that this is necessary and that the cascade at the critical points of α_k and β_k is not polylogarithmic, though we cannot prove this. This is in contrast to $\gamma = 2$ where a transition also occurs.

4. LOWER BOUNDS

In this section, we first describe our three lower bound theorems and the general idea behind each of them. The proof of the first theorem appears in Appendix B and the other two proofs are presented in this section.

What enabled us to prove the polylogarithmic upper bounds in Section 3, was the abundance of weak ties in all the distance ranges: from short weak ties of constant length to long weak ties of length $\Omega(\sqrt{n})$. Such an abundance ceases to exist when γ is outside of $[2, \alpha_k)$ for $K_{m,\gamma}^W(n)$, and outside of $[2, \beta_k)$ for $K_{m,\gamma}^I(n)$. When $\gamma \in [0, 2)$ weak ties become too random and in Appendix B, we show that too much randomness causes the complex contagion to be considerably slower. The intuition is that there is lack of coherence to enable complex contagion to generate *new seeds* until the contagion has grown to a polynomially large portion of the graph. The following theorem works for both graph models and for all possible values of k.

THEOREM 7. *Fix $k, m = O(1)$, $0 < \varepsilon$, let $\mathrm{CC}(K_{m,\gamma}^*(n), k, \mathcal{I})$ be a k-complex contagion in Kleinberg's model $K_{m,\gamma}^*(n)$ where $0 \leq \gamma < 2$, and let $\mathcal{I}$ be a k-seed cluster. With probability at least $1 - O(n^{1-\varepsilon})$ it takes a k-complex contagion, $\mathrm{CC}(K_{m,\gamma}^*(n), k, \mathcal{I})$, $\Omega(n^\delta)$ rounds to infect the entire graph; and*
$$\delta < \min\left(\frac{k-2+\varepsilon/2}{2k}, \frac{k-\gamma/2-1+\varepsilon}{2+2k-k\gamma}\right).$$

When $\gamma > 2$, there is a more subtle situation. As γ becomes big, weak ties become shorter. When the weak ties become too *short*, one might suspect that the complex contagion might take a long time to travel *long* distances in the graph. Our first attempt in formalizing this intuition appears in Theorem 8 below. The theorem applies to k-complex contagions on both variations of the Kleinberg's model (with and without multi-edges) for $\gamma \in (\beta_k, \infty)$, where $\beta_k = \frac{2(k+1)}{k}$. The proof divides the graph into a polynomial number of blocks (of polynomial size) and shows that the k-complex contagion will travel only through adjacent blocks. We show that if adjacent blocks of a block, like B, are not already infected, with high probability no node inside block B gets infected.

THEOREM 8. *Fix $k, m = O(1)$, let $\mathrm{CC}(K_{m,\gamma}^*(n), k, \mathcal{I})$ be a k-complex contagion in Kleinberg's model $K_{m,\gamma}^*(n)$, and let $\mathcal{I}$ be a k-seed cluster. For every k and for every $\gamma > \beta_k = \frac{2(k+1)}{k}$, there exists $\delta, \beta > 0$ such that for any constant $m > k$, with probability $1 - 1/n^\beta$, it takes $\Omega(n^\delta)$ rounds for $\mathrm{CC}(K_{m,\gamma}^*(n), k, \mathcal{I})$ to spread to the entire graph.*

We have proved an upper bound in $K_{m,\gamma}^W(n)$, the model which does not allow multi-edges, for $\gamma \in [2, \alpha_k)$ and an upper bound in $K_{m,\gamma}^I(n)$, the model which allows multi-edges, for $\gamma \in [2, \beta_k)$. Theorem 8 gives a lower bound for the range of $\gamma \in (\beta_k, \infty)$ for both $K_{m,\gamma}^W(n)$ and $K_{m,\gamma}^I(n)$ models.

We are left with one case: What is the speed of k-complex contagions in $K_{m,\gamma}^W(n)$ when $\gamma \in (\alpha_k, \beta_k]$? This proves to be the trickiest case of them all, because it turns out that when $\gamma \in (\alpha_k, \beta_k]$, long ties are still abundant in the $K_{m,\gamma}^W(n)$ graph. This means that infections can occur between parts of the graph that are far from each other. And that is why the argument of Theorem 8 cannot be extended to solve the case of $\gamma \in (\alpha_k, \beta_k]$ for $K_{m,\gamma}^W(n)$.

A better dissection of the nature of a complex contagion is needed to solve this case. We prove a polynomial lower bound for the $K_{m,\gamma}^W(n)$ model when $\gamma \in (\alpha_k, \infty) = (\alpha_k, \beta_k] \cup (\beta_k, \infty)$. We achieve this by carefully analyzing the possible scenarios that could lead to generation of *new seed clusters* in far-away distances. We show that despite the existence of infections occurring over large distances, new seed clusters do not appear in these distances with high probability.

THEOREM 9. *Let* $CC(K_{m,\gamma}^W(n), k, \mathcal{I})$ *be a k-complex contagion in Kleinberg's model $K_{m,\gamma}^W(n)$ (without multi-edges) where $\gamma > \alpha_k = \frac{2(k^2+k+2)}{k(k+1)}$, and let $\mathcal{T}$ be a k-seed cluster. With probability at least $1 - O(n^\zeta)$, a k-complex contagion, $CC(K_{m,\gamma}^W(n), k, \mathcal{I})$, takes at least $n^\epsilon/3$ rounds to spread to the entire graph; where $0 < \epsilon < \frac{1-\alpha_k/\gamma}{2}$, and $1 + \binom{k+1}{2}(1 - \gamma(1/2 - \epsilon)) < \zeta < 0$.*

4.1 Proof of Theorem 8

Fix k and $\gamma > \beta_k$. Define $\epsilon > 0$ so that $\gamma = \frac{2(k+\epsilon+1)}{k}$. Let $\delta = \frac{\epsilon}{4(1+\epsilon)}$, $\beta = \epsilon/3$ and then fix a constant m.

The basic proof strategy is to divide the 2-dimensional $\sqrt{n} \times \sqrt{n}$ grid into $n^{1/2-\delta} \times n^{1/2-\delta}$ sized blocks. We call two blocks adjacent if they are next to each other, or are diagonally adjacent. Any two vertices for two non-adjacent blocks are of distance at least $n^{1/2-\delta}$. We show that the probability that any vertex in a block has k neighbors in non-adjacent blocks on the grid is at most $n^{-\beta}$. We then show that the k-complex contagion must spread via adjacent blocks. If this is the case, then it will take time $\Omega(n^\delta)$ to cross from the block containing the initial seeds to the block furthest away on the grid (wrapped up to a torus).

We will use the following two facts:

1. The probability that a weak tie issued by a node u has Manhattan distance greater than $n^{1/2-\delta}$ is at most

$$P_1 = \int_{n^{\frac{1}{2}-\delta}}^{\sqrt{n}} x^{-\gamma} x\, dx = O\left(1/n^{(\frac{1}{2}-\delta)(\gamma-2)}\right).$$

2. The probability that any vertex has k neighbors of distance greater than $n^{1/2-\delta}$ is at most

$$O\left(1/n^{k(\frac{1}{2}-\delta)(\gamma-2)-1}\right).$$

The outgoing edges of a node are independent of each other in $K_{m,\gamma}^I(n)$, but not in $K_{m,\gamma}^W(n)$. While the out going edges of a node are not completely independent, they are close enough: No matter what configuration the first (up to) $j-1$ ties have, the next tie has a $O(P_1)$ probability of being longer than $n^{1/2-\delta}$. Thus, the probability that any given vertex has j long-range ties is bounded by $O((P_1)^j)$. Consider a vertex u which issues m weak ties. Each one has probability at most $O\left(1/n^{(1/2-\delta)(\gamma-2)}\right)$ of being longer than $n^{1/2-\delta}$. Thus, the probability that k weak ties are longer than $n^{1/2-\delta}$ is at most

$$O\left(\binom{m}{k}\left(1/n^{(\frac{1}{2}-\delta)(\gamma-2)}\right)^k\right) = O\left(1/n^{k(\frac{1}{2}-\delta)(\gamma-2)}\right).$$

Taking a union bound over n vertices, the claim is proved.

Now, by manipulations we see that $O\left(1/n^{(1/2-\delta)(\gamma-2)-1}\right) \subseteq O\left(1/n^\beta\right)$ because $\gamma - 2 = \frac{2+2\epsilon}{k}$ and $\delta = \frac{\epsilon}{4(1+\epsilon)}$ so we get

$$O\left(1/n^{(\frac{1}{2}-\frac{\epsilon}{4(1+\epsilon)})(2+2\epsilon)-1}\right) = O\left(1/n^{\epsilon/2}\right) \subseteq O\left(1/n^\beta\right).$$

If no vertex has k weak ties of distance at least $n^{1/2-\delta}$, in one round the k-complex contagion can only spread to blocks that are adjacent to those blocks already containing infected vertices. By the above claim, this is true with probability at least $1 - n^{-\beta}$. In this

case, the number of steps required is at least $\frac{\sqrt{n}}{(2k+1)n^{1/2-\delta}} > \frac{n^\delta}{3k}$. Initially, at most k rows of the grid are infected. At each step, the infection can only move one row to the right or left of the infected regions. After r rounds there are at most $(2r+1)k$ infected rows. So, to infect n^δ rows, it takes $\Omega\left(n^\delta/(2k+1)\right)$ rounds. $\square$

4.2 Proof of Theorem 9

We say that a weak tie is **long** if its length is at least $n^{1/2-\epsilon}$ and it is **short** otherwise. The definition of short ties also includes *grid edges*. Let $G = K_{m,\gamma}^W(n)$ denote the graph.

DEFINITION 3. *We create a **DAG**, $D(G, A)$, out of the route of infection on a graph G starting from A: There is an **edge from any node (not in A) to the k nodes that** first caused it to be infected. In the case that a node had more than k neighbors at the time of infection, arbitrarily choose k.*

For any subset of nodes S, define $\mathcal{A}(S)$ to be the nodes reachable from S using only short ties in the $D(G, A)$. $\mathcal{A}(S)$ includes S and the edges must be traversed in accord with their orientation.

Let $\mathcal{L}(S)$ be the number of long range ties connected to nodes in $\mathcal{A}(S)$. We overload notation and use $\mathcal{A}$ and $\mathcal{L}$ on singleton vertices.

PROPOSITION 1. *Let nodes u and v be connected by a (directed) path in $D(G, A)$; the time difference between when u, v are infected is at least the length of the path.*

PROOF. Follows from the fact that any two nodes connected by an edge were infected ≥ 1 round apart. $\square$

LEMMA 10. *Let a contagion start from k-seed cluster A and let B be another k-seed cluster:*

- *Either $A \cap \mathcal{A}(B) \neq \emptyset$;*
- *or there exists a connected subset of nodes of size $k^2 - k + 1$ in $K_{m,\gamma}^W(n)$, that has at least $\binom{k+1}{2}$ long ties connected to its vertices.*

The proof of the following lemma is based on computation and is presented in Appendix C.

LEMMA 11. *Let $\alpha_k < \gamma$, $0 < \epsilon < \frac{1-\alpha_k/\gamma}{2}$, and $1 + \binom{k+1}{2}(1 - \gamma(\frac{1}{2} - \epsilon)) < \zeta < 0$. Then with probability at least $1 - O(n^\zeta)$, no connected subset of nodes of size $k^2 - k + 1$ in $K_{m,\gamma}^W(n)$, has at least $\binom{k+1}{2}$ long ties connected to its vertices.*

We now use Proposition 1, Lemma 10, and Lemma 11 to prove Theorem 9.

PROOF OF THEOREM 9. Assume that the k-complex contagion starts from k-seed cluster A. Let B be a k-seed cluster that has distance $n^{1/2}/3$ from A. By Lemma 11, we know that with probability $1 - O(n^\zeta)$, no connected subset of nodes of size $k^2 - k + 1$ in G has at least $\binom{k+1}{2}$ *long* ties connected to its vertices. However, if this is the case, then by Lemma 10 we know that $A \cap \mathcal{A}(B) \neq \emptyset$.

If $A \cap \mathcal{A}(B) \neq \emptyset$, then there is a path of short edges from A to B over which the contagion is transmitted. However, because A and B are distance $n^{1/2}/3$ apart, such a path travels a distance of $n^{1/2}/3$ using edges that span at most distance $n^{1/2-\epsilon}$ (they are *short* edges) and thus has at least $n^\epsilon/3$ edges. A is infected at time 0, so by Proposition 1 this implies that B is not infected until round $n^\epsilon/3$.

Thus, with probability $1 - O(n^\zeta)$, it takes $\geq n^\epsilon/3$ rounds to infect the entire graph. $\square$

It remains to prove Lemma 10 and the the following Proposition will help.

PROPOSITION 2. *Fix $s \leq k$ and let $S \subseteq \mathcal{A}(B)$ where $|\mathcal{A}(S)| \geq s$. If $A \cap \mathcal{A}(B) = \emptyset$, then*

$$\mathcal{L}(S) \geq \sum_{i=0}^{s-1}(k-i) = k + (k-1) + ... + (k-s+1).$$

PROOF OF PROPOSITION 2. We prove it by induction: it is true for $s = 0$. Assume the proposition is true for $s \leq \ell < k$. Let $|\mathcal{A}(S)| \geq \ell + 1$. Topologically order the vertices in $\mathcal{A}(S)$ and let T be the set of the first ℓ vertices, and v be the $(\ell + 1)$-st vertex in this ordering.

Then $|\mathcal{A}(T)| \geq \ell$ and so by the inductive hypothesis, we have that $\mathcal{L}(T) \geq \sum_{i=0}^{\ell-1}(k-i) = k + (k-1) + ... + (k-\ell + 1)$. However, v has at most ℓ vertices before it in the ordering. Thus, it necessarily has $k - \ell$ long-range ties because it required k neighbors to be infected, but had at most ℓ short-range neighbors that contributed to this k. So $\mathcal{A}(T \cup \{v\}) = \mathcal{A}(T) \cup \{v\} \subseteq \mathcal{A}(S)$ has $k + (k-1) + ... + (k-\ell+1) + (k-\ell)$ long-range ties. And this completes the inductive step. $\square$

PROOF OF LEMMA 10. Assume that $A \cap \mathcal{A}(B) = \emptyset$. We must find a connected subset of nodes of size $k^2 - k + 1$ in G, that has at least $\binom{k+1}{2}$ *long* ties connected to its vertices. We consider two cases:

1. There exists a node $v \in B$, such that $|\mathcal{A}(v)| \geq k$.
   Sort $\mathcal{A}(v)$ in topological ordering and consider the first node in the ordering, $v_0 \in \mathcal{A}(v)$, such that $|\mathcal{A}(v_0)| \geq k$.

   We will show $\mathcal{A}(v_0)$ is a connected subset of nodes of size at most $k^2 - k + 1$ in $K_{m,\gamma}^W(n)$, that has at least $\binom{k+1}{2}$ *long* ties connected to its vertices. By v_0's minimality, we have that $\forall u \in \mathcal{A}(v_0), |\mathcal{A}(u)| \leq k - 1$. Since the in-degree of v_0 is at most k, we have that

   $$|\mathcal{A}(v_0)| \leq k(k-1) + 1 = k^2 - k + 1.$$

   Also, because $|\mathcal{A}(v_0)| \geq k$, by Proposition 2, we know that

   $$\mathcal{L}(v_0) \geq k + (k-1) + \cdots + 1 + 0 = \binom{k+1}{2}.$$

2. For all $v \in B$, $|\mathcal{A}(v)| \leq k - 1$.
   We will show $\mathcal{A}(B)$ is a connected subset of nodes of size at most $k^2 - k + 1$ in $K_{m,\gamma}^W(n)$, that has at least $\binom{k+1}{2}$ *long* ties connected to its vertices. Now we have that $k \leq |\mathcal{A}(B)| \leq k(k-1)$. The lower bound follows because $|B| = k$ and $B \subseteq \mathcal{A}(B)$. The upper bound follows because $\mathcal{A}(B) = \bigcup_{v \in B} \mathcal{A}(v)$. Because of the lower bound, by Proposition 2 , we know that

   $$\mathcal{L}(B) \geq k + (k-1) + \cdots + 1 = \binom{k+1}{2}.$$

Hence, in either cases, we find a connected subset of nodes of size at most $k^2 - k + 1$ in G, that has at least $\binom{k+1}{2}$ *long* ties connected to its vertices. $\square$

5. RELATED WORK

Our model of k-complex contagions belongs to the general family of *threshold models*, in which each node may have a different threshold on the number of infected edges/neighbors needed to become infected [12]. The threshold model is motivated by

certain coordination games studied in the economics literature in which a user maximizes its payoff when adopting the behavior as the majority of its neighbors. Many of the studies focus on the stable states, and structural properties that prevent complete adoption of the advanced technology (better behaviors) [17]. Montanari and Saberi [16] analyzed a particular dynamics and show that the convergence time is exponential in a quantity called the 'tilted cutwidth' of the graph and characterized the convergence time for Kleinberg's small world model. The main difference in our model, compared to the coordination game, is that we do not have a competing old behavior and all users once infected will remain infected.

Complex contagions on time-evolving graphs. In our recent work to be reported elsewhere [10], we analyzed the behavior of complex contagions in time evolved networks, one of which is the famous preferential attachment model [5]. We proved that a k-complex contagion can spread in $O(\log n)$ number of rounds in such graphs.

Complex contagions with randomly chosen seeds. In *bootstrap percolation* [8, 1], all nodes have the same threshold but initial seeds are randomly chosen. Here, the focus is to examine the threshold of the number of initial seeds with which the infection eventually 'percolates', i.e. diffuses to the entire network. Studies have been done on the random Erdos-Renyi graph [13] , the random regular graphs [4], and the configuration model [2], etc [3]. All of these results show that for a complex contagion to percolate, the number of initial seeds is a growing function of the network size and in many cases a constant fraction of the entire network. In contrast, we always start with a constant number of seeds and we would like to examine whether a fast spreading is possible.

6. REFERENCES

[1] J. Adler. Bootstrap percolation. *Physica A: Statistical and Theoretical Physics*, 171(3):453–470, Mar. 1991.

[2] H. Amini. Bootstrap percolation and diffusion in random graphs with given vertex degrees. *Electr. J. Comb.*, 17(1), 2010.

[3] H. Amini and N. Fountoulakis. What I tell you three times is true: bootstrap percolation in small worlds. In *Proceedings of the 8th international conference on Internet and Network Economics*, pages 462–474, 2012.

[4] J. Balogh and B. Pittel. Bootstrap percolation on the random regular graph. *Random Structures and Algorithms*, 30:257–286, 2007.

[5] A. Barabási and R. Albert. Emergence of scaling in random networks. *Science*, 286:509–512, 1999.

[6] D. Centola. The spread of behavior in an online social network experiment. *Science*, 329(5996):1194, 2010.

[7] D. Centola and M. Macy. Complex Contagions and the Weakness of Long Ties. *American Journal of Sociology*, 113(3):702–734, 2007.

[8] J. Chalupa, P. L. Leath, and G. R. Reich. Bootstrap percolation on a bethe lattice. *Journal of Physics C: Solid State Physics*, 12(1):L31, 1979.

[9] J. S. Coleman, E. Katz, and H. Menzel. *Medical Innovation: A Diffusion Study*. Bobbs-Merrill Co, 1966.

[10] R. Ebrahimi, J. Gao, G. Ghasemiesfeh, and G. Schoenebeck. How complex contagions spread and spread quickly. http://arxiv.org/abs/1404.2668, 2014.

[11] G. Ghasemiesfeh, R. Ebrahimi, and J. Gao. Complex contagion and the weakness of long ties in social networks:

revisited. In *Proceedings of the fourteenth ACM conference on Electronic Commerce*, pages 507–524, 2013.

[12] M. Granovetter. Threshold models of collective behavior. *The American Journal of Sociology*, 83(6):1420–1443, 1978.

[13] S. Janson, T. Luczak, T. Turova, and T. Vallier. Bootstrap percolation on the random graph $G_{n,n}$. *Annals of Applied Probability*, 22(5):1989–2047, 2012.

[14] J. Kleinberg. The small-world phenomenon: an algorithm perspective. In *Proceedings of the 32-nd annual ACM symposium on Theory of Computing*, pages 163–170, 2000.

[15] C. Martel and V. Nguyen. Analyzing kleinberg's (and other) small-world models. In *Proceedings of the twenty-third annual ACM symposium on Principles of Distributed Computing*, pages 179–188, 2004.

[16] A. Montanari and A. Saberi. Convergence to equilibrium in local interaction games. *SIGecom Exch.*, 8(1):11:1–11:4, July 2009.

[17] S. Morris. Contagion. *Review of Economic Studies*, 67:57–78, 2000.

[18] M. E. J. Newman and D. J. Watts. Scaling and percolation in the small-world network model. *Physical Review E*, 60(6):7332–7342, 1999.

[19] V. Nguyen and C. Martel. Analyzing and characterizing small-world graphs. In *Proceedings of the Sixteenth Annual ACM-SIAM Symposium on Discrete Algorithms*, SODA '05, pages 311–320, 2005.

[20] D. M. Romero, B. Meeder, and J. Kleinberg. Differences in the mechanics of information diffusion across topics: idioms, political hashtags, and complex contagion on twitter. In *Proceedings of the 20th international conference on World Wide Web*, pages 695–704, 2011.

[21] J. Ugander, L. Backstrom, C. Marlow, and J. Kleinberg. Structural diversity in social contagion. *Proc. National Academy of Sciences*, 109(16):5962–5966, April 2012.

[22] D. J. Watts and S. H. Strogatz. Collective dynamics of 'small-world' networks. *Nature*, pages 440–442, 1998.

APPENDIX

A. OMITTED PROOFS IN SECTION 3

In this section, we first provide the proof of Lemma 3 for general k; and then we prove Lemma 5. Both of these lemmas are computational tasks and follow from definitions of $K_{m,\gamma}^W(n)$, $K_{m,\gamma}^I(n)$, and Definition 2. As before $\alpha_k = \frac{2(k^2+k+2)}{k(k+1)}$ and $\beta_k = \frac{2(k+1)}{k}$.

Statement of of Lemma 3. *Fix constants* $2 < \gamma < \alpha_k$, $0 < \delta < 1 - \alpha_k\gamma$, $c \geq \frac{1-\delta}{(\binom{k+1}{2}+1)(1-\delta)+\binom{k+1}{2}\gamma/2}$, *and* $d > 2$. *Then the* $K_{m,\gamma}^W(n)$ *model is* (δ, c, d, k)-*recursively spreading.*

PROOF. Let $r = \left(\frac{d2^k \prod_{i=1}^k i^{k-i+1}}{\lambda^{\binom{k+1}{2}}}\right)^c$. Fix $\ell > (r\log^c n)^{\frac{1}{1-\delta}}$, and ℓ-sized square S and two disjoint $\ell^{(1-\delta)}$-sized subsquares A and B, and partition B into $\ell^{(1-\delta)}/k$ disjoint pairs of (grid) neighbor nodes $(u_1, \ldots, u_k)$. Assume that $a \in A$. Let $d(u, a)$ be the Manhattan distance of u and a.

i) $P_1(\ell) = \Pr\{u \text{ has a weak tie to } a \in A, \text{ via a particular edge}\}$

ii) $P_2(\ell) = \Pr\{u \text{ has a weak tie to } A, \text{ via a particular edge}\} \geq |A| \times P_1(\ell)$

iii) $Q_s(\ell) = \Pr\{u \text{ is connected to } A, \text{ via } s \text{ distinct weak ties}\}$

iv) $P_4(\ell) = \Pr\{(u_1, \ldots, u_k) \text{ form a } new\ seed \text{ in } B\}$

v) $P_5(\ell) = \Pr\{\text{a new seed forms in } B\}$

$$P_1(\ell) \geq \frac{\lambda}{(d(u,a))^\gamma} = \frac{\lambda}{\sqrt{\ell^\gamma}};$$

$$P_2(\ell) \geq |A| \times P_1(\ell) = \lambda\ell^{1-\delta-\gamma/2};$$

$$Q_s(\ell) \geq |\{(a_1, \ldots, a_s)|a_1, \ldots, a_s \in A\}|$$
$$\times \Pr\{u \text{ has a weak tie to } a_1, \ldots, a_s\}$$
$$\geq \binom{|A|}{s} P_1(\ell)^s \geq \frac{\lambda^s \ell^{s(1-\delta-\gamma/2)}}{2s!};$$

$$P_4(\ell) \geq Q_k(\ell) \times Q_{k-1}(\ell) \times \cdots \times Q_1(\ell)$$
$$\geq \frac{\lambda^{\binom{k+1}{2}} \ell^{\binom{k+1}{2}(1-\delta-\gamma/2)}}{2^k \prod_{i=1}^k i^{k-i+1}};$$

$$P_5(\ell) \geq 1 - (1 - P_4(\ell))^{|B|/2} \geq 1 - e^{-P_4(\ell)|B|/2}$$
$$= 1 - e^{-\frac{\lambda^{\binom{k+1}{2}}}{2^k \prod_{i=1}^k i^{k-i+1}} \ell^{(\binom{k+1}{2}+1)(1-\delta)-\binom{k+1}{2}\gamma/2}}$$

We want $P_5(\ell)$ to be very close to 1 and that means that we want the power of $\ell > 0$, which gives us:

$$\left(\binom{k+1}{2}+1\right)(1-\delta) - \binom{k+1}{2}\gamma/2 > 0$$
$$\Rightarrow \gamma < \alpha_k, \ \delta < 1 - \frac{\gamma}{\alpha_k}.$$

Also, note that P_5 is increasing in ℓ. Therefore, the smallest probability happens when then size of ℓ is the smallest; that is $\ell^{1-\delta} = r\log^c n$ and $\ell = (r\log^c n)^{1/(1-\delta)}$. We want $1 - P_5(\ell)$ to be polynomially small even when ℓ takes on its smallest value. This requires that the power of $\log n$ be ≥ 1:

$$\frac{c}{1-\delta}\left(\left(\binom{k+1}{2}+1\right)(1-\delta) - \binom{k+1}{2}\gamma/2\right) \geq 1$$
$$\Rightarrow c \geq \frac{1-\delta}{(\binom{k+1}{2}+1)(1-\delta) - \binom{k+1}{2}\gamma/2};$$

and by replacing $r = \left(\frac{d2^k \prod_{i=1}^k i^{k-i+1}}{\lambda^{\binom{k+1}{2}}}\right)^c$, we get that

$$P_5(\ell) \geq 1 - e^{-\frac{\lambda^{\binom{k+1}{2}}\left((r\log^c n)^{\frac{1}{1-\delta}}\right)^{(\binom{k+1}{2}+1)(1-\delta)-\binom{k+1}{2}\gamma/2}}{2^k \prod_{i=1}^k i^{k-i+1}}}$$
$$\geq 1 - e^{-d\log n} \geq 1 - n^{-d}.$$

$\square$

Statement of of Lemma 5. *Fix constants* $2 < \gamma < \beta_k$, $0 < \delta < 1 - \frac{\gamma}{\beta_k}$, $d > 2$, *and* $c \geq \frac{1-\delta}{(k+1)(1-\delta)-k\gamma/2}$. *Then the* $K_{m,\gamma}^I(n)$ *model is* (δ, c, d, k)-*recursively spreading.*

PROOF. Let $r = \left(\frac{dk^{(k^2\gamma+1)}}{\lambda^{k^2}}\right)^c$ Fix $\ell > (r\log^c n)^{\frac{1}{1-\delta}}$, an ℓ-sized square S and two disjoint $\ell^{(1-\delta)}$-sized subsquares A and B, and partition B into $\ell^{(1-\delta)}/k$ disjoint pairs of (grid) neighbor nodes $(u_1, \ldots, u_k)$. Assume that $a \in A$. Let $d(u, a)$ be the Manhattan distance of u and a.

i) $P_1(\ell) = \Pr\{u \text{ has a weak tie to } a \in A, \text{ via a particular edge}\}$

ii) $P_2(\ell) = \Pr\{u \text{ has a weak tie to } A, \text{ via a particular edge}\} \geq |A| \times P_1(\ell)$

iii) $Q_1(\ell) = \Pr\{u_1 \text{ is connected to } A, \text{ via } k \text{ distinct weak ties}\}$

iv) $Q_s'(\ell) = \Pr\{u_s \text{ has } k \text{ ties to } u_1\}$

v) $P_4(\ell) = \Pr\{(u_1, \ldots u_k) \text{ form a } new\ seed \text{ in } B\}$

vi) $P_5(\ell) = \Pr\{\text{a new seed forms in } B\}$

$$P_1(\ell) \geq \frac{\lambda}{(d(u,a))^\gamma} = \frac{\lambda}{\sqrt{\ell}^\gamma};$$

$$P_2(\ell) \geq |A| \times P_1(\ell) = \lambda \ell^{1-\delta-\gamma/2};$$

$$Q_1(\ell) \geq P_2^k \geq \lambda^k \ell^{k(1-\delta-\gamma/2)};$$

$$Q_s'(\ell) \geq \left(\frac{\lambda}{k^\gamma}\right)^k;$$

$$P_4(\ell) \geq Q_1(\ell) \times Q_2'(\ell) \times \cdots \times Q_k'(\ell) = \frac{\lambda^{(k^2)} \ell^{k(1-\delta-\gamma/2)}}{k^{(\gamma k^2)}};$$

$$P_5(\ell) \geq 1 - (1 - P_4(\ell))^{|B|/2} \geq 1 - e^{-P_4(\ell)|B|/k}$$

$$= 1 - e^{-\frac{\lambda^{(k^2)}}{k^{(\gamma k^2 + 1)}} \ell^{(k+1)(1-\delta)-k\gamma/2}}$$

We want $P_5(\ell)$ to be very close to 1 and that means that we want the power of $\ell > 0$, which gives us:

$$(k+1)(1-\delta) - k\gamma/2 > 0 \Rightarrow \gamma < \beta_k, \ \delta < 1 - \frac{\gamma}{\beta_k}.$$

Also, note that P_5 is increasing in ℓ. Therefore, the smallest probability happens when then size of ℓ is the smallest; that is $\ell^{1-\delta} = r \log^c n$ and $\ell = (r \log^c n)^{1/(1-\delta)}$. We want $1 - P_5(\ell)$ to be polynomially small even when ℓ takes on its smallest value. This requires that the power of $\log n$ be ≥ 1:

$$\frac{c}{1-\delta}((k+1)(1-\delta) - k\gamma/2) \geq 1$$

$$\Rightarrow c \geq \frac{1-\delta}{(k+1)(1-\delta) - k\gamma/2};$$

and by replacing $r = \left(\frac{dk^{(k^2\gamma+1)}}{\lambda^{(k^2)}}\right)^c$, we get that

$$P_5(\ell) \geq 1 - e^{-\frac{\lambda^{(k^2)}}{k^{(\gamma k^2+1)}}\left((r \log^c n)^{\frac{1}{1-\delta}}\right)^{(k+1)(1-\delta)-k\gamma/2}}$$

$$\geq 1 - e^{-d \log n} \geq 1 - n^{-d}.$$

□

B. LOWER BOUND PROOF WHEN $0 \leq \gamma < 2$

Recall that when $0 \leq \gamma < 2$, the normalization factor $\lambda = \Theta(n^{\gamma/2-1})$. That is, the probability that node p chooses node q as a neighbor through a random edge is $\lambda/|pq|^\gamma = \Theta(n^{\gamma/2-1}/|pq|^\gamma)$.

Statement of of Theorem 7. *Let* $CC(K_{m,\gamma}^*(n), k, \mathcal{I})$ *be a k-complex contagion in Kleinberg's model $K_{m,\gamma}^*(n)$ where $0 \leq \gamma < 2$, and let $\mathcal{I}$ be a k-seed cluster. With probability at least $1 - O(n^{1-\varepsilon})$ it takes a k-complex contagion, $\Omega(n^\delta)$ rounds to infect the entire graph; where $m \geq k$ is a constant, $0 < \varepsilon < 1$, and $\delta < \min\left(\frac{k-2+\varepsilon/2}{2k}, \frac{k-\gamma/2-1+\varepsilon}{2+2k-k\gamma}\right)$.*

PROOF. Recall that in $K_{m,\gamma}^*(n)$ each node has m strong ties to the m closest nodes in the grid, and m weak ties randomly distributed to other nodes by the specified distribution. Assume that s is a node in the graph. The initial seeds are a k-seed cluster which includes s along with the closest k nodes on the grid to s. Consider the set D of nodes within Manhattan distance n^δ from s. We prove that the contagion inside D would not utilize weak ties and can only spread along the strong ties until D is completely covered. Since propagation along strong ties is local, it would require $\Omega(n^\delta)$ rounds to just cover D.

We say a node u has a wide bridge to D, if u issues at least k weak ties to nodes in D. We are going to show the following two statements:

1. The expected number of nodes in the annulus $A(2n^\delta, \sqrt{n})$, defined as the set of nodes whose Manhattan distance to s is within the range $(2n^\delta, \sqrt{n}]$, with wide bridges to D, denoted as Z_1, is small;

2. The expected number of nodes in the disk $B(2n^\delta)$, defined as the nodes whose Manhattan distance is at most $2n^\delta$ from s, that have wide bridges to D, denoted as Z_2, is small.

First, we compute Z_1. Let u be a node in the annulus $A(2n^\delta, \sqrt{n})$. Then the distance of u to any node q inside D, $|uq|$, is bounded by constant factors of the distance from u to the center s, $|us|$. That is, $c_1|us| < |uq| < c_2|us|$, with two constants $c_1 < c_2$. Let $y = |us|$ be the Manhattan distance of u to s. One can easily verify that

$$Q_1 = \Pr\left\{\text{Node } u \in A(2n^\delta, \sqrt{n}) \text{ has 1 weak tie to } D\right\}$$

$$= O\left(\frac{\lambda}{y^\gamma} n^{2\delta}\right);$$

$$Q_2 = \Pr\left\{\text{Node } u \in A(2n^\delta, \sqrt{n}) \text{ has at least } k \text{ weak ties to } D\right\}$$

$$= O\left(\left(\frac{\lambda}{y^\gamma} n^{2\delta}\right)^k\right).$$

We explain the second equation. Note that the outgoing edges of a node are independent of each other in $K_{m,\gamma}^I(n)$, but not in $K_{m,\gamma}^W(n)$. While the out going edges of a node are not completely independent, they are close enough: No matter what configuration the first (up to) $j-1$ ties have, the next tie has a $O(Q_1)$ probability of connecting to D. Thus, the probability that any given vertex has j long-range ties is bounded by $O((Q_1)^j)$.

Now, we compute Z_1 using linearity of expectation:

$$Z_1 = \int_{2n^\delta}^{\sqrt{n}} O\left(\left(\frac{\lambda}{y^\gamma} \cdot n^{2\delta}\right)^k\right) \Theta(y) dy$$

$$= O\left(\lambda^k n^{2k\delta}\right) \int_{2n^\delta}^{\sqrt{n}} y^{1-k\gamma} dy$$

$$= \begin{cases} O\left(1/n^{k-1-2k\delta}\right) & 0 \leq \gamma < 2/k \\ O\left(\log n/n^{k-1-2k\delta}\right) & \gamma = 2/k \\ O\left(1/n^{k(\frac{1}{2}-\delta)(2-\gamma)-2\delta}\right) & 2/k < \gamma < 2 \end{cases}$$

Now, we bound Z_2. Consider a node u in $B(2n^\delta)$. Notice that D is contained in the disk D' of radius $3n^\delta$ from u. Thus, the probability that one weak tie issued by u falls inside D is no greater than the probability P of this weak tie connecting to nodes in D'. The latter can be bounded from above:

$$P \leq \int_1^{3n^\delta} \frac{\lambda}{y^\gamma} y \, dy = \lambda(3n^\delta)^{2-\gamma} = O\left(1/n^{(\frac{1}{2}-\delta)(2-\gamma)}\right).$$

Hence, we get that the probability that node $u \in B(2n^\delta)$ has k weak tie to D is at most P^k. We bound Z_2:

$$Z_2 = O\left((2n^\delta)^2/n^{k(\frac{1}{2}-\delta)(2-\gamma)}\right) = O\left(1/n^{k(\frac{1}{2}-\delta)(2-\gamma)-2\delta}\right).$$

We can verify that $Z_1 = O(1/n^{1-\varepsilon})$ and $Z_2 = O(1/n^{1-\varepsilon})$ for $0 < \varepsilon < 1$ when

$$\delta < \min\left(\frac{k-2+\varepsilon/2}{2k}, \frac{k-\gamma/2-1+\varepsilon}{2+2k-k\gamma}\right).$$

Now, by Markov inequality, $Z_1 \geq 1$ and $Z_2 \geq 1$ only happen with small probability. By union bound, we have that $Z_1 = Z_2 = 0$ with probability at least $1 - O(1/n^{1-\varepsilon})$.

If there are no wide bridges to/from D, the contagion inside D can only utilize the strong ties and it will take it $\Omega(n^\delta)$ rounds to cover D. Hence, the contagion speed is $\Omega(n^\delta)$ with probability at least $1 - O(1/n^{1-\varepsilon})$. □

C. PROOF OF LEMMA 11

Statement of of Lemma 11. *Let $\alpha_k < \gamma$, $0 < \epsilon < \frac{1-\alpha_k/\gamma}{2}$, and $1 + \binom{k+1}{2}(1 - \gamma(\frac{1}{2} - \epsilon)) < \zeta < 0$. Then with probability at least $1 - O\left(n^\zeta\right)$, no connected subset of nodes of size $k^2 - k + 1$ in $K_{m,\gamma}^W(n)$, has at least $\binom{k+1}{2}$ long ties connected to its vertices.*

PROOF. Consider a specific set of $k^2 - k + 1$ connected nodes in $K_{m,\gamma}^W(n)$, $S = \{u_1, \ldots, u_{k^2-k+1}\}$. We compute the probability that nodes of S have collectively $\binom{k+1}{2}$ long range ties to other nodes in $K_{m,\gamma}^W(n)$.

i) $P_1 = \Pr\left\{\text{Node } u_1 \text{ has 1 long tie to any node in } K_{m,\gamma}^W(n)\right\}$

ii) $P_2 = \text{Prob }\{\text{Nodes in } S \text{ have collectively } \binom{k+1}{2} \text{ long ties to other nodes in } K_{m,\gamma}^W(n)\}$

$$P_1 = \sum_{\forall\, a \in G: d(u,a) \geq n^{1/2-\epsilon}} \frac{\lambda}{(d(u,a))^\gamma} \in O\left(\frac{n}{(n^{\frac{1}{2}-2\epsilon})^\gamma}\right)$$
$$= O\left(n^{1-(1/2-\epsilon)\gamma}\right);$$
$$P_2 \leq \sum_{i=\binom{k+1}{2}}^{m(k^2-k+1)} \binom{m(k^2-k+1)}{i} O\left(P_1^i\right)(1-P_1)^{m(k^2-k+1)-i}$$
$$\leq \sum_{i=\binom{k+1}{2}}^{m(k^2-k+1)} \binom{m(k^2-k+1)}{i} O\left(P_1^i\right)$$
$$\in O\left(P_1^{\binom{k+1}{2}}\right)$$
$$= O\left(\left(n^{1-(1/2-\epsilon)\gamma}\right)^{\binom{k+1}{2}}\right).$$

The outgoing edges of different nodes in S are independent of each other. While the outgoing edges of a single node are not completely independent, they are close enough: No matter what configuration the first (up to) $j-1$ ties have, the next tie has a $O(P_1)$ probability of being a long range tie. Thus, the probability that any given vertex has j long-range ties is bounded by $O((P_1)^j)$.

We know that the highest degree of nodes in the graph, $H(n)$, is at most $\log n$ with probability at least $1 - n^{-m\log\log n+1}$.

Consider all connected subsets of size $k^2 - k + 1$ in B. If $H(n) \leq \log n$, then there are at most $n \times \left((k^2 - k)\log n\right)^{k^2-k}$ such connected subsets in the graph, because there are n choices for the first node and at most $(k^2 - k)\log n$ choices for each of the next $k^2 - k$ nodes. If $H(n) > \log n$, the number n^{k^2-k+1} gives a trivial bound on the number of all such subsets. We want to compute the following probability:

$P_3 = \text{Prob }\{\text{Any set of } k^2 - k + 1 \text{ connected nodes has more than}$

$$\binom{k+1}{2}$$

long ties connected to its vertices$\}$

We condition P_3 on $H(n)$ being less/bigger than $\log n$.

$$P_3 \leq P_2 \times n\left((k^2-k)\log n\right)^{k^2-k} \times (1 - n^{-m\log\log n+1})$$
$$+ P_2 \times n^{k^2-k+1} \times n^{-m\log\log n+1}$$
$$= O\left(n^{\binom{k+1}{2}(1-(1/2-\epsilon)\gamma)} \times n\log^{k^2-k} n\right) \subseteq O\left(n^\zeta\right).$$

We want P_3 to be polynomially small, so we require that:

$$1 + \binom{k+1}{2}\left(1 - \frac{\gamma}{2} + \gamma\epsilon\right) < \zeta < 0$$
$$\Rightarrow \quad 1 + \binom{k+1}{2} - \binom{k+1}{2}\gamma/2 < 0$$
$$\Rightarrow \gamma > \frac{2(k^2 + k + 2)}{k(k+1)} = \alpha_k.$$

But this means that this inequality can be satisfied because

$$1 + \binom{k+1}{2}(1 - (1/2 - \epsilon)\gamma)$$
$$< 1 + \binom{k+1}{2}\left(1 - \gamma/2 + \frac{\gamma(1 - \alpha_k/\gamma)}{2}\right)$$
$$\text{since } \epsilon < \frac{1 - \alpha_k/\gamma}{2};$$
$$= 1 + \binom{k+1}{2}(1 - \alpha_k/2)$$
$$\leq 1 + \binom{k+1}{2}\left(1 - \left(1 + \frac{1}{\binom{k+1}{2}}\right)\right)$$
$$\text{since } \alpha_k/2 = 1 + \frac{1}{\binom{k+1}{2}};$$
$$= 0.$$

□

Natural Selection as an Inhibitor of Genetic Diversity

Multiplicative Weights Updates Algorithm and a Conjecture of Haploid Genetics [Working Paper Abstract]*

Ruta Mehta[†]
Georgia Institute of Technology
rmehta@cc.gatech.edu

Ioannis Panageas[‡]
Georgia Institute of Technology
ioannis@gatech.edu

Georgios Piliouras[§]
California Institute of Technology
gpiliour@caltech.edu

ABSTRACT

In a recent series of papers [3, 4, 2] a surprisingly strong connection was discovered between standard evolutionary models of natural selection and Multiplicative Weights Updates Algorithm, a ubiquitous model of online learning and optimization. These papers establish that, under specific assumptions, mathematical models of biological evolution can be reduced to studying discrete replicator dynamics [7, 5], a close variant of MWUA [6], in coordination games. This connection allows for introducing insights from game theoretic dynamics into the field of mathematical biology.

Using these results as a stepping stone, we show that mathematical models of haploid evolution imply the extinction of genetic diversity in the long term limit, a widely believed conjecture in genetics [1]. In game theoretic terms we show that in the case of coordination games, under minimal genericity assumptions, discrete replicator dynamics converge to pure Nash equilibria for all but a zero measure of initial conditions. This result holds despite the fact that mixed Nash equilibria can be exponentially (or even uncountably) many, completely dominating in number the set of pure Nash equilibria. Thus, in haploid organisms the long term preservation of genetic diversity needs to be safeguarded by other evolutionary mechanisms such as mutations and speciation.

[†]Affiliated with College of Computing, Georgia Institute of Technology. Supported by NSF Grants CCF-0914732 and CCF-1216019.
[‡]Affiliated with College of Computing, Georgia Institute of Technology. Supported by ARC fellowship, and NSF grants CCF-1415498 and DMS-1407657.
[§]Affiliated with Center for the Mathematics of Information, California Institute of Technology. Supported by CMI Wally Baer and Jeri Weiss postdoctoral fellowship and Linde-SISL postdoctoral fellowship.
*A full version of this working paper is available at http://arxiv.org/abs/1408.6270.

ITCS'15, January 11–13, 2015, Rehovot, Israel.
ACM 978-1-4503-3333-7/15/01.
http://dx.doi.org/10.1145/2688073.2688118.

Categories and Subject Descriptors

F.0 [Theory of Computation]: General; F.2.2 [Analysis of Algorithms and Problem Complexity]: Miscellaneous

General Terms

Theory, Economics

Keywords

Algorithmic Game Theory, Multiplicative Weight Updates, Evolution, Stability of Equilibria, Replicator Dynamics

1. REFERENCES

[1] N. H. Barton, S. Novak, and T. Paixão. Diverse forms of selection in evolution and computer science. *Proceedings of the National Academy of Sciences (PNAS)*, 111(29):10398–10399, 2014.

[2] E. Chastain, A. Livnat, C. Papadimitriou, and U. Vazirani. Algorithms, games, and evolution. *Proceedings of the National Academy of Sciences (PNAS)*, 111(29):10620–10623, 2014.

[3] E. Chastain, A. Livnat, C. H. Papadimitriou, and U. V. Vazirani. Multiplicative updates in coordination games and the theory of evolution. *CoRR*, abs/1208.3160, 2012.

[4] E. Chastain, A. Livnat, C. H. Papadimitriou, and U. V. Vazirani. Multiplicative updates in coordination games and the theory of evolution. In *ITCS*, pages 57–58, 2013.

[5] J. Hofbauer and K. Sigmund. *Evolutionary Games and Population Dynamics*. Cambridge University Press, Cambridge, 1998.

[6] R. Kleinberg, G. Piliouras, and É. Tardos. Multiplicative updates outperform generic no-regret learning in congestion games. In *ACM Symposium on Theory of Computing (STOC)*, 2009.

[7] V. Losert and E. Akin. Dynamics of games and genes: Discrete versus continuous time. *Journal of Mathematical Biology*, 17(2):241–251, 1983.

Fractal structures in Adversarial Prediction

Rina Panigrahy[*]
Google Inc.
Mountain View, CA
rinapy@gmail.com

Preyas Popat[†]
Google Inc.
Mountain View, CA
preyas.p@gmail.com

ABSTRACT

Fractals are self-similar recursive structures that have been used in modeling several real world processes. In this work we study how "fractal-like" processes arise in a prediction game where an adversary is generating a sequence of bits and an algorithm is trying to predict them. We will see that under a certain formalization of the predictive payoff for the algorithm it is most optimal for the adversary to produce a fractal-like sequence to minimize the algorithm's ability to predict. Indeed it has been suggested before that financial markets exhibit a fractal-like behavior [FP98, Man05]. We prove that a fractal-like distribution arises naturally out of an optimization from the adversary's perspective.

In addition, we give optimal trade-offs between predictability and expected deviation (i.e. sum of bits) for our formalization of predictive payoff. This result is motivated by the observation that several time series data exhibit higher deviations than expected for a completely random walk.

Categories and Subject Descriptors

F.2 [**Analysis Of Algorithms And Problem Complexity**]: Nonnumerical Algorithms and Problems

General Terms

Theory

Keywords

Fractal Brownian motion, Adversarial prediction

1. INTRODUCTION

Consider an adversary who is producing a sequence of bits (each bit is $+1$ or -1) and an algorithm having seen a certain number of bits is interested in predicting the next x bits. Say the algorithm gets a payoff of 1 for every bit that it predicts correctly and -1 for

---

[*]This work was done while the author was at Microsoft.

[†]This work was done while the author was at Microsoft.

every bit where it is wrong. This is like an idealized stock market where each day the price changes by $+1$ or -1 percent and the algorithm is required to make a bet on the daily direction. We ask what is the most adversarial distribution on sequence of bits so as to minimize the algorithm's payoff. Clearly the uniform distribution where every bit is chosen independently and uniformly at random is the most adversarial, since the expected payoff of any algorithm is always exactly 0.

Given a sequence s of bits, let $h(s)$ be the sum of the bits in s i.e. the *height* of the sequence when plotted cumulatively. We will refer to the magnitude of height as deviation. For $s \in \{-1, 1\}^T$ chosen uniformly at random the typical deviation s is $\Theta(\sqrt{T})$.

The question we study here is: what is the most adversarial distribution on sequences if the distribution is required to be heavy-tailed, say the typical height should be $k\sqrt{T}$ where $k > 1$. Indeed it has been observed in several studies that the distribution of financial time series is heavy-tailed [BT03, RMF+05]. A natural heavy-tailed distribution is to pick a random string conditioned on its height being at least $k\sqrt{T}$. This is essentially the highest entropy distribution with the property that the typical height is around $k\sqrt{T}$. However the highest entropy distribution is not the least predictable. Indeed for large k, it tends to rise/drop rather linearly to its final height. Thus by observing the initial segment of bits, the algorithm can easily infer the direction of the remaining bits to get a large payoff.

One distribution that has been suggested for financial markets is the Fractional Brownian Motion (FBM) [MVN68, NR06] which is a generalization of the Brownian motion. For our purposes, the Brownian motion can be thought of as a continuous variant of the uniform distribution on bits. FBM is characterized by a single parameter H which is called the Hurst parameter, and the typical height achieved by sequences drawn from $\text{FBM}(H)$ is around T^H. For $H > 1/2$, the increments of FBM are positively correlated while the case $H = 1/2$ corresponds to Brownian motion.

To make our question precise we introduce a measure of unpredictability for a distribution which is motivated by the notion that the expected payoff of an algorithm on an interval I having observed the previous bits should be small compared to the standard deviation of height in I. Intuitively, we are enforcing a low signal-to-noise ratio.

DEFINITION 1.1. *Let D be a distribution which produces bits in an online fashion and s be the sequence of bits that have been produced immediately preceding an interval I. Let $\mathbb{E}[A_s(I)]$ denote the expected payoff of an algorithm A on interval I (where the bits in I are produced according to D conditioned on having produced s immediately before I). Note that A must fix its prediction for I based solely on s and before looking at any bits within I.*

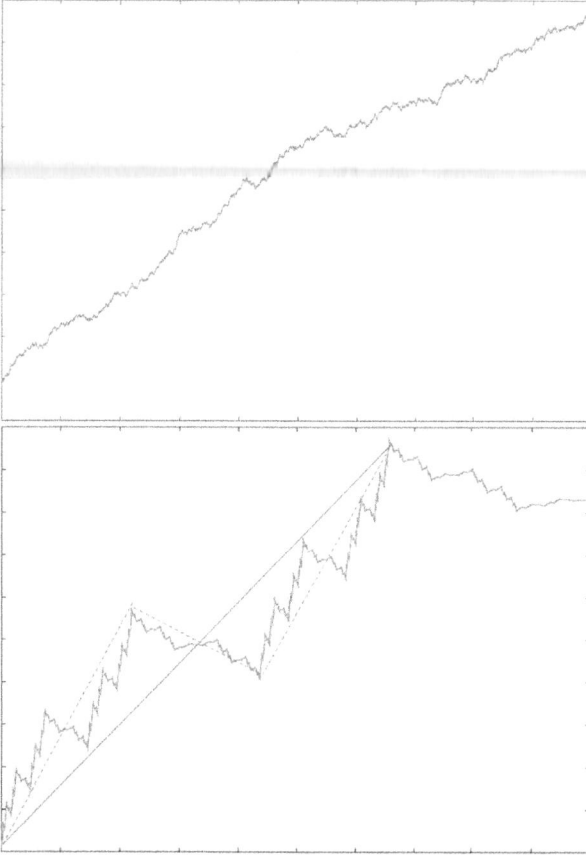

Figure 1: Growth charts for two different types of adversarial sequences. The first is the cumulative plot of a random i.i.d sequence with a constant upward bias. The second is a fractal generated by recursively replacing a line segment with a certain slope by three (shown dotted) line segments in a fixed ratio, where the middle segment slopes in the opposite direction. It is an α-inverting sequence as in Definition 1.2 for α about 0.2. Note that the latter plots seems to change direction more significantly than the former.

We say that D is δ-unpredictable if for all A, s and I, $\mathbb{E}[A_s(I)] \leq \delta \cdot \sqrt{|I|}$.

For example an algorithm may notice a high density of $+1$'s and may decide to predict $+1$ for the next few bits (this would correspond to a "buying" a stock) for the next x bits. Note that $\sqrt{x}$ is the standard deviation in the payoff of an algorithm for the uniform distribution on x bit sequences and thus we are asking that the payoff of the algorithm for a δ-unpredictable distribution is negligible compared to this standard deviation (we will in fact construct distributions where the standard deviation is much higher than $\sqrt{x}$). Roughly, this is equivalent to saying that the signal to noise ratio in any interval is negligible.

We ask what is the maximum deviation that can be achieved by a δ-unpredictable distribution D. We will look at maximizing measures such as median deviation or mean deviation: $\mathbb{E}_{s \sim D}[|h(s)|]$ (we will show that our claims hold with respect to any of these measures).

We show that there is a δ-unpredictable distribution which achieves a deviation of $\sqrt{T}(1 + \Omega(\delta \log T))$. Thus, the deviation can be $\omega(\sqrt{T})$ for $\delta = o(1)$. (Also note that for very small δ, $T^{1/2+\delta} =$

$\sqrt{T}(1 + \Theta(\delta \log T))$ as $\sqrt{T}T^{\delta} = \sqrt{T}(e^{\delta \log T}) = \sqrt{T}(1 + \Theta(\delta \log T))$. The distribution we construct is a variant of a discretization of FBM. We also show that the highest deviation that can be achieved by a δ-unpredictable distribution is $\sqrt{T}(1 + O(\delta \log T))$. In addition, we construct a distribution which is a simple discretization of FBM and show that the deviation achieved by this distribution is $T^{1/2+\Theta(\delta)}$. Though this distribution is not δ-unpredictable, it satisfies a similar but weaker property.

A nice property of δ-unpredictable distributions is that they are "fractal-like" in the sense that they have a recursive "inverting" property. To formalize this property, we first define a notion of inversion for a deterministic sequence. It essentially says that if in any interval there is a huge rise, then there must be a sub-interval where there must be a proportionally big fall and vice versa.

DEFINITION 1.2 (α-INVERSION). *Given a sequence $s \in \{-1, 1\}^T$, it is said to be α-inverting if for every interval X within $[1, T]$ (of at least some constant length) there is a sub interval Y such that $h(s_X)$ and $h(s_Y)$ are of opposite sign and $|h(s_Y)|/|h(s_X)| \geq \alpha$. Here by s_I we mean the sequence s restricted to interval I.*

We refer to the largest feasible α as the inversion ratio of s.

It turns out that for deterministic sequences that are α-inverting, the maximum deviation is achieved by a fractal similar to the one in Figure 1; that is, a line segment has been replaced (recursively) by three segments in a fixed ratio with the middle one sloping in the opposite direction (see Theorem 1.4). Further observe that any α-inverting sequence resembles a fractal: to see this, note that a sequence s such that $h(s) > 0$, may be divided into three parts $s_1 s_2 s_3$ where s_2 has a net downward slope and s_1, s_3 have a positive slope each. But one can recurse and divide each of the three substrings further into three parts each and thus the sequence has a recursive, self-similar structure. Thus it will resemble the fractal shown in Figure 1 and hence we will say that such sequences are "fractal-like".

We show that any δ-unpredictable distribution is α-inverting in a certain sense. Since we are dealing with a distribution rather than a deterministic sequence we need an appropriate generalization of Definition 1.2 which is stated in Section 1.1. It will be clear from the definition that the highest entropy sequence we discussed earlier has a very small inversion ratio compared to δ-unpredictable distributions.

1.1 Main results

In this section we describe our main results in more detail. As we mentioned earlier, the adversarial distributions we construct are closely related to and inspired from FBM.

FBM with parameter H is the unique continuous time, Gaussian process $B_H(t)$ which satisfies $B(0) = 0$, $\mathbb{E}[B_H(t)] = 0$ for all t and has covariance function:

$$\mathbb{E}[B_H(t)B_H(s)] = \frac{1}{2}(|t|^{2H} + |s|^{2H} - |t-s|^{2H})$$

The process B_H is translation invariant and is self-similar in the sense that $\{B_H(at) : t \in \mathbb{R}\}$ is identical in distribution to $\{a^H B_H(t) : t \in \mathbb{R}\}$ for all $a > 0$. Furthermore, $B_H(t)$ is normally distributed with variance t^{2H}. Thus any interval of length t has deviation about t^H. The case $H = 0.5$ corresponds to the standard Brownian motion.

The analysis of the FBM usually requires an understanding of integrated Wiener processes. The first adversarial distribution we construct is a discrete variant of the FBM that produces bits instead of real numbers. We denote this distribution as FRACTAL RANDOM WALK (FRW).

The sequence is constructed recursively in lengths that are powers of 2. To produce a sequence of length $2n$, we concatenate two recursively constructed sequences of length n each, and change the height of the second sequence by a factor proportional to the height h of the first sequence. This is done by flipping approximately δh (-1)'s to $+1$'s if $h > 0$ (and $+1$'s to -1 otherwise.) A formal description of the construction appears in Section 3.

While this lacks the translation invariance and the exact self-similarity properties of the FBM, it still has the property that any interval of size t has deviation $t^{1/2+\Theta(\delta)}$.

To see this, note that if h_1, h_2 denote the heights of the two sequences that are concatenated to produce the sequence of length $2n$ after altering the second string then $E[h_1 h_2] = 2\delta\mathbb{E}[h_1^2] = 2\delta\mathbb{E}[H(n)^2]$ where $H(n)$ is a random variable that denotes the height of a random sequence of length n drawn from FRW. So $\mathbb{E}[H(2n)^2] = E[(h_1+h_2)^2] = E[h_1^2] + E[h_2^2] + 2E[h_1 h_2] = (2+\delta)E[H(n)^2]$. The recurrence works out to a root mean square deviation $(\sqrt{E[H(n)^2]})$ of about $n^{1/2+\Theta(\delta)}$.

This informal description skips over technical issues such as discretization. Furthermore, extending this argument to show that the high deviation is achieved with constant probability is more complicated and is done in Theorem 3.1. Note that a constant probability bound for achieving a particular deviation is stronger than showing a high deviation in expectation (using Markov's inequality). We note that this distribution is not δ-unpredictable but satisfies a weaker property (Theorem 7.1). For completeness, we show in the full version[PP13] that the FBM (continuous version) with $H = 1/2 + \delta$ is also not δ-unpredictable in the strict sense; further we show that the highest entropy distribution is very poor in terms of δ-unpredictability.

We construct another distribution, which we call OPTIMAL FRACTAL RANDOM WALK (OPT-FRW) which has optimal trade-offs between deviation and predictability. The distribution OPT-FRW is a simple but important twist on the above process where instead of flipping $\delta \cdot h$ bits, we flip $\delta \cdot \sqrt{n}$ bits in the direction of h.

THEOREM 1.3. *(Theorems 3.10, 3.5 and 4.1) The distribution* OPT-FRW *is $O(\delta)$-unpredictable and achieves a deviation of $\sqrt{T}(1+\Omega(\delta\log T))$ with constant probability. Further, no δ-unpredictable distribution can achieve an expected deviation higher than $\sqrt{T}(1+O(\delta\log T))$.*

We now turn to formalizing the relationship between δ-unpredictability and recursively inverting "fractal-like" property of a distribution.

For a deterministic sequence we show that an α-inverting sequence with the highest deviation is a fractal.

THEOREM 1.4. *(Claim 5.2)*
Let s be an α-inverting sequence of length t (Definition 1.2), where α is bounded above by a constant. Then the highest deviation that can be achieved by s for large t is t^θ where θ is the solution to the equation $1 = 2((1+\alpha)/2)^{1/\theta} + \alpha^{1/\theta}$. Furthermore, this deviation is actually achieved by an appropriately designed fractal where a line segment has been divided recusively into three segments in a fixed ratio with the middle segment sloping in the opposite direction.

The following claim computes the box-counting dimension [Fal] of the above fractal. Note that it matches the dimension of an FBM with Hurst parmeter H which turns out to be equal to $2 - H$.

CLAIM 1.5. *(Claim 5.3) The above fractal has a box-counting dimension of $2 - \theta$.*

For distributions D over sequences we define the following variant of the earlier inversion rule.

DEFINITION 1.6. *((α, q)-INVERSION). A distribution D is said to be (α, q)-inverting if for any interval X of at least some constant length) with median deviation $\Delta = \Omega(\delta\sqrt{|X|})$, with probability at least q there is a sub interval Y such that $h(s_X)$ and $h(s_Y)$ are of opposite sign and $|h(s_Y)| \geq \alpha \cdot \Delta$. Here by s_I we mean the sequence s restricted to interval I. This should hold even if one conditions on a given history of bits seen before the interval X.*

We note (see full version [PP13]) that a uniform random sequence is (α, q) inverting for some constants α, q. Further the probability parameter q can be made as high as $1 - \varepsilon$ by reducing the inversion ratio α to $\Theta(1/\log(1/\varepsilon))$.

The following theorem establishes that every δ-unpredictable distribution must be fractal-like in the sense that it is $(\Omega(1), \Omega(1))$ inverting.

THEOREM 1.7. *(Theorems 6.3 and 6.4) For δ small enough, any δ-unpredictable distribution is also (α, q)-inverting for some constants α, q. Further by dropping the inversion ratio α to $\Theta(1/\log T)$ the probability q can be made as high as $1 - 1/T^{\Omega(1)}$ for all intervals of length at least $\Omega(\log T)$. Thus the condition holds with high probability simultaneously for all such intervals.*

1.2 Related Work

Many studies support the thesis that fractals occur naturally in several real world processes in diverse fields such as physics, finance and geography [MPP84, DSS90, Man04]. Ralph Elliot [FP98], suggested the use of fractal like "waves" in understanding financial markets. Fractal models for finance have also been studied widely in the academic community. Fractional Brownian Motion (FBM) was introduced as a variant to the well known Brownian Motion by Mandelbrot and van Ness in [MVN68]. In addition to financial time series modeling, FBM has also found applications in the study of network traffic and fluid turbulence [Nor95, NR06].

The reason for considering FBM rather than the standard Brownian motion for financial modelling was the observation that the distribution of financial time series is heavy-tailed [BT03, RMF+05]. This means that the deviations achieved are a bit higher than those expected for Brownian motion. It has been argued that modeling S&P500 price data according to FBM produces an estimated value of the Hurst parameter H to be slightly over the 0.5 value that corresponds to the standard Brownian Motion [BPS04]. Values of $H > 0.5$ allow for long range (positive) correlations in the time series that results in a higher than normal deviation. Besides FBM other models such as p-stable distributions and levy distributions [Voi05, RMF+05, Nol03] provide an alternate explanation for the heavy tailed nature of time series data by allowing heavier tails for the price changes *in each unit time* that are *independent* across time. In contrast, the FBM uses normally distributed price changes in each unit time, and the high deviations are achieved by correlations across time.

Works such as [Rog02, SV03] have analyzed the level of arbitrage present in FBM. The authors in [GN96] have analyzed the predictability of the FBM using a different loss function from ours. Other researchers [SV, AFW12] have studied the prediction problem as a game between an algorithm and an adversary, and derived that the optimal strategy for the adversary resembles a Brownian Motion. The work in [AFW12] was inspired by [DKM06] where the authors provide robust upper and lower bounds for pricing European call options, under the no-arbitrage assumption when the price process is assumed to be *discrete and discontinuous* as opposed to the Black Scholes model [BS73] where the price process is taken to be continuous.

1.3 Discussion and Future work

Note that our notion of δ-unpredictable requires the algorithm to fix its prediction for an entire interval I before looking at any of its bits. A stronger notion of unpredictability is to allow the algorithm to change its prediction for the interval after looking at bits within I. In other words, at every point the algorithm tries to simply predict the next bit, based on the bits it has seen so far. One could ask what is most adversarial distribution in this setting which achieves a high deviation. In this setting, for any sequence s, a bounded regret algorithm such as Weighted Majority can achieve a payoff of $|h(s)| - c\sqrt{|s|}$ where $c := \sqrt{2/\pi}$ [LW89, Cov65]. So for a distribution D which achieves typical deviation $k\sqrt{T}$, it is always possible to get a payoff of $(k-c)\sqrt{T}$. It is also fairly straightforward to construct a distribution D such that no algorithm can achieve an expected payoff better than $(k-c)\sqrt{T}$ even when it predicts one bit at a time. We also note that while the distributions inspired by FBM have some guarantees in terms of δ-unpredictability, they perform poorly in this model when one is allowed to predict based on all previous bits (see full version [PP13]).

One possible justification for our notion of δ-unpredictability is that changing predictions very often may have a cost associated with it. Although this may be a reasonable assumption (at least for financial markets), it is only a conjecture at this point and we invite further comments on this issue.

An interesting direction for further research is to look for natural constraints on real world processes which provably result in the formation of fractal-like processes.

2. PRELIMINARIES

Here is some common notation we use throughout the paper. For a sequence of bits $s \in \{-1, 1\}^T$, $h(s)$ denotes the sum of bits in s i.e. the *height* of s. We refer to the magnitude of height as deviation.

We will be working with several aggregate measures of deviation for a distribution such as median deviation (or generalized median), mean deviation and root-mean-squared deviation ($\sqrt{\mathbb{E}_{s \sim D}[h(s)^2]}$). Note that mean deviation is no more than root-mean-squared deviation and the generalized median is bounded by mean deviation up to constant factors using Markov's inequality (as long as the probability in generalized median is at least a constant). We will prove our upper bounds for root-mean-squared deviation and lower bounds for generalized median and so they will hold for all measures up to constants.

We will typically denote random variables by capital letters and fixed sequences by small letters.

3. CONSTRUCTION OF ADVERSARIAL DISTRIBUTIONS

In this section we formally construct our adversarial distributions. Each of these distributions has two parameters, l which is the length of the sequence in the base case and $\delta > 0$.

We will construct the distributions inductively: having constructed $D_\delta(n)$ we will show how to construct $D_\delta(2n)$ (the base case for $n = l$ is simply a random sequence in $\{-1, 1\}^l$). In both cases below, we describe the distribution $D_\delta(2n)$ in terms of how to generate a sequence $s \sim D_\delta(2n)$ given access to distribution $D_\delta(n)$.

FRACTAL RANDOM WALK (FRW$_{l,\delta}$) $(2n)$

1. Generate sequences s_1, s_2 independently according to FRW$_{l,\delta}(n)$

2. If height of s_1 is positive, change exactly $\delta \cdot h(s_1)$ -1's in s_2 to 1 arbitrarily (if they exist, otherwise change as many as possible). Similarly, if height of s_1 is negative, change exactly $\delta \cdot h(s_1)$ 1's in s_2 to -1 (if they exist). Call the resulting sequence s_2'.

3. Set $s = s_1 \cdot s_2'$ i.e. the concatenation of s_1 and s_2'

OPTIMUM FRACTAL RANDOM WALK (OPT-FRW$_{l,\delta}$)$(2n)$

1. Generate sequences s_1, s_2 independently according to OPT-FRW$_{l,\delta}(n)$

2. If height of s_1 is positive, change exactly $\delta\sqrt{n}$ -1's in s_2 to 1 arbitrarily (if they exist, otherwise change as many as possible). Similarly, if height of s_1 is negative, change exactly $\delta\sqrt{n}$ 1's in s_2 to -1 (if they exist). Call the resulting sequence s_2'.

3. Set $s = s_1 \cdot s_2'$ i.e. the concatenation of s_1 and s_2'

Note: Note that both distributions involve changing exactly r bits in s_2 where r is a real number. Intuitively, we want to change each bit of the appropriate sign in s_2 with probability r/n. However, it is simpler to analyze the deviation of the distributions when we change exactly r bits. The fact that r is a real number and not an integer will not make much difference since our base case l will be an increasing function of T (total number of bits to be produced) and so the discretization errors can be safely ignored.

3.1 High deviation

In this section we show that the distributions we constructed achieve high deviation with constant probability. What follows is a proof sketch for high deviation of distribution FRW$_{i,\delta}$. Next we will show this for for OPT-FRW$_{i,\delta}$.

THEOREM 3.1. *The distribution* FRW$_{l,\delta}(T)$ *achieves a deviation of* $T^{1/2+\Theta(\delta)}$ *with probability at least* $1/2 - \varepsilon$ *where* $\varepsilon \leq T^{-10}$.

Proof: To analyze the height distribution of FRW$_{l,\delta}$ it will be more convenient to define another process which is similar to FRW$_{l,\delta}$ but which can assume integer values instead of bits.

AUGMENTED FRACTAL RANDOM WALK (AFRW$_{l,\delta}$) $(2n)$

1. Generate sequences s_1, s_2 independently according to AFRW$_{l,\delta}(n)$

2. If height of s_1 is positive, change exactly $\delta \cdot h(s_1)$ -1's in s_2 to 1 (if they exist). Similarly, if height of s_1 is negative, change exactly $\delta \cdot h(s_2)$ 1's in s_2 to -1 (if they exist). Call the resulting sequence s_2'.

3. **Augment:** If there aren't enough -1's to flip in s_2, then add 2 to some of the numbers so that the increase in height is exactly $\delta \cdot h(s_1)$. Similarly for 1's.

4. Set $s = s_1 \cdot s_2'$ i.e. the concatenation of s_1 and s_2'

For the random variable $S \sim$ AFRW$_{l,\delta}$, we can exactly characterize the distribution of $h(S)$.

CLAIM 3.2. *(Claim 7.2) For* $n = 2^i \cdot l$, $S \sim$AFRW$_{l,\delta}(n)$,

$$h(S) = \sum_{U \subseteq [i]} r^{|U|} h(X_U) \qquad (1)$$

where $r = (1 + \delta)$ *and each* X_U *is independently and uniformly distributed in* $\{-1, 1\}^l$.

We then apply the Berry-Esseen theorem (see full version [PP13]) to show that the deviation of $|h(\text{AFRW}_{l,\delta})|$ is high.

LEMMA 3.3. *(proof in full version [PP13]) Median of* $|h(\text{AFRW}_{l,\delta}(n))|$ *is* $n^{1/2+\Omega(\delta)}$.

Next we show that the probability of executing step **Augment** in $\text{AFRW}_{l,\delta}$ is exponentially small. Note that when constructing a sequence of size T, the inductive steps of distribution $\text{AFRW}_{l,\delta}$ are executed at most $2T$ times. We show that when starting with sequences of size l where $l = 100 \log T$, the probability that sequence s_2 doesn't have enough 1's or -1's to flip at a particular stage is at most T^{-10}. Thus, taking a union bound over all inductive steps, we get the desired result.

CLAIM 3.4. *(proof in full version [PP13]) The probability that step* **Augment** *is executed at a particular step is at most* T^{-10}.

When the step **Augment** is not executed, the distributions AFRW and FRW are identical. Thus, the probability that the distribution $\text{FRW}_{l,\delta}(T)$ achieves a deviation of $T^{1/2+\Theta(\delta)}$ is at least $1/2 - T^{-10}$.

∎

THEOREM 3.5. *The distribution* $\text{OPT-FRW}_{l,\delta}(T)$ *achieves a deviation of* $\sqrt{T}(1 + \Omega(\delta \log T))$ *with constant probability for* $l := T^{-3/4}$.

Proof:
To prove the theorem it will be more convenient to define another process which is similar to $\text{OPT-FRW}_{l,\delta}$ but which can assume integer values instead of bits.

AUGMENTED OPTIMUM FRACTAL RANDOM WALK (AOPT-$\text{FRW}_{l,\delta})(2n)$

1. Generate sequences $s_1, s_2 \in \{-1, 1\}^n$ independently according to $\text{AOPT-FRW}_{l,\delta}(n)$

2. If height of s_1 is positive, change exactly $\delta \cdot \sqrt{n}$ -1's in s_2 to 1 (if they exist). Similarly, if height of s_1 is negative, change exactly $\delta \cdot \sqrt{n}$ 1's in s_2 to -1 (if they exist). Call the resulting sequence s_2'.

3. **Augment:** If there aren't enough (-1)'s to flip in s_2, then add 2 to some of the numbers so that the increase in height is exactly $\delta \cdot \sqrt{n}$. Similarly for 1's.

4. Set $s = s_1 \cdot s_2'$ i.e. the concatenation of s_1 and s_2'

First we observe that when $l = T^{-3/4}$, the probability of executing step **Augment** is exponentially small in T. To see this note that if all the base sequences of length l have at least $c(T) := \delta\sqrt{T} \log T$ (-1)'s and at least $c(T)$ 1's then the step **Augment** is never called. This is because every inductive step removes at most $\delta\sqrt{T}$ 1's or -1's at each stage and the number of times a base sequence is modified is at most $\log(T/l) \leq \log T$. Now note that by Chernoff bound, probability that a given base sequence does not have $c(T)$ 1's or (-1)'s is exponentially small in T. Finally note that the number of base sequences is at most T/l, so we can simply take a union bound over all of them.

For brevity, let $D := \text{OPT-FRW}_{l,\delta}$ and $D' := \text{AOPT-FRW}_{l,\delta}$. The next observation is that it suffices to prove that $\mathbb{E}[|h(D')|]$ is $\sqrt{T}(1 + \Omega(\delta \log T))$ and $\mathbb{E}[h(D')^2] = O(\mathbb{E}[|h(D')|]^2)$ to prove the theorem. To see this, let NA be the event that the step **Augment** is never executed at any point in the construction, then we have:-

$$
\begin{aligned}
\mathbb{E}_{s \sim D}[|h(s)|] &\geq \mathbb{E}_{s \sim D}[|h(s)| \mid NA] \\
&= \mathbb{E}_{s \sim D'}[|h(s)| \mid NA] \\
&= \mathbb{E}_{s \sim D'}[|h(s)|] - \Pr[NA] \cdot \max_{s \in D'} |h(s)|
\end{aligned}
$$

We already saw that $\Pr[NA]$ is exponentially small in T. Note that the maximum value of $|h(s)|$ is at most $T + \delta(\sqrt{T/2} + 2\sqrt{T/4}) + 4\sqrt{T/8} + \ldots + 2^{T/l-1}\sqrt{l}$ which is bounded by a polynomial in T. Thus, if $\mathbb{E}[|h(D')|]$ is $\sqrt{T}(1 + \Omega(\delta \log T))$ then so is $\mathbb{E}[|h(D)|]$. It is also easy to see that the maximum value of $h(s)^2$ is polynomial in T. This fact combined with our assumption about D', $\mathbb{E}[h(D')^2] = O(\mathbb{E}[|h(D')|]^2)$ implies that $\mathbb{E}[h(D)^2] = O(\mathbb{E}[|h(D)|]^2)$. Applying Lemma 7.4 to distribution D we get that deviation $\sqrt{T}(1 + \Omega(\delta \log T))$ is achieved with constant probability as required.

So to reiterate, we need to prove two things:-

- $\mathbb{E}[|h(D')|]$ is $\sqrt{T}(1 + \Omega(\delta \log T))$
- $\mathbb{E}[h(D')^2] = O(\mathbb{E}[|h(D')|]^2)$

From now on, we denote by S_T a random sequence S drawn from the distribution $D'(T)$. The random variable $h(S_T)$ can be written as $h(A_{T/2}) + h(B_{T/2}) + R$ where R is $\delta\sqrt{T/2}$ if $h(A_{T/2}) > 0$ and $-\delta\sqrt{T/2}$ otherwise. Here the pairs of variables $(A_{T/2}, B_{T/2})$ and $(B_{T/2}, R)$ are independent. Now define $h_T := h(S_T)$. We see that,

$$
\begin{aligned}
\mathbb{E}[h_T^2] &= \mathbb{E}[h(S_T)^2] \\
&= \mathbb{E}[(h(A_{T/2}) + h(B_{T/2}) + R)^2] \\
&= \mathbb{E}[h(A_{T/2})^2] + \mathbb{E}[h(B_{T/2})^2] + \mathbb{E}[R^2] + 2\mathbb{E}[h_A R] \\
&= 2\mathbb{E}[h_{T/2}^2] + \delta^2\sqrt{T/2} + 2\delta\sqrt{T/2}\mathbb{E}[|h_A|] \\
&\geq 2\mathbb{E}[h_{T/2}^2] + \delta\sqrt{2T}\mathbb{E}[|h_{T/2}|]
\end{aligned}
$$

The following claim gives a lower bound for $\mathbb{E}[|h_T|]$.

CLAIM 3.6.
$$
\mathbb{E}[|h_T|] \geq \frac{\mathbb{E}[h_T^2]^2}{\mathbb{E}[h_T^4]^{3/4}}
$$

Proof: Let the random variables X, Y be defined as $X := |h_T|^{1/2}$, $Y := |h_T|^{3/2}$. By Cauchy-Schwartz,

$$
\begin{aligned}
\mathbb{E}[XY]^2 &\leq & \mathbb{E}[X^2] \cdot \mathbb{E}[Y^2] \\
\implies \mathbb{E}[h_T^2]^2 &\leq & \mathbb{E}[|h_T|] \cdot \mathbb{E}[|h_T|^3] \\
&\leq & \mathbb{E}[|h_T|] \cdot \mathbb{E}[h_T^4]^{3/4} \\
\implies \mathbb{E}[|h_T|] &\geq & \frac{\mathbb{E}[h_T^2]^2}{\mathbb{E}[h_T^4]^{3/4}}
\end{aligned}
$$

∎

Thus, we can say that

$$
\begin{aligned}
\mathbb{E}[h_T^2] &\geq 2\mathbb{E}[h_{T/2}^2] + \delta\sqrt{2T}\mathbb{E}[|h_{T/2}|] \\
&\geq 2\mathbb{E}[h_{T/2}^2] + \delta\sqrt{2T}\frac{\mathbb{E}[h_{T/2}^2]^2}{\mathbb{E}[h_{T/2}^4]^{3/4}} \\
&= 2\mathbb{E}[h_{T/2}^2] + \delta\sqrt{2T}\sqrt{\mathbb{E}[h_{T/2}^2]}\left(\frac{\mathbb{E}[h_{T/2}^2]}{\mathbb{E}[h_{T/2}^4]}\right)^{3/4}
\end{aligned}
$$

First, let's complete the proof assuming that $\frac{\mathbb{E}[h_T^2]^2}{\mathbb{E}[h_T^4]} \geq C$ for all T where C is an absolute constant. Let's substitute $g_T^2 := \mathbb{E}[h_T^2]/T$. Then,

$$\mathbb{E}[h_T^2] \geq 2\mathbb{E}[h_{T/2}^2] + \Omega(\delta)\sqrt{2T}\sqrt{\mathbb{E}[h_{T/2}^2]}$$

$$\implies T \cdot g_T^2 \geq 2 \cdot (T/2) \cdot g_{T/2}^2 + \Omega(\delta) \cdot \sqrt{2T} \cdot \sqrt{T/2} \cdot \sqrt{g_{T/2}^2}$$

$$\implies g_T^2 \geq g_{T/2}^2 + \Omega(\delta) \cdot g_{T/2}$$

$$= (g_{T/2} + \Omega(\delta))^2 - O(\delta^2)$$

$$\implies g_T \geq g_{T/2} + \Omega(\delta)$$

For the base case, we have $\mathbb{E}[h_l^2] = l$, thus $g_l^2 = 1$. Thus,

$$g_T \geq 1 + \Omega(\delta) \cdot \log(T/l) = 1 + \Omega(\delta) \cdot \log T^{1/4} = 1 + \Omega(\delta \log T)$$

Thus, $\mathbb{E}[h_T^2] \geq T \cdot g_T^2 = T(1 + \Omega(\delta \log T)^2)$. By Lemma 3.6 and Lemma 3.7, this implies $\mathbb{E}[|h_T|] \geq \sqrt{T}(1 + \Omega(\delta \log T))$. These statements together imply both the guarantees we set out to prove about D'.

It remains to prove the following lemma.

LEMMA 3.7. $\frac{\mathbb{E}[h_T^2]^2}{\mathbb{E}[h_T^4]} \geq C$ for all T where C is an absolute constant.

Proof: Recall that for S_T drawn according to $\text{AOPT-FRW}_{l,\delta}(T)$, we have $h(S_T) = h(A_{T/2}) + h(B_{T/2}) + R$. We already saw that $\mathbb{E}[h_T^2] \geq 2\mathbb{E}[h_{T/2}^2]$. Let $r_T := \frac{\mathbb{E}[h_T^4]}{\mathbb{E}[h_T^2]^2}$. We need to show that $r_T \leq C$. We have,

$$r_T = \frac{\mathbb{E}[h_T^4]}{\mathbb{E}[h_T^2]^2} \geq \frac{\mathbb{E}[h_T^4]}{4\mathbb{E}[h_{T/2}^2]^2}$$

Now, let's write a recurrence for $\mathbb{E}[h_T^4]$.

$$\mathbb{E}[h_T^4] = \mathbb{E}[h(S_T^4)]$$

$$= \mathbb{E}[(h_A + h(s_1) + R)^4]$$

$$= \mathbb{E}[h_A^4] + \mathbb{E}[h(s_1)^4] + \mathbb{E}[R^4] + 6\mathbb{E}[h_A^2 h(s_1)^2]$$

$$+ 6\mathbb{E}[h_A^2 R^2] + 6\mathbb{E}[h(s_1)^2 R^2]$$

$$+ 4\mathbb{E}[h_A R^3] + 4\mathbb{E}[h_A^3 R]$$

$$= 2\mathbb{E}[h_{T/2}^4] + \delta^4 (T/2)^2 + 6\mathbb{E}[h_{T/2}^2]^2$$

$$+ 12\delta^2 (T/2)\mathbb{E}[h_{T/2}^2] + 4\delta^3 (T/2)^{3/2}\mathbb{E}[|h_{T/2}|]$$

$$+ 4\delta\sqrt{T/2}\mathbb{E}[|h_{T/2}|^3]$$

$$\leq 2\mathbb{E}[h_{T/2}^4] + O(\delta^4 T^2) + 6\mathbb{E}[h_{T/2}^2]^2$$

$$+ O(\delta^2 T\mathbb{E}[h_{T/2}^2])$$

$$+ O(\delta^3 T^{3/2})\sqrt{\mathbb{E}[h_{T/2}^2]} + O(\delta\sqrt{T})\mathbb{E}[h_{T/2}^4]^{3/4}$$

Dividing both sides by $4\mathbb{E}[h_{T/2}^2]^2$ and using the fact that $\mathbb{E}[h_T^4] \geq \mathbb{E}[h_T^2]^2 \geq T^2$, we get:-

$$r_T \leq \frac{\mathbb{E}[h_T^4]}{4\mathbb{E}[h_{T/2}^2]^2}$$

$$\leq (1/2) \cdot r_{T/2} + O(\delta^4) + (3/2) + O(\delta^2) + O(\delta^3) + O(\delta)r_{T/2}^{3/4}$$

$$\leq (3/4) \cdot r_{T/2} + O(1)$$

which is clearly bounded above by an absolute constant for all T.

∎

Thus, the theorem is proved.

∎

3.2 Unpredictability

In this section we show that the distribution $\text{OPT-FRW}_{l,\delta}$ is δ-unpredictable.

We first observe that it suffices to work with *aligned* intervals i.e. intervals which start and end at appropriate powers of 2.

DEFINITION 3.8. *(Aligned interval)*
We assume here that T is a power of 2. An aligned interval is one which is obtained by breaking $[1, T]$ into 2^i equal parts for $i \in [0, \log T]$ and picking one of the parts. So for instance the first part is always $[1, 2^i]$.

In other words, an interval $[p + 1, p + x]$ given by $p \in [0, T]$, $x \in [1, T - p]$ is said to be an aligned interval if $p = j \cdot 2^i$ and $x = 2^i$ for some $i \in [0, \log T]$ and $j \in [0, T - 2^i]$.

CLAIM 3.9. *If distribution $D(T)$ is ε-unpredictable with respect to all aligned intervals then it is $c \cdot \varepsilon$-unpredictable with respect to all intervals, where $c := \frac{\sqrt{2}}{\sqrt{2}-1}$.*

The proof of Claim 3.9 is fairly straightforward and is moved to the appendix (Claim 7.3).

THEOREM 3.10. *The distribution $\text{OPT-FRW}_{l,\delta}$ is $O(\delta)$-unpredictable.*

Proof: [Sketch]

It can be shown that the process $\text{OPT-FRW}_{l,\delta}$ has very similar properties if in Step 2 of the construction, instead of changing exactly $\delta \cdot \sqrt{n}$ bits in s_2 we change each bit (of appropriate sign) in s_2 with probability $\frac{\delta}{\sqrt{n}}$. Here we assume this fact without proving it.

We need to show that for every A, s and I, $\mathbb{E}[A_s(I)] \leq O(\delta) \cdot \sqrt{|I|}$ where s and I are as in Definition 1.1. We may assume that I is an aligned interval (Claim 3.9).

From the construction it is clear that $\mathbb{E}[A_s(I)]$ is largest when $h(s) = |s|$ or $h(s) = -|s|$ i.e. all the bits before I are of the same sign. Without loss of generality assume $h_s = s$. Also, if there were no prefix (i.e. $|s| = 0$) then $\mathbb{E}[A_s(I)] = 0$ since the construction is symmetric. To provide an upper bound on $\mathbb{E}[A_s(I)]$ we simply need to bound the expected number of -1's which are changed to $+1$'s due to the existence of s. We will use a simple union bound on the total probability of changing a -1 to a 1 according to the construction. This probability can be split into 2 parts, the first which occurs because of bit sequences immediately preceding I of length less than I and the second because of bit sequences immediately preceding I of length more than I. For sequences of the first kind, the number of bits changed in I is exactly $\delta \cdot \sqrt{l}$ while for sequences of the second kind we may assume that the expected number of bits changed in I is $\frac{\delta \cdot |I|}{\sqrt{l}}$ where l is the length of the bit sequence under discussion. Thus, the total probability is bounded by:-

$$\sum_{i=1}^{\infty} (\min(|I|, 2^i) \cdot \delta)/\sqrt{2^i} = \sum_{i=1}^{\log |I|} \delta \cdot \sqrt{2^i} + \sum_{i=\log |I|+1}^{\infty} \delta \cdot \frac{|I|}{\sqrt{2^i}}$$

Both terms can be bounded by $\delta \cdot \sqrt{|I|} \cdot \sum_{i=0}^{\infty} 1/\sqrt{2^i}$ and so the combined sum is at most $O(\delta) \cdot \sqrt{|I|}$. ∎

4. DEVIATION UPPER BOUND FOR ADVERSARIAL DISTRIBUTIONS

In this section we prove that the deviation achieved by OPT-FRW is essentially the best possible for a δ-unpredictable distribution up to a constant factor.

THEOREM 4.1. *The highest Root-Mean-Square deviation that can be achieved by a δ-unpredictable distribution on sequences of length T is $\sqrt{T}(1 + O(\delta \log T))$.*

Proof:

Let $\mathcal{D}_\delta(T)$ be the set of all δ-unpredictable distributions over sequences of length T, and let $h_n = \max_{D \in \mathcal{D}_\delta(n)} \mathbb{E}_{s \sim D}[h(s)^2]$. Clearly, $h_1 = 1$. We need to show that $\sqrt{h_T} = \sqrt{T}(1 + O(\delta \log T))$.

Let $D(T)$ be a δ-unpredictable distribution which maximizes $\mathbb{E}_{s \sim D}[h(s)^2]$. Given a sequence $s \sim D$, we write $s = s_1 s_2$ where s_1 and s_2 are of length $n/2$ each. Then we have,

$$
\begin{aligned}
h_n &= \mathbb{E}_{s \sim D}[h(s)^2] \\
&= \mathbb{E}[(h(s_1) + h(s_2))^2] \\
&= \mathbb{E}[h(s_1)^2] + \mathbb{E}[h(s_2)^2] + 2\mathbb{E}[h(s_1)h(s_2)] \\
&\leq 2h_{n/2} + 2 \sum_{x=0}^{n/2} \Pr[h(s_1) = x] \cdot x \cdot \mathbb{E}[h(s_2) \mid h(s_1) = x] \\
&\leq 2h_{n/2} + 2\delta\sqrt{n/2} \sum_{x=0}^{n/2} \Pr[h(s_1) = x] \cdot |x| \\
&= 2h_{n/2} + \delta \cdot \sqrt{2n} \cdot \mathbb{E}[|h(s_1)|] \\
&\leq 2h_{n/2} + \delta \cdot \sqrt{2n} \cdot \sqrt{\mathbb{E}[h(s_1)^2]} \\
&\leq 2h_{n/2} + \delta \cdot \sqrt{2n} \cdot \sqrt{h_{n/2}}
\end{aligned}
$$

The first inequality follows from the definition of $h_{n/2}$. The second inequality follows from the fact that the distribution of s_2 is also δ-unpredictable.

Let's substitute, $g_n^2 := h_n/n$. Then $h_{n/2} = (ng_{n/2}^2)/2$ and $\sqrt{h_{n/2}} = \sqrt{n/2}\sqrt{g_n^2/2}$. Thus, we get

$$
\begin{aligned}
ng_n^2 &\leq & ng_{n/2}^2 + \delta n \sqrt{g_{n/2}^2} \\
\implies g_n^2 &\leq & g_{n/2}^2 + \delta\sqrt{g_{n/2}^2} \\
&\leq & \left(\sqrt{g_{n/2}^2} + \delta/2\right)^2 \\
\implies g_n &\leq & g_{n/2} + \delta/2
\end{aligned}
$$

Since $g_1 = 1$, this gives the upper bound $g_n \leq 1 + (\delta/2)\log n$. This implies $\sqrt{h_n} = \sqrt{\mathbb{E}_{A \sim D}[h_A^2]} \leq \sqrt{n}(1 + \delta/2 \log n)$. ∎

5. FRACTAL NATURE OF DETERMINISTIC INVERTING SEQUENCES

We will argue that the optimal sequence with height h and inversion ratio α is achieved by the following fractal-like recursive process. To construct a sequence of height h, recursively generate a sequence s_1 of height $(1 + \alpha/2) \cdot h$ and s_2 of height $\alpha \cdot h$ respectively. Concatenate s_1, an inverted copy of s_2 followed by another copy of s_1. For simplicity for explanation we will ignore rounding errors from the discretization.

It turns out that for large h, the ratio of lengths of s_1 and s_2 is fixed to $\left(\frac{1+\alpha}{2}\right)^{1/\theta} : \alpha^{1/\theta}$ where θ is a constant defined below.

CLAIM 5.1. *The above process produces an α-inverting sequence for α smaller than some constant.*

Proof: Observe that by recurrence any interval that is contained within s_1 or s_2 is α-inverting. The full interval consisting of the three concatenated strings also has an α-inversion; and so are the intervals that span the first two and the last two strings. So we only need to argue about intervals that span parts of multiple of these pieces. Consider for example an interval that spans across some suffix of s_1 and some prefix of the inverted copy of s_2. Now for small enough α, the two parts of the interval have heights of opposite signs. So the α-inversion in the piece with the larger absolute height suffices to produce an α-inversion in the interval. The same argument can be applied for intervals that span part of the first and the third sequence. ∎

CLAIM 5.2. *Let s be an α-inverting sequence of length t (Definition 1.2), where α is bounded above by a constant. Then the highest deviation that can be achieved by s for large t is t^θ where θ is the solution to the equation $1 = 2((1 + \alpha)/2)^{1/\theta} + (\alpha)^{1/\theta}$. Furthermore, this deviation is actually achieved by the above process.*

Proof: [Sketch] We will compute the amount of time $t(h)$ when the process described above first achieves a height $h > 0$. By the construction, $t(h)$ satisfies the recurrence $t(h) = 2t \cdot ((1 + \alpha)h/2) + t(\alpha h)$. In the limit, if this recurrence has a solution of the form $h^{1/\theta}$ then note that $h^{1/\theta} = 2((1 + \alpha)h/2)^{1/\theta} + (\alpha h)^{1/\theta}$ which means that $1 = 2((1 + \alpha)/2)^{1/\theta} + (\alpha)^{1/\theta}$. The proof can be formalized by sandwiching the solution to the recurrence in the limit between the functions h^{1/θ_1} and h^{1/θ_2} where θ_1 and θ_2 approach θ from above and below.

To prove the lower bound, let $t(h)$ denote the required time to produce a height of absolute value h for any α-inverting sequence. We will prove that for large h, $t(h)$ approaches $h^{1/\theta}$. We know that for large enough t there must be an inversion with ratio α. So to achieve height h in time t there must be a sub-interval with height less than $-\alpha h$. So t can be broken into three segments of lengths t_1, t_2, t_3 with heights h_1, h_2, h_3 such that $h = h_1 + h_2 + h_3$ where $h_2 \leq -\alpha h$. We wish to minimize $t(h) = t_1 + t_2 + t_3 \geq t(h_1) + t(h_2) + t(h_3)$. Since $t(h)$ is non-decreasing in h, we may set $h_2 = -\alpha h$ and $h_1 + h_3 = h - h_2 = (1 + \alpha)h$ giving $t(h) = \min t(h_1) + t(h_2) + t(\alpha h)$ where $h_1 + h_3 = (1 + \alpha)h$.

Note that if $t(h)$ is of the form $h^{1/\theta}$ then it is convex and so $t(h_1) + t(h_2)$ is minimized when $h_1 = h_3 = \frac{(1+\alpha) \cdot h}{2}$ giving $t(h) = 2t(\frac{(1+\alpha) \cdot h}{2}) + t(\alpha h)$ whose solution approaches $h^{1/\theta}$ in the limit. That the solution must approach $h^{1/\theta}$, by looking at the behavior of $\log_t h$ in the limit and sandwiching it between θ_1 and θ_2 that approach θ from above and below. ∎

The above sequence when plotted a graph becomes a fractal in the limit for $t \to \infty$. For large t look at the graph obtained for the cumulative plot of the above sequence scaled by a factor of t in the x-axis and t^θ in the y-axis. The box-counting-dimension of the is fractal is $2 - \theta$. This matches the fractal-dimension of the corresponding Fractional Brownian Motion.

CLAIM 5.3. *In the limit the cumulative plot of the above sequence (scaled appropriately) is a fractal with box-counting dimension $2 - \theta$.*

Proof: [Sketch] The box counting dimension is given by $\lim_{\varepsilon \to 0} \log N(\varepsilon) / \log(1/\varepsilon)$, where $N(\varepsilon)$ is the number of boxes of size ε by ε required to cover the plot when plotted on a graph with grid size ε. The plot is obtained by recursively replaing a line segment by three segment. We continue the recursion until the plot is divided into segments which stride a length $O(\varepsilon)$ along the x-axis. In each segment the plot will span a change of $O(\varepsilon^\theta)$ along the y-axis. The number of boxes required to cover the plot along that segment is $O(\varepsilon^\theta)/\varepsilon$. So the total number of boxes required is $N(\varepsilon) = \frac{1}{O(\varepsilon)} \frac{O(\varepsilon^\theta)}{\varepsilon} = (1/\varepsilon)^{2-\theta}$. ∎

6. FRACTAL NATURE OF ADVERSARIAL DISTRIBUTIONS

Here we show that any distribution which is δ-unpredictable must have a fractal like nature (Theorem 1.7). We will first show that δ-unpredictable distributions are also unpredictable in a slightly stronger sense.

DEFINITION 6.1 (ADAPTIVE INTERVAL ALGORITHM). *An interval prediction algorithm is said to be adaptive if it can choose to stop making predictions on interval I at any point within I based on the bits it has seen so far. Note that we do not allow the prediction of the algorithm to depend on the bits in I, the only decision the algorithm can make based on bits in I is to stop predicting earlier than the end point of I.*

DEFINITION 6.2 (ADAPTIVELY δ-UNPREDICTABLE). *A distribution D is said to be adaptively δ-unpredictable if for any adaptive algorithm A, sequence of bits s and interval I, $\mathbb{E}[A_s(I)] \leq \delta \cdot \sqrt{l}$ where l is the expected time for which A continues making a prediction in I.*

Here the bits in I are produced according to D conditioned on having produced s immediately before I, similarly as in Definition 1.1.

THEOREM 6.3. *A δ-predictable distribution is also adaptively $O(\delta)$-unpredictable.*

Proof:
Let D be a δ-predictable distribution and A' an adaptive interval algorithm. We first show that $\mathbb{E}[A'_s(I)] \leq 2\delta \cdot \sqrt{|I|}$ i.e. we replace the *expected* time for which A' continues making a prediction in I by the *maximum* time for which it makes a prediction.

We will construct a non-adaptive algorithm A such that $\mathbb{E}[|A_s(I) - A'_s(I)|] \leq \delta \cdot \sqrt{|I|}$. Since $\mathbb{E}[A_s(I)] \leq \delta \cdot \sqrt{|I|}$ (D is δ-unpredictable) this implies that $\mathbb{E}[A'_s(I)] \leq 2\delta \cdot \sqrt{|I|}$

Let p_u be the probability of producing a sequence of bits u as a prefix in I according to distribution D. Let E be the set of sequences u such that the algorithm A' stops making predictions on seeing u. Then $\sum_{u \in E} p_u = 1$.

Let $P_u(A)$ denote the expected payoff of A on the remaining part of I conditioned on the event that A' has stopped making

predictions. Then $P_u(A) \leq \delta \cdot \sqrt{|I| - |u|} \leq \delta \cdot \sqrt{|I|}$. Thus, $\mathbb{E}[|A_s(I) - A'_s(I)|] \leq \sum_{u \in E} p_u \cdot \delta \cdot \sqrt{|I|} = \delta \cdot \sqrt{|I|}$.

Now we extend the proof to the case where A' makes a prediction for expected time x rather than maximum time x.

Let q_i be the probability that A' makes a prediction for time more thant $2^i x$. By Markov's inequality, $q_i < 2^{-i}$. Also, $q_i = \sum_{u \in E:|u|=2^i} p_u$, where p_u is as defined above. We will bound the payoff of A' in phases where the ith phase consists of bits between $2^i x$ to $2^{i+1} x$ from the start of I, and show that it is at most $2\delta \cdot q_i \cdot \sqrt{2^i x}$. For a fixed sequence u, the payoff of algorithm A' in phase i conditioned on having seen u is at most $2\delta\sqrt{2^i x}$ (proved above). Thus, the total payoff of A' in phase i is at most $2\delta \cdot q_i \cdot \sqrt{2^i x}$. Finally, the expected payoff of A' over all phases is at most:

$\sum_i 2\delta q_i \sqrt{2^i x} \leq 2\delta \cdot \sum_i \sqrt{2^i x}/2^i \leq O(\delta) \cdot \sqrt{x}$

which proves that D is adaptively $O(\delta)$-unpredictable. ∎

Now we turn to showing that any adaptively δ-unpredictable distribution has a fractal like nature.

THEOREM 6.4. *If a distribution over T bit sequences is adaptively δ-unpredictable (Definition 6.2) then it is (α, q)-inverting for some constants α, q. Further by dropping the inversion ratio α to $\Theta(1/\log T)$ the probability q can be made as high as $1 - 1/T^{\Omega(1)}$ for all intervals of length at least $\Omega(\log T)$. Thus the condition holds with high probability simultaneously for all such intervals.*

Proof:
For a certain given history of bits consider the interval I. Let $h(I)$ denote the random variable that denotes the height of this interval. Let θ, p be such that the deviation in I exceeds θ with constant probability p (this generalizes the case when θ is the median deviation.)

We will show that some prefixes of I must achieve height at least $\alpha\theta$ and $-\alpha\theta$ each with constant probability (where $\alpha < 1/2$ is a constant). To show this, note that either $h \geq \theta$ or $h \leq -\theta$ with probabiity at least $p/2$. Assume it is the former without loss of generality. So we only need to prove that $h \leq -\alpha\theta$ with probability at least $p/4$. Assume the contrary and we will see that the interval cannot be δ-unpredictable.

Consider a prediction algorithm that predicts $+1$ for the interval but adaptively terminates its betting if the height drops to $-\alpha\theta$ or if the height exceeds θ, whichever happens first. Since the algorithm hits the lower limit of $-\alpha\theta$ only with probability at most $p/4$, so with at least probability $p/4$ it must realize the upper limit (payoff) of θ (since $2\alpha < 1$). In all remaining cases the payoff is at least $-\alpha\theta$. So the expected payoff is at least $(p/4)(2\alpha\theta) - (1 - p/4)(\alpha\theta)$ which needs to be at most $\delta\sqrt{x}$. This is not possible if $\alpha = \Theta(1/p)$ and $\theta = \Omega(\delta \cdot \sqrt{|I|})$. Thus if the height in an interval has high magnitude with constant probability, it must reach in either direction with constant probability.

To convert this into a high probabililty argument, we will use (at most) s iterations of the above prediction algorithm each with limits that depend on θ/s instead of θ. Each iteration has limits of θ/s and $-\alpha\theta/s$ on the sum of bits seen during its execution. The next iteration is initiated only if either of the upper or lower limit is reached in the previous iteration and if not all $|I|$ bits in the full interval are exhausted. From the previous argument, conditioned on the event that a certain iteration is initiated, if an iteration is executed for expected time $O(|I|/s)$ and hits the upper limit with probability $p/2$ then it must also hit the lower limit with probability $p/4$. Since the final height exceeds θ with constant probability $p/2$, in such cases all s iterations have been initiated. Since there are at most s iterations and all are initated with constant probability, at least half of them must have an expected length of $O(|I|/s)$ conditioned on the event that they are initiated; otherwise the total expected time of all the s iterations will exceed $|I|$. Conditioned on the event that the ith iteration is initiated, with probability $p/4$ it must hit at least one of its two limits; otherwise the total height will not reach θ with probability $p/2$. So conditioned on the event that the ith iteration is initiated, for at least half the iterations, it must hit the lower limit (and upper limit) with probability at least $p/4$. So conditioned on the event that all s iterations are initiated the probability that none of them hit the lower limit and also the upper limit is at most $(p/4)^{s/2}$.

Thus, it follows that by choosing $s = \Theta(1)$, we get an α inversion for constant α with constant probability. This proves the first part of the theorem. For the second part, note that with probability at least $1 - (p/4)^{s/2}$ either the final height is less than θ or some subinterval has height $-\alpha\theta/s$. For $s = \Theta(\log T)$ the probability that the final height exceeds θ and there is no inversion of height $\leq -\alpha/s\theta$ is negligible. ∎

7. MISCELLANEOUS THEOREMS

THEOREM 7.1. *The distribution $D := \mathrm{FRW}_{l,\delta}$ is $O(\delta)$-unpredictable in a weak sense i.e. $\mathbb{E}_{s,I}[A_s(I)] \leq O(\delta) \cdot h_{|I|}$ where $h_n := \mathbb{E}_{s\sim D(n)}[|h(s)|]$. Here s, I and A are as in Definition 1.1. Note that the expectation on the left is taken over I as well as the prefix s as opposed to Definition 1.1 where s is fixed and the expectation is over I only.*

Proof: [Sketch]

It can be shown that the process $\mathrm{FRW}_{l,\delta}$ has very similar properties if in Step 2 of the construction, instead of changing exactly $\delta \cdot h(s_1)$ bits in s_2 we change each bit (of appropriate sign) in s_2 with probability $\frac{\delta \cdot h(s_1)}{n}$. Here we assume this fact without proving it.

We need to show that $\mathbb{E}_{s,I}[A_s(I)] \leq O(\delta) \cdot h_{|I|}$. We may assume that I is an aligned interval (Claim 3.9). Let $s(i)$ be the suffix of length i in s. Then,

$$\mathbb{E}_s[\mathbb{E}_I[A_s(I)]$$

$$\leq \sum_{i=0}^{\log|I|} \delta \cdot \mathbb{E}_s[|h(s(2^i))|] + \sum_{i=\log|I|+1}^{\infty} \frac{\delta \cdot \mathbb{E}_s[|h(s(2^i)|] \cdot |I|}{2^i}$$

$$\leq O(\delta) \cdot \mathbb{E}_s[|h(s(|I|))|] +$$

$$O(\delta) \cdot \mathbb{E}_s[|h(s(|I|))|](1/2^{1/4} + 1/4^{1/4} + \ldots)$$

$$\leq O(\delta) \cdot \mathbb{E}_s[|h(s(|I|))|]$$

$$= O(\delta) \cdot h_{|I|}$$

where the second inequality uses $h_T = T^{1/2+\Theta(\delta)} \leq T^{3/4}$ (Theorem 3.1). ∎

CLAIM 7.2. *For $n = 2^i \cdot l$, $S \sim \mathrm{AFRW}_{l,\delta}(n)$,*

$$h(S) = \sum_{U \subseteq [i]} r^{|U|} h(X_U) \tag{2}$$

where $r = (1+\delta)$ and each X_U is independently and uniformly distributed in $\{-1,1\}^l$.

Proof: We will prove the claim by induction on i. For $i = 0$, the claim clearly holds.

Assume that the claim holds for $i = k$, and let $n := 2^{i+1} \cdot l$. Let $S = S_1 \cdot S_2'$ be the sequence produced by the distribution as described above where S_1 and S_2' are random sequences of length $n/2$ each. Because of step **Augment**, it is clear that $h(S_2') = h(S_2) + \delta h(S_1)$ which means $h(S) = (1+\delta)h(S_1) + h(S_2)$. Thus,

$$h(S) = rh(S_1) + h(S_2)$$

$$= \sum_{U \subseteq [k]} r(r^{|U|} h(X_U)) + \sum_{V \subseteq [k]} r(r^{|V|} h(X_V))$$

$$= \sum_{U \subseteq [k]} r^{|U \cup \{k+1\}|} h(X_{U \cup \{k+1\}})$$

$$+ \sum_{V \subseteq [k]} r(r^{|V|} h(X_V))$$

$$= \sum_{U \subseteq [k+1]} (r^{|U|} h(X_U))$$

∎

CLAIM 7.3. *If distribution $D(T)$ is ε-unpredictable with respect to all aligned intervals then it is $c \cdot \varepsilon$-unpredictable with respect to all intervals, where $c := \frac{\sqrt{2}}{\sqrt{2}-1}$.*

Proof: Consider an interval I of size x. If I is an aligned interval we are done, otherwise we write it as the minimal union of aligned intervals (take out the largest aligned interval in I and repeat). There are three possibilities:-

1. $I = I_1 \cup I_2$ is a union of two intervals of size $x/2$ each (eg. the interval $[T/4 + 1, 3T/4]$)

2. $I = I_1 \cup I_2 \cup \ldots \cup I_k$, where each I_j is of a different size. Note that all interval sizes on the right are powers of 2 and strictly less than x

3. $I = J \cup J'$ where each J can be written as a union of intervals as in 1 or 2 above

In the first case,

$$|\mathbb{E}[h_I]| \leq |\mathbb{E}[h_{I_1}]| + |\mathbb{E}[h_{I_1}]| \leq 2 \cdot \varepsilon \cdot \sqrt{x/2} = \sqrt{2} \cdot \varepsilon \cdot \sqrt{x}$$

In the second case,

$$|\mathbb{E}[h_I]| \leq \sum_{j=1}^{k} |\mathbb{E}[h_{I_j}]| \leq \varepsilon \cdot \sqrt{x} \cdot \sum_{j=1}^{\infty} \sqrt{1/2^j} = \frac{1}{\sqrt{2}-1} \cdot \varepsilon \cdot \sqrt{x}$$

In the third case,

$$|\mathbb{E}[h_I]| \leq |\mathbb{E}[h_J]| + |\mathbb{E}[h_J']| \leq \frac{1}{\sqrt{2}-1} \cdot \varepsilon \cdot \sqrt{|J|} +$$

$$\frac{1}{\sqrt{2}-1} \cdot \varepsilon \cdot \sqrt{|J'|} \leq \frac{\sqrt{2}}{\sqrt{2}-1} \cdot \varepsilon \cdot \sqrt{|I|}$$

∎

CLAIM 7.4. *For any random variable X that only takes non negative values and $E[X^2] = O((E[X])^2)$, $Pr[X \geq \Omega(E[X])] = \Omega(1)$*

Proof: Let $\mu = E[X]$. The the standard deviation $\sigma = O(\mu) = c\mu$ (say) where c is at most some constant. We will bound $E[X|X \geq \mu + rc\mu]$ for any $r \in \mathbb{N}$. Note that $Pr[X \geq \mu + rc\mu] \leq 1/r^2$.

So $E[X|X \geq \mu + rc\mu] \leq (\mu + rc\mu) + \mu \sum_{i>r} 1/i^2 \leq (\mu + rc\mu) + c\mu/r$.

Now $\mu = E[X] = Pr[X < \mu + rc\mu]E[X|X < \mu + rc\mu] + Pr[X \geq \mu + rc\mu]E[X|X \geq \mu + rc\mu] \leq (1 - 1/r^2)E[X|X < \mu + rc\mu] + (1/r^2)(\mu + rc\mu + c\mu/r)$.

By setting r to be a constant that is at least some large multiple of c, we can conclude that $E[X|X < \mu + rc\mu] = \Omega(\mu)$. So this conditioned random variable X has maximum value and mean value that are the same upto constant factors. Thus it must exceed $\Omega(\mu)$ with constant probability. So the unconditioned random variable X must also exceed $\Omega(\mu)$ with a smaller constant probability. ∎

8. ACKNOWLEDGEMENTS

We thank Alex Andoni and Samuel Ieong for useful discussions.

9. REFERENCES

[AFW12] J. Abernethy, R.M. Frongillo, and A. Wibisono. Minimax option pricing meets black-scholes in the limit. In *Proceedings of the 44th symposium on Theory of Computing*, pages 1029–1040. ACM, 2012.

[BPS04] E. Bayraktar, H.V. Poor, and K.R. Sircar. Estimating the fractal dimension of the s&p 500 index using wavelet analysis. *International Journal of Theoretical and Applied Finance*, 7(05):615–643, 2004.

[BS73] F. Black and M. Scholes. The pricing of options and corporate liabilities. *The journal of political economy*, pages 637–654, 1973.

[BT03] B.O. Bradley and M.S. Taqqu. Financial risk and heavy tails. *Handbook of Heavy-Tailed Distributions in Finance*, pages 35–103, 2003.

[Cov65] T. Cover. Behaviour of sequential predictors of binary sequences. *Transactions of the Fourth Prague Conference on Information Theory, Statistical Decision Functions, Random Processes*, 1965.

[DKM06] P. DeMarzo, I. Kremer, and Y. Mansour. Online trading algorithms and robust option pricing. 2006.

[DSS90] P. Davy, A. Sornette, and D. Sornette. Some consequences of a proposed fractal nature of continental faulting. *Nature*, 348(6296):56–58, 1990.

[Fal] Kenneth Falconer. Front matter. *Fractal Geometry: Mathematical Foundations and Applications, Second Edition*, pages i–xxvii.

[FP98] A.J. Frost and R.R. Prechter. *Elliott wave principle: key to market behavior*. Bookworld Services, 1998.

[GN96] G. Gripenberg and I. Norros. On the prediction of fractional brownian motion. *Journal of Applied Probability*, pages 400–410, 1996.

[LW89] N. Littlestone and M.K. Warmuth. The weighted majority algorithm. *FOCS*, 1989.

[Man04] B. Mandelbrot. *Fractals and Chaos: the Mandelbrot set and beyond*, volume 3. Springer, 2004.

[Man05] B.B. Mandelbrot. The inescapable need for fractal tools in finance. *Annals of Finance*, 1(2):193–195, 2005.

[MPP84] B.B. Mandelbrot, D.E. Passoja, and A.J. Paullay. Fractal character of fracture surfaces of metals. 1984.

[MVN68] B.B. Mandelbrot and J.W. Van Ness. Fractional brownian motions, fractional noises and applications. *SIAM review*, 10(4):422–437, 1968.

[Nol03] J. Nolan. *Stable distributions: models for heavy-tailed data*. Birkhauser, 2003.

[Nor95] I. Norros. On the use of fractional brownian motion in the theory of connectionless networks. *Selected Areas in Communications, IEEE Journal on*, 13(6):953–962, 1995.

[NR06] D. Nualart Rodón. Fractional brownian motion: stochastic calculus and applications. In *Proceedings oh the International Congress of Mathematicians: Madrid, August 22-30, 2006: invited lectures*, pages 1541–1562, 2006.

[PP13] Rina Panigrahy and Preyas Popat. Fractal structures in adversarial prediction. *CoRR*, abs/1304.7576, 2013.

[RMF+05] S.T. Rachev, C. Menn, F.J. Fabozzi, et al. *Fat-tailed and skewed asset return distributions: Implications for risk management, portfolio selection, and option pricing*, volume 139. Wiley, 2005.

[Rog02] L.C.G. Rogers. Arbitrage with fractional brownian motion. *Mathematical Finance*, 7(1):95–105, 2002.

[SV] G. Shafer and V. Vovk. *Probability and finance: it's only a game!*, volume 373. Wiley-Interscience.

[SV03] T. Sottinen and E. Valkeila. On arbitrage and replication in the fractional black–scholes pricing model. *Statistics & Decisions/International mathematical Journal for stochastic methods and models*, 21(2/2003):93–108, 2003.

[Voi05] J. Voit. *The statistical mechanics of financial markets*. Springer, 2005.

On Learning Mixture Models for Permutations

Flavio Chierichetti*
Sapienza University of Rome
Rome, Italy
flavio@di.uniroma1.it

Anirban Dasgupta
IIT
Gandhinagar, India
anirban.dasgupta@gmail.com

Ravi Kumar
Google
Mountain View, CA
ravi.k53@gmail.com

Silvio Lattanzi
Google
New York, NY
silviolat@gmail.com

ABSTRACT

In this paper we consider the problem of learning a mixture of permutations, where each component of the mixture is generated by a stochastic process. Learning permutation mixtures arises in practical settings when a set of items is ranked by different sub-populations and the rankings of users in a sub-population tend to agree with each other. While there is some applied work on learning such mixtures, they have been mostly heuristic in nature.

We study the problem where the permutations in a mixture component are generated by the classical Mallows process in which each component is associated with a center and a scalar parameter. We show that even when the centers are arbitrarily separated, with exponentially many samples one can learn the mixture, provided the parameters are all the same and known; we also show that the latter two assumptions are information-theoretically inevitable. We then focus on polynomial-time learnability and show bounds on the performance of two simple algorithms for the case when the centers are well separated.

Conceptually, our work suggests that while permutations may not enjoy as nice mathematical properties as Gaussians, certain structural aspects can still be exploited towards analyzing the corresponding mixture learning problem.

1. INTRODUCTION

Mixture models have been studied for more than a century [35]. In a mixture model setting, we postulate a probabilistic process for generating samples from a convex combination of a small set of distributions, where the distributions in this set are usually from the same underlying family. The parameters of these distributions are typically unknown. Given a set of independently generated samples

---

*This author was supported by a Google Focused Award.

from this process, the question is to learn the hidden parameters of the distributions and cluster the samples. Mixture model learning is a standard way to interpret data in many machine learning and data mining applications [30,37]. This elegant notion has enormously influenced widely-used algorithms in computer science including the expectation-maximization and the k-means algorithms.

A large body of literature exists on learning mixtures where the underlying family is the Gaussian distribution. For applications with real-valued data, the Gaussian distribution is a natural candidate to model the vagaries of the data. There are several heuristics (including versions of the expectation-maximization algorithm and versions of the k-means algorithm) for this learning problem; however very little [15] can be said about these heuristics formally. For more details, see the section on related work.

Much less theoretical work has been done on the problem of learning a mixture of permutations. Permutation mixture models arise in many real-world settings where a set of objects is implicitly or explicitly ranked. As a motivating example, consider a user population that (fully) ranks a small set of local restaurants. The population could be composed of several sub-populations where the users in each sub-population might rank the restaurants in a similar manner. For example, a sub-population that places a lot of emphasis on ambiance will choose a ranking where the restaurant ambiance attribute is highlighted. Similarly, a sub-population with an Italian cuisine preference might rank all Italian restaurants above non-Italian restaurants. These characteristics of such sub-populations may or may not be known a priori. Of course, the members within a sub-population need not necessarily agree with each other about the entire ranking; they might have a few disagreements. From an application point of view, say for restaurant recommendation or for targeted advertisement, it is important to identify these sub-populations, the aggregated ranking of a sub-population, and cluster the entire population into such meaningful sub-populations.

A way to model the above scenario is to use a mixture of distributions on permutations. An important question is which family of distributions on permutations is best suited for this purpose, both from theoretical and practical points of view. A compelling candidate is the *Mallows model* [28]: in this model, a center (a permutation) and a parameter (a real number) induce a distribution on the space of all permutations, where the probability mass on a particular permutation depends on its (Kendall) distance from the center, scaled by the parameter. Mallows model can be thought of as an analog of Gaussians for permutations, where the center plays the role of the mean and the parameter plays the role of the variance. However, unlike multidimensional Gaussian distributions, Mallows model is much less well-behaved with less nice properties and much less is known about the model. Meila and Chen [31] used such a Mallows mixture model for clustering rankings, but their work is restricted to empirical analysis. In particular, they do not have any provable bounds on the performance of their algorithm. There has been other work in the statistics and machine learning community to model rankings as mixtures of other choice models such as the Plackett–Luce and Benter models [9, 20, 21], but it is unclear if these models are easily amenable to algorithmic treatment.

1.1 Our contributions

In this paper we study the problem of learning a mixture of distributions on permutations where each distribution in the mixture generated by a Mallows model, with its own center and parameter. As in the Gaussian case, it is unsurprising that the learnability of the problem can heavily depend on how well-separated are the mixture centers. We first address the following question: assuming the centers are arbitrarily placed and assuming the algorithm has access to an unlimited number of samples, what are the conditions under which the mixture can be learned? We show that for learnability, it is information-theoretically necessary that the following two conditions hold: the Mallows parameter is the *same* for all distributions in the mixture and this (single) parameter must be *known* to the learning algorithm. We complement this non-learnability by obtaining an algorithm for learning the centers from (exponentially) many samples, provided the Mallows parameters are all the same and the algorithm knows its value. In fact, we show that this learnability result holds for any exponential distribution of a distance function that is embeddable into ℓ_2^2; this may be of independent interest.

Next, we focus on the cases where the centers are well-separated, where our goal is to use only a polynomial number of samples for learning. We first obtain an algorithm based on single-linkage clustering that can learn the centers, provided the centers are well-separated. The algorithm works by first clustering the samples and then using an existing algorithm to infer the centers for each cluster. We next obtain a different algorithm based on the nearest-neighbor criterion for clustering the samples. This algorithm needs a quadratically-weaker center separation assumption compared to the single-linkage clustering, but uses a stronger assumption of knowing the position of the centers. While both these algorithms are very simple, the difficulty is in proving that their performance can be tied to the separation of the centers.

Our work illustrates that while permutations and the Mallows model are more cumbersome to work with than multidimensional real-valued distributions because of the finite discrete nature of the permutation space (e.g., even counting the number of permutations at a certain distance is not fully resolved), we can use their structural properties (e.g., embeddability, a simple generative process, alternative equivalent representations such as the insertion vector) in order to

analyze popular and practically used heuristics and obtain provable bounds. On the other hand, the discrete nature of the space also enables us to establish non-learnability for the most general cases of the mixture model, unlike the Gaussian models, and a larger separation between centers is necessitated due to the lack of independence of the "element-wise perturbations" in the Mallows setting.

1.2 Related work

Given a set of permutations generated according to the Mallows model, the permutation that maximizes the likelihood of this set is in fact the center [39]; finding this permutation is the well-known rank aggregation problem. Braverman and Mossel [8] obtained an algorithm for learning the center given a set of samples from a Mallows distribution; our work can be thought of as a natural extension of this work to a mixture setting. Chierichetti et al. [12] studied the problem of reconstructing the center from samples, where each sample is obtained from a Mallows model with the same center but different parameter. Very recently, Awasthi et al. [5] has considered learning the parameters of Mallows model mixtures and obtained a polynomial time algorithm for the case of two mixtures, by using a clever tensor decomposition. However, [5] considers the case of only two components, and settles the polynomial time learnability question for arbitrary separation of the centers. We, on the other hand, present an existential identifiability result for arbitrary number of components, as well as polynomial time algorithms for well-separated centers.

For the problem of learning a mixture of Gaussians, a tremendous amount of progress has been made on the theoretical front over the last few years, starting with the groundbreaking work of S. Dasgupta [14], followed by a series of impressive results [4, 15, 27, 38], culminating with the recent work on the provably learning Gaussian mixtures via the method of moments [6, 22, 24, 25, 32]. See the recent survey article by Kalai, Moitra, and Valiant [26] for an almost up-to-date overview of this research area.

There have been some work on learning mixtures of other distribution families. With the increasing role of heavy-tailed distributions in contemporary applications, the mixture learning problem has also been studied for such distributions [11, 13]. The results here are somewhat weaker than for the Gaussian case. Another topic that has attracted a lot of attention is learning a mixture of product distributions [19, 33]. The problem of learning mixtures of distributions when the domain is discrete but the distribution itself is allowed to be arbitrary has also been studied: the structured case was investigated by Chan et al. [34] and the unstructured case was investigated by Rabani et al. [36] and Anandkumar et al. [3]. Learning mixture of tree graphical models was considered by Anandkumar et al. [2]. None of the tools/techniques developed in these papers seems to apply to the Mallows mixture problem in particular and to permutations in general. While there has been some empirical work [?, ?], mostly using EM, in learning Mallows mixtures, these do not come with theoretical guarantees.

2. PRELIMINARIES

Let S_n be the symmetric group on $[n] = \{1, \ldots, n\}$. For a permutation $\sigma \in S_n$ and an element i, let $\sigma(i)$ denote the rank of the ith element. For two permutations $\pi, \sigma \in S_n$, let $\mathbb{K}(\pi, \sigma)$ denote the *Kendall tau* distance, which is the number of inversions between π and σ.

Let $\beta \in (0, \infty)$ be a parameter and let $\sigma \in S_n$ be a fixed permutation. In the *Mallows* model $\mathcal{M}(\sigma, \beta)$ of generating permutations [28], the parameter β and the permutation σ induce a distribution on S_n as follows:

$$\Pr_{\mathcal{M}(\sigma, \beta)}[\pi] = \frac{e^{-\beta \mathbb{K}(\pi, \sigma)}}{Z_\beta},$$

where Z_β is the normalization constant defined as $Z_\beta = \sum_{\pi \in S_n} e^{-\beta \mathbb{K}(\pi, \sigma)}$. We use $\pi \sim \mathcal{M}(\sigma, \beta)$ to denote that π is generated according to $\mathcal{M}(\sigma, \beta)$. When σ is the identity permutation, we simply denote $\mathbb{K}(\sigma, \pi)$ by $\mathbb{K}(\pi)$ and $\mathcal{M}(\sigma, \beta)$ by $\mathcal{M}(\beta)$.

Let $k > 1$ be an integer. Let $\boldsymbol{\sigma} = \{\sigma_1, \ldots, \sigma_k\}$ be a set of distinct permutations and let $\beta_1, \ldots, \beta_k$ be their corresponding *parameters*. In the Mallows mixture model setting with k centers, a sample permutation is generated by the following mixture process: pick $\sigma_i \in \boldsymbol{\sigma}$ according to a probability distribution (called *weight* distribution) $\mathcal{W}$ on $\boldsymbol{\sigma}$ and output the permutation generated according to $\mathcal{M}(\sigma_i, \beta_i)$. Here, the $\boldsymbol{\sigma}$ is the set of hidden *centers*. In the mixture model learning problem, we are given a set S of samples generated according to the mixture process and the goal is find the hidden centers. In a variant of the problem, in addition to the samples, we are also given the set $\boldsymbol{\sigma}$ of centers and the goal is to assign each sample to the center it came from. The complexity of the learning task is measured in terms of the size $|S|$ of the samples, the running time of the algorithm, and the quality of inferred centers (i.e., their distance to the true hidden centers). Sometimes, we will deal with the case when $\mathcal{W}$ is the uniform distribution on $\boldsymbol{\sigma}$; we call this the uniform Mallows mixture learning problem.

We need the following two tail bounds from [7], which show that no element deviates too far off from its original position and that the Kendall distance of the sample to the center is also bounded.

THEOREM 1 (BHATNAGAR AND PELED [7]). *For all $\beta > 0$, $i \geq 1$ and $t \geq 1$ if $\pi \sim \mathcal{M}(\beta)$, then*

$$(a) \quad \Pr_\pi[|\pi(i) - i| \geq t] \leq 2e^{-\beta t},$$

and for all $c > 0$,

$$(b) \quad \Pr_\pi\left[\mathbb{K}(\pi) > c\frac{n}{\beta}\ln(2nt)\right] < (nt)^{-c}.$$

3. ARBITRARY MIXTURES

In this section we consider the problem of learning the mixtures when the centers can be arbitrarily placed, in particular, when they can be very close to each other. In such settings, we first show that it is necessary to assume that the Mallows parameter β's are the same and are known, for otherwise it is not feasible to identify the components of the mixture. Next, we show that if the β's are the same, then we can learn the mixture for arbitrary separation between the centers provided we have access to sufficiently many samples from the mixture. Note that such a result is not obvious, even for Gaussian mixture models.

3.1 Non-learnability

We first show two easy non-learnability results: the first considers the case of when the parameters can be different and the second considers the case when the parameters, even if all same, are not known to the learning algorithm. Note that in both these results, we will need the centers to sometimes be placed very close (within $\mathbb{K}(\cdot, \cdot) = \Theta(1)$) to each other, i.e., these results are not necessarily true when we assume a super-constant separation between the centers.

First we note that for learnability, the parameters should all be positive for otherwise there is a very simple instance that is not learnable. Indeed, the following two worlds are indistinguishable. In the first world, there are $n!$ centers, all with same β, and $\mathcal{W}$ is uniform. In the second world, there is one center with $\beta = 0$. It is easy to see that both these worlds induce the uniform distribution on S_n.

Therefore, in what follows, we assume that β's are all positive. We now show that if the β's are not all the same, then there are instances of the mixture learning problem that are information-theoretically impossible to learn. We show that this holds in a very strong sense: even if there are only two centers $\{\sigma_1, \sigma_2\}$ and the weight distribution $\mathcal{W}$ is uniform on this set of centers.

LEMMA 2. *The uniform Mallows mixture learning problem with two centers cannot solved in general, without a knowledge of k, β_1 and β_2, regardless of the number of samples.*

PROOF. Suppose that we select the world uniformly at random between the following two possible worlds:

World 1: $k = 1$ with $\sigma = (1, 2)$, $\beta = \ln 2$.

World 2: $k = 2$ with $\sigma_1 = (1, 2)$, $\beta_1 = \ln(14)$ and $\sigma_2 = (2, 1)$, $\beta_2 = \ln(3/2)$; $\mathcal{W}$ is uniform on $\{\sigma_1, \sigma_2\}$.

The mixture distribution $P_1(\cdot)$ in World 1 is

$$P_1(1, 2) = \frac{1}{1 + e^{-\beta}} \quad \text{and} \quad P_1(2, 1) = 1 - P_1(1, 2).$$

In World 2, since $\mathcal{W}$ is uniform, the mixture distribution $P_2(\cdot)$ is

$$P_2(1, 2) = \frac{1}{2} \cdot \left(\frac{1}{1 + e^{-\beta_1}} + \frac{e^{-\beta_2}}{1 + e^{-\beta_2}}\right) = \frac{1}{1 + e^{-\beta}} = P_1(1, 2).$$

Since the two distributions are identical, no algorithm can distinguish between the two worlds. Note that this argument can work for any $\beta_1 > 0$. Then, for any $0 < \beta < \ln\left(3 - \frac{8}{e^{\beta_1} + 3}\right)$, set $\beta_2 = \ln \frac{1 - e^\beta + 2e^{\beta_1}}{e^{\beta_1} \cdot (e^\beta - 1) + 2e^\beta}$. $\square$

We next show that even if all the parameters are the same, if the algorithm does not know the value of the parameter, the Mallows mixture problem cannot be solved in general.

LEMMA 3. *Let $n \geq 2$ and let all the centers have the same $\beta > 0$. The Mallows mixture learning problem cannot be solved in general if β is unknown, regardless of the number of samples.*

PROOF. Fix any $\beta > 0$. Let $p_e(\sigma, \beta)$ be the probability of obtaining a permutation from $\mathcal{M}(\sigma, \beta)$ that has an even Kendall τ distance to σ. Then,

$$p_e(\sigma, \beta) = \sum_{\pi \mid \mathbb{K}(\pi, \sigma) \in 2\mathbb{Z}} \frac{e^{-\beta \mathbb{K}(\pi, \sigma)}}{Z_\beta} = p_e(\beta),$$

since the sum has the same terms and hence the same value for any choice of σ. Note that $\frac{1}{2} < p_e(\beta) < 1$. It is also easy to see that $p_e(\beta)$ is continuous and increasing in β, $p_e(0) = \frac{1}{2}$, and $\lim_{\beta \to \infty} p_e(\beta) = 1$.

Let $0 < \beta_1 < \beta_2$ be chosen arbitrarily. Let

$$\alpha = \frac{p_e(\beta_1) + p_e(\beta_2) - 1}{2p_e(\beta_2) - 1}; \quad \frac{1}{2} < \alpha < 1.$$

Let $A_n \subseteq S_n$ be the set of the *even* permutations on $[n]$, i.e., permutations π such that $\mathbb{K}(\pi, \mathbf{1})$ is even where $\mathbf{1}$ is the identity permutation. It follows $|A_n| = |S_n|/2$.

We select the world uniformly at random between the following two possible worlds:

World 1: create a center for each $\sigma \in A_n$ and each center has the parameter β_1; $\mathcal{W}$ is uniform on A_n.

World 2: create a center for each $\sigma \in S_n$ and each center has the parameter β_2. $\mathcal{W}$ is defined as:

$$\mathcal{W}(\pi) = \begin{cases} \alpha/|A_n| & \pi \in A_n, \\ (1-\alpha)/|A_n| & \pi \in S \setminus A_n. \end{cases}$$

We now calculate the probability of any given even permutation in both worlds. The probability of any given even permutation in World 1 is $p_e(\beta_1)/|A_n|$ and in World 2 is

$$\begin{aligned}
&\frac{\alpha}{|A_n|} \cdot p_e(\beta_2) + \frac{(1-\alpha)}{|A_n|} \cdot (1 - p_e(\beta_2)) \\
&= \frac{1}{|A_n|} \cdot (\alpha(2p_e(\beta_2) - 1) + 1 - p_e(\beta_2)) \\
&= \frac{p_e(\beta_1)}{|A_n|},
\end{aligned}$$

by our choice of α. Analogously, it can be seen that the probability of any given odd permutation in both worlds is $\frac{1 - p_e(\beta_1)}{|A_n|}$. Since both these worlds induce the same distribution on S_n, no algorithm can distinguish between the two worlds. $\square$

Note that even though $k = n!/2$ in the above proof, since it holds for any $n \geq 2$, k need not be particularly large for the instance. Also, even though we defined $\mathcal{W}$ to be non-uniform in World 2, this was for simplicity: for infinitely many β's, by replicating the centers appropriately, we can create an equivalent instance for World 2 where $\mathcal{W}$ is uniform.

3.2 Uniform parameters

In this section we obtain algorithms that can learn Mallows mixtures for arbitrary separation between centers as long as all the parameters are the *same* and are *known*. In conjunction with the non-learnability results in Lemma 2 and Lemma 3, these assumptions about the parameters are inevitable. The main idea in the algorithm is to use the invertibility of a certain Gram matrix.

Let $|X| = n$, and let $d : X \times X \to [0, \infty)$ be a function. We say d is isometrically embeddable into ℓ_2^2 if and only if there exists n vectors $x_1, \dots, x_n$ such that $d(i, j) = ||x_i - x_j||^2$. The Kendall distance can be isometrically embedded into ℓ_1, and therefore into ℓ_2^2. Indeed, let $I(\sigma)$ be the $\binom{n}{2}$ length vector that in the $\{i, j\}$th position is 1 if and only if $i < j$ and $\sigma(i) > \sigma(j)$; it follows $\mathbb{K}(\pi, \sigma) = |I(\pi) - I(\sigma)|$.

A real matrix M is *positive definite* (resp., positive semidefinite) if, for every non-zero real vector x, it holds $xMx^T > 0$ (resp., $xMx^T \geq 0$). We denote $M \succ 0$ (resp., $M \succeq 0$) to denote M is positive definite (resp., positive semidefinite). The *Gram matrix* of the real vectors $x_1, \dots, x_n$ is defined as $G_{i,j} = \langle x_i, x_j \rangle$ and the *Hadamard exponential* $\widehat{A}$ of a matrix A is defined as $\widehat{A}_{i,j} = e^{A_{i,j}}$. We will use the following folklore results.

FACT 4. *If G is a Gram matrix, then $G \succeq 0$.*

LEMMA 5 (THEOREM 7.5.9 [23]). *If A is a positive semidefinite matrix and if A does not contain two equal rows, then its Hadamard exponential satisfies $\widehat{A} \succ 0$ and hence it is non-singular.*

Using these, we now prove the following.

THEOREM 6. *Let $x_1, \dots, x_k$ be pairwise different vectors and let M be the $k \times k$ matrix such that:*

$$M_{i,j} = \frac{e^{-\beta ||x_i - x_j||^2}}{\sum_{\ell=1}^k e^{-\beta ||x_i - x_\ell||^2}}.$$

Then, M is non-singular.

Therefore, the $n! \times n!$ matrix $N_{i,j} = \frac{e^{-\beta \mathbb{K}(\sigma_i, \sigma_j)}}{\sum_{\ell=1}^{n!} e^{-\beta \mathbb{K}(\sigma_i, \sigma_\ell)}}$ is non-singular.

PROOF. The latter claim follows from the former since the Kendall tau distance is isometrically embeddable into ℓ_2^2, and since $\mathbb{K}(\sigma_i, \sigma_j) = 0$ if and only if $i = j$. We now prove the former claim for an arbitrary matrix M.

Let M'' be the Gram matrix corresponding to the vectors $x_1, \dots, x_k$, i.e., $M''_{i,j} = \langle x_i, x_j \rangle$. We use two properties of M''. First, from Fact 4, we know that $M'' \succeq 0$ and hence for any $\beta > 0$, we have

$$2\beta M'' \succeq 0. \tag{1}$$

Second, we argue that M'' does not contain two equal rows. Indeed, assume the contrary and let the ith and the jth row ($j \neq i$) of M'' be equal, i.e., $\langle x_i, x_\ell \rangle = \langle x_j, x_\ell \rangle$ for all ℓ. By choosing $\ell = i$, we have that $||x_i||^2 = \langle x_i, x_i \rangle = \langle x_j, x_i \rangle$ and by choosing $\ell = j$, we have $\langle x_i, x_j \rangle = \langle x_j, x_j \rangle = ||x_j||^2$. Thus, $||x_i||^2 = \langle x_i, x_i \rangle = \langle x_i, x_j \rangle = ||x_j||^2$. By the Cauchy–Schwarz inequality, we know that for $\langle x_i, x_j \rangle^2$ to equal $||x_i||^2 \cdot ||x_j||^2$, we need x_i and x_j to be linearly dependent. Since $||x_i||^2 = ||x_j||^2$, this implies $x_i = x_j$, which is a contradiction, since we assumed that the x_ℓ's are pairwise different.

Let $M' = \widehat{2\beta M''}$, i.e., the Hadamard exponential of $2\beta M''$ given by $M'_{i,j} = e^{2\beta \langle x_i, x_j \rangle}$. By (1) and since M'' (and hence $2\beta M''$) has no two identical rows, using Lemma 5, we get

$$M' \succ 0 \implies \det M' > 0. \tag{2}$$

Finally, using these, we will show M is non-singular by showing its determinant is non-zero. The determinant of M can be written as:

$$\begin{aligned}
\det M &= \sum_{\pi \in S_n} \text{sgn}(\pi) \cdot \frac{e^{-2\beta \sum_{i=1}^n ||x_i||^2 + 2\beta \sum_{i=1}^n \langle x_i, x_{\pi(i)} \rangle}}{\prod_{i=1}^n \sum_{\sigma_\ell \in \sigma} e^{-\beta \mathbb{K}(\sigma_i, \sigma_\ell)}} \\
&= \frac{e^{-2\beta \sum_{i=1}^n ||x_i||^2}}{\prod_{i=1}^n \sum_{\sigma_\ell \in \sigma} e^{-\beta \mathbb{K}(\sigma_i, \sigma_\ell)}} \\
&\quad \cdot \sum_{\pi \in S_n} \text{sgn}(\pi) \cdot e^{2\beta \sum_{i=1}^n \langle x_i, x_{\pi(i)} \rangle}.
\end{aligned}$$

Note that the first term in this product is positive and the second term is precisely $\det M'$, which is also positive using (2). $\square$

THEOREM 7. *If $\beta > 0$ is known and is the same for all the centers and if sufficiently many samples are given, then we can learn the Mallows mixture model with probability $1 - o(1)$.*

PROOF. Consider the matrix N of Theorem 6. Since it is invertible, let

$$u = \left|\left| N^{-1} \right|\right|_\infty.$$

For any i, j, since $\mathbb{K}(\sigma_i, \sigma_j) \leq \binom{n}{2}$, we have

$$
\begin{aligned}
N_{i,j} &= \frac{e^{-\beta \, \mathbb{K}(\sigma_i, \sigma_j)}}{\sum_{\sigma_\ell \in \sigma} e^{-\beta \, \mathbb{K}(\sigma_i, \sigma_\ell)}} \\
&\geq \frac{e^{-\beta \binom{n}{2}}}{\sum_{\sigma_\ell \in \sigma} e^{-\beta \, \mathbb{K}(\sigma_i, \sigma_\ell)}} \\
&\geq \frac{1}{n!} \cdot e^{-\beta \binom{n}{2}} \geq e^{-(1+\beta)\, n^2} \\
&= v.
\end{aligned}
$$

Finally, let η be the minimum non-zero probability in $\mathcal{W}$:

$$\eta = \min_{\sigma \in \sigma, \mathcal{W}(\sigma) > 0} \mathcal{W}(\sigma).$$

Now, let C_t be the column vector of length $n!$ indexed by $\pi \in S_n$ such that the πth entry contains the fraction of times that the permutation π was produced by the mixture model, if it were sampled t times. Let $\mathcal{M}$ be the vector of length $n!$ such that the πth entry is the expected number of times the mixture model outputs π.

By the Chernoff bound, for each $\epsilon > 0$, there exists $\gamma = \gamma(\epsilon)$ such that if $t \geq v^{-\gamma} = e^{\gamma(1+\beta)n^2}$, then with probability $1 - o(1)$, we will have

$$(1 - \epsilon)\mathcal{M}(\pi) \leq C_t(\pi) \leq (1 + \epsilon)\mathcal{M}(\pi),$$

uniformly for each $\pi \in S_n$. By choosing t, the number of samples, to be $O\left(\frac{(3u \cdot n!)^2 \log n}{v \eta^3} \right)$, we can assume $\epsilon = \frac{\eta}{3u \cdot n!}$.

Let $\overline{\mathcal{W}} = N^{-1} C_t$. Observe that, since $N \cdot \mathcal{W} = \mathcal{M}$, we have

$$\overline{\mathcal{W}(\pi)} = N^{-1}\mathcal{M} + \xi,$$

where $|\xi| \leq \epsilon u \cdot n! = \frac{\eta}{3}$. Therefore, the set of π's such that $\overline{\mathcal{W}(\pi)} \geq \frac{2}{3}\eta$, is the correct set of unknown centers with probability $1 - o(1)$. $\square$

In fact, the above proof naturally extends to the following more general setting. Given a set X of elements, let $d : X \times X \to [0, \infty)$ be a semi-metric, i.e., let $d(x, y) = d(y, x)$ for each $x, y \in X$, and $d(x, y) = 0$ iff $x = y$. Given $X, d, \beta > 0$, and some $x \in X$, we define the probability distribution $P_x = P_{x, X, d, \beta}$ as follows:

$$P_x(y) = \frac{e^{-\beta \, d(x, y)}}{\sum_{z \in X} e^{-\beta \, d(x, z)}} \qquad \forall y \in X.$$

Given a set $C \subseteq X$, and a probability distribution $\mathcal{W}$ over C, we define the mixture E of the $\{P_x\}_{x \in C}$ as:

$$E(y) = \sum_{x \in C} \mathcal{W}(x) \cdot P_x(y) \qquad \forall y \in X.$$

Observe that E is a probability distribution over X. The proof of Theorem 7 can be extended to show that if d can be isometrically embedded into ℓ_2^2, if all the centers' parameters are equal to $\beta > 0$, and if β is known, then given sufficiently many samples, it is possible to guess exactly the set C of centers that make up the mixture E with probability $1 - o(1)$.

4. WELL-SEPARATED MIXTURES

Theorem 7 in Section 3 states that with enough samples, one can learn the Mallows mixture model for arbitrary centers if all the β's are the same and known. Unfortunately, the resulting algorithm requires a superpolynomial number of samples and hence has a superpolynomial running time.

In this section we focus on developing efficient algorithms that are provably correct if the centers are well-separated, i.e., there is a minimal Kendall tau distance between every pair of centers. We focus on two cases: in the first, the algorithm does not know the position of the centers. In the second case, the algorithm knows the centers and the goal is to cluster the given samples with respect to the given centers.

4.1 Unknown centers

In this section we assume that the algorithm does not know the location of the centers (or the parameters). Nevertheless, we show that we can reconstruct clusters corresponding to different centers and then use the samples in the clusters to estimate the respective centers.

Let $\beta_1 \leq \cdots \leq \beta_k$ be the Mallows parameters, and let $\sigma_1, \ldots, \sigma_k \in S_n$ be the respective centers.

THEOREM 8. *Let t be the number of samples. If for each $1 \leq i < j \leq k$ we have $\mathbb{K}(\sigma_i, \sigma_j) \geq \Omega\left(\frac{n \log(nt)}{\beta_1} \right)$, then we can learn the Mallows mixture model with probability $1 - \frac{1}{(nt)^{\Theta(1)}}$.*

PROOF. The algorithm we use is the so-called single-linkage clustering, which is a popular practical heuristic. Each of the t samples starts as a singleton. Repeat the following until we obtain k clusters: select clusters C_1, C_2 such that $\min_{\pi_1 \in C_1} \min_{\pi_2 \in C_2} \mathbb{K}(\pi_1, \pi_2)$ is the minimum and merge C_1 and C_2 into a single cluster.

To prove the correctness of this algorithm, we appeal to Theorem 1(b). From this, if the minimum distance between the centers is at least $c' \frac{n}{\beta_1} \ln(2nt)$, for $c' > 2c$, then we are guaranteed that no two samples coming from different centers will end up in the same cluster. Thus, it is possible to guess correctly for each pair of samples if they were produced by the same center (by the mixture process) with probability at least $1 - 1/(nt)^{\Theta(1)}$.

After obtaining this clustering, for the final step of computing the centers themselves, we use the polynomial algorithm of Braverman and Mossel [8, Theorem 7] to use the samples in each cluster in order to estimate the centers. $\square$

4.2 Known centers

In this section we still focus on the case of well-separated centers, when the centers are known in advance to the algorithm; the parameters β. need not be known to the algorithm. Interestingly we can show that it is possible to obtain an algorithm that for some parameters outperforms the algorithm in Theorem 8.

The core intuition behind the algorithm is that even if the average distance between a center and a sample is large, a sample should be closer to the center that generated it than to any other center. In particular, we analyze the following natural algorithm: assign each sample to its nearest center. In the rest of this section we show that, under a separation assumption, this algorithm recovers the correct clustering.

Before describing our results, we recall some properties of the Mallows model. It is well known that a permutation can be sampled from the Mallows distribution using a simple process. For completeness, we describe the process; a full proof of why it corresponds to the $\mathcal{M}(\beta)$ distribution is available in [17].

Insertion process P. Define $q = e^{-\beta}$. We consider the elements $1, \ldots, n$ in this order. For each i, π_i will denote a permutation over the elements 1 to i. Define $\pi_1(1) = 1$. We then define π_i in terms of π_{i-1} as follows. First the entry at the ith position of π_i, i.e., $\pi_i(i)$ is chosen using the following random process:

$$\Pr[\pi_i(i) = j] = \frac{(1/q)^{j-1}}{1 + 1/q + \cdots + (1/q)^{i-1}}, \text{ for } j \in \{1, \ldots, i\}. \quad (3)$$

Then, for s such that $\pi_{i-1}(s) < \pi_i(i)$, set $\pi_i(s) = \pi_{i-1}(s)$ and else set $\pi_i(s) = \pi_{i-1}(s) + 1$. Finally, $\pi = \pi_n$.

We first state the following result from [12]. Let $s_{\beta,k,i}$ be the probability that $\pi(i) > \pi(i+k)$ and let $s'_{\beta,k,i} = \frac{1}{2} - s_{\beta,k,i}$.

THEOREM 9 (LEMMA 4 [12]). $s_{\beta,k,i}$ is independent of i and for all k, $s_{\beta,k} \leq s_{\beta,1} < \frac{\beta + e^{-\beta} - 1}{e^{\beta} + e^{-\beta} - 2}$. Furthermore, for $\beta > 0$, $s'_{\beta,k} \geq s'_{\beta,1} \geq \Theta(\min(\beta, 1))$. If $\beta = \Omega(1)$, $s'_{\beta,k} > 1 - \Theta(\beta e^{-\beta})$.

Finally, we will also need the following form of the method of bounded differences [18]; the original result is due to McDiarmid [29].

THEOREM 10. Let f be a function of n random variables $X_1, \ldots, X_n$, each X_i taking values in a set A_i, such that $E[f]$ is bounded. Assume that

$$m \leq f(X_1, \ldots, X_n) \leq M.$$

Let $\mathcal{B}$ be any event and let c_i be maximum effect of f assuming $\mathcal{B}$, i.e.,

$$|E[f \mid \mathbf{X}_{i-1}, X_i = a_i, \mathcal{B}] - E[f \mid \mathbf{X}_{i-1}, X_i = a'_i, \mathcal{B}]| \leq c_i.$$

Then

$$\Pr[f > E[f] + t] \leq \exp\left(-\frac{2t^2}{\sum_i c_i^2}\right) + \Pr[\mathcal{B}^c],$$

and

$$\Pr[f < E[f] - t] \leq \exp\left(-\frac{t^2}{\sum_i c_i^2}\right) + \Pr[\mathcal{B}^c].$$

Now we are ready to prove our main result: when the centers are known, then with only a $\tilde{O}(\sqrt{n}/\beta s'_{\beta,1})$ separation between the permutations, it is possible to label most points accurately. We first show a claim for two centers, one of them being the identity permutation. Then we extend the result to an arbitrary set of permutations.

LEMMA 11. Let $k = 2$ with σ_1 being the identity permutation and $\sigma_2 = \sigma$. For any permutation $\pi \sim \mathcal{M}(\beta)$, consider the following random variable Δ:

$$\Delta = \mathbb{K}(\pi, \sigma) - \mathbb{K}(\pi).$$

If

$$\mathbb{K}(\sigma) \geq \frac{\log(1/\delta)}{s'_{\beta,1}} \min\left(n^{3/2}, \frac{c\sqrt{n}\log n}{\beta}\right),$$

then with probability $1 - \delta - n^{-c}$, $\Delta > 0$.

PROOF. We analyze the expectation of Δ and then use Theorem 10 to obtain the high probability result. Let $\pi \sim \mathcal{M}(\beta)$ and consider the random variable $\Delta = \mathbb{K}(\pi, \sigma) - \mathbb{K}(\pi)$. Let the indicator variables x_{ij} and y_{ij} be defined as follows: for $j < i$, $x_{ij} = \mathbb{1}[\sigma(j) > \sigma(i)]$ and $y_{ij} = \mathbb{1}[\pi(j) > \pi(i)]$. Also, abusing notation, let $x_i = \sum_{j<i} x_{ij}$ be the ith coordinate of the inversion vector of σ. Now, consider that the Mallows permutation π has been generated according the Mallows process P. Thus, each random variable x_i depends solely on the position of the ith element in the corresponding step. Hence the random variable x_i's are mutually independent. Thus,

$$\begin{aligned}
\Delta &= \sum_i \sum_{j<i} \mathbb{1}[\sigma(j) < \sigma(i) \text{ and } \pi(j) > \pi(i))] \\
&\quad + \mathbb{1}[\sigma(j) > \sigma(i) \text{ and } \pi(j) < \pi(i))] - \mathbb{1}[\pi(j) > \pi(i))] \\
&= \sum_i \sum_{j<i} (1 - x_{ij}) y_{ij} + x_{ij}(1 - y_{ij}) - y_{ij} \\
&= \sum_i \sum_{j<i} x_{ij} - 2 x_{ij} y_{ij} \\
&= \mathbb{K}(\sigma) - 2 \sum_i \sum_{j<i} x_{ij} y_{ij}.
\end{aligned}$$

Consider the random variable $S = \sum_i \sum_{j<i} x_{ij} y_{ij}$. Using Theorem 9, for $j < i$, $E[y_{ij}] = s_{\beta, i-j} \leq s_{\beta,1}$. Hence,

$$E[S] = \sum_i \sum_{j<i} x_{ij} y_{ij} \leq s_{\beta,1} \sum_i \sum_{j<i} x_{ij} = s_{\beta,1} \mathbb{K}(\sigma).$$

Note that $E[S]$ is the number of inversion on which both π and σ agree. In the following we prove that S is concentrated using Theorem 10. The core intuition is to consider the process P and to show that after each insertion step, S changes by at most $\log n$ w.h.p.

More formally, for each i, the number of inversion with elements $j < i$ on which both σ and π agree is upper bounded by $y_i = i - \pi_i(i)$ (recall the definition of $\pi_i(i)$ in process P), that is the number of inversion with elements $j < i$ of π.

Now let the event A be defined as the following: for all $i \in [1, n]$, $|\pi(i) - i| < \min(n - 1, c \log(n)/\beta)$. Using Theorem 1, $\Pr[A] > 1 - n^{-c}$. Let us condition on event A happening. Note that, since the final position of each element change at most of $(c \log n)/\beta$, then y_i is bounded by:

$$|y_i| \leq \min\left(n - 1, \frac{2c \log n}{\beta}\right).$$

Thus, after conditioning on A, for each i the number of inversion with elements $j < i$ on which both σ and π agree is upper bounded by $|y_i| \leq \min(n - 1, (2c \log n)/\beta)$. Furthermore $\sum_i y_i^2 \leq \min(n^3, (4c^2 n \log^2 n)/\beta^2)$.

Now we can apply Theorem 10. Conditioned on A, we get that

$$\begin{aligned}
\Pr[\Delta < 0] &\leq \Pr[S > \mathbb{K}(\sigma)/2] \\
&\leq \exp\left(-\frac{(\frac{1}{2}\mathbb{K}(\sigma) - E[S])^2}{2\min(n^3, \frac{4c^2 n \log^2(n)}{\beta^2})}\right) \\
&\leq \exp\left(-\frac{(s'_{\beta,1}\mathbb{K}(\sigma))^2}{2\min(n^3, \frac{4c^2 n \log^2(n)}{\beta^2})}\right).
\end{aligned}$$

Hence, when

$$\mathbb{K}(\sigma) \geq \frac{\log(1/\delta)}{s'_{\beta,1}} \min\left(n^{3/2}, \frac{2c\sqrt{n}\log n}{\beta}\right),$$

by applying the union bound, we have the total probability of $\Delta < 0$ to be at most $\delta + n^{-c}$. $\square$

The previous result gives us a bound for two centers and a single sample. It is easy to extend it to more than two centers (up to a polynomial number in n) and more than one sample (up to a polynomial number in n). By appropriately setting δ and c and by using the union bound we can get that for each sample is closer to the center it was sampled from than any other center. Hence, we obtain the following.

COROLLARY 12. *Suppose we have k centers $\{\sigma_1, \ldots, \sigma_k\}$, and the parameters $\beta_1 \leq \cdots \leq \beta_k$. Let $\mathcal{W}$ be an arbitrary set of weights for choosing each center. Let $m = poly(n)$ be the number of samples taken from this mixture. Suppose all pairs σ_i, σ_j satisfy*

$$\mathbb{K}(\sigma_i, \sigma_j) \geq \frac{C\log(m)}{s'_{\beta_1,1}} \min\left(n^{3/2}, \frac{2\sqrt{n}\log n}{\beta_1}\right),$$

for some constant $C > 0$. If the σ_i are known, then all sample points can be assigned to their closest center and we would have the correct clustering with probability $1 - n^{-c}$ for some constant c.

PROOF. For each sample $\pi \sim \mathcal{M}(\sigma_i, \beta_i)$, using the above Lemma 11, we can guarantee that for any other center σ_j, since by assumption $\mathbb{K}(\sigma_i, \sigma_j)$ satisfies the inter-center separation of Lemma 11, $\mathbb{K}(\pi, \sigma_i) < \mathbb{K}(\pi, \sigma_j)$ with probability $1 - n^{-c}$ for some c. By using the union bound, the proof is complete. $\square$

It is useful to note if the centers were known in the Gaussian mixture case, for an analogous claim to Lemma 11, we would only need a separation between the centers that is $\Omega(\log n)$ times the maximum variance.

5. CONCLUSIONS

In this work we initiated the formal study of mixtures of Mallows distributions and prove the impossibility of learning arbitrary mixtures in the most general case when the parameters are different and the learnability of the components are identifiable when the Mallows parameter is the same and known. We point out that the setting where the centers are well-separated is an algorithmically easier setting. Our work suggests that while permutations may not enjoy as nice mathematical properties as Gaussians, they still posses structural characteristics such as embeddability that can still be exploited towards analyzing the corresponding mixture learning problem.

It would be interesting to investigate the feasibility of polynomial time algorithms for learning mixtures when $k = \Theta(1)$, center separation is $\tilde{\Theta}(\sqrt{n}/\beta^c)$ and neither the centers nor the parameters is known. While [5] has settled the question for $k = 2$, it would be interesting to see whether we can develop algorithms requiring polynomial number of samples for arbitrary k, as has been done for other well-behaved distributions [1,10,16]. As we mentioned earlier, it will also be interesting to study the learnability of other choice models in the mixture setting.

6. REFERENCES

[1] J. Acharya, A. Jafarpour, A. Orlitsky, and A. T. Suresh. Near-optimal-sample estimators for spherical Gaussian mixtures. In *NIPS*, 2014.

[2] A. Anandkumar, D. Hsu, F. Huang, and S. Kakade. Learning mixtures of tree graphical models. In *NIPS*, pages 1061–1069, 2012.

[3] A. Anandkumar, D. Hsu, and S. M. Kakade. A method of moments for mixture models and hidden Markov models. In *COLT*, pages 1–34, 2012.

[4] S. Arora and R. Kannan. Learning mixtures of arbitrary Gaussians. In *STOC*, pages 247–257, 2001.

[5] P. Awasthi, A. Blum, O. Sheffet, and A. Vijayaraghavan. Learning mixtures of ranking models. In *NIPS*, 2014.

[6] M. Belkin and K. Sinha. Polynomial learning of distribution families. In *FOCS*, pages 103–112, 2010.

[7] N. Bhatnagar and R. Peled. Lengths of monotone subsequences in a Mallows permutation. *Probability Theory and Related Fields*, To appear.

[8] M. Braverman and E. Mossel. Sorting from noisy information. *CoRR, abs/0910.1191*, 2009.

[9] L. M. Busse, P. Orbanz, and J. M. Buhmann. Cluster analysis of heterogeneous rank data. In *ICML*, pages 113–120, 2007.

[10] S.-O. Chan, I. Diakonikolas, R. A. Servedio, and X. Sun. Efficient density estimation via piecewise polynomial approximation. In *STOC*, pages 604–613, 2014.

[11] K. Chaudhuri and S. Rao. Beyond Gaussians: Spectral methods for learning mixtures of heavy-tailed distributions. In *COLT*, volume 4, page 1, 2008.

[12] F. Chiericetti, A. Dasgupta, R. Kumar, and S. Lattanzi. On reconstructing a hidden permutation. In *RANDOM*, pages 604–617, 2014.

[13] A. Dasgupta, J. Hopcroft, J. Kleinberg, and M. Sandler. On learning mixtures of heavy-tailed distributions. In *FOCS*, pages 491–500, 2005.

[14] S. Dasgupta. Learning mixtures of Gaussians. In *FOCS*, pages 634–644, 1999.

[15] S. Dasgupta and L. J. Schulman. A probabilistic analysis of EM for mixtures of separated, spherical Gaussians. *Journal of Machine Learning Research*, 8:203–226, 2007.

[16] C. Daskalakis and G. Kamath. Faster and sample near-optimal algorithms for proper learning mixtures of Gaussians. In *COLT*, pages 1183–1213, 2014.

[17] J. Doignon, A. Pekec, and M. Regenwetter. The repeated insertion model for rankings: Missing link between two subset choice models. *Psychometrika*, 69(1):33–54, 2004.

[18] D. Dubhashi and A. Panconesi. *Concentration of Measure for the Analysis of Randomised Algorithms*. Cambridge University Press, 2009.

[19] Y. Freund and Y. Mansour. Estimating a mixture of two product distributions. In *COLT*, pages 53–62, 1999.

[20] I. C. Gormley and T. B. Murphy. Exploring voting blocs within the Irish electorate: a mixture modeling approach. *J. Am. Stat. Assoc.*, 103(483):1014–1027, 2008.

[21] I. C. Gormley and T. B. Murphy. A mixture of experts model for rank data with applications in election studies. *Ann. Appl. Stat.*, 2(4):1452–1477, 2008.

[22] M. Hardt and E. Price. Sharp bounds for learning a mixture of two Gaussians. Technical Report 1404.4997v1, ArXiv, 2014.

[23] R. Horn and C. Johnson. *Matrix Analysis*. Matrix Analysis. Cambridge University Press, 2012.

[24] D. Hsu and S. M. Kakade. Learning mixtures of spherical Gaussians: moment methods and spectral decompositions. In *ITCS*, pages 11–20, 2013.

[25] A. T. Kalai, A. Moitra, and G. Valiant. Efficiently learning mixtures of two Gaussians. In *STOC*, pages 553–562, 2010.

[26] A. T. Kalai, A. Moitra, and G. Valiant. Disentangling Gaussians. *Commun. ACM*, 55(2):113–120, 2012.

[27] R. Kannan, H. Salmasian, and S. Vempala. The spectral method for general mixture models. *SIAM J. Comput.*, 38(3):1141–1156, 2008.

[28] C. L. Mallows. Non-null ranking models I. *Biometrika*, 44(1-2):114–130, 1957.

[29] C. McDiarmid. Concentration. In M. Habib, C. McDiarmid, J. Ramirez-Alfonsin, and B. Reed, editors, *Probabilistic Methods for Algorithmic Discrete Mathematics*. Springer, 1998.

[30] G. J. McLachlan and D. Peel. *Finite Mixture Models*. Wiley, 2000.

[31] M. Meila and H. Chen. Dirichlet process mixtures of generalized Mallows models. In *UAI*, pages 358–367, 2010.

[32] A. Moitra and G. Valiant. Settling the polynomial learnability of mixtures of Gaussians. In *FOCS*, pages 93–102, 2010.

[33] R. O'Donnell and R. A. Servedio. Learning mixtures of product distributions over discrete domains. *SIAM J. Comput.*, 37(5):1536–1564, 2008.

[34] S. on Chan, I. Diakonikolas, R. A. Servedio, and X. Sun. Learning mixtures of structured distributions over discrete domains. In *SODA*, pages 1380–1394, 2013.

[35] K. Pearson. Contributions to the mathematical theory of evolution. *Philosophical Transactions of the Royal Society of London. A*, 185:71–110, 1894.

[36] Y. Rabani, L. J. Schulman, and C. Swamy. Learning mixtures of arbitrary distributions over large discrete domains. In *ITCS*, pages 207–224, 2014.

[37] D. Titterington and U. Smith, A.; Makov. *Statistical Analysis of Finite Mixture Distributions*. Wiley, 1985.

[38] S. Vempala and G. Wang. A spectral algorithm for learning mixture models. *J. Comput. Syst. Sci.*, 68(4):841–860, 2004.

[39] H. P. Young. Optimal voting rules. *The Journal of Economic Perspectives*, 9(1):51–64, 1995.

Restricted Distribution Automatizability in PAC-Semantics*

Brendan Juba[†]
Washington University in St. Louis
1 Brookings Dr.
St. Louis, MO 63130
bjuba@wustl.edu

ABSTRACT

We consider the proof search (*"automatizability"*) problem
for propositional proof systems in the context of *knowledge
discovery* (or *data mining* and *analytics*). Discovered knowledge necessarily features a weaker semantics than usually
employed in mathematical logic, and in this work we find
that these weaker semantics may result in a proof search
problem that seems easier than the classical problem, but
that is nevertheless nontrivial. Specifically, if we consider
a knowledge discovery task corresponding to the unsupervised learning of parities over the uniform distribution from
partial information, then we find the following:

- Proofs in the system *polynomial calculus with resolution (PCR)* can be detected in quasipolynomial time,
  in contrast to the $n^{O(\sqrt{n})}$-time best known algorithm
  for classical proof search for PCR.

- By contrast, a quasipolynomial time algorithm that
  distinguishes whether a formula of PCR is satisfied a
  $1 - \epsilon$ fraction of the time or merely an ϵ-fraction of the
  time (for polynomially small ϵ) would give a randomized quasipolynomial time algorithm for NP, so the use
  of the promise of a small PCR *proof* is essential in the
  above result.

- Likewise, if integer factoring requires subexponential
  time, we find that bounded-depth Frege proofs cannot
  be detected in quasipolynomial time.

The final result essentially shows that negative results based
on the hardness of interpolation [31, 13, 11] persist under
this new semantics, while the first result suggests, in light
of negative results for PCR [22] and resolution [2] under the
classical semantics, that there are intriguing new possibilities for proof search in the context of knowledge discovery
and data analysis.

---

*Combines and largely subsumes two earlier technical re-
ports, [26] and [25]

[†]Work performed while the author was affiliated with Harvard University and supported by ONR grant number
N000141210358.

Categories and Subject Descriptors

F.4.1 [**Theory of Computation**]: Mathematical Logic—
Mechanical theorem proving, Proof theory; I.2.6 [**Artificial
Intelligence**]: Learning—*Knowledge acquisition*

General Terms

Theory

Keywords

learning; proof complexity; automatizability; PAC-Semantics

1. INTRODUCTION

Consider the following *goal-driven knowledge discovery (data
mining and analytics)* problem proposed by Juba [24], building on earlier work by Khardon and Roth [29, 30]. We have
access to a data set consisting of partially specified examples
$\rho^{(1)}, \ldots, \rho^{(m)}$, i.e., each $\rho^{(i)} \in \{0, 1, *\}^n$, where $*$ is an un-
specified value. We assume that these examples have been
produced by first drawing a complete example $x^{(i)} \in \{0, 1\}^n$
from an unknown, "ground truth" distribution D, and that
some of the attributes have been hidden by a second random
process M. That is, each $\rho^{(i)}$ is drawn i.i.d. from a distribution $M(D)$ with some well-defined "ground truth" $x^{(i)}$ for
the values of all of the attributes. We are now given a *query*
Boolean formula φ, and our objective is to decide whether
the data set *provides empirical evidence* that φ is satisfied
with high probability over D in the following sense. We
wish to guarantee that whenever there are some formulas
$\psi_1, \ldots, \psi_k$ that can be verified to simultaneously hold with
high probability on D using our partial examples,[1] that then
complete a *proof* of the query φ, that we then *certify* φ as
satisfied with high probability under D. At the same time,
we also wish to guarantee that if the query φ is not satisfied with high probability under D, then we are unlikely to
certify it as being so.

We will discuss the motivation for this problem in Section 1.2: as we will review there, this *integrated* data analytics approach is not only sufficient to capture a variety of
applications, but moreover provides more power (in multiple
respects) than a standard, two-stage, "learn-then-analyze"
approach. The previous work [24] considered the advantages
of this integrated formulation of learning and reasoning from

---

[1]Verified by plugging in the partial example for the variables
of the formulas, performing the natural connective-wise simplification, and checking if the result is the constant "true."
See Section 2 for a full definition.

the perspective of learning theory: it enables reliable knowledge discovery and tolerance to adversarial noise. In this work, we will be considering this problem from the angle of *proof complexity*: if our query testing problem can be solved (relatively) efficiently for a proof system, we will say that the proof system is *"PAC-automatizable"* (the formal definition appears in Section 1.1.1). We will see evidence that there may be advantages to the use of integrated algorithms from the standpoint of the power of the proof systems possessing fast algorithms: For a *limited* but *demonstrably nontrivial special case* of distributions over partial examples $M(D)$, we obtain a substantial speedup for query testing using the proof system *"polynomial calculus with resolution"* (PCR), which reasons about the solutions to systems of (arbitrary-degree) polynomial equations. As we will argue, this suggests that data-driven applications will benefit from a deeper integration of learning into the core algorithms.

1.1 Setting and results

In this work, we will focus primarily on a single, common family of query representations against a class of distributions encoding a common family of learning problems. We will obtain positive and negative results for this same class by varying the strength of the proofs we aim to test for. The primary class of queries we consider are given by a system of multivariate polynomial constraints, where the polynomials have rational coefficients. We restrict our attention to the Boolean solutions to these polynomials by assuming that for each indeterminate x_i there is a constraint $[x_i^2 - x_i = 0]$. Naturally, the query is satisfied when the complete example drawn from the distribution D satisfies this system of equations, and we wish to test whether or not the query is satisfied with high probability, given only access to partial examples. That is, whether or not it is $(1 - \epsilon)$-*valid*:

DEFINITION 1 ($(1 - \epsilon)$-VALID [40]). *Given a distribution D over $\{0,1\}^n$, we say that a Boolean formula φ is $(1 - \epsilon)$-valid if $\Pr_{x \in D}[\varphi(x) = 1] \geq 1 - \epsilon$.*

Given the way our query testing problem is set up – we distinguish queries that we can "certify true" using our partial examples from queries that are "inconclusive" – a partial information model in which *all* information may be hidden is trivially equivalent to classical logical reasoning. The "data" in such a case is essentially nonexistent, which is clearly not the setting we had originally envisioned. We wish to restrict our attention to cases where the data for the learning problem provides some information. In the primary special case we consider, our partial examples will be produced in the following, standard way. For each ith attribute of each complete example drawn from the ground truth distribution D, a μ-biased coin (for some constant $\mu \in (0,1)$) is tossed to determine whether or not the attribute is replaced by a $*$ in the resulting partial example. This model first appeared in learning theory in the work of Decatur and Gennaro [18], and more recently was employed as the partial information model for *Population Recovery* [20, 41, 5, 35] (which we will discuss later). Elsewhere, this model is known as *"masking completely at random (MCAR)."*

The main learning problems we consider are an "unsupervised" version of *uniform distribution parity learning*. Recall that in the usual, supervised PAC-learning model [39], there is a distinguished "label" attribute x_ℓ that is guaranteed to be determined by some function f of the other attributes,

where f is adversarially chosen from some pre-determined "concept class" $\mathcal{C}$. "Parity learning" then means that $\mathcal{C}$ is the class of parity functions: $x_\ell = \bigoplus_{i \in S} x_i$ for some $S \subseteq [n]$. In "uniform distribution" learning (in contrast to the original "distribution-free" model), the examples $x_1, \ldots, x_n$ are chosen uniformly at random, and x_ℓ is then determined by the unknown parity function. Equivalently, we could say that there is a *rule* (or *constraint*) $[\bigoplus_{i \in S \cup \{\ell\}} x_i = 0]$ and our examples $(x_1, \ldots, x_n, x_\ell)$ are chosen uniformly at random from the (Boolean) satisfying assignments to this rule. In this formulation, there is no longer any distinguished "label" bit. Indeed, we can naturally consider a *system* of such parity constraints, more generally of the form $[\bigoplus_{i \in S_j} x_i = b_j]$ for $S_j \subseteq [n]$ and $b_j \in \{0, 1\}$, which define an $\mathbb{F}_2$-affine subspace. Our examples are now drawn uniformly at random from this affine subspace. We will simply refer to the distributions underlying these unsupervised learning problems as *"affine distributions"*.

DEFINITION 2 (AFFINE DISTRIBUTION). *For any solvable linear system over $\mathbb{F}_2$ $Ax = b$, the distribution over $\{0,1\}^n$ that is uniform over solutions to the linear system is an affine distribution.*

We chose to focus on this family of problems because it is mathematically simple and problems involving parity learning or parity formulas have provided hard examples in both proof complexity [38] and learning theory (in particular, here, in the work of Ben-David and Dichterman [8] on learning from partial information). Our choice is vindicated by the existence of both positive and negative results for the same learning problem, for different choices of the strength of reasoning problem. We briefly note that our positive result applies to a somewhat broader class of problems that we defer to the body of the work.

1.1.1 Statement and discussion of results

We can now state the results. Recall that we assume that we are given as inputs a query formula (given by a system of multivariate polynomial constraints) and partial examples drawn from some common distribution $M(D)$. We wish to soundly certify when the query is satisfied with high probability by the underlying distribution D over complete examples, and we will seek quasipolynomial time algorithms for these problems. (We discuss this choice in Section 1.2.) We first note that this is NP-hard in general, even for affine distributions masked completely at random:

THEOREM 3. *Let $M(D)$ be an affine distribution masked completely at random (with constant $\mu \in (0,1)$). Unless NP has quasipolynomial-time randomized algorithms, there is no quasipolynomial time algorithm (in n and $1/\epsilon$) that uses examples from $M(D)$ to distinguish systems of multivariate polynomials that are satisfied with probability $1 - \epsilon$ by D from those that are satisfied with probability at most ϵ.*

By contrast, if we only seek to test for the existence of a small proof from some rules (premises) that are verifiable from the partial information, then a quasipolynomial time algorithm sometimes *does* exist, depending on the strength of the proof system. Precisely, we will say that the proof system is *PAC-automatizable* (in time T) if there is a sufficiently fast algorithm to test whether or not a proof exists using rules that simplify to true on the masked examples[2]:

---

[2] A full definition of this operation is deferred to Section 2.

DEFINITION 4 (PAC-AUTOMATIZABILITY). *When we say that a proof system is* PAC-*automatizable in time* $T(N, 1/\epsilon, 1/\gamma, 1/\delta)$, *we mean that there is an algorithm that is given* φ, $\epsilon, \gamma, \delta > 0$, *and N as input and obtains samples from $M(D)$ for a given distribution D. This algorithm runs in time $T(N, 1/\epsilon, 1/\gamma, 1/\delta)$ and with probability $1 - \delta$ distinguishes φ that are $(\epsilon + \gamma)$-valid from φ that have a refutation of size N in the system from additional premises $\psi_1, \ldots, \psi_k$ such that $\psi_1 \wedge \cdots \wedge \psi_k$ simplifies to true under partial examples drawn from $M(D)$ with probability at least $1 - \epsilon + \gamma$.*[3]

In this way, the algorithm implicitly learns some $\psi_1, \ldots, \psi_k$ using examples from $M(D)$, and tests for a proof of the query from such learnable formulas.

THEOREM 5. *Polynomial calculus with resolution (PCR) is PAC-automatizable in quasipolynomial time for affine distributions masked completely at random.*

Comparing Theorems 3 and 5, we see that the *promise* of some structure, such as provided by a small PCR proof, crucially reduces the complexity of our query testing problem, even under a rather benign partial information model and limited family of learning problems. This stands in contrast to Khardon and Roth's *complete* information setting [29] in which entailment queries for relatively rich representations could be answered without the need for any considerations of proof complexity.

We stress that the *"integrated"* formulation of this problem is crucial: in certifying a query, the algorithm is not required to produce either an explicit representation of the learned premises $\psi_1, \ldots, \psi_k$, or an explicit proof of the query from these formulas. Whereas in Section 1.2 we will recall the advantages of such an integrated formulation from the standpoint of learning theory (shown by Juba [24]), here we note that it provides a means to avoid difficulties in proof complexity. In particular, Galesi and Lauria [22] (building on earlier work by Alekhnovich and Razborov for resolution [2]) gave evidence that the proof search problem for PCR is intractable.[4] These works rely on a reduction that uses the *size of the smallest proof* to solve a hard optimization problem. Since the integrated formulation (as we will see) avoids producing an explicit, complete proof of the query, it cannot be invoked in such reductions in any obvious way.

Nevertheless, we can also show that some of the stronger negative results for proof search, namely those based on the infeasibility of "interpolation," as pioneered by Krajíček and Pudlák [31], can be carried over to negative results for our PAC-automatizability problem. Specifically, Bonet et al. [11], building on earlier work by Bonet, Pitassi, and Raz [13], showed that the proof search problem for *"bounded depth Frege systems"* (recalled in Section 2.2) is intractable if factoring requires subexponential time. We obtain an analogue of this result, even when given examples from an affine distribution that is masked completely at random.

THEOREM 6. *If integer factoring requires subexponential time, then bounded-depth Frege is not PAC-automatizable in quasipolynomial time for affine distributions masked completely at random.*

Contrasting Theorem 6 with Theorem 5, we observe that the *strength* of the proof complexity promise given to our algorithm crucially affects its time complexity. Although bounded-depth Frege is a proof system in which the lines of the proof are each given by an AC_0-circuit[5] and so the queries addressed by such proofs are *not* a system of multivariate polynomial constraints, we note that this is not the source of the difficulty. Indeed, these formulas comprising the proof (and therefore the corresponding class of queries) can be translated into a system of quasipolynomial-size multivariate polynomial constraints at the cost of a small increase in the error. This is accomplished by a technique presented by Aspnes et al. [3] for characteristic zero fields, building on an earlier, classic work by Razborov [37] that used such a transformation of AC_0 circuits to polynomials over fields of finite characteristic. Thus, the promise of a small bounded-depth Frege proof of a query implies that the query has an encoding as a system of multivariate polynomials, and so the difficulty does not lie in the use of a different query representation.

Relationship to Population Recovery.

Population recovery was first studied by Dvir et al. [20] and essentially solved in a sequence of later works [41, 5, 35]. In these works, partial examples drawn from an unknown distribution are presented, and the objective is to reconstruct the distribution (or merely the "heavy" portion of the distribution, in the case of the work by Batman et al. [5]) up to some additive error. As mentioned previously, we use the same partial information model as employed in these works. Naturally, if one can recover a sufficient measure of the distribution, then one can solve our approximate query testing problem directly, so whenever these algorithms apply, no proof complexity promise is required. On the other hand, population recovery is only efficient when either the support of the distribution is small (e.g., in Wigderson and Yehudayoff [41] or Moitra and Saks [35]) or when the distribution has almost all of its mass concentrated on a small number of heavy assignments, in the work by Batman et al. [5]. In general, our affine distributions can have high entropy and large support, and hence these algorithms for population recovery are not efficient in the setting we consider here. Indeed, we know that the query testing problem is sometimes NP-hard for affine distributions (in the absence of a proof complexity promise), so we don't expect the population recovery algorithms to solve our problem in general in any straightforward way. The bottom line is that PAC-automatizability and population recovery, in spite of presenting learning tasks for the same partial information model, are generally incomparable problems.

1.2 Motivation and context

In *knowledge discovery* and *data analytics*, the extraction of *knowledge* from a data set is not an end goal, only an in-

---

[3]It turns out to be more convenient to state this definition in terms of refutations of φ since this is how we will use the algorithms in most circumstances. We could equivalently have said that we were distinguishing when $\neg\varphi$ has a proof from when $\neg\varphi$ is *not* $(1 - \epsilon - \gamma)$-valid (where φ is the query actually provided to the algorithm).

[4]Although the technique used in those works cannot address the question of whether or not quasipolynomial-time algorithms for the proof search problem exist, the authors explicitly conjecture that such algorithms do not exist.

[5]Where, recall AC_0 is the class of polynomial-size, unbounded fan-in circuit families of *constant depth*; here, we mean that we consider proofs with some externally fixed constant depth bound.

termediate step. The final goal is to make a *decision* based on the data, perhaps about the allocation of resources in a business or course of treatment in medicine. In this work, we are modeling such decisions as a Boolean query formula. Even for the relatively simple proof system of *resolution* in which these queries are DNFs, such a representation is rich enough to capture some relatively interesting problems such as *planning in a STRIPS environment* [27]. Also, although we do not directly address such proof systems in this work, this broader perspective allows us to consider integer linear program queries against the *cutting planes* proof system, for example, which would capture a variety of real-world optimization problems (and thus presents an intriguing challenge for future work).

The current state of the art in *data science* is not a "closed loop," however. The business of extracting knowledge from the data is the responsibility of a human "data scientist" who, at his or her discretion, opts to invoke one or more of the usual machine learning algorithms on a given data set. These algorithms may be a "supervised" algorithm like linear regression, in search of a linear relationship among some of the data attributes, or perhaps an "unsupervised" algorithm that searches for deviations from a product distribution or some other ad-hoc measure of "interestingness" of properties of the data. In each case, the algorithms can be viewed as producing a *rule* satisfied by the data, e.g., $\psi(x, \vec{y}) = [x = \langle \vec{\beta}, \vec{y} \rangle + \beta_0 \pm \epsilon]$ (properly, a pair of linear inequalities) in the case of linear regression. There may be exponentially many such rules, so the data scientist cannot realistically hope to list them all. Without further guidance, there is therefore no guarantee that the data scientist will manage to discover all of the *relevant* rules necessary to inform the final decision, even when there exists a (polynomially) small list of such rules.

Moreover, the machine learning algorithms employed by the data scientist may be fundamentally incapable of producing the rules required to inform a decision. Recent work by Daniely et al. [15] provides new evidence that DNF/CNF representations may not be learnable by *any* efficient algorithm. Moreover, this result implies [28] that supervised learning algorithms, even for the relatively weak class of *conjunctions*, may be incapable of tolerating adversarial noise ("*agnostic*" learning). This is troubling, as there is no reason to expect that the kinds of simple representations that can be efficiently learned and reasoned about actually capture the "ground truth" (meaning here, hold with probability 1 over D). For example, in the case of STRIPS environments (originally proposed by Fikes and Nilsson [21]) that we mentioned previously, an environment is modeled as a list of deterministic rules of the form "(partial) state and action implies effect" (each formally encoded as clauses). We would only expect these rules to serve as *approximations* to the complicated, true dynamics of any real-world environment [33]. This is, nearly verbatim, the setup assumed in agnostic learning [28], and so seems to be beyond the reach of (stand-alone) learning algorithms.

Perhaps surprisingly, it turns out that these difficulties are an artifact of the separation of the learning algorithm from the query. A result by Juba [24], building on earlier work by Khardon and Roth [29], shows that for nearly every proof system in the literature (those that are "*natural*" in the sense of Beame et al. [6]), the problem of ("*implicitly*") learning all of the relevant rules to certify a query is no harder than the proof search alone, even under an agnostic learning model, *provided that we give up on identifying the rules explicitly*. Indeed, even in an "agnostic" model, the query itself presents merely a problem of *approximate counting* or *testing* using examples: we are only asking the probability that a query φ is satisfied on the complete examples from D. This approximate counting/testing problem then does not require that one actually solve the (often intractable) optimization problem of identifying rules with a near-optimal error rate. Nevertheless, we stress again, *logical queries* against such implicitly learned representations suffice to solve other problems, such as producing plans for STRIPS environments [27] for example.

Khardon and Roth [29] were the first to observe that such integration of logical queries and learning may be beneficial. They showed that, in a *complete* information setting (where the examples are taken from D directly), one can efficiently answer *all* $O(\log n)$-CNF *entailment queries* against any DNF representation that is always satisfied over D, even though it is not known how to learn DNFs in such a model, and such queries may be NP-hard. We stress that their formulation makes *no* reference to *proofs* of the queries from the "learned" DNF: their algorithm decides whether the query is entailed (by such a DNF) or falsified with noticeable probability. While their result is therefore quite striking from both the standpoint of learning theory and automated reasoning, its applicability is severely limited by the requirement of complete examples. This not only denies us the ability to model data sets in which some "ground truth" attributes cannot be directly observed, as for example the presence of a disease might not be in the case of medicine or the true preferences of a user might not be in the case of internet advertising. It also prevents us from setting up an optimization problem in which some attributes, capturing an optimal allocation (say), are likewise unknown. Khardon and Roth, keeping in the spirit of their first approach, proposed an algorithm for using partial examples [30] that avoided the use of theorem-proving techniques. This approach could only efficiently handle queries consisting of k-CNFs (for small k), however.

Khardon and Roth's work raises the question of whether or not the consideration of proof systems and theorem-proving are essential to our query testing problem. Although Juba [24] showed how to make use of partial examples for richer query representations by restricting our attention to testing for the existence of proofs of the query, it is not immediately clear that this introduction of proofs was essential in general. In this work, we address this question by showing that even for rather benign partial information settings, the strength of proof we are testing for may impact the complexity of the problem dramatically: for the same query representation, the query testing problem may be NP-hard without any proof complexity promise (Theorem 3), as hard as breaking Diffie-Hellman key exchange[6] under a weak proof complexity promise (Theorem 22), and solvable in quasipolynomial time under the stronger proof complexity promise of having a (quasi)polynomial size PCR proof (Theorem 5).

We view this final result as particularly significant for two reasons. First, it stands in contrast to what is believed to be possible for classical proof search, i.e., without access to partial examples: The best known algorithm for

---

[6]Therefore, as hard as integer factoring [10].

PCR theorem-proving, due to Clegg et al. [14], runs in time $n^{O(\sqrt{n})}$ for polynomial-size proofs over n variables. Even the weaker system of resolution is conjectured to not have such quasipolynomial-time theorem-proving algorithms (cf. Alekhnovich and Razborov [2]). Therefore, it suggests that the setting in which learning from partial examples is integrated into proof search is significantly different from the classical setting, and specifically that proof search may actually become easier in such an integrated setting. Second, in the context of theorem-proving (or "automatizability" in the usual language of proof complexity), a quasipolynomial time algorithm is relatively efficient. Even the relatively weak system of treelike resolution, in which intermediate derivations are not reused, is only known to have quasipolynomial time algorithms [7, 9]. Nevertheless, until the development of modern "clause learning" SAT-solvers, algorithms for finding treelike resolution proofs (via variants of DPLL [17, 16] which are not necessarily even so efficient) were widely used. Even quasipolynomial-time algorithms (as opposed to truly polynomial time algorithms) for richer proof systems may be of great significance.

2. BACKGROUND AND PRELIMINARIES

In this work, we consider a variety of proof systems under a weaker semantics than usual. It is not hard to show (by a union bound) that any classical logical inference can be applied to formulas possessing $(1 - \epsilon)$-validity, as long as we allow for further loss in the approximation.[7]

PROPOSITION 7 (CLASSICAL REASONING [24]). *Let $\psi_1, \ldots, \psi_k$ be formulas such that each ψ_i is $(1 - \epsilon_i)$-valid under a common distribution D for some $\epsilon_i \in [0, 1]$. Suppose that $\{\psi_1, \ldots, \psi_k\} \models \varphi$ (in the classical sense). Then φ is $1 - \epsilon'$-valid under D for $\epsilon' = \sum_i \epsilon_i$.*

We are therefore safe in considering arbitrary kinds of propositional proof systems in this new setting.

An important notion in proof complexity is that of a *restriction* of a formula; we can naturally interpret our partial examples as restrictions as follows:

DEFINITION 8 (RESTRICTION). *Given a formula φ defined over linear threshold and parity connectives and a partial example $\rho \in \{0, 1, *\}^n$ we define the restriction of φ under ρ, denoted $\varphi|_\rho$, as follows by induction on the construction of φ:*

- *For any Boolean constant b, $b|_\rho = b$.*
- *For any variable x_i, if $\rho_i = *$, then $x_i|_\rho = x_i$, and otherwise (for $\rho_i \in \{0, 1\}$), $x_i|_\rho = \rho_i$.*
- *For a parity connective over $\psi_1, \ldots, \psi_k$, if $\ell \geq 1$ of the ψ_i (indexed by $i_1, \ldots i_\ell$) do not simplify to Boolean values under ρ, then (indexing the rest by $j_1, \ldots, j_{k-\ell}$)*

$$\oplus(\psi_1, \ldots, \psi_k)|_\rho = \oplus\left(\psi_{i_1}|_\rho, \ldots, \psi_{i_\ell}|_\rho, \bigoplus_{r=1}^{k-\ell} \psi_{j_r}|_\rho\right)$$

and otherwise it simplifies to a Boolean constant, $\oplus(\psi_1, \ldots, \psi_k)|_\rho = \psi_1|_\rho \oplus \cdots \oplus \psi_k|_\rho$.
- *A linear threshold $[\sum_{i=1}^k c_i \psi_i \geq b]$ $(c_1, \ldots, c_k, b \in \mathbb{Q})$ simplifies to 1 if $\sum_{i:\psi_i|_\rho = 1} c_i + \sum_{i:\psi_i|_\rho \notin \{0,1\}} \min\{0, c_i\} \geq$*

---

[7]It also is not hard to show that as long as the distributions are arbitrary, the union bound is tight here [24].

b, to 0 if $\sum_{i:\psi_i|_\rho = 1} c_i + \sum_{i:\psi_i|_\rho \notin \{0,1\}} \max\{0, c_i\} < b$, and otherwise is given by

$$\left[\sum_{i:\psi_i|_\rho \notin \{0,1\}} c_i(\psi_i|_\rho) \geq \left(b - \sum_{i:\psi_i|_\rho = 1} c_i\right)\right].$$

That is, $\varphi|_\rho$ is a formula over the variables x_i such that $\rho_i = *$. We chose to define partial evaluation over this atypical basis of connectives because it enables us to define partial evaluation of *both* arithmetic formulas (which play a central role here) and the standard Boolean basis in a natural way. Recalling that our domain is Boolean, we define a monomial to be the AND of the literals, where we define AND and OR using the threshold connective and NOT using the parity connective in the natural way. We can now define a polynomial constraint $P(x) = 0$ using the conjunction of two linear-threshold connectives, $[P(x) \geq 0] \wedge [-P(x) \geq 0]$.

2.1 Polynomial calculus

In polynomial calculus, originally introduced by Clegg et al. [14], formulas have the form of polynomial equations over an arbitrary nontrivial field $\mathbb{F}$ (for the present purposes, assume $\mathbb{F}$ is $\mathbb{Q}$, the field of rationals), and we are interested in their Boolean solutions. A set of hypotheses is thus a system of equations, and polynomial calculus enables us to derive new constraints that are satisfied by any Boolean solutions to the original system. More formally, for our Boolean variables $x_1, \ldots, x_n$, our formulas are equations of the form $[P(x) = 0]$ for $P \in \mathbb{F}[x_1, \ldots, x_n]$ (i.e., formal multivariate polynomials over the field $\mathbb{F}$ with indeterminates given by the variables). We require that the polynomials are represented as a sum of monomials: that is, every line is of the form $\sum_{\vec{\alpha} \in \mathbb{N}^n} c_{\vec{\alpha}} \prod_{i:\alpha_i \neq 0} x_i^{\alpha_i} = 0$ for coefficients $c_{\vec{\alpha}} \in \mathbb{F}$, where the products $\prod_{i:\alpha_i \neq 0} x_i^{\alpha_i}$ are the *monomials* corresponding to the degree vector $\vec{\alpha}$. For each variable, the proof system has a *Boolean axiom* $[x^2 - x = 0]$ (asserting that $x \in \{0, 1\}$). The rules of inference are *linear combination*, which asserts that for equations $[P(x) = 0]$ and $[Q(x) = 0]$, for any coefficients a and b from $\mathbb{F}$, we can infer $[a \cdot P(x) + b \cdot Q(x) = 0]$; and *multiplication*, which asserts that for any variable (indeterminate) x and polynomial equation $[P(x) = 0]$, we can derive $[x \cdot P(x) = 0]$. A *refutation* in polynomial calculus is a derivation of the polynomial 1, i.e., the contradictory equation $[1 = 0]$. We note that without loss of generality, we can restrict our attention to formulas in which no indeterminate appears in a monomial with degree greater than one—such monomials are *multilinear*. Intuitively this is so because the Boolean axioms assert that a larger power can be replaced by a smaller one.

In this work, we focus on an extension of polynomial calculus that can simulate resolution, known as *polynomial calculus with resolution (PCR)* that first appeared in the work of Alekhnovich et al. [1]. We introduce a new indeterminate $\bar{x}$ for each variable x, related by the *complementarity axiom* $[x + \bar{x} - 1 = 0]$ (forcing $\bar{x} = \neg x$). That is, roughly speaking, our indeterminates now correspond to *literals* (and we will abuse notation by speaking of the monomials as products of literals elsewhere). Monomials now can encode clauses, with the degree of the (multilinear) monomial equal to the width of the clause. We can *simulate a resolution step* (i.e., the cut rule) between one monomial of the form $\ell x^{\vec{\alpha}}$ from a larger polynomial constraint $[P(x) = 0]$ and a second monomial constraint of the form $[\neg \ell x^{\vec{\beta}} = 0]$ where $\vec{\beta} \leq \vec{\alpha}$ by adding an appropriate multiple of $[\neg \ell x^{\vec{\alpha}} = 0]$ to $[P(x) = 0]$, and then subtracting the same multiple of $[\ell x^{\vec{\alpha}} + \neg \ell x^{\vec{\alpha}} - x^{\vec{\alpha}} = 0]$ from the result: We then obtain the constraint $[P'(x) = 0]$ in which the monomial $x^{\vec{\alpha}}$ is substituted for the monomial $\ell x^{\vec{\alpha}}$ i.e., ℓ is eliminated. Notice, we can obtain $[P(x) = 0]$ from $[P'(x) = 0]$ and the monomial constraint $\neg \ell x^{\vec{\beta}}$ again by repeating the derivation except subtracting the multiple of $\neg \ell x^{\vec{\beta}}$ and adding the mutiple of $[\ell x^{\vec{\alpha}} + \neg \ell x^{\vec{\alpha}} - x^{\vec{\alpha}} = 0]$, thus "reversing" the elimination of ℓ. This will be important since we can't freely use multiplication to simulate weakening of the monomials of $P(x)$ independently.

Following a standard convention, we define the *size* of a PCR proof to be the *number of monomials* appearing in the proof. We also define the *degree* of the proof to be the maximum degree of any monomial appearing in the proof. The main result of Clegg et al. [14] establishes that the degree-d fragment of polynomial calculus (and PCR) is automatizable in time $n^{O(d)}$.

We will be interested in the result of "plugging in" a partial assignment to each step of a PCR refutation:

DEFINITION 9 (RESTRICTED PROOF). *Given a PCR refutation Π and partial assignment ρ, the restriction of Π under ρ, denoted $\Pi|_\rho$, is the proof obtained by substituting $\varphi|_\rho$ for each line φ of Π.*

A property shared by most propositional proof systems is that a restriction maps a proof to a proof of the restriction of the initial premises—indeed, Beame et al. [6] called such proof systems "natural." It is not hard to show that PCR has this property:

PROPOSITION 10. *For any PCR refutation Π and any partial assignment ρ, the restriction $\Pi|_\rho$ is also a PCR refutation.*

2.2 Bounded-depth Frege

We will use the standard bounded-depth Frege sequent systems of propositional logic defined by Maciel and Pitassi [32]. In these systems, each line is of the form $A_1, \ldots, A_s \rightarrow B_1, \ldots, B_t$ (that is, the conjunction of the A_i's implies the disjunction of the B_j's) where each A_i and B_j is a bounded-depth formula from the appropriate class; we will consider two such classes in this work, AC_0 and TC_0. These classes both use the connectives $\vee$, $\wedge$, and $\neg$, and TC_0 additionally features the $\oplus_b$ connectives that are true iff the number of inputs that are true modulo 2 is $b \in \{0, 1\}$, and the Th_k connective, a threshold connective that is true iff at least k of the inputs are true. All of these connectives (except $\neg$) have unbounded fan-in. We define the *depth* of a formula to be the maximum depth of nesting of these connectives; the depth of a proof is then the maximum depth of any formula appearing in the proof. The *size* of the proof is the sum of the sizes of all of the formulas appearing in the proof. In the systems we consider, the depths will be bounded by some absolute constant (independent of the number of variables n) and the size of the proofs (and hence also their lengths) will be bounded by some polynomial in the number of variables.

The main result of Bonet et al. [11] is essentially a translation from TC_0-Frege proofs to AC_0-Frege proofs:

THEOREM 11 (THEOREM 6.1 OF BONET ET AL. [11]). *Suppose that $\Gamma \rightarrow \Delta$ has a TC_0-Frege proof of size polynomial in n in which the threshold and parity connectives all*

have fan-in bounded by $O(\log^k n)$. *Then there is an AC_0 formula equivalent to $\Gamma \rightarrow \Delta$ that is polynomial-time computable from $\Gamma \rightarrow \Delta$ and has an AC_0-Frege proof of size greater by a factor of at most $O(n^K)$ where K depends only on k.*

Actually, Bonet et al. give specific definitions of such threshold and parity connectives. They do not explicitly state or argue for the efficient computation of the transformation (of the conclusion $\Gamma \rightarrow \Delta$) but this is immediate. This translation enables non-automatizability for (sufficiently simple) specific TC_0-Frege formulas to be carried over to non-automatizability for AC_0-Frege formulas.

Substitutions.

A *substitution* is a mapping from formulas to formulas defined by its action on free variables, taking them to arbitrary propositional formulas. For a substitution θ and propositional formula φ, we typically denote the result of applying θ to φ by $\theta\varphi$. Since the rules of inference for Frege systems remain instances of the same rules under any substitution, the following (essentially standard) fact is easily established:

PROPOSITION 12. *Let θ be any substitution taking variables to depth-d_1 formulas, and suppose that there is a depth-d_2 Frege proof of φ from $\{\psi_1, \ldots, \psi_k\}$. Then there is a depth-$(d_1 + d_2)$ Frege proof of $\theta\varphi$ from $\{\theta\psi_1, \ldots, \theta\psi_k\}$.*

In particular, we will be substituting formulas consisting of a parity connective over variables for the variables of the original formula. This increases the depth of a formula by one and increases the size by at most a factor of n' (where there are n' variables in the substitutions). It thus takes TC_0-Frege proofs to TC_0-Frege proofs.

3. TECHINCAL OVERVIEW

We now provide an overview of how our results are obtained, highlighting the techniques involved. In what follows, we will denote examples drawn from a distribution D masked completely at random with bias μ by $M_\mu(D)$.

3.1 Sketch of Theorem 5

The starting point for our positive results are the prior work by Juba [24], showing how PAC-automatizability can be reduced to classical automatizability whenever the proof system is closed under restrictions (*natural* in the sense of Beame, Kautz, and Sabharwal [6]). That is: it provides a simple technique for searching over conjunctions of premises ψ such that $\psi|_\rho$ simplifies to the constant 1 for $\rho \in M_\mu(D)$ with probability $(1 - \epsilon + \gamma)$ (we say ψ is $(1 - \epsilon + \gamma)$-*testable*) and such that there is a proof of the query φ from ψ in the given proof system. The observation is that for a restriction-closed proof system, when every step of the proof is hit by the restriction ρ, the desired premises ψ will vanish from the proof with high probability. Thus, it suffices to check the provability of $\varphi|_\rho$ on various partial examples ρ drawn from $M_\mu(D)$, and the testable premises are incorporated "for free." We won't focus further on these classes of testable premises in this work; instead, our focus in this work will be on how these restrictions drawn from $M_\mu(D)$ cause polynomial calculus with resolution proofs to simplify.

The uniform distribution provides an informative special case of how such simplification occurs. Consider any monomial of degree at least d: in a partial example ρ drawn from

$M_\mu(U_n)$, each literal ℓ_i in the monomial is set to 0 with probability $\mu/2$. Therefore, when the monomial is hit by the restriction ρ, it simplifies to 0 with probability $1-(1-\mu/2)^d$; if $d \geq \frac{2}{\mu} \ln \frac{1}{\gamma}$, then the monomial only "survives" with probability γ. So, in a polynomial calculus proof of size $P(n)$ (consisting of $P(n)$ monomials), a union bound over the monomials yields that with probability $1 - \delta$, only monomials of degree at most $O(\frac{1}{\mu} \ln \frac{n}{\delta})$ survive. The algorithm of Clegg, Edmonds, and Impagliazzo [14] shows that degree-d polynomial calculus is automatizable in time $n^{O(d)}$; therefore, the basic reduction of our PAC-automatizability problem (for the uniform distribution) produces (YES-)instances which are automatizable in quasipolynomial time.

Affine distributions are not quite so simple. Nevertheless, we show that when polynomial calculus proofs are hit with restrictions from affine distributions, the surviving monomials have a special structure that similarly allows the proofs to be simulated in low degree. We observe that affine distributions feature a *"bias gap"*—the (conditional) biases of variables is either strong or weak (and not of moderate strength):

DEFINITION 13 (BIAS GAP). *We will say that a distribution D over $\{0,1\}^n$ has a width-w $(\beta, 1 - \gamma)$ bias gap if for any monomial of $k \leq w$ literals $\prod_{i=1}^{k} \ell_i$ that takes value 1 with nonzero probability and any variable x, either $\Pr[x = 1| \prod_{i=1}^{k} \ell_i = 1] \geq \beta$ and $\Pr[x = 0| \prod_{i=1}^{k} \ell_i = 1] \geq \beta$ or else for some $b \in \{0,1\}$, $\Pr[x = b| \prod_{i=1}^{k} \ell_i = 1] \geq 1 - \gamma$. In the former case, we say that x is β-balanced for the monomial $\ell_1 \cdots \ell_k$, and in the latter we say that, respectively, x (for $b = 1$) or $\neg x$ (for $b = 0$) is $1 - \gamma$-implied by $\ell_1 \cdots \ell_k$.*

Bias gap distributions are reasonably natural. For example, we note that the simple *"pure document"* probabilistic corpus model introduced by Papadimitriou et al. [36] to analyze Latent Semantic Indexing generally features a nontrivial bias gap. It will turn out that our results will apply to $(\beta, 1 - \eta)$-bias gap distributions where β is any constant and η is quasipolynomially small.

Affine distributions turn out to have a bias gap, since intuitively, if a monomial determines the value of another variable in a linear constraint, that literal is easily seen to be 1-implied, and otherwise the literal turns out to be uniformly distributed (and thus, 1/2-balanced).

DEFINITION 14 (CONSTRAINTS ON MONOMIALS). *We say that there is a constraint on a monomial $x^{\vec{\alpha}}$ in an affine distribution given by the linear system $Ax = b$ if there is a linear combination of the rows of A such that the only nonzero entries are in indices i for which the corresponding variable appears in a variable of $x^{\vec{\alpha}}$.*

LEMMA 15. *Let $x^{\vec{\alpha}}$ be a monomial and D be an affine distribution such that there are no constraints on $x^{\vec{\alpha}}$. Then the marginal distribution over the variables appearing in $x^{\vec{\alpha}}$ is uniform.*

On account of a bias gap, we show that a monomial of logarithmic degree can only survive (with probability $\delta/P(n)$ for a size $P(n)$ proof, again) when, conditioned on partial assignments that set $O(\log n/\delta)$ of the indeterminates to 1, other indeterminates are also fixed to take value 1. This property follows from a couple of lemmas. The first lemma generalizes our observation about the uniform distribution to monomials in which the variables are unbiased:

LEMMA 16. *Let $x^{\vec{\alpha}}$ be a monomial of degree at least $\frac{2}{\mu} \ln \frac{1}{\delta}$ such that for any literal ℓ of $x^{\vec{\alpha}}$ and any submonomial $x^{\vec{\alpha}'}$ of $x^{\vec{\alpha}}$ without ℓ, ℓ is unbiased conditioned on $x^{\vec{\alpha}'}$ surviving. Then $x^{\vec{\alpha}}|_\rho = 0$ on $\rho \in M_\mu(D)$ with probability $1 - \delta$.*

The second lemma considers when the variables may be fixed to take value 0:

LEMMA 17. *Let $x^{\vec{\alpha}}$ be a monomial of degree $2d$ for $d \geq \frac{1}{\mu} \ln \frac{1}{\delta}$ such that for every submonomial of $x^{\vec{\alpha}}$ of degree d there is some further submonomial $\ell x^{\vec{\alpha}'}$ such that conditioned on $x^{\vec{\alpha}'}$ surviving, ℓ is set to 0. Then with probability $1 - \delta$, there is an unmasked variable of $x^{\vec{\alpha}}$ that is fixed to zero under $\rho \in M_\mu(D)$.*

Together, these simple lemmas indeed establish our claimed "structure" of the surviving monomials: As a consequence of the bias gap in affine distributions, every sufficient degree $(\frac{4}{\mu} \ln \frac{P(n)}{\delta})$ submonomial of a surviving monomial in our polynomial calculus proof must have some variable that is fixed to 1, conditioned on the rest of the submonomial surviving. Indeed, otherwise either there is a degree $\frac{2}{\mu} \ln \frac{P(n)}{\delta}$ submonomial satisfying the conditions of the first lemma, or else the conditions of the second lemma are satisfied, and either way the monomial cannot survive with probability greater than $\delta/P(n)$, so by a union bound, none survive.

We can exploit this structure of the monomials now by learning *all* of the small-degree monomial constraints on the distribution's support. Learning these monomials is fairly straightforward: Logarithmic-degree monomials are simultaneously unmasked (under M_μ) with inverse-polynomial probability, and since the masking is independent of the underlying assignment drawn from D, we can obtain unbiased "complete" examples for each monomial, which allows us to apply standard learning techniques, summarized below:

LEMMA 18. *Suppose D is a distribution with a width-d $(\beta, 1 - \frac{\gamma}{4(2n+1)^d})$ bias gap. Let ψ be the conjunction of constraints $[x^{\vec{\alpha}} = 0]$ for all monomials $x^{\vec{\alpha}}$ of degree at most d that simplify to the value 1 in at most a $\frac{\gamma\mu^d}{2(2n+1)^d}$-fraction of a sample of m_0 partial examples from $M_\mu(D)$ (for $m_0 = \frac{2d(2n+1)^{2d}}{\mu^{2d}\gamma^2} \ln \frac{4(2n+1)}{\delta}$). Then with probability at least $1 - \delta/2$, ψ is $1 - \gamma$-valid and contains all $1 - \frac{\gamma}{4(2n+1)^d}$-valid monomial constraints of degree at most d, including specifically all $\neg \ell x^{\vec{\alpha}}$ such that ℓ is implied by $x^{\vec{\alpha}}$.*

The heart of our analysis now is that we show that these small monomial constraints allow us to simulate (the surviving portion of) an arbitrary PCR proof in low degree: We know that every logarithmic-width submonomial of the surviving monomials has a member that is fixed to 1 conditioned on the rest of the monomial surviving; then taking the *complement* of this member (recalling that this is PCR, so we have such complement indeterminates) yields a logarithmic-width monomial that is consistently 0, and hence is among the learned monomial constraints. We can therefore eliminate these variables that are fixed to 1 by resolution steps using our learned monomial constraints. That is, if we quotient out the ideal generated by the small-degree monomial constraints, every step of the restricted PCR proof has a low-degree representative.

The only complication now is that we need to ensure that we can derive the low-degree representatives of subsequent steps of the (restricted) proof by a low-degree PCR derivation. For example, we might try to maintain the same "reduced" monomials across different parts of the proof—say some canonical reduction such as lex. order. The difficulty with this approach is that the multiplication rule of polynomial calculus may change the canonical reduction substantially. What turns out to work is that we suppose that we only make greedy reduction steps on each monomial of the proof according to *some* arbitrary order using our low-degree monomials of the ideal, and we are given that the resulting representative is of low degree. We then show that there is a low-degree PCR derivation of one reduction ordering from any other

LEMMA 19. *Let ψ be a conjunction of constraints of the form $x^{\vec{\alpha}} = 0$ of degree at most d. Let any two submonomials of degree at most d of a common monomial of a constraint be given that have been derived by successively eliminating one variable at a time by simulating resolution steps with monomials from ψ. Then there is a derivation of one from the other of degree at most $3d$.*

We prove Lemma 19 by showing that the *product* of two corresponding reduced monomials of a proof step can be derived in low degree by following one reduction order in reverse and eliminating those indeterminates missing from the product from the rest of the learned, low-degree monomial constraints of the ideal. Either of the reduced monomials can be derived in low degree from their product using these modified monomials from the ideal (with the unnecessary variables eliminated) to perform the reduction. If the reduced monomials and the learned monomial constraints all have degree d, then the overall derivation requires only degree $3d$.

This completes the proof: there is a low-degree simulation of the surviving PCR proof, which is therefore automatizable by the algorithm of Clegg, Edmonds, and Impagliazzo [14]. As we obtain a degree bound of $d = O(\frac{1}{\mu} \log \frac{n}{\delta})$ on the polynomials involved, it turns out that the overall algorithm runs in time $m \cdot n^{O(d)}$, where $m = \frac{2}{\gamma^2} \ln \frac{2}{\delta}$; the initial learning of all of the degree-d monomials can be done using $n^{O(d)}$ time and examples, so the time spent on the proof search dominates. In full generality, we obtain:

THEOREM 20 (CF. THEOREM 5). *Given an input system of polynomial equations φ, a bound $p(n)$, $\mu, \epsilon, \gamma, \delta, \beta \in (0, 1)$, and access to examples from $M_\mu(D)$ for a distribution D that has a width-d $\left(= \frac{1}{\mu\beta} \ln \frac{2m_1 \cdot p(n)}{\delta} \right)$ $\left(\beta, 1 - \frac{\gamma}{4n(2n+1)^d} \right)$ bias gap, (where $m_1 = \frac{1}{2\gamma^2} \ln \frac{2}{\delta}$) and given that either*

- *φ is satisfied by D with probability at least $\epsilon + 2\gamma$ or*
- *there exist systems of polynomial equations ψ_0 and ψ_1 such that*
  - *ψ_0 consists of $1 - \frac{\gamma}{4n(2n+1)^d}$-valid monomials and*
  - *ψ_1 simplifies to 1 with probability $1 - \epsilon + 2\gamma$ under $M_\mu(D)$*

and there is a PCR refutation of size $p(n)$ of $\psi_0 \wedge \psi_1 \wedge \varphi$ there is an algorithm that decides which case holds with probability $1 - \delta$, and runs in time $n^{O(\frac{1}{\mu\beta} \log \frac{p(n)}{\gamma\delta})}$.

3.2 Sketch of Theorems 3 and 6

The main observation underlying both of the negative results is that affine distributions present hard examples because parity constraints are invisible when even one variable

participating in the parity is masked: formally, if all of the constraints are sufficiently large, then the masked affine distribution is indistinguishable from masked examples of the uniform distribution. (Indeed, this is the main content of Ben-David and Dichterman's result for the RFA model [8].) When the query can compute the corresponding large parities, these parity functions are constrained to take a hidden value (depending on the choice of affine distribution) with probability 1. Intuitively, since settings of the parities are hidden from an algorithm that only has access to partial examples, and they can encode an arbitrary fixed assignment, the algorithm will need to somehow "rule out" the possibility that *any* such hidden assignment falsifies the query.

The formalization of this intuition proceeds, naturally, by showing (in Lemma 21) that for any fixed setting of hidden variables we desire, an algorithm that has no access to any examples can always simulate access to masked examples of an affine distribution with parity encodings of these hidden values by simply masking examples of the uniform distribution. Precisely, for any given setting of Boolean values for some basic variables $x_1, \ldots, x_n$, we substitute a parity of a vector of $k(n)$ new variables for each basic variable, and let $D_n^{\oplus k(n)}$ be the distribution in which these parities are constrained to take the same values as the underlying (secret) values of the basic variables.

LEMMA 21. *Let $x^* \in \{0,1\}^n$ and ρ consistent with x^* be given. Let θ be a substitution that takes each variable x_i such that $\rho_i = *$ to a parity of $k(n)$ new variables, $y_1^{(i)}, \ldots, y_{k(n)}^{(i)}$, and leaves all other variables fixed. Let $D^{\oplus k(n)}$ be the distribution over this new set of variables such that the variables left fixed by θ take the same value as in x^* and the new variables are uniformly distributed over values satisfying $y_1^{(i)} \oplus \cdots \oplus y_{k(n)}^{(i)} = b$ where $x_i^* = b$. Then for any p-valid formula φ under the point distribution for x^*, $\theta\varphi$ is also p-valid under $D^{\oplus k(n)}$. Moreover, there is a distribution that can be sampled in linear time given ρ that is $1 - n\mu^{k(n)}$-statistically close to $M_\mu(D^{\oplus k(n)})$.*

Towards showing the NP-hardness of polynomial queries, we take an arbitrary 3DNF and substitute parity encodings for each of the variables: if the 3DNF is a tautology, so is this substitution instance, and otherwise there is an affine distribution (indistinguishable from the uniform distribution under masking) in which it is falsified with probability 1. It is immediate that distinguishing whether such substitution instances are satisfied with probability 1 or 0 is NP-hard, even given masked examples. To fool quasipolynomial-time algorithms, we only need polylogarithmic-size parity constraints, and the work of Bonet et al. [11] in particular establishes that polylogarithmic size parity formulas have AC_0 circuits. We then convert these AC_0 circuits down to polynomial queries using randomized polynomial encodings (of Razborov for finite characteristic [37] and Aspnes et al. for characteristic zero [3]), at the cost of introducing some small error ϵ and an increase to quasipolynomial size monomial expansion representations. The result is a randomized quasipolynomial-time reduction, showing that it is NP-hard to distinguish whether the resulting polynomial queries are satisfied with probability at least $1 - \epsilon$ or at most ϵ. This is Theorem 3.

The argument that bounded depth Frege is not PAC-automatizable in quasipolynomial time is similar: the basic building block is the result by Bonet, Pitassi, and Raz [13] that automatizing TC_0-Frege gives an attack that breaks the Diffie-Hellman key exchange protocol [19], which in turn yields integer factoring [10]. Here, we use parity encodings to hide the unknown values of the Diffie-Hellman protocol.[8] Again, Lemma 21 is indeed saying that there is a simulator that generates such "leakage" as provided by our parital examples, so any algorithm that PAC-automatizes these substitution instances (using examples) can be combined with the simulator to break the security of the Diffie-Hellman protocol. This is summarized in Theorem 22, showing a range of hardness results for PAC-automatizing TC_0-Frege for a corresponding range of security assumptions for Diffie-Hellman key exchange.

THEOREM 22. *Suppose TC_0-Frege is PAC-automatizable for affine distributions under M_μ for constant μ in time $T(N, 1/\epsilon, 1/\gamma, 1/\delta)$ for $T(N, 2, 3, 1/\delta) \geq \Omega(N^c)$ and $T(N, 2, 3, 1/\delta) < 2^{o((N \log \frac{1}{\delta})^{1/c})}$ for sufficiently large c. Then for some polynomial P, there is an algorithm running in time $\tilde{O}(nT(P(n) \cdot \log \frac{1}{\delta}, 2, 3, \frac{n}{\delta}))$ that recovers $g^{ab} \bmod p$ with probability $1 - \delta$ from any n-bit p, generator g of $\mathbb{Z}_p^*$, $g^a \bmod p$, and $g^b \bmod p$, where a and b are arbitrary.*

Now, to obtain the promised hardness of bounded-depth Frege based on integer factoring requiring subexponential time, we consider the reduction of Bonet et al. [11], showing how TC_0-Frege proofs in which the parity and threshold gates have polylogarithmic fan-in can be converted to bounded-depth Frege proofs. With a little more care, we show that the reduction can convert *quasipolynomial-time* algorithms for automatizing bounded-depth Frege to arbitrarily good subexponential-time algorithms for integer factoring. By invoking Lemma 21 again to simulate access to the affine distributions encoding the secret values in the Diffie-Hellman instances used in the factoring reduction, we therefore show that quasipolynomial time PAC-automatizing bounded-depth Frege indeed likewise yields $2^{O(n^\eta)}$-time algorithms for factoring for every $\eta > 0$. As in the original result for classical non-automatizability of bounded-depth Frege by Bonet et al., this contradicts an assumption that there is some lower bound for $\eta > 0$, and Theorem 6 follows.

4. DIRECTIONS FOR FUTURE RESEARCH

Several problems present themselves as natural directions for future work. The most pressing of these is, *can the restriction to distributions with a bias gap be lifted?* That is, how can we efficiently reason about "medium-strength" biases? Although the ultimate objective of such work would be to strengthen these results to the distribution-free PAC setting, any work that handled a class of distributions that exhibited such biases would also be of interest. A similar direction would be to obtain results for a more general class of masking processes [34]; although it seems that our results generalize to masking distributions that simultaneously reveal any width-w set of literals with non-negligible probability (for $w = \Omega(\log n)$) such as w-wise independent distributions (Wigderson and Yehudayoff [41] make a similar

---

[8]The intuition here is that our masking process is "leaking" some of the secrets of the two parties, so we use a leakage-resilient encoding of these values. Since the masking completely at random is such a weak form of leakage, the parity encoding is secure. This use of the parity encoding originally appeared in the work by Ishai, Sahai, and Wagner [23].

observation about their algorithm for population recovery, which uses the same partial-information setup), it would be desirable to find other, perhaps weaker properties that would also permit relatively efficient algorithms.

Of course, the results of this work beg the question so far as the classical (quasi)automatizability of PCR (and resolution) is concerned. Although there are families of counterexamples [12, 4] showing that a purely width (and/or treelike) based approach to finding small resolution proofs such as pursued by Ben-Sasson and Wigderson [9] cannot beat the current best-known bound of $n^{O(\sqrt{n \log n})}$ (for both resolution and PCR), it does not rule out other approaches. Since our algorithm and analysis essentially establish that every PCR proof over distributions with a bias gap has a low-degree approximate version using the learned monomials, it seems significant for our algorithm that the learned formula ψ may not have a small-degree derivation. Unfortunately, it is not clear how one might hope to exploit this in the absence of a distribution. Still, if *any* algorithm could find PCR (resp. resolution) derivations in quasipolynomial time, then using the results of our previous work [24], this would also immediately resolve both of the questions suggested in the previous paragraph.

Along these lines in the other direction, we note that the nonautomatizability results for resolution and PCR (first obtained from the work of Alekhnovich and Razborov [2] and Galesi and Lauria [22], respectively) merely show that such algorithms cannot be too sensitive to the length of the proof. This is too weak to obtain non-PAC-automatizability as our no-instances merely need to detect false queries, not queries requiring long proofs. It seems reasonable to conjecture that resolution and PCR are nonautomatizable in this stronger sense (and that therefore *some* restriction on the masking process is needed at a minimum) and it would be interesting if this could be shown.

The other natural direction in which one might hope to strengthen our results involves extending them to proof systems incomparable with PCR, such as cutting planes or k-DNF resolution. We already observed in previous work [24] that there are natural fragments of these proof systems (already well studied in the case of k-RES) that are PAC-automatizable. The question would be whether, as with degree-restricted PCR, we could use these algorithms as a starting point to obtain algorithms for the unrestricted proof system in the context of reasoning about a distribution.

Acknowledgements

The author thanks Paul Beame, Eli Ben-Sasson, and Leslie Valiant for conversations that helped shape this work. The author also thanks the anonymous reviewers for their constructive comments.

5. REFERENCES

[1] M. Alekhnovich, E. Ben-Sasson, A. A. Razborov, and A. Wigderson. Space complexity in propositional calculus. *SIAM J. Comput.*, 31(4):1184–1211, 2002.

[2] M. Alekhnovich and A. A. Razborov. Resolution is not automatizable unless W[P] is tractable. *SIAM J. Comput.*, 38(4):1347–1363, 2008.

[3] J. Aspnes, R. Beigel, M. Furst, and S. Rudich. The expressive power of voting polynomials. *Combinatorica*, 14(2):135–148, 1994.

[4] A. Atserias and M. L. Bonet. On the automatizability of resolution and related propositional proof systems. *Inf. Comp.*, 189:182–201, 2004.

[5] L. Batman, R. Impagliazzo, C. Murray, and R. Paturi. Finding heavy hitters from lossy or noisy data. In P. Raghavendra et al., editor, *Proc. APPROX/RANDOM 2013*, number 8096 in LNCS, pages 347–362. Springer, 2013.

[6] P. Beame, H. Kautz, and A. Sabharwal. Towards understanding and harnessing the potential of clause learning. *JAIR*, 22:319–351, 2004.

[7] P. Beame and T. Pitassi. Simplified and improved resolution lower bounds. In *Proc. 37th FOCS*, pages 274–282, 1996.

[8] S. Ben-David and E. Dichterman. Learning with restricted focus of attention. *JCSS*, 56(3):277–298, 1998.

[9] E. Ben-Sasson and A. Wigderson. Short proofs are narrow – resolution made simple. *J. ACM*, 48(2):149–169, 2001.

[10] E. Biham, D. Boneh, and O. Reingold. Breaking generalized Diffie-Hellman modulo a composite is no easier than factoring. *Inform. Process. Lett.*, 70:83–87, 1999.

[11] M. L. Bonet, C. Domingo, R. Gavaldá, A. Maciel, and T. Pitassi. Non-automatizability of bounded-depth Frege proofs. *Comput. Complex.*, 13:47–68, 2004.

[12] M. L. Bonet and N. Galesi. Optimality of size-width tradeoffs for resolution. *Comput. Complex.*, 10(4):261–276, 2001.

[13] M. L. Bonet, T. Pitassi, and R. Raz. On interpolation and automization for Frege proof systems. *SIAM J. Comput.*, 29(6):1939–1967, 2000.

[14] M. Clegg, J. Edmonds, and R. Impagliazzo. Using the Gröbner basis algorithm to find proofs of unsatisfiability. In *Proc. 28th STOC*, pages 174–183, 1996.

[15] A. Daniely, N. Linial, and S. Shalev-Shwartz. From average case complexity to improper learning complexity. In *Proc. 46th STOC*, pages 441–448, 2014.

[16] M. Davis, G. Logemann, and D. W. Loveland. A machine program for theorem-proving. *Communications of the ACM*, 5(7):394–397, 1962.

[17] M. Davis and H. Putnam. A computing procedure for quantification theory. *J. ACM*, 7(3):201–215, 1960.

[18] S. E. Decatur and R. Gennaro. On learning from noisy and incomplete examples. In *Proc. 8th COLT*, pages 353–360, 1995.

[19] W. Diffie and M. Hellman. New directions in cryptography. *IEEE Trans. Inform. Theory*, 22:423–439, 1976.

[20] Z. Dvir, A. Rao, A. Wigderson, and A. Yehudayoff. Restriction access. In *Proc. 3rd ITCS*, pages 19–33, 2012.

[21] R. E. Fikes and N. J. Nilsson. STRIPS: a new approach to the application of theorem proving to problem solving. *Artificial Intelligence*, 2(3–4):189–208, 1971.

[22] N. Galesi and M. Lauria. On the automatizability of polynomial calculus. *Theory Comput. Sys.*, 47(2):491–506, 2010.

[23] Y. Ishai, A. Sahai, and D. Wagner. Private circuits: Securing hardware against probing attacks. In D. Boneh, editor, *Proc. CRYPTO 2003*, volume 2729 of *LNCS*, pages 463–481. Springer, Berlin, 2003.

[24] B. Juba. Implicit learning of common sense for reasoning. In *Proc. 23rd IJCAI*, pages 939–946, 2013. Preliminary version: *Learning implicitly in reasoning in PAC-Semantics*, arXiv:1209.0056v1 [cs.AI].

[25] B. Juba. On non-automatizability in pac-semantics. Technical Report TR13-094, ECCC, 2013.

[26] B. Juba. PAC quasi-automatizability of resolution over restricted distributions. Technical Report 1304.4633 [cs.DS], arXiv, 2013.

[27] B. Juba. Integrated common sense learning and planning in POMDPs. Submitted, 2014.

[28] M. J. Kearns, R. E. Schapire, and L. M. Sellie. Towards efficient agnostic learning. *Machine Learning*, 17(2-3):115–141, 1994.

[29] R. Khardon and D. Roth. Learning to reason. *J. ACM*, 44(5):697–725, 1997.

[30] R. Khardon and D. Roth. Learning to reason with a restricted view. *Machine Learning*, 35:95–116, 1999.

[31] J. Krajíček and P. Pudlák. Some consequences of cryptographical conjectures for S_2^1 and EF. In D. Leivant, editor, *Logic and Computational Complexity*, volume 960 of *LNCS*, pages 210–220. Springer, Berlin, 1995.

[32] A. Maciel and T. Pitassi. Towards lower bounds for bounded-depth Frege proofs with modular connectives. In P. Beame and S. Buss, editors, *Proof Complexity and Feasible Arithmetics*, number 39 in DIMACS Ser. Discrete Math. Theoret. Comput. Sci., pages 195–227. AMS, 1998.

[33] J. McCarthy and P. J. Hayes. Some philosophical problems from the standpoint of artificial intelligence. In B. Meltzer and D. Michie, editors, *Machine Intelligence*, volume 4, pages 463–502. Edinburgh University Press, 1969.

[34] L. Michael. Partial observability and learnability. *Artificial Intelligence*, 174(11):639–669, 2010.

[35] A. Moitra and M. Saks. A polynomial time algorithm for lossy population recovery. In *Proc. 54th FOCS*, pages 110–116, 2013.

[36] C. Papadimitriou, P. Raghavan, H. Tamaki, and S. Vempala. Latent semantic indexing: A probabilistic analysis. *JCSS*, 61(2):217–235, 2000.

[37] A. A. Razborov. Lower bounds on the size of bounded-depth networks over a complete basis with logical addition. *Math. Notes Acad. of Sci. USSR*, 41(4):333–338, 1987.

[38] G. S. Tseitin. On the complexity of derivation in propositional calculus. In A. O. Slisenko, editor, *Studies in constructive mathematics and mathematical logic, part 2*, pages 115–125. Consultants Bureau, New York, 1970.

[39] L. G. Valiant. A theory of the learnable. *Communications of the ACM*, 18(11):1134–1142, 1984.

[40] L. G. Valiant. Robust logics. *Artificial Intelligence*, 117:231–253, 2000.

[41] A. Wigderson and A. Yehudayoff. Population recovery and partial identification. In *Proc. 53rd FOCS*, 2012.

A Multiprover Interactive Proof System
for the Local Hamiltonian Problem

[Extended Abstract] [*]

Joseph Fitzsimons
Singapore University of Technology and Design
Centre for Quantum Technologies,
National University of Singapore
Singapore
joe.fitzsimons@nus.edu.sg

Thomas Vidick
California Institute of Technology
Pasadena, USA
vidick@cms.caltech.edu

ABSTRACT

We give a quantum interactive proof system for the local Hamiltonian problem on n qubits in which (i) the verifier has a single round of interaction with five entangled provers, (ii) the verifier sends a classical message on $O(\log n)$ bits to each prover, who replies with a constant number of qubits, and (iii) completeness and soundness are separated by an inverse polynomial in n. As the same class of proof systems, without entanglement between the provers, is included in QCMA, our result provides the first indication that quantum multiprover interactive proof systems with entangled provers may be strictly more powerful than unentangled-prover interactive proof systems. A distinguishing feature of our protocol is that the completeness property requires honest provers to share a large entangled state, obtained as the encoding of the ground state of the local Hamiltonian via an error-correcting code. Our result can be interpreted as a first step towards a multiprover variant of the quantum PCP conjecture.

Categories and Subject Descriptors

F.1 [**Computation by abstract devices**]: Miscellaneous

Keywords

Local Hamiltonian, Quantum Interactive Proofs, Entanglement

1. INTRODUCTION

The PCP theorem [6, 5] asserts that any language in NP admits proofs of membership that can be efficiently verified using a randomized procedure which makes the correct

---

[*]A full version of this paper is available as `arXiv:1409.0260`

decision with high probability while only ever reading a constant number of bits of the proof. An equivalent formulation of the PCP theorem, that has been particularly useful in applications to hardness of approximation [15] as well as in devising further improvements to the theorem [27], uses the language of multiplayer games. A two-player game G is specified by question sets Q, Q', answer sets A, A', a distribution π on $Q \times Q'$ and a verification criterion $V \subseteq (A \times A') \times (Q \times Q')$. The value ω of G is defined as the maximum, over all assignments $f : Q \to A$, $f' : Q' \to A'$, of the average number of valid answers given by the assignments: $\omega(G) = \sup_{f,f'} \sum_{q,q'} \pi(q,q') V(f(q), f'(q'); q, q')$. The PCP theorem is equivalent to the statement that $\omega(G)$ is NP-hard to approximate to within a constant additive factor, even for the case of answer sets A, A' of constant size. To see the connection, consider the following "consistency game": the verifier, instead of directly reading bits $i_1, \ldots, i_k$ of the proof, asks a first player for the entries at those locations and a second player for the entry corresponding to a single location i_j, where j is chosen uniformly at random in $\{1, \ldots, k\}$. The verifier accepts if and only if the first player's answers correspond to entries that he would have accepted had he read them directly from the proof, *and* the second player's answer is consistent with the first'. It is not hard to see that the value of the consistency game is directly related to the fraction of checks satisfied by the optimal PCP proof, so that the respective complexities of deciding whether either is close to 1 (under the appropriate gap promise) are identical. The NP-hardness statement for games can in turn be "scaled up" to obtain the inclusion NEXP $\subseteq$ MIP, where MIP is the class of languages having multiprover interactive proof systems. (In fact, historically the equality NEXP = MIP [7] predates the PCP theorem and constituted an important step forward in its proof.)

The quantum analogue of the local proof checking problem was introduced by Kitaev [21]. An instance of the k-local Hamiltonian problem (LH) with parameters a, b, where a, b are functions $\mathbb{N} \to \mathbb{N}$ such that $b > a$, is specified by m local Hamiltonians $H_1, \ldots, H_m$, where each H_i is a Hermitian matrix acting on at most k out of a total of n qubits. The instance is positive if there exists a quantum proof (a quantum state $|\Psi\rangle$ on the n qubits) satisfying a fraction at least $(1 - a)$ of the constraints; precisely, if $H = \sum_i H_i$ (where each H_i is implicitly tensored with the identity on the remaining qubits) has an eigenvalue at most am. If all eigenvalues of H are larger than bm the instance is negative. The introduction of the local Hamiltonian problem initiated what is now the burgeoning field of Hamiltonian complexity [26, 13], expanding well beyond the initial formal connection with classical constraint satisfaction problems to encompass the computational study of a range of problems motivated by condensed-matter physics.

Kitaev proved the "quantum Cook-Levin theorem": he introduced the class QMA of languages that admit efficiently verifiable quantum proofs, and showed that the local Hamiltonian problem is QMA-complete for some a, b satisfying $b - a = \Theta(\text{poly}^{-1}(n))$. The natural question of whether a quantum analogue of the PCP theorem holds was first posed informally in [4], and subsequently formalized in [2]; it asks whether the local Hamiltonian problem remains QMA-hard for values $b - a = \Omega(1)$. This problem has captured the imagination of many researchers [1, 16, 12], but very little is known. If anything recent results [9, 3] place strong limitations on the parameters, including the locality k or the degree of the constraint graph, for which the conjecture may be valid, showing that it may only hold for ranges of parameters that appear to be much more limited than those for which the classical PCP theorem is known to be true.

In this paper we shed new light on the complexity of the local Hamiltonian problem by recasting it in the language of quantum interactive proofs with entangled provers. In doing so we are motivated by the existing classical connection between local proof verification and multiplayer games, which as already mentioned has been instrumental both in the development of the PCP theorem (and in particular its second proof by Dinur [10]) and for applications. Does this connection extend to the quantum setting? While quantum multiprover interactive proof systems have been intensely studied for their own sake [22, 20, 17], prior to our work no nontrivial relation was known between the class QMA_{EXP}, the exponentially scaled-up version of QMA, and the classes QMIP^* or QMIP of languages having quantum interactive proof systems with entangled or unentangled provers respectively. Building on Babai et al.'s characterization MIP = NEXP [7], Kobayashi and Matsumoto showed that QMIP = NEXP [22], while Ito and the second author recently showed the inclusion NEXP $\subseteq \text{QMIP}^*$ [17]. However, no upper bound on QMIP^* is known, so that one may ask — could QMIP^* be a *larger* class than QMIP = NEXP? The only distinction between the two classes is the presence of entanglement between the provers, which until now (and with some rare exceptions [20]) has for the most part been understood as a nefarious resource that could be used by the provers in order to break a protocol's soundness. Giving a positive answer to the question, however, requires finding a *beneficial* use of entanglement, as it entails devising a protocol in which even honest provers are *required* to share an entangled state over a superpolynomial number of qubits in order to succeed on positive instances.[1]

A natural target for going beyond NEXP $\subseteq \text{QMIP}^*$ consists in devising protocols establishing the inclusion of QMA_{EXP} in QMIP^*. Proving such inclusion, however, immediately runs into a number of serious difficulties. To see why, con-

sider the following attempt at designing a quantum interactive proof system for the local Hamiltonian problem that mimics the classical construction of the consistency game (which, as described earlier, easily leads to a proof of NEXP $\subseteq$ MIP assuming the PCP theorem). Suppose thus that the first player is asked to provide a constant-sized subset of the proof qubits, corresponding to a local constraint H_j which the verifier can then check. In the classical case, the second player is asked for just one of the bits asked to the first player; this is used to verify that the first players' answers to any of the bits he was asked about depends on that bit only, and not on the subset of which it is part. In the quantum case this approach is all but ruled out by the no-cloning principle: any given proof qubit can be placed in the hands of one player only, but it cannot be duplicated! Hence the direct quantum analogue of the consistency game does not have *completeness*: even satisfiable instances of the local Hamiltonian problem may not lead to a winning strategy for the players.

Natural workarounds to this difficulty run into different obstacles. For instance, consider splitting the proof (e.g. the ground state of the local Hamiltonian instance) qubits into two (or more) sets S_1 and S_2, and only asking prover i for qubits coming from set S_i. While this leads to a game which does have perfect completeness, the fact that the sets need to be specified a priori can, at least in some cases, prevent the *soundness* property from holding. To see why, consider the simple example of a one-dimensional nearest-neighbor Hamiltonian in which each term is a projection on the orthogonal complement of an EPR pair split across two adjacent qubits. This Hamiltonian is highly frustrated, as any qubit can only form an EPR pair with its left *or* right neighbor, not both. Nevertheless, the corresponding game in which S_1 (resp. S_2) is the set of all even-numbered (resp. odd-numbered) qubits has a perfect strategy: the players share a single EPR pair and systematically send back their respective half, independently of the question they are asked! Although in this particular case the issue is easily fixed by choosing a different splitting of the proof qubits, in general it seems like any such splitting will be arbitrary and could be taken advantage of by the provers.

1.1 Results

Our main result is the design of an interactive proof system for the local Hamiltonian problem which circumvents the aforementioned difficulties. This is the first time a multiprover interactive proof system is given for a QMA-complete, instead of NP-complete, problem, and it provides strong indication that entangled proof systems may be strictly more powerful than their unentangled counterparts. Formally, we show the following.

THEOREM 1. *Let k be an integer. There exists constants $C, c > 0$ depending on k only such that the following holds. Let $H = \sum_{i=1}^{m} H_i$ be an instance of the k-local Hamiltonian problem with promise parameters $a < b$, such that the number of constraints is $m = \text{poly}(n)$, where n is the number of qubits. There exists a one-round interactive protocol between a quantum polynomial-time verifier and $r = 5$ entangled quantum provers such that:*

- *The verifier sends $O(\log n)$-bit classical messages to each prover,*

- *The provers respond with at most k qubits each,*

---

[1]The class $\text{QMIP}^{(l.e.)}$ of languages having quantum multiprover interactive proof systems in which the provers share an entangled state on at most a polynomial number of qubits is also known to be included in NEXP[22].

- *If there exists a state $|\Gamma\rangle$ such that $\langle\Gamma|H|\Gamma\rangle \leq am$ then there is a strategy for the provers that is accepted with probability at least $1 - a/2$,*

- *If for every state $|\Psi\rangle$, $\langle\Psi|H|\Psi\rangle \geq bm$ then any strategy of the provers is accepted with probability at most $1 - Cb/n^c$.*

The local Hamiltonian problem is known to be QMA-complete for $k = 2$, a that is exponentially small and b at least an inverse polynomial [19]. The following corollary, which we state using the language of multiplayer games, is thus a direct consequence of Theorem 1:

COROLLARY 2. *The problem of approximating, to within an additive inverse polynomial, the referee's maximum acceptance probability in a quantum multiplayer game in which questions from the referee are classical on $O(\log n)$-bits and answers from the players are quantum on $O(1)$ qubits is QMA-hard. Furthermore the same holds when restricted to games in which there is a single round of interaction between the referee and at most 5 players.*

The same problem but with no entanglement between the players is contained in QCMA: the players' constant-sized quantum answers can be described using a classical proof, from which a quantum verifier can reconstruct quantum states on which to run the original verifier's circuit. It is also known to be NP-hard, even allowing for entanglement and when restricted to classical answers from the players and for constant additive approximations [30]. However, no *upper bound* is known on the complexity of the problem considered in Corollary 2, which is not even known to be decidable [29, 18] (and there is no known a priori bound on the amount of entanglement that may be beneficial to the players). Corollary 2 provides the first indication that entanglement indeed *increases* the verifying power of the referee, at least in the range of inverse-polynomial approximations, showing that unless QCMA = QMA the complexity of entangled (quantum) games is strictly *larger* than that of non-entangled (quantum) games.

Consequences for interactive proof systems with entangled provers..

We can scale up our result to QMA$_{\text{EXP}}$, the exponential-witness size version of QMA (see Section 2 for the definition) to obtain a formal separation between quantum multiprover interactive proof systems with and without entanglement between the provers. Let QMIP*(r, t, c, s) be the class of languages that have quantum interactive-proof systems with r provers, t rounds of interaction, completeness c and soundness s (see Section 2 for the complete definition).

COROLLARY 3. *There exists a polynomial q such that*

$$\text{QMA}_{\text{EXP}} \subseteq \text{QMIP}^*(5, 1, 1 - 2^{-(q+1)}, 1 - 2^{-q})$$

and hence

$$\text{QMIP}(5, 1, 1 - 2^{-(q+1)}, 1 - 2^{-q}) \subsetneq \text{QMIP}^*(5, 1, 1 - 2^{-(q+1)}, 1 - 2^{-q})$$

unless NEXP = QMA$_{\text{EXP}}$.

The corollary follows from the fact that QMIP$(5, 1, 1 - 2^{-(q+1)}, 1 - 2^{-q}) \subseteq$ NEXP [22] and NEXP $\subseteq$ MIP*$(3, 1, 1, 1-$

$1/\text{poly})$ [17] together with the observation MIP*$(3, 1, 1, 1 - 1/\text{poly}) \subseteq$ QMIP*$(5, 1, 1 - 2^{-(q+1)}, 1 - 2^{-q})$.

We note that even though it is known that MIP* = QMIP* [28] the above corollary falls short of proving a separation between MIP = QMIP = NEXP and MIP*. The reason is that the transformation from a QMIP* to a MIP* protocol in [28] requires the completeness and soundness parameters of the QMIP* protocol to be separated by an inverse polynomial in the input size, whereas our construction only gives an inverse exponential separation.

1.2 Proof idea

Suppose given an instance $H = \sum H_j$ of the local Hamiltonian problem, where each term H_j acts on a subset $S_j = \{i_1, \ldots, i_k\}$ of at most k of the n qubits. Given an explicit description of H, the goal of the verifier is to decide whether there exists a "proof" $|\Psi\rangle$ that satisfies most terms H_j, i.e. such that the total "energy" $\langle\Psi|H|\Psi\rangle$ is below a certain threshold value. As already mentioned, the main challenge in achieving this is that the verifier will only ever receive, at best, a constant number of qubits of the proof from the provers. Although this easily allows him to estimate the energy $\langle\Psi|H_j|\Psi\rangle$ of any local term H_j, the difficulty is to ensure that the qubits received in response to different queries, associated with different local terms H_j, are *globally consistent* — that they can be "patched together" into an actual proof $|\Psi\rangle$ that has low energy with respect to H. This difficulty is unique to the case of quantum proofs: if we were working with classical assignments, as explained earlier a simple consistency check would be sufficient to enforce that the provers' answers can be combined into a single assignment satisfying most clauses. But how does one devise a consistency check for quantum proofs, when in general it is not even possible to check whether two quantum states agree locally?[2]

We suggest the following workaround. Our main goal is to ensure that, when a prover is asked for its share of a certain qubit i_ℓ, or $i_{\ell'}$, of the proof, the actual qubits that it sends back to the verifier in the one case or the other do indeed correspond to distinct physical qubits — that they do not "overlap", or even correspond to the same physical qubit, as was the case in our description of a strategy for the frustrated Hamiltonian projecting on overlapping EPR pairs. To enforce this, instead of asking the (honest) provers to directly split the qubits of the original proof in-between themselves we ask them to share an *encoding* of the proof: each "logical" qubit of $|\Psi\rangle$ should be individually encoded into five "physical" qubits using a quantum error-correcting code. Each of five provers should then be given one of the five shares associated with each of the original proof's qubits.

Given this (presumed) splitting of the proof, we introduce the following protocol, comprised of two tests each applied with probability $1/2$ by the verifier. The first test consists in estimating the energy of a randomly chosen k-local term H_j, as follows. The verifier chooses an index j uniformly at random and asks each of the five provers for its correspond-

---

[2]Pure quantum states $|\Psi\rangle$ and $|\Phi\rangle$ can be compared using the so-called SWAP test. However, for mixed states this test no longer works, and in fact checking consistency of reduced density matrices, even when specified explicitly, is itself a QMA-complete problem [24]. We refer to [3] for more on the difficulties posed by locally checking consistency of quantum states.

ing share of each qubit on which H_j acts. The verifier then decodes the provers' answers and measures the energy of the resulting qubits with respect to H_j. This only requires each prover to send back k qubits to the verifier.

Next consider the following additional test. The verifier again chooses a term H_j uniformly at random; let $S_j = \{i_1, \ldots, i_k\}$ be the qubits on which it acts. The verifier chooses an index $\ell \in \{1, \ldots, k\}$ at random and asks four out of the five provers (again chosen at random) for their respective share of qubit i_ℓ only. To the last prover he asks for its respective shares of all qubits in S_j (so the last prover cannot distinguish whether it is this test or the first that is being performed). The verifier checks that all shares that he received associated with qubit i_ℓ lie in the codespace, and rejects the provers if not.

In this second test the messages sent back by the first four provers only depend on qubit i_ℓ. The key point is that, informally, given their four respective answer qubits there can exist at most one additional qubit that is entangled with them in a way that completes a valid codeword; indeed this follows from the fact that the code we use corrects (or even just detects) all single-qubit errors. Thus this additional test enforces that the qubit sent back by the fifth prover in response to query i_ℓ is uniquely specified by the query i_ℓ; this is acheived by "locking" the qubit with the other four provers' answers via the codespace.

Although the above provides some intuition, proving soundness of the protocol remains technically challenging. We need to show how, from prover strategies that are successful in the protocol, can be extracted (at least in principle) a complete proof $|\Psi\rangle$ serving as a witness for the energy of the Hamiltonian H. Formally each prover's strategy is specified by a pair of unitaries, one for each type of query from the verifier. The difficulty is that these unitaries may not be "compatible": a priori there is no straightforward way to simultaneously apply all of them to the provers' initial state in order to extract all n qubits of a witness $|\Psi\rangle$ for the local Hamiltonian instance.

Nevertheless, our proof explicitly specifies a density matrix σ to serve as a witness for the local Hamiltonian instance. σ is defined as the result of applying a circuit constructed out of the provers' unitaries to their initial (entangled) private space. The unitaries are applied sequentially to "extract" the qubits of the witness one by one. There are two main difficulties:

First, we need to find a way of composing the provers' unitaries associated with different questions from the verifier. Our idea consists in applying the unitary U, swapping out the qubit that would be sent to the verifier as an answer, replacing it by the totally mixed state, and applying $U^\dagger$. Note that, by virtue of the code used to encode the witness qubits the reduced state of the qubit, when all other provers are traced out, *is* the totally mixed state. Thus the triplet of applying U, swapping, and applying $U^\dagger$ behaves as the identity map on the reduced state of any single prover. We repeat this operation sequentially for the unitaries associated to the witness' n qubits. (See Figure 3 for a representation of the circuit used to define σ.)

Second, one needs to analyze the energy of σ with respect to the local Hamiltonian instance and show that, provided the provers' strategies were accepted with high probability in the protocol, this energy is low enough. To show this we fix a local term H_j of the Hamiltonian and show that the reduced density of the state σ defined above is sufficiently close to the state that would be provided by the provers as answer to the query associated with H_j in the protocol. Proving this involves relating the provers' unitaries used for the two types of queries, using again properties of the error-correcting code, and showing that the effect of unitaries used in defining σ but not involved in any of the qubits on which H_j acts is small enough to not affect the energy much. Unfortunately our proof is limited to showing that this error scales polynomially with the total number of unitaries; it is ultimately this which leads to the polynomial dependence of the soundness parameter on the number of qubits of the witness.

1.3 Open questions

Our work gives the first indication that multi-prover interactive proof systems with entangled provers may be strictly more powerful than their purely classical counterparts. Our protocol relies on the use of quantum communication from the provers to the verifier. Although it is known that quantum communication does not increase the power of entangled-prover interactive proof systems, $\mathrm{QMIP}^* = \mathrm{MIP}^*$ [28], the technique used in [28] to replace quantum messages by classical ones introduce a polynomial amount of error that, at least if applied naïvely, would close the completeness/soundness gap of our protocol. We thus leave the possibility of achieving the same results as our ours through a purely classical interaction as an interesting open question.

Our protocol requires 5 provers, and this is a direct consequence of the 5-qubit error correcting code used in the protocol. Replacing this code by a 4-qubit error detecting code should allow one to extend our result to a 4-prover protocol without difficulty. Further reducing to 3 or even 2 provers may be more challenging, and we leave this as an open question.

The main drawback of our protocol is the scaling of the completeness/soundness gap with the size of the local Hamiltonian instance. The most important question that we leave open for future work is to increase this gap from inverse exponential to inverse polynomial, leading to the inclusion $\mathrm{QMA}_{\mathrm{EXP}} \subseteq \mathrm{QMIP}^*$. Together with $\mathrm{QMIP}^* = \mathrm{MIP}^*$ [28] such a result would in particular reprove the main result of [17], and we expect it to pose a significant challenge. Of importance in itself, research on this question could lead to the development of techniques useful to the study of the quantum PCP conjecture [3]. To stimulate its exploration we propose that the inclusion $\mathrm{QMA}_{\mathrm{EXP}} \subseteq \mathrm{QMIP}^*$ be taken as a second variant of "quantum PCP conjecture" — one we could call the "interactive-proof QPCP", in contrast to the "proof-checking QPCP" that has so far been the accepted formulation (see e.g. Conjecture 1.4 in [3]). No implication is known between the two conjectures; our work provides a first step towards the former, making it potentially more approachable than the latter.

Acknowledgments.

This work was started while both authors were hosted by the Simons Institute in Berkeley, whose financial support we gratefully acknowledge. The second author is grateful to Dorit Aharonov and Umesh Vazirani for pressing him to expose the question investigated in this paper during an open problems session organized at the institute. Joseph Fitzimons' research is supported in part by the Singapore

- If there exists a state $|\Gamma\rangle$ such that $\langle\Gamma|H|\Gamma\rangle \le am$ then there is a strategy for the provers that is accepted with probability at least $1 - a/2$,

- If for every state $|\Psi\rangle$, $\langle\Psi|H|\Psi\rangle \ge bm$ then any strategy of the provers is accepted with probability at most $1 - Cb/n^c$.

The local Hamiltonian problem is known to be QMA-complete for $k = 2$, a that is exponentially small and b at least an inverse polynomial [19]. The following corollary, which we state using the language of multiplayer games, is thus a direct consequence of Theorem 1:

COROLLARY 2. *The problem of approximating, to within an additive inverse polynomial, the referee's maximum acceptance probability in a quantum multiplayer game in which questions from the referee are classical on $O(\log n)$-bits and answers from the players are quantum on $O(1)$ qubits is QMA-hard. Furthermore the same holds when restricted to games in which there is a single round of interaction between the referee and at most 5 players.*

The same problem but with no entanglement between the players is contained in QCMA: the players' constant-sized quantum answers can be described using a classical proof, from which a quantum verifier can reconstruct quantum states on which to run the original verifier's circuit. It is also known to be NP-hard, even allowing for entanglement and when restricted to classical answers from the players and for constant additive approximations [30]. However, no *upper bound* is known on the complexity of the problem considered in Corollary 2, which is not even known to be decidable [29, 18] (and there is no known a priori bound on the amount of entanglement that may be beneficial to the players). Corollary 2 provides the first indication that entanglement indeed *increases* the verifying power of the referee, at least in the range of inverse-polynomial approximations, showing that unless QCMA = QMA the complexity of entangled (quantum) games is strictly *larger* than that of non-entangled (quantum) games.

Consequences for interactive proof systems with entangled provers..

We can scale up our result to QMA_{EXP}, the exponential-witness size version of QMA (see Section 2 for the definition) to obtain a formal separation between quantum multiprover interactive proof systems with and without entanglement between the provers. Let $\text{QMIP}^*(r, t, c, s)$ be the class of languages that have quantum interactive-proof systems with r provers, t rounds of interaction, completeness c and soundness s (see Section 2 for the complete definition).

COROLLARY 3. *There exists a polynomial q such that*

$$\text{QMA}_{\text{EXP}} \subseteq \text{QMIP}^*(5, 1, 1 - 2^{-(q+1)}, 1 - 2^{-q})$$

and hence

$$\text{QMIP}(5, 1, 1 - 2^{-(q+1)}, 1 - 2^{-q}) \subsetneq \text{QMIP}^*(5, 1, 1 - 2^{-(q+1)}, 1 - 2^{-q})$$

unless $\text{NEXP} = \text{QMA}_{\text{EXP}}$.

The corollary follows from the fact that $\text{QMIP}(5, 1, 1 - 2^{-(q+1)}, 1 - 2^{-q}) \subseteq \text{NEXP}$ [22] and $\text{NEXP} \subseteq \text{MIP}^*(3, 1, 1, 1 - $ $1/\text{poly})$ [17] together with the observation $\text{MIP}^*(3, 1, 1, 1 - 1/\text{poly}) \subseteq \text{QMIP}^*(5, 1, 1 - 2^{-(q+1)}, 1 - 2^{-q})$.

We note that even though it is known that $\text{MIP}^* = \text{QMIP}^*$ [28] the above corollary falls short of proving a separation between $\text{MIP} = \text{QMIP} = \text{NEXP}$ and MIP^*. The reason is that the transformation from a QMIP^* to a MIP^* protocol in [28] requires the completeness and soundness parameters of the QMIP^* protocol to be separated by an inverse polynomial in the input size, whereas our construction only gives an inverse exponential separation.

1.2 Proof idea

Suppose given an instance $H = \sum H_j$ of the local Hamiltonian problem, where each term H_j acts on a subset $S_j = \{i_1, \dots, i_k\}$ of at most k of the n qubits. Given an explicit description of H, the goal of the verifier is to decide whether there exists a "proof" $|\Psi\rangle$ that satisfies most terms H_j, i.e. such that the total "energy" $\langle\Psi|H|\Psi\rangle$ is below a certain threshold value. As already mentioned, the main challenge in achieving this is that the verifier will only ever receive, at best, a constant number of qubits of the proof from the provers. Although this easily allows him to estimate the energy $\langle\Psi|H_j|\Psi\rangle$ of any local term H_j, the difficulty is to ensure that the qubits received in response to different queries, associated with different local terms H_j, are *globally consistent* — that they can be "patched together" into an actual proof $|\Psi\rangle$ that has low energy with respect to H. This difficulty is unique to the case of quantum proofs: if we were working with classical assignments, as explained earlier a simple consistency check would be sufficient to enforce that the provers' answers can be combined into a single assignment satisfying most clauses. But how does one devise a consistency check for quantum proofs, when in general it is not even possible to check whether two quantum states agree locally?[2]

We suggest the following workaround. Our main goal is to ensure that, when a prover is asked for its share of a certain qubit i_ℓ, or $i_{\ell'}$, of the proof, the actual qubits that it sends back to the verifier in the one case or the other do indeed correspond to distinct physical qubits — that they do not "overlap", or even correspond to the same physical qubit, as was the case in our description of a strategy for the frustrated Hamiltonian projecting on overlapping EPR pairs. To enforce this, instead of asking the (honest) provers to directly split the qubits of the original proof in-between themselves we ask them to share an *encoding* of the proof: each "logical" qubit of $|\Psi\rangle$ should be individually encoded into five "physical" qubits using a quantum error-correcting code. Each of five provers should then be given one of the five shares associated with each of the original proof's qubits.

Given this (presumed) splitting of the proof, we introduce the following protocol, comprised of two tests each applied with probability $1/2$ by the verifier. The first test consists in estimating the energy of a randomly chosen k-local term H_j, as follows. The verifier chooses an index j uniformly at random and asks each of the five provers for its correspond-

---

[2] Pure quantum states $|\Psi\rangle$ and $|\Phi\rangle$ can be compared using the so-called SWAP test. However, for mixed states this test no longer works, and in fact checking consistency of reduced density matrices, even when specified explicitly, is itself a QMA-complete problem [24]. We refer to [3] for more on the difficulties posed by locally checking consistency of quantum states.

ing share of each qubit on which H_j acts. The verifier then decodes the provers' answers and measures the energy of the resulting qubits with respect to H_j. This only requires each prover to send back k qubits to the verifier.

Next consider the following additional test. The verifier again chooses a term H_j uniformly at random; let $S_j = \{i_1, \ldots, i_k\}$ be the qubits on which it acts. The verifier chooses an index $\ell \in \{1, \ldots, k\}$ at random and asks four out of the five provers (again chosen at random) for their respective share of qubit i_ℓ only. To the last prover he asks for its respective shares of all qubits in S_j (so the last prover cannot distinguish whether it is this test or the first that is being performed). The verifier checks that all shares that he received associated with qubit i_ℓ lie in the codespace, and rejects the provers if not.

In this second test the messages sent back by the first four provers only depend on qubit i_ℓ. The key point is that, informally, given their four respective answer qubits there can exist at most one additional qubit that is entangled with them in a way that completes a valid codeword; indeed this follows from the fact that the code we use corrects (or even just detects) all single-qubit errors. Thus this additional test enforces that the qubit sent back by the fifth prover in response to query i_ℓ is uniquely specified by the query i_ℓ; this is acheived by "locking" the qubit with the other four provers' answers via the codespace.

Although the above provides some intuition, proving soundness of the protocol remains technically challenging. We need to show how, from prover strategies that are successful in the protocol, can be extracted (at least in principle) a complete proof $|\Psi\rangle$ serving as a witness for the energy of the Hamiltonian H. Formally each prover's strategy is specified by a pair of unitaries, one for each type of query from the verifier. The difficulty is that these unitaries may not be "compatible": a priori there is no straightforward way to simultaneously apply all of them to the provers' initial state in order to extract all n qubits of a witness $|\Psi\rangle$ for the local Hamiltonian instance.

Nevertheless, our proof explicitly specifies a density matrix σ to serve as a witness for the local Hamiltonian instance. σ is defined as the result of applying a circuit constructed out of the provers' unitaries to their initial (entangled) private space. The unitaries are applied sequentially to "extract" the qubits of the witness one by one. There are two main difficulties:

First, we need to find a way of composing the provers' unitaries associated with different questions from the verifier. Our idea consists in applying the unitary U, swapping out the qubit that would be sent to the verifier as an answer, replacing it by the totally mixed state, and applying $U^\dagger$. Note that, by virtue of the code used to encode the witness qubits the reduced state of the qubit, when all other provers are traced out, *is* the totally mixed state. Thus the triplet of applying U, swapping, and applying $U^\dagger$ behaves as the identity map on the reduced state of any single prover. We repeat this operation sequentially for the unitaries associated to the witness' n qubits. (See Figure 3 for a representation of the circuit used to define σ.)

Second, one needs to analyze the energy of σ with respect to the local Hamiltonian instance and show that, provided the provers' strategies were accepted with high probability in the protocol, this energy is low enough. To show this we fix a local term H_j of the Hamiltonian and show that the

reduced density of the state σ defined above is sufficiently close to the state that would be provided by the provers as answer to the query associated with H_j in the protocol. Proving this involves relating the provers' unitaries used for the two types of queries, using again properties of the error-correcting code, and showing that the effect of unitaries used in defining σ but not involved in any of the qubits on which H_j acts is small enough to not affect the energy much. Unfortunately our proof is limited to showing that this error scales polynomially with the total number of unitaries; it is ultimately this which leads to the polynomial dependence of the soundness parameter on the number of qubits of the witness.

1.3 Open questions

Our work gives the first indication that multi-prover interactive proof systems with entangled provers may be strictly more powerful than their purely classical counterparts. Our protocol relies on the use of quantum communication from the provers to the verifier. Although it is known that quantum communication does not increase the power of entangled-prover interactive proof systems, $\text{QMIP}^* = \text{MIP}^*$ [28], the technique used in [28] to replace quantum messages by classical ones introduce a polynomial amount of error that, at least if applied naïvely, would close the completeness/soundness gap of our protocol. We thus leave the possibility of achieving the same results as our ours through a purely classical interaction as an interesting open question.

Our protocol requires 5 provers, and this is a direct consequence of the 5-qubit error correcting code used in the protocol. Replacing this code by a 4-qubit error detecting code should allow one to extend our result to a 4-prover protocol without difficulty. Further reducing to 3 or even 2 provers may be more challenging, and we leave this as an open question.

The main drawback of our protocol is the scaling of the completeness/soundness gap with the size of the local Hamiltonian instance. The most important question that we leave open for future work is to increase this gap from inverse exponential to inverse polynomial, leading to the inclusion $\text{QMA}_{\text{EXP}} \subseteq \text{QMIP}^*$. Together with $\text{QMIP}^* = \text{MIP}^*$ [28] such a result would in particular reprove the main result of [17], and we expect it to pose a significant challenge. Of importance in itself, research on this question could lead to the development of techniques useful to the study of the quantum PCP conjecture [3]. To stimulate its exploration we propose that the inclusion $\text{QMA}_{\text{EXP}} \subseteq \text{QMIP}^*$ be taken as a second variant of "quantum PCP conjecture" — one we could call the "interactive-proof QPCP", in contrast to the "proof-checking QPCP" that has so far been the accepted formulation (see e.g. Conjecture 1.4 in [3]). No implication is known between the two conjectures; our work provides a first step towards the former, making it potentially more approachable than the latter.

Acknowledgments.

This work was started while both authors were hosted by the Simons Institute in Berkeley, whose financial support we gratefully acknowledge. The second author is grateful to Dorit Aharonov and Umesh Vazirani for pressing him to expose the question investigated in this paper during an open problems session organized at the institute. Joseph Fitzimons' research is supported in part by the Singapore

National Research Foundation under NRF Award No. NRF-NRFF2013-01. Thomas Vidick's research was supported in part by the Simons Institute and the Ministry of Education, Singapore under the Tier 3 grant MOE2012-T3-1-009.

2. PRELIMINARIES

Notation.

Given a string x we let $|x|$ denote its length. For a set S, $|S|$ is its cardinality. For a positive integer n we abbreviate $\{1, \ldots, n\}$ by $[n]$. We use a calligraphic $\mathcal{H}$ to denote finite-dimensional Hilbert spaces, and roman letters $Q, R, \ldots$ to denote quantum registers. The Hilbert space associated with register R is $\mathcal{H}_R$. We will often, though not always, index kets and bras for quantum states by the names of the registers on which the state lies, e.g. $|\Psi\rangle_{QR}$ means that $|\Psi\rangle$ is a bipartite state on $\mathcal{H}_Q \otimes \mathcal{H}_R$. $L(\mathcal{H}_Q, \mathcal{H}_R)$ is the set of all linear maps $\mathcal{H}_Q \to \mathcal{H}_R$. $\text{Pos}(\mathcal{H})$ is the set of positive operators on $\mathcal{H}$; $D(\mathcal{H})$ the set of density matrices. Given $\mathcal{F}, \mathcal{G} \in L(\mathcal{H}, \mathcal{H})$ we let $\mathcal{F} \circ \mathcal{G}$ denote their composition. If there are s such maps $\mathcal{F}_\ell$, we let $\bigcirc_{\ell=1}^s \mathcal{F}_\ell := \mathcal{F}_s \circ \cdots \circ \mathcal{F}_1$.

Given two registers Q and R associated to isomorphic Hilbert spaces $\mathcal{H}_Q$, $\mathcal{H}_R$ respectively we let SWAP_{QR} be the unitary that swaps their contents: for any two orthonormal bases $|u_i\rangle$ for $\mathcal{H}_Q$ and $|v_j\rangle$ for $\mathcal{H}_R$, $\text{SWAP}_{QR} = \sum_{i,j} |v_i, u_j\rangle\langle u_j, v_i|$.

Complexity classes.

We give relatively informal definitions of the quantum interactive proof classes considered in this paper. For formal definitions we refer the reader to the book [21] and the survey [31].

QMA is the class of all promise problems $L = (L_{yes}, L_{no})$ such that there exists a polynomial p and a quantum polynomial-time verifier V such that:

- (completeness) For every $x \in L_{yes}$, there exists a state $|\Psi\rangle$ on $p(|x|)$ qubits such that $V(x, |\Psi\rangle)$ accepts with probability at least $2/3$,

- (soundness) For every $x \in L_{no}$ and every $|\Psi\rangle$ on $p(|x|)$ qubits, $V(x, |\Psi\rangle)$ accepts with probability at most $1/3$.

We further note that using an amplification technique of Marriott and Watrous [25] one can show that for any fixed polynomial q the completeness and soundness parameters can be replaced by $1 - 2^{-q(|x|)}$ and $2^{-q(|x|)}$ respectively without changing the definition of QMA. Furthermore the amplification procedure in [25] preserves the witness length, so that the polynomial p does not need to grow if one increases q (only the complexity of the verification procedure increases). We define the exponential-size version of QMA, QMA_{EXP}, by allowing the witness to be on $2^{p(|x|)}$ qubits and the verifier to run in quantum exponential time.

$\text{MIP}(r, t, c, s)$ is the class of all promise problems $L = (L_{yes}, L_{no})$ such that there exists a polynomial p and a classical polynomial-time verifier V, interacting with r non-communicating provers through t rounds of interaction in each of which at most $p(|x|)$ bits of communication are exchanged between the verifier and the provers, such that:

- (completeness) For every $x \in L_{yes}$, there exists a strategy for the provers that is accepted by the verifier with probability at least c,

- (soundness) For every $x \in L_{no}$ any strategy of the provers is accepted by the verifier with probability at most s.

$\text{QMIP}(r, t, c, s)$ is defined in the same way, except the verifier and communication exchanged are allowed to be quantum. $\text{MIP}^*(r, t, c, s)$ (resp. $\text{QMIP}^*(r, t, c, s)$) is defined as $\text{MIP}(r, t, c, s)$ (resp. $\text{QMIP}(r, t, c, s)$) but the provers are allowed to share an arbitrary entangled state as part of their strategy. (In this paper we only consider protocols for which the number of rounds of interaction is $t = 1$.)

It follows from [7, 22] that, for any polynomials p_1, p_2 and p_3,

$$\text{MIP}(p_1, p_2, 2/3, 1/3) = \text{QMIP}(p_1, p_2, 2/3, 1/3)$$
$$= \text{MIP}(2, 1, 1, 2^{-p_3}) = \text{QMIP}(2, 1, 1, 2^{-p_3}) = \text{NEXP}.$$

In fact, [22] even show that the same equalities hold for QMIP^* when the provers are limited to a polynomial number of qubits of entanglement.

The local Hamiltonian problem.

Let k be a fixed integer and $a, b : \mathbb{N} \to [0, 1]$ such that $a(n) < b(n)$ for all integers n. The k-local Hamiltonian problem (LH) is defined as follows. The input is a classical description of a local Hamiltonian $H = \sum_{i=1}^m H_i \in L\left(\mathbb{C}^{d^n}, \mathbb{C}^{d^n}\right)$ acting on n qudits of dimension d each. Here each H_i is a positive semidefinite matrix of norm at most 1 acting on at most k out of the n qudits, and can thus be represented by a matrix of dimension $d^k \times d^k$; when we write $H = \sum_i H_i$ we implicitly mean that each H_i should be tensored with the identity acting on the remaining $(n - k)$ qudits. We label the qudits from 1 to n, and denote by S_j the set of k qudits on which H_j acts. The problem is to determine which of the following two cases holds:

1. (YES) There exists a n-qudit state $|\Gamma\rangle$ such that $\langle\Gamma|H|\Gamma\rangle \leq am$,

2. (NO) For all states $|\Psi\rangle$, $\langle\Psi|H|\Psi\rangle \geq bm$.

Kempe, Kitaev and Regev showed the following:

THEOREM 4 ([19]). *For any fixed polynomial q, there is a polynomial p such that the k-local Hamiltonian problem, where the number of qubits n is specified in unary, is QMA-complete for $k = 2$, $d = 2$, $a = 2^{-q(n)}$ and $b = 1/p(n)$.*

For the case of QMA_{EXP} essentially the same construction yields the following (see also [14]):

THEOREM 5 ([19]). *For any fixed polynomial q, there is a polynomial p such that the k-local Hamiltonian problem, where the number of qubits N is specified in binary (hence can be exponential in the input size), is QMA_{EXP}-complete for $k = 2$, $d = 2$, $a = 2^{-q(N)}$ and $b = 1/p(N)$.*

Error-correcting codes.

Our protocol relies on the use of a quantum error-correcting code C that has the following properties:

- C encodes 1 logical qubit into r physical qubits.

- C detects and corrects all Pauli errors on at most e qubits.

Protocol P

Let $H = \sum_{i=1}^{m} H_i$ be an instance of the k-local Hamiltonian problem given as input, and n the number of qubits on which H acts. Let C be an error-correcting code which encodes 1 logical qubit into r physical qubits and satisfies the three conditions described at the end of Section 2.

The verifier performs each of the following tests with probability $1/2$ each:

Test (a) Select a $j \in [m]$ uniformly at random, and let $S_j \subseteq [n]$ be the set of k qubits on which the local term H_j acts. Ask the provers for their respective share of all qubits in S_j. Upon receiving the shares, apply the decoding map independently to each of the k groups of r shares and measure the resulting state using $\{H_j, \text{Id} - H_j\}$. Reject if the outcome is 'H_j'.

Test (b) Select a qubit $i \in [n]$ uniformly at random, and a set $S \subseteq [n]$ uniformly at random among all sets of size k that contain i. With probability $1/2$, ask one of the provers at random for his share of all qubits in S, and the remaining $r-1$ provers for their respective share of the i-th qubit only. With probability $1/2$, ask all provers for their respective share of the i-th qubit. In both cases, verify that all provers' shares of the i-th qubit together lie in the codespace. Reject if not.

Figure 1: Protocol for the verification of an instance of the local Hamiltonian problem.

- The reduced density matrix of any codewords in C on a single qubit is the totally mixed state $\text{Id}/2$.

An example of a code satisfying all three conditions for $r = 5$ and $e = 1$ is the 5-qubit stabilizer code [8, 23]. Given r single-qubit registers $R_1, \ldots, R_r$ we let $\text{DEC}_{R_1 \cdots R_r} : D((\mathbb{C}^2)^{\otimes r}) \to D(\mathbb{C}^2)$ be the completely positive trace-preserving (CPTP) map corresponding to the decoding operation. We also let $\text{CHECK}_{R_1 \cdots R_r} \in \text{Pos}((\mathbb{C}^2)^{\otimes r})$ be the projection onto the code space.

3. PROOF OF THEOREM 1

In this section we prove Theorem 1. The protocol is described in Figure 1. The first two properties claimed in the theorem, on the structure of the protocol, are clear: there is a single round of interaction, and using the 5-qubit stabilizer code for C the protocol can be executed with $r = 5$ provers. Messages from the verifier to the provers are either the label of a qubit or the description of a set of size k, which require $O(\log n)$ bits to specify. Messages from any prover to the verifier are either 1 or k qubits. In Section 3.1 we establish the completeness property of the protocol; soundness is proved in Section 3.2.

3.1 Completeness analysis

LEMMA 6. *Suppose that there exists a state $|\Gamma\rangle$ such that $\langle\Gamma|H|\Gamma\rangle \leq am$. Then there exists a strategy for the provers in Protocol P that is accepted with probability at least $1 - a/2$.*

PROOF. We describe a strategy for the provers. Let $|\Gamma\rangle$ be such that $\langle\Gamma|H|\Gamma\rangle \leq am$. Before the protocols start, the provers generate a shared entangled state $|\Psi\rangle$ over rn qubits by independently encoding each qubit of $|\Gamma\rangle$ into r qubits using the code C prescribed by the protocol. Each of the r provers keeps n qubits of $|\Psi\rangle$, corresponding to a share of each of the encoded qubits of $|\Gamma\rangle$. When asked for its share of any set of qubits, the prover complies and sends it to the verifier. It is clear that this strategy is accepted with probability 1 in item (b), and with probability

$$\frac{1}{m} \sum_{i=1}^{m} \langle\Gamma|(\text{Id} - H_i)|\Gamma\rangle \geq 1 - a$$

in item (a). Using that each test is performed with probability $1/2$, the overall success probability for the strategy is at least $1 - a/2$. $\square$

3.2 Soundness analysis

In this section we analyze the soundness of protocol P. In section 3.2.1 we introduce the notation used to describe the most general strategy that the provers may employ in the protocol. In section 3.2.2 we show that, provided that all eigenvalues of H are larger than some inverse polynomial, any strategy for the provers is rejected by the verifier with inverse polynomial probability.

3.2.1 The provers' strategies

We denote an arbitrary strategy for the r provers in protocol P via a triplet $(U_i^j, V_S^j, |\Psi\rangle)$ (or sometimes (U_i^j, V_S^j, ρ)). Here $|\Psi\rangle$ (or ρ) denotes the initial r-partite entangled state shared by the provers, and U_i, V_S the unitaries that they apply upon receiving questions i, S respectively. More precisely, in the protocol a prover is asked two types of questions. Either it is asked for a single qubit i, in which case we call the unitary U_i^t (where t indexes the prover), or it is asked for a set of k qubits S, in which case we call the unitary V_S^t. We sometimes omit the superscript t, as the labeling of the provers will often be clear from context. We denote the associated completely positive trace-preserving (CPTP) maps by $\mathcal{U}_i^t : \sigma \mapsto U_i^t \sigma(U_i^t)^\dagger$ and $\mathcal{V}_S^t : \sigma \mapsto V_S^t \sigma(V_S^t)^\dagger$.

For $t \in [r]$ we write P^t for the register containing the t-th prover's share of $|\Psi\rangle$. After application of the unitary U_i^t or V_S^t, we relabel registers associated to the prover as $S^t, Q_1^t, \ldots, Q_n^t$. Here the n registers $Q_1^t, \ldots, Q_n^t$ are each single-qubit registers such that register Q_i^t (resp. registers $Q_{i_1}^t \cdots Q_{i_k}^t$) is sent back to the verifier when the prover is asked for qubit i (resp. set of qubits $S = \{i_1, \ldots, i_k\}$). Note that all registers Q_i^t may not exist simultaneously; which ones do depends on the unitary U_i^t or V_S^t that was applied. The remaining register S^t is an auxiliary register of arbitrary dimension. In addition, for each prover $t \in \{1, \ldots, r\}$ we introduce $2n$ auxiliary registers $R_1^t, \ldots, R_n^t$ and $\overline{R}_1^t, \ldots, \overline{R}_n^t$, and define

$$|\tilde{\Psi}\rangle := |\Psi\rangle \bigotimes_{t=1}^{r} \bigotimes_{i=1}^{n} \frac{1}{\sqrt{2}}\left(|00\rangle_{R_i^t \overline{R}_i^t} + |11\rangle_{R_i^t \overline{R}_i^t}\right), \quad (1)$$

i.e. $|\tilde{\Psi}\rangle$ is $|\Psi\rangle$ adjoined with n EPR pairs for each prover, created in the auxiliary registers. We note that the sole role of these EPR pairs will be to create the totally mixed state on the R_i^t registers; the role played by this register will become apparent in the soundness analysis. We write $\rho = |\Psi\rangle\langle\Psi|$ and $\tilde{\rho} = |\tilde{\Psi}\rangle\langle\tilde{\Psi}|$. See Figure 2 for a summary of

	Register	Use
Before application of U_i, V_S.	P^t	Prover t's register in state $|\Psi\rangle$
After application of U_i, V_S	Q_i^t	Sent back by prover t if asked for the i-th qubit.
	S^t	Prover's remaining registers.
Auxiliary registers	R_i^t, $\overline{\mathrm{R}}_i^t$	Initialized as an EPR pair.

Figure 2: Notation for the provers' registers.

our nomenclature for registers. We will often abbreviate Q_i for the union of the Q_i^j, $j \in [r]$, and write $\mathrm{Q}_i^{\neq t}$ for the union of all Q_i^j for $j \in [r]\backslash\{t\}$.

We introduce a new set of unitaries which act on a prover's share of $|\tilde{\Psi}\rangle$ as

$$C_i^t := (U_i^t)^\dagger (\mathrm{SWAP}_{\mathrm{Q}_i^t \mathrm{R}_i^t} \otimes \mathrm{Id})U_i^t,$$

$$D_{i,S}^t := (V_S^t)^\dagger (\mathrm{SWAP}_{\mathrm{Q}_i^t \mathrm{R}_i^t} \otimes \mathrm{Id})V_S^t, \qquad (2)$$

where U_i^t and V_S^t are implicitly tensored with the identity on the auxiliary registers. We denote the associated CPTP maps by $\mathcal{C}_i^t : \sigma \mapsto C_i^t \sigma (C_i^t)^\dagger$ and $\mathcal{D}_{i,S}^t : \sigma \mapsto D_{i,S}^t \sigma (D_{i,S}^t)^\dagger$. In order not to overload the notation we often do not specify precisely on which registers the identity acts (sometimes we even omit the symbol Id altogether), as it should always be clear from context. In words, C_i^t corresponds to applying U_i^t, swapping the register Q_i^t containing the output qubit with the i-th ancilla register R_i^t, and applying $(U_i^t)^\dagger$. For $i \in S$, $D_{i,S}^t$ is defined as C_i^t but from the unitary V_S^t instead of U_i^t, while still swapping the output qubit in register Q_i^t only (and not the others). For any subset $T \subseteq S$ we define $D_{T,S}^t$ in the same ways as $D_{i,S}^t$ except all qubits in the subset T are swapped out; in particular $D_{\{i\},S}^t = D_{i,S}^t$ and $D_{\emptyset,S}^t = \mathrm{Id}$. The following observation, which follows from $V_S^t(V_S^t)^\dagger = \mathrm{Id}$, will be useful:

$$\forall T \subsetneq S, \forall i \in S\backslash T, \qquad D_{i,S}^t D_{T,S}^t = D_{T,S}^t D_{i,S}^t = D_{T\cup\{i\},S}^t. \qquad (3)$$

Since $\mathrm{SWAP} = \mathrm{SWAP}^\dagger$ it also holds that $(C_i^t)^\dagger = C_i^t$ and $(D_{T,S}^t)^\dagger = D_{T,S}^t$.

Finally, we define an n-qubit mixed state

$$\sigma := \left(\bigotimes_{i=1}^n \mathrm{DEC}_{\mathrm{R}_i^1 \cdots \mathrm{R}_i^r} \right) \left(\mathrm{Tr}_{\cup_t ((\cup_i \overline{\mathrm{R}}_i^t \mathrm{Q}_i^t)\mathrm{S}^t)} \left(\left(\bigotimes_{t=1}^r C_n^t \cdots C_2^t C_1^t \right) |\tilde{\Psi}\rangle\langle\tilde{\Psi}| \left(\bigotimes_{t=1}^r (C_1^t)^\dagger \cdots (C_n^t)^\dagger \right) \right) \right), \qquad (4)$$

i.e. σ is the state obtained by, first applying unitaries $C_1^t, \ldots, C_n^t$, for $t = 1, \ldots, r$, to the original state $|\Psi\rangle$ and the auxiliary registers (initialized as EPR pairs), then tracing out all but the nr auxiliary registers $\mathrm{R}_1^t, \ldots, \mathrm{R}_n^t$ for $t = 1, \ldots, r$, and finally applying the decoding map for code C independently to each group of r auxiliary registers $\mathrm{R}_i^1 \cdots \mathrm{R}_i^r$. See Figure 3 for a representation of the state σ.

The intuition for our definition is that the provers' unitaries U_i^t, for $i \in [n]$, are supposed to "extract" the i-th proof qubit from $|\Psi\rangle$. However, in general these unitaries may be incompatible: there is no direct way of simply applying the tensor product, over all i, of the U_i^t to the state $|\Psi\rangle$. Instead, our definition for σ attempts to extract the qubits one at a

time, from $i = 1$ to $i = n$. Each time a qubit has been extracted by application of U_i^t it is swapped out, replaced by the totally mixed state (this is the role of R_i^t), and $(U_i^t)^\dagger$ is applied to "restore" $|\Psi\rangle$. (These three operations are described by C_i^t.) This "restoration" is of course not strictly correct, as even in the case of "honest" unitaries U_i^t the i-th qubit *has* been removed from $|\Psi\rangle$ by the swapping operator. But our analysis will show that, insofar as only the action of the U_j^t for $j \neq i$ is considered, then indeed the new state and $|\Psi\rangle$ are all but indistinguishable from each other.

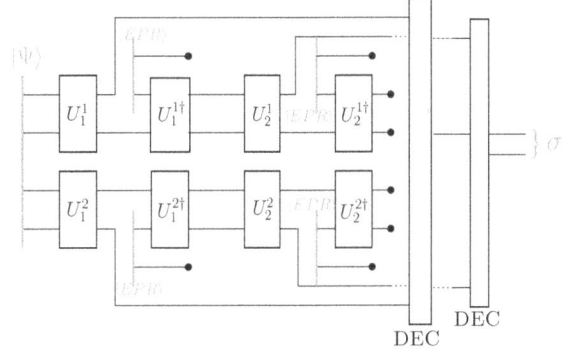

Figure 3: Representation of the circuit used to define the state σ, for $n = t = 2$. A solid black circle represents a set of qubits that is being traced out. A vertical orange line represents a pure state used to initialize the circuit.

3.2.2 Analysis of the strategy

In this section we prove the following lemma, which establishes soundness of protocol P.

LEMMA 7. *There exists a universal constant $c_3 > 0$ (depending on k only) such that the following holds. Suppose a strategy for the provers is accepted with probability at least $1 - \varepsilon$ in each of the tests of protocol P, for some $\varepsilon > 0$. Then the state σ defined in (4) satisfies $\frac{1}{m} \mathrm{Tr}(H\sigma) = O(n^{c_3}\varepsilon)$.*

The proof of the lemma follows from a sequence of claims. The first draws a useful consequence of the condition that the provers succeed in test (b) with high probability.

CLAIM 8. *Suppose the strategy $(U_i^j, V_S^j, |\Psi\rangle)$ succeeds in test (b) with probability at least $1 - \varepsilon$. For any $t \in [r]$, $i \in [n]$ and $S \subseteq [n]$ of cardinality k such that $i \in S$,*

$$\left\| (C_i^t - D_{i,S}^t) \otimes \mathrm{Id} \, |\tilde{\Psi}\rangle \right\|^2 = O(n^k \varepsilon), \qquad (5)$$

where $|\tilde{\Psi}\rangle$ is defined from $|\Psi\rangle$ in (1). Furthermore, for any set $S' \subseteq [n]$ of cardinality k and $T \subseteq S \cap S'$,

$$\left\| (D_{T,S}^t - D_{T,S'}^t) \otimes \mathrm{Id} \, |\tilde{\Psi}\rangle \right\|^2 = O(n^k \varepsilon). \qquad (6)$$

PROOF. For any $t \in [r]$, $i \in [n]$ and set $S \subseteq [n]$ such that $i \in S$ let

$$|\varphi_i\rangle := \bigotimes_{p=1}^r C_i^p |\tilde{\Psi}\rangle \qquad \text{and} \qquad |\varphi_{i,S}\rangle := D_{i,S}^t \left(\bigotimes_{p \neq t} C_i^p \right) |\tilde{\Psi}\rangle, \qquad (7)$$

where for ease of notation the dependence on t of $|\varphi_i\rangle$ and $|\varphi_{i,S}\rangle$ is left implicit. By definition, this strategy's success probability in test (b) of the protocol is exactly

$$\frac{1}{r}\sum_{t=1}^{r}\frac{1}{n}\sum_{i=1}^{n}\frac{1}{\binom{n-1}{k-1}}\sum_{S:i\in S}\frac{1}{2}$$

$$\left(\langle\Psi|\Big(\bigotimes_{p=1}^{r}U_i^p\Big)^{\dagger}\mathrm{CHECK}_{\mathrm{Q}_i^1\cdots\mathrm{Q}_i^r}\Big(\bigotimes_{p=1}^{r}U_i^p\Big)|\Psi\rangle\right.$$

$$\left.+\langle\Psi|\Big(V_S^t\bigotimes_{p\neq t}U_i^p\Big)^{\dagger}\mathrm{CHECK}_{\mathrm{Q}_i^1\cdots\mathrm{Q}_i^r}\Big(V_S^t\bigotimes_{p\neq t}U_i^p\Big)|\Psi\rangle\right).$$

Let $\mathrm{CK}_i := \mathrm{CHECK}_{\mathrm{R}_i^1\cdots\mathrm{R}_i^r}$, where CHECK is the projection on the codespace. Note we will use CK_i for the check operator on the R registers; when we consider the operator on the Q registers these will be specified explicitly. Given the definition of C_i^t and $D_{i,S}^t$ in (2), success $1-\varepsilon$ in test (b) of the protocol can be rewritten as

$$\frac{1}{n}\sum_{i=1}^{n}\frac{1}{\binom{n-1}{k-1}}\sum_{S:i\in S}\frac{1}{2}\Big(\langle\varphi_i|\mathrm{CK}_i|\varphi_i\rangle+\langle\varphi_{i,S}|\mathrm{CK}_i|\varphi_{i,S}\rangle\Big)\geq 1-\varepsilon_t,$$
(8)

where the ε_t satisfy $(1/t)(\varepsilon_1+\cdots+\varepsilon_t)=\varepsilon$. Decompose the action of the unitary $D_{i,S}^t(C_i^t)^{\dagger}$ as

$$D_{i,S}^t(C_i^t)^{\dagger} = \mathrm{Id}_{\mathrm{R}_i^t}\otimes W_{i,S}^1+X_{\mathrm{R}_i^t}\otimes W_{i,S}^2+Y_{\mathrm{R}_i^t}\otimes W_{i,S}^3+Z_{\mathrm{R}_i^t}\otimes W_{i,S}^4,$$
(9)

where the Pauli operators $\{\mathrm{Id},X,Y,Z\}$ act on the i-th auxiliary register R_i^t associated with the t-th prover, and the $W_{i,S}^\ell$ are arbitrary operators (not necessarily unitary) of norm at most 1 acting on the remaining registers $\mathrm{Q}_1^t\cdots\mathrm{Q}_n^t$ and S^t. Note that both C_i^t and $D_{i,S}^t$ are such that $\mathrm{Tr}_{\mathrm{R}_i^t}(C_i^t)=\mathrm{Tr}_{\mathrm{R}_i^t}(D_{i,S}^t)=\mathrm{Id}_{\mathrm{Q}_1^t\cdots\mathrm{Q}_n^t\mathrm{S}^t}$, hence $W_{i,S}^1=\mathrm{Id}$. Let $|\varphi_i^s\rangle := \big(\mathrm{CK}_i\otimes\mathrm{Id}\big)|\varphi_i\rangle$ and $|\varphi_i^f\rangle := \big(\big(\mathrm{Id}-\mathrm{CK}_i\big)\otimes\mathrm{Id}\big)|\varphi_i\rangle$, so that $|\varphi_i\rangle=|\varphi_i^s\rangle+|\varphi_i^f\rangle$. By assumption the code C corrects all single-qubit Pauli errors, and since by definition the reduced density of $|\varphi_i^s\rangle$ on registers $\mathrm{R}_i^1\cdots\mathrm{R}_i^r$ is in the codespace, for any single-qubit Pauli error $E_{\mathrm{R}_i^t}\in\{X,Y,Z\}$ acting on register R_i^t,

$$\mathrm{CHECK}_{\mathrm{R}_i^1\cdots\mathrm{R}_i^r}\big(E_{\mathrm{R}_i^t}\otimes\mathrm{Id}\big)|\varphi_i^s\rangle = 0.$$
(10)

As a consequence, starting from the definition of $|\varphi_{i,S}\rangle$ and using the decomposition (9) we get

$$\mathrm{CK}_i|\varphi_{i,S}\rangle = \mathrm{CK}_i\cdot\Big(D_{i,S}^t\big(C_i^t\big)^{\dagger}\otimes\mathrm{Id}\Big)|\varphi_i\rangle$$

$$= \mathrm{CK}_i\cdot\Big(\mathrm{Id}_{\mathrm{R}_i^t}\otimes\mathrm{Id}+X_{\mathrm{R}_i^t}\otimes W_{i,S}^2$$

$$+Y_{\mathrm{R}_i^t}\otimes W_{i,S}^3+Z_{\mathrm{R}_i^t}\otimes W_{i,S}^4\Big)|\varphi_i\rangle$$

$$= \mathrm{CK}_i\otimes\mathrm{Id}|\varphi_i\rangle+\big(\mathrm{CK}_i\cdot X_{\mathrm{R}_i^t}\otimes W_{i,S}^2$$

$$+\mathrm{CK}_i\cdot Y_{\mathrm{R}_i^t}\otimes W_{i,S}^3+\mathrm{CK}_i\cdot Z_{\mathrm{R}_i^t}\otimes W_{i,S}^4)|\varphi_i^s\rangle$$

$$+\big(\mathrm{CK}_i\cdot X_{\mathrm{R}_i^t}\otimes W_{i,S}^2+\mathrm{CK}_i\cdot Y_{\mathrm{R}_i^t}\otimes W_{i,S}^3$$

$$+\mathrm{CK}_i\cdot Z_{\mathrm{R}_i^t}\otimes W_{i,S}^4)|\varphi_i^f\rangle$$

$$= \mathrm{CK}_i\otimes\mathrm{Id}|\varphi_i\rangle+\big(\mathrm{CK}_i\cdot X_{\mathrm{R}_i^t}\otimes W_{i,S}^2$$

$$+\mathrm{CK}_i\cdot Y_{\mathrm{R}_i^t}\otimes W_{i,S}^3+\mathrm{CK}_i\cdot Z_{\mathrm{R}_i^t}\otimes W_{i,S}^4)|\varphi_i^f\rangle,$$
(11)

where the last equality follows from (10) and the fact that the $W_{i,S}$ do not act on R_i^t. Eq. (8) implies that both

$$\frac{1}{n}\sum_{i=1}^{n}\frac{1}{\binom{n-1}{k-1}}\sum_{S:i\in S}\big\||\varphi_i^f\rangle\big\|^2 \leq 2\varepsilon_t$$
(12)

and

$$\frac{1}{n}\sum_{i=1}^{n}\frac{1}{\binom{n-1}{k-1}}\sum_{S:i\in S}\big\|(\mathrm{Id}-\mathrm{CHECK}_{\mathrm{R}_i^1\cdots\mathrm{R}_i^r})|\varphi_{i,S}\rangle\big\|^2 \leq 2\varepsilon_t,$$
(13)

where we used that $\mathrm{CHECK}_{\mathrm{R}_i^1\cdots\mathrm{R}_i^r}$ is a projection. Using the triangle inequality as

$$\big\||\varphi_{i,S}\rangle-|\varphi_i\rangle\big\| \leq \big\||\varphi_{i,S}\rangle-\mathrm{CK}_i|\varphi_{i,S}\rangle\big\|$$

$$+\big\|\mathrm{CK}_i|\varphi_{i,S}\rangle-\mathrm{CK}_i|\varphi_i\rangle\big\|+\big\|\mathrm{CK}_i|\varphi_i\rangle-|\varphi_i\rangle\big\|$$

we get

$$\frac{1}{n}\sum_{i=1}^{n}\frac{1}{\binom{n-1}{k-1}}\sum_{S:i\in S}\big\||\varphi_{i,S}\rangle-|\varphi_i\rangle\big\|^2 \leq 3\big(2\varepsilon_t+9\cdot 2\varepsilon_t+2\varepsilon_t\big),$$
(14)

where the first bound is obtained from (13), the second from (11), (12) and $\|\mathrm{CK}_i\|,\|W_{i,j}^\ell\|\leq 1$, and the third from the definition of $|\varphi_i^f\rangle$ and (12). Recalling the definition of $|\varphi_i\rangle$ and $|\varphi_{i,S}\rangle$ in (7), (5) is proved by noting that the operator $(\mathrm{Id}\otimes_{p\neq t}C_i^p)$ is unitary and hence its application does not modify the Euclidean norm.

The proof of (6) follows the same steps. Defining vectors $|\varphi_{T,S}\rangle$ and $|\varphi_{T,S'}\rangle$ and using that (8) is satisfied for every $i\in T$ we can decompose $D_{T,S}^t(D_{T,S'}^t)^{\dagger}$ as in (9), except now the decomposition involves all $|T|$-qubit Pauli operators on registers R_i^t for $i\in T$. The different qubits are checked independently, and we can define $|\varphi_{T,S'}^s\rangle := (\otimes_{i\in T}\mathrm{CK}_i)|\varphi_{T,S'}\rangle$. The remainder of the derivation follows the same steps, leading to (6) (where factors polynomial in k are hidden in the $O(\cdot)$ notation, using that k is a constant independent of n). $\square$

For any $i\in[n]$ let $\mathcal{F}_i$ be the completely positive trace non-increasing map, acting on all provers' registers, defined by

$$\mathcal{F}_i:\sigma\mapsto\left(\Big(\bigotimes_{j=1}^{r}X_i^j\Big)^{\dagger}\mathrm{CK}_{\mathrm{Q}_i}\Big(\bigotimes_{j=1}^{r}X_i^j\Big)\right)\sigma$$

$$\left(\Big(\bigotimes_{j=1}^{r}X_i^j\Big)\mathrm{CK}_{\mathrm{Q}_i}\Big(\bigotimes_{j=1}^{r}X_i^j\Big)^{\dagger}\right). \quad (15)$$

Here we use the symbol X_i^j to represent any of U_i^j or V_S^j for any S containing i; we leave the dependence of $\mathcal{F}_i$ on the choice of X_i^j implicit as all bounds proved will hold irrespective of that choice. We also write $\mathcal{X}_i^j:\sigma\to X_i^j\sigma(X_i^j)^{\dagger}$ for the CPTP map associated with X_i^j. Note that, in addition to the presence of the CK operator, the difference between the maps $\mathcal{F}_i$ and e.g. $\otimes_j\mathcal{C}_i^j$ is that in the former the t registers Q_i and R_i are not swapped; in particular $\mathcal{F}_i$ acts as identity on R_i.

Our second claim shows that the property that the qubits extracted from the provers' strategies through the maps X_i^j are in the codespace remains preserved even after many layers of application of the $\mathcal{F}_i$.

CLAIM 9. *Suppose the strategy $(U_i^j, V_S^j, |\Psi\rangle)$ succeeds in test (b) with probability at least $1 - \varepsilon$. Let s be an integer and $i_1, \ldots, i_s \in [n]$. Then*

$$Tr\left(\left(\bigcirc_{\ell=1}^s \mathcal{F}_{i_\ell}\right)(\tilde{\rho})\right) = 1 - O(sn^k\varepsilon). \tag{16}$$

PROOF. We prove (16) by induction on s. For $s = 1$ it follows immediately by first applying Claim 8 (at most) r times to replace each $X_{i_1}^j$ in the definition of $\mathcal{F}_{i_1}$ by $U_{i_1}^j$, and then using the assumption of success in the test, which ensures that the extracted qubits are close to the code space. Suppose (16) verified for some s, and let K be the constant implicit in the $O(\cdot)$ notation; we show it for $s + 1$. Writing $\mathrm{CK}_{i_1} = \mathrm{Id} - (\mathrm{Id} - \mathrm{CK}_{i_1})$,

$$\mathrm{Tr}\left(\left(\bigcirc_{\ell=1}^{s+1} \mathcal{F}_{i_\ell}\right)(\tilde{\rho})\right)$$

$$= \mathrm{Tr}\left(\left(\bigcirc_{\ell=2}^{s} \mathcal{F}_{i_\ell}\right)(\tilde{\rho})\right) - \mathrm{Tr}\left(\left(\bigcirc_{\ell=2}^{s+1} \mathcal{F}_{i_\ell}\right)\right.$$

$$\left. \circ \left(\bigotimes_{j=1}^r \mathcal{X}_{i_1}^j\right)^\dagger\left((\mathrm{Id} - \mathrm{CK}_{i_1})\left(\bigotimes_{j=1}^r \mathcal{X}_{i_1}^j\right)(\tilde{\rho})(\mathrm{Id} - \mathrm{CK}_{i_1})\right)\right)$$

$$\geq 1 - Ksn^k\varepsilon - \mathrm{Tr}\left((\mathrm{Id} - \mathrm{CK}_{i_1})\left(\bigotimes_{j=1}^r \mathcal{X}_{i_1}^j\right)(\tilde{\rho})\right)$$

$$\geq 1 - Ksn^k\varepsilon - O(n^k\varepsilon),$$

where the first inequality uses the induction hypothesis for the first term, and that the $\mathcal{F}_{i_1}$ are trace non-increasing for the second, and the last follows from the case $s = 1$ of (16). Provided K is chosen large enough this establishes the induction step and proves the claim. $\square$

The next claim has a similar flavor as the previous one, that the qubits extracted from the provers' strategies lie in the codespace is preserved even after application of a sequence of maps $\mathcal{C}_i^t$ or $\mathcal{D}_{i,S}^t$ on one of the provers' registers.

CLAIM 10. *There exists a constant $c_1 > 0$ depending on k only such that the following holds. Suppose the strategy $(U_i^j, V_S^j, |\Psi\rangle)$ succeeds in test (b) with probability at least $1 - \varepsilon$. Let s be an integer and $i_1, \ldots, i_s \in [n]$. Then for any $t \in [r]$ and choice of $\mathcal{Y}_{i_\ell}^j \in \{\mathcal{C}_{i_\ell}^j, \mathcal{D}_{i_\ell, S_\ell}^j \,|\, i_\ell \in S_\ell\}$ for $j \in [r]$ and $\ell \in [s]$,*

$$Tr\left(CK_{i_s}\left(\left(\bigcirc_{\ell=1}^s \mathcal{Y}_{i_\ell}^t\right)\bigotimes_{j \neq t} \mathcal{Y}_{i_s}^j\right)(\tilde{\rho})\right) = 1 - O(s^2 n^{c_1}\varepsilon). \tag{17}$$

For lack of space we omit the proof from this extanded abstract; it can be found in the full version [11].

The following corollary is a simple consequence of Claim 8.

COROLLARY 11. *Suppose the strategy $(U_i^j, V_S^j, |\Psi\rangle)$ succeeds in test (b) with probability at least $1 - \varepsilon$. Let s be an integer and $i_1, \ldots, i_s \in [n]$. Then for any $t \in [r]$, set S containing i_s, and choice of $\mathcal{Y}_{i_\ell}^t \in \{\mathcal{C}_{i_\ell}^t, \mathcal{D}_{i_\ell, S_\ell}^t \,|\, i_\ell \in S_\ell\}$ for $\ell \in [s-1]$,*

$$\left\|\left(\left(\mathcal{C}_{i_s}^t \bigcirc_{\ell=1}^{s-1} \mathcal{Y}_{i_\ell}^t\right) \otimes \mathrm{Id}\right)(\tilde{\rho}) - \left(\left(\mathcal{D}_{i_s,S}^t \bigcirc_{\ell=1}^{s-1} \mathcal{Y}_{i_\ell}^t\right) \otimes \mathrm{Id}\right)(\tilde{\rho})\right\|_1$$
$$= O(s^2 n^{c_1+k}\varepsilon), \tag{18}$$

where c_1 is as in Claim 10.

PROOF. Using the freedom in the choice of the operators $\mathcal{Y}$, (17) from Claim 10 shows that the strategy $(U_i^j, V_S^j, (\bigcirc_{\ell=1}^{s-1}\mathcal{Y}_{i_\ell}^t) \otimes \mathrm{Id})(\tilde{\rho}))$ succeeds with probability $1 - O(s^2 n^{c_1}\varepsilon)$ in test (b) of the protocol. The corollary then follows directly from Claim 8. $\square$

Our final claim shows that if the provers have a high success probability in both tests of protocol P the state σ defined in (4) must have low energy with respect to the local Hamiltonian H.

CLAIM 12. *There exists a constant $c_2 > 0$ depending on k only such that the following holds. Let $\delta, \varepsilon > 0$ be such that the provers succeed in test (a) of protocol P with probability at least $1 - \delta$, and in test (b) with probability at least $1 - \varepsilon$. Then*

$$\frac{1}{m}\,Tr(H\sigma) = O(\delta + n^{c_2}\varepsilon).$$

For lack of space we omit the proof from this extanded abstract; it can be found in the full version [11].

Lemma 7 now follows directly from Claim 12 and the fact that any strategy with success $1 - \varepsilon$ in Protocol P must have success probability at least $1 - 2\varepsilon$ in each of the two tests (a) and (b) of the protocol.

4. REFERENCES

[1] S. Aaronson. The quantum PCP manifesto, 2006. Blog entry available at http://www.scottaaronson.com/blog/?p=139.

[2] D. Aharonov, I. Arad, Z. Landau, and U. Vazirani. The detectability lemma and quantum gap amplification. In *Proc. 41st STOC*, pages 417–426, New York, NY, USA, 2009. ACM.

[3] D. Aharonov, I. Arad, and T. Vidick. The quantum PCP conjecture. Technical report, arXiv:1309.7495, 2013. Appeared as guest column in ACM SIGACT News archive Volume 44 Issue 2, June 2013, Pages 47–79.

[4] D. Aharonov and T. Naveh. Quantum NP – a survey. Technical report, arXiv:quant-ph/0210077, 2002.

[5] S. Arora, C. Lund, R. Motwani, M. Sudan, and M. Szegedy. Proof verification and the hardness of approximation problems. *J. ACM*, 45(3):501–555, 1998.

[6] S. Arora and S. Safra. Probabilistic checking of proofs: A new characterization of NP. *J. ACM*, 45(1):70–122, 1998.

[7] L. Babai, L. Fortnow, and C. Lund. Non-deterministic exponential time has two-prover interactive protocols. *Comput. Complexity*, 1:3–40, 1991.

[8] C. H. Bennett, D. P. DiVincenzo, J. A. Smolin, and W. K. Wootters. Mixed-state entanglement and quantum error correction. *Phys. Rev. A*, 54(5):3824, 1996.

[9] F. G. Brandao and A. W. Harrow. Product-state approximations to quantum ground states. In *Proc. 45th STOC*, 2013.

[10] I. Dinur. The PCP theorem by gap amplification. *J. ACM*, 54(3), June 2007.

[11] J. Fitzsimons and T. Vidick. A multiprover interactive proof system for the local Hamiltonian problem. Technical report, arXiv:1409.0260, 2014.

[12] M. H. Freedman and M. B. Hastings. Quantum systems on non-k-hyperfinite complexes: A generalization of classical statistical mechanics on expander graphs. *arXiv preprint arXiv:1301.1363*, 2013.

[13] S. Gharibian, Y. Huang, and Z. Landau. Quantum hamiltonian complexity. Technical report, arXiv:1401.3916, 2014.

[14] D. Gottesman and S. Irani. The quantum and classical complexity of translationally invariant tiling and hamiltonian problems. In *Proc. 50th FOCS*, pages 95–104, Oct 2009.

[15] J. Håstad. Some optimal inapproximability results. *J. ACM*, 48:798–859, 2001.

[16] M. B. Hastings. Trivial low energy states for commuting Hamiltonians, and the quantum PCP conjecture. *Quantum Information and Computation*, 13(5 & 6):393–429, 2013.

[17] T. Ito and T. Vidick. A multi-prover interactive proof for NEXP sound against entangled provers. *Proc. 53rd FOCS*, pages 243–252, 2012.

[18] M. Junge, M. Navascues, C. Palazuelos, D. Perez-Garcia, V. B. Scholz, and R. F. Werner. Connes' embedding problem and tsirelson's problem. *J. Math. Physics*, 52(1):–, 2011.

[19] J. Kempe, A. Kitaev, and O. Regev. The complexity of the local hamiltonian problem. *SIAM J. Comput.*, 35(5):1070–1097, May 2006.

[20] J. Kempe, H. Kobayashi, K. Matsumoto, and T. Vidick. Using entanglement in quantum multi-prover interactive proofs. *Computational Complexity*, 18:273–307, 2009.

[21] A. Y. Kitaev, A. H. Shen, and M. N. Vyalyi. *Classical and Quantum Computation*, volume 47 of *Graduate Studies in Mathematics*. American Mathematical Society, 2002.

[22] H. Kobayashi and K. Matsumoto. Quantum multi-prover interactive proof systems with limited prior entanglement. *Journal of Computer and System Sciences*, 66(3):429–450, 2003.

[23] R. Laflamme, C. Miquel, J. P. Paz, and W. H. Zurek. Perfect quantum error correcting code. *Phys. Rev. Lett.*, 77(1):198, 1996.

[24] Y.-K. Liu. Consistency of local density matrices is QMA-complete. In J. Diaz, K. Jansen, J. D. Rolim, and U. Zwick, editors, *Approximation, Randomization, and Combinatorial Optimization. Algorithms and Techniques*, volume 4110 of *Lecture Notes in Computer Science*, pages 438–449. Springer Berlin Heidelberg, 2006.

[25] C. Marriott and J. Watrous. Quantum Arthur—Merlin games. *Comput. Complexity*, 14(2):122–152, June 2005.

[26] T. J. Osborne. Hamiltonian complexity. *Reports on Progress in Physics*, 75(2):022001, 2012.

[27] R. Raz. A parallel repetition theorem. *SIAM J. Comput.*, 27:763–803, 1998.

[28] B. Reichardt, F. Unger, and U. Vazirani. A classical leash for a quantum system: Command of quantum systems via rigidity of CHSH games. *Nature*, 496(7446):456–460, 2013.

[29] V. B. Scholz and R. F. Werner. Tsirelson's problem. Technical report, arXiv:0812.4305v1 [math-ph], 2008.

[30] T. Vidick. Three-player entangled XOR games are NP-hard to approximate. In *Proc. 54th FOCS*, 2013.

[31] J. Watrous. Quantum computational complexity. In *Encyclopedia of complexity and systems science*, pages 7174–7201. Springer, 2009.

Zero-Information Protocols and Unambiguity in Arthur–Merlin Communication

[Extended Abstract]*

Mika Göös
Department of Computer Science
University of Toronto
mgoos@cs.toronto.edu

Toniann Pitassi
Department of Computer Science
University of Toronto
toni@cs.toronto.edu

Thomas Watson
Department of Computer Science
University of Toronto
thomasw@cs.toronto.edu

ABSTRACT

We study whether information complexity can be used to attack the long-standing open problem of proving lower bounds against Arthur–Merlin (AM) communication protocols. Our starting point is to show that—in contrast to plain randomized communication complexity—every boolean function admits an AM communication protocol where on each yes-input, the distribution of Merlin's proof leaks no information about the input and moreover, this proof is unique for each outcome of Arthur's randomness. We posit that these two properties of *zero information leakage* and *unambiguity on yes-inputs* are interesting in their own right and worthy of investigation as new avenues toward AM.

- **Zero-information protocols (ZAM).** Our basic ZAM protocol uses exponential communication for some functions, and this raises the question of whether more efficient protocols exist. We prove that all functions in the classical space-bounded complexity classes NL and ⊕L have polynomial-communication ZAM protocols. We also prove that ZAM complexity is lower bounded by conondeterministic communication complexity.

- **Unambiguous protocols (UAM).** Our most technically substantial result is a $\Omega(n)$ lower bound on the UAM complexity of the NP-complete *set-intersection* function; the proof uses information complexity arguments in a new, indirect way and overcomes the "zero-information barrier" described above. We also prove that in general, UAM complexity is lower bounded by the classic discrepancy bound, and we give evidence that it is *not* generally lower bounded by the classic corruption bound.

*All proofs appear in the full version of this work [23].

Categories and Subject Descriptors

F.0 [**Theory of Computation**]: General; F.1.3 [**Computation by Abstract Devices**]: Complexity Measures and Classes.

General Terms

Theory

Keywords

Communication complexity, Information complexity, Arthur–Merlin protocols

1. INTRODUCTION

What is AM communication? Arthur–Merlin (AM) games [5] are a type of randomized proof system where a computationally-unbounded prover, Merlin, wishes to convince a skeptical and computationally-bounded verifier, Arthur, that some boolean function f evaluates to 1 on a given input. In this work, we study the communication complexity variant of AM [4, 36, 39] where "Arthur" now consists of two parties, Alice and Bob, and the input is split between them: Alice holds x, Bob holds y, and they wish to verify that $f(x, y) = 1$.

In an execution of an AM communication protocol, Alice and Bob start by tossing some coins, then Merlin produces a proof string that may depend on the input and the outcomes of the coin tosses, and finally Alice and Bob independently decide whether to accept based on their own input, the outcome of the coin tosses, and Merlin's proof string.

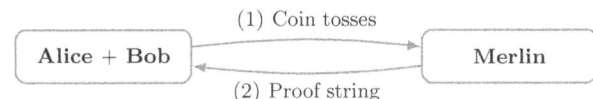

(1) Coin tosses
Alice + Bob ⟷ Merlin
(2) Proof string

The *completeness* criterion is that for every 1-input, with high probability over the coin tosses there exists a proof string that *both* Alice and Bob accept. The *soundness* criterion is that for every 0-input, with high probability over the coin tosses there does not exist a proof string that both Alice and Bob accept. The *communication cost* is the worst-case length of Merlin's proof string.

In short, an AM protocol is a probability distribution over nondeterministic protocols, together with a bounded-error acceptance criterion. That is, AM = BP·NP in standard notation [55]. The model is also robust to changes in its definition; for example, allowing Alice and Bob to communicate after Merlin's proof is published does not increase the power of the model: we can simply include the transcript of the subsequent communication in Merlin's proof.

For a more formal definition of the AM communication model, see Section 2.

Why study AM communication? The Arthur–Merlin communication model marks one of the frontiers of our understanding of communication complexity: no nontrivial lower bounds are known on the amount of communication required by AM protocols for any explicit function.

The desirability of such lower bounds stems from a variety of sources. For one, AM communication has turned out to be closely related to models of streaming delegation [13, 41, 26, 12, 14, 42]. Also, AM lower bounds would be a first step toward proving lower bounds against the communication polynomial hierarchy [4], which is necessary for obtaining strong rank rigidity lower bounds for explicit matrices [51, 46, 47, 59] (as well as margin complexity rigidity lower bounds [45]), which in turn is related to circuit complexity [56]. Lower bounds against the polynomial hierarchy are also related to graph complexity [49, 34]. Another motivation comes from the *algebrization* framework [1, 28], which converts communication lower bounds (such as for AM) into barriers to proving relations among classical, time-bounded complexity classes. The absence of and need for nontrivial AM communication lower bounds has been explicitly pointed out in [46, 45, 48, 42, 40].

For MA, the weaker variant where Merlin sends his proof *before* the coins are tossed, strong lower bounds are known [36, 50, 21, 39, 26] (with applications to property testing [27]). Other powerful subclasses of the polynomial hierarchy for which communication lower bounds are known include SBP (which lies between MA and AM) [24] and P^{NP} [29, 48].

1.1 New models UAM and ZAM

The aim of this work is to study restricted complexity measures that capture some of the difficulty of proving AM lower bounds, and to create new proof techniques and explore the power of existing ones with regard to AM communication complexity. Our results revolve around two new complexity measures UAM and ZAM that we introduce below. We proceed rather informally in this introduction; for precise definitions, see Section 2.

Unambiguous protocols (UAM). A natural restriction on any proof system is *unambiguity*, meaning that the verifier accepts at most one proof on a given input. In the context of AM one can consider three types of unambiguity: (1) *unambiguous completeness*, where for each 1-input and each outcome of the coin tosses, Arthur accepts at most one of Merlin's possible proofs; (2) *unambiguous soundness*, which is the same as above but for 0-inputs; and (3) *two-sided unambiguity*, where both unambiguous completeness and soundness hold.

Lower bounds for models (2) and (3) can be proved using known techniques. In case of (2) it is not difficult to show that lower bounds follow from the classic corruption bound, which is known to characterize the complexity class SBP [24]. In case of (3) the complexity class corresponding to the model is BP·UP. Klauck [38] showed that even the smooth

rectangle bound (introduced in [31]) suffices to lower bound BP·UP communication complexity.

In this work we study the remaining case of unambiguous completeness, henceforth simply called *unambiguous*. We call an unambiguous AM protocol a UAM protocol for short, and we let UAM(f) denote the minimum cost of a UAM protocol for f. As is customary, we also use UAM to denote the class of two-party functions that admit polylog cost UAM protocols. We will see that UAM exhibits new phenomena not captured by SBP or BP·UP. For starters, the model supports *zero-information* protocols as introduced next.

Zero-information protocols (ZAM). One very successful approach for proving communication lower bounds against randomized protocols is the *information complexity* methodology [16, 6, 33, 15, 25, 32, 18, 11, 10, 9, 24]. In this approach one argues that the transcripts of correct protocols must necessarily "leak" information about the input; the amount of information leaked automatically lower bounds the communication.

A natural question is whether information complexity has any bearing on AM. One of the main conceptual contributions of this work is that information complexity, in its standard form, cannot be used to prove lower bounds against UAM protocols (much less against AM protocols). Specifically, we show that every boolean function admits a private-coin UAM protocol satisfying the following:

> **Zero-information:** *The distribution of Merlin's unique proof (which serves as the protocol transcript) is identical across all 1-inputs.*

We call a zero-information UAM protocol a ZAM protocol for short, and we let ZAM(f) denote the minimum cost of a ZAM protocol for f. We posit that ZAM protocols are interesting in their own right, both combinatorially and as a natural model of private computation in which Alice and Bob enlist Merlin's help in computing a function but do not want an external observer to learn anything about their inputs.

When talking about information complexity, it is most natural to consider *private-coin* protocols, where Alice and Bob only know the outcomes of their own coins (and Merlin sees everything), rather than *public-coin* protocols, where Alice and Bob share a source of randomness. Indeed, private-coin protocols arise naturally in the direct sum methodology of information complexity.

1.2 Two examples of ZAM protocols

For the sake of concreteness, let us get acquainted with zero-information protocols by studying two basic examples. Figure 1 defines private-coin AM protocols for the 2-bit functions NAND and XOR. The outer 2×2 grids correspond to the inputs x and y, while the 2×2 grid within each input block corresponds to the outcomes of the private coins (each party uses 1 bit of randomness). Both protocols use four different proofs with labels a, b, c, and d; each proof corresponds to a rectangle in the figures.

To execute such an AM protocol on an input $(x, y) \in \{0, 1\}^2$ we first choose outcomes for the private coins: Alice chooses $r \in \{0, 1\}$ at random and Bob chooses $q \in \{0, 1\}$ at random. The input and the coin tosses now define a point (i.e., a smallest square) $P = ((x, r), (y, q))$ inside our figure. If the point P is covered by some rectangle $R \in \{a, b, c, d\}$, then Merlin can make Alice and Bob accept: he provides the label

$$
\begin{array}{c}
\qquad 0 \qquad 1 \\
\begin{array}{|cc|cc|}
\hline
a & d & a & d \\
c & b & b & c \\
\hline
a & b & a,b & \\
c & d & & c,d \\
\hline
\end{array}
\end{array}
\qquad\qquad
\begin{array}{c}
\qquad 0 \qquad 1 \\
\begin{array}{|cc|cc|}
\hline
a,c & & a & c \\
& b,d & b & d \\
\hline
a & b & a,b & \\
c & d & & c,d \\
\hline
\end{array}
\end{array}
$$

$$\text{NAND} \qquad\qquad\qquad \text{XOR}$$

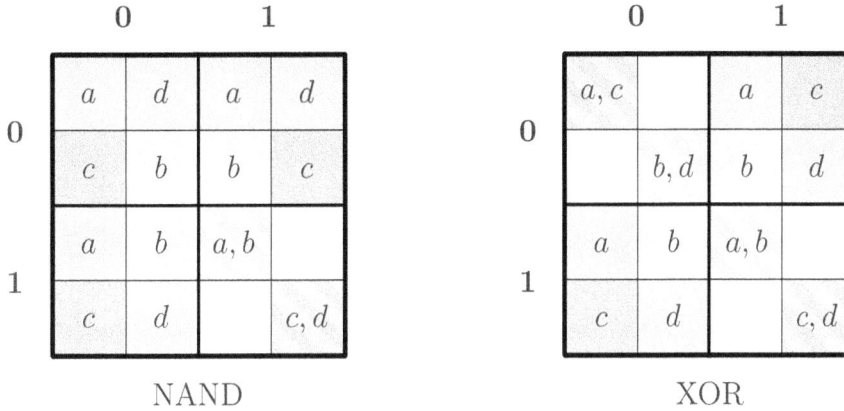

Figure 1: Two examples of ZAM protocols.

Function f	(notation)	Bounds on $\mathsf{ZAM}(f)$	Bounds on $\mathsf{UAM}(f)$
equality	EQ	$\Theta(\log n)$	$\Theta(\log n)$
non-equality	NEQ	$\Theta(n)$	$\Theta(\log n)$
greater-than	GT	$\Theta(n)$	$\Theta(\log n)$
set-disjointness	DISJ	$\Omega(\log n)$ and $O(n)$	$\Omega(\log n)$ and $O(n)$
set-intersection	INTER	$\Theta(n)$	$\Theta(n)$
inner-product	IP	$\Theta(n)$	$\Theta(n)$
random functions		$\Omega(n)$ and $O(2^n)$	$\Theta(n)$
functions in NL or $\oplus$L		$O(\mathrm{poly}(n))$	

Table 1: Bounds on the ZAM and UAM complexities of basic problems.

of the rectangle R as proof and both Alice and Bob can verify that $P \in R$ by checking that this holds from their own perspective. If the point P is not covered by any rectangle, then there is no way for Merlin to make both Alice and Bob accept simultaneously.

The two protocols are unambiguous since no two rectangles intersect inside a 1-block (block corresponding to a 1-input). The protocols make no errors on 1-inputs, i.e., they achieve *perfect completeness*, since they cover each 1-block fully. They are also zero-information, because all rectangles appear with the same "area" (i.e., same probability) inside each of the 1-blocks; hence, for each 1-input, Merlin's unique proof will be uniformly distributed over the set $\{a, b, c, d\}$ (though the definition of zero-information does not require the distribution to be uniform). On 0-inputs, the protocols can erroneously accept with probability $1/2$, i.e., their *soundness* is $1/2$, since in each 0-block the protocols cover half of the points. On uncovered points, Alice or Bob will reject, regardless of which proof Merlin sends. Some points are covered multiple times; e.g., in the case of $(1,1) \in \text{NAND}^{-1}(0)$ the rectangles a and b intersect, as do c and d.

If we want to obtain protocols with soundness $1/2^k$ we can repeat the protocols independently k times in parallel and require that all k iterations accept. In a k-fold protocol the proofs are labeled with k-tuples from $\{a, b, c, d\}^k$. Note also that the iterated protocols retain their unambiguity, zero-information, and perfect completeness properties.

1.3 Results for ZAM

Our starting point is to show that there exists a ZAM protocol for any two-party function $f \colon \mathcal{X} \times \mathcal{Y} \to \{0, 1\}$. Unlike most communication complexity measures, it is not obvious that linear communication suffices for a ZAM protocol, and in fact, our general ZAM protocol uses exponential communication, i.e., we only obtain $\mathsf{ZAM}(f) \leq O(2^n)$ in general when $\mathcal{X} = \mathcal{Y} = \{0, 1\}^n$. We can improve on this general upper bound in case f can be computed in *small space*. To express this result we use a certain measure of parity branching program size $\oplus\mathsf{BP}(f)$ that is tailored for two-party functions; we postpone the precise definition until the proof.

Theorem 1. $\mathsf{ZAM}(f) \leq O(\oplus\mathsf{BP}(f))$ for all f.

In particular, Theorem 1 implies $O(n)$-communication ZAM protocols for all the natural functions listed in Table 1. All functions in the classical space-bounded nonuniform complexity class $\oplus$L/poly have polynomial-size parity branching programs by definition. It is known that NL $\subseteq \oplus$L/poly [20] (moreover, NL/poly equals its unambiguous analogue UL/poly [53]), and thus all functions in the classical classes NL and $\oplus$L have polynomial-communication ZAM protocols. Although Theorem 1 does not seem to yield interesting examples of ZAM protocols with sublinear communication, we show that such a protocol exists at least for the equality function: $\mathsf{ZAM}(\text{EQ}) \leq O(\log n)$.

As for lower bounds, we prove the following.

Theorem 2. $\mathsf{ZAM}(f) \geq \Omega(\mathsf{coNP}(f))$ for all f.

In particular, Theorem 2 allows us to derive matching lower bounds on the ZAM complexity of almost all the functions listed in Table 1; the exceptional DISJ function is discussed shortly. Interestingly, NEQ and GT demonstrate that privacy can come at a huge cost, since $\mathsf{UAM}(\text{NEQ}) \leq \mathsf{BPP}(\text{NEQ}) \leq$

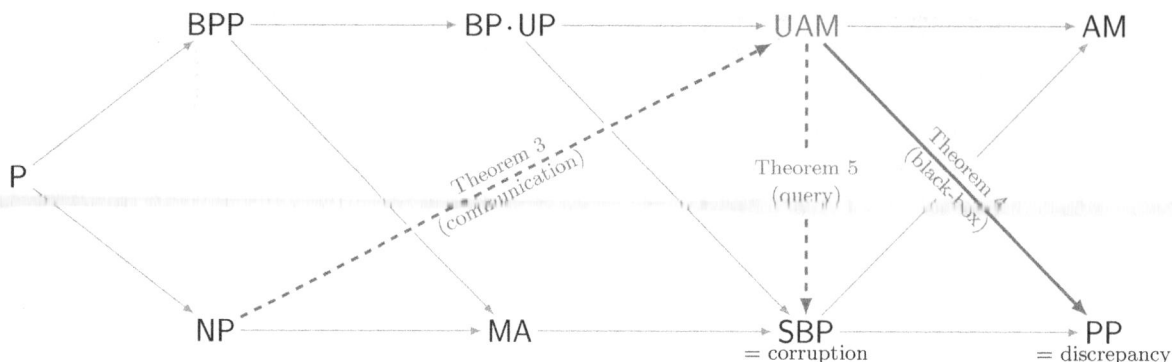

Figure 2: Our results for UAM at a glance. In this diagram, solid arrows A ⟶ B indicate class inclusions A ⊆ B, and dashed arrows A - - ▸ B indicate non-inclusions A ⊄ B.

$O(\log n)$ and similarly for GT, and thus there is an exponential separation between ZAM and UAM.

It remains open to show that there exists a function (even a random one!) that requires superlinear ZAM communication, or prove that all functions have subexponential-communication ZAM protocols. This situation is similar to [19], which studies a different model of private two-party computation, and where the best upper and lower bounds are also exponential and linear. In a similar spirit, [2] proves that in a communication model of approximate privacy called PAR (based on [43]), privacy can come at an exponential cost.

1.4 Results for UAM

Our results for UAM are summarized in Figure 2. Our most technically substantial contribution is a linear lower bound on the UAM complexity of *set-intersection* INTER: $\{0,1\}^n \times \{0,1\}^n \to \{0,1\}$ defined by INTER$(x,y) = 1$ iff x and y intersect when viewed as subsets of $[n]$. Recall that INTER is the canonical NP-complete problem in communication complexity.

Theorem 3. UAM(INTER) $= \Theta(n)$.

Because of the existence of ZAM protocols for INTER, it is not possible to prove Theorem 3 by lower bounding the standard measure of information complexity. Nevertheless, we develop a technique for employing information complexity tools in an *indirect* way, which is inspired by our ZAM lower bounds. Theorem 3 strengthens a result of Klauck [38], who proved that BP·UP(INTER) $= \Theta(n)$ using the smooth rectangle bound of [31] (recall that BP·UP is *two-sided* unambiguous AM). By the methods of [1], a corollary to Theorem 3 is that proving NP $\subseteq$ UAM in the classical time-bounded world would require non-algebrizing techniques. We remark that Theorem 3 also holds for the promise problem where the input sets x and y are guaranteed to intersect in at most two coordinates. This is tight: the UAM complexity of INTER is $O(\log n)$ under the promise that x and y intersect in at most a single coordinate.

One of the most classical lower bound techniques in communication complexity is *discrepancy*, which characterizes PP [37]. Klauck [39] showed that discrepancy does not yield AM lower bounds in general, in other words AM $\not\subseteq$ PP (for promise problems). We prove that discrepancy *can* be used for UAM.

Theorem 4. UAM$(f) \geq \Omega(\text{PP}(f))$ *for all* f.

The proof of Theorem 4 is via a general "black-box" simulation, in the sense that it does not exploit any specific properties of communication complexity and works equally well for other models such as time-bounded computation. Note that Theorem 3 does not follow from Theorem 4, since PP(INTER) $= \Theta(\log n)$. However, all the other UAM lower bounds in Table 1 can be derived as corollaries of Theorem 4.

Since discrepancy can be used for UAM lower bounds, it is natural to ask whether the similarly-prominent *corruption* bound (a one-sided version of discrepancy) can also be used. Since corruption characterizes SBP [24], this is equivalent to asking whether UAM(f) can be reasonably lower bounded in terms of SBP(f), for all f. If so, this would be very significant as it would lead to a lower bound on the UAM complexity of *set-disjointness* DISJ $= \neg$INTER (which is conjectured to require linear AM communication) by the corruption bound for DISJ due to [52]. Currently we cannot even prove that ZAM(DISJ) $\geq \omega(\log n)$. However, we conjecture[1] that corruption alone is *not* sufficient to lower bound UAM complexity, i.e., we conjecture that UAM $\not\subseteq$ SBP. While we are unable to prove this separation for communication complexity, we prove it for *query complexity* (which is a necessary step in order for the communication complexity separation to hold).

In general, an SBP computation (introduced in [8]) is a randomized computation where the acceptance probability is at least α on 1-inputs and at most $\alpha/2$ on 0-inputs, for some arbitrarily small threshold $\alpha > 0$ which may depend on the input size. We provide formal definitions of the query complexity measures UAM$^{\text{dt}}(f)$ and SBP$^{\text{dt}}(f)$ in the full version [23], but for now it suffices to say that they are natural decision tree analogues of the corresponding communication measures. We define a partial function called GUT (short for *gap-unique-tribes*) and prove the following separation.

Theorem 5. UAM^{dt}(GUT) $\leq O(1)$ *and* SBP^{dt}(GUT) $\geq \Omega(n^{1/4})$.

We note that this result yields (by standard techniques) an alternative proof that there exists an oracle separating the classical time-bounded complexity classes MA and AM, which was first proved in [54]. We also note that the composed two-party function GUT $\circ$ AND^n is a natural candidate to witness our conjectured communication separation UAM $\not\subseteq$ SBP.

---

[1]This conjecture has been subsequently settled in [22].

2. DEFINITIONS

We let $\mathbb{P}$ denote probability, $\mathbb{E}$ denote expectation, $\mathbb{H}$ denote Shannon entropy, $\mathbb{I}$ denote mutual information, and $[k]$ denote $\{1, 2, \ldots, k\}$.

2.1 Communication complexity

We assume some familiarity with basic definitions of communication complexity; see [44, 35]. We consider two-party functions $f \colon \mathcal{X} \times \mathcal{Y} \to \{0, 1\}$, where Alice is given the first part of the input $x \in \mathcal{X}$ and Bob is given the second part of the input $y \in \mathcal{Y}$. For $b \in \{0, 1\}$, a b-input is a pair $(x, y) \in f^{-1}(b)$. We adopt the convenient notation of using complexity class names as complexity measures. For example:

- $\mathsf{P}(f)$ is the minimum over all deterministic protocols for f of the maximum number of bits communicated on any input.
- $\mathsf{coNP}(f)$ is the ceiling of the log of the minimum number of rectangles needed to cover the 0's of the communication matrix of f.
- $\mathsf{PP}(f)$ is the minimum over all $\epsilon > 0$ and all randomized protocols computing f with error $\le 1/2 - \epsilon$ of the communication cost of the protocol plus $\log(1/\epsilon)$; see also [4].
- $\mathsf{SBP}(f)$ is the minimum over all $\alpha > 0$ and all randomized protocols that accept 1-inputs with probability $\ge \alpha$ and 0-inputs with probability $\le \alpha/2$ of the communication cost of the protocol plus $\log(1/\alpha)$; see also [24].

We let $\mathrm{EQ}_n, \mathrm{NEQ}_n, \mathrm{GT}_n, \mathrm{DISJ}_n, \mathrm{INTER}_n, \mathrm{IP}_n$ denote the n-bit equality, non-equality, greater-than, set-disjointness, set-intersection, and inner-product modulo 2 functions, respectively. We have that $\mathrm{DISJ}_n(x, y) = \bigwedge_i \neg(x_i \wedge y_i) = \mathrm{AND}_n \circ \mathrm{NAND}^n(x, y)$ is coNP-complete, $\mathrm{INTER}_n(x, y) = \bigvee_i (x_i \wedge y_i) = \mathrm{OR}_n \circ \mathrm{AND}^n(x, y)$ is NP-complete, and $\mathrm{IP}_n(x, y) = \bigoplus_i (x_i \wedge y_i) = \mathrm{XOR}_n \circ \mathrm{AND}^n(x, y)$ is $\oplus\mathsf{P}$-complete. In all cases, we may omit the subscript n when there is no confusion.

2.2 AM, UAM, and ZAM

We work exclusively with *private-coin* AM protocols. Private-coin protocols are essentially equally powerful to their *public-coin* counterparts; see Remark 1 below. We stress that Merlin can always see all the outcomes of coin tosses, and "private" and "public" refer only to whether Alice and Bob can see each other's randomness. (This is in contrast to classical time-bounded complexity where private and public often refer to whether Merlin can see Arthur's randomness.)

In an AM protocol Π, Alice is given a uniform sample from some finite set $\mathcal{R}$ and Bob is independently given a uniform sample from some finite set $\mathcal{Q}$, and there is a collection of rectangles $\tau_1, \ldots, \tau_m \subseteq (\mathcal{X} \times \mathcal{R}) \times (\mathcal{Y} \times \mathcal{Q})$. (Recall that a rectangle τ_i is of the form $A \times B$ for some $A \subseteq \mathcal{X} \times \mathcal{R}$ and $B \subseteq \mathcal{Y} \times \mathcal{Q}$, or equivalently that for all u and u' in $\mathcal{X} \times \mathcal{R}$ and all v and v' in $\mathcal{Y} \times \mathcal{Q}$, if (u, v') and (u', v) are in τ_i, then so are (u, v) and (u', v').) The acceptance probability of Π on input (x, y) is defined to be $\mathbb{P}_{r \in \mathcal{R}, q \in \mathcal{Q}}[\exists i \colon ((x, r), (y, q)) \in \tau_i]$, and we refer to the set $(\{x\} \times \mathcal{R}) \times (\{y\} \times \mathcal{Q})$ as the *block* corresponding to input (x, y). The index i of a rectangle τ_i can be thought of as a message sent from Merlin to Alice and Bob, who then independently decide whether they accept. The output of the protocol is 1 iff they both accept. We use the terminology "rectangles", "transcripts", and "proofs"

interchangeably (τ stands for "transcript"). We define the *communication cost* of Π to be $|\Pi| := \lceil \log m \rceil$, the length of Merlin's proof. The protocol has *completeness* c and *soundness* s if the acceptance probability is at least c on 1-inputs and at most s on 0-inputs. *Perfect completeness* means $c = 1$. We define $\mathsf{AM}_{c,s}(f)$ to be the minimum of $|\Pi|$ over all AM protocols Π for f with completeness c and soundness s.

We say an AM protocol Π is *unambiguous* (more precisely: has unambiguous completeness), or that Π is a UAM protocol, if for every 1-input and every outcome of the randomness, there is at most one proof of Merlin that causes Alice and Bob to accept (and on 0-inputs, in the unlikely event that there exists a proof that is accepted, there can be any number of such proofs). In other words, rectangles do not overlap on 1-inputs; more formally, $((x, r), (y, q)) \notin \tau_i \cap \tau_j$ holds for all $(x, y) \in f^{-1}(1)$, $r \in \mathcal{R}$, $q \in \mathcal{Q}$, and $i \ne j$. We define $\mathsf{UAM}_{c,s}(f)$ to be the minimum of $|\Pi|$ over all UAM protocols Π for f with completeness c and soundness s.

On 1-inputs, a UAM protocol Π can be viewed as a function that maps each $((x, r), (y, q))$ with $(x, y) \in f^{-1}(1)$ to the unique $i \in \{1, \ldots, m\}$ such that $((x, r), (y, q)) \in \tau_i$, or to $\perp$ if no such i exists. We say a UAM protocol Π is *zero-information*, or that Π is a ZAM protocol, if the distribution of the output of this function over random $r \in \mathcal{R}$, $q \in \mathcal{Q}$ is the same for all $(x, y) \in f^{-1}(1)$. We define $\mathsf{ZAM}_{c,s}(f)$ to be the minimum of $|\Pi|$ over all ZAM protocols Π for f with completeness c and soundness s.

The connection to information complexity is that a protocol is zero-information iff for any or all joint random variables (X, Y) whose support is $f^{-1}(1)$, we have $\mathbb{I}(\Pi \colon X, Y) = 0$ (where Π stands for the unique proof function, viewed as a random variable jointly distributed with (X, Y) and with Alice's and Bob's randomness). We consider only distributions over 1-inputs (rather than over all inputs) since (i) the proof function is not uniquely defined on 0-inputs, (ii) the known communication lower bounds via information complexity only need distributions over 1-inputs, and (iii) from a privacy perspective, this is analogous to the situation in cryptographic zero-knowledge, in which the prover's zero-knowledge property is only required to hold on 1-inputs since on 0-inputs, the prover could misbehave and send any message he wants (including ones that reveal too much information).

We assume by default that protocols have perfect completeness and soundness $1/2$, so we define $\mathsf{AM} = \mathsf{AM}_{1,1/2}$ and $\mathsf{UAM} = \mathsf{UAM}_{1,1/2}$ and $\mathsf{ZAM} = \mathsf{ZAM}_{1,1/2}$. Note that $\mathsf{AM}(f) \le \mathsf{UAM}(f) \le \mathsf{ZAM}(f)$ for all f. Our upper bounds all have perfect completeness, and our lower bounds all work even for imperfect completeness (as will be clarified in the proofs).

Remark 1. We note here the well-known fact that by studying a private-coin model (e.g., $\mathsf{UAM} = \mathsf{UAM}^{\mathsf{priv}}$) we lose little generality over analogous public-coin models (e.g., $\mathsf{UAM}^{\mathsf{pub}}$). In a public-coin AM protocol, the randomness is sampled uniformly from some finite set $\mathcal{R}$, and for each $r \in \mathcal{R}$ there is a collection of rectangles $\tau_1^r, \tau_2^r, \ldots, \tau_m^r \subseteq \mathcal{X} \times \mathcal{Y}$. The acceptance probability is $\mathbb{P}_{r \in \mathcal{R}}[\exists i \colon (x, y) \in \tau_i^r]$, and for unambiguity we require that $(x, y) \notin \tau_i^r \cap \tau_j^r$ holds for all $(x, y) \in f^{-1}(1)$, $r \in \mathcal{R}$, and $i \ne j$. For all f we have $\mathsf{UAM}_{c',s'}^{\mathsf{priv}}(f) \le \mathsf{UAM}_{c,s}^{\mathsf{pub}}(f) + O(\log \log |\mathcal{X} \times \mathcal{Y}|)$ by standard sparsification techniques [44, §3.3], provided c, s, c', s' are constants such that $s < s'$ and either $c' < c$ or $c = 1$.

For AM, the same sparsification fact holds, and standard amplification renders the exact values of the constants c and s immaterial. In contrast, for UAM it is not known how to amplify c while preserving the unambiguity property (though s can be amplified if $c = 1$).

3. OVERVIEW OF PROOFS

The proofs of our Theorems 1–5 appear in the full version of this work [23]. Here we only describe the intuitions underlying the proofs.

3.1 Theorem 1

The simple but non-obvious fact that every two-party function f *has* a ZAM protocol (moreover, one of cost $O(2^n)$) follows by combining a generic reduction from f to DISJ with a ZAM protocol for DISJ that runs the ZAM protocol for NAND (from Figure 1) independently for each coordinate.

To prove the stronger Theorem 1, we use a two-step process: (i) we reduce the function f to the evaluation of a determinant of a matrix of a certain form, and (ii) we design a ZAM protocol for the latter task.

We recall that Valiant [57] showed how to reduce any function in NC^1 to the evaluation of a determinant, and subsequently it was shown that mod-2 determinant is actually complete for $\oplus L$ [17]. In [30, 3], a generalization of a reduction from $\oplus L$ to determinant was used (employing the parity branching program model for $\oplus L$ computations). To achieve (i), we use essentially the same reduction, and we describe a simple and combinatorial (as opposed to linear-algebraic as in [30, 3]) proof of the reduction.

To achieve (ii), the basic idea is to pick a random vector and challenge Merlin to find a preimage under the linear transformation of the matrix. If the matrix has nonzero determinant then its linear transformation is a bijection, which means Merlin's proof is in one-to-one correspondence with the challenge vector and is hence uniformly distributed regardless of the matrix. If the determinant is zero then the range of the linear transformation is a proper subspace, so with probability at least half, the challenge vector has no preimage. The matrix needs to be of a certain form to enable Alice and Bob to jointly multiply the matrix by Merlin's claimed preimage without further communication.

The idea for showing $ZAM(EQ) \leq O(\log n)$ is just the standard approach of using an error-correcting code for a downward-random-self-reduction from equality on n bits to equality on 1 bit, and then invoking a 1-bit protocol. The reduction preserves the necessary properties.

3.2 Theorem 2

Many classical lower bound methods in communication complexity (such as discrepancy and corruption) examine the properties of *individual* rectangles. A key departure here is that we consider how *pairs* of rectangles interact with each other.

We need to show how to convert an arbitrary ZAM protocol into a conondeterministic protocol without increasing the cost by more than a constant factor. Thus, we need to be able to find rectangles that cover 0-inputs. The first key idea is the observation that for any unambiguous protocol, the intersection of two different proof rectangles is contained within the blocks of 0-inputs. Thus if we take such an intersection and "project" it to the inputs, we get a 0-monochromatic rectangle in $\mathcal{X} \times \mathcal{Y}$. We call the collection of rectangles that arise in this way the *double cover*. If we knew that the double cover covered *all* the 0-inputs, then it would be a conondeterministic protocol (with cost at most twice the cost of the ZAM protocol) and we would be done.

How can we say anything about *which* 0-inputs get covered by the double cover? This is where the zero-information assumption comes in. As a simple example, consider an arbitrary ZAM protocol for the NAND function. A proof rectangle has the same area within the $(0,0)$ and $(0,1)$ blocks, and this actually forces it to have the same *shape* (height and width) within these blocks. Similarly, the proof has the same shape within the $(0,0)$ and $(1,0)$ blocks. Hence it has the same shape in $(0,1)$ and $(1,0)$ and thus also in $(1,1)$. So every proof has the same shape (in particular, area) in all four blocks! If the proofs were pairwise disjoint in the $(1,1)$ block then we could add up their areas to find that the acceptance probability on this 0-input is the same as the acceptance probability on the 1-inputs, a contradiction.

After generalizing this idea (for an arbitrary function f), what we find is that the 0-inputs *not* covered by the double cover can be organized into a coarse "non-equality-like" structure, and can hence be covered by few rectangles, which we add to the double cover to get a low-cost conondeterministic protocol.

3.3 Theorem 3

By Theorem 2, we know that $ZAM(\text{INTER}) \geq \Omega(n)$. The basic intuition for Theorem 3 is as follows: Building on the ideas in the proof of Theorem 2, we can prove a "robust" version for INTER, showing that $\Omega(n)$ communication is required by UAM protocols whose transcripts leak a sublinear amount of information about the input (which is a weaker assumption than zero-information). This leads to a dichotomy: Either a protocol leaks a linear amount of information, or it does not. If it does, we are done (since information cost trivially lower bounds communication cost). If it does not, we are done by the above argument. In either case, the protocol must use $\Omega(n)$ communication. However, there are several technical obstacles that need to be overcome to get this approach to work.

Similarly to Theorem 2, the basic strategy for proving that "low information implies high communication" is to find a huge number of 0-inputs that all get "double-covered" by Merlin's rectangles, and then use the fact that every 0-monochromatic rectangle is small for INTER (hence there must be many pairs of rectangles of Merlin). However, using information complexity techniques, what we can find is a huge number of special "windows" (which are certain submatrices of the communication matrix) such that each of these windows contains a 0-input that gets double-covered. But what if different windows share the same double-covered 0-input? Then we might not have a huge number of double-covered 0-inputs as required. This problem goes away if the special windows are disjoint. Hence, we define the distribution over inputs (with respect to which information cost is measured) in a careful, nonstandard way to enable us to get a large number of *disjoint* special windows.

Another issue is that our argument requires information cost to be measured with respect to a distribution over 1-inputs, whereas in the standard framework of [6] the distribution is over 0-inputs of INTER. This necessitates using the (somewhat more complicated) framework of [33] for analyzing the so-called *partial information cost* with respect to a distribution over 1-inputs of INTER.

3.4 Theorem 4

We first describe a way to prove a quantitatively weaker version of Theorem 4. Consider a UAM protocol, and let us say a 0-input is unambiguous if no rectangles overlap within its block, and is ambiguous otherwise. Then 1-inputs can be distinguished from ambiguous 0-inputs by a PP (indeed, coNP) protocol à la the proof of Theorem 2, and 1-inputs can be distinguished from unambiguous 0-inputs by a PP (indeed, SBP) protocol by treating the nondeterminism as randomness. Hence 1-inputs can be distinguished from all 0-inputs by using the fact that PP is closed under intersection [7, 58].

The disadvantages of the above proof are that it incurs a quadratic loss in efficiency (from the closure under intersection), and it relies on the somewhat-heavy machinery of [7]. We provide a direct proof that overcomes both of these disadvantages.

Since the acceptance probability on any input can be expressed as the area of the union of rectangles within the block, it can also be expressed in terms of the areas of *intersections* of rectangles using the inclusion–exclusion formula. For 1-inputs, there are no nonempty intersections of two or more rectangles, so the formula can safely be truncated. For 0-inputs, truncating the formula at an *even* level (say, the second) gives an underestimate of the acceptance probability, which is fine for our purpose. Then we can use standard techniques to construct a PP protocol whose acceptance probability is related to the value of the truncated inclusion-exclusion formula. This argument automatically handles AM protocols with "bounded ambiguity" on 1-inputs, simply by truncating the inclusion-exclusion formula at an appropriate level.

3.5 Theorem 5

Our approach to lower bound the SBP decision tree complexity of GUT is analogous to a corruption-style argument in communication complexity. We consider a hard pair of distributions, one over 1-inputs and the other over 0-inputs, and we argue that for any root-to-leaf path in a deterministic decision tree, the path's acceptance probability under the 1-input distribution cannot be more than a small constant factor greater than its acceptance probability under the 0-input distribution. Arguing the latter is more-or-less a direct, technical calculation. For the corruption analogy, a root-to-leaf path in a decision tree plays the role of a transcript/rectangle in a communication protocol.

4. OPEN PROBLEMS

Some speculative open problems include finding applications of our results or techniques to streaming delegation or to other topics. It is also open to consider multi-party versions of any of the topics considered in this work (though we note that our upper bounds generalize straightforwardly to the number-in-hand model). We now discuss some more concrete open problems related to our complexity measures.

ZAM complexity. One or both of the following must hold, but it is open to prove either: $\mathsf{ZAM}(f) \leq 2^{o(n)}$ for all $f : \{0,1\}^n \times \{0,1\}^n \to \{0,1\}$, or $\mathsf{ZAM}(f) \geq \omega(n)$ for some f (even a random f). Proving a superpolynomial ZAM lower

bound for an explicit function would also yield a superlogarithmic lower bound against every level of the communication polynomial hierarchy (hence is probably an unrealistically ambitious goal): By definition, every function in the polynomial hierarchy has a constant-depth circuit whose size is exponential in the communication bound, and where each input bit is an arbitrary function of one party's input. Such a circuit can be straightforwardly converted into a two-party (parity) branching program, and then Theorem 1 can be applied to get a ZAM protocol. Proving a superpolynomial ZAM lower bound for a random function may be a more realistic goal, since it would not have nontrivial consequences for the polynomial hierarchy.

A particularly conspicuous open problem is to prove that $\mathsf{ZAM}(\mathrm{DISJ}) \geq \omega(\log n)$. The function INDEX: $\{0,1\}^n \times [n] \to \{0,1\}$ defined by $\mathrm{INDEX}(x,y) = x_y$ is no harder than DISJ, and yet we conjecture that $\mathsf{ZAM}(\mathrm{INDEX}) = \Theta(n)$. Proving the latter would be a step toward showing that ZAM complexity can be superlinear, since it would show that ZAM complexity can be exponential in *one* party's input length (which cannot happen for deterministic communication complexity).

It would be interesting to show that $\mathsf{ZAM}(f) \geq \omega(\mathsf{coNP}(f))$ for some f. This would require new techniques for understanding ZAM protocols. It would also be interesting to prove new lower bounds even for the special case of ZAM where for each 1-input there is a *bijection* between Merlin's proofs and the outcomes of the randomness; note that all of our ZAM upper bounds have this property. One possible approach for obtaining new ZAM lower bounds is to use information complexity tools to lower bound the information cost—not of the distribution of transcripts (obviously) but of some related distribution, such as correlated tuples of transcripts.

UAM complexity. It is open[2] to prove, in the communication world, that UAM $\not\subseteq$ SBP (which would show that the corruption bound does not automatically lower bound UAM complexity) or even UAM $\not\subseteq$ MA, even for a partial function. It would be very interesting to develop techniques for converting SBP query lower bounds into analogous SBP communication lower bounds. It would also be interesting to compare UAM with other lower bound techniques in the literature (like how Klauck [38] showed that the smooth rectangle bound lower bounds BP·UP complexity).

Another direction for exploring the power of UAM is to design interesting protocols. Here is a framework for designing UAM protocols that might be useful: Suppose Alice can construct from her input x a matrix A, and Bob can construct from his input y a matrix B, such that $f(x,y) = 1$ iff $\det(A + B) \neq 0$. If no row is nonzero in both A and B, then of course $A + B$ is a two-party matrix and the proof of Theorem 1 yields a ZAM protocol. Otherwise, we can at least get a UAM protocol: Alice generates a random vector $\boldsymbol{v}$, and Merlin sends a claimed preimage $\boldsymbol{u}$ and claimed vectors $A\boldsymbol{u}$ and $B\boldsymbol{u}$. Alice checks that the latter vectors sum to $\boldsymbol{v}$ and that $A\boldsymbol{u}$ is as claimed, and Bob checks that $B\boldsymbol{u}$ is as claimed. If the matrices have size $k \times k$, then we would need $k \cdot \log |\mathbb{F}| \leq o(n)$ for the protocol to be nontrivial. Furthermore, this approach would yield a *conondeterministic* protocol of cost $O(k \cdot \log |\mathbb{F}|)$ (Merlin sends distinct vectors with the same image under $A + B$, and sends the images of

---

[2]As mentioned before, this problem has been settled in [22].

119

these vectors under A and B) and hence would not be useful for functions with $\mathsf{coNP}(f) = \Theta(n)$.

One odd property of UAM is that it does not seem conducive to efficient amplification of the completeness probability. Taking a threshold of several independent executions raises the level of ambiguity (number of rectangles that may simultaneously intersect for a 1-input), and our proof of Theorem 3 shows that ambiguity cannot, in general, be efficiently decreased: INTER is hard for UAM under the promise that at most two coordinates intersect; yet this promise problem has a trivial efficient NP protocol where at most 2 rectangles intersect for a 1-input. It would be interesting to have formal evidence for or against the possibility of completeness amplification for UAM.

AM complexity. The principal open problem here is to prove that $\mathsf{AM}(f) \geq \omega(\log n)$ for some explicit f. The only known AM lower bounds follow from the observation that $\mathsf{AM}(f) \geq \Omega(\log \mathsf{BPP}(f))$ for all f. This implies that $\mathsf{AM}(\mathrm{EQ}), \mathsf{AM}(\mathrm{NEQ}), \mathsf{AM}(\mathrm{GT}) \geq \Omega(\log \log n)$, and in fact it is an open problem to prove a $\omega(\log \log n)$ lower bound for any of these three problems.

One possible approach for proving AM lower bounds is to try to reduce to a situation with some amount of unambiguity by using an isolation lemma, and then combine this with our techniques for proving UAM lower bounds. However, we do not see a straightforward way to make this work.

A less ambitious goal might be to prove an explicit linear lower bound for the communication complexity measure that combines the completeness condition of MA and the soundness condition of AM. Such protocols are weaker than *both* MA and AM protocols, so $\Omega(\sqrt{n})$ lower bounds follow from known MA lower bounds. Whereas there seems to be little hope for linear MA lower bounds ([1] gives a $O(\sqrt{n} \log n)$ upper bound for many interesting problems), there may be hope for these weaker protocols.

Finally, we highlight the lurking prospect of designing AM protocols that defy our intuitions.

Acknowledgements

We thank Petteri Kaski, Venkatesh Medabalimi, and Robert Robere for discussions.

5. REFERENCES

[1] S. Aaronson and A. Wigderson. Algebrization: A new barrier in complexity theory. *ACM Transactions on Computation Theory*, 1(1), 2009. doi:10.1145/1490270.1490272.

[2] A. Ada, A. Chattopadhyay, S. Cook, L. Fontes, M. Koucký, and T. Pitassi. The hardness of being private. *ACM Transactions on Computation Theory*, 6(1), 2014. doi:10.1145/2567671.

[3] B. Applebaum, Y. Ishai, and E. Kushilevitz. Cryptography in NC^0. *SIAM Journal on Computing*, 36(4):845–888, 2006. doi:10.1137/S0097539705446950.

[4] L. Babai, P. Frankl, and J. Simon. Complexity classes in communication complexity theory. In *Proceedings of the 27th Symposium on Foundations of Computer Science (FOCS)*, pages 337–347. IEEE, 1986. doi:10.1109/SFCS.1986.15.

[5] L. Babai and S. Moran. Arthur–Merlin games: A randomized proof system, and a hierarchy of complexity classes. *Journal of Computer and System Sciences*, 36(2):254–276, 1988. doi:10.1016/0022-0000(88)90028-1.

[6] Z. Bar-Yossef, T. Jayram, R. Kumar, and D. Sivakumar. An information statistics approach to data stream and communication complexity. *Journal of Computer and System Sciences*, 68(4):702–732, 2004. doi:10.1016/j.jcss.2003.11.006.

[7] R. Beigel, N. Reingold, and D. Spielman. PP is closed under intersection. *Journal of Computer and System Sciences*, 50(2):191–202, 1995. doi:10.1006/jcss.1995.1017.

[8] E. Böhler, C. Glaßer, and D. Meister. Error-bounded probabilistic computations between MA and AM. *Journal of Computer and System Sciences*, 72(6):1043–1076, 2006. doi:10.1016/j.jcss.2006.05.001.

[9] M. Braverman, F. Ellen, R. Oshman, T. Pitassi, and V. Vaikuntanathan. A tight bound for set disjointness in the message-passing model. In *Proceedings of the 54th Symposium on Foundations of Computer Science (FOCS)*, pages 668–677. IEEE, 2013. doi:10.1109/FOCS.2013.77.

[10] M. Braverman, A. Garg, D. Pankratov, and O. Weinstein. From information to exact communication. In *Proceedings of the 45th Symposium on Theory of Computing (STOC)*, pages 151–160. ACM, 2013. doi:10.1145/2488608.2488628.

[11] M. Braverman and A. Moitra. An information complexity approach to extended formulations. In *Proceedings of the 45th Symposium on Theory of Computing (STOC)*, pages 161–170. ACM, 2013. doi:10.1145/2488608.2488629.

[12] A. Chakrabarti, G. Cormode, N. Goyal, and J. Thaler. Annotations for sparse data streams. In *Proceedings of the 25th Symposium on Discrete Algorithms (SODA)*, pages 687–706. ACM-SIAM, 2014. doi:10.1137/1.9781611973402.52.

[13] A. Chakrabarti, G. Cormode, and A. McGregor. Annotations in data streams. In *Proceedings of the 36th International Colloquium on Automata, Languages, and Programming (ICALP)*, pages 222–234. Springer, 2009. doi:10.1007/978-3-642-02927-1_20.

[14] A. Chakrabarti, G. Cormode, A. McGregor, J. Thaler, and S. Venkatasubramanian. On interactivity in Arthur–Merlin communication and stream computation. Technical Report TR13-180, Electronic Colloquium on Computational Complexity (ECCC), 2013. URL: http://eccc.hpi-web.de/report/2013/180/.

[15] A. Chakrabarti, S. Khot, and X. Sun. Near-optimal lower bounds on the multi-party communication complexity of set disjointness. In *Proceedings of the 18th Conference on Computational Complexity (CCC)*, pages 107–117. IEEE, 2003. doi:10.1109/CCC.2003.1214414.

[16] A. Chakrabarti, Y. Shi, A. Wirth, and A. Yao. Informational complexity and the direct sum problem for simultaneous message complexity. In *Proceedings of the 42nd Symposium on Foundations of Computer Science (FOCS)*, pages 270–278. IEEE, 2001. doi:10.1109/SFCS.2001.959901.

[17] C. Damm. Problems complete for ⊕L. *Information Processing Letters*, 36(5):247–250, 1990. doi:10.1016/0020-0190(90)90150-V.

[18] A. Dasgupta, R. Kumar, and D. Sivakumar. Sparse and lopsided set disjointness via information theory. In *Proceedings of the 16th International Workshop on Randomization and Computation (RANDOM)*, pages 517–528. Springer, 2012. doi:10.1007/978-3-642-32512-0_44.

[19] U. Feige, J. Kilian, and M. Naor. A minimal model for secure computation. In *Proceedings of the 26th Symposium on Theory of Computing (STOC)*, pages 554–563. ACM, 1994. doi:10.1145/195058.195408.

[20] A. Gál and A. Wigderson. Boolean complexity classes vs. their arithmetic analogs. *Random Structures & Algorithms*, 9(1-2):99–111, 1996. doi:10.1002/(SICI)1098-2418(199608/09)9:1/2<99:: AID-RSA7>3.0.CO;2-6.

[21] D. Gavinsky and A. Sherstov. A separation of NP and coNP in multiparty communication complexity. *Theory of Computing*, 6(1):227–245, 2010. doi:10.4086/toc.2010.v006a010.

[22] M. Göös, S. Lovett, R. Meka, T. Watson, and D. Zuckerman. Rectangles are nonnegative juntas. Technical Report TR14-147, Electronic Colloquium on Computational Complexity (ECCC), 2014. URL: http://eccc.hpi-web.de/report/2014/147/.

[23] M. Göös, T. Pitassi, and T. Watson. Zero-information protocols and unambiguity in Arthur–Merlin communication. Technical Report TR14-078, Electronic Colloquium on Computational Complexity (ECCC), 2014. Full version. URL: http://eccc.hpi-web.de/report/2014/078/.

[24] M. Göös and T. Watson. Communication complexity of set-disjointness for all probabilities. In *Proceedings of the 18th International Workshop on Randomization and Computation (RANDOM)*, pages 721–736. Schloss Dagstuhl, 2014. doi:10.4230/LIPIcs.APPROX-RANDOM.2014.721.

[25] A. Gronemeier. Asymptotically optimal lower bounds on the NIH-multi-party information complexity of the AND-function and disjointness. In *Proceedings of the 26th International Symposium on Theoretical Aspects of Computer Science (STACS)*, pages 505–516. Schloss Dagstuhl, 2009. doi:10.4230/LIPIcs.STACS.2009.1846.

[26] T. Gur and R. Raz. Arthur–Merlin streaming complexity. In *Proceedings of the 40th International Colloquium on Automata, Languages, and Programming (ICALP)*, pages 528–539. Springer, 2013. doi:10.1007/978-3-642-39206-1_45.

[27] T. Gur and R. Rothblum. Non-interactive proofs of proximity. Technical Report TR13-078, Electronic Colloquium on Computational Complexity (ECCC), 2013. URL: http://eccc.hpi-web.de/report/2013/078/.

[28] R. Impagliazzo, V. Kabanets, and A. Kolokolova. An axiomatic approach to algebrization. In *Proceedings of the 41st Symposium on Theory of Computing (STOC)*, pages 695–704. ACM, 2009. doi:10.1145/1536414.1536509.

[29] R. Impagliazzo and R. Williams. Communication complexity with synchronized clocks. In *Proceedings of the 25th Conference on Computational Complexity (CCC)*, pages 259–269. IEEE, 2010. doi:10.1109/CCC.2010.32.

[30] Y. Ishai and E. Kushilevitz. Perfect constant-round secure computation via perfect randomizing polynomials. In *Proceedings of the 29th International Colloquium on Automata, Languages, and Programming (ICALP)*, pages 244–256. Springer, 2002. doi:10.1007/3-540-45465-9_22.

[31] R. Jain and H. Klauck. The partition bound for classical communication complexity and query complexity. In *Proceedings of the 25th Conference on Computational Complexity (CCC)*, pages 247–258. IEEE, 2010. doi:10.1109/CCC.2010.31.

[32] T. Jayram. Hellinger strikes back: A note on the multi-party information complexity of AND. In *Proceedings of the 13th International Workshop on Randomization and Computation (RANDOM)*, pages 562–573. Springer, 2009. doi:10.1007/978-3-642-03685-9_42.

[33] T. Jayram, R. Kumar, and D. Sivakumar. Two applications of information complexity. In *Proceedings of the 35th Symposium on Theory of Computing (STOC)*, pages 673–682. ACM, 2003. doi:10.1145/780542.780640.

[34] S. Jukna. On graph complexity. *Combinatorics, Probability, & Computing*, 15(6):855–876, 2006. doi:10.1017/S0963548306007620.

[35] S. Jukna. *Boolean Function Complexity: Advances and Frontiers*, volume 27 of *Algorithms and Combinatorics*. Springer, 2012.

[36] H. Klauck. Rectangle size bounds and threshold covers in communication complexity. In *Proceedings of the 18th Conference on Computational Complexity (CCC)*, pages 118–134. IEEE, 2003. doi:10.1109/CCC.2003.1214415.

[37] H. Klauck. Lower bounds for quantum communication complexity. *SIAM Journal on Computing*, 37(1):20–46, 2007. doi:10.1137/S0097539702405620.

[38] H. Klauck. A strong direct product theorem for disjointness. In *Proceedings of the 42nd Symposium on Theory of Computing (STOC)*, pages 77–86. ACM, 2010. doi:10.1145/1806689.1806702.

[39] H. Klauck. On Arthur Merlin games in communication complexity. In *Proceedings of the 26th Conference on Computational Complexity (CCC)*, pages 189–199. IEEE, 2011. doi:10.1109/CCC.2011.33.

[40] H. Klauck and S. Podder. Two results about quantum messages. In *Proceedings of the 39th International Symposium on Mathematical Foundations of Computer Science (MFCS)*, pages 445–456. Springer, 2014. doi:10.1007/978-3-662-44465-8_38.

[41] H. Klauck and V. Prakash. Streaming computations with a loquacious prover. In *Proceedings of the 4th Innovations in Theoretical Computer Science Conference (ITCS)*, pages 305–320. ACM, 2013. doi:10.1145/2422436.2422471.

[42] H. Klauck and V. Prakash. An improved interactive streaming algorithm for the distinct elements problem. In *Proceedings of the 41st International Colloquium on Automata, Languages, and Programming (ICALP)*, pages 919–930. Springer, 2014. doi:10.1007/978-3-662-43948-7_76.

[43] E. Kushilevitz. Privacy and communication complexity. *SIAM Journal on Discrete Mathematics*, 5(2):273–284, 1992. doi:10.1137/0405021.

[44] E. Kushilevitz and N. Nisan. *Communication Complexity*. Cambridge University Press, 1997.

[45] N. Linial and A. Shraibman. Learning complexity vs communication complexity. *Combinatorics, Probability, & Computing*, 18(1–2):227–245, 2009. doi:10.1017/S0963548308009656.

[46] S. Lokam. Spectral methods for matrix rigidity with applications to size-depth trade-offs and communication complexity. *Journal of Computer and System Sciences*, 63(3):449–473, 2001. doi:10.1006/jcss.2001.1786.

[47] S. Lokam. Complexity lower bounds using linear algebra. *Foundations and Trends in Theoretical Computer Science*, 4(1–2):1–155, 2009. doi:10.1561/0400000011.

[48] P. Papakonstantinou, D. Scheder, and H. Song. Overlays and limited memory communication. In *Proceedings of the 29th Conference on Computational Complexity (CCC)*, pages 298–308. IEEE, 2014. doi:10.1109/CCC.2014.37.

[49] P. Pudlák, V. Rödl, and P. Savický. Graph complexity. *Acta Informatica*, 25(5):515–535, 1988. doi:10.1007/BF00279952.

[50] R. Raz and A. Shpilka. On the power of quantum proofs. In *Proceedings of the 19th Conference on Computational Complexity (CCC)*, pages 260–274. IEEE, 2004. doi:10.1109/CCC.2004.1313849.

[51] A. Razborov. On rigid matrices. Technical report, Steklov Mathematical Institute, 1989. In Russian.

[52] A. Razborov. On the distributional complexity of disjointness. *Theoretical Computer Science*, 106(2):385–390, 1992. doi:10.1016/0304-3975(92)90260-M.

[53] K. Reinhardt and E. Allender. Making nondeterminism unambiguous. *SIAM Journal on Computing*, 29(4):1118–1131, 2000. doi:10.1137/S0097539798339041.

[54] M. Santha. Relativized Arthur–Merlin versus Merlin–Arthur games. *Information and Computation*, 80(1):44–49, 1989. doi:10.1016/0890-5401(89)90022-9.

[55] U. Schöning. Probabilistic complexity classes and lowness. *Journal of Computer and System Sciences*, 39(1):84–100, 1989. doi:10.1016/0022-0000(89)90020-2.

[56] L. Valiant. Graph-theoretic arguments in low-level complexity. In *Proceedings of the 6th Symposium on Mathematical Foundations of Computer Science (MFCS)*, pages 162–176. Springer, 1977. doi:10.1007/3-540-08353-7_135.

[57] L. Valiant. Completeness classes in algebra. In *Proceedings of the 11th Symposium on Theory of Computing (STOC)*, pages 249–261. ACM, 1979. doi:10.1145/800135.804419.

[58] H. Wunderlich. A note on a problem in communication complexity. Technical report, arXiv, 2012. arXiv:1205.0903.

[59] H. Wunderlich. On a theorem of Razborov. *Computational Complexity*, 21(3):431–477, 2012. doi:10.1007/s00037-011-0021-5.

Information Causality, Szemerédi-Trotter and Algebraic Variants of CHSH

[Extended Abstract] [*]

Mohammad Bavarian[†]
M.I.T.
77 Massachusetts Avenue,
Cambridge, MA 02139, USA.
bavarian@mit.edu

Peter W. Shor[‡]
M.I.T.
77 Massachusetts Avenue,
Cambridge, MA 02139, USA.
shor@mit.edu

ABSTRACT

In this paper, we consider the following family of two prover one-round games. In the CHSH_q game, two parties are given $x, y \in \mathbb{F}_q$ uniformly at random, and each must produce an output $a, b \in \mathbb{F}_q$ without communicating with the other. The players' objective is to maximize the probability that their outputs satisfy $a + b = xy$ in $\mathbb{F}_q$. This game was introduced by Buhrman and Massar [7] as a large alphabet generalization of the CHSH game—which is one of the most well-studied two-prover games in quantum information theory, and which has a large number of applications to quantum cryptography and quantum complexity. Our main contributions in this paper are the first asymptotic and explicit bounds on the entangled and classical values of CHSH_q, and the realization of a rather surprising connection between CHSH_q and geometric incidence theory.

Categories and Subject Descriptors

F.0 [**Theory of Computation**]: General.

General Terms

Theory.

Keywords

Two player refereed games; the CHSH game; point-line incidences; Bell inequalities and Tsirelson bounds.

---

[*]A full version of this paper including some of the omitted results is available at http://arxiv.org/abs/1311.5186.

[†]Supported by NSF-STC Award 0939370, and NSF CCF-1065125

[‡]Supported by NSF grant CCF-0829421, and by the STC award for Science of Information under NSF grant CCF-0939370.

1. INTRODUCTION

In this work, we study a certain family of two prover one-round games. The study of multiprover one-round games (from now on, simply referred to as games) began in the late 20th century in the context of multiprover interactive proof systems in computer science [2], and also in the context of the Bell inequalities in physics [1] with the topic continuing to be of significant interest in both computer science and quantum physics to this day (see for example [5, 8, 11, 17, 27]). The particular family of games we shall study was first introduced by Buhrman and Massar [7] nearly a decade ago. It is defined as follows.

DEFINITION 1.1. *Let q be a prime, or a prime power, and $\mathbb{F}_q$ the unique field of size q. In the CHSH_q game, two non-communicating parties Alice and Bob are each given an input x and y from $\mathbb{F}_q$ chosen uniformly at random. Their objective is to maximize the probability that their outputs $a, b \in \mathbb{F}_q$ satisfy $a + b = xy$.*

The celebrated CHSH game, named after its inventors Clauser, Horne, Shimony and Holt [9], is the case $q = 2$ of the above definition. It is arguably the most well-studied game in quantum information theory [33], and has many applications in the study of entanglement ([6, 33]) and also in quantum cryptography [12] and quantum complexity [28]. Given the major role CHSH plays in many aspects of quantum information theory, it has been of great interest to find well-structured asymptotic generalizations of CHSH, as this could have much impact in the study of non-locality in general, and in the above applications of CHSH in particular. In this paper we focus on Buhrman and Massar's generalization, described in Definition 1.1, since we expect that the algebraic form of CHSH_q would lead to a interesting and useful structure for this family of games. In fact one of the main results of our work is the realization of a strong connection between the CHSH_q game and some remarkable mathematical results in incidence geometry and arithmetic combinatorics. This surprising connection combined with our other results further supports the intuition about the rich structure of these games.

Despite the simple form of this family of games and our precise understanding of the case $q = 2$, it turns out that analyzing CHSH_q beyond the $q = 2$ case is a rather difficult task. This difficulty is not restricted to analyzing CHSH_q; it is actually an instance of a more general phenomenon, and is essentially shared with any game with $q \geq 3$. The main issue here is that we do not know a large alphabet generalization of the foundational result of Tsirelson on SDP characterization of the entangled value of XOR games (which are a subclass of games with $q = 2$). This result of Tsirelson, combined with the tools of convex analysis such as complementary slackness and strong duality, gives a powerful path toward analyzing the entangled value and the optimal strategies for XOR games. The unavailability of the above powerful tool has resulted in a scarcity of results for analyzing the games in the case $q \neq 2$— which is regarded as one of the central challenges in the study of non-local games (see [6, 13]). Indeed, a major goal of this work is to expand on the set of examples and tools available for analyzing games beyond the relatively well-understood case of XOR games, which we do in the context of studying CHSH$_q$. We note that our results do not go far on addressing the fundamental problems regarding the complexity of entangled two prover non-XOR games. However, we believe that for tackling this fundamental problem, a certain amount of preparatory work in the form of establishment of new tools and examples is a definite prerequisite. We hope that our work constitutes an advance in the foundation necessary for tackling the aforementioned fundamental problems.

1.1 Results

For a game G, we denote by $\omega(G)$ and $\omega^*(G)$ the maximum winning probability of classical and quantum strategies, respectively. These are usually referred to as the classical and entangled values, in short. Recall that since the quantum strategies contain the classical ones as a subset, it is clear that $\omega(G) \leq \omega^*(G)$.

Regarding the entangled value of CHSH$_q$, we give two different proofs of the following theorem, which generalizes the well-known upper bound of Tsirelson [30] for the original CHSH game.

THEOREM 1.2. *For any prime or prime power q we have*

$$\omega^*(\mathsf{CHSH_q}) \leq \frac{1}{q} + \frac{q-1}{q}\frac{1}{\sqrt{q}} .$$

Despite advances due to several researchers [7, 14, 20, 32] in analyzing the value of CHSH$_q$ games, prior to our work there was no result, even in conjectured form, known for the asymptotic behavior of the classical and entangled value of CHSH$_q$. Even for small values of q, most results, with the exception of the original $\frac{1}{3} + \frac{2}{3}\frac{1}{\sqrt{3}}$ upper bound of Buhrman and Massar for $q = 3$, were obtained using numerical methods. Thus, our work is the first to obtain asymptotic results on these games.

One interesting fact about the bound in Theorem 1.2 is the striking similarity of the bound $1/q + (q-1)/(q\sqrt{q})$ here, with the influential tight upper bound of Tsirelson [30] of $1/2 + 1/2\sqrt{2}$ for CHSH. This striking resemblance gives rise to the natural question of asymptotic (or exact) tightness of the bound in Theorem 1.2. Although we cannot answer the above questions in full, we provide some answers which clarify the situation to some extent, and highlight some of the relevant issues.

THEOREM 1.3. *There exists a universal constant $\epsilon_0 > 0$ such that for any prime p and $k \geq 1$ we have*

$$\omega(\mathsf{CHSH_q}) = \begin{cases} \Omega(q^{-\frac{1}{2}}) & for \quad q = p^{2k} \\ O(q^{-\frac{1}{2}-\epsilon_0}) & for \quad q = p^{2k-1} . \end{cases}$$

To prove this theorem, we adopt a new view of CHSH$_q$. The main insight here is the following.

FACT 1.4. *A classical strategy for CHSH$_q$ is in direct correspondence with a configuration of q non-vertical lines and q points in $\mathbb{F}_q^2$, with no two lines having the same slope, and no two points lying on the same vertical line. Given such a configuration of lines and points, the winning probability of the corresponding strategy for CHSH$_q$ is proportional to the number of point-line incidences.*

The correspondence in Fact 1.4 allows us access to some powerful results in arithmetic combinatorics where questions related to the incidences of collections of points and lines over finite fields have seen much progress recently. Most relevant to our problem is the celebrated finite field Szemerédi-Trotter theorem of Bourgain, Katz and Tao [4] which states that, under a certain size restriction satisfied in our case, the number of incidences between a collection of points P and a collection of lines L is at most of the size $|P|^{\frac{3}{4}-\epsilon_0}|L|^{\frac{3}{4}-\epsilon_0}$ for some $\epsilon_0 > 0$. This result combined with Fact 1.4 is essentially sufficient to prove the upper bound in Theorem 1.3.

In fact, the relation between CHSH$_q$ and the finite field Szemerédi-Trotter theorem is closer than it might first appear to be. As we show in Section 3, understanding the classical value of CHSH$_q$ is in some sense equivalent to the finite field Szemerédi-Trotter theorem with the appropriate parameters. We show this by proving that the restrictions on the points and lines in Fact 1.4, which is crucial in order to translate the geometric configuration to a legal CHSH$_q$ strategy, can actually be relaxed without losing much in the bounds.

Going back to the quantum and classical values of CHSH$_q$, it is important to notice that our classical lower bound in Theorem 1.3 shows that there is no asymptotic separation between the quantum and classical values of the game for $q = p^{2k}$, while the classical upper bound of $O(q^{-1/2-\epsilon_0})$ leaves open the possibility of such a separation in the setting of $q = p^{2k-1}$. Hence the most obvious gap in our bounds is captured by the following problem.

PROBLEM 1.5 (OPEN). *Does there exists an infinite family of $q = p^{2k-1}$ such that $\omega^*(\mathsf{CHSH_q}) = \Omega(q^{-\frac{1}{2}})$, or some $\delta > 0$ and an infinite family of $q = p^{2k-1}$ such that $\omega^*(\mathsf{CHSH_q}) = O(q^{-\frac{1}{2}-\delta})$? (It is possible that the answer to both questions above are positive. In fact this would be the best possible outcome from the point of view of applications.)*

Given the geometric picture in Fact 1.4, we observe that our main open problem, Problem 1.5, is related to a question of Kempe and Kasher [18] about the security of Bourgain's two-source extractor [3, 26] in the presence of quantum memory. The main point is that Bourgain's extractor consists of two main ingredients: The first is a crucial preprocessing step, which (roughly-speaking) makes sure the two sources are in generic position with respect to each other. The second is an application of a Hadamard extractor on the two preprocessed sources. It was shown by Kasher and Kempe that the bare Hadamard extractor remains secure in the presence of quantum adversaries. Hence, the missing part in the analysis of Bourgain's extractor in the presence of quantum memory is the first step, analysis of which heavily relies on Szemerédi-Trotter theorem on finite fields. Thus, the core of both Kasher and Kempe's question and that of ours seem to be the extent to which finite-field Szemerédi-Trotter theorem can be (or fails to be) extended to the quantum setting.

1.2 Techniques

Let us start by giving more detail on our two different proofs of Theorem 1.2. A common aspect of both these methods is that they avoid a direct analysis of the norms of associated game operators. Instead, they take a novel indirect approach via reductions. In order to rule out a certain winning probability p for G, we show that the ability to win instances of G with probability greater than p would allow us to achieve a winning probability p' for a more generic game G', one which we already know to be impossible.

Both our methods for proving the upper bound on the entangled value of $\mathsf{CHSH_q}$ game work by a reduction to another generic result: the first method uses a reduction to a large alphabet variant of the result of Linden et al. on quantum and classical strategies for certain distributed tasks [21]. This approach has the advantage of being self-contained and quite simple. The main idea here is to analyze a slightly different variant of $\mathsf{CHSH_q}$ game, called $\mathsf{CHSH_q^{dist}}$, in which two parties receive $(\alpha, \gamma) \in \mathbb{F}_q^2$ and $(\beta, \delta) \in \mathbb{F}_q^2$, and their objective is to produce outputs a and b satisfying $a + b = (\alpha + \beta)(\gamma + \delta)$.

The other approach is by a reduction to a new form of the principle of information causality which in basic form is due to Pawłowski and Winter [24] and is further generalized here. An interesting feature of this approach is that executing it naturally leads us to an open problem of Pawłowski and Winter [24] regarding a generalization of their principle of information causality to larger alphabets which we in fact resolve. To discuss the above, it is best to first recall the standard scenario for information causality (IC) [23].

DEFINITION 1.6 (IC). *In an information causality game, Alice is given an input* $\mathbf{X} = (X_1, X_2, \ldots, X_N)$ *from a known distribution* π, *and Bob an index* $b \in [N]$. *After making a measurement on her system, Alice sends a message* $\alpha \in \Sigma$ *to Bob. After receiving* α *from Alice, Bob makes a measurement on his system producing an output* $Z \in \Lambda$. *Alice and Bob's goal is to maximize the quantity* $IC(A, B) = \sum_{i=1}^{N} I(X_i; Z | b = i)$.[1]

The main idea behind the *principle of information causality* is that assuming a certain form of independence among Alice's inputs (i.e. $\{X_i\}_{i=1}^N$), there is a stringent limit to the amount of correlation, as quantified by $IC(A, B)$, that the two parties can create by limited communication—even given arbitrarily entanglement between Alice and Bob. Our main result about the information causality game is as follows.

THEOREM 1.7 (PAIRWISE INDEPENDENT IC). *Consider an information causality game as in Definition 1.6. Assume Alice's input* $\mathbf{X} = (X_1, X_2, \ldots, X_N)$ *is drawn from an unbiased (i.e. with uniform marginals) pairwise independent distribution. Then we have*

$$IC(A, B) = \sum_{i=1}^{N} I(X_i; Z | b = i) = O_{|\Sigma|, |\Lambda|}(1),$$

where $O_{|\Sigma|, |\Lambda|}(1)$ *is a quantity depending only on the sizes of the alphabets of Alice's message to Bob and Bob's output, and not* N.[2]

The original setting of information causality from [23] is the case where $\{X_i\}_{i=1}^N$ are fully independent. Pawłowksi and Winter in [24] strengthened the original information causality by showing that a similar bound holds even if the full independence condition is *relaxed* to pairwise independence, under the restriction that both Z and α have only two outcomes. They posed as an open problem to extend their result to larger alphabets. As it turns out such a theorem is precisely what we need to prove Theorem 1.2 by our information theoretic approach. The proof of this theorem, though interesting from technical point of view, is somewhat independent of the rest of the paper and hence is omitted from this version of the paper due to space constraints; however the proof can be found in the full version of the work at http://arxiv.org/abs/1311.5186.

1.3 Prior work

Buhrman and Massar were the first to study $\mathsf{CHSH_q}$ for $q \neq 2$ obtaining the upper bound of $1/3 + 2/3\sqrt{3}$ for $q = 3$ using information theoretic methods (different from the ones used here). Although the algebraic view of CHSH is in retrospect more or less clear, this was not the language originally used to describe the CHSH game. Hence, the contribution of Buhrman and Massar was to both realize this view, and to tackle the next interesting case after the original CHSH, which was the case of $q = 3$. In the same work, they mentioned that their method seemed not to work for higher values of q. After the work of Buhrman and Massar, the problem was attacked for small values of q by Ji et al. [14] and then by Liang, Lim and Deng [20] who, through a mix of numerical work and analytic insights, obtained several upper and lower bounds for quantum and classical value of the games for q's up to 13. Since the approach in the above line of work is mostly numerical, it is hard to infer much about the asymptotic questions of interest from the bounds there. The only work prior to ours to obtain some general results about $\mathsf{CHSH_q}$ is [32]. There, Wang proved various interesting results including a large alphabet generalization of a result of van Dam [10], on the collapse of communication complexity in the presence of perfect $\mathsf{CHSH_q}$ oracle boxes (this is a natural higher alphabet analogue of the well-known Popescu-Rohlich box [25]). He also approached the problem of analyzing the value of $\mathsf{CHSH_q}$ using the principle of information causality; however, the arguments there did not seem to provide explicit bounds.

2. A TSIRELSON BOUND FOR $\mathsf{CHSH_q}$

The aim of this section is to prove Theorem 1.2. We have two different proofs of this result which we present in the following two subsections.

In both proofs of Theorem 1.2, we can substantially simplify the arguments by assuming the optimal strategy $\mathcal{P}$ for $\mathsf{CHSH_q}$ always produces different types of error with equal probability. This is formalized as follows.

---

[1] A moment of reflection shows that the distribution of Bob's input $b \in [N]$ does not play any role here. Hence, it can be taken to be uniform over $[N]$ for simplicity.

[2] In most applications of information causality type theorems, including ours, the exact dependence on $|\Sigma|$ and $|\Lambda|$ is not important. The bound here is linear in $|\Sigma||\Lambda|$.

DEFINITION 2.1. *A classical or quantum strategy for* CHSH$_q$ *is called* regular *if the following holds:*

$$\Pr_{a,b \leftarrow \mathcal{P}^*}[a + b = xy + k | x, y] = \frac{1}{q} - \frac{E}{q} \qquad \forall k \in \mathbb{F}_q^*.$$

Here, a, b are the outputs of Alice and Bob's strategies given x, y as inputs, respectively. The symbol $a, b \leftarrow \mathcal{P}$ means that the outputs a, b of Alice and Bob's strategies are produced via the protocol $\mathcal{P}$ (given x, y as inputs). The symbol E as usual denotes the bias of the game defined as in Definition ??. In some occasions, for the ease of notation, we do not write out $a, b \leftarrow \mathcal{P}$ fully, and instead simply write $\mathcal{P}$ to represent the fact that the players follow the particular strategy $\mathcal{P}$ for producing their outputs.

It turns out that we can without loss of generality assume any protocol $\mathcal{P}$ for CHSH$_q$ is regular which is the content of the following lemma.

LEMMA 2.2 (REGULARIZATION LEMMA). *Given any protocol $\mathcal{P}$ for* CHSH$_q$, *there exists a generic method to obtain a regular protocol $\mathcal{P}^*$ from $\mathcal{P}$ without changing the winning probability.*

PROOF. Given any quantum strategy $\mathcal{P}$ for CHSH$_q$ game, define its regularized version $\mathcal{P}^*$ as follows: On inputs x and y, A and B use shared randomness to agree upon $\alpha, \beta \in \mathbb{F}_q^*$ and $\gamma, \delta \in \mathbb{F}_q$ uniformly at random. Then, they follow the original strategy on inputs $\tilde{x} = (\alpha x + \gamma)$, $\tilde{y} = (\beta y + \delta)$. Let $\tilde{a}$ and $\tilde{b}$ be their outputs here. Finally, A outputs $a = \frac{1}{\alpha\beta}(\tilde{a} - \delta\alpha x - \gamma\delta)$ and B outputs $\frac{1}{\alpha\beta}(\tilde{b} - \beta\gamma y)$. We show $\mathcal{P}^*$ satisfies the properties we wanted.

First, notice that $\mathcal{P}^*$ has the same winning probability as $\mathcal{P}$ since the input distribution remains uniform on $\mathbb{F}_q \times \mathbb{F}_q$, i.e. $\Pr_{\mathcal{P}^*}[a + b = xy | x, y] = \Pr_{\mathcal{P}, x', y'}[a' + b' = x'y'] = p_{win}$. It is not too hard to see that

$$\Pr_{a,b \leftarrow \mathcal{P}^*}[a + b = xy + s | x, y] = \Pr_{a', b' \leftarrow \mathcal{P}, x', y'}[a' + b' = x'y' + s\,\alpha\beta].$$

The key here is that quadruple (x', y', α, β) have a uniform product distribution over its domain $(\mathbb{F}_q)^2 \times (\mathbb{F}_q^*)^2$. For $s \in \mathbb{F}_q^*$, we have that $s\alpha\beta$ is uniformly distributed over $\mathbb{F}_q^*$. This and the fact that the input (x', y') is uniform on $\mathbb{F}_q \times \mathbb{F}_q$ imply the regularity property. □

2.1 Reduction to pairwise independent information causality

Let m be a positive integer which will be a parameter taken to be sufficiently large in our proof. We want to instantiate Theorem 1.7 by a subcode of generalized Hadamard code over $\mathbb{F}_q$. Let us recall the definition of this code:

DEFINITION 2.3. *The generalized Hadamard code corresponds to an m-dimensional subspace of a $q^m - 1$ dimensional vector space over $\mathbb{F}_q$. Given a seed $\mathbf{Y} = (Y_1, Y_2, \ldots, Y_m) \in \mathbb{F}_q^m$ we have a coordinate per each $\xi \in \mathbb{F}_q^m \setminus \{0\}$ defined by*

$$\mathrm{Had}_\xi = \xi_1 Y_1 + \xi_2 Y_2 + \ldots + \xi_m Y_m.$$

Hence, a codeword is a point in the above subspace and it is given by the list of $q^m - 1$ coordinates defined as above.

The overall plan is to let Alice's input be a random codeword from $\{\mathrm{Had}_\xi\}_{\xi \in \mathbb{F}_q^m \setminus \{0\}}$, and Bob's input to be some $\xi \in \mathbb{F}_q^m \setminus \{0\}$ which is an index to one of the coordinates of Alice's input. This, however, does not quite work as

the generalized Hadamard codeword is not pairwise independent. To fix this issue, we instead take Alice's input to be a proper subset $U_m \subseteq \mathbb{F}_q^m \setminus \{0\}$ such that $\{\mathrm{Had}_\xi\}_{\xi \in U_m}$ is pairwise independent. Concretely, we take U_m to consist of $a \in \mathbb{F}_q^m \setminus \{0\}$ with their first non-zero coordinate equal to 1. [3] With this setup we have $n = \frac{q^m - 1}{q - 1}$, Bob's input is some $b \in U_m$, and Alice's input is a uniformly random word from $\{\mathrm{Had}_\xi\}_{\xi \in U_m}$.

Now we need a proposition.

PROPOSITION 2.4. *Let $\mathcal{P}$ be a regular protocol for* CHSH$_q$ *with bias E. Assume Alice is given $(c_1, c_2, \ldots, c_m) \in \mathbb{F}_q^m$ and Bob $(d_1, d_2, \ldots, d_m) \in \mathbb{F}_q^m$. Assume Alice and Bob use the protocol $\mathcal{P}$ once per input pair $\{(c_k, d_k)\}_{k=1}^m$ to produce $\{a_k\}_{k=1}^m$ and $\{b_k\}_{k=1}^m$, i.e. using $(a_k, b_k) \leftarrow \mathcal{P}(c_k, d_k)$. Let $Z = \sum_{i=1}^m a_k + \sum_{i=1}^m b_k$. We have*

$$\Pr\left[Z = \sum_{i=1}^m c_i d_i\right] = \frac{1}{q} + \frac{q-1}{q} E^m.$$

Also, for all $e \in \mathbb{F}_q^*$ we have

$$\Pr\left[Z = \sum_{i=1}^m c_i d_i + e\right] = \frac{1}{q} - \frac{1}{q} E^m.$$

PROOF. The proof is by induction on m. For $m = 1$ this is clear. Assume the result for $m - 1$. Notice that for $Z = \sum_{i=1}^m c_i d_i$ to occur, it must be the case that the error in level $m - 1$, i.e. $\sum_{i=1}^{m-1} c_i d_i - a_i - b_i$, exactly cancels out the error occurred in the last step, which is $a_m + b_m - c_m d_m$. Now by the assumptions,

$$Pr\left[Z = \sum_{i=1}^m c_i d_i\right] = \left(\frac{1}{q} + \frac{q-1}{q} E^{m-1}\right)\left(\frac{1}{q} + \frac{q-1}{q} E\right)$$
$$+ (q-1)\left(\frac{1}{q} - \frac{1}{q} E^{m-1}\right)\left(\frac{1}{q} - \frac{1}{q} E\right)$$
$$= \frac{1}{q} + \frac{q-1}{q} E^m.$$

This finishes the first claim of the theorem. The second claim of the theorem follows from the first one and the symmetry. □

We apply this proposition to the setting where Alice is given $\{\mathrm{Had}_\xi\}_{\xi \in U_m}$ and Bob $\xi^* \in U_m$. Alice and Bob want to compute $\mathrm{Had}_{\xi^*} = \xi_1^* Y_1 + \xi_2^* Y_2 + \ldots + \xi_m^* Y_m$. Here, Y_i's are given to Alice as part of her inputs as any coordinate of the form $(0, 0, \ldots, 1, 0, \ldots, 0)$ is in U_m and ξ^* is precisely the input to Bob. Hence by following the above protocol, Alice ends up sending $\sum_{i=1}^m a_i$ to Bob as the message and Bob outputs $Z = \sum_{i=1}^m (a_i + b_i)$. The resulting output Z will satisfy the following:

$$I(X_\xi; Z | b = \xi) = \left(\frac{1}{q} + \frac{q-1}{q} E^m\right) \log_2(1 + (q-1)E^m)$$
$$+ \frac{q-1}{q^2}(1 - E^m) \log_2(1 - E^m).$$

Notice that the calculation above was not too hard because the regularity guaranteed from Proposition 2.4 specifies the exact joint distribution of (X_ξ, Z). Now we take m large enough such that $E^m \ll \frac{1}{q}$. In this regime, it is easy to

---

[3] This is chosen such that the map $\pi : (\xi_1, \xi_2, \ldots, \xi_m) \mapsto (\xi_1 : \xi_2 : \ldots : \xi_m)$ injects onto $\mathbb{PF}_q^{m-1}$.

see that above expression is always larger than $\frac{E^{2m}}{\text{poly}(q)}$ for a fixed polynomial independent of m. Using $I(X_\xi; Z | b = \xi) \geq \frac{E^{2m}}{\text{poly}(q)}$ in Theorem 1.7, and noticing that $|U_m| = (q^m - 1)/(q-1)$, we see that $\frac{q^m-1}{q-1} \frac{E^{2m}}{\text{poly}(q)} = O_q(1)$. For this to hold for arbitrarily large m, we must have

$$E \leq \frac{1}{\sqrt{q}},$$

which is our desired result.

2.2 Reduction to distributed nonlocal computation

Here we give an alternative proof of Theorem 1.2 by establishing a higher alphabet variant of powerful result of Linden et al. [21]. The main result of their work is that for a certain broad class of games, quantum and classical strategies are equivalent in their power. This class of games, called distributed non-local computation games, is defined as follows.

DEFINITION 2.5. *Let* $f : \mathbb{F}_2^n \to \mathbb{F}_2$ *be any function and* $\mathcal{D}$ *any distribution on* $\mathbb{F}_2^n$. *In the 2-party non-local computation of* $(f, \mathcal{D})$, *Alice receives* $x \in \mathbb{F}_2^n$ *uniformly at random and Bob receives* $y \stackrel{\text{def}}{=} z - x$ *where* z *is chosen according to* $\mathcal{D}$. *Alice and Bob succeed if their outputs* $\alpha, \beta \in \mathbb{F}_2$ *satisfy* $\alpha + \beta = f(z)$.

THEOREM 2.6 (LINDEN ET AL.). *For any binary distributed computation problem* S, *given by* $(f, \mathcal{D})$, *the entangled value and the classical value of the game coincide to the best linear approximation of* f.

$$\omega^*(S) = \omega(S) = \max_{l \in \mathcal{L}} \Pr_{z \in \mathcal{D}} [f(z) = l(z)],$$

where $\mathcal{L} = \{l : \mathbb{F}_2^n \to \mathbb{F}_2 \mid l(x+y) = l(x) + l(y)\}$ *is the set of all linear functions.*

Now we can naturally define the distributed version of the CHSH_q game following the above recipe.

DEFINITION 2.7. *In* $\mathsf{CHSH}_q^{\text{dist}}$, *Alice and Bob receive* $(\alpha, \gamma) \in \mathbb{F}_q^2$ *and* $(\beta, \delta) \in \mathbb{F}_q^2$. *Their objective is to produce outputs* a *and* b *satisfying* $a + b = (\alpha + \beta)(\gamma + \delta)$.

Any strategy $\mathcal{P}$ for CHSH_q results in a natural strategy $\mathcal{P}^{\text{dist}}$ for $\mathsf{CHSH}_q^{\text{dist}}$ as follows: assume Alice and Bob have a strategy $\mathcal{P}$ succeeding in CHSH_q game with probability $p_{win} = 1/q + E(q-1)/q$. In $\mathcal{P}^{\text{dist}}$, first Alice and Bob use $\mathcal{P}$ on inputs (α, δ) to produce a_1 and b_1, and then use $\mathcal{P}$ for a second time to produce a_2 and b_2 for inputs (γ, β). Finally Alice outputs $a = a_1 + a_2 + \alpha\gamma$, and Bob outputs $b = b_1 + b_2 + \beta\delta$.

We have the following proposition about $\mathcal{P}^{\text{dist}}$ which is straightforward to establish.

PROPOSITION 2.8. *Let* $\mathcal{P}$ *be a regular protocol for* CHSH_q *with bias* E. *Let* $\mathcal{P}^{\text{dist}}$ *be the resulting distributed protocol obtained through above procedure from* $\mathcal{P}$. *The winning probability of Alice and Bob in the protocol* $\mathcal{P}^{\text{dist}}$ *has bias* E^2, *i.e. we have*

$$p_{win} = \frac{1}{q} + \frac{q-1}{q} E^2.$$

Moreover, the resulting protocol for $\mathsf{CHSH}_q^{\text{dist}}$ *is itself regular.*

The fact that $\mathcal{P}^{\text{dist}}$ is regular when $\mathcal{P}$ is regular because of the symmetry all elements of $\mathbb{F}_q^*$. To see the statement about the winning probability of $\mathcal{P}^{\text{dist}}$, notice that $\mathcal{P}^*$ succeeds if and only if the type of errors produced in two uses of $\mathcal{P}$ in $\mathcal{P}^{\text{dist}}$ give errors of opposite sign. Hence, the following calculation confirms the above proposition.

$$\left(\frac{1}{q} + \frac{q-1}{q}E\right)^2 + \sum_{k=1}^{q} \left(\frac{1}{q} - \frac{E}{q}\right)^2 = \frac{1}{q} + \frac{q-1}{q}E^2.$$

Because of Proposition 2.8, it suffices to prove an upper bound of $2/q - 1/q^2$ for the winning probability of regular strategies in $\mathsf{CHSH}_q^{\text{dist}}$ to finish the proof of Theorem 1.2. Notice that, as hinted before, this value is exactly the winning probability achieved by the trivial strategy in which both players just output 0. This can be seen to be the best linear approximation to the polynomial $f(x,y) = xy$ which is aligned with the philosophy of Linden et al. [21] on equivalence of quantum and classical players for the distributed version of the game.

Now we proceed to the proof of Theorem 1.2. For simplicity, throughout this proof we shall assume q is a prime. However, essentially the same argument works in general with some small modifications mentioned at the end of the section. First we need the following lemma.

LEMMA 2.9. *Let* ω *be a* q^{th} *primitive root of unity. For any set of unit vector* $u_x, v_y \in \mathbb{C}^n$ *we have*

$$\left| \sum_{x,y} \omega^{-xy} \langle u_x, v_y \rangle \right| \leq q^{3/2}. \qquad (1)$$

PROOF. Since the discrete Fourier transform matrix $H_{x,y} = \frac{1}{\sqrt{q}} \omega^{-xy}$ is unitary it follows that for any $f : \mathbb{F}_q \to \mathbb{C}$ and $g : \mathbb{F}_q \to \mathbb{C}$ then

$$\left| \sum_{x,y} \omega^{-xy} f(x) g(y) \right| \leq \sqrt{q} \|f\|_2 \|g\|_2.$$

Here we used Cauchy-Schwarz inequality between $\hat{f}(y)$ and $g(y)$. To finish the proof of the lemma, we apply the above fact to the n coordinate functions $f_i, g_i : \mathbb{F}_q \to \mathbb{C}$ defined by $f_i(x) = \bar{u}_x(i)$ and $g_i(x) = v_y(i)$. Combining that with another Cauchy-Schwarz we get

$$\left| \sum_{x,y} \omega^{-xy} \langle u_x, v_y \rangle \right| = \left| \sum_{i,x,y} \omega^{-xy} f_i(x) g_i(y) \right|$$

$$\leq \sqrt{q} \sum_{i=1}^{n} \left(\sum_{x \in \mathbb{F}_q} |u_x(i)|^2 \right)^{\frac{1}{2}} \left(\sum_{y \in \mathbb{F}_q} |v_y(i)|^2 \right)^{\frac{1}{2}}$$

$$\leq \sqrt{q} \left(\sum_{i,x} |u_x(i)|^2 \right)^{\frac{1}{2}} \left(\sum_{i,y} |v_y(i)|^2 \right)^{\frac{1}{2}}$$

$$= q^{3/2}.$$

$\square$

We also need the following convenient notation for quantifying the probability of different types of error.

NOTATION 2.10. *We let* $p_k = \Pr_{a,b \leftarrow \mathcal{P}^{\text{dist}}} [a+b = k + (\alpha + \beta)(\gamma + \delta)]$ *according to* $\mathcal{P}^{\text{dist}}$ *(defined after definition 2.7).*

PROOF OF THEOREM 1.2. Let ω be a primitive q^{th} root of unity. First notice that since $p_0 = \frac{1}{q} + \frac{q-1}{q}E^2$ and $p_k = \frac{1}{q} - \frac{1}{q}E^2$ for $k \in \mathbb{F}_q^*$, it follows that

$$\sum_{k=0}^{q-1} p_k \, \omega^k = E^2 + \left(\frac{1}{q} - \frac{E^2}{q}\right)\sum_{k=0}^{q-1}\omega^k = E^2. \qquad (2)$$

Denote by $x = (\alpha, \gamma)$ the input of Alice, and by $y = (\beta, \delta)$ the input of Bob. Let P_x^a and Q_y^b be the measurement operators for Alice and Bob given inputs x and y. Define $U_x = \sum_{a=0}^{q-1}\omega^a P_x^a$ and $V_y = \sum_{b=0}^{q-1}\omega^b Q_y^b$. Since we have not assumed any bound on the dimension of Alice and Bob's system, we can assume the operators P_x^a and Q_y^b are projections. This implies that the operators U_x and V_y's are unitary. Now we have

$$
\begin{aligned}
E^2 &= \sum_{k=0}^{q-1} p_k \omega^k = \sum_{k=0}^{q-1} \mathbb{E}_{x,y}\left[\sum_{a+b=k+xy}\langle\psi|P_x^a \otimes Q_y^b|\psi\rangle\right]\omega^k \\
&= \langle\psi|\mathbb{E}_{x,y}\left[\sum_{a,b=0}^{q-1}\omega^{a+b-xy}P_x^a \otimes Q_y^b\right]|\psi\rangle \\
&= \frac{1}{q^2}\sum_{x,y\in F_q^2}\omega^{-xy}\langle\psi|U_x \otimes V_y|\psi\rangle \\
&= \frac{1}{q^2}\sum_{x,y\in F_q^2}\omega^{-xy}\langle u_x|v_y\rangle,
\end{aligned}
$$

where $U_x^\dagger \otimes I|\psi\rangle = |u_x\rangle$ and $I \otimes V_y|\psi\rangle = |v_y\rangle$ are unit vectors. So Lemma 2.9 implies $E \le \frac{1}{\sqrt{q}}$ which establishes the desired result. $\square$

2.2.1 General prime powers

In the above discussion we assumed q was a prime. Here we present the slight modifications necessary in the more general case of $q = p^s$ with s not necessarily 1.

Suppose we have a function $\chi : \mathbb{F}_q \to \mathbb{C}$ with the following properties:

1. For all $x \in \mathbb{F}_q$ we have $|\chi(x)| = 1$.

2. $\chi(x+y) = \chi(x)\chi(y)$.

3. $\sum_{x\in\mathbb{F}_q}\chi(x) = 0$.

Now if we replace the function $x \mapsto \omega^x$ with $x \mapsto \chi(x)$ in our argument we claim that the argument goes through exactly the same as before. To check this, first note that the $q \times q$ matrix $M_{xy} = \frac{1}{\sqrt{q}}\chi(xy)$ is again unitary. This is because for any $y \ne y' \in \mathbb{F}_q^*$ we have

$$\sum_{x\in\mathbb{F}_q}\overline{\chi(xy)}\cdot\chi(xy') = \sum_{x\in\mathbb{F}_q}\chi(x(y'-y)) = 0,$$

where we used the second and third properties of χ. This establishes that the analogue of equation (1) holds.

Next note that the main property we used in equation (2) was the fact that $\sum_{k\in\mathbb{F}_q}\chi(k) = 0$ which again holds here. Similarly, from the fact that $|\chi(a)| = 1$ it follows that operators of the form $U_x = \sum_{a\in\mathbb{F}_q}\chi(a)P_x^a$ are again unitary. It is easy to check the rest of our calculations are similarly valid given properties 1-3 of χ.

Finally, we shall note that a function such as χ is easy to construct using an additive isomorphism between $\mathbb{F}_q$ and

$\mathbb{F}_p^s$ where p is the characteristic of $q = p^s$. A particularly common choice is $\omega^{\text{Tr}(\cdot)}$ where ω is p^{th} root of unity and $\text{Tr}(\cdot)$ denotes the trace function given by $\alpha \mapsto \alpha + \alpha^p + \ldots + \alpha^{p^{s-1}}$ which can be shown to be a map from $\mathbb{F}_q$ to $\mathbb{F}_p$.

3. CLASSICAL ASPECTS OF CHSH$_q$ AND POINT-LINE INCIDENCES

In this section, we present our results regarding the classical value of CHSH$_q$. This includes Theorem 1.3 and various other results.

We begin by a short introduction to some notions from geometric incidence theory. Let $\Pi = \mathbb{F}^2$ be the plane over a field $\mathbb{F}$. For a collection of lines L and points P over a plane Π we define the set of incidences as

$$I(P,L) = \{(p,l) \in P \times L \,, p \in l\}.$$

A central question in geometric incidence theory is the following: Given $|P|$ and $|L|$, what can be said about the size $|I(P,L)|$? If $|P|$ and $|L|$ are of roughly the same size, it is hard to imagine a configuration where every line in L would contain every point in P. Hence $|I(P,L)| \le |P||L|$ seems a rather pessimistic upper bound. In fact, using the fact that there is at most one line through two distinct points and one point at the intersection of two distinct lines suffices to get a better upper bound of $|P|^{3/4}|L|^{3/4} + |P| + |L|$. As shown by Szemerédi and Trotter [29] the above bound can be improved when $\mathbb{F} = \mathbb{R}$ to $|P|^{2/3}|L|^{2/3} + |P| + |L|$. The proof of this result is very geometric and relies on localization techniques that do not work in the finite field settings. The situation over finite fields remained unclear until about a decade ago; finally Bourgain, Katz and Tao [4] used tools from arithmetic combinatorics to show an improved upper bound on $|I(P,L)|$ as long as the sets P and L are not too large. More specifically we have:

THEOREM 3.1 (BKT). *For any $\delta > 0$, there exists some $\epsilon > 0$ such that for any prime field $\mathbb{F}_p$ and any collection of points P and lines L over $\mathbb{F}_p^2$ satisfying $p^\delta \le |P|, |L| \le p^{2-\delta}$, we have*

$$|I(P,L)| = O\left(|P|^{\frac{3}{4}-\epsilon}|L|^{\frac{3}{4}-\epsilon}\right).$$

Although the theorem of Bourgain et al. as stated above only holds for prime fields, it is not too hard to see that essentially the same argument goes through whenever $|P|, |L|$ are large compared to the proper subfields of $\mathbb{F}_q$. This is made explicit in the work of Jones [15, 16]. Although what is proved in [15, 16] is more general, we just need the following corollary.

COROLLARY 3.2 (JONES). *Let q be an odd power of a prime, and assume P and L are sets of points and lines in $\mathbb{F}_q^2$ of size $\Theta(q)$. There exists a universal constant $\epsilon > 0$ such that*

$$I(P,L) \le q^{\frac{3}{2}-\epsilon}.$$

The framework of geometric-incidences can also be used to give an improved lower bound for general q's. For this, the key is the following lemma which allows to relax the restrictions on the points and lines in Fact 1.4.

LEMMA 3.3. *Let P, L be a set of points and lines in $\mathbb{F}_q^2$ with $|P| = \Theta(q)$ and $|L| = \Theta(q)$. There exists a set of points*

P', and a set of lines L', satisfying the conditions of Fact 1.4 with $|P'| \leq |P|$ and $|L'| \leq |L|$ such that

$$|I(P', L')| = \Omega\left(|I(P, L)|\right).$$

The main idea for proving this lemma is to start from the given configuration of P and L, and apply a random projective transformation to them. The proof requires some preparation and some technical work which is presented in Appendix A.

3.1 From Point- Line Incidences to CHSH$_q$

Given the above results, Theorem 1.3 can be proved rather quickly. To see why, recall Fact 1.4 from the introduction where it was claimed that the winning probability of any classical strategy for CHSH$_q$ corresponds to the number of point-line incidences among q lines and q points in $\mathbb{F}_q^2$ under some restrictions on the points and lines. Hence, the result of Jones immediately implies the lower bound in Theorem 1.3.

Before proving Theorem 1.3 we need to establish some useful notation.

DEFINITION 3.4. *Let $\mathbb{F}_q^2 = \mathbb{F}_q[z_1, z_2]$ be the plane. We denote by $\ell_{a,b}$ the line*

$$\ell_{a,b} = \{(z_1, z_2) \in \mathbb{F}_q^2 : z_2 = a z_1 - b\}.$$

PROOF OF THEOREM 1.3 AND FACT 1.4. The optimal classical strategies for CHSH$_q$ are given by two functions $f, g : \mathbb{F}_q \to \mathbb{F}_q$ corresponding to Alice and Bob's strategies maximizing

$$|\{x, y \in \mathbb{F}_q \mid f(x) + g(y) = xy\}|.$$

Given $f : \mathbb{F}_q \to \mathbb{F}_q$ corresponding to Alice's strategy, let P be the collection of q points of the form $(x, f(x)) \in \mathbb{F}_q^2$. To Bob's strategy $g : \mathbb{F}_q \to \mathbb{F}_q$, we associate a collection L of q lines $\{\ell_{y, g(y)}\}$. Observe in this language any pair $(x, y) \in \mathbb{F}_q^2$ satisfying CHSH$_q$ correspond to a point-line incidence. Hence, we have

$$f(x) + g(y) = xy \quad \Leftrightarrow \quad (x, f(x)) \in \ell_{y, g(y)},$$

which means that

$$\sum_{x, y \in \mathbb{F}_q} 1_{f(x) + g(y) = xy} = I(P, L).$$

The upper bound for $q = p^{2k-1}$ now follows from Corollary 3.2.

Now assume $q = p^{2k}$. Recall that in this case there exists a subfield $K \cong \mathbb{F}_{\sqrt{q}}$ such that $K \subset \mathbb{F}_q$. Let $P = \{(a, b) \in \mathbb{F}_q^2 : a, b \in K\}$ and $L = \{\ell_{c,d} : c, d \in K\}$. Notice that $|P| = |L| = q$, and $|I(P, L)| = q^{3/2}$. Combined with Lemma 3.3, this proves the lower bound. $\square$

THEOREM 3.5. *There exists a strategy for CHSH$_q$ achieving a winning probability $\Omega(q^{-2/3})$.*

Let us note that the above lower bound was somewhat counterintuitive to us at first. The point is that we expected that the function $(x, y) \mapsto xy$ to be in some sense *maximally psuedorandom* against the function $(a, b) \mapsto a + b$. Given this, it was reasonable to assume that the best classical strategy for CHSH$_q$ would achieve a winning probability of $\widetilde{O}(q^{-1})$ which is up to polylogarithmic factor the same as that of a random strategy. The logarithmic advantages can be seen

to be achievable using a simple balls-and-bins analysis by taking a random function $f : \mathbb{F}_q \to \mathbb{F}_q$ as Alice's strategy, and optimizing Bob's strategy $g : \mathbb{F}_q \to \mathbb{F}_q$ given that of Alice. In fact, numerical experiments which looked for locally optimal solutions confirmed the above intuition.[4] Despite all this, Theorem 3.5 states that much better lower bounds are achievable in general.

PROOF OF THEOREM 3.5. This follows from Lemma 3.3 applied to the next proposition. $\square$

PROPOSITION 3.6. *For any finite field field $\mathbb{F}_q$, there exists a set of at most q lines and at most q points over $\mathbb{F}_q^2$ with $\Omega(q^{4/3})$ incidences.*

PROOF. Let $q = p^s$. First we handle the case $s = 1$, then we give a construction for $s \geq 2$. Since we are concerned with an asymptotic statement, we can assume q is sufficiently large. As a result, we can safely ignore the ceiling and floor signs as they do not affect the asymptotic. For the prime case $s = 1$, the construction is very simple: let $P = \left[q^{1/3}\right] \times \left[q^{2/3}\right]$. Let L be the collection of lines $\ell_{c,d}$ of the form $y = cx + d$ with $c \in [q^{1/3}/2]$ and $d \in [q^{2/3}/2]$. It is clear that this achieves $I(P, L) = \Theta(q^{4/3})$ with $|P|, |L| \leq q$.

For the case $s \geq 2$, we choose our set P to be a product set, $P = A \times B$ where $A, B \subset \mathbb{F}_q$ are both subspaces. Let g be a primitive element of $\mathbb{F}_q$ so $\{1, g, g^2, \ldots, g^{s-1}\}$ form a basis of $\mathbb{F}_q$ as a vector space over $\mathbb{F}_p$.

Let $b \leq s$ be a positive integer, close to $2s/3$, to be specified later. Let $a = s - b$ (the condition $s \geq 2$ will turn out to be sufficient for $a \geq 1$ which we require). Define

$$A = \mathbb{F}_p + g\mathbb{F}_p + g^2\mathbb{F}_p + \ldots + g^{a-1}\mathbb{F}_p$$

and

$$B = \mathbb{F}_p + g\mathbb{F}_p + g^2\mathbb{F}_p + \ldots + g^{b-1}\mathbb{F}_p$$

and

$$C = \mathbb{F}_p + g\mathbb{F}_p + g^2\mathbb{F}_p + \ldots + g^{b-a}\mathbb{F}_p.$$

Notice that $|P| = |A||B| = q$.

Let $\ell_{c,d} \subset \mathbb{F}_q^2$ to be the line corresponding to $\{(x, y) \in \mathbb{F}_q^2 : y = cx + d\}$. Define

$$L = \{\ell_{c,d} : c \in C, d \in B\}.$$

Given this we can see

$$I(P, L) = |A||B||C| \quad , \quad |L| = |B||C|.$$

We want $|L| = O(q)$ while $I(P, L) = \Omega(q^{4/3})$. Since $|A||B| = q$, it suffices to choose b such that

$$|C| = p^{2b-s+1} = \Omega(p^{\frac{s}{3}}) \quad , \quad |B||C| = p^{3b-s+1} = O(p^s).$$

Now if $s \bmod 3 = 2$ then

$$\mathbb{Z} \cap \left[\frac{2s}{3} - \frac{1}{2}, \frac{2s}{3} - \frac{1}{3}\right] \neq \emptyset.$$

Hence, we are done by taking b to be the integer in that interval. For, $s = 3k$, $s = 3k + 1$ we take $b = 2k$ and $b =$

---

[4]More precisely, the algorithm used was the following: we start from two random strategies $f, g : \mathbb{F}_q \to \mathbb{F}_q$, and in every iteration we fix one of the functions and update the other one to the optimal strategy taking the other function as fixed.

$2k+1$ respectively. In $s = 3k$ case, we have $|I(P, L) = p^{4k+1}$ and $|L| = p^{3k+1}$. The important thing is that although $|L|$ is larger than its desired size by a factor of p, we are also exceeding the desired $|I(P, L)|$ lower bound by a factor p. A moment of though reveals that choosing L' to be the subset of L of size p^{3k} with maximum number incidences will finish the proof in this case. The situation in $s = 3k + 2$ case is analogous: if we choose L' be the the subset of L of size p^{3k+1} with the maximum number of incident points from P that will finish the construction. $\square$

4. CONCLUDING REMARKS

In this work, we initiated the study of $\mathsf{CHSH_q}$ in the asymptotic setting. We developed the theory of both quantum and classical values of this family of games, and outlined the connection to the problem of point-line incidences over finite fields. The fact that $\mathsf{CHSH_q}$ is a natural problem to consider in the study of non-XOR games (which is the original motivation of our work as well as Burhman and Massar's) while exhibiting intimate connections to above mathematical topics indicates that this problem deserves further investigation in the future. This is especially boosted by the fact that guaranteed progress can be made by using better numerical methods to investigate higher values of q, and also by attempting to quantize the results in arithmetic combinatorics. An investigation of the extent to which the results in additive and arithmetic combinatorics quantize could certainly have much further impact beyond the problems considered here.

One goal of our study was to further develop the techniques available for analyzing the entangled value of nonbinary non-local games. We believe that by giving two rather different proofs of Theorem 1.2, we demonstrated the power of the indirect approach of analyzing non-local games.

Future directions. As discussed previously, Problem 1.5 remains the most clear open problem given the bounds proved here. As mentioned before, its resolutions is likely to also resolve to Kasher and Kempe's problem regarding the security of Bourgain's two-source extractor in the presence of entanglement[18]. We can think of two possible routes for resolving this problem: one is by trying to quantize the arguments in the paper of Bourgain, Katz and Tao [4], and the other is by investigating the SDP hierarchies of Navascués et al. [22] to see whether they could lead to any improvement to Theorem 1.2 or lead to tightness results via some rounding scheme. In the hierarchy approach, it might be useful to keep in mind the rounding scheme of Kempe et al. [19] (though their result seem more relevant when the game value is close to 1 which is not the case here). Currently, with some collaborators, we are pursuing the latter direction via the SDP hierarchies.

We finish by recounting perhaps the most intriguing (and rather open-ended) future direction along this work. This is the question of the extent to which the relatively wellunderstood theory of XOR games extends to larger alphabets. A related question is to find a better explanation for the absence of any analogue of a large alphabet generalization of Tsirelson's theorem [31] for even slight variants of non-XOR games (say q-XOR games for $q = 3$) in the literature. A better understanding of the above issues would certainly constitute a major advance in our understanding of two prover games and non-locality in general.

5. REFERENCES

[1] J. S. Bell. On the Einstein-Podolsky-Rosen paradox. *Physics*, 1(3), 1964.

[2] M. Ben-Or, S. Goldwasser, J. Kilian, and A. Wigderson. Multi-prover interactive proofs: How to remove intractability assumptions. In *Proceedings of the twentieth annual ACM symposium on Theory of computing(STOC)*, 1988.

[3] J. Bourgain. More on the sum-product phenomenon in prime fields and its applications. *International Journal of Number Theory*, 1(01):1–32, 2005.

[4] J. Bourgain, N. Katz, and T. Tao. A sum-product estimate in finite fields, and applications. *Geometric & Functional Analysis*, 14(1), 2004.

[5] J. Briët and T. Vidick. Explicit lower and upper bounds on the entangled value of multiplayer XOR games. *Communications in Mathematical Physics*, 321(1):181–207, 2013.

[6] N. Brunner, D. Cavalcanti, S. Pironio, V. Scarani, and S. Wehner. Bell nonlocality. *quant-ph:1303.2849*, 2013.

[7] H. Buhrman and S. Massar. Causality and Tsirel'son bounds. *Physical Review A, 72(5), 052103*, 2005.

[8] H. Buhrman, O. Regev, G. Scarpa, and R. de Wolf. Near-optimal and explicit Bell inequality violations. In *IEEE 26th Annual Conference on Computational Complexity (CCC)*, pages 157–166, 2011.

[9] J. F. Clauser, M. A. Horne, A. Shimony, and R. A. Holt. Proposed experiment to test local hidden-variable theories. *Physical Review Letters*, 23(15):880–884, 1969.

[10] W. v. Dam. Implausible consequences of superstrong nonlocality. *Natural Computing*, 12(1), 2013.

[11] I. Dinur and D. Steurer. Analytical approach to parallel repetition. In *Proceedings of the 46th Annual ACM Symposium on Theory of Computing*, STOC, pages 624–633, 2014.

[12] A. K. Ekert. Quantum cryptography based on Bell's theorem. *Physical Review Letters*, 67(6):661–663, 1991.

[13] N. Gisin. Bell inequalities: Many questions, a few answers. *The Western Ontario Series in Philosophy of Science*, 73, 2009.

[14] S.-W. Ji, J. Lee, J. Lim, K. Nagata, and H.-W. Lee. Multisetting Bell inequality for qudits. *Physical Review A*, 78(5):052103, 2008.

[15] T. G. Jones. Explicit incidence bounds over general finite fields. *arXiv preprint arXiv:1009.3899*, 2010.

[16] T. G. Jones. New quantitative estimates on the incidence geometry and growth of finite sets. *PhD Thesis, University of Bristol. arXiv:1301.4853*, 2013.

[17] M. Junge and C. Palazuelos. Large violation of Bell inequalities with low entanglement. *Communications in Mathematical Physics*, 306(3):695–746, 2011.

[18] R. Kasher and J. Kempe. Two-source extractors secure against quantum adversaries. *Theory of Computing*, 8(21), 2012.

[19] J. Kempe, O. Regev, and B. Toner. Unique games with entangled provers are easy. In *49th Annual IEEE Symposium on Foundations of Computer Science (FOCS)*. IEEE, 2008.

[20] Y.-C. Liang, C.-W. Lim, and D.-L. Deng. Reexamination of a multisetting Bell inequality for qudits. *Physical Review A*, 80(5), 2009.

[21] N. Linden, S. Popescu, A. J. Short, and A. Winter. Quantum nonlocality and beyond: limits from nonlocal computation. *Physical Review Letters*, 99(18):180502, 2007.

[22] M. Navascués, S. Pironio, and A. Acín. A convergent hierarchy of semidefinite programs characterizing the set of quantum correlations. *New Journal of Physics*, 10(7), 2008.

[23] M. Pawłowski, T. Paterek, D. Kaszlikowski, V. Scarani, A. Winter, and M. Zukowski. Information causality as a physical principle. *Nature*, 461, 2009.

[24] M. Pawłowski and A. Winter. Hyperbits: The information quasiparticles. *Physical Review A*, 85(2), 2012.

[25] S. Popescu and D. Rohrlich. Quantum nonlocality as an axiom. *Foundations of Physics*, 24(3):379–385, 1994.

[26] A. Rao. An exposition of Bourgain's 2-source extractor. *Electronic Colloquium on Computational Complexity (ECCC)*, 14(034), 2007.

[27] R. Raz. A counterexample to strong parallel repetition. *SIAM Journal on Computing*, 40(3):771–777, 2011.

[28] B. W. Reichardt, F. Unger, and U. Vazirani. A classical leash for a quantum system: command of quantum systems via rigidity of CHSH games. In *Proceedings of the 4th conference on Innovations in Theoretical Computer Science (ITCS)*, 2013.

[29] E. Szemerédi and W. T. Trotter Jr. Extremal problems in discrete geometry. *Combinatorica*, 3(3-4):381–392, 1983.

[30] B. S. Tsirel'son. Quantum generalizations of Bell's inequality. *Letters in Mathematical Physics*, 4(2), 1980.

[31] B. S. Tsirel'son. Quantum analogues of the Bell inequalities. the case of two spatially separated domains. *Journal of Soviet Mathematics*, 36(4), 1987.

[32] G. Wang. Functional boxes, communication complexity and information causality. *arXiv preprint arXiv:1109.4988*, 2011.

[33] R. F. Werner and M. M. Wolf. Bell inequalities and entanglement. *Quantum Information and Computation (QIC)*, (3), 2001.

APPENDIX

A. PROJECTIVE TRANSFORMATIONS AND THE CLASSICAL VALUE OF CHSH$_q$

The goal of this section is to give a proof of Lemma 3.3. To do so we need to introduce some basic concepts from projective geometry. The major advantages of working over the projective plane as opposed to the affine plane for our purposes here is that firstly, the duality between points and lines becomes quite transparent and clean over the projective plane, and secondly (and more importantly), it turns out that set of *projective transformations*, while still preserving the point-line incidence structure, is much larger and richer than the group of affine transformations.

Recall that the points of the projective plane $\mathbb{PF}_q^2$ are given by the triples $(x : y : z)$, with at least one coordinate non-zero, where we identify any two points $(x : y : z)$ and $(\lambda x : \lambda y : \lambda z)$ for $\lambda \in \mathbb{F}_q^*$. The lines in the projective plane are given by triples $(l : m : n)$ consisting of all point $(x : y : z)$ satisfying $lx + my + nz = 0$. Hence, $\mathbb{PF}_q^2$ consists of a total of $q^2 + q + 1$ points and lines, where each line contains $q + 1$ points, and similarly each point is contained in $q + 1$ lines. One can go from the projective plane to the affine plane by discarding all the points on the "line at infinity", which consists of points of the form $(a : b : 0)$. Any point remaining can then be put in the form $(a : b : 1)$ which corresponds to the point (a, b) of the affine plane. Two points lying on the same a vertical line in the affine plane are $(a : b : 1)$ and $(a : b' : 1)$. These lie on the projective line $(1 : 0 : -a)$. These projective lines all go through the point $(0 : 1 : 0)$, or the "vertical infinity".

Next we describe the concept of a projective transformation. Any 3×3 invertible matrix A induces a map on $\mathbb{PF}_q^2$ by its action on $\mathbb{F}_q^3$. Two matrices A and B induce the same action on $\mathbb{PF}_q^2$, if they are related to by $A = \lambda B$ by some $\lambda \in \mathbb{F}_q^*$. Each element of this equivalence class represents a projective transformation on the projective plane.

Now we are almost ready to prove Lemma 3.3. The main idea of the proof is to start from the given sets of points P and lines L with large $I(P, L)$ which possibly are far from satisfying the conditions of Fact 1.4 and apply a projective transformation. After, this we discard some of our points and lines so that the hypothesis of Fact 1.4 is satisfied. We argue that a good portion of our incidences would remain after the above deletion process finishing the proof. The details are as follows.

PROOF OF LEMMA 3.3. Let P and L in $\mathbb{PF}_q^2$ be the set of points and lines given by the hypothesis. In the argument we shall operate under the assumption that $|P|, |L| \leq \frac{q}{2}$. Indeed, one can cut the sizes of P and L by any constant factor without losing much in $|I(P, L)|$ as follows: first we shrink $|P|$ by keeping the $\frac{q}{2}$ points with the most number of incident lines—which shrinks $|I(P, L)|$ only by a factor of $\frac{2|P|}{q} = O(1)$ factor—and after keeping those lines with the most number incident points (among the $\frac{q}{2}$ size points that we kept).

Now we apply a random projective transformation to $\mathbb{PF}_q^2$ which can be seen to be equivalent to the following operation: Take a line l from all $q^2 + q + 1$ lines in $\mathbb{PF}_q^2$ uniformly at random to be the new line at the infinity. Choose a random point on l to be the new vertical point at infinity (and a random points from the remaining q points on the line at the infinity to be the new horizontal point at infinity, but this latter point plays no role for us). Next we discard all but a single line from any subset of L that are parallel after this operation. Similarly, we discard all but one point from any set of points in P that are on the same vertical line after this operation. We also discard any point of P on the new line at infinity; this puts us back in the case of the affine plane $\mathbb{F}_q^2$. Let P' and L' be the set of points and lines in $\mathbb{F}_q^2$ obtained after the above operation. To finish the proof, it suffices to show that in expectation P', L' and $I(P', L')$ would remain within constant factors of their original sizes.

Let us first compute the probability that two given lines ℓ_1 and ℓ_2 have the same slope. If we choose a random line as ℓ_∞, two lines will have the same slope if they intersect the line ℓ_∞ at the same point. The probability of this event for a specific pair of lines is $1/(q+1)$ (assuming that neither is the line at infinity), as this happens exactly when ℓ_∞ intersects ℓ_1 at the same point that ℓ_2 intersects ℓ_1. We now compute the probability that a given line survives. The probability that it is not the line at infinity is $\frac{q^2+q}{q^2+q+1}$, and given that it is not the line at infinity, it is eliminated with probability at most $\frac{q-1}{2(q+1)}$, since there are $\frac{q-1}{2}$ other lines that would eliminate it by having the same slope. This gives a total probability that it is eliminated of $\frac{q(q+3)}{2(q^2+q+1)} < \frac{1}{2}$. This shows that the expected number of lines that survive is at least $\frac{q+1}{4}$.

We next need to analyze the effect of choosing the point at vertical infinity at random and throwing out points lying on the same vertical line. The argument is analogous to the above. Again, the probability that a given two points lie on a vertical is $1/(q+1)$. The probability that a point is not on the line at infinity is $\frac{q^2}{q^2+q+1}$. By the same argument as before, we have that the expectation that a given point survives is at least $\frac{q^2(q+3)}{2(q^2+q+1)(q+1)}$. Thus, the expected number of points that survive is also $\Theta(q)$. Furthermore the process of throwing out points and the process of throwing out lines are independent. Thus, the probability that we keep a point-line incidence is at least $\Omega(1)$ which finishes the proof. $\square$

Non-Interactive Proofs of Proximity

[Extended Abstract] [*]

Tom Gur
Weizmann Institute of Science
tom.gur@weizmann.ac.il

Ron D. Rothblum
Weizmann Institute of Science
ron.rothblum@weizmann.ac.il

ABSTRACT

We initiate a study of *non-interactive* proofs of proximity. These proof-systems consist of a verifier that wishes to ascertain the validity of a given statement, using a short (sublinear length) explicitly given proof, and a sublinear number of queries to its input. Since the verifier cannot even read the entire input, we only require it to reject inputs that are far from being valid. Thus, the verifier is only assured of the proximity of the statement to a correct one. Such proof-systems can be viewed as the $\mathcal{NP}$ (or more accurately $\mathcal{MA}$) analogue of *property testing*.

We explore both the power and limitations of non interactive proofs of proximity. We show that such proof-systems can be exponentially stronger than property testers, but are exponentially weaker than the *interactive* proofs of proximity studied by Rothblum, Vadhan and Wigderson (STOC 2013). In addition, we show a natural problem that has a full and (almost) tight multiplicative trade-off between the length of the proof and the verifier's query complexity. On the negative side, we also show that there exist properties for which even a linearly-long (non-interactive) proof of proximity cannot significantly reduce the query complexity.

Categories and Subject Descriptors

F.2.0 [**Theory of Computation**]: Analysis of Algorithms and Problem Complexity — General

Keywords

Probabilistic Proof Systems; Property Testing

1. INTRODUCTION

Understanding the power and limitations of sublinear algorithms is a central question in the theory of computation. The study of *property testing*, initiated by Rubinfeld and

[*]The full version [31] is available at `http://eccc.hpi-web.de/report/2013/078/`

Sudan [38] and Goldreich, Goldwasser and Ron [21], aims to address this question by considering highly-efficient randomized algorithms that solve approximate decision problems, while only inspecting a small fraction of the input. Such algorithms, commonly referred to as *property testers*, are given oracle access to some object, and are required to determine whether the object has some predetermined property, or is far (say, in Hamming distance) from every object that has the property. Remarkably, it turns out that many natural properties can be tested by making relatively few queries to the object.

Once a model of computation has been established, a fundamental question that arises is to understand the power of *proof-systems* in this model. Recall that a proof-system consists of a powerful prover that wishes to convince a weak verifier, which does not trust the prover, of the validity of some statement. Since verifying is usually easier than computing, using the power of proofs, it is often possible to overcome limitations of the basic model of computation. In this paper we study proof-systems in the context of property testing, with the hope that by augmenting testers with proofs we can indeed overcome inherent limitations of property testers.

Thus, we are interested in proof-systems in which the verifier reads only a small fraction of the input. Of course we cannot hope for such a verifier to reject *every* false statement. Instead, as is the case in property testing, we relax the soundness condition and only require that it be impossible to convince the verifier to accept statements that are *far* from true statements. Such proof-systems were first introduced by Ergün, Kumar and Rubinfeld [15] and were recently further studied by Rothblum, Vadhan and Wigderson [37] who were motivated by applications to *delegation of computation* in sublinear time. Rothblum *et al.* [37] showed that by allowing a property tester to interact with an untrusted prover (who can read the *entire* input), sublinear time verification is indeed possible for a wide class of properties. As in the property testing framework, the tester is only assured of the proximity of the input to the property and hence such protocols are called *interactive proofs of proximity* ($\mathcal{IPP}$s).

1.1 The Notion of $\mathcal{MAP}$

In this work, we also consider proofs of proximity, but restrict the verification process to be *non-interactive*. In other words, we augment the property testing framework by allowing the tester full and free access to an (alleged) proof. Such a proof-aided tester for a property Π, is given oracle access to an input x and free access to a proof string w, and should distinguish between the case that $x \in \Pi$ and the case that x is far from Π while using a sublinear number of queries. We require that for inputs $x \in \Pi$, there exist a proof that the tester accepts with high probability, and for inputs x that are *far* from Π no proof will make the tester accept, except with some small probability of error.

This type of proof-system can be viewed as the property testing analogue of an $\mathcal{NP}$ proof-system (whereas $\mathcal{IPP}$ is the property testing analogue of $\mathcal{IP}$). However, in contrast to polynomial-time algorithms, sublinear time algorithms inherently rely on *randomization*.[1] Since an $\mathcal{NP}$ proof-system in which the verifier is randomized is known as a *Merlin-Arthur* ($\mathcal{MA}$) proof-system, we call these sublinear non-interactive proof-systems *Merlin-Arthur proofs of proximity* or simply $\mathcal{MAP}$s.

Following the property testing literature, we consider the number of queries that the tester makes as the main computational resource. We ask whether non-interactive proofs can reduce the number of queries that property testers make, and if so by how much. (We note that [37] showed that it is possible to significantly reduce the query complexity of property testers using interactive proofs, but their proof systems rely fundamentally on two-way interaction.)

Given the (widely believed) power of proofs in the context of *polynomial-time* computation, one would hope that proofs can help decrease the number of queries that is needed to test various properties. This is indeed the case. In fact, for every property Π, consider a proof-system for the statement $x \in \Pi$, wherein the proof w is simply equal to x. In order to verify the statement, the tester need only verify that indeed $w \in \Pi$ and that w is close to x (i.e., that the relative Hamming distance between w and x is a small constant). The former check can be carried out without any queries to x, whereas for the latter a constant number of queries suffice. Thus, using a proof of length linear in the input size, *any* property can be tested using a constant number of queries (furthermore, the tester has one-sided error). In contrast, there exist properties for which *linear* lower bounds on the query complexity of standard property testers are known (cf. [21]).

The foregoing discussion leads us to view the proof length, in addition to the number of queries, as a central computational resource, which we should try to minimize. Thus, we measure the complexity of an $\mathcal{MAP}$ by the total amount of information available to the tester, namely, the sum of the $\mathcal{MAP}$s query complexity (i.e., the number of queries that the tester makes) and proof complexity (i.e., the length of the proof). In this work we study the complexity of $\mathcal{MAP}$s in comparison to property testers and to the recently introduced $\mathcal{IPP}$s.

A Concrete Motivation. We note that the non interactive nature of such proof-systems may have significant importance to applications such as *delegation of computation*. Specifically, consider a scenario wherein a computationally weak client has reliable query access to a massive dataset x. The client wishes to compute a function f on x, but its limited power, along with the massive size of the dataset, prevents it from doing so. In this case, the client can use a powerful server (e.g., a cloud computing provider) to compute $f(x)$ for it. However, the client may be distrustful of the server's answer (as it might cheat or make a mistake).

Thus, an $\mathcal{MAP}$ for f can be used to verify the correctness of the computation delegated to the server: Given access to x, the server can send the value $y = f(x)$, together with a proof of proximity that ascertains that x is close to a dataset x' for which $f(x') = y$. The latter can be verified using an $\mathcal{MAP}$ verifier that makes only a small number of queries to x.

We emphasize that the advantage in using *non-interactive* proofs of proximity (rather than interactive ones) is not only in removing the need for two-way communication, but also: (1) the proof can be "annotated" to the dataset by the server in a cheap off-line phase; and (2) the proof can be re-used for multiple clients.

The Computational Complexity of Generating and Verifying the Proof. As noted above, we view the number of queries and proof length as the main computational resources. It is natural to also consider the computational complexity of generating and verifying the proof. However, in this work our main focus is on the query and proof complexities. Still, we note that unless stated otherwise, our protocols can be implemented efficiently; that is, the proof can be generated in *polynomial-time* and verified in *sublinear-time*.

Comparison with $\mathcal{PCP}$s of Proximity. $\mathcal{PCP}$s of proximity ($\mathcal{PCPP}$s), first studied by Ben-Sasson *et al.* [5] and by Dinur and Reingold [14] (where they are called **assignment testers**) are also non-interactive proof-systems in which the verifier has oracle access to an object, and needs to decide whether the object is close to having a predetermined property. However, $\mathcal{PCPP}$s differ from $\mathcal{MAP}$s in that the verifier is only given *query* (i.e., oracle) access to the proof, whereas in $\mathcal{MAP}$s, the verifier has free (*explicit*) access to the proof. Indeed, in contrast to $\mathcal{MAP}$s, the proof string in $\mathcal{PCPP}$s is typically of super-linear length (but only a small fraction of it is actually read at random). Thus, $\mathcal{PCPP}$s may be thought of as the $\mathcal{PCP}$ analogue of property testing, whereas $\mathcal{MAP}$s are the $\mathcal{NP}$ analogue of property testing.

In fact, considering a variety of non-interactive proof-systems that differ in whether the main input and the proof are given explicitly or implicitly (i.e., via query access or free access), leads to the taxonomy depicted in Table 1. Interestingly, the three other variants, corresponding to $\mathcal{NP}, \mathcal{PCP}$ and $\mathcal{PCPP}$, have all been well studied. Thus, we view the notion of $\mathcal{MAP}$s as completing this taxonomy of non-interactive proof-systems.

1.2 The Power of $\mathcal{MAP}$

The first question that one might ask about the model of $\mathcal{MAP}$s is whether proofs give a significant savings in the query complexity of property testers (indeed, such savings are the main reason to introduce a proof-system in the first place). Given the above discussion on the importance of bounding the proof length, we seek savings in the query complexity while using only a relatively short proof. Our first result shows that indeed there exists a property for which a dramatic saving is possible:

INFORMAL THEOREM 1. *There exists a (natural) property that has an $\mathcal{MAP}$ that uses a logarithmic-length proof and only a* constant *number of queries, but requires $n^{0.999}$ queries for every property tester.*

---

[1]It is not difficult to see that the sublinear time *deterministic* computation or even verification is limited to trivial properties (cf. [26]).

Access to Main Input	Access to Proof		
	No Proof	**Free Access**	**Oracle Access**
Free Access	$\mathcal{P}$	$\mathcal{NP}$ or $\mathcal{MA}$	$\mathcal{PCP}$
Oracle Access	Property Testers	$\mathcal{MAP}$ (**this work**)	$\mathcal{PCPP}$

Table 1: Taxonomy of non-interactive proof-systems.

Here and throughout this work, n denotes the length of the object being tested.

Having established an exponential separation between the power of property testers and $\mathcal{MAP}$s, we continue our study of $\mathcal{MAP}$s by asking how many queries can be saved by slightly increasing the length of the proof. The following result shows a property for which a smooth *multiplicative* trade-off, which is (almost) tight, between the number of queries and length of the proof holds:

INFORMAL THEOREM 2. *There exists a (natural) property* Π *such that, for every* $p \geq 1$, *there is an* $\mathcal{MAP}$ *for* Π *that uses a proof of length* p *and makes* $\frac{n^{0.999}}{p}$ *queries. Furthermore, for every* p, *the trade-off is (almost) tight.*

Recall that for property testers huge gaps may exist between the query complexity of testers that have *one-sided error* and the query complexity of testers that have two-sided error (where a one-sided tester is one that accepts every object that has the property with probability 1). Notable examples for properties for which such gaps are known are *Cycle-Freeness* in the bounded degree graph model (see [13]) and ρ-*Clique* in the dense graph model (see [21]). In contrast, we observe that *such gaps can not exist in the case of* $\mathcal{MAP}$s.

INFORMAL THEOREM 3. *Any two-sided error* $\mathcal{MAP}$ *can be converted to have* one-sided error *with only a polylogarithmic overhead to the query and proof complexities.*

Since every property tester can be viewed as an $\mathcal{MAP}$ that uses an empty proof, as an immediate corollary, we obtain a transformation from every two-sided error *property tester* into a one sided $\mathcal{MAP}$ that uses a proof of only polylogarithmic length (with only a polylogarithmic increase in the query complexity). Moreover, since (as noted above) there are well-known properties for which *one-sided error* property testing is exponentially harder than *two-sided error* property testing, Informal Theorem 3 implies an exponential separation between $\mathcal{MAP}$s (with polylogarithmically long proofs) and *one-sided error* property testing. We note that Informal Theorem 1 shows such a separation for the more general case of two-sided error.

We note that all of the explicit properties that were discussed thus far are properties "with distance"; that is, properties for which every two objects that have the property are far apart. In other words, the set of objects forms an error-correcting code. This distance, along with a form of local *self-correction*, is a crucial ingredient of the foregoing $\mathcal{MAP}$s. In contrast, all of the properties described next are properties "without distance". Hence, the power of $\mathcal{MAP}$s is not limited to properties with distance.

$\mathcal{MAP}$s **for parameterized concatenation problems.** We identify a family of natural properties, for which it is possible to construct efficient $\mathcal{MAP}$s, by using a generic scheme. Specifically, for every problem that can be expressed as a parameterized concatenation problem, we show how to construct an efficient $\mathcal{MAP}$ that allows a trade-off between the query and proof complexity. Loosely speaking, a property Π is a parameterized concatenation problem if $\Pi = \Pi_{\alpha_1} \times \cdots \times \Pi_{\alpha_k}$, for some integer k, where each property Π_{α_i} is a property parameterized by α_i.

Using this generic scheme, we obtain $\mathcal{MAP}$s for a couple of natural problems, including: (1) approximating the Hamming weight of a string, and (2) graph orientation problems.

$\mathcal{MAP}$s **for graph properties.** To see that $\mathcal{MAP}$s are also useful for testing graph properties, we consider the problem of testing bipartiteness in the *bounded-degree* graph model. We construct an $\mathcal{MAP}$ protocol for verifying bipartiteness of *rapidly-mixing graphs*, with proof complexity p and query complexity q, *for every* p and q such that $p \cdot q \geq N$ (where N is the number of vertices in the graph). In particular, we obtain an $\mathcal{MAP}$ verifier that uses a proof of length $N^{2/3}$ and makes only $N^{1/3}$ queries. This stands in contrast to the $\Omega(\sqrt{N})$ lower bound on the query complexity of property testers (which do not use a proof), shown by Goldreich and Ron [23], which also holds for *rapidly-mixing graphs*. We remark that in [37] a (multi-round) $\mathcal{IPP}$ was given for the same problem.

We note that in the *dense* graph model, testing bipartiteness (or more generally k-colorability) can be easily done using only $O(1/\varepsilon)$ queries (where ε represents the desired proximity to the object) when given a proof that is simply the k-coloring of the graph (which can be represented by $N \log_2 k$ bits where N is the number of vertices and k is the number of colors).[2] In contrast, for standard property testers such query complexity is impossible (see [8]). We note that a similar protocol (described as a $\mathcal{PCPP}$) for testing bipartiteness in the dense graph model was suggested in [15] and in [5].

$\mathcal{MAP}$s **for sparse properties.** If a property is relatively sparse, in the sense that it contains only t objects, then a proof of length $\log_2 t$ (which fully describes the object) can be used, and only $O(1/\varepsilon)$ queries suffice to verify the proof's consistency with the object. Using this observation we note that testing k-juntas and k-linearity can be verified using only $O(1/\varepsilon)$ queries and a proof of length $O(k \log n)$, whereas a lower bound of $\Omega(k)$ queries is well-known for standard property testers (cf. [6]).

1.3 The Limitations of $\mathcal{MAP}$

In the previous section, we described results that exhibit the power of $\mathcal{MAP}$s. But what about the limitations of $\mathcal{MAP}$s? As discussed above, a proof of linear length suf-

---

[2]Note that the size of the tested object is N^2, and so $N \log_2 k$ is sublinear in the input size. In order to verify this proof, the verifier chooses $O(1/\varepsilon)$ edges at random and accepts if all are properly colored.

fices to reduce the query complexity to $O(1/\varepsilon)$. Moreover, Informal Theorem 1 shows that even a logarithmically long proof can be extremely useful for a specific property. Thus, it is natural to ask whether a *sublinear* proof can reduce the query complexity for *every* property. The following result shows that for *almost all* properties, even a proof of length n/100 cannot improve the query complexity by more than a constant factor.

INFORMAL THEOREM 4. *For almost all properties, every* $\mathcal{MAP}$ *verifier that uses a proof of length* $n/100$ *must make* $\Omega(n)$ *queries.*[3]

Although Informal Theorem 4 holds for most properties, finding an *explicit* property for which a similar statement holds remains an interesting open question. We note that Informal Theorem 4 improves upon a result of Fischer *et al.* [16] (see discussion in Section 1.5).

Since Informal Theorem 4 shows that even a relatively long proof cannot help in general for *every* property, one might ask whether there are specific properties for which short proofs do suffice. As was shown in Informal Theorem 1, this is indeed the case and a logarithmically long proof allows for an exponential improvement in the query complexity for a specific property. But can an even shorter, say constant-size proof, help? Unfortunately, the answer is negative since an $\mathcal{MAP}$ with query complexity q and proof complexity p can be emulated by a property tester that enumerates all possible proofs and makes a total of $\tilde{O}(2^p \cdot q)$ queries. Still, are there any further limits to how proofs can help a tester?

We first note that the ability to query the object in a way that depends on the proof is essential to the power of $\mathcal{MAP}$. In contrast, consider *proof-oblivious queries* $\mathcal{MAP}$s, which are $\mathcal{MAP}$s in which the verifer's queries are independent of the provided proof. Such $\mathcal{MAP}$s can be viewed as a two step process in which the verifier first (adaptively) queries the object and only then it receives the proof and decides whether to accept or reject based on both the answers and the proof. We say that such $\mathcal{MAP}$s have **proof oblivious queries**. The following result shows that $\mathcal{MAP}$s with *proof-oblivious queries* can provide at most a *quadratic* improvement over standard property testers.

INFORMAL THEOREM 5. *If a property* Π *has an* $\mathcal{MAP}$ *that makes* q *proof oblivious queries and uses a proof of length* p, *then* Π *has a property tester that makes* $O(q \cdot p)$ *queries.*

By Informal Theorem 1, the restriction to *proof oblivious queries* is a necessary precondition for Informal Theorem 5 (and indeed, the $\mathcal{MAP}$ verifier of Informal Theorem 1 must make proof-dependent queries).

Having inspected the relationship between $\mathcal{MAP}$s and property testing, we proceed to consider the relationship between $\mathcal{MAP}$s and $\mathcal{IPP}$s. Recall that $\mathcal{MAP}$s are actually a special case of $\mathcal{IPP}$s in which the interaction is limited to a single message sent from the prover to the verifier. When comparing $\mathcal{MAP}$s and $\mathcal{IPP}$s it is natural to compare both the query complexity and the total amount of communication with the prover (which in the case of $\mathcal{MAP}$s is simply the length of the proof).

The following theorem shows that $\mathcal{IPP}$s are stronger than $\mathcal{MAP}$s not only syntactically but also in essence. We show that even 3-message $\mathcal{IPP}$s may have exponentially better query complexity than $\mathcal{MAP}$s (while using the same amount of communication). Moreover, we show that $\mathcal{IPP}$s with *polylogarithmically* many messages of polylogarithmic length can also have exponentially better communication complexity.

INFORMAL THEOREM 6. *There exists a property* Π *such that on the one hand, any* $\mathcal{MAP}$ *for* Π *with proof of length* $n^{0.499+o(1)}$ *has query complexity* $n^{0.499+o(1)}$, *and on the other hand,* Π *has:*

1. *A 3-message* $\mathcal{IPP}$ *that makes* $\mathsf{polylog}(n)$ *queries while using a total of* $n^{0.499+o(1)}$ *communication.*

2. *An* $\mathcal{IPP}$ *with only* $\mathsf{polylog}(n)$ *query and communication complexities but using a* polylogarithmic *number of messages.*

1.4 Techniques

Several of our results (in particular Informal Theorems 2 and 6) are based on a specific algebraic property, which we call *Sub-Tensor Sum* and denote by $\mathsf{TensorSum}$ (c.f. [36]). Let $\mathbb{F}$ be a finite field and let $H \subset \mathbb{F}$ be an arbitrary subset. We consider m-variate polynomials over $\mathbb{F}$ that have individual degree d. The $\mathsf{TensorSum}$ property contains all such polynomials whose sum on H^m equals 0.[4] That is, $\mathsf{TensorSum}$ contains all polynomials $P : \mathbb{F}^m \to \mathbb{F}$ of individual degree d such that

$$\sum_{x \in H^m} P(x) = 0.$$

Selecting $|\mathbb{F}|, m, d$ and $|H|$ suitably (as polylogarithmic functions in the input size $n = |\mathbb{F}|^m$), we obtain the following roughly stated upper and lower bounds for $\mathsf{TensorSum}$ (for the formal statements, see the technical sections):

1. $\mathcal{PT}$: The query complexity of testing the $\mathsf{TensorSum}$ property (without a proof) is $\Theta(n^{0.999\pm o(1)})$ queries.

2. $\mathcal{MAP}$: The $\mathcal{MAP}$ complexity of the $\mathsf{TensorSum}$ problem is $\Theta\left(n^{0.499\pm o(1)}\right)$. Moreover, for every $p \geq 1$, the $\mathcal{MAP}$ query complexity of $\mathsf{TensorSum}$ with respect to proofs of length p is $\Theta\left(\frac{n^{0.999\pm o(1)}}{p}\right)$.

3. $\mathcal{IPP}[3]$: $\mathsf{TensorSum}$ has a 3-*message* $\mathcal{IPP}$ with query complexity $\mathsf{polylog}(n)$ and communication complexity $O\left(n^{0.499+o(1)}\right)$.

4. $\mathcal{IPP}$: $\mathsf{TensorSum}$ has an $\mathcal{IPP}$ with query and communication complexities $\mathsf{polylog}(n)$. However, in contrast to Item 3, this $\mathcal{IPP}$ uses *polylogarithmically* many messages.

To get a taste of our proofs, consider the (relatively) simple case wherein we restrict the $\mathsf{TensorSum}$ property to dimension $m = 2$ and a field $\mathbb{F}$ of size $\sqrt{n}$ (i.e., bivariate polynomials over a field of size $\sqrt{n}$). Naturally, we call this variant the *Sub-Matrix Sum* property and denote it by

---

[3]In fact, we show a general additive tradeoff between proof and query complexities, that is, every $\mathcal{MAP}$ verifier that uses a proof of length p must make $\tilde{\Omega}(n - p)$ queries.

[4]The choice of the constant 0 is arbitrary.

MatrixSum. Note that MatrixSum contains all polynomials $P : \mathbb{F}^2 \to \mathbb{F}$ of individual degree $d = |\mathbb{F}|/10$ such that

$$\sum_{x,y \in H} P(x,y) = 0.$$

As an $\mathcal{MAP}$ proof to the claim that the polynomial P is in MatrixSum, consider the univariate polynomial $Q(x) \overset{\text{def}}{=} \sum_{y \in H} P(x,y)$. To verify that P is indeed in MatrixSum the verifier acts as follows:

1. If $\sum_{x \in H} Q(x) \neq 0$, then reject.

2. Verify that P is (close to) a low degree polynomial and reject if not. This can be done with $O(d)$ queries via the classical low degree test.

3. Verify that Q is consistent with P. Since both are low degree polynomials, it suffices for the verifier to check that $Q(r) = \sum_{y \in H} P(r,h)$ for a random $r \in \mathbb{F}$.

   Actually, a technical difficulty arises from the fact that P can only be verified to be *close* to a low degree polynomial. The naive solution of reading every point via self correction is too expensive in the case of the MatrixSum property. While it is possible to overcome this difficulty using a slightly more sophisticated technique (to appear in a forthcoming revision), the naive solution suffices for our actual setting of parameters (for TensorSum) and so we ignore this difficulty here.

By setting $|H| = O(|\mathbb{F}|)$ we obtain an $\mathcal{MAP}$ with proof and query complexity $O(\sqrt{n})$ (since $n = |\mathbb{F}|^2$). Using more sophisticated techniques in the same spirit, we obtain both $\mathcal{MAP}$ and $\mathcal{IPP}$ upper bounds for the TensorSum problem.[5]

Parameterized Concatenation Problems. Our techniques for showing $\mathcal{MAP}$s for properties that do not have distance (and a structure that allows for self-correction) differ from the above. One class of problems that we consider is that of *parameterized concatenation problems*. Such properties consists of strings that are a concatenation of substrings, where each substring satisfies a particular parameterized property. The actual parameterization is not known a priori to the tester, and so an $\mathcal{MAP}$ proof that simply provides this parameterization turns out to be quite useful. Given this parameterization, the $\mathcal{MAP}$ verifier can simply test each substring individually (or a random subset of these substrings). Actually, in order to solve the problem more efficiently, the different substrings are tested with respect to different values of the proximity parameter by using a technique known as *precision sampling* (see survey [20, Appendix A]).

Verifying Bipartiteness of Rapidly-Mixing Graphs. Our $\mathcal{MAP}$ protocol for proving bipartiteness of a given *well-mixing* graph $G = (V, E)$ of size $N = |V|$ proceeds as follows. The proof consists of a subset $W \subseteq V$ of vertices that are allegedly on the same side of the graph. The verifier selects a random vertex $s \in V$ and takes roughly $N/|W|$ random walks of length $\Theta(\log n)$, starting at s. The verifier rejects if two of the walks pass through vertices of the set W, where

the lengths of the paths from s to these vertices of W have opposite parities. Indeed, such walks cannot occur in bipartite graphs, assuming that all vertices in S are on the same side.

We show that if the graph is rapidly mixing and far from bipartite, then, for a $O(1/\log(N))$ fraction of vertices $s \in W$, the probability that a random walk starting in s will end in W with odd (respectively, even) parity is roughly $|W|/N$. Since the verifier takes $N/|W|$ random walks starting in s, with constant probability, it will detect a violation and reject. The analysis of our protocol is inspired by [23]. Interestingly, in contrast to the analysis of the rapidly-mixing case in [23], our analysis crucially relies on the random selection of the starting vertex.

Lower Bounds via $\mathcal{MA}$ Communication Complexity. As for our property testing *lower bounds*, we base these on the recently introduced technique of Blais, Brody and Metulef [7]. The [7] methodology enables one to obtain property testing lower bounds from *communication complexity* lower bounds. To obtain $\mathcal{MAP}$ lower bounds, we extend the [7] framework. We show that lower bounds on the $\mathcal{MA}$ *communication complexity* of a communication complexity problem related to a property Π can be used to derive lower bounds on the $\mathcal{MAP}$ *complexity* of Π.

The notion of $\mathcal{MA}$ communication complexity, introduced by Babai, Frankl and Simon [4], extends standard communication complexity by adding a third player, Merlin, who sees both the input x of Alice and y of Bob and attempts to convince them that $f(x,y) = 1$ where f is the function that they are trying to compute. We require that if $f(x,y)$ indeed equals 1, then there exist a proof for which Alice and Bob output the correct value (with high probability), but if $f(x,y) = 0$, then no proof will cause them to output a wrong value (except with some small error probability).

In order to show lower bounds for $\mathcal{MAP}$ we are thus left with the task of showing lower bounds for related $\mathcal{MA}$ communication complexity problems. Fortunately, Klauck [33] showed a strong lower bound for the set-disjointness problem, which we use in our reductions. Additionally, we extend a recent result of Gur and Raz [30] who give an $\mathcal{MA}$ communication complexity lower bound on the classical problem of *Gap Hamming Distance*.

We note that nearly all of the lower bounds shown in [7] are proved via reductions from the communication complexity problems of *set-disjointness* and *gap Hamming distance*. Since these communication complexity problems have known $\mathcal{MA}$ communication complexity lower bounds (cf. [33, 30]), these reductions, together with our extension of the [7] framework to $\mathcal{MAP}$s, gives $\mathcal{MAP}$ *lower bounds for the problems studied in [7]* (e.g., testing juntas, Fourier degree, sparse polynomials, monotonicity, etc.).

Lower Bounds via the Probabilistic Method. Finally, to prove Informal Theorem 4, which shows a property that requires $\Omega(n)$ queries even from an $\mathcal{MAP}$ that has access to a proof of length $n/100$, we use a technique that is inspired by [21], and also uses ideas from [37]. In more detail, we note that $\mathcal{MAP}$s can be represented by a relatively small class of functions. Since this class of functions is small, using the probabilistic method, we argue that a "random property" (chosen from an adequate distribution) fools every $\mathcal{MAP}$ verifier in the sense that the verifier cannot distinguish be-

---

[5]We use TensorSum rather than MatrixSum because we do not know how to obtain an $\mathcal{IPP}$ nor a *full* trade-off between proof and query complexities for MatrixSum.

tween a random input that has the property and a totally random input (which will be far from the property).

Separating Property Testing from $\mathcal{MAP}$. The separation is heavily based on error correcting codes. Recall that a code is an injective function $C : \Sigma^k \to \Sigma^n$ over an alphabet Σ. The relative distance of the code is the minimal relative distance between every two (distinct) codewords, and the stretch of the code is n when viewed as a function of k.

Recall that the complexities of property testers and $\mathcal{MAP}$ verifiers with *proof oblivious queries* are polynomially related (see Informal Theorem 5). Thus, in order to show an *exponential* separation between $\mathcal{PT}$ and $\mathcal{MAP}$, one has to use an $\mathcal{MAP}$ for which the queries inherently depend on the proof. That is, the property Π should satisfy the following:

1. Π can be efficiently verified by an $\mathcal{MAP}$ in which the queries are "strongly affected" by the proof;

2. Π is hard for property testers (and hence for $\mathcal{MAP}$s with proof oblivious queries).

Thus, intuitively, we seek a property that is based on a "hidden structure" that can be tested locally if one knows where to look but cannot be tested locally otherwise.

As a first (naive) candidate, consider the property containing the set of all non-zero strings. A short proof for this property could direct us to the exact location of a non-zero bit, which can then be verified by a single query. However, the aforementioned property is (almost) trivial — as all strings are close to a string with a non-zero bit. Hence, we seek a robust version of this property.

This naturally leads us to consider an encoded version of the foregoing naive property. Fix an error-correcting code C and consider the property that contains all codewords that encode non-zero strings. Assuming that the code is both locally testable and locally decodable, it is easy to test this property using an $\mathcal{MAP}$ that simply specifies a non-zero coordinate of the encoded message. However, this property may also be easy to test without a proof since all one needs to do is test that the string is not the (single) encoding of the zero message but is (close to) a codeword.

To overcome this difficulty, we consider a "twist" of the foregoing property in which we consider two codewords that must be non-zero on the same coordinate. That is, for every code C, we define the encoded intersecting messages property, denoted by EIM_C as:

$$\mathsf{EIM}_C \overset{\text{def}}{=} \Big\{ \big(C(x), C(y)\big) \ : \ x, y \in \Sigma^k, \ k \in \mathbb{N}$$
$$\text{and } \exists i \in [k] \text{ s.t. } x_i \neq 0 \text{ and } y_i \neq 0 \Big\},$$

where we assume that $0 \in \Sigma$. We note that we could have slightly modified our definition by requiring that $x_i = y_i = 1$ (where the choice of 1 is arbitrary) rather than $x_i, y_i \neq 0$. Another notable variant is obtained by requiring that $\Sigma = \{0, 1\}$; then the property EIM_C contains all pairs of codewords whose corresponding encoded messages (viewed as sets) intersect (i.e., are not disjoint).

For the lower bound, we only require that C have constant relative distance and the quality of the lower bound is directly related to the stretch of the code. For the upper bound, in addition to the constant relative distance, we need C to be both an LTC and an LDC with small query complexities. Indeed, the query complexity of the $\mathcal{MAP}$

that we construct is proportional to the number of queries required by the LTC and LDC procedures.

It is well-known that (a proper instantiation of) the Reed-Muller code is both an LTC and LDC with $\mathrm{polylog}(n)$ query complexities, and almost linear stretch. By instantiating EIM with this code, we obtain a property that has an $\mathcal{MAP}$ with a proof of length $O(\log n)$ and $\mathrm{polylog}(n)$ query complexity, but requires an almost linear number of queries by any (standard) property tester.

In order to obtain a result with *constant* $\mathcal{MAP}$ query complexity, we need a code that is both an LTC and an LDC, with constant query complexities. While LTCs with constant query complexity (and almost linear stretch) are known, constructing LDCs with constant query complexity (and polynomial stretch) is a major open problem in the theory of computation. However, we observe that for our construction it actually suffices that C be a *relaxed*-LDC. Relaxed-LDCs, introduced by Ben-Sasson *et al.* [5], are a weaker form of LDCs in which the decoder is allowed to output a special abort symbol $\perp$ in case it is unable to decode a corrupt codeword. However, the decoder is not allowed to abort when given as input a correct codeword.

Ben-Sasson *et al.* [5] used $\mathcal{PCPP}$s to construct an $O(1)$-relaxed-LDC with almost linear stretch. Furthermore, [5] argue that their relaxed-LDC is also a $\mathrm{poly}(1/\varepsilon)$-LTC. However, the LTC property only holds for proximity parameter $\varepsilon > 1/\mathrm{polylog}(n)$. In addition, by combining ideas and results of [5] and [27] we construct an $O(1)$-relaxed-LDC that is also a $\mathrm{poly}(1/\varepsilon)$-LTC *for general values of $\varepsilon > 0$*, albeit with polynomial (rather than almost linear) stretch. We remark that the latter result may be of independent interest.

1.5 Related Works

The notion of interactive proofs of proximity was first considered by Ergün, Kumar and Rubinfeld [15] (where it was called approximate interactive proofs). More recently, Rothblum, Vadhan and Wigderson [37] initiated a systematic study of the power of this notion. Their main result is that all languages in $\mathcal{NC}$ have interactive proofs of proximity with query and communication complexities roughly $\sqrt{n}$, and $\mathrm{polylog}(n)$ communication rounds. On the negative side, [37] show that there exists a language in $\mathcal{NC}^1$ for which the sum of queries and communication in any constant-round interactive proof of proximity must be polynomially related to n.

The study of interactive proofs systems (in the polynomial time setting), of which the class $\mathcal{MA}$ is a special case, was initiated in the seminal works of Goldwasser, Micali and Rackoff [29] and Babai [3]. In the last decade, $\mathcal{MA}$ proof-systems were introduced for various computational models. There is a rich body of work in the literature addressing $\mathcal{MA}$ communication complexity protocols (e.g., [33, 17, 34, 39]). Aaronson and Wigderson [1] used $\mathcal{MA}$ communication complexity lower bounds to show that, for many fundamental questions in complexity theory, any solution will require "non-algebraizing" techniques. In addition, in a recent line of research, the data stream model was extended to support several interactive and non-interactive proof systems. The model of streaming algorithms with non-interactive proofs was first introduced in [10] and extended in [12, 30, 9]. Moreover, Cormode *et al.* [11] made a major step toward a practical implementation of the interactive proof-system of Goldwasser *et al.* [28] for delegation of streaming computation.

Relation to Partial Testing [16]. Independently of this work, Fischer, Goldhirsh and Lachish [16] introduced the notion of *partial testing*, which is closely related to the notion of $\mathcal{MAP}$. A property Π is a said to be Π'-partially testable, for $\Pi' \subseteq \Pi$, if inputs in Π' can be distinguished from inputs that are far from Π by a tester that makes only few queries. As pointed out by [16], an $\mathcal{MAP}(p, q)$ for a property Π is equivalent to the existence of sub-properties $\Pi_1, \ldots, \Pi_{2^p} \subseteq \Pi$ such that $\cup_{i \in [2^p]} \Pi_i = \Pi$ and for every $i \in [2^p]$, the property Π is Π_i-partially testable using q queries.

In our terminology, the main result of [16] is that there exists a (natural) property Π such that every $\mathcal{MAP}(p, q)$ for Π must satisfy that $p \cdot q = \Omega(n)$. In contrast, Informal Theorem 2 shows a different property Π' for which $p \cdot q = \Omega(n^{0.999})$. However, we also show an (almost) matching *upper* bound for our property Π' (see Informal Theorem 2). We also note that Informal Theorem 4, which was discovered following the publication of [16], shows a property for which every $\mathcal{MAP}(p, q)$ must satisfy $p + q = \Omega(n)$; that is, if $p = n/100$, then $q = \Omega(n)$. We note that the latter result also resolves (a natural interpretation of) a question asked by [16, Open Question 1.4].[6]

Applications of our Work and Follow-Up Works. Our work has also found applications in unrelated studies. For example, in the study of *sample-based testers*, Goldreich and Ron [24] used the separation between the power of $\mathcal{MAP}$s and property testers in order to show that proximity-oblivious testers do not necessarily imply *fair* proximity-oblivious testers (where fair proximity-oblivious testers are such in which every query is almost uniformly distributed). Another example is an application for *testing dynamic environments*. Specifically, the separation between the power of standard $\mathcal{MAP}$s and $\mathcal{MAP}$s with *proof-oblivious queries* was used to show that time-conforming testers can be exponentially weaker than their non-time-conforming counterparts (see [25] for details). In addition, following the publication of this work, Goldreich, Gur, and Komargodski [22] improved on Informal Theorem 1 by tightening the separation between $\mathcal{MAP}$s and testers.

Non-Deterministic Testing of Graphs Last, we note that Alon *et al.* [2] discussed the notion of *non-deterministic property testing of graphs*, which was formally stated recently by Lovász and Vesztergombi [35], and further studied by Gishboliner and Shapira *et al.* [18]. This model is a form of $\mathcal{PCP}$ of proximity in which both the proof and verification procedure are restricted to be of a particular form.

Organization

In this extended abstract, we only define $\mathcal{MAP}$s (in Section 2) and give a high level overview of Informal Theorem 1 (in Section 3). See the full version [31] for all proofs and further details.

2. DEFINITIONS

---

[6]Loosely speaking, in the terminology of [16], Informal Theorem 4 implies that for every r there exists a property Π that can be tested with r queries, but every partition of Π into k properties $\Pi_1, \ldots, \Pi_k$, such that Π is P_i-partially testable with $O(1)$ queries, must satisfy that $k = 2^{\Omega(r)}$.

In this section we formally define Merlin-Arthur proofs of proximity. We start by introducing some relevant notations and standard definitions.

A property may be defined as a set of strings. However, since we mostly consider properties that consist of (non-Boolean) functions, it will be useful for us to use the following (also commonly used) equivalent definition.

For every $n \in \mathbb{N}$, let D_n and R_n be sets. For simplicity we use the convention that $D_n = [n]$ (and R_n will usually be of size much smaller than n). Let $\mathcal{F}_n$ be the set of all functions from D_n to R_n. A **property** is an ensemble $\Pi = \cup_{n \in \mathbb{N}} \Pi_n$, where $\Pi_n \subseteq \mathcal{F}_n$.

We say that the string $x \in \Sigma^n$ is ε-close to a non-empty set $S \subseteq \Sigma^n$ if $\min_{y \in S} |\{x_i \neq y_i : i \in [n]\}| \leq \varepsilon \cdot n$. We extend this definition from strings to functions, by identifying a function with its truth table.

Notation. We denote by $A^f(x)$ the output of algorithm A given an explicit input x and implicit (i.e., oracle) access to the function f.

2.1 Merlin-Arthur Proofs of Proximity

We are now ready to define Merlin-Arthur proofs of proximity.

DEFINITION 2.1. *A* Merlin-Arthur proof of proximity *(in short, $\mathcal{MAP}$) for a property $\Pi = \cup_{n \in \mathbb{N}} \Pi_n$ consists of a probabilistic algorithm V, called the verifier, that is given as explicit inputs an integer $n \in \mathbb{N}$, a proximity parameter $\varepsilon > 0$, and a proof string $w \in \{0, 1\}^*$; in addition, it is given oracle access to a function $f \in \mathcal{F}_n$. The verifier satisfies the following two conditions:*

1. *Completeness: For every $n \in \mathbb{N}$ and $f \in \Pi_n$, there exists a string w (referred to as a proof or witness) such that for every proximity parameter $\varepsilon > 0$:*

$$\Pr\left[V^f(n, \varepsilon, w) = 1\right] \geq 2/3.$$

where the probability is over the random coin tosses of the verifier V.

2. *Soundness: For every $n \in \mathbb{N}$, function $f \in F_n$, string w, and proximity parameter $\varepsilon > 0$, if f is ε-far from Π_n, then:*

$$\Pr\left[V^f(n, \varepsilon, w) = 1\right] \leq 1/3.$$

where the probability is over the random coin tosses of the verifier V.

If the completeness condition holds with probability 1, then we say that the $\mathcal{MAP}$ has a one-sided error and otherwise we say that it has two-sided error.

We note that $\mathcal{MAP}$s can be viewed as a restricted form of the *interactive* proofs of proximity, studied by [37].

An $\mathcal{MAP}$ is said to have **query complexity** $q : \mathbb{N} \times \mathbb{R}^+ \to \mathbb{N}$ if for every $n \in \mathbb{N}$, $\varepsilon > 0$, $f \in \mathcal{F}_n$ and any $w \in \{0, 1\}^*$, the verifier makes at most $q(n, \varepsilon)$ queries to f. The $\mathcal{MAP}$ is said to have **proof complexity** $p : \mathbb{N} \to \mathbb{N}$ if for every $n \in \mathbb{N}$ and $f \in \Pi_n$ there exists $w \in \{0, 1\}^{p(n)}$ for which the completeness condition holds.[7] If the $\mathcal{MAP}$ has query complexity q and

---

[7]Without loss of generality, using adequate padding, we assume that there is a fixed proof length $p(n)$ for objects of

proof complexity p, we say that it has complexity $t(n, \varepsilon) \overset{\text{def}}{=} q(n, \varepsilon) + p(n)$.

Note that we defined $\mathcal{MAP}$s such that the proofs do not depend on the proximity parameter ε. Since our focus is on demonstrating the power of $\mathcal{MAP}$s (and our lower bounds refer to fixed valued of the proximity parameter), this makes our results stronger.

3. EXPONENTIAL SEPARATION BETWEEN $\mathcal{PT}$ AND $\mathcal{MAP}$

In this section we show a high level overview of our *exponential* separation between the power of property testing and $\mathcal{MAP}$ (i.e., Informal Theorem 1). Roughly speaking, we show a property that requires roughly $n^{0.999}$ queries for every property tester but has an $\mathcal{MAP}$ that, while using a proof of only *logarithmic* length, requires only a *constant* number of queries.

The proof of Informal Theorem 1 is heavily based on error correcting codes. Recall that a code is an injective function $C : \Sigma^k \to \Sigma^n$ over an alphabet Σ. The relative distance of the code is the minimal relative distance between every two (distinct) codewords, and the stretch of the code is n when viewed as a function of k. (For further background, see [31, Appendix A].)

As discussed in the introduction, the complexities of property testers and $\mathcal{MAP}$ verifiers with *proof oblivious queries* are polynomially related (see Informal Theorem 5). Thus, in order to show an *exponential* separation between $\mathcal{PT}$ and $\mathcal{MAP}$, one has to use an $\mathcal{MAP}$ for which the queries inherently depend on the proof. That is, the property Π should satisfy the following:

1. Π can be efficiently verified by an $\mathcal{MAP}$ in which the queries are "strongly affected" by the proof;

2. Π is hard for property testers (and hence for $\mathcal{MAP}$s with proof oblivious queries).

Thus, intuitively, we seek a property that is based on a "hidden structure" that can be tested locally if one knows where to look but cannot be tested locally otherwise.

As a first (naive) candidate, consider the property containing the set of all non-zero strings. A short proof for this property could direct us to the exact location of a non-zero bit, which can then be verified by a single query. However, the aforementioned property is (almost) trivial — as all strings are close to a string with a non-zero bit. Hence, we seek a robust version of this property.

This naturally leads us to consider an encoded version of the foregoing naive property. Fix an error-correcting code C and consider the property that contains all codewords that encode non-zero strings. Assuming that the code is both

locally testable[8] and locally decodable[9] (i.e., both an LTC and an LDC), it is easy to test this property using an $\mathcal{MAP}$ that simply specifies a non-zero coordinate of the encoded message. However, this property may also be easy to test without a proof since all one needs to do is test that the string is not the (single) encoding of the zero message but is (close to) a codeword.

To overcome this difficulty, we consider a "twist" of the foregoing property in which we consider two codewords that must be non-zero on the same coordinate. That is, for every code C, we define the encoded intersecting messages property, denoted by EIM_C as:

$$\mathsf{EIM}_C \overset{\text{def}}{=} \Big\{ \big(C(x), C(y) \big) \: : x, y \in \Sigma^k, \; k \in \mathbb{N} \text{ and}$$
$$\exists i \in [k] \text{ s.t. } x_i \neq 0 \text{ and } y_i \neq 0 \Big\},$$

where we assume that $0 \in \Sigma$. We note that we could have slightly modified our definition by requiring that $x_i = y_i = 1$ (where the choice of 1 is arbitrary) rather than $x_i, y_i \neq 0$. Another notable variant is obtained by requiring that $\Sigma = \{0, 1\}$; then the property EIM_C contains all pairs of codewords whose corresponding encoded messages (viewed as sets) intersect (i.e., are not disjoint).

For the lower bound, we only require that C have constant relative distance and the quality of the lower bound is directly related to the stretch of the code. For the upper bound, in addition to the constant relative distance, we need C to be both an LTC and an LDC with small query complexities. Indeed, the query complexity of the $\mathcal{MAP}$ that we construct is proportional to the number of queries required by the LTC and LDC procedures.

It is well-known that (a proper instantiation of) the Reed-Muller code is both an LTC and LDC with $\mathrm{polylog}(n)$ query complexities, and almost linear stretch. By instantiating EIM with this code, we can obtain a variant of Informal Theorem 1 with a property that has an $\mathcal{MAP}$ with a proof of length $O(\log n)$ and $\mathrm{polylog}(n)$ query complexity, but requires an almost linear number of queries by any (standard) property tester.

In order to obtain a result with *constant* $\mathcal{MAP}$ query complexity , we need a code that is both an LTC and an LDC, with constant query complexities. While LTCs with constant query complexity (and almost linear stretch) are known, constructing LDCs with constant query complexity (and polynomial stretch) is a major open problem in the theory of computation. However, we observe that for our construction it actually suffices that C be a *relaxed*-LDC.

[8]We say that the code C is a t-locally testable code (LTC), where $t : [0, 1] \to \mathbb{N}$, if there exists a probabilistic algorithm T that given oracle access to $w \in \Sigma^n$ and a proximity parameter $\varepsilon > 0$ makes at most $t(\varepsilon)$ queries. The algorithm accepts every codeword with probability 1, and rejects every string that is ε-far from the code with probability at least $1/2$. For further details on LTCs, see [27, 19].

[9]We say that the code C, with relative distance δ_0, is a t-locally decodable code (t-LDC), where $t \in \mathbb{N}$, if there exists a constant $\delta \in (0, \delta_0/2)$ called the decoding radius, and a probabilistic algorithm D that given $i \in [k]$ and oracle access to a string $w \in \{0, 1\}^n$ that is δ-close to a codeword $w' = C(m)$ for some $m \in \{0, 1\}^k$, makes at most t queries to the oracle and outputs m_i (i.e., the ith bit of m) with probability at least $2/3$. Moreover, if w is a *codeword*, then the algorithm outputs m_i with probability 1. For further details on LDCs, see [32].

size n. The latter can be complemented by restricting the soundness condition to hold only for strings of length $p(n)$ (rather than strings of arbitrary length), since the verifier can immediately reject proofs that have length that is not $p(n)$.

Relaxed-LDCs, introduced by Ben-Sasson *et al.* [5], are a weaker form of LDCs in which the decoder is allowed to output a special abort symbol $\perp$ in case it is unable to decode a corrupt codeword. However, the decoder is not allowed to abort when given as input a correct codeword. We refer the reader to the full version [31, Appendix A] for the formal definition.

Ben-Sasson *et al.* [5] used $\mathcal{PCPP}$s to construct an $O(1)$-relaxed-LDC with almost linear stretch. Furthermore, [5] argue that their relaxed-LDC is also a poly$(1/\varepsilon)$-LTC. However, the LTC property only holds for proximity parameter $\varepsilon > 1/\mathsf{polylog}(n)$. Thus, using the [5] code, we (only) obtain variant of Informal Theorem 1 for limited values of the proximity parameter. In addition, by combining ideas and results of [5] and [27] we construct an $O(1)$-relaxed-LDC that is also a poly$(1/\varepsilon)$-LTC *for general values of* $\varepsilon > 0$, albeit with polynomial (rather than almost linear) stretch. Using the latter result, which may be of independent interest, we obtain an additional variant of Informal Theorem 1.

We refer the reader to the full version [31] for the formal statement of all results and proofs and further discussion.

Follow-Up Work. Following the publication of this work, Goldreich, Gur, and Komargodski [22] improved the separation between $\mathcal{MAP}$s and testers, obtaining a separation for all values of the proximity parameter, with constant query complexity for the $\mathcal{MAP}$s, and nearly-linear query complexity for testers.

Acknowledgments

This research was partially supported by the Israel Science Foundation (grant No. 671/13). We thank our advisor, Oded Goldreich, for his encouragement and guidance. We also thank Oded for multiple technical and conceptual suggestions that greatly improved both the results and presentation of this work.

4. REFERENCES

[1] S. Aaronson and A. Wigderson. Algebrization: A new barrier in complexity theory. *ACM Trans. Comput. Theory*, 1:2:1–2:54, February 2009.

[2] N. Alon, E. Fischer, I. Newman, and A. Shapira. A combinatorial characterization of the testable graph properties: it's all about regularity. In *STOC*, pages 251–260, 2006.

[3] L. Babai. Trading group theory for randomness. In *Proceedings of the seventeenth annual ACM symposium on Theory of computing*, pages 421–429. ACM, 1985.

[4] L. Babai, P. Frankl, and J. Simon. Complexity classes in communication complexity theory. In *Proceedings of the 27th Annual Symposium on Foundations of Computer Science*, pages 337–347, Washington, DC, USA, 1986. IEEE Computer Society.

[5] E. Ben-Sasson, O. Goldreich, P. Harsha, M. Sudan, and S. P. Vadhan. Robust PCPs of proximity, shorter PCPs, and applications to coding. *SIAM J. Comput.*, 36(4):889–974, 2006.

[6] E. Blais. Testing juntas: A brief survey. In *Property Testing*, pages 32–40, 2010.

[7] E. Blais, J. Brody, and K. Matulef. Property testing lower bounds via communication complexity. In *IEEE Conference on Computational Complexity*, pages 210–220, 2011.

[8] A. Bogdanov and L. Trevisan. Lower bounds for testing bipartiteness in dense graphs. In *IEEE Conference on Computational Complexity*, pages 75–81, 2004.

[9] A. Chakrabarti, G. Cormode, N. Goyal, and J. Thaler. Annotations for sparse data streams. *arXiv preprint arXiv:1304.3816*, 2013.

[10] A. Chakrabarti, G. Cormode, and A. Mcgregor. Annotations in data streams. In *Proceedings of the 36th International Colloquium on Automata, Languages and Programming: Part I*, ICALP '09, pages 222–234, Berlin, Heidelberg, 2009. Springer-Verlag.

[11] G. Cormode, M. Mitzenmacher, and J. Thaler. Practical verified computation with streaming interactive proofs. In *Proceedings of the 3rd Innovations in Theoretical Computer Science Conference*, pages 90–112. ACM, 2012.

[12] G. Cormode, M. Mitzenmacher, and J. Thaler. Streaming graph computations with a helpful advisor. *Algorithmica*, 65(2):409–442, 2013.

[13] A. Czumaj, O. Goldreich, D. Ron, C. Seshadhri, A. Shapira, and C. Sohler. Finding cycles and trees in sublinear time. *Random Structures & Algorithms*, 2012.

[14] I. Dinur and O. Reingold. Assignment testers: Towards a combinatorial proof of the PCP theorem. *SIAM J. Comput.*, 36(4):975–1024, 2006.

[15] F. Ergün, R. Kumar, and R. Rubinfeld. Fast approximate probabilistically checkable proofs. *Inf. Comput.*, 189(2):135–159, 2004.

[16] E. Fischer, Y. Goldhirsh, and O. Lachish. Partial tests, universal tests and decomposability. In *Innovations in Theoretical Computer Science, ITCS'14, Princeton, NJ, USA, January 12-14, 2014*, pages 483–500, 2014.

[17] D. Gavinsky and A. A. Sherstov. A separation of NP and coNP in multiparty communication complexity. *arXiv preprint arXiv:1004.0817*, 2010.

[18] L. Gishboliner and A. Shapira. Deterministic vs non-deterministic graph property testing. *Electronic Colloquium on Computational Complexity (ECCC)*, 20:59, 2013.

[19] O. Goldreich. Short locally testable codes and proofs: A survey in two parts. In *Property Testing*, pages 65–104, 2010.

[20] O. Goldreich. On multiple input problems in property testing. *Electronic Colloquium on Computational Complexity (ECCC)*, 20:67, 2013.

[21] O. Goldreich, S. Goldwasser, and D. Ron. Property testing and its connection to learning and approximation. *Journal of the ACM (JACM)*, 45(4):653–750, 1998.

[22] O. Goldreich, T. Gur, and I. Komargodski. Strong locally testable codes with relaxed local decoders. *Electronic Colloquium on Computational Complexity (ECCC)*, 21:25, 2014.

[23] O. Goldreich and D. Ron. Property testing in bounded degree graphs. *Algorithmica*, 32(2):302–343, 2002.

[24] O. Goldreich and D. Ron. On sample-based testers. *Electronic Colloquium on Computational Complexity (ECCC)*, 20:109, 2013.

[25] O. Goldreich and D. Ron. On learning and testing dynamic environments. *Electronic Colloquium on Computational Complexity (ECCC)*, 21:29, 2014.

[26] O. Goldreich and O. Sheffet. On the randomness complexity of property testing. *Computational Complexity*, 19(1):99–133, 2010.

[27] O. Goldreich and M. Sudan. Locally testable codes and PCPs of almost-linear length. *J. ACM*, 53(4):558–655, 2006.

[28] S. Goldwasser, Y. T. Kalai, and G. N. Rothblum. Delegating computation: interactive proofs for muggles. In *STOC*, pages 113–122, 2008.

[29] S. Goldwasser, S. Micali, and C. Rackoff. The knowledge complexity of interactive proof systems. *SIAM J. Comput.*, 18(1):186–208, 1989.

[30] T. Gur and R. Raz. Arthur-Merlin streaming complexity. In *Proceedings of the 40th International Colloquium on Automata, Languages and Programming (ICALP)*, 2013.

[31] T. Gur and R. Rothblum. Non-interactive proofs of proximity. *Electronic Colloquium on Computational Complexity (ECCC)*, 20:78, 2013.

[32] J. Katz and L. Trevisan. On the efficiency of local decoding procedures for error-correcting codes. In *STOC*, pages 80–86, 2000.

[33] H. Klauck. Rectangle size bounds and threshold covers in communication complexity. In *Computational Complexity, 2003. Proceedings. 18th IEEE Annual Conference on*, pages 118–134. IEEE, 2003.

[34] H. Klauck. On Arthur Merlin games in communication complexity. In *Computational Complexity (CCC), 2011 IEEE 26th Annual Conference on*, pages 189–199. IEEE, 2011.

[35] L. Lovász and K. Vesztergombi. Nondeterministic graph property testing. *arXiv preprint arXiv:1202.5337*, 2012.

[36] C. Lund, L. Fortnow, H. J. Karloff, and N. Nisan. Algebraic methods for interactive proof systems. *J. ACM*, 39(4):859–868, 1992.

[37] G. N. Rothblum, S. Vadhan, and A. Wigderson. Interactive proofs of proximity: Delegating computation in sublinear time. In *Proceedings of the 45th annual ACM Symposium on Theory of Computing (STOC)*, 2013.

[38] R. Rubinfeld and M. Sudan. Robust characterizations of polynomials with applications to program testing. *SIAM J. Comput.*, 25(2):252–271, 1996.

[39] A. A. Sherstov. The multiparty communication complexity of set disjointness. In *Proceedings of the 44th symposium on Theory of Computing*, pages 525–548. ACM, 2012.

Arithmetic Cryptography

[Extended Abstract] [*]

Benny Applebaum
Tel-Aviv University
bennyap@post.tau.ac.il

Jonathan Avron
Tel-Aviv University
avron@mail.tau.ac.il

Christina Brzuska[†]
Microsoft Cambridge
christina.brzuska@gmail.com

ABSTRACT

We study the possibility of computing cryptographic primitives in a fully-black-box arithmetic model over a finite field $\mathbb{F}$. In this model, the input to a cryptographic primitive (e.g., encryption scheme) is given as a sequence of field elements, the honest parties are implemented by arithmetic circuits which make only a black-box use of the underlying field, and the adversary has a full (non-black-box) access to the field. This model captures many standard information-theoretic constructions.

We prove several positive and negative results in this model for various cryptographic tasks. On the positive side, we show that, under reasonable assumptions, computational primitives like commitment schemes, public-key encryption, oblivious transfer, and general secure two-party computation can be implemented in this model. On the negative side, we prove that garbled circuits, homomorphic encryption, and secure computation with low online complexity cannot be achieved in this model. Our results reveal a qualitative difference between the standard model and the arithmetic model, and explain, in retrospect, some of the limitations of previous constructions.

Categories and Subject Descriptors

F.1.2 [**Modes of Computation**]: Interactive and reactive computation

General Terms

Theory of Computation

Keywords

Cryptography; computational complexity; arithmetic circuits

1. INTRODUCTION

This paper studies the possibility of solving cryptographic problems in a way which is independent from the underlying algebraic domain. We start by describing a concrete motivating example.

Consider the problem of computing over encrypted data where Alice wishes to store her private data $x = (x_1, \ldots, x_n)$ encrypted on a server while allowing the server to run some program f on the data. Let us assume that each data item x_i is taken from some large algebraic domain $\mathbb{F}$ (e.g., finite-precision reals) and, correspondingly, the program f is described as a sequence of arithmetic operations over $\mathbb{F}$. Naturally, Alice would like to employ a *fully homomorphic encryption* (FHE) [27]. However, standard FHE constructions typically assume that the data is represented as a binary string and the computation f is represented by a Boolean circuit.

One way to solve the problem is to translate x and f to binary form. Unfortunately, this solution suffers from several limitation. First, such a translation is typically expensive as it introduces a large overhead (typically much larger than $\log |\mathbb{F}|$).[1] Secondly, such an emulation is not modular as it strongly depends on the bit-representation of x. Finally, in some scenarios Boolean emulation is simply not feasible since the parties do not have an access to the bit-wise representation of the field elements. For example, the data items $(x_1, \ldots, x_n)$ may be already "encrypted" under some algebraic scheme (e.g., given at the exponent of some group generator or represented by some graded encoding scheme [26]).

A better solution would be to have an FHE that supports $\mathbb{F}$-operations. Striving for full generality, we would like to have an FHE that treats the field or ring $\mathbb{F}$ as an oracle which can be later instantiated with any concrete domain. In this paper we explore the feasibility of such schemes. More generally, we study the following natural question:

> Which cryptographic primitives (if any) can be implemented *independently* of the underlying algebraic domain?

[*]A full version of this paper is available at http://www.eng.tau.ac.il/ bennyap/publications.html. This research was supported by ISF grant 1155/11, Israel Ministry of Science and Technology (grant 3-9094), GIF grant 1152/2011, and by the Check Point Institute for Information Security.

[†]Work done while being a postdoctoral fellow at Tel Aviv University.

---

[1]For example, for the case of finite fields with n-bit elements, the size of the best known Boolean multiplication circuits is $\omega(n \log n)$.

We formalize the above question via the following notion of *arithmetic constructions* of cryptographic primitives.

1.1 The Model

Cryptographic constructions.

Standard cryptographic constructions can be typically described by a tuple of efficient (randomized) algorithms P that implement the *honest* parties. The inputs to these algorithms consist of a binary string $x \in \{0,1\}^*$ (e.g., plaintext/ciphertext) and a security parameter 1^λ which, by default, is taken to be polynomial in the length of the input x. These algorithms should satisfy some syntactic properties (e.g., "correctness") as well as some security definition. We assume that the latter is formulated via a game between an adversary and a challenger. The construction is *secure* for a class of adversaries (e.g., polynomial-size Boolean circuits) if no adversary in the class can win the game with probability larger than some predefined threshold.

Arithmetic constructions.

In our arithmetic model, the input $x = (x_1, \ldots, x_n)$ to the honest parties P is a vector of generic field elements. The honest parties can manipulate field elements by applying field operations (addition, subtraction, multiplication, division, and zero-testing). There is no other way to access the field elements. In particular, the honest parties do not have an access to the bit representation of the inputs or even to the size of $\mathbb{F}$. We allow the honest parties to generate the field's constants 0 and 1, to sample random *field elements*, and to sample random *bits*. Overall, honest parties can be described by efficiently computable randomized *arithmetic circuits*.

In contrast to the honest parties, the adversary is non-arithmetic and is captured, as usual, by some class of probabilistic Boolean circuits (e.g., uniform circuits of polynomial-size). Security should hold for any (adversarial) realization of $\mathbb{F}$. Formally, the standard security game is augmented with an additional preliminary step in which the adversary is allowed to specify a field by sending to the challenger a Boolean circuit which implements the field operations with respect to some (adversarially-chosen) binary representation. The game is continued as usual, where the adversary is now attacking the construction $P^{\mathbb{F}}$. Note that once $\mathbb{F}$ is specified, $P^{\mathbb{F}}$ can be written as a standard Boolean circuit. Hence security in the arithmetic setting guarantees that the construction $P^{\mathbb{F}}$ is secure for any concrete field oracle $\mathbb{F}$ which is realizable by our class of adversaries.[2]

EXAMPLE 1.1 (ONE-TIME ENCRYPTION). *We illustrate the model by defining an arithmetic perfectly-secure one-time encryption scheme. Syntactically, such a scheme consists of a key-generation algorithm* KGen, *encryption algorithm* Enc, *and decryption algorithm* Dec *which satisfy the perfect correctness condition:*

$$\Pr_{k \overset{R}{\leftarrow} \mathsf{KGen}(1^n)} [\mathsf{Dec}_k(\mathsf{Enc}_k(m)) = m] = 1,$$

for every message $m \in \mathbb{F}^n$. Perfect security can be defined via the following indistinguishability game: (1) For a security parameter 1^n, the adversary specifies a field $\mathbb{F}$ and a pair of messages $m_0, m_1 \in \mathbb{F}^n$; (2) The challenger responds with a ciphertext $c = \mathsf{Enc}_k(m_b)$ where $k \overset{R}{\leftarrow} \mathsf{KGen}(1^n)$ and $b \overset{R}{\leftarrow} \{0,1\}$; (3) The adversary outputs a bit b' and wins the game if $b' = b$. The scheme is perfectly-secure if no (computationally-unbounded) adversary can win the game with more than probability $\frac{1}{2}$.

A simple generalization of the well-known one-time pad gives rise to an arithmetic one-time encryption scheme. The key generation algorithm samples a random key $k \overset{R}{\leftarrow} \mathbb{F}^n$, to encrypt a message $m \in \mathbb{F}^n$ we output $m + k$ and to decrypt a ciphertext $c \in \mathbb{F}^n$ we output the message $c - k$. All the above operations can be implemented by randomized arithmetic circuits. It is not hard to see that the scheme is perfectly-secure. Namely, for any field $\mathbb{F}$ (or even group) chosen by a computationally-unbounded adversary, the winning probability cannot exceed $\frac{1}{2}$.

1.2 Our Contribution

Our goal in this paper is to find out which cryptographic primitives admit arithmetic constructions. We begin by observing that, similarly to the case of one-time pad, typical information-theoretic constructions naturally arithmetize. Notable examples include various secret sharing schemes [47, 21, 17], and classical information-theoretic secure multiparty protocols [10, 15]. (See Section 1.4 for a detailed account of related works.) This raises the natural question of constructing computationally secure primitives in the arithmetic model. We give an affirmative answer to this question by providing arithmetic constructions of several computational primitives.

INFORMAL THEOREM 1.1. *There are arithmetic constructions of public-key encryption, commitment scheme, oblivious linear evaluation (the arithmetic analog of oblivious transfer), and protocols for general secure multiparty computation without honest majority (e.g., two-party computation), assuming intractability assumptions related to linear codes.*

We emphasize that our focus here is on feasibility rather than efficiency, and so we did not attempt to optimize the complexity of the constructions. The underlying intractability assumption essentially assumes the pseudorandomness of a matrix-vector pair $(M, \tilde{y})$ where M is a random $m \times n$ generating matrix and $\tilde{y} \in \mathbb{F}^m$ is obtained by choosing a random codeword $y \in \mathsf{Span}(M)$ and replacing a random εm-subset of y's coordinates with random field elements.[3] This Random-Linear-Code assumption, which is denoted by $\mathsf{RLC}_{\mathbb{F}}(n, m, \varepsilon)$,

---

[2] Note that the computational complexity of the field representation is limited by the computational power of the adversary. Specifically, if the primitive is secure against polynomial-size circuits then the underlying field must be implementable by a polynomial-size circuit. This limitation is inherent (for computationally-secure schemes), as otherwise, one can use an inefficient field representation to break the scheme (e.g., by embedding an **NP**-complete oracle).

[3] This is contrasted with the more standard Learning-With-Errors (LWE) assumption [46] in which *each* coordinate of y is perturbed with some "small" element from the ring $\mathbb{Z}_p$, e.g., drawn from the interval $\pm \alpha \cdot p$. Note that in the arithmetic setting it is unclear how to sample an element from an interval which grows with p, and so LWE constructions do not seem to arithmetize. See Section 1.3 for further discussion.

was previously considered in [39]. If $\mathbb{F}$ is instantiated with the binary field, we get the standard *Learning Parity with Noise* (LPN) assumption [30, 12]. Indeed, some of the primitives in the above theorem can be constructed by extending various LPN-based schemes from the literature.

Theorem 1.1 shows that the arithmetic model is rich enough to allow highly non-trivial computational cryptography such as general secure two-party protocols. As a result, one may further hope to arithmetize *all* Boolean primitives. Our main results show that this is impossible. That is, we show that there are several cryptographic tasks which can be achieved in the standard model but cannot be implemented arithmetically. This include garbled circuits, secure computation protocols with "low" online communication, and multiplicative homomorphic encryption schemes. Details follow.

Garbled circuits.

Yao's *garbled circuit* (GC) construction [50] maps any boolean circuit $C : \{0,1\}^n \to \{0,1\}^m$ together with secret randomness into a "garbled circuit" $\hat{C}$ along with n "key" functions $K_i : \{0,1\} \to \{0,1\}^k$ such that, for any (unknown) input x, the garbled circuit $\hat{C}$ together with the n keys $K_x = (K_1(x_1), \ldots, K_n(x_n))$ reveal $C(x)$ but give no additional information about x. The latter requirement is formalized by requiring the existence of an efficient *decoder* which recovers $C(x)$ from $(\hat{C}, K_x)$ and an efficient *simulator* which, given $C(x)$, samples from a distribution which is computationally indistinguishable from $(\hat{C}, K_x)$. The keys are *short* in the sense that their length, k, depends only in the security parameter and does not grow with the input length or the size of C. Yao's celebrated result shows that such a transformation can be based on the existence of any pseudorandom generator [13, 49], or equivalently a one-way function [34].

The definition of *arithmetic garbled circuits* naturally generalizes the Boolean setting. The target function $C : \mathbb{F}^n \to \mathbb{F}^m$ is now a formal polynomial (represented by an arithmetic circuit), and we would like to *encode* it into a garbled circuit $\hat{C}$, along with n arithmetic key functions $K_i : \mathbb{F} \to \mathbb{F}^k$, such that $\hat{C}$ together with the n outputs $K_i(x_i)$ reveal $C(x)$ and no additional information about x. As in the Boolean case, we require the existence of an arithmetic decoder and simulator. We say that the garbling is *short* if the key-length depends only in the security parameter (i.e., can be taken to be n^ε for an arbitrary $\varepsilon > 0$). A more relaxed notion is *online efficiency*, meaning that the key-length should be independent of the circuit complexity of C but may grow with the input length. (The latter requirement is typically viewed as part of the definition of garbling schemes, cf. [9].)

The question of garbling arithmetic circuits has been open for a long time, and only recently some partial progress has been made [5]. Still, so far there has been no fully arithmetic construction in which both the encoder and the decoder make a black-box use of $\mathbb{F}$. We show that this is inherently impossible answering an open problem from [35].

INFORMAL THEOREM 1.2. *There are no short arithmetic garbled circuits. Furthermore, assuming the existence of (standard) one-way functions, even online efficient arithmetic garbled circuits do not exist.*[4]

---

[4]The theorem holds even if the simulator is allowed to be non-arithmetic or even inefficient. The latter case corresponds to an indistinguishability notion of security.

Recall that in the Boolean setting short garbled circuits can be constructed based on any one-way function, hence, Theorem 1.2 "separates" the Arithmetic model from the Boolean model.

Secure computation with low online complexity.

Generalizing the above result, we prove a non-trivial lower-bound on the online communication complexity of semi-honest secure computation protocols. Roughly speaking, we allow the parties to exchange all the messages which solely depend on internal randomness at an "offline phase", and then move to an "online phase" in which the parties receive their inputs and may exchange messages based on their inputs (as well as their current view). Such an online/offline model was studied in several works [8, 38, 11, 19, 37]. In the standard Boolean setting, there are protocols which achieve highly efficient online communication complexity. For example, for efficient deterministic two-party functionalities $f : \{0,1\}^n \times \{0,1\}^n \to \{0,1\}^m$ which deliver the output to one of the parties (hereafter referred to as simple functionalities), one can obtain semi-honest protocols with online communication of $n^{1+\varepsilon}$ based on Yao's garbled circuit, or even $n + o(n)$ based on the succinct garbled circuit of [6]. In contrast, we show that in the arithmetic model the online communication complexity must grow with the complexity of the function.

INFORMAL THEOREM 1.3. *Assume that standard one-way functions exist. Then, for every constant $c > 0$ there exists a simple arithmetic two-party functionality $f : \mathbb{F}^n \times \mathbb{F}^n \to \mathbb{F}^{n^c}$ which cannot be securely computed by an arithmetic semi-honest protocol with online communication smaller than $\Omega(n^c)$ field elements.*

The theorem generalizes to the multiparty setting including the case of honest majority.

Multiplicative homomorphic encryption.

A multiplicative homomorphic encryption scheme is a standard public-key encryption scheme in which, given only the public key, one can transform a ciphertext $c = \mathsf{Enc}_{\mathsf{pk}}(x)$ and a scalar $a \in \mathbb{F}$ (given in the clear) into a fresh encryption c' of the product $a \cdot x$. Formally, we require an efficient transformation T such that, for every messages $x, a \in \mathbb{F}$ and almost all public keys pk, the distributions

$$(c, c') \quad \text{and} \quad (c, c''), \quad (1)$$

where $c = \mathsf{Enc}_{\mathsf{pk}}(x), c' = T(\mathsf{pk}, c, a))$ and $c'' = \mathsf{Enc}_{\mathsf{pk}}(a \cdot x)$, are identical.[5] Two well known examples for such schemes (over different fields) are Goldwasser-Micali cryptosystem [33] and ElGamal cryptosystem [23].

We show that multiplicative homomorphic encryption cannot be implemented arithmetically. Unlike the previous theorems, our proof holds only in a *strict* arithmetic model where the honest algorithms are not allowed to use zero-testing gates and division gates.

INFORMAL THEOREM 1.4. *There are no perfectly-correct multiplicative homomorphic encryption schemes in the strict*

---

[5]For technical reasons, we further require the encryption to be *regular*, meaning that the distribution of a random encryption $\mathsf{Enc}_{\mathsf{pk}}(x)$ of a random field element $x \xleftarrow{R} \mathbb{F}$ should be (close to) uniform over the image of $\mathsf{Enc}_{\mathsf{pk}}$.

arithmetic setting. Furthermore, this holds even if the decryption algorithm is non-arithmetic or even inefficient.

The case of inefficient decryption algorithm corresponds to non-interactive perfectly binding *commitments* with multiplicative homomorphism. Interestingly, the commitments constructed in Theorem 1.1 (which are strictly arithmetic, non-interactive, perfectly binding, and regular) enjoy *weak multiplicative homomorphism*. Namely, only the marginals c' and c'', defined in (1), are identically distributed. So the main issue seems to be *strong* homomorphism, which cannot be achieved arithmetically, but can be easily achieved (for scalar multiplication) in the Boolean setting.

1.3 Discussion

Taken together, our positive and negative results suggest that the arithmetic model is highly non-trivial yet significantly weaker from the standard model. Beyond the natural interest in arithmetic constructions, our negative results explain, in retrospect, some of the limitations of previous results.

For example, [5] show that arithmetic garbled circuits can be constructed based on a special "key-shrinking" gadget, which can be viewed as a symmetric encryption over $\mathbb{F}$ with some homomorphic properties. They also provide an implementation of this gadget over the integers. This allows to garble circuits over the ring $\mathbb{Z}_p$ in a "semi-arithmetic" model, in which the encoder can treat the inputs as integers and the decoder is non-arithmetic. Theorem 1.2 shows that these limitations are inherent. Specifically, we can conclude that there are no arithmetic constructions of the key-shrinking gadget. Similarly, Theorem 1.3 explains the high communication complexity of arithmetic MPC protocols such as the ones from [10, 15, 18, 39].

Moreover, we believe that our results have interesting implications regarding the standard *Boolean* model. Inspired by computational complexity theory [7, 45, 1], one can view our negative results as some form of a barrier.

> **The Arithmetization Barrier:** If your construction "arithmetize" then it faces the lower-bounds.

LPN/RLC vs. LWE.

As an example, it seems that constructions which are based on the Learning-Parity-with-Noise assumption typically extend to the arithmetic setting under the RLC assumption. Therefore, "natural" LPN-based constructions are deemed to face our lower-bounds. Specifically, Theorem 1.4 suggests that it may be hard to design an LPN-based commitment with (strong) multiplicative homomorphism. Since such schemes can be easily constructed under Regev's Learning-With-Errors (LWE) assumption [46], this exposes a qualitative difference between the two assumptions. Indeed, this gap between strong LWE-type homomorphism (as in Eq. 1) which can be applied repeatedly, and weak LPN-type homomorphism which can be applied only a small number of times, seems to be crucial. This gap may also explain why LWE has so many powerful applications (e.g., fully homomorphic encryption [14]), while LPN is restricted to very basic primitives. The weak homomorphism supplied by typical LPN-based schemes was probably noticed by several researchers. The new insight,

supplied by our arithmetic lower-bound, is that the lack of strong homomorphism is not just a limitation of a *concrete* construction, but it is, in fact, inherent to *all* arithmetic constructions. Quoting Pietrzak [44] one may wonder: "... is there a fundamental reason why the more general LWE problem allows for such objects, but LPN does not?" A simple answer would be: "LPN arithmetize but LWE doesn't."

IT constructions.

Another example, for which the arithmetization barrier kicks in, is the case of information-theoretic (IT) constructions. Most of the standard techniques in this domain (e.g., polynomial-based error correcting codes) arithmetize, and so these constructions are deemed to be restricted by our lower-bounds. We mention that, in the area of IT-secure primitives, proving lower-bounds (even non-constructively) is notoriously hard.[6] The arithmetic model restricts the honest parties, and as a result makes lower-bounds much more accessible while still capturing most existing schemes. We therefore view the arithmetic setting as a new promising starting point for proving lower-bounds for information-theoretic primitives.

From a more constructive perspective, instead of thinking of arithmetic lower-bounds as barriers, we may view them as road signs saying that in order to achieve some goals (e.g., basing homomorphic encryption on LPN), one must take a non-arithmetic route.

1.4 Previous Work

As already mentioned many information-theoretic primitives admit an arithmetic implementation. Notable examples include one-time MACs based on affine functions, Shamir's secret-sharing scheme [47], the classical information-theoretic secure multiparty protocols of [10, 15] and the randomized encodings of [36]. Extensions of these results to generic black-box *rings* were given in [21, 17, 18].

Much less is known for computationally secure primitives. To the best of our knowledge, previous works only considered arithmetic models in which the honest parties have *richer* interface with the underlying field. (See below.) Therefore the resulting constructions do not satisfy our arithmetic notion.

The IPS model.

Most relevant to our work is the model suggested by Ishai, Prabhakaran and Sahai [39] (hereafter referred to as the IPS model) in the context of secure multiparty computation. In this model the parties are allowed to access the bit-representation of field elements, where the field and its representation are chosen by the adversary. This allows the honest parties to learn an upper-bound on the field size, and to feed field elements into a standard (Boolean) cryptographic scheme (e.g., encryption, or oblivious transfer). In contrast, such operations cannot be applied in our model.[7] The work of Naor and Pinkas [43] yields semi-honest secure two-party protocols in the IPS model. Security against

---

[6] A classical example is the share size of secret-sharing schemes for general access structure. The situation becomes even more involved when it comes to more complicated objects such as secure multiparty protocols.

[7] For example, in the IPS model a party can trivially commit to a field element $x \in \mathbb{F}$ by applying a binary commitment to the bit-representation of x. This is not possible in our model as x can be manipulated only via the field operations.

malicious adversaries (as well as generalization to general rings and efficiency improvements) were given by [39]. Both works rely on the existence of a Boolean Oblivious Transfer primitive.

Arithmetic reductions.

Another line of works provides arithmetic constructions of high-level primitives P (e.g., secure computation protocol) by making use of a lower-level primitive Q (e.g., arithmetic oblivious-transfer) which is defined with respect to the field $\mathbb{F}$. This can be viewed as an *arithmetic reduction* from P to Q. Arithmetic reductions from secure multiparty computation to Threshold Additive Homomorphic Encryption were given by [25] for the semi-honest model, and were extended by [16] to the malicious model (assuming that the underlying encryption is equipped with special-purpose zero-knowledge protocols). Similarly, the results of [5] can be viewed as an arithmetic reduction from garbling arithmetic circuits to the design of a special symmetric encryption over $\mathbb{F}$.

The Generic Group Model.

It is instructive to compare our arithmetic model to the Generic Group Model (GGM) and its extensions [48, 42, 41, 2]. The generic group model is an idealized model, where the adversary's computation is independent of the representation of the underlying cryptographic group (or ring). In contrast, in our model the *honest players* are arithmetic (independent of the field), while the adversary is non-arithmetic and has the power to specify the field and its representation. These two models also serve very different purposes: The GGM allows to prove unconditional hardness results against "generic attacks", while our model allows to increase the usability of cryptographic constructions by making them "field independent". Perhaps the best way to demonstrate the difference between the models is to see what happens when the ideal oracle is instantiated with a concrete field or ring. In our model, the resulting Boolean construction will remain secure by definition, whereas in the GGM the resulting scheme may become completely insecure [20].

2. TECHNIQUES: NEGATIVE RESULTS

In a high level, our main (negative) results are obtained by reducing the task of attacking arithmetic primitives to the task of "analyzing" arithmetic circuits. We solve the latter problem by making a novel use of tools (most notably partial derivatives) that were originally developed in the context of arithmetic complexity theory. In a sense, our lower-bounds show that *algorithms for arithmetic circuits can be used to attack arithmetic constructions*. Below we give an outline of the proofs of the main negative results.

For ease of presentation, we sketch (in Section 2.1) a version of Theorems 1.2 and 1.3 in the Private Simultaneous Messages (PSM) model of [24], which is conceptually simpler than garbled circuits and general secure computation protocols. Section 2.2 contains an overview of the proof of Theorem 1.4.

2.1 Lower Bounds in the PSM model

The PSM model.

Consider two parties Alice and Bob that have private inputs x and y, respectively, and a shared random string r.

Alice and Bob are each allowed to send a single message to a third party Carol, from which Carol is to learn the value of $f(x, y)$ for some predefined function f, but nothing else. The goal is to minimize the communication complexity. In the standard (Boolean) setting, one can use garbled circuits to obtain a protocol in which Alice's communication depends only on her input length and the security parameter k, and is independent of Bob's input length or the complexity of f. Specifically, under standard cryptographic assumptions, Alice's message $A(x; r)$ can be of length $|x| \cdot k$ [24], or even $|x| + k$ [6]. In contrast, we will prove that, in the arithmetic model, the length of Alice's message $A(x; r)$ must grow with Bob's input.

Let Alice's input $x \in \mathbb{F}$ be a single field element, let Bob's input y consist of two column vectors $y_1, y_2 \in \mathbb{F}^n$, and let $f(x, (y_1, y_2)) = x \cdot y_1 + y_2$ be the target function. We will show that if Alice's message is shorter than n, Carol can learn some non-trivial information about Bob's input. In patricular, Carol will output a non-zero vector which is orthogonal to y_1. (This clearly violates privacy as it allows Carol to exclude $1/|\mathbb{F}|$ fraction of all possible inputs for Bob.) Let us assume, for now, that the parties do not use division or zero-testing gates, and so all the parties are simply polynomials over $\mathbb{F}$.

We begin with a few observations. Fix the shared randomness $\mathbf{r}$, Bob's input $\mathbf{y}$, and Bob's message $\mathbf{b} = B(\mathbf{y}; \mathbf{r})$, and consider the residual polynomials of Alice and Carol.[8] Alice computes a vector of univariate polynomials $A_{\mathbf{r}}(x) : \mathbb{F} \to \mathbb{F}^{n-1}$ which takes her input $x \in \mathbb{F}$ and outputs a message $a \in \mathbb{F}^{n-1}$, and Carol computes a vector of multivariate polynomials $C_{\mathbf{b}}(a) : \mathbb{F}^{n-1} \to \mathbb{F}^n$ which maps Alice's message $a \in \mathbb{F}^{n-1}$ to a vector of field elements $z \in \mathbb{F}^n$. By the correctness of the protocol, we have that

$$f_{\mathbf{y_1}, \mathbf{y_2}}(x) = C_{\mathbf{b}}(A_{\mathbf{r}}(x)), \qquad \text{for every } x \in \mathbb{F}, \qquad (2)$$

where $f_{\mathbf{y_1}, \mathbf{y_2}}(x) = x \cdot \mathbf{y_1} + \mathbf{y_2}$. Let us fix a field $\mathbb{F}$ whose characteristic is larger than the degree of the polynomial $C_{\mathbf{b}}(A_{\mathbf{r}}(x))$.[9] Over such a large field, the univariate polynomial in the RHS of (2) and the univariate polynomial in the LHS are *formally equivalent*, namely, they represent the same polynomial in $\mathbb{F}[X]$. As a result, their formal partial derivatives are also equivalent:

$$\partial f_{\mathbf{y_1}, \mathbf{y_2}}(x) \equiv \partial C_{\mathbf{b}}(A_{\mathbf{r}}(x)). \qquad (3)$$

By the definition of f the LHS simplifies to $\mathbf{y_1}$, and by applying the chain rule to the RHS we get

$$\mathbf{y_1} \equiv \mathcal{J} C_{\mathbf{b}}(A_{\mathbf{r}}(x)) \cdot \partial A_{\mathbf{r}}(x). \qquad (4)$$

Syntactically, $\partial A_{\mathbf{r}}(x)$ is a (column) vector of $n-1$ univariate polynomials that contains, for each output of $A_{\mathbf{r}}(x) : \mathbb{F} \to \mathbb{F}^{n-1}$, the derivative with respect to the formal variable x. Similarly, the Jacobian matrix $\mathcal{J} C_{\mathbf{b}}(a) : \mathbb{F}^{n-1} \to \mathbb{F}^{n \times n-1}$ is a matrix of multivariate polynomials whose (i, j)-th entry is the partial derivative of the i-th output of $C_{\mathbf{b}}(a) : \mathbb{F}^{n-1} \to \mathbb{F}^n$ with respect to the j-th input (the formal variable a_j).

Let us now get back to Carol's attack. Carol does not know $\mathbf{r}$ and therefore she cannot compute neither $A_{\mathbf{r}}(x)$ nor

---

[8]We use bold fonts for fixed value, and standard fonts for non-fixed values which are treated as formal variables.
[9]Since the polynomial $C_{\mathbf{b}}(A_{\mathbf{r}}(x))$ can be computed by a circuit of size $s = \text{poly}(n)$, its degree is at most 2^s and so we can just use the field $\text{GF}(p)$ where p is a prime of bit length $2s = \text{poly}(n)$.

its derivative $\partial A_{\mathbf{r}}(x)$. However, she knows $\mathbf{b}$ and therefore can compute a circuit for $C_{\mathbf{b}}$, which, by using standard techniques, can be transformed into a circuit for the Jacobian $\mathcal{J}C_{\mathbf{b}}$. Carol also received from Alice a message $\mathbf{a} = A_{\mathbf{r}}(\mathbf{x})$, where $\mathbf{x}$ is Alice's input, and so Carol can evaluate the circuit $\mathcal{J}C_{\mathbf{b}}$ at the point $\mathbf{a}$ and obtain the matrix $\mathbf{M} = \mathcal{J}C_{\mathbf{b}}(\mathbf{a}) \in \mathbb{F}^{n \times (n-1)}$. Now, the key observation is that

$$\mathbf{y}_1 = \mathbf{M} \cdot \mathbf{v}, \qquad \text{for some (unknown) vector } \mathbf{v}.$$

Indeed, this follows by evaluating the RHS of (4) at the point $\mathbf{x}$ (and taking $\mathbf{v} = \partial A_{\mathbf{r}}(\mathbf{x})$). Overall, Carol now holds a matrix $\mathbf{M}$ whose columns span Bob's input $\mathbf{y}_1 \in \mathbb{F}^n$. Since $\mathbf{M}$ has only $n-1$ columns, Carol can find a non-zero vector which is orthogonal to $\mathbf{y}_1$ and break the security of the protocol.

Handling zero-test gates.

If the parties use zero-test gates then the functions computed by Alice and Carol are not polynomials anymore. As a result, (3) does not hold since the partial derivative of the function $P(x) = C_{\mathbf{b}}(A_{\mathbf{r}}(x))$ is not defined. To solve the problem we show that it is possible to remove the zero-test gates. Assume, for simplicity, that the circuit $P(x)$ contains a single zero-test gate which is applied to the expression $Q(x)$. Note that $Q(x)$ is a polynomial of degree d which is much smaller than the field. We distinguish between two cases: If Q is the zero polynomial we remove the gate and replace its outcome with the constant 0; otherwise, we replace the gate with the constant 1. This transformation changes the value of P on at most d points (the roots of Q), and therefore, the resulting polynomial P' agrees with the polynomial $f_{\mathbf{y}_1, \mathbf{y}_2}$ on all but d points. Since both functions are low degree polynomials we conclude that they must be equal. The above argument easily generalizes to a large number of zero-test gates.

Some technicality arises due to the fact that the attacker Carol does not have an access to P, and can only compute its "outer part" $C_{\mathbf{b}}$. To see the problem, imagine that $C_{\mathbf{b}}$ contains a zero-check gate which is applied to a non-zero polynomial Q which vanishes over the image of $A_{\mathbf{r}}$. In this case, the above procedure (applied to $C_{\mathbf{b}}$ alone) will fail miserably. We solve this issue by showing that, given a random point in the image of $A_{\mathbf{r}}$, one can remove the zero-test gates from $C_{\mathbf{b}}$ in a way which is consistent with the "inner part" $A_{\mathbf{r}}$. Since Carol can get such a point $a = A_{\mathbf{r}}(x)$ from Alice the attack goes through. The more general setting in which the parties may also use division gates is handled similarly (except for some minor technicalities).

Extensions.

The above argument shows that Alice's communication grows with the length of Bob's input. A stronger result would say that Alice's communication grows with the complexity of the function (even if Bob's input is also short). We can prove such a result via the use of a standard (Boolean) pseudorandom generator (PRG). Roughly speaking, we embed a binary PRG in the function f such that a low communication protocol allows to break the pseudorandomness of the PRG. This approach extends to the setting of arithmetic garbled circuits and general secure multiparty protocols yielding Theorems 1.2 and 1.3.

2.2 Impossibility of Multiplicative Homomorphic Encryption

To prove Theorem 1.4 we show that in order to attack multiplicative homomorphic encryption, it suffices to estimate the entropy of some probability distribution which is represented by a given arithmetic circuit. The idea is simple: given a public key pk and an encryption $C = \mathrm{Enc}_{\mathrm{pk}}(y)$ of an unknown plaintext $y \in \{0, 1\}$, we use the multiplicative homomorphism to construct the circuit $f_{C, \mathrm{pk}}(x)$ which maps a plaintext $x \in \mathbb{F}$ into a fresh encryption of $x \cdot y$. Consider the probability distribution of $f_{C, \mathrm{pk}}(x)$ induced by a uniform choice of $x \xleftarrow{R} \mathbb{F}$ and the internal randomness of the homomorphic evaluator (here C and pk are viewed as fixed constants). If C is an encryption of 0 then $f_{C, \mathrm{pk}}(x)$ is simply a fresh encryption of the zero element. In contrast, if C is an encryption of 1 (or any non-zero element) then $f_{C, \mathrm{pk}}(x)$ is a fresh encryption of a random field element. Intuitively, the latter distribution should have larger entropy than the first one. At this point we employ the algorithm of Dvir et al. [22] which, given an arithmetic circuit f, estimates the *min-entropy* of the distribution sampled by f.[10]

3. TECHNIQUES: POSITIVE RESULTS

Our positive results (Theorem 1.1) are based on three different approaches – outlined below.

3.1 Arithmetic/Binary Symmetric Encryption

One main approach is based on a new abstract notion of *arithmetic/binary symmetric encryption* (ABE). An ABE is an arithmetic symmetric encryption scheme which allows to encrypt a field element using a binary key. That is, while the scheme works in the arithmetic model, the key is essentially a string of bits given as a sequence of 0-1 field elements. Such an encryption scheme allows us to import binary constructions to the arithmetic setting, and can be therefore viewed as a bridge between the binary world to the arithmetic world.

Given, for example, a standard *binary* public-key encryption scheme we obtain a new *arithmetic* public-key encryption by working in a hybrid mode. Namely, to encrypt a message $x \in \mathbb{F}$, encrypt x via the ABE under a fresh private binary key k, and then use the binary public-key encryption to encrypt the binary message k. Conveniently, for this purpose it suffices to have a *one-time* secure ABE.[11]

Similarly to the case of public-key encryption, ABE can be used to obtain arithmetic constructions of CPA-secure symmetric-key encryption, and commitment schemes. In order to achieve arithmetic secure computation protocols, we will need an additional "weak homomorphism property": Given a ciphertext $E_k(x)$ and field elements $a, b \in \mathbb{F}$, it should be possible to generate a new ciphertext c' which decrypts to $ax + b$. (The new ciphertext c' does not have to look like a fresh ciphertext – hence the term "weak homomorphism" – and so this does not contradict our negative results.) For technical reasons, we also require a "simple" de-

---

[10]The min-entropy of a probability distribution D measures (in logarithmic scale) the weight of the heaviest element in D.

[11]Although only one-time security is required, ABE cannot be achieved unconditionally as the message space (the size of $\mathbb{F}$) is larger than the key space which depends only on the security parameter and cannot grow with $\mathbb{F}$.

cryption algorithm (e.g., one that can be implemented by a polynomial-size arithmetic formula or branching program).

ABE based on RLC.

We show that such a one-time secure ABE can be obtained under the (generalized) Random Linear Code assumption $\mathsf{RLC}_{\mathbb{F}}(n, m, \varepsilon)$. To encrypt a message x, sample a random generating matrix $A \xleftarrow{R} \mathbb{F}^{m \times n}$ together with a random ε-noisy codeword y, encode the message x via a repetition code, and use the noisy codeword y to mask the encoded message $x \cdot \mathbf{1}_m$. The resulting ciphertext consists of the pair $(A, y + x \cdot \mathbf{1}_m)$. The private-key is the set of all noisy coordinates, described as a binary vector. Decryption can be implemented by ignoring the noisy coordinates and solving a set of linear equations over $\mathbb{F}$. For properly chosen constants m/n and ε, the system will have a unique solution, with all but negligible probability.

From ABE to secure computation.

Let us explain how to construct secure arithmetic two-party computation from an ABE with weak homomorphism. The construction can be viewed as a variant of the construction of [39]. Recall that a (binary) one-out-of-two oblivious transfer ($\binom{2}{1}$-OT) is a two-party functionality which takes two inputs $a_0, a_1 \in \{0,1\}^n$ from a sender, and a selection bit $x \in \{0,1\}$ from the receiver and delivers to the receiver the value a_x.

We begin by converting a maliciously-secure binary $\binom{2}{1}$-OT into a maliciously-secure $\binom{2}{1}$ *arithmetic* oblivious transfer ($\binom{2}{1}$-AOT) in which the sender's inputs $a_0, a_1 \in \mathbb{F}$ are two field elements. The transformation uses an ABE in the natural way: The sender encrypts the arithmetic messages a_0 and a_1 under binary keys k_0, k_1, and sends the ciphertexts to the receiver; then the receiver uses the binary $\binom{2}{1}$-OT to select one of two keys k_0, k_1.

Next, we convert $\binom{2}{1}$-AOT to Oblivious Linear Evaluation (OLE). The latter functionality takes two field elements $a, b \in \mathbb{F}$ from a sender, and another field element $x \in \mathbb{F}$ from the receiver and delivers to the receiver the value $ax + b$. The construction makes use of the ABE again, this time exploiting the weak homomorphism. Specifically, the receiver sends the ciphertext $c = E_k(x)$, and the sender uses the homomorphism to generate a ciphertext c' which decrypts to $ax+b$. This ciphertext cannot be sent back to the receiver as it leaks information on a and b. Instead, a secure two-party computation protocol for decrypting c' is invoked. Since the input of the receiver is binary (and decryption has low-complexity), such a protocol can be implemented efficiently via a $\binom{2}{1}$-AOT (e.g., via the protocols of [18]).[12] This gives a semi-honest OLE.

At this point, we can use the semi-honest OLE together with an arithmetic variant of the classical GMW protocol [32] to obtain an arithmetic secure computation protocol for general arithmetic functions in the semi-honest model. This protocol can be transformed to the malicious setting using the IPS compiler [38]. To make the compiler work in our arithmetic setting, we need two additional tools: arithmetic multiparty protocol with security against a constant fraction of malicious parties (which can be constructed based

---

[12]For our concrete ABE, one can directly use $\binom{2}{1}$-AOT to securely deliver a re-randomized version of c'.

on [10] or [18]), and a maliciously-secure $\binom{2}{1}$-AOT (which we already constructed).

3.2 Alternative approaches

Let us briefly mention two alternative approaches that can be used to derive arithmetic constructions for some of the primitives mentioned in Theorem 1.1.

Arithmetizing LPN-based scheme.

As already mentioned, existing LPN-based schemes easily extend to the arithmetic setting under the (generalized) Random Linear Code assumption. This gives alternative arithmetic constructions for primitives like symmetric encryption [28], commitments [4, 40], and even public-key encryption [3] and $\binom{2}{1}$-AOT. This "direct approach" is inferior to the first (ABE-based) approach in terms of the strength of the underlying assumption. For example, using the direct approach, in order to obtain an arithmetic public-key encryption, we have to assume $\mathsf{RLC}(n, m, \varepsilon)$ for constant-rate code $m = O(n)$ and sub-constant noise rate $\varepsilon = O(1/\sqrt{n})$. In the case of CPA-secure symmetric encryption, the direct approach requires hardness for *any* polynomial $m = m(n)$ and constant noise ε. In contrast, for both primitives, the ABE-based approach requires only hardness for constant rate codes $m = O(n)$ and constant noise rate ε. While all three assumptions are consistent with our knowledge, the third assumption is formally weaker than (i.e., implied by) the first two.

Arithmetizing Cryptographic Transformations.

Another way to construct arithmetic primitives is to start with some direct construction of a simple primitive P, and then use a standard (binary) cryptographic transformation from P to a more complex primitive Q. For this, we have to translate the binary transformation to the arithmetic setting. Indeed, in some cases, existing binary transformations have a straightforward arithmetic analog. For example, we already mentioned that the classical GMW construction [32] of semi-honest secure computation from oblivious transfer (OT) naturally extends to the arithmetic setting [39]. Similarly, we show that Naor's transform from PRGs to commitments has an arithmetic analog. This provides another arithmetic construction of commitments whose security can be reduced to the RLC assumption.

Interestingly, some binary cryptographic transforms do not seem to arithmetize. This typically happens if the construction inspects some input $x_i \in \{0,1\}$ and applies different operations depending on whether x_i equals to zero or x_i equals to one. This kind of arbitrary conditioning cannot be implemented in the arithmetic setting as x_i varies over a huge (possibly exponential size) domain. As a typical example, consider the classical GGM construction [29] of pseudorandom functions (PRFs) from pseudorandom generators (PRGs). In the GGM construction, the value of the PRF F_k on a point $x \in \{0,1\}^n$ is computed by walking on an exponential size tree of length-doubling PRGs, where the i-th step is chosen based on the i-th bit of the input. It is not clear how to meaningfully adopt such a walk to the arithmetic case in which $x_i \in \mathbb{F}$. Similar "conditioning structure" appears in the Goldreich-Levin construction of hardcore predicates [31], and Yao's construction of garbled circuits from one-way functions. In fact, in the latter case our negative results show that finding an arithmetic analog of the binary construction is *provably impossible*. The problem of proving a similar negative result for the case of PRF, or, better yet, coming up with an arithmetic construction of a PRF, is left open for future research.

Acknowledgment

We thank Yuval Ishai for useful discussions.

4. REFERENCES

[1] S. Aaronson and A. Wigderson. Algebrization: a new barrier in complexity theory. In R. E. Ladner and C. Dwork, editors, *40th ACM STOC*, pages 731–740. ACM Press, May 2008.

[2] D. Aggarwal and U. Maurer. Breaking RSA generically is equivalent to factoring. In A. Joux, editor, *EUROCRYPT 2009*, volume 5479 of *LNCS*, pages 36–53. Springer, Apr. 2009.

[3] M. Alekhnovich. More on average case vs approximation complexity. In *44th FOCS*, pages 298–307. IEEE Computer Society Press, Oct. 2003.

[4] B. Applebaum, Y. Ishai, and E. Kushilevitz. Cryptography by cellular automata or how fast can complexity emerge in nature? In A. C.-C. Yao, editor, *ICS 2010*, pages 1–19. Tsinghua University Press, Jan. 2010.

[5] B. Applebaum, Y. Ishai, and E. Kushilevitz. How to garble arithmetic circuits. In R. Ostrovsky, editor, *52nd FOCS*, pages 120–129. IEEE Computer Society Press, Oct. 2011.

[6] B. Applebaum, Y. Ishai, E. Kushilevitz, and B. Waters. Encoding functions with constant online rate or how to compress garbled circuits keys. In R. Canetti and J. A. Garay, editors, *CRYPTO 2013, Part II*, volume 8043 of *LNCS*, pages 166–184. Springer, Aug. 2013.

[7] Baker, Gill, and Solovay. Relativizations of the P =? NP question. *SICOMP: SIAM Journal on Computing*, 4, 1975.

[8] D. Beaver. Precomputing oblivious transfer. In D. Coppersmith, editor, *CRYPTO'95*, volume 963 of *LNCS*, pages 97–109. Springer, Aug. 1995.

[9] M. Bellare, V. T. Hoang, and P. Rogaway. Foundations of garbled circuits. In T. Yu, G. Danezis, and V. D. Gligor, editors, *ACM CCS 12*, pages 784–796. ACM Press, Oct. 2012.

[10] M. Ben-Or, S. Goldwasser, and A. Wigderson. Completeness theorems for non-cryptographic fault-tolerant distributed computation (extended abstract). In *20th ACM STOC*, pages 1–10. ACM Press, May 1988.

[11] R. Bendlin, I. Damgård, C. Orlandi, and S. Zakarias. Semi-homomorphic encryption and multiparty computation. In K. G. Paterson, editor, *EUROCRYPT 2011*, volume 6632 of *LNCS*, pages 169–188. Springer, May 2011.

[12] A. Blum, M. L. Furst, M. J. Kearns, and R. J. Lipton. Cryptographic primitives based on hard learning problems. In D. R. Stinson, editor, *CRYPTO'93*, volume 773 of *LNCS*, pages 278–291. Springer, Aug. 1993.

[13] M. Blum and S. Micali. How to generate cryptographically strong sequences of pseudo random bits. In *23rd FOCS*, pages 112–117. IEEE Computer Society Press, Nov. 1982.

[14] Z. Brakerski and V. Vaikuntanathan. Efficient fully homomorphic encryption from (standard) LWE. In R. Ostrovsky, editor, *52nd FOCS*, pages 97–106. IEEE Computer Society Press, Oct. 2011.

[15] D. Chaum, C. Crépeau, and I. Damgård. Multiparty unconditionally secure protocols (extended abstract). In *20th ACM STOC*, pages 11–19. ACM Press, May 1988.

[16] R. Cramer, I. Damgård, and J. B. Nielsen. Multiparty computation from threshold homomorphic encryption. In B. Pfitzmann, editor, *EUROCRYPT 2001*, volume 2045 of *LNCS*, pages 280–299. Springer, May 2001.

[17] R. Cramer and S. Fehr. Optimal black-box secret sharing over arbitrary Abelian groups. In M. Yung, editor, *CRYPTO 2002*, volume 2442 of *LNCS*, pages 272–287. Springer, Aug. 2002.

[18] R. Cramer, S. Fehr, Y. Ishai, and E. Kushilevitz. Efficient multi-party computation over rings. In E. Biham, editor, *EUROCRYPT 2003*, volume 2656 of *LNCS*, pages 596–613. Springer, May 2003.

[19] I. Damgård, V. Pastro, N. P. Smart, and S. Zakarias. Multiparty computation from somewhat homomorphic encryption. In R. Safavi-Naini and R. Canetti, editors, *CRYPTO 2012*, volume 7417 of *LNCS*, pages 643–662. Springer, Aug. 2012.

[20] A. W. Dent. Adapting the weaknesses of the random oracle model to the generic group model. In Y. Zheng, editor, *ASIACRYPT 2002*, volume 2501 of *LNCS*, pages 100–109. Springer, Dec. 2002.

[21] Y. Desmedt and Y. Frankel. Shared generation of authenticators and signatures (extended abstract). In J. Feigenbaum, editor, *CRYPTO'91*, volume 576 of *LNCS*, pages 457–469. Springer, Aug. 1991.

[22] Z. Dvir, A. Gabizon, and A. Wigderson. Extractors and rank extractors for polynomial sources. In *48th FOCS*, pages 52–62. IEEE Computer Society Press, Oct. 2007.

[23] T. ElGamal. A public key cryptosystem and a signature scheme based on discrete logarithms. In G. R. Blakley and D. Chaum, editors, *CRYPTO'84*, volume 196 of *LNCS*, pages 10–18. Springer, Aug. 1984.

[24] U. Feige, J. Kilian, and M. Naor. A minimal model for secure computation (extended abstract). In *26th ACM STOC*, pages 554–563. ACM Press, May 1994.

[25] M. K. Franklin and S. Haber. Joint encryption and message-efficient secure computation. In D. R. Stinson, editor, *CRYPTO'93*, volume 773 of *LNCS*, pages 266–277. Springer, Aug. 1993.

[26] S. Garg, C. Gentry, and S. Halevi. Candidate multilinear maps from ideal lattices. In T. Johansson and P. Q. Nguyen, editors, *EUROCRYPT 2013*, volume 7881 of *LNCS*, pages 1–17. Springer, May 2013.

[27] C. Gentry. Fully homomorphic encryption using ideal lattices. In M. Mitzenmacher, editor, *41st ACM STOC*, pages 169–178. ACM Press, May / June 2009.

[28] H. Gilbert, M. J. B. Robshaw, and Y. Seurin. How to encrypt with the LPN problem. In L. Aceto, I. Damgård, L. A. Goldberg, M. M. Halldórsson, A. Ingólfsdóttir, and I. Walukiewicz, editors, *ICALP 2008, Part II*, volume 5126 of *LNCS*, pages 679–690. Springer, July 2008.

[29] O. Goldreich, S. Goldwasser, and S. Micali. How to construct random functions. *Journal of the ACM*, 33:792–807, 1986.

[30] O. Goldreich, H. Krawczyk, and M. Luby. On the existence of pseudorandom generators. In S. Goldwasser, editor, *CRYPTO'88*, volume 403 of *LNCS*, pages 146–162. Springer, Aug. 1988.

[31] O. Goldreich and L. A. Levin. A hard-core predicate for all one-way functions. In *21st ACM STOC*, pages 25–32. ACM Press, May 1989.

[32] O. Goldreich, S. Micali, and A. Wigderson. How to play any mental game or A completeness theorem for protocols with honest majority. In A. Aho, editor, *19th ACM STOC*, pages 218–229. ACM Press, May 1987.

[33] S. Goldwasser and S. Micali. Probabilistic encryption. *Journal of Computer and System Sciences*, 28(2):270–299, 1984.

[34] J. Håstad, R. Impagliazzo, L. A. Levin, and M. Luby. A pseudorandom generator from any one-way function. *SIAM Journal on Computing*, 28(4):1364–1396, 1999.

[35] Y. Ishai. Randomization techniques for secure computation. In M. Prabhakaran and A. Sahai, editors, *Secure Multi-Party Computation*, volume 10 of *Cryptology and Information Security Series*, pages 222–248. IOS press, Amsterdam, 2012.

[36] Y. Ishai and E. Kushilevitz. Randomizing polynomials: A new representation with applications to round-efficient secure computation. In *41st FOCS*, pages 294–304. IEEE Computer Society Press, Nov. 2000.

[37] Y. Ishai, E. Kushilevitz, S. Meldgaard, C. Orlandi, and A. Paskin-Cherniavsky. On the power of correlated randomness in secure computation. In A. Sahai, editor, *TCC 2013*, volume 7785 of *LNCS*, pages 600–620. Springer, Mar. 2013.

[38] Y. Ishai, M. Prabhakaran, and A. Sahai. Founding cryptography on oblivious transfer - efficiently. In D. Wagner, editor, *CRYPTO 2008*, volume 5157 of *LNCS*, pages 572–591. Springer, Aug. 2008.

[39] Y. Ishai, M. Prabhakaran, and A. Sahai. Secure arithmetic computation with no honest majority. In O. Reingold, editor, *TCC 2009*, volume 5444 of *LNCS*, pages 294–314. Springer, Mar. 2009.

[40] E. Kiltz, K. Pietrzak, D. Cash, A. Jain, and D. Venturi. Efficient authentication from hard learning problems. In K. G. Paterson, editor, *EUROCRYPT 2011*, volume 6632 of *LNCS*, pages 7–26. Springer, May 2011.

[41] U. M. Maurer. Abstract models of computation in cryptography (invited paper). In N. P. Smart, editor, *10th IMA International Conference on Cryptography and Coding*, volume 3796 of *LNCS*, pages 1–12. Springer, Dec. 2005.

[42] U. M. Maurer and S. Wolf. Lower bounds on generic algorithms in groups. In K. Nyberg, editor, *EUROCRYPT'98*, volume 1403 of *LNCS*, pages 72–84. Springer, May / June 1998.

[43] M. Naor and B. Pinkas. Oblivious transfer and polynomial evaluation. In *31st ACM STOC*, pages 245–254. ACM Press, May 1999.

[44] K. Pietrzak. Cryptography from learning parity with noise. In *SOFSEM 2012: Theory and Practice of Computer Science - 38th Conference on Current Trends in Theory and Practice of Computer Science, Špindlerův Mlýn, Czech Republic, January 21-27, 2012. Proceedings*, pages 99–114, 2012.

[45] A. A. Razborov and S. Rudich. Natural proofs. In *26th ACM STOC*, pages 204–213. ACM Press, May 1994.

[46] O. Regev. On lattices, learning with errors, random linear codes, and cryptography. In H. N. Gabow and R. Fagin, editors, *37th ACM STOC*, pages 84–93. ACM Press, May 2005.

[47] A. Shamir. How to share a secret. *Communications of the Association for Computing Machinery*, 22(11):612–613, Nov. 1979.

[48] V. Shoup. Lower bounds for discrete logarithms and related problems. In W. Fumy, editor, *EUROCRYPT'97*, volume 1233 of *LNCS*, pages 256–266. Springer, May 1997.

[49] A. C.-C. Yao. Theory and applications of trapdoor functions (extended abstract). In *23rd FOCS*, pages 80–91. IEEE Computer Society Press, Nov. 1982.

[50] A. C.-C. Yao. How to generate and exchange secrets (extended abstract). In *27th FOCS*, pages 162–167. IEEE Computer Society Press, Oct. 1986.

The Hidden Graph Model: Communication Locality and Optimal Resiliency with Adaptive Faults[*]

Nishanth Chandran
Microsoft Research, India
nichandr@microsoft.com

Wutichai Chongchitmate
UCLA
wutichai@math.ucla.edu

Juan A. Garay
Yahoo Labs
garay@yahoo-inc.com

Shafi Goldwasser[†]
MIT and The Weizmann
Institute of Science
shafi@theory.csail.mit.edu

Rafail Ostrovsky[‡]
UCLA
rafail@cs.ucla.edu

Vassilis Zikas[§]
ETH Zurich, Switzerland
vzikas@inf.ethz.ch

ABSTRACT

The vast majority of works on secure multi-party computation (MPC) assume a full communication pattern: every party exchanges messages with *all* the network participants over a complete network of point-to-point channels. This can be problematic in modern large scale networks, where the number of parties can be of the order of millions, as for example when computing on large distributed data.

Motivated by the above observation, Boyle, Goldwasser, and Tessaro [TCC 2013] recently put forward the notion of *communication locality*, namely, the total number of point-to-point channels that each party uses in the protocol, as a quality metric of MPC protocols. They proved that assuming a public-key infrastructure (PKI) and a common reference string (CRS), an MPC protocol can be constructed for computing any n-party function, with communication locality $\mathcal{O}(\log^c n)$ and round complexity $\mathcal{O}(\log^{c'} n)$, for appropriate constants c and c'. Their protocol tolerates a static

(i.e., non-adaptive) adversary corrupting up to $t < (\frac{1}{3} - \epsilon)n$ parties for any given constant $0 < \epsilon < \frac{1}{3}$. These results leave open the following questions:
(1) Can we achieve low communication locality and round complexity while tolerating *adaptive* adversaries?
(2) Can we achieve low communication locality with *optimal resiliency* $t < n/2$?

In this work we answer both questions affirmatively. We consider the Boyle *et al.* model, where we replace the CRS with a symmetric-key infrastructure (SKI). In this model we give a protocol with communication locality and round complexity polylog(n) (similarly to Boyle *et al.*) which tolerates up to $t < n/2$ *adaptive* corruptions, under a standard intractability assumption for adaptively secure protocols, namely, the existence of trapdoor permutations whose domain has invertible sampling. This is done by using the SKI to derive a sequence of random *hidden communication graphs* among players. A central new technique shows how to use these graphs to emulate a complete network in polylog(n) rounds while preserving polylog(n) locality. We also show how to remove the SKI setup assumption at the cost, however, of increasing the communication locality (but not the round complexity) by a factor of $\sqrt{n}$.

Categories and Subject Descriptors

F.1.2 [**Modes of Computation**]: Interactive and reactive computation; G.2.2 [**Graph Theory**]: Graph algorithms

General Terms

Theory

1. INTRODUCTION

Secure multi-party computation (MPC for short) allows a set of n parties to securely compute any given function f on their private data. Ensuing the seminal works in the area [40, 26, 2, 14], the systematic study of the problem over the last decades has lead to great improvements regarding several efficiency measures, such as communication complexity (number of exchanged messages), round complexity, and computation complexity. Until recently, however, essentially all MPC results required all parties to communicate directly with each other over a complete network of point to point channels, or by having access to a broadcast channel. While

[*]The full version of this paper is available at the Cryptology ePrint Archive, http://eprint.iacr.org/2014/615 .

[†]Supported in part by NSF Eager CNS-1347364, NSF Frontier CNS-1413920 and Air Force FA8750-11-2-0225.

[‡]Supported in part by NSF grants CCF-0916574; IIS-1065276; CCF-1016540; CNS-1118126; CNS-1136174; US-Israel BSF grant 2008411, OKAWA Foundation Research Award, IBM Faculty Research Award, Xerox Faculty Research Award, B. John Garrick Foundation Award, Teradata Research Award, and Lockheed-Martin Corporation Research Award. This material is also based upon work supported by the Defense Advanced Research Projects Agency through the U.S. Office of Naval Research under Contract N00014-11-1-0392. The views expressed are those of the author and do not reflect the official policy or position of the Department of Defense or the U.S. Government.

[§]Supported in part by Swiss National Science Foundation (SNF) Ambizione grant PZ00P-2142549.

this requirement may be harmless when the number of participants is small compared to the complexity of the function f, it is highly problematic in settings where the number of parties is a dominant factor[1].

Communication locality in MPC. Recently, Boyle, Goldwasser, and Tessaro [6], building on work by King et al. on Byzantine agreement [31, 32][2], introduced a new efficiency metric called *communication locality* to address such settings. Informally, the communication locality of a protocol is the total number of different point-to-point channels that each party uses in the protocol. The protocols provided in [6] for the computation of any polynomial time function f achieve a communication locality of $\mathsf{polylog}(n)$ assuming a public-key infrastructure (PKI), a common reference string (CRS), and the existence of a semantically secure public-key encryption and existentially unforgeable signatures. An example of a scenario where the complexity of the function may be much smaller than the number of parties, is when securely computing the output of a sublinear algorithm, which takes inputs from a small subset of $q = o(n)$ of parties. (Sublinear algorithms are particularly useful for computing statistics on large populations.) By assuming, in addition to the PKI and semantically secure public-key encryption, the existence of a multi-signature scheme [37, 36], a (certifiable) fully homomorphic encryption (FHE) [7, 8], and simulation-sound adaptive non-interactive zero-knowledge (NIZK) [4, 23], the authors also obtain a protocol for computing sublinear functions, which communicates $\mathcal{O}((\kappa + n) \cdot \mathsf{polylog}(n))$-bit messages[3] and terminates in $\mathsf{polylog}(n) + \mathcal{O}(q)$ rounds.

The solution of [6], however, has the following limitations:

(1) It cannot tolerate an *adaptive* adversary who may choose the parties to corrupt on the fly during the protocol execution; it only tolerates a static adversary who decides on the faulty parties prior to the protocol execution.

(2) It achieves a sub-optimal resiliency of $t < (1/3 - \epsilon)n$ corrupted parties, for any given constant $0 < \epsilon < 1/3$, whereas traditional MPC protocols in the computational setting (without the low communication locality requirement) can tolerate up to $t < n/2$ corruptions.

Our results. In this paper, we first show that by replacing the CRS with a slightly different setup assumption, namely, a *symmetric-key infrastructure (SKI)* [21] where every pair of participants shares a uniformly random key that is unknown to other participants, we can overcome both of the above limitations. Specifically, we construct *adaptively secure* MPC protocols with communication locality $\mathsf{polylog}(n)$ tolerating any $t < n/2$ corruptions. (As mentioned above, this is the optimal number of corruptions that can be tolerated, even in the complete communication setting without the extra requirement of communication locality [26, 15].) Looking ahead, we will show how the SKI can be interpreted as a special type of random initial communication graph which dictates which pairs of players can send point-

to-point messages to each other to start with. The graph is shared but "hidden:" each player will only know the restricted subset of $\mathsf{polylog}(n)$ players it can send messages to and receive messages from.[4]

Next, we show that we can remove the additional SKI assumption at the cost of increasing the communication locality by a factor of $\sqrt{n}$. Both our constructions assume the existence of a family of trapdoor permutations which has a *reversed domain sampler* [18, 25]. This is the weakest known general assumption which is sufficient for *non-committing encryption* [10, 18], and thus for adaptively secure MPC over non-private channels. Such families are known to exists under standard number-theoretic assumptions such as the hardness of the decisional Diffie-Hellmann problem (DDH) or the RSA assumption [18].

We remark that in order to circumvent the shortcomings in [6] we need to develop new and quite different techniques, as the limitations to sub-optimal resiliency and non-adaptive adversaries seem to be inherent in their approach. This can be seen as follows. In [6], the parties elect n *input committees* $\mathcal{C}_1, \ldots, \mathcal{C}_n$, as well as one "supreme" committee $\mathcal{C}$—all of size $\mathsf{polylog}(n)$—in a way that ensures that (with high probability) at least a $2/3$ fraction of the parties in each committee are honest. Each protocol message of party p_i is then secret-shared to committee $\mathcal{C}_i$, which re-shares it to the parties of the supreme committee $\mathcal{C}$. Subsequently, the members of $\mathcal{C}$ compute the output of the given function on the shared inputs and return it to the users (by sharing it to the input committees, which then reconstruct to their associated input parties). All sharings are private and robust so long as the adversary does not corrupt more than $1/3$ of a committee members.

Clearly, the above cannot work if the adversary is allowed to adaptively corrupt parties depending on his view of the election process. Such an adversary might choose to corrupt more than a $1/3$ fraction of the parties in some committee[5] and thus violate the privacy of the protocol. Furthermore, even for a static adversary, the above approach cannot yield an optimally resilient (i.e., $t < n/2$) protocol, as an adversary who non-adaptively corrupts $\lceil n/2 \rceil - 1$ of the parties has a noticeable probability of corrupting $1/3$ (or even $1/2$) of the parties in some committee.

Note that under the additional assumptions of FHE and multi-signatures, [6] obtains better communication complexity for computing sublinear algorithms than directly applying our approach. Improving the communication complexity of our protocols is an enthralling direction for future research.

Other related work. Our result should be contrasted with the work of Dani et al. [20], which provides MPC in the information-theoretic setting assuming perfectly private communication channels with communication complexity of $O(\sqrt{n})$, but only offers security against a static adversary and $t < n/3$ corruptions. For the problem of Byzantine agreement (BA), King and Saia [30] show how to construct a protocol that is secure against adaptive corruptions, and where the communication complexity of every party is

---

[1] Interestingly, recent implementation results report remarkable performance of the state-of-the-art solutions for small instances of the problem such as three-party computation [5] or in a lab environment when broadcast is assumed for free (e.g., [3, 35, 16, 17, 19, 29]).

[2] [31, 32] in fact achieve "almost-everywhere" Byzantine agreement [22], which does not guarantee that all honest players will receive an output.

[3] κ is the security parameter.

---

[4] In fact, one may alternatively state our setup as having the players share an initial hidden random graph, and our result as a reduction from this setup.

[5] Recall that the adversary has a linear corruption "budget" $t < (1/3 - \epsilon)n$ and the committees are of size $\mathsf{polylog}(n)$.

$\tilde{\mathcal{O}}(\sqrt{n})$. This leads to a BA protocol with $\tilde{\mathcal{O}}(\sqrt{n})$ communication locality; their protocol, however, tolerates only $t < (\frac{1}{3} - \epsilon)n$ corruptions (and is specific to agreement).

Another related body of work is on conducting Byzantine agreement and MPC when players are not connected via a point-to-point network but rather via a sparse, public network. This has been studied both in the context of BA [22, 39, 12, 13] and of MPC [24, 31, 32]. These results inevitably only achieve the so called *almost-everywhere* versions of the problems, as the protocols "give up" a number $x = \omega(1)$ of honest parties (and provide no guarantees for them). The interested reader may refer to the full version [11] for a short survey of the corresponding literature.

1.1 Overview of our results and techniques

In this paper we establish the feasibility of secure multiparty computation with low (i.e., $\mathsf{polylog}(n)$) communication locality both for static and for adaptive adversaries corrupting any $t < n/2$ parties. Our constructions assume a PKI and a symmetric-key infrastructure (SKI—see details below). Furthermore, our protocols have $\mathsf{polylog}(n)$ round complexity. In more detail, we show the following:

THEOREM 1. *Assuming a PKI, an SKI, and trapdoor permutations with a reversed domain sampler, there exists an MPC protocol secure against an* adaptive *adversary corrupting up to $t < n/2$ parties and satisfying the following properties with overwhelming probability:*

— *(Polylogarithmic communication locality) Every party communicates with at most $\mathcal{O}(\log^{1+\epsilon} n)$ other parties, for some constant $\epsilon > 0$.*

— *(Polylogarithmic round complexity) The protocol terminates after $\mathcal{O}(\log^{\epsilon'} n)$ rounds, for some constant $\epsilon' > 0$.*

Since we wish to obtain MPC with guaranteed output delivery for all honest players, our bound on $t < \frac{n}{2}$ is optimal.

Next, we show that we can completely get rid of the SKI setup (while still guaranteeing adaptive security) at the cost of increasing the communication locality (but not the round complexity). That is, we show:

THEOREM 2. *Assuming a PKI and trapdoor permutations with a reversed domain sampler, there exists an MPC protocol secure against an* adaptive *adversary corrupting up to $t < n/2$ parties and satisfying the following conditions with overwhelming probability:*

— *Every party communicates with at most $\mathcal{O}(\sqrt{n} \log^{1+\epsilon} n)$ other parties, for some constant $\epsilon > 0$.*

— *The protocol terminates after $\mathcal{O}(\log^{\epsilon'} n)$ rounds for some constant $\epsilon' > 0$.*

In the remainder of this section we summarize our main techniques and provide a high-level overview of our MPC construction. Before we do that, we describe our model in a bit more detail. All parties are connected via a complete network of point-to-point channels. For simplicity, we assume that the channels are secure; however, as we assume a public-key infrastructure (PKI), these channels can be implemented by encryption and authentication [26]. Furthermore, we assume *synchronous* communication, i.e., our protocols proceed in rounds where messages send in any round are delivered by the end of the round. An adversary can adaptively corrupt $t < n/2$ parties and cannot observe whether or not

two honest parties communicated. In addition, our construction assumes a *symmetric-key infrastructure* (denoted SKI), where every pair (i, j) of parties shares a uniformly random key $\mathsf{sk}_{i,j} \in \{0, 1\}^\kappa$ for some security parameter κ. Note that there does not seem to be a direct way of getting rid of the SKI assumption without increasing the communication locality, as the direct approach of using the PKI for fair exchange would require (at least) a round where every party communicates with all other parties to exchange the pairwise keys keys. Removing the SKI assumption without increasing the locality is an intriguing open problem.

SKI as a hidden graph setup. Central to our results is a novel way of interpreting/transforming a symmetric key-infrastructure into a special type of setup, which we refer to as *hidden-graph setup* (HG).

Let $G = (V, E)$ be an undirected graph, where $V = [n]$ is the vertex set and E is the set of edges in G. In slight abuse of notation, we also use E to denote the adjacency matrix of G, i.e., $E(i, j) = E(j, i) = 1$ if there is an edge in G connecting vertices i and j; otherwise $E(i, j) = E(j, i) = 0$. We let $G(n, p) = (V, E)$ denote the Erdős-Rényi random graph on n vertices where for every $i, j \in V$, $\Pr[(i, j) \in E] = p$. We refer to such a graph as a *p-random graph*.

We say that the parties in $[n]$ hold a *hidden p-random graph setup* (p-HG)[6] if, after sampling $G = G(n, p)$, every party $i \in [n]$ is given his corresponding row $E(i, j)$ for $j \in [n]$ and no other information on E. Note that instead of the naïve encoding which would require n bits (i.e., give each party the full vector corresponding to his row in E), we can simply give each party i a vector $\Gamma(i)$ which includes the parties i communicates with over the bilateral secure channel. Thus if party i communicates with q parties, his p-HG setup will be of size $q \log(n)$.[7]

We now show how such a HG can be efficiently (and locally) computed from a SKI: Recall that in an SKI every pair of parties i and j is given a uniformly random key $\mathsf{sk}_{i,j}$. We use this key as a seed to a pseudo-random function (PRF). Parties i and j will use the PRF (keyed with $\mathsf{sk}_{i,j}$) to (locally) compute the random coins needed to sample (i, j) for the graph G; i.e., i and j will use the output of the PRF as coins in a sampling algorithm which picks a bit b to be 1 with probability p. If $b = 1$, then i and j will communicate with each other directly in the protocol and (i, j) will be an edge in the communication graph G. The security of the PRF ensures that the bit b computed as above is distributed indistinguishably from the output of the sampling algorithm on uniformly random coins. Without loss of generality, we will henceforth assume that the PRF keys that parties share can be used to sample as many random graphs as needed[8].

Our adaptively secure construction will make use of several ($\mathsf{polylog}(n)$-many) independent HG's. A sequence of ℓ-many HG's that is indistinguishable from a sequence of ℓ independent p-HG's can be generated as above, by querying the PRF on distinct (fixed) inputs.

---

[6] Throughout this paper we only consider $p = \frac{\log^{1+\epsilon}(n)}{n}$ for some $\epsilon > 0$. Whenever ϵ is clear from the context we might omit p and just refer to the setup as a "(hidden) random graph setup."

[7] In our setting $q = \mathsf{polylog}(n)$ with overwhelming probability, thus, our hidden graph setup is also of size $\mathsf{polylog}(n)$.

[8] Note here, that we can eliminate the need for PRFs by increasing the size of the shared secret key.

155

Overview of our construction. At the heart of our construction lies a protocol for reliable message transmission (RMT) in this communication-constrained setting. Such a protocol allows a sender i to reliably send a message to a receiver j. Note that as we assume a completely connected network, a trivial way of implementing RMT would be for party i to use the point-to-point channel he shares with each $j \in [n]$. However, our goal is to achieve RMT where each party utilizes only a polylogarithmic number of its direct point-to-point channels. Clearly, in such a setting we cannot allow the adversary to know the neighbors of an honest party $i \in [n]$ as this would enable the adversary to "cut-off" (i.e., isolate) party i from the rest of the parties by corrupting all of its neighbors.

This is where the hidden-graph setup comes in handy: Every party will only exchange messages with its neighbors in this hidden graph and ignore all other interfaces.[9] As we show, an adversary who corrupts up to any constant fraction $q < 1$ of parties cannot make the length of the shortest honest path between any two honest parties to be greater than $\log^{\epsilon'}(n)$, for some $\epsilon' > 0$, except with negligible probability. In particular, we show that if G' denotes the graph that is obtained by deleting from G all parties/nodes that such an adversary corrupts, then with overwhelming probability, every two nodes in G' (i.e., every two honest parties) are connected (in G') by a path of length at most $\log^{\epsilon'} n$. Thus, parties can achieve RMT by simply "flooding" the network; i.e., party i will simply send message m, signed under its signing key, to all its neighbors; then, for $\log^{\epsilon'}(n)$ rounds, all parties in every round, will simply forward (the first validly signed) message that they receive to all its neighbors. Since i and j are connected by a path of length $N = \log^{\epsilon'} n$ in G', then after N rounds, j will receive at least one copy of m that is signed under i's signing key and hence will reliably receive the message m. Observe that the above RMT protocol tolerates any constant fraction $q < 1$ of corruptions (i.e., up to $t \leq qn$ corrupted parties) and requires a standard PKI for digital signatures (in addition to the HG). We assume standard digital signatures secure against chosen-plaintext attacks. Further, since the message is guaranteed to reach all honest parties within N rounds, the above RMT protocol can be used to have a message sent to *all* honest parties.[10]

Unfortunately, the above approach only works for a static adversary. The reason is that, while corrupting parties (even adaptively) and learning their setup, does not reveal anything about the hidden graph (other than the neighbors of corrupted parties themselves), the protocol itself might reveal whether or not $(i, j) \in E$ for honest parties $i, j \in [n]$. For example, if an adversarial party i sends a message to another adversarial party j, and j receives this message in 3 rounds, then it must be the case that there exists a path of length 3 between i and j. One might think that we can get around this problem by simply having i encrypt the message under j's public key; this, however, is completely useless in the case when j is corrupted. Another idea might be to have i delay sending its message; however, this too is useless when

i is corrupted.[11] As a result, constructing an RMT protocol for the adaptive-corruption case ends up being much more challenging than in the static case.

The high-level idea behind the protocol for the adaptive case is to sample a new Erdős-Rényi random graph $G = G(n, p)$, with $p = \frac{\log^\epsilon n}{n}$, at *every round* of the protocol. As long as the total number of rounds of the protocol is polylogarithmic, so will be the total number of point-to-point channels that an honest party uses (since in each round, every honest party might speak to at most $\mathsf{polylog}(n)$—potentially new—neighbors). The intuition for choosing a different HG for each round is that any corruptions made by the adversary before round i are independent of the graph selected in round i and hence this would be equivalent to the static adversary case. However, now proving that honest parties can communicate reliably (and that there exists a path of bounded length between any two honest parties) is delicate, constituting the crux of our technical result.

Having RMT, the next step is to design the MPC protocol. Recall that our goal is a protocol with full security (i.e., including fairness) and optimal resiliency (i.e., tolerating $t < n/2$ corruptions) [15, 26]. One idea to achieve this is as follows: Since we have already established RMT between any two honest parties, we can invoke any known MPC protocol Π secure for $t < n/2$ assuming authenticated channels, over the virtual network induced by RMT. Whenever party i is instructed in Π to send a message m to party j, we invoke RMT for this purpose. This approach would give an MPC protocol tolerating up to $t < n/2$ corruptions, but does not work generically (for any protocol Π) in combination with our simulated communication channels.

To see why, observe that in our adaptively secure protocol, an increase of the round complexity implies the same (asymptotic) increase of the honest parties' communication locality. Indeed, since using our RMT, every party communicates with $\mathcal{O}(\log^c n)$ (potentially new) parties in every round $1 \leq \ell \leq D$, we can only afford to run a protocol that runs in $\log^{c'} n$ number of rounds for some $c' > 0$. Thus, in order for the above idea to work we need an adaptive MPC protocol over point-to-point authenticated channels which terminates in $\mathsf{polylog}(n)$ rounds. Such a protocol can be obtained by taking any constant-round MPC protocol that utilizes a point-to-point network of secure channels and a broadcast channel (e.g., the protocol in [1]), and modifying it as follows: (1) transmission over the point-to-point secure channels are emulated by calls to our RMT protocol where the message is encrypted using non-committing encryption, and (2) calls to the broadcast channel are emulated by a (randomized, authenticated) broadcast protocol which terminates in $\mathsf{polylog}(n)$ rounds (cf. the protocol in [28]).

REMARK 1 (STATIC SECURITY). *Our primary goal in this paper is adaptive security. However, in the static security setting our approach yields a protocol with $\mathsf{polylog}(n)$ locality which relies only on semantically secure public-key encryption and existentially unforgeable signatures (as in [6]). The protocol tolerates an optimal number of $t < n/2$ cor-*

---

[9]Note that the adversary might try to send messages to honest parties using all the corrupted parties. However, the honest parties will ignore messages from all parties that are not their neighbors in their hidden graphs.

[10]Note, however, that if the sender is corrupted, there is no guarantee that the message is sent consistently.

[11]Note that we want to use RMT for *every* pair of parties; thus, the adversary might use information on the HG learned in an execution of RMT with a corrupted sender and/or receiver to attack another RMT with honest sender and receiver.

ruptions and assumes a PKI and a (single) hidden graph setup[12] (instead of the PKI and CRS assumed in [6]).

Finally, we show (Section 5) how to avoid the SKI assumption, at the expense of an increased communication locality (but not round complexity)—cf. Theorem 2. In a nutshell, the parties will compute a random graph setup by having each party *locally* decide which of his n point-to-point channels he will use; a channel between two (honest) parties $i, j \in [n]$ is then used only if both parties choose it. By adequately setting the probability of the honest parties' decisions, the resulting communication graph will include an Erdős-Rényi graph which will allow us to use our ideas from the SKI-based construction, with a guaranteed $\mathcal{O}(\sqrt{n} \log^\delta n)$ communication locality, for some constant $\delta > 0$.

2. MODEL, DEFINITIONS AND BUILDING BLOCKS

As already mentioned earlier, we assume all parties share a public-key infrastructure (PKI) as well as a symmetric-key infrastructure (SKI). In other words, every party has a public-key, secret-key pair (for a digital signature scheme); every party $i \in [n]$ receives party j's public-key (for all $j \in [n]$). In addition, every pair of parties $i, j \in [n]$ share a secret key $\mathsf{sk}_{i,j}$. Parties are connected by a fully connected *synchronous* network; however, in our constructions every party will only communicate with $\mathsf{polylog}(n)$ other parties.

We allow up to $t < \frac{n}{2}$ parties to be *adaptively* corrupted by a *rushing* adversary (meaning that the adversary is allowed to corrupt parties dynamically during the protocol execution and depending on his view, and that the adversary is able to postpone the sending of any given round's messages until after he receives the messages from the honest parties, resp.).

We consider the standard simulation-based notion of security for multiparty protocols via the real/ideal world paradigm. In other words (and informally), we require that for every probabilistic-polynomial time adversary $\mathcal{A}$ (that corrupts t of the parties) in a real-world execution of the protocol, there exists a corresponding PPT adversary $\mathcal{S}$ in the ideal world who can simulate the output of $\mathcal{A}$ given only access to the ideal world where $\mathcal{S}$ only learns the output of the evaluated function. We prove our results for standalone security. We refer the reader to [9] for further details on this notion of security for multiparty computation. Throughout, we assume that $n > \kappa$, the security parameter.

Our constructions rely on the standard intractability assumption for adaptively secure multi-party protocols, namely, the existence of a family of trapdoor permutations with a reversed domain sampler [18, 25]. Informally, these are trapdoor permutations with an extra property that there exists an algorithm (the reversed domain sampler) which given an input and output can reconstruct (sample) the corresponding random bits used by the function. This assumption is sufficient for all the primitives used in this paper, namely: Pseudo-random functions (PRFs) [27], existentially unforgeable signatures (assuming a PKI setup) [27], constant-round non-committing encryption (informally, this is encryption which transforms an authenticated channel into a secure one in the presence of an adaptive adversary [18]), and constant-

round adaptively secure MPC over a point-to-point network with (authenticated) broadcast [1] (see below).

DEFINITION 3 ([38, 33]). *A protocol for parties* $\mathcal{P} = P_1, \cdots, P_n$, *where a distinguished player (called the dealer)* $P^* \in \mathcal{P}$ *holds an initial input* m, *is a* broadcast protocol *tolerating* t *malicious parties if the following conditions hold for any adversary controlling at most* t *parties:*

— **Agreement:** *All honest parties output the same* v.
— **Validity:** *If the dealer is honest, then* $v = m$.

Broadcast protocols that assume a public-key infrastructure are usually termed authenticated.

We also make use of the following fact about expected-constant-round broadcast and Byzantine agreement protocols, implicit in [28].

THEOREM 4 ([28]). *Assuming a PKI, there exists a protocol* Π_{BC} *which achieves broadcast with overwhelming probability against* $t < n/2$ *adaptive corruptions, running for* $\log^{1+c}(n)$ *rounds (constant* $c > 0$) *on a complete network.*

3. RELIABLE COMMUNICATION IN THE LOCALITY MODEL

In this section we prove our results for Reliable Message Transmission (RMT) between every pair of honest parties in our communication-constrained setting, assuming a standard PKI (for digital signatures) as well as an SKI, as defined above. The constructions in this section tolerate any constant fraction of corrupted parties; that is, we only assume that the number of corrupted parties in $t \leq qn$, for constant $q < 1$ (arbitrarily close to 1).

3.1 Static security

We first show an RMT protocol that is secure against static corruptions. This will illustrate some of the ideas that are needed for our adapively secure construction.

Setup phase. Recall that we work in a model in which parties share a public-key as well as a symmetric-key infrastructure. That is, in the setup phase, party i receives a private key sk_i for a signature scheme, and every party j receives the public key vk_i corresponding to sk_i, for all $i \in [n]$. The SKI allows for a hidden p-random graph setup (p-HG), with $p = \frac{\log^{1+\epsilon} n}{n}$ (for appropriately chosen $\epsilon > 0$), as explained above. Note that, because in this section we assume only a single shared hidden graph, it is sufficient (in fact equivalent) that the keys in the SKI are one-bit long.

Construction idea. The hidden graph setup ensures that the adversary does not get to know whether party i communicates with party j, unless he corrupts one of them. We show that given such a p-HG, an adversary who (non-adaptively) corrupts any constant fraction q of the parties cannot isolate any of the honest parties. In fact, we show a much stronger property for the graph G' formed by removing (in the hidden graph) $t = qn$ corrupted nodes; namely, that with overwhelming probability (in n), every pair (i, j) of honest parties is connected by a path of length at most $N = \log^{\epsilon'}(n)$, for some $\epsilon' > 0$ which depends only on ϵ. Note that since parties start with a PKI, we only require that honest parties $i, j \in [n]$ are connected by a path of length $N = \log^{\epsilon'}(n)$, for some $\epsilon' > 0$ in graph G'. Parties

---

[12]Instead of an SKI, a single copy of our hidden graph can be represented as $\mathsf{polylog}(n)$ bits held by each party corresponding to the vector of the indices of its neighbours.

can then achieve RMT by simply "flooding" the network; i.e., party i will simply send message m, signed under its signing key, to all its neighbors. Next, each party in every round simply forwards the (first validly signed) message that it receives to all of its neighbors. A formal description of the non-adaptively secure protocol for a sender i to reliably send a message m to a receiver j, denoted by $\mathsf{RMT}_{i,j}(m)$, is as follows. (Let $\Gamma(i)$ denote party i's neighbors in G.)

Protocol $\mathsf{RMT}_{i,j}(m)$

1. Round 1: Party i sends $(m, \mathsf{sig}_{\mathsf{sk}_i}(m))$ to all nodes in $\Gamma(i)$.

2. For each round $\rho = 2, \ldots, \log^{\epsilon'}(n)$:
   - For every party $k \in [n] \setminus \{i, j\}$: If a message (m, σ), where σ is party i's valid signature on m, was received *for the first time* from some of its neighbors, i.e., some node in $\Gamma(i)$, in the previous round, then party k sends (m, σ) to all its neighbors and halts. (If multiple validly signed pairs were received in that round for the first time, then take the first one in a lexicographic order.)
   - For receiver j: If a message (m, σ), where σ is party i's valid signature on m, is received *for the first time* from some node in $\Gamma(j)$ then output m and halt. (If multiple validly signed pairs are received in that round for the first time, then take the first one in a lexicographic order.)

The security of protocol $\mathsf{RMT}_{i,j}(m)$ (stated in Theorem 7) can be argued as follows: If i and j are connected by a path of length N in G', then after N rounds j will receive at least one copy of m that is signed under i's signing key, and hence will reliably receive the message m. Thus we simply need to argue that the above holds for some $N = \mathsf{polylog}(n)$. To this direction, we first prove the following lemma, which implies RMT between i and j for all honest $i, j \in [n]$.

LEMMA 5. *Let $G = (V, E)$ be a hidden p-random graph, and let $\mathcal{A}$ be an adversary who non-adaptively chooses a set of parties to corrupt and by doing so learns all their neighbors in G. Denote by $U \subseteq V$ the set of corrupted nodes, and by G' the subgraph on $V \setminus U$ resulting from erasing all nodes in U. If for some constant $q < 1$, $|U| \leq qn$ and $p = \frac{d}{n} = \frac{\log^{1+\epsilon} n}{n}$, then, for any constant $0 < k < \frac{1-q}{2}$, G' is an expander graph with edge expansion kd (except with probability negligible in n).*

PROOF. Since each pair of vertices in G' is still connected with probability p independently of U, G' is a random graph $G((1-q)n, p)$. Let $n' = (1-q)n$ and $0 < k < \frac{1-q}{2}$. Then, for each $S \subseteq V' = V \setminus U$, $|S| = r \leq \frac{n'}{2}$, we have

$$e_{G'}(S, \overline{S}) = \sum_{v \in S, v' \in \overline{S}} X_{v, v'},$$

where $X_{v, v'}$ is the indicator whether there exists an edge between v and v'. Then

$$\mathbb{E}[e_{G'}(S, \overline{S})] = \sum_{v \in S, v' \in \overline{S}} \mathbb{E}[X_{v, v'}] = |S||\overline{S}|p = r(n' - r)p.$$

By the Chernoff bound,

$$\Pr[e_{G'}(S, \overline{S}) < kd|S|] \leq e^{-\left(1 - \frac{kn}{n' - r}\right)^2 r(n' - r)p}$$

$$= \left(e^{-\frac{\left(1 - \frac{kn}{n' - r}\right)^2 (n' - r)}{2n}}\right)^{rd} = \left(e^{-\frac{\left(\frac{n' - r}{n} - k\right)^2}{2 \cdot \frac{n' - r}{n}}}\right)^{rd}.$$

Since $0 < r < \frac{n'}{2}$, we have

$$\frac{1 - q}{2} = \frac{n'}{2n} \leq \frac{n' - r}{n} \leq \frac{n'}{n} = 1 - q < 1.$$

Thus,

$$\frac{\left(\frac{n' - r}{n} - k\right)^2}{2 \cdot \frac{n' - r}{n}} \geq \frac{1}{2} \cdot \left(\frac{1 - q}{2} - k\right)^2 = c > 0.$$

For $d = \log^{1+\epsilon} n$, we have

$$\Pr[e_{G'}(S, \overline{S}) < kd|S|] \leq \left(e^{-c}\right)^{rd} = \left(\frac{1}{n^{c' \log^\epsilon n}}\right)^r,$$

and by the union bound, the probability that $e_{G'}(S, \overline{S}) < kd|S|$ for some subset S, $|S| \leq |V'|/2$ is bounded by

$$\sum_{r=1}^{\frac{n'}{2}} \sum_{S, |S| = r} \Pr[e_{G'}(S, \overline{S}) < kd|S|] \leq \sum_{r=1}^{\frac{n'}{2}} \binom{n'}{r} \left(\frac{1}{n^{c' \log^\epsilon n}}\right)^r$$

$$< \frac{\frac{1}{n^{c' \log^\epsilon n - 1}}}{1 - \frac{1}{n^{c' \log^\epsilon n - 1}}} = \lambda(n),$$

where $\lambda(n)$ represents a function that is negligible in n. Therefore, G' is an expander with edge expansion kd with overwhelming probability. $\square$

The next corollary follows immediately from Lemma 5, by using the fact that an expander graph as above has polylogarithmic diameter except with negligible probability. We make use of the following intuitive terminology: for a given graph $G = ([n], E)$ we say that two parties i and j in $[n]$ are G-*connected by an honest path of length* ℓ if there exists a sequence of connected nodes $\mathsf{PATH}(i, j)$ from i to j in G such that for every node $k \in \mathsf{PATH}(i, j)$, node k is honest, and $|\mathsf{PATH}(i, j)| = \ell$.

COROLLARY 6. *Let $\epsilon > 0$, $p = \frac{\log^{1+\epsilon} n}{n}$, and G be a hidden p-random graph. For any adversary who (non-adaptively) corrupts at most $t = qn$ parties, the following holds except with negligible (in n) probability: there exists some $\epsilon' > 0$ which depends only on ϵ such that any two honest parties are G-connected by an honest path of length at most $\log^{\epsilon'}(n)$.*

The security of protocol $\mathsf{RMT}_{i,j}(m)$ follows now easily from the above corollary, as no matter how the (static) adversary chooses the corrupted parties he cannot increase the diameter of the graph defined by the honest parties and the hidden graph setup to more than $\mathsf{polylog}(n)$.

THEOREM 7. *Let $0 < q < 1$, and $T \subset [n]$ be the set of (non-adaptively) corrupted parties, $|T| = t \leq qn$. Assuming a PKI and an SKI, then $\mathsf{RMT}_{i,j}$ is a secure RMT protocol between any two honest nodes $i, j \in [n] \setminus T$ satisfying the following two conditions with overwhelming probability:*

1. *Every party communicates with at most $\mathcal{O}(\log^{1+\epsilon} n)$ other parties;*

2. *the protocol terminates after $\mathcal{O}(\log^{\epsilon'} n)$ rounds, $\epsilon' > 0$.*

PROOF. Since Lemma 5 shows that any message sent by an honest i will reach every honest j within $\mathcal{O}(\log^{\epsilon'}(n))$ rounds, it follows from the unforgeability property of the signature scheme that j will always accept the message sent by honest i. Hence, the above protocol is a secure RMT protocol. The communication locality of the protocol follows from the degree of $G = G(n, p)$ which is $\mathcal{O}(\log^{1+\epsilon} n)$, except with negligible probability. $\square$

Parallel composition of RMT. In our MPC construction, we will require all nodes to execute their respective RMT protocols in parallel (simultaneously). That is, let $m_{i,j}$ be the message that node i wishes to send to j via the RMT protocol, denoted $\mathsf{RMT}_{i,j}(m_{i,j})$ as above. Now, let $\mathsf{RMT}_{\mathsf{all}}(\mathbf{m})$ denote the protocol executed by all parties when $\mathsf{RMT}_{i,j}(m_{i,j})$ for all $i, j \in [n]$ are executed in parallel. (That is, in round k of $\mathsf{RMT}_{\mathsf{all}}(\mathbf{m})$, all parties execute the kth round of protocol $\mathsf{RMT}_{i,j}(m_{i,j})$, for all $i, j \in [n]$). $\mathsf{RMT}_{\mathsf{all}}(\cdot)$ is composed of n^2 individual RMT protocols. We have the following corollary.

COROLLARY 8. *For all honest $i, j \in [n]$, $\mathsf{RMT}_{\mathsf{all}}(\mathbf{m})$ is a reliable message transmission protocol for sending $m_{i,j}$ from i to j, satisfying the following properties:*

1. *Every party communicates with at most $\mathcal{O}(\log^{1+\epsilon} n)$ other parties in the protocol.*

2. *The protocol terminates in $\mathcal{O}(\log^{\epsilon'} n)$ rounds, $\epsilon' > 0$.*

PROOF. From Lemma 5 we have that any message sent by any honest i will reach every honest j within $\mathcal{O}(\log^{\epsilon'} n)$ rounds. Hence, from this and the unforgeability of the underlying signature scheme, it follows by a standard hybrid argument that every honest j will always accept the message sent by any honest i at the end of $\mathsf{RMT}_{\mathsf{all}}(\mathbf{m})$. Furthermore, note that the protocol's round complexity is equal to the maximum round complexity of its components, which equals $\mathcal{O}(\log^{\epsilon'} n)$. Further, note that the communication locality of every party in $\mathsf{RMT}_{\mathsf{all}}(\mathbf{m})$ is equal to the communication locality of the party in $\mathsf{RMT}_{i,j}(m_{i,j})$, for any $i, j \in [n]$. Hence, the corollary follows. $\square$

3.2 Adaptively secure RMT

As discussed in the Section 1.1 the above proof technique fails against adaptive adversaries. Informally, the issue is that an adversary can use the round in which a corrupted party/relayer receives a message to deduce information on the communication graph (see Section 1.1 for more details and a concrete example). In this section we describe an RMT protocol that is secure against such an *adaptive* adversary. The idea is have the parties use a different, independent communication graph for each round in the transmission scheme. As long as the transmission scheme does not have more than $\mathsf{polylog}(n)$ rounds and in each round, every party communicates with at most $\mathsf{polylog}(n)$ (additional) parties, the overall locality with be $\mathsf{polylog}(n)$.

The main challenge in the above idea is to prove that in this dynamically updated communication graph, the message will reach each recipient through an honest path in at most $\mathsf{polylog}(n)$ rounds. Proving this constitute the main technical contribution of our work. The (adaptively secure) RMT protocol AdRMT is similar to the protocol in the static case, except that in round ρ parties forward messages received in the previous round to their neighbours in the communication graph G_ρ. We first describe the corresponding setup that it requires.

Setup phase. As in the static case, the parties share both a PKI and an SKI. The SKI will be used here in the same spirit, except that instead of generating one Erdős-Rényi

graph, $G = G(n, p)$ with $p = \frac{\log^\epsilon n}{n}$, it will be used to generate D such graphs, denoted $\tilde{\mathcal{G}} = (G_1, \ldots, G_D)$. These graphs can be sampled using the same PRF key $\mathsf{sk}_{i,j}$ that parties i and j share. As before, every node only knows its own neighbors, and when the adversary corrupts a node j, he only learns j's neighbors in $G_1, \ldots, G_D$.

The protocol is described below, followed by security statement and a high-level description of its proof. (The formal proof can be found in the full version.)

Protocol $\mathsf{AdRMT}_{i,j}(m)$

1. Round 1: Party i sends $(m, \mathsf{sig}_{\mathsf{sk}_i}(m))$ to all its neighbors in graph G_1.

2. For each round $\rho = 2, \ldots, \log^{\epsilon'}(n)$:
   - For every party $k \in [n] \setminus \{i, j\}$: If a message (m, σ), where σ is party i's valid signature on m was received *for the first time* from some of its neighbours in $G_{\rho-1}$ in the previous round, then party k sends (m, σ) to all its neighbors in graph G_ρ and halts. (If multiple validly signed pairs were received in that round for the first time, then take the first one in a lexicographic order.)
   - For receiver j: If a message (m, σ), where σ is party i's valid signature on m is received *for the first time* from some of party j's neighbours in G_ρ, then output m and halt. (If more than one validly signed pair is received in that round for the first time, then take the first one in a lexicographic order.)

THEOREM 9. *Let $T \subset [n]$ be the set of adaptively corrupted parties, $|T| = t \leq qn$, for any constant $0 < q < 1$. Assuming a PKI and an SKI, protocol $\mathsf{AdRMT}_{i,j}(m)$ is a secure RMT protocol between any two honest nodes $i, j \in [n] \setminus T$, satisfying the following two properties with overwhelming probability:*

1. *Every party communicates with at most $\mathcal{O}(\log^{1+\epsilon} n)$ other parties.*

2. *The protocol terminates in $\mathcal{O}(\log^{\epsilon'} n)$ rounds, $\epsilon' > 0$.*

Proof idea. As in the static case, we show that there exists a path of length at most $\mathcal{O}(\log^{\epsilon'}(n))$ between any two honest nodes $i, j \in [n]$ when we consider the collection of communication graphs $\mathcal{G}$ that selects graph G_i as the communication graph in hop i. We prove this in three steps:

First, we prove that at every step of the protocol, even if an adversary corrupts a constant fraction of the nodes in the random graph, the honest neighbors of any set S of size $\leq \frac{n}{d}$ that are not in S, will be at least of size $kd|S|$, for some appropriate constant k (except with negligible probability). More concretely, in the full version, we prove the following lemma, where we let $\epsilon > 0, 0 < q < 1$ be constants, $d = \log^{1+\epsilon} n$, $p = \frac{d}{n} = \frac{\log^{1+\epsilon} n}{n}$, and $D = O(\log n)$.

LEMMA 10. *Let $G = G(n, p)$ be graph on $V = [n]$, and $U \subseteq V$, $|U| \leq qn$, chosen adaptively while only learning edges connecting to U. Let G' be the induced subgraph on $V' = V \setminus U$. Then, for any constant $0 < k < \frac{1-q}{2}$, there exists a constant $c > 0$ such that, for sufficiently large n and for any $S \subseteq V'$ with $|S| = r \leq \frac{n}{d} = \frac{1}{p}$, the set of all neighbors of S that are not in S, $\Gamma(S)$, has size at least $kd|S|$ except with negligible probability $P_r = \left(\frac{1}{n^{c \log^\epsilon n}}\right)^r$.*

Next, via an application of Hoeffding's inequality, we prove that as long as the adversarial set of parties (of size at most qn for some constant $0 < q < 1$) are chosen independently of the random neighbors chosen by any party, a constant fraction of the party's neighbors will be honest, except with negligible probability. Thus, we get:

LEMMA 11. *Let $V = [n]$ and $\mathcal{U} \subseteq V$, $|\mathcal{U}| = m$, be a subset chosen uniformly at random. Let $0 < q < 1$ be a constant and $U \subseteq V$, $|U| = qn$, be a subset chosen independently of C. Then, for all $0 < \delta < 1 - q$, $|C \setminus U| > (1 - q - \delta)m$ except with probability $e^{-2m\delta^2}$. In particular, for $m = \log^{1+\epsilon'} n$, $|C \setminus U| > \left(\frac{1-q}{2}\right)m$ except with negligible probability. Further, for $q = \frac{1}{2} - \epsilon$, $|C \setminus U| > \frac{1}{2}m$ except with negligible probability.*

Finally, using Lemmas 10 and 11, we show that even when an adaptive adversary corrupts parties in every round of the protocol, if the parties select a random graph at each round of the protocol, there exists a path of length at most $D = \mathcal{O}(\log n)$ between any two honest nodes in $[n]$. Formally:

LEMMA 12. *Let $G_1, \ldots, G_D$ be graphs on $V = [n]$ constructed independently as $G(n, p)$. Let $U_1, U_2, \ldots, U_D \subseteq V$ be disjoint subsets with $U = \cup_{i=j}^{D} U_j$ such that $|U| = qn$ where U_j is chosen independently from $G_{j+1}, \ldots, G_D$, but adaptively, after learning the neighbors of U_i in G_i for $i \le j$. Let G_i' be the induced subgraph on $V_i = V \setminus (\cup_{j=1}^{i} U_j)$. Then, except with negligible probability, any pair of vertices $v, v' \in V' = V \setminus U$ are reachable with respect to $\mathcal{G}' = (G_1', \ldots, G_D')$ by a path of length at most D.*

Combining these gives us our main theorem (Theorem 9). □

Parallel composition of adaptively secure RMT. Once again, we will require all nodes $i, j \in [n]$ to execute their respective RMT protocols in parallel simultaneously. Let $\mathsf{AdRMT}_{\mathtt{all}}(\mathbf{m})$ denote the protocol executed by all parties when $\mathsf{AdRMT}_{i,j}(m_{i,j})$ for all $i, j \in [n]$ are executed in parallel. That is, in round k of $\mathsf{AdRMT}_{\mathtt{all}}(\mathbf{m})$, all parties execute the kth round of protocol $\mathsf{AdRMT}_{i,j}(m_{i,j})$ (for all $i, j \in [n]$). Note that the graph G_k used in the kth round of the protocol depends only on the round k and not on i and j; hence, we use the same graph G_k to send all the messages of protocol $\mathsf{AdRMT}_{\mathtt{all}}(\mathbf{m})$. We have the following corollary:

COROLLARY 13. *For all honest $i, j \in [n]$, $\mathsf{AdRMT}_{\mathtt{all}}(\mathbf{m})$ is a reliable message transmission protocol for sending $m_{i,j}$ from i to j, satisfying the following properties:*

1. *Every party communicates with at most $\mathcal{O}(\log^{1+\epsilon} n)$ other parties in the protocol.*
2. *The protocol terminates in $\mathcal{O}(\log^{\epsilon'} n)$ rounds, $\epsilon' > 0$.*

The proof of this corollary is similar to Corollary 8's.

4. SECURE MULTI-PARTY COMPUTATION WITH LOW COMMUNICATION

We are now ready to describe our MPC protocol for securely evaluating any given (even reactive) n-party function in the comunication-locality model. Our protocol is secure against $t < n/2$ adaptive corruptions. The idea behind our MPC protocol is to use a constant-round adaptively secure MPC protocol for $t < n/2$ working over point-to-point secure channels and broadcast (e.g., [1]), where those resources are emulated via our RMT protocol of Section 3.2.

We let Π_{BC} denote the authenticated broadcast protocol guaranteed by Theorem 4 (Section 2). The protocol achieves broadcast with overwhelming probability against $t < n/2$ adaptive corruptions, running for $\log^{1+c} n$ rounds on a complete network, for some constant $c > 0$. As pointed out in [28], assuming unique process and message ID's as in [34], Π_{BC} remains secure under parallel composition.

Let Π_{BC}^* denote the protocol which results by having the parties execute Π_{BC} where in each round instead of using the point-to-point channels for exchanging their messages, the parties invoke $\mathsf{AdRMT}_{\mathtt{all}}$ from Section 3.2. Then it follows immediately from the security of $\mathsf{AdRMT}_{\mathtt{all}}$ (Corollary 13) and the fact that each message transmission requires $\mathsf{polylog}(n)$ rounds that protocol Π_{BC}^* is also a secure broadcast protocol with polylogarithmic round complexity and communication locality.

LEMMA 14. *Protocol Π_{BC}^* described above achieves broadcast against $t < n/2$ adaptive corruptions and satisfies the following conditions with overwhelming probability:*

1. *Every party communicaties with at most $\mathcal{O}(\log^{1+\epsilon} n)$ parties.*
2. *The protocol terminates in $\mathcal{O}(\log^{\epsilon'} n)$ rounds, $\epsilon' > 0$.*

PROOF. The security of Π_{BC}^* follows directly from the security of protocols Π_{BC} and $\mathsf{AdRMT}_{\mathtt{all}}$. The (asymptotic) round complexity is computed as follows: for each round ℓ of Π_{BC}, protocol Π_{BC}^* executes $\mathsf{AdRMT}_{\mathtt{all}}$ to have the parties exchange their round ℓ messages; thus, for each round in Π_{BC} we need $\mathcal{O}(\log^{\epsilon''} n)$ rounds in Π_{BC}^*. Because Π_{BC} runs in $\mathcal{O}(\log^{\epsilon'} n)$ rounds, the total round complexity of Π_{BC}^* is $\mathcal{O}(\log^{\epsilon'+\epsilon''} n)$ rounds. We next argue the communication locality: With overwhelming probability, in each round of Π_{BC}^*, every party might communicate with at most to $\mathcal{O}(\log^{1+\epsilon} n)$ (potentially different) parties (for executing $\mathsf{AdRMT}_{\mathtt{all}}$). Thus, since the total number of rounds is $\mathcal{O}(\log^{\epsilon'+\epsilon''} n)$, then with overwhelming probability (by the union bound) the total number of parties that each $i \in [n]$ exchanges messages with using the point-to-point channels is $\mathcal{O}(\log^{1+\epsilon+\epsilon'+\epsilon''} n)$. □

The next step is to construct a *secure* message transmission protocol (SMT) which allows a sender i to securely (i.e., authentically and privately) send a message $m_{i,j}$ to a receiver j. Since we have a PKI and an adaptively secure broadcast protocol, we can use the standard reduction of secure channels to broadcast: The sender i encrypts $m_{i,j}$ under the receiver's public key and broadcasts the corresponding ciphertext $c_{i,j}$. Upon receiving $c_{i,j}$, party j decrypts it using his secret key and recovers $m_{i,j}$. However, for the above reduction to be secure (in a simulation-based manner) against an adaptive adversary, we must ensure that a simulator can "open" a ciphertext to any message of its choice. This can be achieved by the use of a *non-committing encryption* for computing $c_{i,j}$ [10]. As proved in [18] constant-round non-committing encryption can be constructed assuming the existence of families of trapdoor permutations with a reversed domain sampler. We use $\mathsf{AdSMT}_{i,j}$ to denote the above SMT protocol, and $\mathsf{AdSMT}_{\mathtt{all}}$ to denote the protocol composed of n^2 individual $\mathsf{AdSMT}_{i,j}(m_{i,j})$ protocols (for all $i, j \in [n]$), run in parallel, where $\mathbf{m} = (m_{1,1}, m_{1,2}, \ldots, m_{nn})$. We now prove Theorem 1.

PROOF. Let Π_{MPC} denote a constant-round MPC protocol which is secure against adaptive corruptions of up to

$t < n/2$ parties, where parties communicate over a complete network of point-to-point channels and broadcast. (Such protocols are known to exist under the assumption in the theorem, e.g., [1].) Furthermore, let Π_{MPC}^* denote the protocol that results by instantiating in Π_{MPC} the calls to the secure channels and broadcast by invocations of protocols Π_{BC}^* and AdSMT, respectively. We argue that Π_{MPC}^* satisfies all the properties claimed in the theorem. The security of Π_{MPC}^* follows immediately from the security of the underlying protocol Π_{MPC} and the security of protocols Π_{BC}^* and $\text{AdSMT}_{\text{all}}$. For the round complexity: For each round in Π_{MPC}, all message exchanges (i.e., point-to-point transmissions or broadcast calls) are exchanged in Π_{MPC}^* by appropriate (parallel) executions of protocols Π_{BC}^* and $\text{AdSMT}_{\text{all}}$, where the executions have unique round, protocol, and message IDs.[13] Thus, for every round in Π_{MPC} we need $\mathcal{O}(\log^{\epsilon'} n)$ rounds in Π_{MPC}^*, for some given constant $\epsilon' > 0$. Because Π_{MPC} terminates in a constant number of rounds, the round complexity of Π_{MPC}^* is also $\mathcal{O}(\log^{\epsilon'} n)$. In each of these rounds, every party might communicate with at most $\mathcal{O}(\log^{1+\epsilon} n)$ (potentially different) parties, (Recall that all parallel executions of Π_{BC}^* and $\text{AdSMT}_{\text{all}}$ use the same sequence of graph setups.) Thus, the total number of parties that each $i \in [n]$ talks directly to (i.e., via its point-to-point channels) is $\mathcal{O}(\log^{1+\epsilon+\epsilon'} n)$. □

5. GETTING RID OF THE SKI

In this section we show how to get rid of the symmetric-key setup assumption, at the cost, however, of increasing the communication-locality (but not the round complexity) by a factor of $\sqrt{n}$. The idea for getting rid of the SKI is to have the parties compute some kind of an alternative random graph setup. This is done as follows: each party $i \in [n]$ locally decides which of his n point-to-point channels he will use; a channel between two (honest) parties $i, j \in [n]$ is then used only if both parties choose it. (This is similar in spirit to the way the work of Chandran et al. [13] handles "edge corruptions" in sparse networks.) By having each party decide to use each of his channels with probability $p = \frac{\log^\epsilon n}{\sqrt{n}}$ for some given constant $\epsilon > 1$ (and ignore all other channels) we ensure that, with overwhelming probability, each (honest) party uses at most $\mathcal{O}(\sqrt{n} \log^\delta n)$ of its point-to-point channels for some constant $\delta > 0$. Furthermore, each edge between two honest parties i and j is chosen with probability $p' = p^2 = \frac{\log^{2\epsilon} n}{n}$, thus the resulting communication graph will include Erdős-Rényi graph $G(n, p')$ which will allow us to use our ideas from the previous sections. Note, that as the adversarial nodes might choose to communicate with all their neighbors, the communication locality is no longer guaranteed to be $\mathcal{O}(\log^\epsilon n)$; notwithstanding, it is guaranteed to be $\mathcal{O}(\sqrt{n} \log^\delta n)$ with overwhelming probability.

RMT protocol. We now describe a reliable message transmission protocol that tolerates up to $t < qn$ adaptive corruptions, for any constant $q < 1$. Our protocol is similar to the corresponding protocol from Section 3.2, the only difference being that the parties choose their neighbors in a setup procedure as above instead of sampling them through their SKI-keys. We then obtain the following theorem: the proof of communication locality follows from an application of the

Chernoff bound and the proof of round complexity is similar to the proof of Theorem 9 (see the full version for details).

Protocol $\text{AdRMT}_{i,j}^{\text{noSKI}}(m)$

1. Round 1 (Computing the setup): The parties execute the following code for every $(i, j, \rho) \in [n] \times [n] \times [\log^{\epsilon'} n]$ *in parallel* (where $\epsilon' > 1$ is a given constant):
   - Party i samples a bit $b_{i,j}^\rho$ where $b_{i,j}^\rho = 1$ with probability $p = \frac{\log^\epsilon n}{\sqrt{n}}$ for some given constant $\epsilon > 1$; and $b_{i,j}^\rho = 0$ otherwise.
   - If $b_{i,j}^\rho = 0$ for all $\rho \in [\log^{\epsilon'} n]$, then party i ignores all messages on the point-to-point channel between i and j.
   - If $b_{i,j}^\rho = 1$ then i sends $(b_{i,j}^\rho, \rho)$ to j.

2. Round 2: For each $(i, j, \rho) \in [n] \times [n] \times [\log^{\epsilon'} n]$: If $b_{i,j}^\rho = 1$ but party i received no message (b, ρ) from party j in the previous round then i sets $b_{i,j}^\rho := 0$. For $\rho = 1, \ldots, \log^{\epsilon'} n$: Party i sets $\Gamma(i)^\rho := \{j \mid b_{i,j}^\rho = 1\}$ to be the set of parties/neighbors p_i will communicate with in round ρ.

3. Round 3: Party i sends $(m, \text{sig}_{\text{sk}_i}(m))$ to parties in $\Gamma(i)^\rho$.

4. For each round $\rho = 3, \ldots, \log^{\epsilon'} n$:
   - For every party $k \in [n] \setminus \{i, j\}$: If a message (m, σ), where σ is party i's valid signature on m was received *for the first time* in the previous round $\rho - 1$ from some party in $\Gamma(k)^{\rho-1}$, then party k sends (m, σ) to all parties in $\Gamma(k)^\rho$ and halts. (If multiple validly signed pairs were received in that round for the first time, then take the first one in a lexicographic order.)
   - For the receiver j: If a message (m, σ), where σ is party i's valid signature on m is received *for the first time* from some party in $\Gamma(j)^\rho$, then output m and halt. (If more than one validly signed pair is received in that round for the first time, then take the first one in a lexicographic order.)

THEOREM 15. *Let $T \subset [n]$ be the set of adaptively corrupted parties, $|T| = t \leq qn$, for any constant $0 < q < 1$. Assuming a PKI, protocol $\text{AdRMT}_{i,j}^{\text{noSKI}}(m)$ is a secure RMT protocol between any two honest nodes $i, j \in [n] \backslash T$, satisfying the following tow properties with overwhelming probability:*

1. *Every party communicates with at most $\mathcal{O}(\sqrt{n} \log^{1+\delta} n)$ other parties, for some constant $\delta > 0$.*

2. *The protocol terminates in $\mathcal{O}(\log^{\epsilon''} n)$ rounds, for some constant $\epsilon'' > 0$.*

Given Theorem 15, an MPC protocol with the desired communication locality and round complexity can be obtained by replacing in protocol Π_{MPC}^* all invokations of $\text{AdRMT}_{i,j}$ with invocations of $\text{AdRMT}_{i,j}^{\text{noSKI}}$. The proof of Theorem 2 is similar to the proof of Theorem 1.

6. REFERENCES

[1] D. Beaver, S. Micali, and P. Rogaway. The round complexity of secure protocols (extended abstract). In *STOC*, pages 503–513, 1990.

[2] M. Ben-Or, S. Goldwasser, and A. Wigderson. Completeness theorems for non-cryptographic fault-tolerant distributed computation (extended abstract). In *STOC*, pages 1–10, 1988.

[3] R. Bendlin, I. Damgård, C. Orlandi, and S. Zakarias. Semi-homomorphic encryption and multiparty computation. In *EUROCRYPT*, pages 169–188, 2011.

---

[13] Recall that the ID's are needed to ensure security of Π_{BC}^* under parallel composition [34].

[4] M. Blum, P. Feldman, and S. Micali. Non-interactive zero-knowledge and its applications (extended abstract). In *STOC*, pages 103–112, 1988.

[5] D. Bogdanov, S. Laur, and J. Willemson. Sharemind: A framework for fast privacy-preserving computations. In *ESORICS*, pages 192–206, 2008.

[6] E. Boyle, S. Goldwasser, and S. Tessaro. Communication locality in secure multi-party computation - how to run sublinear algorithms in a distributed setting. In *TCC*, pages 356–376, 2013.

[7] Z. Brakerski, C. Gentry, and V. Vaikuntanathan. (leveled) fully homomorphic encryption without bootstrapping. In *ITCS*, pages 309–325, 2012.

[8] Z. Brakerski and V. Vaikuntanathan. Efficient fully homomorphic encryption from (standard) LWE. In *FOCS*, pages 97–106, 2011.

[9] R. Canetti. Security and composition of cryptographic protocols: a tutorial (part i). *SIGACT News*, 37(3):67–92, 2006.

[10] R. Canetti, U. Feige, O. Goldreich, and M. Naor. Adaptively secure multi-party computation. In *STOC*, pages 639–648, 1996.

[11] N. Chandran, W. Chongchitmate, J. A. Garay, S. Goldwasser, R. Ostrovsky, and V. Zikas. Optimally resilient and adaptively secure multi-party computation with low communication locality. Cryptology ePrint Archive, Report 2014/615, 2014.

[12] N. Chandran, J. A. Garay, and R. Ostrovsky. Improved fault tolerance and secure computation on sparse networks. In *ICALP*, pages 249–260, 2010.

[13] N. Chandran, J. A. Garay, and R. Ostrovsky. Edge fault tolerance on sparse networks. In *ICALP*, pages 452–463, 2012.

[14] D. Chaum, C. Crépeau, and I. Damgård. Multiparty unconditionally secure protocols (extended abstract). In *STOC*, pages 11–19, 1988.

[15] R. Cleve. Limits on the security of coin flips when half the processors are faulty (extended abstract). In *STOC*, pages 364–369, 1986.

[16] I. Damgård, M. Keller, E. Larraia, C. Miles, and N. Smart. Implementing AES via an actively/covertly secure dishonest-majority MPC protocol. In *SCN*, pages 241–263, 2012.

[17] I. Damgård, M. Keller, E. Larraia, V. Pastro, P. Scholl, and N. Smart. Practical covertly secure MPC for dishonest majority - or: Breaking the SPDZ limits. In *ESORICS*, pages 1–18, 2013.

[18] I. Damgård and J.B. Nielsen. Improved non-committing encryption schemes based on a general complexity assumption. In *CRYPTO*, pages 432–450, 2000.

[19] I. Damgård, V. Pastro, N. Smart, and S. Zakarias. Multiparty computation from somewhat homomorphic encryption. In *CRYPTO*, pages 643–662, 2012.

[20] V. Dani, V. King, M. Movahedi, and J. Saia. Brief announcement: breaking the o(nm) bit barrier, secure multiparty computation with a static adversary. In *PODC*, pages 227–228, 2012.

[21] Y. Dodis, J. Katz, A. Smith, and S. Walfish. Composability and on-line deniability of authentication. In *TCC*, pages 146–162, 2009.

[22] C. Dwork, D. Peleg, N. Pippenger, and E. Upfal. Fault tolerance in networks of bounded degree (preliminary version). In *STOC*, pages 370–379, 1986.

[23] U. Feige, D. Lapidot, and A. Shamir. Multiple non-interactive zero knowledge proofs based on a single random string (extended abstract). In *FOCS*, pages 308–317, 1990.

[24] J. A. Garay and R. Ostrovsky. Almost-everywhere secure computation. In *EUROCRYPT*, pages 307–323, 2008.

[25] O. Goldreich. Basing non-interactive zero-knowledge on (enhanced) trapdoor permutations: The state of the art. In *Studies in Complexity and Cryptography*, pages 406–421. Springer-Verlag, 2011.

[26] O. Goldreich, S. Micali, and A. Wigderson. How to play any mental game or A completeness theorem for protocols with honest majority. In *STOC*, pages 218–229, 1987.

[27] R. Impagliazzo and M. Luby. One-way functions are essential for complexity based cryptography (extended abstract). In *FOCS*, pages 230–235, 1989.

[28] J. Katz and C. Y. Koo. On expected constant-round protocols for byzantine agreement. In *CRYPTO*, pages 445–462, 2006.

[29] M. Keller, P. Scholl, and N. Smart. An architecture for practical actively secure MPC with dishonest majority. In *CCS*, pages 549–560, 2013.

[30] V. King and J. Saia. Breaking the $O(n^2)$ bit barrier: scalable byzantine agreement with an adaptive adversary. In *PODC*, pages 420–429, 2010.

[31] V. King, J. Saia, V. Sanwalani, and E. Vee. Scalable leader election. In *SODA*, pages 990–999, 2006.

[32] V. King, J. Saia, V. Sanwalani, and E. Vee. Towards secure and scalable computation in peer-to-peer networks. In *FOCS*, pages 87–98, 2006.

[33] L. Lamport, R. E. Shostak, and M. C. Pease. The byzantine generals problem. *ACM Trans. Program. Lang. Syst.*, 4(3):382–401, 1982.

[34] Y. Lindell, A. Lysyanskaya, and T. Rabin. On the composition of authenticated byzantine agreement. In *STOC*, pages 514–523, 2002.

[35] Y. Lindell, E. Oxman, and B. Pinkas. The IPS compiler: Optimizations, variants and concrete efficiency. In *CRYPTO*, pages 259–276, 2011.

[36] S. Lu, R. Ostrovsky, A. Sahai, H. Shacham, and B. Waters. Sequential aggregate signatures and multisignatures without random oracles. In *EUROCRYPT*, pages 465–485, 2006.

[37] S. Micali, K. Ohta, and L. Reyzin. Accountable-subgroup multisignatures: extended abstract. In *CCS*, pages 245–254, 2001.

[38] M. C. Pease, R. E. Shostak, and L. Lamport. Reaching agreement in the presence of faults. *J. ACM*, 27(2):228–234, 1980.

[39] E. Upfal. Tolerating linear number of faults in networks of bounded degree. In *PODC*, pages 83–89, 1992.

[40] A. C. Yao. How to generate and exchange secrets (extended abstract). In *FOCS*, pages 162–167, 1986.

On the Communication Complexity
of Secure Function Evaluation with Long Output

Pavel Hubáček
Department of Computer Science
Aarhus University
Aabogade 34
8200 Aarhus N, Denmark
hubacek@cs.au.dk

Daniel Wichs
Department of Computer Science
Northeastern University
360 Huntington Av., #202 WVH
Boston, MA 02115
wichs@ccs.neu.edu

ABSTRACT

We study the communication complexity of secure function evaluation (SFE). Consider a setting where Alice has a short input x_A, Bob has an input x_B and we want Bob to learn some function $y = f(x_A, x_B)$ with large output size. For example, Alice has a small secret decryption key, Bob has a large encrypted database and we want Bob to learn the decrypted data without learning anything else about Alice's key. In a trivial insecure protocol, Alice can just send her short input x_A to Bob. However, all known SFE protocols have communication complexity that scales with size of the output y, which can potentially be much larger. Is such "output-size dependence" inherent in SFE?

Surprisingly, we show that output-size dependence can be avoided in the *honest-but-curious* setting. In particular, using indistinguishability obfuscation (iO) and fully homomorphic encryption (FHE), we construct the first honest-but-curious SFE protocol whose communication complexity only scales with that of the best insecure protocol for evaluating the desired function, independent of the output size. Our construction relies on a novel way of using iO via a new tool that we call a "somewhere statistically binding (SSB) hash", and which may be of independent interest.

On the negative side, we show that output-size dependence is inherent in the *fully malicious* setting, or even already in an *honest-but-deterministic* setting, where the corrupted party follows the protocol as specified but fixes its random tape to some deterministic value. Moreover, we show that even in an offline/online protocol, the communication of the online phase must have output-size dependence. This negative result uses an incompressibility argument and it generalizes several recent lower bounds for functional encryption and (reusable) garbled circuits, which follow as simple corollaries of our general theorem.

Categories and Subject Descriptors

F.0 [**Theory of Computation**]: GENERAL

ITCS'15, January 11–13, 2015, Rehovot, Israel.
Copyright © 2015 ACM 978-1-4503-3333-7/15/01 ...$15.00.
http://dx.doi.org/10.1145/2688073.2688105.

Keywords

Secure Function Evaluation; Communication Complexity; Indistinguishability Obfuscation; Fully Homomorphic Encryption; Merkle Hash Tree

1. INTRODUCTION

We study the communication complexity of secure function evaluation (SFE). For simplicity, we focus on the case of a two-party functionality $y = f(x_A, x_B)$, where Alice and Bob start with inputs x_A, x_B respectively and we want Bob to learn the output y. Alice should not learn anything about Bob's input x_B or the output y, and Bob should not learn anything about Alice's input x_A *beyond* learning the output $y = f(x_A, x_B)$.

Traditional approaches to SFE, for example based on Yao garbled circuits [24], have communication complexity which is proportional to the circuit size of the function f. The breakthrough results on fully-homomorphic encryption (FHE) by Gentry [13] and follow-up works (e.g., [8, 7, 15]) gave the first general SFE solutions whose communication complexity is independent of the circuit size of f, and only scales with the input and output size of f.[1]

COMMUNICATION COMPLEXITY OF SFE USING FHE. Using FHE, we can get SFE solutions whose communication complexity only scales with the *input* and *output* size of the function f being computed. For example, in the honest-but-curious setting, we get a solution where Bob encrypts his input x_B to Alice via a compact and circuit-private FHE for which he knows the secret key, Alice then runs the computation homomorphically on the received ciphertext and her input x_A to get an encryption of y which she sends back to Bob, and Bob decrypts and learns y. This achieves communication complexity that scales with $|x_B| + |y|$. Alternatively, we can get a similar protocol with communication complexity that scales with $|x_A| + |y|$.

More generally, we can take any *insecure* protocol evaluating a function f with low communication complexity and convert it into a secure protocol as follows. Alice and Bob first run a secure distributed key-generation protocol for an FHE scheme, which gives them a common public-key pk and secret-shares sk_A, sk_B of the secret key $sk = sk_A \oplus sk_B$. They then encrypt their inputs under pk and execute the insecure protocol for evaluating f, by running

---

[1]Prior to FHE, it was known how to beat the circuit-size barrier in many interesting cases, but not in general. See for example Naor and Nissim [23].

it homomorphically under the FHE scheme, so that Bob eventually learns an encryption of the output y. Alice and Bob can then run a secure distributed decryption procedure using their shares sk_A, sk_B and the encryption of y so that Bob learns the decrypted output y (but nothing else). The distributed key-generation and decryption protocols can be implemented generically using an arbitrary SFE scheme.[2] If there exists an efficient protocol π evaluating f *without* any security requirements with communication complexity $\mathbf{CC}(\pi)$ and λ is the security parameter, then the above approach yields an SFE with communication complexity $\mathsf{poly}(\lambda)(\mathbf{CC}(\pi)+|y|)$ where the $\mathsf{poly}(\lambda)$ term is some fixed polynomial independent of the function f. Moreover, using succinct zero-knowledge arguments of Kilian [21], we can even make the above protocols secure in the fully malicious setting without asymptotically increasing the communication complexity.

However, in all known SFE protocols, including the above-described solutions, the communication complexity of the protocol exceeds the output size $|y|$ of the computation. We say that such protocols have *"output-size dependence"*. As the main question of the paper, we ask if output-size dependence is inherent in SFE.

IS OUTPUT-SIZE DEPENDENCE INHERENT IN SFE? If we didn't require any security, then there is a trivial protocol where Alice just sends her input x_A to Bob who computes $y = f(x_A, x_B)$ himself, with communication $|x_A|$ independent of the output size $|y|$. Can we achieve this type of efficiency while maintaining security? For example, imagine that Alice has a short seed x for a pseudorandom generator (PRG) G, Bob does not have any input, and we want Bob to learn a huge PRG output $y = G(x)$. Can we do this with communication complexity which only depends on $|x|$ but not on $|y|$? Alternatively, imagine Alice has a small secret decryption key sk, Bob has a large encrypted database $c = \mathsf{Enc}_{pk}(\mathsf{DB})$ and we want Bob to learn the plaintext database $\mathsf{DB} = \mathsf{Dec}_{sk}(c)$ without learning anything else about sk. Can we do this with communication complexity independent of $|\mathsf{DB}|$? In all of these cases, we would like to have an SFE protocol that avoids output-size dependence.

OUR RESULTS. On the negative side, we show that output-size dependence is inherent for SFE in the *fully malicious* setting. In fact, it is already required even in an *honest-but-deterministic* setting, where the corrupted party follows the protocol as specified but fixes its random tape to some deterministic value (say, all 0s). More specifically, we show that in any honest-but-deterministic SFE scheme, the communication from Alice to Bob must exceed the "Yao incompressibility entropy" of Bob's output conditioned on his input, and in general, this can be as large as Bob's output size. Moreover, we extend this result to protocols in the offline/online setting, where the parties can run an offline phase before knowing their inputs.[3] We show that, no matter how much communication takes place in the offline phase, the com-

munication of the online phase must still satisfy output-size dependence. This negative result uses an "incompressibility argument" which has been used in several recent works giving negative results and/or lower bounds for functional encryption, garbled circuits and some classes of SFE [3, 1, 10, 16, 14, 22]. Our main contribution is to give a (relatively straightforward) generalization of this technique to prove lower bounds on the communication complexity of general SFE, and then show that all of the prior uses of this technique follow as simple corollaries of our general theorem.

On the positive side, we show that output-size dependence can surprisingly be avoided in the *honest-but-curious* setting. In particular, using indistinguishability obfuscation (iO) and fully-homomorphic encryption (FHE), we construct the first general honest-but-curious SFE protocols that avoid output-size dependence. We give two such protocols for evaluating an arbitrary function f where Bob learns the output. The first protocol achieves communication $\mathsf{poly}(\lambda) + |x_A|$, where x_A is Alice's input. The second protocol takes any insecure protocol π for evaluating f and compiles it into a *secure* protocol that achieves communication $\mathsf{poly}(\lambda)\mathbf{CC}(\pi)$ which only scales with the communication-complexity $\mathbf{CC}(\pi)$ of the protocol π. In both cases, the $\mathsf{poly}(\lambda)$ term is some fixed polynomial in the security parameter λ, independent of the function f. Since there is always a simple insecure protocol where Alice sends her input to Bob, we have $\mathbf{CC}(\pi) \leq |x_A|$, and there are functions for which the gap is large $\mathbf{CC}(\pi) \ll |x_A|$. Therefore the latter protocol may be better in some instances, although it incurs a multiplicative rather than additive overhead in the security parameter. Using either of these protocols, we get an SFE solution to the problem where Bob has a large encrypted database and wants to securely learn the decryption under a short key held by Alice, using communication complexity which is independent of the database size.

1.1 Our Techniques: Negative Result

Let us begin by describing the technique behind the negative result.[4] For concreteness, consider a two-party computation protocol where Alice has a secret key k for a pseudorandom function (PRF) $f_k : \mathbb{N} \to \{0,1\}$, Bob does not have any input, and we want Bob to learn the PRF outputs $y_1 = f_k(1), \ldots, y_L = f_k(L)$ for some large integer L. For contradiction, assume that we had an SFE protocol for this task where the communication complexity from Alice to Bob is $L' < L$ bits. Let's look at the case where Alice is honest and has a uniformly random key k as her input, while a corrupted Bob uses an *honest-but-deterministic* strategy, meaning that he follows the specified protocol but fixes his random tape to some deterministic value (say, all 0s). The security of the SFE protocol implies that there is a simulator which gets Bob's output $y_1 = f_k(1), \ldots, y_L = f_k(L)$ and must simulate the view of Bob, denoted $\mathsf{view}_\mathsf{Bob}$. The simulated $\mathsf{view}_\mathsf{Bob}$ consists of messages from Alice to Bob (of size L') that cause Bob to output $y_1, \ldots, y_L$. But this means that the simulator can *efficiently compress* the outputs $y_1, \ldots, y_L$ into a shorter string $\mathsf{view}_\mathsf{Bob}$ of size $L' < L$ bits from which we can efficiently recover the output (by

---

[2] Alternatively, there are much simpler and more efficient distributed key-generation and decryption procedures using the algebraic structure of specific FHE schemes. See for example [4].

[3] We require the offline phase to be simulatable on its own, prior to the online inputs being specified. This differs from previous works that considered a weaker model of offline/online SFE where our impossibility result does not apply (see Remark 1 for additional details).

[4] A similar argument was formalized as Theorem 5.7 in the work of Lindell, Nissim and Orlandi [22], however their claimed negative result is incorrect since it is stated with respect to honest-but-curious adversaries that is shown possible in this work.

running Bob's protocol with the fixed randomness). This in turn contradicts the fact that the outputs are pseudorandom and therefore incompressible, showing that such an SFE cannot exist.

As mentioned, our actual result generalize the above example in several ways. Firstly, we show that the communication from Alice to Bob in any SFE for any function f must exceed the "Yao incompressibility entropy" [25, 19] of Bob's output given Bob's input. In the above example, the incompressibility entropy of the output is L bits. Secondly, we extend this result to protocols in the offline/online setting, where we show that the same lower-bound applies to the online phase, no matter how much communication takes place in the offline phase. In this setting, we require that the simulator can simulate the offline phase before the online inputs are chosen, and therefore without knowing the output of the computation.

Lastly, we show that the above negative result implies many prior lower-bounds on functional encryption and/or (reusable) garbled circuits. In particular, all of these results follow by showing that the desired primitive would immediately yield an SFE protocol (possibly in the offline/online setting) whose communication complexity would beat our lower bound.

1.2 Our Techniques: Positive Result

Surprisingly, we show that it is possible to avoid the negative result in the honest-but-curious setting.[5] Before we describe our solution, it is instructive to see where the negative result fails. In the negative result, we relied on the fact that the simulated view of an *honest-but-deterministic* Bob, denoted view$_{Bob}$, can be used to reconstruct the output of the function, which consists of pseudorandom values $y_1 = f_k(1), \ldots, y_L = f_k(L)$. Since this view only contained the communication from Alice to Bob, which we assumed to be shorter than the output size L, this served as a compression of the output leading to a contradiction. In the "honest-but-curious" setting, the view of Bob also contains all of his random coins used during the protocol execution, which may be arbitrarily long. Therefore, in this setting, view$_{Bob}$ is no longer compressing even if the communication complexity is small, and the negative result fails.

At first it may appear that the above observation cannot help us. In the real protocol execution, Bob's coins are truly random and independent of the output; how can we use the random coins to represent/reconstruct the output $y_1, \ldots, y_L$? We rely on the fact that the simulator can choose the "simulated random coins" for Bob in a way that is not truly random, and in fact can somehow embed into the random coins information about the outputs $y_1, \ldots, y_L$, while still making the coins appear random to a distinguisher.

We now describe our positive result in several steps, focusing on the above example of PRF evaluation for concreteness. This high-level overview doesn't match the actual constructions in the paper, but it elucidates the main ideas.

FIRST ATTEMPT: JUST OBFUSCATE. As a first attempt, consider a protocol where Alice constructs a small circuit $C_k(i)$ with a hard-coded key k which gets as input an in-

dex $i \in \{1, \ldots, L\}$ and outputs $f_k(i)$. Alice obfuscates this circuit and sends it to Bob who then evaluates it on the values $1, \ldots, L$ to get his output. Since the size of the circuit is independent of L (ignoring logarithmic factors), so is the communication complexity of this protocol. On the positive side, the use of obfuscation might already hide some information about Alice's input k. On the negative side, there is no hope of simulating this protocol. Indeed, since Bob does not send any communication to Alice, there is no difference between proving the security of this protocol for an honest-but-curious Bob vs. a fully malicious Bob, and our negative result rules this out.

SECOND ATTEMPT: HASH RANDOMNESS THEN OBFUSCATE. Our main idea for overcoming the negative result is to incorporate the random coins of Bob into the protocol. Let's consider the following modification. Bob first chooses L random bits $r_1, \ldots, r_L$ and hashes them using a Merkle Tree to derive $z = H(r_1, \ldots, r_L)$. A Merkle Tree has the property that Bob can efficiently "open" any bit r_i of the pre-image by providing a short opening π_i. Bob sends the hash z to Alice. Alice now constructs a small circuit $C_{k,z}(i, r_i, \pi_i)$ that has k, z hard-coded, gets as input $i \in \{1, \ldots, L\}, r_i \in \{0, 1\}$ and a short opening π_i, verifies that π_i is a valid opening of the i'th pre-image bit to r_i, and if so outputs $f_k(i)$ (if not outputs 0). Alice obfuscates this circuit $C_{k,z}$ and sends it to Bob, who then evaluates it on the values $i \in \{1, \ldots, L\}$ by also providing the correct bit r_i and the opening π_i for each evaluation. The size of the circuit $C_{k,z}$ is independent of L and therefore so is the communication complexity of this protocol.

Notice that Bob commits himself ahead of time to providing some random bits r_i to the obfuscated circuit on each evaluation. The circuit checks that it gets the right bit, but then essentially ignores it afterwards. The main idea of the simulation strategy is to choose the random coins r_i on behalf of Bob in a way that embeds information about the outputs y_i and to change the circuit being obfuscated so that it uses the inputs r_i to compute the output without knowing k. The simulator chooses his own PRF key k' (unrelated to Alice's key k which the simulator does not know) and sets the simulated random coins to $r_i := f_{k'}(i) \oplus y_i$. Then it creates an obfuscation of the circuit $C'_{k',z}(i, r_i, \pi_i)$ which checks the opening π_i as before, and if the opening is valid, it now outputs $r_i \oplus f_{k'}(i)$ instead of $f_k(i)$. In both cases, if the circuits $C_{k,z}$ and $C'_{k',z}$ get the correct inputs (i, r_i, π_i) they produce the same outputs y_i.

The indistinguishability of simulation boils down to showing that one cannot distinguish an obfuscation of $C_{k,z}$ and $C'_{k',z}$ even given $r_1, \ldots, r_L$, k and k', where $z = H(r_1, \ldots, r_L)$. Functionally, these circuits only differ on inputs of the form (i, r'_i, π'_i) where $r'_i \neq r_i$ differs from the bit that was hashed to create z and π'_i is a valid opening. By the security of the Merkle Tree, such inputs are hard to find. Therefore, we could already show the security of the above construction by relying on differing-inputs obfuscation (diO) [5, 2, 6]. However, diO is a strong assumption and there is some evidence that it may not hold in general [12]. Therefore, we would like a solution based on the weaker and better studied notion of indistinguishability obfuscation (iO) [5, 11].[6]

[6]In both notions of obfuscation, we want to ensure that the obfuscations of two different circuits C, C' are indistinguishable. For iO, we assume that C, C' agree on all inputs,

FINAL ATTEMPT: HASH CAREFULLY AND USE iO. It turns out that we can also prove the security of the above construction using only iO, by being more careful and relying on special type of hash function. We believe that this technique may have broader applicability.

Abstracting out the above construction, we have two circuits C, C' which have a hard-coded hash output $z = H(r_1, \ldots, r_L)$ and they only differ on inputs of the type (i, r_i', π_i') where $r_i' \neq r_i$ differs from the hashed bit in position i, and π_i' is a valid opening for r_i'. Since the hash is compressing, such inputs necessarily exist. However, we'd like to rely on iO to show that obfuscations of C and C' are indistinguishable. We show that we can do this if the hash function satisfies a new notion of security which we call a *"somewhere statistically binding"* (SSB) hash.

An SSB hash H_{hk} has a short public "hashing key" hk. Just like in a Merkle Tree, we can take $z = H_{hk}(r_1, \ldots, r_L)$ and, for any position i, produce a short opening π_i to certify r_i as the correct bit of the pre-image in that position. Moreover, there is now a method of choosing the hash key hk with a special "binding index" i^* and we require the following two security properties:

- $z = H_{hk}(r_1, \ldots, r_L)$ is statistically binding for position i^*, meaning that there does not exist a valid opening π_{i^*}' that would open position i^* to the wrong bit $r_{i^*}' \neq r_{i^*}$.

- The hash key hk does not reveal anything about which index i^* is the binding index.

We show how to construct such SSB hash functions by combining the idea of a Merkle Tree with fully homomorphic encryption. We believe that this primitive may find other applications.

Using an SSB hash, we show that obfuscations of C and C' are indistinguishable via a careful hybrid argument. We can define hybrid circuits $C_{i^*}(i, r_i, \pi_i)$ that evaluate C' when $i \leq i^*$ and C otherwise, so that $C_0 = C$ and $C_L = C'$. For $i^* = 1, \ldots, L$ we define a series of hybrid distributions where we first change the way we choose hk to be binding on index i^* and then we change the circuit being obfuscated to C_{i^*}. Each time we change the circuit being obfuscated from C_{i^*-1} to C_{i^*}, the two circuits being considered are functionally equivalent since the SSB hash is binding on index i^*. Therefore, we get a proof of security using only iO rather than diO.

GENERAL RESULT. So far, we described a specific example for our positive result where we avoid output-size dependence in the concrete case of PRF evaluation. However, the above ideas generalize to providing a general honest-but-curious two-party SFE protocol for any function f, so as to achieve the positive results we described previously.

CAN OBFUSCATION BE AVOIDED? We do not know if iO can be avoided in the above positive result but, in the full version, we present some evidence that at least a weak flavor of obfuscation is inherent. It remains an interesting problem to explore this further and to see what are the minimal assumptions under which we can avoid "output-size dependence" in the honest-but-curious setting.

FULL VERSION. This is an extended abstract and the full version of the paper with all proofs appears in [20].

_____

whereas for diO we only assume that it is computationally infeasible to find an input on which they disagree.

2. DEFINITIONS FOR SFE

Let $f : \{0,1\}^{\ell_A(\lambda)} \times \{0,1\}^{\ell_B(\lambda)} \to \{0,1\}^{L(\lambda)}$ be a function family. We consider the *secure function evaluation problem* with two parties Alice and Bob, where Alice has a private input $x_A \in \{0,1\}^{\ell_A}$, Bob has a private input $x_B \in \{0,1\}^{\ell_B}$, and Bob wishes to obtain the evaluation $y = f(x_A, x_B)$.

HONEST-BUT-CURIOUS SFE. For our positive result, we will rely on the notion of honest-but-curious adversaries, where the adversarial party is assumed to follow the protocol specification completely and hopes to learn some unintended information. For an *honest-but-curious* Bob, we define a random variable denoting his view of the protocol by $\mathsf{view}_B^\Pi(x_A, x_B, \lambda) = (x_B, r_B, m_1, \ldots, m_t)$ where r_B are the random coins used by Bob, and $m_1, \ldots, m_t$ are the messages from Alice to Bob. We define the view of an honest-but-curious Alice, $\mathsf{view}_A^\Pi(x_A, x_B, \lambda)$, analogously.

Definition 1. We say that two-party protocol Π *securely evaluates* $f : \{0,1\}^{\ell_A} \times \{0,1\}^{\ell_B} \to \{0,1\}^L$ *in the presence of honest-but-curious adversaries,* if there exists a PPT simulator $S = (S_A, S_B)$ such that for all $x_A \in \{0,1\}^{\ell_A}$ and $x_B \in \{0,1\}^{\ell_B}$ it holds that

$$\{\mathsf{sim}_{A,\lambda}\}_{\lambda \in \mathbb{N}} \overset{c}{\approx} \{\mathsf{view}_A^\Pi(x_A, x_B, \lambda)\}_{\lambda \in \mathbb{N}} , \quad (1)$$

$$\{\mathsf{sim}_{B,\lambda}\}_{\lambda \in \mathbb{N}} \overset{c}{\approx} \{\mathsf{view}_B^\Pi(x_A, x_B, \lambda)\}_{\lambda \in \mathbb{N}} , \quad (2)$$

where $\mathsf{sim}_{A,\lambda} \leftarrow S_A(1^\lambda, x_A)$ and $\mathsf{sim}_{B,\lambda} \leftarrow S_B(1^\lambda, x_B, f(x_A, x_B))$. We sometimes consider "one-sided" security against honest-but-curious Bob, in which case we only require (2) to hold.

HONEST-BUT-DETERMINISTIC SFE. For our negative results, we will rely on a notion of *honest-but-deterministic* adversaries, where the adversarial party follows the protocol specification, *except* that it refuses to choose truly random coins, and instead sets its random tape to some fixed/deterministic value – say, the all 0 string. This adversarial model is much weaker than the fully malicious one, making our negative results stronger. We will also only consider one-sided security against an honest-but-deterministic Bob, but not require any security against an adversarial Alice. Again, this weakening of the security model makes our results stronger. Lastly, we consider offline/online protocols $\Pi = (\Pi^{\mathsf{off}}, \Pi^{\mathsf{on}})$, comprising of two phases:

- The *offline phase* protocol Π^{off} is run independently of the inputs x_A, x_B and it allows the parties to do some preprocessing. Both parties receive their respective inputs only after the end of the offline phase.

- The *online phase* protocol Π^{on} is run by the parties using their inputs x_A, x_B and any state retained from the offline phase. It results in Bob outputting $y = f(x_A, x_B)$.

We can think of standard SFE protocols as only containing an online phase. We will give a lower-bound on the communication complexity of the online phase in an offline/online protocol, no matter how much communication takes place in the online phase.

The execution of a protocol $\Pi = (\Pi^{\mathsf{off}}, \Pi^{\mathsf{on}})$ between Alice and honest-but-deterministic Bob defines a random variable for Bob's view of the protocol: $(\mathsf{detview}_B^{\Pi^{\mathsf{off}}}, \mathsf{detview}_B^{\Pi^{\mathsf{on}}})(x_A, x_B, \lambda) = ((m_1^{\mathsf{off}}, \ldots, m_s^{\mathsf{off}}), (x_B, m_1^{\mathsf{on}}, \ldots, m_t^{\mathsf{on}}))$, where the offline part consists of the protocol messages from Alice to

Bob in the offline phase, and the online part consists of Bob's input and the protocol messages from Alice to Bob in the online phase. The protocol messages chosen by Alice follow the protocol with true randomness, while those from Bob follow the protocol with the random tape set to the all 0s string.[7]

Definition 2. We say that an offline/online two-party protocol $\Pi = (\Pi^{\text{off}}, \Pi^{\text{on}})$ *evaluates* $f : \{0,1\}^{\ell_A} \times \{0,1\}^{\ell_B} \to \{0,1\}^L$ *with security against honest-but-deterministic Bob,* if there exists a simulator $S = (S^{\text{off}}, S^{\text{on}})$ such that for all $x_A \in \{0,1\}^{\ell_A}$ and $x_B \in \{0,1\}^{\ell_B}$ it holds that

$$\{\text{sim}_{B,\lambda}^{\text{off}}, \text{sim}_{B,\lambda}^{\text{on}}\}_{\lambda \in \mathbb{N}} \overset{c}{\approx} \{(\text{detview}_B^{\Pi^{\text{off}}}, \text{detview}_B^{\Pi^{\text{on}}})(x_A, x_B, \lambda)\}_{\lambda \in \mathbb{N}},$$

where $(\text{sim}_{B,\lambda}^{\text{off}}, \text{state}) \leftarrow S^{\text{off}}(1^\lambda)$ and $\text{sim}_{B,\lambda}^{\text{on}} \leftarrow S^{\text{on}}(x_B, f(x_A, x_B), \text{state})$.

Remark 1. A crucial but subtle aspect of the above definition for offline/online SFE is that the simulator S^{off} must simulate the offline phase without knowing Bob's input x_B or the output $f(x_A, x_B)$. For example, this is required if the inputs can be chosen (e.g., by the adversary/environment) adaptively after the offline phase. In fact, our lower bound in Section 4.2 can be overcome if the simulator is allowed to know the output when simulating the offline part. Indeed Yao garbled circuits (discussed further in Section 4.3) give such an offline/online protocol with low communication complexity in the online part if the offline simulator is given the output.

3. POSITIVE RESULTS IN THE HONEST-BUT-CURIOUS SETTING

We now describe our positive results, giving general SFE protocols in the honest-but-curious setting, whose communication complexity is independent of the output size of the function being computed. As explained in the introduction, we will rely on a new type of security for hash functions and we begin by describing this new primitive.

3.1 Somewhere Statistically Binding Hash Functions

DEFINITION. A *somewhere statistically binding (SSB) hash function* allows us to create a *short* hash $y = H_{\text{hk}}(x)$ of some *long* value $x = (x[0], \ldots, x[L-1])$ and later efficiently "prove" that the i'th block of x takes on some particular value $x[i] = u$ by providing a *short* opening π. The size of the hash $y = H_{\text{hk}}(x)$, the size of the opening π and the time to verify π should be bounded by some fixed polynomials in the security parameter and unrelated to the potentially huge size of x. So far, this problem can be solved using Merkle Trees, where such an opening consists of the hash values of all the sibling nodes along the path from the root of the tree to the i'th leaf. However, the definition of SSB hash has an additional statistical requirement: it allows us to choose the *hashing key* hk with respect to some special "binding index" i in such a way that the hash $y = H_{\text{hk}}(x)$ is statistically binding on the i'th block of the input, meaning

that there only exists a valid opening for a single choice of $x[i]$. The index i on which the hash is statistically binding should remain hidden by the hashing key hk. The formal definition is below.

Definition 3. A *somewhere statistically binding (SSB) hash* consists of PPT algorithms (Gen, H, Open, Verify) along with a block alphabet $\Sigma = \{0,1\}^{\ell_{blk}}$, output size ℓ_{hash} and opening size ℓ_{opn}, where $\ell_{blk}(\lambda), \ell_{hash}(\lambda), \ell_{opn}(\lambda)$ are some fixed polynomials in the security parameter. The algorithms have the following syntax:

- hk $\leftarrow$ Gen$(1^\lambda, L, i)$ takes as input an integer $L \leq 2^\lambda$ and index $i \in \{0, \ldots, L-1\}$ (both of these are in binary) and outputs a public hashing key hk.
- $H_{\text{hk}} : \Sigma^L \to \{0,1\}^{\ell_{hash}}$ is a deterministic polynomial time algorithm that takes as input $x = (x[0], \ldots, x[L-1]) \in \Sigma^L$ and outputs $H_{\text{hk}}(x) \in \{0,1\}^{\ell_{hash}}$.
- $\pi \leftarrow$ Open(hk, x, j): Given the hash key hk, $x \in \Sigma^L$ and an index $j \in \{0, \ldots, L-1\}$, creates an opening $\pi \in \{0,1\}^{\ell_{opn}}$.
- Verify(hk, y, j, u, π): Given a hash key hk and a value $y \in \{0,1\}^{\ell_{hash}}$, an integer index $j \in \{0, \ldots, L-1\}$, a value $u \in \Sigma$ and an opening $\pi \in \{0,1\}^{\ell_{opn}}$, outputs a decision $\in \{\text{accept}, \text{reject}\}$. This is intended to verify that a pre-image x of $y = H_{\text{hk}}(x)$ has $x[j] = u$.

We require the following properties:

Correctness: For any integers $L \leq 2^\lambda$ and $i, j \in \{0, \ldots, L-1\}$, any hk $\leftarrow$ Gen$(1^\lambda, L, i)$, $x \in \Sigma^L$, $\pi \leftarrow$ Open(hk, x, j): we have Verify(hk, $H_{\text{hk}}(x), j, x[j], \pi$) = accept.

Index Hiding: We consider the following game between an attacker $\mathcal{A}$ and a challenger:

- The attacker $\mathcal{A}(1^\lambda)$ chooses an integer L and two indices $i_0, i_1 \in \{0, \ldots, L-1\}$.
- The challenger chooses a bit $b \leftarrow \{0,1\}$ and sets hk $\leftarrow$ Gen$(1^\lambda, L, i_b)$.
- The attacker $\mathcal{A}$ gets hk and outputs a bit b'.

We require that for any PPT attacker $\mathcal{A}$ we have $|\Pr[b = b'] - \frac{1}{2}| \leq \text{negl}(\lambda)$ in the above game.

Somewhere Statistically Binding: We say that hk is *statistically binding for an* index i if there do not exist any values $y, u \neq u', \pi, \pi'$ s.t. Verify(hk, y, i, u, π) = Verify(hk, y, i, u', π') = accept. We require that for any integers $L \leq 2^\lambda$, $i \in \{0, \ldots, L-1\}$ the key hk $\leftarrow$ Gen$(1^\lambda, L, i)$ is statistically binding for i.

Remark 2. Notice that the output size and the opening size of SSB hash are bounded by some fixed polynomials ℓ_{hash}, ℓ_{opn} and independent of the size of the input x. Also, we note that an SSB hash function is necessarily collision resistant. Intuitively, if an attacker can find $x \neq x'$ such that $H_{\text{hk}}(x) = H_{\text{hk}}(x')$ then there must be some index i such that $x[i] \neq x'[i]$ and therefore the attacker knows with certainty that the key hk is not binding on index i. This would contradict index hiding. We only make an informal note of this and do not explicitly rely on this property. Finally, note that achieving both the property of statistical binding for a specific index and efficient local opening is what makes constructing an SSB hash non-trivial.[8]

---

[7] Our results would hold even if we modified the definition so that an honest-but-deterministic Bob uses true randomness in the offline phase but is deterministic in the online phase. We choose to omit this for simplicity.

[8] For example any Private Information Retrieval scheme can be used to attain the former but not the latter.

OVERVIEW OF CONSTRUCTION. Our construction combines the ideas behind Merkle Hash Trees with fully homomorphic encryption (FHE, a formal definition is given in the full version). Let's assume we want to hash some data $x = x[0], \ldots, x[L-1]$ where $L = 2^\alpha$ is a power-of-2. We construct a full binary tree of height α sitting on top of the data x. Each node of the tree is associated with a ciphertext under an FHE scheme. The L leaf nodes are associated with encryptions of $x[0], \ldots, x[L-1]$ respectively, where these ciphertexts are computed deterministically using some fixed random coins. The hashing key $\mathsf{hk} \leftarrow \mathsf{Gen}(1^\lambda, L, i)$ consists of an encrypted path in the tree going to a leaf i. Hashing will consist of homomorphically computing a ciphertext for each node of the tree using the ciphertexts associated with its children and the ciphertexts contained in hk. This is done in a way that ensures that all of the ciphertexts on the path from the root to leaf i contain encryptions of $x[i]$. The output of the hash function is the ciphertext associated with the root of the tree, which is an encryption of $x[i]$ and therefore statistically committing to this value. Analogously to Merkle Trees, opening the hash for some particular block i consists of revealing the ciphertexts associated with all of the siblings along the path from the root to i, which is sufficient to recompute the ciphertext associated with the root. One difficulty is that an adversarial opening may consist of "incorrectly generated ciphertexts" and we cannot guarantee the correctness of homomorphic evaluation over such ciphertexts. Therefore, homomorphic evaluation will only operate on the honestly generated ciphertexts provided as part of the hashing key hk, while the ciphertexts associated with the nodes of the tree will only be used to define the function being evaluated.

CONSTRUCTION. Let $\mathcal{E} = (\mathsf{KeyGen}, \mathsf{Enc}, \mathsf{Dec}, \mathsf{Eval})$ be an FHE scheme. For any polynomial block-size $\ell_{blk} = \ell_{blk}(\lambda)$, we construct an SSB hash function $(\mathsf{Gen}, H, \mathsf{Open}, \mathsf{Verify})$ with alphabet $\Sigma = \{0,1\}^{\ell_{blk}}$ as follows.

- $\mathsf{hk} \leftarrow \mathsf{Gen}(1^\lambda, L, i)$: Assume w.l.o.g. that $L = 2^\alpha$ is a power-of-2 for some integer $\alpha \leq \lambda$. For $j = 0, \ldots, \alpha$: create $(pk_j, sk_j) \leftarrow \mathsf{KeyGen}(1^\lambda)$. Let $(b_\alpha, \ldots, b_1)$ be the binary representation of the index $i \in \{0, \ldots, 2^\alpha - 1\}$.[9] For $j = 1, \ldots, \alpha$, compute $c_j \leftarrow \mathsf{Enc}_{pk_j}((sk_{j-1}, b_j))$. Let $\mathsf{hk} = (pk_0, \ldots, pk_\alpha, c_1, \ldots, c_\alpha)$.

- $y = H_{\mathsf{hk}}(x)$: Let $x = (x[0], \ldots, x[L-1])$. Let T be a binary tree of height α with L leaves. We think of the leaves as being at level 0 and the root of the tree as being at level α. We inductively and deterministically associate a ciphertext ct_v with each vertex $v \in T$. Intuitively, the encrypted bits b_j contained in hk will ensure that the data item $x[i]$ is propagated up the tree in encrypted form. Formally, we define the ciphertexts ct_v inductively as follows:

  - If v is the j'th leaf, we associate to it the ciphertext $ct_v := \mathsf{Enc}_{pk_0}(x[j]; \bar{0})$ to be a deterministically computed encryption of $x[j]$ using fixed randomness $\bar{0}$.

  - Let $v \in T$ be a non-leaf vertex at level $j \in [\alpha]$ with children v_0, v_1 having associated ciphertexts ct_0, ct_1, and let c_j be the ciphertext contained in hk for level j. We associate with v the ciphertext $ct_v = \mathsf{Eval}_{pk_j}(f_{ct_0, ct_1}, c_j)$

---

[9] It is useful to think of the bits b_i as tracing out a path in a binary tree going from the root to the leaf i.

where we define the function:

$$
f_{ct_0, ct_1}(sk, b) : \left\{ \begin{array}{r} \text{Compute: } x_0 = \mathsf{Dec}_{sk}(ct_0), \\ x_1 = \mathsf{Dec}_{sk}(ct_1). \\ \text{Output: } x_b. \end{array} \right\}
$$

Note that the function f_{ct_0, ct_1} is homomorphically evaluated only over the ciphertext $c_j = \mathsf{Enc}_{pk_j}((sk_{j-1}, b_j))$ contained in hk, whereas the ciphertexts ct_0, ct_1 only serve to define the function being evaluated. The output ciphertext ct_v is an encryption under the key pk_j.

The above ensures that for any node v which lies on the path from the root to the leaf at the statistically binding index i, the associated ciphertext ct_v is an encryption of $x[i]$. The output of the hash is the ciphertext ct_v where v is the root of the tree T.

- $\mathsf{Open}(\mathsf{hk}, x, j)$: Perform the computation of $H_{\mathsf{hk}}(x)$ as described above and output the ciphertexts ct_v for each vertex v that's a sibling of some vertex along the path from the root to the leaf at position j.

- $\mathsf{Verify}(\mathsf{hk}, y, j, u, \pi)$: Perform the computation of $H_{\mathsf{hk}}(x)$ as described above using only the provided ciphertexts. In particular, for each vertex v along the path from the root of the tree to leaf j, inductively compute a ciphertext ct_v. In the base case, when v is the j'th leaf, set $ct_v = \mathsf{Enc}_{pk_0}(u; \bar{0})$. Otherwise, if v is not a leaf, then one of its children lies on the path to leaf j in which case the corresponding ciphertext was computed in the previous step, and the sibling ciphertex is provided in the opening π. Therefore, we can compute $ct_v = \mathsf{Eval}_{pk_j}(f_{ct_0, ct_1}, c_j)$ where ct_0, ct_1 are the ciphertexts associated with the children of v and c_j is contained in the hash key hk. Finally, compute the ciphertext ct_v associated with the root of the tree and check that $y \overset{?}{=} ct_v$.

THEOREM 1. *If $\mathcal{E} = (\mathsf{KeyGen}, \mathsf{Enc}, \mathsf{Dec}, \mathsf{Eval})$ is an FHE scheme then, for any polynomial block-size $\ell_{blk}(\lambda)$, the above construction $(\mathsf{Gen}, H, \mathsf{Open}, \mathsf{Verify})$ is an SSB hash with block-alphabet $\Sigma = \{0,1\}^{\ell_{blk}}$.*

PROOF (SKETCH). To argue index hiding security, we use the semantic security of the FHE scheme. For the somewhere statistically binding property, we rely on correctness of the homomorphic evaluation of the FHE scheme. A complete proof is given in the full version. $\square$

3.2 One-Sided SFE for Multi-Decryption

In the introduction, we gave an example of a functionality where Alice has a short secret key, Bob has a large encrypted database and we want Bob to learn the decryption without learning anything else about Alice's secret key. We now show how to do this in the honest-but-curious setting with communication complexity independent of the database size. Then, in the next section, we will leverage this protocol to build general SFE schemes.

MULTI-DECRYPTION. Let $\mathcal{E} = (\mathsf{KeyGen}, \mathsf{Enc}, \mathsf{Dec})$ be a bit-encryption scheme with ciphertext size $\ell_{ctx} = \ell_{ctx}(\lambda)$. We begin by describing an SFE protocol for the "multi-decryption" functionality where Alice has as input a secret key $sk \in \{0,1\}^{\ell_{sk}}$ and Bob has as input some "database" of L ciphertexts $c_0, \ldots, c_{L-1} \in \{0,1\}^{\ell_{ctx}}$ where L is some polynomial in the security parameter. The functionality gives Bob the decryptions $m_0 = \mathsf{Dec}_{sk}(c_0), \ldots, m_{L-1} = \mathsf{Dec}_{sk}(c_{L-1})$

with $m_i \in \{0, 1\}$. In other words, we want an SFE for the function $f^{\mathcal{E},L}_{\text{multi-dec}}(sk, (c_0, \ldots, c_{L-1})) = (m_0, \ldots, m_{L-1})$ where Bob gets the output. We only ask for one-sided security against an honest-but-curious Bob and do not require any security against a corrupt Alice – she may learn something about Bob's ciphertexts $c_0, \ldots, c_{L-1}$ during the course of the protocol.

Our protocol makes use of an SSB hash function $\mathcal{H} = (\text{Gen}, H, \text{Open}, \text{Verify})$ with alphabet $\Sigma = \{0, 1\}^{\ell_{blk}}$ where $\ell_{blk} := \ell_{ctx} + 1$. Assume the SSB hash has some corresponding output size ℓ_{hash} and opening size ℓ_{opn} (all polynomials in the security parameter λ). The protocol relies on an indistinguishability obfuscation (iO) scheme $\mathcal{O}$ (see the full version for a formal definition). The protocol is given in Figure 1.

PROTOCOL 1. SFE for multi-decryption:
$f^{\mathcal{E},L}_{\text{multi-dec}}(sk, (c_0, \ldots, c_{L-1})) = (m_0, \ldots, m_{L-1})$.

- Alice chooses $\text{hk} \leftarrow \text{Gen}(1^\lambda, L, 0)$ and sends hk to Bob.

- Bob chooses randomness $(r_0, \ldots, r_{L-1}) \leftarrow \{0, 1\}^L$. Let $x[i] = (c_i, r_i) \in \Sigma$ and $x = (x[0], \ldots, x[L-1]) \in \Sigma^L$. Bob computes $y \leftarrow H_{\text{hk}}(x)$ and sends y to Alice.

- Alice creates a circuit $C = C[\text{hk}, y, sk]$ as described below and obfuscates it by computing $\widetilde{C} \leftarrow \mathcal{O}(1^\lambda, C)$. She sends $\widetilde{C}$ to Bob.

- For $i = 0, \ldots, L-1$, Bob computes $\pi_i = \text{Open}(\text{hk}, x, i)$ and $m_i := \widetilde{C}(i, c_i, r_i, \pi)$.

Figure 1: Protocol for multi-decryption.

Given values hk (hash key), y (hash output) and sk (decryption key) define the circuit $C = C[\text{hk}, y, sk]$ as follows.

$C[\text{hk}, y, sk](i, c, r, \pi)$:
Hard-coded: hash key hk, hash value y, decryption key sk.
Input: $i \in [L-1]$, $c \in \{0, 1\}^{\ell_{ctx}}$, $r \in \{0, 1\}$, $\pi \in \{0, 1\}^{\ell_{opn}}$.
1. If $\text{Verify}(\text{hk}, y, i, (c, r), \pi) \neq \text{accept}$ output 0.
2. Output $\text{Dec}_{sk}(c)$.

In addition, we assume that the circuit C includes some polynomial-size padding to make it sufficiently large. In particular, we also define an augmented circuit $C^{aug} = C^{aug}[\text{hk}, y, sk, k, i^*]$ below, which is not used in the protocol, but is used in the proof of security. We will need to pad C so that its size matches that of C^{aug}. For the definition of C^{aug}, we assume that $f_k(x)$ is a PRF with key $k \in \{0, 1\}^\lambda$, input $x \in \{0, \ldots, L-1\}$ and output $f_k(x) \in \{0, 1\}$.

$C^{aug}[\text{hk}, y, sk, k, i^*](i, c, r, \pi)$:
New values: PRF key k, index $i^* \in \{0, \ldots, L-1\}$.
1. If $\text{Verify}(\text{hk}, y, i, (c, r), \pi) \neq \text{accept}$ output 0.
2. If $i \geq i^*$ output $\text{Dec}_{sk}(c)$, else output $f_k(i) \oplus r$.

THEOREM 2. *If $\mathcal{H}$ is an SSB hash and $\mathcal{O}$ is an iO scheme then Protocol 1 is a secure SFE for the functionality $f^{\mathcal{E},L}_{\text{multi-dec}}$ with one-sided security against an honest-but-curious Bob. Furthermore, for any choice of encryption scheme $\mathcal{E}$, there is some polynomial $p(\lambda)$ such that for every polynomial $L(\lambda)$ the communication complexity of the above protocol for the functionality $f^{\mathcal{E},L}_{\text{multi-dec}}$ is bounded by $p(\lambda)$ and is independent of $L(\lambda)$.*

PROOF (SKETCH). In order to simulate the view of an honest-but-curious Bob, the simulator uses the PRF to generate Bob's random coins, generates a new hashing key, and obfuscates the program $C^{aug}[\text{hk}, y, \perp, k, i^* = L]$ containing $\perp$ in place of Alice's secret key sk. As discussed in the introduction, we show by a sequence of carefully constructed hybrids that the simulated view and real view are indistinguishable. We leverage the information theoretical guarantee of the SSB hash that allows us to rely on indistinguishability obfuscation, rather than on differing inputs obfuscation. A complete proof is given in the full version. □

3.3 General SFE Constructions

We now leverage the protocol for multi-decryption from the previous section to get generic SFE protocols in the honest-but-curious setting. Let

$$f = \{f_\lambda : \{0, 1\}^{\ell_A(\lambda)} \times \{0, 1\}^{\ell_B(\lambda)} \to \{0, 1\}^{L(\lambda)}\}_{\lambda \in \mathbb{N}}$$

be any efficiently computable function with ℓ_A, ℓ_B, L being some polynomials in the security parameter λ. We focus on SFE schemes where Alice has input x_A, Bob has input x_B and Bob learns the output $y = f(x_A, x_B)$.

We give two constructions. The first one achieves communication complexity $\text{poly}(\lambda) + \ell_A(\lambda)$, where $\text{poly}(\lambda)$ is some fixed polynomial independent of the choice of f or its parameters. In particular, the communication complexity only depends on Alice's input size ℓ_A but is independent of Bob's input-size ℓ_B or output-size L. The second construction achieves communication complexity $\text{poly}(\lambda) \mathbf{CC}(\pi, \lambda)$ where $\mathbf{CC}(\pi, \lambda)$ is the communication complexity of an arbitrary insecure protocol π for evaluating the function f and $\text{poly}(\lambda)$ is some fixed polynomial independent of the choice of f or its parameters. Since there is always a simple insecure protocol where Alice sends her input to Bob, we have $\mathbf{CC}(\pi, \lambda) \leq \ell_A(\lambda)$ and in general, it may be much smaller than Alice's input size. Unfortunately, in this construction we pay with a multiplicative polynomial overhead rather than an additive one as before.

FIRST CONSTRUCTION. Let $\mathcal{E} = (\text{KeyGen}, \text{Enc}, \text{Dec}, \text{Eval}, \text{Rerand})$ be an FHE scheme with rerandomization. As discussed in the full version, by relying on hybrid encryption we can assume without loss of generality that a ciphertext produced by $c \leftarrow \text{Enc}_{pk}(x)$ is of size $|x| + \text{poly}(\lambda)$, meaning that there is only an additive polynomial overhead. Our protocol is given in Figure 2.

THEOREM 3. *Assuming that $\mathcal{E} = (\text{KeyGen}, \text{Enc}, \text{Dec}, \text{Eval}, \text{Rerand})$ is an FHE scheme with rerandomization, and that the conditions of Theorem 2 (Protocol 1) hold, Protocol 2 gives a secure SFE scheme for any polynomial-time computable functionality f. Furthermore, there is some fixed polynomial $p(\lambda)$ such that for every such functionality f where Alice's input size is $\ell_A(\lambda)$, the communication complexity of the protocol is given by $p(\lambda) + \ell_A(\lambda)$.*

PROOF (SKETCH). Protocol 2 can be simulated by relying on semantic security of the FHE scheme, the security of the rerandomization, and the simulation-security of Protocol 1. A complete proof is given in the full version. □

SECOND CONSTRUCTION. Let $\pi^f_{insec} = (\pi^A, \pi^B)$ be any (insecure) protocol between Alice and Bob that evaluates the function $y = f(x_A, x_B)$ so that Bob learns y at the

PROTOCOL 2. General SFE Protocol for $f = \{f_\lambda : \{0,1\}^{\ell_A(\lambda)} \times \{0,1\}^{\ell_B(\lambda)} \to \{0,1\}^{L(\lambda)}\}$. Alice has input x_A, Bob has input x_B and Bob learns $y = f(x_A, x_B)$.

- Alice computes $(pk, sk) \leftarrow \mathsf{KeyGen}(1^\lambda)$, $c_A \leftarrow \mathsf{Enc}_{pk}(x_A)$ and sends pk, c_A to Bob.

- Bob computes $c_{out} = \mathsf{Eval}_{pk}(f(\cdot, x_B), c_A)$. Bob chooses a "one-time-pad" $k \leftarrow \{0,1\}^L$ and sets $c_{pad} = \mathsf{Eval}_{pk}(\mathsf{OTP}_k, c_{out})$ where $\mathsf{OTP}_k(y) := y \oplus k$. Finally, Bob computes $c_{frsh} \leftarrow \mathsf{Rerand}_{pk}(c_{pad})$. Let $c_{frsh} = (c_0, \ldots, c_{L-1})$ where c_i are bit-encryptions.

- Alice and Bob execute Protocol 1 for the functionality $f^{\mathcal{E},L}_{\mathsf{multi-dec}}$ where Alice has input sk and Bob has input $c_{frsh} = (c_0, \ldots, c_{L-1})$. Bob receives the output $z \in \{0,1\}^L$ and sets $y := k \oplus z$ as the output of the protocol.

Figure 2: First Construction – general protocol for $y = f(x_A, x_B)$.

end of the protocol. We assume that it has some fixed round complexity $q = q(\lambda)$ and fixed communication-length in each round, independent of the particular inputs. Without loss of generality, the protocol π works as follows: Alice and Bob start out with a state that just consists of their inputs $\mathsf{state}_0^A = x_A, \mathsf{state}_0^B = x_B$. The protocol proceeds in q rounds where, in each round i, Alice computes $(\mathsf{msg}_i^A, \mathsf{state}_i^A) = \pi^A(\mathsf{msg}_{i-1}^B, \mathsf{state}_{i-1}^A)$, sends msg_i^A to Bob, and Bob computes $(\mathsf{msg}_i^B, \mathsf{state}_i^B) = \pi^B(\mathsf{msg}_i^A, \mathsf{state}_{i-1}^B)$ and sends msg_i^B to Alice (we define msg_0^B to be the empty string). At the end of the protocol, Bob's state $\mathsf{state}_q^B = f(x_A, x_B)$ contains the output of the computation.

Our SFE protocol will rely on the idea of "double encryption" using two FHE public keys pk_A, pk_B and ciphertexts of the form $c = \mathsf{Enc}_{pk_B}(\mathsf{Enc}_{pk_A}(x))$. To simplify notation, we let $\mathsf{Eval}_{pk_B, pk_A}(f, c)$ denote $\mathsf{Eval}_{pk_B}(\mathsf{Eval}_{pk_A}(f, \cdot), c)$. This corresponds to a homomorphic evaluation of the function f on the message x hidden under two layers of encryption. In particular if c is as above and $c^* = \mathsf{Eval}_{pk_B, pk_A}(f, c)$ then $\mathsf{Dec}_{pk_B}(\mathsf{Dec}_{pk_A}(c^*)) = f(x)$. The main idea of our construction is to execute the protocol π under two layers of FHE encryption with public keys pk_A, pk_B chosen by Alice and Bob respectively.[10] The protocol is given in Figure 3.

THEOREM 4. *Assume that $\mathcal{E} = (\mathsf{KeyGen}, \mathsf{Enc}, \mathsf{Dec}, \mathsf{Eval}, \mathsf{Rerand})$ is an FHE scheme with rerandomization, and that the conditions of Theorem 2 (Protocol 1) hold. Let f be any polynomial-time functionality and let π be any (insecure) protocol correctly evaluating f with communication complexity $\mathbf{CC}(\pi, \lambda)$. Then Protocol 3 gives a secure SFE scheme for f. Furthermore, there is some fixed polynomial $p(\lambda)$ such that for every choice of f and π as above, the communication complexity of Protocol 3 is bounded by $p(\lambda)\mathbf{CC}(\pi, \lambda)$.*

PROOF (SKETCH). Protocol 3 can be simulated by relying on semantic security of the FHE scheme, the security of the rerandomization, and the simulation-security of Protocol 1. A complete proof is given in the full version. $\square$

---

[10]We note that an alternate approach avoiding double-encryption and instead using distributed key-generation where Alice and Bob agree on a common FHE public key pk and get secret shares sk_A, sk_B of the corresponding secret key $sk = sk_A \oplus sk_B$ for pk is also possible.

PROTOCOL 3. General SFE Protocol for $f = \{f_\lambda : \{0,1\}^{\ell_A(\lambda)} \times \{0,1\}^{\ell_B(\lambda)} \to \{0,1\}^{L(\lambda)}\}$. Alice has input x_A, Bob has input x_B and Bob learns $y = f(x_A, x_B)$.

- Alice chooses $(pk_A, sk_A) \leftarrow \mathsf{KeyGen}(1^\lambda)$ and sends pk_A to Bob. Bob chooses $(pk_B, sk_B) \leftarrow \mathsf{KeyGen}(1^\lambda)$ and sends pk_B to Alice.

- Alice locally computes a double-encryption $c_{\mathsf{state},0}^A \leftarrow \mathsf{Enc}_{pk_B}(\mathsf{Enc}_{pk_A}(x_A))$ and Bob locally computes $c_{\mathsf{state},0}^B \leftarrow \mathsf{Enc}_{pk_B}(\mathsf{Enc}_{pk_A}(x_B))$.

- For $i = 1, \ldots, q$:

  - Alice computes $(c_{\mathsf{msg},i}^A, c_{\mathsf{state},i}^A) = \mathsf{Eval}_{pk_B, pk_A}(\pi^A, (c_{\mathsf{msg},i-1}^B, c_{\mathsf{state},i-1}^A))$ and sends $c_{\mathsf{msg},i}^A$ to Bob. (We define $c_{\mathsf{msg},0}^B$ to be the empty string.)

  - Bob computes $(c_{\mathsf{msg},i}^B, c_{\mathsf{state},i}^B) = \mathsf{Eval}_{pk_B, pk_A}(\pi^B, (c_{\mathsf{msg},i-1}^A, c_{\mathsf{state},i-1}^B))$ and sends $c_{\mathsf{msg},i}^B$ to Alice.

- Bob computes $c_{out} = \mathsf{Dec}_{sk_B}(c_{\mathsf{state},q}^B)$.
  Bob chooses a 'one-time pad' key $k \leftarrow \{0,1\}^L$ and sets $c_{pad} = \mathsf{Eval}_{pk_A}(\mathsf{OTP}_k, c_{out})$ where $\mathsf{OTP}_k(y) := y \oplus k$.
  Finally, Bob computes $c_{frsh} \leftarrow \mathsf{Rerand}_{pk_A}(c_{pad})$. Let $c_{frsh} = (c_0, \ldots, c_{L-1})$ where c_i are bit-encryptions.

- Alice and Bob execute Protocol 1 for the functionality $f^{\mathcal{E},L}_{\mathsf{multi-dec}}$ where Alice has input sk_A and Bob has input $c_{fin} = (c_0, \ldots, c_{L-1})$. Bob receives the output $z \in \{0,1\}^L$ and sets $y := k \oplus z$ as the output of the protocol.

Figure 3: Second Construction– general protocol for $y = f(x_A, x_B)$.

OUTPUT FOR ALICE. Note that our positive results also extend to the case where both Alice and Bob get the same output y or where they get different outputs y_A, y_B respectively. In particular, we can just run two sequential copies of our SFE where we reverse the roles of Alice and Bob. Using the first construction, this results in communication complexity $\mathsf{poly}(\lambda) + |x_A| + |x_B|$. Using the second construction, this results in communication complexity $\mathsf{poly}(\lambda)\mathbf{CC}(\pi, \lambda)$ where $\mathbf{CC}(\pi, \lambda)$ is now the communication complexity of any insecure protocol π evaluating f where both Alice and Bob get their correct outputs.

4. LOWER BOUNDS IN THE HONEST-BUT-DETERMINISTIC SETTING

We now give a lower bound for communication complexity of offline/online SFE in the presence of honest-but-deterministic adversaries. In particular, we show that the online communication complexity in any such SFE protocol must exceed the Yao incompressibility entropy of the output distribution of the evaluated function f.

4.1 Yao Incompressibility Entropy

The traditional notion of Shannon entropy corresponds to how well a distribution can be compressed (on average). The notion of *Yao incompressibility entropy* [25, 19] extends this to the computational setting by measuring how well a distribution can be compressed when the compressor and decompressor are required to be *efficient*. Roughly speaking, the *Yao incompressibility entropy* of a distribution X is at least k if X cannot be efficiently compressed to fewer than k bits. We will rely on a version of *conditional* Yao incompressibility entropy due to Hsiao, Lu and Reyzin [19]. It was shown by [19] that the (conditional) Yao incompressibility entropy of a distribution X is always at least as large as its HILL pseudo-entropy [18], which is in turn at least as large as its min-entropy, and the gaps between these entropies can be large. Therefore, giving a lower bound in terms of Yao entropy yields the strongest results.

Definition 4. Let $k = k(\lambda)$ be an integer-valued function of security parameter λ. A probability ensemble $X = \{X_\lambda\}_{\lambda \in \mathbb{N}}$ has *Yao incompressibility entropy at least k conditioned on* $Z = \{Z_\lambda\}_{\lambda \in \mathbb{N}}$, denoted by $\mathrm{H}^{\mathrm{Yao}}(X|Z) \geq k$, if for every pair of circuit-ensembles $C = \{C_\lambda\}$, $D = \{D_\lambda\}$ (called "compressor" and "decompressor") of size $\mathsf{poly}(\lambda)$ where C_λ has output-size at most $k(\lambda) - 1$, there exists a negligible function $\varepsilon(\cdot)$ such that

$$\Pr_{(x,z) \leftarrow (X_\lambda, Z_\lambda)}[D_\lambda(C_\lambda(x,z), z) = x] \leq \frac{1}{2} + \varepsilon(\lambda) \ .$$

We note that the above definition is actually somewhat weaker than the one of [19]. The latter required that, if the output of the compressor has length ℓ, then the success probability of the compressor/decompressor should be at most $2^{\ell-k} + \varepsilon(\lambda)$. In our case, we only require this to hold for $\ell = k - 1$. Since considering a weaker definition makes our lower bound stronger, we will use our weaker variant which is also simpler to define and use.

Let $f : \{0,1\}^{\ell_A(\lambda)} \times \{0,1\}^{\ell_B(\lambda)} \to \{0,1\}^{L(\lambda)}$. We define the Yao incompressibility entropy of the function f as a natural extension of the concept of the above Yao incompressibility entropy for probability ensembles (Definition 4). In particular, it measures the incompressibility of Bob's output $Y = f(X_A, X_B)$ conditioned on Bob's input X_B, for the choice of distributions X_A, X_B which maximizes this quantity.

Definition 5. We say that a function $f : \{0,1\}^{\ell_A(\lambda)} \times \{0,1\}^{\ell_B(\lambda)} \to \{0,1\}^{L(\lambda)}$ has *Yao incompressibility entropy at least k*, denoted by $k \leq \mathrm{H}^{\mathrm{Yao}}(f)$, if there exist

- a probability ensemble $X_A = \{X_{A,\lambda}\}_{\lambda \in \mathbb{N}}$ of distributions over $\{0,1\}^{\ell_A(\lambda)}$ and
- a probability ensemble $X_B = \{X_{B,\lambda}\}_{\lambda \in \mathbb{N}}$ of distributions over $\{0,1\}^{\ell_B(\lambda)}$,

such that the ensemble $Y = \{Y_\lambda\}_{\lambda \in \mathbb{N}}$ defined via $Y = f(X_A, X_B)$ satisfies $k \leq \mathrm{H}^{\mathrm{Yao}}(Y|X_B)$; i.e., the Yao incompressibility entropy of Y conditioned on X_B is at least k.

4.2 Communication Complexity vs. Incompressibility Entropy

We now show a lower bound on the communication complexity of any (offline/online) SFE protocol evaluating f in the honest-but-deterministic setting in terms of the Yao incompressibility entropy of f.

THEOREM 5. *Let* $f : \{0,1\}^{\ell_A(\lambda)} \times \{0,1\}^{\ell_B(\lambda)} \to \{0,1\}^{L(\lambda)}$, *and let* $\Pi = (\Pi^{\mathrm{off}}, \Pi^{\mathrm{on}})$ *be an offline/online protocol evaluating f with one-sided security against honest-but-deterministic*

Bob. If the Yao incompressibility entropy of f is $\mathrm{H}^{\mathrm{Yao}}(f) \geq k$ *then the communication complexity from Alice to Bob during the online phase of Π is at least k.*

PROOF (SKETCH). The simulator for any protocol for f (secure against an honest-but-deterministic Bob) with communication complexity lower than k can be used to construct an efficient compressor/decompressor pair contradicting the Yao incompressibility entropy of f. A complete proof is given in the full version. □

As an immediate corollary, we get that the communication complexity during the online phase must be at least as large as the output-size for any functionality with pseudorandom output. For example, we state the following for the example of PRF evaluation discussed in Section 1.1.

COROLLARY 1. *Let* $f = \{f_k : \{0,1\}^\lambda \to \{0,1\}\}_{k \in \{0,1\}^\lambda}$ *be a pseudorandom function. Consider an SFE functionality for "L PRF Evaluations" where Alice has a key $k \in \{0,1\}^\lambda$, Bob has no input, and Bob gets the output $y = (f_k(1), \ldots, f_k(L))$ for some polynomial $L = L(\lambda)$. In any offline/online protocol $\Pi = (\Pi^{\mathrm{off}}, \Pi^{\mathrm{on}})$ for the above functionality, with one-sided security against honest-but-deterministic Bob, the online communication from Alice to Bob must be at least L bits.*

EXTENSION TO MULTI-PARTY SFE. Our negative results also extend to multi-party SFE. In particular, for an n-party functionality $(y_1, \ldots, y_n) = f(x_1, \ldots, x_n)$ where party P_i has input x_i and output y_i, we can define the i'th output entropy of f as being at least k if there exists some distribution $(X_1, \ldots, X_n)$ such that $\mathrm{H}^{\mathrm{Yao}}(Y_i|X_i) \geq k$ where $Y = f(X_1, \ldots, X_n)$. In that case, in any offline/online n-party SFE protocol that has one-sided security against a single honest-but-deterministic party P_i, the communication-complexity from all other parties to P_i must be at least k bits. This simply follows by thinking of party P_i as Bob and thinking of all of the other parties as Alice in a two-party SFE protocol.

4.3 Applications

LOWER BOUNDS FOR FUNCTIONAL ENCRYPTION The impossibility of functional encryption with simulation based security for general circuits was first shown by Agrawal et al. [1]. This result was later extended to prove lower bounds for various related notions of functional encryption [10, 9, 16]. In the full version we show that the above lower bounds for functional encryption follow from our lower bound on communication complexity in offline/online SFE secure against honest-but-deterministic Bob.

LOWER BOUNDS FOR GARBLED CIRCUITS In the full version we also discuss the known lower bounds for garbled circuits [3, 17, 14] that follow from our lower bound on communication complexity of offline/online SFE from Section 4.2.

5. CONCLUSIONS

We explored the communication complexity of SFE for functions with long output. We showed that the honest-but-curious setting allows for general protocols whose communication is smaller than the output size while the malicious or even honest-but-deterministic settings do not. There are several interesting open problems left to explore. One interesting problem would be to consider weaker security notions than simulation-based security. For example, perhaps we get around "output-size dependence" in the malicious setting if we allowed for an unbounded or super-polynomial simulator. We leave this question for future work.

6. ACKNOWLEDGMENTS

The first author was supported by ERC Starting Grant 279447 and the CFEM and CTIC research centers. Part of this work was done while the first author was visiting the Northeastern University. The second author was supported by NSF grants 1347350, 1314722.

The second author would like to thank Craig Gentry and Vinod Vaikuntanathan for bringing the question of output-size dependence to his attention in a conversation several years back. We are also thankful to Claudio Orlandi, Yuval Ishai, and the anonymous ITCS reviewers for valuable feedback that helped improve the paper.

7. REFERENCES

[1] S. Agrawal, S. Gorbunov, V. Vaikuntanathan, and H. Wee. Functional encryption: New perspectives and lower bounds. In R. Canetti and J. A. Garay, editors, *CRYPTO (2)*, volume 8043 of *LNCS*, pages 500–518. Springer, 2013.

[2] P. Ananth, D. Boneh, S. Garg, A. Sahai, and M. Zhandry. Differing-inputs obfuscation and applications. *IACR Cryptology ePrint Archive*, 2013:689, 2013.

[3] B. Applebaum, Y. Ishai, E. Kushilevitz, and B. Waters. Encoding functions with constant online rate or how to compress garbled circuits keys. In R. Canetti and J. A. Garay, editors, *CRYPTO (2)*, volume 8043 of *LNCS*, pages 166–184. Springer, 2013.

[4] G. Asharov, A. Jain, A. López-Alt, E. Tromer, V. Vaikuntanathan, and D. Wichs. Multiparty computation with low communication, computation and interaction via threshold FHE. In D. Pointcheval and T. Johansson, editors, *EUROCRYPT*, volume 7237 of *LNCS*, pages 483–501. Springer, 2012.

[5] B. Barak, O. Goldreich, R. Impagliazzo, S. Rudich, A. Sahai, S. P. Vadhan, and K. Yang. On the (im)possibility of obfuscating programs. In J. Kilian, editor, *CRYPTO*, volume 2139 of *LNCS*, pages 1–18. Springer, 2001.

[6] E. Boyle, K.-M. Chung, and R. Pass. On extractability obfuscation. In Y. Lindell, editor, *TCC*, volume 8349 of *LNCS*, pages 52–73. Springer, 2014.

[7] Z. Brakerski, C. Gentry, and V. Vaikuntanathan. (Leveled) fully homomorphic encryption without bootstrapping. In S. Goldwasser, editor, *ITCS*, pages 309–325. ACM, 2012.

[8] Z. Brakerski and V. Vaikuntanathan. Efficient fully homomorphic encryption from (standard) LWE. In R. Ostrovsky, editor, *FOCS*, pages 97–106. IEEE, 2011.

[9] A. De Caro and V. Iovino. On the power of rewinding simulators in functional encryption. *IACR Cryptology ePrint Archive*, 2013:752, 2013.

[10] A. De Caro, V. Iovino, A. Jain, A. O'Neill, O. Paneth, and G. Persiano. On the achievability of

[11] S. Garg, C. Gentry, S. Halevi, M. Raykova, A. Sahai, and B. Waters. Candidate indistinguishability obfuscation and functional encryption for all circuits. In *FOCS, pages 40–49. IEEE Computer Society, 2013.*

[12] S. Garg, C. Gentry, S. Halevi, and D. Wichs. On the implausibility of differing-inputs obfuscation and extractable witness encryption with auxiliary input. In J. A. Garay and R. Gennaro, editors, *CRYPTO (1)*, volume 8616 of *LNCS*, pages 518–535. Springer, 2014.

[13] C. Gentry. Fully homomorphic encryption using ideal lattices. In M. Mitzenmacher, editor, *STOC*, pages 169–178. ACM, 2009.

[14] C. Gentry, S. Halevi, M. Raykova, and D. Wichs. Outsourcing private RAM computation. *IACR Cryptology ePrint Archive*, 2014:148, 2014.

[15] C. Gentry, A. Sahai, and B. Waters. Homomorphic encryption from learning with errors: Conceptually-simpler, asymptotically-faster, attribute-based. In R. Canetti and J. A. Garay, editors, *CRYPTO (1)*, volume 8042 of *LNCS*, pages 75–92. Springer, 2013.

[16] S. Goldwasser, V. Goyal, A. Jain, and A. Sahai. Multi-input functional encryption. *IACR Cryptology ePrint Archive*, 2013:727, 2013.

[17] S. Goldwasser, Y. T. Kalai, R. A. Popa, V. Vaikuntanathan, and N. Zeldovich. Reusable garbled circuits and succinct functional encryption. In D. Boneh, T. Roughgarden, and J. Feigenbaum, editors, *STOC*, pages 555–564. ACM, 2013.

[18] J. Håstad, R. Impagliazzo, L. A. Levin, and M. Luby. A pseudorandom generator from any one-way function. *SIAM J. Comput.*, 28(4):1364–1396, 1999.

[19] C.-Y. Hsiao, C.-J. Lu, and L. Reyzin. Conditional computational entropy, or toward separating pseudoentropy from compressibility. In M. Naor, editor, *EUROCRYPT*, volume 4515 of *LNCS*, pages 169–186. Springer, 2007.

[20] P. Hubáček and D. Wichs. On the communication complexity of secure function evaluation with long output. *IACR Cryptology ePrint Archive*, 2014:669, 2014.

[21] J. Kilian. A note on efficient zero-knowledge proofs and arguments (extended abstract). In S. R. Kosaraju, M. Fellows, A. Wigderson, and J. A. Ellis, editors, *STOC*, pages 723–732. ACM, 1992.

[22] Y. Lindell, K. Nissim, and C. Orlandi. Hiding the input-size in secure two-party computation. In K. Sako and P. Sarkar, editors, *ASIACRYPT*, volume 8270 of *LNCS*, pages 421–440. Springer, 2013.

[23] M. Naor and K. Nissim. Communication preserving protocols for secure function evaluation. In J. S. Vitter, P. G. Spirakis, and M. Yannakakis, editors, *STOC*, pages 590–599. ACM, 2001.

[24] A. C.-C. Yao. Protocols for secure computations (extended abstract). In *FOCS*, pages 160–164. IEEE Computer Society, 1982.

[25] A. C.-C. Yao. Theory and applications of trapdoor functions (extended abstract). In *FOCS*, pages 80–91. IEEE Computer Society, 1982.

Privacy-Preserving Public Information for Sequential Games

Avrim Blum,* Jamie Morgenstern,† and
Ankit Sharma
Computer Science Department
Carnegie Mellon University
Pittsburgh, PA
avrim@cs.cmu.edu,
jamiemmt@cs.cmu.edu,
ankits@cs.cmu.edu

Adam Smith ‡
Computer Science and Engineering Department
Pennsylvania State University
State College, PA
asmith@cse.psu.edu

ABSTRACT

In settings with incomplete information, players can find it difficult to coordinate to find states with good social welfare. For instance, one of the main reasons behind the recent financial crisis was found to be the lack of market transparency, which made it difficult for financial firms to accurately measure the risks and returns of their investments. Although regulators may have access to firms' investment decisions, directly reporting all firms' actions raises confidentiality concerns for both individuals and institutions. The natural question, therefore, is whether it is possible for the regulatory agencies to publish some information that, on one hand, helps the financial firms understand the risks of their investments better, and, at the same time, preserves the privacy of their investment decisions. More generally, when can the publication of privacy-preserving information about the state of the game improve overall outcomes such as social welfare?

In this paper, we explore this question in a sequential resource-sharing game where the value gained by a player on choosing a resource depends on the number of other players who have chosen that resource in the past. Without any knowledge of the actions of the past players, the social welfare attained in this game can be arbitrarily bad. We show, however, that it is possible for the players to achieve good social welfare with the help of *privacy-preserving, publicly-announced information*. We model the behavior of players in this imperfect information setting in two ways – greedy and undominated strategic behaviours, and we prove guarantees about the social welfare that certain kinds of privacy-preserving information can help attain. To achieve the social welfare guarantees, we design a counter with improved privacy guarantees under continual observation. In addition to the resource-sharing game, we study the main question for other games including sequential versions of the cut, machine-scheduling and cost-sharing games, and games where the value attained by a player on a particular action is not only a function of the actions of the past players but also of the actions of the future players.

Categories and Subject Descriptors

F.m [**Theory of Computation**]: Miscellaneous

Keywords

Privacy; Game Theory

1. INTRODUCTION

Multi-agent settings that are non-transparent (where players cannot see the current state of the system) have the potential to lead to disastrous outcomes. For example, in examining causes of the recent financial crisis and subsequent recession, the Financial Crisis Inquiry Commission [4, p. 352] concluded that "The OTC derivatives market's lack of transparency and of effective price discovery exacerbated the collateral disputes of AIG and Goldman Sachs and similar disputes between other derivatives counterparties." Even though regulators have access to detailed confidential information about financial institutions and (indirectly) individuals, current statistics and indices are based only on public data, since disclosures based on confidential information are restricted. However, forecasts based on confidential data can be much more accurate[1], prompting regulators to

*Blum, Morgenstern, and Sharma were partially supported by NSF grants CCF-1116892 and CCF-1101215.
†Morgenstern was partially supported by an NSF GRFP award and a Simons Award for Graduate Students in Theoretical Computer Science.
‡Smith was funded by NSF awards #0747294 and #0941553. Some of this work was done while on sabbatical at Boston University's Hariri Center for Computation, and at Harvard University's Center for Research on Computation & Society, supported by a Simons Investigator grant to Salil Vadhan.

[1]For example, Oet et al. [12] compared an index based on both public and confidential data with an analogous index based only on publicly available data. The former index would have been a significantly more accurate predictor of financial stress during the recent financial crisis (see Oet et al. [11, Figure 4]). See Flood et al. [5] for further discussion.

ask whether aggregate statistics can be economically useful while also providing rigorous privacy guarantees [5].

In this work, we show that such *privacy-preserving public information*, in an interesting class of sequential decision-making games, can achieve (nearly) the best of both worlds. In particular, the goal is to produce information about actions taken by previous agents that can be posted publicly, preserves all agents' (differential) privacy, and can significantly improve worst-case social-welfare. While our models do not directly speak to the highly complex issues involved in real-world financial decision-making, they do indicate that in settings involving contention for resources and first-mover advantages, privacy-preserving public information can be a significant help in improving social welfare. In the following sections, we describe the game setting and the information model.

1.1 Game Model

Consider a setting in which there are m resources and n players. The players arrive online, in an *adversarial* order, one at a time[2]. Each player i has some set A_i of resources she is interested in and that is known only to herself. An action a_i of player i is of the form $(a_{i,1}, \ldots, a_{i,m})$, where $a_{i,r} \geq 0$ represents the amount that player i invests in resource r, and moreover, $\sum_{j \in [m]} a_{i,j} = 1$. For simplicity, we assume that all $a_{i,r}$ are in $\{0, 1\}$ i.e, the unit-demand setting (we study the continuous version where $a_{i,r}$'s can be fractional, but still sum to 1, in the full version of this paper). Furthermore, we do not make the assumption that players have knowledge of their position in the sequence, that is, a player need not know how many players have acted before her.

Each resource r has some non-increasing function $V_r : \mathbb{Z}^+ \rightarrow \mathbb{R}^+$ indicating the *value, or utility, of this resource to the kth player who chooses it*. Therefore, the utility of player i is $u_i(a_i, a_{1,\ldots,i-1}) = \sum_r a_{i,r} V_r(x_{i,r})$, where $x_{i,r} = \sum_{j=1}^{i-1} a_{j,r}$ for each r. In this **resource sharing** setting, the utility for a player of choosing a certain resource is a function of the resource and (importantly) the number of players who have invested in the resource before her (and not after her)[3].

Illustrative Example.

For each resource, suppose $V_r(k) = V_r(0)/k$, where $V_r(0)$ is the initial value of resource r. The value of each resource r drops rapidly as a function of the number of players who have chosen it so far. If each player i has *perfect information* about the investment choices made by the players before her, the optimal action for player i is to greedily select the action in A_i of highest utility based on the number of players who have selected each resource so far. As shown in Section 3, the resulting social welfare of this behavior is within a factor of 4 of the optimal. In the case where each player has *no information* about other players' behaviors, some particularly disastrous sequences of actions might reasonably occur, leading to very low social welfare. For example, if each player i has access to a public resource r where $V_r(0) = 1$ and a private resource r_i where $V_{r_i}(0) = 1 - \epsilon$, each might reasonably choose greedily according to $V.(0)$, selecting the

resource of highest initial value (in this case, r). This would give social welfare of $\ln(n)$, whereas the optimal assignment would give $n(1 - \epsilon)$. Without information about the game state, therefore, the players may achieve only a $O\left(\frac{\ln(n)}{n}\right)$ fraction of the possible welfare.

1.2 Information Model

In resource sharing games, players' decisions about their actions will be best when they know how many players have chosen each resource when they arrive. The mechanisms we consider, therefore, will publicly announce some estimate of these counts. We consider the trade-off between the privacy lost by publishing these estimates and the accuracy of the counters in terms of social welfare. We consider three categories of counters for publicly posting the estimate of resource usage: perfect, private and empty counters.

Perfect Counters: At all points, the counters display the exact usage of each resource.

Privacy-preserving public counters: At all points, the counters display an approximate usage of the resources while maintaining privacy for each player. We define the privacy guarantee in Section 2.

Empty Counters: At all points, every counter displays the value 0.

1.3 Players' Behavior

Each player is a utility-maximizing agent and will choose the resource that, given their beliefs about actions taken by previous players and the publicly displayed counters, gives them maximum value. We analyze the game play under two classes of strategies – greedy and undominated strategies.

1. **Greedy strategy:** Under the greedy strategy, a player has no outside belief about the actions of previous players and chooses the resource that maximizes her utility given the *currently displayed (or announced) values of the counters*. Greedy is a natural choice of strategy to consider since it is the utility-maximizing strategy when the usage counts posted are *perfect*.

2. **Undominated Strategy(UD):** Under undominated strategies, we allow players to have any beliefs about the actions of the previous players that are consistent with the displayed value of the counters[4], and they are allowed to play *any* undominated strategy a_i under this belief. A strategy a_i is *undominated* under a belief, if no other a_i' get a strictly higher utility.[5]

---

[2]For ease of exposition, we rename players such that player i is the ith to arrive.

[3]In Section 5, we consider a generalization where the utility to a player of investing in a particular resource is a function of the total number of players who have chosen that resource, including those who have invested after her.

[4]As will become clear in Section 2, we work with privacy-preserving public counters that display values that can be off from the true usage only in a *bounded* range. Hence with these counters, a player's belief is consistent as long as the belief implies the usage of the resource to be a number that is within the bounded range of the displayed value. Moreover, with empty counters, any belief about the actions of previous players is a consistent belief.

[5]For each counter mechanism we consider, there exists at least one undominated strategy. For example, with perfect counters, the only consistent belief is that the true value is equal to the displayed value and here the greedy strategy is always undominated; moreover, if the counter mechanism has a nonzero probability of outputting the true value, then again the greedy strategy is undominated under the belief that the displayed value is the true value; if the counter mechanism can display values that are arbitrarily off from the true value, then for equal initial values *every* strategy is undominated.

We analyze the social welfare $SW(a) = \sum_i u_i(a)$ generated by an announcement mechanism $\mathcal{M}$ for a set of strategies D and compare it to the optimal social welfare OPT. For a game setting g, constituted of a collection of players $[n]$ and their allowable actions A_i (as defined in Section 1.1), $OPT(g)$ is defined as the optimal social welfare that can be achieved by any allocation of resources to the players, where the space of feasible allocations is determined by the setting g. In the unit-demand setting, $OPT(g)$ is the maximum weight matching in the bipartite graph $G = (U \cup V, E)$ where U is the set of the n players, V has n vertices for each resource r, one of value $V_r(k)$ for each $k \in [n]$, and there is an edge between player i and all vertices corresponding to resource r if and only if $r \in A_i$ (Note that the weights are on the vertices in V). The object of our study is $CR_D(g, \mathcal{M})$, the *worst case competitive ratio* of the optimal social welfare to the welfare achieved under strategy D and counter mechanism $\mathcal{M}$. As mentioned earlier, D will either be the greedy (GREEDY) or the undominated (UNDOM) strategy, and $\mathcal{M}$ will be either the perfect ($\mathcal{M}_{Full}$), the privacy-preserving or the empty ($\mathcal{M}_\emptyset$) counter. When $\mathcal{M}$ uses internal random coins, our results will either be worst-case over all possible throws of the random coins, or will indicate the probability with which the social welfare guarantee holds.

1.4 Statement of Main Results

For sequential resource-sharing games, we prove that for all nonincreasing value curves, the greedy strategy following privacy-preserving counters has a competitive ratio *polylogarithmic* in the number of players (Theorem 5). This should be contrasted with the competitive ratio of 4 achieved by greedy w.r.t. perfect counters (Theorem 1) and the nearly-linear (in the number of players) competitive ratio of greedy with empty counters (as shown in the illustrative example in Section 1.1). For the case of undominated strategies, when the marginal values of resources drop slowly, (for example, at a polynomial rate, $V_r(k) = V_r(0)/k^p$ for constant $p > 0$), we bound the competitive ratio (w.r.t. privacy-preserving counters) (Theorem 7). With empty counters, the competitive ratio for undominated strategies is unbounded (Theorem 2) for arbitrary curves and is at least quadratic (in the number of players) if the value curve drops slowly (Theorem 3). We note here that for many of our positive results for privacy preserving counters state the competitive ratio in terms of parameters of the counter vector α and β (as detailed in Section 2) and for a particular implementation of the counter vectors, the values of α and β are mentioned in Section 4.

The key privacy tool we use is the differentially private counter under continual observation [3], which we use to publish estimates of the usage of each resource. We improve upon the existing error guarantees of differentially private counters and design a new differentially private counter in Section 4. The new counter provides a tighter additive guarantee at the price of introducing a constant multiplicative error.

In Section 5, we consider other classes of games – specifically, we analyze Unrelated Machine Scheduling, Cut, and Cost Sharing games. The work of Leme et al. [10] showed these games have improved *sequential* price of anarchy over the *simultaneous* price of anarchy. For these games, we ask the question: if players do not have perfect information to make decisions, but instead have only noisy approximations (due to privacy considerations), does sequentiality still im-

prove the quality of play? We prove that the answer is affirmative in many cases.

1.5 Related Work

A great deal of work has been done at the intersection of mechanism design and privacy; Pai and Roth [13] have an extensive survey. Our work is similar to much of the previous work in that it considers maintaining differential privacy to be a constraint. The focus of our work however is on *how useful information can be provided to players in games of imperfect information* to help achieve a good social objective while respecting the privacy constraint of the players. The work of Kearns et al. [9] is close in spirit to ours. Kearns et al. [9] consider games where players have incomplete information about other players' types and behaviors. They construct a privacy-preserving mechanism which collects information from players, computes an approximate correlated equilibria, and then advises players to play according to this equilibrium. The mechanism is approximately incentive compatible for the players to participate in the mechanism and to follow its suggestions. Several later papers [14, 7] privately compute approximate equillibria in different settings. Our main privacy primitive is the differentially private counters under continual observation [3, 2], also used in much of the related work on private equilibrium computation.

Our investigation of cut games, unrelated machine scheduling, and cost-sharing (Section 5) is inspired by work of Leme et al. [10]. Their work focuses on the improvement in social welfare of equilibria in the *sequential* versus the *simultaneous* versions of certain games. We ask a related question: when we consider sequential versions of games, and only *private, approximate information about the state of play* (as opposed to perfect) is given to players, how much worse can social welfare be?

As mentioned in Section 1.3, one class of player behavior for which we analyze the games is *greedy*. Our analysis of greedy behavior is in part inspired by the work of Balcan et al. [1], who study best response dynamics with respect to noisy cost functions for potential games. An important distinction between their setting and ours is that the noisy estimates we consider are *estimates of state, not value*, and may for natural value curves be quite far from correct in terms of the *values* of the actions.

2. PRIVACY-PRESERVING PUBLIC COUNTERS

We design announcement mechanisms $\mathcal{M}_i$ which give approximate information about actions made by the previous players to player i. Let Δ_m denote the action space for each player (the m-dimensional simplex $\Delta_m = \{a \in [0,1]^m \mid \|a\|_1 \leq 1\}$). Mechanism $\mathcal{M}_i : (\Delta_m)^{i-1} \times R \to \Delta_m$ depends upon the actions taken before i (specifically, the usage of each resource by each player), and on internal random coins R. When player i arrives, $m_i(a_1, \ldots, a_{i-1}) \sim \mathcal{M}_i(a_1, \ldots, a_{i-1})$ is publicly announced. Player i plays according to some strategy $d_i : \Delta_m \to A_i$, that is $a_i = d_i(m_1, \ldots, m_i(a_1, \ldots, a_{i-1}))$, a random variable which is a function of this announcement. When it is clear from context, we denote $m_i(a_1, \ldots, a_{i-1})$ by m_i. Formally, the counters used in this paper satisfy the following notion of privacy.

DEFINITION 1. *An announcement mechanism $\mathcal{M}$ is (ϵ, δ)-differentially private under adaptive[6] continual observation in the strategies of players if, for each d, for each player i, each pair of strategies d_i, d'_i, and every $S \subseteq (\Delta_m)^n$:*

$$\mathbb{P}[(m_1, \ldots, m_n) \in S] \le e^\epsilon \mathbb{P}[(m_1, \ldots, m_i, m'_{i+1} \ldots, m'_n) \in S] + \delta,$$

where $a_j = d_j(m_1, \ldots, m_j)$, $a'_i = d'_i(m_1, \ldots, m_i)$, $m_j \sim \mathcal{M}_j(a_1, \ldots, a_{j-1})$, $m'_j \sim \mathcal{M}_j(a_1, \ldots, a_{i-1}, a'_i, a'_{i+1}, \ldots, a'_{j-1})$ and for all $j > i$, $a'_j = d_j(m_1, \ldots, m_{i-1}, m_i, m'_{i+1}, \ldots, m'_j)$

This definition requires that two worlds which differ in a single player changing her strategy from d_i to d'_i have statistically close joint distributions over all players' announcements (and thus their joint distributions over actions). Note that the distribution of $j > i$'s announcement can change slightly, causing j's distribution over actions to change slightly, necessitating the cascaded m'_j, a'_j for $j > i$ in our definition. The mechanisms we use maintain approximate use counters for each resource. The values of the counters are *publicly announced* throughout the game play. We now define the notion of accuracy used to describe these counters.

DEFINITION 2 ((α, β, γ)-ACCURATE COUNTER VECTOR). *A set of counters $y_{i,r}$ is defined to be (α, β, γ)-accurate if with probability at least $1 - \gamma$, at all points of time, the displayed value of every counter $y_{i,r}$ lies in the range $[\frac{x_{i,r}}{\alpha} - \beta, \alpha x_{i,r} + \beta]$ where $x_{i,r}$ is the true count for resource i, and is monotonically increasing in the true count.*

We refer to a set of $(\alpha, \beta, 0)$-accurate counters as (α, β)-counters for brevity. It is possible to achieve $\gamma = 0$ (which is necessary for undominated strategies, which assumes the multiplicative and additive bounds on y are worst-case), taking an appropriate loss in the privacy guarantees for the counter (Proposition 1). Counters satisfying Definitions 1 and 2 with $\alpha = 1$ and $\beta = O(\log^2 n)$ were given in Dwork et al. [3], Chan et al. [2]; we give a different implementation in Section 4 which gives a tighter bound on $\alpha\beta$ by taking α to be a small constant larger than 1. Furthermore, the counters in Section 4 are *monotonic* (i.e., the displayed values can only increase as the game proceeds) and we use monotonicity of the counters in some of our results.

In some settings we require counters we a more specific utility guarantee:

DEFINITION 3 ((α, β, γ)-ACCURATE UNDERESTIMATOR). *A set of counters $y_{i,r}$ is defined to be (α, β, γ)-accurate underestimator if with probability at least $1 - \gamma$, at all points of time, the displayed value of every counter $y_{i,r}$ lies in the range $[\frac{x_{i,r}}{\alpha} - \beta, x_{i,r}]$ where $x_{i,r}$ is the true count for resource i.*

The following observation states that a counter vector can be converted to an undercounter with small loss in accuracy.

OBSERVATION 1. *We can convert a (α, β)-counter to an $(\alpha^2, \frac{2\beta}{\alpha})$-underestimating counter vector.*

PROOF. We can shift the counter, $\frac{1}{\alpha}x - \beta \le y \le \alpha x + \beta$ implies $y' = \frac{y-\beta}{\alpha} \le x$ and $\frac{1}{\alpha^2}x - \frac{2\beta}{\alpha} \le y'$. □

---

[6] Adaptivity is needed in this case because the announcements are arguments to the actions of players: when a particular action changes, this modifies the distribution over the future announcements, which in turn changes the distribution over future selected actions.

3. RESOURCE SHARING

In this section, we consider resource sharing games – the utility to a player is completely determined by the resource she chooses and the number of players who have chosen that resource before her. This section considers the case where players' actions are discrete: $a_i \in \{0, 1\}^m$ for all $i, a_i \in A_i$. We defer the analysis of the case where players' actions are continuous to the full version of this paper.

3.1 Perfect counters and empty counters

Before delving into our main results, we point out that, with perfect counters, greedy is the only undominated strategy, and the competitive ratio of greedy is a constant.

THEOREM 1. *With perfect counters, greedy behavior is dominant-strategy and all other behavior is dominated for any sequential resource-sharing game g; and $CR_{\text{GREEDY}}(\mathcal{M}_{Full}, g) \le 4$.*

The proof of this Theorem follows from the connection between future-independent resource-sharing and online vertex-weighted matching, which we mention below.

OBSERVATION 2. *In the setting where $\|a_i\|_1 = 1$ for all $a_i \in A_i$, for all i, full-information, discrete resource-sharing reduces to online, vertex-weighted bipartite matching.*

PROOF. Construct the following bipartite graph $G = (U, V, E)$ as an instance of online vertex-weighted matching from an instance of the future-independent resource sharing game. For each resource r, create n vertices in V, one with weight $V_r(t)$ for each $t \in [n]$. As players arrive online, they will correspond to vertices in $u_i \in U$. For each $a_i \in A_i$ corresponding to a set of resources S, u_i is allowed to take any subset of V with a single copy of each $r \in S$. □

The proof of the social welfare is quite similar to the one-to-one, online vertex-weighted matching proof of [8], with the necessary extension for many-to-one matchings (losing a factor of $1/2$ in the process).

PROOF OF THEOREM 1. Consider any instance of $G = (U, V, E)$, a vertex-weighted bipartite graph. Let μ be the optimal many-to-one matching, which can be applied to nodes in both U and V (where $u \in U$ has potentially multiple neighbors in V). Consider μ', the greedy many-to-one matching for a particular sequence of arrivals σ.

Consider a particular $u \in U$, and the time it arrives $\sigma(u)$ as μ' progresses. If at least $1/2$ the value of $\mu(u)$ is available at that time, then $w(\mu'(u)) \ge \frac{1}{2} w(\mu(u))$ (since u can be matched to any subset of $\mu(u)$, by the downward closed assumption). If not, then $w(\mu'(\mu(u))) \ge \frac{1}{2} w(\mu(u))$ (at least half the value was taken by others). Thus, we know that, for all u,

$$w(\mu'(u)) + w(\mu'(\mu(u))) \ge \frac{1}{2} w(\mu(u))$$

summing up over all u, we get

$$\sum_u w(\mu'(u)) + w(\mu'(\mu(u))) = 2w(\mu') \ge \frac{1}{2} \sum_u w(\mu(u)) = \frac{1}{2} w(\mu)$$

Rearranging shows that $w(\mu') \ge \frac{1}{4} w(\mu)$.

Finally, the utility to a player is clearly greatest when they are greedy, so that is a dominant strategy (thus implying any non-greedy strategy is dominated). □

Recall, from our example in the introduction, that both greedy and undominated strategies can perform poorly with respect to empty counters. We defer the proof of the following results to the full version of the paper. Recall that $\mathcal{M}_\emptyset$ refers to the empty counter mechanism.

THEOREM 2. *There exist games g such that $CR_{\text{UNDOM}}(\mathcal{M}_\emptyset, g)$ cannot be bounded by any function of n.*

THEOREM 3. *There exists g such that $CR_{\text{UNDOM}}(\mathcal{M}_\emptyset, g) \geq \Omega(\frac{n^2}{\log(n)})$, when $V_r(t) = \frac{V_r(0)}{t}$.*

3.2 Privacy-Preserving Counters and Greedy Behavior

THEOREM 4. *With (α, β)-accurate underestimator counter mechanism $\mathcal{M}$, $CR_{\text{GREEDY}}(\mathcal{M}, g) = O(\alpha\beta)$ for all resource-sharing games g.*

Before we prove Theorem 4, we need a way to compare players' utilities with the utility they *think* they get from choosing resources greedily with respect to approximate counters. Let a player's *perceived value* be $V_r(y_{i,r})$ where r is the resource she chose (the value of a resource if the counter was correct, which may or may not be the *actual* value of the resource).

LEMMA 1. *Suppose players choose greedily according to a (α, β)-underestimator. Then, the sum of their actual values is at least a $\frac{1}{2\alpha\beta}$-fraction of the sum of their perceived values.*

PROOF. Suppose k players chose a given resource r. For ease of notation, let these be players 1 through k. We wish to bound the ratio

$$\frac{\sum_{i=1}^k V_r(y_{i,r})}{\sum_{c=1}^k V_r(c)}.$$

We start by "grouping" the counter values: it cannot take on values that are small for more than a certain number of steps. In particular, if $x_{i,r} > T\alpha\beta$, for some $T \in \mathbb{N}$,

$$y_{i,r} \geq \frac{1}{\alpha}x_{i,r} - \beta \geq \frac{T\alpha\beta}{\alpha} - \beta = (T-1)\beta$$

Now, we bound the ratio from above using this fact.

$$\frac{\sum_{i=1}^k V_r(y_{i,r})}{\sum_{c=1}^k V_r(c)} \leq \frac{2\alpha\beta \sum_{T=1}^{\lceil \frac{k}{\alpha\beta} \rceil} V_r((T-1)\beta)}{\sum_{c=1}^k V_r(c)}$$

$$\leq \frac{2\alpha\beta \sum_{T=1}^{\lceil \frac{k}{\alpha\beta} \rceil} V_r((T-1)\beta)}{\sum_{T=1}^{\lceil \frac{k}{\alpha\beta} \rceil} V_r((T-1)\beta)} \leq 2\alpha\beta$$

where the first inequality came from the fact that the value curves are non-increasing and the lower bound on the counter values from above, and the second because all terms are non-negative. □

PROOF OF THEOREM 4. The optimal value of the resource-sharing game g, denoted by $OPT(g)$, is the maximum weight matching in the bipartite graph $G = (U \cup V, E)$ where U is the set of the n players and V has n vertices for each resource r, one of value $V_r(k)$ for each $k \in [n]$. There is an edge between player i and all vertices corresponding to resource r if and only if $r \in A_i$. Note that the weights are on the vertices in V.

We now define a complete bipartite graph G' which has the same set of nodes but whose node weights differ for some nodes in G. Consider some resource r, and the collection of players who chose r in g. If there were t_k players i who chose resource r when $y_{i,r} = k$, make t_k of the nodes corresponding to r have weight $V_r(k)$. Finally, if there were F_k players who chose resource r, let the remaining $n - F_k$ nodes corresponding to r have weight $V_r(F_k + 1)$.

We first claim that the perceived utility of players choosing greedily according to the counters is identical to the weight of the greedy matching in G' (where nodes arrive in the same order). We prove, in fact, that the corresponding matching will be identical by induction. Since the counters are monotone, earlier copies of a resource appear more valuable. So, when the first player arrives in G', the most valuable node she has access to is exactly the first node corresponding to the resource she took according to the counters. Now, assume that prior to player i, all players have chosen nodes corresponding to the resource they chose according to the counters. By our induction hypothesis and monotonicity of the counters and value curves, there is a node n_i corresponding to i's selection r according to counters of weight $V_r(y_{i,r})$, and no heavier node corresponding to r. Likewise, for all other resources r', all nodes corresponding to r' have weight more than $V_{r'}(y_{i,r'})$. Thus, i will take n_i for value $V_r(y_{i,r})$. Thus, the weight of the greedy matching in G' equals the perceived utility of greedy play according to the counters.

Let GREEDY$_{\text{COUNTERS}}$ denote the set of actions players make playing greedily with respect to the counters. By Lemma 1, the social welfare of GREEDY$_{\text{COUNTERS}}$ is a $\frac{1}{\alpha\beta}$-fraction of the perceived social welfare. By our previous argument, the perceived social welfare of greedy play according to the counters is the same as the weight of the greedy matching in G'. By Theorem 1, the greedy matching in G' is a 4-approximation to the max-weight matching in G'. Finally, since the counters are underestimators, the weight of the max-weight matching in G' is at least as large as $OPT(g)$. Thus, that the social welfare of greedy play with respect to counters is a $\frac{1}{2\alpha\beta}$ fraction of the optimal welfare of g. □

THEOREM 5. *There exists (ϵ, δ)-privacy-preserving mechanism $\mathcal{M}$ such that*

$$CR_{\text{GREEDY}}(\mathcal{M}, g) \leq \min\left(O\left(\frac{\log n \log \frac{nm}{\delta}}{\epsilon}\right), O\left(\frac{m \log n \log \log \frac{1}{\delta}}{\epsilon}\right)\right)$$

for all resource-sharing games g.

PROOF. In Section 4, we prove Corollary 2 that says that we can achieve an (ϵ, δ)-differentially private counter vector achieving the better of $(1, O(\frac{(\log n)(\log(nm/\delta))}{\epsilon}))$-accuracy and $(\alpha, \tilde{O}_\alpha(\frac{m \log n \log \log(1/\delta)}{\epsilon}))$-accuracy for any constant $\alpha > 1$. This along with Theorem 4 proves the result. □

Observation 3 (whose proof can be found in the full version) states that players acting greedily according to any estimate that is *deterministically* more accurate than the values provided by the private counters also achieve similar or better social welfare guarantees. Moreover, we show that if the estimates used by the players are more accurate only in expectation, as opposed to deterministically, then we cannot make a similar claim (Observation 4).

OBSERVATION 3. *Suppose that $\mathcal{M}$ is a (α, β, γ) underestimator, giving estimates $y_{i,r}$. Furthermore, assume each player i is playing greedily with respect to a revised estimate $z_{i,r}$ such that, for each r, i, and value of $z_{i,r}$ is always in the range $[y_{i,r}, x_{i,r}]$. Then, for g, a discrete resource-sharing game, with probability $1 - \gamma$, the ratio of the optimal to the achieved social welfare is $\Omega(\alpha\beta)$.*

PROOF. The proof follows from the proof of Theorem 4, along with the following observation. Since $z_{i,r}$'s is deterministically more accurate than the COUNTERS, we have for each i that the value gained by greedily choosing according to the estimates $z_{i,r}$ is at least as much as the value gained by greedily choosing using $y_{i,r}$. Therefore, summing over all the players, the achieved social welfare is at least as much as it would be if everyone had played greedily according to $y_{i,r}$. □

OBSERVATION 4. *There exists a resource-sharing game g, such that if the players play greedily according to estimates $z_{i,r}$ that are more accurate than the displayed value only in expectation – specifically for each r, i, and value of $x_{i,r}$, $\mathbb{P}[z_{i,r} < x_{i,r}] \geq 1/2$ and also $\mathbb{E}[|z_{i,r} - x_{i,r}|] = 1$, then the ratio of the optimal to the achieved social welfare can be as bad as $\Omega(\sqrt{n})$.*

PROOF. Let there be $n + \sqrt{n}$ resources, with resources $r*_{1,\ldots,\sqrt{n}}$ having $V_{r*_f}(0) = H$, $V_{r*_f}(t) = 0$ for all $t > 0$, and resource r_i such that $V_{r_i}(t) = H - \epsilon$ for all t. Player i has access to all resources $r*_f$ and r_i. Then, $OPT = H\sqrt{n} + (H - \epsilon)(n - \sqrt{n}) = Hn - (n - \sqrt{n})\epsilon$.
Consider the counter vector which is exactly correct with probability $1 - \frac{1}{\sqrt{n}}$ and undercounts by $\sqrt{n}$ with probability $\frac{1}{\sqrt{n}}$ (note that the expected error is just 1 and it undercounts with probability 1). Then, greedy behavior with respect to this counter will (in expectation) have $\sqrt{n}$ players choose $r*_f$ for each f, achieving welfare $\sqrt{n}H$. Thus, the competitive ratio is $\Omega(\sqrt{n})$ as $\epsilon \to 0$, as desired. □

3.3 Privacy-Preserving Counters and Undominated behavior

We begin with an illustration of how undominated strategies can perform poorly for arbitrary value curves, as motivation for the restricted class of value curves we consider in Theorem 7. In the case of greedy players, we were able to avoid the problem of players undervaluing resources rather easily, by forcing the counters to only underestimate $x_{i,r}$. This won't work for undominated strategies: players who know the counts are shaded downward can compensate for that fact.

THEOREM 6. *For an (ϵ, δ)-differentially private announcement mechanism $\mathcal{M}$, there exist games g for which*

$$CR_{\text{UNDOM}}(g, \mathcal{M}) = \Omega\left(\frac{1}{\delta}\right).$$

PROOF. Suppose there are two players 1 and 2, and resources r, r'. Let r have $V_r(0) = 1$, $V_r(1) = 0$, and $V_{r'}(k) = \rho$, for all $k \geq 0$. Furthermore, let player 1 have access only to resource r' but player 2 has access to both r and r'. Player 1 will choose r'. Let player 2's strategy be d_2, such that if she determines there was nonzero chance that player 1 chose r according to her signal m_2, she will choose resource r'. This is undominated: if 1 *did* choose r, r' will be more valuable

for 2. Thus, if 2 sees any signal that can occur when r is chosen by 1, she will choose r'. The collection of signals 2 can see if 1 chooses r has probability 1 in total. So, because m_2 is (ϵ, δ)-differentially private in player 1's action, the set of signals *reserved* for the case when 1 chooses r' (that cannot occur when r is chosen by 1) may occur with probability at most δ (they can occur with probability 0 if I chose r, implying they can occur with probability at most δ when 1 chooses r'). Thus, with this probability $1 - \delta$, player 2 will choose r', implying $\mathbb{E}[SW] \leq (1 - \delta)2\rho + \delta(1 + \rho) = \delta + (2 - \delta)\rho$, which for ρ sufficiently small approaches δ, while $1 + \rho$ is the optimal social welfare. □

Given the above example, we cannot hope to have a theorem as general as Theorem 4 when analyzing undominated strategies with privacy-preserving counters. Instead, we show that, for a class of well-behaved value curves, we can bound the competitive ratio of undominated strategies (Theorem 7).
Again, along the lines of the greedy case, we show that any player who chooses any undominated resource r' over resource r gets a reasonable fraction of the utility she would get from choosing r. Then, by the analysis of greedy players, we have an analogous argument implying the bound of Theorem 7.

THEOREM 7. *If each value curve V_r has the property that $\psi(\alpha, \beta)V_r(x) \geq V_r((\max\{0, \frac{x}{\alpha^2} - \frac{2\beta}{\alpha}\}))$ and also $V_r((\alpha^2 x + 2\alpha\beta)) \geq \phi(\alpha, \beta)V_r(x)$, then an action profile a of undominated strategies according to (α, β)-counter vector $\mathcal{M}$ has $CR_{\text{UNDOM}}(g, \mathcal{M}) = O(\psi(\alpha, \beta)\phi(\alpha, \beta))$.*

In particular, Theorem 7 shows that, for games where $V_r(i) = \frac{V_r(0)}{g_r(x_{i,r})}$, where g_r is a polynomial, the competitive ratio of undominated strategies degrades gracefully as a function of the maximum degree of those polynomials. A simple calculation implies the following corollary, whose proof we relegate to the full version.

COROLLARY 1. *Suppose for a resource-sharing game g, each resource r has a value curve of the form $V_r(x) = \frac{V_r(0)}{g_r(x)}$, where g_r is a monotonically increasing degree-d polynomial and $V_r(0)$ is some constant. Then, $CR_{\text{UNDOM}}(g, \mathcal{M}) \leq O(2\alpha^3\beta)^d$ with $\mathcal{M}$ providing (α, β)-counters.*

4. PRIVATE COUNTERS WITH SMALLER ERROR AT SMALLER VALUES

In this section, we describe a counter for the model of differential privacy under continual observation that has improved guarantees when the value of the counter is small. Recall the basic counter problem: given a stream $\vec{a} = (a_1, a_2, \ldots, a_n)$ of numbers $a_i \in [0, 1]$, we wish to release at every time step t the partial sum $x_t = \sum_{i=1}^{t} a_i$. We require a generalization, where one maintains a vector of m counters. Each player's update contribution is now a vector $a_i \in \Delta_m = \{a \in [0, 1]^m \mid \|a\|_1 \leq 1\}$. That is, a player can add non-negative values to all counters, but the total value of her updates is at most 1. The partial sums x_t then lie in $(\mathbb{R}^+)^m$ and have ℓ_1 norm at most t.
Given an algorithm $\mathcal{M}$, we define the output stream $(y_1, \ldots, y_n) = \mathcal{M}(\vec{a})$ where $y_t = \mathcal{M}(t, a_1, \ldots, a_{t-1})$ lies in $\mathbb{R}^m$. We seek counters that are private (Definition 1) and satisfy a mixed multiplicative and additive accuracy guarantee

(Definition 2). Proofs of all the results in this section can be found in the full version of this paper.

The original works on differentially private counters [3, 2] concentrated on minimizing the additive error of the estimated sums, that is, they sought to minimize $\|x_t - y_t\|_\infty$. Both papers gave a binary tree-based mechanism, which we dub "TreeSum", with additive error approximately $(\log^2 n)/\epsilon$. Some of our algorithms use TreeSum, and others use a new mechanism (FTSum, described below) which gets a better additive error guarantee at the price of introducing a small multiplicative error. Formally, they prove:

LEMMA 2. *For every $m \in \mathbb{N}$ and $\gamma \in (0,1)$: Running m independent copies of TreeSum [3, 2] is $(\epsilon, 0)$-differentially private and provides an $(1, C_{tree} \cdot \frac{\log n \log \frac{nm}{\gamma}}{\epsilon}, \gamma)$-approximation to partial vector sums, where $C_{tree} > 0$ is an absolute constant.*

Even for $m = 1, \alpha = 1$, this bound is slightly tighter than those in Chan et al. [2] and Dwork et al. [3]; however, it follows directly from the tail bound in Chan et al. [2].

Our new algorithm, FTSum (for Flag/Tree Sum), is described in Algorithm 1. For small m ($m = o(log(n))$), it provides lower additive error at the expense of introducing an arbitrarily small constant multiplicative error.

LEMMA 3. *For every $m \in \mathbb{N}$, $\alpha > 1$ and $\gamma \in (0,1)$, FTSum (Algorithm 1) is $(\epsilon, 0)$-differentially private and $(\alpha, \tilde{O}_\alpha(\frac{m \log \frac{n}{\gamma}}{\epsilon}), \gamma)$-approximates partial sums (where $\tilde{O}_\alpha(\cdot)$ hides polylogarithmic factors in its argument, and treats α as constant).*

FTSum proceeds in two phases. In the first phase, it increments the reported output value only when the underlying counter value has increased significantly. Specifically, the mechanism outputs a public signal, which we will call a "flag", roughly when the true counter achieves the values $\log n$, $\alpha \log n$, $\alpha^2 \log n$ and so on, where α is the desired *multiplicative* approximation. The reported estimate is updated each time a flag is raised (it starts at 0, and then increases to $\log n$, $\alpha \log n$, etc). The privacy analysis for this phase is based on the "sparse vector" technique of Hardt and Rothblum [6], which shows that the cost to privacy is proportional to the number of times a flag is raised (but not the number of time steps between flags).

When the value of the counter becomes large (about $\frac{\alpha \log^2 n}{(\alpha-1)\epsilon}$), the algorithm switches to the second phase and simply uses the TreeSum protocol, whose additive error (about $\frac{\log^2 n}{\epsilon}$) is low enough to provide an α multiplicative guarantee (without need for the extra space given by the additive approximation).

If the mechanism were to raise a flag *exactly* when the true counter achieved the values $\log n$, $\alpha \log n$, $\alpha^2 \log n$, etc, then the mechanism would provide a $(\alpha, \log n, 0)$ approximation during the first phase, and a $(\alpha, 0, 0)$ approximation thereafter. The rigorous analysis is more complicated, since flags are raised only near those thresholds.

Enforcing Additional Guarantees.

Finally, we note that it is possible to enforce to additional useful properties of the counter. First, we may insist that the accuracy guarantees be satisfied with probability 1 (that is, set $\gamma = 0$), at the price of increasing the additive term δ in the privacy guarantee:

Algorithm 1: FTSum — A Private Counter with Low Multiplicative Error

Input: Stream $\vec{a} = (a_1, ..., a_n) \in ([0,1]^m)^n$, parameters $m, n \in \mathbb{N}$, $\alpha > 1$ and $\gamma > 0$

Output: Noisy partial sums $y_1, ..., y_n \in \mathbb{R}^m$

$k \leftarrow \lceil \log_\alpha(\frac{\alpha}{\alpha-1} \cdot C_{tree} \cdot \frac{\log(nm/\gamma)}{\epsilon}) \rceil$;

/* C_{tree} is the constant from Lemma 2 */

$\epsilon' \leftarrow \frac{\epsilon}{2m(k+1)}$;

for $r = 1$ **to** m **do**

  flag$_r \leftarrow 0$;

  $x_{0,r} \leftarrow 0$;

  $\tau_r \leftarrow (\log n) + \mathsf{Lap}(2/\epsilon')$;

for $i = 1$ **to** n **do**

  for $r = 1$ **to** m **do**

    if $flag_r \leq k$ **then** (First phase still in progress for counter r)

      $x_{i,r} \leftarrow x_{i-1,r} + a_{i,r}$;

      $\tilde{x_{i,r}} \leftarrow x_{i,r} + \mathsf{Lap}(\frac{2}{\epsilon'})$;

      if $\tilde{x_{i,r}} > \tau_r$ **then** (Raise a new flag for counter r)

        flag$_r \leftarrow$ flag$_r + 1$;

        $\tau_r \leftarrow (\log n) \cdot \alpha^{flag_r} + \mathsf{Lap}(2/\epsilon')$;

      Release $y_{i,r} = (\log n) \cdot \alpha^{flag_r - 1}$;

    else (Second phase has been reached for counter r)

      Release $y_{i,r} = r$-th counter output from TreeSum$(\vec{a}, \epsilon/2)$;

PROPOSITION 1. *If $\mathcal{M}$ is (ϵ, δ)-private and (α, β, γ)-accurate, then one can modify $\mathcal{M}$ to obtain an algorithm $\mathcal{M}'$ with the same efficiency that is $(\epsilon, \delta + \gamma)$-private and $(\alpha, \beta, 0)$-accurate.*

Second, as in [3], we may enforce the requirement that the reported values be monotone, integral values that increase at each time step by at most 1. The idea is to simply report the nearest integral, monotone sequence to the noisy values (starting at 0 and incrementing the reported counter only when the noisy value exceeds the current counter).

PROPOSITION 2 ([3]). *If $\mathcal{M}$ is (ϵ, δ)-private and (α, β, γ)-accurate, then one can modify $\mathcal{M}$ to obtain an algorithm $\mathcal{M}'$ which reports monotone, integral values that increase by 0 or 1 at each time step, with the same privacy and accuracy guarantees as $\mathcal{M}$.*

COROLLARY 2. *Algorithm 1 is an (ϵ, δ)-differentially private vector counter algorithm providing a*

1. *$(1, O(\frac{(\log n)(\log(nm/\delta))}{\epsilon}), 0)$-approximation (using modified TreeSum); or*

2. *$(\alpha, \tilde{O}_\alpha(\frac{m \log n \log \log(1/\delta)}{\epsilon}), 0)$-approximation for any constant $\alpha > 1$ (using FTSum).*

5. EXTENSIONS

In the full version of this paper, we also consider settings where players' utility when choosing a resource r depends upon the *total number* of players choosing r, not just the players who chose r before. In addition, we study several other classes of games: namely, cut games, consensus games, and unrelated machine scheduling, and consider whether or not private synopses of the state of play is sufficient to improve social welfare over simultaneous play, as perfect synopses have been proven to be in Leme et al. [10].

6. DISCUSSION AND OPEN PROBLEMS

In this work, we considered how public dissemination of information in sequential games can guarantee a good social welfare while maintaining differential privacy of the players' strategies. We considered two 'extreme' cases – the greedy strategy and the class of all undominated strategies. While analyzing the class of undominated strategies gives guarantees that are robust, in many games that we considered, the competitive ratios were significantly worse than greedy strategies, and in some cases they were unbounded. It is interesting to note that many of the examples in this paper that show the poor performance with undominated strategies also hold when the players know their position in the sequence, an assumption we have not made for any of the positive results in this work. It is an interesting direction for future research to consider classes of strategies that more restricted than undominated strategies yet are general enough to be relevant for games where players play with imperfect information.

As mentioned in the introduction, we note here that, while players are making choices subject to approximate information, our results are not a direct extension of the line of thought that approximate information implies approximate optimization. In particular, for greedy strategies, while there may be a bound on the error of the counters, that *does not imply*, for arbitrary value curves, playing greedily according to the counters will be *approximately optimal for each individual*. In particular, consider one resource r with value H for the first 10 investors, and value 0 for the remaining investors, and a second resource r' with value $H/2$ for all investors. With (α, β, γ), as many as β players might have unbounded ratio between their value for r as r', but will pick r over r'. The analysis of greedy shows, despite this anomaly, the total social welfare is still well-approximated by this behavior.

All of our results relied on using differentially private counters for disseminating information. For the differentially-private counter, a main open question is "what is the optimal trade-off between additive and multiplicative guarantees?". Furthermore, as part of future research, one can consider other privacy techniques for announcing information that can prove useful in helping players achieve a good social welfare. And more generally, we want to understand what features of games lend themselves to be amenable to public dissemination of information that helps achieve good welfare and simultaneously preserves privacy of the players' strategies.

References

[1] Maria-Florina Balcan, Avrim Blum, and Yishay Mansour. The Price of Uncertainty. In *Proceedings of the 10th ACM Conference on Electronic Commerce*, EC '09, pages 285–294, 2009.

[2] T.-H. Hubert Chan, Elaine Shi, and Dawn Song. Private and Continual Release of Statistics. *ACM Trans. Inf. Syst. Secur.*, 14(3):26, 2011.

[3] Cynthia Dwork, Moni Naor, Toniann Pitassi, and Guy N Rothblum. Differential Privacy under Continual Observation. In *Symposium on Theory of Computing*, STOC '10, pages 715–724. ACM, 2010.

[4] Financial Crisis Inquiry Commission. *The Financial Crisis Inquiry Report: Final Report of the National Commission on the Causes of the Financial and Economic Crisis in the United States*. U.S. Government Printing Office, 2011. URL http://fcic.law.stanford.edu/report.

[5] Mark D. Flood, Jonathan Katz, Stephen J. Ong, and Adam Smith. Cryptography and the Economics of Supervisory Information: Balancing Transparency and Confidentiality. Working Paper #11, Office of Financial Research, US Department of Treasury, August 2013.

[6] Moritz Hardt and Guy N. Rothblum. A Multiplicative Weights Mechanism for Privacy-Preserving Data Analysis. In *FOCS '10*, 2010.

[7] Justin Hsu, Zhiyi Huang, Aaron Roth, Tim Roughgarden, and Zhiwei Steven Wu. Private Matchings and Allocations. *CoRR*, abs/1311.2828, 2013.

[8] Richard M. Karp, Umesh V. Vazirani, and Vijay V. Vazirani. An Optimal Algorithm for On-line Bipartite Matching. In *STOC '90*, pages 352–358, 1990.

[9] Michael Kearns, Mallesh M. Pai, Aaron Roth, and Jonathan Ullman. Mechanism Design in Large Games: Incentives and privacy. *CoRR*, abs/1207.4084, 2012.

[10] Renato Paes Leme, Vasilis Syrgkanis, and Éva Tardos. The Curse of Simultaneity. In *Proceedings of the 3rd Innovations in Theoretical Computer Science Conference*, ITCS '12, pages 60–67, 2012.

[11] Mikhail V. Oet, Timothy Bianco, Dieter Gramlich, and Stephen J. Ong. Safe: An early warning system for systemic banking risk. Working Paper 11-29, Federal Reserve Bank of Cleveland, 2011. URL http://www.clevelandfed.org/research/workpaper/2011/wp1129.pdf.

[12] Mikhail V. Oet, Timothy Bianco, Dieter Gramlich, and Stephen J. Ong. Financial Stress Index: A Lens for Supervising the Financial System. Working Paper 12-37, Federal Reserve Bank of Cleveland, 2012. URL http://www.clevelandfed.org/research/workpaper/2012/wp1237.pdf.

[13] Mallesh M. Pai and Aaron Roth. Privacy and mechanism design. *CoRR*, abs/1306.2083, 2013.

[14] Ryan M Rogers and Aaron Roth. Asymptotically Truthful Equilibrium Selection in Large Congestion Games. In *Proceedings of the fifteenth ACM conference on Economics and computation*, pages 771–782. ACM, 2014.

Uniform Sampling for Matrix Approximation

Michael B. Cohen
micohen@mit.edu

Yin Tat Lee
yintat@mit.edu

Cameron Musco
cnmusco@mit.edu

Christopher Musco
cpmusco@mit.edu

Richard Peng
rpeng@mit.edu

Aaron Sidford
sidford@mit.edu

Departments of EECS and Mathematics
Massachusetts Institute of Technology
Cambridge, MA 02139

ABSTRACT

Random sampling has become a critical tool in solving massive matrix problems. For linear regression, a small, manageable set of data rows can be randomly selected to approximate a tall, skinny data matrix, improving processing time significantly. For theoretical performance guarantees, each row must be sampled with probability proportional to its *statistical leverage score*. Unfortunately, leverage scores are difficult to compute. A simple alternative is to sample rows uniformly at random. While this often works, uniform sampling will eliminate critical row information for many natural instances.

We take a fresh look at uniform sampling by examining what information it *does* preserve. Specifically, we show that uniform sampling yields a matrix that, in some sense, well approximates a large fraction of the original. While this weak form of approximation is not enough for solving linear regression directly, it *is* enough to compute a better approximation.

This observation leads to simple iterative row sampling algorithms for matrix approximation that run in input-sparsity time and preserve row structure and sparsity at all intermediate steps. In addition to an improved understanding of uniform sampling, our main proof introduces a structural result of independent interest: we show that every matrix can be made to have low coherence by reweighting a small subset of its rows.

Categories and Subject Descriptors

F.2.1 [**Analysis of Algorithms and Problem Complexity**]: Numerical Algorithms and Problems—*Computations on matrices*; G.1.3 [**Numerical Analysis**]: Numerical Linear Algebra—*Sparse, structured, and very large systems*

General Terms

Algorithms, Theory

Keywords

Regression, leverage scores, matrix sampling, randomized numerical linear algebra

1. INTRODUCTION

Many fast, randomized algorithms for solving massive regression problems rely on the fundamental building block of *spectral approximation*. For a tall, narrow data matrix $\mathbf{A}$, these methods find a shorter approximate data matrix, $\tilde{\mathbf{A}}$, such that, for all vectors $\mathbf{x}$, $\|\tilde{\mathbf{A}}\mathbf{x}\|_2 \approx \|\mathbf{A}\mathbf{x}\|_2$. A recent explosion in work on this problem has lead to extremely fast algorithms, all of which rely on variations of Johnson-Lindenstrauss random projections [4, 20, 24, 18].

By re-examining uniform sampling, a heuristic that works for *low coherence* data, we give spectral approximation algorithms that avoid random projection entirely. Our methods are the first to match state-of-the-art runtimes while preserving row structure and sparsity in all matrix operations.

It is known that for a data matrix $\mathbf{A} \in \mathbb{R}^{n \times d}$, a spectral approximation can be obtained by sampling $O(d \log d)$ rows, each with probability proportional to its *statistical leverage score* [12, 10, 27]. The leverage score of $\mathbf{A}$'s i^{th} row, $\mathbf{a}_i$, is $\tau_i = \mathbf{a}_i^\top (\mathbf{A}^\top \mathbf{A})^+ \mathbf{a}_i$, where $\mathbf{M}^+$ denotes the Moore-Penrose pseudoinverse of $\mathbf{M}$. A higher leverage score indicates that $\mathbf{a}_i$ is more important in composing the spectrum of $\mathbf{A}$.

Unfortunately, leverage scores are difficult to calculate – finding them involves computing the pseudoinverse $(\mathbf{A}^\top \mathbf{A})^+$, which is as slow as solving our regression problem in the first place! In practice, data is often assumed to have *low coherence* [23], in which case simply selecting rows uniformly at random works [1, 17]. However, uniform sampling could be disastrous – if $\mathbf{A}$ contains a row with some component orthogonal to all other rows, removing it will reduce the rank of $\mathbf{A}$ and thus we cannot possibly preserve all vector products ($\|\tilde{\mathbf{A}}\mathbf{x}\|_2$ will start sending some vectors to 0). Any uniform sampling scheme is likely to drop any such single row.[1]

Possible fixes include randomly "mixing" data points to avoid degeneracies [1]. However, this approach sacrifices sparsity and structure in our data matrix, increasing storage and runtime costs. Is there a more elegant fix? First note that sampling $\mathbf{A}$ by *approximate* leverage scores is fine, but we may need to select more than the optimal $O(d \log d)$ rows. With that in mind, consider the following straightforward algorithm for iterative sampling, inspired by [18]:

---

[1]On the other hand, when leverage score sampling, such a row would have the highest possible leverage score of 1.

Step 1 Reduce $\mathbf{A}$ significantly by sampling uniformly.

Step 2 Approximate $(\mathbf{A}^\top\mathbf{A})^+$ using the smaller matrix and estimate leverage scores for $\mathbf{A}$.

Step 3 Resample rows from $\mathbf{A}$ using these estimates, obtaining a spectral approximation $\tilde{\mathbf{A}}$.

Step 4 Repeat from **Step 1** to reduce $\tilde{\mathbf{A}}$ further and obtain a smaller approximation.

While intuitive, this scheme was not previously known to work! Our main result is proving that it does. This process (and related schemes) will quickly converge on a small spectral approximation to $\mathbf{A}$, i.e. with $O(d\log d)$ rows.

A few results come close to an analysis of such a routine – in particular, two iterative sampling schemes are analyzed in [18]. However, the first ultimately requires Johnson-Lindenstrauss projections that mix rows, something we were hoping to avoid. The second almost maintains sparsity and row structure (except for possibly including rows of the identity in $\tilde{\mathbf{A}}$), but its convergence rate depends on the condition number of $\mathbf{A}$.

More importantly, both of these results are similar in that they rely on the primitive that a (possibly poor) spectral approximation to $\mathbf{A}$ is sufficient for approximately computing leverage scores, which are in turn good enough for obtaining an even better spectral approximation. As mentioned, uniform sampling will not in general give a spectral approximation – it does not preserve information about all singular values. Our key contribution is a better understanding of what information uniform sampling *does* preserve. It turns out that, although weaker than a spectral approximation, the matrix obtained from uniform sampling can nonetheless give leverage score estimates that are good enough to obtain increasingly better approximations to $\mathbf{A}$.

1.1 Our Approach

Suppose we compute a set of leverage score estimates, $\{\tilde{\tau}_i\}$, using $(\tilde{\mathbf{A}}^\top\tilde{\mathbf{A}})^+$ in place of $(\mathbf{A}^\top\mathbf{A})^+$ for some already obtained matrix approximation $\tilde{\mathbf{A}}$. As long as our leverage score approximations are *upper bounds* on the true scores ($\tilde{\tau}_i \geq \tau_i$) we can use them for sampling and still obtain a spectral approximation to $\mathbf{A}$ [18]. The number of samples we take will be

$$c \cdot \log d \cdot \sum_{i=1}^n \tilde{\tau}_i$$

where c is some fixed constant. When sampling by exact leverage scores, it can be shown that $\sum_{i=1}^n \tau_i \leq d$ so we take $c \cdot d\log d$ rows.

Thus, to prove that our proposed iterative algorithm works, we need to show that, if we uniformly sample a relatively small number of rows from $\mathbf{A}$ (**Step 1**) and estimate leverage scores using these rows (**Step 2**), then the sum of our estimates will be small. Then, when we sample by these estimated leverage scores in **Step 3**, we can sufficiently reduce the size of $\mathbf{A}$. Note that we will *not* aim to reduce $\mathbf{A}$ to $O(d\log d)$ height in one shot – we just need our leverage estimates to sum to say, $n/(2c\log d)$, which allows us to cut the large matrix in half at each step.

In prior work, the sum of overestimates was bounded by estimating *each* leverage score to within a multiplicative factor. This requires a spectral approximation, which is why

previous iterative sampling schemes could only boost poor spectral approximations to better spectral approximations. Of course, a "for each" statement is not required, and we will not get one through uniform sampling. Thus, our core result avoids this technique. Specifically, we show,

Theorem 1 (Leverage Score Approximation via Uniform Sampling). *For any m, we can select $O(m)$ rows uniformly at random from $\mathbf{A}$ to obtain $\tilde{\mathbf{A}}$. Then, letting $\{\tilde{\tau}_i\}$ be a set of leverage score estimates for $\mathbf{A}$ computed using $\tilde{\mathbf{A}}$[2], both of the following hold:*

$$\forall i, \ \tilde{\tau}_i \geq \tau_i,$$

$$\mathbb{E}\left[\sum_{i=1}^n \tilde{\tau}_i\right] \leq \frac{nd}{m}.$$

The validity of our proposed iterative sampling scheme immediately follows from Theorem 1. For example, if we set $m = O(d\log d)$ with a high enough constant, $c\log d\sum\tilde{\tau}_i \leq \frac{n}{2}$, allowing us to cut our matrix in half. Alternatively, if we uniformly sample $m = O(n)$ rows (say n/2) then $c\log d\sum\tilde{\tau}_i \leq O(d\log d)$, so we can cut our matrix down to $O(d\log d)$ rows. There is a convenient tradeoff – the more rows uniformly sampled in **Step 1**, the more we can cut $\mathbf{A}$ down by in **Step 3**. This tradeoff leads to natural recursive and iterative algorithms for row sampling.

We give a proof of Theorem 1 using a simple expectation argument that bounds $\mathbb{E}\,\tilde{\tau}_i$ for all i. We also prove alternative versions of Theorem 1 with slightly different guarantees (Theorems 3 and 4) using a technique that we believe is of independent interest. It is well known that, if $\mathbf{A}$ has low coherence – that is, has a low maximum leverage score – then uniform sampling from the matrix is actually sufficient for obtaining a full spectral approximation. The uniform rate will upper bound the leverage score rate for every row. With this in mind, we show a powerful fact: while many matrices do not have low coherence, for any $\mathbf{A}$, we can decrease the weight on a small subset of rows to make the matrix have low coherence. Specifically,

Lemma 1 (Coherence Reducing Reweighting). *For any $\mathbf{A} \in \mathbb{R}^{n\times d}$ and any coherence upper bound $\alpha > 0$, there exists a diagonal reweighting matrix $\mathbf{W} \in \mathbb{R}^{n\times n}$ with all entries in $[0, 1]$ and just (d/α) entries not equal to 1, such that:*

$$\forall i, \ \tau_i(\mathbf{W}\mathbf{A}) \leq \alpha.$$

Intuitively, this lemma shows that uniform sampling gives a matrix that spectrally approximates a large sub-matrix of the original data. It follows from our more general Theorem 2, which describes exactly how leverage scores of $\mathbf{A}$ can be manipulated through row reweighting.

We never actually find $\mathbf{W}$ explicitly – simply its existence implies our uniform sampling theorems! As explained, since $\mathbf{W}\mathbf{A}$ has low coherence, uniform sampling would give a spectral approximation to the reweighted matrix and thus a multiplicatively good approximation to *each* leverage score. Thus, the sum of estimated leverage scores for $\mathbf{W}\mathbf{A}$ will be low, i.e. $< O(d)$. It can be shown that, for any row that is not reweighted, the leverage score in $\mathbf{A}$ computed using a

---

[2] We describe exactly how each $\tilde{\tau}_i$ is computed when we prove Theorem 1 in Section 4.

182

uniformly sampled $\tilde{\mathbf{A}}$, is never greater than the corresponding leverage score in $\mathbf{WA}$ computed using a uniformly sampled $\widetilde{\mathbf{WA}}$. Thus, the sum of approximate leverage scores for rows in $\mathbf{A}$ that are not reweighted is small by comparison to their corresponding leverage scores in $\mathbf{WA}$. How about the rows that *are* reweighted in $\mathbf{WA}$? Lemma 1 claims there are not too many of these – we can trivially bound their leverage score estimates by 1 and even then the total sum of estimated leverage scores will be small.

This argument gives the result we need: even if a uniformly sampled $\tilde{\mathbf{A}}$ cannot be used to obtain good per row leverage score upper bounds, it is sufficient for ensuring that the sum of all leverage score estimates is not too high. Varying α and setting $m = \alpha \log d/n$ leads to a range of iterative schemes, as described under Theorem 1.

1.2 Road Map

Section 2 Survey prior work on randomized linear algebra and spectral matrix approximation.

Section 3 Review frequently used notation and important foundational lemmas.

Section 4 Prove that uniform sampling is sufficient for leverage score estimation (Theorem 1).

Section 5 Show the existence of small, coherence-reducing reweightings (Theorem 2, Lemma 1).

Section 6 Use this result to prove alternative versions of Theorem 1 (Theorems 3 and 4).

Section 7 Describe simple and efficient iterative algorithms for spectral matrix approximation.

2. BACKGROUND

2.1 Randomized Numerical Linear Algebra

In the past decade, fast randomized algorithms for matrix problems have risen to prominence. Numerous results give improved running times for matrix multiplication, linear regression, and low rank approximation – helpful surveys of this work include [19] and [14]. In addition to asymptotic runtime gains, randomized alternatives to standard linear algebra tools tend to offer significant gains in terms of data access patterns and required working memory.

Algorithms for randomized linear algebra often work by generically reducing problem size – large matrices are compressed (using randomness) to smaller approximations which are processed deterministically via standard linear algebraic methods. Methods for matrix reduction divide roughly into two categories – random projection methods [3, 4, 20, 24, 26] and sampling methods [7, 8, 9, 13, 11, 18].

Random projection methods recombine rows or columns from a large matrix to form a much smaller problem that approximates the original. Descending from the Johnson-Lindenstrauss Lemma [15] and related results, these algorithms are impressive for their simplicity and speed – reducing a large matrix simply requires multiplication by an appropriately chosen random matrix.

Sampling methods, on the other hand, seek to approximate large matrices by judiciously selecting (and reweighting) few rows or columns. Sampling itself is even simpler

and faster than random projection – the challenge becomes efficiently computing the correct measure of "importance" for rows or columns. More important rows or columns are selected with higher probability.

2.2 Approximate Linear Regression

We focus on linear regression, i.e. solving overdetermined systems, which requires our matrix reduction step to produce a spectral approximation $\tilde{\mathbf{A}}$ to the data matrix $\mathbf{A}$. One possibility is to obtain a $(1 \pm \epsilon)$ approximation with $O(d \log d/\epsilon^2)$ rows and to solve regression on the smaller problem to give an approximate solution.[3] To improve stability and achieve $\log(1/\epsilon)$ dependence, randomized schemes can be combined with known iterative regression algorithms. These methods only require a constant factor spectral approximation with $O(d \log d)$ rows [1, 5, 4, 21, 25].

When random projections are used, $\tilde{\mathbf{A}} = \mathbf{\Pi A}$ for some randomly generated matrix $\mathbf{\Pi}$ which is known as a *subspace embedding*. Recent progress has significantly sped up the process of computing $\mathbf{\Pi A}$, leading to the first *input-sparsity time* algorithms for linear regression (or nearly input-sparsity time if iterative methods are employed) [4, 20, 24].

2.3 Row Sampling

An alternative route to spectral matrix approximation is importance sampling. Specifically, $O(d \log d/\epsilon^2)$ rows can be sampled with probability proportional to their leverage scores [12, 10, 27]. In [27], Spielman and Srivastava specifically focus on spectral approximations for the edge-vertex incidence matrix of a graph. This is more commonly referred to as *spectral graph sparsification*, a primitive that has become important in research on graph algorithms. Each row in a graph's (potentially tall) edge-vertex incident matrix corresponds to an edge and the row's leverage score is exactly the edge's *weighted effective resistance*, which is used as the sampling probability in [27].

This application illustrates an important point: for spectral sparsification, it is critical that $\mathbf{A}$ is compressed via sampling instead of random projection. Sampling ensures that $\tilde{\mathbf{A}}$ contains only reweighted rows from $\mathbf{A}$, so it remains an edge-vertex incidence matrix. In general, sampling is interesting because it preserves row structure. Even if that structure is just a certain level of sparsity, it can reduce memory requirements and accelerate matrix operations.

While leverage scores for the edge-vertex incidence matrix of a graph can be computed quickly [16, 28], in general, computing leverage scores requires evaluating $(\mathbf{A}^{\top} \mathbf{A})^{+}$, which is as difficult as solving regression in the first place. Li, Miller, and Peng address this issue with methods for iteratively computing good row samples [18]. Their algorithms achieve input-sparsity time regression, but are fairly involved and rely on intermediate operations that ultimately require Johnson-Lindenstrauss projections, mixing rows and necessitating dense matrix operations. An alternative approach from [18] does preserve row structure (except for possible additions of rows from the identity to intermediate matrices) but converges in a number of steps that depends on $\mathbf{A}$'s condition number.

---

[3] In fact, it is possible to improve this dependence to $O(d \log d/\epsilon)$ for solving regression [26]. In general, however, a $(1 + \epsilon)$ spectral approximation requires an $\tilde{\mathbf{A}}$ with dimension dependent on $1/\epsilon^2$.

3. NOTATION AND PRELIMINARIES

3.1 SVD and Pseudoinverse

For $\mathbf{A} \in \mathbb{R}^{n \times d}$ with rank r, we write the reduced singular value decomposition (SVD), $\mathbf{A} = \mathbf{U}\boldsymbol{\Sigma}\mathbf{V}^\top$. $\mathbf{U} \in \mathbb{R}^{n \times r}$ and $\mathbf{V} \in \mathbb{R}^{d \times r}$ have orthonormal columns and $\boldsymbol{\Sigma} \in \mathbb{R}^{r \times r}$ is diagonal and contains the nonzero singular values of $\mathbf{A}$. $\mathbf{A}^\top \mathbf{A} = \mathbf{V}\boldsymbol{\Sigma}\mathbf{U}^\top \mathbf{U}\boldsymbol{\Sigma}\mathbf{V}^\top = \mathbf{V}\boldsymbol{\Sigma}^2\mathbf{V}^\top$. Let $(\mathbf{A}^\top \mathbf{A})^+$ denote the Moore-Penrose pseudoinverse of $\mathbf{A}^\top \mathbf{A}$. $(\mathbf{A}^\top \mathbf{A})^+ = \mathbf{V}(\boldsymbol{\Sigma}^{-1})^2\mathbf{V}^\top$.

3.2 Spectral Approximation

For any $\lambda \geq 1$, we say that $\tilde{\mathbf{A}} \in \mathbb{R}^{n' \times d}$ is a λ-*spectral approximation* of $\mathbf{A} \in \mathbb{R}^{n \times d}$ if, $\forall \boldsymbol{x} \in \mathbb{R}^d$

$$\frac{1}{\lambda}\|\mathbf{A}\mathbf{x}\|^2 \leq \|\tilde{\mathbf{A}}\mathbf{x}\|^2 \leq \|\mathbf{A}\mathbf{x}\|^2, \text{ or equivalently}$$

$$\frac{1}{\lambda}\mathbf{x}^\top \mathbf{A}^\top \mathbf{A}\mathbf{x} \leq \mathbf{x}^\top \tilde{\mathbf{A}}^\top \tilde{\mathbf{A}}\mathbf{x} \leq \mathbf{x}^\top \mathbf{A}^\top \mathbf{A}\boldsymbol{x}. \quad (1)$$

Letting σ_i denote the ith singular value of a matrix, λ-spectral approximation implies:

$$\forall i, \frac{1}{\lambda}\sigma_i(\mathbf{A}) \leq \sigma_i(\tilde{\mathbf{A}}) \leq \sigma_i(\mathbf{A}).$$

So, a spectral approximation preserves the magnitude of matrix-vector multiplication with $\mathbf{A}$, the value of $\mathbf{A}^\top \mathbf{A}$'s quadratic form, and consequently, each singular value of $\mathbf{A}$. For conciseness, we sometimes use the Loewner ordering, writing $\frac{1}{\lambda}\mathbf{A}^\top \mathbf{A} \preceq \tilde{\mathbf{A}}^\top \tilde{\mathbf{A}} \preceq \mathbf{A}^\top \mathbf{A}$ where $\mathbf{C} \preceq \mathbf{D}$ indicates that $\mathbf{D} - \mathbf{C}$ is positive semidefinite. Even more succinctly, $\tilde{\mathbf{A}}^\top \tilde{\mathbf{A}} \approx_\lambda \mathbf{A}^\top \mathbf{A}$ denotes the same condition.

3.3 Leverage Scores

The leverage score of the ith row $\mathbf{a}_i^\top$ of $\mathbf{A}$ is:

$$\tau_i(\mathbf{A}) \overset{\text{def}}{=} \mathbf{a}_i^\top (\mathbf{A}^\top \mathbf{A})^+ \mathbf{a}_i. \quad (2)$$

We also define the related *cross leverage score* as $\tau_{ij}(\mathbf{A}) \overset{\text{def}}{=} \mathbf{a}_i^\top (\mathbf{A}^\top \mathbf{A})^+ \mathbf{a}_j$. Let $\boldsymbol{\tau}(\mathbf{A})$ be a vector containing $\mathbf{A}$'s n leverage scores. $\boldsymbol{\tau}(\mathbf{A})$ is the diagonal of $\mathbf{A}(\mathbf{A}^\top \mathbf{A})^+ \mathbf{A}^\top$, which is a projection matrix. Thus, $\tau_i(\mathbf{A}) = \mathbb{1}_i^\top \mathbf{A}(\mathbf{A}^\top \mathbf{A})^+ \mathbf{A}^\top \mathbb{1}_i \leq 1$. Futhermore, since $\mathbf{A}(\mathbf{A}^\top \mathbf{A})^+ \mathbf{A}^\top$ is a projection matrix, the sum of $\mathbf{A}$'s leverage scores is equal to the matrix's rank:

$$\sum_{i=1}^n \tau_i(\mathbf{A}) = \text{tr}(\mathbf{A}(\mathbf{A}^\top \mathbf{A})^+ \mathbf{A}^\top) = \text{rank}(\mathbf{A}(\mathbf{A}^\top \mathbf{A})^+ \mathbf{A}^\top)$$

$$= \text{rank}(\mathbf{A}) \leq d. \quad (3)$$

A row's leverage score measures how important it is in composing the row space of $\mathbf{A}$. If a row has a component orthogonal to all other rows, its leverage score is 1. Removing it would decrease the rank of $\mathbf{A}$, completely changing its row space. If all rows are the same, each has leverage score d/n. The *coherence* of $\mathbf{A}$ is $\|\boldsymbol{\tau}(\mathbf{A})\|_\infty$. If $\mathbf{A}$ has low coherence, no particular row is especially important. If $\mathbf{A}$ has high coherence, it contains at least one row whose removal would significantly affect the composition of $\mathbf{A}$'s row space. A characterization that helps with this intuition follows:

Lemma 2. *For all* $\mathbf{A} \in \mathbb{R}^{n \times d}$ *and* $i \in [n]$ *we have that*

$$\tau_i(\mathbf{A}) = \min_{\mathbf{A}^\top \mathbf{x} = \mathbf{a}_i} \|\mathbf{x}\|_2^2.$$

Let $\mathbf{x}_i$ *denote the optimal* $\mathbf{x}$ *for* $\mathbf{a}_i$. *The* j^{th} *entry of* $\mathbf{x}_i$ *is given by* $\mathbf{x}_i^{(j)} = \tau_{ij}(\mathbf{A})$.

Proof. For the solution $\mathbf{x}_i$ to have minimal norm, we must have $\mathbf{x}_i \perp \ker(\mathbf{A}^\top)$. Thus, $\mathbf{x}_i \in \text{im}(\mathbf{A})$ and we can write $\mathbf{x}_i = \mathbf{A}\mathbf{c}$ for some $\mathbf{c} \in \mathbb{R}^d$. Using the constraints of the optimization problem we have that $\mathbf{A}^\top \mathbf{x}_i = \mathbf{A}^\top \mathbf{A}\mathbf{c} = \mathbf{a}_i$. Thus $\mathbf{c} = (\mathbf{A}^\top \mathbf{A})^+ \mathbf{a}_i$, so $\mathbf{x}_i = \mathbf{A}(\mathbf{A}^\top \mathbf{A})^+ \mathbf{a}_i$. This gives $x_i^{(j)} = \mathbf{a}_j^\top (\mathbf{A}^\top \mathbf{A})^+ \mathbf{a}_i = \tau_{ij}(\mathbf{A})$. Furthermore:

$$\|\mathbf{x}_i\|_2^2 = \mathbf{a}_i^\top (\mathbf{A}^\top \mathbf{A})^+ \mathbf{A}^\top \mathbf{A}(\mathbf{A}^\top \mathbf{A})^+ \mathbf{a}_i$$

$$= \mathbf{a}_i^\top (\mathbf{A}^\top \mathbf{A})^+ \mathbf{a}_i = \tau_i(\mathbf{A}). \qquad \square$$

We often approximate the leverage scores of $\mathbf{A}$ by computing them with respect to some other matrix $\mathbf{B} \in \mathbb{R}^{n' \times d}$. We define the *generalized leverage score*:

$$\tau_i^\mathbf{B}(\mathbf{A}) \overset{\text{def}}{=} \begin{cases} \mathbf{a}_i^\top (\mathbf{B}^\top \mathbf{B})^+ \mathbf{a}_i & \text{if } \mathbf{a}_i \perp \ker(\mathbf{B}), \\ \infty & \text{otherwise.} \end{cases} \quad (4)$$

If $\mathbf{a}_i$ has an component in $\ker(\mathbf{B})$, we set its generalized leverage score to ∞, since it might be the only row in $\mathbf{A}$ pointing in this direction. Thus, when sampling rows, we cannot remove it. We could set the generalized leverage score to 1, but using ∞ simplifies notation in some of our proofs. If $\mathbf{B}$ is a spectral approximation for $\mathbf{A}$, then every generalized leverage score is a good multiplicative approximation to its corresponding true leverage score:

Lemma 3 (Leverage Scores via Spectral Approx. – Lemma 4.3 in [18]). *If* $\mathbf{B}$ *is a* λ-*spectral approximation of* $\mathbf{A}$, *so* $\frac{1}{\lambda}\mathbf{A}^\top \mathbf{A} \preceq \mathbf{B}^\top \mathbf{B} \preceq \mathbf{A}^\top \mathbf{A}$, *then* $\tau_i(\mathbf{A}) \leq \tau_i^\mathbf{B}(\mathbf{A}) \leq \lambda \cdot \tau_i(\mathbf{A})$.

Proof. This follows from the definition of leverage scores and generalized leverage scores and the fact that $\frac{1}{\lambda}\mathbf{A}^\top \mathbf{A} \preceq \mathbf{B}^\top \mathbf{B} \preceq \mathbf{A}^\top \mathbf{A}$ implies $\lambda(\mathbf{A}^\top \mathbf{A})^+ \succeq (\mathbf{B}^\top \mathbf{B})^+ \succeq \mathbf{A}^\top \mathbf{A}^+$. $\square$

3.4 Leverage Score Sampling

Sampling rows from $\mathbf{A}$ according to their exact leverage scores gives a spectral approximation for $\mathbf{A}$ with high probability. Sampling by leverage score overestimates also suffices:

Lemma 4 (Spectral Approximation via Leverage Score Sampling). *Given an error parameter* $0 < \epsilon < 1$, *let* $\mathbf{u}$ *be a vector of leverage score overestimates, i.e.,* $\tau_i(\mathbf{A}) \leq u_i$ *for all* i. *Let* α *be a sampling rate parameter and let* c *be a fixed positive constant. For each row, we define a sampling probability* $p_i = \min\{1, \alpha \cdot u_i c \log d\}$. *Furthermore, let* $\texttt{Sample}(\mathbf{u}, \alpha)$ *denote a function which returns a random diagonal matrix* $\mathbf{S}$ *with independently chosen entries.* $\mathbf{S}_{ii} = \frac{1}{\sqrt{p_i}}$ *with probability* p_i *and 0 otherwise.*

$\mathbf{S} = \texttt{Sample}(\mathbf{u}, \epsilon^{-2})$ *has at most* $\sum_i \min\{1, \alpha \cdot u_i c \log d\} \leq \alpha c \log d \|\mathbf{u}\|_1$ *non-zero entries and* $\frac{1}{\sqrt{1+\epsilon}}\mathbf{S}\mathbf{A}$ *is a* $\frac{1+\epsilon}{1-\epsilon}$-*spectral approximation for* $\mathbf{A}$ *with probability at least* $1 - d^{-c/3}$.

We prove Lemma 4 in Appendix A of the full version of this paper [6] using a matrix concentration result of [29].

4. LEVERAGE SCORE ESTIMATION VIA UNIFORM SAMPLING

In this section, we use a simple expectation argument to prove Theorem 1, which is restated in full below:

Theorem 1 (Full Statement). *Given any* $\mathbf{A} \in \mathbb{R}^{n \times d}$. *Let S denote a uniformly random sample of m rows from $\mathbf{A}$ and* let $\mathbf{S} \in \mathbb{R}^{n \times n}$ be its diagonal indicator matrix (i.e. $\mathbf{S}_{ii} = 1$ for $i \in S$, $\mathbf{S}_{ii} = 0$ otherwise). Define

$$\tilde{\tau}_i \overset{\text{def}}{=} \begin{cases} \tau_i^{\mathbf{SA}}(\mathbf{A}) & \text{if } i \in S, \\ \frac{1}{1 + \frac{1}{\tau_i^{\mathbf{SA}}(\mathbf{A})}} & \text{otherwise.} \end{cases}$$

Then, $\tilde{\tau}_i \geq \tau_i(\mathbf{A})$ for all i and

$$\mathbb{E}\left[\sum_{i=1}^n \tilde{\tau}_i\right] \leq \frac{nd}{m}.$$

Proof. First we show that our estimates are valid leverage score upper bounds, i.e. $\tilde{\tau}_i \geq \tau_i(\mathbf{A})$. Let $\mathbf{S}^{(i)}$ be the diagonal indicator matrix for $S \cup \{i\}$. We claim that, for all i,

$$\tilde{\tau}_i = \tau_i^{\mathbf{S}^{(i)}\mathbf{A}}(\mathbf{A}). \tag{5}$$

This is proved case-by-case:

1. When $i \in S$, $\mathbf{S} = \mathbf{S}^{(i)}$ so it holds trivially.

2. When $i \notin S$ and $\mathbf{a}_i \not\perp \ker(\mathbf{SA})$, then by definition, $\tau_i^{\mathbf{SA}}(\mathbf{A}) = \infty$ and $\tilde{\tau}_i = \frac{1}{1 + \frac{1}{\infty}} = 1 = \tau_i^{\mathbf{S}^{(i)}\mathbf{A}}(\mathbf{A})$.

3. When $i \notin S$ and $\mathbf{a}_i \perp \ker(\mathbf{SA})$ then by the Sherman-Morrison formula for pseudoinverses [22, Thm 3],

$$\tau_i^{\mathbf{S}^{(i)}\mathbf{A}}(\mathbf{A}) = \mathbf{a}_i^\top \left(\mathbf{A}^\top \mathbf{S}^2 \mathbf{A} + \mathbf{a}_i \mathbf{a}_i^\top\right)^+ \mathbf{a}_i$$
$$= \mathbf{a}_i^\top \left(\left(\mathbf{A}^\top \mathbf{S}^2 \mathbf{A}\right)^+ - \frac{\left(\mathbf{A}^\top \mathbf{S}^2 \mathbf{A}\right)^+ \mathbf{a}_i \mathbf{a}_i^\top \left(\mathbf{A}^\top \mathbf{S}^2 \mathbf{A}\right)^+}{1 + \mathbf{a}_i^\top \left(\mathbf{A}^\top \mathbf{S}^2 \mathbf{A}\right)^+ \mathbf{a}_i}\right) \mathbf{a}_i$$
$$= \tau_i^{\mathbf{SA}}(\mathbf{A}) - \frac{\tau_i^{\mathbf{SA}}(\mathbf{A})^2}{1 + \tau_i^{\mathbf{SA}}(\mathbf{A})} = \frac{1}{1 + \frac{1}{\tau_i^{\mathbf{SA}}(\mathbf{A})}} = \tilde{\tau}_i.$$

By (5) and the fact that $\mathbf{A}^\top \mathbf{S}^{(i)2} \mathbf{A} \preceq \mathbf{A}^\top \mathbf{A}$ (see Lemma 3), we have $\tilde{\tau}_i = \tau_i^{\mathbf{S}^{(i)}\mathbf{A}}(\mathbf{A}) \geq \tau_i(\mathbf{A})$, so our estimates are upper bounds as desired. It remains to upper bound the expected sum of $\tilde{\tau}_i$. We can break down the sum as:

$$\sum_{i=1}^n \tilde{\tau}_i = \sum_{i \in S} \tilde{\tau}_i + \sum_{i \notin S} \tilde{\tau}_i.$$

The first term is simply the sum of $\mathbf{SA}$'s leverage scores, so it is equal to $\text{rank}(\mathbf{SA}) \leq d$ by (3). To bound the second term, consider a random process that first selects $\mathbf{S}$, then selects a random row $i \notin S$ and returns $\tilde{\tau}_i$. There are always exactly $n - m$ rows $\notin S$, so the value returned by this random process is, in expectation, exactly equal to $\frac{1}{n-m} \cdot \mathbb{E} \sum_{i \notin S} \tilde{\tau}_i$.

This random process is *also* equivalent to randomly selecting a set S' of $m + 1$ rows, then randomly choosing a row $i \in \mathbf{S}'\mathbf{A}$ and returning its leverage score! In expectation it is therefore equal to the average leverage score in $\mathbf{S}'\mathbf{A}$. $\mathbf{S}'\mathbf{A}$ has $m + 1$ rows and its leverage scores sum to its rank, so we can bound its average leverage score by $\frac{d}{m+1}$. Overall:

$$\mathbb{E}\left[\sum_{i=1}^n \tilde{\tau}_i\right] \leq d + (n - m) \cdot \frac{d}{m+1} \leq \frac{d(n+1)}{m+1} \leq \frac{nd}{m}. \quad \square$$

5. COHERENCE-REDUCING WEIGHTING

In this section, we prove Theorem 2, which shows that we can reweight a small number of rows in any matrix $\mathbf{A}$ to make it have low coherence. This structural result may be of independent interest. It is also fundamental in proving Theorem 3, a slightly stronger and more general version of Theorem 1 that we will prove in Section 6.

Actually, for Theorem 2 we prove a more general statement, studying how to select a diagonal row reweighting matrix $\mathbf{W}$ to arbitrarily control the leverage scores of $\mathbf{WA}$. One simple conjecture would be that, given a vector $\mathbf{u}$, there always exists a $\mathbf{W}$ such that $\tau_i(\mathbf{WA}) = u_i$. This conjecture is unfortunately not true - if $\mathbf{A}$ is the identity matrix, then $\tau_i(\mathbf{WA}) = 0$ if $\mathbf{W}_{ii} = 0$ and $\tau_i(\mathbf{WA}) = 1$ otherwise. Instead, we show the following:

Theorem 2 (Leverage Score Bounding Row Reweighting). *For any $\mathbf{A} \in \mathbb{R}^{n \times d}$ and any vector $\mathbf{u} \in \mathbb{R}^n$ with $u_i > 0$ for all i, there exists a diagonal matrix $\mathbf{W} \in \mathbb{R}^{n \times n}$ with $\mathbf{0} \preceq \mathbf{W} \preceq \mathbf{I}$ such that:*

$$\forall i, \ \tau_i(\mathbf{WA}) \leq u_i, \tag{6}$$

and

$$\sum_{i: \mathbf{W}_{ii} \neq 1} u_i \leq d. \tag{7}$$

Note that (6) is easy to satisfy – it holds if we set $\mathbf{W} = \mathbf{0}$. Hence, the main result is the second claim. Not only does a $\mathbf{W}$ exist that gives the desired leverage score bounds, but it is only necessary to reweight rows in $\mathbf{A}$ with a low total weight in terms of $\mathbf{u}$.

For any incoherence parameter α, if we set $u_i = \alpha$ for all i, then this theorem shows the existence of a reweighting that reduces coherence to α. Such a reweighting has $\sum_{i: \mathbf{W}_{ii} \neq 1} \alpha \leq d$ and therefore $|\{i : \mathbf{W}_{ii} \neq 1\}| \leq \frac{d}{\alpha}$. So, we see that Lemma 1 follows as a special case of Theorem 2.

In order to prove Theorem 2, we first give two technical lemmas which are proved in Appendix A of the full version of this paper [6]. Lemma 5 describes how the leverage scores of $\mathbf{A}$ evolve when a single row of $\mathbf{A}$ is reweighted. We show that, when we decrease the weight of a row, that row's leverage score decreases and the leverage score of all other rows increases.

Lemma 5 (Leverage Score Changes Under Rank 1 Updates). *Given any $\mathbf{A} \in \mathbb{R}^{n \times d}$, $\gamma \in (0, 1)$, and $i \in [n]$, let $\mathbf{W}$ be a diagonal matrix such that $\mathbf{W}_{ii} = \sqrt{1 - \gamma}$ and $\mathbf{W}_{jj} = 1$ for all $j \neq i$. Then,*

$$\tau_i(\mathbf{WA}) = \frac{(1 - \gamma)\tau_i(\mathbf{A})}{1 - \gamma \tau_i(\mathbf{A})} \leq \tau_i(\mathbf{A}),$$

and for all $j \neq i$,

$$\tau_j(\mathbf{WA}) = \tau_j(\mathbf{A}) + \frac{\gamma \tau_{ij}(\mathbf{A})^2}{1 - \gamma \tau_i(\mathbf{A})} \geq \tau_j(\mathbf{A}).$$

Next we claim that, with respect to weightings of $\mathbf{A}$'s rows, leverage scores are lower semi-continuous.

Lemma 6 (Leverage Scores are Lower Semi-continuous). *$\boldsymbol{\tau}(\mathbf{WA})$ is lower semi-continuous in the diagonal matrix $\mathbf{W}$, i.e. for any sequence $\mathbf{W}^{(k)} \to \overline{\mathbf{W}}$ with $\mathbf{W}_{ii}^{(k)} \geq 0$ for all k and i, we have*

$$\tau_i(\overline{\mathbf{W}}\mathbf{A}) \leq \liminf_{k \to \infty} \tau_i\left(\mathbf{W}^{(k)}\mathbf{A}\right).$$

With Lemmas 5 and 6 in place, we are ready to prove the main reweighting theorem.

Proof of Theorem 2. We prove the existence of the required $\mathbf{W}$ by considering the limit of the following algorithm for computing a reweighting matrix.

Algorithm 1 COMPUTE REWEIGHTING (a.k.a the whack-a-mole algorithm)

Initialize $\mathbf{W} = \mathbf{I}$
while true **do**
  for $i = 1$ to n **do**
    if $\tau_i(\mathbf{WA}) \geq u_i$ **then**
      if $\tau_i(\mathbf{WA}) < 1$ **then**
        Decrease $\mathbf{W}_{ii}$ so that $\tau_i(\mathbf{WA}) = u_i$.
      else
        Set $\mathbf{W}_{ii} = 0$
      end if
    end if
  end for
end while
return $\mathbf{W}$

For all $k \geq 0$, let $\mathbf{W}^{(k)}$ be the value of $\mathbf{W}$ after the kth update to the weight. We show that $\overline{\mathbf{W}} = \lim_{k\to\infty} \mathbf{W}^{(k)}$ meets the conditions of Theorem 2. First note that Algorithm 1 is well defined and that all entries of $\mathbf{W}^{(k)}$ are non-negative for all $k \geq 0$. To see this, suppose we need to decrease $\mathbf{W}_{ii}^{(k)}$ so that $\tau_i(\mathbf{W}^{(k+1)}\mathbf{A}) = u_i$. Note that the condition $\tau_i(\mathbf{W}^{(k)}\mathbf{A}) < 1$ gives

$$\lim_{\gamma\to 1} \frac{(1-\gamma)\,\tau_i\left(\mathbf{W}^{(k)}\mathbf{A}\right)}{1-\gamma\tau_i\left(\mathbf{W}^{(k)}\mathbf{A}\right)} = 0.$$

Therefore, Lemma 5 shows that we can make $\tau_i(\mathbf{W}^{(k+1)}\mathbf{A})$ arbitrary small by setting γ close enough to 1. Since the leverage score for row i is continuous, this implies that $\mathbf{W}^{(k+1)}$ exists as desired.

Since, the entries of $\mathbf{W}^{(k)}$ are non-negative and decrease monotonically by construction, clearly $\overline{\mathbf{W}}$ exists. Furthermore, since setting $\mathbf{W}_{ii} = 0$ makes $\tau_i(\mathbf{WA}) = 0$, we see that, by construction,

$$\liminf_{k\to\infty} \tau_i\left(\mathbf{W}^{(k)}\mathbf{A}\right) \leq u_i \text{ for all } i \in [n].$$

Therefore, by Lemma 6 we have that $\tau_i(\overline{\mathbf{W}}\mathbf{A}) \leq u_i$.

It only remains to show that $\sum_{i:\overline{\mathbf{W}}_{ii}\neq 1} u_i \leq d$. Let k be the first iteration such that $\mathbf{W}_{ii}^{(k)} \neq 1$ for any i such that $\overline{\mathbf{W}}_{ii} \neq 1$. Let $S \subseteq [n]$ be the set of rows such that $\mathbf{W}_{ii}^{(k)} = 0$ and let $T = \{i : \overline{\mathbf{W}}_{ii} \neq 1\} - S$. Since decreasing the weight of one row increases the leverage scores of all other rows, we have

$$\sum_{i \in T \cup S} u_i \;\leq\; \sum_{i \in T} \tau_i\left(\mathbf{W}^{(k)}\mathbf{A}\right) + \sum_{i \in S} 1$$
$$\leq\; \text{rank}\left(\mathbf{W}^{(k)}\mathbf{A}\right) + |S|.$$

When we set $\mathbf{W}_{ii} = 0$, it must be the case that $\tau_i(\mathbf{WA}) = 1$. In this case, removing the ith row decreases the rank of $\mathbf{WA}$ by 1 and hence $\text{rank}(\mathbf{W}^{(k)}\mathbf{A}) \leq d - |S|$. Therefore,

$$\sum_{i:\overline{\mathbf{W}}_{ii}\neq 1} u_i = \sum_{i \in T \cup S} u_i \leq d. \qquad \square$$

6. LEVERAGE SCORE ESTIMATION VIA UNDERSAMPLING

Theorem 1 alone is enough to prove that a variety of iterative methods for spectral matrix approximation work. However, in this section we prove Theorem 3, a slight strengthening and generalization that improves runtime bounds, proves correctness for some alternative sampling schemes, and gives some more intuition for why uniform sampling allows us to obtain leverage score estimates with low total sum.

Theorem 3 relies on Theorem 2, which intuitively shows that a large fraction of our matrix $\mathbf{A}$ has low coherence. Sampling rows uniformly will give a spectral approximation for this portion of our matrix. Then, since few rows are reweighted in $\mathbf{WA}$, even loose upper bounds on the leverage scores for those rows will allow us to bound the total sum of estimated leverage scores when we sample uniformly.

Formally, we show an upper bound on the sum of estimated leverage scores obtained from *undersampling* $\mathbf{A}$ according to any set of leverage score upper bounds. Uniform sampling $\mathbf{A}$ can simply be viewed as undersampling $\mathbf{A}$ when all we know is that each leverage score is upper bounded by 1. That is, in the uniform case, we set $\mathbf{u} = \mathbf{1}$.

The bound in Theorem 3 holds with high probability, rather than in expectation like the bound in Theorem 1. This gain comes at a cost of requiring our sampling rate to be higher by a factor of $\log d$. At the end of this section we show how the $\log d$ factor can be removed at least in the case of uniform sampling, giving a high probability statement that matches the bound of Theorem 1.

Theorem 3 (Leverage Score Approximation via Undersampling). *Let $\mathbf{u}$ be a vector of leverage score overestimates, i.e. $\tau_i(\mathbf{A}) \leq u_i$ for all i. For some undersampling parameter $\alpha \in (0,1]$, let $\mathbf{S}' = \sqrt{\alpha}\sqrt{3/4} \cdot \mathtt{Sample}\,(\mathbf{u}, 9\alpha)$. Let $u_i^{(new)} = \min\{\tau_i^{\mathbf{S}'\mathbf{A}}(\mathbf{A}), u_i\}$. Then, with high probability, $\mathbf{u}^{(new)}$ is a vector of leverage score overestimates, i.e. $\tau_i(\mathbf{A}) \leq u_i^{(new)}$, and*

$$\sum_{i=1}^{n} u_i^{(new)} \leq \frac{3d}{\alpha}.$$

Furthermore, $\mathbf{S}'$ has $O\left(\alpha \left\|\mathbf{u}\right\|_1 \log d\right)$ nonzeros.

Proof. Let $\mathbf{S} = \sqrt{3/4} \cdot \mathtt{Sample}\,(\mathbf{u}, 9)$. Since $\mathbf{u}$ is a set of leverage score overestimates, Lemma 4 (with $\epsilon = 1/3$) shows that, with high probability,

$$\mathbf{A}^\top \mathbf{S}^2 \mathbf{A} \preceq \mathbf{A}^\top \mathbf{A}.$$

In $\mathtt{Sample}$, when we include a row, we reweight it by $1/\sqrt{p_i}$. For $\mathbf{S}' = \sqrt{\alpha}\sqrt{3/4} \cdot \mathtt{Sample}\,(\mathbf{u}, 9\alpha)$, we sample at a rate lower by a factor of α as compared with $\mathbf{S}$, so we weight rows by a factor of $1/\sqrt{\alpha}$ higher. The $\sqrt{\alpha}$ multiplied by $\mathbf{S}'$ makes up for this difference. Thus, $\mathbf{S}'$ is equivalent to $\mathbf{S}$ with some rows removed. Therefore:

$$\mathbf{A}^\top \mathbf{S}'^2 \mathbf{A} \preceq \mathbf{A}^\top \mathbf{S}^2 \mathbf{A} \preceq \mathbf{A}^\top \mathbf{A}.$$

So, for all i, $\tau_i(\mathbf{A}) \leq \tau_i^{\mathbf{S}'\mathbf{A}}(\mathbf{A})$. By assumption $\tau_i(\mathbf{A}) \leq u_i$, so this proves that $\tau_i(\mathbf{A}) \leq u_i^{(new)}$.

By Theorem 2, there is a diagonal matrix $\mathbf{W}$ such that $\tau_i(\mathbf{WA}) \leq \alpha u_i$ for all i and $\sum_{i:\mathbf{W}_{ii}\neq 1} \alpha u_i \leq d$. For this $\mathbf{W}$, using the fact that $u_i^{(new)} = \min\{\tau_i^{\mathbf{S}'\mathbf{A}}(\mathbf{A}), u_i\}$, we have

$$\sum_{i=1}^{n} u_i^{(new)} \leq \sum_{i:\mathbf{W}_{ii} \neq 1} u_i + \sum_{i:\mathbf{W}_{ii}=1} \tau_i^{\mathbf{S}'\mathbf{A}}(\mathbf{A})$$

$$\leq \frac{d}{\alpha} + \sum_{i:\mathbf{W}_{ii}=1} \tau_i^{\mathbf{S}'\mathbf{A}}(\mathbf{A})$$

$$= \frac{d}{\alpha} + \sum_{i:\mathbf{W}_{ii}=1} \tau_i^{\mathbf{S}'\mathbf{A}}(\mathbf{W}\mathbf{A}). \qquad (8)$$

Using $\mathbf{W} \preceq \mathbf{I}$, we have

$$\tau_i^{\mathbf{S}'\mathbf{A}}(\mathbf{W}\mathbf{A}) \leq \tau_i^{\mathbf{S}'\mathbf{W}\mathbf{A}}(\mathbf{W}\mathbf{A}). \qquad (9)$$

Now, note that $\mathbf{S}' = \sqrt{\alpha}\sqrt{3/4} \cdot \texttt{Sample}\,(\mathbf{u}, 9\alpha) = \sqrt{\alpha}\sqrt{3/4} \cdot \texttt{Sample}\,(\alpha\mathbf{u}, 9)$. Since $\alpha\mathbf{u}$ is an overestimate of leverage scores for $\mathbf{W}\mathbf{A}$, Lemma 4 (again with $\epsilon = 1/3$) shows that $\alpha \cdot \frac{1}{2}\mathbf{A}^{\top}\mathbf{W}^2\mathbf{A} \preceq \mathbf{A}^{\top}\mathbf{W}\mathbf{S}'^2\mathbf{W}\mathbf{A}$. Hence (9) along with Lemma 3 shows that

$$\tau_i^{\mathbf{S}'\mathbf{A}}(\mathbf{W}\mathbf{A}) \leq \frac{2}{\alpha}\tau_i(\mathbf{W}\mathbf{A}).$$

Combining with (8), we have

$$\sum_{i=1}^{n} u_i^{(new)} \leq \frac{d}{\alpha} + \frac{2}{\alpha}\sum_{i:\mathbf{W}_{ii}=1} \tau_i(\mathbf{W}\mathbf{A})$$

$$\leq \frac{d}{\alpha} + \frac{2d}{\alpha} \leq \frac{3d}{\alpha}. \qquad \square$$

Choosing an undersampling rate α is equivalent to choosing a desired sampling rate and setting α accordingly. From this perspective, it is clear that Theorem 3 gives an extremely simple way to iteratively improve leverage scores. Start with $\mathbf{u}^{(1)}$ with $\|\mathbf{u}^{(1)}\|_1 = s_1$. Undersample at rate $\frac{6d}{s_1}$ to obtain a sample of size $O(d \log d)$, which gives new leverage score estimates $\mathbf{u}^{(2)}$ with $\|\mathbf{u}^{(2)}\|_1 = \frac{3d}{6d/s_1} = \frac{s_1}{2}$. Repeat this process, cutting the sum of leverage score estimates in half with each iteration. Recall that we restrict $\alpha < 1$, so once the sum of leverage score estimates converges on $O(d)$, this halving process halts – as expected, we cannot keep cutting the sum further.

This procedure corresponds to Algorithm 3 in Section 7 and differs somewhat from approaches discussed earlier (e.g. our proposed algorithm from Section 1). It always maintains a sample of just $O(d \log d)$ rows that is improved iteratively.

6.1 Improved Bound for Uniform Sampling

Now, consider instead sampling few rows from $\mathbf{A}$ with the goal of estimating leverage scores well enough to obtain a spectral approximation with $n/2$ rows. In the uniform sampling case, when $\mathbf{u} = \mathbf{1}$, if we set $\alpha = d \log d / 6n$ for example, then sampling $O(\alpha\|\mathbf{u}\|_1 \log d) = O(d \log^2 d)$ rows uniformly will give us leverage score estimates summing to $n/2 \log d$. This is good enough to cut our original matrix in half. However, we see that we have lost a $\log d$ factor to Theorem 1, which let us cut down to *expected* size $\frac{n}{2}$ by sampling just $O(d \log d)$ rows uniformly.

At least when $\mathbf{u} = \mathbf{1}$, this $\log d$ factor can be eliminated. In Theorem 3, we set $\mathbf{S}' = \sqrt{\alpha}\sqrt{3/4} \cdot \texttt{Sample}\,(\mathbf{u}, 9\alpha)$, meaning that rows selected for $\mathbf{S}'$ are included with weight $\sqrt{\alpha}\sqrt{3/4} \cdot \frac{1}{\sqrt{p_i}} = \sqrt{\frac{3\alpha}{4\cdot\min\{1,9\alpha c \log d\}}}$. Instead of reweighting rows, consider simply setting all non-zero values in $\mathbf{S}'$ to be 1. We

know that our leverage score estimates will still be overestimates as we still have $\mathbf{S}' \preceq \mathbf{I}$ and so $\mathbf{A}^{\top}\mathbf{S}'^2\mathbf{A} \preceq \mathbf{A}^{\top}\mathbf{A}$. Formally, consider two cases:

1. $(1 \leq 9\alpha c \log d)$. In this case, $\mathbf{S}'\mathbf{A}$ is simply $\mathbf{A}$ itself, so we know our leverage score estimates are exact and thus their sum is $\leq d$. We can use them to obtain a spectral approximation with $O(d \log d)$ rows.

2. $(1 > 9\alpha c \log d)$. In this case, we reweight rows by $\sqrt{\alpha}\sqrt{3/4} \cdot \frac{1}{\sqrt{p_i}} = \sqrt{\frac{3\alpha}{4\cdot9\alpha c \log d}} = \sqrt{\frac{3}{4\cdot9c \log d}}$. Thus, increasing weights in $\mathbf{S}'$ to 1 will reduce leverage score estimates by a factor of $\frac{3}{4\cdot9c \log d}$. So overall we have:

$$\sum_{i=1}^{n} u_i^{(new)} \leq \sum_{i:\mathbf{W}_{ii} \neq 1} u_i + \sum_{i:\mathbf{W}_{ii}=1} \tau_i^{\mathbf{S}'\mathbf{A}}(\mathbf{A})$$

$$\leq |\{i : \mathbf{W}_{ii} \neq 1\}| + \frac{3}{4\cdot9c \log d} \cdot \frac{2d}{\alpha}.$$

Recall from Lemma 4 that sampling by $\mathbf{u}^{(new)}$ actually gives a matrix with $\sum_i \min\{1, u_i^{(new)} \cdot \epsilon^{-2}c \log d\}$ rows. Thus, we obtain a $\frac{1+\epsilon}{1-\epsilon}$-spectral approximation to $\mathbf{A}$ with the following number of rows:

$$|\{i : \mathbf{W}_{ii} \neq 1\}| + \epsilon^{-2}c \log d \cdot \frac{3}{4\cdot9c \log d} \cdot \frac{2d}{\alpha} \leq \frac{d}{\alpha} + \frac{\epsilon^{-2}d}{6\alpha}.$$

Setting $\alpha = \frac{m}{n\cdot9c \log d}$ for some $m \leq n$ so that $\texttt{Sample}(\mathbf{1}, 9\alpha)$ samples rows at rate m/n yields the following theorem:

Theorem 4. *Given* $\mathbf{A} \in \mathbb{R}^{n\times d}$, *suppose we sample rows uniformly and independently at rate* $\frac{m}{n}$, *without reweighting, to obtain* $\mathbf{S}\mathbf{A}$. *Computing* $\tilde{\tau}_i = \min\{1, \tau_i^{\mathbf{S}\mathbf{A}}(\mathbf{A})\}$ *for each row and resampling from* $\mathbf{A}$ *by these estimates will, with high probability, return a* $\frac{1+\epsilon}{1-\epsilon}$-*spectral approximation to* $\mathbf{A}$ *with at most* $O(\frac{nd \log d\epsilon^{-2}}{m})$ *rows.*

Choosing $m = O(d \log d)$ allows us to find a spectral approximation of size $n/2$, as long as $O(d \log d) < n$. This matches Theorem 1, but holds with high probability.

7. ROW SAMPLING ALGORITHMS

As discussed in the introduction, Theorems 1, 3, and 4 immediately yield new, extremely simple algorithms for spectral matrix approximation. For clarity, we initially present versions running in *nearly* input-sparsity time. However, we later explain how our first algorithm can be modified with standard techniques to remove log factors, achieving input-sparsity time and thus matching state-of-the-art results [4, 20, 24]. Our algorithms rely solely on row sampling, which preserves matrix sparsity and structure, possibly improving space usage and runtime for intermediate system solves.

7.1 Algorithm Descriptions

The first algorithm we present, REPEATED HALVING, is a simple recursive procedure. We uniformly sample $\frac{n}{2}$ rows from $\mathbf{A}$ to obtain $\mathbf{A}'$. By Theorems 1 and 4, estimating leverage scores of $\mathbf{A}$ with respect to this sample allows us to immediately find a spectral approximation to $\mathbf{A}$ with $O(d \log d)$ rows. Of course, $\mathbf{A}'$ is still large, so computing these estimates would be slow. Thus, we *recursively* find a spectral approximation of $\mathbf{A}'$ and use this to compute the estimated leverage scores.

Algorithm 2 REPEATED HALVING

input: $n \times d$ matrix $\mathbf{A}$
output: spectral approximation $\tilde{\mathbf{A}}$ consisting of $O(d \log d)$ rescaled rows of $\mathbf{A}$

1: Uniformly sample $\frac{n}{2}$ rows of $\mathbf{A}$ to form $\mathbf{A}'$
2: If $\mathbf{A}'$ has $> O(d \log d)$ rows, **recursively** compute a spectral approximation $\tilde{\mathbf{A}}'$ of $\mathbf{A}'$
3: Compute approximate generalized leverage scores of $\mathbf{A}$ w.r.t. $\tilde{\mathbf{A}}'$
4: Use these estimates to sample rows of $\mathbf{A}$ to form $\tilde{\mathbf{A}}$
5: **return** $\tilde{\mathbf{A}}$

The second algorithm, REFINEMENT SAMPLING, makes critical use of Theorem 3, which shows that, given a set of leverage score upper bounds, we can undersample by these estimates and still significantly improve their quality with each iteration. We start with all of our leverage score upper bounds set to 1 so we have $\|\tilde{\boldsymbol{\tau}}\|_1 = n$. In each iteration, we sample $O(d \log d)$ rows according to our upper bounds, meaning that we undersample at rate $\alpha = O\left(\frac{d}{\|\tilde{\boldsymbol{\tau}}\|_1}\right)$. By Theorem 3, we cut $\|\tilde{\boldsymbol{\tau}}\|_1$ by a constant fraction in each iteration. Thus, within $\log(n)$ rounds, $\|\tilde{\boldsymbol{\tau}}\|_1$ will be $O(d)$ and we can simply use our estimates to directly obtain a spectral approximation to $\mathbf{A}$ with $O(d \log d)$ rows.

Algorithm 3 REFINEMENT SAMPLING

input: $n \times d$ matrix $\mathbf{A}$
output: spectral approximation $\tilde{\mathbf{A}}$ consisting of $O(d \log d)$ rescaled rows of $\mathbf{A}$

1: Initialize a vector of leverage score upper bounds, $\tilde{\boldsymbol{\tau}}$, to **1**
2: **while** $\|\tilde{\boldsymbol{\tau}}\|_1 > O(d)$ **do**
3: Undersample $O(d \log d)$ rows of $\mathbf{A}$ with probabilities proportional to $\tilde{\boldsymbol{\tau}}$ to form $\tilde{\mathbf{A}}$
4: Compute a vector $\mathbf{u}$ of approximate generalized leverage scores of $\mathbf{A}$ w.r.t. $\tilde{\mathbf{A}}$
5: Set $\tilde{\tau}_i = \min(\tilde{\tau}_i, u_i)$
6: **end while**
7: Use the final $\tilde{\boldsymbol{\tau}}$ to sample $O(d \log d)$ rows from $\mathbf{A}$ to form $\tilde{\mathbf{A}}$
8: **return** $\tilde{\mathbf{A}}$

7.2 Runtime Analysis

In analyzing the runtimes of these algorithms, we assume $n = O(\text{poly}(d))$, which is a reasonable assumption for any practical regression problem.[4] Furthermore, we use the fact that a $d \times d$ system can be solved in time d^ω, where ω is the matrix multiplication exponent. However, we emphasize that, depending on the structure and sparsity of $\mathbf{A}$, alternative system solving methods may yield faster results or runtimes with different trade offs. For example, if the rows of $\mathbf{A}$ are sparse, solving a system in $\tilde{\mathbf{A}}$, where $\tilde{\mathbf{A}}$ consists of $O(d \log d)$ rescaled rows from $\mathbf{A}$ may be accelerated by using iterative conjugate gradient, or other Krylov subspace methods (which can also avoid explicitly computing $\tilde{\mathbf{A}}^\top \tilde{\mathbf{A}}$). It is best to think of d^ω as the runtime of the fastest available system solver in your domain, and the quoted runtimes

---

[4]A simple method for handling even larger values of n is outlined in [18].

as general guidelines that will change somewhat depending on exactly how the above algorithms are implemented.

First, we give an important primitive showing that estimates of generalized leverage scores can be computed efficiently. Computing exact generalized leverage scores is slow and we only need constant factor approximations, which will only increase our sampling rates and hence number of rows sampled by a constant factor.

Lemma 7. *Given* $\mathbf{B}$ *containing* $O(d \log d)$ *rescaled rows of* $\mathbf{A}$, *for any* $\theta > 0$, *it is possible to compute an estimate of* $\boldsymbol{\tau}^{\mathbf{B}}(\mathbf{A})$, $\tilde{\boldsymbol{\tau}}$, *in* $O(d^\omega \log d + \text{nnz}(\mathbf{A})\theta^{-1})$ *time such that, w.h.p. in* d, *for all* i, $\tilde{\tau}_i \geq \tau_i^{\mathbf{B}}(\mathbf{A})$ *and* $\tilde{\tau}_i \leq d^\theta \tau_i^{\mathbf{B}}(\mathbf{A})$.

Setting $\theta = O(\frac{1}{\log d})$ gives constant factor generalized leverage score approximations in $O(d^\omega \log d + \text{nnz}(\mathbf{A}) \log d)$ time.

Proof Sketch. Lemma 7 follows from a standard technique that uses Johnson-Lindenstrauss projections [2, 18, 27]. Presuming $\mathbf{a}_i \perp \ker(\mathbf{B})$, the general idea is to write $\tau_i^{\mathbf{B}}(\mathbf{A}) = \mathbf{a}_i^\top (\mathbf{B}^\top \mathbf{B})^+ \mathbf{a}_i = \|\mathbf{B}(\mathbf{B}^\top \mathbf{B})^+ \mathbf{a}_i\|_2^2$. If we instead compute $\|\mathbf{G}\mathbf{B}(\mathbf{B}^\top \mathbf{B})^+ \mathbf{a}_i\|_2^2$, where $\mathbf{G}$ is a random Gaussian matrix with $O(\theta^{-1})$ rows, then by Johnson-Lindenstrauss lemma, with high probability, the approximation will be within a d^θ factor of $\|\mathbf{B}(\mathbf{B}^\top \mathbf{B})^+ \mathbf{a}_i\|_2^2$ for all i (See [18] Lemma 4.5).

The naive approach requires multiplying every row by $(\mathbf{B}^\top \mathbf{B})^+$, which has height d and would incur cost $\text{nnz}(\mathbf{A})d$. Computing $\mathbf{G}\mathbf{B}(\mathbf{B}^\top \mathbf{B})^+$ takes $O(\text{nnz}(\mathbf{A})\theta^{-1})$ time to compute $\mathbf{G}\mathbf{B}$ and at most $O(d^\omega \log d)$ time to compute $(\mathbf{B}^\top \mathbf{B})$ and invert it. It then takes $O(d^\omega)$ time to multiply these matrices. With $\mathbf{G}\mathbf{B}(\mathbf{B}^\top \mathbf{B})^+$ in hand, we just need to multiply by each row in $\mathbf{A}$ to obtain generalized leverage scores, which takes time $O(\text{nnz}(\mathbf{A})\theta^{-1})$. If we use an alternative system solver instead of explicitly computing $(\mathbf{B}^\top \mathbf{B})^+$, the JL reduction means we only need to solve $O(\theta^{-1})$ systems in $\mathbf{B}$ to compute $\mathbf{G}\mathbf{B}(\mathbf{B}^\top \mathbf{B})^+$ (one for each row of $\mathbf{G}$).

When $\mathbf{a}_i \not\perp \ker(\mathbf{B})$, its generalized leverage score should be ∞ – see (4). So, we need to check whether each $\mathbf{a}_i$ has a component in the null-space of $\mathbf{B}$. This can be done in a variety of ways. For example, we can choose a random gaussian vector $\mathbf{g}$ and compute $\mathbf{g} - \mathbf{B}^\top (\mathbf{B}\mathbf{B}^\top)^+ \mathbf{B}\mathbf{g}$, which is the same as $\mathbf{g} - (\mathbf{B}^\top \mathbf{B})^+ \mathbf{B}^\top \mathbf{B}\mathbf{g}$. This gives a random vector in the null space of $\mathbf{B}$, so computing its dot product with any row $\mathbf{a}_i$ will tell us (with probability 1) whether $\mathbf{a}_i$ is orthogonal to the null space or not. $\square$

With Lemma 7 in place, we can analyze the runtime of our algorithms. For simplicity, we give runtimes for computing a constant factor spectral approximation to $\mathbf{A}$, which can be used as a preconditioner in iterative regression algorithms [1, 4, 25] or used to compute leverage scores of $\mathbf{A}$ up to a constant factor. We could sample $O(d \log d\epsilon^{-2})$ rows to directly obtain a $(1 + \epsilon)$ approximation. By Lemma 7 the runtime of this final refinement is just $O(\text{nnz}(\mathbf{A}) \log d + d^\omega \log d)$.

Lemma 8. REPEATED HALVING *(Algorithm 2) runs in time* $O(\text{nnz}(\mathbf{A}) \log d + d^\omega \log(n/d) \log d)$, *outputting a matrix with* $\tilde{\mathbf{A}}$ *with* $O(d \log d)$ *rows such that* $\tilde{\mathbf{A}}^\top \tilde{\mathbf{A}} \approx_2 \mathbf{A}^\top \mathbf{A}$.

Proof. The proof is by induction – it suffices to show that the work done at the top level is $O(\text{nnz}(\mathbf{A}) \log d + d^\omega \log d)$. At each of the $O(\log(n/d))$ levels of recursion, we cut our matrix in half uniformly so $\text{nnz}(\mathbf{A})$ will also be cut approximately in half with high probability.

By Theorem 4, sampling by $\tau_i^{\mathbf{A}'}(\mathbf{A})$ allows us to obtain $\tilde{\mathbf{A}}$ with $O(d \log d)$ rows. If we instead use $\tilde{\mathbf{A}}'$, our estimated leverage scores increase by at most a constant factor (since $\tilde{\mathbf{A}}'$ is a constant factor spectral approximation to $\mathbf{A}'$). Furthermore, using Lemma 7 to approximate generalized leverage scores increases our estimates by another constant factor at most. Overall, $\tilde{\mathbf{A}}$ will have $O(d \log d)$ rows as desired and our runtime at the top level is just the runtime of estimating leverage scores from Lemma 7 – $O(\mathrm{nnz}(\mathbf{A}) \log d + d^\omega \log d)$. □

Lemma 9. REFINEMENT SAMPLING *(Algorithm 3) runs in time* $O(\mathrm{nnz}(\mathbf{A}) \log(\frac{n}{d}) \log d + d^\omega \log(\frac{n}{d}) \log d)$, *outputting a matrix with* $\tilde{\mathbf{A}}$ *with* $O(d \log d)$ *rows such that* $\tilde{\mathbf{A}}^\top \tilde{\mathbf{A}} \approx_2 \mathbf{A}^\top \mathbf{A}$.

Proof. $\tilde{\mathbf{A}}$'s row count and the fact that it spectrally approximates $\mathbf{A}$ follows from the termination condition and Lemma 4. By Lemma 7, each iteration takes time $O(\mathrm{nnz}(\mathbf{A}) \log d + d^\omega \log d)$. Thus it suffices to show that the algorithm terminates after $O(\log(n/d))$ iterations. At each iteration, we undersample by a factor $\alpha = \frac{c \cdot d}{\|\tilde{\tau}\|_1}$ for some constant c. So by Theorem 3, $\|\tilde{\tau}\|_1$ decreases to $\frac{3d}{\alpha} = \frac{3\|\tilde{\tau}\|_1}{c}$. Setting $c = 6$, we cut $\|\tilde{\tau}\|_1$ in half each time. Since we start with $\|\tilde{\tau}\|_1 = n$ and stop when $\|\tilde{\tau}\|_1 = O(d)$, we terminate in $O(\log(n/d))$ iterations. □

7.3 Achieving Input Sparsity Time

We briefly note that, using techniques from [18], it is possible to remove the $\log d$ factor on the $\mathrm{nnz}(\mathbf{A})$ term to achieve true input-sparsity time with REPEATED HALVING. Instead of using Lemma 7 to estimate generalized leverage scores from up to a constant factor using $\mathbf{A}'$, we only estimate them up to a d^θ factor for some constant $0 < \theta < 1$. Using these rough estimates, we obtain $\tilde{\mathbf{A}}$ with $O(d^{1+\theta} \log d)$ rows. Then, for the rows in $\tilde{\mathbf{A}}$, we can again compute generalized leverage scores with respect to $\mathbf{A}'$, now up to constant factors, and reduce down to just $O(d \log d)$ rows. In total, each iteration will take time $O(\theta^{-1} \mathrm{nnz}(\mathbf{A}) + d^\omega \log d + d^{2+\theta} \log^2 d)$, so obtaining a constant factor approximation to $\mathbf{A}$ takes time $O(\theta^{-1} \mathrm{nnz}(\mathbf{A}) + d^\omega \log^2 d + d^{2+\theta} \log^3 d)$. Recall that we assume $n = \mathrm{poly}(d)$, so we have $\log(n/d) = O(\log d)$ iterations.

In order to obtain a $(1 + \epsilon)$-spectral approximation with only $O(d \log d\epsilon^{-2})$ rows, we first obtain a constant factor approximation, $\tilde{\mathbf{A}}$, with $O(d \log d)$ rows. We then use leverage scores estimated with $\tilde{\mathbf{A}}$ to compute a $(1 + \epsilon/2)$ approximation to $\mathbf{A}$ with $O(d^{1+\theta} \log d\epsilon^{-2})$ rows. Finally, we again use leverage scores estimated with $\tilde{\mathbf{A}}$ and Lemma 7 with $\theta = O(1/\log d)$ to a compute a $(1 + \epsilon/2)$ approximation to this smaller matrix with only $O(d \log d\epsilon^{-2})$ rows. This takes total time $O(\theta^{-1} \mathrm{nnz}(\mathbf{A}) + d^\omega \log d + d^{2+\theta} \log^2 d\epsilon^{-2})$. The $d^{2+\theta} \log^2 d\epsilon^{-2}$ comes from applying Lemma 7 to refine our second approximation, which has $O(d^{1+\theta} \log d\epsilon^{-2})$ rows and thus at most $O(d^{2+\theta} \log d\epsilon^{-2})$ nonzero entries. Overall, the technique yields:

Lemma 10. *Given any constant* $0 < \theta \leq 1$, *and any error* $0 \leq \epsilon < 1^5$, *w.h.p. in* d *we can compute a matrix* $\tilde{\mathbf{A}}$ *with* $O(d \log d\epsilon^{-2})$ *rows such that* $\tilde{\mathbf{A}}^\top \tilde{\mathbf{A}} \approx_{1+\epsilon} \mathbf{A}^\top \mathbf{A}$ *in* $O(\mathrm{nnz}(\mathbf{A}) + d^\omega \log^2 d + d^{2+\theta}\epsilon^{-2})$ *time.*

---

[5]If $\epsilon < 1/\mathrm{poly}(d)$, then $O(d \log d\epsilon^{-2}) > n$, so we can trivially return $\tilde{\mathbf{A}} = \mathbf{A}$ in $O(\mathrm{nnz}(\mathbf{A}))$ time.

As is standard, $\log d$ factors on the $d^{2+\theta}$ term are 'hidden' as we can just slightly increase the value of θ to subsume them. The full tradeoff parameterized by θ is:

$$O(\theta^{-1} \mathrm{nnz}(\mathbf{A}) + d^\omega \log^2 d + d^{2+\theta}(\log^3 d + \log^2 d\epsilon^{-2})).$$

7.4 General Sampling Framework

It is worth mentioning that Algorithms 2 and 3 are two extremes on a spectrum of algorithms between halving and refinement sampling. Generically, the full space of algorithms can be summarized using the pseudocode in Algorithm 4. For notation, note that $\mathbf{A}$ always refers to our *original* data matrix. $\hat{\mathbf{A}}$ is the data matrix currently being processed in the recursive call to Algorithm 4.

Algorithm 4 Generic Row Sampling Scheme

input: original $n \times d$ matrix $\mathbf{A}$, current $\bar{n} \times d$ matrix $\hat{\mathbf{A}}$.
output: approximation $\tilde{\mathbf{A}}$ consisting of $O(d \log d)$ rescaled rows of $\mathbf{A}$

1: Uniform sample n_1 rows of $\hat{\mathbf{A}}$, $\mathbf{A}_1$
2: Approximate $\mathbf{A}_1$ with a row sample, $\mathbf{A}_2$, **recursively**
3: Estimate generalized leverage scores using $\mathbf{A}_2$ and use them to sample n_3 rows of either $\hat{\mathbf{A}}$ or $\mathbf{A}$ itself to obtain $\mathbf{A}_3$
4: Approximate $\mathbf{A}_3$ with a row sample, $\mathbf{A}_4$, **recursively**
5: **return** $\mathbf{A}_4$

Different choices for n_1 and n_3 lead to different algorithms. Note that the last recursion to approximate $\mathbf{A}_4$ has error build up incurred from sampling to create $\mathbf{A}_3$. As a result, this generic scheme has error buildup, but it can be removed by sampling w.r.t. $\mathbf{A}$ instead of $\hat{\mathbf{A}}$.

Note that if we choose $n_1 = O(d \log d)$, we can simply set $\mathbf{A}_2 \leftarrow \mathbf{A}_1$, and the first recursive call in Line 2 is not necessary. Also, Theorem 3 gives that, if we pick n_1 sufficiently large, n_3 can be bounded by $O(d \log d)$. This would then remove the last recursive call to compute $\mathbf{A}_4$. Such modifications lead to head and tail recursive algorithms, as well as a variety of intermediate forms:

1. Head recursive algorithm, $n_1 = n/2$, giving Algorithm 2 (REPEATED HALVING).

2. Tail recursive algorithm, $n_1 = d \log d$, $n_3 = \frac{n}{2}$, sampled w.r.t. $\hat{\mathbf{A}}$. At each step error compounds so setting error to $\frac{1}{\log n}$ per step gives a constant factor approximation.

3. $n_1 = d \log d$, $n_3 = d \log d$, sampled w.r.t. $\mathbf{A}$, giving Algorithm 3 (REFINEMENT SAMPLING).

4. For situations where iterations are expensive, e.g. MapReduce, a useful choice of parameters is likely $n_1 = n_3 = O(\sqrt{nd \log d})$, This allows one to compute $\mathbf{A}_2$ and $\mathbf{A}_4$ without recursion, while still giving speedups.

8. ACKNOWLEDGEMENTS

We would like to thank Jonathan Kelner and Michael Kapralov for helpful discussions. This work was partially supported by NSF awards 0843915, 1111109, and 0835652, CCF-AF-0937274, CCF-0939370, and CCF-1217506, NSF Graduate Research Fellowship grant 1122374, Hong Kong RGC grant 2150701, AFOSR grant FA9550-13-1-0042, and the Defense Advanced Research Projects Agency (DARPA).

9. REFERENCES

[1] H. Avron, P. Maymounkov, and S. Toledo. Blendenpik: Supercharging LAPACK's least-squares solver. *SIAM J. Scientific Computing*, 32(3):1217–1236, 2010.

[2] H. Avron and S. Toledo. Effective stiffness: Generalizing effective resistance sampling to finite element matrices. *Computing Research Repository (CoRR)*, abs/1110.4437, 2011. arXiv:1110.4437.

[3] K. Clarkson and D. Woodruff. Numerical linear algebra in the streaming model. In *Proceedings of the 41st Annual ACM Symposium on Theory of Computing (STOC)*, pages 205–214, 2009.

[4] K. L. Clarkson and D. P. Woodruff. Low rank approximation and regression in input sparsity time. In *Proceedings of the 45th Annual ACM Symposium on Theory of Computing (STOC)*, pages 81–90, 2013.

[5] E. S. Coakley, V. Rokhlin, and M. Tygert. A fast randomized algorithm for orthogonal projection. *SIAM J. Scientific Computing*, 33(2):849–868, 2011.

[6] M. B. Cohen, Y. T. Lee, C. Musco, C. Musco, R. Peng, and A. Sidford. Uniform sampling for matrix approximation. *Computing Research Repository (CoRR)*, abs/1408.5099, 2014. arXiv:1408.5099.

[7] P. Drineas, R. Kannan, and M. W. Mahoney. Fast Monte Carlo algorithms for matrices I: Approximating matrix multiplication. *SIAM J. Comput.*, 36(1):132–157, 2006. Preliminary version in the 42nd Annual IEEE Symposium on Foundations of Computer Science (FOCS).

[8] P. Drineas, R. Kannan, and M. W. Mahoney. Fast Monte Carlo algorithms for matrices II: Computing a low-rank approximation to a matrix. *SIAM J. Comput.*, 36(1):158–183, 2006.

[9] P. Drineas, R. Kannan, and M. W. Mahoney. Fast Monte Carlo algorithms for matrices III: Computing a compressed approximate matrix decomposition. *SIAM J. Comput.*, 36(1):184–206, 2006. Preliminary version in the 14th Annual ACM-SIAM Symposium on Discrete Algorithms (SODA).

[10] P. Drineas, M. Mahoney, and S. Muthukrishnan. Subspace sampling and relative-error matrix approximation: Column-based methods. In *Proceedings of the 10th International Workshop on Randomization and Computation (RANDOM)*, pages 316–326, 2006.

[11] P. Drineas and M. W. Mahoney. Effective resistances, statistical leverage, and applications to linear equation solving. *Computing Research Repository (CoRR)*, abs/1005.3097, 2010. arXiv:1005.3097.

[12] P. Drineas, M. W. Mahoney, and S. Muthukrishnan. Sampling algorithms for ℓ_2 regression and applications. In *Proceedings of the 17th Annual ACM-SIAM Symposium on Discrete Algorithms (SODA)*, pages 1127–1136, 2006.

[13] P. Drineas, M. W. Mahoney, and S. Muthukrishnan. Relative-error CUR matrix decompositions. *SIAM J. Matrix Anal. Appl.*, 30(2):844–881, 2008.

[14] N. Halko, P. G. Martinsson, and J. A. Tropp. Finding structure with randomness: Probabilistic algorithms for constructing approximate matrix decompositions. *SIAM Review*, 53(2):217–288, 2011.

[15] W. Johnson and J. Lindenstrauss. Extensions of Lipschitz mappings into a Hilbert space. In *Conference on modern analysis and probability*, volume 26 of *Contemporary Mathematics*, pages 189–206. 1984.

[16] I. Koutis, G. L. Miller, and R. Peng. Approaching optimality for solving SDD linear systems. In *Proceedings of the 51st Annual IEEE Symposium on Foundations of Computer Science (FOCS)*, pages 235–244, 2010.

[17] S. Kumar, M. Mohri, and A. Talwalkar. Sampling methods for the Nystrom method. *Journal of Machine Learning Research*, 13(1):981–1006, 2012.

[18] M. Li, G. L. Miller, and R. Peng. Iterative row sampling. In *Proceedings of the 54th Annual IEEE Symposium on Foundations of Computer Science (FOCS)*, pages 127–136, 2013.

[19] M. W. Mahoney. Randomized algorithms for matrices and data. *Foundations and Trends in Machine Learning*, 3(2):123–224, 2011.

[20] M. W. Mahoney and X. Meng. Low-distortion subspace embeddings in input-sparsity time and applications to robust linear regression. In *Proceedings of the 45th Annual ACM Symposium on Theory of Computing (STOC)*, pages 91–100, 2013.

[21] X. Meng, M. A. Saunders, and M. W. Mahoney. LSRN: A parallel iterative solver for strongly over- or under-determined systems. *SIAM J. Scientific Computing*, 36(2), 2014.

[22] C. D. Meyer, Jr. Generalized inversion of modified matrices. *SIAM J. Appl. Math*, 24(3):315–323, 1973.

[23] M. Mohri and A. Talwalkar. Can matrix coherence be efficiently and accurately estimated? In *Proceedings of the 14th International Conference on Artificial Intelligence and Statistics (AISTATS)*, pages 534–542, 2011.

[24] J. Nelson and H. L. Nguyen. OSNAP: Faster numerical linear algebra algorithms via sparser subspace embeddings. In *Proceedings of the 54th Annual IEEE Symposium on Foundations of Computer Science (FOCS)*, pages 117–126, 2013.

[25] V. Rokhlin and M. Tygert. A fast randomized algorithm for overdetermined linear least-squares regression. *Proc. Natl. Acad. Sci. USA*, 1005(36):13212–7, 2008.

[26] T. Sarlos. Improved approximation algorithms for large matrices via random projections. In *Proceedings of the 47th Annual IEEE Symposium on Foundations of Computer Science (FOCS)*, pages 143–152, 2006.

[27] D. A. Spielman and N. Srivastava. Graph sparsification by effective resistances. *SIAM Journal on Computing*, 40(6):1913–1926, 2011. Preliminary version in the 40th Annual ACM Symposium on Theory of Computing (STOC).

[28] D. A. Spielman and S.-H. Teng. Nearly linear time algorithms for preconditioning and solving symmetric, diagonally dominant linear systems. *SIAM Journal on Matrix Analysis and Applications*, 35(3):835–885, 2014. Preliminary version in the 36th Annual ACM Symposium on Theory of Computing (STOC).

[29] J. A. Tropp. User-friendly tail bounds for sums of random matrices. *Foundations of Computational Mathematics*, 12(4):389–434, 2012.

Relax, No Need to Round: Integrality of Clustering Formulations

Pranjal Awasthi[*]
Department of Computer
Science
Princeton University
pawasthi@cs.cmu.edu

Afonso S. Bandeira[†]
Program in Applied and
Computational Mathematics
Princeton University
ajsb@math.princeton.edu

Moses Charikar[‡]
Department of Computer
Science
Princeton University
moses@cs.princeton.edu

Ravishankar Krishnaswamy[§]
Department of Computer
Science
Princeton University
ravishan@cs.cmu.edu

Soledad Villar[¶]
Department of Mathematics
University of Texas at Austin
mvillar@math.utexas.edu

Rachel Ward[¶]
Department of Mathematics
University of Texas at Austin
rward@math.utexas.edu

ABSTRACT

We study exact recovery conditions for convex relaxations of point cloud clustering problems, focusing on two of the most common optimization problems for unsupervised clustering: k-means and k-median clustering. Motivations for focusing on convex relaxations are: (a) they come with a certificate of optimality, and (b) they are generic tools which are relatively parameter-free, not tailored to specific assumptions over the input. More precisely, we consider the distributional setting where there are k clusters in $\mathbb{R}^m$ and data from each cluster consists of n points sampled from a symmetric distribution within a ball of unit radius. We ask: what is the minimal separation distance between cluster centers needed for convex relaxations to exactly recover these k clusters as the optimal integral solution? For the k-median linear programming relaxation we show a tight bound: exact recovery is obtained given arbitrarily small pairwise separation $\epsilon > 0$ between the balls. In other words, the pairwise center separation is $\Delta > 2 + \epsilon$. Under the same distributional model, the k-means LP relaxation fails to recover such clusters at separation as large as $\Delta = 4$. Yet, if we enforce PSD constraints on the k-means LP, we get exact cluster recovery at separation as low as $\Delta > \min\{2 + \sqrt{2k/m}, 2 + \sqrt{2 + 2/m}\} + \epsilon$. In contrast, common heuristics such as Lloyd's algorithm (a.k.a. the k-means algorithm) can *fail* to recover clusters in this setting; even with arbitrarily large cluster separation, k-means++ with overseeding by any constant factor fails with high probability at exact cluster recovery. To complement the theoretical analysis, we provide an experimental study of the recovery guarantees for these various methods, and discuss several open problems which these experiments suggest.

[*]Supported by a Princeton CCI postdoctoral fellowship.

[†]supported by AFOSR Grant No. FA9550-12-1-0317.

[‡]Supported by NSF grants CCF-1218687 and CCF-1302518.

[§]Supported by a Simons postdoctoral fellowship.

[¶]Supported by an NSF CAREER grant.

1. INTRODUCTION

Convex relaxations have proved to be extremely useful in solving or approximately solving difficult optimization problems. In theoretical computer science, the "relax and round" paradigm is now standard: given an optimization problem over a difficult (non-convex) feasible set, first *relax* the feasible set to a larger (convex) region over which the optimization problem is convex, then *round* the resulting optimal solution back to a point in the feasible set. Such convex relaxations generally serve a dual purpose: (i) they can be solved efficiently, and thus their solution gives a good starting point for the rounding step [56], and (ii) the value of the optimal solution to the convex relaxation serves as a good bound on the true optimal solution, and this can be used to certify the performance of the overall algorithm. Often, the feasible set is non-convex due to integral constraints of the form $x_i \in \{0, 1\}$, so that the relaxed convex set is given by the *interval* constraints $x_i \in [0, 1]$.

The study of convex relaxations in theoretical computer science has typically focused on how well such relaxations can approximate the objective function. This is captured by the *approximation factor* that can be obtained, i.e., how much worse in cost the integer rounded solution can be be in terms of the cost of the optimal fractional solution to the convex relaxation. However, in many practical scenarios, the choice of using a particular objective function is only a means to recovering the true hidden solution. For instance, when solving a clustering problem, the goal is to find the underlying ground truth clustering of the given data set. Modeling this problem via minimizing a particular objective function (such as k-median, k-means etc.) is a convenient mathematical choice, albeit the true goal still being to approximate the ground truth rather than the objective. In such scenarios, it is natural to ask if one can use convex relaxations directly to obtain the underlying ground truth solution and bypass the rounding step. In practice, it is often observed that optimal solutions of convex relaxations are also optimal for the original problem. As a result, one no longer needs the rounding step and the optimal solution can be recovered directly from solving the relaxed problem [54, 52]. We refer to this occurrence as exact recovery, tightness, or integrality, of the convex relaxation. Currently, there is very little theoretical understanding of this phenomenon (see e.g. [54, 52]). Motivated by this question, our goal in this work is to understand *whether and when convex relaxations can in fact lead to exact recovery, i.e. yield the optimum solution for the underlying discrete optimization problem.* This question also motivates the study and comparison of different relaxations for the same problem, in terms of their ability to produce integral optimum solutions. This is different from the typical goal of choosing the relaxation which yields algorithms with the best approximation factor. We believe that this is an interesting lens for examining convex relaxations that yields different insights into their strengths and weaknesses.

The phenomenon of exact recovery is understood in certain cases: a classical result says that *network flow* problems (e.g. maximum flow or minimum cost flow problems), or more generally any integer programming problem whose constraints are totally unimodular, all vertex solutions in the feasible set of the linear programming relaxation are integral, and hence the optimal solution (necessarily a vertex solution) is also integral [53]. Integrality of convex relaxations have also been studied in LP decoding, where linear programming techniques are used to decode LDPC codes [32, 31, 26, 7]. More recently, in the statistical signal procressing community, the seminal papers on compressive sensing [19, 28] started a trend towards "with high probability" tightness results: many optimization problems, while NP hard in the worst case, have tight convex relaxations with high probability over a distributions on input parameters. Subsequently, similar phenomena and guarantees have also emerged in low-rank matrix completion problems [51, 20, 34, 50, 22], and in graph partition problems [5, 23, 6, 30, 24, 27, 1]. Some other examples include multireference alignment and the study of MIMO channels [44, 15]. Among these works, the graph partitioning problems are most closely related to the clustering problems considered here; still, there are fundamental differences as discussed in Section 1.5. Convex relaxations have also been shown to recover optimal solutions to certain "stable" instances of graph partitioning problems such as Max-Cut [43] and for inference in graphical models [54, 55, 52, 39].

1.1 Geometric clustering

We will focus on integrality for convex relaxations of *geometric* clustering problems: given an initial set of data, map the data into a metric space, define an objective function over the points and solve for the optimal or an approximately optimal solution to the objective function. Then we can assume we are given a finite set of points $P = \{x_1, \ldots, x_n\}$ in a metric space (X, d) which we would like to partition into k disjoint clusters. Two of the most commonly studied objective functions in the literature are *k-median* and *k-means*, depicted in Figure 1. In the *k-median* (also known as *k-medoid*) problem, clusters are specified by *centers*: k representative points *from within the set P* denoted by $c_1, c_2, \ldots, c_k$. The corresponding partitioning is obtained by assigning each point to its closest center. The cost incurred by a point is the distance to its assigned center, and the goal is to find k center points that minimize the sum of the costs of the points in P:

$$\underset{\{c_1, c_2, \ldots, c_k\} \subset P}{\text{minimize}} \sum_{i=1}^{n} \min_{j=1, \ldots, k} d(x_i, c_j) \qquad (k\text{-median})$$

Alternatively, in the euclidean *k-means* problem, the points are in $\mathbb{R}^m$ and the distance $d(x_i, x_j)$ is the euclidean distance. The goal is to partition a finite set $P = \{x_1, \ldots, x_n\}$ in k clusters such that the sum of the squared euclidean distances to the *average point* of each cluster is minimized. Let $A_1, A_2, \ldots, A_k$ denote a partitioning of the the n points into k clusters; if $c_t = \frac{1}{|A_t|} \sum_{x_j \in A_t} x_j$, then the

k-means problem reads

$$\underset{A_1 \cup \cdots \cup A_k = P}{\text{minimize}} \sum_{t=1}^{k} \sum_{x_i \in A_t} d^2(x_i, c_t)$$

The identity $\sum_{x_i \in A_t} d^2(x_i, c_t) = \frac{1}{2} \frac{1}{|A_t|} \sum_{x_i, x_j \in A_t} d^2(x_i, x_j)$, allows us to re express the k means problem as the following optimization problem:

$$\underset{A_1 \cup \cdots \cup A_k = P}{\text{minimize}} \sum_{t=1}^{k} \frac{1}{|A_t|} \sum_{x_i, x_j \in A_t} d^2(x_i, x_j) \qquad (k\text{-means})$$

1.2 Prior work

The k-median and the k-means problems and their LP relaxations have been extensively studied from an approximation point of view. Both problems can be expressed as integer programming problems – see (1) and (2) below – which are NP-hard to optimize [4, 35]. There exist, for both problems, approximation algorithms which achieve a constant factor approximation [38, 41]. The k-median objective is closely related to the well studied facility location problem [10, 35] and the best known algorithms use convex relaxations via a rounding step. For k-means there also exist very effective heuristics [42] that although having provable guarantees in some cases [40, 21], may, in general, converge to local minima of the objective function. SDP relaxations of the k-means optimization problem were previously introduced [49, 48], albeit without exact recovery guarantees.

The question of *integrality* for convex relaxations of geometric clustering problems –in which case no rounding step needed – seems to have first appeared only recently in [29], where integrality for an LP relaxation of the k-median objective was shown, provided the set of points P admits a partition into k clusters of equal size, and the separation distance between any two clusters is sufficiently large. The paper [46] also studied integrality of an LP relaxation to the k-median objective (with squared Euclidean distances $d^2(\cdot)$ in the objective), and introduced a distribution on the input $\{x_1, x_2, \ldots, x_n\}$ which we will also consider here: Fix k balls in $\mathbb{R}^m$ of unit radius in arbitrary position, with a specified minimum distance between centers $\Delta > 2$. Draw n/k random points uniformly[1] and independently from each of the k balls. In [46], it was shown that the LP relaxation of k-median will recover these clusters as its global solution with high probability once $\Delta \geq 3.75$ and n is sufficiently large. Note that once $\Delta \geq 4$, any two points within a particular cluster are closer to each other than any two points from different clusters, and so simple thresholding algorithms can also work for cluster recovery in this regime. In Theorem 1, we contribute to these results, showing that the LP relaxation of k-median will recover clusters generated as such w.h.p. at *optimal* separation distance $\Delta \geq 2 + \varepsilon$, for n sufficiently large given ε.

1.3 Our contribution

We study integrality for three different convex relaxations of the k-median and k-means objectives:

(i) A standard linear programming (LP) relaxation of the k-median integer program,

(ii) A linear programming (LP) relaxation of the k-means integer program, and

---

[1] More generally, any rotationally-symmetric distribution where every neighborhood of 0 has a positive measure.

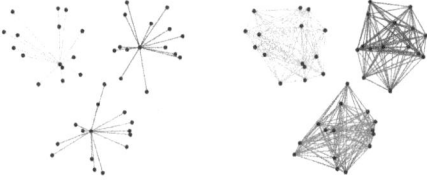

Figure 1: The k-median objective (left) minimizes the sum of distances from points to their representative data points. The k-means objective (right) minimizes the average of the squared euclidean distances of all points within a cluster.

$$\min_{z \in \mathbb{R}^{n \times n}} \quad \sum_{p,q \in P} d(p,q) z_{pq} \qquad (1)$$

$$\text{subject to} \quad \sum_{p \in P} z_{pq} = 1 \ \forall q \in P$$
$$z_{pq} \leq y_p \ \forall p, q \in P$$
$$\sum_{p \in P} y_p = k$$
$$z_{pq}, y_p \in \{0, 1\}$$

$$\min_{z \in R^{n \times n}} \quad \sum_{p,q \in P} d^2(p,q) z_{pq} \qquad (2)$$

$$\text{subject to} \quad \sum_{q \in P} z_{pq} = 1 \ \forall p \in P$$
$$z_{pq} \leq z_{pp} \ \forall p, q \in P$$
$$\sum_{p \in P} z_{pp} = k$$
$$z_{pq} \in \{0, \tfrac{1}{|A_p|}\}$$

Figure 2: IP formulations for the k-median (1) and k-means (2) problems. In the k-median formulation, the variable y_p indicates whether the point p is a center or not, while z_{pq} is 1 if the point q is assigned to p as center, and 0 otherwise. The solution for this integer programming problem corresponds to the adjacency matrix for a graph consisting of disjoint star-shaped graphs like the one shown in Figure 1. For k-means, an integral solution means that $z_{pq} = \frac{1}{|A_p|}$ if both p and q are in the cluster A_p, otherwise $z_{pq} = 0$. So in fact we are using the word "integral" in a broader sense. The solution corresponds to the adjacency matrix of k disjoint complete graphs, were each edge is weighted by the inverse of the number of vertices in its connected component as shown in Figure 1.

(iii) A semidefinite programming (SDP) relaxation of the k-means integer program (closely related to a previously proposed SDP relaxation for k-means [48]),

Each of these relaxations produces integer solutions if the point set partitions into k clusters and the intra-cluster separation distance (distance between cluster centers) is sufficiently large. As the separation distance decreases to 2 (at which point clusters begin to overlap and the "cluster solution" is no longer well-defined), a phase transition occurs for the k-means relaxations, and we begin to see fractional optimal solutions. For the k-median LP, it is actually difficult to generate fractional solutions, even as the cluster centers become arbitrarily close. We now present informal statements of our main results; see specific sections for more details.

THEOREM 1. *For any constant $\epsilon > 0$, and k balls of unit radius in $\mathbb{R}^m$ whose centers are separated by at least $\Delta > 2 + \epsilon$, there exists n sufficiently large that if n random points are drawn uniformly and independently from each ball, then with high probability, the natural k-median LP relaxation is integral and recovers the true clustering of the points.*

THEOREM 2. *Under the same setting as above and with high probability, a simple LP relaxation for the k-means objective fails to recover the exact clusters at separation $\Delta < 4$, even for $k = 2$ clusters.*

THEOREM 3. *Under the same setting as above, an SDP relaxation for the k-means objective recovers the clusters up to separation $\Delta > \min\{2+\sqrt{\frac{2k}{m}}, 2+\sqrt{2+\frac{2}{m}}\} + \epsilon$. Here k is the number of clusters points are sampled from balls of unit radius in $\mathbb{R}^m$.*

Theorems 1 and 2 are tight in their dependence on the cluster separation Δ. Theorem 3 is also tight in Δ in the limit as the ambient dimension $m \to \infty$. In fact, for Theorem 3 we can provide quantitative rates for exact recovery in terms of n, m, and k: the SDP will recover k clusters with inter-center separation $\Delta > 2 + \sqrt{(1+\frac{1}{\log n})^2 \frac{2k}{m} + \frac{8\log(kn)}{\sqrt{n}}}$ with probability greater than $1 - 2mk \exp(-cn^{1-\gamma}/m) - \frac{1}{2kn}$ (where c is a universal constant and $\gamma > 0$). See Section 4 for details.

REMARK 1. *As an addition to Theorem 1 we show that the popular Primal-Dual approximation algorithm for k-median [36] also recovers the true clustering under the same assumptions. In fact, in this case, when executing the algorithm one does not need to run the second stage of choosing independent sets among the set of potential centers. See the full version for details.*

REMARK 2. *Under the assumptions of the theorems above, popular heuristic algorithms such as* Partitioning around Medoids (PAM) *and* Lloyd's algorithm *(for k-median and k-means, respectively) can fail with high probability. See Section 5 for details.*

The main mathematical ingredients to establish the results above consist in the use of concentration of measure results, both scalar and matrix versions, to build appropriate dual certificates for these problems. That is, we construct deterministic sufficient conditions for the convex relaxations to be integral, and then demonstrate that with high probability, such conditions are satisfied for the random input at sufficiently high cluster separation. At the same time, the complementary slackness conditions for the k-means LP reveal that exact recovery for the k-means LP is possible if and only if the cluster separation satisfies $\Delta \geq 4$.

1.4 Why Study Convex Relaxations?

At this point, we reiterate why we focus on exact recovery guarantees for convex relaxations in particular, as opposed to other popular algorithms, such as the k-means heuristic (a.k.a. Lloyd's algorithm [42]). In fact, there has been substantial work on studying exact recovery conditions for such heuristics [47, 40, 9, 3]. However, one disadvantage of using these heuristics is that there is typically no way to *guarantee* that the heuristic is computing a good solution. In other words, even if such a heuristic is recovering an optimal solution to the underlying combinatorial optimization problem, we cannot ascertain such optimality just by looking at the output of the heuristic. Indeed, a crucial advantage of convex relaxations over other heuristics is that they come with a *certificate* that the produced solution is optimal, when this is the case. This property makes convex relaxations appealing over other iterative heuristics. There is also a large body of work on studying clustering problems under distributional or deterministic stability conditions [12, 25, 8, 18, 13, 37, 37, 2, 14]. However, the algorithms designed are usually tailored to specific assumptions on the input. On the other hand, the convex relaxation algorithms we study are not tied to any particular data distribution, and only depend on k, the number of clusters.

Nevertheless, it is natural to ask how well the commonly-used heuristics for k-means and k-median perform on the instances we analyze. Toward this end, we show (see Section 5) that heuristics such as Lloyd's algorithm and kmeans ++ (even with initialization procedures like overseeding) can fail to recover clusters with exponentially high probability, even when the cluster separation is *arbitrarily high*, far within the regime where Theorems 1 and 3 imply that the k-means and k-median convex relaxations are guaranteed (with high probability) to recover the clusters correctly.

1.5 Comparison with stochastic block models

The stochastic block model (SBM) with k communities is a simple random graph model for graph with a community behavior. Each edge is random (similarly to an Erdős Rényi graph) where the edges are independent and the probability of each depends on wether it is a intra- or inter-community edge. The task consists of recovering the hidden communities, and is often known as community detection or graph partitioning; in the particular case of two communities this is also known as planted bisection. Recently, [1] and [45] have obtained sharp thresholds for which problem parameters it is, in the $k = 2$ case, possible to correctly recover the labels of every point. Moreover an SDP relaxation is proposed in [1] and shown to be integral and perform exact recovery close to the optimal threshold. Although sharing many characteristics with our problem, the stochastic block model differs from the clustering problems we consider in many fundamental ways. Our objective is to cluster a point cloud in *euclidean* space. Although our results are for specific models, they are obtained from establishing conditions on the point clouds that could potentially be established for other, perhaps even deterministic, point clouds as the methods we analyze are not tied to the point model; they are clustering methods widely used in many settings. In contrast, the convex relaxation mentioned above for the SBM is based on the maximum likelihood estimator for the graph model. Moreover, while the SBM produces graphs whose edges are independent, our random model is on the vertices, which creates non-trivial dependencies in the edges (distances). Another technical difficulty in the clustering problems we study, that is not present in the SBM, is the inhomogeneity of the points; the points in the SBM are fairly uniform, even though there might be small variations, the inner and outer degree of every node will be comparable. On the other hand, in our setting, points close to other clusters have a very different distance profile from points near the center of their own cluster.

2. INTEGRALITY FOR THE K-MEDIAN LP RELAXATION

The k-median problem, expressed in the form of an integer programming problem (1), has a natural linear programming relaxation given by relaxing the integral constraints to interval constraints. This linear program is given in (3); its dual linear program is given in (4).

In the integer programming problem (1) the variable $y_p \in \{0, 1\}$ indicates whether the point $p \in P$ is a center or not. The variable $z_{pq} \in \{0, 1\}$ for $p, q \in P$ indicates whether or not the point p is the center for the point q. Each point has a unique center, and a cluster is the set of points sharing the same center. The solution $z \in \mathbb{R}^{n \times n}$ of (3) is a clustering if and only if it is integral (i.e. z_{pq} are integers for all $p, q \in P$). This solution is generically unique since no constraint is parallel to the objective function, hence motivating the following definitions.

$$\min_{z \in \mathbb{R}^{n \times n}} \sum_{p,q \in P} d(p,q) z_{pq} \tag{3}$$

$$\text{subject to} \quad \sum_{p \in P} z_{pq} = 1, \quad \forall q \in P$$

$$z_{pq} \leq y_p, \quad \forall p, q \in P$$

$$\sum_{p \in P} y_p = k$$

$$z_{pq}, y_p \in [0, 1], \quad \forall p, q \in P$$

$$\max_{\alpha \in \mathbb{R}^n} \sum_{q \in P} \alpha_q - kz \tag{4}$$

$$\text{subject to} \quad \alpha_q \leq \beta_{pq} + d(p,q) \quad \forall p, q \in P$$

$$\sum_q \beta_{pq} \leq \xi \quad \forall p \in P$$

$$\beta_{pq} \geq 0 \quad \forall p, q \in P$$

DEFINITION 1. *For $A_j \subseteq P$, let c_j the center of A_j*

$$c_j = \text{argmin}_{p \in A_j} \sum_{q \in A_j} d(p,q) \text{ and } \text{OPT}_j = \min_{p \in A_j} \sum_{q \in A_j} d(p,q).$$

We will ensure optimality of a particular integral solution to (3) by showing the existence of a feasible solution to the dual problem (4) whose dual objective value matches the primal objective value of the intended integral solution - a so-called *dual certificate*. When the solution of (3) is integral, it is also degenerate, since most of the variables are zero. In fact we experimentally observed that the dual (4) has multiple solutions. Indeed, motivated by this observation and experimental evidence, we can essentially enforce an extra constraint in the dual by asking that the variables α be constant within each cluster. Given α's as such, the β's and ξ's are then easily identified. We now formulate a sufficient condition for integrality based on these observations:

LEMMA 4. *Consider sets $A_1, \ldots, A_k$ with $n_1, \ldots, n_k$ points respectively. If $\exists \alpha_1, \ldots, \alpha_k$ s.t for each $s \in A_1 \cup \ldots \cup A_k$,*

$$\frac{1}{k} \left(\sum_{i=1}^{k} \left[n_i \alpha_i - \min_{p \in A_i} \sum_{q \in A_i} d(p,q) \right] \right) \geq$$
$$\sum_{q \in A_1} (\alpha_1 - d(s,q))_+ + \ldots + \sum_{q \in A_k} (\alpha_k - d(s,q))_+, \quad (5)$$

then the k-median LP (3) is integral and the partition in clusters $A_1, \ldots, A_k$ is optimal.

PROOF. By strong duality, the intended cluster solution is optimal if the corresponding LP objective value

$$\min_{p \in A_1} \sum_{q \in A_1} d(p,q) + \ldots + \min_{p \in A_k} \sum_{q \in A_k} d(p,q)$$

is less than or equal to the dual objective for some feasible point in the dual problem. By restricting the dual variables α_q to be constant within each cluster, and by setting ξ to be equal to the RHS of the Lemma statement, we can verify that the dual objective is at least the cost of the intended clustering. Moreover, it is also easy to see that for this setting of ξ and α_q's, the dual constraints are trivially satisfied. $\square$

Note that the sufficient condition in (4) is similar to the sufficient condition considered in [46], but turns out to be more powerful

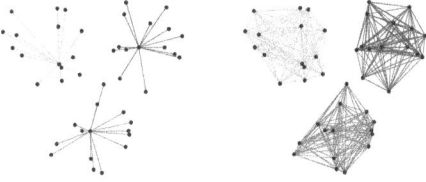

Figure 1: The k-median objective (left) minimizes the sum of distances from points to their representative data points. The k-means objective (right) minimizes the average of the squared euclidean distances of all points within a cluster.

(iii) A semidefinite programming (SDP) relaxation of the k-means integer program (closely related to a previously proposed SDP relaxation for k-means [48]),

Each of these relaxations produces integer solutions if the point set partitions into k clusters and the intra-cluster separation distance (distance between cluster centers) is sufficiently large. As the separation distance decreases to 2 (at which point clusters begin to overlap and the "cluster solution" is no longer well-defined), a phase transition occurs for the k-means relaxations, and we begin to see fractional optimal solutions. For the k-median LP, it is actually difficult to generate fractional solutions, even as the cluster centers become arbitrarily close. We now present informal statements of our main results; see specific sections for more details.

THEOREM 1. *For any constant $\epsilon > 0$, and k balls of unit radius in $\mathbb{R}^m$ whose centers are separated by at least $\Delta > 2 + \epsilon$, there exists n sufficiently large that if n random points are drawn uniformly and independently from each ball, then with high probability, the natural k-median LP relaxation is integral and recovers the true clustering of the points.*

THEOREM 2. *Under the same setting as above and with high probability, a simple LP relaxation for the k-means objective fails to recover the exact clusters at separation $\Delta < 4$, even for $k = 2$ clusters.*

THEOREM 3. *Under the same setting as above, an SDP relaxation for the k-means objective recovers the clusters up to separation $\Delta > \min\{2 + \sqrt{\frac{2k}{m}}, 2 + \sqrt{2 + \frac{2}{m}}\} + \epsilon$. Here k is the number of clusters points are sampled from balls of unit radius in $\mathbb{R}^m$.*

Theorems 1 and 2 are tight in their dependence on the cluster separation Δ. Theorem 3 is also tight in Δ in the limit as the ambient dimension $m \to \infty$. In fact, for Theorem 3 we can provide quantitative rates for exact recovery in terms of n, m, and k: the SDP will recover k clusters with inter-center separation $\Delta > 2 + \sqrt{(1 + \frac{1}{\log n})^2 \frac{2k}{m} + \frac{8 \log(kn)}{\sqrt{n}}}$ with probability greater than $1 - 2mk \exp(-cn^{1-\gamma}/m) - \frac{1}{2kn}$ (where c is a universal constant and $\gamma > 0$). See Section 4 for details.

REMARK 1. *As an addition to Theorem 1 we show that the popular Primal-Dual approximation algorithm for k-median [36] also recovers the true clustering under the same assumptions. In fact, in this case, when executing the algorithm one does not need to run the second stage of choosing independent sets among the set of potential centers. See the full version for details.*

REMARK 2. *Under the assumptions of the theorems above, popular heuristic algorithms such as* Partitioning around Medoids *(PAM) and* Lloyd's algorithm *(for k-median and k-means, respectively) can fail with high probability. See Section 5 for details.*

$$\min_{z \in \mathbb{R}^{n \times n}} \quad \sum_{p,q \in P} d(p,q) z_{pq} \tag{1}$$
$$\text{subject to} \quad \sum_{p \in P} z_{pq} = 1 \; \forall q \in P$$
$$z_{pq} \le y_p \; \forall p, q \in P$$
$$\sum_{p \in P} y_p = k$$
$$z_{pq}, y_p \in \{0,1\}$$

$$\min_{z \in R^{n \times n}} \quad \sum_{p,q \in P} d^2(p,q) z_{pq} \tag{2}$$
$$\text{subject to} \quad \sum_{q \in P} z_{pq} = 1 \; \forall p \in P$$
$$z_{pq} \le z_{pp} \; \forall p, q \in P$$
$$\sum_{p \in P} z_{pp} = k$$
$$z_{pq} \in \{0, \frac{1}{|A_p|}\}$$

Figure 2: IP formulations for the k-median (1) and k-means (2) problems. In the k-median formulation, the variable y_p indicates whether the point p is a center or not, while z_{pq} is 1 if the point q is assigned to p as center, and 0 otherwise. The solution for this integer programming problem corresponds to the adjacency matrix for a graph consisting of disjoint star-shaped graphs like the one shown in Figure 1. For k-means, an integral solution means that $z_{pq} = \frac{1}{|A_p|}$ if both p and q are in the cluster A_p, otherwise $z_{pq} = 0$. So in fact we are using the word "integral" in a broader sense. The solution corresponds to the adjacency matrix of k disjoint complete graphs, were each edge is weighted by the inverse of the number of vertices in its connected component as shown in Figure 1.

The main mathematical ingredients to establish the results above consist in the use of concentration of measure results, both scalar and matrix versions, to build appropriate dual certificates for these problems. That is, we construct deterministic sufficient conditions for the convex relaxations to be integral, and then demonstrate that with high probability, such conditions are satisfied for the random input at sufficiently high cluster separation. At the same time, the complementary slackness conditions for the k-means LP reveal that exact recovery for the k-means LP is possible if and only if the cluster separation satisfies $\Delta \ge 4$.

1.4 Why Study Convex Relaxations?

At this point, we reiterate why we focus on exact recovery guarantees for convex relaxations in particular, as opposed to other popular algorithms, such as the k-means heuristic (a.k.a. Lloyd's algorithm [42]). In fact, there has been substantial work on studying exact recovery conditions for such heuristics [47, 40, 9, 3]. However, one disadvantage of using these heuristics is that there is typically no way to *guarantee* that the heuristic is computing a good solution. In other words, even if such a heuristic is recovering an optimal solution to the underlying combinatorial optimization problem, we cannot ascertain such optimality just by looking at the output of the heuristic. Indeed, a crucial advantage of convex relaxations over other heuristics is that they come with a *certificate* that the produced solution is optimal, when this is the case. This property makes convex relaxations appealing over other iterative heuristics. There is also a large body of work on studying clustering problems under distributional or deterministic stability conditions [12, 25, 8, 18, 13, 37, 37, 2, 14]. However, the algorithms designed are usually tailored to specific assumptions on the input. On the other hand, the convex relaxation algorithms we study are not tied to any particular data distribution, and only depend on k, the number of clusters.

Nevertheless, it is natural to ask how well the commonly-used heuristics for k-means and k-median perform on the instances we analyze. Toward this end, we show (see Section 5) that heuristics such as Lloyd's algorithm and kmeans ++ (even with initialization procedures like overseeding) can fail to recover clusters with exponentially high probability, even when the cluster separation is *arbitrarily high*, far within the regime where Theorems 1 and 3 imply that the k-means and k-median convex relaxations are guaranteed (with high probability) to recover the clusters correctly.

1.5 Comparison with stochastic block models

The stochastic block model (SBM) with k communities is a simple random graph model for graph with a community behavior. Each edge is random (similarly to an Erdős Rényi graph) where the edges are independent and the probability of each depends on wether it is a intra- or inter-community edge. The task consists of recovering the hidden communities, and is often known as community detection or graph partitioning; in the particular case of two communities this is also known as planted bisection. Recently, [1] and [45] have obtained sharp thresholds for which problem parameters it is, in the $k = 2$ case, possible to correctly recover the labels of every point. Moreover an SDP relaxation is proposed in [1] and shown to be integral and perform exact recovery close to the optimal threshold. Although sharing many characteristics with our problem, the stochastic block model differs from the clustering problems we consider in many fundamental ways. Our objective is to cluster a point cloud in *euclidean* space. Although our results are for specific models, they are obtained from establishing conditions on the point clouds that could potentially be established for other, perhaps even deterministic, point clouds as the methods we analyze are not tied to the point model; they are clustering methods widely used in many settings. In contrast, the convex relaxation mentioned above for the SBM is based on the maximum likelihood estimator for the graph model. Moreover, while the SBM produces graphs whose edges are independent, our random model is on the vertices, which creates non-trivial dependencies in the edges (distances). Another technical difficulty in the clustering problems we study, that is not present in the SBM, is the inhomogeneity of the points; the points in the SBM are fairly uniform, even though there might be small variations, the inner and outer degree of every node will be comparable. On the other hand, in our setting, points close to other clusters have a very different distance profile from points near the center of their own cluster.

2. INTEGRALITY FOR THE K-MEDIAN LP RELAXATION

The k-median problem, expressed in the form of an integer programming problem (1), has a natural linear programming relaxation given by relaxing the integral constraints to interval constraints. This linear program is given in (3); its dual linear program is given in (4).

In the integer programming problem (1) the variable $y_p \in \{0,1\}$ indicates whether the point $p \in P$ is a center or not. The variable $z_{pq} \in \{0,1\}$ for $p, q \in P$ indicates whether or not the point p is the center for the point q. Each point has a unique center, and a cluster is the set of points sharing the same center. The solution $z \in \mathbb{R}^{n \times n}$ of (3) is a clustering if and only if it is integral (i.e. z_{pq} are integers for all $p, q \in P$). This solution is generically unique since no constraint is parallel to the objective function, hence motivating the following definitions.

$$\min_{z \in \mathbb{R}^{n \times n}} \sum_{p,q \in P} d(p,q) z_{pq} \qquad (3)$$

$$\text{subject to} \quad \sum_{p \in P} z_{pq} = 1, \quad \forall q \in P$$
$$z_{pq} \leq y_p, \quad \forall p, q \in P$$
$$\sum_{p \in P} y_p = k$$
$$z_{pq}, y_p \in [0,1], \quad \forall p, q \in P$$

$$\max_{\alpha \in \mathbb{R}^n} \sum_{q \in P} \alpha_q - kz \qquad (4)$$

$$\text{subject to} \quad \alpha_q \leq \beta_{pq} + d(p,q) \quad \forall p, q \in P$$
$$\sum_q \beta_{pq} \leq \xi \quad \forall p \in P$$
$$\beta_{pq} \geq 0 \quad \forall p, q \in P$$

DEFINITION 1. *For $A_j \subseteq P$, let c_j the center of A_j*

$$c_j = \text{argmin}_{p \in A_j} \sum_{q \in A_j} d(p,q) \text{ and } \text{OPT}_j = \min_{p \in A_j} \sum_{q \in A_j} d(p,q).$$

We will ensure optimality of a particular integral solution to (3) by showing the existence of a feasible solution to the dual problem (4) whose dual objective value matches the primal objective value of the intended integral solution - a so-called *dual certificate*. When the solution of (3) is integral, it is also degenerate, since most of the variables are zero. In fact we experimentally observed that the dual (4) has multiple solutions. Indeed, motivated by this observation and experimental evidence, we can essentially enforce an extra constraint in the dual by asking that the variables α be constant within each cluster. Given α's as such, the β's and ξ's are then easily identified. We now formulate a sufficient condition for integrality based on these observations:

LEMMA 4. *Consider sets $A_1, \ldots, A_k$ with $n_1, \ldots, n_k$ points respectively. If $\exists \alpha_1, \ldots, \alpha_k$ s.t for each $s \in A_1 \cup \ldots \cup A_k$,*

$$\frac{1}{k} \left(\sum_{i=1}^{k} \left[n_i \alpha_i - \min_{p \in A_i} \sum_{q \in A_i} d(p,q) \right] \right) \geq$$
$$\sum_{q \in A_1} (\alpha_1 - d(s,q))_+ + \ldots + \sum_{q \in A_k} (\alpha_k - d(s,q))_+, \quad (5)$$

then the k-median LP (3) is integral and the partition in clusters $A_1, \ldots, A_k$ is optimal.

PROOF. By strong duality, the intended cluster solution is optimal if the corresponding LP objective value

$$\min_{p \in A_1} \sum_{q \in A_1} d(p,q) + \ldots + \min_{p \in A_k} \sum_{q \in A_k} d(p,q)$$

is less than or equal to the dual objective for some feasible point in the dual problem. By restricting the dual variables α_q to be constant within each cluster, and by setting ξ to be equal to the RHS of the Lemma statement, we can verify that the dual objective is at least the cost of the intended clustering. Moreover, it is also easy to see that for this setting of ξ and α_q's, the dual constraints are trivially satisfied. $\square$

Note that the sufficient condition in (4) is similar to the sufficient condition considered in [46], but turns out to be more powerful in the sense that it allows us to get down to cluster separation $\Delta = 2 + \epsilon$.

A possible interpretation for the dual variables (which has been exploited by the current primal-dual based approximation algorithms for the k-median problem described in the full version) is as distance thresholds. In the RHS of equation (5) in $\sum_{q \in A_j} (\alpha_j - d(s, q))_+$ a point $s \in P$ gets positive contribution from points $q \in A_j$ that are at a distance smaller than α_j. In this sense, a point in the set A_j can only "see" other points within a distance α_j.

Following this intuition, one way to prove that inequality (5) holds is to show that we can choose feasible dual variables $\alpha_1, \dots, \alpha_k$ to satisfy

- Each center sees exactly its own cluster
  i.e. $(\alpha_j - d(c_j, q))_+ > 0$ if and only if $q \in A_j$.

- The RHS of (5) attains its maximum in the centers $c_1, \dots, c_k$.

- Each of the terms $n_i \alpha_i - \min_{p \in A_i} \sum_{q \in A_i} d(p, q)$ in the average in the LHS of (5) are the same.

Our strategy is to provide a set of conditions in our data points that guarantee such feasible dual variables exist. Assume the sets $A_1, \dots, A_k$ are contained in disjoint balls $B_{r_1}(c_1), \dots, B_{r_k}(c_k)$ respectively (where we use the notation $B_r(c)$ to indicate a ball of radius r centered at c), and suppose that $\alpha_1, \dots, \alpha_k$, $\alpha_j > r_j$, are such that for all $i \neq j$, $B_{\alpha_j}(c_j) \cap B_{r_i}(c_i) = \emptyset$. Given the α's there exist $\tau_1, \dots, \tau_k > 0$ sufficiently small that any $x \in B_{\tau_j}(c_j)$ is seen only by points in its own ball (see Definition 3 for a precise statement). We now define conditions on the sets $A_1, \dots, A_k$ which imply integrality of the linear programming relaxation (3). For simplicity, we assume for the remainder of the section $n_1 = \dots = n_k = n$ and $r_1 = \dots = r_k = 1$. Roughly speaking, our conditions ask that a) The clusters are separated, being contained in disjoint balls, b) Outside of a certain neighborhood of the center, no point is a good center for its own cluster and c) No point gets too much contribution from any other cluster. More precisely, we require the following *separation* and *center dominance* conditions:

DEFINITION 2 (SEPARATION). *Let the sets* $A_1, \dots, A_k$ *in* X, $|A_1| = \dots = |A_k| = n$, *such that*

$$\mathrm{OPT}_1 \leq \dots \leq \mathrm{OPT}_k$$

We say such sets satisfy the separation condition if they are included in k disjoint balls: $A_1 \subset B_1(c_1), \dots, A_k \subset B_1(c_k)$, $d(c_i, c_j) = 2 + \delta_{ij}$ *for* $i \neq j$ *where* $\delta_{ij} > 0$, *and the distance between* $B_1(c_i)$ *and* $B_1(c_j)$ *satisfies:*

$$\Theta := \min_{1 \leq i, j \leq k} \delta_{ij} > \frac{\mathrm{OPT}_k - \mathrm{OPT}_1}{n}. \quad (6)$$

REMARK 3. *The expression* $\frac{\mathrm{OPT}_k - \mathrm{OPT}_1}{n}$ *provides a way of measuring how different the clusters are from each other. For example, if the clusters are symmetric, then* $\frac{\mathrm{OPT}_k - \mathrm{OPT}_1}{n} = 0$. *This condition requires bigger separation when clusters are different.*

We also require a *center dominance* condition. Consider the contribution function $P^{(\alpha_1, \dots, \alpha_k)} : X \to \mathbb{R}$ as the sum of all contributions that a point can get:

$$P^{(\alpha_1, \dots, \alpha_k)}(y) = \sum_{i=1}^{k} \sum_{x \in A_i} (\alpha_i - d(y, x))_+.$$

The center dominance condition essentially says that the contribution function attains its maximum in a small neighborhood of the

center of each ball, as long as the parameters α are chosen from some small interval.

DEFINITION 3 (CENTER DOMINANCE). $A_1, \dots, A_k$ *satisfy center dominance in the interval* $(a, b) \subset (1, 1 + \Theta)$ *if*

$$b - a > \frac{\mathrm{OPT}_k - \mathrm{OPT}_1}{n} \quad (7)$$

and for all $\alpha_1, \dots, \alpha_k \in (a, b)$ *there exist* $\tau_1, \dots, \tau_k > 0$ *such that for all* $x \in B_{\tau_j}(c_j)$, $j = 1, \dots, k$

$$B_{\alpha_i}(x) \cap B_{r_i}(c_i) = \begin{cases} B_{r_j}(c_j) & \text{if } i = j \\ \emptyset & \text{otherwise} \end{cases} \quad (8)$$

$$\max_{y \in A_j \setminus B_{\tau_j}(c_j)} P^{(\alpha_1, \dots, \alpha_k)}(y) < \max_{y \in B_{\tau_j}(c_j)} P^{(\alpha_1, \dots, \alpha_k)}(y) \quad (9)$$

Note that, in particular this condition requires the existence of a point of A_j in $B_{\tau_j}(c_j)$.

We now state our main recovery theorem, and show that very natural distributions satisfy the conditions.

THEOREM 5. *If* $A_1, \dots, A_k$ *are k sets in a metric space* (X, d) *satisfying separation and center dominance, then there is an integral solution for the k-median LP and it corresponds to separating* $P = A_1 \cup \dots \cup A_k$ *in the clusters* $A_1, \dots, A_k$.

Indeed, a broad class of distributions are likely to satisfy these conditions. The following theorem shows that with high probability, such conditions are satisfied by a set of nk points in $\mathbb{R}^m$ (for n sufficiently large) drawn from k clusters which have the same (but shifted) rotationally symmetric probability distribution which is such that the probability of any ball containing 0 is positive.

THEOREM 6. *Let μ be a probability measure in $\mathbb{R}^m$ supported in $B_1(0)$, continuous and rotationally symmetric with respect to 0 such that every neighborhood of 0 has positive measure. Then, given points $c_1, \dots, c_k \in \mathbb{R}^m$ such that $d(c_i, c_j) > 2$ if $i \neq j$, let μ_j be the translation of the measure μ to the center c_j. Now consider the data set* $A_1 = \left\{ x_i^{(1)} \right\}_{i=1}^{n}, \dots, A_k = \left\{ x_i^{(k)} \right\}_{i=1}^{n}$, *each point drawn randomly and independently with probability given by $\mu_1, \dots, \mu_k$ respectively. Then, $\forall \gamma < 1$, $\exists N_0$ such that, $\forall n > N_0$, the k-median LP (3) is integral with prob. at least γ.*

The proof of this theorem can be found in the full version of the paper [11]. The main idea is that given k balls with the same continuous probability distribution, for large values of n, the separation condition is just a consequence of the weak law of large numbers. And one can see that center dominance holds in expectation, so it will hold with high probability if the number of points n is large enough. Note that the condition that all measures be the same and rotationally symmetric can be dropped as long as the expectation of the contribution function attains its maximum in a point close enough to the center of the ball and $\lim_{n \to \infty} \frac{\mathrm{OPT}_k - \mathrm{OPT}_1}{n} < d(c_i, c_j) - 2$ for all $i \neq j$.

3. AN INTEGRALITY GAP FOR THE K-MEANS LP RELAXATION

We now show that, in contrast to the LP relaxation for the k-median clustering problem, the natural LP relaxation for k-means does not attain integral solutions for the clustering model presented in Theorem 6, unless the separation between cluster centers exceeds $\Delta = 4$. In particular, this shows that the k-median LP relaxation performs better (as a clustering criterion) for such data sets.

The natural LP relaxation for k-means uses the formulation of the objective function given by equation (k-means). The natural LP relaxation for (2) is given by (10) below, whose dual LP is (11):

$$\min_{z \in \mathbb{R}^n \times \mathbb{R}^n} \sum_{p,q \in P} d^2(p,q) z_{pq}$$

$$\text{subject to} \quad \sum_{q \in P} z_{pq} = 1, \qquad \forall p \in P$$

$$r_{pq} \leq r_{pp}, \qquad \forall p, q \in P \qquad (10)$$

$$\sum_{p \in P} z_{pp} = k$$

$$z_{pq} \in [0,1]$$

$$\max_{\substack{\alpha \in \mathbb{R}^n, \xi \in \mathbb{R} \\ \beta \in \mathbb{R}^{n \times n}}} \sum_{p \in P} \alpha_p - k\xi$$

$$\text{subject to} \quad \alpha_p \leq d^2(p,q) + \beta_{pq}, \qquad \forall p, q \in P$$

$$\sum_{q \in P} \beta_{pq} = \xi, \qquad \forall p \in P \qquad (11)$$

$$\beta_{pq} \geq 0$$

In an intended integral solution to (10), the variable $z_{pq} = 1/|C|$ if p, q belong to the same cluster C in an optimal clustering, and $z_{pq} = 0$ otherwise. It is easy to see that such a solution satisfies all the constraints, and that the objective exactly measures the sum of average distances within every cluster. The following theorem completely characterizes when this LP relaxation can recover the optimum k-means cluster solution: if the distance between any two points in the same cluster is smaller than the distance between any two points in different clusters.

THEOREM 7. *Given a set of points $P = A_1 \cup \ldots \cup A_k$, the solution of (10) is integral and divides the set P in k clusters $A_1, \ldots, A_k$ if and only if for all p, q in the same cluster A_i and r in a different cluster A_j,*

$$d(p,q) < d(p,r). \qquad (12)$$

PROOF. If the solution of (10) is integral and divides the set P in the clusters $A_1, \ldots, A_k$, complementary slackness tells us that

$$\alpha_p = d^2(p,q) + \beta_{pq} \quad \text{if } p, q \text{ are in the same cluster} \quad (13)$$
$$\beta_{pr} = 0 \quad \text{if } p, r \text{ are in different clusters} \quad (14)$$

if and only if α, β are corresponding optimal dual variables. Combining (11), (13) and (14), since $\beta_{pq} > 0$ we obtain that if p, q are in the same cluster and r is in a different cluster,

$$d^2(p,q) + \beta_{pq} = \alpha_p \leq d^2(p,r).$$

Conversely, if (12) holds then there exist dual feasible variables satisfying (13) and (14) for the corresponding cluster solution, indicated by $z_{pq} \in \{0, \frac{1}{|A_i|}\}$. Indeed, for any dual feasible solution, $\sum_{q \in P} \beta_{pq} = \xi \; \forall p \in P$ implies $\sum_{p,q \in P} \beta_{pq} z_{pq} = k\xi$; we also have $\alpha_p = \sum_{q \in P}(d^2(p,q) + \beta_{pq}) z_{pq}$. Then for any dual feasible solution,

$$\sum_{p,q \in P} d^2(p,q) z_{pq} = \sum_{p \in P} \alpha_p - k\xi$$

which gives the integrality of (11). The solution is generically unique because no constraint in (10) is parallel to the objective function. $\square$

The following is a direct consequence of Theorem 7.

THEOREM 8. *Fix k balls of unit radius in $\mathbb{R}^m$, and draw n points from any distribution supported in these balls. If n is sufficiently large, then the LP relaxation of k-means (10) is not inte-gral with high probability, unless the centers of any two balls are separated by a distance $\Delta \geq 4$.*

4. INTEGRALITY FOR THE K-MEANS SDP RELAXATION

In contrast to the negative results for the k-means LP relaxation, we now show that by adding positive semidefinite constraints, the resulting SDP relaxation of the k-means problem is integral at much closer range: for unit-radius clusters whose centers are separated by distance as low as $2 + \sqrt{\frac{2k}{m}} + \epsilon$ for any $\epsilon > 0$. To fix notation for this section, we have k clusters in $\mathbb{R}^m$, each containing n points, so that the total number of points is $N = kn$. We index a point with (a,i) where $a = 1, \ldots, k$ represents the cluster it belongs to and $i = 1, \ldots, n$ the index of the point in that cluster. The distance between two points is represented by $d_{(a,i),(b,j)}$. We define the $N \times N$ matrix D given by the squares of these distances. It consists of blocks $D^{(a,b)}$ of size $n \times n$ such that $D_{ij}^{(a,b)} = d_{(a,i),(b,j)}^2$. For ease of dual notation, the k-means SDP (15) and dual (16) are presented using slightly unconventional notation:

$$\max_{X \in \mathbb{R}^{N \times N}} -\text{Tr}(DX) \qquad (15)$$

$$\text{subject to} \quad \text{Tr}(X) = k$$
$$X1 = 1$$
$$X \geq 0$$
$$X \succeq 0.$$

$$\min_{z \in \mathbb{R}, \alpha} kz + \sum_{a=1}^{k} \sum_{i=1}^{n} \alpha_{a,i} \qquad (16)$$

$$\text{subject to } Q = zI_{N \times N} + \sum_{a=1}^{k} \sum_{i=1}^{n} \alpha_{a,i} A_{a,i}$$

$$\sum_{a,b=1}^{k} \sum_{i,j=1}^{n} \beta_{i,j}^{(a,b)} E_{(a,i),(b,j)} + D$$

$$\beta_{i,j} \geq 0$$
$$Q \succeq 0$$

Here, $1 \in \mathbb{R}^{N \times 1}$ has unit entries, and $e_{a,i} \in \mathbb{R}^{N \times 1}$ is the indicator function for index (a,i). Also, $A_{a,i} = \frac{1}{2}(1e_{a,i}^T + e_{a,i}1^T)$ and $E_{(a,i),(b,j)} = \frac{1}{2}(e_{b,j}e_{a,i}^T + e_{a,i}e_{b,j}^T)$.

The intended primal optimal solution $X \in \mathbb{R}^{N \times N}$ which we will construct a dual certificate for is block-diagonal, equal to $1/n$ in the $n \times n$ diagonal blocks for each of the clusters, and 0 otherwise. Defining 1_a as the indicator function of cluster a (that is, it has a 1 in coordinates corresponding to the points in cluster a), we can write the intended solution as $X = \frac{1}{n} \sum_{a=1}^{k} 1_a 1_a^T$.

Recall the dual certificate approach: if we can construct a set of feasible dual variables (z, α, β, Q) with dual objective function (16) equal to the primal objective (15) corresponding to X, then we can be assured that X is an optimal solution. If, in addition, $\text{rank}(Q) + \text{rank}(X) = N$, then we can be assured that X is the unique optimal solution. Towards this end, complementary slackness tells us that $QX = 0$, which means that

$$Q1_a \equiv 0, \qquad \forall_a. \qquad (17)$$

Complementary slackness also tells us that, over each $n \times n$ diagonal block,

$$\beta^{(a,a)} \equiv 0, \qquad \forall_a. \qquad (18)$$

We thus have, for each $n \times n$ diagonal block of Q,

$$Q^{(a,a)} = zI_{n \times n} + \frac{1}{2} \sum_{i=1}^{n} \alpha_{a,i} \left(1 e_i^T + e_i 1^T \right) + D^{(a,a)}. \quad (19)$$

Note that here e_i are n-length vectors and before they were N-length (we shall switch between vectors of length n and N when necessary, this makes our notations easier).

In fact, these constraints implied by complementary slackness suffice to specify the $\alpha_{(a,i)}$ values. Since the total dual objective is equal to the clustering cost of the intended solution, it remains to complete the Q matrix and the β matrix such that $\beta \geq 0$ (entry wise), and $Q \succeq 0$ (in the positive definite sense). To this end, consider the non-diagonal $n \times n$ blocks:

$$Q^{(a,b)} = \frac{1}{2} \sum_{i=1}^{n} (\alpha_{a,i} e_i 1^T + \alpha_{b,i} 1 e_i^T) - \frac{1}{2} \beta^{(a,b)} + D^{(a,b)}, \quad a \neq b$$

Since we want to ultimately arrive at a sufficient condition for integrality which depends on within- and between-cluster pairwise distances, and we know that Q must be positive semi-definite and satisfy the constraints (17), we guess that the submatrix $Q^{(a,b)}$ ($a \neq b$) as follows: the $(r,s)^{th}$ entry of $Q(a,b)$ is set to $\frac{1}{n} e_r^T D^{(a,b)} 1 + \frac{1}{n} 1^T D^{(a,b)} e_s - e_r^T D^{(a,b)} e_s - \frac{1}{n^2} 1^T D^{(a,b)} 1$. Writing $Q^{(a,b)}$ also in terms of the $\beta^{(a,b)}$ and solving for $\beta^{(a,b)}$, the non-negativity of β gives us the following constraints that these parameters need to satisfy: for all clusters $a \neq b$, and all $r \in a, s \in b$,

$$2 D_{rs}^{(a,b)} - \frac{e_r^T D^{(a,b)} 1}{n} - \frac{1^T D^{(a,b)} e_s}{n} + \frac{1^T D^{(a,b)} 1}{n^2} \geq$$
$$\frac{e_r^T D^{(a,a)} 1}{n} + \frac{e_s^T D^{(b,b)} 1}{n} - \frac{1}{2} \left(\frac{1^T D^{(a,a)} 1}{n^2} + \frac{1^T D^{(b,b)} 1}{n^2} \right) + \frac{1}{n} z.$$

Notice that the above constraints essentially compare (for two points r, s in clusters a, b respectively) (i) the average distance of r to the cluster b, the average distance of s to cluster a, the distance between r and s, and finally the average distance between the two clusters, indicating that these are reasonable conditions. Now, note by (19) that $Q \succeq 0$ automatically holds once z is sufficiently large; It remains to find a lower bound on z for which this holds. Since $Q1_a = 0$ for all a, it is sufficient to check that $x^T Q x \geq 0$ for all x perpendicular to Λ; that is, for all x in the span of $\{1_a, a \in [k]\}$. But if x is perpendicular to these cluster indicator vectors, $x^T Q x \geq 0$ greatly simplifies to[2] $z x^T x + 2 x^T (\sum_a D^{(a,a)}) x - x^T D x > 0$. This suggests setting $z > z^* = \left(2 \max_a \max_{x \perp 1} \left| \frac{x^T D^{(a,a)} x}{x^T x} \right| + \max_{x \perp \Lambda} \left| \frac{x^T D x}{x^T x} \right| \right)$, so that the null space of Q only consists of Λ, thus ensuring that $\text{rank}(Q) + \text{rank}(X) = N$. This combined with the non-negativity of β gives us the following deterministic separation condition:

DEFINITION 4 (AVERAGE SEPARATION). *A clustering instance satisfies average separation if for all clusters a, b, and all $r \in a, s \in b$:*

$$2 D_{rs}^{(a,b)} - \frac{e_r^T D^{(a,b)} 1}{n} - \frac{1^T D^{(a,b)} e_s}{n} + \frac{1^T D^{(a,b)} 1}{n^2} >$$
$$\frac{e_r^T D^{(a,a)} 1}{n} + \frac{e_s^T D^{(b,b)} 1}{n} - \frac{1}{2} \left(\frac{1^T D^{(a,a)} 1}{n^2} + \frac{1^T D^{(b,b)} 1}{n^2} \right) + \frac{1}{n} z^*,$$

where $z^* = \left(2 \max_a \max_{x \perp 1} \left| \frac{x^T D^{(a,a)} x}{x^T x} \right| + \max_{x \perp \Lambda} \left| \frac{x^T D x}{x^T x} \right| \right)$.

[2]this uses our choice of $Q^{(a,b)}$ above, which ensures that most terms cancel

The above condition essentially compares (for two points r, s in clusters a, b respectively) (i) the average distance of r to the cluster b, the average distance of s to cluster a, the distance between r and s, and finally the average distance between the two clusters. Hence, we have the following theorem.

THEOREM 9. *If an euclidean clustering instance with the squared distance matrix D satisfies average separation, then the corresponding k-means SDP for the instance has unique integral solution equal to the k-means optimal solution, and corresponding to this clustering.*

We may show that for our distributional instances consisting of clusters whose centers are separated by $2 + \sqrt{\frac{2k}{m}} + \epsilon$, average separation is satisfied for large enough n. This involves delicate tail bounds on the spectrum of matrices where the rows correspond to points sampled from isotropic distributions supported on the unit ball, and also on the average between- and across-cluster distances. Putting this together, we get the following:

THEOREM 10. *For the k-means objective, if n points are drawn from k distributions in $\mathbb{R}^m$, where each distribution is isotropic and supported on a ball of radius 1, and if the centers of these balls are separated at a distance of $2 + \sqrt{\frac{2k}{m}} + \epsilon$ for some $\epsilon > 0$, then there exists n_0 such that for all $n \geq n_0$, the k-means SDP recovers the exact clusters with probability exceeding $1 - 2mk \exp(-cn^{1-\varepsilon}/m) - \frac{1}{2kn}$.*

REMARK 4. *A slightly different dual certificate shows that under the same hypothesis the SDP recovers the exact clusters when the centers are separated by a distance $2 + \sqrt{2 + 2/m} + \epsilon$, which is better in the regime $k > m$. Therefore our recovery result holds for separation $\min\{2 + \sqrt{2k/m}, 2 + \sqrt{2 + 2/m}\} + \epsilon$.*

Refer to the full version of our paper [11] for complete details.

5. WHERE CONVEX RELAXATIONS SUCCEED, LLOYD'S METHOD CAN FAIL

The well-known heuristic algorithm for solving the k-means optimization problem known as *Lloyd's algorithm*[3] (also known as the k-means algorithm or Voronoi iteration) can *fail* in the setting of separated isotropic clusters where, as shown in Theorem 6, the k-median LP is guaranteed to be integral. The construction of a bad scenario for Lloyd's algorithm consists of 3 balls of unit radius, such that the centers of the first two are at a distance of $\Delta > 2$ from each other, and the center of the third is far away (at a distance of $D \gg \Delta$ from each of the first two balls). Generate the data by sampling n points from each of these balls. Now we create l copies of this group of 3 clusters such that each copy is very far from other copies. In the full version of our paper [11] we will show that with overwhelming probability Lloyd's algorithm will pick initial centers such that either (1) some group of 3 clusters does not get 3 centers initially, or (2) some group of 3 clusters will get 3 centers in the following configuration: 2 centers in the far away cluster and only one center in the two nearby clusters. In such a case it is easy to see the the algorithm will never recover the true clustering.

[3]We recap how the Lloyds algorithm proceeds: initialize k centers *uniformly at random* from among the data points. Then, in each iteration, two steps occur: (i) using the currently chosen centers, each point assigns itself to the nearest center; (ii) now, given the assignment of data points to clusters, new centers are computed as being the means of each cluster (i.e., the average of the data points assigned to a cluster). The algorithm terminates at the first step when the clustering does not change in successive iterations.

The same example can also be extended to show that the well known kmeans++ algorithm [9] which uses a clever initialization will also fail with high probability when the number of clusters and the dimension of the space is large enough, even in the setting with overseeding proposed in [47]. A complete statement and proof of this theorem is available at the full version of our paper [11].

THEOREM 11. *Given an overseeding parameter $c \geq 1$ and minimum separation $\Delta > 2$, there exist inputs with center separation at least Δ, for which kmeans++ with overseeding [47] with ck centers selected initially, fails with high probability to exactly recover the clusters.*

6. SIMULATIONS

In this section we report on experiments conducted regarding the integrality of k-median LP (3), k-means LP (10), and k-means SDP (15). Our input consists of k disjoint unit-radius balls in $\mathbb{R}^m$ such that the centers of distinct balls are separated by distance $\Delta \geq 2$. We then randomly draw $N = kn$ points; n points i.i.d. uniformly within each ball. We implement and solve the convex optimization problems using Matlab and CVX [33]. An experiment is considered successful if the solution of the convex optimization is integral and separates the balls into their respective clusters. Note that this is the same experimental set-up as in [46]. For each value of Δ and n we repeat the experiment 10 times and plot, in a gray scale, the empirical probability of success.

Figure 3 shows the simulation results for $k = 2$ clusters in $\mathbb{R}^3$. The number of points N ranges from 4 to 50 and Δ ranges from 2 to 3.5. It is clear that the k-median LP and k-means SDP are superior to the k-means LP in achieving exact recovery at lower threshold Δ. In fact, as predicted by our theoretical analysis, the k-means LP integrality is very infrequent for $\Delta < 3$. The k-median LP and k-means SDP seem to have comparable performance, but the k-median LP is much faster than the k-means SDP.

REMARK 5. *If instead requiring integrality and recovery of the planted clusters, we only test our results for integrality (i.e. the result of the simulation should just be some clustering, not necessarily the clustering corresponding to the disjoint supports from which we draw the points) we see a very interesting behavior:*

k-**median LP** *We observe that k-median LP obtains integral solutions for every instance of our experiments. That is, the failure instances in our experiments shown in Figures 4 and 3 still coincide with clusterings, just not the clusters corresponding to the planted disjoint supports. Indeed, a different clustering can make sense as being more "optimal" than the planted distribution when N is small. We refer to Section 7 for a discussion of an open problem regarding this.*

k-**means SDP and LP** *For all instances of our experiments, every time we obtain an integral solution, the integral solution corresponded to the underlying expected clustering. The failure instances in Figures 4 and 3 correspond to matrices that do not represent any clustering as represented in Figure 5. We have not explored whether it is possible to recover the expected clustering via rounding such a fractional solution.*

7. CONCLUSIONS AND FUTURE WORK

In this work we studied convex relaxations for popular clustering objectives and gave sufficient conditions under which such relaxations lead to exact recovery thereby bypassing the traditional rounding step in approximation algorithms. Our results also shed

light on differences between different relaxations. For instance, our theoretical and empirical results show that the k-median LP is much better at recovering optimal solutions than the k-means LP. In fact, we show that the k-means LP is integral only in the regime $\Delta \geq 4$ where a simple thresholding algorithm could also be used to distinguish clusters.

Our analysis for the k-means SDP shows that for any cluster center separation $\Delta \geq 2 + \sqrt{2k/m}$, the solution corresponds to a clustering for n sufficiently large, where we give a precise bound on n. In contrast, for the k-median LP, we know that for any separation $2 + \epsilon$ and any number of clusters k, the solution of the k-median LP is integral if n is large enough. It remains to quantify how large n needs to be in terms of the other parameters.

Several possible future research directions come out of this work. Although we study only a specific distribution over data – points drawn i.i.d. from disjoint balls of equal radius – it is of interest to investigate further to determine if the exact recovery trends we observe are more general, for example, by relaxing certain assumptions such as equal radii, equal numbers of points within clusters, etc. A particularly interesting direction is the setting where the balls overlap and/or when the points are drawn according to a mixture of Gaussians. These two examples share the difficulty that there is no longer a "ground truth" clustering to recover, and hence it is not even clear how to build a dual certificate to certify an integral solution. Despite this difficulty, we observe in experiments that the k-median LP relaxation still remains integral with high probability, even in extreme situations such as when the points are drawn i.i.d from a single isotropic distribution but parameter $k > 1$ clusters are sought in the LP relaxation! As in most practical applications, hoping for ground truth recovery is overly optimistic; understanding the integrality phenomenon beyond the exact recovery setting is an important problem. Recently, the same phenomenon was observed [16] in the context of the Procrustes, alignment, and angular synchronization problems and referred to as *rank recovery*.

A third direction would be to relax the notion of integrality, asking instead that a convex relaxation produce a *near*-optimal solution. There has been recent work on this for the k-means++ algorithm [3]. Another by-product of our analysis is a sufficient condition under which the popular primal-dual algorithm for k-median leads to exact recovery. It would be interesting to prove similar exact recovery guarantees for other approximation algorithms.

Finally, convex relaxations are a very powerful tool not just for clustering problems but in many other domains. The questions that we have asked in this paper can also be studied for various other domains such as inference in graphical models [54], graph partitioning [17, 43], and more.

8. ACKNOWLEDGEMENTS

We would like to thank Ulas Ayaz and Abhinav Nellore along with the anonymous referees for helpful comments which greatly improved this paper. Part of this work was done while ASB and RW were participating in Oberwolfach's workshop "Mathematical Physics meets Sparse Recovery"; these authors thank Oberwolfach's hospitality.

9. REFERENCES

[1] E. Abbe, A. S. Bandeira, and G. Hall. Exact recovery in the stochastic block model. *arXiv preprint arXiv:1405.3267*, 2014.

[2] D. Achlioptas and F. McSherry. On spectral learning of mixtures of distributions. In *Proceedings of the Eighteenth Annual Conference on Learning Theory*, 2005.

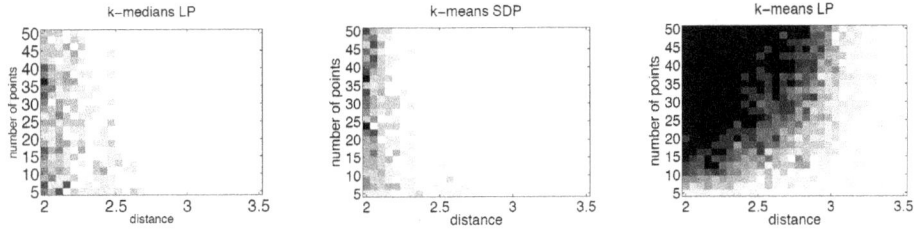

Figure 3: Empirical probability of integrality of convex relaxation-based clustering. Lighter color corresponds to higher probability of success. We consider 2 clusters in $\mathbb{R}^3$, $4 \le N \le 50$, $2 \le \Delta \le 3.5$.

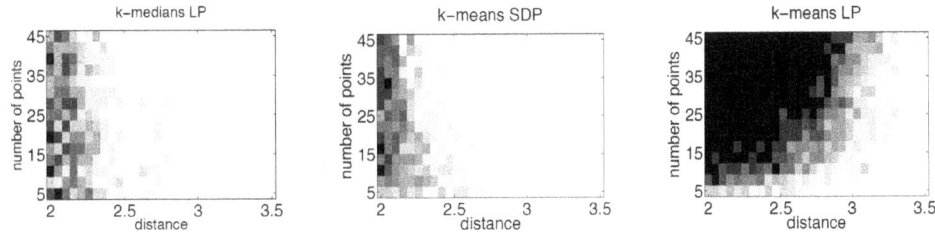

Figure 4: For this simulation we generate 3 clusters in $\mathbb{R}^3$, $6 \le N \le 42$, $2 \le \Delta \le 3.5$. Lighter color corresponds to higher probability of success.

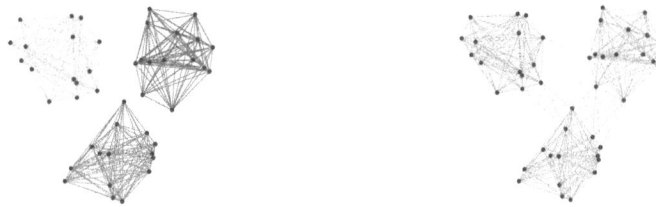

Figure 5: A solution of k-means LP or SDP that corresponds to a clustering can be seen as the adjacency matrix of a graph with k complete connected components as represented in the left image. In this graph each edge has weight $1/|C|$ and $|C|$ is the number of vertices in its connected component. When the solution of k-means LP or SDP is not the expected clustering, we observe cliques corresponding to the ground truth clustering and extra edges between clusters as represented in the right figure.

[3] M. Agarwal, R. Jaiswal, and A. Pal. k-means++ under approximation stability. *The 10th annual conference on Theory and Applications of Models of Computation*, 2013.

[4] D. Aloise, A. Deshpande, P. Hansen, and P. Popat. NP-hardness of euclidean sum-of-squares clustering. *Mach. Learn.*, 75(2):245–248, May 2009.

[5] B. Ames. Guaranteed clustering and biclustering via semidefinite programming. *Mathematical Programming*, pages 1–37, 2012.

[6] B. Ames. Robust convex relaxation for the planted clique and densest k-subgraph problems. *arXiv preprint arXiv:1305.4891*, 2013.

[7] S. Arora, C. Daskalakis, and D. Steurer. Message passing algorithms and improved LP decoding. In *Proceedings of the Forty-first Annual ACM Symposium on Theory of Computing*, STOC, 2009.

[8] S. Arora and R. Kannan. Learning mixtures of arbitrary gaussians. In *STOC*, 2005.

[9] D. Arthur and S. Vassilvitskii. k-means++: the advantages of careful seeding. In *Proceedings of the eighteenth annual ACM-SIAM symposium on Discrete algorithms*, 2007.

[10] V. Arya, N. Garg, R. Khandekar, A. Meyerson, K. Munagala, and V. Pandit. Local search heuristics for k-median and

facility location problems. *SIAM Journal on Computing*, 33(3):544–562, 2004.

[11] P. Awasthi, A. Bandeira, M. Charikar, K. Ravishankar, S. Villar, and R. Ward. Relax, no need to round: Integrality of clustering formulations. *http://arxiv.org/abs/1408.4045*, 2014.

[12] M. Balcan, A. Blum, and A. Gupta. Approximate clustering without the approximation. In *SODA*, 2009.

[13] M. Balcan, A. Blum, and S. Vempala. A discriminative framework for clustering via similarity functions. In *STOC*, 2008.

[14] M.-F. Balcan and Y. Liang. Clustering under perturbation resilience. *ICALP*, 2012.

[15] A. S. Bandeira, M. Charikar, A. Singer, and A. Zhu. Multireference alignment using semidefinite programming. *ITCS 2014*, 2014.

[16] A. S. Bandeira, Y. Khoo, and A. Singer. Open problem: Tightness of maximum likelihood semidefinite relaxations. *Conference on Learning Theory (COLT 2014), Open problem session*, 2014.

[17] Y. Bilu and N. Linial. Are stable instances easy? In *Proceedings of the First Symposium on Innovations in Computer Science*, 2010.

[18] S. C. Brubaker and S. Vempala. Isotropic PCA and affine-invariant clustering. In *Proceedings of the 2008 49th Annual IEEE Symposium on Foundations of Computer Science*, 2008.

[19] E. J. Candès, J. Romberg, and T. Tao. Robust uncertainty principles: Exact signal reconstruction from highly incomplete frequency information. *IEEE Trans. Inf. Theor.*, 2006.

[20] E. J. Candès and T. Tao. The power of convex relaxation: Near-optimal matrix completion. *IEEE Trans. Inf. Theor.*, 56(5), May 2010.

[21] K. Chaudhuri, S. Dasgupta, and A. Vattani. Learning mixtures of gaussians using the k-means algorithm. *arXiv preprint arXiv:0912.0086*, 2009.

[22] Y. Chen, S. Bhojanapalli, S. Sanghavi, and R. Ward. Coherent matrix completion. *Proceedings of The 31st International Conference on Machine Learning*, pages 674–682, 2014.

[23] Y. Chen, S. Sanghavi, and H. Xu. Clustering sparse graphs. In *NIPS*, pages 2204–2212, 2012.

[24] Y. Chen and J. Xu. Statistical-computational tradeoffs in planted problems and submatrix localization with a growing number of clusters and submatrices. *arXiv preprint arXiv:1402.1267*, 2014.

[25] S. Dasgupta. Learning mixtures of gaussians. In *Foundations of Computer Science, 1999. 40th Annual Symposium on*, pages 634–644. IEEE, 1999.

[26] C. Daskalakis, A. Dimakis, R. M. Karp, and M. Wainwright. Probabilistic analysis of linear programming decoding. *Information Theory, IEEE Trans. on*, 54(8), Aug 2008.

[27] A. Decelle, F. Krzakala, C. Moore, and L. Zdeborová. Asymptotic analysis of the stochastic block model for modular networks and its algorithmic applications. *Phys. Rev. E*, 84:066106, 2011.

[28] D. Donoho. Compressed sensing. *Information Theory, IEEE Transactions on*, 52(4):1289–1306, April 2006.

[29] E. Elhamifar, G. Sapiro, and R. Vidal. Finding exemplars from pairwise dissimilarities via simultaneous sparse recovery. *Advances in Neural Information Processing Systems*, pages 19–27, 2012.

[30] L. Elkin, T. Pong, and S. Vavasis. Convex relaxation for finding planted influential nodes in a social network. *arXiv preprint arXiv:1307.4047*, 2013.

[31] J. Feldman, T. Malkin, R. Servedio, C. Stein, and M. Wainwright. LP decoding corrects a constant fraction of errors. *Information Theory, IEEE Trans. on*, 53(1), Jan 2007.

[32] J. Feldman, M. Wainwright, and D. Karger. Using linear programming to decode binary linear codes. *Information Theory, IEEE Transactions on*, 51(3):954–972, March 2005.

[33] M. Grant and S. Boyd. CVX: Matlab software for disciplined convex programming, version 2.1. http://cvxr.com/cvx, Mar. 2014.

[34] D. Gross. Recovering low-rank matrices from few coefficients in any basis. *Information Theory, IEEE Transactions on*, 57(3):1548–1566, 2011.

[35] K. Jain, M. Mahdian, and A. Saberi. A new greedy approach for facility location problems. In *Proceedings of the 34th Annual ACM Symposium on Theory of Computing*, 2002.

[36] K. Jain and V. V. Vazirani. Approximation algorithms for metric facility location and k-median problems using the primal-dual schema and lagrangian relaxation. *JACM*, 48(2):274 – 296, 2001.

[37] R. Kannan, S. Vempala, and A. Vetta. On clusterings: good, bad and spectral. *JACM*, 51(3):497–515, 2004.

[38] T. Kanungo, D. M. Mount, N. S. Netanyahu, C. D. Piatko, R. Silverman, and A. Y. Wu. A local search approximation algorithm for k-means clustering. In *Proceedings of the eighteenth annual symposium on Computational geometry*, New York, NY, USA, 2002. ACM.

[39] N. Komodakis and N. Paragios. Beyond loose lp-relaxations: Optimizing mrfs by repairing cycles. In *Computer Vision–ECCV 2008*, pages 806–820. Springer, 2008.

[40] A. Kumar and R. Kannan. Clustering with spectral norm and the k-means algorithm. In *FOCS*, 2010.

[41] S. Li and O. Svensson. Approximating k-median via pseudo-approximation. In *STOC*, 2013.

[42] S. Lloyd. Least squares quantization in pcm. *Information Theory, IEEE Transactions on*, 28(2):129–137, 1982.

[43] K. Makarychev, Y. Makarychev, and A. Vijayaraghavan. Bilu-linial stable instances of max cut and minimum multiway cut. In *SODA*, 2014.

[44] A. Man-Cho So. Probabilistic analysis of the semidefinite relaxation detector in digital communications. In *SODA*, 2010.

[45] E. Mossel, J. Neeman, and A. Sly. Consistency thresholds for binary symmetric block models. *arXiv preprint arXiv:1407.1591*, 2014.

[46] A. Nellore and R. Ward. Recovery guarantees for exemplar-based clustering. *arXiv:1309.3256*, 2013.

[47] R. Ostrovsky, Y. Rabani, L. Schulman, and C. Swamy. The effectiveness of lloyd-type methods for the k-means problem. In *Proceedings of the 47th Annual IEEE Symposium on Foundations of Computer Science*, 2006.

[48] J. Peng and Y. Wei. Approximating k-means-type clustering via semidefinite programming. *SIAM Journal on Optimization*, 18(1):186–205, 2007.

[49] J. Peng and Y. Xia. A new theoretical framework for k-means-type clustering. In *Foundations and advances in data mining*, pages 79–96. Springer, 2005.

[50] B. Recht. A simpler approach to matrix completion. *JMLR*, 12:3413–3430, 2011.

[51] B. Recht, M. Fazel, and P. A. Parrilo. Guaranteed minimum-rank solutions of linear matrix equations via nuclear norm minimization. *SIAM review*, 52(3):471–501, 2010.

[52] A. M. Rush, D. Sontag, M. Collins, and T. Jaakkola. On dual decomposition and linear programming relaxations for natural language processing. In *Proceedings of the 2010 Conference on Empirical Methods in Natural Language Processing (EMNLP)*, 2010.

[53] A. Schrijver. *Theory of Linear and Integer Programming*. John Wiley & Sons, Inc., New York, NY, USA, 1986.

[54] D. Sontag, T. Meltzer, A. Globerson, T. Jaakkola, and Y. Weiss. Tightening LP relaxations for MAP using message passing. In *UAI*, 2008.

[55] D. A. Sontag. *Approximate inference in graphical models using LP relaxations*. PhD thesis, Massachusetts Institute of Technology, 2010.

[56] V. V. Vazirani. *Approximation Algorithms*. Springer-Verlag New York, Inc., New York, NY, USA, 2001.

On Multiplicative Weight Updates for Concave and Submodular Function Maximization

[Extended Abstract]

Chandra Chekuri [*]
Dept. of Computer Science
Univ. of Illinois
Urbana, IL 61801, USA
chekuri@illinois.edu

T.S. Jayram
IBM Almaden Research
Center
San Jose, CA 95120, USA
jayram@us.ibm.com

Jan Vondrák
IBM Almaden Research
Center
San Jose, CA 95120, USA
jvondrak@us.ibm.com

ABSTRACT

We develop a continuous-time framework based on multiplicative weight updates to approximately solve continuous optimization problems. The framework allows for a simple and modular analysis for a variety of problems involving convex constraints and concave or submodular objective functions. The continuous-time framework avoids the cumbersome technical details that are typically necessary in actual algorithms. We also show that the continuous-time algorithms can be converted into implementable algorithms via a straightforward discretization process. Using our framework and additional ideas we obtain significantly faster algorithms compared to previously known algorithms to maximize the multilinear relaxation of a monotone or non-monotone submodular set function subject to linear packing constraints.

Categories and Subject Descriptors

G.1.6 [**Optimization**]: Constrained Optimization

Keywords

submodular function, multiplicative weight updates

1. INTRODUCTION

The "multiplicative weight updates (MWU) method" has a wide variety of applications in computer science and can be considered a meta-algorithm. The excellent survey of Arora, Hazan and Kale [2] takes this point of view and describes several applications that follow from the basic method and its analysis. One of the key applications of the MWU method is to obtain fast near-optimal algorithms for a large class of continuous optimization problems such as fractional packing

and covering and mixed packing/covering problems. Plotkin, Shmoys and Tardos [35], and Grigoriadis and Khachiyan [22] initiated this line of work and subsequently there has been a large amount of literature on this topic; see [38, 19, 20, 17, 39, 8, 18, 27, 29, 1, 3, 26, 40].

Linear functions and constraints have been primarily the setting of interest, but recent applications have shown the usefulness of considering more general objectives as well, such as concave or submodular. Our aim in this paper is to develop a versatile framework that allows the inclusion of concave or submodular objectives under convex constraints. A concrete goal is to obtain faster algorithms for submodular objective functions. We define the relevant notions first. A set function $f : 2^N \to \mathbb{R}$ over a finite ground set N is *submodular* if for all $A, B \subseteq N$ it satisfies $f(A) + f(B) \geq f(A \cup B) + f(A \cap B)$. It is *monotone* if $f(A) \leq f(B)$ for all $A \subseteq B$. In this paper we consider only non-negative submodular functions and use the term non-monotone to refer to a function that may not be monotone. There are many applications for constrained submodular function maximization. The meta-problem of interest here is $\max_{S \in \mathcal{S}} f(S)$ where $\mathcal{S} \subseteq 2^N$ is a collection of feasible sets that model the constraints (typically $\mathcal{S}$ is a down-closed family of sets[1]). Most of the problems here are NP-Hard and the main focus has been on developing approximation algorithms.

The multilinear extension F of f is a continuous function that extends f to the domain $[0, 1]^N$; for a point $\mathbf{x} \in [0, 1]^n$ where N is identified with $\{1, 2, \ldots, n\}$, the function F is defined as $F(\mathbf{x}) = \sum_{S \subseteq N} f(S) \prod_{i \in S} x_i \prod_{i \notin S} (1 - x_i)$. Equivalently, $F(\mathbf{x}) = \mathbb{E}[f(R)]$ where R is a random set obtained by picking each element $i \in N$ independently with probability x_i. The multilinear relaxation for the discrete optimization problem $\max_{S \in \mathcal{S}} f(S)$ is the continuous optimization problem $\max\{F(\mathbf{x}) : \mathbf{x} \in P\}$ where P is a convex relaxation for the constraint set $\mathcal{S}$ (that is, P contains the convex hull of the characteristic vectors of the sets in $\mathcal{S}$). A solution to the multilinear relaxation has to be then suitably rounded. This paradigm has led to a number of new algorithmic results for constrained submodular function maximization [10, 37, 11, 33, 30, 13, 16]. The multilinear extension F is neither convex nor concave. In fact it is NP-Hard to solve the multilinear relaxation to within a $(1 - 1/e - \epsilon)$ factor for any fixed $\epsilon > 0$ even for the simple cardinality constraint polytope $\{\mathbf{x} \in [0, 1]^n : \sum_i x_i \leq k\}$ and when f is an explicitly given monotone function f. This follows from a reduction from

---

[*]Work on this paper supported in part by an IBM Faculty Award and NSF grant CCF-1319376.

ITCS'15, January 11–13, 2015, Rehovot, Israel.
Copyright 2015 ACM 978-1-4503-3333-7/15/01 ...$15.00.
http://dx.doi.org/10.1145/2688073.2688086 .

---

[1]We say $\mathcal{S}$ is down-closed if $A \subset B, B \in \mathcal{S} \Rightarrow A \in \mathcal{S}$

the maximum k-coverage problem [10]. Nevertheless constant factor approximation algorithms are known via continuous versions of greedy [37, 11, 16] and local-search [33, 13]. In particular, there is a $(1 - 1/e)$-approximation for the monotone case [37, 11] and a $1/e$-approximation for the non-negative case [16] assuming that P is a solvable polytope[2]. Although the methodology is powerful and has shown promise in some empirical work [21], one of the limitations is the slow running time of the algorithms. One of our motivations for considering MWU-based algorithms for the multilinear relaxation is the work of Azar and Gamzu [4]. They developed a MWU-based greedy algorithm for monotone submodular function maximization subject to linear packing constraints; we discuss more details of their work later in the paper.

An MWU algorithm can be viewed as a black-box Turing reduction of an optimization problem to a simpler problem which can be solved faster. For instance the problem we desire to solve could be the maximum s-t flow problem and the simpler problem could be the s-t shortest path problem. Typically the MWU approach reduces optimization with many constraints to optimization with one constraint. Since the reduction uses the algorithm for the simpler problem in a black-box fashion it is common to refer to it as an "oracle". Clearly, several considerations influence this approach, the main ones being (i) the objective function (ii) the type of constraints, and (iii) the "oracle" that is available to the algorithm. A significant effort has been devoted to obtain running times that are "width independent" (independent of the numerical values of coefficients present in the constraints), either by width reduction techniques as suggested in [35], or via the idea of variable-sized (non-uniform) increments [19, 20].

1.1 Our Results

We introduce a continuous-time framework for optimization of concave and submodular functions based on MWU which is motivated by the desire to obtain a clean high-level analysis. We analyze algorithms in the framework using simple differential equations. The advantage is that we can initially sidestep the discretization issues involved in actual implementations. After the high-level analysis we are able to derive implementable algorithms by discretizing the continuous process. A key advantage is that the discretization process is systematic; we choose the (variable) step sizes to ensure that the the continuous process can be approximated by the discrete process. In particular, it allows us to cleanly integrate the issues involved in handling the constraints and the objective function.

In this version of the paper we focus on maximization problems subject to packing constraints. Our framework yields width-independent algorithms for maximizing linear, concave and submodular functions. The framework and several results also apply to minimizing convex objectives, covering constraints, and mixed packing and covering constraints; these will be discussed in detail in a future version of the paper. Several previous results including the work of Garg and Könemann on variable-sized increments [19, 20] can be explained cleanly in our framework.

After we present the generic framework, we focus on deriving fast algorithms for the problem of maximizing the

multilinear extension F of a submodular function f defined over a ground set of n elements subject to m explicitly given linear packing constraints. We will assume that f is available via a value oracle and our main metric for the efficiency of an algorithm will be the number of calls it makes to f or to an oracle that returns the partial derivatives of F. The special properties of F and the sampling issues in evaluating $F(\mathbf{x})$ make it non-trivial to adapt the MWU method to solve the multilinear relaxation.

We obtain the following results. Our first result applies to maximization of the multilinear extension of a monotone submodular function.

THEOREM 1. *Let F be the multilinear extension of a monotone submodular function $f : 2^N \to \mathbb{R}_+$. Given $\epsilon \in (0, \frac{1}{2})$, $A \in \mathbb{R}_+^{m \times n}$, there is an algorithm that computes a solution $\mathbf{y}$ to the problem $\max\{F(\mathbf{x}) : 0 \le \mathbf{x} \le \mathbf{1}, A\mathbf{x} \le \mathbf{1}\}$ such that $F(\mathbf{y}) \ge (1 - 1/e - \epsilon)\mathsf{OPT}$ and:*

- *the algorithm makes $O(\frac{n}{\epsilon^2} polylog(m, n))$ value oracle calls to partial derivatives of F,*

- *and in addition makes $O(\frac{(m+n)^2}{\epsilon^2} polylog(m, n))$ arithmetic steps.*

If F is accessible through a value oracle to f, the algorithm can be implemented so that the number of calls to the value oracle for f is $\tilde{O}(n^2/\epsilon^4)$.

Our second result applies to non-negative (possibly non-monotone) submodular functions. More precisely it holds for *smooth submodular* functions [37], i.e., twice-differentiable functions with the property that $\frac{\partial^2 F}{\partial x_i \partial x_j} \le 0$ for all $i, j \in [n]$ and $\mathbf{x} \in [0, 1]^n$. Smooth submodular functions arise naturally as multilinear extensions of submodular functions, but they can also arise in other ways (see [21] for a maximization problem involving a smooth submodular function which is not multilinear).

THEOREM 2. *Let F be a non-negative smooth submodular function. Given $\epsilon \in (0, \frac{1}{2})$, $A \in \mathbb{R}_+^{m \times n}$, there is an algorithm that computes a solution $\mathbf{y}$ to the problem $\max\{F(\mathbf{x}) : 0 \le \mathbf{x} \le \mathbf{1}, A\mathbf{x} \le \mathbf{1}\}$, such that $F(\mathbf{y}) \ge (1/e - \epsilon)\mathsf{OPT}$ and:*

- *$O(mn^2/\epsilon^2)$ value oracle calls to the partial derivatives of F,*

- *and in addition makes $O(m^2 n^2/\epsilon^2)$ arithmetic steps.*

If F is the multilinear extension of a non-negative submodular function f the algorithm can be implemented such that the number of calls to the value oracle to f is $\tilde{O}(mn^3/\epsilon^4)$.

We remark that the approximation ratios match the best known bounds while the running times are significantly improved. We briefly compare the run-times we obtain with those from prior work. The previous polynomial-time approximation algorithms for solving the multilinear relaxation based on continuous greedy [37, 11, 16] and local search [13] are polynomial-time but very slow. Moreover, the running times are not explicitly stated, partly due to the fact that the algorithms assume an oracle to optimize a linear function over the underlying polytope P. Faster variants of continuous greedy (with near-quadratic running times) have been developed in recent work by Badanidiyuru and Vondrák [6]

---

[2]We say that $P \subseteq [0, 1]^n$ is solvable if there is an efficient algorithm to optimize any linear function over P.

but these are for specific polytopes such as the matroid polytope or the knapsack polytope (1 linear constraint). When the polytope P is induced by m linear packing constraints we could use a MWU based algorithm for linear optimization that provides a $(1-\epsilon)$-approximation in $\tilde{O}(n+m)$ time [29]; even with this optimization the overall running time of the algorithms for the multilinear relaxation can be conservatively estimated to be $\Omega(n^5)$ both in terms of value oracle calls to f and arithmetic operations. The algorithms we describe in this paper yield significant improvements and point towards practical feasibility of multilinear relaxation based algorithms.

Azar and Gamzu [4] gave an MWU-based greedy algorithm for the discrete setting $\max\{f(S) : A\mathbf{x} \le \mathbf{1}, \mathbf{x} \in \{0,1\}^n\}$. The number of oracle class to f in their algorithm can be $\Omega(n^2)$ and the number of arithmetic operations can be $\Omega(mn)$. Among other results they obtain a $(1-1/e-\epsilon)$-approximation for the monotone case when the width[3] of the system is $\Omega(\log m/\epsilon^2)$; the width is defined as $\min_{i,j}\lceil\frac{1}{A_{ij}}\rceil$. Our algorithm for the monotone case is similar in spirit to theirs although we optimize the multilinear relaxation while they directly optimize f. We derive our algorithm organically from a general framework; to obtain good running-times while dealing with the multilinear extension F we need to use several ideas, some borrowed from recent work [6]. Further, our framework extends naturally to non-monotone submodular functions, unlike the discrete greedy approach.

Applications: Several approximation algorithms for constrained submodular function maximization are based on solving the multilinear relaxation followed by rounding; for some problems this is the only known approach or gives better bounds than any other method. A general framework for rounding is via contention resolution schemes [13]. A number of interesting constraints can be modeled by linear packing systems of the form $A\mathbf{x} \le 1$ including several types of useful matroids such as uniform, partition and laminar matroids and their intersections.[4] For many of these problems the bottleneck, in terms of the run-time of the algorithm, is solving the multilinear relaxation. The contention resolution schemes are typically based on randomized rounding followed by simple pruning rules. Thus, we obtain algorithms for a large number of problems that are faster by factors of n^3 or more. Since these specific applications are not the focus of this paper we do not go into details, however, we briefly discuss two concrete examples to illustrate the advantage of using the multilinear relaxation.

First, consider the problem $\max\{f(S) : A\mathbf{x} \le 1, \mathbf{x} \in \{0,1\}^n\}$ where the matrix A is k-column sparse (the maximum number of non-zero entries in each column is at most k). Such column-sparse problems capture several important problems; for instance matchings in general graphs are captured by 2-sparse matrices. The multilinear relaxation based approach yields an $\Omega(\frac{1}{k^{1/W}})$ approximation for both monotone and non-monotone submodular functions [7, 13] where W is the width of system. The combinatorial approach of Azar and Gamzu [4], even though it is based on MWU, gives

a weaker bound of $\Omega(\frac{1}{Wk^{1/W}})$ for only the monotone case. In contrast, since we solve the multilinear relaxation, we are able to match the previous bounds with a run-time that is essentially the same as the combinatorial greedy algorithm of [4].

Second, consider the problem of routing pairs in a capacitated path or tree (called UFP on the line/tree) to maximize a submodular function of the routed pairs [13]. The constraints can be modeled via simple linear packing constraints. There is a constant factor approximation for these problems via the multilinear relaxation. Even when the objective function is a linear function, the only way to obtain a constant factor approximation is via a linear programming relaxation.

Multiple Submodular and Concave Objectives: We can show that our continuous-time framework extends to handle multiple objective functions. A standard approach is to convert the objectives into constraints with lower bounds on each constraint. This is relatively easy to do for concave objectives, however, handling multiple submodular objectives is less straighforward. Multiple monotone submodular objectives were considered in [12] with an application to an a fair-allocation problem; an algorithm based on adapting the continuous greedy was described in the same paper. The continuous-time MWU algorithm and the details of discretization and the run-time analysis are deferred to a later version of the paper.

Other Related Work: Submodular functions are playing an increasingly important role in various applications, in particular machine learning. There are several efforts is to obtain faster algorithms for both maximization and minimization. Here we focus on maximization. There is a spectrum of results ranging from the more theoretical settings [14, 4, 31, 6, 9] where the goal is obtain provable guarantees on the running time, as well as in applied settings with motivations coming from machine learning applications [21, 24, 5].

Continuous-time variants of the multiplicative weight update method have been considered in the past, e.g. in the context of packing/covering LPs [34], and regret minimization in online learning [36, 32]. Khandekar [27] and the survey of Arora *et al.* [2] apply the discrete-time experts framework for online optimization and the corresponding regret bounds in designing and analyzing fast algorithms. Our continuous-time analysis and discretization is similar in spirit to some of the ideas in [32]. Our framework and results are more explicit and in particular we address optimization problems involving submodular functions which are not considered in [32].

Fast algorithms for packing, covering and mixed packing and covering problems have also been designed via the logarithmic potential function [23, 15, 25]. It will be interesting to see whether a continuous-time framework can be developed for the logarithmic potential function.

Due to space limitations in this version of the paper, we omit some proofs and the implementation details of the algorithms that yield Theorems 1 and 2.

2. MWU FOR OPTIMIZATION: A CONTINUOUS POINT OF VIEW

In this section we present a continuous-time framework of multiplicative weight updates for optimization. This point

---

[3]For a system of packing constraints $A\mathbf{x} \le \mathbf{b}$, *width* is the minimum ratio b_i/A_{ij} over all i,j.

[4]The matroid polytope has an exponential number of constraints in general, while these special cases have simple descriptions with a linear (in n) number of explicit constraints.

of view eliminates some of the issues which are important in the eventual implementation - namely discretization and running time. On the positive side, the continuous presentation is cleaner and highlights the main conceptual ideas in multiplicative weight updates, without cumbersome technical details. Our main purpose here is to use the continuous framework to show how different variants of multiplicative weight updates can be tied together and unified in a simple manner.

2.1 MWU template for optimization

We consider the following generic optimization problem.

$$\max f(\mathbf{x}) :$$
$$g_i(\mathbf{x}) \leq 1; \quad 1 \leq i \leq m;$$
$$\mathbf{x} \in P$$

where $g_i : \mathbb{R}^n \to \mathbb{R}$, $1 \leq i \leq m$ are convex functions and $f : \mathbb{R}^n \to \mathbb{R}$ is a generic continuous function. P is a convex (polyhedral) constraint (like a box constraint) which is assumed to be "simple" — we know how to optimize over it quickly. We will assume that the feasible region is bounded and f is bounded in the feasible region and that an optimum solution exists. The MWU method effectively collapses the "complicated" constraints $g_i(x) \leq 1$ into a single convex constraint that can be dealt with more efficiently. Let $\mathbf{x}^* = \arg\max\{f(\mathbf{y}) : \mathbf{y} \in P, g_i(\mathbf{y}) \leq 1 \ \forall i\}$ denote an optimal solution and let $\mathsf{OPT} = f(\mathbf{x}^*)$.

The continuous framework that we present below has the following template. It uses a parameter $\eta > 0$ and involves two time-varying vectors: a weight vector $\mathbf{w}(t) \in \mathbb{R}_+^m$ and a domain point $\mathbf{v}(t) \in \mathbb{R}^n$, for $t \in [0, 1]$. These two vectors are jointly related to each other. The vector $\mathbf{v}(t)$ is related to $\mathbf{w}(t)$ via a carefully designed optimization problem depending on f. The important feature of this optimization problem is that $\mathbf{v}(t)$ is a solution satisfying $\mathbf{v}(t) \in P$ and a single convex constraint $\sum_{i=1}^m w_i(t) g_i(\mathbf{v}(t)) \leq \sum_{i=1}^m w_i(t)$. The weight vector $\mathbf{w}(t)$ is related to $\mathbf{v}(t)$ via a differential equation. We describe this system of equations below as an algorithm and can be interpreted as a limit of a process where the functions are evaluated at discrete points of t going from 0 to 1.

Algorithm 1 MWU template

1: **procedure** MWU$(f, g_1, \ldots, g_m, P, \eta)$:
2:    $\mathbf{w}(0) = 1$ $\triangleright \mathbf{w}(t) \in \mathbb{R}^m$ for all t
3:    **for** $t \in [0, 1]$ **do**
4:       Solve an appropriate optimization problem and obtain $\mathbf{v}(t)$
5:       $\triangleright \mathbf{v}(t) \in P$ and $\sum_{i=1}^m w_i(t) g_i(\mathbf{v}(t)) \leq \sum_{i=1}^m w_i(t)$
6:       **for** $i \in [m]$ **do**
7:          $\frac{dw_i}{dt} = \eta w_i(t) g_i(\mathbf{v}(t))$
8:       **end for**
9:    **end for**
10:   **return** $\mathbf{x}_{\mathrm{out}} = \int_0^1 \mathbf{v}(t) \, dt$
11: **end procedure**

The key result of the continuous-time framework is that implies the near-feasibility of the output.

THEOREM 3. *The point $\mathbf{x}_{\mathrm{out}}$ returned by Algorithm 1 satisfies $\mathbf{x}_{\mathrm{out}} \in P$ and $g_i(\mathbf{x}_{\mathrm{out}}) \leq 1 + \frac{\ln m}{\eta}$ for $1 \leq i \leq m$. In particular if $\eta \geq \frac{\ln m}{\epsilon}$, $g_i(\mathbf{x}_{\mathrm{out}}) \leq 1 + \epsilon$ for all i.*

Further, suppose there is a point $\mathbf{x}_0 \in P$ such that $g_i(\mathbf{x}_0) = 0 \ \forall i$. Then the modified solution $\mathbf{x}'_{\mathrm{out}} = \theta \mathbf{x}_{\mathrm{out}} + (1 - \theta)\mathbf{x}_0$, where $\theta = 1/(1 + \frac{\ln m}{\eta})$, is feasible.

Given any point $\mathbf{x}_0$ in the interior of the feasible set, we can assume in fact by a suitable transformation to the g_i's, e.g., $\tilde{g}_i(\mathbf{x}) = \frac{g_i(\mathbf{x}) - g_i(\mathbf{x}_0)}{1 - g_i(\mathbf{x}_0)}$, that $g_i(\mathbf{x}_0) = 0$ while applying Algorithm 1.

PROOF. First, observe that $\mathbf{x}_{\mathrm{out}} = \int_0^1 \mathbf{v}(t) dt$ is a convex combination of points in P, and therefore also in P. Secondly, we analyze the constraints $g_i(\mathbf{x}) \leq 1$. By the convexity of g_i, we have:

$$g_i(\mathbf{x}_{\mathrm{out}}) = g_i \left(\int_0^1 \mathbf{v}(t) \, dt \right) \leq \int_0^1 g_i(\mathbf{v}(t)) \, dt.$$

By the update rule for $w_i(t)$, we get

$$\int_0^1 g_i(\mathbf{v}(t)) \, dt = \frac{1}{\eta} \int_0^1 \frac{1}{w_i(t)} \frac{dw_i}{dt} \, dt = \frac{1}{\eta} \ln w_i(1) \quad (1)$$

since $w_i(0) = 1$. We also have

$$\frac{d}{dt} \sum_{i=1}^m w_i(t) = \sum_{i=1}^m \frac{dw_i}{dt} = \eta \sum_{i=1}^m w_i(t) g_i(\mathbf{v}(t)) \leq \eta \sum_{i=1}^m w_i(t),$$

by the constraints on $\mathbf{v}(t)$. Solving this differential inequality, we obtain

$$\sum_{i=1}^m w_i(t) \leq e^{\eta t} \sum_{i=1}^m w_i(0) = e^{\eta t} m.$$

Thus, for each fixed i, $w_i(1) \leq e^\eta m$. By eq. (1), $g_i(\mathbf{x}_{\mathrm{out}}) \leq \frac{1}{\eta} \ln w_i(1) \leq 1 + \frac{\ln m}{\eta}$.

Finally, consider $\mathbf{x}'_{\mathrm{out}} = \theta \mathbf{x}_{\mathrm{out}} + (1 - \theta)\mathbf{x}_0$ where $\theta = 1/(1 + \frac{\ln m}{\eta})$ and $\mathbf{x}_0 \in P$, $g_i(\mathbf{x}_0) = 0$. By convexity, $\mathbf{x}'_{\mathrm{out}} \in P$, and we have $g_i(\mathbf{x}'_{\mathrm{out}}) \leq \theta g_i(\mathbf{x}_{\mathrm{out}}) + (1 - \theta)g_i(\mathbf{x}_0) \leq 1$. □

REMARK 1. *The analysis did not assume non-negativity of the g_i's. In particular, a covering constraint of the form $h(\mathbf{x}) \geq 1$ where h is a concave function can be modeled as $g(\mathbf{x}) \leq 1$ where $g(\mathbf{x}) = -h(\mathbf{x}) + 2 \leq 1$ is a convex function. The continuous-time process, unlike the discrete time experts framework, does not have an error term that depends on range of the functions g_i. Finally, the error terms can be made $(1 + \epsilon)$ by choosing $\eta = \frac{\ln m}{\epsilon}$ which does not depend on n but only on the number of constraints m.*

REMARK 2. *Let $\phi(t) = \sum_{i=1}^m w_i(t)$ be the potential function at time t; note that $\frac{1}{\eta} \ln \frac{\phi(t)}{m} \leq t$ by the proof above. Several algorithms/analyses work with this quantity as a proxy for "time". We believe that fixing the time evolution to be the fixed interval of length 1 allows for a cleaner separation of the analysis of optimality and feasibility, and makes it easier to integrate the analysis of the continuous greedy algorithm (for submodular maximization) with multiplicative weight updates.*

2.2 Concave and linear objective functions

We apply the framework to maximize a concave function f. Suppose $\mathbf{v}(t)$ is an optimal solution to a concave maximization problem with a single constraint:

$$\mathbf{v}(t) = \arg\max_{\mathbf{y} \in P} \left\{ f(\mathbf{y}) : \sum_{i=1}^m w_i(t) g_i(\mathbf{y}) \leq \sum_{i=1}^m w_i(t) \right\} \quad (2)$$

We analyze the objective value $\mathbf{x}_{\text{out}}$ returned by the algorithm as follows. By concavity of f:

$$f(\mathbf{x}_{\text{out}}) = f\left(\int_0^1 \mathbf{v}(t)dt\right) \geq \int_0^1 f(\mathbf{v}(t))dt$$

At each time t, $\mathbf{x}^*$ is a candidate solution for the optimization problem given by eq. (2). Therefore, $f(\mathbf{v}(t)) \geq f(\mathbf{x}^*)$ for all t and we conclude that $f(\mathbf{x}_{\text{out}}) \geq \mathsf{OPT}$.

Now suppose further that f is non-negative and consider the modified solution $\mathbf{x}'_{\text{out}} = \theta \mathbf{x}_{\text{out}} + (1-\theta)\mathbf{x}_0$ given by Theorem 3, with $\theta = \frac{1}{1+\epsilon}$, which we showed to be completely feasible. By concavity, $f(\mathbf{x}'_{\text{out}}) \geq \theta f(\mathbf{x}_{\text{out}}) + (1-\theta)f(\mathbf{x}_0) \geq \theta f(\mathbf{x}_{\text{out}}) \geq \mathsf{OPT}/(1+\epsilon)$. We summarize these observations as follows:

THEOREM 4. *Let f be a concave function. The point $\mathbf{x}_{\text{out}}$ returned by Algorithm 1 where $\mathbf{v}(t)$ obeys eq. (2) satisfies $f(\mathbf{x}_{\text{out}}) \geq \mathsf{OPT}$, $\mathbf{x}_{\text{out}} \in P$ and $g_i(\mathbf{x}_{\text{out}}) \leq 1 + \epsilon$ for all i. Moreover, if f is non-negative, then the modified solution $\mathbf{x}'_{\text{out}}$ is completely feasible with $f(\mathbf{x}'_{\text{out}}) \geq \mathsf{OPT}/(1+\epsilon)$.*

Linear objective with linear packing constraints: An important special case is when $f(\mathbf{x}) = \mathbf{c}^T\mathbf{x}$ is a linear function and all the constraints are linear, that is, the feasible region is defined as $A\mathbf{x} \leq \mathbf{1}$. The oracle required in this case is to solve $\max \mathbf{c}^T\mathbf{x}$ subject to a single constraint of the form $\mathbf{a}^T\mathbf{x} \leq 1$. An optimum solution to this problem can be easily computed by finding the i that maximizes the ratio c_i/a_i. Moreover, we observe that this optimum solution has a single non-zero coordinate. We note that number of variables can be much larger than m as long as the oracle can compute the best coordinate in each iteration efficiently. For instance in the maximum throughput multicommodity flow problem the variables correspond to paths between source-sink pairs and the constraints correspond to edges; the Garg-Könemann algorithm corresponds to picking a shortest path among the source-sink pairs in each iteration.

2.3 Monotone submodular functions

Next, we show how the framework can be adapted to the case of a monotone submodular objective functions. Let the objective function $F: \mathbb{R}^n \to \mathbb{R}_+$ be a monotone smooth submodular function; in particular, we require that $\frac{\partial F}{\partial x_i} \geq 0$ (via monotonicity) and $\frac{\partial^2 F}{\partial x_i \partial x_j} \leq 0$ for all $i, j \in [n]$ (via submodularity) over $[0,1]^n$. We assume that $P \subseteq [0,1]^n$.

For ease of notation, let $\mathcal{G}_t = \{\mathbf{y} : \sum_{i=1}^m w_i(t)g_i(\mathbf{y}) \leq \sum_{i=1}^m w_i(t)\}$ at time t denote the set defined by combining all the constraints g_i using the weight vector $\mathbf{w}(t)$.

Let $\mathbf{x}(t) \in \mathbb{R}^n$ for all $t \in [0,1]$ such that $\mathbf{x}(0) = 0$ and for $t \in [0,1]$:

$$\begin{aligned} \mathbf{v}(t) &= \arg\max_{\mathbf{y} \in P}\left\{\mathbf{y} \cdot \nabla F|_{\mathbf{x}(t)} : \mathbf{y} \in \mathcal{G}_t\right\} \\ \frac{d\mathbf{x}}{dt} &= \mathbf{v}(t) \end{aligned} \quad (3)$$

Observe that is a linear optimization problem, with one additional convex constraint. In case the g_i's are linear constraints, this is just a linear programming problem.

We state an abstract inequality that relies only on the continuous submodularity of F.

LEMMA 5. *Let $\mathbf{x}(t) \in [0,1]^n$, $\mathbf{v}(t)$ and $\mathbf{z}(t)$ be such that (a) $\frac{d\mathbf{x}}{dt} = \mathbf{v}(t)$, (b) $\mathbf{z}(t) \geq 0$, and (c) $\mathbf{z}(t) \cdot \nabla F|_{\mathbf{x}(t)} \leq \mathbf{v}(t) \cdot \nabla F|_{\mathbf{x}(t)}$. Then:*

$$\frac{d}{dt}F(\mathbf{x}(t)) \geq F(\mathbf{x}(t) + \mathbf{z}(t)) - F(\mathbf{x}(t)).$$

PROOF. By submodularity, F is concave along the non-negative direction $\mathbf{z}(t)$, therefore:

$$F(\mathbf{x}(t) + \mathbf{z}(t)) - F(\mathbf{x}(t)) \leq \mathbf{z} \cdot \nabla F|_{\mathbf{x}(t)}$$
$$\leq \mathbf{v}(t) \cdot \nabla F|_{\mathbf{x}(t)} = \frac{d\mathbf{x}}{dt} \cdot \nabla F|_{\mathbf{x}(t)} = \frac{d}{dt}F(\mathbf{x}(t)).$$

This concludes the proof. $\square$

THEOREM 6. *Let F be monotone smooth submodular function with $F(0) = 0$. The point $\mathbf{x}_{\text{out}}$ returned by Algorithm 1 with $\eta = \frac{\ln m}{\epsilon}$ and F as the objective function where the subproblem is solved using eq. (3) satisfies $F(\mathbf{x}_{\text{out}}) \geq (1 - \frac{1}{e})\mathsf{OPT}$, $\mathbf{x}_{\text{out}} \in P$ and $g_i(\mathbf{x}_{\text{out}}) \leq 1 + \epsilon$ for all i. Further, suppose F is non-negative, $0 \in P$ and $g_i(0) = 0$. Then the modified solution $\mathbf{x}'_{\text{out}}$ of Theorem 3 with $x_0 = 0$ obeys all the constraints and satisfies $F(\mathbf{x}'_{\text{out}}) \geq (1 - \frac{1}{e} - \epsilon)\mathsf{OPT}$.*

PROOF. The (near) feasibility of $\mathbf{x}_{\text{out}}$ follows from Theorem 3.

Because $\mathbf{x}(0) = 0$, we have $\mathbf{x}(t) = \int_0^t \mathbf{v}(\tau)\,d\tau$. Since $\mathbf{v}(t) \in [0,1]^n$, we have $\mathbf{x}(t) \in [0,t]^n$ for all $t \in [0,1]$. We analyze the optimality of the returned value $\mathbf{x}_{\text{out}} = \mathbf{x}(1)$.

Define the non-negative vector $\mathbf{z}(t) = (\mathbf{x}(t) \vee \mathbf{x}^*) - \mathbf{x}(t)$, where $\vee$ denotes coordinate-wise maximum. Both $\mathbf{x}^* \geq 0$ and $\mathbf{x}(t) \geq 0$, so $\mathbf{z}(t) \leq \mathbf{x}^*$. Because $\mathbf{x}(t) \in [0,1]^n$, the gradient at $\mathbf{x}(t)$ is non-negative (since F is monotone), hence $\mathbf{z}(t) \cdot \nabla F|_{\mathbf{x}(t)} \leq \mathbf{x}^* \cdot \nabla F|_{\mathbf{x}(t)} \leq \mathbf{v}(t) \cdot \nabla F|_{\mathbf{x}(t)}$, since $\mathbf{x}^*$ a candidate solution for the optimization problem given by eq. (3). Applying Lemma 5:

$$\begin{aligned} \frac{d}{dt}F(\mathbf{x}(t)) &\geq F(\mathbf{x}(t) + \mathbf{z}(t)) - F(\mathbf{x}(t)) \\ &= F(\mathbf{x}(t) \vee \mathbf{x}^*) - F(\mathbf{x}(t)) \geq \mathsf{OPT} - F(\mathbf{x}(t)), \end{aligned}$$

by monotonicity. This has the solution $F(\mathbf{x}(t)) \geq (1 - e^{-t})\mathsf{OPT}$, proving the theorem with $t = 1$.

Suppose F is non-negative. By Theorem 3, the modified solution $\mathbf{x}'_{\text{out}}$ is completely feasible and by submodularity, $F(\mathbf{x}'_{\text{out}}) \geq \frac{1}{1+\epsilon}F(\mathbf{x}_{\text{out}}) \geq \frac{1}{1+\epsilon}(1 - \frac{1}{e})\mathsf{OPT} \geq (1 - \frac{1}{e} - \epsilon)\mathsf{OPT}$. $\square$

2.4 Non-negative submodular functions

For non-negative (non-monotone) submodular functions, we need only a minor adjustment which is based on the $1/e$-approximation algorithm of Feldman, Naor and Schwartz [16]. Here too we will only require that F is a smooth submodular function. The added ingredient here is that we increase the coordinates less aggressively than in the monotone case, because increasing coordinates too much can possibly hurt the solution. This is expressed by the following simple lemma (paraphrasing [16])[5].

LEMMA 7. *If $\theta \in (0,1)$, $\mathbf{x} \in [0,\theta]^N$ and $\mathbf{x}^* \in [0,1]^N$, then $F(\mathbf{x} \vee \mathbf{x}^*) \geq (1-\theta)F(\mathbf{x}^*)$.*

---

[5]Note that since F is not necessarily monotone, $F(\mathbf{x} \vee \mathbf{x}^*)$ could be less than $F(\mathbf{x}^*)$. In [16] the lemma is shown when $\mathbf{x}^*$ is an optimum integer solution, while we show it with respect to a fractional solution $\mathbf{x}^*$.

PROOF. Let $\mathbf{y} = (\mathbf{x} \vee \mathbf{x}^*) - \mathbf{x}^*$ and consider the ray $\mathbf{r}(\lambda) = \mathbf{x}^* + \lambda \mathbf{y}$, $\lambda \geq 0$. This ray lies in the non-negative orthant because $\mathbf{y} \geq 0$. Consider the point $\mathbf{z} = \mathbf{r}(\lambda')$ where $\lambda' = \frac{1}{\theta}$; note that $\lambda' \geq 1$. Fix a coordinate i. If $x_i \leq x_i^*$ then $y_i = 0$ and $z_i = x_i^* \leq 1$. Otherwise, $z_i = x_i^* + \lambda' y_i = x_i^* + \frac{1}{\theta}(x_i - x_i^*) \leq \frac{1}{\theta} x_i \leq 1$, by the assumption that $x_i \leq \theta$. Thus, $\mathbf{z} \in [0,1]^n$, and by nonnegativity, $F(\mathbf{z}) > 0$. We have $\mathbf{x} \vee \mathbf{x}^* = \mathbf{r}(1) = (1-\theta)\mathbf{r}(0) + \theta \mathbf{r}(\frac{1}{\theta}) = (1-\theta)\mathbf{x}^* + \theta \mathbf{z}$, and so by concavity along the ray $\mathbf{r}(\lambda)$ we obtain:

$$F(\mathbf{x} \vee \mathbf{x}^*) \geq (1-\theta)F(\mathbf{x}^*) + \theta F(\mathbf{z}) \geq (1-\theta)F(\mathbf{x}^*).$$

This concludes the proof. □

In other words, we can lower-bound the value of $\mathbf{x} \vee \mathbf{x}^*$ if the coordinates of $\mathbf{x}$ are not too large. To limit the speed at which coordinates increase, we move along a direction $\mathbf{v}(t)$ that is additionally constrained by $\mathbf{v}(t) \leq \mathbf{1} - \mathbf{x}(t)$; this still allows us to find a direction of sufficient marginal gain.

We assume that $g_i : \mathbb{R}^n \to \mathbb{R}$ are *non-decreasing* convex functions and $P \subseteq [0,1]^n$ is a down-closed convex polyhedral constraint; i.e., the full constraint set is down-closed. Let $\mathbf{x}(0) = 0$ and for $t \in [0,1]$:

$$\boxed{\begin{aligned} \mathbf{v}(t) &= \arg\max_{\mathbf{y} \in P}\left\{ \mathbf{y} \cdot \nabla F|_{\mathbf{x}(t)} : \mathbf{y} \leq \mathbf{1} - \mathbf{x}(t), \mathbf{y} \in \mathcal{G}_t \right\} \\ \frac{d\mathbf{x}}{dt} &= \mathbf{v}(t) \end{aligned}} \quad (4)$$

where $\mathcal{G}_t = \{\mathbf{y} : \sum_{i=1}^m w_i(t) g_i(\mathbf{y}) \leq \sum_{i=1}^m w_i(t)\}$ is defined as before. The following lemma bounds each coordinate as a function of time.

LEMMA 8. *At time t, we have $x_i(t) \leq 1 - e^{-t}$.*

PROOF. From the differential equaltion $\frac{dx_i}{dt} = v_i(t) \leq 1 - x_i$, we obtain $\frac{d}{dt}(e^t x_i(t)) = e^t x_i(t) + e^t \frac{dx_i}{dt} \leq e^t$. Using the initial condition $x_i(0) = 0$, we get $e^t x_i(t) \leq e^t - 1$ and hence $x_i(t) \leq 1 - e^{-t}$. □

We note that without the constraint $\mathbf{v}(t) \leq \mathbf{1} - \mathbf{x}(t)$, we would obtain $x_i(t) \leq t$ which also leads to a constant factor, but a smaller one than $1/e$. The analysis of the objective value is just a bit more involved than in the monotone case.

THEOREM 9. *Let F be a non-negative smooth submodular function with $F(0) = 0$. The point $\mathbf{x}_{\text{out}}$ returned by Algorithm 1 with $\eta = \frac{\ln m}{\epsilon}$, F as the objective function where the subproblem is solved using eq. (4) satisfies $F(\mathbf{x}_{\text{out}}) \geq \frac{1}{e}\text{OPT}$, $\mathbf{x}_{\text{out}} \in P$ and $g_i(\mathbf{x}_{\text{out}}) \leq 1 + \epsilon$ for all i. Further, suppose F is non-negative, $0 \in P$ and $g_i(0) = 0$. Then the modified solution $\mathbf{x}'_{\text{out}}$ of Theorem 3 with $x_0 = 0$ obeys all the constraints and satisfies $F(\mathbf{x}'_{\text{out}}) \geq \frac{1}{e}(1-\epsilon)\text{OPT}$.*

PROOF. The direction vector $\mathbf{z}(t) = \mathbf{x}(t) \vee \mathbf{x}^* - \mathbf{x}(t)$ is feasible for the optimization problem given by eq. (4): $\mathbf{z}(t) \leq \mathbf{1} - \mathbf{x}(t)$, $\mathbf{z}(t) \leq \mathbf{x}^* \in P$ and also $g_i(\mathbf{z}(t)) \leq g_i(\mathbf{x}^*) \leq 1$ by the monotonicity of g_i. Therefore, $\mathbf{z}(t) \cdot \nabla F(\mathbf{x}(t)) \leq \mathbf{v}(t) \cdot \nabla F|_{\mathbf{x}(t)}$. Applying Lemma 5, we obtain: $\frac{d}{dt}F(\mathbf{x}(t)) \geq F(\mathbf{x}(t) + \mathbf{z}(t)) - F(\mathbf{x}(t)) = F(\mathbf{x}(t) \vee \mathbf{x}^*) - F(\mathbf{x}(t)) \geq e^{-t}\text{OPT} - F(\mathbf{x}(t))$, by Lemma 7 and Lemma 8. Rewriting, we have $\frac{d}{dt}(e^t F(\mathbf{x}(t))) = e^t(F(\mathbf{x}(t)) + \frac{dF}{dt}) \geq \text{OPT}$. We obtain $e^t F(\mathbf{x}(t)) \geq t \cdot \text{OPT}$. At time $t = 1$, we obtain $F(\mathbf{x}(1)) \geq \frac{1}{e}\text{OPT}$.

The (near) feasibility of $\mathbf{x}_{\text{out}}$ follows from Theorem 3. The modified solution $\mathbf{x}'_{\text{out}}$ is feasible via Theorem 3. By submodularity, $F(\mathbf{x}'_{\text{out}}) \geq \frac{1}{1+\epsilon}F(\mathbf{x}_{\text{out}}) \geq \frac{1}{e}(1-\epsilon)\text{OPT}$. □

3. WIDTH-INDEPENDENT DISCRETIZATION

We describe a modified version of the basic MWU template where we solve the subproblem only at certain discrete time steps. Namely, suppose we solve the subproblem at a certain time $t_\diamond$. Now consider the differential equation $\frac{dw_i}{dt} = \eta w_i(t) g_i(\mathbf{v}(t_\diamond))$, $t \geq t_\diamond$, for each $i \in [m]$ using the initial value $w(t_\diamond)$. This is just an approximation to the original differential equation since we have avoided computing $\mathbf{v}(t)$ for $t > t_\diamond$. On the other hand, we can solve for this analytically to get $w_i(t) = w_i(t_\diamond)\exp((t - t_\diamond)\eta g_i(\mathbf{v}(t_\diamond)))$. We show that there is a good interval $[t_\diamond, t_\diamond + \delta]$, for some step size δ, such that the degradation in the quality of the solution is not severe compared to the continuous-time process. The important point is that the largest step size δ that can be taken at $t_\diamond$ is a function of $\mathbf{v}(t_\diamond)$ and the g_i's and is variable. Moreover, it will result in a width-independent algorithm. The width-independent analysis via the variable-sized steps is not novel. However we believe that the view point of discretizing a fixed time interval $[0,1]$ to closely follow the differential equation based analysis is novel in the context of MWU.

REMARK 3. *We will assume that $g_i(x)$ is non-negative on P for $1 \leq i \leq m$, that is, we focus on packing problems. Covering constraints and mixed packing and covering constraints can also be handled in a similar fashion, however we need the idea of dropping covered constraints [28, 39]. We defer these details for a later version.*

Algorithm 2 MWU template with discretization

1: **procedure** MWU-DISCRETE($f, g_1, \ldots, g_m, P, \eta, \epsilon$):
2:     $\mathbf{w}(0) = 1$
3:     $\mathbf{x} = 0$
4:     $t = 0$
5:     **while** $t < 1$ **do**
6:         Solve subproblem and obtain $\mathbf{v}(t) \in P$
7:         $\triangleright \sum_{i=1}^m w_i(t) g_i(\mathbf{v}(t)) \leq \sum_{i=1}^m w_i(t)$
8:         $\delta = \min\{\frac{\epsilon}{\eta} \cdot \frac{1}{\max_i g_i(\mathbf{v}(t))}, 1 - t\}$
9:         $\triangleright \delta$ is positive since $g_i(\mathbf{v}(t)) \geq 0 \,\forall i$
10:        $\mathbf{x} = \mathbf{x} + \delta \mathbf{v}(t)$
11:        **for** $i \in [m]$ **do**
12:           $w_i(t + \delta) = w_i(t)\exp(\eta \delta g_i(\mathbf{v}(t)))$
13:        **end for**
14:        $t = t + \delta$
15:     **end while**
16:     **return** $\mathbf{x}_{\text{out}} = \mathbf{x}$
17: **end procedure**

LEMMA 10. *Let $\epsilon \in [0, 1/2)$. Fix any iteration of the while loop, and let $t_\diamond$ be the value of t at the start of the iteration and δ be the step size for that iteration. Then, $\sum_i w_i(t_\diamond + \delta) \leq \exp(\eta\delta(1+\epsilon))\sum_i w_i(t_\diamond)$.*

PROOF. Extend $\mathbf{w}(t)$ to $t \in [t_\diamond, t_\diamond + \delta]$, via $w_i(t) = w_i(t_\diamond)e^{(t-t_\diamond)\eta g_i(\mathbf{v}(t_\diamond))}$ for all i. Since $g_i(\mathbf{v}(t_\diamond)) \geq 0$, it follows that $\eta g_i(\mathbf{v}(t_\diamond)) \leq \epsilon/\delta$. Hence $w_i(t) \leq w_i(t_\diamond)\exp((t - t_\diamond)\epsilon/\delta)$.

$$\frac{d}{dt}\sum_{i=1}^m w_i(t) = \eta \sum_{i=1}^m w_i(t) g_i(\mathbf{v}(t_\diamond))$$
$$\leq \eta e^{(t-t_\diamond)\epsilon/\delta} \sum_{i=1}^m w_i(t_\diamond) g_i(\mathbf{v}(t_\diamond)) \leq \eta e^{(t-t_\diamond)\epsilon/\delta} \sum_{i=1}^m w_i(t_\diamond),$$

because $\mathbf{v}(t_\diamond)$, obtained via the subproblem, satisfies the weighted combination of the constraints with $\mathbf{w}(t_\diamond)$. Integrating both sides in the interval $[t_\diamond, t_\diamond + \delta]$, and rearranging, we obtain

$$
\begin{aligned}
\sum_{i=1}^m w_i(t_\diamond + \delta) &\leq \left(1 + \frac{\eta\delta(e^\epsilon - 1)}{\epsilon}\right) \sum_{i=1}^m w_i(t_\diamond) \\
&\leq \exp\left(\frac{\eta\delta(e^\epsilon - 1)}{\epsilon}\right) \sum_{i=1}^m w_i(t_\diamond).
\end{aligned}
$$

Using the approximation, $e^\epsilon \leq 1 + \epsilon + \epsilon^2$ for $\epsilon \in [0, 1/2]$, we obtain the desired bound. $\quad\square$

THEOREM 11. *Let $\epsilon \in [0, 1/2)$. If $\eta = \ln m / \epsilon$ the point $\mathbf{x}_{\mathrm{out}}$ returned by Algorithm 2 satisfies $\mathbf{x}_{\mathrm{out}} \in P$ and $g_i(\mathbf{x}_{\mathrm{out}}) \leq 1 + 2\epsilon$ for all i. The number of iterations is $O\left(\frac{m \ln m}{\epsilon^2}\right)$.*

PROOF. We set up some notation. The number of iterations of the while loop is given by T. Let δ_j be the step size chosen in the j-th iteration for $j \in \{0, 1, \dots, T-1\}$. Let $t_j = \sum_{\ell=0}^{j-1} \delta_\ell$ denote the value of t at the start of the j-th iteration. Thus $t_0 = 0$ and define $t_T = \sum_{j=0}^{T-1} \delta_j = 1$. We use $w_i(t_j)$ and $\mathbf{v}(t_j)$ to refer to the values of the appropriates quantities at time t_j. For each j:

1. $\ln w_i(t_{j+1}) = \ln w_i(t_j) + \eta\delta_j g_i(\mathbf{v}(t_j)) \geq \ln w_i(t_j) \; \forall i$;

2. $\ln\left(\sum_i w_i(t_{j+1})\right) \leq \ln\left(\sum_i w_i(t_j)\right) + \eta\delta_j(1+\epsilon)$, by Lemma 10.

The output $\mathbf{x}_{\mathrm{out}}$ equals $\sum_{j=0}^{T-1} \delta_j v(t_j)$. By convexity, $\mathbf{x}_{\mathrm{out}} \in P$. Fix $i \in [m]$. Applying the fact that g_i is convex followed by the identity in 1) above, we have:

$$
\begin{aligned}
g_i(\mathbf{x}_{\mathrm{out}}) &= g_i\left(\sum_{j=0}^{T-1} \delta_j v(t_j)\right) \leq \sum_{j=0}^{T-1} \delta_j g_i(\mathbf{v}(t_j)) \\
&= \frac{1}{\eta}\sum_{j=0}^{T-1} \ln w_i(t_{j+1}) - \ln w_i(t_j) = \frac{\ln w_i(1)}{\eta}.
\end{aligned}
$$

To bound the right side above, we sum the inequality in 2) above over all j. Since $\sum_i w_i(0) = m$, we obtain:

$$
\ln\left(\sum_i w_i(1)\right) \leq \sum_{j=0}^{T-1} \eta(1+\epsilon)\delta_j + \ln m = \eta(1+\epsilon) + \ln m \quad (5)
$$

Thus, $g_i(\mathbf{x}_{\mathrm{out}}) \leq 1 + \epsilon + \frac{\ln m}{\eta} = 1 + 2\epsilon$, for the choice of η.

We now bound the number of iterations. Fix an iteration j. Note that if $\delta_j = 1 - t_j$, then the algorithm will terminate at the end of that iteration. Therefore, $\eta\delta_j \max_i g_i(\mathbf{v}(t_j)) = \epsilon$ for all $j < T-1$. If equality is achieved at $i \in [m]$, then by (i) above, $\ln w_i(t_{j+1}) = \ln w_i(t_j) + \epsilon$. Since the weights never decrease, aggregated over all $j < T-1$, there is at least one $i \in [m]$ such that $\ln w_i(1) \geq (T-1)\epsilon/m + \ln w_i(0) = (T-1)\epsilon/m$. Therefore, by eq. (5) above:

$$
T \leq \frac{m}{\epsilon}(\eta(1+\epsilon) + \ln m) + 1 = O\left(\frac{m \ln m}{\epsilon^2}\right),
$$

for the choice of η. $\quad\square$

Discretization to handle the objective function: We have seen a discretization step that ensures that the weigth updates track the differential equation. This also results in a width-independent number of iterations. So far we have ignored the objective function. For linear objectives with pure

linear packing constraints the step-size is not constrained by the objective function, and as we mentioned in Section 2.2, there is an optimum solution to the oracle with only one non-zero coordinate. For more complicated objective functions such as concave functions and submodular functions we may use an oracle based on gradient of f. In such cases the step size may be constrained to be smaller than what is necessary for the weight update in line 8 of Algorithm 2. For instance, to keep things simple, suppose the step size cannot be more than some fixed quantity α in order to preserve the objective to some desired accuracy. Then line 8 can be changed to $\delta = \min\{\alpha, \frac{\epsilon}{\eta} \cdot \frac{1}{\max_i g_i(\mathbf{v}(t))}, 1 - t\}$. Then one can prove that the number of iterations of the algorithm will be $O(\frac{m \ln m}{\epsilon^2} + \frac{1}{\alpha})$. Of course, one could also choose variable step sizes depending on the objective function and one needs to do a corresponding analysis to bound the overall number of iterations.

3.1 Discretization for multilinear relaxation of monotone submodular functions

Here we consider the problem $\max\{F(\mathbf{x}) : \mathbf{x} \geq 0, A\mathbf{x} \leq \mathbf{1}\}$ where $F : [0,1]^N \to \mathbb{R}_+$ is the multilinear extension of a monotone submodular function[6], and $A\mathbf{x} \leq \mathbf{1}$ is a system of m linear packing constraints ($A \geq 0$). We assume that these constraints include in particular the constraint $\mathbf{x} \leq \mathbf{1}$, so that $\mathbf{x} \in [0,1]^N$ for any feasible solution. We also assume for now that F and its first partial derivatives $\frac{\partial F}{\partial x_i}$ are accessible directly through a value oracle. (Which is the case in certain applications where F has an explicit form.) Later, we discuss the issue of estimating $F(\mathbf{x})$ from values oracle for f by random sampling.

For monotone submodular functions, the multilinear extension satisfies $\frac{\partial F}{\partial x_i} \geq 0$ and $\frac{\partial^2 F}{\partial x_i \partial x_j} \leq 0$ for all $i, j \in N$. Moreover, it is linear in each coordinate, i.e. $\frac{\partial^2 F}{\partial x_i^2} = 0$ for all $i \in N$. The general framework for applying multiplicative weight updates to this problem was given in Section 2.3. We use Algorithm 2 where the subproblem to be solved is implemented via an appropriate discretization of eq. (3). At time t with step size δ, we have

$$
\begin{aligned}
\mathbf{v}(t) &= \arg\max_{\mathbf{y} \in P}\left\{\mathbf{y} \cdot \nabla F|_{\mathbf{x}(t)} : \sum_{i,j} w_i(t) A_{ij} y_j \leq \sum_i w_i(t)\right\} \\
\mathbf{x}(t + \delta) &= \mathbf{x}(t) + \delta\,\mathbf{v}(t)
\end{aligned}
$$

We note some simplifications due to the special case that we consider here: the polyhedron P is the non-negative orthant and the constraint functions are linear. This implies that the rule for selecting an optimal direction in each iteration becomes much simpler here. Since we have only one linear constraint per iteration here, the optimal direction is simply $\mathbf{v}(t) = \frac{\sum_i w_i(t)}{\sum_i w_i(t) A_{ij^*}} \mathbf{e}_{j^*}$ for the coordinate j^* that maximizes the benefit/cost ratio $\frac{\sum_i w_i(t)}{\sum_i w_i(t) A_{ij^*}} \frac{\partial F}{\partial x_j}$. Following the general framework, the time step is chosen as $\delta = \min_i \frac{\epsilon}{\eta A_{ij^*} v_{j^*}}$. (Here we run from time 0 to $1 - 2\epsilon$, to ensure feasibility of the final solution.) Therefore, if coordinate x_{j^*} is chosen then it is incremented by $\Delta_{j^*} = \delta v_{j^*} = \min_i \frac{\epsilon}{\eta A_{ij^*}}$. Note

---

[6]The continuous framework in Section 2.3 is applicable for any monotone smooth submodular function. However, one can algorithmically exploit the multilinearity of F when it is the extension of a discrete set function f.

that this quantity depends only on j^*. From here, the corresponding time increment can be written as $\delta = \Delta_{j^*}/v_{j^*} = \frac{\sum_i w_i(t) A_{ij^*}}{\sum_i w_i(t)} \Delta_{j^*}$. We obtain the following algorithm.

Algorithm 3 MWU for Monotone Submodular Functions with Linear Constraints

1: **procedure** MWU-MONOSUBMOD(F, N, A, η, ϵ):
2:     $\mathbf{x} = 0$
3:     **for** $i = 1$ to m **do**
4:         $w_i = 1$
5:     **end for**
6:     **for** $j \in N$ **do**
7:         $\Delta_j = \min_i \frac{\epsilon}{\eta A_{ij}}$
8:     **end for**
9:     $t = 0$
10:    **while** $t < 1 - 2\epsilon$ **do**
11:        $j^* = \arg\max_{j \in N} \left(\frac{1}{\sum_i A_{ij} w_i} \frac{\partial F}{\partial x_j} \Big|_{\mathbf{x}} \right)$
12:        $x_{j^*} = x_{j^*} + \Delta_{j^*}$
13:        $t = t + \frac{\sum_i w_i A_{ij^*}}{\sum_i w_i} \Delta_{j^*}$
14:        **for** $i = 1$ to m **do**
15:            $w_i = w_i e^{\eta A_{ij^*} \Delta_{j^*}}$
16:        **end for**
17:    **end while**
18:    **return** $\mathbf{x}$
19: **end procedure**

We analyze the algorithm as follows. Note that the algorithm stops at time $t = 1 - 2\epsilon$. This ensures that the output solution is feasible. This follows from the analysis in the proof of Theorem 11. Next, because F is multilinear and $\mathbf{v}(t)$ is a basis vector, $F(\mathbf{x}(t+\delta)) - F(\mathbf{x}(t)) = \delta \mathbf{v}(t) \cdot \nabla F|_{\mathbf{x}(t)}$. (Here, δ denotes the appropriate time step, which is $\delta = \frac{\sum_i w_i A_{ij^*}}{\sum_i w_i} \Delta_{j^*}$ whenever x_{j^*} is being incremented.) Similar to the proof of Theorem 6, the vector $\mathbf{z}(t) = (\mathbf{x}(t) \vee \mathbf{x}^*) - \mathbf{x}(t)$ is a candidate solution to the optimization problem, so $\mathbf{v}(t) \cdot \nabla F|_{\mathbf{x}(t)} \geq \mathbf{z}(t) \cdot \nabla F|_{\mathbf{x}(t)}$. By monotonicity and submodularity, $\mathbf{z}(t) \cdot \nabla F|_{\mathbf{x}(t)} \geq F(\mathbf{x}(t) + \mathbf{z}(t)) - F(\mathbf{x}(t)) \geq \mathsf{OPT} - F(\mathbf{x}(t))$. Thus, $\mathbf{v}(t) \cdot \nabla F(\mathbf{x}(t)) \geq \mathsf{OPT} - F(\mathbf{x}(t))$. Therefore, $F(\mathbf{x}(t + \delta)) - F(\mathbf{x}(t)) = \delta(\mathsf{OPT} - F(\mathbf{x}(t)))$. Rewriting we get $\mathsf{OPT} - F(\mathbf{x}(t) + \delta) \leq (1 - \delta)(\mathsf{OPT} - F(\mathbf{x}(t)))$.

Using the notation in the proof of Theorem 11, if $\mathbf{x}_{\text{out}}$ is the solution and t_{out} is the time at termination of the algorithm, we obtain

$$\mathsf{OPT} - F(\mathbf{x}_{\text{out}}) \leq (\mathsf{OPT} - F(\mathbf{x}(0))) \cdot \prod_j (1 - \delta_j) \leq \mathsf{OPT} \cdot e^{-t_{\text{out}}}.$$

We have $t_{\text{out}} \geq 1 - 2\epsilon$ and hence $F(\mathbf{x}_{\text{out}}) \geq (1 - e^{-1+2\epsilon})\mathsf{OPT} \geq (1 - 1/e - \epsilon)\mathsf{OPT}$.

Implementation details that yield the claimed running time are deferred to a longer version of the paper.

3.2 Discretization for non-monotone submodular functions

Now let us turn to the case of non-monotone submodular functions. We only assume here that F arises as a multilinear extension from a non-negative submodular function. Again, we follow the continuous-time framework from Section 2.4. We recall that the subproblem to solve in the

continuous framework is as follows:

$$\mathbf{v}(t) = \arg\max_{0 \leq \mathbf{y} \leq \mathbf{1} - \mathbf{x}} \{ \mathbf{y} \cdot \nabla f|_{\mathbf{x}(t)} : \sum_{i,j} w_i(t) A_{ij} y_j \leq \sum_i w_i(t) \} \quad (6)$$

(see Section 2.4). Here, the optimal direction $\mathbf{v}(t)$ is not necessarily a single coordinate, which makes the analysis somewhat more involved and the running time slower. The main added issue is that the objective function is no longer linear when moving along a general direction $\mathbf{v}(t)$, and hence we have another reason to be careful about the step size. (This was already an issue in the original implementation of the continuous greedy algorithm [37, 11].) To ensure that we get sufficient gains on the objective function, we force the time steps to be bounded by $\min_i \frac{\epsilon}{\eta n \sum_j A_{ij} v_j}$ where $n = |N|$, instead of $\min_i \frac{\epsilon}{\eta \sum_j A_{ij} v_j}$. We obtain the following algorithm.

Algorithm 4 MWU for Nonmonotone Submodular Functions with Linear Constraints

1: **procedure** MWU-NONMONOSUBMOD(F, N, A, η, ϵ):
2:     $\mathbf{x} = 0$
3:     **for** $i = 1$ to m **do**
4:         $w_i = 1$
5:     **end for**
6:     **for** $j \in N$ **do**
7:         $\Delta_j = \min\{\min_i \frac{\epsilon}{\eta n A_{ij}}, \frac{\epsilon}{\eta n}\}$
8:     **end for**
9:     $t = 0$
10:    **while** $t < 1 - 2\epsilon$ **do**
11:        $\mathbf{v} = \arg\max_{\mathbf{y}} \{ \mathbf{y} \cdot \nabla F|_{\mathbf{x}+\Delta} : 0 \leq \mathbf{y} \leq \mathbf{1} - \mathbf{x}, \sum_{i,j} w_i A_{ij} y_j \leq \sum_i w_i \}$
12:        $\delta = \min\{\min_i \frac{\epsilon}{\eta n \sum_j A_{ij} v_j}, \frac{\epsilon}{\eta n}, 1 - t\}$
13:        $\mathbf{x} = \mathbf{x} + \delta \mathbf{v}$
14:        $t = t + \delta$
15:        **for** $i = 1$ to m **do**
16:            $w_i = w_i e^{\eta \delta \sum_j A_{ij} v_j}$
17:        **end for**
18:    **end while**
19:    **return** $\mathbf{x}$
20: **end procedure**

LEMMA 12. *The total number of iterations is at most $(2 + \epsilon)mn\eta/\epsilon$.*

PROOF. Suppose that the number of iterations is $T > (2+\epsilon)mn\eta/\epsilon$. Clearly, there are at most $n\eta/\epsilon \leq mn\eta/\epsilon$ steps where the step size is $\delta = \frac{\epsilon}{\eta n}$. Therefore, there must be at least $(1+\epsilon)mn\eta/\epsilon$ steps where the step size is $\delta = \frac{\epsilon}{\eta \sum_j A_{ij} v_j}$ for some $i \in [m]$, and by the pigeonhole principle there is a particular $i \in [m]$ for which there are at least $(1+\epsilon)n\eta/\epsilon$ such steps. By the multiplicative weight update, w_i increases by a factor of $e^{\epsilon/n}$ in such a step. Therefore, w_i would reach a value of $e^{(1+\epsilon)\eta}$, which cannot happen by the proof of Theorem 11. $\square$

LEMMA 13. *For $\eta = \frac{\ln m}{\epsilon}$, at termination we have $\mathbf{x} \in P$ and $\sum_j A_{ij} x_j \leq 1 + 2\epsilon$ for each i.*

LEMMA 14. *At time t, we have $x_j \leq 1 - e^{-(1+\epsilon/\eta)t}$ for each $j \in N$.*

PROOF. Note that at each step, we have $v_j(t) \leq 1 - x_j(t)$, and we increment $x_j(t)$ to $x_j(t+\delta) = x_j(t) + \delta v_j(t)$. Therefore, $1 - x_j(t+\delta) = 1 - x_j(t) - \delta v_j(t) \geq 1 - x_j(t) - \delta(1 - x_j(t)) = (1 - \delta)(1 - x_j(t))$. Using $\delta \leq \epsilon/\eta$, we get $1 - \delta \geq e^{-(1+\epsilon/\eta)\delta}$, and $1 - x_j(t+\delta) \geq e^{-(1+\epsilon/\eta)\delta}(1 - x_j(t))$. By induction, starting from $x_j(0) = 0$, we obtain $1 - x_j(t) \geq e^{-(1+\epsilon/\eta)t}$. □

Next, we prove a lower bound on the gain that the algorithm makes in one step. Note that instead of considering the gradient at the current point $\mathbf{x}(t)$, the algorithm considers a slightly higher point $\mathbf{x}(t) + \Delta$. First, we show that the increment Δ is chosen so that it upper-bounds any possible step that the algorithm could make at this point.

LEMMA 15. *Define $\Delta \in \mathbb{R}_+^n$ as*

$$\Delta_j = \min \left\{ \min_i \frac{\epsilon}{\eta n A_{ij}}, \frac{\epsilon}{\eta n} \right\}.$$

Then at any time t, if the current solution is $\mathbf{x}(t)$, then after one step the solution is $\mathbf{x}(t+\delta) \leq \mathbf{x}(t) + \Delta$.

PROOF. Given a direction vector $\mathbf{v}(t)$ found by the algorithm, the step size is chosen as

$$\delta = \min \left\{ \min_i \frac{\epsilon}{\eta n \sum_j A_{ij} v_j}, \frac{\epsilon}{\eta n}, 1 - t \right\}.$$

Therefore, the increment δv_j in coordinate x_j is upper-bounded by $\frac{\epsilon}{\eta n}$ (since $v_j \leq 1$) and also by

$$\delta v_j \leq \min_i \frac{\epsilon v_j}{\eta n \sum_{j'} A_{ij'} v_{j'}} \leq \min_i \frac{\epsilon}{\eta n A_{ij}}.$$

This completes the proof. □

LEMMA 16. *If the current solution is $\mathbf{x}(t)$, then there is a vector $0 \leq \mathbf{v} \leq \mathbf{1} - \mathbf{x}(t)$ such that $\sum_{i,j} w_i A_{ij} v_j \leq \sum_i w_i$ and*

$$\mathbf{v} \cdot \nabla F \Big|_{\mathbf{x}(t)+\Delta} \geq \left(e^{-t} - \frac{2\epsilon}{\eta} \right) OPT - F(\mathbf{x}(t) + \Delta).$$

PROOF. Consider the optimum $\mathbf{y}^*$, $OPT = F(\mathbf{y}^*)$. The direction vector

$$\mathbf{v} = ((\mathbf{x}(t) + \Delta) \vee \mathbf{y}^*) - (\mathbf{x}(t) + \Delta)$$

satisfies $0 \leq \mathbf{v} \leq \mathbf{1} - \mathbf{x}(t)$ and $\sum_{i,j} w_i A_{ij} v_j \leq \sum_i w_i$, by the feasibility of $\mathbf{y}^*$.

Next, by the concavity of F along non-negative directions,

$$
\begin{aligned}
\mathbf{v} \cdot \nabla F \Big|_{\mathbf{x}(t)+\Delta} &\geq F(\mathbf{x}(t) + \Delta + \mathbf{v}) - F(\mathbf{x}(t) + \Delta) \\
&= F((\mathbf{x}(t) + \Delta) \vee \mathbf{y}^*) - F(\mathbf{x}(t) + \Delta).
\end{aligned}
$$

Since we have $x_j(t) \leq 1 - e^{-(1+\epsilon/\eta)t}$ by Lemma 14, we have $x_j(t) + \Delta_j \leq 1 - e^{-(1+\epsilon/\eta)t} + \frac{\epsilon}{\eta n}$. Therefore, by Lemma 7, $F((\mathbf{x}(t)+\Delta) \vee \mathbf{y}^*) \geq (e^{-(1+\epsilon/\eta)t} - \frac{\epsilon}{\eta n})F(\mathbf{y}^*) = (e^{-(1+\epsilon/\eta)t} - \frac{\epsilon}{\eta n})OPT$. We estimate $e^{-(1+\epsilon/\eta)t} \leq (1 - \epsilon t/\eta)e^{-t} \geq e^{-t} - \epsilon/\eta$ which finishes the proof. □

We need one more bound, comparing the values of $F(\mathbf{x}')$ for $\mathbf{x} \leq \mathbf{x}' \leq \mathbf{x} + \Delta$. Since Δ was chosen to be "small", we prove that these values cannot differ by too much.

LEMMA 17. *For any pair of points such that $0 \leq \mathbf{x}' - \mathbf{x} \leq \Delta$, we have $F(\mathbf{x}') - F(\mathbf{x}) \leq \frac{\epsilon}{\eta} OPT$.*

LEMMA 18. *For each time step, define $\phi : [t, t+\delta] \to \mathbb{R}$ as $\phi(t + \lambda) = F(\mathbf{x}(t) + \lambda \mathbf{v}(t))$ for $\lambda \in [0, \delta]$. If $\eta \geq 3$, then for each $\tau \in (t, t+\delta)$, we have*

$$\phi'(\tau) \geq (e^{-\tau} - \epsilon)OPT - \phi(\tau).$$

LEMMA 19. *At time $t = 1$, we obtain*

$$F(\mathbf{x}(1)) \geq \left(\frac{1}{e} - \epsilon \right) OPT.$$

COROLLARY 20. *For $\eta = \ln m/\epsilon$, the algorithm runs in $O(mn \log m/\epsilon^2)$ iterations and returns a solution of value $F(\mathbf{x}) \geq (1/e - \epsilon)OPT$.*

Implementation details that yield the claimed running time are deferred to a longer version of the paper.

Acknowledgments: We thank Ken Clarkson and Neal Young for several helpful discussions.

4. REFERENCES

[1] S. Arora, E. Hazan, and S. Kale. Fast algorithms for approximate semidefinite programming using the multiplicative weights update method. In *Proc. 46th FOCS*, pages 339–348. IEEE Comp. Soc. Press, 2005.

[2] S. Arora, E. Hazan, and S. Kale. The multiplicative weights update method: a meta-algorithm and applications. *Theory of Computing*, 8(6):121–164, 2012.

[3] S. Arora and S. Kale. A combinatorial, primal-dual approach to semidefinite programs. In *Proc. 39th STOC*, pages 227–236. ACM Press, 2007.

[4] Y. Azar and I. Gamzu. Efficient submodular function maximization under linear packing constraints. In A. Czumaj, K. Mehlhorn, A. M. Pitts, and R. Wattenhofer, editors, *ICALP (1)*, volume 7391 of *Lecture Notes in Computer Science*, pages 38–50. Springer, 2012.

[5] A. Badanidiyuru, B. Mirzasoleiman, A. Karbasi, and A. Krause. Streaming submodular maximization: Massive data summarization on the fly. In *Proceedings of the 20th ACM SIGKDD International Conference on Knowledge Discovery and Data Mining, KDD '14*, pages 671–680. ACM, 2014.

[6] A. Badanidiyuru and J. Vondrák. Fast algorithms for maximizing submodular functions. In *SODA*, pages 1497–1514, 2014.

[7] N. Bansal, N. Korula, V. Nagarajan, and A. Srinivasan. Solving packing integer programs via randomized rounding with alterations. *Theory of Computing*, 8(1):533–565, 2012.

[8] D. Bienstock. *Potential Function Methods for Approximately Solving Linear Programming Problems: Theory and Practice*. Springer, 2002.

[9] C. Borgs, M. Brautbar, J. T. Chayes, and B. Lucier. Maximizing social influence in nearly optimal time. In *SODA*, pages 946–957. SIAM, 2014.

[10] G. Călinescu, C. Chekuri, M. Pál, and J. Vondrák. Maximizing a submodular set function subject to a matroid constraint (extended abstract). In M. Fischetti and D. P. Williamson, editors, *IPCO*, volume 4513 of *Lecture Notes in Computer Science*, pages 182–196. Springer, 2007.

[11] G. Călinescu, C. Chekuri, M. Pál, and J. Vondrák. Maximizing a monotone submodular function subject to a matroid constraint. *SIAM J. Comput.*, 40(6):1740–1766, 2011.

[12] C. Chekuri, J. Vondrak, and R. Zenklusen. Dependent randomized rounding via exchange properties of combinatorial structures. In *Foundations of Computer Science (FOCS), 2010 51st Annual IEEE Symposium on*, pages 575–584. IEEE, 2010.

[13] C. Chekuri, J. Vondrák, and R. Zenklusen. Submodular function maximization via the multilinear relaxation and contention resolution schemes. In L. Fortnow and S. P. Vadhan, editors, *STOC*, pages 783–792. ACM, 2011.

[14] F. Chierichetti, R. Kumar, and A. Tomkins. Max-cover in map-reduce. In M. Rappa, P. Jones, J. Freire, and S. Chakrabarti, editors, *WWW*, pages 231–240. ACM, 2010.

[15] F. Diedrich and K. Jansen. Faster and simpler approximation algorithms for mixed packing and covering problems. *Theoretical computer science*, 377(1):181–204, 2007.

[16] M. Feldman, J. Naor, and R. Schwartz. A unified continuous greedy algorithm for submodular maximization. In R. Ostrovsky, editor, *FOCS*, pages 570–579. IEEE, 2011.

[17] L. Fleischer. Approximating fractional multicommodity flow independent of the number of commodities. *SIAM Journal on Discrete Mathematics*, 13(4):505–520, 2000.

[18] N. Garg and R. Khandekar. Fractional covering with upper bounds on the variables: Solving LPs with negative entries. In *Proc. 12th Ann. Europ. Symp. on Algorithms (ESA'04)*, pages 371–382, 2004.

[19] N. Garg and J. Könemann. Faster and simpler algorithms for multicommodity flow and other fractional packing problems. In *Proc. 39th FOCS*, pages 300–309. IEEE Comp. Soc. Press, 1998.

[20] N. Garg and J. Könemann. Faster and simpler algorithms for multicommodity flow and other fractional packing problems. *SIAM J. Comput.*, 37:630–652, 2007.

[21] J. Gillenwater, A. Kulesza, and B. Taskar. Near-optimal map inference for determinantal point processes. In *Advances in Neural Information Processing Systems*, pages 2735–2743, 2012.

[22] M. Grigoriadis and L. Khachiyan. Fast approximation schemes for convex programs with many blocks and coupling constraints. *SIAM Journal on Optimization*, 4(1):86–107, 1994.

[23] M. D. Grigoriadis, L. G. Khachiyan, L. Porkolab, and J. Villavicencio. Approximate max-min resource sharing for structured concave optimization. *SIAM Journal on Optimization*, 11(4):1081–1091, 2001.

[24] R. Iyer, S. Jegelka, and J. Bilmes. Fast semidifferential-based submodular function optimization. In *Proceedings of The 30th International Conference on Machine Learning*, pages 855–863, 2013.

[25] K. Jansen and H. Zhang. Approximation algorithms for general packing problems and their application to the multicast congestion problem. *Mathematical Programming*, 114(1):183–206, 2008.

[26] S. Kale. *Efficient Algorithms Using The Multiplicative Weights Update Method*. PhD thesis, Princeton University, 2006. Technical Report TR-804-07.

[27] R. Khandekar. *Lagrangian Relaxation based Algorithms for Convex Programming Problems*. PhD thesis, Indian Institute of Technology, Delhi, 2004.

[28] J. Könemann. Fast combinatorial algorithms for packing and covering problems. Master's thesis, Universitat des Saarlandes, 1998. Available at: http://www.math.uwaterloo.ca/jochen/docs/diplom.ps.

[29] C. Koufogiannakis and N. E. Young. Beating simplex for fractional packing and covering linear programs. In *FOCS*, pages 494–504. IEEE Computer Society, 2007.

[30] A. Kulik, H. Shachnai, and T. Tamir. Approximations for monotone and nonmonotone submodular maximization with knapsack constraints. *Mathematics of Operations Research*, 38(4):729–739, 2013.

[31] R. Kumar, B. Moseley, S. Vassilvitskii, and A. Vattani. Fast greedy algorithms in mapreduce and streaming. In G. E. Blelloch and B. Vöcking, editors, *SPAA*, pages 1–10. ACM, 2013.

[32] J. Kwon and P. Mertikopoulos. A continuous-time approach to online optimization. *arXiv preprint arXiv:1401.6956*, 2014.

[33] J. Lee, V. S. Mirrokni, V. Nagarajan, and M. Sviridenko. Maximizing nonmonotone submodular functions under matroid or knapsack constraints. *SIAM J. Discrete Math.*, 23(4):2053–2078, 2010.

[34] M. Luby and N. Nisan. A parallel approximation algorithm for positive linear programming. In *ACM STOC*, pages 448–457, 1993.

[35] S. A. Plotkin, D. B. Shmoys, and É. Tardos. Fast approximation algorithm for fractional packing and covering problems. *Math. Oper. Res.*, 20:257–301, 1995. Preliminary version in FOCS'91.

[36] S. Sorin. Exponential weight algorithm in continuous time. *Mathematical Programming*, 116(1-2):513–528, 2009.

[37] J. Vondrák. Optimal approximation for the submodular welfare problem in the value oracle model. In C. Dwork, editor, *STOC*, pages 67–74. ACM, 2008.

[38] N. E. Young. Randomized rounding without solving the linear program. In *Proc. 6th Ann. ACM-SIAM Symp. on Discrete Algorithms (SODA'95)*, pages 170–178. ACM Press, 1995.

[39] N. E. Young. Sequential and parallel algorithms for mixed packing and covering. In *Proceedings of 42nd IEEE Symposium on Foundations of Computer Science*, pages 538–546. IEEE, 2001.

[40] N. E. Young. Nearly linear-time approximation schemes for mixed packing/covering and facility-location linear programs. *ArXiv e-prints*, July 2014.

Robust Hierarchical k-Center Clustering

Silvio Lattanzi
Google Research, New York
silviol@google.com

Stefano Leonardi*
Sapienza University of Rome
leonardi@dis.uniroma1.it

Vahab Mirrokni
Google Research, New York
mirrokni@google.com

Ilya Razenshteyn†
MIT
ilyaraz@mit.edu

ABSTRACT

One of the most popular and widely used methods for data clustering is hierarchical clustering. This clustering technique has proved useful to reveal interesting structure in the data in several applications ranging from computational biology to computer vision. Robustness is an important feature of a clustering technique if we require the clustering to be stable against small perturbations in the input data. In most applications, getting a clustering output that is robust against adversarial outliers or stochastic noise is a necessary condition for the applicability and effectiveness of the clustering technique. This is even more critical in hierarchical clustering where a small change at the bottom of the hierarchy may propagate all the way through to the top.

Despite all the previous work [2, 3, 6, 8], our theoretical understanding of robust hierarchical clustering is still limited and several hierarchical clustering algorithms are not known to satisfy such robustness properties. In this paper, we study the limits of robust hierarchical k-center clustering by introducing the concept of *universal hierarchical clustering* and provide (almost) tight lower and upper bounds for the robust hierarchical k-center clustering problem with outliers and variants of the stochastic clustering problem. Most importantly we present a constant-factor approximation for optimal hierarchical k-center with at most z outliers using a universal set of at most $O(z^2)$ set of outliers and show that this result is tight. Moreover we show the necessity of using a universal set of outliers in order to compute an approximately optimal hierarchical k-center with a different set of outliers for each k.

1. INTRODUCTION

As the amount of data available in many different domains (social sciences, text classification, bioinformatics, image processing) is increasing every day, the development of computationally efficient data clustering techniques that are also effective, accurate, and robust to noise has become increasingly important. As one of the most popular and widely used methods for data clustering, hierarchical clustering aims to describe the structure of the data at different scale levels. This clustering technique is applied as a standard tool by statisticians, computer scientists, bio-scientists and more recently data scientists.

Hierarchical clustering provides partitions of the input data at different levels where every partition is obtained by refining a partition at a higher level. The structure of the solution of a hierarchical clustering algorithm is conveniently represented by a tree. More specifically, the top partitioning is formed by the whole set of input points, the partitioning of level k is obtained by refining one of the clusters of the partition at level $k - 1$, and the partitioning at the lowest level is the one with each of the points in a separate cluster. The quality of a partitioning is mathematically described by some measures of the internal cohesiveness of the clustering, every measure giving rise to a different clustering problem. In this paper we consider the k-center clustering problem, i.e., the problem of partitioning data into k clusters while minimizing the maximum radius of a cluster.

The k-center clustering problem is NP-hard, and admits simple aproximation algorithms with a ratio of 2 [11, 14]. An approximation algorithm for hierarchical k-center clustering problem outputs a tree of partitions that contains, for every integer k, a k-cluster partitioning that is a good approximation of the optimum k-center clustering. For hierarchical k-center clustering, Dasgupta and Long [8] presented an algorithm that for every k induces a k-clustering with maximum radius at most 8 times the optimal k-center clustering. A wealth of methods for computing a hierarchical clustering has been proposed in the literature (see for instance [3, 6, 8, 10, 16, 17].) These methods are either based on a top-down recursive partitioning or more often based on a bottom-up agglomerative method that merges the two closest clusters according to some measure.

Most of the standard hierarchical clustering algorithms are not tolerant to noise [20] meaning that the output solution is very sensible to size and position of the outliers. In other words, the insertion of a few outliers in the metric space may determine a complete alteration of the clustering structure, thus leaving the question of whether the computed clustering is meaningful at all. In order to deal with issue, several practical and theoretical algorithms have been proposed. Some well-known practical techniques are the Ward's method [21], the Wishart's method [22], and CURE [13]. These algorithms however do not have a theoretical guarantee. Various attempts for a theoretical analysis of these problems have also been made, e.g., Balcan et. al [2] studied a certain type of separation property, and presented an agglomerative procedure that clusters instances that possess this property.

*Work partially done while at Google Research NY. Partially supported from Google Focused Research Award "Algorithms for Large-scale Data Analysis", EU projects FET MULTIPLEX 317532 and ERC PAAI 259515.
†Work partially done while at Google Research NY.

ITCS'15, January 11–13, 2015, Rehovot, Israel.
Copyright 2015 ACM 978-1-4503-3333-7/15/01...$15.00.
http://dx.doi.org/10.1145/2688073.2688104.

In this paper, we study a variant of the robust hierarchical k-center clustering. Specifically, we seek hierarchical clustering algorithms that are tolerant against *outliers*, i.e., we aim to find, for each k, a solution to the k-center problem that is approximately optimal for a large portion of the data points excluding a small number of outliers (considered as noise in the data). In particular, our goal is to compute a k-center hierarchical clustering that is robust against outliers using a small set of *universal outliers*, i.e., a set of outliers whose removal allows to find an approximately optimal solution for the k-center problem for all values of k. Although dealing with outliers has been extensively considered already in the context of k-center and other clustering problems[4, 5, 19], the question of finding a universal set of outliers for all k has not been formally studied. In fact, in our study, we will show that a universal set of outliers is needed if we want to obtain a good approximation for all values of k, since an outlier used for one partition of the hierarchy may be used as a center for another partition. In this paper, we aim to study this problem by answering the following question: Does there exist a set of *universal outliers* whose removal allows to compute a k-center hierarchical clustering on the remaining points that is approximately optimal for all values of k?

We also investigate another aspect of robustness related to clustering. In applications with large-scale data it is often impossible to observe the whole input data, but it is available some knowledge on the distribution that generates the input. It is relevant in these cases to compute a clustering that is good on average for most of the input instances generated by the distribution. Achieving a similar result requires to discard some outliers, for instance those points that have a big influence on the solution but appear in the input data with small probability. In this work, we address for the first time the problem of computing an *hierarchical stochastic k-center clustering with outliers* that provides, on average, a good solution for (almost) any sample of the metric space.

Our Contributions. We study the robust hierarchical k-center clustering problem. One of our main contributions is to introduce the concept of *universal hierarchical clustering* and provide lower and upper bounds for the hierarchical clustering problem with outliers and variants of the stochastic clustering problem.

To achieve this result, we first study the existence of a set of *universal outliers*, O, that can be used for k-center solution for all k, $k = 1, \ldots, n$, to obtain a solution that compares with the optimal solution of the k-center clustering with z outliers. In particular, we present the following structural results on the set of *universal outliers*:

1. There does not exist a constant-factor approximation algorithm for all possible k using a set of universal outliers with less than $\Omega\left(z^2\right)$ points.

2. There does not exist a constant-factor approximation algorithm for the problem without deciding in advance a universal set of outliers.

We also present the following nearly matching upper bound:

3. There exists a set of universal outliers, O, with $O\left(z^2\right)$ points, such that the k-center solution computed with O as a set of outliers is an $O(1)$ approximation of the optimal k-center with z outliers for all possible k(where the z outliers can change with k).

4. The set of universal outliers can be computed in polynomial time.

The above result is somehow surprising as it implies that the total number of points in the set of *universal outliers* does not depend on n, or on the number of levels of the hierarchical clustering, but only on z.

We next consider the problem of designing a stochastic hierarchical k-center clustering with outliers that provides a good hierarchical solution for every subset of h points independently sampled from a metric space of n points.

5. There exists an $O(1)$-approximation algorithm for *stochastic hierarchical k-center clustering* on inputs of size h and $k \leq K$ that uses at most $z = \frac{2K(K-1)\ln n}{h} n$ outliers.

The above result is obtained by computing an *a-priori* solution that is used for all subsets sampled from the metric space. In order for this result to be non-trivial, K should be bounded by $O\left(\sqrt{\frac{n \times h}{\ln n}}\right)$. In our stochastic model, all points are sampled with equal probability. However, we observe that a non-uniform distribution can be simulated by repeating more points at nearby locations of the metric space. With suitable discretization, this leads only to a small loss in the approximation for the k-center problem.

2. RELATED WORK

Hierarchical or agglomerative clustering is a popular clustering techniques widely studied in data mining and machine learning [8, 15, 18].

We study the k-center clustering problem with outliers. The first work in this direction was by Charikar et al. [4] that develops a 3-approximation algorithm for the problem. If one is interested in hierarchical k-center clustering (without outliers), [8] then gives a procedure for finding a hierarchical clustering that is 8-approximated for every $k = 1, \ldots, n$. This paper is to the best of our knowledge the first theoretical work which combines both hierarchical k-center clustering and the notion of outliers. Our construction for universal outliers is somewhat similar conceptually to [19], where a streaming algorithm for k-center clustering with outliers is presented. Finally, universal stochastic optimization has been considered for network design and set cover problems in [12, 9]. The problem of universal stochastic optimization with outliers for network design has also been addressed in [1].

3. PRELIMINARIES

In this section, we give a formal definition of the hierarchical k-center with z outliers, and introduce some notation that will be used throughout the paper.

Let $M = (X, d)$ be a metric space, S be a subset of X and $n = |X \setminus S|$. Let $c_1, c_2, \ldots, c_n$ be an ordering of the points in $X \setminus S$ and π be a function from $\{c_2, \ldots, c_n\} \to \{c_1, \ldots, c_n\}$ such that for every c_i we have $\pi(c_i) = c_j$, with $j < i$. Note that using the function π, we can define a tree on $c_1, c_2, \ldots, c_n$ where each node c_i points to $\pi(c_i)$ and c_1 is the root of the tree.

For every point $c_i \in X \setminus S$ with $i > 1$, we say that the node c_j is the ancestor of c_i in $c_1, c_2, \ldots, c_k$, with $1 \leq k \leq i - 1$, and denote it by $a_k(c_i) = c_j$, if $c_j \in \{c_1, c_2, \ldots, c_k\}$ is the closest node in π to c_i.

Note that we can define a recursive partition of the points in $X \setminus S$, using $c_1, c_2, \ldots, c_n$ and π. More precisely, for every $1 \leq k \leq n$ we can use the first $c_1, \ldots, c_k$ points as centers of the clusters in the partition and we can assign each node c_i with $i > k$ to the cluster whose center is its ancestor. Furthermore, we can define the cost of such a partition at level k as $C(c_1, c_2, \ldots, c_k, \pi, X \setminus S) = \max_{i > k} d(c_i, a_k(c_i))$.

For $1 \leq k \leq n$, let O_k denote the optimal set of z outliers for k-center clusterings, and OPT_k^z denote the cost of the optimal solution for k-center with z outliers and with $\mathrm{OPT}_k(X \setminus S)$ be the cost of the optimal k-center solution for the points in $X \setminus S$. In the hierarchical k-center problem with z outliers, we want to find an ordering of points in $X \setminus S$, $c_1, c_2, \ldots, c_n$, and a function π such that $C(c_1, c_2, \ldots, c_k, \pi, X \setminus S) \leq \alpha \mathrm{OPT}_k^z$ for any $1 \leq k \leq n$ where α is minimized.

In the rest of the paper, we denote by $B(u, C)$ the ball centered in u and with radius C. Also we often refer to S as universal set of outliers.

4. OUTLIERS AND HIERARCHICAL K-CENTER

In this section, we analyze the structural properties of hierarchical k-center clustering with outliers. We know from the work of Das and Mathieu [7](Theorem 4) that no randomized algorithm can achieve an approximation better than 3/2 for the hierarchical k-center clustering problem even when we allow unbounded computational power so in the paper we focus on finding a constant factor approximation for our problem.

In particular we are able to show that it is possible to compute a hierarchical k-center clustering that uses a set of universal outliers S of size $O\left(z^2\right)$ and that gives a constant approximation for the k-center problem with z outliers for all values of k. Furthermore, we show that this result is asymptotically tight, i.e., in order to get a constant factor approximation for all k, we need to use a universal set of outliers and such a universal set of outlier has to be of size at least $\Omega\left(z^2\right)$.

In the next subsections, we first present the two structural lower bounds, and then we describe our positive result.

4.1 Lower bounds

4.1.1 Size of the set of universal outliers

Given that we cannot hope to have an approximation better than 3/2, we focus on obtaining a constant-factor approximation. Here we show that in order to get a constant-factor approximation algorithm with a set of universal outliers S, we need S to be of size $\Omega\left(z^2\right)$.

LEMMA 1. There exists a layout of the points in a 1-dimensional euclidian space such that it is impossible to obtain a constant approximation for all possible k using a set of universal outliers with less than $\Omega\left(z^2\right)$ points.

PROOF. We partition the n points in t sets $U_0, U_1, \ldots, U_{t-1}$. All the sets U_j, for j in $1 \leq j \leq t - 1$, contain $j + 1$ points, the set U_0 contains the remaining points. All the points in U_0 lie in $[0, 1]$, in all the other sets U_j, for j in $1 \leq j \leq t - 1$, there is one point in position $-\log^j(n)$ and j points in $[\log^j(n) - 1, \log^j(n)]$.

Consider the 1 center solution for the problem with z outliers. The optimal solution in this case is to select one center in U_0 and to select as outliers all points in U_{z-1}, this solution has cost $O(\log^{z-2} n)$. Furthermore note that all the solutions with cost $O(\log^{z-2} n)$ select U_{z-1} as set of outlier so the universal set of outliers contains U_{z-1}. The optimal solution with 2 centers and z outliers has one center in U_0 one center in the positive points of U_{z-1}, and the outliers' set is composed by the negative point in U_{z-1} and the points in U_{z-2}, this solution has cost $O(\log^{z-3} n)$. Also in this case it is possible to check that there is no solution of cost $O(\log^{z-3} n)$ with a different set of outliers so the universal set of outliers contains $U_{z-1} \cup U_{z-2}$. More generally, the solution with j centers and z

outliers, for $1 \leq j \leq z - 1$, has one center in U_0, one center between the positive points in U_{z-1}, one center between the positive points in $U_{z-2}, \ldots$, one center between the positive points in U_{z-j+1} and the set of outliers for such solution is composed by the negative points of $U_{z-1}, U_{z-2}, \ldots, U_{z-j+1}$ and all the points in U_{z-j} (refer to figure 1 for an example for $k = 1, 2, 3$ and $z = 4$). This solution has cost $O(\log^{z-j-1} n)$ and one can check that it is possible to get a $O(\log^{z-j-1} n)$ solution only using the described set of outliers, so the universal set of outliers contains $U_{z-1} \cup U_{z-2} \cup \cdots \cup U_{z-j}$.

Thus we have that the cardinality of the universal set of outliers U is lower bounded by

$$|U| \geq \left| \cup_{j=1}^{z-1} U_j \right| = \sum_{j=1}^{z-1} |U_j| = \sum_{j=1}^{z-1} j + 1 \in O(z^2).$$

The claim follows. $\square$

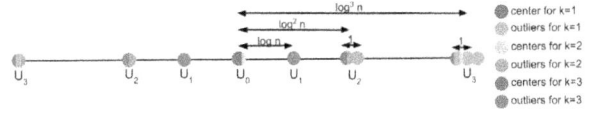

Figure 1: Visualization of the layout for $z = 4$. The different set of outliers and centers are represented using different colors. Nodes with multiple colors are outliers or centers for multiple values of k.

4.1.2 A universal set of outliers is necessary

We just proved that the size of the set of universal outliers needed to get a constant-factor approximation is at least of size $\Omega\left(z^2\right)$. In this subsection, we show that a universal set of outliers is necessary if we want to construct a robust hierarchical k-center solution. More precisely, we show that it is impossible to obtain a constant-factor approximation for the problem without deciding in advance a universal set of outliers to be excluded since the beginning of the execution of a hierarchical clustering algorithm. To prove it we exhibit an example where one of the centers in a k-center solution computed for a value of k must later be turned into an outlier if we like to maintain a constant approximation for another value of k (note that this is impossible in a hierarchical solution). Our result holds also if we are allowed to use a different set of outliers for different values of k.

LEMMA 2. There exists a layout of the points in a 1-dimensional Euclidian space such that for $z = 4$ it is impossible to obtain an approximate solution for all possible k without using a set of universal outliers.

PROOF. Consider the following layout of the points, point v_1 is in position $\log^2 n$, point v_2 in position $\log^2 n + 1$, point v_3 in position $-\log^2 n$, point v_4 in position $-\log^2 n - 1$, point v_5, v_6, v_7 and v_8 are respectively in positions $\log^3 n, \log^3 n + \log n, \log^3 n + 2\log n$ and $\log^3 n + 3\log n$, all the remaining points are in the set U_0 and in positions in $[0, 1]$.

All the constant approximations with 2 centers and 4 outliers have one center in $[0, 1]$, one center between v_5, v_6, v_7 or v_8 and the outliers are v_1, v_2, v_3 and v_4. Instead all the constant approximations with 3 centers and 4 outliers have one center in $[0, 1]$, one center between v_1 or v_2, one center between v_3 or v_4 and the outliers are v_5, v_6, v_7 and v_8. So if we do not use universal outliers a point between v_5, v_6, v_7 or v_8 is a center for the solution with 2 centers and an outlier for the solution for 3 centers, but this is impossible in hierarchical solution (refer to figure 2 for a visual representation). In fact, in hierarchical solution if a point is a center for some k it has to remain center for all the larger values of k. Thus it is impossible to have a robust hierarchical solution without a set of universal outliers. □

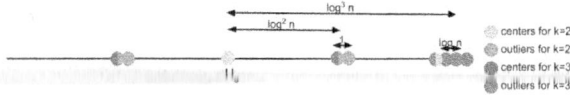

Figure 2: Visual representation for $k = 2, 3$ and $z = 4$. The different set of outliers and centers are represented using different colors. Nodes with multiple colors are outliers or centers for multiple values of k.

4.2 Upper bound

In this section, we prove that the lower bound of Lemma 1 is asymptotically tight. In particular, we present a constructive proof for the existence of a set of universal outliers of size $O(z^2)$ that once removed allow the existence of algorithms that achieves an $O(1)$ approximation for hierarchical k-center. In particular, thanks to the result of Dasgupta and Long [8] on hierarchical k-center clustering it suffices to prove that there is a set S of size $O(z^2)$ such that for every k $\text{OPT}_k(X \setminus S) \leq O(1) \cdot \text{OPT}_k^z$.

Note that in this section our construction will not be algorithmic, in particular we assume to know the optimal solution and the optimal set of outliers, O_k, for each k. In the next section we will show how to turn this existential result into a polynomial time algorithm that identifies the set of universal outliers and produces the hierarchical clustering on the remaining points.

The main idea behind the construction is to include a node in the set of universal outliers only if by including it the optimal solution improves significantly and only if it does not have too many "close" points. More formally, the algorithm to find the universal set of outliers is shown in Algorithm 1.

Algorithm 1 Finding universal outliers

1: Let $0 < \alpha \leq 1/12$ be a parameter that we will choose later.
2: $t \leftarrow 0$
3: $k_0 \leftarrow 1$
4: $S_0 \leftarrow O_1$
5: **for** $2 \leq k \leq n$ **do**
6:     **if** $\text{OPT}_k^z < \alpha \cdot \text{OPT}_k(X \setminus S_t)$ **then**
7:         $t \leftarrow t + 1$
8:         $k_t \leftarrow k$
9:         $U_t \leftarrow S_{t-1} \cup O_k$
10:         $A_t \leftarrow \left\{ u \in U_t \mid B\left(u, 2 \cdot \text{OPT}_k^z\right) \cap X \subseteq U_t \right\}$
11:         $B_t \leftarrow \left\{ u \in U_t \mid \left|B\left(u, 2 \cdot \text{OPT}_k^z\right) \cap X\right| \leq z \right\}$
12:         $S_t \leftarrow A_t \cap B_t$
13:     **end if**
14: **end for**
15: $S \leftarrow S_t$

In the remaining of this section we prove that Algorithm 1 constructs a good universal set of outliers. More formally we show the following theorem:

THEOREM 3. *For every metric space $\mathcal{M} = (X, d)$ with $|X| = n$ and $z > 0$ there exists a subset $S \subseteq X$ such that*

- $|S| \leq z^2$,

- *for every $1 \leq k \leq n$, $\text{OPT}_k(X \setminus S) \leq 28 \cdot \text{OPT}_k^z$.*

In order to prove the main theorem of the section we first show a series of technical lemma that we use to get the approximation guarantee. We start by showing that the cardinality of S is small:

LEMMA 4. *For the resulting set S one has $|S| \leq z^2$.*

PROOF. We prove that if for every t the size of S_t is at most z^2. Consider the optimal k-center clustering of $X \setminus O_{k_t}$ (with all the clusters having radii at most $\text{OPT}_{k_t}^z$). Consider all the clusters that consist of points from S_{t-1} exclusively and have cardinality at most z. Note that there are less than z such clusters otherwise, we could remove them and add all the points from O_{k_t} as singletons and this would contradict the invariant $\text{OPT}_{k_t}^z < \alpha \cdot \text{OPT}_{k_t}(X \setminus S_{t-1})$. So, in total there are at most $(z-1)z$ points in all these clusters. Moreover, all the points from S_{t-1} outside these clusters are filtered from S_t.

Thus, overall the total size of S_t is at most z^2. □

Now we focus on proving the approximation factor, the core idea of the proof is to show that $\text{OPT}_{k_t}(X \setminus S_t)$ and $\text{OPT}_{k_t}^z$ are a constant factor away and also $\text{OPT}_{k_t}^z$ and $\text{OPT}_{k_{t-1}}^z$ are a constant factor away and combine this two facts to prove the approximation. We start by introducing a lemma bounding the difference between the optimal k-center solutions on two set $P, Q \subseteq X$.

LEMMA 5. *For every $P, Q \subseteq X$*

$$\text{OPT}_k(P) \leq 2 \cdot \left(\text{OPT}_k(Q) + \max_{p \in P} d(p, Q) \right).$$

PROOF. First, note that

$$\text{OPT}_k(P) \leq 2 \cdot \text{OPT}_k(P \cup Q). \tag{1}$$

Indeed, consider the optimal k-center clustering for $P \cup Q$. First, we remove all the clusters that do not contain points from P. Second, in each of the remaining clusters we move the center to any point in P. Thus, the cost of the clustering can at most double.

Second, note that

$$\text{OPT}_k(P \cup Q) \leq \text{OPT}_k(Q) + \max_{p \in P} d(p, Q). \tag{2}$$

Indeed, consider the optimal k-center clustering for Q, attach all the points from $P \setminus Q$ to the closest clusters and apply the triangle inequality.

Finally, combining (1) and (2) we get the desired inequality. □

Using the previous Lemma we are now able to prove a relationship between $\text{OPT}_{k_t}(X \setminus S_t)$ and $\text{OPT}_{k_t}^z$.

LEMMA 6. *For every t, $\text{OPT}_{k_t}(X \setminus S_t) \leq 6 \cdot \text{OPT}_{k_t}^z$.*

PROOF. By Lemma 5 and the definition of O_{k_t}

$$\text{OPT}_{k_t}(X \setminus S_t) \leq 2 \cdot \left(\text{OPT}_{k_t}^z + \max_{u \in X \setminus O_{k_t}} d(u, X \setminus O_{k_t}) \right).$$

Thus, it is sufficient to prove that for every $u \in X \setminus S_t$ one has $d(u, X \setminus O_{k_t}) \leq 2 \cdot \text{OPT}_{k_t}^z$. If $u \notin O_{k_t}$, then the required distance is zero. So, we can assume wlog that $u \in O_{k_t} \setminus S_t$. Since $O_{k_t} \subseteq U_t$, u was filtered out in the line 9 of the code. This means that one of the two possibilities holds. The first is that $B\left(u, 2 \cdot \text{OPT}_{k_t}^z\right) \cap X \not\subseteq U_t$, but since $O_{k_t} \subseteq U_t$, we have $d(u, X \setminus O_{k_t}) \leq 2 \cdot \text{OPT}_{k_t}^z$. The second possibility is that $\left|B\left(u, 2 \cdot \text{OPT}_{k_t}^z\right) \cap U_t\right| > z$. But since $|O_{k_t}| \leq z$ it again means that $d(u, X \setminus O_{k_t}) \leq 2 \cdot \text{OPT}_{k_t}^z$. □

Now we focus on the relationship between $\text{OPT}_{k_t}^z$ and $\text{OPT}_{k_{t-1}}^z$.

LEMMA 7. *For every* $t \geq 1$, $\mathrm{OPT}^z_{k_t} < 6\alpha \cdot \mathrm{OPT}^z_{k_{t-1}}$.

PROOF.

$$\mathrm{OPT}^z_{k_t} < \alpha \cdot \mathrm{OPT}_{k_t}(X \backslash S_{t-1}) \leq \alpha \cdot \mathrm{OPT}_{k_{t-1}}(X \backslash S_{t-1}) \leq 6\alpha \cdot \mathrm{OPT}^z_{k_{t-1}}$$

The first step is due to the condition in the "for" loop. The last inequality is due to Lemma 6. □

After studying the relationship between $\mathrm{OPT}_{k_t}(X \backslash S_t)$ and $\mathrm{OPT}^z_{k_t}$ and between $\mathrm{OPT}^z_{k_t}$ and $\mathrm{OPT}^z_{k_{t-1}}$, we are now ready to prove that $\mathrm{OPT}_{k^*}(X \backslash S)$ and $\mathrm{OPT}^z_{k^*}$ are close.

LEMMA 8. *For every* $1 \leq k^* \leq n$

$$\mathrm{OPT}_{k^*}(X \backslash S) \leq \left(\frac{2}{\alpha} + \frac{24\alpha}{1 - 6\alpha} \right) \cdot \mathrm{OPT}^z_{k^*}.$$

Let λ be the largest integer such that $k_\lambda \leq k^*$. Let $\tilde{S} = S_\lambda$. Before showing the previous lemma, we prove two lemmas about $\tilde{S}$.

LEMMA 9.

$$\mathrm{OPT}_{k^*}(X \backslash \tilde{S}) \leq \frac{1}{\alpha} \cdot \mathrm{OPT}^z_{k^*}.$$

PROOF. If $k_\lambda < k^*$, then we are done due to the invariant we test in the "for" loop.

If $k_\lambda = k^*$, then by Lemma 6

$$\mathrm{OPT}_{k^*}(X \backslash \tilde{S}) \leq 6 \cdot \mathrm{OPT}^z_{k^*} \leq \frac{1}{\alpha} \cdot \mathrm{OPT}^z_{k^*}.$$

The last inequality is true, because $\alpha \leq 1/12$. □

LEMMA 10. *For every* $u \in X \backslash S$

$$d(u, X \backslash \tilde{S}) \leq \frac{12\alpha}{1 - 6\alpha} \cdot \mathrm{OPT}^z_{k^*}.$$

PROOF. If $u \in X \backslash \tilde{S}$, then the inequality is true. So we can assume that $u \in \tilde{S} \backslash S$. There exists $t > \lambda$ such that $u \in S_{t-1} \backslash S_t$. Let us prove that

$$d(u, X \backslash \tilde{S}) \leq 2 \cdot \sum_{i=\lambda+1}^{t} \mathrm{OPT}^z_{k_i}. \qquad (3)$$

Let us prove this inequality via induction on t. Since $u \in S_{t-1} \backslash S_t$, there are two possible explanations of this fact. First, it could be that $B\left(u, 2 \cdot \mathrm{OPT}^z_{k_t}\right) \cap X \not\subseteq U_t$. If $B\left(u, 2 \cdot \mathrm{OPT}^z_{k_t}\right) \cap X \not\subseteq \tilde{S}$, then (3) is true. So, we can focus on the case where $B\left(u, 2 \cdot \mathrm{OPT}^z_{k_t}\right) \cap X \subseteq \tilde{S}$. Thus, there exists $u' \in \tilde{S} \backslash S_{t-1}$ such that $d(u, u') \leq 2 \cdot \mathrm{OPT}^z_{k_t}$ (otherwise the point would be in S_t). But if is the case we can invoke the induction hypothesis and the triangle inequality to get equation (3). The second possibility is that $\left| B\left(u, 2 \cdot \mathrm{OPT}^z_{k_t}\right) \cap U_t \right| > z$. But since $u \in \tilde{S}$, we have $\left| B\left(u, 2 \cdot \mathrm{OPT}^z_{k_t}\right) \cap \tilde{S} \right| \leq z$ and so there is a point in $X \backslash \tilde{S}$ with at most distance $2 \cdot \mathrm{OPT}^z_{k_t}$ from u. (Note that here we use that $t > \lambda$ and thus by Lemma 18 one has $2 \cdot \mathrm{OPT}^z_{k_t} \leq 12\alpha \cdot \mathrm{OPT}^z_{k_\lambda} \leq \mathrm{OPT}_{k_\lambda}$ since $\alpha \leq 1/12$). Finally, from (3), Lemma 7 and the fact that $k_{\lambda+1} > k^*$ we get

$$
\begin{aligned}
d(u, X \backslash \tilde{S}) &\leq 2 \cdot \mathrm{OPT}^z_{k_{\lambda+1}} \cdot \sum_{i=0}^{\infty} (6\alpha)^i \leq \mathrm{OPT}^z_{k_{\lambda+1}} \cdot \frac{2}{1 - 6\alpha} \\
&\leq \frac{12\alpha}{1 - 6\alpha} \cdot \mathrm{OPT}^z_{k^*}.
\end{aligned}
$$

□

Using the previous two lemma we can prove Lemma 8.

PROOF. (of Lemma 8)
By combining Lemma 5, Lemma 9 and Lemma 10 we get

$$
\begin{aligned}
\mathrm{OPT}_{k^*}(X \backslash S) &\leq 2 \cdot \left(\mathrm{OPT}_{k^*}(X \backslash \tilde{S}) + \max_{u \in X \backslash S} d(u, X \backslash \tilde{S}) \right) \\
&\leq \left(\frac{2}{\alpha} + \frac{24\alpha}{1 - 6\alpha} \right) \cdot OPT^z_{k^*}.
\end{aligned}
$$

□

We are now ready to show our main theorem in fact by using the result of Lemma 4 and Lemma 8 and by choosing choose $\alpha = 1/12$ we get Theorem 3.

5. HIERARCHICAL CLUSTERING WITH OUTLIERS

In this section we give a polynomial time algorithm that constructs a hierarchical clustering that uses a set S of universal outliers of size $O(z^2)$ and for every k gives a constant approximation to OPT^z_k.

The core idea of the algorithm is to use the same schema of our constructive proof for the universal set of outliers to find the outliers and then to apply a hierarchical k-center clustering on the remaining points. For $1 \leq k \leq n$ let O_k denote the set of z outliers for k-center clusterings of X computed by a 3-approximation algorithm. Note that O_k can be computed in polynomial time using the algorithm from [4]. Let $\mathrm{cost}_k(U)$ be the cost of a k-center clustering of $U \subseteq X$, found by the farthest-point traversal. To find S we now use Algorithm 2.

Algorithm 2 Finding a hierarchical universal k-center

1: $t \leftarrow 0$
2: $k_0 \leftarrow 1$
3: $S_0 \leftarrow O_1$
4: **for** $2 \leq k \leq n$ **do**
5:     **if** $\mathrm{cost}_k(X \backslash O_k) < \alpha \cdot \mathrm{cost}_k(X \backslash S_t)$ **then**
6:         $t \leftarrow t + 1$
7:         $k_t \leftarrow k$
8:         $U_t \leftarrow S_{t-1} \cup O_k$
9:         $A_t \leftarrow \{ u \in U_t \mid B(u, 2 \cdot \mathrm{cost}_k(X \backslash O_k)) \cap X \subseteq U_t \}$
10:         $B_t \leftarrow \{ u \in U_t \mid |B(u, 2 \cdot \mathrm{cost}_k(X \backslash O_k)) \cap X| \leq z \}$
11:         $S_t \leftarrow A_t \cap B_t$
12:     **end if**
13: **end for**
14: $S \leftarrow S_t$

Using the previous algorithm we can show that:

THEOREM 11. *For every metric space* $\mathcal{M} = (X, d)$ *with* $|X| = n$ *and* $z > 0$ *there exists a subset* $S \subseteq X$

- $|S| \leq z^2$,

- *for every* $1 \leq k \leq n$, $\mathrm{OPT}_k(X \backslash S) \leq O(1) \cdot \mathrm{OPT}^z_k$.

- S *can be found in polynomial time*

The full proof of Theorem 11 is given in Appendix A. The proof follows the lines of Theorem 3. The blow up in the approximation factor is given by the use of the 3-approximation polynomial time algorithm from [4] to compute a set O_k of outliers and by the 2-approximation farthest-first traversal polynomial time algorithm for computing $\mathrm{cost}_k(X \backslash O_k)$.

Note that once we have found the universal set of outliers we can use the hierarchical k-center algorithm of Dasgupta and Long [8] on the remaining points to get a hierarchical k-center clustering with z outliers that uses a set of universal outliers of size $O(z^2)$. More formally:

COROLLARY 12. *There is a polynomial algorithm for the hierarchical k-center clustering with z outliers that uses a set S of universal outliers of size $O\left(z^2\right)$ and that compute a set of centers $c_1, c_2, \ldots, c_n$ and a function π such that, for every $1 \le k \le n$,*
$$C(c_1, c_2, \ldots, c_k, \pi, X \setminus S) \le O(1) \cdot \mathrm{OPT}_k^z.$$

6. STOCHASTIC HIERARCHICAL CLUSTERING

We define the *stochastic* variant of hierarchical k-center with outliers: find a hierarchical k-center solution on the metric space $M = (X, d)$ which is good on average for any subset of h randomly selected points. Unfortunately this goal cannot always be achieved, for instance if the metric space contains $k + 1$ points that are far away from each other.

For this reason, it is important to allow the presence of outliers also in the stochastic setting. [1] More precisely, we answer the following question: does it exist a small set of outliers that allows to compute a good *stochastic* and *hierarchical k-center* solution for a range of values $k = 1, \ldots, K$? We answer this question by finding a set S of outliers such that the expectation, over a random subset of h points from X, of the cost of an a-priori hierarchical clustering of X is for any fixed $k \in \{1, \ldots, K\}$ close to the expected cost of the optimal k-clustering. We show the following theorem:

THEOREM 13. *There exists a 48-approximation algorithm for* stochastic hierarchical k-center on inputs of size h and maximum number of centers equal to K that uses at most $z = \frac{2K(K-1)\ln n}{h} n$ outliers.

We remark that the solution computed on $X \setminus S$ is an a-priori solution which is good on average for any subset of h points sampled from X.

To show our Theorem we first prove some technical lemmas. We start by proving that there exists a set of outliers S of small size such that there exists a stochastic k-center solution for $X \setminus S$ that is on average also a good solution for $Y \setminus S$, where Y is randomly selected set of h points from X (possibly with repetitions). Initially we focus on the setting where k is fixed then we generalize the result for k between $1, 2, \ldots, K$.

Let us first fix a value of k. Let us also denote by $OPT_k^{X \setminus S}(Y \setminus S)$ the cost of the optimal k-center solution computed for $X \setminus S$ when applied to set $Y \setminus S$. We also denote by $OPT_k(Y)$ the cost of the optimal k-center solution computed for Y.

The goal is to determine a set of outliers S of minimum cardinality such that:

$$E_{Y \in X^h}[\mathrm{OPT}_k^{X \setminus S}(Y \setminus S)] / E_{Y \in X^h}[\mathrm{OPT}_k(Y)] = O(1).$$

Let $r = E_{Y \in X^h} OPT_k(Y)$ the expected cost of the k-center solution on a random set Y of size h. In the following we prove a claim on the existence of a set of k balls of radius $2r$ that cover most of the points of the metric space. This lemma will provide us with an

[1]Note that in order to have a hierarchical clustering we need to have an assignment of all points to their centers and this assignment cannot be based only on d [8] so we need to assume to know X in advance.

upper bound on the size of the set of outliers that is needed in order to obtain a good *stochastic* solution. Note in fact that the existence of a good solution for $X \setminus S$ implies the existence of a good solution for $Y \setminus S$ since $Y \subseteq X$. A similar lemma is also proved in [12] for the universal stochastic set cover problem.

LEMMA 14. *There exists a set of k balls of radius $2r$ that cover all but a fraction $\delta = \frac{2k \log n}{h}$ of X.*

PROOF. Since the expected optimal cost is r, we know that at least $\frac{1}{2}n^h$ input instances, i.e., half of the input instances, will lead to a solution of radius at most $2r$. Moreover, there exists at most $p = n^k = e^{k \ln n}$ solutions of k balls of radius $2r$. Denote by X_i the set of points covered from solution i within radius $2r$. We prove that there must exist at least one solution X_i such that $|X_i| \ge (1-\delta)n$ for $\delta = \frac{2k \log n}{h}$. In order to prove this claim, assume by contradiction that all the solutions X_i have $|X_i| < (1-\delta)n \le ne^{-\delta}$.

All the subsets of h points with a solution of radius at most $2r$ must have been selected among all subsets of h points covered from one of the solutions X_i. We therefore have the following inequality:

$$\sum_{i=1}^{p} |X_i|^h \ge \frac{1}{2} n^h.$$

Since there are at most $e^{k \ln n}$ solutions, and by contradiction $|X_i| < ne^{-\delta}$ for all solutions, we obtain $e^{k \ln n}(n^{-\delta})^h \ge \frac{1}{2}n^h$ and therefore $e^{k \ln n - h\delta} \ge \frac{1}{2}((1-\delta)n)^h$. This is leads to a contradiction if $\delta \ge 2\frac{k \ln n}{h}$ since

$$e^{-k \ln n} < \frac{1}{2}n^h,$$

for $k, n, h > 1$. $\square$

The previous lemma allows to claim the existence of set S of $z = \frac{2k \ln n}{h} n$ outliers such that a solution for k-center on $X \setminus S$ of value $2r$ is also a solution a good *stochastic solution* for $Y \setminus S$ since $Y \subseteq X$.

Now for a fixed k, we compute a 3-approximation solution [4] with set S of

$$z = \frac{2k \ln n}{h} n$$

outliers on metric space X. The returned solution provides a k-center solution to be used for any randomly chosen subset Y of h points with set of outliers S. Given Lemma 14, this algorithm is a 6 approximation of the expected cost of a k-center for a random subset Y of h randomly chosen points of the metric space. This solution is meaningful as long as as

$$h = \Omega(k \ln n).$$

We therefore conclude with the following:

LEMMA 15. *There exists a 6-approximation algorithm for k-center for fixed k and sample size h that uses at most $z = \frac{2k \ln n}{h} n$ outliers.*

We now extend this solution to a *stochastic hierarchical k-center* problem with outliers for a number of centers in a range $k = 1, \ldots, K$. We take the union of the set of outliers for each value of $k = 1, \ldots, K$. We obtain a total number of outliers equal to

$$\frac{2K(K-1)\ln n}{h} n$$

that is meaningful as long as

$$h = \Omega(K(K-1) \ln n).$$

The algorithm for the *stochastic* variant of hierarchical k-center is as follows:

We run an 8-approximation hierarchical algorithm [8] for the whole metric space after we remove a set of universal outliers of cardinality $\frac{2K(K-1)\ln n}{h} n$ (we remove $z = \frac{2k \ln n}{h} n$ outliers for each k as in the previous algorithm), note that by removing the universal set of outliers we loose at most a factor of 3 in the optimal solution. This algorithm provides a 24-approximation of the optimal solution $\mathrm{OPT}_k^S(X)$ that we know it is at most equal to $2r = 2E_Y[OPT_k(Y)]$ for input set Y of cardinality h. Thus we get the main theorem of this section Theorem 13.

7. REFERENCES

[1] ANAGNOSTOPOULOS, A., GRANDONI, F., LEONARDI, S., AND SANKOWSKI, P. Online network design with outliers. In *Proceedings of the 37th International Colloquium Conference on Automata, Languages and Programming* (Berlin, Heidelberg, 2010), ICALP'10, Springer-Verlag, pp. 114–126.

[2] BALCAN, N., AND GUPTA, P. Robust hierarchical clustering. In *COLT* (2010).

[3] BRYANT, D., AND BERRY, V. A structured family of clustering and tree construction methods. *Advances in Applied Mathematics 27*, 4 (2001), 705 – 732.

[4] CHARIKAR, M., KHULLER, S., MOUNT, D. M., AND NARASIMHAN, G. Algorithms for facility location problems with outliers. In *Proceedings of the Twelfth Annual ACM-SIAM Symposium on Discrete Algorithms* (Philadelphia, PA, USA, 2001), SODA '01, Society for Industrial and Applied Mathematics, pp. 642–651.

[5] CHARIKAR, M., O'CALLAGHAN, L., AND PANIGRAHY, R. Better streaming algorithms for clustering problems. In *Proceedings of the 35th Annual ACM Symposium on Theory of Computing, STOC03* (2003), pp. 30–39.

[6] CHENG, D., KANNAN, R., VEMPALA, S., AND WANG, G. A divide-and-merge methodology for clustering. *ACM Trans. Database Syst. 31*, 4 (Dec. 2006), 1499–1525.

[7] DAS, A., AND KENYON, C. On hierarchical diameter-clustering and the supplier problems. In *In Proc. WAOAÕ06, 4th Workshop on Approximation and Online Algorithms, September 2006* (2006), Springer.

[8] DASGUPTA, S., AND LONG, P. M. Performance guarantees for hierarchical clustering. *Journal of Computer and System Sciences 70*, 4 (2005), 555–569.

[9] GARG, N., GUPTA, A., LEONARDI, S., AND SANKOWSKI, P. Stochastic analyses for online combinatorial optimization problems. In *Proceedings of the Nineteenth Annual ACM-SIAM Symposium on Discrete Algorithms* (Philadelphia, PA, USA, 2008), SODA '08, Society for Industrial and Applied Mathematics, pp. 942–951.

[10] GOLLAPUDI, S., KUMAR, R., AND SIVAKUMAR, D. Programmable clustering. In *Proceedings of the Twenty-fifth ACM SIGMOD-SIGACT-SIGART Symposium on Principles of Database Systems* (New York, NY, USA, 2006), PODS '06, ACM, pp. 348–354.

[11] GONZALEZ, T. F. Clustering to minimize the maximum intercluster distance. *Theoretical Computer Science 38*, 0 (1985), 293 – 306.

[12] GRANDONI, F., GUPTA, A., LEONARDI, S., MIETTINEN, P., SANKOWSKI, P., AND SINGH, M. Set covering with our eyes closed. *SIAM J. Comput. 42*, 3 (2013), 808–830.

[13] GUHA, S., RASTOGI, R., AND SHIM, K. Cure: an efficient clustering algorithm for large databases. In *Proceedings of the 24th Annual ACM SIGMOD* (1998).

[14] HOCHBAUM, D. S., AND SHMOYS, D. B. A best possible heuristic for the k-center problem. *Mathematics of operations research 10*, 2 (1985), 180–184.

[15] JAIN, A., MURTY, M., AND FLYNN, P. Data clustering: a review. *ACM computing surveys* (1999).

[16] JAIN, A. K., AND DUBES, R. C. *Algorithms for Clustering Data.* Prentice-Hall, Inc., Upper Saddle River, NJ, USA, 1988.

[17] JAIN, A. K., MURTY, M. N., AND FLYNN, P. J. Data clustering: A review. *ACM Comput. Surv. 31*, 3 (Sept. 1999), 264–323.

[18] JOHNSON., S. C. Hierarchical clustering schemes. *Psychometrika* (1967).

[19] MCCUTCHEN, R. M., AND KHULLER, S. Streaming algorithms for k-center clustering with outliers and with anonymity. In *Proceedings of the 11th International Workshop on Approximation Algorithms for Combinatorial Optimization Problems (APPROX '2008)* (2008), pp. 165–178.

[20] NARASIMHAN, M., JOJIC, N., AND BILMES, J. Q-clustering. In *Advances in Neural Information Processing Systems (NIPS)* (2006), pp. 348–354.

[21] WARD, J. H. Hierarchical grouping to optimize an objective function. *Journal of the American Statistical Association,* (1963).

[22] WISHART., D. Mode analysis: a generalization of nearest neighbour which reduces chaining effects. *Numerical Taxonomy* (1969).

APPENDIX

A. PROOFS OF SECTION 5

Here we give the proof of Theorem 11, before proving it we restate it:

THEOREM 16. *For every metric space $M = (X, d)$ with $|X| = n$ and $z > 0$ there exists a subset $S \subseteq X$*

- $|S| \leq z^2$,
- *for every $1 \leq k \leq n$, $\mathrm{OPT}_k(X \setminus S) \leq O(1) \cdot \mathrm{OPT}_k^z$.*
- *S can be found in polynomial time*

The proof follows from the same scheme of the techniques of the constructive proof, the main difference is that here we will handle suboptimal solutions and outliers.

PROOF. Let $0 < \alpha \leq 1/360$ be a parameter that we will choose later.

LEMMA 17. *For every t, $\mathrm{OPT}_{k_t}(X \setminus S_t) \leq 30 \cdot \mathrm{OPT}_{k_t}^z$.*

PROOF. By Lemma 5 and the definition of O_{k_t}

$$\mathrm{OPT}_{k_t}(X \setminus S_t) \leq 2(3 \cdot \mathrm{OPT}_{k_t}^z + \max_{u \in X \setminus S_t} d(u, X \setminus O_{k_t})).$$

Thus, it is sufficient to prove that for every $u \in X \setminus S_t$ one has $d(u, X \setminus O_{k_t}) \leq 12 \cdot \mathrm{OPT}_{k_t}^z$. If $u \notin O_{k_t}$, then the required distance is zero. So, we can assume wlog that $u \in O_{k_t} \setminus S_t$. Since $O_{k_t} \subseteq U_t$, u was filtered out in the line 9 of the code. This means that one of the two possibilities holds. The first is that $B(u, 2 \cdot \mathrm{cost}_{k_t}(X \setminus O_{k_t})) \cap X \not\subseteq U_t$, but since $O_{k_t} \subseteq U_t$, we have

$$d(u, X \setminus O_{k_t}) \leq 2 \cdot \mathrm{cost}_{k_t}(X \setminus O_{k_t}) \leq 4 \cdot \mathrm{OPT}_{k_t}(X \setminus O_{k_t}) \leq 12 \cdot \mathrm{OPT}_{k_t}^z.$$

The inequality above follows since $\text{cost}_{k_t}(X \setminus O_{k_t})$ is computed by a 2-approximation k-center algorithm whereas O_{k_t} is computed with a 3-approximation algorithm for k-center with outliers.

The second possibility is that $|B(u, 2 \cdot \text{cost}_{k_t}(X \setminus O_{k_t})) \cap U_t| > z$. But since $|O_{k_t}| \leq z$ it again means that $d(u, X \setminus O_{k_t}) \leq 12 \cdot \text{OPT}^z_{k_t}$. $\square$

LEMMA 18. *For every $t \geq 1$, $\text{OPT}^z_{k_t} < 60\alpha \cdot \text{OPT}^z_{k_{t-1}}$.*

PROOF.

$$
\begin{aligned}
\text{OPT}^z_{k_t} \leq \text{cost}_{k_t}(X \setminus O_{k_t}) \quad &< \quad \alpha \cdot \text{cost}_{k_t}(X \setminus S_{t-1}) \\
&\leq \quad 2\alpha \cdot \text{OPT}_{k_t}(X \setminus S_{t-1}) \\
&\leq \quad 2\alpha \cdot \text{OPT}_{k_{t-1}}(X \setminus S_{t-1}) \\
&\leq \quad 60\alpha \cdot \text{OPT}^z_{k_{t-1}}.
\end{aligned}
$$

The second step is due to the condition in the "for" loop. The last inequality is due to Lemma 17. $\square$

Now we prove that the resulting set S is relatively good for every k.

LEMMA 19. *For every $1 \leq k^* \leq n$*

$$\text{OPT}_{k^*}(X \setminus S) \leq 2163 \cdot \text{OPT}^z_{k^*}.$$

PROOF. Let λ be the largest integer such that $k_\lambda \leq k^*$. Let $\tilde{S} = S_\lambda$.
We prove two lemmas about $\tilde{S}$.

LEMMA 20. $\text{OPT}_{k^*}(X \setminus \tilde{S}) \leq \frac{6}{\alpha} \cdot \text{OPT}^z_{k^*}.$

PROOF. If $k_\lambda < k^*$, then we are done due to the invariant we test in the "for" loop. Indeed,

$$
\begin{aligned}
\text{OPT}_{k^*}(X \setminus \tilde{S}) \quad &\leq \quad \text{cost}_{k^*}(X \setminus \tilde{S}) \leq \frac{1}{\alpha} \cdot \text{cost}_{k^*}(X \setminus O_{k^*}) \\
&\leq \quad \frac{2}{\alpha} \cdot \text{OPT}_{k^*}(X \setminus O_{k^*}) \leq \frac{6}{\alpha} \cdot \text{OPT}^z_{k^*}.
\end{aligned}
$$

If $k_\lambda = k^*$, then by Lemma 17

$$\text{OPT}_{k^*}(X \setminus \tilde{S}) \leq 30 \cdot \text{OPT}^z_{k^*} \leq \frac{6}{\alpha} \cdot \text{OPT}^z_{k^*}.$$

The last inequality is true, because $\alpha < 1/5$. $\square$

LEMMA 21. *For every $u \in X \setminus S$*

$$d(u, X \setminus \tilde{S}) \leq \frac{720}{1 - 60\alpha} \cdot \text{OPT}^z_{k^*}.$$

PROOF. If $u \in X \setminus \tilde{S}$, then the inequality is true. So we can assume that $u \in \tilde{S} \setminus S$. There exists $t > \lambda$ such that $u \in S_{t-1} \setminus S_t$. Let us prove that

$$d(u, X \setminus \tilde{S}) \leq 2 \cdot \sum_{i=\lambda+1}^{t} \text{cost}_{k_i}(X \setminus O_{k_i}). \qquad (4)$$

Let us prove this inequality via induction on t. Since $u \in S_{t-1} \setminus S_t$, there are two possible explanations of this fact. First, it could be that $B(u, 2 \cdot \text{cost}_{k_t}(X \setminus O_{k_t})) \cap X \nsubseteq U_t$. If $B(u, 2 \cdot \text{cost}_{k_t}(X \setminus O_{k_t})) \cap X \nsubseteq \tilde{S}$, then (4) is true. So, we can assume that $B(u, 2 \cdot \text{cost}_{k_t}(X \setminus O_{k_t})) \cap X \subseteq \tilde{S}$. Thus, there exists $u' \in \tilde{S} \setminus S_{t-1}$ such that $d(u, u') \leq 2 \cdot \text{cost}_{k_t}(X \setminus O_{k_t})$. In this case we can invoke the induction hypothesis and the triangle inequality. The second

possibility is that $|B(u, 2 \cdot \text{cost}_{k_t}(X \setminus O_{k_t})) \cap U_t| > z$. Note that since $u \in \tilde{S}$ and thus $|B(u, 2 \cdot \text{cost}_{k_t}(X \setminus O_{k_t})) \cap \tilde{S}| \leq z$. (Note that here we use that $t > \lambda$ and thus by Lemma 18 one has

$$2 \cdot \text{cost}_{k_t}(X \setminus O_{k_t}) < 12 \cdot \text{OPT}^z_{k_t} \leq 720\alpha \text{OPT}^z_{k_\lambda}$$

$$\leq 720\alpha \cdot \text{cost}_{k_\lambda}(X \setminus O_{k_\lambda}) \leq 2 \cdot \text{cost}_{k_\lambda}(X \setminus O_{k_\lambda}),$$

since $\alpha \leq 1/360$. So in this case $d(u, X \setminus \tilde{S}) \leq 2 \cdot \text{cost}_{k_t}(X \setminus O_{k_t})$.
Finally, from (4), Lemma 18 and the fact that $k_{\lambda+1} > k^*$ we get

$$d(u, X \setminus \tilde{S}) \leq 12 \cdot \text{OPT}^z_{k_{\lambda+1}} \cdot \sum_{i=0}^{\infty} (60\alpha)^i \leq \text{OPT}^z_{k_{\lambda+1}} \cdot \frac{12}{1 - 60\alpha}$$

$$\leq \frac{720\alpha}{1 - 60\alpha} \cdot \text{OPT}^z_{k^*}.$$

$\square$

Finally, combining Lemma 5, Lemma 20 and Lemma 21 we get

$$\text{OPT}_{k^*}(X \setminus S) \leq \text{OPT}_{k^*}(X \setminus \tilde{S}) + \max_{u \in X \setminus S} d(u, X \setminus \tilde{S})$$

$$\leq \left(\frac{6}{\alpha} + \frac{720\alpha}{1 - 60\alpha} \right) \cdot OPT^z_{k^*}.$$

We can choose $\alpha = 1/360$ to get a 2163-approximation.
Finally we prove that S is relatively small.

LEMMA 22. *For the resulting set S one has $|S| \leq z^2$.*

PROOF. We prove that if for every t the size of S_t is at most z^2.
Consider a k-center clustering of $X \setminus O_{k_t}$ with all the clusters having radii at most $\text{cost}_{k_t}(X \setminus O_{k_t})$. Consider all the clusters that consist of points from S_{t-1} exclusively and have cardinality at most z. Clearly, there are less than z such clusters. Indeed, otherwise we could upper bound

$$\text{OPT}_{k_t}(X \setminus S_{t-1}) \leq \text{cost}_{k_t}(X \setminus O_{k_t})$$

by removing these clusters and attaching points from $O_{k_t} \setminus S_{t-1}$ as singletons. But since

$$\text{OPT}_{k_t}(X \setminus S_{t-1}) \geq \frac{1}{2} \cdot \text{cost}_{k_t}(X \setminus S_{t-1}),$$

we would get

$$\text{cost}_{k_t}(X \setminus O_{k_t}) \geq \frac{1}{2} \cdot \text{cost}_{k_t}(X \setminus S_{t-1}),$$

which contradicts the invariant

$$\text{cost}_{k_t}(X \setminus O_{k_t}) < \alpha \cdot \text{cost}_{k_t}(X \setminus S_{t-1})$$

(here we use that $\alpha \leq 1/2$). So, in total there are at most $(z - 1)z$ points in all these clusters. Moreover, all the points from S_{t-1} outside these clusters are filtered from S_t.
Thus, overall the total size of S_t is at most z^2. $\square$

The Computational Benefit of Correlated Instances

Irit Dinur[*]
Weizmann Institute of Science
Rehovot, Israel
irit.dinur@weizmann.ac.il

Shafi Goldwasser[†]
MIT
Boston, USA
Weizmann Institute of Science
Rehovot, Israel
shafi@theory.csail.mit.edu

Huijia Lin
UCSB
Santa Barbara, USA
rachel.lin@cs.ucsb.edu

ABSTRACT

The starting point of this paper is that instances of computational problems often do not exist in isolation. Rather, multiple and correlated instances of the same problem arise naturally in the real world. The *challenge* is how to gain computationally from instance correlations when they exist. We will be interested in settings where significant computational gain can be made in solving a single primary instance by having access to additional auxiliary instances which are correlated to the primary instance via the solution space.

We focus on Constraint Satisfaction Problems (CSPs), a very expressive class of computational problems that is well-studied both in terms of approximation algorithms and NP-hardness and in terms of average case hardness and usage for cryptography, e.g. Feige's random 3-SAT hypothesis, Goldreich's one way function proposal, learning-parity-with-noise, and others.

To model correlations between instances, we consider *generating processes* over search problems, where a primary instance I is first selected according to some distribution D (e.g. worst case, uniform, etc); then auxiliary instances $I_1, ..., I_T$ are generated so that their underlying solutions $S_1, ..., S_T$ each are a "perturbation" of a primary solution S for I. For example, S_t may be obtained by the probabilistic process of flipping each bit of S with a small constant probability.

We consider a variety of naturally occurring worst case and average case CSPs, and show how availability of a small number of auxiliary instances generated through a natural generating process, radically changes the complexity of solving the primary instance, from intractable to expected polynomial time. Indeed, at a high-level, knowing a logarithmic number of auxiliary instances enables a close polynomial time approximation of the primary solution, and when in addition the "difference vector" between the primary and the auxiliary solution is known, the primary solution can be exactly found. Furthermore, knowing even a single auxiliary instance already enables finding the exact primary solution for a large class of CSPs.

Categories and Subject Descriptors

F.2.0 [**Theory of computation**]: Analysis of algorithms and problem complexity—*General*

General Terms

Theory

Keywords

Correlated instances; Constraint satisfaction problem; Complexity

1. INTRODUCTION

The integer factorization problem has fascinated mathematicians for centuries and computer scientists for decades. It has helped us illucidate some of the key concepts at the heart of the theory of computation, providing arguably the most elegant example of an NP problem which is hard to solve but easy to verify by grade school mathematics, the basis for the first public key encryption scheme, and the impetus for much of modern day research into the power of quantum over classical computation.

Recently, [34] pointed out a simple but pervasive problem with using integer factorization as a basis for public-key cryptography. Many composite and hard to factor numbers used in practice, are obtained by first generating their prime divisors using the outputs of weak pseudo random number generators with correlated seeds. As a result, one can obtain *multiple instances* of composite numbers with correlated prime divisors, which render the composite number instances trivial to factor. At the extreme, two instances $n = pq$ and $n' = pq'$ share a prime factor. It is trivial to then factor n and n' by computing their greatest common divisor.

This example of problem instances which are hard when they stand alone, but are easy when given correlated instances, may seem anecdotal. Our thesis is that the situation may be quite to the contrary. Instances of computational problems with correlated solutions seem to arise naturally in many scenarios. *The challenge is not to find settings which present correlated instances, but how to take advantage of correlations when they exist.*

[*]Irit Dinur's research is supported by ERC-Stg grant number 239985.
[†]Shafi Goldwasser's reseach is supported by NSF CNS-1347364, Simons Investigator Award, FA8750-11-2-0225.

To mention a few "real world" examples. In biology, the problem of learning the mapping from DNA (genotype) to the observable characteristics (phenotype) of an organism, draws on data from multiple specimens with highly correlated DNA providing multiple correlated inputs. In coding theory, the objective is to recover from as many possible errors as possible: to this end, one may well take advantage of the fact that a typical hard-drive contains error-correcting encodings of multiple files that are within small edit-distance from each other. In learning theory, one well-studied goal is to classify future examples from known examples of a hidden concept class. It is likely, that many concepts to be learned are correlated, and access to examples from correlated concepts can reduce the number of examples necessary to learn any one of them.

In this paper, we focus on the complexity of constraint satisfaction problems (CSPs) with access to multiple instances with correlated solutions. The class of constraint satisfaction problems is a very rich and well-studied class of computational problems. This class includes many NP-hard problems (such as 3SAT, max-cut, 3-coloring) whose precise approximation behavior has been extensively studied. It is also believed that random instances of CSPs (under an appropriately defined distribution) are hard and this has been the content of several influential conjectures including Goldreich's one way function proposal [31], Feige's random 3SAT hypothesis [27], learning parity with noise hypothesis [37, 20, 1], and various extensions and follow up works e.g. [4, 10, 24]. We show that in various settings, hard CSP instances become easy when correlated instances are available.

We view this work as a first step in a wider study of how to exploit correlations in available inputs.

Correlation. To model correlation between problem instances, we think of a *generating process* over search problems: In the process, a primary instance I (e.g., a CSP instance) with an underlying hidden solution S (e.g., an assignment satisfying all constraints) is selected according to some distribution Pri (e.g. worst case, uniform, etc.). Next, some auxiliary instances $\{I_1, I_2, \ldots\}$ are selected according to another distribution $\mathsf{Aux}(I, S)$ depending on the primary instance I and solution S. The algorithmic goal is to recover a solution $\tilde{S}$ to the primary instance I, given additionally the collection of auxiliary instances (but not their solutions).

What types of correlation between instances are interesting to study? We first observe that if the auxiliary instances can be sampled efficiently given the primary instance but not the solution (that is, $I_j \xleftarrow{\$} \mathsf{Aux}(I)$ can be sampled efficiently); then access to such auxiliary instances can at most lead to a polynomial-time speedup. In this work, we are interested in qualitative computational gains so we naturally consider correlation based also on the *solution* of the primary instance. Two natural and interesting models are the *randomly-perturbed-solution model* and the *known-differences model*. Below we explain the two models in the context of CSP.

CSPs. Formally, a constraint satisfaction problem (CSP) is parameterized by a predicate $P : \{0,1\}^d \to \{0,1\}$, and a density parameter $D \geq 1$. An instance of this problem on n input variables $x = x_1, \ldots x_n$ is a set of $m = nD$ constraints specified by a bi-partite graph $G = ([n], [m], E)$ and a string $y \in \{0,1\}^m$. The graph connects each "output vertex" y_k (for $k = 1, \ldots, m$) to d "input vertices" which we index by $G(k,1), G(k,2), \ldots, G(k,d)$. Each output vertex specifies an equation constraint on the input variables: $\forall k \in [m]$, $P(x_{G(k,1)}, \ldots, x_{G(k,d)}) = y_k$. Given a CSP instance, represented succinctly as a pair (G, y), the goal is to find a solution, i.e., an assignment $\tilde{x}$ maximizing the fraction of satisfied constraints. Throughout this paper, we focus on CSPs whose solution satisfies all of the constraints.

This definition of a CSP is "functional" in the sense that the graph G and the predicate P together define a function mapping inputs x to outputs y, such that the CSP problem is to invert this function on a given output string y. This differs from the more standard definition of a P-CSP (for example think of 3-SAT) where the instance is a collection of d-tuples of variables on which the predicate P should evaluate always to *true*. The advantage in our functional definition is that it allows efficient sampling of a pair of instance and solution while at the time remaining to be (conjectured) hard. In contrast, sampling satisfiable 3-SAT formulae, for example, is a process that is notoriously hard to analyze[1].

Correlated CSPs. In the randomly-perturbed-solution model, the underlying solutions of the auxiliary instances are "random perturbations" of the primary solution. In the context of CSP, in addition to a primary instance (G, y), multiple *auxiliary* instances $(G^1, y^1), \ldots (G^T, y^T)$ correlated with (G, y) are generated according to the following process $Gen_{\mathsf{Pri},\mathsf{Aux}}$:

On input n, T, ε where N is the length of the primary instance, T the number of auxiliary instances, and $\varepsilon \in (0, 1/2]$ the perturbation parameter, do:

1. Choose a primary instance and solution (G, y, x) from the distribution Pri.

2. Perturb the solution: For each $t = 1, 2, \ldots, T$, let x^t be an ε-noisy copy of x derived by flipping each bit of x with probability ε independently.

3. Choose T auxiliary instances: For each $t = 1, 2, \ldots, T$, choose an instance (G, y^t) from the distribution $\mathsf{Aux}(x^t)$ of instances with solution x^t.

Output $(G, y), (G, y^1), (G, y^2), \ldots, (G, y^T)$.

Observe that in our model all instances have the exact same G. The distributions Pri and $\mathsf{Aux}(x^t)$ specify how the primary instance and auxiliary instance with solution x_t are chosen in Step 1 and 3. Naturally, different instantiations of these distributions lead to different variants of the randomly-perturbed-solution model. For instance, Pri could be choosing a worst-case CSP instance or a random one, leading to the question of solving worst-case or random CSP, given

---

[1]There are two average case distributions for satisfiable SAT formulae that are studied in the literature: "conditional" and "planted". In the "conditional" distribution one samples a random k-SAT formula with given number of clauses and variables, conditioned on it being satisfiable. In the "planted" distribution one chooses a random solution, and then samples satisfied clauses independently at random. The conditional distribution is notoriously hard to analyze, so instead significant effort has been devoted to the planted distribution, resulting in polynomial time algorithms for example for finding a solution in a 3-SAT instance with large enough constant clause-to-variable ratio [29]. This means that even without correlated inputs, the problem is easy; and this directs our efforts elsewhere.

auxiliary instances[2]. The algorithmic goal is to recover a solution $\tilde{x}$ for (G, y), given $(G, y), (G, y^1), (G, y^2), \ldots, (G, y^T)$.

A tampering-oriented model of correlated instances would allow the algorithm itself to control the perturbation process (by algorithm we always mean the algorithm whose goal is to recover a solution to the primary instance (G, y)). This however may give undue power to the algorithm designer, and make results less interesting. We instead consider a second model which can be considered as an intermediate model between tampering and the randomly-perturbed-solution model above. In this model the perturbation is still performed randomly, but the algorithm is given, in addition to the auxiliary instance, the exact coordinates in which bits were flipped although not the values of the bits. Formally, the algorithm is given $\{(G, y_t)\}_t$ and $\{\Delta_t = x_t \oplus x\}_t$ generated by $Gen_{\text{Pri,Aux}}$. The algorithmic task is easier in this model compared to the randomly-perturbed-solution model and harder than the tampering model. This model turns out to be technically interesting and useful because it pinpoints an intermediate step in a natural class of algorithms that search for a solution $\tilde{x}$ by first trying to estimate the difference $\Delta_t = x \oplus x_t$ for each t.

Organization. Next we proceed to describe our main results on using correlated instances in the CSP domain in Section 2. We describe our techniques in Section 3. Section 4 contains additional results: showing how access to examples of correlated learning with parity (LPN) instances can speed up algorithms solving the underlying LPN, showing some limits on the benefit of correlated instances, showing the need for some "diversity" as well as correlation, and a proposal of a general complexity measure for algorithms which have access to auxiliary instances correlated via the solution space; Section 4 also offers some discussion and interpretation of our work. Due to the lack of space, our results and techniques are stated informally, we refer the reader to the full version [25] for formal description of our theorems, algorithms, and proofs.

2. MAIN RESULTS

Our main results are algorithms for solving CSP instances that come from widely-believed hard-to-solve distributions, given a number of correlated instances. Our results suggest that significant computational gains can be made when we can find multiple instances of search problems whose solutions are highly correlated *but not identical* – diversity pays off. The phenomenon of turning problems from intractable to efficiently solvable, goes way beyond exploiting coincidental algebraic structure to a wide setting of correlations in the realm of combinatorial problems.

We have different results for solving correlated instances of CSPs when the primary instance is a worst case instance and when it is an average case instance. In both cases, we focus our attention to CSP instances that are fully satisfiable. [3]

The average case distribution is based on a proposed one way function of Goldreich [31]:

Random CSP distribution rCSP: *Select at random a right-d-regular bipartite graph* $G = ([n], [m], E)$, $m = Dn$, *and an input string* $x \in \{0, 1\}^n$, *and compute* y *according to the mapping* $f_{G,P}(x) = P \circ G(x)$ *that computes each output bit by* $y_k = P(x_{G(k,1)}, \ldots, x_{G(k,d)})$ *for* $k \in [m]$. *Pictorially, we place the bits of* x *as labels to the input vertexes* $[n]$, *and then compute each output bit* $k \in [m]$ *of* $P \circ G(x)$ *by applying the predicate* P *to the substring obtained from the labels of its* d *neighbors.*

This is a natural distribution on pairs of CSP instance and solution (where the solution satisfies all of the clauses) We point to an ongoing line of work studying average case CSPs as well as their approximate version, either conjecturing their hardness [27, 1, 4, 3, 10], or studying various aspects of these problems [21, 3, 38, 23, 21]. In particular, Goldreich [31] conjectured that for some predicates P, it is hard to invert the image $f_{G,P}(x)$ with any non-negligible probability for a randomly chosen graph G and input x, and for $D = 1$. Subsequent works [21, 23] also considered this construction for larger values of D.

The generating process we consider, $Gen_{\text{Pri,Aux}}$, samples (G, y) from a primary distribution Pri which will either be some arbitrary worst-case distribution over satisfiable instances, or the average-case distribution rCSP. The generating process then generates each auxiliary instance (G, y^t) by perturbing x to obtain x^t, and then setting $y_t = \text{Aux}(x_t) = G \circ P(x_t)$.

Algorithms using *many* correlated instances Our first result is that for a primary instance drawn at random, and for a large enough number of correlated instances $T = O(\log n)$, there is a randomized polynomial time algorithm that recovers a solution that satisfies $1 - \delta$ fraction of the constraints in an *average-case* primary instance, for arbitrarily small $\delta > 0$.

Informal Theorem 1 - random CSP *Fix any non-constant predicate* $P : \{0, 1\}^d \to \{0, 1\}$ *and constant* $\delta > 0$. *For small enough constant* $\varepsilon = \varepsilon(d) > 0$ *and large enough* $D = D(d, \varepsilon, \delta)$ *there is some* $T = O(\log n)$ *such that the following holds. There is a polynomial time algorithm that on input* $(G, y), (G, y^1), \cdots, (G, y^t)$ *finds a string* $\tilde{x}$ *that satisfies at least* $1 - \delta$ *fraction of the constraints in* (G, y), *with probability* $1 - O(1/n)$. *The instances* $G, y, y^1, \cdots y^T$ *are generated at random by the process* $Gen_{\text{Pri,Aux}}(n, T, \varepsilon)$ *with* Pri = rCSP *and* Aux = $P \circ G$ *(this notation means that* Aux *perturbs the solution* x *to get* x^t *and then applies* $G \circ P$ *on* x^t*).* [4]

Note that besides having sufficiently many correlated instances, the algorithm also requires the correlation between instances to be sufficiently high (that is, ε is sufficiently small), and the density D of the instances to be sufficiently large.

We next show that knowing the differences $\{\Delta_t = x_t \oplus x\}_{t=1,\ldots,T}$ between the hidden solutions of the primary and auxiliary instances grants the algorithm surprising power. It allows the algorithm to find an exact solution to any *worst-case* primary instance (with high probability over the random coins for generating the auxiliary instances). Moreover,

---

[2]We also remark that in the above model each auxiliary instance for $t = 1, \ldots, T$ is generated independently of the others. Other models may allow different dependency structures, e.g. the t-th instance may "evolve" by perturbation of the $t - 1$-st instance.

[3]The advantage of working with CSP instances that are 100% satisfiable is that it makes it easier to reason about how perturbation on the optimal solution affects the constraints. Studying CSP instances that are only, say 99%, satisfiable is an interesting open question.

---

[4]In fact, the algorithm additionally finds such an $(1 - \delta)$-approximate solution for each auxiliary instance.

the algorithm works with *arbitrary* correlation parameter $0 < \varepsilon < 1/2$ and density $D \geq 1$, as long as the number of auxiliary instances T is sufficiently large, but still logarithmic. Needless to say, without auxiliary correlated instances this problem is NP-hard even to approximate, due to the PCP theorem [8, 7].

Informal Theorem 2 - worst case CSP, known differences *For every $\varepsilon \in (0, 1/2)$, there is a polynomial time algorithm, such that for every predicate P, density $D \geq 1$, graph G, $y = P \circ G(x)$, and constant $r > 0$, the algorithm on input $(G, y, y_1, \cdots, y_T, \Delta_1, \cdots, \Delta_T)$ finds a solution $\tilde{x}$ for (G, y) with probability $1 - O(n^{-r})$, provided that $T = O(\log n)$ is a sufficiently large multiple of $\log n$. All instances are generated by the process $\mathrm{Gen}_{\mathrm{Pri},\mathrm{Aux}}(n, T, \varepsilon)$ with Pri is fixed to output (G, y) and $\mathrm{Aux} = P \circ G$ and where $\Delta_t = x_t \oplus x$ for each t.*

The algorithm in Theorem 2 can be easily extended to inverting arbitrary computation $y = f(x)$ in $\mathcal{NC}^0$ given a logarithmic number of correlated instances (i.e. images $y^1, \ldots, y^t$) and the differences between hidden solutions (or pre-images). The intuition behind this is that finding a pre-image of y with respect to f is equivalent to solving CSPs with a more general form where every constraint is with respect to a possibly different predicate. More generally, we show an algorithm that inverts any function f with low output locality $d = O(\log n)$ in the "worst case", if a sufficiently large number $T = O(\varepsilon^{-d} \log n)$ of auxiliary instances and the difference between their hidden solutions are available. The algorithm runs in $\mathrm{poly}(2^d n)$ steps. From the perspective of tampering, this result states that every function with low output locality, in particular Goldreich's OWF, is easy to invert under a very weak model of tampering; we refer the reader to Section 5 for a comparison with cryptographic tampering results.

Interestingly, the limitation of $d \leq O(\log n)$ is optimal. Our next result shows that there is no algorithm that solves worst case instances with larger arity, even with access to correlated instances, unless $NP \subseteq BPP$.

Claim 1 - NP-hardness of solving worst case CSP with arity $d = \Omega(\log n)$, known differences *There is a predicate P with arity $O(\log n)$ such that unless $NP \subseteq BPP$, there is no probabilistic polynomial time algorithm for solving the P-CSP problem when given an additional correlated instance.*

The proof of the lemma is simple. Take an NP-hard CSP, and replace each Boolean variable by a cloud of $c \log n$ new variables. Replace each predicate by a new one that reads all $d \cdot c \log n$ variables encoding the original d variables, and that accepts if the majority decoding of each cloud would have satisfied the original predicate. One can see that any solution x_0 for the original CSP gives rise to a solution x to the new CSP, in which the value of all members of a cloud is the same. A perturbation x' of this solution would, with probability $1 - 1/\mathrm{poly}(n)$ yield the exact same y, i.e. with high probability $P \circ G(x') = P \circ G(x)$. Thus, under our randomly-perturbed-solution correlation model, the correlated instance (G, y') will be identical to the primary instance (G, y) with probability $1/\mathrm{poly}(n)$, in which case, it does not help to receive the correlated instance and the difference between the hidden solutions x' and x. This holds with high probability $1 - 1/\mathrm{poly}(n)$, even when $O(\log n)$ auxiliary instances are available.

This lemma demonstrates an interesting threshold of $\log n$ in the arity of computations for which correlation is helpful.

Algorithms using *a single* auxiliary correlated instance The previous two theorems demonstrate the power of having many correlated auxiliary instances. The next natural question that arises is "does correlation help when only a few auxiliary instances are available?" Our next two results investigate this case, and show that when the primary instance is drawn from the random CSP distribution, then the availability of even *one more* auxiliary instance, already gives a non-trivial computational advantage, albeit only for a *subclass of predicates*. These results extend previous work by Bogdanov and Qiao [21] who showed that in the random CSP distribution certain classes of predicates can be solved or approximated (even with no auxiliary correlated instances, and when the density is sufficiently high). Our results show that the class of solvable predicates grows with the addition of an auxiliary correlated instance.

Again we separate two cases, depending on whether we know the difference $\Delta = x' \oplus x$ between the primary solution x and the perturbed solution x'. Our results are based on *derivatives* of the predicate P. The derivative in direction σ is defined by $P^\sigma(a) := P(a) + P(a + \sigma)$. We limit ourselves to CSPs with predicates that come from the class $\mathcal{P}$ of predicates $P : \{0, 1\}^d \rightarrow \{0, 1\}$ for which there is some direction σ, and index $i^* \in [d]$ for which P^σ is γ-correlated with its i^*-th input bit (i.e., the output of the derivative $P^\sigma(a)$ equals to a_{i^*} with probability at least $1/2 + \gamma$ for a random a).

We show that for this class $\mathcal{P}$ of special predicates, a random CSP instance becomes easy to solve, given only a single auxiliary instance and the difference (between the two solutions). Interestingly, this algorithm requires the hidden solutions to be either sufficiently correlated, or sufficiently *anti-correlated*, depending on the predicate under consideration. More specifically, for a special predicate P satisfying the above condition w.r.t. direction σ and index i^*, if $\sigma_{i^*} = 0$, the perturbation flipping probability $p^* = \varepsilon$ must be sufficiently small, and otherwise the flipping probability $p^* = 1 - \varepsilon$ must be sufficiently large.

Informal Theorem 3 - random CSP, with a single auxiliary instance and known difference *Let $P \in \mathcal{P}$ be as above with parameters σ, i^*, and γ. For any $\varepsilon \in (0, 1/2)$, let the flipping probability p^* be set to ε if $\sigma_{i^*} = 0$, and $1 - \varepsilon$ otherwise.*

Assume that ε is sufficiently small, and D is sufficiently large. For every constant $r \geq 1$, there is a polynomial time algorithm $\mathcal{A}$ that on input $(G, y, y^1\Delta)$ finds a solution $\tilde{x}$ for (G, y) with probability $1 - O(n^{-r})$. All variables are generated by the process $\mathrm{Gen}_{\mathrm{Pri},\mathrm{Aux}}(n, 1)$ with $\mathrm{Pri} = \mathrm{rCSP}$ and $\mathrm{Aux} = P \circ G$ with perturbation parameter p^* and $\Delta = x^1 \oplus x$.

Furthermore, we show that even when the difference is not given, correlation still helps to solve random CSP with the above special predicates of the case $\sigma_{i^*} = 0$. In this case, the algorithm simply requires the correlation between the hidden solutions to be sufficiently large.

Informal Theorem 4 - random CSP, with a single auxiliary instance *Let P be a special predicate as defined above with parameters σ, i^*, and γ, **and** $\sigma_{i^*} = 0$. Assume that ε is sufficiently small, and D is sufficiently large. For every constant $r \geq 1$, there is a polynomial time algorithm $\mathcal{A}'$ that on input (G, y, y^1) finds a solution $\tilde{x}$ for (G, y) with* probability $1 - O(n^{-r})$. *All variables are generated by the process* $Gen_{\mathsf{Pri},\mathsf{Aux}}(n,1)$ *with* $\mathsf{Pri} = \mathsf{rCSP}$ *and* $\mathsf{Aux} = P \circ G$ *and with perturbation parameter* ε.

Algorithms for well-known "hard-by-design" instances, using a single additional correlated instance The gain from one more auxiliary correlated instance is not limited only to solving random CSP instances. We next show two algorithms for solving well-known families of CSP instances, with the aid of a single auxiliary correlated instance. Our first result solves a family of NP-hard 3SAT instances generated by Håstad's PCP reduction [33]. These instances are the hardest known instances in terms of approximation, yet, they become easy in the presence of correlation.

Informal Theorem 5 - Håstad's 3SAT instances, with a single auxiliary instance *Let* $L \in NP$ *and let* $\delta, \varepsilon > 0$. *There is a polynomial time reduction* H *(due to Håstad) mapping instances of* L *to instances of 3SAT such that given a yes instance* $\varphi \in$ 3SAT *it is NP-hard to find an assignment* x *satisfying more than* $\frac{7}{8} + \delta$ *fraction of the clauses of* φ. *Nevertheless, given also an auxiliary correlated instance* $\varphi' \in$ 3SAT *there is a polynomial time algorithm that finds an assignment satisfying 99% of the clauses in* φ *with high probability over the choice of* φ'. *The correlated instance* φ' *is generated as follows*

1. *Let* $x \in \{0,1\}^n$ *be a satisfying assignment for* φ. *Flip each bit of* x *independently with probability* ε, *obtaining* x'.

2. *Let* φ' *be the 3SAT formula obtained by deleting from* φ *all of the clauses that are unsatisfied by the assignment* x'.

Our focus on 3SAT is for explicitness only. Similar results probably hold for other predicates.

Our second result inverts randomized encodings of [6]. The notion of randomized encodings allows to "encode" a complex deterministic function f by a simple randomized function $\hat{f}$. From the output of the randomized encoding $\hat{f}(x;r)$ one can reconstruct the output of $f(x)$, and at the same time no other information of x is revealed; the latter is called the privacy property. Applebaum, Ishai, and Kushilevitz [6] showed in a celebrated work how to represent any $\mathcal{NC}^1$ computable function by an $\mathcal{NC}^0$ function with output locality 4, denoted by $\mathcal{NC}^0_4$. This encoding is referred to as the AIK randomized encoding henceforth. By the privacy property, images $\hat{f}(x;r)$ of AIK encodings are hard to invert on the average over the random choices of r, as long as the original function image $f(x)$ is hard to invert.

AIK thus constructs cryptographic primitives such as stream-ciphers and commitment-schemes which have low depth and constant output locality yet are still hard to invert. (See the survey by Applebaum [2] for more details.)

If we view both x and r as the input variables to the encoded function $\hat{f}$, then inverting $y = \hat{f}(x;r)$ corresponds exactly to solving a CSP instance, where every output bit is a constraint over 4 input bits that belong to x or r. The randomly-perturbed-solution model for CSP naturally extends to this setting, where the generating process $Gen_{\mathsf{Pri},\mathsf{Aux}}$ samples a primary instance $(\hat{f}, y = \hat{f}(x;r))$ together with many auxiliary instances $(\hat{f}, y^t = \hat{f}(x^t;r^t))$ with (x^t, r^t) perturbed from (x,r) by flipping each bit independently with

probability ε. The algorithmic goal is still to invert the image $f(x)$ of the original function.

We show that if the original function f is "well formed" (see full version [25] for a precise definition, we mention only that any function can easily be modified to possess this property) then, its encoding is easy to invert in the worst-case when given a single auxiliary instance $y^1 = \hat{f}(x^1; r^1)$

Informal Theorem 6 - AIK randomized encodings, with a single auxiliary instance *For every function* f *in* $\mathcal{NC}^1$, *let* $\hat{f}$ *be the AIK randomized encoding of* f. *Fix any* $\varepsilon \in (0, 1/2)$ *and any constant* $\alpha > 0$. *There is a polynomial time algorithm, such that, for every* well-formed *function* f, *string* x, *and sufficiently long* r, *the algorithm on input* $(\hat{f}, y, y^1)$ *inverts* $f(x)$ *with probability* $1 - n^{-\alpha}$, *where all variables are generated by the process* $Gen_{\mathsf{Pri},\mathsf{Aux}}(n,1)$ *with* Pri *fixed to output* $(\hat{f}, y = \hat{f}(x;r))$ *and* $\mathsf{Aux} = \hat{f}$.

We compare this result with Theorem 3 and 4 for solving random CSPs with a single auxiliary instance. There, the predicate under consideration comes from a special class, but the CSP graph is chosen at random with the only constraint that it must have high density. Here, given the original function f, the AIK encoding scheme determines the set of predicates and the graph based on f; in particular, the graph is not random and does not have high density. Therefore, Theorem 5 can be view as another demonstration that even a single correlated instance helps solving special classes of CSPs.

To summarize, these results demonstrate that access to several correlated instances gives significant more algorithmic power than considering one instance alone, and it can turn a conjectured intractable problem into a provably tractable one.

3. TECHNIQUES

We next describe the high-level techniques that we have used for the results outlined above.

The shift encoding. We start with the easiest algorithmic setting, where to solve a primary instance G, y, the algorithm is given multiple auxiliary instances $(G, y^1, \cdots, y^T)$ *and* the differences $(\Delta^1, \cdots, \Delta^T)$ where $\Delta^t = x \oplus x^t$ is the difference between the primary solution x and the perturbed solution x^t. In this setting, we are able to recover x completely even if the primary instance is a worst case instance, and for any correlation $\varepsilon \in (0, 1/2)$ and density $D \geq 1$.

The key observation is that given sufficiently many correlated instances, a fixed output vertex $k \in [m]$ will eventually see all perturbation patterns: Its value in the tth instance is equal to $y_k^t = P(x_{G(k)}^t) = P(x_{G(k)} \oplus \Delta_{G(k)}^t)$, where we denote by $x_{G(k)}$ the restriction of x to the d indexes neighboring k. For every instance t, the difference $\Delta_{G(k)}^t$ (restricted to the neighbors of k) is a d-bit string, where every bit $\Delta_{G(k,l)}^t$ is independently Bernoulli distributed with probability ε of being 1. Given sufficiently many auxiliary instances, every possible "shift" $a \in \{0,1\}^d$ will appear (i.e., for every $a \in \{0,1\}^d$, $\exists t$ s.t. $\Delta_{G(k)}^t = a$). Since the differences $\{\Delta_{G(k)}^t\}$ are known, the algorithm can collect the values of P on every possible shift a from $x_{G(k)}$, which form an encoding of $x_{G(k)}$; we call it the *shift-P-encoding* of $x_{G(k)}$.

More specifically, let

$$\text{Encode}(z) \triangleq (P(z \oplus a))_{a \in \{0,1\}^d}$$
$$\triangleq P(z \oplus \underbrace{0 \cdots 0}_{d}), P(z \oplus \underbrace{0 \cdots 0}_{d-1} 1) \cdots, P(z \oplus \underbrace{1 \cdots 1}_{d})$$

Given the shift-P-encoding $\text{Encode}(x_{G(k)})$, if the predicate P satisfies that the encoding for every $z \in \{0,1\}^d$ is unique, then we can uniquely recover $x_{G(k)}$. (This can be done efficiently, since the encoding has constant size 2^d.) Then using the same procedure for every output bit k, the algorithm uncovers the unique value of $x_{G(k)}$ for every k. By stitching them together, it obtains the unique string x consistent with y as well as all $\{\Delta^t\}_t$ and $\{y^t\}_t$.

Does this approach handle all predicates? No, there are predicates P for which the shift P encoding is not unique. The next challenge is *how to go beyond predicates that admit unique shift encoding and handle all non-constant predicates.* The difficulty lies in that for a general predicate P, there may exist different strings $z \neq z'$ that have the same encoding $\text{Encode}(z) = \text{Encode}(z')$. Then, from the encoding $\text{Encode}(x_{G(k)})$, the algorithm can only deduce that there are multiple candidates for the value of $x_{G(k)}$. However, given a collection of candidates for all sub-strings $\{x_{G(k)}\}$, it is not clear how to find a single string $\tilde{x}$ that simultaneously satisfies all constraints on all sub-strings $\{x_{G(k)}\}$.

We overcome this problem by showing that given a valid encoding E (for which there exists a pre-image), all the pre-images of E form a unique affine space Λ. Then, given encoding $\text{Encode}(x_{G(k)})$, the constraints on $x_{G(k)}$—that is, $\{P(x_{G(k)} \oplus \Delta_{G(k)}^t) = y_k^t\}_t$—are equivalent to a set of linear constraints on $x_{G(k)}$, that is, $x_{G(k)} \in \Lambda$. Now, given the collection of linear constraints for all k, the algorithm can solve the linear system efficiently to recover a string $\tilde{x}$ consistent with all constraints. These are the main ingredients in the proof of Theorem 2.

Estimating the differences, and then estimating the estimation error. For Theorem 1, we adapt the algorithm above to the case where the differences Δ^t are not given. Here the natural approach is to *estimate* the differences, and obtain $\tilde{\Delta}^1, \ldots, \tilde{\Delta}^T$ such that $\tilde{\Delta}^t \approx \Delta^t$ for $t = 1, \ldots, T$. The estimation is possible because by knowing which output bits have flipped we get a reasonable guess as to which input bits have flipped. The smaller the arity d, and the higher the density D, the better this estimate is.

However, replacing Δ^t by $\tilde{\Delta}^t$ is reasonable only if our algorithm above is resilient to the noise introduced by the approximation. This does not hold, unfortunately, because the second step of the algorithm relies on solving linear equations, a procedure that is infamously non-robust to noise. Nevertheless, we overcome this problem by taking advantage of the fact that our primary instance comes from the random CSP distribution. We add an estimate-verification step that marks the indices $i \in [n]$ that suffered from unbounded estimation errors (informally, this refers to the case where errors in the i-th bit occur for Δ^t across too many t's). Then, we prove that this verification procedure will, with very high probability, not make mistakes, assuming that the primary instance is drawn from the random CSP distribution. Finally, by avoiding these problematic indices we can correctly recover most of the solution.

Directional derivatives. In case only a single auxiliary correlated instance is available, we cannot expect to learn the shift-encoding of any substring of x. Instead, we observe that by getting an evaluation, for each $k \in [m]$, of $P(x_{G(k)})$ and $P(x'_{G(k)}) = P(x_{G(k)} + \Delta_{G(k)})$, we can directly compute $P^\sigma(x_{G(k)})$ for $\sigma = \Delta_{G(k)}$. The extra information provided by P^σ allows us, in Theorems 3 and 4, to solve a broader class of CSPs. We rely on the randomness of the primary instance to ensure that our difference estimation is correct, without which the derivatives will be useless.

Solving NP-hard instances using the structure of the solution space. In Theorem 5 we solve instances that come from PCP reductions, with the help of an extra correlated instance. Here the given primary instance is not random and so difference estimation as in the previous results will not necessarily work. Our approach is to rely on the fact that the satisfying assignment, if it exists, is highly structured. In particular, the variables are partitioned into constant-size blocks (corresponding to long code encodings) and on each block there is only a small number of possible assignments. It is feasible to enumerate all possible legal assignments on a pair of blocks and to check if they are likely to give rise to a given difference pattern. We prove that this works by analyzing the precise long code test and showing that certain difference patterns are more likely for certain assignments than for others.

Inverting AIK randomized encoding by cascading from many break points. In Theorem 5, we invert the AIK randomized encoding given a single auxiliary instance. The first step of the inverting algorithm is similar to the algorithms for solving CSP: By crucially relying on the low output-locality feature of AIK, it recovers some "local" information about the hidden solution. (In the case of CSP, the local information pieces pertain to the substrings $\{x_{G(k)}\}$; similarly, in AIK, these local information pieces are about subsets of bits in x and/or r influencing different output bits.) However, unlike the case of CSP, these local information pieces are not sufficient for generating the global solution. The graph corresponding to the AIK encoding is not random and its density is very low, so this first step can only recover an ε fraction of the solution. In remedy, the algorithm in a second phase, relying on the concrete structure of the AIK encoding, uses the partial information as *break points* for starting many iterative *cascading steps*. In each step given the appropriate information associated with one input bit, the value and associated information of the input bit "next to" it are found; thus, the information recovered propagates, until the whole input is found.

The concrete procedure for recovering the initial local information and cascading information requires heavy engineering on the specifics of the AIK encoding. Nevertheless, the overall structure of the inverting algorithm is the key and demonstrates that the ways to leverage correlation can vary from problem to problem.

4. MORE RESULTS AND DISCUSSION

A Complexity Measure for Correlated-Instances. One of the goals of research in the design and analysis of algorithms is to develop algorithms which work well in practice, by taking into account all available data. In the CSP domain, we demonstrated that access to multiple problem instances with correlated solutions can change the complexity of problems from intractable to tractable. It is similarly possible that access to correlated instances can lead to faster and different algorithms for problems which are already solvable in polynomial time.

To this end, we propose a new *correlated-instance* complexity measure. Correlated-instance complexity measures the performance of an algorithm on a primary instance given as auxiliary input a tuple of correlated instances where the correlation is over the solution space. We emphasize that the measure does not restrict the distribution of the primary instance, which can be worst-case or average-case, but introduces the new dimension of correlation, and can be used to analyze the behavior of algorithms that utilizes multiple correlated instances. See full version [25].

Correlation versus Diversity We have demonstrated that correlation between instances is helpful. Yet, interestingly, "too much correlation" is not good either. Clearly, if the auxiliary instance at hand is identical, thus 100% correlated, to the primary instance, it is of no use, as it brings no additional information. Hence, some amount of diversity is necessary.

We further observe that in the randomly-perturbed solution model of CSP, the amount of "diversity", i.e. the perturbation parameter ε, should be some positive constant for the auxiliary instances to be useful. Indeed, we observe that this follows from the *exponential-time-hypothesis* [35] which conjectures that for every $k > 2$ the best algorithm for k-SAT requires time $2^{s_k n}$ for some constant s_k.

Claim 2 - hardness of solving correlated kSAT, when correlation is too high *Assuming the exponential time hypothesis, there is no polynomial-time algorithm for solving a primary kSAT instance φ even if given a randomly perturbed[5] correlated instance φ' obtained by perturbing the solution of φ with perturbation parameter $\varepsilon = o(1)$ and then modifying the affected clauses to make φ' satisfiable.*

The reason is that an algorithm can generate the correlated instance (G, y') on its own in time that is $\exp(\tilde{o}(n))$ (simply by cycling through all possibilities of having $o(n)$ affected clauses).

Going back to our techniques, intuitively we are using the differences between the two instances (i.e diversity) to our advantage, to get a handle on the derivative *in addition* to the original function, which allows us to approximate it better. Too large a correlation would not yield enough information about the derivative, whereas too little correlation is hard to tell apart from noise. We find the non-monotonic behavior of the problem very interesting and worthy of more careful examination.

Does Correlation Always Help? We have demonstrated that significant computational gains can be made for solving CSPs, given access to correlated instances. One basic question that arises immediately is "do *all* search problem become easy, given $I, I_1, \cdots, I_T$ for sufficiently and naturally correlated x_i's?"

Restricting the question to the context of CSPs, although we described a number of algorithms for solving CSPs, these do not cover all possible cases. In particular, they do not address the case of CSPs whose optimal solution does not satisfy all constraints. Here, for the 3LIN predicate, we have the following hardness result.

Claim 3 - hardness of solving correlated 3LIN instances that are $1 - \delta$ satisfiable *Unless $P = NP$, there is no polynomial-time algorithm that gets as input a 3LIN instance (G, y) whose optimal solution satisfies at least $1 - \delta$ of the clauses, and a correlated instance (G, y') generated using $\mathsf{Aux} = P \circ G$ (where $P = 3LIN$), and finds a solution that satisfies more than $1/2 + \delta$ of the clauses.*

The claim follows from the following arguments: We know [33] that it is NP-hard to decide if a given instance (G, y) has a solution satisfying at least $1 - \delta$ of the clauses, or no more than $1/2 + \delta$. Given an instance G, y, we can use A to solve it, by simulating the instance y'. First we generate a random difference vector $\Delta \in \{0, 1\}^n$ by setting each bit independently to 1 with probability ε, and then we let $y' = y + P \circ G(\Delta)$. The answer of A on (G, y, y') is a solution to the original instance. It remains to observe that for $x' := x + \Delta$ we have $y' = P \circ G(x')$ so (G, y') is distributed exactly according to $\mathsf{Aux} = P \circ G$.

One wonders whether a similar hardness result exists for a CSP with perfect completeness.

This result shows that there are some CSP-based problems for which there is no algorithmic gain from looking at additional correlated instances. In contrast, we remark that for every function f, there is another "equivalent" function f' that is susceptible to correlated instances. More accurately, f' is as hard to invert as f, and yet becomes easy to invert when given an additional auxiliary instance. The reduction is as follows[6]. Given any function $f(x)$, we define the corresponding randomized function $f'(x; r, s)$ as follows: f' on input x and $2kn$ bits (k is set later) of random coins $r = \{r_{ij}\}_{i \in [n], j \in [k]}$ and $s = \{s_{ij}\}_{i \in [n], j \in [k]}$, outputs $f(x)$ and an "encoding" $\{y_{ij}, r_{ij}\}_{i \in [n], j \in [k]}$ of the input x using the random coins r and s, where every input bit x_i is encoded as $\{(y_{ij}, r_{ij})\}_{j \in [k]}$ with $y_{ij} = x_i \cdot r_{i,j} + s_{i,j}$. It is easy to see that given uniform random coins r_{ij}'s and s_{ij}'s, the encoding hides the input x information theoretically; thus, the randomized function $f'(x; r, s)$ has the same inversion complexity as $f(x)$ (when r, s are random).

We show that $f'(x; r, s)$ becomes easy to invert given a single correlated instance $f'(x'; r', s')$ with ε-perturbed x', r', s', for a constant ϵ. The inversion procedure simply tries to recover the x from the two input encodings $\{y_{ij}, r_{ij}\}$ and $\{y'_{ij}, r'_{ij}\}$ contained in the two instances as follows: Collect the j's for which $r_{i,j} = 1$ but $r'_{i,j} = 0$. For these j's, the value $y_{i,j} \oplus y'_{i,j} = x_i + s_{i,j} + s'_{i,j}$ is correlated with x_i, and can be viewed as vote for the value of x_i. Thus by taking a majority vote, x_i can be recovered with high probability $1 - O(1/n)$, provided that k is a sufficiently large logarithmic number. Therefore, we are likely to recover all the bits of x.

We remark that key of the above transformation from f to f' is the encoding of the input, which is information theoretically hiding given one encoding, but easy to decode given two. It is easy to see that this encoding can also be used to transform any search problem to another search prob-

---

[5]We remark that the distribution of φ' conditioned on φ is not exactly the same as in our model, but this difference is not important. In particular, it is reasonable to expect the ETH to hold for CSPs (G, y) as in our definition, for some predicate P, in which case an equivalent formulation could be made in which the correlated instances are exactly as in our model.

[6]We thank an anonymous referee for pointing out a simpler proof of this claim.

lem with the same complexity (under an input distribution where the random coins used for the encodings are indeed random), which becomes easy to solve given a correlated instance.

The Benefit of Correlation in Learning Theory Access to correlated instances is a wider phenomenon beyond improving time complexity of algorithms. In particular, it seems that in sub-areas as varied as *learning theory, coding theory* and *biological experiments*, correlated problem instances come up naturally. Does the benefit of correlation extend as well? We suggest an affirmative answer showing an example in learning theory.

The classical PAC learning [41], considers an underlying hidden concept C (for example, C can be a DNF, a junta, or a parity function), a learning algorithm is given multiple labelled examples of the form $(x, C(x))$, and the goal is finding a hypothesis that labels future examples correctly with high probability (w.r.t. a distribution on examples). In the commonly used random-query model, the learning algorithm sees only a sequence of examples $(x_1, C(x_1)), (x_2, C(x_2)), \ldots$ where each x_i is independently drawn from a probability distribution.

Two degrees of correlation may be incorporated into the random query model. First, the examples may be correlated. Formally, a generating process Gen_C produces a sequence of pairs (I_i, S_i) where $S_i = C$ for all i, and $I_i = (x_i, C(x_i))$ for correlated x_i's. This model has been studied in the learning literature (e.g.[22]). However, not only the examples may be correlated, in actuality, many concepts to be learned are potentially correlated themselves, and leveraging this correlation may reduce the complexity of learning any one of them in isolation. Think of multiple specimens (the concepts to be learned) which are highly correlated but not identical, all exposed to a battery of experimental conditions, as a researcher/learner is trying to learn hidden variables governing their reaction. Put in our framework, there is a generating process Gen that generates correlated concepts $C_0, C_1, \ldots, C_T$, and then provides a list of examples $I_t = \{x_i, C_t(x_i)\}_{i=1}^k$ for each $t = 1, \ldots, T$, with the corresponding solutions $S_t = C_t$. This is best imagined as a table whose rows are indexed by the examples and whose columns are indexed by the various correlated concepts. The learner gets to see the entries of this table, describing the behavior of each concept $C_1, \ldots, C_T$ on the same set of examples $\{x_i\}$ (corresponding to the experimental conditions), and tries to find a hypothesis for each of the hidden concepts.

We illustrate the strength of this model for the learning parity with noise (LPN) problem. In the standard LPN, there is a hidden function $C(x) = \langle s, x \rangle \mod 2 = \sum_{i=1}^n s_i x_i \mod 2$, and the learner gets noisy samples of the form $x, C(x) + b$ for independently drawn $x \in \{0,1\}^n$ and a random biased bit b that equals 1 with probability $\frac{1}{2} - \delta$. The goal is to find $s \in \{0,1\}^n$. In our correlated concept model, there is a random string s_0 and T ε-noisy copies of it, $s_1 \ldots, s_T$; these strings describe $T+1$ parity functions $C_t(x) = \langle s_t, x \rangle \mod 2$. The learning algorithm gets as input a table Y whose rows are indexed by the queries $x_1, \ldots, x_k$ and whose columns are indexed by $s_0, \ldots, s_T$ such that $Y_{it} = \langle x_i, s_t \rangle +$ b_{it}, where b_{it} are independent biased noise bits[7], and the goal is to find the strings $s_0, \ldots, s_T$.

We show that when the underlying parity functions are sufficiently correlated, with $\varepsilon = 1/n$, the LPN problem becomes easy to solve. The same statement can also be shown for larger ε using a similar approach, with the running time growing exponentially in εn. For simplicity, we only analyze the case with $\varepsilon = 1/n$.

Claim 4 - learning correlated parities *There is a polynomial time algorithm that, given access to $k = O(\log n)$ samples from $T = O(n \log n)$ parities with $1/n$-noise, learns s_0 with high probability.*

Let us sketch a proof of this claim. Let Y be the input arranged in a table, so that $Y_{it} = \langle x_i, s_t \rangle + b_{it}$. Our first step will be to find the difference $s_0 + s_t$ for many t's, by a guess-and-check strategy. Note that by our choose of $\varepsilon = 1/n$, it is likely that $s_0 + s_t$ has very low weight. Let $v_i = \langle x_i, s_0 \rangle + b_{i0} + \langle x_i, s_t \rangle + b_{it} = \langle x_i, s_0 + s_t \rangle + (b_{i0} + b_{it})$. Let $\Delta_{0,t}$ be a guess for $s_0 + s_t$. We will check whether our guess is correct by computing v' defined by $v'_i = v_i - \langle x_i, \Delta_{0,t} \rangle$. This vector will be biased towards 0 only if the guess is correct (since in that case the i-th entry equals $b_{i0} + b_{it}$ which is 1 with probability $\frac{1}{2} - 2\delta^2$). Searching among all difference vectors of weight 1 we will succeed with constant probability and thus be able to find the difference for many "good" columns t. For simplicity let us pretend all differences had weight 1.

Our second step will be to find s_0. Fix i, and observe that for each "good" t we know $s_0 + s_t$ so can check if $\langle s_0 + s_t, x_i \rangle = 0$. For each such t, the entry Y_{it} in the input is an independent noisy copy of $\langle s_0, x_i \rangle$. Taking majority, we can get a guess for $\langle s_0, x_i \rangle$ that is correct with probability $1 - 1/\text{poly}(n)$. Collecting such equations for various x_i we can solve a linear system to recover s_0. This also immediately gives s_t for all good t's.

A Possible Interpretation: Why do we Collaborate? Finally, we mention that the computational benefit of access to instances which are correlated via the solution space may give computational insight on a fundamental "human" question: why do we interact and collaborate with each other?

Collaboration between different entities which have access to different information has been an over riding theme in theoretical computer science research in the last few decades. Famous examples include *communication complexity* and *multi party secure computation*. In both of these examples, interaction and collaboration is built-in the definition of the problem, as the goal is to compute a function of the information held by "the other party". However, as individuals and scientists it seems that we benefit from collaboration not only as a means to find out functions of what our partners know but in order to be able to understand ourselves better and achieve more than we could on our own. A fascinating question is: why and when is collaboration beneficial from a computational point of view?

One interpretation of our results (and actually an initial motivator for our work) is that *correlation* between the inputs of the different parties may be by itself a major driving force for interaction and collaboration. We may view col-

---

[7]Note that if b_{it} are identical for all t rather than being independent then this model reduces back to the standard LPN problem. The reason is that upon receiving $x, C_1(x)$ the learner can always generate $C_1(x) + \langle x, \Delta s \rangle + b_1$ for any string Δs of his choice. This clearly equals $C_2(x) + b_2$ for $\Delta s = s_2 - s_1$.

laborating parties A and B as holding respectively inputs $y = f(x)$ and $y' = f(x')$. Each party knows her own y (and y' respectively) but doesn't know the hidden variables (or *internal state*) x (and x' respectively). They collaborate by exchanging $f(x)$ and $f'(x')$ to engage in "self discovery". If their internal states are sufficiently similar (correlated) but not identical, collaboration will result in successful computation of x and x'. Similarly, collaboration with multiple entities can be of further benefit.

We do note that in our setting, once A and B exchange $y = f(x)$ and $y' = f(x')$, they do not need to interact further. It would be highly interesting to find examples where more complex interaction would be useful for discovering the hidden internal state. In other words, settings in which the algorithms of A and B would benefit from the adaptivity of the interaction. For example, a variant of the above would be a setting in which the access to y is limited compared to the length of x and y. Say x, y are exponentially long in the running time allowed to the recovery algorithm. Then, the recovery algorithm may be given "oracle" access to the tuple (f, y, y_i'). Given a set of indices $J = \{j\}$, the goal would be to recover the j-th bit of x for all $j \in J$. We leave as an open question to exhibit functions for which an adaptive inverting algorithm can be more powerful than non-adaptive inverting algorithms, necessitating a multi-round interaction.

5. OTHER RELATED WORK

On Correlation in Cryptanalysis Our work assumed that the CSP-solving algorithms *magically* have access to correlated solutions, in some settings, one may imagine being able to actively obtain such instances. One such setting studied in the cryptographic literature is called *tampering* attacks. The tampering attack was first introduced in a beautiful paper by Boneh, DeMillo and Lipton in 1997 "On the Importance of Checking Cryptographic Protocols for Faults" who asked whether one may tamper the secret key by inducing hardware faults. More recently, the works of [26, 9] consider adaptive tampering attacks on the randomness used by a cryptographic algorithm. We note that the correlation models we considered for CSPs are by and large, much weaker than the tampering considered in the cryptographic literature.

Another body of cryptanalytic work in which correlated instances play a crucial role is differential cryptanalysis (for example [16, 19, 18, 17, 14] and many more) which has been extensively applied to symmetric key encryption schemes such as AES, with the goal of recovering the secret key. The analysis works on the premise that the cryptanalyst has access to many correlated (*plaintext, ciphertext*) pairs, which are analogous to our correlated instances.

Yet another related body of work is on related-key attacks in the cryptography literature, where the adversary may even *choose* the correlation between the secret key or inputs [15, 36, 13, 30, 11, 12, 5, 42].

Cryptanalysis on Goldreich's OWF The work of Bogdanov and Qiao [21] showed that Goldreich's OWFs are easy to invert *in the standard model* (where algorithm is given only one instance) in two restricted settings: The first is for arbitrary predicates but assumes that the algorithm is given a 'hint' which is a string x' that is correlated to x. The second is an inversion algorithm that works for predicates correlated with one or two of their input bits. In comparison, our first algorithm (for Theorem 1) addresses arbitrary predicates given hints of a much weaker nature, that is $f(x')$ rather than x'. Our third algorithm (from Theorem 3) which takes a single $f(x')$ hint is limited to predicates in $\mathcal{P}$. For the predicates in this class, not covered in the first result of [21], one additional correlated instance already makes a difference.

The Study of Correlated Examples in Learning Theory In section 1.3 we showed how receiving examples of correlated concepts to be learned can be beneficial. Access to correlated examples of the *same concept* have been previously studied. For example Bshouty et. al. [22] show an efficient learning algorithm for DNFs in the, so called, random walk query model, where the $i + 1^{\text{th}}$ query x_{i+1} is derived from x_i by performing a random bit flip. In contrast, learning DNFs in the random query model is a notoriously hard problem. Thus, the correlation between the queries x_i's seems to give the learner significantly more power.

The Study of Correlated Examples in the Planted Independent Set Model In work inspired by this paper, Holmogren (private communication) recently examines correlated instances in the context of the planted independent-set semi-random graph model of Feige and Kilian [28].

The semi-random graph model [28] was initially proposed to try to "mediate between the unstructured 'uninteresting' graphs produced by the purely random models and the worst-case graphs that are seemingly beyond the heuristics's ability to solve." To this end, the model first plants in their graphs a solution to an underlying graph problem (e.g. independent set, coloring, graph bisection) as in the random graph world. Next, *subject to this planted solution remaining intact*, the model adds edges to the graph in a random fashion followed by a final adversarial step in which edges can be added arbitrarily. In the case of planted independent set of size αn for an n node graph, [28] proves a sharp threshold between when it is easy to recover the planted independent set and when it is NP-hard, depending on the probability of adding edges in the random step.

A natural question to ask in the context of studying correlations defined over solutions, is whether access to *two* graphs with correlated planted independent sets (i.e correlated solutions), change the complexity of the problem when it is NP-hard. Indeed, Holmogren presents an algorithm that given a single auxiliary graph, finds an $(1 - \gamma)$-approximate independent set (of size at least $(1 - \gamma)\alpha n$) in the primary graph, for any constant γ. There, the auxiliary graph is correlated with the primary graph in the way that its planted independent set overlaps with that of the primary graph for more than $(1-\delta)\alpha n$ vertexes, for a sufficiently small $\delta = \delta(\gamma)$ (and the rest of the graphs are constructed independently according to the semi-random graph model above).

Correlated Instances in Smooth Analysis The celebrated work on smooth analysis by Spielman and Teng[40] introduced a new measure on the complexity of algorithms, first illustrated via the smooth analysis of the celebrated Simplex algorithm in the realm of real valued inputs. Smooth analysis measure for an input x, is the expected behavior of the algorithm on correlated inputs which are the result of subjecting x to perturbations (e.g. flip its bits with a certain probability). The correlated instance complexity measure we introduce, is different in several aspects. First, we don't consider inputs which correlated to a primary input

x, but rather inputs whose underling solutions correlated to the solution of x. Second, we deviate from the traditional paradigm of an algorithm working on a single input x, toward the design of algorithms which receive input x as well as in addition auxiliary inputs x_i's whose solutions are correlated to the solution to x, to assist in the goal of computing the solution for x.

We mention that Spielman and Teng [39] in a follow up work to their original smooth analysis paper observe that in the discrete input domain, perturbations of the input "should probably be restricted to those which preserve the most significant aspect input with respect to a given situation". To address this, they define property-preserving perturbations to inputs and relate this measure to property testing work [32] and the heuristics of Feige and Kilian [28] for finding cliques on semi-random graphs with planted cliques.

Acknowledgement. We would like to thank the anonymous reviewers for many valuable comments.

6. REFERENCES

[1] M. Alekhnovich. More on average case vs approximation complexity. In *FOCS*, pages 298–307, 2003.

[2] B. Applebaum. Randomly encoding functions: A new cryptographic paradigm (survey). The 5th International Conference on Information Theoretic Security, 2011.

[3] B. Applebaum. Pseudorandom generators with long stretch and low locality from random local one-way functions. In *STOC*, pages 805–816, 2012.

[4] B. Applebaum, B. Barak, and A. Wigderson. Public-key cryptography from different assumptions. In *STOC*, pages 171–180, 2010.

[5] B. Applebaum, D. Harnik, and Y. Ishai. Semantic security under related-key attacks and applications. In *ICS*, pages 45–60, 2011.

[6] B. Applebaum, Y. Ishai, and E. Kushilevitz. Cryptography in nc^0. In *FOCS*, pages 166–175, 2004.

[7] S. Arora, C. Lund, R. Motwani, M. Sudan, and M. Szegedy. Proof verification and intractability of approximation problems. *Journal of the ACM*, 45(3):501–555, 1998.

[8] S. Arora and S. Safra. Probabilistic checking of proofs: A new characterization of NP. *Journal of the ACM*, 45(1):70–122, 1998.

[9] P. Austrin, K.-M. Chung, M. Mahmoody, R. Pass, and K. Seth. On the (im)possibility of tamper-resilient cryptography: Using fourier analysis in computer viruses. *IACR Cryptology ePrint Archive*, 2013:194, 2013.

[10] B. Barak, G. Kindler, and D. Steurer. On the optimality of semidefinite relaxations for average-case and generalized constraint satisfaction. In *ITCS*, pages 197–214, 2013.

[11] M. Bellare and D. Cash. Pseudorandom functions and permutations provably secure against related-key attacks. In *CRYPTO*, pages 666–684, 2010.

[12] M. Bellare, D. Cash, and R. Miller. Cryptography secure against related-key attacks and tampering. In *ASIACRYPT*, pages 486–503, 2011.

[13] M. Bellare and T. Kohno. A theoretical treatment of related-key attacks: Rka-prps, rka-prfs, and applications. In *EUROCRYPT*, pages 491–506, 2003.

[14] I. Ben-Aroya and E. Biham. Differtial cryptanalysis of lucifer. In *CRYPTO*, pages 187–199, 1993.

[15] E. Biham. New types of cryptanalytic attacks using related keys. *J. Cryptology*, 7(4):229–246, 1994.

[16] E. Biham and A. Shamir. Differential cryptanalysis of des-like cryptosystems. In *CRYPTO*, pages 2–21, 1990.

[17] E. Biham and A. Shamir. Differential cryptanalysis of des-like cryptosystems. *J. Cryptology*, 4(1):3–72, 1991.

[18] E. Biham and A. Shamir. Differential cryptanalysis of snefru, khafre, redoc-ii, loki and lucifer. In *CRYPTO*, pages 156–171, 1991.

[19] E. Biham and A. Shamir. Differential cryptoanalysis of feal and n-hash. In *EUROCRYPT*, pages 1–16, 1991.

[20] A. Blum, M. L. Furst, M. J. Kearns, and R. J. Lipton. Cryptographic primitives based on hard learning problems. In *CRYPTO*, pages 278–291, 1993.

[21] A. Bogdanov and Y. Qiao. On the security of goldreich's one-way function. *Computational Complexity*, 21(1):83–127, 2012.

[22] N. H. Bshouty, E. Mossel, R. O'Donnell, and R. A. Servedio. Learning dnf from random walks. *J. Comput. Syst. Sci.*, 71(3):250–265, 2005.

[23] J. Cook, O. Etesami, R. Miller, and L. Trevisan. Goldreich's one-way function candidate and myopic backtracking algorithms. In *TCC*, pages 521–538, 2009.

[24] A. Daniely, N. Linial, and S. Shalev-Shwartz. More data speeds up training time in learning halfspaces over sparse vectors. In *NIPS*, pages 145–153, 2013.

[25] I. Dinur, S. Goldwasser, and H. Lin. The computational benefit of correlated instances. *Electronic Colloquium on Computational Complexity (ECCC)*, 21:83, 2014.

[26] Y. Dodis, S. J. Ong, M. Prabhakaran, and A. Sahai. On the (im)possibility of cryptography with imperfect randomness. In *FOCS*, pages 196–205, 2004.

[27] U. Feige. Relations between average case complexity and approximation complexity. In *STOC*, pages 534–543, 2002.

[28] U. Feige and J. Kilian. Heuristics for semirandom graph problems. *J. Comput. Syst. Sci.*, 63(4):639–671, 2001.

[29] A. Flaxman. A spectral technique for random satisfiable 3cnf formulas. *Random Struct. Algorithms*, 32(4):519–534, 2008.

[30] D. Goldenberg and M. Liskov. On related-secret pseudorandomness. In *TCC*, pages 255–272, 2010.

[31] O. Goldreich. Candidate one-way functions based on expander graphs. *IACR Cryptology ePrint Archive*, 2000:63, 2000.

[32] O. Goldreich, S. Goldwasser, and D. Ron. Property testing and its connection to learning and approximation. In *FOCS*, pages 339–348, 1996.

[33] J. Håstad. Some optimal inapproximability results. *J. ACM*, 48(4):798–859, 2001.

[34] N. Heninger, Z. Durumeric, E. Wustrow, and J. A. Halderman. Mining your Ps and Qs: Detection of widespread weak keys in network devices. In *Proceedings of the 21st USENIX Security Symposium*, Aug. 2012.

[35] R. Impagliazzo and R. Paturi. On the complexity of k-sat. *J. Comput. Syst. Sci.*, 62(2):367–375, 2001.

[36] L. R. Knudsen. Cryptanalysis of loki91. In *AUSCRYPT*, pages 196–208, 1992.

[37] R. J. McEliece. A publickey system based on algebraic coding theory pages. *DSN Progress Report, Jet Propulsion lab*, 44:114–116, 1978.

[38] R. O'Donnell and D. Witmer. Goldreich's prg: Evidence for near-optimal polynomial stretch. Manuscript, 2012.

[39] D. A. Spielman and S.-H. Teng. Smoothed analysis (motivation and discrete models). In *WADS*, pages 256–270, 2003.

[40] D. A. Spielman and S.-H. Teng. Smoothed analysis of algorithms: Why the simplex algorithm usually takes polynomial time. *J. ACM*, 51(3):385–463, 2004.

[41] L. G. Valiant. A theory of the learnable. In *STOC*, pages 436–445, 1984.

[42] H. Wee. Public key encryption against related key attacks. In *Public Key Cryptography*, pages 262–279, 2012.

Why are Images Smooth?

Uriel Feige
Department of Computer Science and Applied Mathematics
the Weizmann Institute
Rehovot, Israel
uriel.feige@weizmann.ac.il

ABSTRACT

It is a well observed phenomenon that natural images are smooth, in the sense that nearby pixels tend to have similar values. We describe a mathematical model of images that makes no assumptions on the nature of the environment that images depict. It only assumes that images can be taken at different scales (zoom levels). We provide quantitative bounds on the smoothness of a typical image in our model, as a function of the number of available scales. These bounds can serve as a baseline against which to compare the observed smoothness of natural images.

Categories and Subject Descriptors

I.2.10 [**Computing Methodologies**]: Artificial Intelligence—*vision and scene understanding*

Keywords

Natural image statistics; local repetition lemma

1. INTRODUCTION

An *image* is a two dimensional array of pixels with n rows and m columns (typically we will take $m = n$), where a pixel p has a real value $x_p \in [0, 1]$. (This naturally corresponds to a grey-scale image, though the results extend in a straightforward way to color images, by applying them separately to each of the the basic colors RGB.) It is common wisdom that in natural images nearby pixels tend to have similar values. One may refer to this property as saying that natural images are *smooth*. Several hypotheses can be made as to why natural images are smooth. For example:

1. Our physical world has the property that environments are smooth, and images merely reflect this physical reality.

2. Physical and technological constraints in generating images (for example, properties of lenses) tend to cre-

ate smooth images, regardless of whether the environment is smooth or not.

3. There is a *selection bias* - the portions of the environment that we tend to depict in images are the smooth portions.

In order to test such hypotheses, it is desirable to compare them against a null hypothesis. One baseline for comparison is that of random arrays of pixels. However, we propose a different baseline for comparisons, that we shall refer to as *images* (in distinction from *natural images*).

We study a formal mathematical model of images that assumes that there are no technological constraints in depicting images of the environment, and assumes that there is no selection bias – any portion of the environment is equally likely to be depicted. We show that in our formal model, some level of smoothness of images is to be expected, regardless of any assumptions on the physical environment that is being depicted.

The key aspect that our model makes use of is that environments are depicted in various scales. For example, our eyes may focus on objects as small as a few centimeters in length (say, an insect), or sceneries spanning many kilometers (say, a distant mountain range). It is common wisdom that the smoothness of an object depends on the scale at which it is depicted. Consider for example a very large black and white checkerboard pattern. Viewed from a large distance, one pixel in the image will average the value of many checkerboard squares, and hence the image may be uniformly grey (very smooth). Viewed from a very short distance, every square may correspond to many pixels, and then nearby pixels will have the same value, so the image will be very smooth almost everywhere (except on the boundary between squares). However, at some intermediate scale, each square will occupy a small number of pixels (say one pixel, or four pixels), and then adjacent pixels will have very different values and the image will not be considered smooth.

In our study we present a formal model, and within this model we provide quantitative results regarding the effect that having multiple scales has on the typical smoothness of images. Our results imply that a nontrivial level of smoothness of images should be attributed to some universal mathematical principles that have nothing to do with the environment that is being depicted.

1.1 Related work

There is a vast body of work on *natural image statistics* (see [2], for example). Smoothness is a well observed aspect of these statistical properties. Moreover, natural images tend to have interesting and useful statistical properties that go much beyond smoothness (see [8], for example). A key aspect of our study is that environments are depicted in various scales. This same aspect appears in existing studies of natural images (see [7, 6, 1, 5], for example), though the focus of work in these references is different from ours: it relates to observed scale invariant properties of natural images, and to statistical models that attempt to explain these phenomena. Our current work does not deal with natural images, but rather with images in some abstract mathematical model. Our results can be contrasted against known results on natural images, but do not directly provide new information about natural images.

The techniques used in our proofs are of the form often used in image processing literature and practice. They are strongly related to a wavelet transform [3] with a Haar basis.

As our results deal with abstract notions of images rather than natural images, the mathematical principles that underlie them are applicable in other settings, and in fact similar principles were used in other settings. Specifically, Theorem 7 is a variation on a certain *local repetition lemma* proved in [4] in the context of sequential decision making, and Proposition 9 is based on an example given in [4] showing the tightness of the parameters in the local repetition lemma.

2. A FORMAL MODEL OF IMAGES

An *image* $I_{n,m}$ is a two dimensional array of pixels with n rows and m columns. We shall sometimes omit the subscripts n, m and simply use I. A pixel p has a real value $x_p \in [0,1]$. Numbering the pixels in $I_{n,m}$ by (i,j) with $0 \le i < n$ and $0 \le j < m$, two pixels (i_1, j_1) and (i_2, j_2) are *adjacent* if either $i_1 = i_2$ and $|j_1 - j_2| = 1$, or $j_1 = j_2$ and $|i_1 - i_2| = 1$. Borrowing standard graph theoretic terminology, we refer to a pair of adjacent pixels as an *edge* in the image, and we denote the set of edges in the image by E. It is not difficult to verify that $|E| = 2nm - n - m$. We remark that the notation E would also be used in order to denote the expectation operator, but the intended use of the notation E (either as set of edges or as expectation) will be clear from the context.

The *discrepancy* of two pixels p and q is a measure of how different their value is. We consider two different ways of measuring discrepancy, *linear discrepancy* $D_1(p,q) = |x_p - x_q|$ and *quadratic discrepancy* $D_2 = (x_p - x_q)^2$. The subscript of D indicates the power to which $|x_p - x_q|$ is raised. D_1 is perhaps the more natural of these two measures, but it is mathematically more convenient to work with D_2.

DEFINITION 1. *The* local discrepancy *of an image* $I_{n,m}$ *is the average discrepancy for pairs of adjacent pixels. It is denoted by* $LD_1(I) = \frac{1}{|E|} \sum_{(p,q) \in E} |x_p - x_q|$ *and* $LD_2(I) = \frac{1}{|E|} \sum_{(p,q) \in E} (x_p - x_q)^2$. *The* global discrepancy *of an image* I *is the average discrepancy over all pairs of pixels whether adjacent or not, including also pairs in which p and q are the same pixel. It is denoted by* $GD_1(I) = \frac{1}{n^2 m^2} \sum_{p \in I; q \in I} |x_p - x_q|$ *and* $GD_2(I) = \frac{1}{n^2 m^2} \sum_{p \in I; q \in I} (x_p - x_q)^2$. *In cases where we do not wish to distinguish between linear and quadratic discrepancy, we shall use the notation $LD(I)$ and $GD(I)$ with no subscript.*

REMARK 2. *Given an arbitrary graph $G(V, E)$ with n vertices and m edges, let L be its Laplacian matrix (a symmetric matrix with $L_{ii} = deg_i$, $L_{ij} = -1$ if $(i,j) \in E$, and $L_{ij} = 0$ otherwise), and let C be the Laplacian matrix of the complete graph on n vertices. Then given a column vector x of vertex values, our notion of local quadratic discrepancy coincides with $\frac{1}{2m} x^t L x$ (specialized to the grid graph, in our context), and our notion of global quadratic discrepancy coincides with $\frac{1}{n^2} x^t C x$. This will be used in the proof of Lemma 13.*

The range of possible values of local and global discrepancy is as specified in the following Proposition.

PROPOSITION 3. *For every image I the following hold: $0 \le LD(I) \le 1$ and $0 \le GD(I) \le \frac{1}{2}$.*

PROOF. Nonnegativity follows immediately from Definition 1.

$LD(I) \le 1$ holds because for every pixel p, $0 \le x_p \le 1$. In a checkerboard pattern with pixel values alternating between 0 and 1 the bound $LD(I) = 1$ is attained. On the same pattern, the bound $GD(I) = \frac{1}{2}$ is attained (if n is even). Convexity of the functions $|x|$ and x^2 implies that to maximize $GD(I)$ one needs $x_p \in \{0, 1\}$ for every p, and one needs the number of 0-pixels to be equal to the number of 1-pixels. In this extreme case $GD(I) = \frac{1}{2}$. □

An image may be smooth in several different senses, and we shall explicitly distinguish between them. One sense of being smooth is that of having low local discrepancy. A consequence of this smoothness is that the image can be compressed: traversing all pixels via some connected path (e.g., row by row in a snakelike fashion), for every new pixel we encounter we already have some prior estimate on its value, based on the pixel preceding it. Another sense of being smooth is by having low global discrepancy. This is a stronger notion than low local discrepancy, due to the following proposition.

PROPOSITION 4. *For every n by n image I, $GD(I) \ge \frac{1}{2} LD(I) - O(\frac{1}{n})$.*

PROOF. Pick a random pixel p, and independently, a random pixel q and a random neighbor q' of q. By the triangle inequality, $|x_p - x_q| + |x_p - x_{q'}| \ge |x_q - x_{q'}|$. Observe that $GD_1(I)$ exactly equals the expectation of $|x_p - x_q|$, and nearly equals the expectation of $|x_p - x_{q'}|$ (up to an $O(1/n)$ term that is the result of boundary effects). Likewise, $LD_1(I)$ nearly equals the expectation of $|x_q - x_{q'}|$ (up to an $O(1/n)$ term that is the result of boundary effects). Hence averaging over all choices of p, q, q' the inequality $GD_1(I) \ge \frac{1}{2} LD_1(I) - O(\frac{1}{n})$ is proved.

A simple modification to the proof above shows that $GD_2(I) \ge \frac{1}{4} LD_2(I) - O(\frac{1}{n})$. The proof of the stronger claim that $GD_2(I) \ge \frac{1}{2} LD_2(I) - O(\frac{1}{n})$ is deferred to Section 4.1. □

Yet another sense of being smooth is by having a high local correlation coefficient.

DEFINITION 5. *The* local correlation *of an image I is $LC(I) = \frac{GD_2(I)}{LD_2(I)}$, where $\frac{0}{0}$ is interpreted as being equal to 1. (Observe that $LD_2(I) = 0$ if and only if $GD_2(I) = 0$.)*

Observe that for an image I in which the values of pixels are chosen as independent identically distributed (i.i.d.)

random variables, one would expect $LC(I) \simeq 1$. An LC value that significantly deviates from 1 is an indication that the image is not just a collection of random pixels, but rather that there are local correlations. High local correlation (LC values larger than 1) relates to the experience of putting together a jigsaw puzzle: it is a good heuristic to try to match together jigsaw pieces of roughly the same color, rather than just trying to match together random pieces. This is because local discrepancy is typically smaller than global discrepancy.

The main claim of this manuscript is that most images are smooth to a noticeable extent. However, the definitions that we gave so far point to the contrary. If an image is just an array of pixels, then a natural interpretation of the term *most* is to select the values of these pixels at random in an i.i.d. fashion, with each pixel value distributed uniformly in the range $[0, 1]$. This will give LC value of roughly 1 which we do not consider as smooth, and also the local discrepancy would not be low (one expects $LD_1(I) \simeq \frac{1}{3}$ in this case, details omitted).

To be able to substantiate a claim of smoothness, we refine the definition of what an image is. This will lead to natural probability distributions over images that are different from the uniform one stated above, and with respect to these probability distributions most images will be smooth.

2.1 The probability distribution D over images

An image, unlike an arbitrary array of pixels, is meant to be an image of "something". That it, we assume that there is some underlying *environment*, and images depict portions of the environment. We shall not make any assumptions about the environment – it can be arbitrarily complex and random looking. However, we shall make one assumption about images, and this is that the portions of the environment that images depict can be of different sizes. We now present our model more formally.

There is an environment U, which is an N by N grid of *cells*. For example, the environment can be a large geographical region (say, of size 100km by 100km), and a cell can be of size corresponding to the smallest unit realistically observable by optical means (say, of side-length 10^{-5} meters). In the case described above, $N = 10^{10} \simeq 2^{33}$. Each cell c has *intensity* $I_c \in [0, 1]$.

Recall that we defined an image to be an n by m two dimensional array composed of pixels. To simplify of the rest of the presentation, we shall assume that $m = n$. We require n to be considerably smaller than N. For example, for images with 4 mega-pixels, $n \simeq 2^{11}$.

In terms of terminology, the terms *grid*, *cell*, *intensity* and N will be associated with environments, whereas the terms *array*, *pixel*, *value* and n will be associated with images.

There is a *scale* associated with an image, which is an integer in the range $[0, k-1]$, where k is some fixed integer satisfying $n2^k \leq N$. An image with scale ℓ describes an $n2^\ell$ by $n2^\ell$ portion of U, where every pixel of the image corresponds to a square of 2^ℓ by 2^ℓ cells of U. The value x_p of a pixel p is the average intensity of the cells that it represents, namely, $x_p = 2^{-2\ell} \sum_{c \in p} I_c$. One may think of an image as an n-pixel by n-pixel photograph of some portion of U, taken at a zoom level determined by ℓ. (This is not meant to be a model that incorporates all optical and technological constraints when describing what a photograph is, but merely a simple approximate model.) Pixels of highest

resolution ($\ell = 0$) in our model correspond to single cells in the environment. This convention simplifies the presentation without significantly affecting our results.

Now we describe our probability distribution D that governs which portion of U is contained in the image. This involves two aspect. One is the *scale* of the image: in D the scale is an integer ℓ chosen uniformly at random in the range $[0, k-1]$. The other aspect is the *location* of the image within U. In D the location is a cell (i, j) chosen uniformly at random in the range $0 \leq i, j \leq N - 1$, and the image extends over those cells (i', j') with $i' - i < n2^\ell$ modulo N and $j' - j < n2^\ell$ modulo N. Observe that under this definition, an image that is close to the boundary of U, "wraps around" and continues at the other side of U. Hence U is treated as a torus rather than as a grid. This is done for technical reasons, so as not to complicate the analysis by boundary effects. It has very little influence on the end results, because a random image is unlikely to be at the boundary of U, and even if it is, only $O(n)$ out of its n^2 pixels are at the boundary of U.

Observe that under the distribution D, every cell of U is equally likely to be part of an image. Each cell of U belongs to at most one pixel in the image, but each pixel in the image in scale ℓ contains $2^{2\ell}$ cells. Observe also that D as described above is simply the uniform distribution over all possible images (portions of U that satisfy the size constraints of images).

DEFINITION 6. *Given an N by N environment U and integers $n, k \geq 2$ satisfying $n2^k < N$, the average local discrepancy of the U, denoted by $LD(U, k)$, is the expected local discrepancy of an image sampled from U according to distribution D. Namely:*

$$LD(U, k) = E_{I \leftarrow D} LD(I)$$

Analogously, the average global discrepancy of U is

$$GD(U, k, n) = E_{I \leftarrow D} GD(I)$$

Observe that given U and k, the average local discrepancy is independent on n, but global discrepancy does depend on n.

3. RESULTS

In this section, the terminology used is as defined in Section 2. In particular, k is the number of scales, and we always assume that $n2^k < N$. For simplicity, we shall assume that n is a power of 2. Throughout, all logarithms are in base 2. Subscripts of 1 or 2 following D denote whether we are referring to linear or quadratic discrepancy.

THEOREM 7. *For every environment U its average local discrepancy satisfies $LD_2(U, k) \leq \frac{1}{k}$.*

PROPOSITION 8. *When $\log n \leq k$, there are environment U for which the average global discrepancy satisfies $GD_2(U, k, n) \geq \frac{\log n}{2k}$, up to low order terms that tend to 0 as n grows.*

Let us contrast Theorem 7 with Proposition 8. Suppose that images can correspond to objects as small as one centimeter in the environment U (say, a photo of an insect), up to objects as large as ten kilometers (say, a photo of a landscape). This gives $k \simeq \log 10^6 \simeq 20$ different scales for images. Suppose that every image has 1024 by 1024 pixels. Then $n = 2^{10}$ and $\log n = 10$. Proposition 8 shows that for a random image (sampled from D), the average global discrepancy might be as high as $\frac{\log n}{2k} = \frac{1}{4}$. Theorem 7 shows that the average local discrepancy is at most $\frac{1}{k} = \frac{1}{20}$.

Theorem 7 concerns quadratic discrepancy and not linear discrepancy. Hence possibly $LD_1(n,k) \simeq \frac{1}{\sqrt{k}}$, even though $LD_2(n,k) \le \frac{1}{k}$.

PROPOSITION 9. *There is some constant $c > 0$ such that for every k, there is an environment U for which $LD_1(U,k) \ge \frac{c}{\sqrt{k}}$.*

The theme of the next theorem is that unless local correlation (in the sense of Definition 5) is significant, then $O(1/k)$ bounds apply not only to quadratic discrepancy, but also to linear discrepancy.

For an environment U and $0 \le \ell \le k-1$, let $LD(\ell)$ denote the average local discrepancy taken only over images of scale ℓ, and let $GD(\ell)$ denote the average global discrepancy taken only over images of scale ℓ.

THEOREM 10. *For an environment U and $1 < \alpha < \frac{\log n}{2}$, suppose that for every $0 \le \ell \le k-1$, $LD_2(\ell) \ge \frac{GD_2(\ell)}{\alpha}$. Let $0 < p < 1$ be such that $\frac{1-p^{\log n}}{1-p} = 2\alpha$. Then $\sum_{\ell=0}^{k-1} LD_1(\ell) \le \frac{1+\sqrt{p}}{\sqrt{1-p}}$. In particular, as n grows, the upper bound on $LD_1(U,k)$ tends to $\frac{\sqrt{2\alpha}+\sqrt{2\alpha-1}}{k}$.*

4. PROOFS

4.1 Some preliminary results

The following propositions collect some properties of discrepancy.

PROPOSITION 11. *For any image I, $LD_2(I) \ge \Omega(\frac{GD_2(I)}{n^2})$. There are images with $LD_2(I) \le O\left(\frac{GD_2(I)}{n^2}\right)$.*

PROOF. One can lower bound $LD_2(I)$ as a function of $GD_2(I)$ by the following procedure for sampling an adjacent pair of pixels. First, sample two pixels p and q uniformly at random (as done for computing $GD_2(I)$). Then follow a canonical path from p to q, first going along the row of p until the column of q is reached, and then along the column of q until p is reached. Thereafter, a random adjacent pair of pixels (u,v) along this path is chosen. As the path is at most of length $2n$, the triangle inequality for distances implies that $E[(x_u - x_v)^2] \ge \frac{(x_p - x_q)^2}{4n^2}$ (the worst case is when the value of every two adjacent pixels along the path differs by $\frac{|x_p - x_q|}{2n}$). The above procedure for sampling adjacent pixels distorts the uniform distribution over adjacent pixels, but only to limited extent. A pair of adjacent pixels can increase its probability of being sampled (compared to the uniform probability) by at most a constant factor. Hence also with respect to the uniform distribution over pairs of adjacent pixels we must have $LD_2(I) \ge \Omega(\frac{GD_2(I)}{n^2})$. (The constants in this proof can be improved by a more careful analysis.)

An example of an image I with $GD_2(I) = \Omega(1)$ and $LD_2(I) = O(\frac{1}{n^2})$ is the following: for every $0 \le i < n$, all pixels in row i have the same value $\frac{i}{n}$. $\square$

For linear discrepancy, the bounds in Proposition 11 should be changed to $LD_1(I) \ge \Omega(\frac{GD_1(I)}{n})$ (proof omitted). In any case, Proposition 11 shows that local discrepancy can be much smaller than global discrepancy. In contrast, global discrepancy cannot be much smaller than local discrepancy, as shown by Proposition 4. We now develop some machinery for proving Proposition 4 for the case of quadratic discrepancy.

PROPOSITION 12. *Given a 2 by 1 image I composed only of two adjacent pixels, $LD(I) = 2GD(I)$.*

PROOF. We prove the proposition for quadratic discrepancy. The proof for linear discrepancy is similar.

Let the two pixels be p and q. Then $LD_2(I) = (x_p - x_q)^2$, whereas
$$GD_2(I)$$
$$= \frac{1}{4}\left((x_p - x_p)^2 + (x_p - x_q)^2 + (x_q - x_p)^2 + (x_q - x_q)^2\right)$$
$$= \frac{1}{2}LD_2(I). \quad \square$$

Given an image I, an *equipartition* P of I partitions the set of its pixels into disjoint equal size subsets. The global discrepancy of an equipartition of I, denoted by $GD(P)$, is the average of the global discrepancies of its parts.

LEMMA 13. *For every image I and every equipartition P of I, $GD_2(P) \le GD_2(I)$.*

PROOF. For convenience of notation, let n denote here (and only here) the total number of pixels in the image I, and suppose that the equipartition P partitions the set of pixels into n/d subsets, each with d pixels. Number the pixels from 1 to n, with each subset occupying d consecutive numbers. Consider now two n by n symmetric matrices. (These matrices are so called *Laplacian* matrices of graphs associated with the way discrepancy is being computed.) Matrix A has $n-1$ along its diagonal, and all other entries are -1. Matrix B is a block matrix with n/d blocks of size d along the diagonal. Each block has $d-1$ along its diagonal, and -1 elsewhere in the block. Outside the diagonal blocks, the matrix B is all 0.

Let x be the vector of values for the pixels of I. We think of x as a column vector, and x^T is its transposed row vector. Then $GD_2(I) = \frac{1}{n^2}x^T A x$, and the average discrepancy of the partition is $GD_2(P) = \frac{1}{dn}x^T B x$. Decompose x into two components, $\alpha y + z$, where y is the all 1 vector, α is the average value of x, and z is a vector orthogonal to y. Observe that y is an eigenvector of eigenvalue 0 both for A and for B. Hence $GP_2(I) = \frac{1}{n^2}z^T A z$ and $GD_2(P) = \frac{1}{dn}z^T B z$. Observe that all eigenvalues of A, except for the unique 0 eigenvalue, have value n. Hence $GP_2(I) = \frac{1}{n^2}z^T A z = \frac{1}{n}|z|^2$ (where $|z|$ is the norm of z). As for B, it has n/d eigenvalues of 0, and each block contributes $d-1$ eigenvalues of value d. Hence $GD_2(P) = \frac{1}{dn}z^T B z \le \frac{1}{n}|z|^2$. This establishes that $GD_2(P) \le GD_2(I)$, as desired. $\square$

We can now prove the quadratic discrepancy part of Proposition 4.

PROOF. Suppose for simplicity that n is even. Observe that the grid graph is nearly 4-regular. Add one edge to each row making that row into a cycle, and one edge to each column making the column into a cycle. Thus $2n$ edges are added, but they form only a $1/n$ fraction of the total number of edges, explaining the $(1/n)$ error term in the statement of Proposition 4. Consider now 4 different partitions of the grid (which by now is a torus), each into $n^2/2$ parts: P_1 takes all even pairs in the rows, P_2 takes all odd pairs in the rows, P_3 takes all even pairs in the columns, P_4 takes all odd pairs in the columns. By Lemma 13, $GD_2(P_i) \leq GD_2(I)$ for every $1 \leq i \leq 4$. Hence the average global discrepancy of a pair of adjacent pixels is at most $GD_2(I)$. Proposition 12 then implies that $LD_2(I) \leq 2GD_2(I)$. $\square$

4.2 Lower bounds on discrepancy

The following proposition shows that the bounds in Theorem 7 are best possible.

PROPOSITION 14. *For some environment U the average local discrepancy satisfies $LD(U, k) \geq \frac{1}{k}$.*

PROOF. The following U attains $LD(U, k) = \frac{1}{k}$. The cells of U form a checkerboard pattern with alternating 0/1 values. In the scale $\ell = 0$ the local discrepancy is 1 (regardless of the location of I), and in every other scale local discrepancy is 0. As $Pr[\ell = 0] = \frac{1}{k}$, the proposition follows. $\square$

We now prove Proposition 8 concerning global discrepancy.

PROOF. Partition U into *mega-cells* where a mega-cell is a 2^k by 2^k array of cells. Within a mega-cell, every cell has the same intensity. The mega-cells are arranged in a checkerboard pattern, with alternating 0/1 intensities.

The distribution D selects a scale $\ell \in [0, k-1]$ uniformly at random. Observe that already when $\ell = k-1$, a random pixel has constant probability of being entirely contained in a mega cell, and this probability tends to 1 at an exponential rate as ℓ decreases. Moreover, when n is even, as long as $\ell \geq k - \log n + 1$, exactly half the cells (not mega cells) contained in an image have intensity 1, and the other half has intensity 0. The combination of these two facts implies that roughly half the pixels of the image have value 1, and roughly half have value 0, giving $GD(I) \simeq \frac{1}{2}$. As this happens at roughly $\log n$ scales out of k possible choices of scales, $E_{I \leftarrow D} GD(I) \simeq \frac{\log n}{2k}$, as desired. $\square$

The bound in Proposition 8 is nearly best possible, though this will not be proved in this manuscript, because we only need the direction of the inequality that is stated in the proposition.

We now prove Proposition 9 concerning linear discrepancy.

PROOF. We shall not try to optimize the constant c in the following proof.

In our proof it will be convenient to allow the intensities of cells to be in the range $[-2\sqrt{\log k}, 2\sqrt{\log k}]$, where for simplicity we assume that $2\sqrt{\log k}$ is integer. Clearly, intensities can be scaled to lie in the range $[0, 1]$, while losing a factor of $4\sqrt{\log k}$ in the value of LD_1.

Let the N by N environment (with $N > 2^k$ a power of 2) be such that the intensity of a cell (i, j) depends only on j but not on i. Specifically, the intensity of cell (i, j) is computed as follows. Write j in binary notation, but with -1 replacing 0. Consider only the k least significant bits in this notation. This gives some string $r \in \{-1, 1\}^k$. For cells that we refer to as *balanced* the intensity of the cell is simply the sum of bits in r. However, there are cells that we refer to as *extreme*. Those are the cells for which for some

$q \leq k$ the sum of the first q bits in r is either $-2\sqrt{\log k}$ or $2\sqrt{\log k}$. For these extreme cells their intensity is the sum of the corresponding prefix (hence the maximum allowed absolute value for the intensity). By Kolmogorov's inequality for partial sums of independent ± 1 random variables, at most one quarter of the cells are extreme.

Consider now a random pixel p at an arbitrary scale $0 \leq \ell < k$. For all the cells within it, the corresponding r share the same $(k-\ell)$-prefix. Observe that when this prefix by itself is not extreme (namely, its sum of values never hits neither $-2\sqrt{\log k}$ nor $2\sqrt{\log k}$ – this happens with probability at least $\frac{3}{4}$) then the value of the pixel (the average over all cells that it contains) is precisely the sum of values of the $(k-\ell)$-prefix. Of the four pixels adjacent to p, one of them is adjacent to it horizontally and agrees with it on an $(k-\ell-1)$-prefix and differs on bit $(k-\ell)$. The linear discrepancy between these two pixels is 2.

This implies that with probability at least $\frac{3}{16}$ the linear discrepancy is at least 2, which after scaling the intensities to lie in $[0, 1]$ shows that $LD_1 \geq \frac{3}{32\sqrt{\log k}}$. $\square$

4.3 Proofs of main theorems

Proof of Theorem 7.

PROOF. In an image of scale ℓ, the side length of a pixel is 2^ℓ cells. Using distribution D, every scale $\ell \in \{0, \ldots, k-1\}$ is chosen with equal probability, and given a scale ℓ, every two adjacent pixels of size 2^ℓ are equally likely to be in the image. We need to prove that the expectation of the discrepancy $(x_p - x_q)^2$ of two adjacent pixels (chosen at random from an image chosen from distribution D) is at most $\frac{1}{k}$. It suffices to prove it for pairs of pixels adjacent horizontally, and by symmetry, the same proof will apply to pairs of pixels adjacent vertically. Hence for the rest of the proof, pixels are considered to be adjacent if and only if they are adjacent horizontally. We may envision a pair of adjacent pixels as a domino piece. We describe now a method of sampling uniformly at random a domino piece.

Consider a "window" W of U with 2^k columns and 2^{k-1} rows. This window is equivalent to a domino piece of scale $k-1$. Subdivide each of its pixels of scale $k-1$ into four pixels of scale $k-2$. These pixels are arranged as two domino pieces of scale $k-2$. Continue subdividing recursively, where for every $\ell \geq 1$, every pixel of scale ℓ gives two domino pieces of scale $\ell-1$. Hence in scale ℓ there are $4^{k-1-\ell}$ disjoint domino pieces. Now to sample a random domino piece, choose W at random, choose a scale ℓ uniformly at random, and within W choose a domino piece of scale ℓ uniformly at random.

To compute the discrepancy of a domino piece of scale ℓ, one needs first to average the value of its left pixel p (by summing all cells and dividing by $2^{2\ell}$) getting a value x_p, to average the value of its right pixel q getting a value x_q, and compute $(x_p - x_q)^2$.

Let W_ℓ denote the set of domino pieces of scale ℓ in W. Let $LD(W)$ denote the weighted average local discrepancy (over horizontal pairs) in W, where the weights are such that each scale is equally likely to be chosen. We have:

$$LD(W) = \frac{1}{k} \sum_{\ell=0}^{k-1} 4^{\ell+1-k} \sum_{(p,q) \in W_\ell} (x_p - x_q)^2 \qquad (1)$$

The intensities of cells in W is a function I from $2^{k-1} \times 2^k$ cells of W to $[0, 1]$. Denoting cells by c, the average intensity $2^{1-2k}\sum_{c\in W} I(c)$ will be denoted by μ, and the average of the squares of the intensities $2^{1-2k}\sum_{c\in W}(I(c))^2$ will be denoted by w^2. We now represent the function I in an orthonormal basis that is very much related to the Haar basis, though not identical to it. The number of basis vectors needs to be 2^{2k-1} (matching the number of cells in W), but we shall specify only some of the basis vectors. The set of basis vectors that we specify will be referred to as the *domino partial basis*. One basis vector v_0 has value $\frac{1}{2^k\sqrt{2}}$ on all cells of W. In addition, each domino piece in W represents a basis vector as follows. Given the scale ℓ of the domino piece, in its left pixel (composed of $2^{2\ell}$ cells), each cell has value $\frac{1}{2^\ell\sqrt{2}}$, each cell in the right pixel has value $-\frac{1}{2^\ell\sqrt{2}}$, and the cells not covered the domino piece have value 0. Hence the norm of every vector in the domino partial basis is 1, and every two vectors are orthogonal.

The inner product of I with a basis vector that corresponds to a domino piece (p,q) at scale ℓ is precisely $\frac{2^\ell}{\sqrt{2}}(x_p-x_q)$. This is the coefficient of the function I according to the basis vector corresponding to the domino piece. The square of this coefficient is $2^{2\ell-1}(x_p-.x_q)^2$. For v_0, the squared value of the coefficient can readily be seen to be $2^{2k-1}\mu^2$. The sum of squares of all coefficients is at most the square of the norm of I (if we had a complete basis, they would be equal, by Parseval's identity), and hence:

$$2^{2k-1}\mu^2 + \sum_{\ell=0}^{k-1}\sum_{(p,q)\in W_\ell} 2^{2\ell-1}(x_p-x_q)^2 \le \sum_{(i,j)\in W}(W_{i,j})^2$$
$$= 2^{2k-1}w^2 \quad (2)$$

Dividing both sides of inequality (2) by 2^{2k-1}, we obtain

$$\mu^2 + \sum_{\ell=0}^{k-1}\sum_{(p,q)\in W_\ell} 4^{\ell-k}(x_p-x_q)^2 \le w^2 \quad (3)$$

Combining Equation (3) with (1) we obtain that $LD(W) \le \frac{4}{k}(w^2-\mu^2)$. As the intensities are in the range $[0,1]$, necessarily $w^2 \le \mu$. The expression $\mu-\mu^2$ is maximized when $\mu = \frac{1}{2}$, and then it evaluates to $\frac{1}{4}$. Hence $LD(W) \le \frac{1}{k}$, as desired. $\square$

For the proof of Theorem 10 we use the following notation. Let $x_\ell = LD_2(\ell)$ for $0 \le \ell \le k-1$ and $x_\ell = 0$ for $\ell \ge k$.

LEMMA 15. *For every $0 \le \ell \le k-1$,*
$2GD_2(\ell) \ge \sum_{\ell'=\ell}^{\ell+\log n-1} x_{\ell'}$.

PROOF. The proof of Lemma 15 is implicit in our proof of Theorem 7. Consider a random window W of U with $n2^{\ell-1}$ rows and $n2^\ell$ columns. It can be thought of as half an image I at scale ℓ, and being half an image, Lemma 13 implies that the expectation over choice of random W satisfies $E[GD_2(W)] \le E[GD_2(I)] = GD_2(\ell)$. The proof of Theorem 7 implies that $\sum_{\ell'=\ell}^{\ell+\log n-1} x_{\ell'} \le 4E[w^2-\mu^2]$, where μ is the average value of a pixel in W and w^2 is the average squared value. As $GD_2[W] = 2(w^2-\mu^2)$, the lemma follows. $\square$

We now prove Theorem 10.

PROOF. Observe that convexity of the function x^2 implies that $LD_1(\ell) \le \sqrt{x_\ell}$. Hence to prove Theorem 10 we shall

bound the maximum possible value of $\sum_{\ell=0}^{k-1}\sqrt{x_\ell}$. As $x_\ell = 0$ for $\ell \ge k$, this is the same as bounding the maximum possible value of $\sum_{\ell \ge 0}\sqrt{x_\ell}$. Relaxing the constraint that $x_\ell = 0$ for $\ell \ge k$, we get the following mathematical program.

Maximize $\sum_{i\ge 0}\sqrt{x_i}$ subject to:

1. $x_i > 0$.

2. $\sum x_i \le 1$.

3. $2\alpha x_i \ge \sum_{j=i}^{i+\log n-1} x_j$.

Constraint 2 is a consequence of Theorem 7. Constraint 3 is a consequence of Lemma 15 together with the premise of Theorem 10.

Consider a feasible (not necessarily optimal) solution to the above mathematical program of the form $x_i = (1-p)p^i$, for some $0 < p < 1$. Then constraint 1 is necessarily satisfied. Constraint 2 is satisfied with equality because $\sum_{i\ge 0}(1-p)p^i = (1-p)\sum_{i\ge 0}p^i = \frac{1-p}{1-p} = 1$. As for Constraint 3, we require that $2\alpha(1-p)p^i \ge \sum_{j=i}^{i+\log n-1}(1-p)p^j$. Dividing both sides by $(1-p)p^i$ we get an upper bound on the maximum possible value of p, implied by the inequality $2\alpha \ge \sum_{j=0}^{\log n+1} p^j = \frac{1-p^{\log n}}{1-p}$.

If x_i is of the form $(1-p)p^i$, then in order to maximize $\sum_{i\ge 0}\sqrt{x_i}$ we need to choose p as large as possible. This follows because

$$\sum_{i\ge 0}\sqrt{x_i} = \sum_{i\ge 0}\sqrt{1-p}(\sqrt{p})^i = \frac{\sqrt{1-p}}{1-\sqrt{p}} = \frac{1+\sqrt{p}}{\sqrt{1-p}}$$

is increasing with p.

Recall that p needs to satisfy the constraint:

$$\frac{1-p^{\log n}}{1-p} \le 2\alpha$$

In particular, when n tends to infinity, we have that $p \le 1-\frac{1}{2\alpha}$. Under the solution $p = 1-\frac{1}{2\alpha}$ the value of the objective function of the mathematical program has the following simple form:

$$\sum_{i\ge 0}\sqrt{x_i} = \frac{1+\sqrt{p}}{\sqrt{1-p}} = \sqrt{2\alpha}+\sqrt{2\alpha-1}$$

It remains to show that the solution $x_i = (1-p)p^i$ is not only feasible but also optimal. Hence fix $\alpha > 1$ and integer $\log n > 2\alpha$ and let $0 < p < 1$ be the solution of $\frac{1-p^{\log n}}{1-p} = 2\alpha$. (The inequality $\log n > 2\alpha$ is required in order to ensure the existence of such a p.)

Consider an optimal solution $X = x_0, x_1, \ldots$, and for the sake of contradiction suppose that there is some i (we take the smallest one) for which $x_i \ne (1-p)p^i$. We consider two cases.

1. $x_i < (1-p)p^i$. Let $i \le j \le i + \log n - 1$ be largest such that $x_j < (1-p)p^j$. Constraint 3 implies that necessarily $j > i$. Likewise, Constraint 3 implies that $\sum_{\ell=i+1}^{j} x_\ell < \sum_{\ell=i+1}^{j}(1-p)p^\ell$. The same argument can be repeated with j replacing i, and thereafter repeated indefinitely. By minimality of i we have that $\sum_{\ell=0}^{i-1} x_\ell = \sum_{\ell=0}^{i-1}(1-p)p^\ell$. Hence we have that

$\sum_{\ell \geq 0} x_\ell < \sum (1-p)p^\ell = 1$. This means that in the solution X one can increase x_i (in fact, at least up to $(1-p)p^i$) without violating any of the constraints, thus contradicting the optimality of X.

2. $x_i > (1-p)p^i$. An argument analogous to Case 1 above implies that it cannot be that for every j Constraint 3 is attained with equality, as then Constraint 2 will be violated. Let j be the smallest index for which there is slackness in Constraint 3, and let ϵ_1 be the amount of slackness. Denote $\epsilon_2 = x_j - x_{j+1}$ and suppose that $\epsilon_2 > 0$. In this case, modify the solution X to a new solution X' in which x_j is replaced by $x_j' = x_j - \frac{1}{2}\min[\epsilon_1, \epsilon_2]$ and x_{j+1} is replaced by $x_{j+1}' = x_{j+1} + \frac{1}{2}\min[\epsilon_1, \epsilon_2]$. One can easily verify that X' is feasible and gives a higher value than X does for the objective function (due to concavity of $\sqrt{x}$). This contradicts the assumed optimality of X.

It remains to deal with the case that $\epsilon_2 \leq 0$. Below we establish that in this case there is some other index $q > j$ such that Constraint 3 has slackness for x_q, and moreover, $x_q > x_{q+1}$. Then the above argument can be applied with q replacing j, completing the proof.

Observe that there are only finitely many indices q with $x_q \geq x_j$ (because $\sum x_i \leq 1$). Let q be the largest index such that $x_q \geq x_j$. By our assumption that $\epsilon_2 \leq 0$ we have that $q > j$. Clearly $x_q > x_{q+1}$. We now show that Constraint 3 has slackness for x_q. There are two cases to consider.

(a) For all $j \leq i \leq q$ it holds that $x_i \geq x_j$. In this case $q < j + \log n - 1$, because Constraint 3 (together with $\log n > 2\alpha$) implies that the average value of x_i for $j \leq i \leq j + \log n - 1$ is less than x_j. It follows that the inequalities implied by Constraint 3, one for x_j and one for x_q, overlap in some terms on the right-hand side. Moreover, for all the terms in which they differ, the right hand side for x_j has strictly higher value (every term at least x_j) than for x_q (every term strictly smaller than x_j). Since $x_q \geq x_j$, there must be slackness for x_q.

(b) For some $j < i < q$ it holds that $x_i < x_j$. Let $i < q$ be the largest such index. Then repeat the argument above with the inequalities implied by Constraint 3, one for x_i (instead of x_j) and one for x_q.

$\square$

5. DISCUSSION

One may think of our work as distinguishing between three concepts.

1. An array of pixels.

2. An image as defined in our abstract model. It depicts a portion of an environment, and may do so in one of several scales. No assumptions are made on the nature of the environment.

3. A natural image. The environment depicted needs to adhere to physical realities of our world, and the selection process of images may be biased, based on the goals of the person taking these images.

The three main principles that underlie our probabilistic model of images are the following:

- The model assumes nothing about the nature of the environment U. As our results are positive (showing some level of smoothness), this aspect strengthens the applicability of our results.

- There is no single scale in which a large fraction of the images are taken. If there was such a scale, then U can be arranged to have large local discrepancy at this scale (e.g., a checkerboard pattern), and on average images would not be smooth.

- The location of the image is chosen independently of the content of U – for a given scale, there is no correlation between the smoothness of U at a certain location and the probability that the image is taken at this location.

We showed that a key statistical property associated with natural images, that of smoothness, already manifests itself to some extent in the abstract model for images. Our study is quantitative, and our quantitative results uncover rather subtle and perhaps counter-intuitive effects. Let us recap one of our conclusions. Arguably, noticeable local correlation in an image (namely, having quadratic local discrepancy that is small compared to the quadratic global discrepancy) is by itself an indication for smoothness. Theorem 10 (contrasted with proposition 9) shows that the *absence* of local correlation (setting α close to 1) leads to improved upper bounds on the expected linear local discrepancy of random images.

Given quantitative values of smoothness of natural images, our work may allow one to assess how much of this value should be attributed already to the abstract image model, and then only the residual smoothness needs to be explained by properties of the natural world.

Our results become more significant as the number k of scales grows. In natural images, due to physical constraints of the real world, k cannot grow indefinitely, and hence we attempted to present our results not only in an asymptotic sense (e.g., $O(1/k)$), but also to provide explicit bounds on the leading constants involved. In particular, the premise of Theorem 10 was chosen in a way that would keep these constants small. The proof technique of Theorem 10 (using a linear program to upper bound the linear discrepancy) is versatile enough to extend to weaker premises, at the cost of resulting in higher leading constants in the $O(1/k)$ upper bound.

Acknowledgements

Work supported in part by the Israel Science Foundation (grant No. 621/12) and by the I-CORE Program of the Planning and Budgeting Committee and the Israel Science Foundation (grant No. 4/11). The author thanks Ronen Basri, Anat Levin and Boaz Nadler for helpful discussions on natural image statistics.

6. REFERENCES

[1] Luis Alvarez, Yann Gousseau, Jean-Michel Morel. The Size of Objects in Natural and Artificial Images. *Advances in Imaging and Electron Physics*, Volume 111, 1999, Pages 167–242.

[2] Aapo Hyvarinen, Jarmo Hurri, Patrik O. Hoyer. *Natural Image Statistics: A probabilistic approach to early computational vision.* Springer-Verlag, 2009.

[3] Ingrid Daubechies. *Ten Lectures on Wavelets.* SIAM, 1992.

[4] Uriel Feige, Tomer Koren, Moshe Tennenholtz. Chasing Ghosts: Competing with Stateful Policies. FOCS 2014.

[5] D. Mumford and B. Gidas. Stochastic models for generic images. *Quarterly of Applied Mathematics,* 54(1):85–111, 2001.

[6] D. Ruderman. Origins of scaling in natural images. *Vision Res.,* Vol. 37, No. 23, pp. 3385–3398, 1997.

[7] Daniel L. Ruderman, William Bialek. Statistics of Natural Images: Scaling in the Woods. *Physical Review Letters,* 73(6), 814–817, 1994.

[8] Maria Zontak, Michal Irani. Internal statistics of a single natural image. *CVPR* 2011: 977–984.

A Physically Universal Cellular Automaton

Luke Schaeffer
Massachusetts Institute of Technology
77 Massachusetts Ave.
Cambridge, MA 02139
lrs@mit.edu

ABSTRACT

Several cellular automata (CA) are known to be universal in the sense that one can simulate arbitrary computations (e.g., circuits or Turing machines) by carefully encoding the computational device and its input into the cells of the CA. In this paper, we consider a different kind of universality proposed by Janzing. A cellular automaton is *physically universal* if it is possible to implement any transformation on a finite region of the CA by initializing the complement of the region and letting the system evolve. We give the first known example of a physically universal CA, answering an open problem of Janzing and opening the way for further research in this area.

Categories and Subject Descriptors

F.1.1 [**Computation by Abstract Devices**]: Models of Computation—*cellular automata*

Keywords

Cellular automata; universality; models of computation

1. INTRODUCTION

Computation with cellular automata (CA) has an interesting history. Early work by von Neumann focused on self-reproducing structures and universal construction in cellular automata [11], although many of the proposed CAs were also computationally universal. In 1982, Berlekamp, Conway and Guy [2] showed that Conway's Game of Life (see also Gardner's article [5]), a particularly simple binary cellular automaton, is Turing-complete. Shortly after, Margolus [8] gave a reversible cellular automaton analogue for Fredkin and Toffoli's (reversible) billiard ball model of computation. More recently, Cook [3] proved rule 110 (a binary, one-dimensional CA) Turing-complete.

A cellular automaton is Turing-complete if it can simulate a Turing machine, but there is a fair amount of latitude in

the details of the simulation. For instance, in Life, the simulation uses multicellular patterns called *gliders* to transmit and manipulate information. Likewise, Margolus's machine is based on "billiard balls" composed of pairs of particles moving along the same trajectory. Rule 110 builds its simulation on multicellular patterns called *spaceships*. In each case, the simulation requires the input tape to be specially formatted (as gliders, spaceships, or pairs of particles) and produces output in a similar format.

Janzing [7] proposed an alternative notion of universality specific to cellular automata. Informally, a CA is *physically universal* if it is possible to implement any transformation on a finite set of cells by initializing the surrounding cells and letting the system evolve (we will see a formal definition in the next section). In other words, computations in a physically universal CA operate directly on cells, without requiring any special input encoding.

For instance, in a physically universal CA, there is some way to configure the cells around a 5-by-5 square region such that after some number of steps, t, the contents of the region will be rotated 90 degrees. Of course, we are not limited to geometric transformations. Given two disjoint 1-by-n regions, we can treat them as n-bit integers, compute their product, and write back the high-order bits of the product in one region and the low-order bits in the other. We can transform the input region by *any* function.

As motivation for physical universality, consider Deutsch's constructor theory [4], which "seeks to express all fundamental scientific theories in terms of a dichotomy between possible and impossible physical transformations". A physically universal CA is a toy universe in which all transformations (on a finite region) are possible. As a special case of physical universality, we can construct any desired pattern, and although this does not imply the existence of self-reproducing machines, it is closely related to von Neumann's work on universal construction. Janzing proposed physically universal CAs as a model of a world in which the boundary between a controller and the physical system it controls can be shifted. He discusses the thermodynamic and Kolmogorov complexity implications of physical universality at length in [7].

Physical universality imposes fairly stringent conditions on a CA. In particular, the CA must be reversible (i.e., it is possible to run the CA backwards), because otherwise information in the input may be lost before we can reach it. For instance, there are exponentially many configurations in Life which evolve to the empty configuration in one step. If one of these configurations occurs in the middle of the input region, there is no way to distinguish it from the others, because we cannot interact with it before it collapses. Reversibility rules out all of the examples above except for Margolus's CA.

Despite being reversible and capable of simulating circuits, Margolus's CA is not physically universal. It is possible to construct immovable, impenetrable walls in Margolus's CA, which contradict physical universality in two different ways. First, information cannot pass through the wall, so input cells within the wall cannot interact with the cells encoding the transformation, and it is impossible to implement an arbitrary transformation. Second, there is no way to move or destroy a wall, so it impossible to construct certain output configurations.

Since these well-known CAs (and many others) are not physically universal, Janzing asks whether physically universal CAs exist. The goal of this paper is to answer this question in two dimensions by presenting an example of a physically universal CA.

In addition to the proof of physical universality presented in this paper, the author has created an implementation of the CA in an open source cellular automaton simulator, available at http://web.mit.edu/lrs/www/physCA/index.html. The reader is encouraged to consult the website for a more concrete discussion of the cellular automaton and proof presented in this paper.

2. PHYSICAL UNIVERSALITY

Consider a cellular automaton where each cell has a state in Σ, a finite set. We will assume the cells are positioned at integer points $\mathbb{Z}^d$ in d dimensions (and eventually specialize to $d = 2$), but many of the following definitions could be generalized to other topologies. Let $\Omega := \mathbb{Z}^d$ be the set of all cells. Given a set $X \subseteq \Omega$, we say $\overline{X} := \Omega \backslash X$ is the *complement of X in Ω*.

A *configuration* of some subset of cells $X \subseteq \Omega$ is a map assigning each cell in X a state in Σ, and we let Σ^X denote the set of all configurations of X. The notation $\gamma \to \gamma'$ indicates that a configuration $\gamma \in \Sigma^\Omega$ changes into $\gamma' \in \Sigma^\Omega$ after one timestep. Similarly, $\gamma \xrightarrow{n} \gamma'$ means that after n timesteps the configuration goes from γ to γ'.

Suppose $Z \subseteq \Omega$ is a set of cells and we partition Z into disjoint subsets X and Y. A configuration $\gamma \in \Sigma^Z$ naturally splits into configurations $\gamma|_X \in \Sigma^X$ and $\gamma|_Y \in \Sigma^Y$ called the *restriction of γ to X (resp. Y)*. Conversely, given configurations $\alpha \in \Sigma^X$ and $\beta \in \Sigma^Y$, we let $\alpha \oplus \beta$ denote the combined configuration of Σ^Z.

Definition 1. Let $X, Y \subseteq \Omega$ be finite sets. Let $f \colon \Sigma^X \to \Sigma^Y$ be an arbitrary function. Then we say a configuration $\phi \in \Sigma^{\overline{X}}$ *implements the transformation f in time T* if for any configuration $x \in \Sigma^X$ there exists a configuration $\psi \in \Sigma^{\overline{Y}}$ such that

$$x \oplus \phi \xrightarrow{T} \psi \oplus f(x).$$

In other words, a configuration ϕ of $\overline{X}$ implements a transformation f if any initial configuration of x, combined with ϕ, evolves (in T timesteps) to a configuration where Y contains $f(x)$. We do not care about the contents of $\overline{Y}$ after T timesteps.

Definition 2. We say a cellular automaton is *physically universal* if for any input region $X \subseteq \Omega$, output region

$Y \subseteq \Omega$, and transformation $f \colon \Sigma^X \to \Sigma^Y$, there exists a configuration ϕ of $\overline{X}$ and constant t_0 such that ϕ implements f in time t_0.

We say the CA is *efficiently* physically universal if the implementation runs in time t_0, where t_0 is polynomial in

- the *diameter* of X (i.e., the width of the smallest hypercube containing the set) and diameter of Y,

- the distance between X and Y, and

- the computational complexity of f under some appropriate model of computation (e.g., the number of logical gates in a circuit for f).

Janzing's definition differs from our definition in two ways, but it turns out the definitions are equivalent. First, he assumes the input and output region are the same, i.e., $X = Y$. Clearly we can take any region Z containing $X \cup Y$ and extend f to a function $\hat{f}$ on the region Z, which does not depend on cells outside X, agrees with f on Y, and takes arbitrary values everywhere else. Janzing also assumes the transformation is bijective, but by a well-known result of Bennett [1], we can embed an arbitrary function f into a reversible function on twice as many bits, such that for some initial configuration of half the bits, f is a restriction of the reversible function to the other half of the bits.

Let us make a few observations about efficient physical universality. First, the time to implement an arbitrary transformation must grow linearly with the diameter of the input, since information can only travel $O(1)$ cells per timestep. For the same reason, information must (in general) travel from X to Y, so the number of steps is at least linear in the distance between them. Finally, there is an enormous number of transformations from X to Y. Even if Y is a single cell, we need at least $|\Sigma|^{|X|}$ bits specify an arbitrary transformation. We do not have that many bits in polynomial space, so we need a third parameter, e.g., computational complexity, to give us more space for some transformations.

3. CELLULAR AUTOMATON

In this section, we define and motivate a cellular automaton; in Section 4 we will prove the CA is physically universal. We use two states, $\Sigma = \{0, 1\}$, in our CA. In figures, we will represent 0 cells as white and 1 cells as black. Our CA is a kind of *block cellular automaton*, meaning that we partition the grid into blocks of cells and update each block according to a *local update rule*. In this case, we use a partition of the grid into 2-by-2 blocks. On the next timestep, we shift the partition one step north and one step east, then back again for the timestep after that. This is known as a *Margolus neighbourhood*.

Let the symbol $\boxplus$ denote a set of four cells in a 2-by-2 square. The state of a block is a function from $\boxplus$ to Σ, so we write $\Sigma^{\boxplus}$ for the set of all configurations of the block. In a Margolus neighbourhood cellular automaton, the local update rule takes the form $\rho \colon \Sigma^{\boxplus} \to \Sigma^{\boxplus}$, which expresses the evolution of a 2-by-2 block over one timestep.

There are some advantages to using a Margolus neighbourhood over the more common *Moore neighbourhood*, where each cell is updated based on its current state and the states of its eight nearest neighbours. It is much easier to express CAs with reversibility and conservation properties in a Margolus neighbourhood. For instance, a Margolus neighbourhood CA is reversible if and only if the update rule ρ is reversible, and the reverse CA has a Margolus neighbourhood. Compare this to a Moore neighbourhood CA, where it is undecidable whether an arbitrary CA is reversible, and the reverse may not be a Moore neighbourhood CA.

Margolus and Toffoli [10] give a very general conversion from block cellular automata to Moore neighbourhood CAs. Their conversion augments the set of states with extra information, so each cells knows its current position within the block (e.g., NE, NW, SE, SW). Then the Moore neighbourhood rule can tell which neighbours of a cell are in the same block, and update accordingly. This is suitable for simulating a block CA, but note that the extra information must have the correct initial configuration (e.g., a "northeast corner" cell should not be next to another cell of the same type) or the CA will fail. The resulting Moore neighbourhood CA is therefore not physically universal, since some configurations of the input region (or output region) are forbidden.

Another way to convert a Maroglus neighbourhood CA to a Moore neighbourhood is to collapse each 2-by-2 block to a cell (with state $\Sigma^{\boxplus}$). The configuration of a block after two timesteps is a function of its current state and the eight surrounding blocks, so we can make one timestep in the Moore neighbourhood CA simulate *two* timesteps of the Margolus neighbourhood CA. It will turn out that our (Margolus neighbourhood) CA takes an even number of steps to implement any transformation, so the corresponding Moore neighbourhood CA is also physically universal.

Let us introduce the local update rules for our CA. We begin with the following two rules:

The rule on the left says that empty (white) space remains empty. If we start with a single black cell in the northwest corner of a block, the rule on the right moves it to the southeast corner. Since the partition also moves one step southeast (or equivalently northeast/northwest/southwest), the black cell is again in the northwest corner and therefore it takes another step southeast. Every step, the black cell will move one unit southeast.

We also have the following three similar rules.

It follows that a lone black cell will move in some direction (northeast, northwest, southeast or southwest as dictated by the corner it starts in) until it encounters another black cell. We think of black cells as *particles* and white cells as empty space, so the remaining update rules describe the interactions between two or more particles. In keeping with the particle metaphor, our CA satisfies the following "physical" laws.

Symmetry: Particle interaction is symmetric. To be precise, given a symmetry $\pi \colon \boxplus \to \boxplus$ of $\boxplus$ (e.g., rotation or reflection), $\rho(x \circ \pi) = \rho(x) \circ \pi$ for all $x \in \Sigma^{\boxplus}$, where $\circ$ denotes function composition.

Conservation: The number of particles is conserved. The number of black cells within a block does not change after one update step, and therefore the number of black cells across the whole grid is constant over time.

Reversibility: The CA is reversible. A Margolus neighbourhood CA is reversible if and only if the update rule, ρ, is bijective.

We argued that reversibility is necessary in a physically universal CA. There is no reason to believe symmetry or conservation are necessary for physical universality, but they are nice properties to have.

Up to symmetry, there are only four kinds of collisions: two opposing particles, two particles at right angles, three particles, and four particles. Particle conservation forces the four-particle rule to be

and severely restricts the two- and three-particle collisions. Symmetry narrows down the set of possible rules even further. For instance, if we have one of these two rules,

then we have both by symmetry, since they are 180 degree rotations of each other. Both rules cannot hold simultaneously because the local update rule is deterministic, therefore neither rule holds. Due to the reversibility of the CA, the reverse situation is similar. That is, we cannot have the rules

since having one would imply the other (by symmetry) and having both contradicts reversibility.

There are eight cellular automata which meet our self-imposed constraints. We will take the CA such that

but at least five of the alternatives have been previously studied, including Margolus's billiard ball CA [8] and Hardy-Pazzis-Pomeau (HPP) gas [6]. The HPP gas is particularly interesting, because it is likely physical universal by a similar proof.

For reference, Figure 1 presents the complete update rule for our CA.

4. PROOF OF PHYSICAL UNIVERSALITY

As discussed earlier, we may assume the input region X and output region Y are the same, and take X to be a $2n \times 2n$ square of cells aligned to the block boundaries. We assume our boolean function is given as a circuit of m NOR gates. Our goal is to produce an initial configuration $\phi \in \Sigma^X$ which implements f in time polynomial in n and m.

We divide the computation into stages chronologically as follows.

1. It turns out that particles in our CA behave somewhat like a gas, in that particles diffuse out of any bounded region. We will show that if all particles are initially in a square box (e.g., X), then after some number of timesteps, all particles will be outside the box, moving away in one of four groups of particles.

2. We place particles in the initial configuration of $\overline{X}$ to intercept the particles as they escape from the box, preserving the information represented by the presence

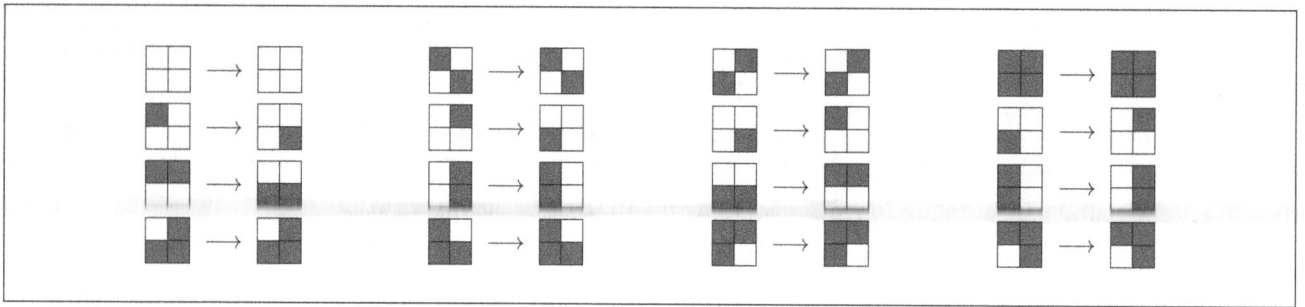

Figure 1: A full description of ρ, the local update rule.

or absence of a particle. We rearrange this information into a column formation for easier computation.

3. Next, we show how to implement a NOR operation on the column of bits. Since the NOR gate is universal, we can implement arbitrary circuits, which we use to perform the following transformations.

   - Simulate the CA in reverse to determine the initial configuration of the input, based on the particles that escaped X.
   - Apply the function f to the initial contents of X.
   - Simulate the CA in reverse again, so we know where to send particles to achieve the desired output configuration.

4. Finally, we carefully position particles such that they converge on X and interact to produce the desired result.

We structure the proof to reflect these stages. For each stage, we place a few more particles in the initial configuration at positions designed to cause collisions between particles at precise locations. By setting up collisions in appropriate locations (and avoiding all other collisions), we can accomplish the objectives for each stage.

4.1 Particle Diffusion

Particles in our CA will tend to diffuse out of any finite region into the empty space surrounding it. The CA is deterministic, so all particles escape after finite time, and we can give an explicit bound on that time. Furthermore, there are exactly $4n^2$ places where the $4n^2$ particles in the input region can escape, so we know where to intercept the particles. We express this more precisely with the following theorem.

THEOREM 1 (DIFFUSION THEOREM). Let $X \subseteq \Omega$ be a $2n$-by-$2n$ square region of cells. Partition X into four groups of cells, C_{NE}, C_{NW}, C_{SE} and C_{SW}. Let C_{NE} consist of the southwest corner of every block in X, because particles in those cells will move northeast in the next timestep (barring interference from other particles). Similarly, C_{NW}, C_{SE} and C_{SW} consist of the southeast, northwest and northeast corners of the blocks.

Let each group evolve as a function of time (i.e., $C_{NE} = C_{NE}(t)$) such that after t timesteps, group C_x is translated t cells in the direction x from its initial position. Let X evolve over time as well by defining

$$X(t) = C_{NE}(t) \cup C_{NW}(t) \cup C_{SE}(t) \cup C_{SW}(t).$$

If we start in a configuration with all particles inside $X(0)$ then all particles will be inside $X(t)$ after t timesteps. For $t \geq n$, no block contains more than one cell in $X(t)$, so it follows that there are no particle interactions after timestep n.

We leave the proof to Appendix A.

The theorem tells us that the information will escape from the region on its own, saving us the trouble of probing into the input region to its contents. The $4n^2$ bits of information stay in $X(t)$, and though the cells in $X(t)$ grow apart over time, the information remains concentrated in the $4n^2$ cells of $X(t)$ at any given time. This is remarkable because most reversible CAs will spread the information over more cells as time passes, creating an urgency to probe the bits before they spread further, but the diffusion theorem tells us we will only ever have $4n^2$ cells to look at. Moreover, the contents of the cells do not change after n timesteps because there are no interactions. This means we can probe the $4n^2$ cells on different timesteps (after step n) and still easily reconstruct the current state. In summary, the diffusion theorem guarantees a number of properties which make it easy to extract information from the input region.

The diffusion theorem has other applications. It helps us prevent unintended collisions between particles by specifying a time after which there are no more collisions. If we know there will be no more collisions between particles in one stage of our construction, then any interaction involving those particles must also involve two particles from a later stage. On the other hand, we cannot perform any useful computation without collisions, so the diffusion theorem bounds the time any given finite region can compute. Finally, observe that the update rule ρ is an involution, so the reverse CA is the same as the original CA, but starting with the opposite block alignment. Therefore, the diffusion theorem tells us we can put the output region into an arbitrary configuration by colliding four groups. This is exactly how we will generate an arbitrary configuration in the output.

4.2 Input Signal Redirection

After $2n$ steps, the input particles are in the four groups, as described above. The presence or absence of particles in the groups encodes $4n^2$ bits of information. Every timestep, each particle in C_{NE} moves one step northeast. Similarly, if there is no particle in some cell of C_{NE} then in the next timestep there will be no particle in the cell one step northeast. Either way, a bit of information moves northeast each timestep. We call this moving piece of information a *signal*.

We need to preserve the signals in order to reconstruct the original input bits, and eventually perform the transformation. It is difficult (if not impossible) to perform any computation while the signals are moving in four different directions. Therefore, our first task is to redirect the signals to all move in the same direction, say, northeast. Then we manipulate the signals so they are in the same column and densely packed. We call this arrangement *column formation*.

We use carefully placed particles (*control particles*) to control the signals. Since there are no interactions between pairs of particles, we need to intercept a signal with at least two other particles to affect it. Nothing useful happens when three particles meet a signal, so we consider the two ways (up to symmetry) for a signal and two particles to meet. We call these cases *reflection* and *deflection*.

Reflection: Suppose two particles meet head-on, with the signal at right angles. The signal will reflect off of the two particles and move in the opposite direction, as shown by the following rules.

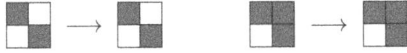

We use reflection to reverse the direction of a particle.

Deflection: Suppose the signal meets one particle head-on and another particle at right angles. The signal will continue on, but the particle at right angles will be reflected or not depending on the signal, effectively copying the signal.

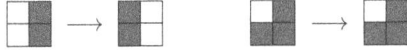

Deflection is useful for creating a duplicate (or inverted) signal at right angles. A deflection can produce particles or signals in all four directions, so we usually follow a deflection with one or more reflections to clean up.

These two operations are the building blocks for all the signal redirection. We also think of the following two operations as primitives, although they are built from deflections and reflections.

Double Deflection: In this maneuver, we deflect the signal 90 degrees, and then deflect it back along its original heading. This changes the diagonal along which the signal is moving, but not the direction. The deflections do not change the path of the original signal, so unless stated otherwise, a double deflection operation also includes a reflection to divert the original signal.

Double Reflection: When we reflect a particle twice, it will end up moving the same direction, along the same diagonal, but further back than before. The time between the two reflections controls how far the particle moves backwards.

Figure 2 illustrates all four basic operations, and shows how a signal x is manipulated by the other particles.

Since each operation requires us to intercept a signal with *two* other particles, we can control the position and time of the operation because those two particles intersect at a single point. If we have a group of signals moving northeast, for instance, we can apply an operation to any one of them

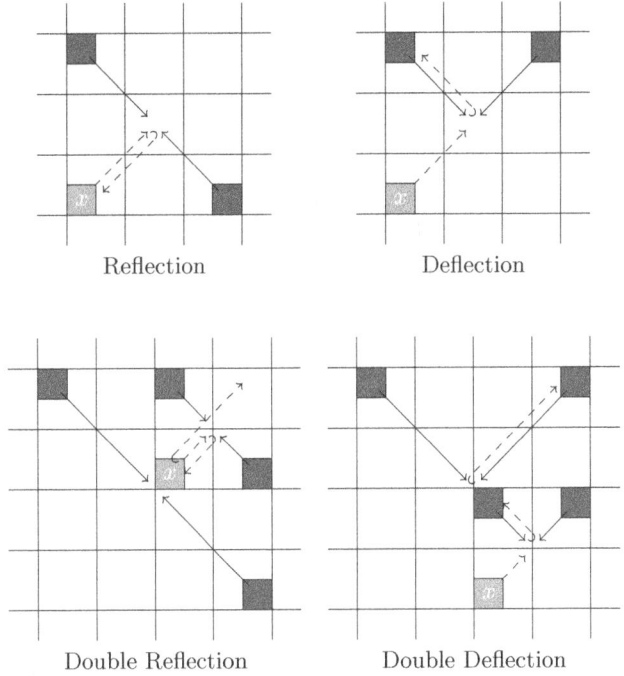

Figure 2: Basic operations for manipulating a signal, x, representing a bit of data. The flow of information is indicated by dashed lines.

without affecting the others, even though each control particle may have to pass several other signals. As long as the signals do not intersect each other, and we are given enough time, we can redirect signals to almost any location, in any arrangement.

In Appendix B, we work out an explicit procedure to transform the four square groups from the input region into a single column. To summarize, we use deflections and reflections to align the signals from the four groups in one direction, double deflections to place each signal in its own diagonal, and then double reflections to align the signals into a column.

4.3 Logical Operations and Computation

Observe that the local update rule $\rho \colon \Sigma^{\boxplus} \to \Sigma^{\boxplus}$ is a function from four bits to four bits. Define a four-input/four-output logical gate, the ρ-gate, based on ρ. The ρ-gate is universal,[1] so we can write our circuit in terms of ρ-gates. Using the redirection techniques from the previous section, we can arrange for four arbitrary signals to meet at an arbitrary block, where they are transformed (in a single step) according to ρ, thereby implementing a ρ-gate. The outputs of this interaction can then be redirected as well, and so on, to build up an arbitrary ρ-gate circuit.

For the sake of computational efficiency, we give a different approach in Appendix C. We start from a column of signals, then show how to compute the NOR of a set of signals and append it to the end. Since NOR is universal, we can repeat this procedure to implement any logical circuit. When it is complete, we have a column with signals representing the

---

[1]One can implement a controlled-controlled-NOT (i.e., a Toffoli gate), for instance, where two of the inputs control a "dual rail" representation of a bit in the other two inputs.

input bits, intermediate computations, and output bits. The cost of the computation is proportional to the length of the column.

We use our ability to perform a sequence of computations, where the original transformation, $f: \Sigma^X \to \Sigma^X$, is somewhere in the middle. Before we can apply f to the initial configuration, $x \in \Sigma^X$, we must decode x from the $4n^2$ signals captured from the four square groups. Similarly, after we have computed the final configuration $f(x) \in \Sigma^X$, we need to encode it as a set of $4n^2$ signals. We arrange the signals into four groups, which converge on X to produce $f(x)$. This last step is the subject of the following section.

4.4 Output Signal Redirection

The final step of the construction is to insert the desired configuration, $f(x)$, into X, the output region. The diffusion theorem tells us we can insert $f(x)$ by making four groups of carefully designed signals meet in the output. The signals in the four groups were computed in the previous section, so the problem is to redirect a column of $4n^2$ signals into four groups, converging on X. This is essentially the reverse of an earlier step, where we redirected the four groups of signals into a single column.

Unfortunately, literally reversing our steps (in an attempt to exploit the reversibility of the CA) is not a practical way to put information into the output. To illustrate, suppose we implement our procedure and let the system evolve up to the point where the contents of the input region are laid out as a column of signals (i.e., just before we begin computation). Then we change some of the signals in the column, and run CA backwards for the same number of timesteps. In this situation, the contents of the input region will not reflect the changes we made to the column. The problem is that many cells, not just the the ones in the column, depend on a given cell of the input. Our construction copies information every time we perform a deflection operation, and we leave intermediate steps around in our computation. We have to change all of these cells to change the value of the input cell. Since there are too many cells to practically change, we must find another way to populate the output.

In Appendix D we describe a procedure to redirect a column of signals into the output. We use reflection and deflection operations to redirect signals, like we did for the input. The only challenge is that the signals must arrive simultaneously, which we ensure by designing "slack" into the paths of the signals, so we can adjust the length of the path to make the signal arrive at the correct time.

4.5 Conclusion

The output step completes the proof that this cellular automaton is physically universal. We have shown how to extract information from the region, perform arbitrary computations, and put arbitrary data back into the output region. Moreover, note that all operations take polynomial time. Redirecting the input takes $O(n^2)$ time where n is the diameter (in blocks) of the input. Performing the computation is $O(m)$ (where the transformation takes m gates), after $O(n^3)$ to decode the input. Encoding the output is $O(n^3)$, then redirecting it to the output takes time proportional to the rest of the computation. It is certainly polynomial in n and m, so we have shown our CA is efficiently physically universal.

There are many unanswered questions and conjectures about physical universality, our cellular automaton, and this specific physical universality construction. To summarize, there are three general questions.

- Give other examples of physically universal CAs, from the literature, in other dimensions, or with different qualitative properties.

- Improve the time or space complexity, with either a different construction or a different cellular automaton.

- Construct a CA with a stronger physical universality property. For instance, implement some notion of physical universality for unitary transformations in quantum cellular automata, or show how to implement unbounded computations.

5. ACKNOWLEDGEMENTS

This research was supported by the National Science Foundation Alan T. Waterman Award, grant number 2745557. The author would also like to thank Scott Aaronson for the problem and help preparing this paper, as well as David Deutsch for his comments.

6. REFERENCES

[1] C. H. Bennett. Logical reversibility of computation. *IBM J. Res. Dev.*, 17(6):525–532, November 1973.

[2] Elwyn Berlekamp, John H. Conway, and Richard K. Guy. *Winning Ways for Your Mathematical Plays*, volume 2. A. K. Peters, 1st edition, 1982.

[3] Matthew Cook. Universality in Elementary Cellular Automata. *Complex Systems*, 15(1):1–40, 2004.

[4] David Deutsch. Constructor Theory. http://arxiv.org/abs/1210.7439, 2012. [Online; accessed 7-August-2014].

[5] Martin Gardner. The fantastic combinations of John Conway's new solitaire game "life". *Scientific American*, 223:120–123, October 1970.

[6] J. Hardy, O. De Pazzis, and Y. Pomeau. Molecular dynamics of a classical lattice gas: Transport properties and time correlation functions. *Physical Review A*, 13(5):1949–1961, 1976.

[7] Dominik Janzing. Is there a physically universal cellular automaton or Hamiltonian? http://arxiv.org/abs/1009.1720, 2010. [Online; accessed 7-August-2014].

[8] Norman Margolus. Physics-like models of computation. *Physica D: Nonlinear Phenomena*, 10(1–2):81–95, 1984.

[9] Luke Schaeffer. A physically universal cellular automaton. http://web.mit.edu/lrs/www/physCA/index.html, 2014. [Online; accessed 7-August-2014].

[10] Tommaso Toffoli and Norman Margolus. *Cellular Automata Machines: A New Environment for Modeling*. MIT Press, Cambridge, MA, USA, 1987.

[11] John von Neumann. *Theory of Self-Reproducing Automata*. University of Illinois Press, Champaign, IL, USA, 1966.

APPENDIX

A. DIFFUSION THEOREM

In this appendix, we will prove a theorem about particles escaping from a bounded region in our CA. Loosely speaking, we show that any configuration of particles in a finite region will eventually escape the region.

In order to prove a theorem about all possible configurations of a region, we need to reason about the evolution of a collection of configurations simultaneously. Our approach is to represent the set of configurations in our original CA, which we call the *concrete CA*, with a single configuration of a new three-state *abstract CA*. We will relate the evolution of a single abstract configuration to the evolution of the collection of concrete configuration. The abstract CA is purely a tool for the proof; it will not be physically universal, or even reversible.

The abstract CA is over a set of three states, $\Gamma = \{0, 1, \top\}$, drawn as white, black and gray in figures. We think of it as in extension of the concrete CA where white and black have the same meaning as before, and gray is used to represent cells with unknown, uncertain or "wildcard" state. Suppose $\phi \in \Sigma^X$ is a concrete configuration and $\Phi \in \Gamma^X$ is an abstract configuration (of the same region). Then we say ϕ is *consistent* with Φ (or sometimes, Φ is *consistent* with ϕ) if every non-gray cell in Φ has the same colour as the corresponding cell in ϕ.

Given a set of concrete configurations, $S \subseteq \Sigma^X$, there is a *minimal consistent configuration* $\Phi_S \in \Gamma^X$ which is consistent with every member of S, and has the minimal number of gray cells. We think of Φ_S as a representation of the entire set S, but we lose a lot of information about the specific correlations between cells. For instance, if S is the set of all 2-by-2 block configurations with exactly one black cell, then we are uncertain about every cell. The minimal consistent configuration Φ_S is an all-gray block, the same as if S was the set of *all* block configurations.

The evolution of the abstract CA is as one might expect. Formally, we define $\rho' \colon \Gamma^{\boxplus} \to \Gamma^{\boxplus}$ such that $\rho'(\Phi)$ is the minimal configuration consistent with $\rho(\phi)$ for all ϕ consistent with Φ. In other words, we fill in the gray cells of Φ as black or white in all possible ways, evolve this collection of concrete configurations forwards one timestep, then let $\rho'(\Phi)$ be the minimal configuration consistent with all the evolutions. For example, ρ' contains the following rule

because the two configurations consistent with evolve as follows,

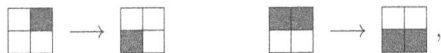

and is the minimal configuration consistent with both outcomes.

We can say a few general things about ρ' based on the conservativity of our CA. Consider the number of black cells, or *population*, of a configuration. For abstract configurations, the population is a *range* from the number of black cells, to the number of black or gray cells. Since our CA is conservative, the range in population for an abstract Φ is contained

in the range for $\rho'(\Phi)$. In particular, if all the cells in Φ are white or gray, then there cannot be any black cells in $\rho'(\Phi)$, since the population could be zero. The width of the range is the number of gray cells, so this also tells us that the number of gray cells cannot decrease as we evolve an abstract configuration (we can also get this from reversibility).

The payoff of these definitions is the following theorem (which we state without proof) relating the evolution of a collection of concrete configurations to the evolution of a single abstract configuration.

THEOREM 2. *Let* $\Phi \in \Gamma^\Omega$ *be an abstract configuration, and suppose* Φ *evolves (in the abstract CA) to* Φ' *after* n *timesteps. Let* $\phi \in \Sigma^\Omega$ *be an concrete configuration, and suppose it evolves (in the concrete CA) to* ϕ' *after* n *timesteps. Then* ϕ' *is consistent with* Φ' *if* ϕ *is consistent with* Φ.

The theorem, and more generally, the idea of creating an abstract CA with an "uncertain" state, is not specific to our CA. We could easily take an arbitrary binary cellular automaton and construct the corresponding abstract CA as above. In most cases, the result is uninformative; the "uncertain" state tends to proliferate, which tells us nothing about the concrete state. For some CAs, Theorem 2 may tell us little more than "non-blank cells may spread up to t steps away in t timesteps". In the abstract version of Conway's Life, for example, aside from two simple patterns[2], it is challenging to construct any configuration where the uncertain cells neither go extinct, nor overwhelm everything else.

Our specific abstract CA does not suffer from the problems described above because interaction between cells is rare. The CA just swaps opposite corners within each block unless exactly three of the cells are black. As a result, ρ' swaps opposite corners with each abstract block unless it is consistent with some three-particle concrete block. This allows us to compute most of the rules on white and gray blocks, shown in Figure 3. Observe that on white and gray blocks, ρ' is identical to ρ, except for the three-particle interactions. It follows that gray cells behave like particles, except when exactly three of them collide.

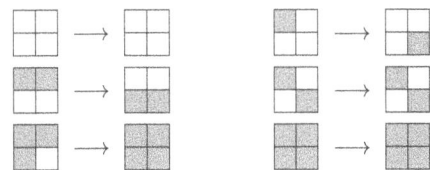

Figure 3: The update rule ρ' (suppressing symmetries) on white and gray blocks.

We will now show that a square of gray cells will diffuse into four groups, without generating any new gray cells. By Theorem 2, any concrete configuration of the square must also diffuse, and the diffusion theorem from the main text follows.

THEOREM 3. *Let* $X \subseteq \Omega$ *be a* $2n$-by-$2n$ *square region of cells. Let* $\phi \in \Gamma^\Omega$ *be the configuration where* $\overline{X}$ *is white and* X *is gray. Then we can partition the gray cells into four groups,* C_{NE}, C_{NW}, C_{SE} *and* C_{SW} *such that*

---

[2]Specifically, a blinker and a block, identical to their counterparts in concrete Life, but with uncertain cells.

- *each group contains n^2 gray particles,*
- *the gray particles in C_x all move in the direction x each step, and*
- *the cells outside $C_{NE} \cup C_{NW} \cup C_{SE} \cup C_{SW}$ are all white.*

It follows (by Theorem 2) that for any concrete configuration ψ consistent with ϕ (i.e., with all particles confined to the box X), the region X will be empty after $2n$ timesteps.

PROOF. The initial abstract configuration ϕ contains only white and gray cells. Since ρ' maps white and gray blocks to white and gray blocks (see Figure 3), the configuration will always be white and gray. Recall that the gray cells behave like particles as long as there are no three-particle interactions.

Divide the gray particles into groups C_{NE}, C_{NW}, C_{SE} and C_{SW}. We let C_{NE} contain particles in the southwest corners of their respective blocks because a particle in the southwest corner will move to the northeast corner (i.e., in the northeast direction) if there are no other particles. Similarly for C_{NW}, C_{SE} and C_{SW}.

We claim that the following blocks do not appear in the evolution of ϕ

,

and all the gray cells are in C_{NE}, C_{NW}, C_{SE}, C_{SW}, which move one cell per timestep in their respective directions.

If the six forbidden blocks do not appear, then it follows from the rules in Figure 3 that the gray cells in the groups move as described and no other gray cells are created.

The forbidden blocks do not appear in the initial configuration, but suppose for a contradiction that one of these six blocks occurs in some timestep. Without loss of generality, let the northeast corner of the block be white, so C_{SW} does not overlap with the block. Since C_{SW} is a square, the block is either too far north/south, or too far east/west to be in C_{SW}. In the former case, the block is also outside C_{SE} (since C_{SE} covers the same north/south range as C_{SW}), so the northwest corner is also white. In the latter case, the block must be outside C_{NE} and therefore the southeast corner of the block is white. In general, if some corner of a block is white then one of the two adjacent corners is also white. All six blocks above violate this condition, so they cannot occur.

A simple induction argument completes the proof. There are no forbidden blocks at $t = 0$, so the cells evolve as described, which implies there are no forbidden blocks in the next timestep, and so on. $\square$

The proof ignores the behaviour of ρ' on the forbidden blocks, so the theorem generalizes to other abstract CAs (and the corresponding concrete CAs). We can change the two-opposing-particle and three-particle interactions in the concrete CA, and it will only affect the two-opposing-particle and three-particle interactions in the abstract CA. In particular, the theorem holds for the HPP gas.

B. REDIRECTING INPUT SIGNALS INTO A COLUMN

Our goal is to redirect the four groups (C_{NE}, C_{NW}, C_{SE}, C_{SW}) from the input into a column of signals. First we need to get a copy of each signal moving northeast. The plan for each group is as follows.

Northeast The signals in C_{NE} are already moving northeast. We do not need to do anything with them until we have all the other signals moving northeast too.

Southwest The group C_{SW} is moving southwest, so we can use reflections to reverse the signals. One could reflect each particle individually, but it is easier to reflect the entire group by having a line of $O(n)$ particles moving southeast meet a line of $O(n)$ particles moving northwest. The two lines form a "mirror" to reflect the group.

Southeast The signals in C_{SE} are moving southeast, so we need to deflect them northeast. There is no shortcut to deflect the entire group at once (as we did for C_{SW}), but a single particle moving northwest may intercept many signals in C_{SE}, and we can reuse it for deflection of all those signals in quick succession.

Northwest The procedure for deflecting C_{NW} is essentially the mirror image of the procedure for C_{SE}. However, particles passing through C_{NW} (going southeast) may meet the particles passing through C_{SE} (going northwest). These intersections are harmless unless they meet a signal from C_{SW} moving northeast (having been redirected by our mirror) and reflect it back southwest. We can avoid this kind of interaction by changing the precise timing of C_{SW}, C_{SE} or C_{NW} redirections, so we will assume it does not happen.

Now suppose the four groups have been redirected and all the information from the input is contained in a collection of $4n^2$ signals moving northeast. We can reflect any other particles or signals moving northeast, so we assume only the input signals are moving northeast, and we redirect these signals into a column as follows.

1. If there are two or more particles moving along the same (northeast/southwest) diagonal then move them to separate diagonals using a double deflection maneuver. The signals from C_{SE} and C_{NW} should already be spread out (over approximately $O(n^2)$ diagonals) by the earlier deflections, but the signals from C_{NE} and C_{SW} are contained in just $O(n)$ diagonals. Computation on the column formation will be relatively efficient whether the signals are consecutive or not.

2. Identify the westmost signal in the group. Use double reflections to move each particle backwards (i.e., southwest) along the northeast/southwest diagonal until it is in the same column as the westernmost signal.

The plan above lists the collisions required to redirect the signals into column formation, but only at a high level. The exact time and coordinates of each collision are too tedious to specify here, so scheduling is left as an exercise to the reader. We make the following observations about scheduling collisions.

- It is easy to determine the initial configuration required to produce a collision at a given time and place, assuming nothing interferes with our particles along the way. We simply work backwards from the collision site.

- Any accidental interaction requires at least three particles (or signals). Each of the three particles is either on the way to an (intentional) interaction, or the product some earlier interaction. In almost all cases, we can move one of the three interactions such that the particles do not coincide.

244

- We have plenty of time and space to spend making sure there are no accidental interactions. We claim that an efficient schedule can perform the redirections above in $O(n^2)$ time, but scheduling becomes much easier if we give ourselves polynomial time. For instance, when we deflect C_{SE}, we can wait $O(n)$ steps after each deflection to ensure the particles and signals from one deflection are completely clear of C_{SE} before we start the next deflection.

- We can apply the diffusion theorem to prevent unintended collisions. For instance, if it takes $O(n^2)$ time to redirect the four groups, then all signals and particles used up to that point must be in a region of size $O(n^2)$. After another $O(n^2)$ steps, none of the particles from that region will ever interact with each other again (by the diffusion theorem).

C. EFFICIENT COMPUTATION

In the main text, we argued that our CA can simulate arbitrary circuits by stringing ρ-gates together with redirection operations. Here we will present an alternative method, which builds on the column formation Appendix B for provably efficient universal computation.

THEOREM 4. *Let* $X = \{x_1, \ldots, x_{n+m}\}$ *be a group of signals moving northeast in column formation, where signals* $x_1, \ldots, x_n$ *encode bits* $b_1, \ldots, b_n \in \{0,1\}$ *respectively, and* $x_{n+1}, \ldots, x_{n+m}$ *are empty.*

Suppose we are given sets $S_1, \ldots, S_m$ *where* S_i *is a subset of* $\{1, \ldots, n+i-1\}$, *for all* i. *Define* $b_{n+1}, \ldots, b_{n+m}$ *such that*

$$b_{n+i} = \overline{\bigvee_{j \in S_i} b_j}.$$

Then we can initialize $\overline{X}$ *such that after* t *timesteps, the signal* x_j *encodes bit* b_j, *for all* $1 \leq j \leq m+n$. *In other words, we can modify the last* m *signals so each one is the NOR of a given set of earlier signals.*

Furthermore, t *is in* $O(n+m)$ *and the number of particles in* $\overline{C}$ *is*

$$3m + \sum_{i=1}^{m} |S_i|.$$

PROOF. Consider an arbitrary signal x_{n+i} where $1 \leq i \leq m$. We construct particles p_i, q_i and r_i, moving southeast, southwest, and northwest respectively. We position the particles so they all meet (at the same time) with x_{i+n}, assuming they are not reflected earlier. Furthermore, we position p_i north of all signals in X and north of $p_1, \ldots, p_{i-1}$. The idea is that if p_i is not reflected back northwest before it meets r_i, then p_i and r_i will reflect q_i into x_{i+n} (i.e., signal x_{i+n} will contain a particle). Otherwise q_i will continue moving southwest and x_{i+n} will continue to be empty.

We also set up a particle s_{ij} for each $1 \leq i \leq m$ and $j \in S_i$. Let s_{ij} move southwest and intercept p_i and x_j at the same time. The result is that p_i will be reflected if $b_j = 1$, unless p_i has already been reflected. Hence, p_i only reaches x_{i+n} if $b_j = 0$ for all $j \in S_i$. It follows that

$$b_{n+i} = \overline{\bigvee_{j \in S_i} b_j},$$

as desired.

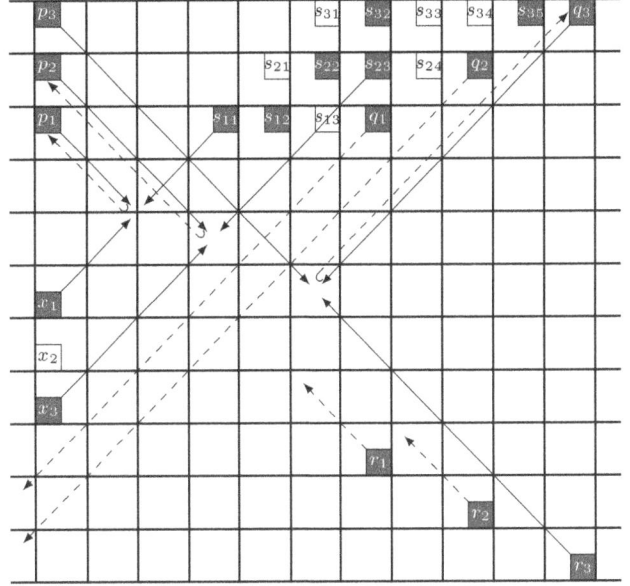

Figure 4: **An example of a small computation on bits** x_1, x_2, x_3.

Observe that only $x_1, \ldots, x_{n+m}$ and $p_1, \ldots, p_m$ are moving eastwards (i.e., northeast or southeast). Each p_i is positioned to collide with the corresponding x_{i+n}, so they must be in the same column. It follows that all eastbound particles are in the same column. Collisions require at least three particles, at least one of which must be eastbound, so all collisions must occur in the same column as the x_js. We positioned the particles (p_i, q_i, r_i and s_{ij}) based on where and when they meet the x_js, so the only collisions are the ones we have already discussed.

Suppose we place p_1 immediately above x_1 and $p_2, \ldots, p_m$ in order above that. Then clearly p_m reaches x_{m+n} in $t = O(m+n)$ time. It is also clear that we use only $3 + |S_i|$ particles to modify x_{i+n}, and hence only $3m + \sum_{i=1}^{m} |S_i|$ particles altogether. $\square$

Figure 4 shows the construction on three bits, $x_1 = 1$, $x_2 = 0$ and $x_3 = 1$. We add $x_4 = \overline{x_1 \vee x_2} = 0$, $x_5 = \overline{x_2 \vee x_3} = 0$ and $x_6 = \overline{x_2 \vee x_5} = 1$ over the course of the computation. The black cells are particles, and white cells are locations where particles are conspicuously absent. For instance, we could place particles at s_{13}, s_{21}, and so on, to specify a different circuit. We use arrows to indicate the motion of key particles, and we use a dashed arrow if the particle does not interact with any other particles. We can see that p_1 and p_2 are deflected (by x_1 and x_3 respectively), but p_3 makes it all the way to q_3 and r_3, so it can reflect q_3 into position as x_6.

D. OUTPUT REDIRECTION

We start with a column of signals from the computation step (see Appendix C), which we wish to insert into a square region X, the output. We divide the signals into four groups, C_{NE}, C_{NW}, C_{SW}, and C_{SE}, where the subscript indicates the direction of motion of the group when it eventually converges on X. Initially, the signals are in column formation, moving northeast, along with signals leftover from the intermediate computations. We make a few preliminary adjustments to the signals as follows.

1. Reflect all signals moving northeast except the $4n^2$ designated signals. We do not want any interference.

2. Use a series of double deflections to move the $4n^2$ designated signals so they are approximately northeast of X. That is, they are not too far from the northeast/southwest diagonal passing through the center of X.

3. Use further double deflections and double reflections to rearrange the signals into four square formations corresponding to the four groups. Within a group, each signal should have the same offset from its intended destination, except within C_{SW}. We will move C_{SW} into final position by reflection, so we expect each signal to have the same offset to the *reflection* (over a northwest/southeast diagonal) of its destination. For C_{SW} and C_{NE}, we expect the offsets to be strictly northeast (no steps northwest or southeast).

At this point, we wait until the signals are, as a group, some suitably large distance D northeast of X. The plan is to have the signals diverge at this point, and converge on X in approximately $3D$ steps, at some target time t. Conceptually, we redirect the four groups as follows.

Southwest Signals in C_{SW} continue northeast until they are $2D$ units from X, and then we reflect them back towards the origin. No other manipulations are necessary because the signals in C_{SW} are already in the correct square formation.

Northeast We reflect signals in C_{NE} back to the southwest, and let them travel $2D$ units before reflecting them northeast again. The two reflections are sufficient because C_{NE} is already in a square formation.

Southeast We deflect signals in C_{SE} northwest for about D units. Then we deflect the signals southwest for D units, and finally southeast for the final approach. The final deflection (to the southeast) is different from the other deflections; we use the incoming signal from the northeast and a particle from the southwest to reflect a particle coming from the northwest because a particle from the southeast would have to pass through X at an awkward time. In other words, there is a group of particles in square formation moving southeast towards X, and the final deflection whittles away particles to form signals, instead of reflecting new particles into empty space.

Northwest We redirect signals in C_{NW} as the mirror image C_{SE}. We will see that it is not an exact mirror image in practice.

There are two practical issues. First, the operations turn out to depend on the "parity"' of the signals. That is, if a particle is x blocks right of its target position and y blocks above, then it will be impossible to maneuver it into position if $x + y$ is odd. Fortunately, we completely control parity in the computation stage, and a more complicated series of collisions could avoid parity issues altogether.

Second, we cannot redirect all four groups simultaneously. Even if we could, deflecting C_{SE} and C_{NW} would likely create unwanted collisions. As a result, there may be some distance (and time) between the ideal initial redirection of a signal, and the actual initial redirection. Each signal still needs to arrive at the right time, so we make corrections as follows.

- Define D so that the path of group C_{SW} does not require correction. The other groups may be delayed, but we assume D is large enough that they will be deflected long before we need to reflect C_{SW}.

- As long as the initial reflection of C_{NE} is less than D steps late, it will pass through X before the designated time t. As the time remaining (until the groups converge) decreases, the distance between C_{NE} and X increases. At some point the time remaining is equal to the distance, and we schedule the second reflection relative to that point.

- We adjust signals in C_{SE} using the second deflection, at a location approximately $2D$ cells north of its final location. Recall that we want each signal in C_{SE} to meet a particle moving southeast, so we must deflect the signal southwest when it is in the same row of cells as the particle. Then the signal is to the east of the particle, so the two will eventually collide.

  Observe that if we delay the first deflection, it does not change the time of the second deflection, since the signal is moving north (either northeast or northwest) at the same rate before and after the first deflection. The delay does move the location of the second deflection east.

Finally, we need to show that there are no unintentional collisions. Any unintentional collision involves three particles, so there are intentional collisions on three sides. If two or more of the signals come from nearby collisions (say, within $\frac{D}{2}$ timesteps) then we say the collision is *local*. The nearby collisions must involve the same group, so we can eliminate a local collision by rescheduling the collisions for a single group, and there is plenty of time and space to do so. We will assume any unintentional collisions are non-local.

There are only two areas where three intentional collisions could occur at the right time to have an unintentional non-local collision.

1. The area D units northeast of the output region is also D units from collisions involving C_{SE}, C_{NW}, and C_{SW}. The concern is that garbage from the C_{SE} and C_{NW} collisions (which deflect those groups to the southwest) will cross in this area and interfere with C_{SW}. This can be corrected by scheduling the initial deflections for C_{SE} and C_{NW} sufficiently far apart, ideally on disjoint northwest/southeast diagonals.

2. The output region itself has intentional collisions on all sides. However, the only collisions to the northwest are the ones which deflect C_{SE} toward the output region. Assuming there are no local collisions, this means any unintentional collision would have to involve C_{SE}. Similarly, an unintentional collision would have to involve C_{NW}. These two groups only meet in the output region, just before time t, so any collision involving C_{SE} and C_{NW} is essential.

Since only intentional collisions occur, we will redirect the signals into four groups, which will converge on X to create the desired configuration at time t. The results in this appendix, along with Appendix A, Appendix B, and Appendix C complete the proof of physical universality.

A New Approach to the Sensitivity Conjecture

Justin Gilmer
Department of Mathematics
Rutgers University
Piscataway, NJ, USA
jmgilmer@math.rutgers.edu

Michal Koucký
Computer Science Institute
Charles University
Prague, Czech Republic
koucky@iuuk.mff.cuni.cz

Michael Saks
Department of Mathematics
Rutgers University
Piscataway, NJ, USA
saks@math.rutgers.edu

ABSTRACT

One of the major outstanding foundational problems about boolean functions is the *sensitivity conjecture*, which (in one of its many forms) asserts that the degree of a boolean function (i.e. the minimum degree of a real polynomial that interpolates the function) is bounded above by some fixed power of its sensitivity (which is the maximum vertex degree of the graph defined on the inputs where two inputs are adjacent if they differ in exactly one coordinate and their function values are different). We propose an attack on the sensitivity conjecture in terms of a novel two-player communication game. A strong enough lower bound on the cost of this game would imply the sensitivity conjecture.

To investigate the problem of bounding the cost of the game, three natural (stronger) variants of the question are considered. For two of these variants, protocols are presented that show that the hoped for lower bound does not hold. These protocols satisfy a certain monotonicity property, and (in contrast to the situation for the two variants) we show that the cost of any monotone protocol satisfies a strong lower bound.

Categories and Subject Descriptors

F.1.3 [**Computation by Abstract Devices**]: Complexity Measures and Classes—*Relations among complexity measures*

Keywords

Sensitivity conjecture; degree of Boolean functions; sensitivity; decision trees; communication complexity

1. INTRODUCTION

1.1 A Communication Game

The focus of this paper is a somewhat unusual cooperative two player communication game. The game is parameterized by a positive integer n and is denoted G_n. Alice receives

a permutation $\sigma = (\sigma_1, \ldots, \sigma_n)$ of $[n] = \{1, \ldots, n\}$ and a bit $b \in \{0,1\}$ and communicates to Bob in a very restricted way (which will be described momentarily). Bob receives the message from Alice and then outputs a subset J of $[n]$ that is required to include σ_n, the last element of the permutation. The cost to Alice and Bob is the size of the set $|J|$.

The communication from Alice to Bob is constrained as follows: Alice has a memory vector $\mathbf{v}$ consisting of n cells which we will refer to as *locations*, where each location v_ℓ is either empty, denoted by $v_\ell = *$, or is set to 0 or 1. Initially all locations are empty. Alice gets the input as a data stream $\sigma_1, \ldots, \sigma_n, b$ and is required to fill the cells of $\mathbf{v}$ in the order specified by σ. After receiving σ_i for $i < n$, Alice fills location σ_i with 0 or 1. Upon receiving σ_n and b, Alice writes b in location σ_n.

Once $\mathbf{v}$ is filled, Bob inspects $\mathbf{v}$ and outputs the subset J.

Given a protocol Π for this game, the cost of the protocol $c(\Pi)$ is the maximum of the output size $|J|$ over all inputs $\sigma_1, \ldots, \sigma_n, b$.

For example, consider the following protocol. Let $k = \lceil \sqrt{n} \rceil$. Alice and Bob fix a partition of the locations of $\mathbf{v}$ into k blocks each of size at most k. Alice fills $\mathbf{v}$ as follows: When σ_i arrives, if σ_i is the last location of its block to arrive then fill the entry with 1 otherwise fill it with 0.

Notice that if $b = 1$ then the final vector $\mathbf{v}$ will have a single 1 in each block. If $b = 0$ then $\mathbf{v}$ will have a unique all 0 block.

Bob chooses J as follows: if there is an all 0 block, then J is set to be that block, and otherwise J is set to be the set of locations containing 1's. It is clear that $\sigma_n \in J$ and so this is a valid protocol. In all cases the size of J will be at most k and so the cost of the protocol is $\lceil \sqrt{n} \rceil$. We will refer to this protocol as the AND-OR protocol. In Section 2.1 we remark on this protocol's connection to the boolean function

$$\text{AND-OR}(x) = \bigwedge_{i=1}^{\sqrt{n}} \bigvee_{j=1}^{\sqrt{n}} x_{ij}.$$

Let us define $C(n)$ to be the minimum cost of any protocol for G_n. We are interested in the growth rate of $C(n)$ as a function of n. In particular, we propose:

QUESTION 1. *Is there a $\delta > 0$ such that $C(n) = \Omega(n^\delta)$?*

1.2 Connection to the Sensitivity Conjecture

Why consider such a strange game? The motivation is that the game provides a possible approach to the well known *sensitivity conjecture* from boolean function complexity.

Recall that the sensitivity of an n-variate boolean function f at an input $\mathbf{x}$, denoted $s_f(\mathbf{x})$, is the number of locations ℓ such that if we flip the bit of $\mathbf{x}$ in location ℓ then the value of the function changes. (Alternatively, this is the number of neighbors of $\mathbf{x}$ in the hamming graph whose f value is different from $f(\mathbf{x})$.) The sensitivity of f, $s(f)$, is the maximum of $s_f(\mathbf{x})$ over all boolean inputs $\mathbf{x}$.

The degree of a function f, $deg(f)$, is the smallest degree of a (real) polynomial p in variables $x_1, \ldots, x_n$ that agrees with f on the boolean cube.

CONJECTURE 2. *(The Sensitivity Conjecture) There is a $\delta > 0$ such that for any boolean function f, $s(f) \geq \Omega(deg(f)^\delta)$.*

An easy argument (given in Section 2) connects the cost function $C(n)$ of the game G_n to the sensitivity conjecture:

PROPOSITION 3. *For any boolean function on n variables, $s(f) \geq C(deg(f))$.*

In particular, an affirmative answer to Question 1 would imply the sensitivity conjecture.

1.3 Background on the Sensitivity Conjecture

Sensitivity and degree belong to a large class of complexity measures for boolean functions that seek to quantify, for each function f, the amount of knowledge about individual variables needed to evaluate f. Other such measures include decision tree complexity and its randomized and quantum variants, certificate complexity, and block sensitivity. The value of such a measure is at most the number of variables. There is a long line of research aimed at bounding one such measure in terms of another. For measures a and b let us write $a \leq_r b$ if there are constants C_1, C_2 such that for every total boolean function f, $a(f) \leq C_1 b(f)^r + C_2$. For example, the decision tree complexity of f, $D(f)$, is at least its degree $deg(f)$ and thus $deg \leq_1 D$. It is also known [8] that $D \leq_3 deg$. We say that a is *polynomially bounded* by b if $a \leq_r b$ for some $r > 0$ and that a and b are *polynomially equivalent* if each is polynomially bounded by the other.

The measures mentioned above, with the notable exception of sensitivity, are known to be polynomially equivalent. For example, in relating block sensitivity, $bs(f)$, to degree Nisan and Szegedy [9] show that $bs(f) \leq_2 deg(f)$. In the other direction, the bound $deg(f) \leq_3 bs(f)$ follows from a result in [1]. For a survey on many of these results, see [2]. The sensitivity conjecture asserts that $s(f)$ is polynomially equivalent to all of the measures mentioned in this section, and for this, it suffices to show that it is polynomially related to $deg(f)$.

There are a number of equivalent formulations of the sensitivity conjecture. For instance [4] give a graph theoretic formulation by exploring a different relationship between sensitivity and degree than what is presented here. The same graph theoretic question also appeared somewhat earlier in [3], however, sensitivity of boolean functions was only mentioned as a related problem and no direct connection was given. For a good survey of many other variations of the sensitivity conjecture, see [5].

The sensitivity conjecture perhaps more commonly appears as a question on the relationship between sensitivity and block sensitivity. For example, Nisan and Szegedy

[9] asked specifically if $bs(f) = O(s^2(f))$ for all functions, and as of this writing no counterexample has been given. The best known bound relating sensitivity to another measure was given by Kenyon and Kutin [6]. They proved that $bs(f) \leq \frac{e}{2\pi} e^{s(f)} \sqrt{s(f)}$ for all boolean functions.

1.4 Outline of the Paper

In Section 2 we prove that a positive answer to Question 1 would imply the sensitivity conjecture. We also describe how protocols relate adversarial methods for proving that boolean functions are evasive (that is have decision tree complexity $D(f) = n$). At the end of the section we prove that it suffices to answer Question 1 for a special subset of protocols called *order oblivious protocols*.

In Section 3 we present three stronger variants of Question 1. We then show that for two of these variants, there are protocols that give negative answers to the questions, and suggest that Question 1 has a negative answer as well. However, these protocols satisfy a property called monotonicity and in Section 4 we prove an $\Omega(n^{1/2})$ lower bound on the cost of any monotone protocol, which shows that any protocol that gives a negative answer to Question 1, must look quite different from the two protocols that refuted the strengthenings. In the same section we prove a rather weak lower bound for a special class of protocols called assignment oblivious protocols. Finally, in Section 5 we give the construction of the lowest cost protocol that we know, whose cost is lower than that of the AND-OR protocol by a constant factor.

2. CONNECTION BETWEEN THE SENSITIVITY CONJECTURE AND THE GAME

In this section we prove Proposition 3, which connects the sensitivity conjecture with the two player game described in the introduction.

We will use $\mathbf{e}_\ell$ to denote the assignment in $\{0,1\}^n$ that is 1 in location ℓ and 0 elsewhere. Given two assignments $\mathbf{v}, \mathbf{w} \in \{0,1\}^n$ we will use $\mathbf{v} \oplus \mathbf{w}$ to denote the assignment for which each coordinate is the mod-2 sum of the corresponding coordinates in $\mathbf{v}$ and $\mathbf{w}$.

Recall that Alice's strategy gives the mapping from the input permutation σ and bit b to a boolean vector $\mathbf{v}$ and Bob's strategy maps the vector $\mathbf{v}$ to a subset of locations in $\mathbf{v}$. We first observe that for each strategy for Alice there is a canonical best strategy for Bob. For a permutation σ, we let $\Pi_A(\sigma)$ denote the vector Alice writes down after receiving $\sigma_1, \cdots, \sigma_{n-1}$ (so the location σ_n is still labeled with a $*$). Thus $\Pi_A(\sigma)$ can be viewed as an edge in the *hamming graph* $\mathbb{H}_n$ whose vertex set is $\{0,1\}^n$, with two vertices adjacent if they differ in one coordinate. The *edge set* $E(\Pi)$ of a protocol Π is the set of edges $\Pi_A(\sigma)$ over all permutations σ. This defines a subgraph of $\mathbb{H}_n$. Given Alice's output $\mathbf{v}$, the possible values for σ_n are precisely those locations ℓ that satisfy $(\mathbf{v}, \mathbf{v} \oplus \mathbf{e}_\ell)$ is an edge in $E(\Pi)$. Thus the best strategy for Bob is to output this set of locations. It follows that $c(\Pi)$ is equal to the maximum vertex degree of the graph $E(\Pi)$.

Proposition 3 will therefore follow by showing the following: Given a boolean function with degree n and sensitivity s, there is a strategy Π for Alice for the game G_n such that the graph $E(\Pi)$ has maximum degree at most s.

We need a few preliminaries. A *subfunction* of a boolean function f is a function g obtained from f by fixing some of the variables of f to 0 or 1. Note it is clear that if g is a subfunction of f then $s(f) \geq s(g)$. We say a function has *full degree* if $deg(f)$ is equal to the number of variables of f. We start by recalling some well known facts.

LEMMA 4. *For any boolean function f there exists a subfunction g on $deg(f)$ variables that has full degree.*

PROOF. If p is the (unique) multilinear real polynomial that agrees with f on the boolean cube, then p contains a monomial $\prod_{\ell \in S} x_\ell$ where $|S| = deg(f)$. Let g be the function obtained by fixing the variables in $[n] \setminus S$ to 0. Then g is a function on $deg(f)$ variables that has full degree. $\square$

LEMMA 5. *Given a function f with full degree and a location ℓ, there exists a bit b such that the function obtained from f by fixing $x_\ell = b$ is also of full degree.*

PROOF. The polynomial (viewed as a function from $\{0,1\}^n \to \{0,1\}$) for f may be written in the form $p_1(x_1, x_2, \cdots, \cancel{x_\ell}, \cdots, x_n) + x_\ell p_2(x_1, x_2, \cdots, \cancel{x_\ell}, \cdots, x_n)$. Here $p_1(x_1, x_2, \cdots, \cancel{x_\ell}, \cdots, x_n)$ indicates that the variable x_ℓ is not an input to the polynomial. If p_1 has a non zero coefficient on the monomial $\prod_{k \neq \ell} x_k$, then we set $x_\ell = 0$ and the resulting function will have full degree. For the other case, note p_2 must have a non zero coefficient on $\prod_{k \neq \ell} x_k$ because f has full degree. Thus, setting $x_\ell = 1$ will work. $\square$

We remark that the argument in the above lemma is essentially the same as the standard argument that the decision tree complexity of any function f is at least $deg(f)$.

We are now ready to prove Proposition 3.

PROOF. Given the function f, let g be a subfunction on $deg(f)$ variables with full degree. We will construct a protocol Π that satisfies $E(\Pi) \subseteq E(g)$, where $E(g)$ denotes the set of sensitive edges for the function g, i.e. the edges of $\mathbb{H}_n$ whose endpoints are mapped to different values by g. This will imply that $c(\Pi) \leq s(g) \leq s(f)$, and thus prove the proposition. As Alice receives $\sigma_1, \sigma_2, \cdots, \sigma_n$, she fills in $\mathbf{v}$ in such a way so that the function f restricted to the partial assignment written on $\mathbf{v}$ remains a full degree function, which is possible by Lemma 5.

Note that after Alice writes a bit in location σ_{n-1}, the function g restricted to $\mathbf{v}$ is now a non-constant function of one variable, and thus the edge $\Pi_A(\sigma)$ is a sensitive edge for the function g. This implies that $E(\Pi) \subseteq E(g)$.

$\square$

Remark: To summarize, the reduction above shows that a degree n Boolean function having sensitivity s can be converted into a strategy for Alice for the game G_n of cost at most s. We don't know whether this connection goes the other way, i.e., we can't rule out the possibility that the answer to Question 1 is negative (there is a very low cost protocol for G_n) but the sensitivity conjecture is still true.

2.1 Connection to Decision Tree Complexity

We note the connection between protocols Π for the game G_n and boolean functions on n variables for which $D(f) = n$ (sometimes referred to as *evasive* functions). A common

method for showing that a function is evasive is to use an *adversary argument*. For example, consider the evasive function

$$\text{AND-OR}(\mathbf{x}) = \bigwedge_{i=1}^{\sqrt{n}} \bigvee_{j=1}^{\sqrt{n}} x_{ij}.$$

To show this function is evasive we simulate the computation of some decision tree on an input $\mathbf{x}$, except when the tree queries a variable x_{ij} the adversary will respond either 0 or 1 in such a way as to keep the value of the function on the input $\mathbf{x}$ unknown until all variables are queried. For the AND-OR function, take the adversary that always answers 0 as long as some other variable in the corresponding OR block remains undetermined, otherwise it answers 1. This adversary is exactly Alice's part of the AND-OR protocol described in the introduction. For more examples of adversary arguments see [7].

Every evasive function by definition admits an adversary argument which in turn defines a protocol Π. In fact a function f is evasive if and only if there exists a protocol Π for which $E(\Pi) \subseteq E(f)$ (recall $E(f)$ is the set of sensitive edges of the function f). This work explores the question, can we use the inherent structure of an arbitrary adversary (or protocol) to exhibit a lower bound on sensitivity? We provide some limited evidence that this may be possible by proving lower bounds for restricted classes of protocols Π (see Section 4).

2.2 Order Oblivious Protocols

In the game G_n, at each step $i < n$, the value written by Alice at location σ_i may depend on her knowledge up to that step, which includes both the sequence $\sigma_1, \cdots, \sigma_i$ and the partial assignment already made to v at locations $\sigma_1, \ldots, \sigma_{i-1}$. A natural way to restrict Alice's strategy is to require that the bit she writes in location σ_i depend only on σ_i and the current partial assignment to v but not on the order in which $\sigma_1, \ldots, \sigma_{i-1}$ arrived. A protocol satisfying this restriction is said to be *order oblivious*. The following easy proposition shows that it suffices to answer Question 1 for order oblivious protocols.

PROPOSITION 6. *Given any protocol Π there exists an order oblivious protocol Π' such that $E(\Pi') \subseteq E(\Pi)$. In particular, $c(\Pi') \leq c(\Pi)$.*

PROOF. First some notation. Given a permutation σ let $\sigma_{\leq k}$ denote the prefix of the first k elements of σ. We let $\Pi_A(\sigma_{\leq k})$ denote the partial assignment written on $\mathbf{v}$ after Alice has been streamed $\sigma_1, \cdots, \sigma_k$.

We give a canonical way of obtaining an order oblivious protocol Π' from Π. We define Π' in steps, where step k refers to what Alice does when she is streamed σ_k. For step 1, when σ_1 arrives, she writes according to what Π does for that value of σ_1. In order to define step $k + 1$, assume Π' is defined for the first k steps. Assume as well that it satisfies for every permutation σ, there is a permutation τ of $\sigma_1, \cdots, \sigma_k$ so that $\Pi_A(\tau) = \Pi'_A(\sigma_{\leq k})$.

Suppose σ_{k+1} arrives and the current state of the vector is $\mathbf{v} := \Pi'(\sigma_{\leq k})$. Note from $\mathbf{v}$ Alice can deduce the set of the first k elements of σ (it is the set of locations not labeled with a *). Alice then considers all permutations τ of $\sigma_1, \cdots, \sigma_k$ such that $\Pi_A(\tau) = \Pi'_A(\sigma_{\leq k})$ and picks the lexicographically smallest permutation (call it τ^*) in that set and writes on location σ_{k+1} according to what Π does after τ^*. Note that the bit written on location σ_{k+1} does not depend on the relative order of $\sigma_1, \sigma_2, \cdots, \sigma_k$. Using this strategy, Alice maintains the invariant that for every permutation σ, there is a permutation τ of $\sigma_1, \cdots, \sigma_k$ so that $\Pi(\tau) = \Pi'(\sigma_{\leq k})$.

Thus, by construction, Π' is assignment oblivious. Also for any permutation σ there is a permutation τ for which $\Pi_A(\tau) = \Pi'_A(\sigma)$. This implies that $E(\Pi') \subseteq E(\Pi)$. $\square$

3. STRONGER VARIANTS OF QUESTION 1

In this question we propose three natural variants of Question 1, and refute two of these variants by exhibiting and analyzing some specific protocols.

The cost function $c(\Pi)$ of a protocol is defined based on the worst case over all choices of $\sigma_1, \ldots, \sigma_n, b$. Alternatively, it is natural to evaluate a protocol based on the average size of the set Bob outputs, where the average is taken over a random permutation $\sigma_1, \ldots, \sigma_n$ and a random bit b. We call this the *expected cost of* Π and denote it by $\tilde{c}(\Pi)$. Let $\tilde{C}(n)$ denote the minimum expected cost of a protocol for G_n.

QUESTION 7. *Is there a $\delta > 0$ such that $\tilde{C}(n) = \Omega(n^\delta)$?*

An affirmative answer to this question would give an affirmative answer to Question 1.

We point out that it is well known that the natural probabilistic version of the sensitivity conjecture, where sensitivity is replaced by average sensitivity (where the average is taken uniformly over $\{0,1\}^n$) is trivially false (for example, for the OR function). For contrast, consider the protocol Π where Alice writes a 0 at each step. This protocol is closely related to the OR function in that Alice's part of this protocol is exactly the adversary argument used to prove that OR is evasive. Note also that $E(\Pi)$ is exactly the set of sensitive edges for the OR function. However, the average cost $\tilde{c}(\Pi)$ is $n/2$ whereas the average sensitivity of the OR function is $o(1)$. We currently know of no protocol Π for which $\tilde{c}(\Pi) = o(\sqrt{n})$.

We also remark that an analog of Proposition 6 holds for the cost function $\tilde{c}(\Pi)$, and therefore it suffices to answer the question for order oblivious protocols. (The proof of the analog is similar to the proof of Proposition 6, except when modifying the protocol τ^* is not selected to be the lexicographically smallest permutation in the indicated set, but rather the permutation in the indicated set that minimizes the expected cost conditioned on the first k steps.)

There is another natural variant of Question 1 based on average case. When we run a fixed protocol Π on a random permutation σ and bit b, we can view the vector $\mathbf{v}$ produced by Alice as a random variable. Let $\tilde{h}(\Pi)$ be the conditional entropy of σ_n given $\mathbf{v}$; intuitively this measures the average number of bits of uncertainty that Bob has about σ_n after seeing $\mathbf{v}$. It is easy to show that this is bounded above by $\log(c(\Pi))$. Let $\tilde{H}(n)$ be the minimum of $\tilde{h}(\Pi)$ over all protocols Π for G_n. The analog of Question 1 in this setting asks whether there is a positive constant δ such that $\tilde{H}(n) = \Omega(\delta \log(n))$? An affirmative answer to this would imply an affirmative answer to Question 1, however it turns out that the answer to this new question is negative.

THEOREM 8. *There is an order oblivious protocol Π for G_n such that $\tilde{h}(\Pi) = O(\log \log(n))$.*

Remark: Earlier we showed one can transform any protocol into an order oblivious protocol with smaller cost. However, it is not clear whether or not this transformation can increase $\tilde{h}$. Instead, we directly provide an example of an order oblivious protocol for which $\tilde{h}(\Pi)$ is small.

PROOF. Before defining the protocol Π we need some setup. Let $k = \lceil \log(n) \rceil$ and associate each integer $\ell \in [n]$ to its binary expansion, viewed as a vector $\mathbf{b}(\ell) \in \mathbb{F}_2^k$. Note that $0 \notin [n]$, and thus each vector $\mathbf{b}(\ell)$ is nonzero. Let $t > k$ be an integer (which we'll choose to be $\log^2(n)$) and for each $S \subseteq [n]$ of size t, let $Z(S)$ be a maximal subset of S such that $\sum_{\ell \in Z(S)} \mathbf{b}(\ell)$ is the 0 vector. Observe that by maximality, $Z(S) \geq |S| - k$ (otherwise $S \setminus Z(S)$ would have a linearly dependent subset which we could add to $Z(S)$). Finally let $\mathcal{H} = \{Z(S) : S \in \binom{[n]}{t}\}$.

Given $T \in \mathcal{H}$ and a partial assignment π, we say T is *compatible* with π if $\pi_i \in \{1, *\}$ for all $i \in T$. The protocol Π is defined as follows. For $i \neq n$ Alice writes a 0 on location σ_i unless doing so makes all $T \in \mathcal{H}$ not compatible with the resulting partial assignment written on $\mathbf{v}$, otherwise she writes a 1.

In an earlier version of this paper, we had defined Π so that Alice writes 1 on location i if and only if $i \in Z(S)$ where S is the set of the last t locations of σ. The cost of this protocol is easier to analyze, but it is not order oblivious. Here we instead analyze the order oblivious protocol you obtain if Alice writes a 0 as long as she remains consistent with some partial assignment in the order sensitive protocol.

We note two properties of Π. First, Alice will write a 0 on the first $n - t$ streamed locations. To see this, let $S(\sigma)$ denote the set of the last t elements of σ. Then $Z(S(\sigma))$ will be compatible with $\mathbf{v}$ for the first $n - t$ steps. We also have:

CLAIM 9. *There is a unique set $F \in \mathcal{H}$ that is compatible with the partial assignment $\Pi_A(\sigma)$.*

PROOF. Recall that $\Pi_A(\sigma)$ will have a $*$ in location σ_n. Suppose that there are two sets F_1, F_2 that are compatible with $\Pi_A(\sigma)$ and let T be their symmetric difference. First suppose $T - \{\sigma_n\}$ is non-empty and pick $i \in T - \{\sigma_n\}$. Then when location i arrived, Alice could have written a 0 since one of F_1 or F_2 would remain compatible. This contradicts the construction of the protocol. Now suppose that $T = \{\sigma_n\}$. In this case, since $\sum_{\ell \in F_1} \mathbf{b}(\ell) = \sum_{\ell \in F_2} \mathbf{b}(\ell) = \vec{0}$, the vector $\mathbf{b}(\sigma_n)$ must be the zero vector. This is also impossible because we defined the protocol to have all $\mathbf{b}(\ell)$ non-zero. $\square$

We will refer to the set promised by Claim 9 as the *final set* and denote it as $F(\sigma)$.

We now obtain an upper bound on the conditional entropy of σ_n given $\mathbf{v}$. Let L be the random variable that is 1 if $\sigma_n \in F(\sigma)$ and 0 otherwise. We have:

$$
\begin{aligned}
H(\sigma_n | \mathbf{v}) &\leq H(\sigma_n, L | \mathbf{v}) \\
&= H(L | \mathbf{v}) + H(\sigma_n | \mathbf{v}, L) \\
&\leq 1 + H(\sigma_n | \mathbf{v}, L) \\
&= 1 + H(\sigma_n | \mathbf{v}, L = 1) \Pr[L = 1] \\
&\quad + H(\sigma_n | \mathbf{v}, L = 0) \Pr[L = 0]
\end{aligned}
$$

We first bound the second term. Note that given $L = 1$ we have that σ_n is in the final set $F(\sigma)$ and that Bob can deduce

$F(\sigma)$ given the vector $\mathbf{v}$. To see this, let W be the set of locations ℓ for which $\mathbf{v}$ is set to 1 and let $\Gamma = \sum_{\ell \in W} \mathbf{b}(\ell)$. If Γ is $\vec{0}$, then $F(\sigma)$ must be the set of locations that are set to 1. Otherwise Γ will be equal to $\mathbf{b}(\ell^*)$ for some unique ℓ^*, and $F(\sigma)$ is then the set of locations set to 1 union ℓ^*. In either case, the number of possible values for σ_n is no more than t and so the second term is at most $H(\sigma_n | \mathbf{v}, L = 1) \leq \log(t)$.

To bound the third term we first show the following:

CLAIM 10. *The probability that $L = 0$ is at most k/t.*

Remark: This claim is very easy to see for the order sensitive version mentioned earlier ($L = 0$ is exactly the event that $\sigma_n \in S - Z(S)$). The fact that it still works for the order oblivious version seems quite intuitive because Alice writing some additional 0's should only help the probability. For completeness, we provide a rigorous proof of this below.

PROOF. Recall that $L = 0$ means that $\sigma_n \in S \setminus F(\sigma)$. As before let $\sigma_{\leq j}$ denote the prefix of the first j elements of σ and let $T(\sigma_{\leq j})$ denote the set of the first j elements of σ. Given a prefix τ of length $n - l$ we let $M(\tau)$ denote $\max_E |T(\tau) - E|$ where the max is over all sets E that are compatible with $\Pi_A(\tau)$. For integers l and m let $f(l, m)$ denote $\min_\tau (\Pr[L = 0 | \sigma_{\leq n-t} = \tau])$ where the minimum is over all prefixes τ of length $n - \ell$ for which $M(\tau) = m$. We will show that $f(\ell, m) \leq m/\ell$ for all ℓ, m. In particular, since every $Z(S)$ has size at least $t - k$, showing that $f(t, k) \leq k/t$ will prove the claim. We proceed by induction on $\ell + m$. As a base case, it is easy to see that if $m = 0$ the probability is 0, and if $\ell = m$ then the probability is 1.

Let τ be any prefix of length $n - \ell$ for which $M(\tau) = m$ and suppose that $\sigma_{\leq (n-\ell)} = \tau$. Note that if Alice writes a 0 next, then $M(\sigma_{\leq(n-\ell+1)}) \leq M(\sigma_{\leq(n-\ell)}) - 1$. Also if Alice writes a 1 next, then $M(\sigma_{\leq(n-\ell+1)}) = M(\sigma_{\leq(n-\ell)})$. Let p denote the probability that Alice will write a 0 on location $\sigma_{n-\ell+1}$. Then $p \geq m/\ell$ (if there is exactly one set T that is compatible then $p = m/\ell$ and with additional sets the probability only increases). Thus

$$f(\ell, m) \leq \Pr[L = 0 | \sigma_{\leq n-\ell} = \tau]$$
$$\leq pf(\ell - 1, m) + (1 - p)f(\ell - 1, m - 1).$$
$$\leq \frac{m}{\ell}\frac{m-1}{\ell-1} + \frac{\ell - m}{\ell}\frac{m}{\ell-1} \quad \text{(by the I.H.)}$$
$$= m/\ell$$

□

Note that trivially $H(\sigma_n | \mathbf{v}, L = 0) \leq \log(n)$, thus the claim implies that the third term is at most $\log(n) \cdot \frac{k}{t}$. By choosing $t = \log^2(n)$ the second term is $O(\log \log(n))$ and the third term is $O(1)$.

For our last variant, suppose Alice can communicate to Bob with a ternary alphabet instead of a binary alphabet. We will show that Question 1 is false in this setting. The setup is the same as before: Alice is streamed a permutation σ, only when σ_i arrives she may write a 0,1, or 2 on location σ_i in $\mathbf{v}$. When $b \in \{0, 1, 2\}$ arrives she is forced to write b at location σ_n. Bob sees $\mathbf{v}$ and has to output a set J which must contain σ_n. The cost is the maximum size of J for any σ and b.

THEOREM 11. *There is a protocol Π using a ternary alphabet that has cost $O(\log(n))$.*

PROOF. Let $t < n$ be a parameter to be chosen later (we will end up showing that the cost is less than t).

Alice begins by writing 0 on the first $n - t$ locations streamed to her. After this, Alice writes only 1's and 2's (as described below). Clearly if the final input b is not 0, Bob will see exactly t locations that are not labeled a 0 and know the last t elements. Consider then the case that $b = 0$. We'll show that Alice can write the 1's and 2's in such a way that Bob can then determine σ_n exactly. In what follows, a binary string will refer to a string of 1's and 2's.

Consider the graph defined on t element sets where two sets are joined if they have symmetric difference 2. The degree of this graph is trivially less than n^2 so it has a proper coloring with at most n^2 colors.

Now let us encode each of these colors by a binary string of length t. Write $E(c)$ for the encoding of color c. We want our encoding to have the following property: for any two colors c, d if you delete any single bit from the encoding of $E(c)$ (which leaves a $t - 1$ bit string) and delete any single bit from the encoding of $E(d)$ then they are still different.

CLAIM 12. *There is such an encoding for $t = 5 \log(n)$.*

PROOF. Consider the graph defined on binary strings of length t, where two strings s_1, s_2 are joined if there is a way of deleting a symbol from s_1 and a symbol from s_2 to arrive at the same string of length $t - 1$. The degree of this graph is trivially less than $2t^2$, thus there is a proper coloring with at most $2t^2$ colors. Thus there is a color class of size at least $\frac{2^t}{2t^2}$ strings. If $t > 5 \log(n)$ then there is a color class of size at least n^2. Picking n^2 strings in this color class will give us the desired encoding $E(c)$. □

After Alice writes the first $(n - t)$ 0's, she knows the final t positions denoted $j_1 < \ldots < j_t$. She determines the color c of that set and the encoding $E(c)$. She then writes the bits of $E(c)$ in the positions $j_1, \ldots, j_t$ (writing the bits in this order and not in the σ order of the last t elements).

If $b = 0$, Bob only sees $t - 1$ of the bits. However, by the property of the encoding, this is enough to recover $E(c)$ and therefore c. Furthermore, knowing c and $t - 1$ out of the last t elements, the property of the coloring allows Bob to recover the missing element, which is σ_n. This concludes the construction.

4. LOWER BOUNDS FOR RESTRICTED PROTOCOLS

In the previous section we formulated two stronger variants of Question 1 that turned out to be false. This may suggest that the original question is also false. In this section however, we will prove a lower bound which implies that any counterexample to Question 1 will need to look quite different from the two protocols provided in the last section.

An order oblivious protocol can be specified by a sequence of maps $A_1, \cdots, A_n$ where each A_i maps partial assignments on the set $[n]$ to a single bit. When location σ_i arrives, the bit Alice writes is $A_{\sigma_i}(\mathbf{v})$. For partial assignments α and β, we say that β is an *extension* of α, denoted as $\beta \geq \alpha$, if β is obtained by starting from α and possibly fixing more variables. An order oblivious protocol is *monotone* if each of the maps $A_1, \cdots, A_n$ are monotone with respect to the extension partial order. That is, if $\beta \geq \alpha$ are partial assignments, then $A_i(\beta) \geq A_i(\alpha)$ for each i. As a remark, when running the protocol there may be assignments that are never written on $\mathbf{v}$, however defining each A_i to have domain all partial assignments is still valid and simplifies notation.

Both the AND-OR protocol described in the introduction and the protocol constructed in Theorem 8 are examples of monotone protocols. This definition easily generalizes to protocols on alphabets of size k, in which case the ternary protocol given in the previous section can be seen to be monotone. Our main result in this section is that monotone protocols on binary alphabets have cost $\Omega(\sqrt{n})$. In particular, Question 1 is true for such protocols. For the rest of the paper, all protocols will be on binary alphabets.

Before proving the theorem we'll need some new definitions. Recall that an edge $e \in \mathbb{H}_n$ may be written as a vector in $\{0, 1, *\}^n$ for which $e_\ell = *$ on exactly one location ℓ. We call this location ℓ the *free location* of that edge. We say two edges e, e' *collide* if $e_\ell = e'_\ell$ for all ℓ that is not a free location of either edge. Equivalently, two edges collide if they share at least one vertex (each edge collides with itself). Both of the lower bounds in this section will follow by finding an edge $e \in E(\Pi)$ that collides with m other edges in $E(\Pi)$. This implies at least one of the vertices in e has degree at least $m/2$ in the graph $E(\Pi)$, which in turn lower bounds the cost of the protocol.

Finally, given a permutation σ we will use $\ell <_\sigma k$ to denote that the element ℓ comes before the element k in σ.

THEOREM 13. *All monotone protocols have cost $\Omega(\sqrt{n})$.*

PROOF. Let Π be a monotone protocol.

For a permutation σ denote by $\mathrm{bump}_k(\sigma)$ the permutation obtained from σ by "bumping" the element k to the end of σ and maintaining the same relative order for the rest of σ. For example, $\mathrm{bump}_1(321654) = 326541$.

We let $w(\sigma)$ denote the vector $\Pi_A(\sigma)$ with the entries sorted in σ order. In other words, $w(\sigma)$ is the vector defined by $w(\sigma)_i = (\Pi_A)_{\sigma_i}$. Our proof follows by repeated application of the following:

CLAIM 14. *Let σ be any permutation and let τ be obtained from σ by performing some sequence of bumps on σ. Suppose that τ and $m < n$ satisfies the following:*

- *The elements $\tau_1, \tau_2, \cdots, \tau_m$ were never bumped.*
- *Alice originally wrote a 0 on the locations $\tau_1, \cdots, \tau_m$, that is $\Pi_A(\sigma)_{\tau_i} = 0$ for all $i \leq m$.*

Then $\Pi_A(\tau)_{\tau_i} = 0$ for all $i \leq m$. Equivalently, $w(\tau)$ begins with m 0's.

PROOF. The claim follows easily by induction on i. Suppose we have already shown that $w(\tau)$ begins with $(i-1)$ 0's. Let $\mathbf{v}(\sigma, k)$ denote the partial assignment written on $\mathbf{v}$ just before Alice receives the index k (here the reader should take care to distinguish this from the partial assignment just before Alice receives σ_k). Consider the partial assignment $\mathbf{v}(\tau, \tau_i)$. It follows from the first assumption and the inductive hypothesis that $\mathbf{v}(\sigma, \tau_i)$ is an extension of $\mathbf{v}(\tau, \tau_i)$. Thus, since Alice originally wrote a 0 on location τ_i, by monotonicity she continues to write a 0 on that location when being streamed τ (that is $\Pi_A(\tau)_{\tau_i} = 0$). $\square$

Let σ be the permutation for which $w(\sigma)$ is lexicographically smallest.

CLAIM 15. *$w(\sigma)$ consists of a string of 0's followed by a string of 1's, followed by a single *.*

PROOF. Suppose for contradiction that there is a a 0 that comes after a 1, and let k be the least index such that $w(\sigma)_k = 1$ and $w(\sigma)_{k+1} = 0$. Let τ be obtained from σ by bumping all of the locations ℓ for which $\ell <_\sigma k$ and $\Pi_A(\sigma)_\ell = 1$. Let m denote the number of locations ℓ for which $\ell <_\sigma k$ and $\Pi_A(\sigma)_\ell = 0$. Then by Claim 14, $w(\tau)$ begins with $(m+1)$ 0's. This contradicts the choice of σ $\square$

Let $n-t$ be the number of initial 0's in $w(\sigma)$ and $t-1$ be the number of 1's. For k between 1 and n, let $\tau^{(k)} = \mathrm{bump}_k(\sigma)$. Let x be the assignment obtained from $\Pi_A(\sigma)$ by setting location σ_n (which is a *) to 1.

CLAIM 16. *The edges $\Pi_A(\tau^{(k)})$ and $\Pi_A(\sigma)$ intersect at the input x for all k among the last t elements of σ. In particular x has degree at least t in the graph $E(\Pi)$.*

PROOF. Fix k among the last t elements of σ. Clearly $w(\tau^{(k)})$ has the first $n-t$ bits 0, and so by the choice of σ all other locations in $w(\tau^{(k)})$ must be labeled 1. Thus $w(\tau^{(k)}) = w(\sigma)$. This means that the edges $\Pi_A(\sigma)$ and $\Pi_A(\tau^{(k)})$ agree at all locations except for σ_n and σ_k (which are the free location of the edges respectively). Since $\Pi_A(\sigma)_{\sigma_k} = \Pi_A(\tau^{(k)})_{\sigma_n} = 1$, the two edges meet at x. $\square$

To conclude the proof of the theorem we will find an assignment y that has degree at least $(n-t)/(t+1)$ in the graph $E(\Pi)$.

CLAIM 17. *For k among the first $n-t$ elements of σ, $w(\tau^{(k)})$ has the first $n-t-1$ bits equal to 0, and has at most one 0 among the next t bits (and last bit *).*

PROOF. The fact that the first $n-t-1$ bits of $w(\tau^{(k)})$ are labeled 0 follows by directly by Claim 14.

Suppose for contradiction that there are at least 2 0's among the next t locations and denote the locations of the first and second 0 to be ℓ_1 and ℓ_2 respectively. Take all of the locations that are labeled 1 in $\Pi_A(\tau^{(k)})$ and bump them to the end and let this new permutation be ρ. Once again by applying Claim 14 we have $\Pi_A(\rho)_{\ell_1} = \Pi_A(\rho)_{\ell_2} = 0$. Thus $w(\rho)$ has the first $n-t+1$ locations set to 0 which contradicts the choice of σ. $\square$

Now classify each of the first $n-t$ elements of σ into $t+1$ types $n-t, \ldots, n$. Element k is of type n if $w(\tau^{(k)})$ has t 1's. Otherwise $w(\tau^{(k)})$ has $(t-1)$ 1's, and the type of k is equal to the index j between $n-t$ and $n-1$ such that $w(\tau^{(k)})_j = 0$.

Some type occurs at least $m := (n-t)/(t+1)$ times, call it j^*, and let $k_1, k_2, \cdots, k_m$ be the m elements that are type j^*. For $1 \leq i \leq m$ let $y^{(i)}$ be the assignment obtained by taking the edge $\Pi_A(\tau^{(k_i)})$ and assigning the * to 0.

CLAIM 18. *The assignments $y^{(i)}$ are all equal.*

PROOF. By the definition of the bump operation the permutations $\tau^{(k_i)}$ all have the same elements at positions

252

$n-t, n-t+1, \cdots, n-1$ (they have the same suffix with the exception of the last element). Since they are all of the same type it follows that the $y^{(i)}$ all agree on locations in the set $\{\tau^{(k_1)}(j) \mid j \in n-t, \cdots, n-1\}$. For all other locations, each $y^{(i)}$ is set to 0, thus they are the same assignment. □

Therefore there are m distinct edges in the graph $E(\Pi)$ that are incident with the assignment $y := y^{(1)}$. Thus y has degree at least $m = (n-t)/(t+1)$. This implies that cost of Π is at least $\max(t, (n-t)/(t+1)) = \Omega(\sqrt{n})$.

As demonstrated by the AND-OR protocol, Theorem 13 is tight up to a constant factor. We remark that the monotone protocols we consider here seem to have no general connection to the class of monotone boolean functions, and our result for monotone protocols seems to be unrelated to the easy and well known fact that the sensitivity conjecture is true for monotone functions.

We conclude this section with a lower bound for a second class of protocols. Although the lower bound is only logarithmic, we point out that proving a logarithmic lower bound for all protocols with a strong enough constant would imply new bounds relating degree and sensitivity.

For a permutation σ let $S_k(\sigma)$ denote the set of elements ℓ that satisfy $\ell <_\sigma k$. For example, if $\sigma = 321654$ then $S_1(\sigma) = \{2, 3\}$. We say a protocol is *assignment oblivious* if the bit written by Alice in location k only depends on the set $S_k(\sigma)$. Such protocols can be described by a collection of n hypergraphs $H_1, H_2, \cdots, H_n$, where each H_ℓ is a hypergraph with vertex set $[n] \setminus \{\ell\}$. When k arrives, Alice writes a 1 if and only if the set $S_k(\sigma)$ is in H_k.

THEOREM 19. *Every assignment oblivious protocol Π has $c(\Pi) \geq \log_2(n)/2$.*

PROOF. Let Π be an assignment oblivious protocol.

Given a permutation $\sigma = \sigma_1 \sigma_2 \cdots \sigma_n$ and $k \in [n]$ we define $\text{swap}_k(\sigma)$ to be the permutation obtained by swapping the positions of the elements k and σ_n within σ and keeping every other element in the same place. For example, $\text{swap}_3(654321) = 654123$. The lemma will follow by constructing a permutation σ such that that $\Pi_A(\sigma)$ and $\Pi_A(\text{swap}_k(\sigma))$ collide for each $k \in \{\sigma_{n-1}, \cdots, \sigma_{n-\lceil \log_2(n) \rceil}\}$

We build up such a σ in a greedy manner. We start with setting $\sigma_{n-1} = 1$. With σ_{n-1} fixed, the bit Alice writes in location 1 is completely determined by σ_n (and does not depend on the values we later choose for $\sigma_1, \cdots, \sigma_{n-2}$). This holds by the assignment oblivious property and because $S_1(\sigma) = \{\ell : \ell \neq 1, \sigma_n\}$. Let R_1 be the locations ℓ for which setting $\sigma_n = \ell$ results in Alice writing a 1 in location 1. At least one of $|R_1|, |R_1^c|$ are bigger than $\lceil (n-1)/2 \rceil$, let T_1 be that set. Now we fix σ_{n-2} to be any element in T_1.

Having fixed σ_{n-1} and σ_{n-2}, the bit Alice writes on location σ_{n-2} also only depends on the value of σ_n. Now let R_2 be the subset of indices j in T_1 such that setting $\sigma_n = j$ would cause Alice to write a 1 in location σ_{n-2}. At least one of $|R_2|, |R_2^c|$ are bigger than $\lceil (|T_1|-1)/2 \rceil$, let $T_2 \subseteq T_1$ be that set. This process is iteratively repeated. At step i we set σ_{n-i} to be an arbitrary element of T_{i-1}. With $\sigma_{n-1}, \cdots, \sigma_{n-i}$ now fixed, the value written in location σ_{n-i} depends only on the value of σ_n. The set R_i is defined to be all such values of σ_n that result in Alice writing a 1 in location σ_{n-i} and $T_i \subseteq T_{i-1}$ is defined to be the larger of $|R_i|$

and $|R_i^c|$. We proceed until the set T_i has only one element in it, in this case we assign σ_n to be that element. This process will take at least $\lceil \log_2(n) \rceil$ steps. We then assign the remaining elements to $\sigma_1, \cdots, \sigma_{n-i-1}$ in an arbitrary order.

We now claim that $\Pi_A(\sigma)$ and $\Pi_A(\text{swap}_k(\sigma))$ collide for $k = \sigma_n, \sigma_{n-1}, \cdots, \sigma_{n-\lceil \log_2(n) \rceil}$.

CLAIM 20. *Let $i < \lceil \log_2(n) \rceil$, and let $k = \sigma_{n-i}$. Then $\Pi_A(\sigma)_\ell = \Pi_A(\text{swap}_k(\sigma))_\ell$ for all $\ell \neq k, \sigma_n$.*

PROOF. Let $\sigma' = \text{swap}_k(\sigma)$. If $\ell <_\sigma k$ then $S_\ell(\sigma) = S_\ell(\sigma')$ and so Alice writes the same bit to location ℓ under both permutations.

Suppose that $\ell >_\sigma k$. Let j be such that $\sigma_{n-j} = \ell$. Note that $\sigma_{n-1} = \sigma'_{n-1}, \cdots, \sigma_{n-j} = \sigma'_{n-j}$. Recall that holding $\sigma_{n-1}, \cdots, \sigma_{n-j}$ fixed, the bit Alice writes at location ℓ depends only on the value of σ_n, and furthermore that bit is the same as for all settings of $\sigma_n \in T_j$. Since both σ_n and $\sigma'_n = k$ are in the set T_j, it follows that $\Pi_A(\sigma)_\ell = \Pi_A(\sigma')_\ell$. □

By the above claim, σ collides with $\text{swap}_k(\sigma)$ for at least $\lceil \log_2(n) \rceil$ values of k. Furthermore, at least one of the vertices in $\Pi_A(\sigma)$ has degree more than $\lceil \log_2(n)/2 \rceil$. This concludes the proof.

5. A PROTOCOL WITH LOWER COST THAN THE AND-OR PROTOCOL

In this section we present a construction of a protocol with $c(\Pi) \leq \sqrt{\frac{999}{1000}} \sqrt{n}$ which is the lowest cost protocol we know. The construction is a variant of the AND-OR protocol defined in the introduction.

Assume n and k are integers where $n - k$ is a perfect square. A set of assignments $\{\mathbf{x}_S \in \{0, 1\}^n \mid S \in \binom{[n]}{k}\}$ is an (n, k)-*proper code* if the hamming distance between any $\mathbf{x}_S, \mathbf{x}_{S'}$ is at least $2\sqrt{n}$ and each $\mathbf{x}_S$ is 0 on the locations $i \in S$. Let $\{\mathbf{x}_S \mid S \in \binom{[n]}{k}\}$ be an (n, k)-proper code. We construct a protocol Π as follows: Alice writes 0 at locations $\sigma_1, \cdots, \sigma_k$. Alice then takes the set $S = \{\sigma_1, \cdots, \sigma_k\}$ and splits $[n] \setminus S$ into $\sqrt{n-k}$ disjoint blocks of size $\sqrt{n-k}$. When Alice continues and receives σ_j (for $k < j < n$) she writes the mod-2 sum of the bit b_j and the bit in location σ_j of $\mathbf{x}_S$, where b_j is 1 if σ_j is the last element in its block, and 0 otherwise.

We claim that upon receiving vector $\mathbf{v}$, Bob knows that the value of σ_n is one of $\sqrt{n-k}$ possible locations. First note that the vector $\mathbf{v}$ is within distance $\sqrt{n-k}$ of the vector $\mathbf{x}_S$, and thus Bob may decode $\mathbf{v}$ to learn the assignment $\mathbf{x}_S$ (and thus the set S as well). Consider the assignment $\mathbf{v} \oplus \mathbf{x}_S$ restricted to the locations outside of S. If the final bit b is 0, then exactly one of the $\sqrt{n-k}$ blocks will be all 0's. Bob can output J to be that block. If the final bit b is 1, then every block will have exactly a single 1 in it. Bob can output J to be the set of locations that are set to 1. In each case $|J| = \sqrt{n-k}$.

To conclude the construction of this protocol we prove the existence of an $(n, n/1000)$-proper code. Consider the following random code indexed by the sets $S \in \binom{[n]}{k}$: Each $\mathbf{x}_S$ is set to 0 on locations in S, and set to an independently and uniformly chosen random bit on locations outside of S. We claim that with nonzero probability this set is a proper code. The second property holds by definition, it only remains to check the pairwise distances of the code words.

Given sets S, S' let $E_{S,S'}$ be the event that $d(\mathbf{x}_S, \mathbf{x}_{S'}) < 2\sqrt{n}$. This may be upper bounded by the probability that $\mathbf{x}_S, \mathbf{x}_{S'}$ differ on less than $2\sqrt{n}$ locations in the set $[n] \setminus (S \cup S')$. This probability is exactly the probability that two random $n - |S \cup S'|$ bit strings are within distance $2\sqrt{n}$. Since $n - |S \cup S'| \geq n/2$ this probability is at most $\exp(-n/32)$ by a standard Chernoff bound. By a union bound the probability of any event $E_{S,S'}$ occurring is at most

$$\binom{n}{n/1000}^2 \exp(-n/32) < 1.$$

Thus with nonzero probability this is a proper code.

COROLLARY 21. *There is an $\epsilon > 0$ and a protocol Π for which $c(\Pi) \leq (1 - \epsilon)\sqrt{n}$.*

6. ACKNOWLEDGEMENTS

We thank Ran Raz for helpful discussions. The first author was supported by NSF grant CCF 083727. The second author was supported in part by (FP7/2007-2013)/ERC Consolidator grant LBCAD no. 616787, a grant from Neuron Fund for Support of Science, and the project 14-10003S of GA ČR. The third author was supported by NSF grants CCF-083727 and CCF-1218711, and the Simons Foundation under award 332622.

7. REFERENCES

[1] R. Beals, H. Buhrman, R. Cleve, M. Mosca, and R. De Wolf. Quantum lower bounds by polynomials. *Journal of the ACM (JACM)*, 48(4):778–797, 2001.

[2] H. Buhrman and R. de Wolf. Complexity measures and decision tree complexity: a survey. *Theor. Comput. Sci.*, 288(1):21–43, 2002.

[3] F. R. Chung, Z. Füredi, R. L. Graham, and P. Seymour. On induced subgraphs of the cube. *Journal of Combinatorial Theory, Series A*, 49(1):180–187, 1988.

[4] C. Gotsman and N. Linial. The equivalence of two problems on the cube. *Journal of Combinatorial Theory, Series A*, 61(1):142–146, 1992.

[5] P. Hatami, R. Kulkarni, and D. Pankratov. *Variations on the Sensitivity Conjecture*. Number 4 in Graduate Surveys. Theory of Computing Library, 2011.

[6] C. Kenyon and S. Kutin. Sensitivity, block sensitivity, and ℓ-block sensitivity of boolean functions. *Information and Computation*, 189(1):43–53, 2004.

[7] L. Lovasz and N. E. Young. Lecture notes on evasiveness of graph properties. *arXiv preprint cs/0205031*, 2002.

[8] G. Midrijanis. Exact quantum query complexity for total boolean functions. *arXiv preprint quant-ph/0403168*, 2004.

[9] N. Nisan and M. Szegedy. On the degree of boolean functions as real polynomials. *Computational Complexity*, 4:301–313, 1994.

Standard Simplices and Pluralities are Not the Most Noise Stable

[Abstract]

Steven Heilman[*]
Department of Mathematics
UCLA
Los Angeles, CA 90095-1555
heilman@math.ucla.edu

Elchanan Mossel[†]
Department of Statistics
University of Pennsylvania and
U.C. Berkeley
mossel@wharton.upenn.edu

Joe Neeman[‡]
Mathematics and Electrical
and Computer Engineering
University of Texas at Austin
Austin, TX 78712
joeneeman@gmail.com

ABSTRACT

The Standard Simplex Conjecture and the Plurality is Stablest Conjecture are two conjectures stating that certain partitions are optimal with respect to Gaussian and discrete noise stability respectively. These two conjectures are natural generalizations of the Gaussian noise stability result by Borell (1985) and the Majority is Stablest Theorem (2004). Here we show that the standard simplex is not the most stable partition in Gaussian space and that Plurality is not the most stable low influence partition in discrete space for every number of parts $k \geq 3$, for every value $\rho \neq 0$ of the noise and for every prescribed measures for the different parts as long as they are not all equal to $1/k$. Our results do not contradict the original statements of the Plurality is Stablest and Standard Simplex Conjectures concerning partitions into sets of equal measure. However, they indicate that if these conjectures are true, their veracity and their proofs will crucially rely on assuming that the sets are of equal measures, in stark contrast to Borell's result, the Majority is Stablest Theorem and many other results in isoperimetric theory.

In other words, the optimal partitions for noise stability are of a different nature than the ones considered for partitions into three parts in isoperimetric theory. In the latter

[*]S. H. was supported by NSF Graduate Research Fellowship DGE-0813964 and a Simons-Berkeley Research Fellowship. Part of this work was completed while S. H. visited the Network Science and Graph Algorithms program at ICERM.

[†]E. M. was supported by NSF grants DMS 1106999 and CCF 1320105, and by grant 328025 from the Simons Foundation.

[‡]J. N. was supported by NSF grant DMS-1106999 and DOD ONR grant N000141110140. Part of this work was carried out while the authors were visiting the Real Analysis in Computer Science program at the Simons Institute for the Theory of Computing.

ITCS'15, January 11–13, 2015, Rehovot, Israel.
ACM 978-1-4503-3333-7/15/01.
http://dx.doi.org/10.1145/2688073.2688076.

case, the standard simplex is the partition of the plane into three sets of smallest Gaussian perimeter, where the sets are restricted to have Gaussian measures $a_1, a_2, a_3 > 0$ respectively, with $a_1 + a_2 + a_3 = 1$ and $|a_i - 1/3| < .04$ for all $i \in \{1, 2, 3\}$. Thus, we now know that the extension of noise stability theory from two to three or more parts is very much different than the extension of isoperimetric theory from two to three or more parts. Moreover, all existing proofs which optimize noise stability of two sets must fail for more than three sets, since these proofs rely on the fact that a half-space optimizes noise stability with respect to any measure restriction. Given our results it is natural to ask for (conjectured) partitions achieving the optimum noise stability.

The main new ingredient in our work shows that the Ornstein-Uhlenbeck operator applied to the indicator function of a simplicial cone becomes holomorphic when restricted to certain lines. This holomorphicity condition, when combined with a first variation argument (i.e. an infinite dimensional perturbative argument of the first order), then shows that any simplicial cone can be perturbed in a volume-preserving manner to improve its noise stability. Such a holomorphicity argument seems unavailable for the isoperimetric problem, since this argument uses the inherent nonlocality of the Ornstein-Uhlenbeck semigroup.

A full version of the paper is available at arXiv:1403.0885.

Categories and Subject Descriptors

Theory of computation [**Analysis of algorithms and problem complexity**]: Nonnumerical algorithms and problems—*Geometrical problems and computations*

General Terms

Theory

Keywords

Plurality; Standard Simplex; Noise Stability

Acknowledgement. Thanks to Oded Regev, Ronen Eldan, Kostya Makarychev, and Assaf Naor for helpful comments. This work was mostly conducted during the semester on "Real Analysis in Computer Science" at the Simons Institute for Theoretical Computer Science. We are grateful to the institute for its hospitality and support.

Communication with Imperfectly Shared Randomness

Clément L. Canonne [*]
Columbia University
New York, NY 10027
ccanonne@cs.columbia.edu

Venkatesan Guruswami [†]
Carnegie Mellon University
Pittsburgh, PA 15213
guruswami@cmu.edu

Raghu Meka
Microsoft Research
1288 Pear Avenue
Mountain View, CA 94043
meka@microsoft.com

Madhu Sudan
Microsoft Research
1 Memorial Drive
Cambridge, MA 02142
madhu@mit.edu

ABSTRACT

The communication complexity of many fundamental problems reduces greatly when the communicating parties share randomness that is independent of the inputs to the communication task. Natural communication processes (say between humans) however often involve large amounts of shared correlations among the communicating players, but rarely allow for perfect sharing of randomness. Can the communication complexity benefit from shared correlations as well as it does from shared randomness? This question was considered mainly in the context of simultaneous communication by Bavarian et al. [1]. In this work we study this problem in the standard interactive setting and give some general results. In particular, we show that every problem with communication complexity of k bits with perfectly shared randomness has a protocol using imperfectly shared randomness with complexity $2^{\Omega(k)}$ bits. We also show that this is best possible by exhibiting a promise problem with complexity k bits with perfectly shared randomness which requires $2^{\Omega(k)}$ bits when the randomness is imperfectly shared. Along the way we also highlight some other basic problems such as compression, and agreement distillation, where shared randomness plays a central role and analyze the complexity of these problems in the imperfectly shared randomness model.

The technical highlight of this work is the lower bound that goes into the result showing the tightness of our general connection. This result builds on the intuition that communication with imperfectly shared randomness needs to be less sensitive to its random inputs than communication with perfectly shared randomness. The formal proof invokes results about the small-set expansion of the noisy hypercube and an invariance principle to convert this intuition to a proof, thus giving a new application domain for these fundamental results.

Categories and Subject Descriptors

E.4 [**Coding and Information Theory**]: Formal models of communication; H.1.1 [**Models and Principles**]: Systems and Information Theory—*Information theory*

General Terms

Theory

1. INTRODUCTION

The availability of shared randomness can lead to enormous savings in communication complexity when computing some basic functions whose inputs are spread out over different communicating players. A basic example of this is Equality Testing, where two players Alice and Bob have inputs $x \in \{0,1\}^n$ and $y \in \{0,1\}^n$ and need to determine if $x = y$. Deterministically this takes n bits of communication. This reduces to $\Theta(\log n)$ bits if Alice and Bob can toss coins and they are allowed some error. But if they share some randomness $r \in \{0,1\}^*$ independent of x and y then the communication cost drops to $O(1)$. (See, for instance, [11]).

A more prevalent example of a communication problem is compression with uncertain priors. Here Alice has a distribution P on a universe $[N] = \{1, \ldots, N\}$, and a message $m \in [N]$ chosen according to the distribution P. Alice is allowed to send some bits to Bob and Bob should output m and the goal is to minimize the expected number of bits that Alice sends Bob (over the random choice of m). If Bob knows the distribution P exactly then this is the classical compression problem, solved for example by Huffman coding. In most forms of natural communication (e.g., think about the next email you are about to send), Alice and Bob are not perfectly aware of the underlying context to their exchange, but have reasonably good ideas about each other. One way to model this is to say that Bob has a distribution Q that is

[*]Research supported in part by NSF CCF-1115703 and NSF CCF-1319788. Some of this work was done when the author was an intern at Microsoft Research New England.

[†]Some of this work was done when the author was visiting Microsoft Research New England. Research supported in part by NSF CCF-0963975.

close to the distribution P that Alice is working with, but is not identical to P. Compressing information down to its entropy in the presence of such uncertainty (i.e., $P \neq Q$) turns out to be possible if Alice and Bob share randomness that is independent of (P, Q, m) as shown by Juba et al. [9]. However it remains open as to whether such compression can be effected deterministically, without the shared randomness — the best known schemes can only achieve a compression length of roughly $O(H(P) + \log \log N)$, where $H(P) = \sum_{i \in [N]} P(i) \log 1/P(i)$ denotes the entropy of P.[1]

In both examples above it is natural to ask the question: can the (presumed) savings in communication be achieved in the absence of perfect sharing of randomness? The question especially makes sense in the latter context where the essential motivation is that Alice and Bob are not in perfect synchrony with each other: If Alice and Bob are not perfectly aware of the distributions P and Q, why should their randomness be identical?

The question of communication with imperfectly shared randomness was considered recently in the work of Bavarian et al. [1]. They consider the setting where Alice and Bob have randomness r and s respectively, with some known correlation between r and s, and study the implications of correlated randomness in the simultaneous message communication model (where a referee gets messages from Alice and Bob and computes some joint function of their inputs). Their technical focus is on the different kinds of correlations possible between r and s, but among basic results they show that equality testing has a $O(1)$ communication complexity protocol with correlated shared randomness.

In this work we are concerned with the setting of general communication protocols, where Alice and Bob interact to determine the value of some function. From some perspectives, this setting does not seem to offer a major difference between "private randomness" and "perfectly shared randomness" — Newman [14] shows that the communication complexity in the former setting can be larger by at most an additive $\log n$ term, where n is the input size. "Imperfectly shared randomness" being in between the two models cannot therefore be too far from them either. However, problems like compression above highlight a different perspective. There N is the size of the universe of all possible messages, and compression to $\log N$ bits of communication is trivial and uninteresting. Even a solution with $\log \log N$ bits of communication is not completely satisfactory. The real target is $O(H(P))$ bits of communication, which may be a constant independent of the universe size N (and for natural communication, the set of possible messages could be thought of as an infinitely large set). Thus the gap between the communication complexity with perfectly shared randomness and imperfectly shared randomness remains a very interesting question, which we explore in this paper.

We provide a formal description of our models and results in the following section, and here give an informal preview. We consider communication complexity in a simplified setting of imperfectly shared randomness: Alice has a uniform binary string $r \in \{0,1\}^m$ and Bob has a string s obtained by flipping each bit of r independently with some tiny probability. (While this setting is not the most general possible, it seems to capture the most interesting aspects of the "lack of prior agreement" between Alice and Bob.) Our main contributions in this work are the introduction of some new problems of interest in the context of communication complexity, and a comparison of their communication complexity with/without perfect sharing of randomness.

The first problem we study is the complexity of *compression with uncertain priors*. We show that any distribution P can be compressed to $O(H(P))$ bits even when the randomness is not perfectly shared. As in the analogous result of Juba et al. [9] this protocol sheds some light on natural communication processes, and introduces an error-correcting element that was not previously explained.

The next problem we mention is that of *agreement distillation*. Here Alice and Bob try to agree on a small random string using little communication. This is a natural problem to study in the context of communication complexity with imperfect randomness, since an efficient solution for this problem would allow Alice and Bob to convert any protocol using perfectly shared randomness into one that relies only on imperfectly shared randomness. It turns out that the zero-communication version of this question, where Alice and Bob are not allowed to communicate at all with each other, was studied by Bogdanov and Mossel [2]. They give a very strong negative result for this problem, showing that the probability that Alice and Bob can agree on a k-bit string is exponentially small in k. By a simple reduction we show that this implies that $o(k)$ bits of communication are insufficient to get agreement on k bits. Conversely, we also show that Alice and Bob can get a constant factor advantage — so they can communicate αk bits for some $\alpha < 1$. Such a result seems implicit in [2].

Returning to our work, we next attempt to get a general conversion of communication protocols from the perfectly-shared setting to the imperfectly-shared setting. We introduce a complete promise problem GAPINNERPRODUCT which captures two-way communication, and use it to show that any problem with k bits of communication with perfectly shared randomness also has a $\min\{\exp(k), k + \log n\}$ bit (one-way) protocol with imperfectly shared randomness. While the protocol is simple, we feel its existence is somewhat surprising; and indeed it yields a very different protocol for equality testing when compared with Bavarian et al. [1].

Lastly, our *main technical result* is a matching lower bound giving a parameterized family of promise problems, SPARSEGAP-INNERPRODUCT, where the k'th problem can be solved with k bits of communication with perfect randomness, but requires $\exp(\Omega(k))$ bits with imperfect sharing. This result builds a new connection between influence of variables and communication complexity, which may be of independent interest. Finally we conclude with a variety of open questions.

---

[1] We stress that the setting of uncertain compression is completely different from that of compression with the "wrong distribution", a well-studied question in information theory. In the "wrong distribution problem" (see, for instance, [4, Theorem 5.4.3]) the sender and receiver agree on the distribution, say P, but both have it wrong and the distribution the message comes from is R. This leads to a compression length of $\mathbb{E}_{m \sim R}[\log(1/P(m))] \approx H(R) + D(R\|P)$. The important aspect here is that while the compression is not as good, there is no confusion between sender and receiver; and the latter is the focus of our problem.

2. MODEL, FORMAL DESCRIPTION OF RESULTS AND MAIN IDEAS

Throughout the paper, we denote by $\mathbb{Z}^+$ the set of positive integers, and by $[n]$ the set $\{1, \ldots, n\}$. Unless specified otherwise, all logarithms are in base 2. We also recall, for $x \in [0,1]$, the definition of the binary entropy function $h(x) = -x \log x - (1-x) \log(1-x)$; furthermore, for any $p \in [0,1]$, we will write $\text{Bern}(p)$ for the Bernoulli distribution on $\{0,1\}$ with parameter p, and $\text{Bern}^n(p)$ for the product distribution on $\{0,1\}^n$ of n independent Bernoulli random variables. For a distribution P over a domain Ω, we write $H(P) = \sum_{x \in \Omega} P(x) \log(1/P(x))$ for its entropy, and $x \sim P$ to indicate that x is drawn from P. $\mathcal{U}_\Omega$ denotes the uniform distribution over Ω.

Finally, for two elements $x, y \in \{+1, -1\}^n$, their *Hamming distance* $\text{dist}(x, y)$ is defined as the number of coordinates in which they differ (and similarly for $x, y \in \{0,1\}^n$).

2.1 Model

We use the familiar model of communication complexity, augmented by the notion of correlated shared randomness. Recall that in the standard model, two players, Alice and Bob, have access to inputs x and y respectively. A protocol Π specifies the interaction between Alice and Bob (who speaks when and what), and concludes with Alice and Bob producing outputs w_A and w_B respectively. A communication problem P is (informally) specified by conditions on the inputs and outputs (x, y, w_A, w_B). In usual (promise) problems this is simply a relationship on the 4-tuple. In sampling problems, this may be given by requirements on the distribution of this output given x and y. For functional problems, $P = (f_A, f_B)$ and the conditions require that $w_A = f_A(x, y)$ and $w_B = f_B(x, y)$. A randomized protocol is said to solve a functional problem P if the outputs are correct with probability at least $2/3$. The (worst-case) complexity of a protocol Π, denoted $cc(\Pi)$ is the maximum over all x, y of the expected number of bits communicated by Π. This is the main complexity measure of interest to us, although distributional complexity will also be considered, as also any mix. (For instance, the most natural measure in compression is a max-average measure.)

We will be considering the setting where Alice and Bob have access to an arbitrarily long sequence of correlated random bits. For this definition it will be convenient to let a random bit be an element of $\{+1, -1\}$. For $\rho \in [-1, +1]$, we say a pair of bits (a, b) are ρ-*correlated (uniform) bits* if $\mathbb{E}[a] = \mathbb{E}[b] = 0$ and $\mathbb{E}[ab] = \rho$. We will consider the performance of protocols when given access to sequences (r, r') where each coordinate pair (r_i, r'_i) are ρ-correlated uniform bits chosen independently for each i. We shall write $r \sim_\rho r'$ for such ρ-correlated pairs.

The *communication complexity of a problem* P with access to ρ-correlated bits, denoted[2] $\text{isr-cc}_\rho(P)$ is the minimum over all protocols Π that solve P with access to ρ-correlated bits of $cc(\Pi)$. For integer k, we let $\text{ISR-CC}_\rho(k)$ denote the collections of problems P with $\text{isr-cc}_\rho(P) \leq k$. The one-way communication complexity and simultaneous message complexities are defined similarly (by restricting to appropriate protocols) and denoted $\text{isr-cc}_\rho^{\text{ow}}(P)$ and $\text{isr-cc}_\rho^{\text{sm}}(P)$ respec-

tively. The corresponding complexity classes are denoted similarly by $\text{ISR-CC}_\rho^{\text{ow}}(k)$ and $\text{ISR-CC}_\rho^{\text{sm}}(k)$.

Note that when $\rho = 1$ we get the standard model of communication with shared randomness. We denote this measure by $\text{psr-cc}(P) = \text{isr-cc}_1(P)$, and write $\text{PSR-CC}(k)$ for the corresponding complexity class. Similarly, when $\rho = 0$ we get communication complexity with private randomness $\text{private-cc}(P) = \text{isr-cc}_0(P)$. We note that $\text{isr-cc}_\rho(P)$ is non-increasing in ρ. Combined with Newman's Theorem [14], we obtain:

PROPOSITION 1. *For every problem P with inputs $x, y \in \{0,1\}^n$ and $0 \leq \rho \leq \rho' \leq 1$ we have*

$$\text{psr-cc}(P) \leq \text{isr-cc}_{\rho'}(P) \leq \text{isr-cc}_\rho(P)$$
$$\leq \text{private-cc}(P) \leq \text{psr-cc}(P) + O(\log n).$$

The proposition also holds for one-way communication, and (except for the last inequality) simultaneous messages.

2.2 Problems, Results and Techniques

We now define some of the new problems we consider in this work and describe our main results.

2.2.1 Compression

Definition 1. For $\delta > 0$, $\Delta \geq 0$ and integers ℓ, n, the *uncertain compression problem* $\text{COMPRESS}_{\Delta, \delta}^{\ell, n}$ is a promise problem with Alice getting as input the pair (P, m), where $P = (P_1, \ldots, P_n)$ is a probability distribution on $[n]$ and $m \in [n]$. Bob gets a probability distribution Q on $[n]$. The promises are that $H(P) \leq \ell$ and for every $i \in [n]$, $|\log(P_i/Q_i)| \leq \Delta$. The goal is for Bob to output m, i.e., $w_B = m$ with probability at least $1 - \delta$. The measure of interest here is the maximum, over (P, Q) satisfying the promise, of the expected one-way communication complexity when m is sampled according to P.

When $\Delta = 0$, this is the classical compression problem and Huffman coding achieves a compression length of at most $\ell + 1$; and this is optimal for "prefix-free" compressions. For larger values of Δ, the work of [9] gives an upper bound of $\ell + 2\Delta + O(1)$ in the setting of perfectly shared randomness (to get constant error probability). In the setting of deterministic communication or private randomness, it is open if this communication complexity can be bounded by a function of ℓ and Δ alone (without dependence on n). (The work of [6] studies the deterministic setting.) Our first result shows that the bound of [9] can be extended naturally to the setting of imperfectly shared randomness.

THEOREM 1 (). *For every $\epsilon, \delta > 0$ and $0 < \rho \leq 1$ there exists $c = c_{\epsilon, \delta, \rho}$ such that for every ℓ, n, we have* $\text{isr-cc}_\rho^{\text{ow}}\left(\text{COMPRESS}_{\Delta, \delta}^{\ell, n}\right) \leq \frac{1+\epsilon}{1-h((1-\rho)/2)}(H(P) + 2\Delta + c)$.

We stress that the notation $\text{isr-cc}_\rho^{\text{ow}}\left(\text{COMPRESS}_{\Delta, \delta}^{\ell, n}\right)$ describes the *worst-case* complexity over P with entropy $H(P) \leq \ell$ of the *expected* compression length when $m \leftarrow P$. The protocol that achieves this bound is a simple modification of the protocol of [9]. Roughly, Alice and Bob use their correlated randomness to define a "redundant and ambiguous dictionary" with words of every length for every message. Alice communicates using a word of appropriate length given the

---

[2]All throughout "isr" stands for *imperfect shared randomness*, while *psr* refers to *perfect* shared randomness.

distribution P, and Bob decodes using maximum likelihood decoding given Q. The main difference in our case is that Alice and Bob work knowing their dictionaries do not match exactly (as if they spelled the same words differently) and so use even longer words during encoding and decoding with some error-correction to allow for spelling errors. Details can be found in the full version [3].

2.2.2 Agreement distillation

Next we turn to a very natural problem in the context of imperfect sharing of randomness. Can Alice and Bob communicate to distill a few random bits from their large collection r and r' (of correlated random bits), bits on which they can agree perfectly?

Definition 2. In the AGREEMENT-DISTILLATION$_\gamma^k$ problem, Alice and Bob have no inputs. Their goal is to output w_A and w_B satisfying the following properties:

(i) $\Pr[w_A = w_B] \geq \gamma$;

(ii) $H_\infty(w_A) \geq k$; and

(iii) $H_\infty(w_B) \geq k$

where $H_\infty(X) = \min_x \log \frac{1}{\Pr[X=x]}$.

The (slightly) special case of this problem where Alice and Bob are not allowed to communicate at all was considered by Bogdanov and Mossel [2]. The setting where some communication is allowed is closely related but we describe the results in our language anyway.

A trivial way to distill randomness would be for Alice to toss random coins and send their outcome to Bob. This would achieve $\gamma = 1$ and communication complexity of k for k bits of entropy. Our first proposition says that with non-trivial correlation, some savings can always be achieved over this naive protocol.

PROPOSITION 2. *For every $\rho > 0$, it is the case that* isr-cc$_\rho^{ow}$(AGREEMENT-DISTILLATION$_\gamma^k$) $= (h(\frac{1-\rho}{2}) + o_k(1)) \cdot k$ *with $\gamma = 1 - o_k(1)$. In particular, for every $\rho > 0$ there exists $\alpha < 1$ such that for every sufficiently large k, we have* isr-cc$_\rho^{ow}$(AGREEMENT-DISTILLATION$_{1/2}^k$) $\leq \alpha k$.

We prove this proposition in the full version [3]. We note that this proposition is similar in spirit to Theorem 4 of [2] with the difference that they use their "better strategy" to improve γ with zero-communication, but γ remains exponentially small. We use communication to increase γ close to 1.

Our next theorem says that these linear savings are the best possible: one cannot get away with $o(k)$ communication unless $\rho = 1$. This theorem follows immediately from Theorem 1 of [2] and a simple reduction that converts protocols with communication to zero-communication protocols with a loss in γ.

THEOREM 2. *For every $\rho > 0$ there exists $\epsilon > 0$ such that* isr-cc$_\rho$(AGREEMENT-DISTILLATION$_\gamma^k$) $\geq \epsilon k - \log \frac{1}{\gamma}$.

The full version [3] contains details of this proof.

2.2.3 General relationships between perfect and imperfect sharing

Our final target in this work is to get some general relationships for communication complexity in the settings of perfect and imperfectly shared randomness. Our upper bounds for communication complexity are obtained by considering a natural promise problem, that we call GAPINNERPRODUCT, which is a "hard problem" for communication complexity. We use a variant, SPARSEGAPINNERPRODUCT, for our lower bounds. We define both problems below.

Definition 3. The GAPINNERPRODUCT$_{c,s}^n$ problem has parameters $n \in \mathbb{Z}^+$ (dimension), and $c > s \in [0,1]$ (completeness and soundness). Both yes- and no-instances of this problem have inputs $x, y \in \{0,1\}^n$. An instance (x,y) is a yes-instance if $\langle x,y \rangle \geq cn$, and a no-instance if $\langle x,y \rangle < sn$. The SPARSEGAPINNERPRODUCT$_{q,c,s}^n$ is a restriction of GAPINNERPRODUCT$_{c,s}^n$ where both the yes- and the no-instances are sparse, i.e., $\|x\|_2^2 \leq n/q$.

In the full version [3] we show that GAPINNERPRODUCT$_{c,s}^n$ is "hard" for PSR-CC(k) with $c = (2/3)2^{-k}$ and $s = (1/3)2^{-k}$. Then we show that this problem is in ISR-CC$_\rho^{ow}$(poly$(1/(c-s))$). Putting the two results together we get the following theorem giving a general upper bound on isr-cc$_\rho^{ow}(P)$ in terms of psr-cc(P) for any promise problem P.

THEOREM 3. $\forall \rho > 0$, $\exists c < \infty$ *such that $\forall k$, we have* PSR-CC(k) $\subseteq$ ISR-CC$_\rho^{ow}(c^k)$.

We prove this theorem in the full version [3].

Theorem 3 is obviously tight already because of known gaps between one-way and two-way communication complexity. For instance, it is well known that the "indexing" problem (where Alice gets a vector $x \in \{0,1\}^n$ and Bob an index $i \in [n]$ and they wish to compute x_i) has one-way communication complexity of $\Omega(n)$ with perfectly shared randomness, while its deterministic two-way communication complexity is at most $\log n + 2$. However one could hope for tighter results capturing promise problems P with low psr-cc$^{ow}(P)$, or to give better upper bounds on isr-cc(P) for P with low psr-cc(P). Our next theorem rules out any further improvements to Theorem 3 when n is sufficiently large (compared to k). We do so by focusing on the problem SPARSEGAPINNERPRODUCT. In the full version [3] we show that psr-cc^{ow}(SPARSEGAPINNERPRODUCT$_{q,c,s}^n$) $= O(\text{poly}(\frac{1}{q(c-s)}) \log q)$ for every q, n and $c > s$. In particular if say $c = 1/(2q)$ and $s = 1/(4q)$ the one-way communication complexity with perfectly shared randomness reduces to $O(\log q)$, in contrast to the poly(q) upper bound on the one-way communication complexity with imperfectly shared randomness.

Our main technical theorem shows that this gap is necessary for every $\rho < 1$. Specifically in the full version we show that

$$\text{isr-cc}_\rho(\text{SPARSEGAPINNERPRODUCT}_{q,c=.9/q,s=.6/q}^n) = \Omega(\sqrt{q}).$$

Putting the two together we get a strong converse to Theorem 3, stated below.

THEOREM 4. *For every k, there exists a promise problem $P = (P_n)_{n \in \mathbb{Z}^+}$ such that psr-cc$^{ow}(P) \leq k$, but for every $\rho < 1$ it is the case that isr-cc$_\rho(P) = 2^{\Omega_\rho(k)}$.*

Remarks on the proofs.

Theorem 3 and Theorem 4 are the technical highlights of this paper and we describe some of the ideas behind them here.

Theorem 3 gives an upper bound for isr-cc$_\rho^{ow}$ for problems with low psr-cc. As such this ought to be somewhat surprising in that for known problems with low probabilistic communication complexity (notably, equality testing), the known solutions are very sensitive to perturbations of the randomness. But the formulation in terms of GAPINNER-PRODUCT suggests that any such problem reduces to an approximate inner product calculation; and the theory of metric embeddings, and examples such as locality sensitive hashing, suggest that one can reduce the dimensionality of the problems here significantly and this may lead to some reduced complexity protocols that are also robust to the noise of the ρ-correlated vectors. This leads us to the following idea: To estimate $\langle x, y \rangle$, where $x, y \in \{0,1\}^n$, Alice can compute $a = \langle g_1, x \rangle$ where g_1 is a random n-dimensional spherical Gaussian and send a (or the most significant bits of a) to Bob. Bob can compute $b = \langle g_2, y \rangle$ and $a \cdot b$ is an unbiased estimator (up to normalization) of $\langle x, y \rangle$ if $g_1 = g_2$. This protocol can be easily shown to be robust in that if g_2 is only ρ-correlated with g_1, $a \cdot b$ is still a good estimator, with higher variance. And it is easy to convert a collection of ρ-correlated bits to ρ-correlated Gaussians, so it is possible for Alice and Bob to generate the g_1 and g_2 as desired from their imperfectly shared randomness. A careful analysis (of a variant of this protocol) shows that to estimate $\langle x, y \rangle$ to within an additive error $\epsilon \|x\|_2 \|y\|_2$, it suffices for Alice to send about $1/\epsilon^2$ bits to Bob, and this leads to a proof of Theorem 3.

Next we turn to the proof of Theorem 4, which shows a roughly matching lower bound to Theorem 3 above. The insight to this proof comes from examining the "Gaussian protocol" above carefully and contrasting it with the protocol used in the perfect randomness setting. In the latter case Alice uses the randomness to pick one (or few) coordinates of x and sends some function of these bits to Bob achieving a communication complexity of roughly $\log(1/\epsilon)$, using the fact that only $O(\epsilon n)$ bits of x are non-zero. In the Gaussian protocol Alice sends a very "non-junta"-like function of x to Bob; this seems robust to the perturbations of the randomness, but leads to $1/\epsilon^2$ bits of communication. This difference in behavior suggests that perhaps functions where variables have low "influence" cannot be good strategies in the setting of perfect randomness, and indeed we manage to prove such a statement in the full version of this paper (see Theorem 6.8 in [3]). The proof of this theorem uses a variant of the invariance principle that we prove (see Theorem 7.1 in [3]), which shows that if a communication protocol with low-influences works in a "product-distributional" setting, it will also work with inputs being Gaussian and with the same moments. This turns out to be a very useful reduction. The reason that SPARSEGAPINNERPRODUCT has nice psr-cc^{ow} protocols is the asymmetry between the inputs of Alice and the inputs of Bob — inputs of Alice are sparse! But with the Gaussian variables there is no notion of sparsity and indeed Alice and Bob have symmetric inputs and so one can now reduce the "disjointness" problem from communication complexity (where now Alice and Bob hold sets $A, B \subseteq [1/\epsilon]$, and would like to distinguish $|A \cap B| = 0$ from $|A \cap B| = 1$) to the Gaussian inner product problem. Using the well-known lower bound on disjointness, we conclude that $\Omega(1/\epsilon)$ bits of communication are necessary and this proves Theorem 6.8 in [3].

Of course, all this rules out only one part of the solution space for the communication complexity problem, one where Alice and Bob use functions of low-influence. To turn this into a general lower bound we note that if Alice and Bob use functions with some very influential variables, then they should agree on which variable to use (given their randomness r and r'). Such agreement on the other hand cannot happen with too high a probability by our lower bound on AGREEMENT-DISTILLATION (from Theorem 2). Putting all these ingredients together gives us a proof of Theorem 4.

The full version of this paper [3] contains proofs of all the theorems mentioned above as also the description of an invariance principle suitable for communication complexity.

3. CONCLUSIONS

In this paper we carried out an investigation of the power of imperfectly shared randomness in the context of communication complexity. There are two important aspects to the perspective that motivated our work: First, the notion that in many forms of natural communication, the communicating parties understand each other (or "know" things about each other) fairly well, but never perfectly. This imperfection in knowledge/understanding creates an obstacle to many of the known solutions and new solutions have to be devised, or new techniques need to be developed to understand whether the obstacles are barriers. Indeed for the positive results described in this paper, classical solutions do not work and the solutions that ended up working are even "provably" different from classical solutions. (In particular they work hard to preserve "low influence").

However, we also wish to stress a second aspect that makes the problems here interesting in our view, which is an aspect of scale. Often in communication complexity our main motivation is to compute functions with sublinear communication, or prove linear lower bounds. Our work, and natural communication in general, stresses the setting where inputs are enormous, and the communication complexity one is considering is tiny. This models many aspects of natural communication where there is a huge context to any conversation which is implicit. If this context were known exactly to sender and receiver, then it would play no significant mathematical role. However in natural communication this context is not exactly known, and resolving this imperfection of knowledge before communicating the relevant message would be impossibly hard. Such a setting naturally motivates the need to study problems of input length n, but where any dependence on n in the communication complexity would be impractical.

We note that we are not at the end of the road regarding questions of this form: Indeed a natural extension to communication complexity might be where Alice wishes to compute $f_A(x, y)$ and Bob wishes to compute $f_B(x, y)$ but Alice does not know f_B and Bob does not know f_A (or have only approximate knowledge of these functions). If x and y are n-bits strings, f_A and f_B might require 2^n bits to describe and this might be the real input size. There is still a trivial upper bound of $2n$ bits for solving any such communication problem, but it would be interesting to study when, and what form of, approximate knowledge of f_A and f_B helps improve over this trivial bound.

Turning to the specific questions studied in this paper a fair number of natural questions arise that we have not been able to address in this work. For instance, we stuck to a specific and simple form of correlation in the randomness shared by Alice and Bob. One could ask what general forms of randomness (r, r') are equally powerful. In particular if the distribution of (r, r') is known to both Alice and Bob, can they convert their randomness to some form of correlation in the sense used in this paper (in product form with marginals being uniform)?

In the AGREEMENT-DISTILLATION problem the goal was for Alice and Bob to agree perfectly on some random string. What if their goal is only to generate more correlated bits than they start with? What is possible here and what are the limits?

In the study of perfectly shared randomness, Newman's Theorem [14] is a simple but powerful tool, showing that $O(\log n)$ bits of randomness suffice to deal with problems on n bit inputs. When randomness is shared imperfectly, such a randomness reduction is not obvious. Indeed for the problem of equality testing, the protocol of [1] uses 2^n bits of randomness, and our Gaussian protocol (which can solve this with one-way communication) uses $\text{poly}(n)$ bits. Do $O(\log n)$ bits of imperfectly shared randomness suffice for this problem? How about for general problems?

Finally almost all protocols we give for imperfectly shared randomness lead to two-sided error. This appears to be an inherent limitation (with some philosophical implications) but we do not have a proof. It would be nice to show that one-sided error with imperfectly shared randomness cannot lead to any benefits beyond that offered by private randomness.

Acknowledgments

We thank Brendan Juba for his helpful notes [8] on the invariance principle. We thank the anonymous referees for their valuable comments and pointers.

References

[1] Mohammad Bavarian, Dmitry Gavinsky, and Tsuyoshi Ito. On the role of shared randomness in simultaneous communication. In Javier Esparza, Pierre Fraigniaud, Thore Husfeldt, and Elias Koutsoupias, editors, *ICALP (1)*, volume 8572 of *Lecture Notes in Computer Science*, pages 150–162. Springer, 2014. ISBN 978-3-662-43947-0.

[2] Andrej Bogdanov and Elchanan Mossel. On extracting common random bits from correlated sources. *CoRR*, abs/1007.2315, 2010. URL http://arxiv.org/abs/1007.2315.

[3] Clément L. Canonne, Venkatesan Guruswami, Raghu Meka, and Madhu Sudan. Communication with imperfectly shared randomness. *CoRR*, abs/1411.3603, 2014. URL http://arxiv.org/abs/1411.3603.

[4] Thomas M. Cover and Joy A. Thomas. *Elements of Information Theory*. Wiley Publishing, New York, 1991.

[5] Venkatesan Guruswami, Johan Håstad, Rajsekar Manokaran, Prasad Raghavendra, and Moses Charikar. Beating the random ordering is hard: Every ordering CSP is approximation resistant. *SIAM J. Comput.*, 40 (3):878–914, 2011.

[6] Elad Haramaty and Madhu Sudan. Deterministic compression with uncertain priors. In *Proceedings of the 5th Conference on Innovations in Theoretical Computer Science*, ITCS '14, pages 377–386, New York, NY, USA, 2014. ACM. ISBN 978-1-4503-2698-8. doi: 10.1145/2554797.2554832. URL http://doi.acm.org/10.1145/2554797.2554832.

[7] Marcus Isaksson and Elchanan Mossel. Maximally stable Gaussian partitions with discrete applications. *Israel Journal of Mathematics*, 189:347–396, June 2012.

[8] Brendan Juba. 18.177 course project: Invariance principles, 2009. URL http://people.seas.harvard.edu/~bjuba/papers/18177-report.pdf.

[9] Brendan Juba, Adam Tauman Kalai, Sanjeev Khanna, and Madhu Sudan. Compression without a common prior: an information-theoretic justification for ambiguity in language. In Bernard Chazelle, editor, *ICS*, pages 79–86. Tsinghua University Press, 2011. ISBN 978-7-302-24517-9.

[10] Bala Kalyanasundaram and Georg Schnitger. The probabilistic communication complexity of set intersection. *SIAM J. Discrete Math.*, 5(4):545–557, 1992. doi: 10.1137/0405044. URL http://dx.doi.org/10.1137/0405044.

[11] Eyal Kushilevitz and Noam Nisan. *Communication Complexity*. Cambridge University Press, New York, NY, USA, 2006. ISBN 9780521029834. URL http://books.google.com/books?id=dHH7rdhKwzsC.

[12] Michel Ledoux and Michel Talagrand. *Probability in Banach spaces: Isoperimetry and processes*. Springer, Berlin, 1991. ISBN 3540520139.

[13] Elchanan Mossel. Gaussian bounds for noise correlation of functions. *Geometric and Functional Analysis*, 19(6):1713–1756, 2010. ISSN 1016-443X. doi: 10.1007/s00039-010-0047-x. URL http://dx.doi.org/10.1007/s00039-010-0047-x.

[14] Ilan Newman. Private vs. common random bits in communication complexity. *Inf. Process. Lett.*, 39(2): 67–71, July 1991. ISSN 0020-0190. doi: 10.1016/0020-0190(91)90157-D. URL http://dx.doi.org/10.1016/0020-0190(91)90157-D.

[15] Ryan O'Donnell. *Analysis of Boolean Functions*. Cambridge University Press, 2014. ISBN 9781107038325. URL http://books.google.com/books?id=5xlvAwAAQBAJ.

The Circuit-Input Game, Natural Proofs, and Testing Circuits With Data[*]

Brynmor Chapman
Stanford
chapmanb@cs.stanford.edu

Ryan Williams
Stanford
rrw@cs.stanford.edu

ABSTRACT

We revisit a natural zero-sum game from several prior works. A *circuit player*, armed with a collection of Boolean circuits, wants to compute a function f with one (or some) of its circuits. An *input player* has a collection of inputs, and wants to find one (or some) inputs on which the circuit player cannot compute f. Several results are known on the existence of small-support strategies for zero-sum games, in particular the above circuit-input game. We give two new applications of these classical results to circuit complexity:

Natural properties useful against self-checking circuits are equivalent to circuit lower bounds. We show how the Natural Proofs barrier may be potentially sidestepped, by simply focusing on analyzing *circuits that check their answers*. Slightly more precisely, we prove $\mathsf{NP} \not\subset \mathsf{P/poly}$ *if and only if* there are natural properties that (a) accept the SAT function and (b) are useful against polynomial-size circuits that never err when they report SAT. (Note, via self-reducibility, any small circuit can be turned into one of this kind!) The proof is very general; similar equivalences hold for other lower bound problems. Our message is that one should search for lower bound methods that are designed to succeed (only) against circuits with "one-sided error."

Circuit Complexity versus Testing Circuits With Data. We reconsider the problem of program testing, which we formalize as deciding if a given circuit computes a (fixed) function f. We define the "data complexity" of f (as a function of circuit size s) to be the minimum cardinality of a *test suite* of inputs: a set of input/output pairs necessary and sufficient for deciding if any given circuit of size at most s computes a slice of f. (This is a "gray-box testing" problem, where the value s is side information.) We prove that designing small test suites for f is equivalent to proving circuit lower bounds on f: the data complexity of

testing f is "small" if and only if the circuit complexity of f is "large." Therefore, circuit lower bounds may be constructively viewed as *data design* circuit-testing problems.

Categories and Subject Descriptors

F.2.m [**Analysis of Algorithms and Problem Complexity**]: Miscellaneous

General Terms

Complexity Theory; Circuit Complexity; Circuit-Input Game; Natural Proofs; Program Testing; Gray-Box Testing

1. INTRODUCTION

We consider the following zero-sum game studied in prior work (e.g., [LY94, FIKU08]), which we call the *circuit-input game*. Fix a Boolean function f. A *circuit player* chooses from a set of Boolean circuits, while an *input player* chooses from a set of inputs. A payoff goes to the circuit player if its chosen circuit computes f on the chosen input; otherwise, the input player is paid.

To our knowledge, the circuit-input game was first explicitly studied by Lipton and Young [LY94], in the context of providing complexity-theoretic applications of strategies for general zero-sum games (see also [Yao77]). Among other results, they (and independently, Newman [New91] and Althöfer [Alt94]) proved that approximate and succinct strategies exist for any zero-sum game in the sense for an $m \times n$ matrix M, there exists a strategy for the row player with support size $O(\log n)$, and a strategy for the column player with support size $O(\log m)$, which together additively approximate the optimal strategy of the game. This result was used to prove the existence of so-called *anti-checkers*: for any function $f : \{0,1\}^n \to \{0,1\}$ with circuit complexity at least s, there exists a set S of $O(s)$ n-bit inputs on which all circuits of size at most s/n fail to compute f correctly on a $1/2 - \varepsilon$ fraction of inputs in S.

In this paper, we start by proving a general extension of these classical results, and we also prove that our extension cannot be improved in a certain technical way. We then use our extension to present two new applications of these classical results to the field of circuit complexity.

Natural Properties Equivalent to Lower Bounds.

In the first part of the paper, we give an alternative view into the Natural Proofs barrier [RR97]; in particular, we suggest a new pathway around it. Recall that Natural Proofs have three properties.

[*]Supported by NSF CCF-1212372. Any opinions, findings, and conclusions or recommendations expressed in this material are those of the author(s) and do not necessarily reflect the views of the National Science Foundation.

- They are *constructive*: they contain an efficient algorithm A from a complexity class Γ for testing Boolean functions given as truth tables,

- They are *large*: algorithm A accepts a large fraction (at least $1/2^{O(n)}$) of all n-bit Boolean functions, and

- They are *useful*: algorithm A rejects all functions which are truth tables of circuits from a circuit class $\mathcal{C}$, for infinitely many input lengths.

Such an algorithm A is called a Γ-*natural property useful against* $\mathcal{C}$, and Razborov-Rudich showed that there are no P/poly-natural properties useful against P/poly unless every pseudorandom function candidate can be broken. Hence a natural proof is not capable of proving P/poly lower bounds, or statements like NP $\not\subset$ P/poly. This ruled out many potential methods for proving circuit lower bounds.

We show that a minor (and in hindsight, obvious) modification to the "useful" condition of Natural Proofs not only makes the barrier disappear, but it makes circuit lower bounds equivalent to the existence of such modified natural properties. Our minor modification is perhaps best illustrated by considering NP vs P/poly and the SAT problem (although any self-reducible NP-complete problem would suffice). We begin with the well-known observation that any polynomial-size circuit C can be assumed, without loss of generality, to never err when it reports satisfiability. That is, given a circuit C that potentially solves SAT, C can be augmented to print a satisfying assignment: create a larger circuit C' that contains copies of C, such that when C reports "SAT" on a formula, C' repeatedly plugs in values for variables of the formula and queries C on the reduced formulas to check if satisfiability still holds. Either C will eventually be in error (in which case C' reports "UNSAT") or C will produce a SAT assignment, in which case C' reports "SAT" without error.

Let C be a Boolean circuit on n inputs. Define C to be a *SAT solver* if for all n-bit formulas F, $C(F) = 1$ implies that F is satisfiable. (We call such circuits "SAT solvers" because one could use these circuits to print satisfying assignments to formulas, when the circuits report "SAT.") The class of functions computable by polynomial-size SAT solvers is an expressive class, including special cases such as 2-SAT, Horn-SAT, etc. By the previous paragraph, to prove NP $\not\subset$ P/poly it suffices to prove that no polynomial-size family of SAT solvers can compute SAT. That is, a lower bound proof only needs to be *useful* against small SAT solvers. But *how* might we prove this? If we used combinatorial or probabilistic methods, we might expect to find an efficient test for Boolean functions, such that random functions (and SAT) pass, but SAT solver circuits do not pass. This looks very much like Natural Proofs, except instead of rejecting all polynomial-size circuits, our test will only try to reject the polynomial-size SAT solvers. It turns out that such tests always exist, if NP $\not\subset$ P/poly. More formally, let SAT$_n$ denote the restriction of SAT to formulas encoded in n bits. We prove:

THEOREM 1.1. NP $\not\subset$ P/*poly if and only if there is an* $\mathrm{AC}^0/n^{o(1)}$-*natural property that is useful against polynomial-size SAT solvers and accepts* SAT$_n$ *for all* n.

Compare with the main theorem of Razborov-Rudich: if there are P/poly-natural properties useful against P/poly,

then there are no strong pseudorandom generators. The above theorem suggests that, to circumvent "naturalness" and prove circuit lower bounds for SAT, we should try to look for proof methods which *fail* on arbitrary polynomial-size circuits, but *succeed* on circuits that try to print full satisfying assignments. This point also gives intuition for why THEOREM 1.1 holds without hurting cryptography: the truth tables of SAT solvers do not look at all like random functions, so a natural property useful against SAT solvers is in no danger of distinguishing pseudorandom functions from truly random ones.[1]

Equivalences similar to THEOREM 1.1 hold for other circuit lower bound problems. In general, for any function f that permits a zero-error or one-sided error corrector in a complexity class $\mathcal{C}$, there is an equivalence between proving $f \notin \mathcal{C}$ and exhibiting natural properties useful against "error-corrected f-solving circuits." We also show how a version of our statement holds for f with (randomized) polynomial-time program checkers [BK95].

Testing Circuits for Functionality Using Data.

In the second part of the paper, we apply succinct strategies for zero-sum games to set a framework that is "dual" to the usual computational view of circuits computing functions on inputs, treating inputs as the "programs" and circuits as the "input data". We generalize Lipton-Young's anti-checkers, showing how the general problem of circuit lower bounds can be seen in a constructive light: as designing small data sets that can be used to conclusively test whether a given circuit computes a particular function. This also yields a complexity-theoretic perspective on the practical problem of software testing (see [Pat05, UL07]).

To describe the results, we need to fix some terminology. Let $\mathcal{C}$ be the collection of Boolean circuits over the standard basis B_2, the set of all two-bit Boolean functions. The *size* of a circuit $C \in \mathcal{C}$ is measured by its number of gates; let $|C|$ denote the size of C. Let $f : \{0,1\}^\star \to \{0,1\}$ be a decision problem. The nth slice of f is the function $f_n : \{0,1\}^n \to \{0,1\}$ that agrees with f on all n-bit inputs. Function f_n is computed by $C_n \in \mathcal{C}$ if for every $x \in \{0,1\}^n$ we have $C_n(x) = f_n(x)$, and the *circuit complexity of* f is the function $g : \mathbb{N} \to \mathbb{N}$ such that $g(n)$ equals the minimum $|C_n|$ over all $C_n \in \mathcal{C}$ computing f_n.

Define the computational problem of TESTING FOR f, which we abbreviate as TEST-f, to be the union (over all n) of the set of *all* circuits C_n which compute f_n. For simplicity, we define the sth slice of TEST-f to be the set of all size-s circuits computing some slice of f (rather than the set of all circuits encoded in s bits that compute some slice).

Let $\{0,1\}^{\leq n}$ be the set of all bit strings of length at most n. Let $X_s \subseteq \{0,1\}^{\leq s} \times \{0,1\}$. That is, X_s is a collection of pairs of ($\leq s$)-bit strings with bit labels.

DEFINITION 1.1. *The set* X_s *is said to test size-s for* f *if:*
- *for all* $(x,b) \in X_s$, $f(x) = b$, *and*
- *for every size-s circuit* $C \in (\mathcal{C} \setminus \text{TEST-}f)$ *with n inputs (that is, $C \neq f_n$), there is a pair* $(x,b) \in X_s$ *such that* $|x| = n$ *and* $C(x) \neq b$.[2]

---

[1] As a reviewer succinctly noted, one might interpret this result as saying, "pseudorandom functions have no hope of computing SAT, so why should we care about them?"

[2] Note that s is the maximal number of input gates in a circuit of size s, so $n \leq s$.

That is, a circuit C of size s and n inputs agrees with f on all n-bit inputs in X_s if and only if the circuit C computes f_n. Hence such a collection X_s can be used to conclusively test whether a given circuit computes the relevant slice of f.

An infinite family of input sets $\{X_s \mid s \in \mathbb{N}^+\}$ is said to *test for* f if for all $s \geq 1$, and for every circuit $C \in (\mathcal{C} \setminus \text{TEST-}f)$ of size s, there is a string $x \in X_s$ such that $C(x) \neq f_{|x|}(s)$. Thinking of TEST-f as a decision problem to be computationally solved, the family $\{X_s\}$ can serve as a *test suite* for deciding this problem, by providing pairs $(x, f(x)) \in X_s$, then verifying that a given circuit C agrees with all pairs.

Using inputs to test for whether a circuit computes f leads to a natural definition of the complexity of testing for f:

DEFINITION 1.2. *The* data complexity of TEST-f *is defined to be the function* $g : \mathbb{N} \to \mathbb{N}$ *such that* $g(s)$ *equals the minimum cardinality of a set* X_s *testing size-s for f.*

(Note that we measure data complexity as a function of the circuit size s, because s measures the "length of the input" to the problem TEST-f.) The design of a test suite $\{X_s\}$ with low complexity is an extremely natural goal that is rather well-motivated practically. It is a *data design* problem, as opposed to the typical algorithm/circuit design problem. Just as there are trivial circuits of $O(n2^n)$ size for every Boolean function on n variables, there are also trivial test suites where each X_s contains $2^{O(s)}$ inputs of length up to s. The theory of circuits becomes interesting when we restrict the complexities of circuits; the theory of test suites becomes similarly interesting when restricting the amount of necessary data.

There is an inherent duality between data complexity and circuit complexity. Our main theorem is that lower bounds on the circuit complexity of f are basically *equivalent* to upper bounds on the data complexity of testing f. This also uses the circuit-input game in a crucial way:

THEOREM 1.2. *Let* $f : \{0,1\}^* \to \{0,1\}$, *and let* $S(n) \geq 2n$ *for all n.*

1. *If f is in* $\mathsf{SIZE}(S(n))$, *then the data complexity of testing size-s circuits for f is at least* $2^{\Omega(S^{-1}(s))}$ *almost everywhere.*

2. *If f is not in* $\mathsf{SIZE}(n \cdot S(n))$, *then the data complexity of testing size-s circuits for f is at most* $O(2^{S^{-1}(s)} + S^{-1}(s) \cdot s^2 \log s)$ *infinitely often.*

As a corollary, we can give a different characterization of the $\mathsf{NP} \not\subset \mathsf{P/poly}$ problem: it is equivalent to the existence of a test suite for testing circuits for SAT with subexponential data complexity:

COROLLARY 1.1. $\mathsf{NP} \not\subset \mathsf{P/poly}$ *(resp.* $\mathsf{NP} \not\subset \mathsf{i.o.P/poly}$*) if and only if for every* $\varepsilon > 0$ *and for infinitely many s (resp. for every* $\varepsilon > 0$ *and for every s), the data complexity of testing size-s circuits for SAT is at most* $O\left(2^{s^{\varepsilon}}\right)$.

We strongly recommend reading (not skipping) the Preliminaries section below, as it introduces notation, background, and intuitions that will be required at key points in the paper.

2. PRELIMINARIES

2.1 Background

Complexity Theory.

We assume standard background in complexity theory, along with the following additional notation: $\mathsf{SIZE}(S(n))$ is the class of functions $f : \{0,1\}^* \to \{0,1\}$ such that f is computable with a size-$S(n)$ circuit family $\{C_n\}$ over the basis B_2 of all two-bit Boolean functions.

Zero-Sum Games and Succinct Strategies.

We think of a zero-sum game as an $m \times n$ matrix M with entries from $[0,1]$ describing the payoff to the row player in a game between a *row player* and *column player*. We now describe the concepts and theorems of Lipton and Young [LY94] relevant to this paper.

DEFINITION 2.1. *Let S be any set, and let* $k \in \mathbb{N}$. *A k-uniform distribution on S is a probability distribution obtained by choosing uniformly from a multiset of k elements from S.*

DEFINITION 2.2. *Let $\mathcal{C}$ be a set of n circuits, let $\mathcal{I}$ be a set of m inputs, and let M be an $m \times n$ matrix with entries in $[0,1]$. (Intuitively, $M(C, x)$ represents some cost of the computation of $C(x)$.) The* circuit-input game w.r.t. M *is the two-player zero-sum game given by the matrix M.*

For a function $f : \{0,1\}^* \to \{0,1\}$, our central game of interest is what we call the *circuit-input game for f on size-s circuits and n inputs*, which is the circuit-input game w.r.t. the following matrix M. M has 2^n rows (for all strings x in $\{0,1\}^n$) and $2^{O(s \log s)}$ columns (for all circuits C of size s), and

$$M(C, x) := \begin{cases} 0 & \text{if } C(x) = f(x) \\ 1 & \text{otherwise} \end{cases}$$

Let $\mathcal{C}$, $\mathcal{I}$, and M be as above. Assume without loss of generality that $\exists C_0, x_0$ such that $M(C_0, x_0) = 0$ and $\exists C_1, x_1$ such that $M(C_1, x_1) = 1$. We shall use the following two theorems saying that approximately optimal strategies with small support exist for every game M:

THEOREM 2.1 ([NEW91, ALT94, LY94]). *Let* $\epsilon > 0$, *let* $k > \dfrac{\ln |\mathcal{I}|}{2\epsilon^2}$, *and let* $\ell > \dfrac{\ln |\mathcal{C}|}{2\epsilon^2}$.

1. *There exists a k-uniform distribution p on $\mathcal{C}$ such that for every* $x \in \mathcal{I}$, *the expectation* $\displaystyle\mathop{\mathbf{E}}_{C \sim p}[M_{C,x}] < \mathcal{V}(M) + \epsilon$, *where $\mathcal{V}(M)$ denotes the value of the circuit-input game w.r.t. M.*

2. *There exists an ℓ-uniform distribution p on $\mathcal{I}$ such that for every* $C \in \mathcal{C}$, *the expectation* $\displaystyle\mathop{\mathbf{E}}_{x \sim p}[M_{C,x}] > \mathcal{V}(M) - \epsilon$, *where $\mathcal{V}(M)$ denotes the value of the circuit-input game w.r.t. M.*

This theorem can be proved using a random sampling argument and standard large deviation (Chernoff-Hoeffding) bounds. From THEOREM 2.1, we may derive the following general consequence which does not appear in prior work:

THEOREM 2.2. *Let $\mathcal{C}_n$ be a set of 2^t circuits where each circuit has n inputs, let $\mathcal{I}_n \subseteq \{0,1\}^n$, and let $f : \{0,1\}^n \to \{0,1\}$. Let $\epsilon : \mathbb{N} \to \mathbb{Q} \cap (0,1]$, and let $p, q : \mathbb{N} \to [0,1]$ with $p + q \leq 1 - \epsilon$. For every $n \in \mathbb{N}$, one of the following must hold:*

1. *There exists an $O(n/\varepsilon(n)^2)$-size multiset $X_n \subseteq \mathcal{C}_n$ such that for every $y \in \mathcal{I}_n$, $C(y) = f(y)$ for more than a $p(n)$ fraction of the circuits $C \in X_n$.*

2. *There exists an $O(t/\varepsilon(n)^2)$-size multiset $Y_n \subseteq \mathcal{I}_n$ such that for every $C \in \mathcal{C}_n$, $C(y) \neq f(y)$ for more than a $q(n)$ fraction of the inputs $y \in Y_n$.*

PROOF. Let M be the circuit-input game for a function f. Let ε, p, q, and n be as in the statement of the theorem. Set a parameter $\delta := \varepsilon(n)/2$, set $k := \dfrac{\ln |\mathcal{I}|}{\delta^2} = \dfrac{n}{\delta^2}$, and set $\ell := \dfrac{\ln |\mathcal{P}|}{\delta^2} = \dfrac{t}{\delta^2}$. Then by THEOREM 2.1, there exists a k-uniform distribution X_n on $\mathcal{C}_n$ such that for all $y \in \mathcal{I}_n$,

$$\mathop{\mathbf{E}}_{C \sim X_n} [M[C,y]] < \mathcal{V}(M) + \delta, \qquad (1)$$

and there exists an ℓ-uniform distribution Y_n on $\mathcal{I}_n$ such that for every $C \in \mathcal{C}_n$,

$$\mathop{\mathbf{E}}_{y \sim Y_n} [M[C,y]] > \mathcal{V}(M) - \delta. \qquad (2)$$

Assume that there exists $y^* \in \mathcal{I}_n$ such that $C(y^*) \neq f(y^*)$ for at least a $1 - p(n)$ fraction of the circuits $C \in X_n$. Since M is a Boolean matrix, we have for every $C^* \in \mathcal{C}_n$ that

$$
\begin{aligned}
q(n) &\leq 1 - p(n) - \varepsilon(n) \\
&\leq \mathop{\mathbf{Pr}}_{C \sim X_n} [C(y^*) \neq f(y^*)] - \varepsilon(n) \quad \text{(by choice of } y^*\text{)} \\
&< \mathcal{V}(M) - \delta \quad \text{(by choice of } \delta \text{ and (1))} \\
&< \mathop{\mathbf{Pr}}_{y \sim Y_n} [C^*(y) \neq f(y)]. \quad \text{(by (2))}
\end{aligned}
$$

This completes the proof. □

That is, we can trade off between the "measure of success" p of the succinct strategy for the circuit player, and the measure of success q of the succinct strategy for the row player. This tradeoff can be exploited for complexity-theoretic purposes as follows: if item 1 does not hold (because of circuit lower bounds for computing f with $\mathcal{C}$ circuits) then there are small multisets "witnessing" this inability to compute. Lipton and Young observed this consequence for the special case of $p = 1/2$ and $q = 1/2 - \varepsilon$, calling such sets *anti-checkers*. In our main results, we shall adjust p and q to different values, as needed. (For example, in our results concerning natural properties, we use the case of $p = 0$ and $q = 1 - \varepsilon$.)

It is natural to ask whether THEOREM 2.2 can be improved, so that $p + q = 1$. We now show that this is not possible, at least not in full generality. In particular, while THEOREM 2.2 holds for all $p + q \leq 1 - \varepsilon$, where $\varepsilon > 0$, it does not hold for $p = q = 1/2$ and all matrices M:

THEOREM 2.3. *THEOREM 2.2 does not hold with $p = q = 1/2$.*

PROOF. Let $f : \{0,1\}^* \to \{0,1\}$ be a Boolean function without circuits of size $c \cdot ns$, for a sufficiently large constant $c \geq 1$. Suppose THEOREM 2.2 holds with $p = q = 1/2$ and the circuit-input game for f on size-s circuits and n inputs. Then at least one of the following holds.

1. There is an $O(n)$-size multiset $\mathcal{C}_n$ of size-s circuits where $\mathop{\mathrm{Pr}}_{C \in \mathcal{C}_n} [C(x) \neq f(x)] < 1/2$ holds for all $x \in \{0,1\}^n$.

2. There exists an $O(s \log s)$-size multiset $\mathcal{X}_n$ of n-bit inputs such that for every circuit C of size s, $\mathop{\mathrm{Pr}}_{x \in \mathcal{X}_n} [C(x) \neq f(x)] \geq 1/2$.

In the first case, f can be implemented with a (strict) MAJORITY circuit on $\mathcal{C}_n$, giving a circuit of size $O(ns)$, contradicting our choice of f.

The second case also leads to a contradiction. For any $\mathcal{X}_n$, we may take a circuit C of size $O(n)$ that has a single input x in $\mathcal{X}_n$ hardwired along with the value $f(x)$. The circuit C outputs $f(x)$ on input x, and otherwise it outputs the bit b maximizing the quantity $\mathop{\mathrm{Pr}}_{x' \in \mathcal{X}_n \setminus \{x\}} [f(x') = b]$. It follows that $\Pr[C(x) \neq f(x)] < \frac{1}{2}$. □

2.2 Additional Prior Work

The problem of approximately solving a zero-sum game has been studied in operations research as well; for example, Grigoriadis and Khachiyan [GK95b] show how to find an approximately optimal strategy with randomness in time sublinear in the size of the game matrix.

Bshouty *et al* [BCG+96] studied the circuit-input game in the context of learning theory, focusing on the complexity of finding succinct strategies in the game. They proved (for example) that if NP $\subset$ P/poly then one can uniformly construct circuits solving SAT in ZPP^{NP} – this gave a new collapse of the polynomial-hierarchy under the assumption that NP $\subset$ P/poly. Dually, if NP $\not\subset$ P/poly, then their results also show that one can uniformly construct multisets of satisfiable formulas that "fool" all small circuits, in ZPP^{NP}: Fortnow, Pavan, and Sengupta applied this consequence to the "two queries" problem in structural complexity [FPS08]. Subsequently, Fortnow *et al* [FIKU08] proved that the problem of finding approximate succinct strategies in an implicitly represented game (such as the circuit-input game) is promise-S_2-complete. Other works on succinct games include [CR08, SV12].

When circuit lower bounds are true, succinct strategy results like THEOREM 2.2 tell us that there are small distributions of inputs that "fool" all small circuits. Another class of related results have focused on a different flavor of hardness result: *given the code* of an efficient algorithm (randomized or otherwise) that's supposed to solve SAT, one can construct even smaller distributions that fool the given algorithm [GSTS05, Ats06, BTW10].

Our ideas for using data to test circuits for a function are vaguely related to the notion of *teaching dimension of a class of concepts*, from learning theory (see Goldman and Kearns [GK95a] and Shinohara and Miyano [SM91]). The teaching dimension is defined with respect to a *collection* of functions, and it bounds the total number of labeled examples needed to identify each concept in the collection (to distinguish it from the other concepts). However, this notion is information-theoretic: there are no computational bounds placed on *what* is distinguishing one function from another. In our setting, we have a collection of *programs* and a specific function f of interest, and wish to know how many labeled examples we need to distinguish "bad" programs which do not compute f from "good" ones which do.

Mulmuley's GCT program [Mul11] has also considered "sets of counterexamples" similar to our test sets, calling them "obstructions."

3. NATURAL PROPERTIES EQUIVALENT TO CIRCUIT LOWER BOUNDS

In this section, we prove that natural properties useful against self-checking circuits are *equivalent* to circuit lower bounds in some important settings.

Let SAT_n denote the restriction of SAT to formulas encoded in n bits.

REMINDER OF THEOREM 1.1 $NP \not\subset P/poly$ *if and only if there is an $AC^0/n^{o(1)}$-natural property that is useful against polynomial-size SAT solvers and accepts SAT_n for all n.*

PROOF. One direction of the equivalence is trivial: if there is any logical property that is false on the truth tables of all polynomial-size SAT_n solvers for infinitely many n, yet the property is true of SAT_n for all n, then no polynomial-size SAT solving circuit can compute SAT_n almost everywhere. Therefore $NP \not\subset P/poly$.

Now we proceed with the other direction. Assume $NP \not\subset P/poly$. Let s be a polynomial in n. For every $n \in \mathbb{N}$, let $\mathcal{C}_n$ denote the set of n-input circuits of size $s(n)$ which are SAT solvers (i.e., they never err on unsatisfiable formulas). Set $\mathcal{I}_n := SAT_n$, i.e., the set of satisfiable formulas encoded in n bits. Consider the circuit-input game M for SAT, over the set of circuits $\mathcal{C}_n$ and set of inputs $\mathcal{I}_n$.

Applying our THEOREM 2.2 to this game M (taking $p(n) = 0$ and $q(n) = 1 - \varepsilon(n)$ for some inverse polynomial $\varepsilon(n)$), either:

1. there is an $poly(s, n)$-size set $X \subseteq \mathcal{C}_n$ such that for every $x \in \mathcal{I}$, at least one $C \in X$ computes $SAT(x)$, or

2. there is an $poly(s, n)$-size set $Y \subseteq \mathcal{I}_n$ such that every circuit $C \in \mathcal{C}_n$ computes SAT correctly on at most an $\epsilon(n)$ fraction of inputs in Y.

In the first case, we may construct a polynomial-size circuit for SAT_n by simply taking the OR of the circuits in X: since the circuits never err on unsatisfiable formulas, this will compute SAT_n. Our assumption $NP \not\subset P/poly$ is therefore contradicted if the first case holds for almost every n.

Suppose the second case holds for infinitely many n. Then we can construct an algorithm A which takes as input the 2^n-bit truth table of a function $f : \{0,1\}^n \to \{0,1\}$ and is armed with Y as advice. Algorithm A accepts f if f outputs 1 on at least a $2\varepsilon(n)$ fraction of the inputs in Y, and rejects f if f outputs 1 on at most an $\varepsilon(n)$ fraction of inputs in Y. This A is implementable in polynomial-size AC^0 (in fact, depth-3 AND-OR-AND circuits), by classical results on distinguishing strings with many 1's from strings with many 0's [Ajt83, Vio11]. Furthermore, A trivially accepts SAT_n for every n, because $SAT_n(y) = 1$ for every input $y \in Y$.

Notice that, while A rejects the truth tables of SAT solving circuits of $s(n)$ size, A will *accept* a randomly chosen Boolean function with probability $1 - o(1)$. Notice that the advice needed is $s(n) \leq O(n^k)$, which is polylogarithmic in the input length, 2^n. Therefore, A is an $AC^0/n^{o(1)}$-natural property that is useful against SAT solving circuits of $s(n)$ size. Such an A can be constructed for every polynomial $s(n)$, assuming $NP \not\subset P/poly$. $\square$

A reviewer pointed out that the above theorem holds not only for SAT solvers, but for any circuit which computes a NP-complete problem with one-sided error, regardless of whether the problem in question exhibits self-reducibility. We consider SAT specifically because self-reducibility allows us to construct a SAT solver from an arbitrary circuit with only polynomial overhead.

3.1 Natural Properties from Circuit Lower Bounds for Checkable Functions

It is easy to extend the previous theorem to general functions f with deterministic one-sided checkers: functions f that allow polynomial-size circuits with oracle gates for f which never err when they output 0 (or never err when they output 1). Now we consider languages which have (randomized) polynomial time program checkers, such as EXP-complete sets [BFL91, BK95], the Permanent [Lip91], etc. Such randomized program checkers can be adapted to give polynomial size circuit families which act as program checkers that *deterministically* check all functions computable by small circuits. These deterministic program checkers can then be used to prove (as above with SAT) equivalences between circuit lower bounds and the existence of natural properties. Here we use the following definition of a program checker.

DEFINITION 3.1. *Let $L \in \{0,1\}^*$. A randomized (polynomial time) program checker for L is a randomized (polynomial time) algorithm with oracle access to an arbitrary function f, which when given an n-bit input x and randomness r will accept with probability greater than $2/3$ (over the choice of r) if $L = f$ and will reject with probability greater than $2/3$ if $L(x) \neq f(x)$.*

In order for a randomized program checker to be adapted to produce a deterministic circuit family, we require that the language L be paddable, so that a circuit computing L on inputs of length n can also compute L on inputs of length less than n. Hence for the rest of the section, we consider only functions which are paddable in the following sense.

DEFINITION 3.2. *A language L is* paddable *if there exists a language L' such that $L = \left\{ x01^k : x \in L', k \in \mathbb{N} \right\}$.*

Note that any language L' can be converted into a paddable language L as above, while preserving both asymptotic circuit complexity (up to a polynomial factor) and the existence of program checkers.

THEOREM 3.1. *Let p and t be polynomials, and let L be a paddable language with a randomized $t(n) - n$ time program checker. Then there exists a polynomial size circuit family which deterministically checks all functions on n inputs computable by circuits of size at most $p(t(n))$.*

PROOF. Let p and t be polynomials in n. Let L be any paddable language with a randomized $t(n) - n$ time program checker, i.e. there exists a randomized $t(n) - n$ time algorithm A such that for every input $x \in \{0,1\}^n$ and every $f : \{0,1\}^{t(n)} \to \{0,1\}$, $A^f(x) = 1$ with probability more than $2/3$ if f is the $t(n)$th slice of L, and $A^f(x) = 0$ with probability more than $2/3$ if $f\left(x1^{t(n)-n}\right) \neq L(x)$.

We may amplify this success probability to $1 - 2^{-q(n)}$ (for some polynomial $q(n) > 2p(t(n)) \log p(t(n)) + n$), by creating another checker A' which runs A independently $18q(n)$

times and returns the MAJORITY of the $18q(n)$ results; appealing to a Chernoff bound yields the higher success probability.

We may simulate A' with a polynomial size family $\{B_n\}$ of oracle circuits which take as input the string $x \in \{0,1\}^n$ and a string of randomness $r \in \{0,1\}^{n^k}$, and which use oracle gates to compute the function f. Since there are at most $2^{2p(t(n))\log p(t(n))}$ circuits of size $p(t(n))$ and 2^n n-bit input strings, we have (using a union bound) with non-zero probability (over the choice of $r \in \{0,1\}^{n^k}$), for every $x \in \{0,1\}^n$ and every f computable by a circuit of size $p(t(n))$,

- $f(z) = L(z)$ for all $z \in \{0,1\}^{t(n)} \implies B_n^f(x,r) = 1$ and

- $f(x) \neq L(x) \implies B_n^f(x,r) = 0.$

Hence there is some choice of randomness $r^* \in \{0,1\}^{n^k}$ for which $B_n(-, r^*)$ is a deterministic program checker (where the randomness r^* is hard coded into the circuit). $\square$

Fix a polynomial p and a circuit family A_n which deterministically checks circuits of size at most $p(n)$. Now for any circuit $\{C\}$ with $t(n)$ inputs and of size $p(t(n))$, we may augment C with $A_{t(n)}$ to create a self-checking circuit C' on n inputs with polynomial overhead. We may treat C' as a ternary circuit which outputs 0 (resp. 1) if $A_{t(n)}$ outputs 1 and C outputs 0 (resp. 1), and which outputs $\perp$ if $A_{t(n)}$ outputs 0. We may treat $\perp$ as 0 or 1, in which case C' gives a circuit with one-sided error (in either direction). Call all such C' the *self-checked circuits* for L.

THEOREM 3.2. *Let L be a paddable language with a randomized polynomial time program checker. If $L \notin \mathsf{P}/\mathrm{poly}$, then for every polynomial s, there exists a natural property computable in $\mathsf{AC}^0/n^{o(1)}$ useful against size-$s(n)$ self-checked circuits for L.*

PROOF. In the case where $\perp = 0$ above, we may take $\mathcal{C}_n$ to be the set of $s(n)$ size circuits, $\mathcal{I}_n := \{0,1\}^n \cap L$, and $M(C,y) := 1 - C(y)$. From THEOREM 2.2 (taking $p(n) = 0$ and $q(n) = 1 - \epsilon(n)$ for some inverse polynomial ϵ), either there is a polynomial size set $X \subseteq \mathcal{C}_n$ such that for every $y \in \mathcal{I}$, at least one $C \in X$ computes $L(y)$, or there is a polynomial size set $Y \subseteq \mathcal{I}_n$ such that every circuit $C \in \mathcal{C}_n$ computes L correctly on at most an $\epsilon(n)$ fraction of inputs in Y. If the former case holds for almost every n, then we may construct a polynomial size circuit family for L by taking the OR of the circuits in X. Otherwise, the latter case holds infinitely often, giving an efficiently computable $(\mathsf{AC}^0/n^{o(1)})$ natural property useful against functions with one-sided error which are computable with $s(n)$ size circuits.

Note that the choice to treat $\perp$ as 0 is arbitrary. We may instead treat $\perp$ as 1, in which case THEOREM 2.2 either gives a polynomial size set of circuits whose AND computes L, or an $\mathsf{AC}^0/n^{o(1)}$-computable natural property useful against functions with $p(n)$ size circuits and which are (bitwise) at least L. $\square$

4. CIRCUIT LOWER BOUNDS AS DATA DESIGN PROBLEMS

We now turn to our results on testing circuits and data complexity. In the following, let $f : \{0,1\}^* \to \{0,1\}$ and let

$S : \mathbb{N} \to \mathbb{N}$ satisfy $S(n) \geq n$ for all n. For simplicity, we prove the main theorem (THEOREM 1.2) only for the class of circuits over the basis B_2 of all two-bit Boolean functions, although analogous statements will hold for any complete basis with minor modifications. For a circuit C, let $n(C)$ be its number of inputs.

Recall that the *data complexity* of testing size-s circuits for f is the minimum cardinality of a set S of labeled examples $(x, f(x))$ (where $|x|$ can range from 1 to s) that suffice to distinguish all size-s circuits which do not compute a slice of f from those which do. Namely, for all size-s circuits C which do not compute $f_{n(C)}$, there is some "witness" in S: a pair $(x, f(x)) \in S$ with $|x| = n(C)$ such that $C(x) \neq f(x)$.

The data complexity of testing size-s circuits is always at most $2^{O(s)}$ for any function f: one can simply include all possible input/output pairs on inputs of length up to s. We are interested to know: for what functions f can the data complexity be much smaller? We prove an equivalence between upper bounds on the data complexity of testing f and lower bounds on the circuit complexity of f:

REMINDER OF THEOREM 1.2 *Let $f : \{0,1\}^* \to \{0,1\}$, and let $S(n) \geq 2n$ for all n.*

1. *If f is in $\mathsf{SIZE}(S(n))$, then the data complexity of testing size-s circuits for f is at least $2^{\Omega(S^{-1}(s))}$ almost everywhere.*

2. *If f is not in $\mathsf{SIZE}(n \cdot S(n))$, then the data complexity of testing size-s circuits for f is at most $O(2^{S^{-1}(s)} + S^{-1}(s) \cdot s^2 \log s)$ infinitely often.*

Since for a uniformly random function $f_n : \{0,1\}^n \to \{0,1\}$, $f_n \notin \mathsf{SIZE}(2^n/n^2)$ with high probability, we have the following corollary:

COROLLARY 4.1. *If $f : \{0,1\}^* \to \{0,1\}$ is uniformly random, then almost certainly the data complexity of testing size-s circuits for f is at most $O(s^2 \log^2 s)$ infinitely often.*

We also note that since the circuit complexities of a function f over any complete bases differ by at most a constant factor (and as noted previously, all results presented hold for an arbitrary complete gate basis with minor modifications to the proofs), the data complexities of TEST-f over any complete bases differ by at most a constant factor.

To get some intuition towards a proof of THEOREM 1.2, notice that if we replace "data complexity" with "time complexity" in the above, one direction of the equivalence is easy to establish. Namely, for functions f computable within exponential time, when the circuit complexity of f is large, the *time complexity* of testing circuits for f will be provably low, as follows.

Suppose $S(n)$ is a lower bound on the circuit complexity of computing f on n-bit inputs. To efficiently test a given circuit C of size s with n inputs, we can immediately reject if $s < S(n)$, otherwise we may try all $2^n < 2^{S^{-1}(s)}$ inputs to C and check whether the truth table obtained for C matches f_n on n-bit inputs. For f computable within $2^{O(n)}$ time, this algorithm takes $2^{O(S^{-1}(s))}$ time; larger $S(n)$ entails a faster running time. (For example, if some f in $2^{O(n)}$ time requires $2^{\varepsilon n}$ size $\mathcal{C}$-circuits, then testing $\mathcal{C}$ for f is in $\mathrm{poly}(s)$ time.) However, this particular connection is not terribly useful: we are basically saying that strong circuit lower bounds happen to make testing circuits for f trivial, because most circuits can be immediately rejected. Moreover we do not know if low time complexity for testing circuits for f will imply analogous circuit lower bounds for f, in general.

The equivalence between circuit complexity and data complexity is far less obvious. We use the following consequence of results on the circuit-input game (THEOREM 2.2 in the Preliminaries): when circuits are too small to compute a function, there are small data sets that will efficiently refute these small circuits.

PROOF OF THEOREM 1.2. (Part 1.) Suppose for all n, there is a circuit C of size $S(n)$ which computes f_n on all inputs of length n. For each n, we claim that every test set T_s for f on circuits of size $S'(n) = S(n) + n$ satisfies $|T_{s'}| \geq 2^n$. Observe that for every circuit C of size $S(n)$ with n inputs and for all x of length n, there is a circuit C_x of size at most $S'(n) = S(n) + n$ which agrees with C on all inputs except x, where C_x and C disagree. In particular, C_x can use a tree of $n-1$ gates that outputs 1 if and only if the input equals x, and take the XOR of this tree's output with the circuit C.

So given an n-input circuit C computing f with size at most $S'(n)$, in order to distinguish C from all of the C_x, x must be included in $T_{s'}$. That is, all x of length $n = \Omega(S^{-1}(s))$ must be in $T_{s'}$.

(Part 2.) Suppose the circuit complexity of f is greater than $n \cdot S(n)$ on inputs of length n. Then there cannot be a collection $\mathcal{D}$ of $O(n/\varepsilon^2)$ size-$S(n)$ circuits such that for all $x \in \{0,1\}^n$, $C(x) = f(x)$ for more than a $1/2$ fraction of C in $\mathcal{D}$: otherwise, taking the MAJORITY of the outputs of circuits in $\mathcal{D}$ would yield a circuit for f of complexity at most $n \cdot S(n)$. Therefore, item 1 of THEOREM 2.2 does not hold with $p = 1/2$, and hence item 2 must hold for $q \leq 1/2 - \varepsilon$ for every sufficiently small ε.

Setting ε appropriately, this implies for all input lengths m ranging from n to $n \cdot S(n)$, there is a set $X_{m,s}$ of m-bit strings x with labels $f(x)$ and cardinality $O(S(n)\log S(n))$, such that every circuit of size $S(n)$ taking m bits of input fails to compute f correctly on at least $1/10$ of the x in the set $X_{m,s}$. By adding all strings in $X_{m,s}$ to the set X_s, we can refute any circuit with more than n inputs and size $S(n)$, with a set of $O(nS(n)^2 \log S(n))$ strings.

For input lengths m that are below n, there may be a size $S(n)$ circuit for f that works on all m-bit strings. To cover this case, we simply include (with labels for the value of f) all bit strings of length up to $n-1$ in the set X_s as well – then, every circuit of size s and at most n inputs can also be checked. In total, we have a test set X_s of cardinality $O(2^n + nS(n)^2 \log S(n))$. For size s circuits, we set $s := S(n)$, i.e., $n = S^{-1}(s)$, so the cardinality is $O(2^{S^{-1}(s)} + S^{-1}(s) \cdot s^2 \log s)$ as a function of the circuit size s. $\square$

In the above theorems, the small cardinality test suites X_s have the following structure: for input sizes which are "too long" to support size-s circuits for f, we have small sets of counterexamples from the circuit-input game, but as the input sizes decrease, we reach a threshold where it's possible to compute f within size s, and must start including all possible inputs and their labels.

When we consider polynomial-size circuits in general, we simply obtain an *equivalence*:

COROLLARY 4.2. *A function f is in P/poly if and only if for some $\varepsilon > 0$, the data complexity of testing circuits for f is greater than 2^{s^ε} for almost every s.*

PROOF. If f is in P/poly, then it is in SIZE(n^k) for some constant k. By Part 1 of THEOREM 1.2, the data complexity of testing circuits for f is at least $2^{\Omega(s^{1/k})}$. On the other hand, if f is not in P/poly, then it is not in SIZE(n^{k+1}) for every k. By Part 2 of THEOREM 1.2, the data complexity of testing circuits for f is then at most $O(s^k \log s + 2^{s^{1/k}})$ for all k. $\square$

REMINDER OF COROLLARY 1.1 NP $\not\subset$ P/poly (resp. NP $\not\subset$ i.o.P/poly) if and only if for every $\varepsilon > 0$ and for infinitely many s (resp. for every $\varepsilon > 0$ and for every s), the data complexity of testing size-s circuits for SAT is at most $O\left(2^{s^\varepsilon}\right)$.

5. CONCLUSION

There are many questions raised by this work that seem worth exploring further, regarding the circumvention of natural proofs and regarding the testing of circuits for computing functions. Here are three questions we particularly like.

1. *Can new circuit lower bounds be proved, based on the guidance of* THEOREM *1.1?* Again, this theorem tells us that we should expect there to be combinatorial properties useful against polynomial-size SAT solving circuits, or in general, circuits which never err when they print solutions to their input instances.

   To be more concrete, let CLIQUE$_{n^2}^{n/2}$: $\{0,1\}^{n^2} \to \{0,1\}^n$ be the function which treats its input as an $n \times n$ adjacency matrix A, and outputs a bit vector specifying a clique of size at least $n/2$ in A, when one exists (otherwise, it outputs the all-zeros vector). Can one prove that computing CLIQUE$_{n^2}^{n/2}$ requires circuits of size at least $4n^2$ over the basis of all fan-in two Boolean functions?

2. *Can the equivalence of* THEOREM *1.2 be tightened further?* Currently there is a gap between the two implications in the equivalence, amounting to a multiplicative factor of n. Could this gap be necessary?

3. *How does the complexity of f relate to the complexity of testing circuits for f?* Here we mean "complexity" in the usual, most generic sense: if f is known to be computable in some particular complexity class, what can we say about the complexity class(es) that support testing for f?

Acknowledgements.
We thank the ITCS reviewers for their helpful comments. In particular, one reviewer improved an earlier version of THEOREM 2.3.

6. REFERENCES

[Ajt83] Miklos Ajtai. Σ_1^1-formulae on finite structures. *Annals of Pure and Applied Logic*, 24:1–48, 1983.

[Alt94]   Ingo Althöfer. On sparse approximations to randomized strategies and convex combinations. *Linear Algebra and its Applications*, 199:339–355, 1994.

[Ats06]   Albert Atserias. Distinguishing SAT from polynomial-size circuits, through black-box queries. In *IEEE Conference on Computational Complexity*, pages 88–95. IEEE, 2006.

[BCG$^+$96] Nader Bshouty, Richard Cleve, Ricard Gavalda, Sampath Kannan, and Christino Tamon. Oracles and queries that are sufficient for exact learning. *J. Comput. Syst. Sci.*, 52(2):268–286, 1996.

[BFL91]   László Babai, Lance Fortnow, and Carsten Lund. Non-deterministic exponential time has two-prover interactive protocols. *Computational Complexity*, 1:3–40, 1991.

[BK95]   Manuel Blum and Sampath Kannan. Designing programs that check their work. *J. ACM*, 42:269–291, 1995.

[BTW10]   Andrej Bogdanov, Kunal Talwar, and Andrew Wan. Hard instances for satisfiability and quasi-one-way functions. In *ICS*, pages 290–300, 2010.

[CR08]   Venkatesan T. Chakaravarthy and Sambuddha Roy. Finding Irrefutable Certificates for S_2^p via Arthur and Merlin. In *25th International Symposium on Theoretical Aspects of Computer Science*, volume 1 of *Leibniz International Proceedings in Informatics (LIPIcs)*, pages 157–168, Dagstuhl, Germany, 2008.

[FIKU08] Lance Fortnow, Russell Impagliazzo, Valentine Kabanets, and Christopher Umans. On the complexity of succinct zero-sum games. *Computational Complexity*, 17(3):353–376, 2008.

[FPS08]   Lance Fortnow, Aduri Pavan, and Samik Sengupta. Proving SAT does not have small circuits with an application to the two queries problem. *J. Comput. Syst. Sci.*, 74(3):358–363, 2008.

[GK95a]   Sally A. Goldman and Michael J. Kearns. On the complexity of teaching. *J. Comput. Syst. Sci.*, 50(1):20–31, 1995.

[GK95b]   M.D. Grigoriadis and L.G. Khachiyan. A sublinear-time randomized approximation algorithm for matrix games. *Operations Research Letters*, 18(2):53–58, 1995.

[GSTS05] Dan Gutfreund, Ronen Shaltiel, and Amnon Ta-Shma. If NP languages are hard on the worst-case, then it is easy to find their hard instances. *Computational Complexity*, 16(4):412–441, 2007. See also CCC'05.

[Lip91]   Richard Lipton. New directions in testing. In *Distributed Computing and Cryptography, vol. 2 of DIMACS Series in Discrete Mathematics and Theoretical Computer Science*, pages 191–202. American Mathematical Society, 1991.

[LY94]   Richard J. Lipton and Neal E. Young. Simple strategies for large zero-sum games with applications to complexity theory. In *STOC*, pages 734–740. ACM, 1994.

[Mul11]   Ketan D. Mulmuley. On P vs. NP and geometric complexity theory: Dedicated to Sri Ramakrishna. *J. ACM*, 58(2):5, 2011.

[New91]   Ilan Newman. Private vs. common random bits in communication complexity. *Information Processing Letters*, 39:67–71, 1991.

[Pat05]   Ron Patton. *Software Testing (2nd Edition)*. Sams, Indianapolis, IN, USA, 2005.

[RR97]   Alexander Razborov and Steven Rudich. Natural proofs. *J. Comput. Syst. Sci.*, 55(1):24–35, 1997.

[SM91]   Ayumi Shinohara and Satoru Miyano. Teachability in computational learning. *New Generation Comput.*, 8(4):337–347, 1991.

[SV12]   Grant Schoenebeck and Salil P. Vadhan. The computational complexity of nash equilibria in concisely represented games. *TOCT*, 4(2):4, 2012.

[UL07]   Mark Utting and Bruno Legeard. *Practical Model-Based Testing: A Tools Approach*. Morgan Kaufmann Publishers Inc., San Francisco, CA, USA, 2007.

[Vio11]   Emanuele Viola. Randomness buys depth for approximate counting. In *FOCS*, pages 230–239. IEEE, 2011.

[Yao77]   Andrew Chi-Chin Yao. Probabilistic computations: Toward a unified measure of complexity. In *FOCS*, pages 222–227. IEEE, 1977.

Separation between Estimation and Approximation

Uriel Feige
uriel.feige@weizmann.ac.il

Shlomo Jozpeh
shlomo.jozeph@weizmann.ac.il

Department of Computer Science and Applied Mathematics
Weizmann Institute of Science
Rehovot, Israel

ABSTRACT

We show (under standard assumptions) that there are NP optimization problems for which estimation is easier than approximation. Namely, one can estimate the value of the optimal solution within a ratio of ρ, but it is difficult to find a solution whose value is within ρ of optimal. As an important special case, we show that there are linear programming relaxations for which no polynomial time rounding technique matches the integrality gap of the linear program.

Categories and Subject Descriptors

F.2.m [**Analysis of Algorithms and Problem Complexity**]: Miscellaneous; F.1.3 [**Computation by Abstract Devices**]: Complexity Measures and Classes

Keywords

Linear Programming; Integrality Gap; Rounding; TFNP

1. INTRODUCTION

We briefly review some basic concepts related to approximation algorithms for optimization problems. For simplicity of the presentation, we shall only deal with maximization problems, though our results can be adapted to minimization problems as well. Given a binary relation (also referred to as *predicate*) R, we say that y is a feasible solution for x if $(x, y) \in R$. Let $|s|$ denote the representation size of input s (e.g., the number of bits in some standard binary representation). We say that R is a polynomial relation if for every x, every feasible y is of size $|y| \leq |x|^{O(1)}$, and furthermore, there is a polynomial time algorithm that for every pair (x, y) decides whether $(x, y) \in R$. Let V be a value function, mapping pairs (x, y) to nonnegative integer values, and computable in polynomial time. For simplicity of the presentation and essentially without loss of generality, let us assume that $V(x, y) = 0$ if y is not feasible for x. An NP-optimization problem is specified by a predicate R and value function V as above. An instance of the problem is an

input x, and the desired goal is to output a y maximizing $V(x, y)$. Given such an x, we refer to such a y as an optimal solution, and to the corresponding value of $V(x, y)$ as the optimum value $\mathrm{opt}(x)$.

For example, in the maximum independent set problem, the input x is a graph, $(x, y) \in R$ iff y is an independent set in x, and $V(x, y)$ outputs the number of vertices in y if y is a feasible solution, and outputs 0 otherwise.

Some NP-optimization problems cannot be solved optimally in polynomial time, unless P=NP. A common approach of coping with this difficulty is via approximation algorithms. Given R and V as above, a polynomial time algorithm A is said to have *approximation ratio* $0 \leq \rho \leq 1$ if for every input x it outputs a solution $A(x)$ whose value satisfies $V(x, A(x)) \geq \rho \cdot \mathrm{opt}(x)$. A polynomial time algorithm B is said to have *estimation ratio* $0 \leq \rho \leq 1$ if for every input x it outputs a value $B(x)$ satisfying $\rho \cdot \mathrm{opt}(x) \leq B(x) \leq \mathrm{opt}(x)$. Clearly, approximation is at least as difficult as estimation, because a ρ-approximation algorithm A can be used as a ρ-estimation algorithm B by taking $B(x) = V(x, A(x))$. The question addressed in this work is whether there are NP-optimization problems for which estimation is easier than approximation, in the sense that the best estimation ratio for the problem is strictly larger than the best approximation ratio. We refer to this as a separation between estimation and approximation.

Observe that if P=NP then every NP-optimization problem can be solved exactly, and there is no separation between estimation and approximation. Hence to establish a separation we need to at least assume that P does not equal NP. In fact, to establish our results, we shall use an even stronger assumption. A polynomial relation R is in TFNP [9] (Total Function NP) if every x has a feasible solution. A TFNP relation is said to be in FP if there is a polynomial time algorithm that on input x finds a feasible solution. It is currently not know whether every TFNP predicate is in FP, and there are several TFNP relations that serve as plausible candidates for not being in FP. Examples include *factoring* (every integer has a prime factorization, but no polynomial time factoring algorithm is known, a fact that serves as the basis of several well known cryptographic schemes, such as RSA), *Nash equilibrium* (every two player game in normal form has a mixed Nash equilibrium, but finding a Nash equilibrium is PPAD-complete [2]), and *maximal cut* (every edge weighted graph has a cut whose size cannot be improved by a single vertex changing size, but finding a maximal cut is PLS-complete [14]).

ITCS'15, January 11–13, 2015, Rehovot, Israel.
Copyright is held by the owner/author(s). Publication rights licensed to ACM.
ACM 978-1-4503-3333-7/15/01 ...$15.00.
http://dx.doi.org/10.1145/2688073.2688101.

We observe that a separation between estimation and approximation can be established under the assumption that TFNP is not in FP. In fact, one can precisely control the gap between estimation and approximation.

THEOREM 1. *For every $0 \leq \alpha < \beta \leq 1$ and $\epsilon > 0$, there is an NP-optimization problem that has a β-estimation algorithm, an α-approximation algorithm, no $(\beta + \epsilon)$-estimation algorithm (unless P=NP), and no $(\alpha + \epsilon)$-approximation algorithm (unless TFNP is in FP).*

The NP-optimization problem in the proof of Theorem 1 is somewhat artificial and was designed specifically for the proof. For natural NP-optimization problems, such a separation can often be proved not to occur. See Section 1.1 for more details.

A common technique for designing approximation algorithms is via linear programming relaxations. One first formalizes the NP-optimization problem π as an integer linear program (IP). This step is typically not difficult, because integer linear programming is NP-hard (and hence other problems in NP can be reduced to it). Thereafter, one relaxes the integrality constraints, thus achieving a linear program (LP) relaxation whose optimal value satisfies $\text{opt}_{LP}(x) \geq \text{opt}(x)$. The smallest possible ratio $\frac{\text{opt}(x)}{\text{opt}_{LP}(x)}$ (over all x) is referred to as the integrality gap ρ_{LP} of the LP. As linear programs can be solved in polynomial time, computing $\text{opt}_{LP}(x)$ (and scaling the result by ρ_{LP}) can serve as a ρ_{LP}-estimation algorithm for π. To obtain an approximation algorithm one designs a *rounding* procedure that takes a (fractional) solution of the LP and "rounds" it to an integer solution to the integer program. Let $\text{rounded}(x)$ denote the value of the solution obtained after rounding the optimal LP solution. Ideally, one can establish that the value $\frac{\text{rounded}(x)}{\text{opt}_{LP}(x)} \geq \rho_{LP}$, which then implies that computing $\text{rounded}(x)$ is a ρ_{LP}-approximation algorithm for π. This approach has been successful numerous times (see [6, 16, 15] for many examples), and hence one might be led to believe that for every LP relaxation there is a polynomial time rounding procedure that matches the integrality gap. Our next theorem specializes Theorem 1 to the context of integer programs, showing that rounding procedures that match the integrality gap do not always exist.

THEOREM 2. *For every $0 \leq \alpha < \beta \leq 1$ and $\epsilon > 0$, there is a family of (maximization) integer programs with nonnegative objective function with the following properties:*

1. *For every integer program its LP-relaxation has an integrality gap of no worse than β.*

2. *For infinitely many integer programs the LP-relaxation has an integrality gap no better than $\beta + \epsilon$.*

3. *There is a polynomial time algorithm that gives a solution whose value approximates the optimal integer program value within a ratio of α.*

4. *There is no $(\alpha + \epsilon)$-approximation algorithm for the optimal solution of the integer program, unless TFNP is in FP.*

The family of integer programs in Theorem 2 defines an NP-optimization problem, and hence Theorem 2 implies Theorem 1.

Our separation between estimation and approximation ratios (Theorems 1 and 2) assumes that TFNP is not contained in FP. This assumption is unavoidable, as otherwise no separation exists.

PROPOSITION 3. *If α-estimation of a value function V is in FP, then α-approximation of V is reducible to a problem in TFNP.*

1.1 Related Work

The current work continues a line of research outlined in [3]. The reader is referred to [3] for a more detailed discussion of the motivations and background (though note that there are more recent developments that are not covered in [3] and are mentioned below). Here we provide a shorter presentation of the background.

The distinction between estimation and approximation is analogous to the distinction between decision (does a solution exist?) and search (find a solution) for NP-problems. For NP-complete problems, due to their self reducible nature, search can be reduced to decision, and there is no separation between decision and search. However, for problems in NP that are not (known to be) NP-complete, it is plausible that such a separation exists. In particular, the class TFNP (mentioned in Section 1) contains problems that always have solutions (hence decision is trivial), but for which the search problem is not known to be solvable in polynomial time. Unlike the class NP which has NP-complete problems (such as SAT), TFNP does not seem to have complete problems (for reasons that we shall not discuss here), and hence many subclasses of TFNP has been introduced (such as PLS [7] and PPAD [11]), and these subclasses do have complete problems. In a sense, our Theorem 2 can be thought of as suggesting for TFNP a problem that can serve the purpose usually attributed to complete problems. Namely, one may think of the problem of rounding LP-relaxations within ratios that match the integrality gap as a problem that is essentially in TFNP (it is reducible to a problem in TFNP, by proposition 3), and every problem in TFNP is reducible to it.

Known NP-hardness of approximation results are in fact (we are not aware of exceptions) hardness of estimation results. Hence in those cases (which are quite common by now) in which the hardness ratio matches the approximation ratio given by known algorithms (such as max 3SAT, where this ratio is 7/8 up to low order terms), there is no separation between estimation and approximation (except possibly in the low order terms, an issue that is beyond the scope of the current paper).

There are only a few optimization problems in which the current state of our knowledge is such that the estimation ratios known are better than the approximation ratios know. Some such problems were discussed in [3], but even for some of these problems there had since been progress in closing the apparent gap between estimation and approximation. Most notable, new algorithmic versions of the local lemma [10, 4], of discrepancy bounds [1, 8] and of local search [13] serve towards this purpose.

2. FORMAL DEFINITIONS AND PROOFS

2.1 Definitions

DEFINITION 4. *For a polynomial h, let $D_h = \bigcup_n \{0,1\}^n \times \{0,1\}^{h(n)}$. A function $V : D_h \to \mathbb{N}$ that is computable in FP (Function Polynomial Time) is a* value function.

We may define a value function on inputs satisfying a certain property with the implicit intention that the function gives a value of zero to all other inputs.

DEFINITION 5. *Given a value function V and an input x, let $M_x^V = \max_y \{V(x,y)\}$. An α-solution for V and x is a string z such that $V(x,z) \geq \alpha M_x^V$*

DEFINITION 6. *α-estimation of a value function is the following problem: given a value function V and a string x, output a value v such that $\alpha M_x^V \leq v \leq M_x^V$.*

DEFINITION 7. *α-approximation of a value function is the following problem: given a value function V and a string x, output an α-solution.*

EXAMPLE 8. *The value function $V_{\text{SAT}}(\varphi, a)$ is defined as follows: interpret φ as an E3SAT formula, and a as an assignment to its variables. Return the number of satisfied clauses. It is known that $7/8$-approximation is in FP, while $(7/8 + \epsilon)$-estimation is NP-hard [5], for any $\epsilon > 0$.*

DEFINITION 9. *A relation R is in the complexity class TFNP (Total Function NP) if there is a polynomial time Turing machine T and a polynomial h such that*

$$R = \{(x,y) \mid |y| \leq h(|x|), T(x,y) = 1\}$$

and for any string x there is a y such that $(x,y) \in R$. The first element of the pair is called the input, and the second element is called the solution. The goal of every problem in TFNP is to find a solution, given an input. Note that given any pair (x,y), it is possible to use T to verify that $(x,y) \in R$ in polynomial time.

DEFINITION 10. *A reduction from a certain relation R to a TFNP problem S is a pair of polynomial time computable functions (f,g). It must hold that for any x, if $(f(x), y) \in S$, then $(x, g(x,y)) \in R$.*

REMARK 11. *Suppose that there is a reduction from a relation R to a TFNP problem S. Then R satisfies one of the requirements for being in TFNP, namely, every input x in R has a solution. However, in might not satisfy the requirement that R is a polynomial time predicate (there might not be a polynomial time Turing machine that given x and arbitrary y determines whether $(x,y) \in R$). Consequently R is not necessarily in TFNP.*

Note that if α-approximation for some value function V is in FP, α-estimation of V is in FP as well. If α-estimation is NP-hard, then α-approximation is also NP-hard. Additionally, For any $\beta \leq \alpha$

- If α-estimation (approximation) of V is in FP, then β-estimation (approximation) of V is in FP.

- If β-estimation (approximation) of V is NP-hard, then α-estimation (approximation) of V is NP-hard

Most hardness of approximation results show that value functions are NP-hard to estimate, which also shows that value functions are NP-hard to approximate. On the other hand, usually algorithms in P approximate, and not just estimate.

2.2 Proofs

Given a value function V, suppose that α-estimation is in P. How hard can α-approximation be? We now prove Proposition 3 which addresses this question.

PROOF. Let V be a value function, and let f be a function in FP that α-estimates V. Define the following relation: $R = \{(x,y) \mid V(x,y) \geq f(x)\}$. Note that for any input x, there is some solution y such that $(x,y) \in R$. Additionally, given x and y, one can verify in polynomial time whether $(x,y) \in R$ or not. Therefore, the relation R is in TFNP. α-approximation of V is reducible to finding a string in the relation R, hence, α-approximation is reducible to TFNP. $\square$

REMARK 12. *The relation $R = \{(x,y) \mid V(x,y) \geq f(x)\}$ is in TFNP. The relation $\hat{R} = \{(x,y) \mid V(x,y) \geq \alpha M_x^V\}$ might not be in TFNP: for a given x it may include solutions y for which $\alpha M_x^V \leq V(x,y) < f(x)$, and then membership of $(x,y) \in \hat{R}$ might not be decidable in polynomial time.*

The following proposition is a special case of Theorem 1 and illustrates the proof techniques that can be used in order to prove Theorem 1. Later, the proof of Theorem 2 will serve as a complete proof for Theorem 1.

PROPOSITION 13. *For any $R \in$ TFNP, there is a value function V_R for which $7/8$-estimation is in P, $(7/8 + \epsilon)$-estimation is NP-hard, $7/16$-approximation is in P, and $(7/16 + \epsilon)$-approximation is as hard as R, for any $\epsilon > 0$.*

PROOF. Given $R \in$ TFNP, we define the following value function V_R: Given (x,y), the input x is interpreted as encoding two sub-inputs $x = (\varphi, r)$, where φ is interpreted as an E3SAT formula and r as an input to R, and the solution y is interpreted as encoding two sub-solutions $y = (a, s)$, where a is an assignment for φ and s is a solution for r.

Let c_φ^a be the number of clauses in φ satisfied by a.

$$V_R(\varphi, r, a, s) = \begin{cases} c_\varphi^a & (r,s) \notin R \\ 2c_\varphi^a & (r,s) \in R \end{cases}$$

By the definition of TFNP, for any string r there is a string s such that $(r,s) \in R$. Thus, if there is an assignment satisfying c clauses in φ, the value function can get value $2c$. Since every E3SAT formula has an assignment satisfying $7/8$ of its clauses, we have that $7/8$-estimation is in FP. Since distinguishing between satisfiable 3SAT formulas and 3SAT formulas that are at most $(7/8 + \epsilon)$-satisfiable is NP-hard [5], $(7/8 + \epsilon)$-estimation is NP-hard.

For any E3SAT formula, it is easy to find an assignment that satisfies $7/8$ of its clauses. This gives $7/16$-approximation to V_R. It remains to show that $(7/16 + \epsilon)$-approximation is as hard as R.

Suppose that a black box gives us β-approximation of V_R, for some $\beta > 7/16$. We show that given an arbitrary r, the blackbox can be used so as to find s such that $(r,s) \in R$. Follow the reduction of [5] to reduce r to a E3SAT formula φ, with the following two properties:

1. φ is satisfiable. This will hold because R being TFNP implies that there is some s such that $(r,s) \in R$.

2. Every assignment of φ that satisfies a fraction of $2\beta > 7/8$ of the clauses can be translated back in polynomial time to a solution s such that $(r,s) \in R$. This will hold because the reduction [5] is reversible. (Technically, reversing the reduction will produce a list of polynomially many candidates s, at least one of which is a solution for r. Given such a list one can test each member of the list because R is a polynomial predicate.)

Querying the blackbox with the above r, φ, the black box outputs a, s such that $V_R(\varphi, r, a, s) \geq \beta M_{\varphi,r}^{V_R}$. Therefore, either $(r,s) \in R$ directly giving a solution for r, or a is a 2β-approximation to the optimal assignment to φ, and a solution s for r can be extracted from a. This proves that β-approximation of V_R is at least as hard as R. □

We now turn to prove Theorem 2. Its proof is broken into several propositions.

PROPOSITION 14. *For any $R \in$ TFNP, there is a set of integer programs (one for each input instance x) where*

- *The integer program has a feasible solution, and a feasible solution can be found in polynomial time.*

- *Every feasible solution has nonnegative value.*

- *The maximum value of the integer program is 1.*

- *The linear program relaxation (that is, replacing the requirement that the variables are in $\{0,1\}$ with the requirement that they are in the range $[0,1]$) has maximal value 1. Hence the integrality gap is 1.*

- *Outputting a solution to the IP of value that is not 0 is as hard as solving R.*

PROOF. Given $R \in$ TFNP let T denote the Turing machine associated with R. For every n, one can associate a circuit C_n that simulates the computation of T on those input pairs (x,y) of size $|x| = n$, and outputs 1 if and only if $(x,y) \in R$. As binary NAND forms a complete basis for logical gates, we may assume that all gates in the circuit are NAND gates. Given an input string x' with $|x'| = n$, let $C_n(x')$ denote the NAND circuit obtained from C_n by simplifying, after the input variables x are fixed to x'. Only the variables y remain as input to $C_n(x')$. We associate a variable name μ with the output of the circuit.

We now associate a 0/1 integer program IP with circuit $C_n(x')$. Every input (a y variable) to the circuit and every output of every gate will have an IP variable associated with it. The variable associated with the output gate of the circuit is called μ, and the objective of the IP is to maximize μ. The constraints are as follows. For every variable z we have the 0/1 constraint $z \in \{0,1\}$. For every NAND gate the IP contains two constraints as follows. Let z_1 and z_2 (which need not be distinct) denote the input variables to the NAND gate, and let the output variable of the gate be z_3. The constraints associated with the gate are:

- $z_1 + z_2 + z_3 \leq 2\mu$.

- $z_1 + z_2 + 2z_3 \geq 2\mu$.

Observe that if $\mu = 0$ the assignment $z_i = 0$ for $i \in \{1,2,3\}$ satisfies the constraints. However, if $\mu = 1$ only assignments consistent with the NAND gate satisfy both constraints. Specifically, if $z_1 = z_2 = 1$ then the second constraint is satisfied and the first constraint requires that $z_3 = 0$. For other assignments to z_1, z_2, the first constraint is satisfied and the second constraint requires that $z_3 = 1$.

The IP is feasible, and assigning all variables to 0 is a feasible solution (of value 0). Every feasible solution has nonnegative value because of the 0/1 constraints. The maximum value of the IP is 1, obtained by considering a solution y such that the output of $C_n(x')$ is 1 (such a y necessarily exists, because $R \in$ TFNP), and assigning the values of variables in the IP according to the computation of $C_n(x')$ on input y. The linear programming relaxation (relaxing $z \in \{0,1\}$ to $0 \leq z \leq 1$ for all variables) has value at most 1 because of the constraint $\mu \leq 1$. Assigning $\mu = 1$ and $z = \frac{1}{2}$ to all other variables is a feasible solution of value 1 for the LP relaxation.

For every feasible solution of value $\mu = 1$ to the IP, the value of the y variables is such that $(x', y) \in R$. Hence finding a solution to the IP of value 1 is as hard as solving R. □

PROPOSITION 15. *For any $0 < \gamma < 1$, there is a set of integer programs satisfying*

- *The integer program is feasible and the value of every feasible solution is nonnegative.*

- *The maximum value of each program is between γ and 1.*

- *A solution with value γ can be found in polynomial time.*

- *The linear program relaxation (that is, replacing the requirement that the variables are in $\{0,1\}$ with the requirement that they are in the range $[0,1]$) has maximal value exactly 1. Hence the integrality gap is no worse than γ.*

- *Estimating the optimal value of the integer programs within a ratio of $\gamma + \epsilon$ is NP-hard.*

PROOF. Consider an arbitrary 3CNF formula with n variables and m clauses. Represent it as an integer program in the following way (which is standard except for our choice of objective function). For every variable x_j of the formula the IP has a corresponding variable, and for every clause j the IP has a variable y_j. All variables are in $\{0,1\}$. For every clause there is a linear constraint that allows the corresponding y variable to be 1 if and only if the clause is satisfied by the x variables. For example, if clause j is $(x_1, \bar{x}_2, x_3)$ then the corresponding constraint is $x_1 + (1 - x_2) + x_3 \geq y_j$. The IP also has an auxiliary variable μ with the constraint $\mu = 1$. The objective function is to maximize $(8\gamma - 7)\mu + \frac{8(1-\gamma)}{m}\Sigma_{j=1}^{m}y_j$, which by the constraint $\mu = 1$ is equivalent to $8\gamma - 7 + \frac{8(1-\gamma)}{m}\Sigma_{j=1}^{m}y_j$. To ensure nonnegativity of the objective value, we add the constraint $\Sigma_{j=1}^{m}y_j \geq 7m/8$.

One easily observes that to maximize the objective function one needs to maximize $\Sigma_{j=1}^{m}y_j$. As for every 3CNF formula with m clauses there is an assignment satisfying at least $7m/8$ clauses, the IP is feasible. Its maximum value is thus at least $8\gamma - 7 + \frac{8(1-\gamma)}{m}\frac{7m}{8} = \gamma$. If the 3CNF formula is satisfiable then the LP has a feasible solution with $\Sigma_{j=1}^{m} y_j = m$, and then the maximum value is $8\gamma - 7 + \frac{8(1-\gamma)}{m} m = 1$. No higher value is possible neither for the IP nor for its LP relaxation because of the constraints $y_j \leq 1$. The LP relaxation has value 1, by taking $x_i = \frac{1}{2}$ for every i, and $y_j = 1$ for every j.

By the construction of the IP, for any 0/1 solution, the x variables are an assignment satisfying Σy_j clauses of the 3CNF instance. Since it is NP-hard to distinguish between satisfiable 3CNF-formulas and those that are at most $\frac{7+\epsilon}{8}$-satisfiable [5], estimating the optimal value of the integer program within a ratio of $\gamma + \epsilon$ is NP-hard. $\square$

We remark (for the purpose of handling a technicality in the proof of Theorem 2) that Proposition 15 also holds when $\gamma = 1$, in a trivial sense. (Take the IP with one constraint $x = 1$ and objective function x. Moreover, estimating the optimal value of the integer program within a ratio of $\gamma + \epsilon = 1 + \epsilon$ is then impossible, rather than just NP-hard, as approximation ratios cannot exceed 1.)

We now prove Theorem 2.

PROOF. The case $\alpha = 0$ and $\beta = 1$ is handled by Proposition 14. Hence we may assume that $1 - \beta + \alpha > 0$.

Suppose that there is $R \in \mathsf{TFNP}$ that is not in P (given x, there is no polynomial time algorithm guaranteed to find y such that $(x, y) \in R$). For such an R and an input x', consider the corresponding integer program from Proposition 14. Call it IP_1 and its objective value v_1. Given a 3CNF formula, consider the corresponding integer program from Proposition 15, with $\gamma = \frac{\alpha}{1-\beta+\alpha}$ (note that necessarily $\gamma \leq 1$). Call it IP_2 and its objective value v_2.

The integer program IP is a concatenation of the constraints of IP_1 and IP_2 on disjoint sets of variables, and its objective function is $\lambda v_1 + (1-\lambda)v_2$, where $\lambda = \beta - \alpha$. We remark that given an IP of this form, one can easily decide which variables originated from IP_1 and which variables originated from IP_2. (For example, the constraints involving the former have a variable whose coefficient is 2.)

Proposition 14 implies that finding a feasible solution (of value at least 0) for IP_1 is easy, and Proposition 15 implies that finding a solution of value γ for IP_2 is easy. Hence finding a solution of value $(1-\lambda)\gamma = \alpha$ for IP is easy. Finding a solution of value above $\alpha + \epsilon$ is as hard as solving R (because it requires either solving R, or approximating 3SAT within a ratio better than 7/8, which is NP-hard and hence at least as hard as solving R). There is always a solution of value 1 for IP_1 and hence a solution of value $\lambda + (1-\lambda)\gamma = \beta$ for IP. The LP-relaxation has value 1 (because this is true for both IP_1 and IP_2), and hence the integrality gap is no worse than β. For infinitely many inputs IP_2 does not have value above $\gamma + \epsilon$ (otherwise estimating its value within this ratio could not be NP-hard), hence there are infinitely many integer programs in the IP family whose LP-relaxation has integrality gap no better than $\beta + O(\epsilon)$. $\square$

2.3 Extensions

There are known reductions between various subclasses of TFNP (see [12]). These subclasses can be incorporated into more elaborate constructions based on the proof method of Proposition 13.

The following construction creates a problem with several approximation hardness jumps. Let $\mathcal{R} = \{R_i\}_{i=1}^{k}$ be relations in TFNP such that there is a reduction from R_i to R_{i+1}.

The problem we construct in this section is R_j-hard to approximate within a factor better than $\frac{7}{2^{4+k-j}}$ and NP-hard to approximate to within a factor of 7/8.

The input and the solution are treated as $k + 1$ strings, $x = (\varphi, r_1, \cdots, r_k)$ and $y = (a, s_1, \cdots, s_k)$. φ is interpreted as a E3SAT formula. Let c be the number of clauses in φ satisfied by a. For all $1 \leq i \leq k$, $p_i = 2$ if $(r_i, s_i) \in R_i$, otherwise $p_i = 1$. We define the value function

$$V_{\mathcal{R}}(\varphi, r_1, \cdots, r_k, a, s_1, \cdots s_k) = c\Pi p_i$$

Since each p_i can be made to be 2, 7/8-estimation is in FP. However, for $1 \leq j \leq k$, $\left(\frac{7}{2^{4+k-j}} + \epsilon\right)$-approximation is at least as hard as R_j: Fix an input for R_j, x_j. For $i > j$ let x_i the reduction of x_j to R_i. For $i < j$, x_i are arbitrary. Let φ be any E3SAT formula.

Suppose that a black box approximates $\mathcal{R}$ to within a factor of $\left(\frac{7}{2^{4+k-j}} + \epsilon\right)$ when given input $(\varphi, x_1, \cdots, x_k)$. Using a similar method to that used in the proof of Proposition 13, such a black box can be used to solve R_{k-j}. Either the black box gives at least j solutions to the x_i's or the black box gives a good approximation to the optimal assignment for φ. In the first case, since there are j solutions, there must be a solution for x_j or one of its reduction, so we can find a solution to any $x_j \in R_j$. In the second case, we can use the black box to decide any NP problem, so we can find a solution to any x_j, using the same method as in Proposition 13 to ensure that a failure of in approximating φ by the black box gives a solution of x_j.

The other direction is trivial: If there is a black box solving R_j, then the black box solves R_i for $i < j$. 7/8-approximation of E3SAT formulas is easy, so using j calls to the black box we can approximate $\mathcal{R}$ to within a factor of $\frac{7}{2^{3+k-j}}$.

2.4 Easily certifiable integrality gaps

Theorem 2 presents a family of integer programs (call this family F_β), such that for every IP in F_β the LP-relaxation has an integrality gap no worse than β (and furthermore, no polynomial time "rounding" algorithm ensures approximation within a ratio better than α, unless TFNP is in FP). Recall (see proof of Proposition 14) that the IPs in F_β are derived from some relation $R \in \mathsf{TFNP}$. We may assume that the Turing machine T (and hence also the circuits C_n) associated with R is publicly known. In this case, for every $IP \in F_\beta$ there is a polynomial size witness (which includes the input x' for R and the chain or reductions leading to the IP) that certifies that indeed the IP is in F_β, and hence that the integrality gap is no worse than β. However, this does not necessarily imply that given an IP in F_β, finding the associated witness for being in F_β is a computationally easy task (this is not required in the statement of Theorem 2). We sketch below how one can modify the proofs in this manuscript so that the resulting family F_β is such that finding witnesses for $IP \in F_\beta$ becomes an easy computational task.

As observed in the proof of Theorem 2, given an IP as in Theorem 2, it is easy to decompose it into IP_1 and IP_2, and to separate the objective function into a part that depends on IP_1 and a part that depends on IP_2. The form of IP_2 makes it self-evident that it represents a 3CNF formula (that can be explicitly reconstructed from the constraints of IP_2). However, without a-priori knowing the instance x', the task of determining that IP_1 is an IP that is derived by a reduction from an instance of R might be difficult. To make this task easy, one can slightly modify the proof of Proposition 14. Namely, first reduce the circuit C_n (rather than the simplified circuit $C_n(x')$) to an IP. Thereafter, given x', for each input bit i the reduction adds either the constraint $x_i = 0$ or the constraint $x_i = 1$, depending on the value of bit i in x'. Finally, the reduction names the variables in the order in which they appear in the circuit C_n. (Alternatively, if we do not wish names of variables to convey information, there are other tricks of associating an index i with a variable z, e.g., by adding a trivially satisfiable constraint $z \leq i$.) Given an IP constructed as above, one can easily reconstruct x' and the circuit C_n, and consequently certify that the integrality gap is no worse than β.

3. ACKNOWLEDGEMENTS

Work supported in part by the Israel Science Foundation (grant No. 621/12) and by the I-CORE Program of the Planning and Budgeting Committee and the Israel Science Foundation (grant No. 4/11).

4. REFERENCES

[1] N. Bansal. Semidefinite optimization in discrepancy theory. *Math. Program.*, 134(1):5–22, Aug. 2012.

[2] X. Chen, X. Deng, and S.-H. Teng. Settling the complexity of computing two-player nash equilibria. *J. ACM*, 56(3):14:1–14:57, May 2009.

[3] U. Feige. On estimation algorithms vs approximation algorithms. In *IARCS Annual Conference on Foundations of Software Technology and Theoretical Computer Science*, volume 2 of *Leibniz International Proceedings in Informatics (LIPIcs)*, pages 357–363. Schloss Dagstuhl–Leibniz-Zentrum fuer Informatik, 2008.

[4] B. Haeupler, B. Saha, and A. Srinivasan. New constructive aspects of the lovász local lemma. *J. ACM*, 58(6):28:1–28:28, Dec. 2011.

[5] J. Håstad. Some optimal inapproximability results. *J. ACM*, 48(4):798–859, July 2001.

[6] D. S. Hochbaum, editor. *Approximation Algorithms for NP-hard Problems*. PWS Publishing Co., 1997.

[7] D. S. Johnson, C. H. Papadimtriou, and M. Yannakakis. How easy is local search? *J. Comput. Syst. Sci.*, 37(1):79–100, Aug. 1988.

[8] S. Lovett and R. Meka. Constructive discrepancy minimization by walking on the edges. In *Proceedings of the 2012 IEEE 53rd Annual Symposium on Foundations of Computer Science*, FOCS '12, pages 61–67. IEEE Computer Society, 2012.

[9] N. Megiddo and C. H. Papadimitriou. On total functions, existence theorems and computational complexity. *Theor. Comput. Sci.*, 81(2):317–324, Apr. 1991.

[10] R. A. Moser and G. Tardos. A constructive proof of the general lovász local lemma. *J. ACM*, 57(2):11:1–11:15, Feb. 2010.

[11] C. H. Papadimitriou. On graph-theoretic lemmata and complexity classes. In *Proceedings of the 31st Annual Symposium on Foundations of Computer Science*, SFCS '90, pages 794–801 vol.2. IEEE Computer Society, 1990.

[12] C. H. Papadimitriou. On the complexity of the parity argument and other inefficient proofs of existence. *J. Comput. Syst. Sci.*, 48(3):498–532, June 1994.

[13] L. Polacek and O. Svensson. Quasi-polynomial local search for restricted max-min fair allocation. In *Proceedings of the 39th International Colloquium Conference on Automata, Languages, and Programming - Volume Part I*, ICALP'12, pages 726–737. Springer-Verlag, 2012.

[14] A. A. Schäffer and M. Yannakakis. Simple local search problems that are hard to solve. *SIAM J. Comput.*, 20(1):56–87, Feb. 1991.

[15] V. V. Vazirani. *Approximation Algorithms*. Springer-Verlag New York, Inc., 2001.

[16] D. P. Williamson and D. B. Shmoys. *The Design of Approximation Algorithms*. Cambridge University Press, 1st edition, 2011.

Deterministic Extractors for Additive Sources

[Extended Abstract] [*]

Abhishek Bhowmick
Department of Computer
Science
The University of Texas at
Austin
Austin, USA
bhowmick@cs.utexas.edu

Ariel Gabizon
Computer Science
Department
Technion
Haifa, Israel
ariel.gabizon@gmail.com

Thái Hoàng Lê
Department of Mathematics
The University of Texas at
Austin
Austin, USA
leth@math.utexas.edu

David Zuckerman
Department of Computer
Science
The University of Texas at
Austin
Austin, USA
diz@cs.utexas.edu

ABSTRACT

We propose a new model of a weakly random source that admits randomness extraction. Our model of additive sources includes such natural sources as uniform distributions on arithmetic progressions (APs), generalized arithmetic progressions (GAPs), and Bohr sets, each of which generalizes affine sources. We give an explicit extractor for additive sources with linear min-entropy over both $\mathbb{Z}_p$ and $\mathbb{Z}_p^n$, for large prime p, although our results over $\mathbb{Z}_p^n$ require that the source further satisfy a list-decodability condition. As a corollary, we obtain explicit extractors for APs, GAPs, and Bohr sources with linear min-entropy, although again our results over $\mathbb{Z}_p^n$ require the list-decodability condition.

We further explore special cases of additive sources. We improve previous constructions of line sources (affine sources of dimension 1), requiring a field of size linear in n, rather than $\Omega(n^2)$ by Gabizon and Raz. This beats the non-explicit bound of $\Theta(n \log n)$ obtained by the probabilistic method. We then generalize this result to APs and GAPs.

Categories and Subject Descriptors

G.2 [**Discrete Mathematics**]: General

General Terms

Theory

[*]A full version of this paper is available at
http://arxiv.org/abs/1410.7253

Keywords

deterministic extractors; additive combinatorics; small doubling sets; arithmetic progressions; Bohr sets; exponential sums

1. INTRODUCTION

High-quality randomness is needed for a variety of applications. However, most physical sources are only weakly random. Moreover, such weak sources arise in cryptography when an adversary learns information about a uniformly random string. It is therefore natural and important to try to extract the usable randomness from a weak source. It is impossible to extract even one bit of randomness from a natural yet large enough class of sources using a single function [24]. There are two ways to counter this. One is to extract with the help of a small amount of randomness; this is called a seeded extractor [19]. Our focus is on the second way: to extract only from more structured sources (and not allow any auxiliary randomness). Such a function is called a *deterministic* (or seedless) extractor.

We now give a formal definition of extractors. In the following definition the term *source* simply refers to a random variable.

DEFINITION 1.1. *A function* Ext $: \{0,1\}^n \to \{0,1\}^m$ *is an ϵ-extractor for a family of sources $\mathcal{X}$ if for every $X \in \mathcal{X}$, the distribution* Ext(X) *is ε-close in statistical (variation) distance to U_m. Here U_m denotes the uniform distribution on m bits.*

We measure the randomness in a source X using min-entropy.

DEFINITION 1.2. *The* min-entropy *of a random variable X is*

$$H_\infty(X) = \min_{x \in \mathrm{supp}(X)} \log_2(1/\mathbf{Pr}[X = x]).$$

If $X \subseteq \{0,1\}^n$, we say that X has entropy rate $H_\infty(X)/n$.

The probabilistic method shows that if $|\mathcal{X}| \leq 2^{2^{.9k}}$, where k is the min-entropy of each source, then there exists a deterministic extractor for $\mathcal{X}$. Constructing such an extractor explicitly is a much harder challenge. One type of source for which deterministic extractors have been constructed is an *affine source* - a uniform distribution over an affine subspace of a vector space [12, 5, 9, 20, 17, 7]. In this paper, we explore generalizations of affine sources with more minimal structure. We show that an explicit deterministic extractor can be constructed for a broad generalization of affine sources that we call *additive sources*.

REMARK 1.3. *Throughout the paper we often abuse notation and refer to a set X as a source. The source is actually the random variable uniformly distributed on the set X.*

Before presenting our general notion of an additive source, it will be instructive to look at two simpler natural generalizations of affine sources that are special cases of our notion. The first generalizes an affine source when viewed as the *image* of a linear map. The second generalizes a linear source when viewed as the *kernel* of a linear map.

Generalized arithmetic progressions.

An affine subspace in $\mathbb{Z}_p^n$ may be viewed as the set of elements $V = \{a_1 \cdot t_1 + \ldots a_r \cdot t_r + b | t_1, \ldots, t_r \in \mathbb{Z}_p\}$ for some fixed $a_1, \ldots, a_r, b \in \mathbb{Z}_p^n$ such that $a_1, \ldots, a_r$ are linearly independent. One relaxation of this definition would be to not insist that $a_1, \ldots, a_r$ be linearly independent, and allow the t_i's to only range through a subset of $\mathbb{Z}_p$ of the form $\{0, \ldots, s-1\}$, rather than all of $\mathbb{Z}_p$. The result is exactly what is known as a *generalized arithmetic progression* (GAP). That is, a (r,s)-GAP is a set of the form

$$A = \{a_1 \cdot t_1 + \ldots a_r \cdot t_r + b | 0 \leq t_1, \ldots, t_r \leq s - 1\}$$

for some fixed $a_1, \ldots, a_r, b \in \mathbb{Z}_p^n$ and $s \leq p$.

Bohr sets.

A linear subspace in $\mathbb{Z}_p^n$ may also be viewed as the set of elements $v \in \mathbb{Z}_p^n$ such that for all $i = 1, \ldots, d$, $L_i(v) = 0$, for some fixed linear functions $L_1, \ldots, L_d : \mathbb{Z}_p^n \to \mathbb{Z}_p$. A relaxation of this definition could be to look at the set of elements $v \in V$ such that $L_i(v)$ is 'close to zero' for every $i \in [d]$. We could define the *distance from zero* of an element $a \in \mathbb{Z}_p$ by looking at a as an integer in $\{0, \ldots, p-1\}$, and taking the minimum of the distances between $|p - a|$ and $|a - 0| = |a|$. Equivalently, we could define it as $\|a/p\|$ where $\| \cdot \|$ denotes the distance to the nearest integer. The resulting definition is what is known as a *Bohr set* in $\mathbb{Z}_p^n$. That is, a (d, ρ)-Bohr set is a set B of the form

$$B = \{v \in \mathbb{Z}_p^n : \|L_i(v)/p\| < \rho, i \in [d]\}$$

for some fixed $0 < \rho < 1$ and linear functions $L_1, \ldots, L_d : \mathbb{Z}_p^n \to \mathbb{Z}_p$.

In fact, as opposed to subspaces GAPs and Bohr sets can be defined not just in $\mathbb{Z}_p^n$ but in any abelian group. See Definitions 2.3 and 2.6 for the definitions in a general abelian group. We proceed to describe our general notion of an additive source.

1.1 Defining additive sources

Before defining an additive source, we give some intuition on the definition we chose and the pitfalls of other natural definitions.

We work in an abelian group G, which is usually $\mathbb{Z}_p$ or $\mathbb{Z}_p^n$ under addition. A first attempt at a minimal structure that generalizes subspaces is to require X to have small doubling: $|X + X| \leq C|X|$ for small $C > 1$. (Here $A + B$ denotes the set $\{a + b | a \in A, b \in B\}$.) The Cauchy-Davenport Theorem implies that for $A \subseteq \mathbb{Z}_p$, $|A+A| \geq \min\{2|A|-1, p\}$. Kneser's theorem, which extends the Cauchy-Davenport theorem, implies the same is true for any $A \subseteq \mathbb{Z}_p^n$ that is not contained in a strict subgroup of $\mathbb{Z}_p^n$. So, for obtaining a large class of sources it makes sense to look at $C \geq 2$. However, even for $C = 2$ we get a class of sources for which deterministic extraction is impossible: For let $f : G \to \{0, 1\}$ be any such purported extractor. Then the uniform distribution on the larger of $f^{-1}(0)$ and $f^{-1}(1)$ gives a counterexample. If this seems artificial and one asks about smaller sets, we could start with any B such that $|B + B| \leq 2|B|$, such as an arithmetic progression, and then the larger of $f^{-1}(0) \cap B$ or $f^{-1}(1) \cap B$ gives a counterexample for $C = 4$. A similar attempt at a definition would be to lower bound the *additive energy* - a quantity that measures how many sums in $X + X$ lead to the same value. However, this is also insufficient, as sets with small doubling have large energy.

In light of the above, we seek to impose an additional condition, besides small doubling. This extra condition involves the notion of symmetry sets from additive combinatorics. A symmetry set for a set $X \subseteq G$ with parameter $\gamma > 0$ is defined as

$$\mathrm{Sym}_\gamma(X) = \{g \in G : |X \cap (X + g)| \geq \gamma|X|\}.$$

In other words, an element is in $\mathrm{Sym}_\gamma(X)$ if it can be expressed as $x - x'$, for $x, x' \in X$, in at least $\gamma|X|$ ways. We shall be interested in the setting where γ is close to 1. The simplest examples of sets with large symmetry sets are subgroups and cosets of subgroups. Specifically, if X is a subgroup or a coset of a subgroup, then $\mathrm{Sym}_1(X) = X$.

We note that large symmetry sets don't imply small doubling. For example, if we start with a set Y with $\mathrm{Sym}_{1-\alpha}(Y)$ large, then we could choose a set T of size $2\alpha|Y|$ with large doubling, such as a Sidon set or random set, and set $X = Y \cup T$. Then $\mathrm{Sym}_{1-3\alpha}(X)$ is large but X has large doubling. Yet this counterexample isn't completely satisfactory, because for extraction it would suffice that whenever X has $\mathrm{Sym}_{1-\alpha}(X)$ large, there exists a large $X' \subseteq X$, $|X'| \geq (1 - \varepsilon)|X|$, where X' has small doubling. We also give a counterexample to this weakened question. To give a counterexample with $p^{1/d}$ large symmetry sets, it's easiest to work in $\mathbb{Z}_p^d$. Pick a large-doubling set T in $\mathbb{Z}_p^{d-1}$, and let $X = T \times \mathbb{Z}_p$. Then $\mathrm{Sym}_1(X)$ contains $\mathbb{Z}_p$, but $X + X$ has size $\Theta(|T|^2 p) = \Theta(|X|^2/p)$. The same is true for large subsets of X. If we worked in $\mathbb{Z}_p$ instead, we could take a union of intervals, which would give slightly weaker parameters.

Thus, we define an additive source to be (the uniform distribution on) a set that has small doubling and has a large symmetry set.

DEFINITION 1.4 (ADDITIVE SOURCE). *A set X in a finite abelian group $(G, +)$ is called an (α, β, τ)-additive source if $|X + X| \leq |X|^{1+\tau}$ and*

$$|\mathrm{Sym}_{1-\alpha}(X)| \geq |X|^\beta.$$

In Sections 3 and 4 we show that GAPs and Bohr sets in $\mathbb{Z}_p$ and $\mathbb{Z}_p^n$ are indeed captured by our definition of additive sources. As far as we know, these have not been studied in the extractor literature.

One can easily see that there are doubly exponentially many (α, β, τ)-additive sources for reasonably small α, τ and any constant $\beta < 1$. Due to this, there is no succinct representation of a general additive source, unlike affine sources. The only other natural family with doubly exponentially many sources is the family of independent sources.

1.2 Related work

We review relevant previous work. The first class of additive sources considered were bit fixing sources by Chor et al [8], and then by Kamp and Zuckerman [16] and Gabizon, Raz and Shaltiel in [13]. Next, in the more general case of affine sources, Bourgain obtained extractors for constant entropy rate [5] over $\mathbb{F}_2$, with improvements to slightly subconstant rate by Yehudayoff [29] and Li [17]. In the case of large fields, extractors for affine sources were given by Gabizon and Raz [12] and more recently by Bourgain, Dvir and Leeman [7]. DeVos and Gabizon [9] gave constructions interpolating between these extreme cases. Generalizations of affine sources have also been studied in the work of Dvir, Gabizon and Wigderson [11] and Ben-Sasson and Gabizon [1] where the authors look at polynomial sources and by Dvir [10] where varieties are considered. Special cases of affine sources have also been studied by Rao [22]. Gabizon and Shaltiel [14] constructed a weaker object called a disperser over large fields for affine sources. Ben-Sasson and Kopparty [2] constructed dispersers for affine sources with min-entropy $6n^{4/5}$ over $\mathbb{F}_2$. Shaltiel [26] improved on this and constructed a disperser for min-entropy $n^{o(1)}$ over $\mathbb{F}_2$.

1.3 Our results

In our main theorem for $\mathbb{Z}_p$ for p a large prime, we construct an extractor for additive sources for any constant entropy rate. More specifically, our construction works whenever p is large enough, and for (α, β, τ)-additive sources whenever α and τ are small enough. Specifically, for p an n-bit prime, we need $\alpha < 1/n$, and we extract about $\log(1/(\alpha n))$ bits. Thus, $\alpha = 1/\text{poly}(n)$ leads to $\Omega(\log n)$ random bits whereas $\alpha = 1/p^\gamma$ leads to $\Omega(n)$ random bits. We now state our main theorem over $\mathbb{Z}_p$.

THEOREM 1. *For every $\delta, \beta > 0$, there exists $\tau > 0$ and p_0 such that for all primes $p > p_0$ and $\alpha > 0$, the following holds. There is an explicit efficient ε-extractor* Ext : $\mathbb{Z}_p \to \{0,1\}^m$, *for (α, β, τ)-additive sources of entropy rate δ in $\mathbb{Z}_p$ where $\varepsilon = \left(3\alpha + p^{-\Omega_{\beta,\delta}(1)}\right) 2^{m/2} \log p$.*

As a corollary, we obtain extractors for GAPs [1] for any constant entropy rate.

COROLLARY 2 (GAP SOURCES). *For all $\delta > 0$, there exists c, p_0 such that for all primes $p \geq p_0$ the following holds. For all integers $r \geq c$, and all primes $p \geq c^{r/\delta}$ the following holds. There exists an explicit efficient ε-extractor* Ext : $\mathbb{Z}_p \to \{0,1\}^m$, *for $(r, p^{\delta/r})$-GAP sources (of entropy rate δ) in $\mathbb{Z}_p$ where $\varepsilon = \left(\frac{3r}{p^{0.9\delta/r}} + p^{-1/2}\right) 2^{m/2} \log p$.*

Observe that the only restriction we put is that $r \geq c$ and $p \geq c^{r/\delta}$ which simply means that the side lengths of

the GAP (that is, $p^{\delta/r}$) have to be larger than some fixed constant c and the dimension has to be larger than a fixed constant c. Thus, if we let r be a constant, then we can extract a constant fraction of the min entropy, that is $\Omega(\delta \log p)$ bits.

As another corollary, we obtain extractors for Bohr sources. We state it for constant ρ for simplicity. It can be easily generalized to any arbitrary ρ.

COROLLARY 3 (BOHR SOURCES). *Let $\rho, \alpha > 0$ and $S \subseteq \mathbb{Z}_p$ with $|S| = d$ be arbitrary. Then for prime $p = \Omega\left(\left(\frac{d}{\alpha}\right)^d\right)$, there exists an explicit efficient ε-extractor* Ext : $\mathbb{Z}_p \to \{0,1\}^m$, *for (d, ρ)-Bohr sources of entropy rate δ in $\mathbb{Z}_p$ where $\varepsilon = \left(3\alpha + p^{-\Omega(1)}\right) 2^{m/2} \log p$.*

Next, we construct an extractor for additive sources in $\mathbb{Z}_p^n$ for large enough p (polynomial in n) and any constant entropy rate, provided the source is sufficiently structured additively and satisfies a certain list decodability property. As a corollary, we give an extractor for GAPs in $\mathbb{Z}_p^n$ and Bohr sets with constant entropy rate, provided they satisfy the list decodability property. For a precise statement, see Theorem 4.2. We note that our extractor works for affine sources even though they may not satisfy the list decodability property. See Section 4.3.

Our extractors for GAPs and Bohr sets over $\mathbb{Z}_p$, and for Bohr sets over $\mathbb{Z}_p^n$, extract a linear number of bits with exponentially small error. We also show that all large sets (min-entropy rate close to 1), most sets (δ min-entropy rate for any $\delta > 0$) and most affine sources (δ min-entropy rate for any $\delta > 0$) satisfy the list decodability condition. See Remark 4.3, 4.4 and 4.5.

In the final two sections, we study special cases of additive sources. First, we give an extractor for one dimensional affine sources (lines) in $\mathbb{F}_q^n$ which requires only that $q > n$. This improves the results of Gabizon and Raz [12], which required $q = \Omega(n^2)$. Surprisingly, it even improves the non-explicit bound obtained via the probabilistic method of $q = \Omega(n \log n)$.

THEOREM 4 (EXTRACTORS FOR LINES). *There is an explicit efficient ε-extractor* Ext : $\mathbb{F}_q^n \to \{0,1\}$ *for all line sources in $\mathbb{F}_q^n$ where $\varepsilon \leq 4(n/q)^{1/2}$.*

We then show the same extractor in fact works for 'partial lines' - i.e., arithmetic progressions in $\mathbb{Z}_p^n$.

THEOREM 5 (EXTRACTORS FOR APs). *There is an explicit efficient ε-extractor* Ext : $\mathbb{F}_p^n \to \{0,1\}^m$ *for all k-AP sources in $\mathbb{F}_p^n$ where $\varepsilon \leq 16 \log^2 p \sqrt{np} 2^{m/2}/k$.*

Therefore, if we have $k = p^{1/2+\delta}$ and $n < p^\delta$, then we can extract $\delta/2 \log p$ bits. Moreover, we show that the general framework of [12] for constructing extractors for affine sources can be generalized to work for GAPs. As a corollary, we extend a result of DeVos and Gabizon [9] to obtain extractors for GAPs in $\mathbb{Z}_p^n$.

THEOREM 6 (EXTRACTORS FOR GAPs). *Fix integers r, s with $s < p$.*
Then we can construct an explicit efficient ε-extractor Ext : $\mathbb{F}_p^n \to \{0,1\}^m$ *for (r, s)-GAP sources where*

$$\varepsilon \leq (34 \log^3 p \cdot \sqrt{p}) \cdot n/(r \cdot \log s \cdot s) \cdot 2^{m/2} + 2^m/p.$$

In particular, when $p = \Omega((r \cdot s/n)^2)$ we can output one bit with constant error.

---

[1] Technically, we prove it for proper GAPs (Definition 2.3). However, we prove a result for general GAPs by reducing to proper GAPs in Section 5.

1.4 Techniques and Proof Overview

1.4.1 Extractors for additive sources in $\mathbb{Z}_p$.

For our proofs it will be convenient to define the notion of a *multiplicative source*. The definition simply corresponds to that of an additive source with multiplicative notation. Formally,

DEFINITION 1.5 (MULTIPLICATIVE SOURCE). *Fix positive constants* $0 < \alpha, \beta, \tau \leq 1$. *Let* Y *be a subset of a finite abelian group* $(G, \cdot)$. *We define the set* $\mathrm{Sym}_{1-\alpha}(Y) \subseteq G$ *by*

$$\mathrm{Sym}_{1-\alpha}(Y) \triangleq \{g \in G : |Y \cap (Y \cdot g)| \geq (1-\alpha) \cdot |Y|\}.$$

We say that Y *is an* (α, β, τ)*-multiplicative source if* $|Y \cdot Y| \leq |Y|^{1+\tau}$ *and* $|\mathrm{Sym}_{1-\alpha}(Y)| \geq |Y|^{\beta}$.

Suppose X is an (α, β, τ)-additive source in $\mathbb{Z}_p$. Our extractor construction is as follows. We describe the construction in detail only for this class of sources. Let q be a large prime, $q = 1 \pmod{p}$ and g be a generator of $\mathbb{Z}_q^*$ of order p. Define $\mathrm{Ext}(x) \triangleq \sigma(g^x)$, where $\sigma : \mathbb{Z}_q \to \mathbb{Z}_m$ is the function from Lemma 2.8. Then, it is enough by Lemma 2.8, to show that $|\mathbb{E}_X e_p(a.g^X)|$ for all $a \neq 0$ is small. The analysis break down into two main steps:

Step 1: 'Encoding' X into a multiplicative source.

As noted before, we fix a prime $q > p$ such that $q = 1 \pmod{p}$. For such q there exists an element $g \in \mathbb{Z}_q^*$ of order p. Fix such an element g and look at the map from $\mathbb{Z}_p$ to $\mathbb{Z}_q^*$ taking x to g^x. Let $Y \subseteq \mathbb{Z}_q^*$ be the image of X under this map. That is, $Y \triangleq \{g^x | x \in X\}$. As the subgroup generated by g in $\mathbb{Z}_q^*$ is isomorphic to $\mathbb{Z}_p$ we can show that Y is an (α, β', τ)-multiplicative source in $\mathbb{Z}_q^*$, where $\beta' \sim \beta$.

Step 2: Applying a character sum bound of Bourgain together with an 'average to worst-case reduction'.

The advantage of the transition to a multiplicative source comes from a theorem of Bourgain that roughly says the following. Suppose Y is a subset of $\mathbb{Z}_q^*$ such that $|Y \cdot Y| \leq |Y|^{1+\tau}$ for appropriate $0 < \tau < 1$. Then, for most $a \in \mathbb{Z}_q$ the sum

$$\widehat{Y}(a) \triangleq \sum_{y \in Y} e_q(a \cdot y)$$

is small in absolute value. If we knew that $|\widehat{Y}(a)|$ is small for *all* $a \in \mathbb{Z}_q^*$ rather than most $a \in \mathbb{Z}_q^*$, we could extract randomness from Y using the XOR lemma (Lemma 2.8). Our main insight is that when $\mathrm{Sym}_{1-\alpha}(Y)$ is large, we can indeed deduce that $|\widehat{Y}(a)|$ is small for all $a \in \mathbb{Z}_q^*$. We sketch why this is the case. Assume for contradiction that there is some $a \in \mathbb{Z}_q^*$ such that

$$|\widehat{Y}(a)| = \left| \sum_{y \in Y} e_q(a \cdot y) \right|$$

is large. Fix any $a' \in \mathrm{Sym}_{1-\alpha}(Y)$. As $|Y \cap a' \cdot Y| \geq (1-\alpha) \cdot |Y|$ and each summand is one in absolute value, the above sum will not change much if we sum over $a' \cdot Y$ rather than Y. That is, the sum

$$\sum_{y \in a' \cdot Y} e_q(a \cdot y)$$

must also be large in absolute value. But this sum is equal to

$$\sum_{y \in Y} e_q(a' \cdot a \cdot y) = \widehat{Y}(a' \cdot a).$$

Thus, $|\widehat{Y}(a' \cdot a)|$ is large for all $a' \in \mathrm{Sym}_{1-\alpha}(Y)$ - a contradiction as we know that $|\widehat{Y}(b)|$ is small for most $b \in \mathbb{Z}_q^*$.

Thus, for all $a \neq 0$, $|\mathbb{E}_X e_p(a.g^X)|$ is small. In summary, the extractor construction is $\mathrm{Ext}(x) \triangleq \sigma(g^x)$, where $\sigma : \mathbb{Z}_q \to \mathbb{Z}_m$ is the function from Lemma 2.8. See Section 3 for full details.

1.4.2 Extractors for additive sources in $\mathbb{Z}_p^n$.

Our construction over $\mathbb{Z}_p^n$ follows similar lines but is more involved. We give a sketch describing the same basic two steps. Let X be an (α, β, τ)-additive source in $\mathbb{Z}_p^n$.

Step 1: 'Encoding' X into a multiplicative source..

We choose n distinct primes $q_1, \ldots, q_n$ such that for all $i \in [n]$, $q_i = 1 \pmod{p}$. Let g_i be an element of order p in $\mathbb{Z}_{q_i}^*$. Let $q = q_1 \cdots q_n$, and let $CRT : \prod_i \mathbb{Z}_{q_i} \to \mathbb{Z}_q$ be the 'Chinese remaindering map'.

We look at the map from $\mathbb{Z}_p^n$ to $\mathbb{Z}_q$ taking $(x_1, \ldots, x_n)$ to $CRT(g_1^{x_1}, \ldots, g_n^{x_n})$. Let Y be the image of X under this map. That is, $Y \triangleq \{CRT(g_1^{x_1}, \ldots, g_n^{x_n}) | (x_1, \ldots, x_n) \in X\}$.

We can show that Y is an (α, β', τ)-multiplicative source in $\mathbb{Z}_q^*$,[2] where $\beta' \sim \beta$ assuming $q = p^{O(1)}$. We show that we can indeed get $q = p^{O(1)}$ by observing that the proof of Linnik's Theorem implies that for large enough p, we can always find appropriate $q_1, \ldots, q_n$ that are all at most $p^{O(1)}$.

Step 2: Applying a character sum bound of Bourgain together with an 'average to worst-case reduction'..

As in the case of $\mathbb{Z}_p$, we would now like to apply a theorem saying that for $Y \subseteq \mathbb{Z}_q^*$ such that $|Y \cdot Y| \leq |Y|^{1+\tau}$, $|\widehat{Y}(a)|$ is small for most $0 \neq a \in \mathbb{Z}_q$. The difference from the case of $\mathbb{Z}_p$ is that now we are dealing with a *composite* q. Bourgain indeed has such a theorem for the case of composite q. However, it requires an additional condition on Y apart from $|Y \cdot Y| \leq |Y|^{1+\tau}$. Roughly speaking, the condition is that if we look at elements of Y modulo a factor q_i of q, they are not too concentrated on any particular element of $\mathbb{Z}_{q_i}$. We show that if X satisfies a certain 'list-decodability' condition, Y satisfies the condition required by Bourgain's theorem. For arbitrary $\gamma > 0$, we also show that a random source of min-entropy γn and a random affine source of min-entropy γn satisfy the list decodability condition with very high probability. Thus, our extractor does not work for all additive sources in $\mathbb{Z}_p^n$. The reduction from the statement about most $0 \neq a \in \mathbb{Z}_q$ to all is similar to the description in the case of $\mathbb{Z}_p$.

We show that for the case of affine sources, we do not need a list decodability condition on X. A potentially useful tool we develop for this is an XOR lemma that guarantees closeness to uniform under a weaker condition than usual. The usual setting, described for example by Rao [21], is when $N > M$ and for all nontrivial characters ψ on $\mathbb{Z}_N$, we have $\mathbb{E}_X[\psi(X)] \leq \varepsilon$. Then there's a simple map $\sigma : \mathbb{Z}_N \to \mathbb{Z}_M$

---

[2]Observe that since the vector $(g_1^{x_1}, \ldots, g_n^{x_n})$ is non-zero in all coordinates, the element $CRT(g_1^{x_1}, \ldots, g_n^{x_n})$ of $\mathbb{Z}_q$ is indeed in $\mathbb{Z}_q^*$.

such that $\sigma(X)$ is close to uniform. We show that a similar result holds under the weaker assumption that $\mathbb{E}_X[\psi(X)] \leq \varepsilon$ only for characters ψ of the form $\psi(x) = e_n(a \cdot x)$ for $a \in \mathbb{Z}_N^*$, i.e., $(a, N) = 1$.

See Section 4 for full details.

1.4.3 Extractors for APs and GAPs.

For the case when the additive source is an AP or GAP in $\mathbb{Z}_p^n$, we give alternate constructions for a wider range of parameters.

For this, we generalize an approach introduced by Gabizon and Raz [12] and used by DeVos and Gabizon [9] for constructing extractors for affine sources. Their approach was to construct a polynomial $f : \mathbb{Z}_p^n \to \mathbb{Z}_p$ guaranteed to be non-constant on any k-dimensional affine subspace. Given such an f of degree d, the Weil bound (Theorem 2.12) can be used to construct an extractor for affine sources of dimension k when $p = \Omega(d^2)$. We show that the same approach works for GAPs: Suppose we can construct an explicit polynomial $f : \mathbb{Z}_p^n \to \mathbb{Z}_p$ of degree d that is non-constant *and of degree larger than one* when restricted to any affine subspace of dimension k. Then we can construct an extractor for GAPs in $\mathbb{Z}_p^n$ of dimension $r \sim k$, assuming p is roughly $\Omega(d^2 \cdot \log^4 d)$. This follows from a generalization of the Weil bound. Let us first recall the Weil bound of Theorem 2.12 says. Suppose we have a univariate polynomial f over $\mathbb{Z}_p$ of degree $d < \sqrt{p}$. Suppose ψ is a non trivial additive character of $\mathbb{Z}_p$. Then the character sum,

$$\left| \sum_{t \in \mathbb{Z}_p} \psi(f(t)) \right|$$

is small; more specifically, it is at most $d \cdot \sqrt{q}$. One may ask what happens when the same sum is taken only on the first s elements of $\mathbb{Z}_p$. Perhaps it is significantly larger than $d \cdot \sqrt{q}$ and becomes smaller only when running over the whole field? We show this is not the case. More precisely, for any $0 \leq s < p$ we have

$$\left| \sum_{0 \leq t \leq s-1} \psi(f(t)) \right| \leq 16 \log^2 p \cdot \sqrt{p} \cdot d$$

(see Lemma 5.5). The proof uses a combination of Theorem 2.12 and Fourier analysis. For example, a central step is to bound the Fourier coefficients of the function $\psi \circ f$ using the Weil bound.

See Section 5.2 for more details.

Extractors for lines over smaller fields..

[12] used the approach mentioned above to construct extractors for line sources in $\mathbb{Z}_p^n$ over fields $\mathbb{Z}_p$ of size $p = \Omega(n^2)$. The main component in their construction was an explicit polynomial $f : \mathbb{Z}_p^n \to \mathbb{Z}_p$ of degree n that is non-constant when restricted to any affine line. We improve on this and construct a polynomial f of degree $O(\sqrt{n})$ that is non-constant on any affine line. As a result we get extractors for line sources in $\mathbb{Z}_p^n$ when $p = \Omega(n)$. We sketch the construction of f.

- The first step is to construct a polynomial $g : \mathbb{Z}_p^n \to \mathbb{Z}_p$ of degree n that is non-constant on any line, and moreover, has the following stronger property: The restriction of g to any affine line will have degree *exactly* n

(rather than just *at most* n). We show that taking g to be a 'norm polynomial' insures this property.

- The second step is to partition the n coordinates into blocks of ascending size $1, 2, \ldots, \ell$ where $\ell = O(\sqrt{n})$. Now, let $g_i : \mathbb{Z}_p^i \to \mathbb{Z}_p$ denote the 'version' of the polynomial g when applied to a domain of i coordinates. We apply g_i to the i'th block. Note that the degree of the g_i's is at most $\deg(g_\ell) = \ell = O(\sqrt{n})$.

- Now we define f to be the sum of the g_i's when applied to the corresponding blocks. Note that $\deg(f) = O(\sqrt{n})$. We claim that f is non-constant on any affine line: Fix any affine line L, and fix the maximal $i \in [\ell]$ such that L is non-constant when restricted to the coordinates of the i'th block. The above-mentioned property of g guarantees that the 'g_i-summand of f' restricted to L will have degree i. All other summands will either be constant or of lower degree. Thus, f restricted to L is non-constant.

See Section 5 for full details.

1.5 Organization

In Section 2, we present basic definitions. In Section 3, we present our deterministic extractor for additive sources in $\mathbb{Z}_p$, and instantiate it in the case of GAPs and Bohr sets. In Section 4, we give our deterministic extractor for sources in $\mathbb{Z}_p^n$ and again instantiate it in the case of GAPs and Bohr sets. In Section 5, we construct deterministic extractors for lines (1 dimensional affine spaces), partial lines in $\mathbb{Z}_p^n$ (APs) and further generalize to GAPs. In most cases, we defer the proofs to the full version.

2. DEFINITIONS

In the following, p will denote a prime number. For $x \in \mathbb{R}$, $\|x\|$ denote the distance to the nearest integer. $e(x)$ denotes the complex number $e^{2\pi i x}$ and $e_m(x)$ denotes $e^{2\pi i x/m}$ for any positive integer m. To avoid clutter, e^y is written is $\exp(y)$.

2.1 Probability Distributions and Extractors

As mentioned earlier, a set X and a source X shall be used interchangeably where a source X denotes the uniform distribution on the set X.

2.2 Additive Combinatorics

We now state some standard terminology from additive combinatorics. We refer the reader to [27] for more details. In this section, let us fix a finite abelian group $(G, +)$.

DEFINITION 2.1 (REPRESENTATION FUNCTION). *Let A be a subset of G. For $g \in G$, we define*

$$rep_{A-A}(g) = |A \cap (A + g)|$$

which is the number of ways to represent g as a difference of two elements in A.

DEFINITION 2.2 (AFFINE SOURCE AND LINE SOURCE). *A δ-affine source in $\mathbb{Z}_p^n$ is an affine source of dimension δn. A dimension 1 affine source is called a line source.*

DEFINITION 2.3 (GAP). *An (r, s)-Generalized arithmetic progression (or GAP for short) in G defined is a set of the form*

$$\left\{ b_0 + \sum_{i=1}^{r} a_i b_i : 0 \leq a_i \leq s - 1 \right\}$$

for fixed elements $b_0, b_1, \ldots, b_r \in G$ (note that the a_i's are integers rather than elements of G). We say that the GAP is proper if all the s^r sums are distinct. The dimension of the GAP is r.

All GAPs are assumed to be proper in this paper unless mentioned otherwise. In fact, we will see in Section 5.2 how to handle general GAPs in $\mathbb{F}_p^n$.

DEFINITION 2.4 (k-AP AND k-LINE). *An arithmetic progression of length k (or k-AP for short) is a $(1, k)$-GAP. A k-AP in $\mathbb{F}_q^n$ is also called a k-line.*

DEFINITION 2.5 (k-HAP). *A homogenous arithmetic progression of length k (or k-HAP for short) is a k-AP with $b_0 = 0$.*

DEFINITION 2.6 (BOHR SET). *Let S be a set of characters of G and let $\rho > 0$. Then we define the Bohr set*

$$\mathbf{Bohr}(S, \rho) = \{ x \in G : \max_{\xi \in S} |\xi(x)| < \rho \}$$

We call the ρ the radius and $|S|$ the rank of the Bohr set. We refer to a Bohr set of rank d and radius ρ as a (d, ρ)-Bohr set.

Bohr sets and GAPs are closely related. In particular, any Bohr set contains a large GAP with small dimension [23, Theorem 7.1].

We say that a Bohr set is *regular* if additionally,

$$\mathbf{Bohr}(S, \rho(1 + \kappa)) \leq (1 + 100\kappa|S|)\mathbf{Bohr}(S, \rho)$$

whenever $\kappa < 1/100|S|$. Regular Bohr sets have the property that increasing the radius of the Bohr set by a little does not make the Bohr set very large. In fact, regular Bohr sets are ubiquitous [27], that is every Bohr set is "close" to a regular Bohr set. More precisely, for every S and ε, there is $\rho \in [\varepsilon, 2\varepsilon]$ such that $\mathbf{Bohr}(S, \rho)$ is regular. In this work, all Bohr sets will be regular Bohr sets.

When $G = \mathbb{Z}_p^n$, we know that the dual of G is isomorphic to G. Thus, in this case, we can consider $S \subseteq \mathbb{Z}_p^n$ and the Bohr set

$$\mathbf{Bohr}(S, \rho) = \left\{ x \in \mathbb{Z}_p^n : \max_{\xi \in S} \left\| \frac{\xi \cdot x}{p} \right\| < \rho \right\}.$$

Here $\| \cdot \|$ denotes the distance to the nearest integer.

Note that if G is a vector space over $\mathbb{F}_q$, then every subspace of G is a Bohr set with radius $1/q$ and rank equal to the codimension of the subspace. Thus, Bohr sets are generalizations of subspaces and are substitutes for the latter when G has no proper subgroups (e.g., when $G = \mathbb{Z}_p$). Bohr sets can also be thought of as the inverse image of a cube in $\mathcal{C}^S$ (where $\mathcal{C}$ is the unit circle in $\mathbb{C}$) if one considers the map $x \mapsto (e_p(\xi \cdot x))_{\xi \in S}$. This is justified by the inequality $4\|\theta\| \leq |e(\theta) - 1| \leq 2\pi\|\theta\|$.

2.3 Characters

Let $f : \mathbb{Z}_m \to \mathbb{C}$ be any function. Recall that, for $0 \leq j \leq m - 1$, the Fourier coefficients of f are given by

$$\widehat{f}(j) = \frac{1}{m} \sum_{x \in \mathbb{Z}_m} f(x) \exp(-2\pi ijx/m).$$

It is well known that the set of functions $\{\exp(2\pi ijx/m)\}_{0 \leq j \leq m-1}$ is an orthonormal basis for all complex functions defined on $\mathbb{Z}_m$, and that f can be expressed as

$$f(x) = \sum_{j=0}^{m-1} \widehat{f}(j) \exp(2\pi ijx/m).$$

Let us consider $f : \mathbb{Z}_m \to [0, 1]$. Thus, Parseval's identity states that

$$\sum_{j=0}^{m-1} \left| \widehat{f}(j) \right|^2 = \frac{1}{m} \sum_{x \in \mathbb{Z}_m} f(x)^2 \leq 1.$$

Exponential/Character sums to extractors. Throughout the paper, ψ and χ denote additive and multiplicative characters respectively and ψ_0 and χ_0 denote the trivial additive and multiplicative characters respectively. We let $e_n(x)$ denote $e^{2\pi ix/n}$. We now state two lemmas that gives a black box construction of deterministic extractors from exponential/character sums. Note that we use the term exponential sum for additive characters and character sums for multiplicative characters.

The following lemma is for exponential sums.

LEMMA 2.7. *Let $X \subseteq \mathbb{F}_p^n$. If $\left| \frac{1}{|X|} \sum_{x \in X} \psi(x) \right| < \varepsilon \; \forall \psi \neq \psi_0$, then there exists an efficient $\sigma : \mathbb{F}_p^n \to \mathbb{F}_p^m$ such that*

$$|\sigma(X) - U| < \varepsilon \sqrt{p^m}$$

We state a similar lemma that works for cyclic groups. A proof of this can be found in [20].

LEMMA 2.8. *Let $X \subseteq \mathbb{Z}_N$. If $\left| \frac{1}{|X|} \sum_{x \in X} \psi(x) \right| < \varepsilon \; \forall \psi \neq \psi_0$, then there exists an efficient $\sigma : \mathbb{Z}_N \to \mathbb{Z}_M$ such that*

$$|\sigma(X) - U| < \varepsilon \sqrt{M} \log N + O(M/N)$$

The next lemma is for character sums.

LEMMA 2.9. *Let $X \subseteq \mathbb{F}_{p^n}^*$. If $\left| \frac{1}{|X|} \sum_{x \in X} \chi(x) \right| < \varepsilon \; \forall \chi \neq \chi_0$, then there exists an efficient $\sigma : \mathbb{F}_{p^n}^* \to \mathbb{F}_{p^m}^*$ such that*

$$|\sigma(X) - U| < \varepsilon \sqrt{p^m}$$

PROOF. Without loss of generality let us assume that m divides n. If not, we can always append 0's to increase the dimension by a factor of at most 2. We have the following standard claim.

CLAIM 2.10. *Let X be a distribution on G such that $|\mathbb{E}[\chi(X)]| \leq \varepsilon \; \forall \chi \neq \chi_0$. Then, X is $\varepsilon\sqrt{|G|}$ close to U.*

With the above claim, we define $\sigma : \mathbb{F}_{p^n}^* \to \mathbb{F}_{p^m}^*$ as $\sigma(x) = x^{\frac{p^n-1}{p^m-1}}$. Now,

CLAIM 2.11. *Given a nontrivial multiplicative character Ψ of $\mathbb{F}_{p^m}^*$, $\Psi \circ \sigma$ is a nontrivial multiplicative character of $\mathbb{F}_{p^n}^*$.*

Thus, by hypothesis, $\left| \frac{1}{|X|} \sum_{x \in X} \Psi \circ \sigma(x) \right| < \varepsilon$. Therefore, $\left| \mathbb{E}_{\sigma(X)} \Psi(\sigma(X)) \right| < \varepsilon$. Thus, $\sigma(X)$ is $\varepsilon p^{m/2}$ close to U. $\square$

The Riemann Hypothesis for curves over finite fields. In 1948 Weil [28] proved the celebrated *Riemann Hypothesis for curves over finite fields*. A consequence of Weil's result is a bound for exponential and character sums over low degree polynomials over a finite field. We state it below. The theorems can also be found in [25].

THEOREM 2.12 (WEIL'S BOUND). *Let ψ be a nontrivial additive character of $\mathbb{F}_q$. Let $f(t) \in \mathbb{F}_q[t]$ be a polynomial of degree m. Let $\gcd(m,q) = 1$. Then*

$$\left| \sum_{t \in \mathbb{F}_q} \psi(f(t)) \right| \leq m q^{1/2}.$$

THEOREM 2.13 (WEIL'S BOUND). *Let χ be a nontrivial multiplicative character of $\mathbb{F}_q$ of order d. Let $f(t) \in \mathbb{F}_q[t]$ be a polynomial of degree m. Suppose that $f(t)$ is not of the form $cg(t)^d$ for any $c \in \mathbb{F}_q$ and $g(t) \in \mathbb{F}_q[t]$. Then*

$$\left| \sum_{t \in \mathbb{F}_q} \chi(f(t)) \right| \leq m q^{1/2}.$$

3. Extractors for additive sources in $\mathbb{Z}_p$

We now state our extractors for additive sources in $\mathbb{Z}_p$.

3.1 An extractor for additive sources

Our main theorem for $\mathbb{Z}_p$ (Theorem 1) follows from the following theorem.

THEOREM 3.1. *Fix any $\delta > 0$ and positive constant C. There exists $p_0 \in \mathbb{N}$ such that for all primes $p \geq p_0$ the following holds. There is an explicit efficient ε-extractor $\text{Ext} : \mathbb{Z}_p \to \{0,1\}^m$, for (α, β, τ)-additive sources of entropy rate δ in $\mathbb{Z}_p$ where $\delta\beta \geq 2t \log_p(1/\alpha) + \delta/C$, $\varepsilon = 3\alpha 2^{m/2} \log p + O(2^m/p)$ and τ, t are constants depending only on δ and C.*

PROOF OF THEOREM 1. Let $C = 2/\beta$ and $\gamma = \frac{\beta\delta}{4t}$. Then the hypothesis of the above theorem is satisfied if $\alpha > p^{-\gamma}$. The $2^m/p$ term can now be dropped by assuming without loss of generality $\gamma < 1/2$. Now, since, any (α, β, τ)-additive source is an (α', β, τ)-additive source for $\alpha < \alpha'$, this finishes the proof. $\square$

We show that GAPs and Bohr sets are indeed additive sources in $\mathbb{Z}_p$. We then use Theorem 3.1 to derive Corollaries 2 and 3.

3.2 Application to GAPs and Bohr sets

We first prove that a GAP source is an additive source with the appropriate parameters. We assume that the GAP is proper in this subsection.

LEMMA 3.2. *For all $\varepsilon > 0$, there exists $c, n_0 \in \mathbb{N}$ such that for all prime $p \geq n_0$ the following holds. If $\delta \geq c/\log p$, then an (r, p^δ)-GAP source is a $(r/p^{0.9\delta}, 0.1, \varepsilon)$-additive source of entropy rate δr in $(\mathbb{Z}_p, +)$.*

Note that the requirement of $\delta \geq c/\log p$ merely means that the sides of the GAP are $p^\delta = \Omega(1)$ in length.

Next, we prove that a Bohr set is an additive source with the appropriate parameters.

LEMMA 3.3. *Let $\beta, \varepsilon, \delta, \rho > 0$ be arbitrary and $S \subseteq \widehat{G}$ be a set of frequencies. Let $B = \mathbf{Bohr}(S, \rho)$ in G where $d = |S|$. Let $0 \leq \kappa \leq \frac{1}{100d}$. A Bohr source is a $(100\kappa d, \beta, \varepsilon)$-additive source of entropy rate δ in G whenever*

$$|G| \geq \max \left\{ \left(\frac{4^{1/\varepsilon}}{\rho} \right)^d, \left(\frac{1}{\rho} \right)^{d/1-\delta}, \left(\frac{1}{\kappa\rho} \right)^{d/1-\beta} \right\}.$$

This proves Corollaries 2 and 3.

We can extract more randomness from GAPs under the Paley Graph Conjecture which we describe in detail in the full version.

4. Extractors for additive sources in $\mathbb{Z}_p^n$

We first show that a GAP source is an additive source with the appropriate parameters.

LEMMA 4.1. *For all $\varepsilon > 0$, there exists $c, n_0 \in \mathbb{N}$ such that for all prime $p \geq n_0$ the following holds. If $\delta \geq (C/\log p)$, then an $(r = \mu n, p^\delta)$-GAP source is a $(\mu n/p^{0.9\delta}, 0.1, \varepsilon)$-additive source of entropy rate $\delta\mu$ in $(\mathbb{Z}_p, +)$.*

Note that the requirement of $\delta \geq (C/\log p)$ merely means that the sides of the GAP are $p^\delta = \Omega(1)$ in length.

We have already shown in Lemma 3.3 that Bohr sets are additive sources. We now proceed with the main theorem of this section.

4.1 The extractor

We say that a set X is (r, B)-list decodable if for any arbitrary r indices $i_1, \cdots i_r$, $c_j \in \mathbb{Z}_p$ for $j \in [r]$, $\left| X_{x_{i_1} = c_1, \ldots x_{i_r} = c_r} \right| \leq B$. We now state the main theorem of this section.

THEOREM 4.2. *There exists $p_0, L_0 \in \mathbb{N}$ such that for all $L \geq L_0$ and primes $p \geq p_0$ the following holds. Let $\gamma, \kappa > 0$ be arbitrary. There exists an efficient ε-extractor $\text{Ext} : \mathbb{Z}_p^n \to \{0,1\}^m$ for $(\alpha, \kappa L/\delta, \tau)$-additive sources of entropy rate δ in $(\mathbb{Z}_p^n, +)$ where $n \leq p^{L-2}$, X is $(r, p^{-r \cdot \gamma \cdot L} \cdot |X|)$-list decodable for every $\tau n/L \leq r \leq n$ and $\varepsilon < (3\alpha + |X|^{-\tau}) 2^{m/2} \log p^n + O(2^m/p^n)$ where τ is a constant depending on γ and κ.*

The following remarks show that the list decodability condition is not too restrictive.

REMARK 4.3 (MIN-ENTROPY $(1 - \varepsilon')n$). *In fact, for high enough min-entropy, we can now eliminate the list decodability assumption altogether. Given L, choose $\gamma = 1/(4L)$, (and fix some $\kappa > 0$ as in Theorem 4.2). Now this fixing of γ and κ also fixes some $\tau > 0$. Denote $a = \tau n/L$. We claim the theorem can now be applied to any source of entropy $k = n - a/2$. Fix such a source X. For $r > a$, and any fixing of any r coordinates, the corresponding list will be of size at most p^{n-r}. We need to show that this is smaller than $p^{-L\gamma r}|X| = p^{-r/4+n-a/2}$ It can be checked that this is indeed the case*

$$n - r < -r/4 + n - a/2 \qquad iff \qquad (3/4)r > a/2$$

REMARK 4.4 (RANDOM SOURCE: MIN-ENTROPY $\varepsilon'n$).
A random set X of size $|X| > p^{2L\gamma n}$ satisfies the list decodability condition with high probability. To see this, fix $r > \tau n/L$, a set of indices S of size r, field values $c_1, \ldots, c_r$ for those indices and a subset W of the set of size $B = p^{-\gamma Lr}|X| + 1$. The probability that all of W has the property that the coordinates in S get values c_i's is $(1/p^r)^B$. A union bound over all W gives $\binom{|X|}{B}(1/p^r)^B < (|X|e/B)^B(1/p^r)^B << 1/p^{0.9rB}$ as γ is arbitrarily small. An outer round of union bound over each of the p^r settings of c_i's and S is too mild to boost up the error probability for large p.

REMARK 4.5 (RANDOM AFFINE: MIN-ENTROPY $\varepsilon'n$).
Let $\gamma < 1/L$ be an arbitrary small constant. A subspace X of dimension $k > 2\gamma Ln$ defined by a random $k \times n$ matrix satisfies the list decodability condition. Indeed, let G be the random $k \times n$ matrix. We know that for any submatrix C of r columns in G, C has rank at least γrL with high probability. To see this, fix a subset of r column indices. Let $a = \gamma rL$. Note that $a < k/2$. Let C be the submatrix of G defined by the r columns. Then, $\mathbf{Pr}[\text{rank}(C) < a] < \binom{r}{a}p^{a-k}$. Here we are saying that some choice of the a columns of C will be linearly independent and then using the bound that a random $s \times t$ matrix has full rank with probability roughly at least $1 - p^{s-t}$ (for $s < t/2$). Continuing with the analysis, $\binom{r}{a}p^{a-k} < 2^r p^{-k/2} < 2^n p^{-k/2}$. Taking a union bound over the choice of r columns, we incur another factor of 2^n, and taking $p \geq 5^{2n/k}$ gives error at most $(4/5)^n$, finishing the proof. Let us continue with the proof. Fix r coordinates $i_1, \ldots, i_r$. Let $c_1, \ldots, c_r$ be r values in the field. Since the corresponding submatrix C has rank at least γrL, the number of strings in X which are c_j in coordinate i_j, $j = 1, \ldots, r$, is at most $p^{-\gamma Lr}|X|$. This satisfies the list decodability condition for all r.

The theorem follows from Lemma 2.8 and the following lemma.

LEMMA 4.6. *There exists $p_0, L_0 \in \mathbb{N}$ such that for all $L \geq L_0$ and primes $p \geq p_0$ the following holds. There exists an efficient $f : \mathbb{Z}_p^n \to \mathbb{Z}_q$ (for $p^n < q < p^{Ln}$) such that if $\gamma, \kappa > 0$ are arbitrary, then there exists $\tau > 0$ such that if*

- *X is an $(\alpha, \frac{\kappa L}{\delta}, \tau)$-additive source of entropy rate δ in $(\mathbb{Z}_p^n, +)$*

- *$n \leq p^{L-2}$*

- *for every integer $\tau n/L \leq r \leq n$, X is $(r, p^{-r \cdot \gamma \cdot L} \cdot |X|)$-list decodable,*

Then, for all $\xi \in \mathbb{Z}_q \setminus \{0\}$,

$$\left| \sum_{x \in X} e_q(\xi f(x)) \right| < 3 \max\{\alpha, 1/|X|^\tau\}|X|.$$

4.2 Application to GAPs and Bohr sets

COROLLARY 4.7 (GAP SOURCE). *Let $C > 0$ be arbitrary. There exists $p_0, L_0 \in \mathbb{N}$ such that for all $L \geq L_0$ and primes $p \geq p_0$ the following holds. Let $\delta, \mu > 0$ be arbitrary. There exists an efficient ε-extractor Ext $: \mathbb{Z}_p^n \to \{0,1\}^m$ for $(\mu n, p^\delta) - GAP$ sources (of entropy rate $\mu\delta$) in $\mathbb{Z}_p^n$ where $n \leq p^{L-2}$, X is $(\tau n/L, |X|^{1-1/C})$-list decodable and*

$\varepsilon < \left(3\frac{\mu n}{p^{0.9\delta}}\right)2^{m/2}\log p^n + O(2^m/p^n)$ *where $\tau < 1$ is a constant depending on $\delta \times \mu, L, C$.*

COROLLARY 4.8 (BOHR SOURCE). *Let $C, \rho, \alpha, \mu > 0$ be arbitrary. There exists $p_0, L_0 \in \mathbb{N}$ such that for all $L \geq L_0$ and primes $p \geq p_0$ the following holds. There exists an efficient ε-extractor Ext $: \mathbb{Z}_p^n \to \{0,1\}^m$ for $(d = \mu n, \rho)$-Bohr sources in $\mathbb{Z}_p^n$ where $p \geq \max\{n^{1/(L-2)}, \Omega\left(\left(\frac{n}{\alpha}\right)^\mu\right)\}$, X is $(\tau n/L, |X|^{1-1/C})$-list decodable and $\varepsilon < \left(3\alpha + |X|^{-\tau}\right)2^{m/2}\log p^n + O(2^m/p^n)$ where $\tau < 1$ is an arbitrarily small constant depending on d, ρ and C.*

4.3 Application to affine sources and a new XOR lemma

We note that extractor for additive sources in $\mathbb{Z}_p^n$ presented above indeed works for arbitrary affine spaces of constant min-entropy without any condition on list decodability. Firstly we need a way of converting exponential sum bounds to extractors. This has been folklore and known as the Vazirani XOR lemma. However, the conditions required for that are too stringent for our character sum bounds and we need a different generalization of the XOR lemma which we state below.

LEMMA 4.9. *Let $M < N$ be integers with M, N coprime and N be the product of n distinct primes all greater than p. Let $\sigma : \mathbb{Z}_N \to \mathbb{Z}_M$ be the function $\sigma(x) = x \mod M$. Let X be a distribution on $\mathbb{Z}_N$ with $|\mathbb{E}_X\psi(X)| \leq \varepsilon$ for every $\psi \in \mathbb{Z}_N^*$. Then,*

$$|\sigma(X) - U| = O\left((\varepsilon + n/p)\log N/M\right)$$

The proof will perform a rather careful analysis of the traditional proof of the XOR lemma. See the full version for details. We believe this might be of independent interest. Using this, we have the following.

THEOREM 4.10. *There exists $p_0, L_0 \in \mathbb{N}$ such that for all $L \geq L_0$ and primes $p \geq p_0$ the following is true. Let $\delta > 0$ be arbitrary. There exists an efficient ε-extractor Ext $: \mathbb{Z}_p^n \to \{0,1\}^m$ for (δ)-affine sources (entropy rate δ) in $\mathbb{Z}_p^n$ where $n \leq p^{L-2}$ and $\varepsilon < \left(1/p^{\tau n} + n/p\right)2^{m/2}\log p^n + O(2^m/p^n)$ where τ is a constant depending on δ/L.*

5. Extractor for APs and GAPs in $\mathbb{F}_q^n$

We first focus our attention to the special case of line sources. We construct an extractor for line sources and later generalize to partial lines (or k-lines).

5.1 Extractor for lines in $\mathbb{F}_q^n$

As mentioned in the introduction, it becomes increasingly harder to construct an extractor for lines for small q (large n), since when n is large enough compared to q, we get a proof of non-existence by the density Hales-Jewett theorem. In this section, we shall focus on 1-bit extractors. Generalizations to more number of bits follows from the XOR lemma (Lemma 2.8). In the following, let q be power of p.

For the sake of completeness, we first show by a simple well known probabilistic argument, the existence of a 1-bit 0.1-extractor for lines sources in $\mathbb{F}_q^n$ as long as $q = \Omega(n \log n)$.

LEMMA 5.1. *There exists a non-explicit 0.1-extractor $f : \mathbb{F}_q^n \to \{0,1\}$ for all line sources in $\mathbb{F}_q^n$ for n large enough as long as $q > 200n \log n$.*

Gabizon and Raz [12] achieved an extractor for $q = \Omega(n^2)$.

THEOREM 5.2 ([12]). *There is an explicit efficient ε-extractor* $\text{Ext} : \mathbb{F}_q^n \to \{0, 1\}$ *for all line sources in* $\mathbb{F}_q^n$ *where* $\varepsilon \leq n/\sqrt{q}$.

In this section, we construct our extractor which beats the randomness argument and works for $q = \Omega(n)$ which is the focus of Theorem 4 now. In order to construct our extractor, we shall be using *Norm Polynomials* (p.272 of [18]).

We state the two main lemmas of this section. The first lemma is for additive characters and works for all q. The second lemma is for the quadratic multiplicative character for odd q.

LEMMA 5.3. *There is an explicit efficient* $f : \mathbb{F}_q^n \to \mathbb{F}_q$ *such that the following holds. Let X be a line in* $\mathbb{F}_q^n$. *Then for any non trivial additive character* ψ,

$$\frac{1}{q} |\sum_{x \in X} \psi(f(x))| \leq 4(n/q)^{1/2}$$

LEMMA 5.4. *Let q be odd. There is an explicit efficient* $f : \mathbb{F}_q^n \to \mathbb{F}_q$ *such that the following holds. Let X be a line in* $\mathbb{F}_q^n$. *Then for the multiplicative quadratic character χ_2 we have*

$$\frac{1}{q} |\sum_{x \in X} \chi_2(f(x))| \leq 4(n/q)^{1/2}$$

To extract more bits, we use the XOR lemma along with the theorem on additive characters. The general form is presented in the next subsection. Let us now focus on the problem of extracting 1 bit. When q is even, we use the trace function for the additive character which gives 1 bit. For odd q, we see that the quadratic character outputs 1 bit. Some care needs to be taken in this case. For a proof, see [12].

5.2 Extractors for APs and GAPs in $\mathbb{Z}_p^n$

We further generalize these techniques to prove Theorem 5 and 6.

The main ingredient in the above proofs apart from the norm polynomials, includes a generalization of the Weil bound for exponential sums (Theorem 2.12) to the case where the sum ranges only over an AP, rather than the whole field.

LEMMA 5.5. *Let $f \in \mathbb{F}_p[t]$ be a polynomial of degree $1 < d < p$. Let X be an s-AP. Let ψ be a non trivial additive character of $\mathbb{F}_p$. Then, for any integer $0 < s \leq p$,*

$$\left| \sum_{t \in X} \psi(f(t)) \right| \leq 4 \log p \cdot \sqrt{p} \cdot d.$$

PROOF. The proof combines the Weil bound with Fourier analysis. It is based on two claims. The first uses the Weil bound to bound the Fourier coefficients of f *composed with an additive character*.

CLAIM 5.6. *Let ψ be the non trivial additive character from the lemma statement. Then for all $\xi \in \mathbb{F}_p$, we have* $\left| \widehat{\psi \circ f}(\xi) \right| \leq \sqrt{d/p}$.

PROOF. Suppose $\psi(x) = e_p(a \cdot x)$ for some $a \in \mathbb{F}_p$. We have

$$\left| \widehat{\psi \circ f}(\xi) \right|$$
$$= 1/p \left| \sum_{t \in \mathbb{F}_p} e_p(a \cdot f(t)) \cdot e_p(-\xi t) \right|$$
$$= 1/p \left| \sum_{t \in \mathbb{F}_p} e_p(a^{-1}(f(t) - a \cdot \xi \cdot t)) \right|$$
$$\leq (d/p)^{1/2}$$

The last line follows from Weil bound and by observing two things: The first is that the sum in the line before is an exponential sum with the character $\phi'(x) = e_p(a^{-1} \cdot x)$ on the polynomial $f'(t) \triangleq f(t) - \xi \psi^{-1} t$. The second is that $f'(t)$ is also a non-constant polynomial of degree $d < p$ so the Weil bound can be used. $\square$

Next, we need the following claim upper bounding the L_1 Fourier norm of a set related to s-APs. Let $A = \{0, 1, \ldots s - 1\}$. Denote by $A(x)$ the indicator set of A.

CLAIM 5.7. $\sum_{0 \leq j \leq p-1} \left| \hat{A}(j) \right| \leq 4 \log p$

PROOF. Note that

$$\hat{A}(j) = 1/p \sum_{i \in A} e(ji)$$
$$= 1/p \frac{e(jk) - 1}{e(j) - 1}$$

Now noting that $|e(\theta) - 1| \geq 4\{\theta\}$ we have $\left| \hat{A}(j) \right| \leq \frac{1}{2p\{j/p\}}$

We now turn to computing the L_1 Fourier norm of A.

$$\sum_{j \in \mathbb{F}_p} \left| \hat{A}(j) \right| = \sum_{j \leq p/2} \left| \hat{A}(j) \right| + \sum_{j > p/2} \left| \hat{A}(j) \right|$$
$$\leq \sum_{j \leq p/2} 1/(2j) + \sum_{j > p/2} 1/2(p - j)$$
$$\leq 4 \log p$$

$\square$

With the above two claims in place, we now turn to proving the lemma.

$$\left| \sum_{0 \leq t \leq s-1} \psi(f(t)) \right| = \left| \sum_{t \in \mathbb{F}_p} A(t)\psi(f(t)) \right|$$
$$= p \left| \sum_{\xi \in \mathbb{F}_p} \overline{\hat{A}(\xi)} \widehat{\psi \circ f}(\xi) \right|$$
$$\leq 4 \log p \cdot \sqrt{p} \cdot d.$$

This finishes the proof.

6. ACKNOWLEDGMENTS

A. Bhowmick and D. Zuckerman acknowledge the support of NSF Grants CCF-0916160 and CCF-1218723. A. Gabizon acknowledges the support of grant agreement number

257575 from the European Community's Seventh Framework Programme (FP7/2007-2013). The authors thank the anonymous referees for their valuable comments to improve the quality of the writeup. We also thank the reviewer who pointed out a problem with the condition of list decodability in Section 4. This led us to make the condition much less restrictive.

7. REFERENCES

[1] E. Ben-Sasson and A. Gabizon. Extractors for polynomial sources over constant-size fields of small characteristic. Technical Report TR11-129, Electronic Colloquium on Computational Complexity, 2011.

[2] E. Ben-Sasson and S. Kopparty. Affine dispersers from subspace polynomials. *SIAM J. Comput.*, 41(4):880–914, 2012.

[3] J. Bourgain. Estimates on exponential sums related to the diffieâĂŞhellman distributions. *Geometric and Functional Analysis GAFA*, 15(1):1–34, 2005.

[4] J. Bourgain. Exponential sum estimates over subgroups of zq*, q arbitrary. *Journal dâĂŹAnalyse MathÂl'matique*, 97(1):317–355, 2005.

[5] J. Bourgain. On the construction of affine extractors. *Geometric and Functional Analysis*, 17:33–57, 2007.

[6] J. Bourgain. SumâĂŞproduct theorems and exponential sum bounds in residue classes for general modulus. *Comptes Rendus Mathematique*, 344(6):349 – 352, 2007.

[7] J. Bourgain, Z. Dvir, and E. Leeman. Affine extractors over large fields with exponential error. *CoRR*, abs/1401.6189, 2014.

[8] B. Chor, J. Friedman, O. Goldreich, J. Hastad, S. Rudich, and R. Smolensky. The bit extraction problem or t–resilient functions. In *Proceedings of the 26th Annual IEEE Symposium on Foundations of Computer Science*, pages 396–407, 1985.

[9] M. DeVos and A. Gabizon. Simple affine extractors using dimension expansion. In *Proceedings of the 25th Annual IEEE Conference on Computational Complexity*, 2010.

[10] Z. Dvir. Extractors for varieties. In *Proceedings of the 24th Annual IEEE Conference on Computational Complexity*, pages 102–113, 2009.

[11] Z. Dvir, A. Gabizon, and A. Wigderson. Extractors and rank extractors for polynomial sources. In *Proceedings of the 48th Annual IEEE Symposium on Foundations of Computer Science*, pages 52–62, 2007.

[12] A. Gabizon and R. Raz. Deterministic extractors for affine sources over large fields. In *Proceedings of the 46th Annual IEEE Symposium on Foundations of Computer Science*, pages 407–418, 2005.

[13] A. Gabizon, R. Raz, and R. Shaltiel. Deterministic extractors for bit-fixing sources by obtaining an independent seed. *SIAM J. Comput.*, 36(4):1072–1094, 2006.

[14] A. Gabizon and R. Shaltiel. Increasing the output length of zero-error dispersers. In A. Goel, K. Jansen, J. Rolim, and R. Rubinfeld, editors, *Approximation, Randomization and Combinatorial Optimization. Algorithms and Techniques*, volume 5171 of *Lecture Notes in Computer Science*, pages 430–443. Springer Berlin Heidelberg, 2008.

[15] H. Iwaniec and E. Kowalski. *Analytic number theory*, volume 53 of *American Mathematical Society Colloquium Publications*. American Mathematical Society, Providence, RI, 2004.

[16] J. Kamp and D. Zuckerman. Deterministic extractors for bit-fixing sources and exposure-resilient cryptography. *SIAM Journal on Computing*, 36:1231–1247, 2006.

[17] X. Li. A new approach to affine extractors and dispersers. In *Proceedings of the 26th Annual IEEE Conference on Computational Complexity*, 2011.

[18] R. Lidl and H. Niederreiter. *Finite Fields*. Addison-Wesley, 1983.

[19] N. Nisan and D. Zuckerman. Randomness is linear in space. *Journal of Computer and System Sciences*, 52(1):43–52, 1996.

[20] A. Rao. Extractors for a constant number of polynomially small min-entropy independent sources. In *Proceedings of the 38th Annual ACM Symposium on Theory of Computing*, pages 497–506, 2006.

[21] A. Rao. An exposition of Bourgain's 2-source extractor. Technical Report TR07-034, Electronic Colloquium on Computational Complexity, 2007.

[22] A. Rao. Extractors for low-weight affine sources. *Electronic Colloquium on Computational Complexity (ECCC)*, 15(015), 2008.

[23] I. Z. Ruzsa. Sumsets and structure. In *Combinatorial number theory and additive group theory*, Adv. Courses Math. CRM Barcelona, pages 87–210. Birkhäuser Verlag, Basel, 2009.

[24] M. Santha and U. V. Vazirani. Generating quasi-random sequences from semi-random sources. *Journal of Computer and System Sciences*, 33:75–87, 1986.

[25] W. Schmidt. *Equations over Finite Fields. An Elementary Approach*, volume 536 of *Lecture Notes in Mathematics*. Springer-Verlag, 1976.

[26] R. Shaltiel. Dispersers for affine sources with sub-polynomial entropy. In *FOCS*, pages 247–256, 2011.

[27] T. Tao and V. Vu. *Additive Combinatorics*. Cambridge University Press, 2006.

[28] A. Weil. On some exponential sums. *Proceedings of the National Academy of Sciences*, 34:204–207, 1948.

[29] A. Yehudayoff. Affine extractors over prime fields. *Combinatorica*, 31(2):245–256, 2011.

It'll Probably Work Out: Improved List-Decoding Through Random Operations[*]

Atri Rudra[†]
Department of Computer Sc. and Engr.
University at Buffalo, SUNY
atri@buffalo.edu

Mary Wootters[‡]
Computer Science Department
Carnegie Mellon University
marykw@cs.cmu.edu

ABSTRACT

In this work, we introduce a framework to study the effect of random operations on the combinatorial list decodability of a code. The operations we consider correspond to row and column operations on the matrix obtained from the code by stacking the codewords together as columns. This captures many natural transformations on codes, such as puncturing, folding, and taking subcodes; we show that many such operations can improve the list-decoding properties of a code. There are two main points to this. First, our goal is to advance our (combinatorial) understanding of list-decodability, by understanding what structure (or lack thereof) is necessary to obtain it. Second, we use our more general results to obtain a few interesting corollaries for list decoding.

Categories and Subject Descriptors

E.4 [**Coding and Information Theory**]: Miscellaneous

Keywords

List decoding, random codes

1. INTRODUCTION

The goal of *error correcting codes* is to enable communication between a sender and receiver over a noisy channel. For this work, we will think of a code $\mathcal{C}$ of block length n and size N over an alphabet Σ as an $n \times N$ matrix over Σ, where each column in the matrix $\mathcal{C}$ is called a *codeword*. The sender and receiver can use $\mathcal{C}$ for communication as follows. Given one of N messages—which we think of as indexing the columns of $\mathcal{C}$—the sender transmits the corresponding codeword over a noisy channel. The receiver gets

a corrupted version of the transmitted codeword and aims to recover the originally transmitted codeword (and hence the original message). Two primary quantities of interest are the fraction ρ of errors that the receiver can correct (the *error rate*); and the redundancy of the communication, as measured by the *rate* $R := \frac{\log_{|\Sigma|} N}{n}$ of the code. The central goal is to design codes $\mathcal{C}$ so that both R and ρ are large.

A common approach to this goal is to first design a code matrix $\mathcal{C}_0$ that is "somewhat good," and to modify it to obtain a better code $\mathcal{C}$. Many of these modifications correspond to row or column operations on the matrix $\mathcal{C}_0$: for example, dropping of rows or columns, taking linear combinations of rows or columns, and combining rows or columns into "mega" rows or columns. In this work, we study the effects of such row- and column-operations on the *list decodability* of the code $\mathcal{C}_0$.

List decoding.

In the list decoding problem [Eli57, Woz58], the receiver is allowed to output a small list of codewords that includes the transmitted codeword, instead of having to pin down the transmitted codeword exactly. The remarkable fact about list decoding is that the receiver may correct twice as many adversarial errors as is possible in the unique decoding problem. Exploiting this fact has led to many applications of list decoding in complexity theory and in particular, pseudorandomness.[1]

Perhaps the ultimate goal of list decoding research is to solve the following problem.

> PROBLEM 1. *For $\rho \in (0, 1 - 1/q)$, construct q-ary codes with rate $1 - H_q(\rho)$ that can correct ρ fraction of errors with linear time encoding and linear time decoding.[2] Above, H_q denotes the q-ary entropy, and $1 - H_q(\rho)$ is known to be the optimal rate.*

Even though much progress has been made in algorithmic list decoding, we are far from answering the problem above in its full generality. If we are happy with polynomial time encoding and decoding (and large enough alphabet size), then the problem was solved by Guruswami and Rudra [GR08], and improved by several follow-up re-

---

[*]Full version at `http://arxiv.org/abs/1408.2237`

[†]AR's research is supported in part by NSF CAREER grant CCF-0844796 and NSF grant CCF-1161196.

[‡]MW's research is supported in part by a Rackham Predoctoral Fellowship from the University of Michigan.

---

[1]See the survey by Sudan [Sud00] and Guruswami's thesis [Gur04] for more on these applications.

[2]One needs to be careful about the machine model when one wants to claim linear runtime. In this paper we consider the RAM model. For the purposes of this paper, it is fine to consider linear time to mean linear number of $\mathbb{F}_q$ operations and the alphabet size to be be small, say polynomial in $1/\varepsilon$.

sults [GW13, Kop12, GX12, GX13, DL12, GK13]. However, even with all of this impressive work on algorithmic list decoding, the landscape of list-decoding remains largely unexplored. First, while the above results offer concrete approaches to Problem 1, we do not have a good characterization of which codes are even *combinatorially* list-decodable at near-optimal rate. Second, while we have polynomial-time encoding and decoding, linear-time remains an open problem. In this work, we make some progress in both of these directions.

New codes from old: random operations.

In this paper, we develop a framework to study the effect of random operations on the list-decodability of a code. Specific instantiations of these operations are a common approach to Problem 1. For example,

1. In the work of [GR08] mentioned above, one starts with a Reed-Solomon code and modifies it by applying a *folding* operation to each codeword. In the matrix terminology, we bunch up rows to construct "mega" rows.

2. In another example mentioned above [GX13], one starts with a Reed-Solomon code and picks certain positions in the codeword, and also throws away many codewords—that is, one applies a *puncturing* operation the codewords, and then considers a *subcode*. In matrix terminology, we drop rows and columns.

3. In [Tre03, IJKW10], the *direct product* operation and the *XOR* operation are used to enhance the list-decodability of codes. In matrix terminology, the direct product corresponds to bunching rows and the XOR operation corresponds to taking inner products of rows.

4. In [GI01, GI03, GI05], the *aggregation* operation is used to construct efficiently list-decodable codes out of list-recoverable codes. In matrix terminology, this aggregation again corresponds to bunching rows.

However, in all of these cases, the operations used are very structured; in the final two, the rate of the code also takes a hit.[3] It is natural to ask how generally these operations can be applied. In particular, if we considered random versions of the operations above, can we achieve the optimal rate/error rate/list size trade-offs? If so, this provides more insight about why the structured versions work.

Recently the authors showed in [RW14] that the answer is "yes" for puncturing of the rows of the code matrix: if one starts with *any* code with large enough distance and randomly punctures the code, then with high probability the resulting code is nearly optimally combinatorially list-decodable. In this work, we extend those results to other operations.

1.1 Our contributions and applications

The contributions of this paper are two-fold. First, the goal of this work is to improve our understanding of (combinatorial) list-decoding. What is it about these structured operations that succeed? How could we generalize? Of course, this first point may seem a bit philosophical without some actual deliverables. To that end, we show how to use our framework to address some open problems in list decoding. We outline some applications of our results below.

In order to state our main results, we pause briefly to set the quantitative stage. There are two main parameter regimes for list-decoding, and we will focus on both in this paper. In the first regime, corresponding the the traditional communication scenario, the error rate ρ is some constant $0 < \rho < 1 - 1/q$. In the second regime, motivated by applications in complexity theory, the error rate ρ is very large. For q-ary codes, these applications require correction from a $\rho = 1 - 1/q - \varepsilon$ fraction of errors, for small $\varepsilon > 0$. In both settings, the best possible rate is given by

$$R^* = 1 - H_q(\rho),$$

where H_q denotes the q-ary entropy. In the second, large-q, regime, we may expand $H_q(1 - 1/q - \varepsilon)$ to obtain an expression

$$R^*(q,\varepsilon) := 1 - H_q(1-1/q-\varepsilon) = \min\left\{\varepsilon, \frac{q\varepsilon^2}{2\log(q)} + O_q(\varepsilon^3)\right\}.$$

For complexity applications it is often enough to design a code with rate $\Omega(R^*(q,\varepsilon))$ with the same error correction capability.

1.1.1 Linear time encoding with near optimal rate

We first consider the special case of Problem 1 that concentrates on the encoding complexity for binary codes in the high error regime:

QUESTION 1. *Do there exist binary codes with rate $\Omega(\varepsilon^2)$ that can be encoded in linear time and are (combinatorially) list-decodable from a $1/2 - \varepsilon$ fraction of errors?*

Despite much progress on related questions, obtaining linear time encoding with (near-)optimal rate is still open. More precisely, for q-ary codes (for q sufficiently large, depending on ε), Guruswami and Indyk showed that linear time encoding and decoding with near-optimal rate is possible for *unique* decoding [GI05]. For list decoding, they prove a similar result for list decoding but the rate is exponentially small in $1/\varepsilon$ [GI03]. This result can be used with code concatenation to give a similar result for binary codes (see the full version for more details) but also suffers from an exponentially small rate. If we allow for super-linear time encoding in Question 1, then it is known that the answer is yes. Indeed, random linear codes will do the trick [ZP82, CGV13, Woo13] and have quadratic encoding time; In fact, near-linear time encoding with optimal rate also follows from known results.[4]

Our results.

We answer Question 1 in the affirmative. To do this, we consider the row-operation on codes given by taking random XORs of the rows of $\mathcal{C}_0$. We show that this operation yields codes with rate $\Omega(\varepsilon^2)$ that are combinatorially list-decodable from $1/2 - \varepsilon$-fraction of errors, provided the

---

[3]It must be noted that in the work of [Tre03, IJKW10] the main objective was to obtain sub-linear time list decoding and the suboptimal rate is not crucial for their intended applications.

[4]For example, Guruswami and Rudra [GR10] showed that folded Reed-Solomon codes—which can be encoded in near-linear time—concatenated with random inner codes with at most logarithmic block length achieve the optimal rate and fraction of correctable errors tradeoff.

original code has constant distance and rate. Instantiating this by taking $\mathcal{C}_0$ to be Spielman's code [Spi96], we obtain a linear-time encodable binary code which is nearly-optimally list-decodable.

1.1.2 The folding operation, and random t-wise direct product

The result of Guruswami and Rudra [GR08] showed that when the *folding* operation is applied to Reed-Solomon codes, then the resulting codes (called folded Reed-Solomon codes) can be list decoded in polynomial time with optimal rate. The folding operation is defined as follows. We start with a q-ary code $\mathcal{C}_0$ of length n_0, and a partition of $[n_0]$ into n_0/t sets of size t, and we will end up with a q^t-ary code $\mathcal{C}$ of length $n = n_0/t$. Given a codeword $c_0 \in \mathcal{C}_0$, we form a new codeword $c \in \mathcal{C}$ by "bunching" together the symbols in each partition set and treating them as a single symbol. A formal definition is given in Section 2. For large enough t, this results in codes that can list decode from $1 - \varepsilon$ fraction of errors with optimal rate [GR08, GX12, GX14] when one starts with Reed-Solomon or certain algebraic-geometric codes.

Folding is a special case of t-wise aggregation of symbols. Given a code $\mathcal{C}_0$ of length n_0, we may form a new code $\mathcal{C}_0$ of length n by choosing n subsets $S_1, \ldots, S_n \subset [n_0]$ and aggregating symbols according to these sets. This operation has been used to good effect in the list-decoding literature: in [GI01, GI03, GI05], the sets S_i are defined using expander codes, and the original code $\mathcal{C}_0$ is chosen to be *list-recoverable*. This results in efficiently list-decodable codes, although not of optimal rate. We can also view this t-wise aggregation as a puncturing of a t-wise direct product (where $n = \binom{n_0}{t}$ and all sets of size t are included).

There is a natural intuition for the effectiveness of the folding operation in [GR08, GR09], and for the t-wise aggregation of symbols in [GI01, GI03, GI05]. In short, making the symbols larger increases the size of the "smallest corruptable unit," which in turn decreases the number of error patterns we have to worry about. (See Section 5.2 for more on this intuition). In some sense, this intuition is the reason that random codes over large alphabets can tolerate more error than random codes over small alphabets: indeed, an inspection of the proof that random codes obtain optimal list-decoding parameters shows that this is the crucial difference. Since a random code over a large alphabet is in fact a folding of a random code over a small alphabet, the story we told above is at work here.

Despite this nice-sounding intuition—which doesn't use anything specific about the code—the known results mentioned above do not use it, and rely crucially on specific properties of the original codes, and on algorithmic arguments. It is natural to wonder if the intuition above can be made rigorous, and to hold for *any* original code $\mathcal{C}_0$. In particular,

QUESTION 2. *Can the above intuition be made rigorous? Precisely, are there constants $\delta_0, c_0 > 0$, so that for any $\varepsilon > 0$, any code with distance at least δ_0 and rate at most $c_0 \varepsilon$ admits a t-wise folding (or other t-wise aggregation of symbols with $n = n_0/t$) for t depending only on ε, such that the resulting code is combinatorially list-decodable from a $1 - \varepsilon$ fraction of errors?*

The first question mimics the parameters of folded Reed-Solomon codes; the second part is for the parameter regime of [GI01, GI03, GI05]. Notice that both the requirements (distance $\Omega(1)$ and rate $O(\varepsilon)$) are necessary. Indeed, if the original code does not have distance bounded below by a constant, it is easy to come up with codes where the answer to the above question is "no." The requirement of $O(\varepsilon)$ on the rate of the original code is needed because folding preserves the rate, and the list-decoding capacity theorem implies that any code that can be list decoded from $1 - \varepsilon$ fraction of errors must have rate $O(\varepsilon)$.

Our results.

We answer Question 2 in the affirmative by considering the operation of random t-wise aggregation. We show that if $n = n_0/t$ (the parameter regime for t-wise folding), the resulting code is list-decodable from a $1 - \varepsilon$ fraction of errors, as long as $t = O(\log(1/\varepsilon))$. Our theory can also handle the case when $n \ll n_0$, and obtain near-optimal rate at the same time.

1.1.3 Taking sub-codes

The result of Guruswami and Rudra [GR08], even though it achieves the optimal tradeoff between rate and fraction of correctable errors is quite far from achieving the best known combinatorial bounds on the worst-case list sizes. Starting with the work of Guruswami [Gur11], there has been a flurry of work on using *subspace evasive subsets* to drive down the list size needed to achieve the optimal list decodability [GW13, DL12, GX12, GX13, GK13]. The basic idea in these works is the following: we first show that some code $\mathcal{C}_0$ has optimal rate vs fraction of correctable tradeoff but with a large list size of L_0. In particular, this list lies in an affine subspace of roughly $\log L_0$ dimensions. A subspace evasive subset is a subset that has a small intersection with any low dimension subset. Thus, if we use such a subset to pick a subcode of $\mathcal{C}_0$, then the resulting subcode will retain the good list decodable properties but now with smaller worst-case lists size. Perhaps the most dramatic application of this idea was used by Guruswami and Xing [GX13] who show that certain Reed-Solomon codes have (non-trivial) exponential list size and choosing an appropriate subcode with a subspace evasive subset reduces the list size to a constant.

However, the intuition that using a subcode can reduce the worst-case list size is not specifically tied to the algebraic properties of the code (i.e, to Reed-Solomon codes and subspace evasive sets). As above, it is natural to ask if this intuition holds more broadly.

QUESTION 3. *Given a code, does there always exist a subcode that has the same list decoding properties as the original code but with a smaller list size? In particular, is this true for random sub-codes?*

Our results.

We answer Question 3 by showing that for any code, a random subcode with the rate smaller only by an additive factor of ε can correct the same fraction of errors as the original code but with a list size of $O(1/\varepsilon)$ as long as the original list size is at most N^ε. Guruswami and Xing [GX13] showed that Reed-Solomon codes defined over (large enough) extension fields with evaluation points coming from a (small enough) subfield has non-trivial list size of N^ε. Thus, our result then implies the random sub-codes of such Reed-Solomon codes are optimally list decodable.[5] We also complement this result by showing that the tradeoff between the loss in rate and the final list size is the best one can hope for in general. We also use the positive result to show another result: given that $\mathcal{C}_0$ is optimally list decodable up to rate ρ_0, its random subcodes (with the appropriate rate) with high probability are also optimally list decodable for any error rate $\rho > \rho_0$.

1.1.4 Techniques

Broadly speaking, the operations we consider fall into two categories: row-operations and column-operations on the matrix $\mathcal{C}$. We use different approaches for the different types of operations.

For row operations (and Questions 1 and 2) we use the machinery of [Woo13, RW14] in a more general context. In those works, the main motivations were specific families of codes (random linear codes and Reed-Solomon codes). In this work, we use the technical framework (implicit in) those earlier papers to answer new questions. Indeed, one of the contributions of the current work is to point out that in fact these previous arguments apply very generally. For column operations, our results follow from a few simple direct arguments (although the construction for the lower bound requires a bit of care).

REMARK 4. *We will specifically handle all row operations on the code matrix mentioned at the beginning of the introduction. For column operations, we handle only column puncturing (taking random subcodes). For many operations, this is not actually an omission: some of the column-analogues of the row-operations we consider are redundant. For example, taking random linear combinations of columns of a linear code has the same distribution as a random column puncturing. We do not handle bunching up of columns into mega columns, which would correspond to designing interleaved codes—see Section 2 for a formal definition—and we leave the solution of this problem as an open question.*

Organization.

In Section 2, we set up our formal framework and present an overview of our techniques in Section 3. In Section 4, we state and prove our results about the list-decodability of codes under a few useful random operations; these serve to give examples for our framework. They also lay the groundwork for Section 5, where we return to the three applications we listed above, and resolve Questions 1, 2, and 3. Finally, we conclude with some open questions.

2. SET-UP

In this section, we set notation and definitions, and formalize our notion of row and column operations on codes. Throughout, we will be interested in codes $\mathcal{C}$ of length n and size N over an alphabet Σ. Traditionally, $\mathcal{C} \subset \Sigma^n$ is a set of codewords. As mentioned earlier, we will treat $\mathcal{C}$ as a matrix in $\Sigma^{n \times N}$, with the codewords as columns. We will abuse notation slightly by using $\mathcal{C}$ to denote both the matrix and the set; which object we mean will be clear from

---

[5]Guruswami and Xing also prove a similar result (since a random subset can be shown to be subspace evasive) so ours gives an arguably simpler alternate proof.

context. For a prime power q, we will use $\mathbb{F}_q$ to denote the finite field with q elements.

For $x, y \in \Sigma^n$, we will use $d(x, y)$ to denote the Hamming distance between x and y, and we will use $\mathrm{agr}(x, y) := n - d(x, y)$ to denote the agreement between x and y. We study the list-decodability of $\mathcal{C}$: we say that $\mathcal{C}$ is (ρ, L)-list-decodable if for all $x \in \Sigma^n$, $|\{c \in \mathcal{C} : d(c, x) \leq \rho\}| < L$. In this work, we will also be interested in the slightly stronger notion of *average-radius list-decodability*.

DEFINITION 1. *A code* $\mathcal{C} \subset \Sigma^n$ *is* (ρ, L)*-average-radius list-decodable if for all sets* $\Lambda \subset \mathcal{C}$ *with* $|\Lambda| = L$,

$$\max_z \sum_{c \in \Lambda} \mathrm{agr}(c, z) \leq (1 - \rho)nL.$$

Average-radius list-decodability implies list-decodability [GN13, RW14]. Indeed, the mandate of average-radius list decodability is that, for any L codewords in $\mathcal{C}$, they do not agree too much on average with their center, z. On the other hand, standard list decodability requires that for any L codewords in $\mathcal{C}$, at least one does not agree too much with z. As the average is always smaller than the maximum, standard list-decodability follows from average-radius list-decodability.

We will create new codes $\mathcal{C} \in \Sigma^{n \times N}$ from original codes $\mathcal{C}_0 \in \Sigma_0^{n_0 \times N_0}$; notice that we allow the alphabet to change, as well as the size and block length of the code. We will consider code operations $f : \Sigma_0^{n_0 \times N_0} \to \Sigma^{n \times N}$ which act on rows and columns of the matrix $\mathcal{C}_0$.

We say that a *basic row operation* takes a code $\mathcal{C}_0$ and produces a row of a new matrix $\mathcal{C}$: that is, it is a function

$$r : \Sigma_0^{n_0 \times N_0} \to \Sigma^{N_0}.$$

Two examples of basic row operations that we will consider in this paper are taking linear combinations of rows or aggregating rows. That is:

(a) When $\Sigma = \Sigma_0 = \mathbb{F}_q$, and for a vector $v \in \mathbb{F}_q^{n_0}$, the row operation corresponding to linear combinations of rows is $r_v^{(\mathrm{ip})} : \mathbb{F}_q^{n_0 \times N} \to \mathbb{F}_q^N$, given by

$$r_v^{(\mathrm{ip})}(\mathcal{C}_0) = v^T \mathcal{C}_0.$$

(b) Let $S \subset [n_0]$ be a set of size t, and let $\Sigma = \Sigma_0^t$. Then the row operation corresponding to aggregating rows is $r_S^{(\mathrm{agg})} : \Sigma_0^{n_0 \times N} \to (\Sigma_0^t)^N$, given by

$$r_S^{(\mathrm{agg})}(M) = \left((M_{i,1})_{i \in S}, (M_{i,2})_{i \in S}, \ldots, (M_{i,N})_{i \in S} \right).$$

(Above, we have replaced $\mathcal{C}_0$ with M to ease the number of subscripts).

We will similarly consider *basic column operations*

$$c : \Sigma_0^{n_0 \times N_0} \to \Sigma^{n_0},$$

which take a code $\mathcal{C}_0$ and produce a new column of a matrix $\mathcal{C}$. Analogous to the row operations, we have the following two examples.

(a) When $\Sigma = \Sigma_0 = \mathbb{F}_q$, and for a vector $w \in \mathbb{F}_q^{N_0}$, we can consider

$$c_w^{(\mathrm{ip})}(\mathcal{C}_0) = \mathcal{C}_0 w.$$

(b) Let $T \subset [N_0]$ be a set of size t, and let $\Sigma = \Sigma_0^t$. Then

$$c_T^{(\mathrm{agg})}(M) = \left((M_{1,j})_{j \in T}, (M_{2,j})_{j \in T}, \ldots, (M_{n,j})_{j \in T} \right).$$

The code operations that we will consider in this paper are distributions over a collection of random basic row operations or collection of random basic column operations:

DEFINITION 2. *A random row operation is a distribution $\mathcal{D}$ over n-tuples of basic row operations. We treat a draw $f = (r_1, \ldots, r_n)$ from $\mathcal{D}$ as a code operation mapping $\mathcal{C}_0$ to $\mathcal{C}$ by defining the ith row of $\mathcal{C} = f(\mathcal{C}_0)$ to be $r_i(\mathcal{C}_0)$. Similarly, a random column operation is a distribution $\mathcal{D}$ over N-tuples of basic column operations.*

We say a random row (column) operation $\mathcal{D}$ has independent symbols *(independent codewords resp.) if the coordinates are independent. We say a random row operation $\mathcal{D}$ has symbols drawn* independently without replacement *if $(r_1, \ldots, r_n)$ are drawn uniformly at random without replacement from some set R of basic row operations.*

Finally, for a random row operation $\mathcal{D}$ and a sample f from $\mathcal{D}$ note that the columns of $f(\mathcal{C})$ are in one-to-one correspondence with the columns of $\mathcal{C}$. Thus, we will overload notation and denote $f(c)$ for $c \in \mathcal{C}$ to denote the column in $f(\mathcal{C})$ corresponding to the codeword $c \in \mathcal{C}$.

Below, we list several specific random row operations that fit into our framework.

1. *Random Sampling:* Let $\Sigma = \Sigma_0$ be any alphabet, and let $\mathcal{D} = (\mathcal{U}_r)^n$, where $\mathcal{U}_r$ is the uniform distribution on the n_0 basic row operations $r_{e_j}^{(\mathrm{ip})}$ for $j \in [n_0]$, where e_j is the jth standard basis vector. Thus, each row of $\mathcal{C}$ is a row of $\mathcal{C}_0$, chosen independently uniformly with replacement.

2. *Random Puncturing:* Same as above except $r_1, \ldots, r_n$ are chosen *without* replacement.

3. *Random t-wise XOR:* Let $\Sigma_0 = \Sigma = \mathbb{F}_2$ and $\mathcal{D} = (\mathcal{U}_{\oplus,t})^n$. $\mathcal{U}_{\oplus,t}$ is the uniform distribution over the $\binom{n_0}{t}$ basic row operations

$$\left\{ r_v^{(\mathrm{ip})} : v \in \mathbb{F}_2^{n_0} \text{ has weight } t \right\}.$$

That is, to create a new row of $\mathcal{C}$, we choose t positions from $\mathcal{C}_0$ and XOR them together.

4. *Random t-wise aggregation:* Let $\Sigma = \Sigma_0^t$, for any alphabet Σ_0, and let $\mathcal{D} = (\mathcal{U}_{t,\mathrm{dp}})^n$, where $\mathcal{U}_{t,\mathrm{dp}}$ is the uniform distribution over the $\binom{n_0}{t}$ basic row operations

$$\left\{ r_S^{(\mathrm{agg})} : S \subset [n_0], |S| = t \right\}.$$

5. *Random t-wise folding:* Let $\Sigma = \Sigma_0^t$, for any alphabet Σ_0. For each partition $\pi = (S_1, \ldots, S_{n_0/t})$ of $[n_0]$ into sets of size t, consider the row operation $f_\pi = (r_1, \ldots, r_n)$ where

$$r_j = r_{S_j}^{(\mathrm{agg})}.$$

Let $\mathcal{D}$ be the uniform distribution over f_π for all partitions π.

The following column operations also fit into this framework; in this paper, we consider only the first. We mention the second operation (random interleaving) in order to parallel the situation with columns. We leave it as an open problem to study the effect of interleaving.

1. *Random sub-code:* Let $\Sigma = \Sigma_0$ be any alphabet, and let $\mathcal{D} = (\mathcal{U}_c)^N$, where $\mathcal{U}_c$ is the uniform distribution on the N_0 basic column operations

$$\left\{ c_w^{(\mathrm{ip})} : w = e_i, i \in [N_0] \right\}.$$

That is, $\mathcal{C}$ is formed from $\mathcal{C}_0$ by choosing codewords independently, uniformly, with replacement from $\mathcal{C}_0$.

Notice that if $\mathcal{C}_0$ is a linear code over $\mathbb{F}_q$, then this operation is the same if we replace $\{w = e_i : i \in [N_0]\}$ with all of $\mathbb{F}_q^n$, or with all vectors of a fixed weight, etc. Thus, we do not separately consider random XOR (or inner products), as we do with rows.

2. *Random t-wise interleaving:* In this case $\mathcal{D} = (\mathcal{U}_{t,\mathrm{dp}}^c)^n$. $\mathcal{U}_{t,\mathrm{dp}}^c$ is the uniform distribution over the $\binom{N_0}{t}$ basic column operations

$$\left\{ c_T^{(\mathrm{agg})} : T \subset [N_0], |T| = t \right\}.$$

3. OVERVIEW OF OUR TECHNIQUES

Random Row Operations.

In addition to answering Questions 1 and 2, one of the contributions of this work is to exhibit the generality of the techniques developed in [RW14]. As such, our proofs follow their framework. In that work, there were two steps: the first step was to bound the list-decodability in expectation (this will be defined more precisely below), and the second step was to bound the deviation from the expectation. In this work, we use the deviation bounds as a black box, and it remains for us to bound the expectation. We would also like to mention that we could have answered Questions 1 and 2 by applying the random puncturing results from [Woo13, RW14] as a black box to the XOR and direct product of the original code. We chose to unpack the proof to illustrate the generality of the proof technique developed in [Woo13, RW14] (and they also seem necessary to prove the generalization to the operation of taking random linear combinations of the rows of the code matrix).

The results on random row operations in this paper build on the approaches of [Woo13, RW14]. While those works are aimed at specific questions (the list-decodability of random linear codes and of Reed-Solomon codes with random evaluation points), the approach applies more generally. In this paper, we interpret the lessons of [Woo13, RW14] as follows:

> If you take a code over Σ_0 that is list-decodable (enough) up to $\rho_0 = 1 - 1/|\Sigma_0| - \varepsilon$, and do some random (enough) stuff to the symbols, you will obtain a new code (possibly over a different alphabet Σ) which is list-decodable up to $\rho = 1 - 1/|\Sigma| - O(\varepsilon)$. If the random stuff that you have done happens to, say, increase the rate, then you have made progress.

First, our notion of a random row operation $\mathcal{D}$ being random enough is the same as $\mathcal{D}$ having independent symbols (or independent symbols without replacement). Now, we will quantify what it means to be "list-decodable enough" in the setup described above. We introduce a parameter $\mathcal{E} = \mathcal{E}(\mathcal{C}_0, \mathcal{D})$, defined as follows:

$$\mathcal{E}(\mathcal{C}_0, \mathcal{D}) := \max_{\Lambda \subset \mathcal{C}_0, |\Lambda| = L} \mathbb{E}_{f \sim \mathcal{D}} \max_{z \in \Sigma^n} \sum_{c \in \mathcal{C}_0} \mathrm{agr}(f(c), z). \quad (1)$$

The quantity $\mathcal{E}$ captures how list-decodable $\mathcal{C}$ is in expectation. Indeed, $\max_z \sum_{c \in \mathcal{C}_0} \mathrm{agr}(f(c), z)$ is the quantity controlled by average-radius list-decodability (Definition 1). To make a statement about the actual average-radius list-decodability of $\mathcal{C}$ (as opposed to in expectation), we will need to understand $\mathcal{E}$ when the expectation and the maximum are reversed:

$$\mathbb{E}_{f \sim \mathcal{D}} \max_{\Lambda \subset \mathcal{C}_0, |\Lambda| = L} \max_{z \in \Sigma^n} \sum_{c \in \mathcal{C}_0} \mathrm{agr}(f(c), z).$$

The work of [Woo13, RW14] shows the following theorem.

THEOREM 2. *Let $\mathcal{C}_0, \mathcal{D}$ and $\mathcal{C}$ be as above, and suppose that $\mathcal{D}$ has independent symbols. Fix $\varepsilon > 0$. Then*

$$\mathbb{E}_f \max_{z \in \Sigma^n} \max_{\Lambda \subset \mathcal{C}_0, |\Lambda| = L} \sum_{c \in \Lambda} \mathrm{agr}(f(c), z) \leq \mathcal{E} + Y + \sqrt{\mathcal{E}Y},$$

where

$$Y = CL \log(N) \log^5(L)$$

for an absolute constant C. For $|\Sigma| = 2$, we have

$$\mathbb{E}_f \max_{x \in \Sigma^n} \max_{\Lambda \subset \mathcal{C}_0, |\Lambda| = L} \sum_{c \in \Lambda} \mathrm{agr}(f(c), z) \leq \mathcal{E} + CL \sqrt{n \ln(N)}.$$

Theorem 2 makes the intuition above more precise: Any "random enough" operation (that is, an operation with independent symbols) of a code with good "average-radius list-decodability" (that is, good $\mathcal{E}(\mathcal{C}_0, \mathcal{D})$) will result in a code which is also list-decodable. In the full version, we show that Theorem 2 in fact implies the same result when "random enough" is taken to be mean that $\mathcal{D}$ has symbols drawn independently at random instead:

COROLLARY 1. *Theorem 2 holds when "independent symbols" is replaced by "symbols drawn independently without replacement".*

In this work, we answer Questions 1 and 2 by coming up with useful distributions $\mathcal{D}$ on functions f and computing the parameter $\mathcal{E}$. To do this, we will make use of some average-radius Johnson bounds; see the full version of the paper for more details.

Random Column Operations.

Our result on random subcodes follows from a simple probabilistic method. The argument for showing that the parameters in this positive result cannot be improved, we construct a specific code $\mathcal{C}_0$. The code $\mathcal{C}_0$ consists of various "clusters", where each cluster is the set of all vectors that are close to some vector in another code C^*. The code C^* has the property that it is list decodable from a large fraction of errors and that for smaller error rate its list size is suitably smaller— the existence of such a code with exponentially many vectors follows from the standard random coding argument. This allows the original code $\mathcal{C}_0$ to even have good average-radius list decodability. The fact that the cluster vectors are very close to some codeword in C^* (as well as the fact that C^* has large enough distance) basically then shows that the union bound used to prove the positive result is tight.

4. GENERAL RESULTS

In this section, we state our results about the effects of some particular random operations—XOR, aggregation, and

subcodes—on list-decodability. In Section 5, we will revisit these operations and resolve Questions 1, 2 and 3.

4.1 Random t-wise XOR

In this section, we consider the row-operation of t-wise XOR. We prove the following theorem.

THEOREM 3. *Let $\mathcal{C}_0 \in \mathbb{F}_2^{n_0 \times N}$ be a code with distance $0 < \delta_0 < 1/2$. Let $\mathcal{D} = (\mathcal{U}_{\oplus, t})^n$, as defined in Section 2, and consider the code operation $f \sim \mathcal{D}$. Suppose that $t = 4 \ln(1/\varepsilon) \delta_0^{-1}$. Then for sufficiently small $\varepsilon > 0$ and large enough n, with probability $1 - o(1)$, $\mathcal{C} = f(\mathcal{C}_0)$ is $(1/2(1 - O(\varepsilon)), \varepsilon^{-2})$-average-radius list decodable and has rate $\Omega(\varepsilon^2)$.*

With the goal of using Theorem 2, we begin by computing the quantity $\mathcal{E}(\mathcal{C}_0, \mathcal{D})$.

LEMMA 1. *Let $\mathcal{C}_0 \in \mathbb{F}_2^{n_0}$ be a code with distance δ_0, and suppose $t \geq \frac{4 \ln(1/\varepsilon)}{\delta_0}$. Then*

$$\mathcal{E}(\mathcal{C}_0, \mathcal{D}) \leq \frac{n}{2} \left(L(1 + \varepsilon) + \sqrt{L} \right).$$

The proof of Lemma 1 follows from an application of an average-radius Johnson bound. See the full version of the paper for more on these bounds and for the proof. Given Lemma 1, Theorem 2 implies that with constant probability,

$$\max_{z \in \mathbb{F}_2^n} \max_{\Lambda \subset \mathcal{C}, |\Lambda| = L} \frac{1}{L} \sum_{c \in \Lambda} \mathrm{agr}(c, z) \leq \frac{\mathcal{E}}{L} + C \sqrt{n \ln(N)}$$

$$\leq \frac{n}{2} \left(1 + \varepsilon + \frac{1}{\sqrt{L}} \right) + C \sqrt{n \ln N}.$$

In particular, if $C \sqrt{n \ln N} \leq \varepsilon n$, then in the favorable case $\mathcal{C}$ is $(\rho, L - 1)$-average-radius list-decodable, for $L = \varepsilon^{-2}$ and $\rho = \frac{1}{2} \cdot (1 - C'\varepsilon)$ for some constant C'.

It remains to verify the rate R of $\mathcal{C}$. Notice that if $|\mathcal{C}| = N$, then we are done, because then the requirement $C \sqrt{n \ln(N)} \leq \varepsilon n$ reads

$$R = \frac{\log_2(N)}{n} \leq \frac{\varepsilon^2}{C \ln(2)}.$$

We argue in the full version that f is injective with high probability, and so in the favorable case $|\mathcal{C}| = N$. This completes the proof of Theorem 3.

REMARK 5 (RANDOM INNER PRODUCTS FOR $q > 2$). *For our application (Question 1), $q = 2$ is the interesting case. However, our arguments go through for $q > 2$.*

4.2 Random t-wise aggregation

Theorem 4 below analyzes t-wise aggregation in two parameter regimes. In the first parameter regime, we address Question 2, and we consider t-wise direct product where $n_0 = nt$. In this case, final code $\mathcal{C}$ will have the same rate as the original code $\mathcal{C}_0$, and so in order for $\mathcal{C}$ to be list-decodable up to radius $1 - \varepsilon$, the rate R_0 of $\mathcal{C}_0$ must be $O(\varepsilon)$. Item 1 shows that if this necessary condition is met (with some logarithmic slack), then $\mathcal{C}$ is indeed list-decodable up to $1 - \varepsilon$. In the second parameter regime, we consider what can happen when the rate R_0 of $\mathcal{C}_0$ is significantly larger. In this case, we cannot hope to take n as small as n_0/t and hope for list-decodability up to $1 - \varepsilon$. The second part of Theorem 4 shows that we may take n nearly as small as the list-decoding capacity theorem allows.

THEOREM 4. *There are constants C_i, $i = 0, \ldots, 5$, so that the following holds. Suppose $q > 1/\varepsilon^2$. Let $\mathcal{C}_0 \subset \mathbb{F}_q^{n_0}$ be a code with distance $\delta_0 \geq C_2 > 0$.*

1. *Suppose $t \geq C_0 \log(1/\varepsilon) \geq 4 \ln(1/\varepsilon)/\delta_0$. Suppose that $\mathcal{C}_0$ has rate*

$$R_0 \leq \frac{C_1 \varepsilon}{\log(q) t \log^5(1/\varepsilon)}.$$

Let $n = n_0/t$, and let $\mathcal{D} = (\mathcal{U}_{t,\mathrm{dp}})^n$ be the t-wise aggregation operation of Section 2. Draw $f \sim \mathcal{D}$, and let $\mathcal{C} = f(\mathcal{C}_0)$. Then with high probability, $\mathcal{C}$ is $(1 - C_3\varepsilon, 1/\varepsilon)$-average-radius list-decodable, and further the rate R of $\mathcal{C}$ satisfies $R = R_0$.

2. *Suppose that $t \geq 4 \ln(1/\varepsilon)/\delta_0$, and suppose that $\mathcal{C}_0$ has rate R_0 so that*

$$R_0 \leq \left(\frac{nt}{n_0}\right)\left(\frac{\log(1/\varepsilon)}{\log(q)}\right).$$

Choose n so that

$$n \geq \frac{\log(N)\log(1/\varepsilon)}{\varepsilon}.$$

Let $\mathcal{D} = (\mathcal{U}_{t,\mathrm{dp}})^n$ be the t-wise aggregation operation of Section 2. Draw $f \sim \mathcal{D}$, and let $\mathcal{C} = f(\mathcal{C}_0)$. Then with high probability, $\mathcal{C}$ is $(1 - C_4\varepsilon, 1/\varepsilon)$-average-radius list-decodable, and the rate R of $\mathcal{C}$ is at least

$$R \geq \frac{C_5 \varepsilon}{t \log(q) \log^5(1/\varepsilon)}.$$

The rest of this section is devoted to the proof of Theorem 4. As before, it suffices to control $\mathcal{E}(\mathcal{C}_0, \mathcal{D})$.

LEMMA 2. *With the set-up above, we have*

$$\mathcal{E}(\mathcal{C}_0, \mathcal{D}) \leq Cn.$$

Again, the proof of Lemma 2 follows from an average-radius Johnson bound and can be found in the full version. Then by Theorem 2, recalling that

$$Y = CL \log(N) \log^5(L),$$

and $N = |\mathcal{C}_0|$, we have with high probability that

$$\mathbb{E}_f \max_{z \in \Sigma^n} \max_{\Lambda \subset \mathcal{C}_0, |\Lambda| = L} \sum_{c \in \Lambda} \mathrm{agr}(f(c), z)$$
$$\leq \mathcal{E}(\mathcal{C}_0, \mathcal{D}) + Y + \sqrt{\mathcal{E}(\mathcal{C}_0, \mathcal{D})Y}$$
$$\leq O\left(L \log(N) \log^5(L) + n\right).$$

In the favorable case,

$$\mathbb{E}_f \max_{z \in \Sigma^n} \max_{\Lambda \subset \mathcal{C}, |\Lambda| = L} \frac{1}{L} \sum_{c \in \Lambda} \mathrm{agr}(c, z)$$
$$\leq O\left(\log(N) \log^5(L) + n/L\right)$$
$$= O\left(\log(N) \log^5(1/\varepsilon) + n\varepsilon\right). \quad (2)$$

As before, $\mathcal{C}$ is $(1 - C\varepsilon, L - 1)$ average-radius list-decodable, for some constant C, as long as the right hand side is no more than $O(n\varepsilon)$. This holds as long as

$$\log(N) \log^5(1/\varepsilon) \leq n\varepsilon. \quad (3)$$

We need to show that (3) holds for our choices of n. First, we prove item 1 and we focus on the case that $n_0 = nt$; this

mimics the parameter regime the definition of folding (which addresses Question 2). Given $n_0 = nt$, we can translate (3) into a condition on R_0, the rate of $\mathcal{C}_0$. We have

$$R_0 = \frac{\log_q(N)}{n_0} = \frac{\log_q(N)}{nt},$$

and so translating (3) into a requirement on $R(\mathcal{C}_0)$, we see that as long as

$$R_0 \lesssim \frac{\varepsilon}{\log(q) t \log^5(1/\varepsilon)} \lesssim \frac{\varepsilon}{\log(q) \log^6(1/\varepsilon)},$$

then with high probability $\mathcal{C}$ is $(1 - C\varepsilon, L)$-list-decodable. Choose n so that this holds. It remains to verify that the rate R of $\mathcal{C}$ is the same as the rate R_0 of $\mathcal{C}_0$. The (straightforward) proof can be found in the full version of the paper.

CLAIM 5. *With $\mathcal{C}_0$ as above and with $n_0 = nt$, $|\mathcal{C}| = N$ with probability at least $1 - o(1)$.*

By a union bound, with high probability both the favorable event (2) occurs, and Claim 5 holds. In this case, $\mathcal{C}$ is $(1 - C\varepsilon, L)$-list-decodable, and the rate R of $\mathcal{C}$ is

$$R = R_0.$$

Next, we consider Item 2, where we may choose $n < n_0/t$, thus increasing the rate. It remains true that as long as (3) holds, then $\mathcal{C}$ is $(1 - C\varepsilon, L)$-list-decodable. Again translating the condition (3) into a condition on $\log_{q^t}(N)/n$, we see that as long as

$$\frac{\log_{q^t}(N)}{n} \leq \frac{\varepsilon}{t \log(q) \log^5(1/\varepsilon)}, \quad (4)$$

then $\mathcal{C}$ is $(1 - C\varepsilon, L)$-list-decodable. Now we must verify that the left-hand-side of (4) is indeed the rate R of $\mathcal{C}$, that is, that $|\mathcal{C}| = N$. As before, the proof is straightforward and can be found in the full version of the paper.

CLAIM 6. *With $\mathcal{C}_0$ as above and with n arbitrary, $|\mathcal{C}| = N$ with probability at least $1 - o(1)$.*

Now, recalling our choice of n in (4), with high probability both (2) occurs and Claim 6 holds. In the favorable case, $\mathcal{C}$ is $(1 - C\varepsilon, L)$-list-decodable, as long as the rate R satisfies

$$R = \frac{\log_{q^t}(|\mathcal{C}|)}{n} = \frac{\log_{q^t}(N)}{n} \leq \frac{C\varepsilon}{t \log^5(1/\varepsilon) \log(q)}.$$

This completes the proof of Theorem 4.

4.3 Random sub-codes

In this section we address the case of random sub-codes. Unlike the previous sections, the machinery of [RW14, Woo13] does not apply, and so we prove the results in this section directly. We have the following proposition.

PROPOSITION 1. *Let $\mathcal{C}_0$ be any (ρ, L_0)-list decodable q-ary code. Let $\mathcal{C}$ be a random sub-code of $\mathcal{C}_0$ with $N = pN_0$ (as in the definition in Section 2), where $p = \frac{1}{q^{\varepsilon n} \cdot L_0}$. With probability $1 - o(1)$, the random subcode $\mathcal{C}$ is $\left(\rho, \frac{3}{\varepsilon}\right)$-list decodable. Further, the number of distinct columns n $\mathcal{C}$ is at least $pN_0/2$.*

The proof of Proposition 1 follows straightforwardly from some Chernoff bounds and can be found in the full version of the paper.

Proposition 1 only works for the usual notion of list decodability. It is natural to wonder if a similar result holds for average-radius list decodability. We show that such a result indeed holds (though with slightly weaker parameters) in the full version.

It is also natural to wonder if one can pick a larger value of p—closer to $1/L_0$ than to $1/(q^{\varepsilon n}L_0)$—in the statement of Proposition 1. In particular, if L_0 is polynomial in n, could we pick $p = q^{-o(\varepsilon n)}$? In the full version of the paper, we show that this is not in general possible. More precisely, we show the following theorem.

THEOREM 7. *For every $\rho > 0$, and for every $0 < \alpha < \frac{1-\rho}{12}$, and for every n sufficiently large, there exists a code $\mathcal{C}_0$ with block length n that is (ρ, n)-average-radius list decodable such that the following holds. Let $\mathcal{C}$ be obtained by picking a random sub-code of $\mathcal{C}_0$ of size $N = pN_0$ where $p = q^{-\alpha n}/n$. Then with high probability if $\mathcal{C}$ is (ρ', L)-list decodable for any $\rho' \geq 1/n$, then $L \geq \Omega(1/\alpha)$.*

5. APPLICATIONS

Finally, we use the results of Section 4 to resolve Questions 1, 2, and 3.

5.1 Linear time near optimal list decodable codes

First, we answer Question 1, and give linear-time encodable binary codes with the optimal trade-off between rate and list-decoding radius. Our codes will work as follows. We begin with a linear-time encodable code with constant rate and constant distance; we will use Spielman's variant on expander codes [Spi96, Theorem 19]. These codes have rate $1/4$, and distance $\delta_0 \geq 0$ (a small positive constant). Notice that a random puncturing of $\mathcal{C}_0$ (as in [Woo13, RW14]) will not work, as $\mathcal{C}_0$ does not have good enough distance—however, a random XOR, as in Section 4.1 will do the trick.

COROLLARY 2. *There is a randomized construction of binary codes $\mathcal{C} \in \mathbb{F}_2^n$ so that the following hold with probability $1 - o(1)$, for any sufficiently small ε and any sufficiently large n.*

1. *$\mathcal{C}$ is encodable in time $O(n\ln(1/\varepsilon))$.*

2. *$\mathcal{C}$ is (ρ, L)-average-radius list-decodable with $\rho = \frac{1}{2}(1 - C\varepsilon)$ and $L = \varepsilon^{-2}$, where C is an absolute constant.*

3. *$\mathcal{C}$ has rate $\Omega(\varepsilon^2)$.*

Indeed, let $\mathcal{C}_0$ be as above. Let $t = 4\ln(1/\varepsilon)\delta_0^{-1}$, and choose $f \sim (\mathcal{U}_{\oplus,t})^n$, as in Theorem 3. Let $\mathcal{C} = f(\mathcal{C}_0)$. Items 2. and 3. follow immediately from Theorem 3, so it remains to verify Item 1 of Theorem 2, that $\mathcal{C}$ is linear-time encodable. Indeed, we have $\mathcal{C}(x) = A\mathcal{C}_0(x)$, where $A \in \mathbb{F}_2^{n \times n_0}$ is a matrix whose rows are binary vectors with at most t nonzeros each. In particular, the time to multiply by A is $nt = O(n\ln(1/\varepsilon))$, as claimed.

5.2 Random Folding

Next, we further discuss Question 2, which asked for a rigorous version of the intuition behind results for folded Reed-Solomon codes and expander-based symbol aggregation. The intuition is that increasing the alphabet size effectively reduces the number of error patterns a decoder has to

handle, thus making it easier to list-decode. To make this intuition more clear, consider the following example when $q = 2$. Consider an error pattern that corrupts a $1 - 2\varepsilon$ fraction of the *odd* positions (the rest do not have errors). This error pattern must be handled by any decoder which can list decode from $1/2 - \varepsilon$ fraction of errors. On the other hand, consider a 2-folding (with partition as above) of the code; now the alphabet size has increased, so we hope to correct $1 - 1/2^2 - \varepsilon = 3/4 - \varepsilon$ fraction of errors. However, the earlier error pattern affects a $1 - 2\varepsilon$ of the new, folded symbols. Thus, in the folded scenario, an optimal decoder need not handle this error pattern, since $1 - 2\varepsilon > 3/4 - \varepsilon$ (for small enough ε).

In Theorem 4, Item 1, we have shown that if $\mathcal{C}_0$ is any code with distance bounded away from 0 and with rate sufficiently small (slightly sublinear in ε), has abundant random t-wise aggregation of symbols which are list-decodable up to a $1 - \varepsilon$ fraction of errors, when $n = n_0/t$ and t is large enough (depending only on ε and q). This is the same parameter regime as folded Reed-Solomon codes (up to logarithmic factors in the rate), and thus the Theorem answers Question 2 insofar as it lends a rigorous way to interpret t-wise aggregation in this parameter regime.

REMARK 6. *While the intuition above applies equally well to folding and more general t-wise symbol aggregation, We note that a random folding and a random symbol aggregation are not the same thing. In the latter, the symbols of the new code may overlap, while in the former they may not. However, allowing overlap makes our computations simple; since the goal was to better understand the intuition above, we have done our analysis for the simpler case of t-wise symbol aggregation. It is an interesting open question to find a (clean) argument for the folding operation, perhaps along the lines of the argument of Corollary 1 for puncturing vs. sampling.*

5.3 Applications of random sub-codes

Finally, we observe that Proposition 1 immediately answers Question 3 in the affirmative. Indeed, suppose that $\mathcal{C}_0$ is (ρ_0, L_0)-list-decodable with rate R_0. Then Proposition 1 implies that with high probability, for any sufficiently small ε, a random subcode of rate

$$R_0 - O\left(\varepsilon \log(q) + \frac{\log(L_0)}{n}\right)$$

is $(\rho_0, 3/\varepsilon)$-list-decodable. In particular, if we start out with a binary code with constant rate and large but subexponential list size, the resulting subcode will also have constant rate, and constant list size.

For example, this has immediate applicatons for Reed-Solomon codes. Guruswami and Xing [GX13] showed that for every real R, $0 < \varepsilon < 1 - R$ and prime power q, there is an integer $m > 1$ such that Reed-Solomon codes defined over $\mathbb{F}_{q^m}$ with the evaluation points being $\mathbb{F}_q$ of rate R can be list decoded from the optimal $1 - R - \varepsilon$ fraction of errors with list size N^ε. Thus, Proposition 1 implies that random sub-codes of these codes are optimally list decodable (in all the parameters). We remark that this result also follows from the work of Guruswami and Xing [GX13]; our argument above is arguably simpler, but does not come with an algorithmic guarantee as results of [GX13] do.

Given Proposition 1, it is natural to ask about the list-decodability of the subcode $\mathcal{C}$ when the error radius ρ may be different than ρ_0. It turns out that this also follows from Proposition 1: below, we will use Proposition 1 to argue that if a code $\mathcal{C}_0$ is optimally list decodable for some fixed $\rho_0 > 0$ fraction of errors, then its random subcodes with high probability are optimally list decodable from ρ fraction of errors for any $\rho_0 \le \rho < 1 - 1/q$. Towards that end, we will make the following simple observation:

LEMMA 3. *Let $\mathcal{C}$ be (ρ, L)-list decodable q-ary code. Then for every $\rho \le \rho' < 1 - 1/q$, $\mathcal{C}$ is also (ρ', L')-list decodable, where*

$$L' \le L \cdot q^{n(H_q(\rho') - H_q(\rho) + o(1))} \cdot 2^n.$$

PROOF. Consider a received word $y \in [q]^n$ such that $|\mathcal{C} \cap B_q(y, \rho'n)| = L'$. Now we claim that there exists a $z \in B_q(y, \rho'n)$ such that

$$|B_q(z, \rho n) \cap \mathcal{C}| \ge L' \cdot \frac{(q-1)^{\rho n}}{|B_q(y, \rho'n)|} \tag{5}$$

$$\ge L' \cdot \frac{q^{H_q(\rho)n - o(n)}}{2^n} \cdot \frac{1}{q^{H_q(\rho'n)}}. \tag{6}$$

In the above the second inequality follows from the following facts: volume of q-ary Hamming balls of radius γn are bounded from above by $q^{H_q(\gamma)n}$ and from below by $q^{H_q(\gamma)n - o(n)}$ (and that $\binom{n}{\rho n}(q-1)^{\rho n} \ge q^{H_q(\rho)n - o(n)}$). (6) along with the fact that $\mathcal{C}$ is (ρ, L)-list decodable proves the claimed bound on L'.

To complete the proof we argue (5): we show the existence of z by the probabilistic method: pick $z \in B_q(y, \rho'n)$ uniformly at random. Fix a $c \in \mathcal{C} \cap B_q(y, \rho'n)$. Then

$$\mathbb{P}\{c \in B_q(z, \rho n)\} = \frac{|B_q(c, \rho n) \cap B_q(y, \rho'n)|}{B_q(y, \rho'n)}.$$

Next we argue that

$$|B_q(c, \rho n) \cap B_q(y, \rho'n)| \ge (q-1)^{\rho n}. \tag{7}$$

Note that the above implies that

$$\mathbb{E}\left[|B_q(z, \rho n) \cap \mathcal{C}|\right] \ge L' \cdot \frac{(q-1)^{\rho n}}{|B_q(y, \rho'n)|},$$

which would prove (5). To see why (7) is true, consider any ρn positions where c and y agree on. Note that if we change all of those values (to any of the $(q-1)^{\rho n}$ possibilities) to obtain c', then we have $d(c', y) \le \rho'n$ and $d(c', c) = \rho n$, which proves (7). $\square$

Lemma 3 along with Proposition 1 implies the following.

COROLLARY 3. *Let $q \ge 2^{1/\varepsilon}$. Let $\mathcal{C}_0$ be a (ρ, L)-list decodable q-ary code with optimal rate $1 - H_q(\rho) - \varepsilon$. Then for any $\rho' \ge \rho$, with probability at least $1 - o(1)$, a random subcode $\mathcal{C}$ of $\mathcal{C}_0$ of rate $1 - H_q(\rho') - O(\varepsilon)$ is $(\rho', O(1/\varepsilon))$-list decodable.*

REMARK 7. *The bound in Lemma 3 is tight up to the $q^{o(n)} \cdot 2^n$ factor. In particular, one cannot have a bound of $L \cdot q^{\gamma n}$ for any $\gamma < H_q(\rho') - H_q(\rho)$ since that would contradict the list decoding capacity bounds.*

6. OPEN QUESTIONS

In this work we have made some (modest) progress on understanding on how random row and column operations change the list decodability of codes. We believe that our work highlights many interesting open questions. We list some of our favorites below:

1. Theorem 4 is proved for random t-wise direct product codes. It would be nice to prove the analog of item 1 in Theorem 4 for random t-wise folding so that we can formally answer Question 2 in the affirmative.

2. We did not present any results for random t-wise interleaving. Gopalan, Guruswami and Raghavendra have shown that for any code $\mathcal{C}_0$ its t-wise interleaved code $\mathcal{C}$ (that is the code that deterministically applies all possible basic column operations that bunch together the $\binom{N_0}{t}$ subsets of columns of size t) the list decodability does not change by much [GGR11]. In particular, they show that if $\mathcal{C}_0$ is (ρ, L)-list decodable then $\mathcal{C}$ is $(\rho, L^{O(1)})$-list decodable. However, for *random t-wise interleaving* the list decoding radius might actually improve.[6] We leave open the question of resolving this possibility.

3. As mentioned above, our work, and the results of Guruswami and Xing [GX13], shows that random subcodes of Reed-Solomon codes over $\mathbb{F}_{q^m}$ (for large enough m) with evaluation points from the sub-field $\mathbb{F}_q$ have optimal list decodable properties. We believe that we should be able to derive such a result even if we start from any Reed-Solomon codes or at the very least if one starts off with a randomly punctured Reed-Solomon codes. Note that even though the results of [RW14] give near optimal list decodability results of Reed-Solomon codes, their results are logarithmic factors off from the optimal rate bounds. Proposition 1 implies that it suffices to prove a non-trivial exponential bound on the list size for list decoding rate R Reed-Solomon codes from $1 - R - \varepsilon$ fraction of errors—a special case of this is proved in [GX13], but the general question is open.

4. All of our results so far only use either just random row operation or just random column operations. An open question is to find applications where random row and column operations could be use together to obtain better results than either on their own. The above point would be such an example, if resolved.

Acknowledgments

We thank Swastik Kopparty and Shubhangi Saraf for initial discussions on Questions 1 and 2 (and for indeed suggesting the random XOR as an operation to consider) and Dagstuhl for providing the venue for these initial discussions. We thank Venkat Guruswami for helpful discussions. Finally, we thank Parikshit Gopalan for pointing the connection of our results to existing results on XOR and direct product codes. MW also thanks the theory group at IBM Almaden for their hospitality during part of this work.

7. REFERENCES

[CGV13] Mahdi Cheraghchi, Venkatesan Guruswami, and Ameya Velingker. Restricted isometry of fourier matrices and list decodability of random linear codes. In *Proceedings of the 24th Annual*

---

[6]If this were to be the case then this could formalize the reason why the Parvaresh-Vardy codes [PV05], which are sub-codes of interleaving of Reed-Solomon codes, have good list decodability properties.

ACM-SIAM Symposium on Discrete Algorithms (SODA), pages 432–442, 2013.

[DL12] Zeev Dvir and Shachar Lovett. Subspace evasive sets. In *Proceedings of the 44th Symposium on Theory of Computing Conference (STOC)*, pages 351–358, 2012.

[Eli57] Peter Elias. List decoding for noisy channels. *Technical Report 335, Research Laboratory of Electronics, MIT*, 1957.

[GGR11] Parikshit Gopalan, Venkatesan Guruswami, and Prasad Raghavendra. List decoding tensor products and interleaved codes. *SIAM J. Comput.*, 40(5):1432–1462, 2011.

[GI01] Venkatesan Guruswami and Piotr Indyk. Expander-based constructions of efficiently decodable codes. In *Proceedings of the 42nd Annual IEEE Symposium on the Foundations of Computer Science (FOCS)*, pages 658–667. IEEE, 2001.

[GI03] Venkatesan Guruswami and Piotr Indyk. Linear time encodable and list decodable codes. In *Proceedings of the 35th Annual ACM Symposium on Theory of Computing (STOC)*, pages 126–135, 2003.

[GI05] Venkatesan Guruswami and Piotr Indyk. Linear-time encodable/decodable codes with near-optimal rate. *IEEE Transactions on Information Theory*, 51(10):3393–3400, 2005.

[GK13] Venkatesan Guruswami and Swastik Kopparty. Explicit subspace designs. In *FOCS*, 2013. To appear.

[GN13] Venkatesan Guruswami and Srivatsan Narayanan. Combinatorial limitations of average-radius list decoding. *RANDOM*, 2013.

[GR08] Venkatesan Guruswami and Atri Rudra. Explicit codes achieving list decoding capacity: Error-correction with optimal redundancy. *IEEE Transactions on Information Theory*, 54(1):135–150, 2008.

[GR09] Venkatesan Guruswami and Atri Rudra. Error correction up to the information-theoretic limit. *Commun. ACM*, 52(3):87–95, 2009.

[GR10] Venkatesan Guruswami and Atri Rudra. The existence of concatenated codes list-decodable up to the hamming bound. *IEEE Transactions on Information Theory*, 56(10):5195–5206, 2010.

[Gur04] Venkatesan Guruswami. *List Decoding of Error-Correcting Codes (Winning Thesis of the 2002 ACM Doctoral Dissertation Competition)*, volume 3282 of *Lecture Notes in Computer Science*. Springer, 2004.

[Gur11] Venkatesan Guruswami. Linear-algebraic list decoding of folded reed-solomon codes. In *IEEE Conference on Computational Complexity*, pages 77–85, 2011.

[GW13] Venkatesan Guruswami and Carol Wang. Linear-algebraic list decoding for variants of reed-solomon codes. *IEEE Transactions on Information Theory*, 59(6):3257–3268, 2013.

[GX12] Venkatesan Guruswami and Chaoping Xing. Folded codes from function field towers and improved optimal rate list decoding. In

Proceedings of the 44th Symposium on Theory of Computing Conference (STOC), pages 339–350, 2012.

[GX13] Venkatesan Guruswami and Chaoping Xing. List decoding reed-solomon, algebraic-geometric, and gabidulin subcodes up to the singleton bound. In *Proceedings of the 45th ACM Symposium on the Theory of Computing (STOC)*, pages 843–852, 2013.

[GX14] Venkatesan Guruswami and Chaoping Xing. Optimal rate list decoding of folded algebraic-geometric codes over constant-sized alphabets. In *Proceedings of the Twenty-Fifth Annual ACM-SIAM Symposium on Discrete Algorithms (SODA)*, pages 1858–1866, 2014.

[IJKW10] Russell Impagliazzo, Ragesh Jaiswal, Valentine Kabanets, and Avi Wigderson. Uniform direct product theorems: Simplified, optimized, and derandomized. *SIAM J. Comput.*, 39(4):1637–1665, 2010.

[Kop12] Swastik Kopparty. List-decoding multiplicity codes. *Electronic Colloquium on Computational Complexity (ECCC)*, 19:44, 2012.

[PV05] Farzad Parvaresh and Alexander Vardy. Correcting errors beyond the guruswami-sudan radius in polynomial time. In *Proceedings of the 46th Annual IEEE Symposium on Foundations of Computer Science (FOCS)*, pages 285–294, 2005.

[RW14] Atri Rudra and Mary Wootters. Every list-decodable code for high noise has abundant near-optimal rate puncturings. In *Proceedings of the 46th annual ACM Symposium on the Theory of Computing (STOC)*, 2014.

[Spi96] Daniel A. Spielman. Linear-time encodable and decodable error-correcting codes. *IEEE Transactions on Information Theory*, 42(6):1723–1731, 1996.

[Sud00] Madhu Sudan. List decoding: algorithms and applications. *SIGACT News*, 31(1):16–27, 2000.

[Tre03] Luca Trevisan. List-decoding using the xor lemma. In *Proceedings of the 44th Symposium on Foundations of Computer Science (FOCS)*, pages 126–135, 2003.

[Woo13] Mary Wootters. On the list decodability of random linear codes with large error rates. In *Proceedings of the 45th annual ACM Symposium on the Theory of Computing (STOC)*, pages 853–860. ACM, 2013.

[Woz58] John M. Wozencraft. List Decoding. *Quarterly Progress Report, Research Laboratory of Electronics, MIT*, 48:90–95, 1958.

[ZP82] Victor V. Zyablov and Mark S. Pinsker. List cascade decoding. *Problems of Information Transmission*, 17(4):29–34, 1981 (in Russian); pp. 236-240 (in English), 1982.

Verifiably Truthful Mechanisms

Simina Brânzei
Computer Science Department
University of Aarhus, Denmark
simina@cs.au.dk

Ariel D. Procaccia
Computer Science Department
Carnegie Mellon University, USA
arielpro@cs.cmu.edu

ABSTRACT

It is typically expected that if a mechanism is truthful, then the agents would, indeed, truthfully report their private information. But why would an agent *believe* that the mechanism is truthful? We wish to design truthful mechanisms that are "simple", that is, whose truthfulness can be verified efficiently (in the computational sense). Our approach involves three steps: (i) specifying the structure of mechanisms, (ii) constructing a verification algorithm, and (iii) measuring the quality of verifiably truthful mechanisms. We demonstrate this approach using a case study: approximate mechanism design without money for facility location.

Categories and Subject Descriptors

F.m [**Theory of Computation**]: Miscellaneous; J.4 [**Social and Behavioral Sciences**]: Economics

Keywords

Mechanism Design, Decision Trees, Verification, Facility Location, Approximation

1. INTRODUCTION

The mechanism design literature includes a vast collection of clever schemes that, in most cases, provably give rise to a specified set of properties. Arguably, the most sought-after property is *truthfulness*, more formally known as *incentive compatibility* or *strategyproofness*: an agent must not be able to benefit from dishonestly revealing its private information. Truthfulness is, in a sense, a prerequisite for achieving other theoretical guarantees, because without it the mechanism may receive unpredictable input information that has little to do with reality. For example, if the designer's goal is to maximize utilitarian social welfare (the sum of agents' utilities for the outcome), but the mechanism is not truthful, the mechanism would indeed maximize social welfare — albeit, presumably, with respect to the wrong utility functions!

An implicit assumption underlying the preceding (rather standard) reasoning is that when a truthful mechanism is used, (rational) agents would participate truthfully. This requires the agents to *believe* that the mechanism is actually truthful. Why would this be the case? Well, in principle the agents can look up the proof of truthfulness.[1] A more viable option is to directly verify truthfulness by examining the specification of the mechanism itself, but, from a computational complexity viewpoint, this problem would typically be extremely hard — even undecidable. This observation is related to the more general principle that the mechanism should be transparent and simple, so that bounded-rational economic agents can reason about it and take decisions efficiently.

Motivated by the preceding arguments, our goal in this paper is to design mechanisms that are *verifiably truthful*. Specifically, we would like the verification to be *efficient* — in the computational sense (i.e., polynomial time), not the economic sense. In other words, the mechanism must be truthful, and, moreover, each agent must be able to efficiently verify this fact.

1.1 Our Approach and Results

Our approach to the design of verifiably truthful mechanisms involves three steps:

(I) *Specifying the structure of mechanisms*: The verification algorithm will receive a mechanism as input — so we must rigorously specify which mechanisms are admissible as input, and what they look like.

(II) *Constructing a verification algorithm*: Given a mechanism in the specified format, the algorithm decides whether the mechanism is truthful.

(III) *Measuring the quality of verifiably truthful mechanisms*: The whole endeavor is worthwhile (if and) only if the family of mechanisms whose truthfulness can be verified efficiently (via the algorithm of Step 2) is rich enough to provide high-quality outcomes.

We instantiate this program in the context of a case study: *approximate mechanism design without money for facility location* [27]. The reason for choosing this specific domain is twofold. First, a slew of recent papers has brought about a good understanding of what quality guarantees are achievable via truthful facility location mechanisms [1, 21, 20, 25,

---

[1]A related, interesting question is: If we told human players that a non-truthful mechanism is provably truthful, would they play truthfully?

13, 14, 15, 29, 30, 8, 32]. Second, facility location has also served as a proof of concept for the approximate mechanism design without money agenda [27], whose principles were subsequently applied to a variety of other domains, including allocation problems [17, 16, 12, 9], approval voting [2], kidney exchange [3, 7], and scheduling [19]. Similarly, facility location serves as an effective proof of concept for the idea of verifiably truthful mechanisms, which, we believe, is widely applicable.

We present our results according to the three steps above:

(I) In §2, we put forward a representation of facility location mechanisms. In general, these are arbitrary functions mapping the reported locations of n agents on the real line to the facility location (also on the real line). We present *deterministic* mechanisms as *decision trees*, which branch on comparison queries in internal nodes, and return a function that is a convex combination of the reported locations in the leaves. Roughly speaking, randomized mechanisms are distributions over deterministic mechanisms, but we use a slightly more expressive model to enable a concise representation for certain randomized mechanisms that would otherwise need a huge representation.

(II) The *cost* of an agent is the distance between its (actual) location, which is its private information, and the facility location. A deterministic mechanism is truthful if an agent can never decrease its cost by reporting a false location. In §3, we show that the truthfulness of a deterministic mechanism can be verified in polynomial time in the size of its decision tree representation and number of agents. We also demonstrate that one cannot do much better: it is necessary to at least inspect all the tree's leaves. We establish that the efficient verification result extends to randomized mechanisms, as long as the notion of truthfulness is *universal truthfulness*: it must be impossible to gain from manipulating one's reported location, regardless of the mechanism's coin tosses.

(III) Building on the results of Step II, we focus on decision trees of polynomial size — if such mechanisms are truthful, their truthfulness can be efficiently verified. In §4, we study the quality of polynomial-size decision trees, via two measures of quality: the *social cost* (the sum of agents' cost functions) and the *maximum cost* (of any agent). Figure 1 summarizes our results. The table on the top shows tight bounds on the (multiplicative, worst-case) approximation ratio that can be achieved by truthful mechanisms [27] — deterministic in the first row, randomized in the second. The (lower) bound for the maximum cost of universally truthful mechanisms is new. The results for efficiently verifiable mechanisms are shown in the bottom table. Our main results pertain to the social cost (left column): while deterministic polynomial-size decision trees only achieve an approximation ratio of $\Theta(n/\log n)$, we construct (for any constant $\epsilon > 0$) a polynomial-size, randomized, universally truthful decision tree approximating the social cost to a factor of $1 + \epsilon$.

1.2 Related Work

Verification is a common theme in algorithmic mechanism design, but in the past it was always the agents' reports that were being verified, not the properties of the mecha-

General Mechanisms	Social Cost	Max Cost
Truthful	1	2
Univ. Truthful	1	2 (*)

Polynomial-size Decision Trees	Social Cost	Max Cost
Truthful	$\Theta\left(\frac{n}{\log n}\right)$	2
Univ. Truthful	$1 + \epsilon$	2

Figure 1: The results of §4, outlined in §1.1. The lower bound (*) for general mechanisms is also shown here

nism itself. In fact, in the eponymous paper by Nisan and Ronen [24], a class of mechanisms with verification (and money) for scheduling was proposed. These mechanisms are allowed to observe both the reported types and the actual types (based on the execution of jobs), and payments may depend on both. Verification of agents' reports has subsequently played a role in a number of papers; of special note is the work of Caragiannis et al. [6], who focused on different notions of verification. They distinguished between *partial verification*, which restricts agents to reporting a subset of types that is a function of their true type (e.g., in scheduling agents can only report that they are slower than they actually are, not faster), and *probabilistic verification*, which catches an agent red handed with probability that depends on its true type and reported type. There are also examples of this flavor of verification in approximate mechanism design without money [19].

A small body of work in multiagent systems [26, 5, 28] actually aims to verify properties of mechanisms and games. The work of Tadjouddine et al. [28] is perhaps closest to ours, as they verify the truthfulness of auction mechanisms. Focusing on the Vickrey Auction [31], they specify it using the Promela process modeling language, and then verify its truthfulness via model checking techniques. This basically amounts to checking all possible bid vectors and deviations in a discretized bid space. To improve the prohibitive running time, abstract model checking techniques are applied. While model checking approaches are quite natural, they inevitably rely on heuristic solutions to problems that are generally very hard. In contrast, we are interested in mechanisms whose truthfulness can be verified *in polynomial time*.

Mu'alem [23] considers a motivating scenario similar to ours and focuses on testing extended monotonicity, which is a property required for truthfulness in the single parameter domain studied therein. In particular, Mu'alem shows that if a function f is ϵ-close to extended monotonicity, then there *exists* an associated payment function p such that the mechanism given by the tuple (f, p) is $(1 - 2\epsilon)$-truthful. She also describes a shifting technique for obtaining almost truthful mechanisms and a monotonicity tester. While studying truthfulness in the context of property testing remains an interesting question for future work, we would like to obtain mechanisms whose truthfulness can be verified exactly and in polynomial time (independent of the size of the domain — in fact, our domain is continuous). On a technical level, we study a setting without payments, which does not admit a close connection between monotonicity and truthfulness.

Kang and Parkes [18] consider the scenario in which multiple entities (e.g. companies, people, network services) can deploy mechanisms in an open computational infrastructure. Like us, they are interested in verifying the truthfulness of mechanisms, but they sidestep the question of how mechanisms are represented by focusing on what they call *passive verification*: their verifier acts as an intermediary and monitors the sequence of inputs and outputs of the mechanism. The verifier is required to be sound and complete; in particular, if the mechanism is not strategyproof, the verifier is guaranteed to establish this fact after observing all the possible inputs and outputs.

Our work is also related to the line of work on *automated mechanism design* [10], which seeks to automatically design truthful mechanisms that maximize an objective function, given a prior distribution over agents' types. In an informal sense, this problem is much more difficult than our verification problem, and, indeed, in general it is computationally hard even when the mechanism is explicitly represented as a function whose domain is all possible type vectors. Automated mechanism design is tractable in special cases — such as when the number of agents is constant and the mechanism is randomized — but these results do not yield nontrivial insights on the design of verifiably truthful mechanisms.

2. STEP I: SPECIFYING THE STRUCTURE OF MECHANISMS

We consider the (game-theoretic) facility location problem [27]. An instance includes a set $N = \{1, \ldots, n\}$ of agents. Each agent $i \in N$ has a location x_i. The vector $\mathbf{x} = \langle x_1, \ldots, x_n \rangle$ represents the location profile. We relegate the presentation of the strategic aspects to Section 3.

2.1 Deterministic Mechanisms

A *deterministic mechanism* (for n agents) is a function $\mathcal{M} : \mathbb{R}^n \to \mathbb{R}$, which maps each location profile $\mathbf{x}$ to a facility location $y \in \mathbb{R}$. We put forward a simple, yet expressive, representation of deterministic mechanisms, via *decision trees*.

In more detail, given input $\mathbf{x} = \langle x_1, \ldots, x_n \rangle$, the mechanism is represented as a tree, with:

- *Internal nodes*: used to verify sets of constraints over the input variables. We focus on a comparison-based model of computation, in which each internal node verifies one constraint, of the form $(x_i \geq x_j)$, $(x_i \leq x_j)$, $(x_i > x_j)$, or $(x_i < x_j)$, for some $i, j \in N$. The node has two outgoing edges, that are taken depending on whether the condition is true or false.

- *Leaves*: store the outcome of the mechanism if the path to that leaf is taken, i.e. the facility location. We require that for each leaf $\mathcal{L}$, the location of the facility at $\mathcal{L}$, $y_{\mathcal{L}}(x)$, is a convex combination of the input locations: $y_{\mathcal{L}}(\mathbf{x}) = \sum_{i=1}^{n} \lambda_{\mathcal{L},i} \cdot x_i$, where the $\lambda_{\mathcal{L},i}$ are constants with $\lambda_{\mathcal{L},i} \geq 0$ and $\sum_{i=1}^{n} \lambda_{\mathcal{L},i} = 1$.

The Average Mechanism   *Dictatorship of Agent i*

For example, the left figure (above) shows the decision tree representation of the average mechanism, which returns the average of the reported locations. It is just a single leaf, with

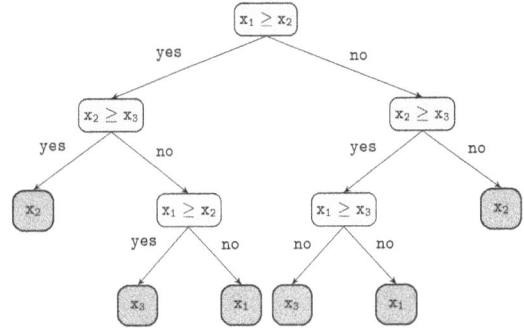

Figure 2: The median mechanism for 3 agents.

coefficients $\lambda_i = 1/n$ for all $i \in N$. The right figure shows a dictatorship of agent i — whatever location is reported by agent i is always selected. Figure 2 shows the median mechanism for $n = 3$, which returns the median of the three reported locations; this mechanism will play a key role later.

We remark that our positive results are based on mechanisms that have the so-called *peaks-only* property: they always select one of the reported locations. However, our more expressive definition of the leaves of the decision tree (as convex combinations of points in $\mathbf{x}$) is needed to compute optimal solutions under one of our two objectives (as we discuss below), and also strengthens our negative results.

2.2 Randomized Mechanisms

Intuitively, randomized mechanisms are allowed to make branching decisions based on coin tosses. Without loss of generality, we can just toss all possible coins in advance, so a randomized mechanism can be represented as a probability distribution over deterministic decision trees. However, this can lead to a large representation of simple mechanisms that consist of the same (fixed) subroutine executed with possibly different input variables. For example, the mechanism that selects a (not very small) subset of agents uniformly at random and computes the median of the subset can be seen as a median mechanism parameterized by the identities of the agents. In order to be able to represent such mechanisms concisely, we make the representation a bit more expressive.

Formally, a randomized mechanism is represented by a decision tree with a chance node of degree K as the root, such that the r'th edge selects a decision tree $\mathcal{T}_r$ and is taken with probability p_r, where $\sum_{i=1}^{K} p_i = 1$. Each tree $\mathcal{T}_r$ is defined as follows:

- There is a set of agents $N_r \subseteq N$, such that the locations x_i for $i \in N$ appear directly in the internal nodes and leaves of the tree.

- There is a set of parameters $Z_r = \{z_{r,1}, \ldots, z_{r,m_r}\}$, that also appear in the internal nodes and leaves of $\mathcal{T}_r$, where $0 \leq m_r \leq |N \setminus N_r|$.

- The description of $\mathcal{T}_r$ includes a probability distribution over tuples of m_r distinct agents from $N \setminus N_r$.

The semantics are as follows. At the beginning of the execution, a die is tossed to determine the index $r \in \{1, \ldots, K\}$ of the function (i.e. tree $\mathcal{T}_r$) to be implemented. Then, the parameters $z_{r,j}$ are bound to locations of agents from $N \setminus N_r$ according to the given probability distribution for $\mathcal{T}_r$; each

$z_{r,j}$ is bound to a different agent. At this point all the parameters in the nodes and leaves of $\mathcal{T}_r$ have been replaced by variables x_i, and we just have a deterministic decision tree, which is executed as described above.

For example, say we want to implement the mechanism that selects three agents uniformly at random from N and outputs the median of these three agents. This mechanism requires a randomized decision tree with a chance node of degree one, that selects with probability $p_1 = 1$ a single decision tree $\mathcal{T}_1$, which is the tree in Figure 2 with the x_i variables replaced by z_i. We set $N_1 = \emptyset$ (thus the tree $\mathcal{T}_1$ is completely parameterized), and the probability distribution over distinct subsets of size 3 from $N \setminus N_1 = N$ is just the uniform distribution over such subsets.

3. STEP II: CONSTRUCTING A VERIFICATION ALGORITHM

In Section 2 we focused on the non-strategic aspects of the facility location game: agents report their locations, which are mapped by a mechanism to a facility location. The potential for strategic behavior stems from the assumption that the agents' locations $\mathbf{x}$ are private information — x_i represents agent i's *ideal* location for the facility (also known as agent i's *peak*). Like Procaccia and Tennenholtz [27], and almost all subsequent papers, we assume that the *cost* of agent i for facility location y is simply the Euclidean distance between (the true) x_i and y,

$$\text{cost}(x_i, y) = |x_i - y|.$$

3.1 Deterministic Mechanisms

A deterministic mechanism $\mathcal{M} : \mathbb{R}^n \to \mathbb{R}$ is *truthful* if for every location profile $\mathbf{x} \in \mathbb{R}^n$, every agent $k \in N$, and every $x'_k \in \mathbb{R}$, $\text{cost}(x_k, \mathcal{M}(\mathbf{x})) \leq \text{cost}(x_k, \mathcal{M}(x'_k, \mathbf{x}_{-k}))$, where $\mathbf{x}_{-k} = \langle x_1, \ldots, x_{k-1}, x_{k+1}, \ldots, x_n \rangle$. Our next goal is to construct an algorithm that receives as input a deterministic mechanism, represented as a decision tree, and verifies that it is truthful.

The verification algorithm is quite intuitive, although its formal specification is somewhat elaborate. Consider a mechanism $\mathcal{M} : \mathbb{R}^n \to \mathbb{R}$ that is represented by a tree $\mathcal{T}$. For a leaf $\mathcal{L}$, denote the location chosen by $\mathcal{M}$ at this leaf by $y_{\mathcal{L}}(\mathbf{x}) = \sum_{i=1}^n \lambda_{\mathcal{L},i} \cdot x_i$. In addition, let $\mathcal{C}(\mathcal{L})$ denote the set of constraints encountered on the path to $\mathcal{L}$. For example, the set of constraints corresponding to the leftmost leaf in Figure 2 is $\{(x_1 \geq x_2), (x_2 \geq x_3)\}$, while the second leaf from the left verifies: $\{(x_1 \geq x_2), (x_2 < x_3), (x_1 \geq x_3)\}$. We define a procedure, BUILD-LEAF-CONSTRAINTS, that gathers these constraints (Algorithm 2). One subtlety is that the procedure "inflates" strict inequality constraints to constraints that require a difference of at least 1; we will explain shortly why this is without loss of generality.

The main procedure, TRUTHFUL (given as Algorithm 1), checks whether there exist location profiles $\mathbf{x}$ and $\mathbf{x}'$ that differ only in the k'th coordinate, such that $\mathbf{x}$ reaches leaf $\mathcal{L}$ (based on the constraints of the BUILD-LEAF-CONSTRAINTS procedure, given as Algorithm 3), $\mathbf{x}'$ reaches leaf $\mathcal{L}'$, and

$$\text{cost}(x_k, y_{\mathcal{L}'}(\mathbf{x}')) + 1 \leq \text{cost}(x_k, y_{\mathcal{L}}(\mathbf{x}))$$

That is, the reduction in cost is at least 1.

So why can we "inflate" strict inequalities by requiring a difference of 1? Assume that we are given a mechanism $\mathcal{T}$ and an agent i such that for some strategy profiles $\mathbf{x}$ and

---

Algorithm 1: TRUTHFUL($\mathcal{T}$) // *Verifier for Deterministic Mechanisms*

Data: mechanism $\mathcal{T}$
Result: *true* if $\mathcal{T}$ represents a truthful mechanism, *false* otherwise

1   BUILD-LEAF-CONSTRAINTS($\mathcal{T}$)
2   **foreach** $k \in N$ **do**
3   **foreach** *leaf* $\mathcal{L} \in \mathcal{T}$ **do**
4   // $y_{\mathcal{L}}(\mathbf{x})$ *is the symbolic expression for the facility at $\mathcal{L}$ on $\mathbf{x}$ and $d_k(\mathbf{x})$ is agent k's distance from the facility*
5   **foreach** $d_k(\mathbf{x}) \in \{x_k - y_{\mathcal{L}}(\mathbf{x}), \ -x_k + y_{\mathcal{L}}(\mathbf{x})\}$ **do**
6   // *two cases, for x_k to the left or right of the facility $y_{\mathcal{L}}(\mathbf{x})$*
7   **foreach** *leaf* $\mathcal{L}' \in \mathcal{T}$ **do**
8   **foreach** $d'_k(\mathbf{x}') \in \{x'_k - y_{\mathcal{L}'}(\mathbf{x}'), -x'_k + y_{\mathcal{L}'}(\mathbf{x}')\}$ **do**
9        $inc(\mathbf{x}, \mathbf{x}') \leftarrow \{(d_k(\mathbf{x}) - d'_k(\mathbf{x}') \geq 1),$ $d_k(\mathbf{x}) \geq 0, d'_k(\mathbf{x}') \geq 0\}$
10   // *utility increase from $\mathbf{x}$ to $\mathbf{x}'$, distances are non-negative*
11   **if** EXISTS-SOLUTION($k, \mathcal{C}_{\mathcal{L}}, \mathcal{C}_{\mathcal{L}'}, inc$) **then**
12   **return** *False*

13   **return** *True*

$\mathbf{x}'$ with $\mathbf{x}_{-i} = \mathbf{x}'_{-i}$, agent i can strictly benefit by switching from $\mathbf{x}$ to $\mathbf{x}'$. Then there exists $\epsilon > 0$ such that agent i's improvement is at least ϵ, and for every strict inequality satisfied by $\mathbf{x}$ and $\mathbf{x}'$, the difference between the terms is at least ϵ; for example, if $x_k > x_l$, then it is the case that $x_k - x_l \geq \epsilon$. Since each facility location is a homogeneous linear function of the input $\mathbf{x}$, all variables can be multiplied by $\frac{1}{\epsilon}$ to obtain that $\mathbf{x}/\epsilon$ and $\mathbf{x}'/\epsilon$ satisfy the more stringent constraints (with a difference of 1) on agent locations and facility locations.

Finally, this algorithm works in polynomial time because the procedure EXISTS-SOLUTION, which checks whether there is a solution to the different constraints (corresponding to a profitable manipulation), just solves a linear program using the procedure SOLVE.

We summarize the preceding discussion with the theorem:

THEOREM 1. *Let $N = \{1, \ldots, n\}$. The truthfulness of a deterministic mechanism $\mathcal{M}$ represented as a decision tree $\mathcal{T}$ can be verified in polynomial time in n and $|\mathcal{T}|$.*

Algorithm 1 essentially carries out a brute force search over pairs of leaves to find a profitable manipulation. Under the decision tree representation, is it possible to verify truthfulness much more efficiently? Our next result answers this question in the negative.

THEOREM 2. *Let $N = \{1, \ldots, n\}$ with $n \geq 2$, and $\ell \leq n!$. Then any algorithm that verifies truthfulness for every deterministic decision tree with ℓ leaves for n agents must inspect all the leaves in the worst case.*

PROOF. Assume by contradiction there exists a verification algorithm that can check truthfulness for every tree

---

Algorithm 2: BUILD-LEAF-CONSTRAINTS($\mathcal{T}$)

Data: mechanism $\mathcal{T}$
Result: set of symbolic constraints $\mathcal{C}$; the location at leaf $\mathcal{L}$ is selected on input $\mathbf{x}$ $\iff$ constraints $\mathcal{C}_{\mathcal{L}}(\mathbf{x})$ hold

1 $\mathcal{C} \leftarrow \emptyset$ // Initialize the set of constraints
2 **foreach** leaf $\mathcal{L} \in \mathcal{T}$ **do**
3    $Q \leftarrow \mathcal{L}$
4   **while** $Q \neq Null$ **do**
5   // Add the constraint that must hold for Q to be reached from parent(Q)
6      $c \leftarrow constraint(parent(Q).Next() = Q)$
7   **switch** c **do**
8   **case** $x_{i_c} \geq x_{j_c}$
9          $\mathcal{C}_{\mathcal{L}}(\mathbf{x}) \leftarrow \mathcal{C}_{\mathcal{L}}(\mathbf{x}) \cup \{x_{i_c} - x_{j_c} \geq 0\}$
10   **case** $x_{i_c} > x_{j_c}$
11          $\mathcal{C}_{\mathcal{L}}(\mathbf{x}) \leftarrow \mathcal{C}_{\mathcal{L}}(\mathbf{x}) \cup \{x_{i_c} - x_{j_c} \geq 1\}$
12   **case** $x_{i_c} \leq x_{j_c}$
13          $\mathcal{C}_{\mathcal{L}}(\mathbf{x}) \leftarrow \mathcal{C}_{\mathcal{L}}(\mathbf{x}) \cup \{x_{j_c} - x_{i_c} \geq 0\}$
14   **case** $x_{i_c} < x_{j_c}$
15          $\mathcal{C}_{\mathcal{L}}(\mathbf{x}) \leftarrow \mathcal{C}_{\mathcal{L}}(\mathbf{x}) \cup \{x_{j_c} - x_{i_c} \geq 1\}$
16      $Q \leftarrow parent(Q)$
17 **return** $\mathcal{C}$

Algorithm 3: EXISTS-SOLUTION($k, \mathcal{C}_{\mathcal{L}}, \mathcal{C}'_{\mathcal{L}'}, inc$)

Data: agent k and symbolic constraint sets $\mathcal{C}_{\mathcal{L}}, \mathcal{C}'_{\mathcal{L}'}$, inc
Result: $true \iff \exists\, x_1, \ldots, x_n, x'_k \in \mathbb{R}^+$ subject to $\mathcal{C}_{\mathcal{L}}(\mathbf{x})$ & $\mathcal{C}'_{\mathcal{L}}(x'_k, \mathbf{x}_{-k})$ & $inc(\mathbf{x}, (x'_k, \mathbf{x}_{-k}))$

1 $\mathbf{x}' \leftarrow (x_1, \ldots, x_{i-1}, x'_i, x_{i+1}, \ldots, x_n)$
2 $W \leftarrow \{\mathcal{C}_{\mathcal{L}}(\mathbf{x}), \mathcal{C}'_{\mathcal{L}}(\mathbf{x}'), inc(\mathbf{x}, \mathbf{x}')\}$
3 $\mathbf{z} \leftarrow (x_1, \ldots, x_n, x'_i)$
4 **return** SOLVE($\mathbf{z}, W, \mathbf{z} \geq 0$) // Linear program solver

---

with ℓ leaves without inspecting all the leaves. Let $\mathcal{T}$ be a decision tree in which every internal node has the form $x_i < x_j$, for $i, j \in N$ such that $i < j$, and the location is set to x_1 in every leaf. Since there are $n!$ possible orders of the agent locations, we can generate such a tree with ℓ leaves. Clearly, $\mathcal{T}$ is truthful since it coincides with the mechanism in which agent 1 is a dictator.

Consider the execution of the verification algorithm on input $\mathcal{T}$ and let $\mathcal{L}$ be a leaf that is not inspected by the algorithm. Construct a tree $\mathcal{T}'$ that is identical to $\mathcal{T}$, with the exception of leaf $\mathcal{L}$, where the selected location is $y_{\mathcal{L}}(\mathbf{x}) = \frac{x_1 + \ldots + x_n}{n}$. First note that mechanism $\mathcal{T}'$ is not truthful. For every leaf of $\mathcal{T}'$, the mechanism cannot enforce that two variables are equal, since that would require comparing $x_i < x_j$ and $x_j < x_i$ (similarly if weak inequalities are used). However, if $i < j$ then $\mathcal{T}'$ can only check if $x_i < x_j$; similarly, if $j < i$, then $\mathcal{T}'$ can only check if $x_j < x_i$. Thus the leaf $\mathcal{L}$ can be reached when the input $\mathbf{x}$ is consistent with some strict ordering π on n elements.

Define $\mathbf{x} \in \mathbb{R}^n$ such that $x_{\pi_1} < x_{\pi_2} < \ldots < x_{\pi_n}$. Then $y_{\mathcal{L}}(\mathbf{x}) = \frac{x_1 + \ldots + x_n}{n}$ and the cost of agent π_n is $\text{cost}(x_{\pi_n}, y_{\mathcal{L}}(\mathbf{x})) = x_{\pi_n} - y_{\mathcal{L}}(\mathbf{x})$. There exists $\delta > 0$ such that by reporting $x'_{\pi_n} = x_{\pi_n} + \delta$, agent π_n ensures that leaf $\mathcal{L}$ is still reached

and the new cost is lower:

$$
\begin{aligned}
\text{cost}(x_{\pi_n}, y_{\mathcal{L}}(x'_{\pi_n}, \mathbf{x}_{-\pi_n})) &= x_{\pi_n} - \frac{\left(\sum_{i \neq \pi_n} x_i\right) + (x_{\pi_n} + \delta)}{n} \\
&< x_{\pi_n} - \frac{x_1 + \ldots + x_n}{n} \\
&= \text{cost}(x_{\pi_n}, y_{\mathcal{L}}(\mathbf{x})).
\end{aligned}
$$

However, since the verification algorithm does not inspect leaf $\mathcal{L}$, it cannot distinguish between $\mathcal{T}$ and $\mathcal{T}'$, and so it decides that $\mathcal{T}'$ is also truthful. This contradicts the correctness of the verification algorithm. $\square$

Crucially, our decision trees are binary trees, so the number of leaves is exactly the number of internal nodes plus one. Theorem 2 therefore implies:

COROLLARY 1. *Let $N = \{1, \ldots, n\}$, $n \geq 2$. Any verification algorithm requires superpolynomial time in n (in the worst-case) to verify the truthfulness of trees of superpolynomial size in n.*

3.2 Randomized Mechanisms

In the context of randomized mechanisms, there are two common options for defining truthfulness: *truthfulness in expectation* and *universal truthfulness*. In our context, truthfulness in expectation means that an agent cannot decrease its expected distance to the facility by deviating; universal truthfulness means that the randomized mechanism is a probability distribution over truthful deterministic mechanisms, i.e., an agent cannot benefit from manipulation regardless of the mechanism's random coin tosses. Clearly, the former notion of truthfulness is weaker than the latter. In some settings, truthful-in-expectation mechanisms are known to achieve guarantees that cannot be obtained through universally truthful mechanisms [11].

We focus on universal truthfulness, in part because we do not know whether truthful-in-expectation mechanisms can be efficiently verified (as we discuss in §5). Using Theorem 1, universal truthfulness is easy to verify, because it is sufficient and necessary to verify the truthfulness of each of the decision trees in the mechanism's support. One subtlety is the binding of agents in $N \setminus N_r$ to the $z_{r,j}$ parameters. However, for the purpose of verifying truthfulness, any binding will do by symmetry between the agents in $N \setminus N_r$. We therefore have the following result:

THEOREM 3. *Let $N = \{1, \ldots, n\}$. The universal truthfulness of a randomized mechanism $\mathcal{M}$ represented as a distribution over K decision trees $\mathcal{T}_1, \ldots, \mathcal{T}_K$ can be verified in polynomial time in n and its representation size, $\sum_{r=1}^{K} |\mathcal{T}_r|$.*

4. STEP III: MEASURING THE QUALITY OF VERIFIABLY TRUTHFUL MECHANISMS

We have shown that the truthfulness of mechanisms represented by decision trees of polynomial size can be verified in polynomial time. This result is encouraging, but it is only truly meaningful if decision trees of polynomial size can describe mechanisms that provide good guarantees with respect to the quality of the solution.

Like Procaccia and Tennenholtz [27], and subsequent papers, we measure solution quality in the facility location domain via two measures. The *social cost* of a facility location

$y \in \mathcal{R}$ for a location profile $\mathbf{x} \in \mathbb{R}^n$ is

$$\mathrm{sc}(\mathbf{x}, y) = \sum_{i=1}^{n} \mathrm{cost}(x_i, y),$$

and the *maximum cost* is

$$\mathrm{mc}(\mathbf{x}, y) = \max_{i \in N} \mathrm{cost}(x_i, y).$$

We denote the optimal solutions with respect to the social cost and maximum cost by $\mathrm{sc}^*(\mathbf{x}) = \min_{y \in \mathbb{R}} \sum_{i=1}^{n} \mathrm{cost}(x_i, y)$, and $\mathrm{mc}^*(\mathbf{x}) = \min_{y \in \mathbb{R}} \max_{i \in N} \mathrm{cost}(x_i, y)$, respectively.

4.1 Deterministic Mechanisms

Let us first review what can be done with deterministic mechanisms represented by decision trees of arbitrary size, without necessarily worrying about verification.

For the maximum cost, the optimal solution is clearly the midpoint between the leftmost and rightmost reported locations. It is interesting to note that the midpoint may not be one of the agents' reported locations — so, to compute the optimal solution, our expressive representation of the leaves as convex combinations of points in $\mathbf{x}$ is required. Procaccia and Tennenholtz [27] have shown that any truthful mechanism cannot achieve an approximation ratio smaller than 2 for the maximum cost. A ratio of 2 is achieved by any solution that places the facility between the leftmost and rightmost reported locations. It follows that the optimal ratio is trivial to obtain truthfully, e.g., by always selecting the location x_1 reported by agent 1. This mechanism is representable via a tiny decision tree with one leaf.

We conclude that, in the context of deterministic mechanisms and the maximum cost objective, truthful mechanisms that are efficiently verifiable can do just as well as any truthful mechanism.

Let us therefore focus on the social cost. For any number of agents n, it is easy to see that selecting the median of the reported locations is the optimal solution. Indeed, if the facility moves right or left, the facility would get further away from a majority of locations, and closer to a minority of locations. The median mechanism was observed by Moulin [22] to be truthful. Intuitively, this is because the only way an agent can manipulate the median's location is by reporting a location that is on the other side of the median — but that only pushes the median away from the agent's actual location. Moreover, the median can be computed by a decision tree in which every internal node contains comparisons between the input locations, and each leaf $\mathcal{L}$ outputs the location of the facility (the median) when $\mathcal{L}$ is reached.

In contrast to the maximum cost, though, the optimal mechanism for the social cost — the median — requires a huge decision tree representation. The number of comparisons required to compute the median has been formally studied (see, e.g., Blum et al. [4]), but, in our case, simple intuition suffices: if there is an odd number of agents with distinct locations, the median cannot be determined when nothing is known about the location of one of the agents, so $(n-1)/2$ comparisons are required *in the best case*, leading to a tall binary tree of exponential size.

Our next result strengthens this insight by giving a lower bound on the approximation ratio achievable by polynomial size decision trees (i.e., trees efficiently verifiable by our algorithm of §3).

THEOREM 4. *For every constant $k \in \mathbb{N}$, every truthful deterministic decision tree for n agents of size at most n^k has an approximation ratio of $\Omega\left(\frac{n}{\log n}\right)$ for the social cost.*

PROOF. Let $\mathcal{M}$ be a deterministic mechanism represented by some decision tree $\mathcal{T}$ of size at most n^k. Recall that every internal node in $\mathcal{T}$ checks the order of two input variables with one of the following inequalities: $\{x_i \geq x_j,\ x_i \leq x_j,\ x_i < x_j,\ x_i > x_j\}$.

Since $\mathcal{T}$ is binary and $|\mathcal{T}| \leq n^k$, there exists at least one leaf $\mathcal{L} \in \mathcal{T}$ of depth

$$d < 2 \cdot \log(|\mathcal{T}|) \leq 2\log(n^k) = 2k\log(n).$$

Let $S_{\mathcal{L}} = \{i_1, \ldots, i_m\}$ be the set of agents whose locations are inspected on the path to $\mathcal{L}$. It holds that $|S_{\mathcal{L}}| = m \leq 2 \cdot d \leq 4k \cdot \log(n)$, since $\mathcal{L}$ has depth d and each node on the path to $\mathcal{L}$ inspects two locations. Note that if $S_{\mathcal{L}} = \emptyset$, then $\mathcal{M}$ is a dictatorship, and so its approximation ratio is no better than $n - 1$. Thus we can assume that $S_{\mathcal{L}} \neq \emptyset$.

Recall that the facility at $\mathcal{L}$ is a convex combination of the input locations; that is, $y_{\mathcal{L}}(\mathbf{x}) = \sum_{i=1}^{n} \lambda_{\mathcal{L},i} \cdot x_i$, where $\lambda_{\mathcal{L},i} \in [0,1], \forall i \in N$ and $\sum_{i=1}^{n} \lambda_{\mathcal{L},i} = 1$. Let π be a weak ordering consistent with the leaf $\mathcal{L}$ and $D_{\mathcal{L}} = \{i_1, \ldots, i_l\}$ a "deduplicated" version of $S_{\mathcal{L}}$, such that $D_{\mathcal{L}}$ contains one representative agent i for each maximal subset $W \subseteq S_{\mathcal{L}}$ with the property that under π, $x_j = x_i, \forall j \in W$. Note that $D_{\mathcal{L}}$ is consistent with some strict ordering σ on l elements.

We distinguish among three cases:

Case 1: The facility at $\mathcal{L}$ is a convex combination of agents in $S_{\mathcal{L}}$ only (i.e., $\lambda_{\mathcal{L},i} = 0, \forall i \notin S_{\mathcal{L}}$).

Let ϵ be fixed such that $0 < \epsilon < \frac{|S_{\mathcal{L}}|}{n}$ and define the following input $\mathbf{x} = \langle x_1, \ldots, x_n \rangle$:

- For each $i \in D_{\mathcal{L}}$, let r_i be the number of agents in $D_{\mathcal{L}}$ strictly to the left of i according to σ; set $x_i \leftarrow \epsilon \cdot \left(\frac{r_i}{n}\right)$.

- For each $j \in S_{\mathcal{L}} \setminus D_{\mathcal{L}}$, set $x_j \leftarrow x_i$, where $i \in D_{\mathcal{L}}$ and $x_i = x_j$ according to π.

- For each $j \notin S_{\mathcal{L}}$, set $x_j \leftarrow 1$.

The optimal location of the facility given $\mathbf{x}$ is $y^* = 1$, since most agents are situated at 1 (except the agents in $S_{\mathcal{L}}$, of which there are at most: $4k\log(n) \ll n/2$). The optimal social cost is:

$$\mathrm{sc}^*(\mathbf{x}) = \sum_{i=1}^{n} \mathrm{cost}(x_i, y^*) = \sum_{i \in S_{\mathcal{L}}} (1 - x_i) \leq 1 \cdot |S_{\mathcal{L}}|.$$

On the other hand, the output of the mechanism is $y_{\mathcal{L}}(\mathbf{x}) = \sum_{i \in S_{\mathcal{L}}} \lambda_{\mathcal{L},i} \cdot x_i \leq \epsilon$; the social cost incurred by $\mathcal{M}$ on $\mathbf{x}$ is:

$$\mathrm{sc}(\mathbf{x}, \mathcal{M}(\mathbf{x})) = \sum_{i=1}^{n} \mathrm{cost}(x_i, y_{\mathcal{L}}(\mathbf{x})) \geq (n - |S_{\mathcal{L}}|) \cdot (1 - \epsilon).$$

Choosing $\epsilon \leq 1/n$, the approximation ratio of $\mathcal{M}$ is no better than:

$$\begin{aligned}
\frac{\mathrm{sc}(\mathbf{x}, \mathcal{M}(\mathbf{x}))}{\mathrm{sc}^*(\mathbf{x})} &\geq \frac{(n - |S_{\mathcal{L}}|) \cdot (1 - \epsilon)}{|S_{\mathcal{L}}|} \\
&= \frac{n}{|S_{\mathcal{L}}|} - \frac{n\epsilon}{|S_{\mathcal{L}}|} - 1 + \epsilon \\
&> \frac{n}{4k\log(n)} - 2 \in \Omega\left(\frac{n}{\log(n)}\right).
\end{aligned}$$

Case 2: The facility coincides with the location of some agent $t \notin S_{\mathcal{L}}$ (i.e. $y_{\mathcal{L}}(\mathbf{x}) = x_t$).

Similarly to Case 1, let ϵ be fixed such that $0 < \epsilon < \frac{|S_{\mathcal{L}}|+1}{n}$ and define $\mathbf{x} = \langle x_1, \ldots, x_n \rangle$ as follows:

- For each $i \in D_{\mathcal{L}}$, let r_i be the number of agents in $D_{\mathcal{L}}$ strictly to the left of i according to σ; set $x_i \leftarrow \epsilon \cdot \left(\frac{r_i}{n} \right)$.

- For each $j \in S_{\mathcal{L}} \setminus D_{\mathcal{L}}$, set $x_j \leftarrow x_i$, where $i \in D_{\mathcal{L}}$ and $x_i = x_j$ according to π.

- Set $x_t = 0$.

- For each $j \notin S_{\mathcal{L}}, j \neq t$, set $x_j \leftarrow 1$.

The optimal location on $\mathbf{x}$ is $y^* = 1$, since most agents are located at 1 (except agent t and the agents in $S_{\mathcal{L}}$). As in Case 1, by also taking agent t into account, we get:

$$\frac{\mathrm{sc}(\mathbf{x}, \mathcal{M}(\mathbf{x}))}{\mathrm{sc}^*(\mathbf{x})} \geq \frac{(n - |S_{\mathcal{L}}| - 1) \cdot (1 - \epsilon)}{|S_{\mathcal{L}}| + 1} \in \Omega \left(\frac{n}{\log(n)} \right).$$

Case 3: The facility is a weighted sum with at least two terms, one of which is an agent $t \notin S_{\mathcal{L}}$. We claim that no mechanism that is truthful on the full domain (i.e. the line) can have such an output at any leaf. Let $\epsilon, \delta > 0$ be such that

$$\delta = \frac{1}{2} \left(\frac{1}{\lambda_{\mathcal{L},t}} - 1 \right) \text{ and } \epsilon = \frac{1 - \lambda_{\mathcal{L},t}(1 + \delta)}{n - 1}.$$

Consider an input $\mathbf{x}$ consistent with the ordering π such that $x_t = 1$ and $x_i \in (0, \epsilon), \forall i \neq t$. Then:

$$y_{\mathcal{L}}(\mathbf{x}) = \sum_{i=1}^{n} \lambda_{\mathcal{L},i} \cdot x_i = \left(\sum_{i \neq t} \lambda_{\mathcal{L},i} \cdot x_i \right) + \lambda_{\mathcal{L},t} \cdot 1.$$

If agent t reports instead $x_t' = 1 + \delta$, the output of $\mathcal{M}$ on $\mathbf{x}' = (x_t', \mathbf{x}_{-t})$ is:

$$y_{\mathcal{L}}(\mathbf{x}') = \left(\sum_{i \neq t} \lambda_{\mathcal{L},i} \cdot x_i \right) + \lambda_{\mathcal{L},t} \cdot (1 + \delta).$$

It can be verified that $0 < y_{\mathcal{L}}(\mathbf{x}) < y_{\mathcal{L}}(\mathbf{x}') < 1$, and so $\mathrm{cost}(x_t, y_{\mathcal{L}}(\mathbf{x}')) < \mathrm{cost}(x_t, y_{\mathcal{L}}(\mathbf{x}))$, which contradicts the truthfulness of $\mathcal{M}$. Thus Case 3 never occurs.

By the cases above, there exists at least one input on which the approximation ratio of $\mathcal{M}$ is $\Omega \left(\frac{n}{\log(n)} \right)$, which completes the proof. $\square$

On the positive side, we show that the lower bound of Theorem 4 is asymptotically tight.

THEOREM 5. *For every $n \in \mathbb{N}$ there is a truthful deterministic decision tree of size $O(n^6)$ that approximates the social cost within a factor of $O \left(\frac{n}{\log(n)} \right)$.*

PROOF. First, we claim that for every $k \in \{1, \ldots, n/2\}$, there exists a truthful, deterministic decision tree of size $O(2^{6k})$ that approximates the social cost within a factor of $O \left(\frac{n-k}{k} \right)$. Given a fixed k, let $\mathcal{M}$ be the mechanism:

- Given $\mathbf{x} = (x_1, \ldots, x_n)$, output median($\{x_1, \ldots, x_k\}$).

That is, $\mathcal{M}$ always outputs the median of the fixed set of agents $\{1, \ldots, k\}$. Computing the median on an input vector of size k requires fewer than $6k$ comparisons [4], and since the decision tree for $\mathcal{M}$ is binary, its size is $O(2^{6k})$.

We next claim that the approximation ratio of $\mathcal{M}$ is $O \left(\frac{n-k}{k} \right)$. Indeed, given any instance $\mathbf{x} \in \mathbb{R}^n$, denote $\tilde{m} = \mathcal{M}(\mathbf{x})$ and $m^* = \mathrm{argmin}_{y \in \mathbb{R}} \mathrm{sc}(\mathbf{x}, y)$. Without loss of generality, assume that $\tilde{m} < m^*$ and let $\Delta = |\tilde{m} - m^*|$. Let $S_l = \{x_i \mid x_i \leq \tilde{m}\}$, $S_r = \{x_i \mid x_i \geq m^*\}$, and $S_m = \{x_i \mid \tilde{m} < x_i < m^*\}$ be the sets of points to the left of $\tilde{m}$, to the right of m^*, and strictly between $\tilde{m}$ and m^*, respectively. Denote the sizes of the sets by $n_l = |S_l|$, $n_r = |S_r|$, and $n_m = |S_m|$, where $n_l + n_m + n_r = n$.

We compute the upper bound by comparing the social cost of $\mathcal{M}$ on $\mathbf{x}$, $\mathrm{sc}(\mathbf{x}, \mathcal{M}(\mathbf{x})) = \sum_{i=1}^{n} \mathrm{cost}(x_i, \tilde{m})$, with $\mathrm{sc}^*(\mathbf{x}) = \sum_{i=1}^{n} \mathrm{cost}(x_i, m^*)$. Observe that for all the points in S_r, the cost increases by exactly Δ when moving the location from m^* to $\tilde{m}$. On the other hand, the change from m^* to $\tilde{m}$ results in a decrease by exactly Δ for the points in S_l. Thus $\mathrm{sc}(\mathbf{x}, \mathcal{M}(\mathbf{x}))$ can be expressed as follows:

$$\mathrm{sc}(\mathbf{x}, \mathcal{M}(\mathbf{x})) = \mathrm{sc}^*(\mathbf{x}) + n_r \cdot \Delta + \sum_{j \in S_m} [\mathrm{cost}(x_j, \tilde{m}) - \mathrm{cost}(x_j, m^*)] - \Delta n_l$$

The ratio of the costs is:

$$\frac{\mathrm{sc}(\mathbf{x}, \mathcal{M}(\mathbf{x}))}{\mathrm{sc}^*(\mathbf{x})} = \frac{\mathrm{sc}^*(\mathbf{x}) + n_r \cdot \Delta}{\mathrm{sc}^*(\mathbf{x})} + $$
$$+ \frac{\sum_{j \in S_m} [\mathrm{cost}(x_j, \tilde{m}) - \mathrm{cost}(x_j, m^*)] - n_l \cdot \Delta}{\mathrm{sc}^*(\mathbf{x})}.$$

We claim that

$$\frac{\mathrm{sc}(\mathbf{x}, \mathcal{M}(\mathbf{x}))}{\mathrm{sc}^*(\mathbf{x})} \leq \frac{3(n-k)}{k}. \quad (1)$$

Inequality (1) is equivalent to:

$$k \cdot n_r \cdot \Delta + k \cdot \sum_{j \in S_m} [\mathrm{cost}(x_j, \tilde{m}) - \mathrm{cost}(x_j, m^*)] - k \cdot n_l \cdot \Delta \leq (3n - 4k) \mathrm{sc}^*(\mathbf{x})$$

Note that for all $j \in S_m$, $\mathrm{cost}(x_j, \tilde{m}) - \mathrm{cost}(x_j, m^*) \leq \Delta$, and so if Inequality (1) holds when $\mathrm{cost}(x_j, \tilde{m}) - \mathrm{cost}(x_j, m^*) = \Delta$, then it also holds for all other instances where the change in cost is smaller for some agents $j \in S_m$. Formally, if:

$$k \cdot n_r \cdot \Delta + k \cdot n_m \cdot \Delta - k \cdot n_l \cdot \Delta \leq (3n - 4k) \mathrm{sc}^*(\mathbf{x}), \quad (2)$$

then Inequality (1) holds. Inequality (2) is equivalent to:

$$\begin{aligned} \mathrm{sc}^*(\mathbf{x}) &\geq \frac{k \cdot n_r \cdot \Delta + k \cdot n_m \cdot \Delta - k \cdot n_l \cdot \Delta}{3n - 4k} \\ &= \frac{k \cdot (n_r + (n - n_l - n_r) - n_l) \cdot \Delta}{3n - 4k} \\ &= \frac{k \cdot (n - 2n_l) \cdot \Delta}{3n - 4k}. \end{aligned} \quad (3)$$

Each of the agents in S_l pays a cost of at least Δ under $\mathrm{sc}^*(\mathbf{x})$, and so $\mathrm{sc}^*(\mathbf{x}) \geq n_l \cdot \Delta$. Moreover, since $\tilde{m}$ is the median of $\{x_1, \ldots, x_k\}$, it follows that $n_l \geq \frac{k}{2}$. We first show that $n_l \cdot \Delta \geq \frac{k \cdot (n-2n_l) \cdot \Delta}{3n - 4k}$:

$$\begin{aligned} n_l \cdot \Delta &\geq \frac{k \cdot (n - 2n_l) \cdot \Delta}{3n - 4k} \\ &\iff n_l(3n - 4k) \geq k(n - 2n_l) \\ &\iff n_l(3n - 2k) \geq kn \\ &\iff n_l \geq \frac{kn}{3n - 2k} \end{aligned} \quad (4)$$

In addition, we have that

$$\frac{k}{2} \geq \frac{kn}{3n - 2k} \iff 3kn - 2k^2 \geq 2kn \iff n \geq 2k. \quad (5)$$

Inequality (5) holds by the choice of k; combining it with $n_l \geq \frac{k}{2}$, we obtain:

$$n_l \geq \frac{k}{2} \geq \frac{kn}{3n - 2k}. \tag{6}$$

By Inequality (3), it follows that $n_l \cdot \Delta \geq \frac{k \cdot (n - 2n_l) \cdot \Delta}{3n - 4k}$. In addition, $\mathrm{sc}^*(\mathbf{x}) > n_l \cdot \Delta$, thus:

$$\mathrm{sc}^*(\mathbf{x}) \geq n_l \cdot \Delta \geq \frac{k \cdot (n - 2n_l) \cdot \Delta}{3n - 4k}.$$

Equivalently, Inequality (2) holds, which gives the worst case bound required for Inequality (1) to always hold. Thus $\frac{\mathrm{sc}(\mathbf{x}, \mathcal{M}(\mathbf{x}))}{\mathrm{sc}^*(\mathbf{x})} \leq \frac{3(n-k)}{k}$, for every input $\mathbf{x}$.

Let $k = \log n$. Then $\mathcal{M}$ can be implemented using a decision tree of size $O(n^6)$ and has an approximation ratio bounded by

$$\frac{\mathrm{sc}(\mathbf{x}, \mathcal{M}(\mathbf{x}))}{\mathrm{sc}^*(\mathbf{x})} \leq \frac{3(n-k)}{k} \in O\left(\frac{n}{\log(n)}\right)$$

This completes the proof of the theorem. $\square$

In summary, polynomial-size decision trees can achieve the best possible approximation ratio (among all truthful deterministic mechanisms) with respect to the maximum cost objective and an approximation ratio of $\Theta(n/\log n)$ with respect to the social cost.

4.2 Randomized Mechanisms

We next turn to randomized mechanisms. In this context, we are interested in the expected social cost, or the expected maximum cost. The latter measure is somewhat subtle, so let us state specifically that, like Procaccia and Tennenholtz [27], we are interested in

$$\mathbb{E}\left[\mathrm{mc}(\mathbf{x}, \mathcal{M}(\mathbf{x}))\right] = \mathbb{E}\left[\max_{i \in N} \mathrm{cost}(x_i, \mathcal{M}(\mathbf{x}))\right].$$

A less stringent alternative would be to take the maximum over agents of the agent's expected cost.

It is immediately apparent that universally truthful, randomized, small decision trees can easily beat the lower bound of Theorem 4 for social cost. To see this, consider the random dictator mechanism, that selects an agent $i \in N$ uniformly at random, and returns the location x_i. This mechanism is clearly universally truthful (it is a uniform distribution over dictatorships), and it is easy to verify that its approximation ratio is $2 - 2/n$.

Our next theorem, which we view as the main result of this section, shows that randomization allows us to get arbitrarily close to 1 using universally truthful, efficiently-verifiable mechanisms.

THEOREM 6. *For every $0 < \epsilon < \frac{1}{10}$ and $n \in \mathbb{N}$, there exists a universally truthful randomized decision tree of size $O(poly(n))$, approximates the social cost to a factor of $1 + \epsilon$.*

PROOF. The idea is the following: we sample a subset of agents of logarithmic size – more exactly $O\left(\frac{\ln(n/\epsilon)}{\epsilon^2}\right)$ – and select the median among their reported locations. To reason about this mechanism, we define the rank of an element x in a set S ordered by $\succ$ to be $\mathrm{rank}(x) = |\{y \in S \mid y \succ x \vee y = x\}|$, and the ϵ-*median* of S to be $x \in S$ such that $(1/2 - \epsilon)|S| < \mathrm{rank}(x) < (1/2 + \epsilon)|S|$. The following lemma is a folklore result when sampling is done with replacement; we include its proof because we must sample without replacement.

LEMMA 1. *Consider the algorithm that samples t elements without replacement from a set S of size n, and returns the median of the sampled points. For all $\epsilon, \delta < 1/10$, if*

$$\frac{100 \ln \frac{1}{\delta}}{\epsilon^2} \leq t \leq \epsilon n,$$

then the algorithm returns an ϵ-median with probability $1 - \delta$.

PROOF. We partition S into three subsets:

$$S_1 = \{x \in S \mid \mathrm{rank}(x) \leq n/2 - \epsilon n\},$$

$$S_2 = \{x \in S \mid n/2 - \epsilon n < \mathrm{rank}(x) < n/2 + \epsilon n\},$$

and

$$S_3 = \{x \in S \mid \mathrm{rank}(x) \geq n/2 - \epsilon n\}.$$

Suppose that t elements are sampled without replacement from S. If less than $t/2$ are sampled from S_1, and less than $t/2$ are sampled from S_3, then the median of the sampled elements will belong to S_2 — implying that it is an ϵ-approximate median.

Let us, therefore, focus on the probability of sampling *at least* $t/2$ samples from S_1. Define a Bernoulli random variable X_i for all $i = 1, \ldots, t$, which takes the value 1 if and only if the i'th sample is in S_1.

Note that $X_1, \ldots, X_t$ are not independent (because we are sampling with replacement), but for all i it holds that

$$\Pr\left[X_i = 1 \mid X_1 = x_1, \ldots, X_{i-1} = x_{i-1}\right] \leq \frac{\frac{n}{2} - \epsilon n}{n - (i-1)}$$

$$\leq \frac{\frac{n}{2} - \epsilon n}{n - \epsilon n} \leq \frac{1}{2} - \frac{\epsilon}{3}$$

for any $(x_1, \ldots, x_{i-1}) \in \{0,1\}^{i-1}$, where the second inequality follows from $i \leq t \leq \epsilon n$.

Let $Y_1, \ldots, Y_t$ be i.i.d. Bernoulli random variables such that $Y_i = 1$ with probability $1/2 - \epsilon/3$. Then for all x,

$$\Pr\left[\sum_{i=1}^{t} X_i \geq x\right] \leq \Pr\left[\sum_{i=1}^{t} Y_i \geq x\right].$$

Using Chernoff's inequality, we conclude that

$$\Pr\left[\sum_{i=1}^{t} X_i \geq \frac{t}{2}\right] \leq \Pr\left[\sum_{i=1}^{t} Y_i \geq \frac{t}{2}\right]$$

$$= \Pr\left[\sum_{i=1}^{t} Y_i \geq \left(1 + \frac{\epsilon}{\frac{3}{2} - \epsilon}\right)\mathbb{E}\left[\sum_{i=1}^{t} Y_i\right]\right]$$

$$\leq \Pr\left[\sum_{i=1}^{t} Y_i \geq \left(1 + \frac{\epsilon}{2}\right)\mathbb{E}\left[\sum_{i=1}^{t} Y_i\right]\right]$$

$$\leq \exp\left(-\frac{\left(\frac{\epsilon}{2}\right)^2 \left(\frac{1}{2} - \frac{\epsilon}{3}\right) t}{3}\right) \leq \frac{\delta}{2}$$

The last inequality follows from the assumption that $t \geq \frac{100 \ln(1/\delta)}{\epsilon^2}$. The proof of the lemma is completed by applying symmetric arguments to S_3, and using the union bound. $\square$

Let $\mathbf{x} = \langle x_1, \ldots, x_n \rangle$ be the set of inputs. For every $k \in N$, define the mechanism $\mathcal{M}_{n,k}$ as follows:

- Select uniformly at random a subset $S_k \subseteq N$, where $|S_k| = k$.

- Output the median of S_k.

Note that $\mathcal{M}_{n,1}$ coincides with random dictator, while $\mathcal{M}_{n,n}$ is the median mechanism. Recall that random dictator, $\mathcal{M}_{n,1}$, has an approximation ratio of $2 - 2/n$ for the social cost, while the median, $\mathcal{M}_{n,n}$, is optimal. The approximation ratio of $\mathcal{M}_{n,k}$ improves as k grows from 1 to n and the mechanism is universally truthful for every k; in particular, we show there exists a choice of k that achieves a good trade-off between the size of the mechanism and its approximation ratio.

First, we describe the implementation of $\mathcal{M}_{n,k}$ as a randomized decision tree. The root has outgoing degree one and selects a function $\mathcal{F}$ that takes k arguments $Z = \{z_1, \ldots, z_k\}$ and computes the median of $z_1, \ldots, z_k$. At execution time, $z_1, \ldots, z_k$ are instantiated using the locations $x_{i_1}, \ldots, x_{i_k}$ of k distinct agents, chosen uniformly at random from k-subsets of N. Note that $\mathcal{F}$ can be implemented with a decision tree of size $O(2^{6k})$.

Let $\epsilon', \delta > 0$ be fixed such that $\epsilon', \delta < \frac{1}{10}$. By Lemma 1, the algorithm that samples without replacement $t = \lceil \frac{100 \ln \frac{1}{\delta}}{(\epsilon')^2} \rceil$ elements from a set of n elements returns an ϵ'-median with probability $1 - \delta$, as long as $t \leq \epsilon' n$.

Let $\mathbf{x} \in \mathbb{R}^n$; without loss of generality $x_1 \leq \cdots \leq x_n$. We wish to compare $\mathbb{E}[\mathrm{sc}(\mathbf{x}, \mathcal{M}_{n,t}(\mathbf{x}))]$ and $\mathrm{sc}^*(\mathbf{x})$. Let us suppose that $\mathcal{M}_{n,t}$ returns an ϵ'-median, call it x_l. Since x_l is an ϵ'-median, we have that $\frac{n}{2} - \epsilon' n < l < \frac{n}{2} + \epsilon' n$. Take the case where $l < \frac{n}{2}$ (the other case, where $l > \frac{n}{2}$, is similar) and let $\Delta = |x_l - x_m|$, where $x_m = \mathrm{median}(\mathbf{x})$. Then by moving the facility from x_m to x_l, the costs of the agents change as follows:

(i) Each agent to the left of x_l (including agent l) has the cost decreased by exactly Δ.

(ii) Each agent strictly between x_l and x_m incurs an increase in cost of at most Δ.

(iii) Each agent to the right of x_m (including agent m) has the cost increased by Δ.

It follows that

$$\mathrm{sc}(\mathbf{x}, x_l) \leq \mathrm{sc}^*(\mathbf{x}) - l \cdot \Delta + (n - l) \cdot \Delta = \mathrm{sc}^*(\mathbf{x}) + (n - 2l) \cdot \Delta.$$

On those instances where $\mathcal{M}_{n,t}$ does not return the median, the social cost is at most $(n-1) \cdot \mathrm{diam}(\mathbf{x})$, where $\mathrm{diam}(\mathbf{x}) = \max_{i,j \in N} |x_i - x_j|$. On the other hand, the optimal cost satisfies: $\mathrm{sc}^*(\mathbf{x}) \geq \mathrm{diam}(\mathbf{x})$ and $\mathrm{sc}^*(\mathbf{x}) \geq l \cdot \Delta$.

Since $\mathcal{M}_{n,t}$ returns an ϵ'-median with probability $1 - \delta$, the ratio of the costs can be bounded by:

$$
\begin{aligned}
\frac{sc_{\mathcal{M}_{n,t}}(\mathbf{x})}{\mathrm{sc}^*(\mathbf{x})} &\leq \frac{(1-\delta)\mathrm{sc}^*(\mathbf{x}) + \Delta(1-\delta)(n - 2l) + \delta(n-1)\mathrm{diam}(\mathbf{x})}{\mathrm{sc}^*(\mathbf{x})} \\
&\leq (1-\delta) + \frac{\Delta(1-\delta)(n-2l)}{\Delta \cdot l} + \frac{\delta(n-1)\mathrm{diam}(\mathbf{x})}{\mathrm{diam}(\mathbf{x})} \\
&= 1 - \delta + (1-\delta)\frac{n}{l} - 2(1-\delta) + \delta(n-1) \\
&\leq \delta \cdot n - 1 + (1-\delta)\frac{2}{1 - 2\epsilon'} \leq 1 + \delta \cdot n + 5\epsilon'.
\end{aligned}
$$

Given $\epsilon < 1/10$, let $\epsilon' = \epsilon/10$ and $\delta = \epsilon/(2n)$, and set $t = \lceil \frac{100 \ln \frac{1}{\delta}}{(\epsilon')^2} \rceil$. Then $\mathcal{M}_{n,t}$ can be represented as a randomized decision tree of size $O(2^{6t})$, which is polynomial in n.

Moreover, for this choice of ϵ', δ, the approximation ratio of $\mathcal{M}_{n,t}$ is bounded by

$$1 + \delta \cdot n + 5\epsilon' = 1 = \frac{\epsilon}{2} + \frac{\epsilon}{2} = 1 + \epsilon.$$

In stark contrast, universal truthfulness does not help obtain a better bound than the trivial approximation ratio of 2 for the maximum cost — even in the case of general mechanisms. The proof is included in the full version of the paper.

THEOREM 7. *For each $\epsilon > 0$, there exists no universally truthful mechanism given by a distribution over countably many deterministic mechanisms that can approximate the maximum cost within a factor of $2 - \epsilon$.*

We have the following corollary for universally truthful decision trees.

COROLLARY 2. *For each $\epsilon > 0$, there exists no universally truthful decision tree mechanism given by a distribution over countably many deterministic decision trees that can approximate the maximum cost within a factor of $2 - \epsilon$.*

5. DISCUSSION

Theorem 7 shows that universally truthful decision trees cannot achieve a nontrivial (better than 2) approximation for the maximum cost. In contrast, Procaccia and Tennenholtz [27] designed a *truthful-in-expectation* mechanism that approximates the maximum cost to a factor of 3/2. This motivates the study of truthful-in-expectation randomized decision trees, as an alternative to universal truthfulness. However, we do not know whether truthfulness in expectation can be efficiently verified (and we believe that it cannot). Intuitively, the main difficulty is that, for every selection of one leaf from each tree in the support of the randomized mechanism, a naïve verification algorithm would need to reason about whether a certain location profile $\mathbf{x}$ can reach this collection of leaves under the constraints imposed by the different trees.

Our work focuses on the case of locating one facility on the line, which is quite simple from the approximate-mechanism-design-without-money viewpoint. Researchers have investigated approximate mechanism design in generalized facility location settings, involving multiple facilities [27, 21, 20, 25, 13, 14, 15], different cost functions [32, 15], metric spaces and graphs [1, 20], and so on. Of these generalizations and extensions, all but one only require a rethinking of our results of §4 — that is, mechanisms can still be represented as polynomial-size decision trees. But moving from the real line to a more general metric space requires a revision of the way mechanisms are represented in our framework.

We conclude by re-emphasizing the main message of our paper. In our view, our main contribution is the three-step approach to the design of verifiably truthful mechanisms. Our technical results provide a proof of concept by instantiating this approach in the context of a well-studied facility location setting, and constructing verifiably truthful mechanisms that achieve good quality guarantees. We firmly believe, though, that the same approach is widely applicable. For example, is there a class of mechanisms for combinatorial auctions that gives rise to verifiably truthful mechanisms providing a good approximation to social welfare? One can ask similar questions in the context of every problem studied in algorithmic mechanism design (with or without money). More generally, how should economic systems be designed so that players can reason efficiently about their decisions?

6. ACKNOWLEDGMENTS

We would like to thank Aris Filos-Ratsikas for a helpful discussion on characterizations of mechanisms for single peaked preferences and Joan Feigenbaum, Kevin Leyton-Brown, Peter Bro Miltersen, and Tuomas Sandholm for useful feedback.

Simina Brânzei acknowledges support from the Danish National Research Foundation and the National Science Foundation of China (under the grant 61361136003) for the Sino-Danish Center for the Theory of Interactive Computation and from the Center for Research in Foundations of Electronic Markets (CFEM), supported by the Danish Strategic Research Council. Simina also acknowledges support from an IBM Ph.D. fellowship.

Ariel D. Procaccia was partially supported by the NSF under grants CCF-1215883 and IIS-1350598.

7. REFERENCES

[1] N. Alon, M. Feldman, A. D. Procaccia, and M. Tennenholtz. Strategyproof approximation of the minimax on networks. *Mathematics of Operations Research*, 35(3):513–526, 2010.

[2] N. Alon, F. Fischer, A. D. Procaccia, and M. Tennenholtz. Sum of us: Strategyproof selection from the selectors. In *TARK*, pages 101–110, 2011.

[3] I. Ashlagi, F. Fischer, I. Kash, and A. D. Procaccia. Mix and match. *Game. Econ. Behav.*, 2014. Forthcoming.

[4] M. Blum, R. W. Floyd, V. Pratt, R. L. Rivest, and R. E. Tarjan. Time bounds for selection. *Journal of Computer and System Sciences*, 7(4):448–461, 1973.

[5] R. H. Bordini, M. Fisher, W. Visser, and M. Wooldridge. Verifying multi-agent programs by model checking. *JAAMAS*, 12:239–256, 2006.

[6] I. Caragiannis, E. Elkind, M. Szegedy, and L. Yu. Mechanism design: from partial to probabilistic verification. In *EC*, pages 266–283, 2012.

[7] I. Caragiannis, A. Filos-Ratsikas, and A. D. Procaccia. An improved 2-agent kidney exchange mechanism. In *WINE*, pages 37–48, 2011.

[8] Y. Cheng, W. Yu, and G. Zhang. Strategy-proof approximation mechanisms for an obnoxious facility game on networks. *Theoretical Computer Science*, 497:154–163, 2013.

[9] R. Cole, V. Gkatzelis, and G. Goel. Mechanism design for fair division: Allocating divisible items without payments. In *EC*, pages 251–268, 2013.

[10] V. Conitzer and T. Sandholm. Complexity of mechanism design. In *UAI*, pages 103–110, 2002.

[11] S. Dobzinski and S. Dughmi. On the power of randomization in algorithmic mechanism design. *SIAM Journal on Computing*, 42(6):2287–2304, 2013.

[12] S. Dughmi and A. Ghosh. Truthful assignment without money. In *EC*, pages 325–334, 2010.

[13] D. Fotakis and C. Tzamos. Winner-imposing strategyproof mechanisms for multiple facility location games. In *WINE*, pages 234–245, 2010.

[14] D. Fotakis and C. Tzamos. On the power of deterministic mechanisms for facility location games. In *ICALP*, pages 449–460, 2013.

[15] D. Fotakis and C. Tzamos. Strategyproof facility location for concave cost functions. In *EC*, pages 435–452, 2013.

[16] M. Guo and V. Conitzer. Strategy-proof allocation of multiple items between two agents without payments or priors. In *AAMAS*, pages 881–888, 2010.

[17] M. Guo, V. Conitzer, and D. Reeves. Competitive repeated allocation without payments. In *WINE*, pages 244–255, 2009.

[18] Laura Kang and David C. Parkes. Passive verification of the strategyproofness of mechanisms in open environments. In *ICEC*, 2006.

[19] E. Koutsoupias. Scheduling without payments. In *SAGT*, pages 143–153, 2011.

[20] P. Lu, X. Sun, Y. Wang, and Z. A. Zhu. Asymptotically optimal strategy-proof mechanisms for two-facility games. In *EC*, pages 315–324, 2010.

[21] P. Lu, Y. Wang, and Y. Zhou. Tighter bounds for facility games. In *WINE*, pages 137–148, 2009.

[22] H. Moulin. On strategy-proofness and single-peakedness. *Public Choice*, 35:437–455, 1980.

[23] Ahuva Mu'alem. A note on testing truthfulness. *ECCC, Report No. 130*, 2005.

[24] N. Nisan and A. Ronen. Algorithmic mechanism design. *Game. Econ. Behav.*, 35(1–2):166–196, 2001.

[25] K. Nissim, R. Smorodinsky, and M. Tennenholtz. Approximately optimal mechanism design via differential privacy. In *ITCS*, pages 203–213, 2012.

[26] M. Pauly and M. Wooldridge. Logic for mechanism design—a manifesto. In *GTDT*, 2003.

[27] A. D. Procaccia and M. Tennenholtz. Approximate mechanism design without money. *ACM Transactions on Economics and Computation*, 2013. Forthcoming; preliminary version in EC'09.

[28] E. M. Tadjouddine, F. Guerin, and W. Vasconcelos. Abstracting and verifying strategy-proofness for auction mechanisms. In *DALT*, pages 197–214, 2009.

[29] N. K. Thang. On (group) strategy-proof mechanisms without payment for facility location games. In *WINE*, pages 531–538, 2010.

[30] T. Todo, A. Iwasaki, and M. Yokoo. False-name-proof mechanism design without money. In *AAMAS*, pages 651–658, 2011.

[31] W. Vickrey. Counter speculation, auctions, and competitive sealed tenders. *J. Financ.*, 16(1):8–37, 1961.

[32] Y. Wilf and M. Feldman. Strategyproof facility location and the least squares objective. In *EC*, pages 873–890, 2013.

Mechanism Design with Strategic Mediators

[Extended Abstract]

Moshe Babaioff
Microsoft Research
Herzliya, Israel
moshe@microsoft.com

Moran Feldman[*]
EPFL
Lausanne, Switzerland
moran.feldman@epfl.ch

Moshe Tennenholtz[†]
Technion
Haifa, Israel
moshet@ie.technion.ac.il

ABSTRACT

We consider the problem of designing mechanisms that interact with strategic agents through *strategic* intermediaries (or mediators), and investigate the cost to society due to the mediators' strategic behavior. Selfish agents with private information are each associated with exactly one strategic mediator, and can interact with the mechanism exclusively through that mediator. Each mediator aims to optimize the combined utility of *his* agents, while the mechanism aims to optimize the combined utility of *all* agents. We focus on the problem of facility location on a metric induced by a publicly known tree. With non-strategic mediators, there is a dominant strategy mechanism that is optimal. We show that when both agents and mediators act strategically, there is no dominant strategy mechanism that achieves *any* approximation. We, thus, slightly relax the incentive constraints, and define the notion of a *two-sided incentive compatible* mechanism. We show that the 3-competitive *deterministic* mechanism suggested by Procaccia and Tennenholtz [12] and Dekel et al. [3] for lines extends naturally to trees, and is still 3-competitive as well as two-sided incentive compatible. This is essentially the best possible [3, 12]. We then show that by allowing randomization one can construct a 2-competitive *randomized* mechanism that is two-sided incentive compatible, and this is also essentially tight. This result also closes a gap left in the work of Procaccia and Tennenholtz [12] and Lu et al. [8] for the simpler problem of designing strategy-proof mechanisms for weighted agents with no mediators on a line, while extending to the more general model of trees. We also investigate a further generalization of the above setting where there are multiple levels of mediators.

[*]Supported by ERC Starting Grant 335288-OptApprox. Part of the work was done while the author was an intern at Microsoft Research, Herzliya.

[†]Work carried out at Microsoft Research, Herzliya.

Categories and Subject Descriptors

F.2.2 [**Theory of Computation**]: Analysis of Algorithms and Problem Complexity—*Nonnumerical Algorithms and Problems*; J.4 [**Computer Applications**]: Social and Behavioral Sciences—*Economics*

General Terms

Algorithms, Economics, Theory

Keywords

Mechanism design; mediators; facility location

1. INTRODUCTION

The Algorithmic Mechanism Design literature is generally interested in the implications of strategic behavior on the quality of social decision making. The usual assumption is that agents interact directly with a mechanism that picks an outcome. Yet, in many complex real world settings the interaction goes through *intermediaries*. If these intermediaries are acting strategically, this can influence the outcome picked by the mechanism, and result with an increase in social cost.

Consider, for example, a political decision taken by indirect voting. There are districts, and each district is represented by a representative. Each citizen has a position, and let us assume the positions of the citizens are points on an interval. A decision is also a point on the interval, and the cost for a citizen of such a point equals to the distance of her position from the decision made. Each representative aims to minimize the total cost for his own constituency, while the global goal is to minimize the total cost of all citizens. Decisions are taken using the reports of the representatives exclusively (there is no direct interaction with the agents), and these representatives have the freedom to manipulate their reports if such a manipulation helps their constituency. We are interested in questions such as: *What is the cost for society of such strategic behavior? How should the society set up the decision process to minimize that cost?*

More generally, we are interested in designing mechanisms that interact with strategic agents through *strategic* intermediaries (which we also call mediators). Agents have private information, and when put in a game, each agent acts to optimize her own utility.[1] The mechanism designer aims to optimize a social goal. The intermediaries do not have

---

[1]Throughout the paper we refer to an agent as "she", and to a mediator as "he".

any private information of their own, rather, each intermediary acts in the mechanism on behalf of the agents associated with him, aiming to optimize the same social goal with respect to his agents only (note that he does *not* have a personal agenda and is completely benevolent). As the intermediaries control the information flow from the agents to the mechanism, the mechanism faces strategic behavior not only of the agents, but also of intermediaries: within the freedom given by the mechanism, an intermediary acts strategically to optimize on behalf of the agents he represents.[2] In this paper we aim to understand the implications of the strategic behavior of intermediaries on the welfare of the agents.

The general framework outlined above can be studied in the context of many specific settings, and might yield very different results in different cases. Here, we focus on one such example and leave the consideration of other settings for future works. The setting we consider is facility location on a metric induced by a publicly known tree, which generalizes the decision making problem on a line introduced above. There are n agents, each located at some private location. The agents are partitioned to k disjoint sets, and each set is represented by a unique mediator. The mechanism (or *center*) should locate one facility. The cost of an agent is her distance from the location of the facility, and she aims to minimize her cost.[3] The social goal considered is the goal of minimizing the total distance of the agents from the facility.

If the center had access to the locations of all agents he could minimize the total cost by locating the facility at a *median* of all locations. While all our results hold for general tree metrics, for the sake of the exposition, in the introduction we mainly discuss the euclidian metric on an interval of the real line. For that metric, if t_i is the i-th left most agent (breaking ties arbitrarily) and n is odd, then there is a unique optimal location at the median location $t_{(n+1)/2}$ (for even n there is an interval of optimal locations, between the two medians). With strategic agents but no mediators (or equivalently, with non-strategic mediators), there is a dominant strategy mechanism that is optimal: locate the facility at a median point, breaking ties to the left. While this result gives a complete picture for the standard model without strategic mediators, we show that with both strategic agents and strategic mediators the picture is much more complicated. We first show that there does not exist a dominant strategy mechanism achieving any approximation. This happens even in a simple setting with two possible locations, a single mediator and a single agent, as if the agent switches between the locations in her report, the mediator should switch them back, and vice versa.

Given the impossibility to achieve a dominant strategy mechanism with good performance, we suggest a slightly weaker solution concept for direct revelation mechanisms (in which each agent reports her location, and each mediator reports the locations of all his agents). Our aim would be to build mechanisms which achieve good approximation (minimize the ratio between the cost of the outcome and the optimal cost). A mechanism is *agent-side incentive compatible (agent-side IC)* if each agent has a dominant strategy to be truthful given that her mediator is truthful (regardless of any parameter of the model, like the number of mediators, and regardless of other players' strategies). A mechanism is *mediator-side incentive compatible (mediator-side IC)* if each mediator has a dominant strategy to be truthful given that all his agents are truthful (again, regardless of any parameter and regardless of other players' strategies). We aim to construct mechanisms that are *two-sided incentive compatible (two-sided IC)*, i.e., they are both agent-side incentive compatible and mediator-side incentive compatible. We construct both deterministic and randomized mechanisms, and prove that they achieve essentially the best possible performance.[4]

One of the settings considered by Procaccia and Tennenholtz [12] is equivalent to designing deterministic mediator-side IC mechanisms on an interval of the real line. Their work implies that the results of Dekel et al. [3] for regression learning induce a 3-competitive *deterministic* mediator-side IC mechanism on an interval, and that this is *essentially* the best possible competitive ratio for such a mechanism. The mechanism induced works as follows: for every mediator, it replaces all points reported by the mediator by the optimal[5] location for that mediator, and then finds an optimal location with this new input (the mechanism essentially computes median of medians, weighted by the number of agents each mediator represents).

We prove the above mechanism is also agent-side IC, and describe a simple extension of it to general trees. This yields the following theorem.

THEOREM 1. *There exists a deterministic two-sided IC mechanism on tree metrics with a competitive ratio of 3. Moreover, for any fixed $\varepsilon > 0$, there is no deterministic two-sided IC mechanism with a competitive ratio of $3 - \varepsilon$.*

Procaccia and Tennenholtz [12] asked whether it is possible to get a better competitive ratio using randomization. They were able to answer affirmatively in the case of two mediators representing a "similar" number of agents. Lu et al. [8] extend the analysis of the mechanism of [12] to the case of multiple mediators representing a "similar" number of agents. However, even if all mediators have equal number of agents, the competitive ratio of this mechanism approaches 3 as the number of mediators increase. On the negative side, [8] gives a hardness result of 1.33 using a complex LP-based proof.

We suggest a new and sophisticated randomized mechanism that is 2-competitive and works for any tree. We also

---

[2] We assume that an intermediary *is able* to manipulate the reports of his agents, and do not consider settings in which there exists an infrastructure for sending messages between the agents and the center through the mediators in a non-manipulable way (*e.g.*, using cryptographic means.)

[3] While the general framework does not preclude transfer of utilities, in this specific model there is no money and utilities cannot be transferred. Thus, our results for facility location can be viewed as part of the literature on approximate mechanism design without money [12].

---

[4] All the mechanisms we construct run in polynomial time, while our lower bounds hold independent of computational consideration. Like in prior literature in approximate mechanism design without money [12], the barrier to optimality is incentives, not computation.

[5] There might be multiple optimal locations, in such cases ties need to be handled carefully to preserve incentives. To simplify the exposition, in the introduction we assume there are no ties.

prove using a simple argument that this is essentially the best possible.[6]

THEOREM 2. *There is a randomized two-sided IC mechanism on tree metrics with a competitive ratio of 2. Moreover, for any fixed $\varepsilon > 0$, there is no randomized two-sided IC mechanism with a competitive ratio of $2 - \varepsilon$.*

This result closes the gap left in the work of Procaccia and Tennenholtz [12] and Lu et al. [8] for the simpler problem of designing strategy-proof mechanisms for weighted agents with no mediators on a line, while extending to the more general model of trees.

For the case of locations on an interval of the real line the mechanism works as follows. For every mediator it replaces all points reported to the mediator by the optimal location for that mediator. For simplicity assume that the number of agents can be divided by 4. Then, it sorts the locations and uses a uniformly selected point among the $n/2$ central points (that is, the points from the $n/4+1$ leftmost location to the $3n/4$ leftmost location).

The randomized mechanism for trees generalizes this idea but is much more involved, and is our main technical contribution. This mechanism chooses from the set of medians (optimal locations of mediators) a "core" subset. This core is the equivalent of the central points from the line case. Each point in the core is assigned some positive probability to become the facility location. However, unlike in the line case, the probabilities assigned to the points of the core are non-uniform, and are carefully chosen to achieve both the competitive ratio and the right incentives. The exact probability distribution depends on the medians of all mediators, including medians outside of the core. If all the reports happen to fall on a single line, then the probability distribution becomes uniform, and the algorithm reduces to the one described above for lines.

We remark that all our mechanisms run algorithms that use only the optimal location for each mediator, and do not need, in addition, access to the exact locations of the agents associated with each mediator. We call an algorithm that satisfies this property a *mediator based* algorithm. We prove that such algorithms, which use *only* the locations of the optimal points of the mediators (and not the locations of their agents), cannot be better than 2-competitive. Interestingly, we show that there exists a deterministic mediator based algorithm that has a competitive ratio of 2, yet that algorithm is *not* two-sided IC. Thus, for deterministic two-sided IC mechanisms, the implications of strategic behavior by the mediators goes beyond the constraint of being mediator based; such mechanisms cannot be better than 3-competitive (which is tight). Thus, there is a gap that is a result of incentives, and is not due to insufficient information.

Tree metrics are a strict generalization of line metrics and capture domains that cannot be reasonably modeled by line metrics. Consider the following toy example. People of three nationalities live in a single country (*e.g.*, Switzerland), and want to elect a president. The candidates for the position differ in two attributes: their nationality and their degree of nationalism (for example, how much are they willing to settle for a compromise when dealing with an issue on which

the different national groups disagree). Each citizen, naturally, wants to elect a president sharing his nationality, but different citizens of the same national group might want to elect candidates with different degrees of nationalism. Notice that a candidate of low nationalism is more acceptable by citizens of other nationalities (regardless of the level of nationalism, every citizen would probably like to have a president of her own nationality), thus, the metric induced by this example is a star with 3 edges (of course, one can think of a country with more nationalities to get a star with more edges).

We also consider a generalization of the above setting allowing multiple levels of mediation. In other words, the center, agents and mediators form a tree, in which the root is the center and the leaves are the agents. Every internal node of the tree is a mediator representing its children in the tree. Unfortunately, the competitive ratio of every mechanism for this setting degrades exponentially with the height of the tree, even when the mechanism is only required to respect a very weak definition of incentive compatibility. This result is consistent with the existence of a symmetric voting system composed of k levels where a minority of size exponentially small in k can control the decisions of the system.[7] Finally, we show that the mechanism that iteratively applies weighted median has a competitive ratio which is essentially optimal and satisfies the weak notion of incentive compatibility.

1.1 Related Work

In this paper we deal with mediators who act as intermediaries between a set of agents and a mechanism. The most related setting studied in the literature is the recent work on auctions with intermediaries [4]. There, as in our setting, both agents and intermediaries are strategic. However, the setting there is Bayesian while ours is Pre-Bayesian. Also, our aim is to address the social welfare issue requiring dominant strategies by the agents when their associated mediator is truthful, rather than revenue maximization.

More generally, our work refers to the study of mediators (see, *e.g.*, [9] for a study in the context of complete information games, and [2] for a study in the context of incomplete information games). However, the typical signature of work on mediators is a single mediator that serves as an arbitration device: the agents are not a captive audience, and each of them can decide to participate in the game directly or work through the mediator. In our setting there are multiple intermediaries, each having his own captive audience, which must play the game through the intermediary. Moreover, the intermediaries are players and try to optimize their own utilities. Our setting nicely fit with situations such as voting by the (already selected) representatives of a geographic area or interest group. Additionally, we would like to mention the work of Leyton-Brown et al. [6] which deals with game theoretic aspects of bidding clubs in which "collusion devices" (cartels) are strategically created in a fixed mechanism (first price auction). In contrast, in our setting the partition of agents to mediators is pre-determined and our focus is on mechanism design given that fact.

The specific example of the framework that we consider is related to the recent literature on approximated mechanism

---

[6]Like the hardness of [8], our hardness holds, in fact, even for mediator-side IC mechanisms.

[7]An example of such a voting system can be found at http://gowers.wordpress.com/2013/10/15/holding-a-country-to-ransom/.

design without money [12]. This literature deals with approximation algorithms which are used to resolve incentive issues for tractable problems rather than overcome computational complexity of intractable problems, when no money transfers are available. An additional conceptual contribution of our work is extending the literature on approximate mechanism design without money to incorporate mediation devices. Indeed, the problem studied in this paper, the facility location problem, is the canonical problem of that literature, which is easily solved (optimally) if no intermediaries are in place.

As pointed out previously, the design of mediator-side incentive compatible mechanisms is equivalent to the design of strategy-proof mechanisms for weighted agents that was studied by Procaccia and Tennenholtz [12], and later also by Lu et al. [8] (these papers only considered the special case of a line metric). The implications of this equivalence to our settings were discussed above.

The literature on facility location on a line based on information provided by strategic agents is classic in the context of mechanism design with single-peaked preferences [10]. The extension of this problem to facility location on a network has been introduced by [13]. It has been shown that there exist non-dictatorial strategy proof algorithms for facility location on trees, and that any graph possessing circles does not allow for that. The study of approximate mechanism design without money for networks [1] discusses the minimization of the maximal distance to a facility on a network using deterministic and probabilistic strategy proof algorithms, yielding some positive approximation results and tight bounds. The problem of approximating the optimal location of two facilities on a line using strategy proof mechanisms has been discussed in [7], while the general case of locating k facilities in an approximately optimal manner using strategy proof mechanisms can be handled for large populations by the general technique given in [11].

2. MODEL AND SOLUTION CONCEPT

Within the general framework of strategic mediators we focus on one specific mechanism design problem: facility location on a metric induced by a publicly known tree $T = (V, E)$ with the following metric on each edge. Each edge $e \in E$ in the tree is mapped to the interval $[0, \ell_e]$ for some $\ell_e > 0$, with the usual Euclidian metric. In our problem there are n agents, each of which has a private position which can be represented by a point on the tree. The position of an agent can be either a node $v \in V$ or a point somewhere along an edge $e \in E$. Each one of the n agents is associated with one of k mediators. For $i \in [k]$, mediator d_i represents a set A_i of n_i agents; we denote these agents by $a_{i,1}, a_{i,2}, \ldots, a_{i,n_i}$. As we assume each agent is associated with exactly one mediator, the sets of agents of any two mediators do not intersect and $\sum_{i=1}^{k} n_i = n$. The position of each agent is only known to the agent herself, and we denote the private position of agent $a_{i,j}$ by $t_{i,j}$. Everything else is common knowledge. In particular, the number of agents represented by each mediator is known to the mechanism.[8] We call a point from the metric induced by T simply a "point".

For example, by saying that "p is a point" we mean that p is a point from the metric induced by T. Particularly, the location of each agent is a point.

The *center* has to pick a position for a single facility. If the center locates the facility at point p, then the *cost of an agent* $a_{i,j}$ is $\mathsf{dist}(p, t_{i,j})$, where $\mathsf{dist}(p, t_{i,j})$ is the distance between p and $t_{i,j}$ along the metric induced by T. The *social cost* of locating the facility at point p is $\sum_{i \in [k], j \in [n_i]} \mathsf{dist}(p, t_{i,j})$, *i.e.*, the sum of all the agents' costs. The objective of the center is to pick a location for the facility that minimizes the social cost. The *cost of a mediator* d_i ($i \in [k]$) is the total cost for the agents he represents, which is $\sum_{j \in [n_i]} \mathsf{dist}(p, t_{i,j})$. Each mediator aims to minimize his cost. We use the term *player* to denote either an agent or a mediator. We assume that the center and players are risk neutral, and for a distribution over locations, they evaluate their cost by the expected cost. Note that in our model there is no money, and utilities cannot be transferred.

An *algorithm* for the center is a mapping from its input, the locations of all agents, to a location for the facility. We say that an algorithm is α-competitive, or has a *competitive ratio* of α, if for any set of locations for the agents, the location picked by the center for the facility induces a cost that is at most α times larger than the minimal possible cost (with respect to its input).

When the agents' locations are private information the center has to come up with a mechanism by which players report their information and this information is used to pick a facility location. We consider *direct revelation mechanisms* in which each agent is asked to report her location (to her mediator), and each mediator is asked to report the location of each of his agents. The mechanism uses the public information and the mediators' reports to locate the facility, with the aim of minimizing the social cost. We say that a mechanism is α-*competitive*, or has a *competitive ratio* of α, if under the solution concept that we consider, the location of the facility picked by the center has cost that is at most α times larger than the minimal possible cost. Crucial to our model is the assumption that the center (or the mechanism) can not interact directly with the agents, and has access to their locations only through their mediators, which can manipulate the agents' reports.

Solution Concept. Any direct revelation mechanism picked by the center puts the agents and the mediators (the players), which are both strategic, into a game. We would like to use mechanisms which induce games with some desired properties.

A direct revelation mechanism is *dominant strategy truthful* if it is a dominant strategy for each agent to report her location truthfully (regardless of the strategies chosen by the mediators and the other agents), and it is a dominant strategy for each mediator to report the locations of all of his agents to the center exactly as reported to him by the agents (again, regardless of the strategies chosen by the agents and the other mediators). We observe that asking a competitive mechanism to be dominant strategy truthful is unrealistic.

OBSERVATION 1. *No direct revelation dominant strategy truthful mechanism has a finite competitiveness, and this is*

---

[8]If the number of agents represented by each mediator is considered private information, then the mechanism has no way to distinguish "important" mediators representing many agents from "unimportant" mediators representing only few agents. This intuitive impossibility can be easily formalized

to show that no constant competitive ratio is possible. The assumption that size of the population represented by each mediator is public is reasonable in many settings, for example, the size of the population of a congressman's district is publicly known.

true even if the center is allowed to charge the mediators and agents.

PROOF. Consider an instance with a single mediator representing a single agent which can take two possible locations x and y. To have finite competitiveness the center must locate the facility at the location of the agent (when both the agent and the mediator are truthful). However, the center gets no information other than the report of the mediator, and therefore, it must *always* locate the facility at the location reported by the mediator. Moreover, the charges collected by the center can depend only on this location.

Let p_x and p_y be the charges that the mediator pays when reporting x and y, respectively. Assume without loss of generality that $p_y \geq p_x$. Now, assume that the agent's strategy is to report y despite the fact that she is located at x. If the mediator switches the location back, then his cost is p_x, while a truthful repetition of the agent's report will result in a cost of $p_y + |y - x| \geq p_x + |y - x| > p_x$. Thus, it is clearly non-optimal for the mediator in this case to truthfully repeat the report of the agent. □

Remark 1. The above impossibility applies to a setting in which all entities have *exactly* the same utility function, so there are no conflicts. It is a result of the sequential nature of information propagation from the agents to the center through the mediators, and the incompatibility of that with dominant strategies.

Given this impossibility result we need to settle for a slightly weaker solution concept, achieving *Incentive Compatibility* (IC) in the following sense. We still want each agent to have an incentive to be truthful, as long as her mediator is truthful (as opposed to playing an "unreasonable" strategy), and we want each mediator to be truthful as long as his agents are truthful. This is captured by the following definition.

Definition 1. A direct revelation mechanism is *agent-side incentive compatible* if for every mediator d_i, in the induced game created by fixing d_i to be truthful, truthful reporting is a dominant strategy for each agent $a_{i,j}$ represented by d_i.

A direct revelation mechanism is *mediator-side incentive compatible* if for every mediator d_i, in the induced game created by fixing all d_i's agents to be truthful, truthful reporting is a dominant strategy for d_i.

A direct revelation mechanism is *two-sided incentive compatible* if it is agent-side incentive compatible and mediator-side incentive compatible.

Note that in any two-sided incentive compatible mechanism, it is in particular an Ex-post Nash for all players to be truthful.

To understand the implication of strategic behavior by the mediators we compare the competitiveness achieved by the best two-sided incentive compatible mechanisms to the competitiveness achieved by the best agent-side incentive compatible mechanisms (we do so both for deterministic and for randomized mechanisms).

2.1 Agent-Side Incentive Compatible Mechanisms

Median points play a significant role both in the optimal algorithm and our mechanisms. We next present some basic definitions and observe that median points exactly characterize optimal locations.

Definition 2. Median points and weighted median points are defined as follows.

- A *weighted point* is a pair (p, x) where p is a point and x is a positive real number. Given a weighted point $\tilde{p} = (p, x)$, we say that x is the weight of $\tilde{p}$, and write $w(\tilde{p}) = x$. We also think of $\tilde{p}$ as located at location p in the metric. Hence, we can talk, *e.g.*, about the distance between two weighted points.[9]

- Given a multi-set S of elements, let $f(p, S)$ be the multiplicity of p in S (*i.e.*, $f(p, S)$ is the number of copies of p in S). Given an additional multi-set S', we denote by $S \cup S'$ and $S \setminus S'$ two multi-set containing $f(p, S) + f(p, S')$ and $\max\{f(p, S) - f(p, S'), 0\}$ copies of every element $p \in S \cup S'$, respectively.

- Given a multi-set S of weighted points and a point p.
  - Let S_p denote the multi-set of weighted points in S that have p as their location. More formally, for every weighted point $\tilde{q} = (q, x) \in S$, the multi-set S_p contains $f(\tilde{q}, S)$ copies of $\tilde{q}$ if $q = p$, and no copy of $\tilde{q}$ otherwise.
  - The weight of S, denoted by $w(S)$, is the total weight of the weighted points in S. More formally, $w(S) = \sum_{\tilde{q} \in S} w(\tilde{q}) \cdot f(\tilde{q}, S)$,
  - Let m_p be the maximum weight of a multi-set $S' \subseteq S \setminus S_p$ such that the path connecting every two weighted points of S' does not go through p.
  - We say that p is a *weighted median* of S if $m_p \leq w(S)/2$.

- Given a multi-set S of points, we say that a point p is a *median* of S if it is a weighted median of the multi-set S' containing $f(p, S)$ copies of $(p, 1)$ for every point $p \in S$.

Informally, a point p is a median of S if removing it splits the tree T into parts, each containing at most $|S|/2$ points of S. The importance of median points stems from the following easy observation, whose proof is deferred to a full version of this paper due to space constraints (simpler versions of this lemma go back to [5]).

OBSERVATION 2. *For every non empty finite multi-set S of weighted points, there is at least one weighted median. Moreover, a point p is a weighted median of S if and only if locating the facility at p minimizes the weighted total cost of a set of agents located at the points of S (i.e., the sum $\sum_{\tilde{q} \in S} w(\tilde{q}) \cdot f(\tilde{q}, S) \cdot \mathsf{dist}(p, \tilde{q})$).*

The mechanism that always picks a median of all the locations of the agents (with a careful tie breaking) is optimal and agent-side incentive compatible. Thus, we have the following observation that naturally extends a well known result for line metrics [12].

OBSERVATION 3. *There exists a deterministic agent-side incentive compatible mechanism which is optimal (i.e., 1-competitive).*

We note that the optimal agent-side IC mechanism is deterministic. Hence, randomization clearly does not help in improving performance when mediators are not strategic. Our results show that this is not the case when mediators are strategic and one aims for two-sided IC mechanisms.

---

[9] In the interest of readability, throughout the paper we put the tilde sign above letters representing weighted points.

2.2 Mediator Based Algorithms

We say that an algorithm for the center is *mediator based* if it uses only an optimal facility location for each mediator (but never uses any other information regarding the positions of the agents themselves). We show that for mediator based algorithms, randomization does not improve performance, as any such randomized α-competitive algorithm can be transformed to a mediator based deterministic algorithm with the same competitive ratio (moreover, the resulting algorithm performs at least as good on every single input). To state this result we first need the following lemma whose proof is deferred to a full version of this paper.

LEMMA 1. *For any tree and any distribution over points F, there exists a point $p(F)$ such that for any finite multi-set S of points:*

$$\mathop{\mathbb{E}}_{p' \sim F} \left[\sum_{q \in S} \mathsf{dist}(p', q) \cdot f(q, S) \right] \geq \sum_{q \in S} \mathsf{dist}(p(F), q) \cdot f(q, S) \ .$$

Moreover, for the euclidian metric on $[a, b]$ (for arbitrary a and b) the expected location according to F can serve as such a point $p(F)$.

Note that $p(F)$ does *not* depend on S, and the same $p(F)$ works for every S. A randomized algorithm maps the locations of all agents to a distribution over locations F. By the above lemma the deterministic algorithm that instead locates the facility deterministically at $p(F)$ can only improve the social cost for every input. Thus, we have the following corollary.

COROLLARY 1. *Given any α-competitive mediator based randomized algorithm, it is possible to construct a mediator based deterministic algorithm with the same competitive ratio α.*

Note that the above transformation does *not* maintain incentives, indeed we show below that there exists a mediator based randomized two-sided IC mechanism which is 2-competitive, but no mediator based deterministic two-sided IC mechanism achieves this competitive ratio. Thus, although randomization does not improve performance for mediator-based *algorithms*, it does improve performance for mediator-based *two-sided IC mechanisms*.

3. DETERMINISTIC TWO-SIDED IC MECHANISMS

In this section we extend the deterministic "median of medians" mechanism of [3, 12] from lines to trees and show that the resulting mechanism, which we call the *Weighted Median Mechanism* (WMM), is a deterministic two-sided IC mechanism. This mechanism is also 3-competitive, which is essentially tight by a lower bound of [3, 12] (given for completeness as Theorem 4). The mechanism essentially elicits from each mediator an optimal location from the mediator's perspective (median of the mediator's agents), and then picks a weighted median of these locations. To create the right incentives for the agents and mediators, tie breaking must be handled carefully in both steps of the mechanism. By breaking ties in a way that is independent of the players' reports, we make sure the players have no incentive to manipulate. The basic idea is that in each step we break ties

in favor of the point closest to an arbitrary predetermined point. To formally describe WMM we need the following observation which proves that the above tie breaking rule is well defined, *i.e.*, whenever the mechanism has to decide between a set of points, there is always a unique point in the set which is closest to the arbitrary predetermined point. The proofs of Observation 4 and the other claims in this section are deferred to a full version of this paper due to space constraints.

OBSERVATION 4. *Given a non-empty finite multi-set S of weighted points and an arbitrary point $z \in V$, the set M of weighted medians of S contains a unique point p closest to z.*

The *Weighted Median Mechanism (WMM)* is a direct revelation mechanism in which the center does the following:
- For each mediator d_i it computes ℓ_i which is the median of the multi-set $\{t'_{i,j} | 1 \leq j \leq n_i\}$ closest to z_i, where $t'_{i,j}$ is the location reported by d_i for agent $a_{i,j}$ and z_i is an arbitrary point chosen independently of the reports received from the mediators (such a median exists, and is unique, by Observation 4).
- Let M be the set of weighted medians of the multi-set $\{(\ell_i, n_i) | 1 \leq i \leq k\}$. Locate the facility at the point of M closest to z, where z is an arbitrary point chosen independently of the reports received from the mediators.

The next theorem summarizes the properties of WMM.

THEOREM 3. *For any tree metric, the Weighted Median Mechanism is a deterministic two-sided IC mechanism with a competitive ratio of 3.*

Note that this direct revelation mechanism can also be executed with much less communication since the only information the center needs from each mediator is a single point (the location of the median closest to some arbitrary point), and not the location of every agent represented by the mediator. Thus, the center can ask each mediator d_i to report a single location ℓ_i, and locate the facility at the weighted median of the multi-set $\{(\ell_i, n_i) | 1 \leq i \leq k\}$ closest to some point z picked in advance. Observe that this algorithm for the center is mediator based. The resulting mechanism clearly achieves the same competitiveness as the direct revelation mechanism when each mediator d_i indeed reports a median location ℓ_i of his agents closets to an arbitrary point z_i since the location is picked using exactly the same method. Moreover, this mechanisms is also two-sided IC since the space of possible deviations for the mediators in this mechanism is more restricted than the corresponding space in the direct revelation mechanism.

On line metrics WMM is essentially identical to a mechanism already known to be 3-competitive and mediator-side IC by an observation of [12] based on a result of [3]. The following theorem proved by [3, 12] shows that WMM has an optimal competitive ratio.

THEOREM 4. *Fix any constant $\varepsilon > 0$. Then, no direct revelation deterministic mechanism that is mediator-side incentive compatible has a competitive ratio of $3 - \varepsilon$, even for line metrics.*

4. RANDOMIZED TWO-SIDED IC MECHANISMS

It is known by [3, 12] that there is no deterministic Two-Sided IC Mechanism that is better than 3-competitive (this result also appears as Theorem 4). In this section we show that we can improve and achieve a competitive ratio of 2 by switching to randomized mechanisms, and that this is the best ratio that can be achieved. All the proofs in this section are deferred to a full version of this paper due to space constraints.

To simplify the exposition of our mechanism, we first describe it for the simple case of line metrics (*i.e.*, for the case where the tree T is simply an interval). A line metric is the Euclidean metric of an arbitrary interval $[a, b]$ (where $a < b$ are real numbers). Notice that a point in the metric is simply a real number from the interval $[a, b]$. The *Two Percentiles Range Mechanism (TPRM)* is a direct revelation mechanism in which the center runs the following algorithm:

- For each mediator d_i compute the median ℓ_i of the multi-set $\{t'_{i,j} | 1 \le j \le n_i\}$ that is closest to z_i, where $t'_{i,j}$ is the location reported by d_i for agent $a_{i,j}$ and z_i is an arbitrary point chosen independently of the reports received from the agents.
- Consider the multi-set S of points, created by adding ℓ_i to the multi-set n_i times, for each i. Let u_i denote the i-th element of this multi-set when sorted in any non-decreasing order.
- Randomly choose a location for the facility from the list: $u_{\lfloor n/4 \rfloor+1}, u_{\lfloor n/4 \rfloor+2}, \ldots, u_{\lceil 3n/4 \rceil}$, where the probability of each value u_i in this list is $(n/2)^{-1}$, except for the first and last values ($u_{\lfloor n/4 \rfloor+1}$ and $u_{\lceil 3n/4 \rceil}$), which have a probability of $(1 - r/4)/(n/2)$ where r is the reminder of dividing n by 4.

Like in the deterministic case, Observation 4 ensures that ℓ_i is well defined for every i. Also similarly to the deterministic case, this direct revelation mechanism can also be executed with much less communication by only asking each mediator to report a single point (the location of the median closest to some arbitrary point) and running a mediator based algorithm that corresponds to the two final steps of TPRM on the reports. The resulting mechanism will have the same properties (competitiveness, incentives) as the direct revelation mechanism.

THEOREM 5. *For any line metric, the* Two Percentiles Range Mechanism *(TPRM) is a randomized two-sided IC mechanism with a competitive ratio of 2.*

The intuition behind the improved competitive ratio of TPRM, as compared to WMM, is as follows. Consider a section s connecting the real locations of two agents separated by no other agent.

- If s is located near the median of all the agents, then it is not very important on which side of it is the facility located, because either way s will contribute to the distance between the facility and about half the agents.
- If s is located very far from the median, then both TPRM and WMM will locate the facility at the "right" side of s.
- If s is not near the median, nor very far from it, then it is important that the mechanism will locate the facility at the right side of s. WMM makes the wrong call for some inputs, and, being deterministic, when it

makes the wrong call it makes it with probability 1. On the other hand, it can be shown that the randomized TPRM always has a significant probability of making the right choice.

Next, we present a mechanism that extends TPRM to general trees, called the *Tree Randomized Mechanism (TRM)*. Like TPRM, TRM defines a distribution over the medians of the sets reported by the mediators, and then chooses the facility location randomly according to this distribution. The distribution is carefully picked to achieve the best possible competitive ratio of 2. More specifically, the mass of the distribution is placed on the "central parts" of the tree, which is analogous to behavior of TPRM. Formally, the TRM is a direct revelation two-sided IC mechanism that is also 2-competitive. The description of TRM consists of two parts. The first part of TRM determines the medians of the sets reported by the mediators, and then splits the edges of T at these points, which allows us to assume that all medians are vertexes of T. Additionally, this part finds a point r which is considered to be the "center" of T. If necessary, an edge is split to make r a vertex of T, and then T is rooted at r.

TRM - Part 1

1. Fix an arbitrary point z independently of the reports of the mediators.
2. Define $\text{size}(p) = \sum_{i|\ell_i = p} n_i$ for every point p, where ℓ_i is the median closest to z of the points reported by d_i.
3. Let $L = \{(p, \text{size}(p)) \mid p$ is a point and $\text{size}(p) > 0\}$.
4. Let r be the weighted median of L closest to z.
5. For every point $p \in \{r\} \cup \{\ell_i \mid 1 \le i \le k\}$ do:
6.   If p is an internal point of an edge e, then:
7.   Split e at point p to two edges.
8. Root T at r.

Clearly we can assume after the first part of TRM that $\{r\} \cup \{\ell_i \mid 1 \le i \le k\} \subseteq V$. Since T is now rooted, we can define additional notation that is used to describe the second part of TRM.

Definition 3.
- children(u) - The set of children nodes of u in the tree.
- subtree(u) - The set of nodes in the subtree of node u, including u itself. More formally, subtree(u) = $\{u\} \cup [\cup_{u' \in \text{children}(u)} \text{subtree}(u')]$.
- treesize(u) - The number of agents represented by a mediator d_i for which $\ell_i \in \text{subtree}(u)$. More formally, treesize(u) = size(u) + $\sum_{u' \in \text{children}(u)} \text{treesize}(u')$.

The second part of TRM defines the probability distribution used to select the facility location. Informally, this distribution has the following property: the probability that the facility location is in the *subtree* of a (non-root) vertex u is proportional to $\max\{\text{treesize}(u) - n/4, 0\}$. An alternative view of this distribution is that the algorithm preprocess the agents by discarding some agents of peripheral vertexes, and "promoting" other agents of these vertexes to be associated with vertexes which are closer to the root. After this preprocessing, the algorithm selects a uniformly random remaining agent, and locates the facility at the location desired by the mediator associated with the selected agent. The preprocessing is done in a way that guarantees the following:

- If only a few agents originally belong to the subtree of a vertex u (*i.e.*, treesize(u) $\le n/4$), then all these agents are either discarded or promoted to some ances-

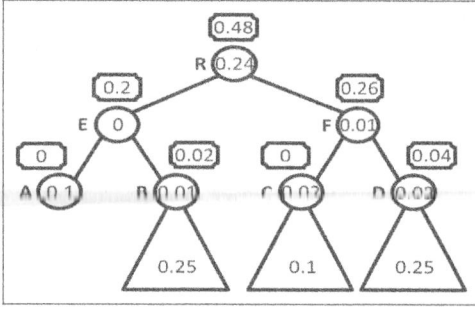

Figure 1: Example of a probability distribution induced by TRM.

tor vertex of u, and thus, u never becomes the facility location.

- If many agents originally belong to the subtree of a vertex u, then the preprocessing reduces the number of agents associated with this subtree by $n/4$ (or $n/2$ if u is the root).

TRM - Part 2

1. Let $X = \{u \in V \mid \text{treesize}(u) \geq n/4\}$.
2. Let $c(u)$ denote the value $n/4$ for every node $u \in X - \{r\}$ and $n/2$ for $u = r$.
3. Pick every node $u \in X$ as the facility location with probability:
$$p(u) = \frac{\text{treesize}(u) - c(u)}{n/2}$$
$$- \frac{\sum_{u' \in X \cap \text{children}(u)} (\text{treesize}(u') - c(u'))}{n/2}.$$

For consistency, define $p(u) = 0$ for every point $u \notin X$.

Note that this direct revelation mechanism can also be viewed (and executed) as a mediator based algorithm as the center only needs from each mediator d_i a location ℓ_i which is optimal from d_i's perspective.

THEOREM 6. *For any tree metric, the* Tree Randomized Mechanism *(TRM) is a randomized two-sided IC mechanism with a competitive ratio of 2.*

Let us get a better understanding of TRM by considering an example input (given as Figure 1) and explaining the probability distribution induced by TRM. The figure depicts the top 7 nodes of an example tree T that can be outputted by the first part of TRM. The number inside each node represents the portion of the agents population represented by mediators whose (sole) median is this node. For example, the number 0.24 appears inside the root node R, hence, in our example, $0.24 \cdot n$ agents are represented by mediators whose median is R. Some of the nodes in the figure have a triangle shape dangling from them. Each triangle represents the subtree of the node it is dangling from, and the number written inside it represents the portion of the agents represented by mediators whose (sole) median is inside the subtree (but is not the root of the subtree). For example, inside the rightmost triangle we have the label 0.25. Hence there are $0.25 \cdot n$ agents represented by mediators whose median is inside the subtree of D, but is not D itself. Finally, outside of each node there is an additional number (in a box). This number represents the probability that TRM selects this node as the facility location.

Following is a short explanation of how (some of) the probabilities in Figure 1 were calculated. We say that a node (subtree) in Figure 1 has a weight of x if x agents are represented by mediators whose median is the node (a node in the subtree). Observe that TRM selects R to be the root node r since its left subtree has a weight of only $0.36 \cdot n < n/2$, and its right subtree has a weight of only $0.4 \cdot n < n/2$. Next, observe that no triangle in the figure represents a subtree with weight of more than 0.25, and therefore, no node in the subtrees represented by these rectangles has a positive probability to be the location of the facility. Consider now a few of the nodes of Figure 1.

- The subtree rooted at A (which contains A alone) has a weight of only $0.1 \cdot n \leq 0.25 \cdot n$, and therefore, $A \notin X$ and thus has 0 probability to be the facility location.
- The subtree rooted at B has a weight of $0.26 \cdot n > 0.25 \cdot n$, and no other node in this subtree has a positive probability to be the facility location. Therefore, B has a probability of $2(0.26 - c(B)) = 2(0.26 - 0.25) = 0.02$ to be the facility location.
- The subtree rooted at E has a weight of $0.36 \cdot n > 0.25 \cdot n$. However, E has a single child B with a positive probability, and the subtree rooted at B has a weight of 0.26. Therefore, E has a probability of $2(0.36 - c(E) - (0.26 - c(B))) = 0.2$ to be the facility location.
- The subtree rooted at R has a weight of $1 \cdot n$. However, R has two children E and F, each associated with a positive probability by the algorithm, whose subtrees have weights of 0.36 and 0.4, respectively. Therefore, R has a probability of $2(1 - c(R) - (0.36 - c(E)) - (0.4 - c(F))) = 0.48$ to be the facility location.

The following theorem shows that TRM and TPRM have optimal competitive ratios.

THEOREM 7. *Fix any constant $\varepsilon > 0$. Then, no direct revelation randomized mechanism that is mediator-side incentive compatible and no mediator based algorithm has a competitive ratio of $2 - \varepsilon$, even for line metrics.*

5. MULTIPLE LEVELS OF MEDIATION

In this section we present results for the case of multiple levels of mediation. We can represent a hierarchy of mediators by a tree (note that this tree is *not* the same tree as the one defining the metric). The root of the tree represents the center, each internal node represents a mediator, and each leaf represents an agent. The tree is common knowledge. Let s be the *depth* of the tree, or the maximal number of edges between the root and a leaf. The case we have studied so far is thus represented by a tree with three levels ($s = 2$), the root represents the center, the internal level represents the mediators, and the leaves represents the agents.

As before, a *player* is either an agent or a mediator. For each player, another player is a *direct kin* if that other player is either a descendent in the tree, or an ancestor in the tree. Recall that a direct revelation mechanism is a mechanism in which each agent reports her location, and each mediator reports all of the locations of the agents below him. In such a mechanism, we say that a player is *truthful* if she is an agent and she reports her location truthfully, or he is a mediator and he reports all of the locations of the agents below him truthfully (as received from his direct descendants). While our results from the previous sections show the existence of competitive mechanisms that are two-sided incentive compatible for trees with a single layer of mediators, the next theorem proves that even for a much weaker solution concept, ex-post incentive compatibility, competitive mechanisms with multiple layers of mediators are impossible.

Definition 4. A direct revelation mechanism is *ex-post incentive compatible* if for every player, being truthful always maximizes the player's utility, assuming that all other players are truthful.

We note that this solution concept is weaker than being two-sided IC (or the natural generalization of this notion to more levels) as it does not require any player to ever have a dominant strategy in an induced game with only part of the other players (his direct kins) being truthful. Unfortunately, it is impossible to construct competitive ex-post IC mechanisms for $s > 2$.

THEOREM 8. *No mechanism with a finite competitive ratio is ex-post IC for instances with $s > 2$.*

PROOF. Consider the following instance on the metric interval $[0, 2]$ with $s = 3$.

- Level 3 contains the center.
- Level 2 contains a single mediator C, reporting to the center.
- Level 1 contains two mediators, which we will call A and B, both reporting to C.
- Level 0 contains five agents:
  - Agents a, b and c are represented by mediator A, and located in $0, 0$ and 1, respectively.
  - Agents d and e are represented by mediator B, and are both located at 2.

Assume for the sake of contradiction that there exists a finite competitive ratio mechanism which is ex-post IC for the above instance. Observe that if the center gets a report stating that all five agents are located at a point p, then the mechanism must locate the facility at p to have a bounded competitive ratio. Assuming all players are truthful, except maybe for C. Then the following observations hold:

- Let S be the multi-set of the positions of the agents as reported to C. Then, S represents the true locations of all the agents.
- The center observes the report of C.

Let m be S's median. By Observation 2, m is the optimal facility location for C. If C deviates and reports that all agents are located at m, the center will have to locate the facility at m, due to the above discussion. Thus, for C to have no incentive to deviate, the center must always locate the facility at the median of the locations it gets.

Consider now the situation that all players are truthful, except maybe for A. Let us considers A's situation. A is reported, correctly, that his agents are located at $0, 0$ and 1. Thus, the optimal facility location for A is 0. If A reports truthfully, the center will get the reports $0, 0, 1, 2$ and 2, and, by the above discussion, will locate the facility at 1. On the other hand, if A deviates, and reports that all his agents are located at 0, the center will get the reports $0, 0, 0, 2$ and 2, and will locate the facility at 0 (which is better from A's point of view). Thus, the mechanism considered is not ex-post IC. □

It seems that in any mechanism that satisfies "minimal" incentive properties, the only "useful" part of the information reported by a player to its ancestor is the optimal location (from the perspective of that player) with respect to

that player's input. That is, the mechanism's output cannot change if the locations reported by a player are all replaced by the optimal location of that player (with respect to that player's input). This observation naturally suggests the following mechanism which generalizes the Weighted Median Mechanism. The mechanism iteratively computes weighted medians (breaking ties in a report-independent way) for each mediator, bottom up, and outputs the final location. Consider the example presented in the proof of Theorem 8. The suggested mechanism would behave as if A reports that all his agents are located at 0, and C reports that all his agents are located at 0 (as this is the median of his input which is $0, 0, 0, 2, 2$). The final outcome would be to locate the facility at 0. Notice that this outcome, while not optimal, is not too far from optimality.

This raises few questions which we address next. First, assuming that all players are truthful, what is the approximation that this mechanism achieves? Second, what kind of incentive property does this mechanism satisfy? And finally, for this incentive property, is there any other mechanism that is substantially better?

We begin by establishing some notation. Let $d_{i,j}$ be the jth node of the ith level in the tree, where the level of the leaves is $i = 0$ (notice that $d_{s,1}$ is the root). For every $0 \leq i \leq s$, let m_i denote the number of nodes appearing in level i of the tree. For every mediator $d_{i,j}$ we denote by $C_{i,j}$ the set of children of $d_{i,j}$ in the tree and by $A_{i,j}$ the set of leaves (agents) that descent from $d_{i,j}$. For consistency, if $d_{i,j}$ is an agent, then $C_{i,j} = \varnothing$ and $A_{i,j} = \{d_{i,j}\}$. Finally, for every agent a, let t_a denote the location of a.

We can now formally define the mechanism. We note that this is not a direct revelation mechanism, but rather, each player is asked to report a single location.

In the *Iterative Weighted Median Mechanism (IWMM)*:

- An agent reports her location.
- A mediator reports the weighted median of the reports he gets. More formally, let $\ell_{i,j}$ be the report of player $d_{i,j}$ and let $z_{i,j}$ be an arbitrary point selected independently of any reports. Then, $\ell_{i,j}$ is the weighted median of the multi-set $\{(\ell_{i-1,j'}, |A_{i-1,j'}|) \mid d_{i-1,j'} \in C_{i,j}\}$ closest to $z_{i,j}$.
- The center locates the facility at the point it would have reported according to the above rule, if it were a mediator.

Notice that IWMM is well defined by Observation 4. The next proposition summarizes the competitiveness of IWMM when viewed as an algorithm (with respect to its input). All proofs in the remining of this section are deferred to a full version of this paper due to space constraints.

PROPOSITION 1. *Assume that in Iterative Weighted Median Mechanism every agent is truthful and every mediator follows the protocol, then the mechanism has a competitive ratio of $2^s - 1$ for any tree metric.*

By Theorem 8, the direct revelation implementation of IWMM is not ex-post IC. Yet, this mechanism satisfies the following, much weaker, incentive property. Informally, every mediator, assuming that all his ascendants follow the protocol, and that the input he received from each of his direct descendants represents the true location of all agents of that direct descendant, will optimize his perceived utility by following the protocol.

Definition 5. A *single-location mechanism* is a non-direct revelation mechanism in which each player is reporting a single location to its direct ascendant.

A player of a single-location mechanism is *straightforward* if she is an agent and is truthful, or if he is a mediator and the location he reports is optimal with respect to his utility function assuming every agent represented by a direct descendant is located at the location reported by that direct descendent.

For a player in a single-location mechanism, we say that being straightforward is *naively optimal*, if being straightforward maximizes the above utility function under the assumption that his ascendants are straightforward.

A single-location mechanism is *naively incentive compatible* if for every player being straightforward is naively optimal.

We note that the term *naive* comes to emphasize that the players do not form Bayesian beliefs regarding the true locations of their agents and they do not try to optimize with respect to that belief, but rather (naively) assume that the reports they receive represent the true locations of the agents. Such a naive behavior is consistent with a mediator that never allows himself to harm his agents in the case when the reported locations are actually the true locations of his agents.

We prove that IWMM is naively incentive compatible. Combining this with Proposition 1 we derive the following theorem which summarizes the properties of IWMM.

THEOREM 9. *The Iterative Weighted Median Mechanism (IWMM) is a naively incentive compatible mechanism with a competitive ratio of $2^s - 1$ for any tree metric.*

Note that although our incentive property is extremely weak, the competitive ratio of IMWW degrades exponentially in s. Can such bad performance be avoided? We conclude this section with a lower bound showing that up to constant factors, it cannot.

THEOREM 10. *Fix any constant $\varepsilon > 0$ and tree depth $s \geq 3$. Then, no mechanism (possibly randomized) that is naively incentive compatible has a competitive ratio of $2^{s-2} - 1 - \varepsilon$ even for line metrics.*

6. CONCLUSION

We studied the impact of strategic mediators on the competitive ratio of IC mechanisms in a facility location setting. Our results show that a single layer of mediation cause a moderate degradation in the competitive ratio, which becomes much worse as additional layers of mediation are introduced. We also showed that randomized mechanisms perform better than deterministic ones.

Strategic mediators appear in many real world scenarios, and we believe it is important to study the implications of their behaviour in various settings. For example, in display advertising, one common practice is for a mediator to buy advertisement space on a web page and split it between multiple advertisers he represents. Assume the mediator gets bids from potential advertisers, and based on these bids decides how to bid for the space (in the ad exchange auction). If he wins the space he also need to decide how to split the newly bought space among his advertisers. The mediator needs a strategy that will incentivize his advertisers to be truthful, which is not a trivial task even if the ad exchange uses a second price auction. Studying the effect on the social welfare and revenue of such mediators is an interesting open problem.

7. REFERENCES

[1] N. Alon, M. Feldman, A. D. Procaccia, and M. Tennenholtz. Strategyproof approximation of the minimax on networks. *Mathematics of Operations Research*, 35(3):513–526, 2010.

[2] I. Ashlagi, D. Monderer, and M. Tennenholtz. Mediators in position auctions. *Games and Economic Behavior*, 67(1):2–21, 2009.

[3] O. Dekel, F. Fischer, and A. D. Procaccia. Incentive compatible regression learning. *J. Comput. Syst. Sci.*, 76(8):759–777, December 2010.

[4] J. Feldman, V. S. Mirrokni, S. Muthukrishnan, and M. M. Pai. Auctions with intermediaries: extended abstract. In *ACM Conference on Electronic Commerce*, pages 23–32, New York, NY, USA, 2010. ACM.

[5] C. Jordan. Sur les assemblages de lignes. *J. Reine Angew. Math.*, 70:185–190, 1869.

[6] K. Leyton-Brown, Y. Shoham, and M. Tennenholtz. Bidding clubs in first-price auctions. In *AAAI/IAAI*, pages 373–378, 2002.

[7] P. Lu, X. Sun, Y. Wang, and Z. Zhu. Asymptotically optimal strategy-proof mechanisms for two-facility games. In *ACM Conference on Electronic Commerce*, pages 315–324, New York, NY, USA, 2010. ACM.

[8] P. Lu, Y.Wang, and Y. Zhou. Tighter bounds for facility games. In *The International Workshop on Internet and Network Economics*, pages 137–148, Berlin, Heidelberg, 2009. Springer-Verlag.

[9] D. Monderer and M. Tennenholtz. Strong mediated equilibrium. *Artif. Intell.*, 173(1):180–195, 2009.

[10] H. Moulin. On strategy-proofness and single-peakedness. *Public Choice*, 35(4):437–455, 1980.

[11] K. Nissim, R. Smorodinsky, and M. Tennenholtz. Approximately optimal mechanism design via differential privacy. In *Innovations of Theoretical Computer Science*, pages 203–212, New York, NY, USA, 2012. ACM.

[12] A. D. Procaccia and M. Tennenholtz. Approximate mechanism design without money. In *ACM Conference on Electronic Commerce*, pages 177–186, New York, NY, USA, 2009. ACM.

[13] J. Schummer and R. V. Vohra. Strategy-proof location on a network. *Journal of Economic Theory*, 104(2):405–428, 2002.

Accuracy for Sale:
Aggregating Data with a Variance Constraint

Rachel Cummings[*]
Caltech

Katrina Ligett[†]
Caltech

Aaron Roth[‡]
University of Pennsylvania

Zhiwei Steven Wu[§]
University of Pennsylvania

Juba Ziani[¶]
Caltech

ABSTRACT

We consider the problem of a data analyst who may purchase an unbiased estimate of some statistic from multiple data providers. From each provider i, the analyst has a choice: she may purchase an estimate from that provider that has variance chosen from a finite menu of options. Each level of variance has a cost associated with it, reported (possibly strategically) by the data provider. The analyst wants to choose the *minimum cost* set of variance levels, one from each provider, that will let her combine her purchased estimators into an aggregate estimator that has variance at most some fixed desired level. Moreover, she wants to do so in such a way that incentivizes the data providers to truthfully report their costs to the mechanism.

We give a dominant strategy truthful solution to this problem that yields an estimator that has optimal expected cost, and violates the variance constraint by at most an additive term that tends to zero as the number of data providers grows large.

Categories and Subject Descriptors

[**Theory of Computation**]: Algorithmic Game Theory and Mechanism Design

[*]Supported in part by NSF grant CNS-1254169 and the US-Israel Binational Science Foundation (grant 2012348).

[†]Supported by NSF grant CNS-1254169, US-Israel Binational Science Foundation (grant 2012348), the Charles Lee Powell Foundation, a Google Faculty Research Award and a Microsoft Faculty Fellowship.

[‡]Supported by NSF grants: CCF-1101389, CNS-1065060, CNS-1253345.

[§]Supported by NSF grant CCF-1101389.

[¶]Supported in part by NSF grant CNS-1254169 and the US-Israel Binational Science Foundation (grant 2012348).

Keywords

Mechanism Design, VCG Mechanism, Buying Data

1. INTRODUCTION

We consider a *data analyst* who wishes to compute an unbiased estimate of some underlying population statistic, by buying and aggregating data from multiple strategic data providers. Each data provider may experience different costs for different levels of data accuracy (variance), and may strategically price access to his data if doing so would benefit him. The analyst must design a mechanism for choosing which level of accuracy to purchase from each provider, and for combining the purchased data into a single aggregate quantity that forms an unbiased estimator of the statistic of interest. Her goal is to do so at minimum cost, given some target level of overall accuracy.

This model captures a number of interesting scenarios. For example:

- Each data provider might in fact be a single individual, who is selling a (possibly perturbed) bit signifying some property of interest to the data analyst (e.g., the cancer status of the individual). Here, the variance of each of these estimates comes from two sources: each individual's bit is the realization of an independent sample from some underlying population distribution, with an inherent variance. A data provider may also add his own perturbation (e.g., noise from a Gaussian or Laplace distribution) in order to guarantee a certain level of (differential) privacy. He can therefore potentially offer the data analyst access to his data at a menu of different variance levels (and costs), corresponding to differing levels of privacy protection. Intuitively, the different costs the individual experiences at different levels of accuracy may correspond to his (potentially arbitrary) preferences for privacy. Since we model data providers as strategic agents, they will report the cost that maximizes their utility, and their reported costs need not necessarily match their true costs. We allow each individual to report an arbitrary cost separately for each variance level, so this approach does not require assuming that agent preferences for privacy respect any fixed functional form.

- Each data provider might be an organization (such as a university) that has the ability to collect a random sample of varying size from a sub-population that it controls (e.g. students, professors, etc). Under the assumption that the individuals in the data provider's populations are sampled i.i.d. from some underlying distribution, the variance of the estimate that they offer is inversely proportional to the number of individuals that they sample. Here, the costs for different levels of variance correspond to the costs required to recruit different numbers of participants to a study. These costs may differ between organizations, and behave in complicated ways: for example, the marginal cost for each additional sample might be decreasing (if there are economies of scale – for example by advertising on a campus TV station), or might be increasing (for example, after exhausting the undergraduate population at a university, obtaining additional samples may require recruiting faculty, which is more difficult). Again, because we allow data providers to report arbitrary cost schedules corresponding to different variance levels, we need make no assumptions about the form that these costs take.

1.1 Our Results and Techniques

We model the data analyst's problem as a combinatorial optimization problem: From each of the data providers, the analyst buys an unbiased estimator of the population statistic of interest, for which she must choose a variance from a fixed, finite menu of options. Given these purchased estimators, the data analyst may then take any convex combination to obtain her final unbiased estimator of the underlying population statistic. The choices made by the data analyst affect both the variance of the final estimator that she derives, as well as the total payment that she must make. We consider the problem of finding the *cheapest* way of constructing an estimator that has variance below some fixed desired level, specified in advance by the data analyst.

Our main tool in solving this problem is linear programming. However, the solution is not straightforward. First, our problem actually consists of two nested optimization problems: we must choose a variance level for each of the estimators, and then we must find the optimal weighted linear combination of these estimators. Rather than solving these problems separately, we use the KKT conditions to derive a closed form for the optimal weights to use in the linear combination of each of the estimators *as a function of their variance*. This allows us to express the problem as a one-shot optimization problem, with decision variables only for the choices of variance for each estimator. Unfortunately, the natural fractional relaxation of this optimization problem (in which the data analyst may fractionally choose different variance levels) is non-convex. Instead, we consider a further (linear) relaxation of the constraint in our problem, which matches the original constraint only for integer solutions. We show that all optimal extreme points of the linear program that result from this relaxation do in fact yield integer choices for all but *at most one* data provider, and then show that if the number of data providers is sufficiently large, then rounding the one fractional assignment to an integer assignment only marginally violates our target variance constraint.

We note that our algorithm chooses the *minimum expected cost* lottery over purchase decisions from among a pre-specified feasible set of lotteries, and hence is *maximal-in-distributional-range* (i.e. it outputs a lottery that maxi-

mizes expected welfare). This means that when paired with VCG payments, truthful reporting of costs is a dominant strategy for each of the data providers. (We recall that although we allow data providers to misreport their costs, they cannot lie about their data or its accuracy.)

In summary, we show the following theorem:

THEOREM 1 (INFORMAL). *Given any finite menu of variance levels, and any feasible aggregate variance level for the data analyst, there exists a dominant strategy truthful mechanism that selects the minimum cost assignment of variance levels to providers, and generates an unbiased linear estimator that satisfies the analyst's variance constraint up to an additive term that tends to 0 as the number of data providers grow large.*

Finally, we observe that VCG payments (although always truthful) do *not* guarantee individual rationality in our setting, because these payments may fail to compensate players for their cost for providing data. We prove an upper bound on the degree to which individual rationality can be violated for any player, and hence can add a fixed amount to the payment given to each player, to guarantee individual rationality for all providers with sufficiently low minimum costs.

1.2 Related Work

There is a growing body of work [7–10, 15, 17, 19] related to our first motivating example: buying sensitive data from individuals. This line of work considers the problem of incentivizing individuals to provide their data to an analyst, when they experience a cost — usually due to privacy loss — from sharing their data. These papers have used differential privacy, defined in [6], to combat this privacy loss, but have generally offered only a single privacy level to participants, or have made assumptions about the functional form of this privacy loss in terms of the differential privacy parameter. Our construction, on the other hand, allows the analyst to offer each data provider a menu of different variance levels, corresponding to different levels of differential privacy, and allows the agents to express *arbitrary* costs for each level independently. This requires no assumptions at all about the functional form of agent costs. As in our setting, these papers all consider the individual data providers to be selfish agents, and thus allow agents to strategically misreport their costs to secure them a higher payment. Recently, [9] considered a setting where individuals have unverifiable data, and can also misreport their data. We restrict to a setting where data is verifiable (as the other papers in this literature do), but allow individuals to lie about their costs for providing data. In this setting, we are making the implicit assumption that the sensitive data held by individuals is independent of their privacy costs. This is motivated by an impossibility result of [10], later strengthened by [17], that when privacy costs are correlated with data, no mechanism can satisfy individual rationality and estimate the statistic of interest with non-trivial accuracy, while making finite payments.

Our paper is also related to the vast body of work on optimal experiment design, in which an analyst wishes to learn parameters of an underlying distribution by optimizing a multi-set of samples to observe from the population, each at some cost. (For a survey of results see [18] or [2]; for a textbook treatment see Section 7.5 of [3].) Each data sample is an "experiment" with observable attributes. The analyst assumes a linear relationship between experiment attributes and outcomes, and wishes to accurately learn the linear parameter by performing a collection of experiments subject to a budget constraint. Although the problem we consider seems to be a special case of experiment design (i.e. with attribute vector of dimension 0), these two problems differ in a few key aspects. First, optimal experiment design allows the analyst to *repeat experiments*, and performing the same experiment multiple times may result in different outcomes. We do not allow this, and we further constrain the problem to require the analyst to buy exactly one "experiment" (i.e. observation of data) from each data provider. The techniques used in this line of work do not generically extend to the more constrained setting that we consider. Additionally, optimal experiment design is a problem in the *full information* setting, so the cost of each experiment is a priori known by the analyst. That is, data providers cannot misreport their costs. The experimental design literature generally gives approximation algorithms which are not maximal in range, and hence do not yield truthful mechanisms. We consider a setting in which data providers are strategic agents, and we must additionally ensure that our optimization process is incentive compatible. Recent work of [13] considered experimental design for strategic agents, but their work considered a different accuracy objective (other than minimizing variance), and their techniques fail under the additional constraint that the analyst can buy at most one estimate from each data provider.

The truthfulness of our mechanism depends on a property called *maximal-in-distributional-range* (MIDR), defined in [4]. MIDR mechanisms are guaranteed to select a distribution over outputs that maximizes expected welfare. Similar properties were also used in [1], [5] and [14]. Dobzinski and Dughmi [4] showed that MIDR mechanisms are *truthful-in-expectation* when paired with VCG payments. That is, with an MIDR mechanism, no player can increase her expected utility by lying about her private information. We first show that our proposed mechanism is MIDR, and then use this result to show that data providers do not have an incentive to misreport their costs.

2. PRELIMINARIES AND MODEL

We consider an analyst who wishes to estimate the expected value μ of some statistic on the underlying population. She has access to a set of n data providers, each of which is capable of providing some unbiased estimate μ_i of the statistic of interest with different levels of variance $\mathbb{E}\left[(\mu_i - \mu)^2\right]$. The provider may also experience some cost for computing the estimate at each variance level. The analyst's goal is to obtain an accurate unbiased estimate for μ, using the estimates from the providers, while minimizing the social cost for computing such data.

We equip the analyst with a mechanism that offers a menu specifying a discrete, finite range of possible variance levels $0 < v_1 < v_2 < \ldots < v_m < \infty$, and asks each provider i to report back a set of costs $\{c_{ij}\}_{j=1}^m$ for computing the estimates at all levels. The mechanism then selects a variance level to purchase from each provider, and generates an estimate for μ that is a weighted sum of the providers' reported estimates μ_i's: $\widehat{\mu} = \sum_i w_i \mu_i$. Note that the expectation $\mathbb{E}[\widehat{\mu}] = \sum_i w_i \mathbb{E}[\mu_i] = \sum_i w_i \mu$, so $\widehat{\mu}$ will be an unbiased estimate as long as $\sum_i w_i = 1$. The following proposition,

often called the Bienaymé formula, allows us to express the variance of $\widehat{\mu}$ as a linear combination of the variances of μ_i.

PROPOSITION 1. *Let $X_1, \ldots, X_n$ be uncorrelated real-valued random variables, and $w_1, \ldots, w_n$ be any real numbers, then*

$$Var\left(\sum_i w_i X_i\right) = \sum_i w_i^2 Var(X_i).$$

The goal of the analyst is to minimize the total cost among all providers, while maintaining a guarantee that the variance of $\widehat{\mu}$ is below some threshold α. This can be expressed in the following program, where each x_{ij} indicates whether we assign provider i to variance level j:

$$\min \sum_{i,j} x_{ij} c_{ij} \tag{1}$$

$$\text{subject to } \sum_i w_i^2 \left(\sum_j x_{ij} v_j\right) \leq \alpha \tag{2}$$

$$\sum_j x_{ij} = 1 \text{ for all } i \tag{3}$$

$$x_{ij} \in \{0,1\} \text{ for all } (i,j) \tag{4}$$

$$\sum_i w_i = 1 \text{ and for all } i, w_i \geq 0 \tag{5}$$

2.1 Mechanism Design Basics

We study our optimization problem in the context of mechanism design, with n players and a set Ω of possible outcomes. In our framework, the analyst wishes to determine a variance level at which to purchase data from each player, so this set Ω corresponds to the set of possible assignments of players to variance levels. Each player also has a cost function $c_i \colon \Omega \to \mathbb{R}$, where $c_i(\omega)$ is player i's cost for outcome ω. Let $c = (c_1, \ldots, c_n)$ denote the profile of cost functions for all players. We want to minimize total cost, so our objective is $\sum_{i=1}^n c_i(\omega)$. We will use Ω_{-i} to denote the set of possible assignments of all players other than i to variance levels, and c_{-i} to denote the vector of reported costs by all players other then i.

A *(direct-revelation) mechanism* $\mathcal{M}$ consists of an *allocation rule* $\mathcal{A}$, a function mapping reported cost profiles to outcomes, and a *payment rule* p, a function mapping cost profiles to a payments to each player. Such a mechanism takes as input reported cost functions from the players, and outputs (possibly randomly) an allocation ω and payments to all the players. Two important desiderata in mechanism design are *truthfulness* and *individual rationality*.

We study our optimization problem in the setting of mechanism design, with n players, and a set Ω of possible outcomes. In particular, this set Ω corresponds to the set of possible assignments of players to variance levels. Each player also has a cost function $c_i \colon \Omega \to \mathbb{R}$, where $c_i(\omega)$ is player i's cost for outcome ω. Let $c = (c_1, \ldots, c_n)$ denote the profile of cost functions for all players. We want to minimize total cost, so our objective is $\sum_i^n c_i(\omega)$.

DEFINITION 1 (TRUTHFUL-IN-EXPECTATION). *A mechanism $\mathcal{M} = (\mathcal{A}, p)$ on n players is (dominant strategy) truthful-in-expectation if for all $i \in [n]$, for any reported cost profile c_{-i} of other players, and any misreport c_i' by* *player i:*

$$\mathbb{E}_{\mathcal{M}}\left[p_i((c_i, c_{-i})) - c_i(\mathcal{A}((c_i, c_{-i})))\right]$$
$$\geq \mathbb{E}_{\mathcal{M}}\left[p_i((c_i', c_{-i})) - c_i\left(\mathcal{A}((c_i', c_{-i}))\right)\right].$$

DEFINITION 2 (INDIVIDUALLY RATIONAL). *A mechanism $\mathcal{M} = (\mathcal{A}, p)$ is individually rational (IR) if for any reported cost profile c and for all $i \in [n]$:*

$$\mathbb{E}_{\mathcal{M}}\left[p_i(c) - c_i(\mathcal{A}(c))\right] \geq 0.$$

We will use *VCG-based mechanisms* to minimize total cost while achieving truthfulness. A *VCG mechanism* is defined by the allocation rule that selects the cost-minimizing outcome $\omega^* \in \arg\min_{\omega \in \Omega} \sum_i c_i(\omega)$ for any reported cost functions, and the payment rule p that rewards each player his "externality":

$$p_i(c) = \min_{\omega \in \Omega_{-i}} \sum_{i' \neq i} c_{i'}(\omega) - \sum_{i' \neq i} c_{i'}(\omega^*). \tag{6}$$

Let $dist(\Omega)$ be the set of all probability distributions over the set of outcomes Ω, and let $\mathcal{R} \subseteq dist(\Omega)$ be a compact subset. Then a *maximal-in-distributional-range* (MIDR) allocation rule is defined as sampling an outcome ω from distribution $D^* \in \mathcal{R}$, where D^* minimizes the expected total cost $\mathbb{E}_{\omega \sim D^*}\left[\sum_i c_i(\omega)\right]$ over all distributions in $\mathcal{R}$. A VCG payment rule can be defined accordingly, where $\mathcal{R}_{-i}$ is the corresponding compact subset of Ω_{-i}:

$$p_i(c) = \min_{D' \in \mathcal{R}_{-i}} \mathbb{E}_{\omega \sim D'}\left[\sum_{i' \neq i} c_{i'}(\omega)\right] - \mathbb{E}_{\omega \sim D^*}\left[\sum_{i' \neq i} c_{i'}(\omega)\right].$$

It is known from [4] that when an MIDR allocation rule is paired with a VCG payment rule, the resulting mechanism is truthful-in-expectation.

To guarantee individual rationality, we pay each player some entrance reward R before running the MIDR mechanism so that $R + \mathbb{E}\left[p_i(c) - c_i(\mathcal{A}(c))\right] \geq 0$ for all players. It suffices to set $R \geq \max_i \mathbb{E}\left[p_i(c) - c_i(\mathcal{A}(c))\right]$, and in Section 4.2 we derive a more refined bound for R to achieve individual rationality.

3. REWRITING THE PROGRAM

The optimization problem introduced in Section 2 is non-convex because the variance constraint (2) contains the product of decision variables x_{ij} and w_i. To achieve convexity, we will transform the program in three steps:

1. First, we will eliminate the decision variables w_i by deriving a closed form solution for the weights w_i that minimize variance, once the variables x_{ij} are fixed. However, this will still leave us with a non-convex optimization problem.

2. Next, we will replace the non-convex constraint derived above with a linear constraint, that is identical whenever the x_{ij} variables take on integral values.

3. Finally in Section 4, we relax the integrality constraint. Because our linear variance constraint is no longer identical to the original "correct" non-convex variance constraint, we must in the end argue that a rounded solution does not substantially violate the original constraint.

First, to simplify notation, for any assignment $\{x_{ij}\}$, let $\widehat{v_i}$ denote the variance level assigned to provider i. We want to write each w_i as a function of the $\widehat{v_k}$'s. In particular, given the variance assignments, we want to choose the weights w_i so that the variance of the aggregate statistic $\widehat{\mu}$ is minimized.

LEMMA 1. *Given a variance level assignment $\{\widehat{v_i}\}$, the weight vector w^* that minimizes the variance of $\widehat{\mu} = \sum_i w_i \mu_i$ satisfies*

$$w_i^* = \frac{1/\widehat{v_i}}{\sum_k 1/\widehat{v_k}} \qquad \text{for all } i.$$

PROOF. The problem can be written as a convex program

$$\min \sum_i w_i^2 \widehat{v_i} \qquad \text{subject to } \sum_i w_i = 1 \text{ and } w_i \geq 0 \text{ for all } i$$

We know that strong duality holds because the program satisfies Slater's condition, and the Lagrangian is given by

$$\mathcal{L}(w, \lambda) = \sum_i \widehat{v_i} \cdot w_i^2 - \lambda\left(1 - \sum_i w_i\right)$$
$$= w^T V w - \lambda(1 - \mathbb{1}^T w),$$

where $V = diag(\widehat{v_1}, \ldots, \widehat{v_n})$. Note that $\nabla_w \mathcal{L}(w, \lambda)^T = 2Vw + \lambda\mathbb{1}$. By KKT conditions, $\nabla_w \mathcal{L}(w^*, \lambda)^T = 0$, and so $w^* = -\frac{\lambda}{2} V^{-1} \mathbb{1}$, which gives $\min_w \mathcal{L}(w, \lambda)^T = -\frac{\lambda^2}{4} \sum_i 1/\widehat{v_i} - \lambda$. Now the dual problem can be written as

$$\max_\lambda \min_{w \geq 0} \mathcal{L}(w, \lambda) = \max_\lambda \left[-\frac{\lambda^2}{4} \sum_i 1/\widehat{v_i} - \lambda\right]$$
$$= \max_\lambda \left[-\left(\sum_i 1/\widehat{v_i}\right)\left(\lambda/2 + \frac{1}{\sum_i 1/\widehat{v_i}}\right)^2\right.$$
$$\left. + \frac{1}{\sum_i 1/\widehat{v_i}}\right].$$

It is easy to see that the maximum is reached at $\lambda^* = \frac{-2}{\sum_i 1/\widehat{v_i}}$. It follows that

$$w^* = \frac{-\lambda^*}{2} V^{-1} \mathbb{1} = \frac{V^{-1}\mathbb{1}}{\sum_i 1/\widehat{v_i}},$$

and so,

$$w_i^* = \frac{1/\widehat{v_i}}{\sum_k 1/\widehat{v_k}} \text{ for all } i$$

as suggested by the lemma. $\square$

Lemma 1 shows that we can rewrite the variance constraint of $\widehat{\mu}$ as

$$\sum_i \left(\frac{1/\widehat{v_i}}{\sum_k 1/\widehat{v_k}}\right)^2 \widehat{v_i} = \sum_i \frac{1/\widehat{v_i}}{\left(\sum_k 1/\widehat{v_k}\right)^2} = \frac{1}{\sum_k 1/\widehat{v_k}} \leq \alpha.$$

Changing indices back to i, plugging in $\widehat{v_i} = \sum_j x_{ij} v_j$, and taking the inverse on both sides, constraint (2) becomes

$$1/\alpha \leq \sum_i \frac{1}{\sum_j x_{ij} v_j} \tag{7}$$

Note that the constraints are not linear, but since each $x_{ij} \in \{0, 1\}$, and only one $x_{ij} = 1$ for each i, we have

$1/\sum_j x_{ij}v_j = \sum_j x_{ij}/v_j$. Thus, we can write our whole program as the following ILP.

$$\min_{x_{ij}} \sum_{i,j} x_{ij}c_{ij} \qquad (8)$$

$$\text{subject to} \quad 1/\alpha \leq \sum_i \sum_j x_{ij}/v_j \qquad (9)$$

$$\sum_j x_{ij} = 1 \text{ for all } i \qquad (10)$$

$$x_{ij} \in \{0,1\} \text{ for all } (i,j) \qquad (11)$$

Remark 1.

Note that our problem is only interesting if the target variance α is in the range of $[v_1/n, v_m/n]$. This is due to the following observation based on constraint (9): if $1/\alpha < n/v_m$, then the problem is trivial since the variance constraint is satisfied by any assignment; if $1/\alpha > n/v_1$, then the problem is infeasible, i.e. even if we assign the lowest variance level to all providers, the variance constraint is still violated.

4. AN MIDR MECHANISM VIA A LINEAR PROGRAMMING RELAXATION

In order to obtain a computationally efficient mechanism, we consider the LP relaxation of the integer linear program we derived in the previous section, by replacing constraint (11) with $x_{ij} \geq 0$ for all (i,j). We interpret a fractional solution $x_i = (x_{i1}, \ldots, x_{im})$ as a lottery over assignments for player i, i.e. the probabilities of getting assigned to different variance levels. Since the objective is to minimize the total cost, the LP gives a maximal-in-distributional-range allocation rule, where the restricted distributional range is,

$$S_\alpha = \{x \geq 0 \mid \sum_j x_{ij} = 1 \text{ for all } i, \text{ and } \sum_{ij} x_{ij}/v_j \geq 1/\alpha\}.$$

Similarly, the restricted distributional range for $n-1$ players, used to compute VCG payments is,

$$(S_\alpha)_{-i} = \{x \geq 0 \mid \sum_j x_{i'j} = 1 \text{ for all } i' \neq i,$$
$$\text{and } \sum_{i' \neq i, \, j} x_{i'j}/v_j \geq 1/\alpha\}.$$

Given a collection of reported costs, our mechanism first computes a distribution x over assignments, based on the MIDR allocation rule defined by the LP. We then pay each provider based on the VCG payment rule, in addition to some entrance reward R. Given the realized variance assignment sampled from x, we ask the providers to compute their estimates μ_i at the corresponding variance levels. Finally, we re-weight the estimates to obtain the linear combination estimator $\widehat{\mu}$ with the minimum variance based on the optimal re-weighting rule in Lemma 1. The formal description of our mechanism is presented in Algorithm 1.

THEOREM 2. *Given n data providers with reported costs $\{c_{ij}\}$ for variance levels $\{v_j\}$ and a feasible target variance level α, Algorithm 1 is a truthful-in-expectation mechanism that selects a minimum expected cost assignment, and,*

Algorithm 1 MIDR Mechanism for Buying Estimates

Input: Data providers' reported costs $\{c_{ij}\}$ for different variance levels $\{v_1, \ldots, v_m\}$, target variance α, initial payment R

Compute assignment and payment based on MIDR allocation rule and VCG payment rule:

$$x^* \in \arg\min_{x \in S_\alpha} \sum_i c_{ij}x_{ij}$$

$$p_i = \min_{x_{-i} \in (S_\alpha)_{-i}} \left[\sum_{i' \neq i} c_{i'}(x) \right] - \sum_{i' \neq i} c_{i'}(x^*) + R$$

Let $\widehat{v} = (\widehat{v_1}, \ldots, \widehat{v_n})$ be the realized variance assignments sampled from x^* and

$$w_i = \frac{1/\widehat{v_i}}{\sum_k 1/\widehat{v_k}} \qquad \text{for all } i.$$

Collect the estimates from providers $\{\mu_i\}$ based on $\widehat{v}$
Output: $\sum_i w_i\mu_i$ as our estimate $\widehat{\mu}$

---

1. *for any $\varepsilon > 0$, computes an estimate $\widehat{\mu}$ with variance $Var(\widehat{\mu}) \leq (1+\varepsilon)\alpha$ as long as*

$$n \geq \left(\frac{v_m}{v_1} - 1\right)\left(\frac{1}{\varepsilon} + 1\right),$$

2. *the mechanism is individually rational if the entrance reward $R \geq \max_i \min_j c_{ij}$.*

The properties of cost minimization and truthfulness follow from the MIDR allocation rule and VCG payments. We show the other two properties in the following subsections.

Remark 2.

To achieve a 2-approximation for the variance (i.e. $\varepsilon = 1$), it will suffice to have $n = 2v_m/v_1$ providers. Plugging in the bound in Remark 1, the meaningful range of target variance should be $v_1^2/2v_m \leq \alpha \leq v_1/2$. Note that $v_1/v_m < 1$, so this range is always non-empty.

4.1 Variance Violation

The fractional solution we obtain could violate the variance constraint (7), as could the final assignment sampled from the fractional solution. Let x be an optimal solution to the LP. Then x violates the variance constraint (7) by at most

$$\Delta(x) = \sum_i \sum_j x_{ij}/v_j - \sum_i 1/\sum_j x_{ij}v_j$$
$$= \sum_i (\sum_j x_{ij}/v_j - 1/\sum_j x_{ij}v_j).$$

The quantity $\Delta(x)$ represents the distance between the "real" desired variance constraint and our linear relaxation. Note that for any agent who happens to receive an integral allocation, the corresponding terms in the two constraints are equal, but they may diverge for agents who have fractional allocations. To simplify and bound this quantity, we show that at any optimal fractional solution, all but at most one agent receives an integral allocation:

LEMMA 2. *At any extreme point x^* of the feasible region for the LP, there are at least $n-1$ indices i such that $x_{ij} \in \{0,1\}$ for all j.*

PROOF. Suppose not. Then let x be a point in the feasible set S_α such that at least two players (without loss of generality, players 1 and 2) are assigned to lotteries. In other words, each of these two players are assigned nonzero weight on at least two different variance levels. Let $a < b, k < l$ be the indices such that $x_{1a}, x_{1b}, x_{2k}, x_{2l} \notin \{0,1\}$. Let $\varepsilon > 0$ be a small enough number such that

$$x_{1a} \pm \varepsilon, x_{1b} \pm \varepsilon, x_{2k} \pm \varepsilon, x_{2l} \pm \varepsilon \in [0,1]$$

and

$$x_{1a} \pm \varepsilon', x_{1b} \pm \varepsilon', x_{2k} \pm \varepsilon', x_{2l} \pm \varepsilon' \in [0,1],$$

where $\varepsilon' = \varepsilon \left(\frac{1/v_a - 1/v_b}{1/v_k - 1/v_l} \right)$. Now consider the following two points that differ from x only in four coordinates:

$$y : \; y_{1a} = x_{1a} + \varepsilon, \; y_{1b} = x_{1b} - \varepsilon,$$
$$y_{2k} = x_{2k} - \varepsilon', \; \text{and} \; y_{2l} = x_{2l} + \varepsilon'n$$
$$z : \; z_{1a} = x_{1a} - \varepsilon, \; z_{1b} = x_{1b} + \varepsilon,$$
$$z_{2k} = x_{2k} + \varepsilon', \; \text{and} \; z_{2l} = x_{2l} - \varepsilon'$$

Note that $x = \frac{1}{2}(y+z)$, and recall that $1/\alpha \le \sum_i \sum_j x_{ij}/v_j$ because $x \in S_\alpha$. Furthermore,

$$\sum_i \sum_j y_{ij}/v_j = \sum_i \sum_j x_{ij}/v_j$$
$$+ \varepsilon(1/v_a - 1/v_b) + \varepsilon'(1/v_l - 1/v_k)$$
$$= \sum_i \sum_j x_{ij}/v_j$$
$$+ \varepsilon \left[1/v_a - 1/v_b + (1/v_l - 1/v_k)\frac{1/v_a - 1/v_b}{1/v_k - 1/v_l} \right]$$
$$= \sum_i \sum_j x_{ij}/v_j \ge 1/\alpha.$$

Similarly, $\sum_{i,j} z_{ij}/v_j = \sum_{i,j} x_{ij}/v_j \ge 1/\alpha$, so both y and z are in the feasible region S_α. Since x is a convex combination of y and z that are both in S_α, we know that x cannot be an extreme point of the feasible region. □

Lemma 2 says that at any extreme point x, at least $n-1$ players have an integral assignment in x. To use this property, we will compute the solution using an (ellipsoid-based) polynomial-time LP solver from [16] that always returns an optimal extreme point solution.[1] Now we can bound the variance of our aggregate estimate $\widehat{\mu}$.

LEMMA 3. *For any $\varepsilon > 0$, the variance of our estimate $Var(\widehat{\mu}) \le (1+\varepsilon)\alpha$, as long as*

$$n \ge \left(\frac{v_m}{v_1} - 1 \right)\left(\frac{1}{\varepsilon} + 1 \right).$$

PROOF. Suppose that n satisfies the bound above. If the solution x is fully integral, then the variance is no more than α. Otherwise let k be the data provider receiving a lottery

---

[1] The algorithm consists of two steps: first compute a sufficiently near optimal solution $\widehat{x}$ using the ellipsoid algorithm; then round the solution $\widehat{x}$ to an optimal extreme point solution x^* using the method of continued fractions. For more details, see [16].

in x. Since for every player i with an integral assignment $\sum_j x_{ij}/v_j = \sum_j 1/\sum_j x_{ij}v_j$, we can further simplify,

$$\Delta(x) = \sum_j x_{kj}/v_j - 1/\sum_j x_{kj}v_j.$$

Then we can bound the violation of (7) by the final assignment $\widehat{v}$:

$$\sum_j x_{kj}/v_j - 1/v_m \le 1/v_1 - 1/v_m.$$

In other words, the resulting variance $Var(\widehat{\mu})$ satisfies

$$\frac{1}{Var(\widehat{\mu})} \ge \frac{1}{\alpha} - \left(\frac{1}{v_1} - \frac{1}{v_m} \right).$$

Since we assume $n > v_m/v_1 - 1$, we have $n/v_m - (1/v_1 - 1/v_m) > 0$. As stated earlier in Remark 1, the only interesting range of α is $v_1/n \le \alpha \le v_m/n$. (Recall that if $\alpha < v_1/n$, then the problem is infeasible; if $\alpha > v_m/n$, then the problem is trivial.) For the remainder of the proof, we assume $\alpha \in [v_1/n, v_m/n]$. By this assumption, $1/\alpha - (1/v_1 - 1/v_m) > 0$, and so,

$$Var(\widehat{\mu}) \le \frac{1}{\frac{1}{\alpha} - \frac{1}{v_1} + \frac{1}{v_m}} = \alpha \left(\frac{1}{1 - \frac{\alpha}{v_1 v_m}(v_m - v_1)} \right)$$
$$\le \alpha \left(\frac{n}{n - \left(\frac{v_m}{v_1} - 1 \right)} \right)$$
$$\le (1 + \varepsilon)\alpha,$$

which recovers our lemma. □

We give an example in Appendix A showing that this analysis cannot be improved, and we do need $n = \Omega(v_m/v_1)$ to approximately satisfy the target variance constraint.

4.2 Individual Rationality

In order to ensure individual rationality, we need to set the entrance reward R large enough, so that for each player i, $R + p_i - c_i \ge 0$, where c_i denotes the cost for player i to provide its assigned estimate. To reason about the payment player i gets, we need to compute the following two costs C_1 and C_2, for all players except i. Let x^* be the optimal (fractional) solution for our LP, and $\widehat{v}_i$ be the expected variance level assigned to player i: $\widehat{v}_i = \sum_j x_{ij}^* v_j$. Let OPT denote the optimal min-cost value of the LP, and C_1 denote the total cost for all players except i in x^*:

$$C_1 = \min \sum_{k \ne i, j} x_{kj} c_{kj}$$
$$\text{subject to} \sum_{k \ne i, j} x_{kj}/v_j \ge 1/\alpha - 1/\widehat{v}_i$$
$$\sum_j x_{kj} = 1 \text{ for all } k$$
$$x_{kj} \ge 0 \text{ for all } (k, j)$$

322

Let C_2 be the minimum cost had we removed agent i from the input:

$$C_2 = \min \sum_{k \neq i, j} x_{kj} c_{kj}$$

$$\text{subject to } \sum_{k \neq i, j} x_{kj}/v_j \geq 1/\alpha$$

$$\sum_j x_{kj} = 1 \text{ for all } k$$

$$x_{kj} \geq 0 \text{ for all } (k, j)$$

The VCG payment given to player i in Algorithm 1 is $p_i = C_2 - C_1$. Note that since the second LP is more constrained than the first, we know $C_2 \geq C_1$ and the payment is always non-negative. We can write down the expected utility of player i:

$$R + p_i - c_i$$
$$= R + C_2 - C_1 - c_i$$
$$= R + C_2 - \text{OPT}.$$

LEMMA 4. *The mechanism in Algorithm 1 is individually rational if the entrance reward satisfies*

$$R \geq \max_i \min_j c_{ij}.$$

PROOF. Let x_{-i} be the optimal assignment for the second program (with optimal objective value at C_2). Now let's add back player i to the problem, and construct an assignment x such that $x = (x_i, x_{-i})$, where x_i assigns player i to the assignment with minimum cost ($\min_j c_{ij}$).

Note that x is a feasible solution to our original problem since x_{-i} already satisfies the variance constraint. It follows that the cost given by x is at least as large as OPT, the optimal solution: $\text{OPT} \leq C_2 + \min_j c_{ij}$.

Therefore, as long as $R \geq \min_j c_{ij}$ for each player i, we have individual rationality. $\square$

We give an example in Appendix A to show that this bound is tight. In particular, our example shows that without an entrance reward, the individual rationality constraint could be violated by up to $\min_j c_{ij}$ for each player i.

Remark 3.

Let $c_{min} = \max_i \min_j c_{ij}$. If costs are drawn from a known distribution, the analyst can set R to ensure that with high probability, all players have $c_{min} \leq R$. If c_{min} is unbounded, it is clear that no Groves mechanism[2] can be individually rational for all players in this setting. The Green-Laffont-Holmström theorem [11, 12] shows that under certain technical conditions, any mechanism which is dominant strategy incentive compatible and maximizes welfare must be a Groves mechanism. Thus without additional information on the players' costs, we should not hope to satisfy individual rationality for all players while still achieving our other desiderata.

---

[2] A *Groves mechanism* is one which selects the welfare maximizing outcome, and each player's payment is his externality plus an amount that is independent of his report. In particular, the payments induced by any Groves mechanism to a player i are shifts of the payments induced by our mechanism, by an amount that is independent of player i's report. Hence by reporting a large enough value of c_{min}, individual rationality can always be violated by a Groves mechanism.

References

[1] Aaron Archer, Christos Papadimitriou, Kunal Talwar, and Éva Tardos. An approximate truthful mechanism for combinatorial auctions with single parameter agents. In *Proceedings of the 14th Annual ACM-SIAM Symposium on Discrete Algorithms*, SODA '03, pages 205–214, 2003.

[2] Anthony Atkinson, Alexander Donev, and Randall Tobias. *Optimum Experimental Designs, with SAS*. Oxford Statistical Science, 2007.

[3] Stephen Boyd and Lieven Vandenberghe. *Convex Optimization*. Cambridge University Press, 2004.

[4] Shahar Dobzinski and Shaddin Dughmi. On the power of randomization in algorithmic mechanism design. In *Proceedings of the 50th Annual IEEE Symposium on Foundations of Computer Science*, FOCS '09, pages 505–514, 2009.

[5] Shahar Dobzinski and Noam Nisan. Limitations of VCG-based mechanisms. In *Proceedings of the 39th Annual ACM Symposium on Theory of Computing*, STOC '07, pages 338–344, 2007.

[6] Cynthia Dwork, Frank McSherry, Kobbi Nissim, and Adam Smith. Calibrating noise to sensitivity in private data analysis. In *Proceedings of the 3rd Conference on Theory of Cryptography*, TCC'06, pages 265–284, 2006.

[7] Lisa K. Fleischer and Yu-Han Lyu. Approximately optimal auctions for selling privacy when costs are correlated with data. In *Proceedings of the 13th ACM Conference on Electronic Commerce*, EC '12, pages 568–585, 2012.

[8] Arpita Ghosh and Katrina Ligett. Privacy and coordination: computing on databases with endogenous participation. In *Proceedings of the 14th ACM conference on Electronic Commerce*, pages 543–560. ACM, 2013.

[9] Arpita Ghosh, Katrina Ligett, Aaron Roth, and Grant Schoenebeck. Buying private data without verification. In *Proceedings of the 15th ACM Conference on Economics and Computation*, EC '14, pages 931–948, 2014.

[10] Arpita Ghosh and Aaron Roth. Selling privacy at auction. In *Proceedings of the 12th ACM Conference on Electronic Commerce*, EC '11, pages 199–208, 2011.

[11] Jerry R. Green and Jean-Jacques Laffont. Characterization of satisfactory mechanisms for the revelation of preferences for public goods. *Econometrica*, 45(2):427–438, 1977.

[12] Bengt Holmström. Groves' scheme on restricted domains. *Econometrica*, 47(5):1137–1144, 1979.

[13] Thibaut Horel, Stratis Ioannidis, and S. Muthukrishnan. Budget feasible mechanisms for experimental design. In Alberto Pardo and Alfredo Viola, editors, *LATIN 2014: Theoretical Informatics*, Lecture Notes in Computer Science, pages 719–730. 2014.

[14] Ron Lavi and Chaitanya Swamy. Truthful and near-optimal mechanism design via linear programming. *J. ACM*, 58(6):1–24, December 2011.

[15] Katrina Ligett and Aaron Roth. Take it or leave it: Running a survey when privacy comes at a cost. In Paul W. Goldberg, editor, *Internet and Network Economics*, volume 7695 of *Lecture Notes in Computer Science*, pages 378–391. 2012.

[16] George L. Nemhauser and Laurence A. Wolsey. *Integer and combinatorial optimization*. Wiley interscience series in discrete mathematics and optimization. Wiley, 1988.

[17] Kobbi Nissim, Salil Vadhan, and David Xiao. Redrawing the boundaries on purchasing data from privacy-sensitive individuals. In *Proceedings of the 5th Conference on Innovations in Theoretical Computer Science*, ITCS '14, pages 411–422, 2014.

[18] Friedrich Pukelsheim. *Optimal Design of Experiments*, volume 50. Society for Industrial and Applied Mathematics, 2006.

[19] Aaron Roth and Grant Schoenebeck. Conducting truthful surveys, cheaply. In *Proceedings of the 13th ACM Conference on Electronic Commerce*, EC '12, pages 826–843, 2012.

APPENDIX

A. TIGHTNESS OF OUR BOUNDS

A.1 Example for Variance Violation Bound

Consider an example where there are only two options of variance levels, v_1 and v_2, and we set the target variance $\alpha = \frac{v_1 v_2}{n v_1 + \delta(v_2 - v_1)}$. Suppose the reported costs $c_{i1} = t_1$ and $c_{i2} = t_2$ for each player $i \in [n-1]$, and $c_{n1} < t_1$ and $c_{n2} = t_2$ for player n. We also assume that $t_2 < t_1$. Let x denote the assignment such that $x_{i1} = 0$ and $x_{i2} = 1$ for each $i \in [n-1]$, and $x_{n1} = \delta \in (0,1)$ and $x_{n2} = 1 - \delta$. That is, the assignment gives v_2 to the first $(n-1)$ players, and give a lottery between the two levels to player n. Note that

$$\frac{1}{\alpha} = \frac{n - \delta}{v_2} + \frac{\delta}{v_1}.$$

We know that the fractional solution x exactly satisfies the variance constraint (7), and is also the optimal min-cost solution. Therefore, with probability $(1-\delta)$, the realized variance satisfies,

$$\frac{1}{\text{Var}(\widehat{\mu})} = \frac{n}{v_2} = \frac{n-\delta}{v_2} + \frac{\delta}{v_1} + \frac{\delta}{v_2} - \frac{\delta}{v_1} = \frac{1}{\alpha} - \delta(\frac{1}{v_1} - \frac{1}{v_2}) > 0.$$

It follows that

$$\text{Var}(\widehat{\mu}) = \frac{\alpha}{1 - \alpha \delta(\frac{1}{v_1} - \frac{1}{v_2})}$$

$$= \alpha \left(1 - \frac{\delta\left(\frac{1}{v_1} - \frac{1}{v_2}\right)}{\frac{n}{v_2} + \delta\left(\frac{1}{v_1} - \frac{1}{v_2}\right)} \right)^{-1}$$

$$= \alpha \left(1 + \frac{\delta\left(\frac{v_2}{v_1} - 1\right)}{n} \right)$$

If we want $\frac{\delta(v_2/v_1 - 1)}{n} \leq \varepsilon$, we would need to have the number of providers

$$n \geq \left(\frac{v_2}{v_1} - 1\right)\frac{\delta}{\varepsilon}.$$

For δ close to 1 and constant ε, the number of providers we need does scale with v_2/v_1, which shows that the $\Omega(v_m/v_1)$ for n is essentially tight.

A.2 Example for Entrance Reward Bound

Consider an example with two providers, two possible variance levels v_1, v_2 such that $v_2 = 2v_1$, and target variance $\alpha = v_1$. Suppose the costs satisfy $c_{11} = c_{21} = t$ and $c_{12} = c_{22} = t - \varepsilon$ for some $\varepsilon > 0$.

Since we need to an estimate from each provider, the optimal solution is to assign v_2 to both players, which yields cost OPT $= 2t - 2\varepsilon$. Now suppose we remove any provider from the mechanism. Then we would assign the remaining provider to v_1, which yield cost $C_2 = t$. Therefore, the utility for each provider is

$$R + C_2 - \text{OPT}$$
$$= R + t - 2(t + \varepsilon)$$
$$= R + 2\varepsilon - t$$
$$= R + \varepsilon - t.$$

In order to ensure non-negative utility, we need $R \geq t - \varepsilon$. Note that the right hand side tends to $\max_i \min_j c_{ij}$ when ε tends to 0. Therefore, the bound in Lemma 4 is tight.

Better Outcomes from More Rationality[*]

Jing Chen
Dept. of Computer Science,
Stony Brook University
Stony Brook, NY 11794, USA
jingchen@cs.stonybrook.edu

Silvio Micali
CSAIL, MIT
Cambridge, MA 02139, USA
silvio@csail.mit.edu

Rafael Pass
Dept. of Computer Science,
Cornell University
Ithaca, NY 14853, USA
rafael@cs.cornell.edu

ABSTRACT

Mechanism design enables a social planner to obtain a desired outcome by leveraging the players' rationality and their beliefs. It is thus a fundamental, but yet unproven, intuition that *the higher the level of rationality of the players, the better the set of obtainable outcomes.*

In this paper we prove this fundamental intuition for players with *possibilistic beliefs*, the traditional model of epistemic game theory. Specifically,

- We define a sequence of *monotonically increasing* revenue benchmarks for single-good auctions, $G^0 \leq G^1 \leq G^2 \leq \cdots$, where each G^i is defined over the players' beliefs and G^0 is the second-highest valuation (i.e., the revenue benchmark achieved by the second-price mechanism).

- We (1) construct a single, interim individually rational, auction mechanism that, *without any clue* about the rationality level of the players, guarantees revenue G^k if all players have rationality levels $\geq k + 1$, and (2) prove that no such mechanism can guarantee revenue even close to G^k when at least two players are at most level-k rational.

Categories and Subject Descriptors

F.2 [**Theory of Computation**]: Computational Game Theory; J.4 [**Computer Applications**]: Social and Behavioral Sciences—*Economics*

General Terms

Theory, Economics, Algorithms

Keywords

epistemic game theory; incomplete information; single-good auctions

[*]The authors thank Shafi Goldwasser, Aviad Heifetz, Andrew Lo, Ron Rivest, several anonymous reviewers and the editor of Econometrica for many helpful comments. The third author thanks Joseph Halpern for introducing him to the area of epistemic game theory, and for hours and hours of enlightening discussions about it. The first two authors have been partially supported by ONR Grant No. N00014-09-1-0597. The third author has been partially supported by an Alfred P. Sloan Fellowship, Microsoft New Faculty Fellowship, NSF Award CNS-1217821, NSF CAREER Award CCF-0746990, NSF Award CCF-1214844, AFOSR YIP Award FA9550-10-1-0093, and DARPA and AFRL under contract FA8750-11-2-0211. A full version of this paper is available at http://www.cs.stonybrook.edu/~jingchen/.

ITCS'15, January 11–13, 2015, Rehovot, Israel.
ACM 978-1-4503-3333-7/15/01.
http://dx.doi.org/10.1145/2688073.2688083.

Direct Sum Testing.

[Extended Abstract] [*]

Roee David
Weizmann Institute of
Science,
Department of Computer
Science and Applied
Mathematics,
234 Herzl St.
Rehovot, Israel
roee.david@weizmann.ac.il

Irit Dinur [†]
Weizmann Institute of
Science,
Department of Computer
Science and Applied
Mathematics,
234 Herzl St.
Rehovot, Israel
irit.dinur@weizmann.ac.il

Elazar Goldenberg [‡]
Charles University in Prague,
Computer Science Institute of
Charles University,
Malostranské námesti 25
118 00 Praha 1, Czech
Republic
elazargold@gmail.com

Guy Kindler [§]
School of Computer Science
and Engineering,
Hebrew University of
Jerusalem,
The Edmond J. Safra Campus
Jerusalem, Israel
gkindler@cs.huji.ac.il.

Igor Shinkar [¶]
Courant Institute of
Mathematical Sciences,
New York University,
251 Mercer Street
New York, NY 10012
ishinkar@cims.nyu.edu

ABSTRACT

The *k-fold direct sum encoding* of a string $a \in \{0,1\}^n$ is a function f_a that takes as input sets $S \subseteq [n]$ of size k and outputs $f_a(S) = \sum_{i \in S} a_i \pmod 2$. In this paper we prove a Direct Sum Testing theorem. We describe a three query test that accepts with probability one any function of the form f_a for some a, and rejects with probability $\Omega(\varepsilon)$ functions f that are ε-far from being a direct sum encoding.

This theorem has a couple of additional guises:

- *Linearity testing:* By identifying the subsets of $[n]$ with vectors in $\{0,1\}^n$ in the natural way, our result can be thought of as a linearity testing theorem for functions whose domain is restricted to the k'th layer of the hypercube (i.e. the set of n-bit strings with Hamming weight k).

- *Tensor power testing:* By moving to $-1, 1$ notation, the direct sum encoding is equivalent (up to a difference that is negligible when $k \ll \sqrt{n}$) to a tensor power. Thus our theorem implies a three query test for deciding if a given tensor $f \in \{-1, 1\}^{n^k}$ is a tensor power of a single dimensional vector $a \in \{-1, 1\}^n$, i.e. whether there is some a such that $f = a^{\otimes k}$.

We also provide a four query test for checking if a given ± 1 matrix has rank 1.

Our test naturally extends the linearity test of Blum, Luby, and Rubinfeld (STOC '90). Our analysis proceeds by first handling the $k = n/2$ case, and then reducing this case to the general $k < n/2$ case, using a recent direct product testing theorem of Dinur and Steurer (CCC '2014). The $k = n/2$ case is proven via a new proof for linearity testing on the hypercube, which we extend to the restricted domain of the $n/2$-th layer of the hypercube.

[*] A full version of this paper is available at http://eccc.hpi-web.de/report/2014/002/

[†] Research was supported by ERC-StG grant number 239985

[‡] Research was supported by Irit Dinur's ERC-StG grant number 239985

[§] Research was supported by ISF grant 1692/13 and by BSF grant 2012220

[¶] Research was supported by Irit Dinur's ERC-StG grant number 239985

Categories and Subject Descriptors

F.2 [**Analysis of algorithms and problems complexity**]: Miscellaneous—*property testing*

General Terms

Theory

Keywords

Property testing, direct sum, linearity testing.

1. INTRODUCTION

The *k-fold direct sum encoding* of a string $a \in \{0,1\}^n$ is the function $f : \binom{[n]}{k} \to \{0,1\}$ which takes as input subsets $S \subseteq [n]$ of size k, and whose output on such an S is $f(S) = \sum_{i \in S} a_i \pmod 2$. Direct sums were originally considered in theoretical computer science in the famous Yao XOR lemma [35] for the purpose of hardness amplification in circuit complexity, and since then have been extensively studied. They can also potentially be used for gap amplification in PCP constructions, provided that we can devise and analyze local tests for them. We thus naturally arrive at the following problem, which is the focus of this paper.

Direct Sum Testing Problem: Efficiently test whether a given a boolean function $f : \binom{[n]}{k} \to \{0,1\}$ is (close to) a k-fold direct sum encoding.

This question is also very much related to that of testing whether a given function is close to a k-fold tensor power and we elaborate on this in Section 1.2.

If we represent subsets $S \in \binom{[n]}{k}$ by strings $x \in \{0,1\}^n$ of weight k, then the direct sum encoding f_a of a can be written as $f_a(x) = \sum_i x_i a_i \pmod 2$. In other words, f is the restriction of the linear function $x \mapsto \sum_{i \in [n]} a_i x_i \pmod 2$ to the k'th layer of the hypercube, which we denote by

$$L_k^n = \{x \in \{0,1\}^n : |x| = k\}.$$

Another definition for a function f to be linear on the hypercube is that it satisfies $f(x) + f(y) = f(x+y)$ for every pair of inputs x, y. This suggests the natural linearity-test considered in the paper of Blum, Luby, and Rubinfeld [9]: Pick a pair of inputs x, y in the hypercube independently and uniformly at random, and check whether $f(x)+f(y) = f(x+y)$. A linear function clearly passes the test with probability 1, and it was shown in [9] that a function that is far from all linear functions passes the test with probability bounded away from 1. This linearity test is quite fundamental and plays an important role in the study of PCPs, locally testable codes, and hardness of approximation. The test is well studied, and has many known proofs and generalizations, including to the case where the domain is a group other than the hypercube. Most proofs, however, use the fact that the elements x and y are chosen by the test independently, and moreover, for all x, y their sum $x+y$ always belongs to the domain of the tested function (see Section 1.5 for more details).

In the direct sum testing problem setting we are interested in functions whose domain is L_k^n. Trying to apply the BLR-test on a function $f : L_k^n \to \{0,1\}$ we face an obstacle: if we pick $x, y \in L_k^n$ independently, often $x+y \notin L_k^n$, and so we cannot query f on that input. Even in the case $k = n/2$, where the expected weight of $x+y$ is also $n/2$, $x+y$ actually belongs to $L_{n/2}^n$ only with probability $O(1/\sqrt{n})$. To overcome this our test picks $x, y \in L_{n/2}^n$ randomly, *conditioned on $x + y$ being in $L_{n/2}^n$*. Since x and y are no longer independent and the domain does not have a group structure, the known linearity testing proofs do not seem to work for this setting.

The following is a formal definition of our direct sum test T_k^n for parameters n and k, where k is assumed to be even and upper bounded by $n/2$.

The Direct Sum Test - T_k^n
Given an oracle access to a function $f : L_k^n \to \{0,1\}$ do:

1. Pick $x, y \in L_k^n$ uniformly at random conditioned on $x + y \in L_k^n$.

2. Accept if and only if $f(x) + f(y) = f(x+y)$.

Step 1 of the test can be implemented by picking first $x \in L_k^n$ uniformly at random, then choosing $k/2$ coordinates inside x, and $k/2$ coordinates outside x uniformly at random, and setting y to be 1 on these k coordinates and 0 elsewhere. Note that the test T_k^n only makes sense for even values of k, since otherwise it is impossible that x, y, and $x + y$ all belong to L_k^n.

THEOREM 1.1 (MAIN THEOREM). *Let $n \in \mathbb{N}$, and let $k \leq n/2$ be an even integer. For any function $f : L_k^n \to \{0,1\}$ the following holds.*

1. *If f is linear, then T_k^n accepts with probability 1.*

2. *For all $\varepsilon > 0$ if $\Pr[T_k^n$ accepts $f] > 1 - \varepsilon$, then there exists a string $a \in \{0,1\}^n$ such that $\Pr_{x \in L_k^n}[f(x) = \sum_{i \in [n]} a_i x_i] > 1 - O(\varepsilon)$.*

1.1 Motivation - hardness amplification

The direct sum encoding was first considered in theoretical computer science in the context of hardness amplification for boolean circuits. Yao's XOR lemma [35] (see also [18]) shows that if a function is slightly hard to compute then its direct sum encoding is significantly harder to compute. In other words, the direct sum encoding amplifies the hardness of a function. Hardness amplification has been the subject of much research (see, e.g., [32, 28, 21, 33, 22]). A closely related building block in the context of hardness amplification is the *direct product encoding*. The direct product encoding of a string $a \in \{0,1\}^n$ is a function $DP_a : \binom{[n]}{k} \to \{0,1\}^k$ that gets as input a k-element subset S and outputs $DP_a(S) := a|_S$.

The area of PCPs and hardness of approximation is another setting where hardness amplification is well studied. Here we deal with optimization problems, and the parameter that is amplified is the gap between the optimal value in the 'yes' and the 'no' cases. In these questions direct products play an important role. The celebrated parallel repetition theorem of Raz [30] shows that very strong amplification can be obtained by applying the direct product operation to games. Dinur's [11] gap amplification proof of the PCP theorem [3, 2] proceeds by repeatedly performing a (derandomized, or punctured) direct product encoding.

In the aforementioned PCP constructions (as well as in other constructions that involve direct products [15, 23, 14]) the analysis involves a so-called *direct product test*. Roughly speaking, a direct product test works by picking two intersecting sets, and checking that the function is consistent on their intersection. The analysis of such tests is far from trivial, and there has been a line of work investigating this [19, 15, 12, 23, 14, 13, 16], especially in relation to PCP constructions.

The direct sum encoding is arguably more natural than the direct product, because it maps a boolean function to another (larger) boolean function. This is in contrast to an undesirable alphabet increase that occurs in the direct product encoding. Indeed, the large size of the alphabet in the direct product encoding makes it less useful in hardness amplification, and arguably the simplest way to reduce the alphabet size is XORing the entries of the output, resulting in the direct sum encoding. For example, in the gap amplification proof of the PCP theorem [11] each direct product step is followed by an alphabet reduction step that is rather complicated. If one were to replace the direct product by a direct sum, this step could potentially be avoided, thus leading to a significant simplification, as well as the potential of improving the parameters of PCP constructions. In order to obtain such constructions we need to devise an efficient test that checks whether a given function is (close to) a direct sum encoding.

Another important related question is that of understanding how the value of a multi-player game behaves under the direct sum operation. Here we imagine a twist on the parallel repetition of games setting, where the players are required to output the XOR of their answers (rather than their concatenation, as in the classical parallel repetition setup). This question is analogous to direct sum testing in a similar way that parallel repetition is analogous to direct product testing. The direct sum operation is particularly meaningful for XOR games, and is the basis of a recent breakthrough work of Chan [10], who constructs a PCP with optimal amortized free bit complexity.

The PCP motivation also drives our quest to find a direct sum test that makes the absolute minimal number of queries, namely three. The fewer queries a test makes, the more useful it is for combination with other gadgets, leading to stronger inapproximability results.

Another related question is the problem of locally testable codes. Note that the BLR linearity testing may be phrased as locally testing the Hadamard code using a 3-query test. Our result gives a step towards derandomizing the Hadamard code, while maintaining the property of being testable with 3 queries. We remark that for every $a, a' \in \{0,1\}^n$ the relative distance between their k-fold direct sum encodings is roughly equal to $\text{dist}(f_a, f_{a'}) = \Theta(\frac{k}{n} \cdot \text{dist}(a, a'))$. In particular, this means that for small values of k the distance of the k-fold direct sum code is small and the rate of the code is polynomial, while for $k = \Omega(n)$ the distance of the code is constant but the rate is exponential. We stress that our testability result hold for both regimes.

1.2 Tensor Power Testing

The direct sum encoding is very much related to the tensor power operation, and our results imply a testing result for deciding whether a given function is a tensor power.

A function $f : [n]^k \to \{-1,1\}$ is a *tensor power* if there is a function $b : [n] \to \{-1,1\}$ such that $f = b^{\otimes k}$, i.e., $f(z) = \prod_{i=1}^{k} b(z_i)$ for all $z \in [n]^k$.

One can see that by moving between $\{-1,1\}$ notation and $\{0,1\}$ notation the tensor power and the direct sum operations are very similar. Indeed, the only difference is that in the direct sum we consider k-element subsets $S \subset [n]$ whereas in the tensor product we consider k-tuples. When $k \ll \sqrt{n}$ this difference is negligible, which implies the testing results for tensor power. We suggest and analyze the following three query test.

The Tensor Power Test - TP_k^n
Given an oracle access to a function $f : [n]^k \to \{-1,1\}$ do:

1. Pick $u, v, w \in [n]^{k/2}$ independently at random.

2. Pick three permutations $\pi_1, \pi_2, \pi_3 : [k] \to [k]$ independently at random.

3. Accept if and only if $f(uv \circ \pi_1) \cdot f(vw \circ \pi_2) = f(uw \circ \pi_3)$.

In the test above for a k-tuple $z \in [n]^k$ and a permutation $\pi : [k] \to [k]$ the notation $z \circ \pi$ denotes the k-tuple permuted by π, namely, $z \circ \pi = (z_{\pi(1)}, z_{\pi(2)}, \ldots, z_{\pi(k)})$.

We prove the following theorem by reduction to Theorem 1.1.

THEOREM 1.2. *Suppose $n, k \in \mathbb{N}$ and $\varepsilon > 0$ are such that $k^2/n = o(\varepsilon)$. Let $f : [n]^k \to \{-1,1\}$ be a function that passes the test TP_k^n with probability at least $1 - \varepsilon$. Then there is some $b : [n] \to \{-1,1\}$ such that*

$$\Pr_{z \in [n]^k}[f(z) = b^{\otimes k}(z) = \prod_{i=1}^{k} b(z_i)] \geq 1 - O(\varepsilon).$$

1.3 Tensor Product Testing

It is natural to try to extend the above result to a test for tensor products. A function $f : [n]^k \to \{-1,1\}$ is a *tensor product* if there are k (possibly distinct) functions $b_1, \ldots, b_k : [n] \to \{-1,1\}$ such that $f = b_1 \otimes \cdots \otimes b_k$, i.e., $f(z) = \prod_{i=1}^{k} b_i(z_i)$ for all $z \in [n]^k$.

It seems that this problem is somewhat different from the problem of testing tensor powers, and there is no natural three query test analogous to Tensor Power Test above. We propose the following four query test for testing tensor product.

The Tensor Product Test - $TProd_k^n$
Given an oracle access to a function $f : [n]^k \to \{-1,1\}$ do:

1. Pick $x, x', y, y' \in [n]^{k/2}$ independently uniformly at random.

2. Pick a permutation π on k elements uniformly at random.

3. Accept if and only if $f(xy \circ \pi) \cdot f(xy' \circ \pi) = f(x'y \circ \pi) \cdot f(x'y' \circ \pi)$.

In the full version of the paper we analyze the foregoing test for the special case $k = 2$. This case is interesting on its own, since it can be phrased as testing whether an $n \times n$-matrix over $\{-1,1\}$ is of rank 1.

THEOREM 1.3. *Let $n \in \mathbb{N}$ and $\varepsilon > 0$. Let $M : [n]^2 \to \{-1,1\}$ be a matrix for which*

$$\Pr_{i,i',j,j' \in [n]}[M(i,j)M(i,j') = M(i',j)M(i',j')] \geq 1 - \varepsilon,$$

Then there are $b_1, b_2 : [n] \to \{-1,1\}$ such that

$$\Pr_{(i,j) \in [n]^2}[M(i,j) = b_1(i) \cdot b_2(j)] \geq 1 - \varepsilon.$$

This looks like a first step towards proving the testing tensor product result for general k. Indeed, consider the Tensor Product Test, and fix a permutation π chosen in the test. If for this choice of π the test passes with probability $1 - \varepsilon$, then by Theorem 1.3 we have $\Pr[f(xy \circ \pi) = h_1(x) \cdot h_2(y)] > 1 - \varepsilon$ for some functions $h_1, h_2 : [n]^{k/2} \to \{-1,1\}$ that may depend on π. Therefore, if f passes the Tensor Product Test with probability $1-\varepsilon$, then for most permutation π the function f has this nice decomposition. However, we do not know how to stitch these decompositions in order to conclude that f is close to a tensor product. We leave this question as an open problem.

1.4 Technical contribution

Our proof of Theorem 1.1 first handles the case $k = n/2$, and then derives the result for $k < n/2$ via a reduction to $k = n/2$. For $k = n/2$ we have the following result.

THEOREM 1.4 (DIRECT SUM TESTING FOR $k = n/2$). Let $n \in \mathbb{N}$ be such that $n \equiv 0 \pmod{4}$, and let $\varepsilon > 0$. For all functions $f : L_{n/2}^n \to \{0,1\}$, if $\Pr[f(x) + f(y) = f(x+y)] > 1 - \varepsilon$ then there exists a string $a \in \{0,1\}^n$ such that $\Pr_{x \in L_{n/2}^n}[f(x) = \sum_{i \in [n]} a_i x_i] > 1 - \delta$, where $\delta = \delta(\varepsilon) = \frac{\varepsilon}{3} \cdot (1 + o_n(1)) + O(\varepsilon^2)$.[1]

In fact, we prove a 3-functions version of the above theorem: Given three functions $f_1, f_2, f_3 : L_{n/2}^n \to \{0,1\}$ the test picks $x, y \in L_{n/2}^n$ with the same distribution as in $T_{n/2}^n$, and checks that $f_1(x) + f_2(y) = f_3(x+y)$.

THEOREM 1.5. Let $n \in \mathbb{N}$ be such that $n \equiv 0 \pmod{4}$, and let $\varepsilon > 0$. Given three functions $f_1, f_2, f_3 : L_{n/2}^n \to \{0,1\}$ if $\Pr[f_1(x) + f_2(y) = f_3(x+y)] > 1 - \varepsilon$, then there exists some $i \in \{1,2,3\}$ and a string $a \in \{0,1\}^n$ such that $\Pr_{x \in L_{n/2}^n}[f_i(x) = \sum_{i \in [n]} a_i x_i] > 1 - O(\varepsilon)$.

This theorem clearly implies Theorem 1.4 with weaker parameters (which we will fix later in the proof). We prove Theorem 1.5 by giving a new analysis for the BLR test on the entire hypercube and generalizing it for L_k^n with $k = n/2$. We give more details below.

Reducing Theorem 1.1 for $k < n/2$ to the case $k = n/2$:.

First, let us describe how the case $k < n/2$ in Theorem 1.1 is obtained by reduction to $k = n/2$. The key of the reduction is to notice that T_k^n actually performs T_k^{2k} on a random subset $u \subset [n]$ of size $2k$. That is, T_k^n is equivalent to a test that first chooses a random set u of $2k$ coordinates, sets x and y to be zero on coordinates outside of u, and on the u coordinates chooses them according to the distribution used by T_k^{2k}.

If a function f passes the test with probability close to 1, then for most choices of u the test passes with high probability when conditioned on the selection of u. By the $n/2$ case (namely Theorem 1.4) for each such u the restriction of f to inputs that are contained in u is close to some linear function $\phi^{(u)}$, i.e., there is a $2k$-string $\sigma^{(u)}$ such that $f(x) = \sum_{j \in u} \sigma_j^{(u)} x_j$ for most such x's. We then show that these "local" linear functions can be stitched together to a "global" linear function ϕ, by finding a global string $a \in \{0,1\}^n$ such that $\sigma^{(u)} = a|_u$. This is done by first showing that for most u, u' the strings $\sigma^{(u)}, \sigma^{(u')}$ are consistent on their common coordinates. Then, using a recent result by of Dinur and Steurer [16] on direct product testing, we conclude that these local consistencies between $\sigma^{(u)}$ and $\sigma^{(u')}$

---

[1] We denote by $o_n(1)$ a function that tends to zero as n tends to infinity.

imply the existence of such a global string. This implies existence of a "global" linear function $\phi : L_k^n \to \{0,1\}$ that is close to f.

A new analysis of linearity testing:.

Below we outline our analysis of linearity testing on the hypercube, and then explain its extension to the direct sum testing. Let $f : \{0,1\}^n \to \{0,1\}$ be a function such that $\Pr_{x,y}[f(x) + f(y) = f(x+y)] > 1 - \varepsilon$, and let δ be the relative distance of f from the nearest linear function. Our goal is to show that $\delta = O(\varepsilon)$.

The proof follows a two step approach. The first step shows a dichotomy: either δ is $O(\varepsilon)$ or it lies in $1/2 \pm O(\varepsilon)$. Indeed, if L is the closest linear function to f and $B_L = \{x \in \{0,1\}^n : f(x) \neq L(x)\}$ is the set of points in which $f(x) \neq L(x)$, the rejection probability of the test can be written as

$$\varepsilon = \Pr[f(x) + f(y) \neq f(x+y)] \qquad (1)$$
$$\geq \Pr[x, y, x + y \in B_L] + 3\Pr[x \in B_L, y, x + y \notin B_L].$$

The first step follows easily from (1). We remark that this step is very similar to Lemma 3.7 in [5]. Nonetheless, we give a proof of this step since later we need to adapt it to functions defined on $L_{n/2}^n$.

It is now left to rule out the possibility of f agreeing with every linear function on $1/2 \pm O(\varepsilon)$ fraction of the domain. This is done in the second step which is carried out by induction on the number of variables n, and works as follows. By averaging, there exist $x_n, y_n \in \{0,1\}$ such that when fixing the last coordinates of x and y to these values the test accepts f with high probability. Fixing the last bit to x_n naturally induces a function $f_1 : \{0,1\}^{n-1} \to \{0,1\}$ defined as $f(x) = f(x \circ x_n)$. Similarly, we define f_2, and f_3 by fixing the last bit to y_n and $x_n + y_n$ respectively. Hence, the functions $f_1, f_2, f_3 : \{0,1\}^{n-1} \to \{0,1\}$ pass the 3-function test with high probability. Our goal is now to prove that (i) If $\Pr[f_1(x) + f_2(y) = f_3(x+y)] > 1 - \varepsilon$, then one of the f_i's is close to a linear function; and (ii) If some f_i is close to a linear function, then f is close to a linear function.

In order to prove (i) we define a function $g : \{0,1\}^{n-1} \to \{0,1\}$ as $g = f_1 + f_2 + f_3$, and show that g passes the linearity test with high probability. By the induction hypothesis g must be close to some linear function $L : \{0,1\}^{n-1} \to \{0,1\}$. We then show that each of the functions f_1, f_2, f_3 is either $O(\varepsilon)$-close to L or is $O(\varepsilon)$-close to $1 + L$. This implies that at least one of the three functions must be close to L, as otherwise the three functions would pass the test with very low probability.

In order to prove (ii) let us suppose for concreteness that f_1 is $O(\varepsilon)$-close to a linear function L. Then f agrees with a linear function L on $(1 - O(\varepsilon))$-fraction of the halfspace obtained by the fixing the last bit to x_n. By taking a random extension of L to the entire space $\{0,1\}^n$, we get that f agrees with some linear function in at least $3/4 - O(\varepsilon)$ fraction of the points. Therefore, the agreement of f with this linear function significantly deviates from $1/2$, and hence by the first step f must be $O(\varepsilon)$ close to a linear function. Note that the first step is crucial for the induction to go through, as it allows us to boost the agreement of f with a linear function from $3/4$ to $1 - O(\varepsilon)$ in the induction step.

Functions defined on $L_{n/2}^n$:.

In the above analysis looked at expressions of the form $\Pr[x \in B, y \in B]$ for some set B (see e.g. (1)). Since in the setting of $L_{n/2}^n$ the vertices x and y are not independent, estimating such a quantity is no longer a straightforward task. Similar estimations are also required in the induction step, although this was not mentioned explicitly in the sketch above.

We estimate this probability by considering the expansion properties of the underlying graph $J_n = (V_n, E_n)$, whose edges are (x, y) chosen by the test. Namely, the vertex set V_n of the graph is $L_{n/2}^n$ and there is an edge between x and y if and only if $x + y \in L_{n/2}^n$. We refer to J_n as the Johnson graph as it closely related to the Johnson scheme. We show that J_n satisfies the following expansion property.

LEMMA 1.6. *Let $A \subseteq V_n$ be a subset of the vertices of J_n of size $|A| = \alpha|V|$. Pick an edge $(x, y) \in E_n$ of J_n uniformly at random. Then*

1. $\Pr[x \in A, y \notin A] = \alpha(1 - \alpha) \pm \alpha(1 - \alpha) \cdot \tilde{O}(n^{-1/4})$.

2. $\Pr[x, y \in A] = \alpha^2 \pm \alpha(1 - \alpha) \cdot \tilde{O}(n^{-1/4})$.

This is proven by showing that J_n has very short mixing time. Specifically, we prove that if we start from an arbitrary vertex and make two random steps on the graph, then the distribution of the walk after two steps is $\tilde{O}(n^{-1/2})$-close to the uniform distribution. This is what we would expect to have from a random graph with such degree. We remark that although the spectrum of J_n is well known (see [20]), the bounds on the expansion of J_n obtained from the spectral analysis are not sufficiently tight for our purpose, and we give a bespoke combinatorial analysis for this graph in order to obtain the result.

1.5 Related work

There has recently been an active line of research in the field of analysis of boolean functions extending known results regarding functions defined on the hypercube to their analogues defined on a fixed layer of the hypercube [29, 34, 17]. In this paper we prove an analogous result for linearity test, which is another classical result in this area.

Since the original proof of [9], the linearity test has received a lot of attention, and was extensively studied and generalized. Generalizations include testing linearity for groups other than the hypercube, testing low degree (rather than degree 1), and finding more randomness-efficient tests. See [6, 7, 4, 31, 1, 24, 8, 26].

Kopparty and Saraf [26] studied linearity testing on the hypercube for a large family of measures on distances between functions. That is, the distance between functions is defined as $\text{dist}(f, g) = \Pr_{x \sim \mu}[f(x) \neq g(x)]$ for some predefined distribution μ, which is not necessarily the uniform measure. In particular, they show a linearity test that works for the distribution μ_p, where each bit of $x \in \{0, 1\}^n$ is chosen to be 1 with probability p, and their proof also applies to the setting of L_k^n. A drawback of their test is that it makes $O(n/k)$ queries, and does not look like the natural "BLR-style" 3 query test.

Kaufman and Lubotzky [25] recently discovered an intriguing connection between high dimensional expanders and testing, a connection that served as a trigger for this work. They show that expansion of a k-dimensional simplicial complex $V \subseteq L_k^n$ on vertex set $[n]$ is equivalent to testing whether

a function $f : V \to \{0, 1\}$ is a linear extension of a function defined on L_{k-1}^n, i.e., whether there is some $g : L_{k-1}^n \to \{0, 1\}$ such that $f(x) = \sum_{y \subseteq x, |y|=|x|-1} g(y)$ for all $x \in V$. The case of $k = 2$ coincides with our result (because a function $g : L_1^n \to \{0, 1\}$ is just an n-bit string), and was analyzed by Linial and Meshulam in [27] in the language of simplicial complexes.

Motivated by constructions of short PCPs Ben-Sasson et al. [7] analyze a linearity test in which, just like in our result, the queries x and y are not independent. Their domain is the hypercube, and their goal was to minimize the number of random bits used by the test. The test works by choosing $x \in \{0, 1\}^n$ uniformly at random, choosing $s \in S$ for some $S \subseteq \{0, 1\}^n$ of size $n^{O(1)}$ uniformly at random, and setting $y = x + s$. The test accepts if and only if $f(x) + f(y) = f(x + y)$. They show that if S is a small biased set, then this indeed gives a good linearity test.

This idea was later generalized by Shpilka and Wigderson [31] to arbitrary groups Γ with generators S of size $|S| = O(1)$, where the Cayley graph $Cay(\Gamma, S)$ is an expander. They showed that the test described above performs nearly as well as the original BLR-test (depending on the expansion of the graph). The main difficulty in their work comes from the fact that x and y are not chosen independently, which is similar to our setting. They overcome this problem using the assumption that the underlying graph is an expander, which implies that if a function f is far from being linear, then the inconsistencies in the $f(x) + f(y) = f(x + y)$ test are "well spread", and hence it rejects such functions with non-negligible probability. Still, in their settings the domain of the function has a group structure, which seems to be crucial in their analysis.

Another natural generalization of linearity testing is checking whether a function is a low-degree polynomial. This was done by Alon et al. in [1], whose analysis was later improved by Bhattacharyya et al. [8]. The proof of Bhattacharyya et al. gives a new analysis of linearity test on the hypercube by induction. It seems to differ from our proof, and, in particular, we do not know if their proof can be extended to the setting of $L_{n/2}^n$.

1.6 Comparison with known proofs

In this section we explain why the BLR decoding-style analysis of linearity testing does not extend to our setting.

The combinatorial proofs of linearity testing, such the ones in [9, 6, 31], take a function $f : \{0, 1\}^n \to \{0, 1\}$ that passes the linearity test with probability $1 - \varepsilon$, and define a *correction* function $g : \{0, 1\}^n \to \{0, 1\}$ by letting $g(x) = MAJ_{y \in \{0,1\}^n}\{f(y) + f(x + y)\}$. It is then claimed that for ε small enough the function g is linear. Then, using the fact that $\text{dist}(f, g) < O(\varepsilon)$ it follows that f is $O(\varepsilon)$-close to a linear function.

In our settings, even for the case $k = n/2$ this analysis does not apply, since if we take a function $f : L_{n/2}^n \to \{0, 1\}$ that passes the $T_{n/2}^n$ test with high probability, and define the correction function $g : L_{n/2}^n \to \{0, 1\}$ analogously, namely,

$$g(x) = MAJ\{f(y) + f(x+y) : y \in L_{n/2}^n \text{ such that } x+y \in L_{n/2}^n\},$$

then we can no longer assure that the function g is linear. To understand why the analysis above cannot work, note that in our setting the correction function g considers for every $x \in L_{n/2}^n$ the "local majority" vote over only a small fraction of the space, namely those vertices that intersect

x on exactly $n/4$ of the coordinates. Therefore we cannot expect the global property of f to propagate after one step of majority voting. One could try to make more steps of corrections. By the expansion properties of the underlying graph J_n this approach could potentially work, but it seems difficult to push through, and our proof takes a different approach.

The multiple-step correction approach looks similar to the work of Shpilka and Wigderson [31] discussed earlier in Section 1.5. In their setting every vertex x is tested only with a tiny fraction of the domain (induced by an underlying expander graph G). For every vertex x they considered the "local majority" of x. They use the expansion of G to show that if f passes the test with high probability, then iterating the "local majority" function would converge to the linear function closest to f. However, in order to prove convergence, they first defined a correction function using "global majority", and then prove the "local majority" converges to the same linear function.

1.7 Structure of the paper

We begin by presenting some notations in Section 2. In Section 3 we show a new analysis for the linearity test on the hypercube. In Section 4 we sketch the proof for our main technical result, namely, Theorem 1.4. This is done by showing how to extend the proof for the hypercube to our setting.

2. NOTATIONS AND PRELIMINARIES

Notations:.

Let $n \in \mathbb{N}$. We denote by $L_k^n \subseteq \{0,1\}^n$ the set

$$L_k^n = \{x \in \{0,1\}^n : |x| = k\},$$

and by $L_{EVEN}^n \subseteq \{0,1\}^n$ the set

$$L_{EVEN}^n = \{x \in \{0,1\}^n : |x| \text{ is even}\}.$$

Note that L_{EVEN}^n is a subgroup of $\{0,1\}^n$.

FACT 2.1. *Let $n \in \mathbb{N}$, and let $k < n$. If k is even, then* $\text{span}\langle L_k^n \rangle = L_{EVEN}^n$. *If k is odd, then* $\text{span}\langle L_k^n \rangle = \{0,1\}^n$.

DEFINITION 2.2. *Let $S \subseteq \{0,1\}^n$ be a subset (S is not necessarily a subgroup). A function $f : S \to \{0,1\}$ is said to be linear if there exists $a = (a_1, \ldots, a_n) \in \{0,1\}^n$ such that $f(x) = \sum_{i \in [n]} a_i x_i \pmod{2}$ for all $x \in S$.*

In particular, as explained above, a function f is a direct sum if and only if it is a linear functions with domain L_k^n.

Note that if $\text{span}\langle S \rangle \neq \{0,1\}^n$, then the choice of $a \in \{0,1\}^n$ in Definition 2.2 may not be unique.

FACT 2.3. *Let $n \in \mathbb{N}$, and let $k < n$ be even. Suppose that $\phi : L_k^n \to \{0,1\}$ is a linear function. Then, there are precisely two strings $a, a' \in \{0,1\}^n$ such that $\phi(x) = \sum_{i \in [i]} a_i x_i \pmod{2}$ and $\phi(x) = \sum_{i \in [n]} a_i' x_i \pmod{2}$ for all $x \in L_k^n$. Specifically, the strings a and a' are complements of each other, i.e., $a_i = 1 - a_i'$ for all $i \in [n]$.*

We will also need the following claim on distances between distinct linear functions on L_k^n. Note that unlike in the hypercube settings this claim is not trivial in the L_k^n settings, and depends on k not being to close to 0 or n.

PROPOSITION 2.4. *Let $p \in (0,1)$, let $n \in \mathbb{N}$ be an integer so that $pn \in \mathbb{N}$, and let $k = pn$. Then, for every pair of distinct linear functions $\phi_1 \neq \phi_2 : L_k^n \to \{0,1\}$ it holds that*

$$c \leq \Pr_{x \in L_k^n}[\phi_1(x) \neq \phi_2(x)] \leq 1 - c$$

for some constant $c = c(p) > 0$ that depends only on p.

In particular, for all $k \in (\varepsilon n, (1-\varepsilon)n)$ the distance between two distinct functions of L_k^n is bounded away above zero. Due to space constraints we omit the proof of Proposition 2.4 and it can be found in the full version of the paper.

We will also need the following definition of a δ-test.

DEFINITION 2.5. *Let $\mathbf{C}$ be a class of functions from a finite domain $\mathbf{D}$ to a finite range Σ. Let $\delta : (0,1] \to (0,1]$ be a function such that $\delta(\varepsilon) \to 0$ as $\varepsilon \to 0$. We say that T is a δ-test for the class $\mathbf{C}$ if*

1. *All functions in $\mathbf{C}$ are accepted by T with probability 1.*

2. *For every $\varepsilon > 0$, any function $f : \mathbf{D} \to \Sigma$ that passes the test T with probability $1 - \varepsilon$ is $\delta(\varepsilon)$-close to $\mathbf{C}$, i.e., there exists some $\phi \in \mathbf{C}$ such that $\Pr_{x \in \mathbf{D}}[f(x) \neq \phi(x)] < \delta(\varepsilon)$.*

Using this definition Theorem 1.1 considers the following class of functions.

DEFINITION 2.6. *Define LIN_k^n to be the class of functions $f : L_k^n \to \{0,1\}$ for which there exists $a \in \{0,1\}^n$ such that for every $x \in L_k^n$ it holds that $f(x) = \sum_{i \in [n]} a_i x_i$.*

Similarly, by identifying k-subsets of $[n]$ with vectors in $\{0,1\}^n$ of weight k, the class of direct product functions can be written as follows.

DEFINITION 2.7. *Define DP_k^n to be the class of functions $F : L_k^n \to \{0,1\}^k$ for which there exists $a \in \{0,1\}^n$ such that $F(x) = a_x$ for every $x \in L_k^n$, where a_x is the substring of a confined to the coordinates in which $x_i = 1$.*

Note that if T is a direct product test in the sense of Definition 2.5 then for any function $F : L_k^n \to \{0,1\}^k$ that passes the test with high probability there exists a string $a \in \{0,1\}^n$ such that $F(x) \equiv a_x$ for most inputs $x \in L_k^n$. This is as opposed to a more relaxed definition of direct product test (such as the ones in [12, 23]), where for most x's the Hamming distance between $F(x)$ and a_x is small.

3. LINEARITY TESTING ON THE HYPERCUBE

In this section we describe the idea behind the proof of Theorem 1.1 by discussing a simpler setting of the hypercube $\{0,1\}^n$. Our approach gives a new proof for linearity testing on $\{0,1\}^n$. In Section 4 we show how this proof can be modified in order to prove linearity testing in the setting of $L_{n/2}^n$.

Recall, the test gets as an oracle access a function $f : \{0,1\}^n \to \{0,1\}$ and tests whether f is close to a linear function. The test is defined as follows.

BLR Linearity Test on the Hypercube:
Given an oracle access to a function $f : \{0,1\}^n \to \{0,1\}$ do:

1. Select $x, y \in \{0,1\}^n$ independently.

2. Accept if and only if $f(x) + f(y) = f(x+y)$.

THEOREM 3.1. *There exists some $\varepsilon_0 > 0$ small enough such that for every $\varepsilon \in (0, \varepsilon_0)$ and for all $n \in \mathbb{N}$ the following holds. Suppose that a function $f : \{0,1\}^n \to \{0,1\}$ passes the BLR test with probability $1 - \varepsilon$. Then f is $(\varepsilon/3 + 8\varepsilon^2/9)$-close to some linear function, namely, there exists a linear function $g : \{0,1\}^n \to \{0,1\}$ such that*

$$\Pr[f(x) \neq g(x)] < \varepsilon/3 + 8\varepsilon^2/9.$$

In fact, we prove a slightly stronger result. Suppose that we are given three functions $f_1, f_2, f_3 : \{0,1\}^n \to \{0,1\}$, and our goal is to check whether the functions are (close to) linear. Consider the following test. Given (an oracle access) to three functions $f_1, f_2, f_3 : \{0,1\}^n \to \{0,1\}$ the test works as follows.

Three Functions Testing Linearity on the Hypercube
Given an oracle access to three functions $f_1, f_2, f_3 : \{0,1\}^n \to \{0,1\}$ do:

1. Select $x, y \in \{0,1\}^n$ independently.

2. Accept if and only if $f_1(x) + f_2(y) = f_3(x+y)$.

Note that if we take a linear function f_1, and let $f_2 = f_3 = f_1 + 1$, then the above test accepts these functions. Therefore, if the test passes with high probability, it does not imply that all functions are close to linear. What we do prove is that at least one of the functions must be close to linear. Specifically, we prove the following theorem.

THEOREM 3.2. *There exists some $\varepsilon_0 > 0$ small enough such that for every $\varepsilon \in (0, \varepsilon_0)$ and for all $n \in \mathbb{N}$ the following holds. Let $f_1, f_2, f_3 : \{0,1\}^n \to \{0,1\}$ be three functions. Suppose that they pass the three functions test with probability $1 - \varepsilon$. Then, there is $i \in \{1,2,3\}$ such that f_i is $2\varepsilon + O(\varepsilon^2)$-close to some linear function.*

3.1 First step towards the proof

Towards proving Theorem 3.1 we show first that if a function passes BLR test with probability $1 - \varepsilon$, then for every linear function $L : \{0,1\}^n \to \{0,1\}$ it holds that either the distance between f and L is either close to 0 or close to $\frac{1}{2}$.

LEMMA 3.3. *Let $f : \{0,1\}^n \to \{0,1\}$ be a boolean function. For every linear function $L : \{0,1\}^n \to \{0,1\}$ let $\delta_L = \mathrm{dist}(L, f)$ be the distance of f from L. If $\Pr[f(x) + f(y) = f(x+y)] = 1 - \varepsilon$, then for every linear function L we have*

- *either $\delta_L \leq \varepsilon/3 + 8\varepsilon^2/9$*

- *or $\frac{1}{2} - (\varepsilon/3 + 8\varepsilon^2/9) \leq \delta_L \leq \frac{1}{2} + \varepsilon$.*

In particular, if $\phi : \{0,1\}^n \to \{0,1\}$ is a linear function such that $\mathrm{dist}(f, \phi) \notin [\frac{1}{2} - (\varepsilon/3 + 8\varepsilon^2/9), \frac{1}{2} + \varepsilon]$, then $\mathrm{dist}(f, \phi) \leq \varepsilon/3 + 8\varepsilon^2/9$.

PROOF. Fix a boolean function $f : \{0,1\}^n \to \{0,1\}$, and suppose that it passes linearity test with probability $\Pr[f(x) + f(y) = f(x+y)] = 1 - \varepsilon$. For any linear function $L : \{0,1\}^n \to \{0,1\}$ define $B_L = \{x \in \{0,1\}^n : f(x) \neq L(x)\}$, and let $G_L = \{0,1\}^n \setminus B_L$. Using this notation the

distance between f and L is $\delta_L = \frac{|B_L|}{2^n}$, and the rejection probability of the test on f can be written as

$$\varepsilon = \Pr[\text{Test rejects } f] \quad \geq \quad \Pr[x, y, x+y \in B_L] \qquad (2)$$
$$+ 3\Pr[x \in B_L, y, x+y \in G_L].$$

Since $\Pr[\cdot] \geq 0$, it follow that each of the two terms is smaller than ε. The first term gives us the following bound.

$$\Pr[x, y, x+y \in B_L] \quad \geq \quad \Pr[x \in B_L] - \Pr[x \in B_L, y \notin B_L]$$
$$- \Pr[x \in B_L, x+y \notin B_L]$$
$$= \quad \Pr[x \in B_L] - 2\Pr[x \in B_L, y \notin B_L]$$
$$\geq \quad \delta_L - 2\delta_L(1 - \delta_L)$$
$$\geq \quad \delta_L(2\delta_L - 1).$$

Solving the inequality $\varepsilon \geq \Pr[x, y, x+y \in B_L] \geq \delta_L(2\delta_L - 1)$ for $\delta_L \geq 0$ we get

$$\delta_L \leq \frac{1}{2} + \varepsilon. \qquad (3)$$

Similarly, the second term gives us

$$\Pr[x \in B_L, y, x+y \in G_L] \quad \geq \quad \Pr[x \in B_L] - \Pr[x \in B_L, y \in B_L]$$
$$- \Pr[x \in B_L, x+y \in B_L]$$
$$= \quad \Pr[x \in B_L] - 2\Pr[x \in B_L, y \in B_L]$$
$$\geq \quad \delta_L - 2\delta_L^2$$
$$\geq \quad \delta_L(1 - 2\delta_L).$$

Solving the quadratic inequality $\varepsilon \geq 3\Pr[x \in B_L, y, x+y \in G_L] \geq 3 \cdot \delta_L(1 - 2\delta_L)$ we get

$$\delta_L \leq \varepsilon/3 + 8\varepsilon^2/9 \quad \text{or} \quad \delta_L \geq \frac{1}{2} - (\varepsilon/3 + 8\varepsilon^2/9). \quad (4)$$

where we use the fact that $\sqrt{1 - 8\varepsilon/3} \geq 1 - 4\varepsilon/3 - 32\varepsilon^2/9$ holds for all $\varepsilon \in [0, 1/8]$. Lemma 3.3 follows by combining Equation (3) with Equation (4). $\square$

3.2 Proof of Theorems 3.1 and 3.2

In this section we prove Theorems 3.1 and 3.2.

PROOF. We prove both Theorems 3.1 and 3.2 by induction of n. For the base case for Theorem 3.1 note that if $n \leq \frac{\log(1/\varepsilon)}{2}$, then $\varepsilon < 2^{-2n}$, and hence for every $x, y \in \{0,1\}^n$ it holds that $f(x) + f(y) = f(x+y)$. This implies that f is a linear function. For the induction step we prove the following two lemmas.

LEMMA 3.4. *Suppose that the statement of Theorem 3.1 holds for $n - 1$. Then, the statement of Theorem 3.2 holds for $n - 1$.*

LEMMA 3.5. *Suppose that for some $n \in \mathbb{N}$ the statement of Theorem 3.2 holds for $n - 1$. Then, the statement of Theorem 3.1 holds for n.*

Therefore, in order to prove Theorems 3.1 and 3.2 it is enough to prove the two foregoing lemmas. $\square$

PROOF OF LEMMA 3.4. We prove the lemma for the n-dimensional hypercube, and not for $n - 1$ as stated in the lemma.

Let $f_1, f_2, f_3 : \{0,1\}^n \to \{0,1\}$ be three functions and suppose that $\Pr[f_1(x) + f_2(y) = f_3(x+y)] \geq 1 - \varepsilon$. Define a function $g : \{0,1\}^n \to \{0,1\}$ as $g(x) = f_1(x) + f_2(x) + f_3(x)$. Note first that g is close to a linear function. Indeed,

$$\Pr[g(x) + g(y) \neq g(x+y)]$$

$$= \Pr \left[\begin{array}{ccc} f_1(x) + f_1(y) & & f_1(x+y) \\ + \ f_2(x) + f_2(y) & \neq & + \ f_2(x+y) \\ + \ f_3(x) + f_3(y) & & + \ f_3(x+y) \end{array} \right]$$

$$= \Pr \left[\begin{array}{ccc} f_1(x) + f_2(y) & & f_3(x+y) \\ + \ f_2(x) + f_3(y) & \neq & + \ f_1(x+y) \\ + \ f_3(x) + f_1(y) & & + \ f_2(x+y) \end{array} \right]$$

$$\leq 3 \Pr[f_1(x) + f_2(y) \neq f_3(x+y)]$$

$$\leq 3\varepsilon,$$

and thus, by Theorem 3.1 for n the function g is $(\varepsilon + 8\varepsilon^2)$-close to some linear function.

CLAIM 3.6. *Let ϕ be a linear function such that* $\mathrm{dist}(g, \phi) \leq \varepsilon + 8\varepsilon^2$. *Then, the function f_1 is $(2\varepsilon + O(\varepsilon^2))$-close to either ϕ or to $\phi + 1$, where $O()$ hides some absolute constant.*

PROOF. We note first that $\Pr[f_1(x) + f_1(y) = g(x+y)] \geq 1 - 3\varepsilon$. Indeed

$$\Pr[f_1(x) + f_1(y) \neq g(x+y)]$$

$$\leq \Pr[(f_2(y) + f_3(x+y)) + (f_3(x) + f_2(x+y)) = g(x+y)] + 2\varepsilon$$

$$\leq \Pr[f_2(y) + f_3(x) = f_1(x+y)] + 2\varepsilon \leq 3\varepsilon.$$

Since $\phi : \{0,1\}^n \to \{0,1\}$ is a linear function such that $\mathrm{dist}(g, \phi) \leq \varepsilon + 8\varepsilon^2$, it follows that

$$\Pr_{x,y}[f_1(x) + \phi(x) = f_1(y) + \phi(y)] \geq 1 - 4\varepsilon - 8\varepsilon^2. \quad (5)$$

We claim that Equation (5) implies that f_1 is either close to ϕ or close to $\phi + 1$. Indeed, let $f_1' : \{0,1\}^n \to \{0,1\}$ be defined as $f_1' = f_1 + \phi$. Then

$$\Pr[f_1'(x) = f_1'(y)] \geq 1 - 4\varepsilon - 8\varepsilon^2.$$

Therefore, by the "collision probability" argument f' is close to a constant function. Indeed, if we denote $p = \Pr[f_1'(x) = 1]$, then $p^2 + (1-p)^2 \geq 1 - 4\varepsilon - 8\varepsilon^2$, which implies that either $p \leq 2\varepsilon + O(\varepsilon^2)$ or $p \geq 1 - (2\varepsilon + O(\varepsilon^2))$. Therefore, f_1' is $(2\varepsilon + O(\varepsilon^2))$-close to a constant function, and hence f_1 is $(2\varepsilon + O(\varepsilon^2))$-close to either ϕ or to $\phi + 1$. $\square$

Similarly, the function f_2 and f_3 are also close to either ϕ or to $\phi + 1$. It is left to prove that one of the f_i's must be linear. Indeed, if all f_i's were $2\varepsilon + C\varepsilon^2$ close to $\phi + 1$, then

$$1 - \varepsilon \ \leq \ \Pr[f_1(x) + f_2(y) = f_3(x+y)]$$
$$\leq \ \Pr[\phi(x) + \phi(y) = \phi(x+y) + 1] + 3(2\varepsilon + C\varepsilon^2)$$
$$= \ 3(2\varepsilon + C\varepsilon^2)$$

contradicting the assumption that ε is sufficiently small. Therefore, there must be some $i \in \{1,2,3\}$ such that f_i is $(2\varepsilon + O(\varepsilon^2))$-close to the linear function ϕ. This completes the proof of Lemma 3.4.

We now turn to proof of Lemma 3.5.

PROOF OF LEMMA 3.5. Let $f : \{0,1\}^n \to \{0,1\}$ be a linear function, and suppose that $\Pr[f(x) + f(y) = f(x+y)] \geq 1 - \varepsilon$. By averaging there are some bits $x_n, y_n \in \{0,1\}$ such that if we pick $x', y' \in \{0,1\}^{n-1}$ independently then

$$\Pr[f(x' \circ x_n) + f(y' \circ y_n) = f((x'+y') \circ (x_n+y_n))] \geq 1-\varepsilon, \quad (6)$$

where $\circ$ denotes the concatenation of strings. Define three functions $f_1, f_2, f_3 : \{0,1\}^{n-1} \to \{0,1\}$ be letting

$$f_1(x') = f(x \circ x_n) \quad f_2(x') = f(x' \circ y_n) \quad f_3(x') = f(x' \circ (x_n + y_n))$$

Then, by Equation (6) we have

$$\Pr[f_1(x') + f_2(y') = f_3(x' + y')] \geq 1 - \varepsilon.$$

By the hypothesis of the lemma it follows that one of the functions f_i is $(2\varepsilon + O(\varepsilon^2))$-close to a linear function $\phi : \{0,1\}^{n-1} \to \{0,1\}$. Let us assume for concreteness that f_1 is this function. Our goal is to extend ϕ to an affine function ψ on $\{0,1\}^n$ so that $\Pr[f(x) = \psi(x)] \geq 3/4 - O(\varepsilon)$. Then, by Lemma 3.3 it will follow that ψ is linear, and f is close to ψ.

Let us assume first that $x_n = 0$. Define ψ randomly by choosing a random bit $b \in \{0,1\}$ and letting $\psi(x_1, \ldots, x_n) = \phi(x_1, \ldots, x_{n-1}) + b \cdot x_n$. Note that ψ agrees with ϕ on the subspace $\{x \in \{0,1\}^n : x_n = 0\}$, and for every $x \in \{0,1\}^n$ such that $x_n = 1$ it holds that $\Pr[\psi(x) = f(x)] = \frac{1}{2}$. Therefore, the expected agreement of f with ψ is

$$\mathbb{E}[\mathrm{agr}(f, \psi)] \geq \frac{1}{2}(\mathrm{agr}(f_1, \psi)) + \frac{1}{2} \cdot \frac{1}{2} \geq 3/4 - O(\varepsilon).$$

The case $x_n = 1$ is similar. Define ψ randomly by choosing a random bit $b \in \{0,1\}$ and letting $\psi(x_1, \ldots, x_n) = \phi(x_1, \ldots, x_{n-1}) + b \cdot (1 + x_n)$. Similarly, ψ agrees with ϕ on the affine subspace $\{x \in \{0,1\}^n : x_n = 1\}$, and for every $x \in \{0,1\}^n$ such that $x_n = 0$ it holds that $\Pr[\psi(x) = f(x)] = \frac{1}{2}$. Hence the expected agreement of f with ψ is

$$\mathbb{E}[\mathrm{agr}(f, \psi)] \geq \frac{1}{2}(\mathrm{agr}(f_1, \psi)) + \frac{1}{2} \cdot \frac{1}{2} \geq 3/4 - O(\varepsilon).$$

Therefore, if ε is sufficiently small, then by Lemma 3.3 the function ψ is linear, and $\mathrm{dist}(f, \psi) \leq \varepsilon/3 + 8\varepsilon^2/9$. The lemma follows. $\square$

4. PROOF OF THEOREM 1.4: DIRECT SUM TESTING FOR $K = N/2$

In this section we prove Theorem 1.4. Recall that for n divisible by 4 the $T_{n/2}^n$ test is defined as follows.

$T_{n/2}^n$ - **Direct Sum Test for $k = n/2$:**
Given an oracle access to $f : L_{n/2}^n \to \{0,1\}$ do:

1. Pick $x, y \in L_{n/2}^n$ uniformly at random so that $x + y \in L_{n/2}^n$.

2. Accept if and only if $f(x) + f(y) = f(x+y)$.

Theorem 1.4 restated:.

Let $n \in \mathbb{N}$ be such that $n \equiv 0 \pmod 4$, and let $\varepsilon > 0$. For all functions $f : L_{n/2}^n \to \{0,1\}$ if $\Pr[f(x) + f(y) = f(x+y)] > 1 - \varepsilon$, then there exists a string $a \in \{0,1\}^n$ such that $\Pr_{x \in L_k^n}[f(x) = \sum_{i \in [n]} a_i x_i] > 1 - \delta$, where $\delta = \delta(\varepsilon) = \frac{\varepsilon}{3} \cdot (1 + O(\sqrt{\gamma_n})) + O(\varepsilon^2)$, and $\gamma_n = \tilde{O}(n^{-1/2})$ is the quantity from Lemma 1.6.

As explained in Section 1.4 we prove a stronger three functions version of this theorem.

Direct Sum Test for three functions:
Given an oracle access to three functions $f_1, f_2, f_3 : L_{n/2}^n \to \{0,1\}$ do:

1. Select $x, y \in L_{n/2}^n$ such that $x + y \in L_{n/2}^n$.

2. Accept if and only if $f_1(x) + f_2(y) = f_3(x + y)$.

Theorem 1.5 restated:.

Let $n \in \mathbb{N}$ be such that $n \equiv 0 \pmod 4$, and let $\varepsilon > 0$. For all functions $f_1, f_2, f_3 : L_{n/2}^n \to \{0, 1\}$ if $\Pr[f_1(x) + f_2(y) = f_3(x + y)] > 1 - \varepsilon$, then there exists $i \in \{1, 2, 3\}$ and a string $a \in \{0, 1\}^n$ such that $\Pr_{x \in L_k^n}[f_i(x) = \sum_{i \in [n]} a_i x_i] > 1 - \delta$, where $\delta = \delta(\varepsilon) = 4\varepsilon + O(\varepsilon^2)$.

The proof is very similar to the proof of Theorems 3.1 and 3.2 from Section 3

PROOF OF THEOREM 1.4. We prove Theorem 1.4 by induction of n, where in each step we increase n by 4, since the theorem assumes that $n \equiv 0 \pmod 4$. The base case $n \leq \frac{\log(1/\varepsilon)}{2}$ holds by Proposition 4.1, stated next:

PROPOSITION 4.1. *Let $n \in \mathbb{N}$ and let $k \leq n$ be even. Let $f : L_k^n \to \{0, 1\}$ be a boolean function. Then f passes the T_k^n test with probability 1 if and only if f is a linear function.*

Due to space limitation we omit the proof of Proposition 4.1. For the induction step we prove the following two lemmas.

LEMMA 4.2. *Suppose that the statement of Theorem 1.4 holds for some $n - 4 \in \mathbb{N}$. Then, the statement of Theorem 1.5 holds for $n - 4$.*

LEMMA 4.3. *Suppose that for some $n \in \mathbb{N}$ the statement of Theorem 1.5 holds for $n - 4$. Then, the statement of Theorem 1.4 holds for n.*

These two lemmas, clearly, prove Theorem 1.4. □

Due to space limitations we omit the proofs of Lemma 4.2 and Lemma 4.3. We stress that in our settings the choices of x and y are not independent, and are chosen such that $|x \cap y| = n/4$. This corresponds to choosing a random edge (x, y) in the graph $J_n = (V_n, E_n)$, whose edges are (x, y) chosen by the test. Namely, the vertex set V_n of the graph is $L_{n/2}^n$ and there is an edge between x and y if and only if $x + y \in L_{n/2}^n$. We use the following corollary from Lemma 1.6 to complete the proof:

COROLLARY 4.4. *Let $A \subseteq V_n$ be a set of vertices of density $\alpha = \frac{|A|}{|V|}$. Suppose that if we pick a random edge $(x, y) \in E$ then the probability that one endpoint is in A and the other is not in A is at most ε for some $\varepsilon > 0$ sufficiently small. Then either $\alpha < \varepsilon + O(\varepsilon^2)$ or $\alpha > 1 - (\varepsilon + O(\varepsilon^2))$.*

5. REFERENCES

[1] N. Alon, T. Kaufman, M. Krivelevich, S. Litsyn, and D. Ron. Testing reed-muller codes. *IEEE Transactions on Information Theory*, 51(11):4032–4039, 2005.

[2] S. Arora, C. Lund, R. Motwani, M. Sudan, and M. Szegedy. Proof verification and the hardness of approximation problems. *J. ACM*, 45(3):501–555, 1998.

[3] S. Arora and S. Safra. Probabilistic checking of proofs: A new characterization of NP. *J. ACM*, 45(1):70–122, 1998.

[4] M. Bellare, D. Coppersmith, J. Håstad, M. A. Kiwi, and M. Sudan. Linearity testing in characteristic two. *IEEE Transactions on Information Theory*, 42(6):1781–1795, 1996.

[5] M. Bellare, S. Goldwasser, C. Lund, and A. Russell. Efficient probabilistic checkable proofs and applications to approximation. In *Proceedings of the 25th Annual ACM Symposium on the Theory of Computing*, pages 294–304, 1993.

[6] M. Ben-Or, D. Coppersmith, M. Luby, and R. Rubinfeld. Non-abelian homomorphism testing, and distributions close to their self-convolutions. *Random Struct. Algorithms*, 32(1):49–70, 2008.

[7] E. Ben-Sasson, M. Sudan, S. Vadhan, and A. Wigderson. Randomness-efficient low degree tests and short pcps via epsilon-biased sets. In *Proceedings of the 35th Annual ACM Symposium on the Theory of Computing*, pages 612–621, 2003.

[8] A. Bhattacharyya, S. Kopparty, G. Schoenebeck, M. Sudan, and D. Zuckerman. Optimal testing of reed-muller codes. In *Proceedings of the 51st Annual IEEE Symposium on Foundations of Computer Science*, 2010.

[9] M. Blum, M. Luby, and R. Rubinfeld. Self-testing/correcting with applications to numerical problems. *J. Comput. Syst. Sci.*, 47(3):549–595, 1993.

[10] S. O. Chan. Approximation resistance from pairwise independent subgroups. In *Proceedings of the 45th Annual ACM Symposium on the Theory of Computing*, pages 447–456, 2013.

[11] I. Dinur. The PCP theorem by gap amplification. *J. ACM*, 54(3), 2007.

[12] I. Dinur and E. Goldenberg. Locally testing direct product in the low error range. In *Proceedings of the 49th Annual IEEE Symposium on Foundations of Computer Science*, pages 613–622, 2008.

[13] I. Dinur and E. Goldenberg. The structure of winning strategies in parallel repetition games. In *Proceedings of the 14th RANDOM*, pages 518–530, 2010.

[14] I. Dinur and O. Meir. Derandomized parallel repetition via structured pcps. *Computational Complexity*, 20(2):207–327, 2011.

[15] I. Dinur and O. Reingold. Assignment testers: Towards a combinatorial proof of the PCP theorem. *SIAM J. Comput.*, 36(4):975–1024, 2006.

[16] I. Dinur and D. Steurer. Direct product testing. In *Proceedings of the 29th Anual IEEE Conference on Computational Complexity*, 2014.

[17] Y. Filmus. Orthogonal basis for functions over a slice of the boolean hypercube. 2014. Available at: http://arxiv.org/pdf/1406.0142v1.pdf.

[18] O. Goldreich, N. Nisan, and A. Wigderson. On Yao's XOR lemma. 1995. http://eccc.hpi-web.de/report/1995/050/.

[19] O. Goldreich and S. Safra. A combinatorial consistency lemma with application to proving the pcp theorem. *SIAM J. Comput.*, 29(4):1132–1154, 2000.

[20] R. L. Graham, M. Grötschel, and L. Lovász, editors. *Handbook of combinatorics (vol. 1)*. MIT Press, Cambridge, MA, USA, 1995.

[21] A. Healy, S. P. Vadhan, and E. Viola. Using nondeterminism to amplify hardness. *SIAM Journal on Computing*, 34(4):903–931, 2006.

[22] R. Impagliazzo, R. Jaiswal, V. Kabanets, and A. Wigderson. Uniform direct product theorems: Simplified, optimized, and derandomized. *SIAM J. Comput.*, 39(4):1637–1665, 2010.

[23] R. Impagliazzo, V. Kabanets, and A. Wigderson. New direct-product testers and 2-query PCPs. In *Proceedings of the 41st Annual ACM symposium on the Theory of computing*, pages 131–140, New York, NY, USA, 2009. ACM.

[24] T. Kaufman, S. Litsyn, and N. Xie. Breaking the epsilon-soundness bound of the linearity test over GF(2). *SIAM Journal on Computing*, 39(5):1988–2003, 2007.

[25] T. Kaufman and A. Luobtzky. High dimensional expanders and property testing. In *Proceedings of the 5th ITCS*, 2014.

[26] S. Kopparty and S. Saraf. Tolerant linearity testing and locally testable codes. In *Proceedings of the 12th RANDOM*, pages 601–614, 2009.

[27] N. Linial and R. Meshulam. Homological connectivity of random 2-complexes. *Combinatorica*, 26(4):475–487, 2006.

[28] R. O'Donnell. Hardness amplification within np. In *Proceedings of the 34th Annual ACM symposium on the Theory of computing*, STOC '02, pages 751–760, New York, NY, USA, 2002. ACM.

[29] R. O'Donnell and K. Wimmer. KKL, Kruskal-Katona, and monotone nets. In *Proceedings of the 50st Annual IEEE Symposium on Foundations of Computer Science*, 2009.

[30] R. Raz. A parallel repetition theorem. *SIAM Journal on Computing*, 27(3):763–803, 1998.

[31] A. Shpilka and A. Wigderson. Derandomizing homomorphism testing in general groups. In *Proceedings of the 36th Annual ACM Symposium on the Theory of Computing*, pages 427–435. ACM, 2004.

[32] M. Sudan, L. Trevisan, and S. P. Vadhan. Pseudorandom generators without the xor lemma. *J. Comput. Syst. Sci.*, 62(2):236–266, 2001.

[33] L. Trevisan. List-decoding using the xor lemma. In *Proceedings of the 44th Annual IEEE Symposium on Foundations of Computer Science*, pages 126–135, Washington, DC, USA, 2003. IEEE Computer Society.

[34] K. Wimmer. Low influence functions over slices of the boolean hypercube are essentially juntas. In *Proceedings of the 29th IEEE Conference on Computational Complexity*, 2014.

[35] A. C. Yao. Theory and application of trapdoor functions. In *Proceedings of the 23rd Annual IEEE Symposium on Foundations of Computer Science*, pages 80–91, Washington, DC, USA, 1982. IEEE Computer Society.

On Sample-Based Testers

[Extended Abstract] [*]

Oded Goldreich
Weizmann Institute of Science
Rehovot, Israel
oded.goldreich@weizmann.ac.il

Dana Ron
Tel Aviv University
Tel Aviv, Israel
danar@eng.tau.ac.il

ABSTRACT

The standard definition of property testing endows the tester with the ability to make arbitrary queries to "elements" of the tested object. In contrast, sample-based testers only obtain independently distributed elements (a.k.a. labeled samples) of the tested object. While sample-based testers were defined by Goldreich, Goldwasser, and Ron (*JACM* 1998), with few exceptions, most research in property testing is focused on query-based testers.

In this work, we advance the study of sample-based property testers by providing several general positive results as well as by revealing relations between variants of this testing model. In particular:

- We show that certain types of query-based testers yield sample-based testers of sublinear sample complexity. For example, this holds for a natural class of proximity oblivious testers.

- We study the relation between distribution-free sample-based testers and one-sided error sample-based testers w.r.t. the uniform distribution.

While most of this work ignores the time complexity of testing, one part of it does focus on this aspect. The main result in this part is a sublinear-*time* sample-based tester in the dense graphs model for k-Colorability, for any $k \geq 2$.

1. INTRODUCTION

In the last couple of decades, the area of property testing has attracted much attention (see, e.g., [7, 20, 21]). Loosely speaking, property testing typically refers to sub-linear complexity probabilistic algorithms for deciding whether a given object has a predetermined property or is far from any object having this property. Such algorithms, called testers, obtain local views of the object by performing queries; that is, the object is seen as a function and the testers get oracle access to this function (and thus may be expected to work in time that is sub-linear in the length of the object).

The standard definition of property testing, which is alluded to above, endows the tester with the ability to make queries. This is the definition presented in [22], and it is also the main definition studied in [9] as well as in most research on property testing. Nevertheless, a weaker notion, where the tester is only provided with uniformly distributed labeled samples (or, equivalently, is only allowed to make uniformly and *independently distributed* queries)[1] was also presented (and briefly studied) in [9]. We call such testers *sample-based*.

While sample-based testers were studied in [9][2] and in some subsequent works (see, e.g., [8]), these studies tend to be negative in nature: Their focus is on showing why the query ability utilized in the main positive results is necessary for efficiently testing the property that is being considered. This amounts to presenting high lower bounds on the sample complexity of sample-based testers for that property. A few positive results on sample-based testers have been obtained in previous work [8, 18, 2], and they are further discussed in Subsection 1.3. We also discuss the relation to testing properties of *distributions* in Subsection 1.2.1.

In this work we aim at a broader study of sample-based property testing, and we obtain several general positive results as well as reveal relations between variants of this testing model. Although sample-based testers are typically much less efficient than general (query-based) testers, in many applications, random labeled samples are easier to obtain than a full query capacity. Hence, we believe that sample-based testers may be of practical value.

1.1 Sample-based testers of sublinear sample complexity

The complexity of testers (of various types) is measured as a function of the size of the object, denoted n, and the

[*]A full version of this paper is available on ECCC [13]. Partially supported by the Israel Science Foundation (grant No. 671/13).

[1]We stress that the canonical testers of graph properties, which are used in many works and are studied explicitly in [15, Section 4], do *not* make uniformly and independently distributed queries. Indeed, they select at random a uniformly distributed set of vertices, but their queries (which correspond to all vertex pairs) are dependent, although each is uniformly distributed. In general, many testers make uniformly distributed queries, but these queries are typically not fully independent of one another. See further discussion following Theorem 1.1.

[2]In fact, the main definition in [9] refers to (distribution-free) sample-based testers (cf. [9, Definition 2.1]).

proximity parameter, denoted ϵ. (Both these parameters are given as input to standard testers.) When we say that a complexity measure is *sublinear*, we mean that it is sublinear as a function of n, when fixing ϵ. (Typically, the query and sample complexities are at least linear in $1/\epsilon$.) We stress that when the tested object is a function, its size is the size of the function's domain, not the length of elements in that domain; for example, the size of $f : \{0, 1\}^\ell \to \{0, 1\}$ is $n = 2^\ell$. With one exception, all our positive results assert sublinear sample complexity for properties that are impossible to learn within such complexity (under the uniform distribution).

One of our results transforms certain Proximity Oblivious Testers (POTs) into sample-based testers of sublinear sample complexity, where the "level of sublinearity" depends on the (constant) query complexity of the POT. Loosely speaking, Proximity Oblivious Testers (POTs) are "basic testers" that do not get a proximity parameter as input, and make only a constant number of queries to the tested object [12]. They are required to reject objects with probability that is lower bounded by a function of the object's distance to the property (see Definition A.2).[3] This function is called the *detection probability function*.

THEOREM 1.1. (Proximity Oblivious Testers with uniformly distributed queries imply sample-based testers of sublinear sample complexity): *Suppose that Π has a q-query POT with detection probability function ϱ that makes uniformly distributed queries. Then, Π has a sample-based tester with sample complexity $s(n, \epsilon) = O(n^{1-(1/q)}/\varrho(\epsilon)^{2+(3/q)})$. Furthermore, if the POT has one-sided error, then so does the sample-based tester.*

We stress that the premise of Theorem 1.1 is merely that each of the queries made by the POT is uniformly distributed, although the queries may be dependent on one another and may even be chosen adaptively. A typical example is the celebrated `linearity` tester of [4], which is based on a three-query POT. This three-query POT selects x and y uniformly and independently in the function's domain (which is a group), and makes the queries x, y and $x + y$.

Theorem 1.1 implies that `linearity` has a sample-based tester with sample complexity $O(n^{2/3}\mathrm{poly}(1/\epsilon))$, but a better (and tight) result can be obtained directly (see Theorem 5.1 in the full version of this paper [13]). In general, POTs that satisfy the "uniform query distribution" condition are quite common; in fact, in the dense graph model, any POT can be converted to one that makes uniformly distributed queries, while at most squaring the number of queries (see [12, Section 4.2], following [15, Section 4]).[4] Actually, we can get stronger results for the dense graph model.

THEOREM 1.2. (on sample-based testers in the dense graph model): *Let n denote the size of the adjacency matrix of a graph, that is, the number of vertex-pairs.*

1. (From quasi-canonical testers to sample-based testers): *Let Π be a graph property and consider the task of*

testing Π in the dense graph model. If Π has a POT with detection probability function ϱ that inspects the subgraph induced by a random set of ν vertices, then Π has a sample-based tester with sample complexity $s(n, \epsilon) = O(n^{1-(1/(\nu-1))}/\varrho(\epsilon)^2)$. Furthermore, if the POT has one-sided error, then so does the sample-based tester.

2. *In the dense graph model, for every $k \geq 2$, k-Colorability has a sample-based tester with sample complexity $s(n, \epsilon) = O(1/\epsilon) \cdot \sqrt{n}$. Furthermore, this tester has one-sided error.*

Note that Bipartiteness (2-Colorability) does not have a POT (cf. [12]). Hence, while Item 1 merely presents a quantitative improvement over Theorem 1.1, Item 2 goes beyond the scope of Theorem 1.1. Two more comments are in order:

1. The square-root dependence on n of the sample complexity in the second item of the theorem is tight for (sample-based) testing of bipartiteness.

2. The tester referred to in the second item of the theorem is not computationally efficient. We address this issue in Subsection 1.4.

1.2 Perspectives on other testing models

Sample-based testing offers interesting perspectives on several notions.

1.2.1 Testing symmetric properties and testing distributions

As argued in [17] (see also [10]), natural families of properties are defined in terms of invariances, where each property in the family is invariant under a group of permutations acting on the functions' domain. (Indeed, testing graph properties in the dense graph model (as in Theorem 1.2) is one famous example, and linearly invariant properties [17] is another.) At the very extreme, one may consider **symmetric properties**, which are properties that are invariant under the symmetric group acting on the functions' domain. We observe that *when testing symmetric properties, samples are essentially as good as queries* (see Theorem 6.1 in the full version of this paper [13]).

We also articulate Sudan's observation that *testing distributions* (for any property of distributions, cf. [3]) *can be tightly reduced to testing symmetric properties* [23, Section 2.1]. In particular, Theorem 6.4 in the full version of this paper [13] formally relates the model of testing distributions[5] to the standard model of property testing (i.e., testing properties of functions w.r.t. the uniform distribution over their domains). While establishing this relation is technically simple, to the best of our knowledge, this is the first time that the model of testing distributions has been formally related to the standard model of property testing, which relates to testing functions (w.r.t. the uniform distribution over their domains).

---

[3] In contrast, standard testers do get a proximity parameter, denoted ϵ, as input, make a number of queries that depend on ϵ, and are required to reject any object that is ϵ-far from the property with probability at least $2/3$.

[4] The resulting POT inspects the subgraph induced by a random set of $O(q)$ vertices, where q is the query complexity of the original POT.

[5] In this model the tested object is a distribution D over some domain X and the algorithm receives points $x \in X$ that are distributed according to D. The goal is to decide whether D has a particular property or is far from any distribution that has the property (where the distance measure between distributions is usually the variation distance).

1.2.2 Distribution-Free Testing and One-Sided Error

The focus on sample-based testers brings us closer to the area of computational learning theory (cf. [25, 19]). Within this mind-frame, it is natural to consider distribution-free testing, which was also defined in [9] but received relatively little attention so far. In distribution-free testing, the sample that the testing algorithm receives is distributed according to an arbitrary and unknown distribution, and distance between functions (and hence distance to having the property) is defined according to the same distribution. Our initial feeling was that there may be a relation between *one-sided error* sample-based testing (under the uniform distribution) and *distribution-free* (sample-based) testing. This feeling was partially confirmed by a general upper bound on the sample complexity of the former in terms of the sample complexity of the latter, but beyond this upper bound the two complexity measures may exhibit different relationships. Our results are summarized in the following theorem, where $\mathsf{OSE}(\Pi)$ denotes the sample complexity of one-sided error sample-based testing Π (under the uniform distribution), and $\mathsf{DF}(\Pi)$ denotes the sample complexity of distribution-free (sample-based) testing Π.

THEOREM 1.3. (distribution-free sample-based testers versus one-sided error sample-based testers under the uniform distribution):

1. *For every property Π, it holds that $\mathsf{OSE}(\Pi) = \widetilde{O}(\mathsf{DF}(\Pi)^2)$.*

2. *There exists a property Π such that $\mathsf{OSE}(\Pi) = \Omega(n)$ but $\mathsf{DF}(\Pi) = \mathrm{poly}(1/\epsilon) \cdot \frac{n}{\log n}$.*

3. *There exists a property Π such that $\mathsf{OSE}(\Pi) = \Theta(\mathsf{DF}(\Pi))$.*

4. *There exists a property Π such that $\mathsf{OSE}(\Pi) = \widetilde{\Theta}(1/\epsilon) \cdot \log \mathsf{DF}(\Pi)$.*

5. *There exists a property Π such that $\mathsf{OSE}(\Pi) = \widetilde{O}(1/\epsilon)$ but $\mathsf{DF}(\Pi) = \Omega(n)$.*

Hence, there exists a general upper bound of OSE in terms of DF (i.e., Item 1), but in specific cases we may see quite different relations ranging from $\mathsf{OSE} = \omega(\mathsf{DF})$, to $\mathsf{OSE} = \Theta(\mathsf{DF})$, to $\mathsf{OSE} = o(\mathsf{DF})$ (cf., Items 2-5). We mention that the properties used in Items 2-4 are natural ones.

1.3 Related work

As mentioned upfront, sample-based testers were considered in several prior works, starting with the work of Goldreich, Goldwasser, and Ron [9]. Ironically, the main definition in their work (i.e. [9, Definition 2.1]), refers to (distribution-free) sample-based testers, whereas the now-standard definition of query-based testers (with respect to the uniform distribution) is presented there as a variant (see Item 3 in [9, Section 2]). However, the bulk of [9] is devoted to the study of query-based testers, and this notion became the standard in the area.

Nevertheless, sample-based testers were considered also in subsequent works, which focused on query-based testers. Typically, the perspective is negative; that is, the focus is on lower bounds on sample complexity, which are presented

as a justification for the use of queries in the main positive results. For example, the first study of testing monotonicity [8] focuses on query-based testers, but also provides a lower bound on the sample complexity of sample-based testers, which is shown to be tight. Indeed, the latter lower bound (i.e., [8, Theorem 5]) is used as justification for the use of queries in the main result (i.e., [8, Theorem 1]), and the sample-based tester (of [8, Theorem 6]) is viewed as indicating that this lower bound is tight.

Two notable exceptions appear in [18, 2], Kearns and Ron [18] consider sample-based testing (under the uniform distribution) for decision trees of a bounded size s over $[0,1]^d$ (for constant d) and for a special class of neural networks with s hidden units. They design testers whose sample complexity is significantly lower than that required for learning the corresponding class of functions. However, their testers are only required to reject functions that are far from a super-class of the tested class (determined by a larger size parameter s'). For the special case of interval functions ($d = 1$), Blum et al. [2] showed how this relaxation of the rejection requirement can be removed, and they obtained optimal (in terms of the dependence on s) sample-based testers. Blum et al. [2] also present sample-based testers (which outperform learning algorithms) for linear threshold functions under the Gaussian distribution.

Actually, the work of Blum et al. [2] puts forward a more refined notion, called active testers. These may be viewed as a generalization of sample-based testers, where the testers are provided with *unlabeled* samples, and may query the function only at points that appear in the given sample. Blum et al. [2] consider both the sample-complexity and the query-complexity of these testers, where the latter is typically smaller (since the tester does not query the function on all the sample points). They view sample-based testers as a special case (which they call *passive testing*) in which the testers query the function on all points in the sample (and so in this case their notion of query-complexity equals the notion of sample-complexity).

1.4 The computational complexity aspect

Throughout most of this work, we ignore the computational complexity aspect (i.e., the running-time of the various testers). This choice seems crucial to some of our results; examples include Proposition A.4, Theorem 2.1 (see also Theorems 1.1 and Theorem 3.5 in the full version of this paper [13]), Theorem 4.5 in [13] (see Item 2 in Theorem 1.2), and Theorem 3.1. In contrast, the following result (i.e., Theorem 1.4) is of interest only because it addresses the computational complexity aspect, which was ignored in Item 2 of Theorem 1.2).

THEOREM 1.4. (on computational efficient sample-based testers in the dense graph model):

1. *Bipartiteness has a (one-sided error) sample-based tester of time complexity $O(1/\epsilon) \cdot \sqrt{n}$.*

2. *For every $k \geq 3$, k-Colorability has a (one-sided error) sample-based tester of time complexity $f_k(\epsilon) \cdot n^{1-(1/2k)}$, where $f_k(\epsilon) \stackrel{\mathrm{def}}{=} \exp(\exp(\widetilde{O}(k/\epsilon)))$.*

We do not know whether for $k \geq 3$, k-Colorability has a sample-based tester of time complexity $\mathrm{poly}(1/\epsilon) \cdot \sqrt{n}$. In order to establish the second item in Theorem 1.4, we build on a technique introduced by Alon and Krivelevich [1]. They showed that if a graph is ϵ-far from being k-colorable, then with high constant probability, a subgraph induced by $\Theta(k \log k / \epsilon^2)$ uniformly selected vertices will not be k-colorable. To this end they introduced (as a mental experiment) a process by which new vertices that are added to the sample *restrict* the legal colorings of previously added vertices.[6] Their analysis uses the fact that with each newly added vertex we get all edges to previously selected vertices (as part of the induced subgraphs). In contrast, for the sample size we use, we cannot expect to obtain so much information, and this is one aspect in which we depart from their analysis. The second aspect is that we need to turn the mental experiment into an efficient algorithm (which finds a small subgraph that is not k-colorable) while the algorithm lacks some of the knowledge that the mental experiment has.

1.5 Organization

In this extended abstract we give a flavor of our results by providing some of the proofs and/or high-level discussion of our results and the ideas behind them. In particular, in Section 2 we establish Theorem 1.1 (relating certain POTs to sample-based testers), and in Section 3 we prove two items from Theorem 1.3 (relating distribution-free (sample based) testing and one-sided error (sample-based) testing under the uniform distribution). We provide formal definitions in the appendix and all missing results and details can be found in the full version of this paper [13].

2. POTS AND SAMPLE-BASED TESTERS: A TASTE OF THE RESULTS

The fact that *certain* POTs yield sample-based testers of sublinear sample complexity was proven implicitly in [6, Apdx. A.2]. The context of that result is of testing graph properties in the bounded-degree model (introduced in [11]). Here we present much more general results.

In what follows we prove Theorem 1.1, or more precisely, a slightly stronger version of it. Specifically, we consider POTs that make queries that are *each* almost uniformly distributed in the domain, although their joint distribution may be very dependent. Stated formally, for $\alpha \in (0, 1]$, a tester (or a POT) is called α-fair if, *for each i and $j \in D_n$ (and for every $f : D_n \to R_n$), the ith query of the tester (when it accesses the oracle f) equals j with probability at most $1/\alpha n$.* We stress that here we consider the marginal distribution of the ith query. Note that by [15, Section 4], we may assume without loss of generality, that any constant-query POT in the dense graphs model is 1-fair. Lastly, we mention that the notion of a fair tester is reminiscent of the notion of a smooth decoder [16].

THEOREM 2.1. (from POTs to sample-based testers – basic version): *Suppose that Π has a q-query POT with detection probability ϱ that is $\Omega(1)$-fair. Then, Π has a sample-based tester with sample complexity $s(n, \epsilon) = O(n^{1-(1/q)}/\varrho(\epsilon)^{2+(3/q)})$. Furthermore, if the POT has one-sided error, then so does the sample-based tester (and the sample complexity can be reduced to $O(n^{1-(1/q)}/\varrho(\epsilon)^{1+(3/q)}))$.*

---

[6] Such a process was introduced previously in [9], but it did not lend itself to our purposes.

Note that the POT in the premise of Theorem 2.1 implies a standard (query-based) tester of query complexity $O(1/\varrho(\epsilon)^b)$, where $b = 2$ in the general case and $b = 1$ in the one-sided error case. The fairness condition is essential to Theorem 2.1; however, it is satisfied by almost all known POTs. See further discussion in the full version of this paper [13, Section 3.2].

PROOF. As in [6, Apdx. A.2], the basic idea is that a random sample of the said size is very likely to contain a sequence of queries that are made by the POT on some setting of its random coins. Furthermore, this setting is almost uniformly distributed among all possible settings of the random coins. The proof is devoted to actually establishing that the above assertions hold, in particular given that the algorithm may be adaptive. We note that the situation here is more complex than in [6, Apdx. A.2], since the property is not necessarily closed under any non-trivial invariance.

Throughout the analysis we fix the POT, denoted T, and *fix the function, denoted f, tested by T.* By the hypothesis, T is α-fair, for some constant $\alpha > 0$. Denoting the randomness complexity of T by r, it follows that $2^r \geq \alpha n$. We consider all possible random strings $\omega \in \{0, 1\}^r$. A key notion is that of the **sequence of queries generated by** ω, which is defined as *the sequence of queries that T makes when using randomness ω and having access to f.*

We start by presenting a sample-based algorithm that emulates the POT up to an $O(\delta)$-deviation, where δ is a parameter to be determined later.[7] For $t = \Theta(n^{1-(1/q)}/\delta^{3/q})$, the sample-based tester that we wish to construct is given a sequence of qt labeled examples $(s_1, f(s_1)), \ldots, (s_{qt}, f(s_{qt}))$, where $\overline{S} = (s_1, \ldots, s_{qt})$ is uniformly distributed in $[n]^{qt}$. For each $i \in [q]$, we let $\overline{S}_i$ denote the subsequence $(s_{(i-1)t+1}, \ldots, s_{it})$.

We say that $(\omega, \overline{S}) \in \{0, 1\}^r \times [n]^{qt}$ is **good** if the sequence generated by ω is in $(\overline{S}_1, \ldots, \overline{S}_q)$ (i.e., for each $i \in [q]$, when given oracle access to f and using coins ω the ith query of T is in $\overline{S}_i$). In such a case we say that $\overline{S}$ is good for ω, and that ω is **good for** $\overline{S}$. For starters, note that for every fixed $\omega \in \{0, 1\}^r$, the probability that a uniformly distributed $\overline{S} \in [n]^{qt}$ is good for ω equals $(1 - (1 - (1/n))^t)^q \approx (t/n)^q$. We shall show that, with high probability, such a random $\overline{S}$ is good for a $(1 \pm o(1)) \cdot (t/n)^q$ fraction of the settings of $\omega \in \{0, 1\}^r$. This will imply that if the sample-based tester selects at random an ω that is good for the sample that it receives, and emulates T using ω as its random coins (while answering T's queries by using the corresponding labels), then this tester emulates the POT quite well. We start with the first claim whose proof can be found in the full version of this paper [13, Section 3].

CLAIM 2.1.1. *Let $\delta > 0$ and $\mu = (1 - (1 - (1/n))^t)^q$. If $\overline{S}$ is uniformly distributed in $[n]^{qt}$, then with probability at least $1 - \frac{q}{\alpha \delta^2 \mu n}$ the sequence $\overline{S}$ is good for a $(1 \pm \delta) \cdot \mu$ fraction of the settings of $\omega \in \{0, 1\}^r$.*

We set δ so as to equate the two errors in Claim 2.1.1; that is, we set $\delta = \frac{q}{\delta^2 \mu \alpha n}$, which implies $\mu n = 1/\alpha \delta^3 = \Theta(1/\delta^3)$. Indeed, this requires that $\mu n > 1$. Since $\mu = (1 - (1 -$

---

[7] This tester is reminiscent of the notion of a relaxed POT, as presented in the full version of this paper [13, Definition A.1], but we shall proceed without any definition regarding this matter.

$(1/n))^t)^q < (t/n)^q$, this implies that $t > n^{(q-1)/q}$. Using Claim 2.1.1, the analysis of the sample-based tester outlined above reduces to the following claim (whose proof is also given in [13, Section 3].

CLAIM 2.1.2. *Let $G = ((X, Y), E)$ be a bipartite graph such that each vertex in X has degree $|E|/|X|$ and at least a $1-\delta$ fraction of the vertices in Y have degree $(1\pm\delta)\cdot|E|/|Y|$, where $\delta \in [0, 0.5)$. Then, uniformly selecting a vertex y in Y, and uniformly selecting a neighbor of y, yields a distribution that is 2δ-close to the uniform distribution on X.*

(We shall apply Claim 2.1.2 with $X = \{0, 1\}^r$ and $Y = [n]^{qt}$, where there is an edge between $x \in X$ and $y \in Y$ if x is good for y.)

The sample-based tester (formalized): On input parameters n, ϵ and a sequence of labeled samples $((s_1, v_1), \ldots, (s_{qt}, v_{qt}))$, where $t = \Theta(n^{1-(1/q)}/\varrho(\epsilon)^{3/q})$, the tester proceeds as follows, with the intention of emulating a single execution of T with statistical deviation of at most $\varrho(\epsilon)/3$.

1. The tester selects uniformly $\omega \in \{0, 1\}^r$ such that ω is good for $\overline{S}$, where $\overline{S} = (s_1, \ldots, s_{qt})$.

   If no such ω exists, then the tester halts and outputs 1 with probability c (and outputs 0 otherwise), where c is the threshold probability of T. (This bad event occurs with probability at most $\varrho(\epsilon)/10$.)

   (The next step is executed only if ω was selected in Step 1.)

2. Let $(i_1, \ldots, i_q) \in [qt]$ be such that $(s_{i_1}, \ldots, s_{i_q})$ is the sequence of queries generated by ω.

   The tester emulates T using randomness ω, while using v_{i_j} as the answer to the jth query, and outputs whatever T does.

Note that for our choice of $t = \Theta(n^{1-(1/q)}/\varrho(\epsilon)^{3/q})$, it holds that $\mu n \approx (t/n)^q \cdot n = \Theta(1/\varrho(\epsilon)^3)$, and so (by Claims 2.1.1 and 2.1.2) this emulation of T deviates from a perfect one by at most $\varrho(\epsilon)/3$. The final sample-based tester is obtained by running $O(1/\varrho(\epsilon)^b)$ copies of the above emulation, where $b = 2$ for the general case and $b = 1$ for the one-sided error case. Details follow.

On input n, ϵ and $((s_1, v_1), \ldots, (s_{qt'}, v_{qt'}))$, where $t' = \Theta(t/\varrho(\epsilon)^b) = \Theta(n^{1-(1/q)}/\varrho(\epsilon)^{b+(3/q)})$, the tester runs $O(1/\varrho(\epsilon)^b)$ copies of the above emulation, when using the subsequence of labeled samples $((s_{(i-1)t+1}, v_{(i-1)t+1}), \ldots, (s_{it}, v_{it}))$, in the ith emulation. In the general case the tester outputs 1 if and only if at least $c - \varrho(\epsilon)/2$ of the emulations returned 1, whereas in the one-sided error case the tester outputs 1 if and only if all the emulations returned 1. ∎

Fairness.

The fairness condition is essential to the foregoing proof of Theorem 2.1: If there exists $i \in [n]$ such that the given POT always makes the query i, then we have no chance to emulate it while using a random sample of size $o(n)$. One might conjecture that *every property that has a q-query POT, also has a q-query POT that is $\Omega(1)$-fair.* We prove (see Proposition 3.2 in the full version of this paper [13]) that this conjecture does not hold.

The fact that a property having a constant-query POT does not have an $\Omega(1)$-fair POT does not imply that the property does not have a sample-based tester with sublinear complexity. Hence, one might weaken the abovementioned conjecture and ask whether every property having a constant-query POT (with sufficiently large detection probability) has a sample-based tester with sublinear complexity. We also falsify this conjecture (see [13, Proposition 3.3]). However, the property used to falsify the conjecture is somewhat contrived, and in particular, has a huge range. In a preliminary version of this work, we wondered whether the result holds also for a class of functions with significantly smaller range (e.g., $|R_n| = n$ or maybe even $|R_n| = 2$). Subsequently, Fischer *et al.* [5, Corollary 1.9] proved that such a result does not hold for Boolean functions (i.e., for $|R_n| = 2$). Specifically, they showed that any property of Boolean functions that has a one-sided error two-query POT also has a sample-based tester with sample complexity $s(n, \epsilon) = O(n^{2/3}/\epsilon)$.

While Propositions 3.2 and 3.3 [13] assert that not every POT can be transformed into a fair one, we give (in [13, Proposition 3.4]) a sufficient condition (related to invariance of the property under 1-transitive permutations) based on which such a transformation does hold. We note that this condition is not necessary: Any POT in the bounded-degree graph model can be transformed into a fair one (cf. [12, Claim 5.5.2]), although the condition does not hold.

A generalization of Theorem 2.1.

Theorem 2.1 considers POTs whose q queries are each (almost) uniformly distributed. A natural generalization is to POTs such that any k of the q queries are (almost) uniformly distributed, for $k > 1$. In [13, Theorem 3.5] we give a generalization of Theorem 2.1 which holds for such testers. The bound on the sample complexity of the sample-based tester is (roughly) of the form $O(n^{1-(k/q)})$.

3. DISTRIBUTION-FREE TESTING: A TASTE OF THE RESULTS

Recall that distribution-free testing is a generalization of the standard notion of testing functions where the distance measure is defined according to an arbitrary distribution over the function's domain. In this case, the tester is given samples drawn according to this (unknown) distribution, where these samples are labeled by the tested function. We stress that the task is to test properties of the function, not of the distribution.[8] For a formal definition, see [13, Definition 7.1] In this section we prove the first two items in Theorem 1.3. We start with Item 1:

THEOREM 3.1. (distribution-free testers imply one-sided error testers under the uniform distribution): *For every property Π, if Π has a sample-based distribution-free tester with sample complexity $s : \mathbb{N} \times (0, 1] \to \mathbb{N}$, then Π has a one-sided error sample-based tester with sample complexity $\tilde{O}(s^2)$ (under the uniform distribution).*

The sample complexity of the one-sided error sample-based tester is actually $O(s^2)$ if $s < \sqrt{n}/25$ and $O(n \log n)$ otherwise. While an upper bound of $O(s^2)$ is quite likely, we

---

[8]The latter subject (i.e., testing distributions) is discussed in Section 6.3 in the full version of this paper [13].

shall show (in Theorem 3.2) that an upper bound of $O(s)$ cannot hold in general. We stress that Theorem 3.1 (as well as the last sentence) refer to an upper bound that holds for *any* property (rather than to specific cases, as studied in [13, Section 7.2]).

PROOF. Let T' be a sample-based distribution-free tester with sample complexity $s : \mathbb{N} \times (0, 1] \to \mathbb{N}$ for Π. Assume that T' has error probability at most $1/6$ (rather than at most $1/3$),[9] and that $s < \sqrt{n}/25$ (to be justified at the end). Consider the following sample-based algorithm T, with sample complexity $t = O(s^2)$. On input parameters n, ϵ and a sequence $((r_1, v_1), \ldots, (r_t, v_t))$, where the v_i's are determined by the tested function, algorithm T accepts if and only if there exists $g \in \Pi_n$ such that $g(r_i) = v_i$ for every $i \in [t]$. We claim that T is a one-sided error tester for Π under the uniform distribution.

By its construction, T accepts every function in Π with probability 1. Hence, if T is not a one-sided error tester for Π (under the uniform distribution), then it must be that it accepts some no-instance (i.e., a function far from Π) with too high probability (i.e., probability exceeding $1/3$). Thus, we assume towards a contradiction that there exist n, ϵ and $f : D_n \to R_n$ such that f is ϵ-far from Π_n (under the uniform distribution) *and* T accepts f with probability at least $1/3$ (when given $t = t(n, \epsilon)$ uniformly distributed samples that are labeled according to f). By the construction of T, it follows that for at least one third of the possible $\bar{r} = (r_1, \ldots, r_t) \in D_n^t$ there exists $g_{\bar{r}} \in \Pi_n$ such that $g_{\bar{r}}(r_i) = f(r_i)$ for every $i \in [t]$. For each such $\bar{r} = (r_1, \ldots, r_t)$, consider the distribution $\mu_{\bar{r}}$ that is uniform over the corresponding (multi)set $\{r_1, \ldots, r_t\}$. The key observation is that T' must accept a sequence of s samples drawn from $\mu_{\bar{r}}$ that are labeled according to f with probability at least $5/6$, since these labels are consistent with $g_{\bar{r}} \in \Pi$. (The fact that f is ϵ-far from Π according to the uniform distribution on D_n is irrelevant here, and in particular $\delta_{\Pi_n}^{\mu_{\bar{r}}}(f) = 0$.)[10] Thus, the following holds.

CLAIM 3.1.1. *Let T and f be as in the foregoing paragraph, and let $X = (X_1, \ldots, X_s)$ denote a random sequence produced by first selecting uniformly $\bar{r} \in D_n^t$, and then picking s independent samples from the distribution $\mu_{\bar{r}}$. Then, on input n, ϵ and $((X_1, f(X_1)), \ldots, (X_s, f(X_s))$, algorithm T' accepts with probability at least $\frac{1}{3} \cdot \frac{5}{6} > \frac{1}{6} + \frac{1}{10}$.*

On the other hand, on input n, ϵ and $((Y_1, f(Y_1)), \ldots, (Y_s, f(Y_s)))$, where the Y_i's are independently and uniformly distributed in D_n, algorithm T' must reject with probability at least $5/6$, because by the hypothesis f is ϵ-far from Π_n (under the uniform distribution). If $t \leq n$, then this yields a contradiction, because (as stated in the next claim, which is proved in Section 7 in the full version of this paper [13]) the two distribution (i.e., X and Y) are 0.1-close.

CLAIM 3.1.2. *Suppose that $500s^2 < t \leq n$, and let $X = (X_1, \ldots, X_s)$ and $Y = (Y_1, \ldots, Y_s)$ be as above; that is, X*

is as defined in Claim 3.1.1 and Y is a sequence of independently and uniformly distributed elements of D_n. Then, the variation distance between X and Y is at most 0.1.

Recall that $t = O(s^2)$ by construction, whereas $t \leq n$ was assumed upfront and will be justified next. Assume, contrary to the claim, that $t > n$. Since $t = O(s^2)$, this implies that $s = \Omega(\sqrt{n})$. But in this case, with high probability, a labeled (uniformly distributed) sample of size $O(s^2 \log s)$ allows to reconstruct the function, and Theorem 3.1 (Item 1 of Theorem 1.3) follows. ∎

We now turn to Item 2 of Theorem 1.3.

THEOREM 3.2. (distribution-free sample-complexity may be lower than the one-sided error sample complexity under the uniform distribution): *There exists a property Π such that*

1. *Any one-sided error tester for Π (under the uniform distribution) must have query complexity $q(n, \epsilon) = \Omega(n)$ for every $\epsilon < 1/2$.*

2. *There exists a (sample-based) distribution-free tester for Π with sample complexity $s(n, \epsilon) = \text{poly}(1/\epsilon) \cdot \frac{n}{\log n}$.*

For example, Π_n may be the set of Boolean functions over $[n]$ that evaluate to 1 more often than to 0.

It follows that there are properties for which the one-sided error sample complexity (under the uniform distribution) is higher than the distribution-free sample complexity. Note that Π is a symmetric property, and so queries are not more powerful for it than samples (see Theorem 6.1 in the full version of this paper [13]).

PROOF. We consider the class, denoted Π_n, of Boolean functions over $[n]$ such that $f : [n] \to \{0, 1\}$ is in Π_n if and only if $|\{i \in [n] : f(i) = 1\}| > n/2$. The proof of the first claim follows directly from the definition of one-sided error testing and the definition of Π_n.

CLAIM 3.2.1. *Any one-sided error tester for Π_n (under the uniform distribution) has query complexity $q(n, \epsilon) \geq n/2$ for any $\epsilon < 1/2$.*

CLAIM 3.2.2. *There exists a (sample-based) distribution-free tester with sample complexity $s(n, \epsilon) = \tilde{O}(1/\epsilon^2) \cdot \frac{n}{\log n}$ for Π.*

Proof: We shall rely on an algorithm of Valiant and Valiant [24], which approximates the support size of an unknown distribution over $[n]$ based on $O(n/\log n)$ samples of the distribution. Specifically, we use the following result.

Theorem 1 in [24] (rephrased): *There exists an algorithm A_{VV} that on input a parameter δ and $\tilde{O}(1/\delta^2) \cdot n/\log n$ samples of a random variable, denoted X_n, that ranges over $[n]$, outputs a representation of a distribution Y_n that with overwhelmingly high probability is δ-close to a distribution X'_n that equals X_n up to relabeling.*

By saying that X equals X' up to relabeling we mean that there exists a permutation $\pi : [n] \to [n]$ such that for every $v \in [n]$ it holds that $\text{Pr}_{x \sim X'}[x = v] = \text{Pr}_{x \sim X}[x = \pi(v)]$.

---

[9]This is justified by straightforward error reduction, which merely increases s by a constant factor.

[10]We stress that our argument is not based on the fact that $\delta_{\Pi_n}^{\mu_{\bar{r}}}(f) = 0$ but rather on the fact that the samples labeled by f can be thought to be labeled by $g_{\bar{r}} \in \Pi$.

(Actually, the representation of Y_n is succinct so as to allow the algorithm to run in time that is linear in the number of samples that it obtains, but this is irrelevant to us here.) Now, suppose that, on input n and ϵ, we get $s = s(n, \epsilon)$ samples drawn according to an unknown distribution μ_n and labeled by an unknown Boolean function f. Our task is to decide whether f is in Π_n or is ϵ-far from Π_n with respect to the distribution μ_n. We propose the following algorithm.

1. The algorithm uses a small portion of the label sample (i.e., $O(1/\epsilon^2)$ samples) in order to approximate the probability $p_0 \overset{\text{def}}{=} \Pr_{r \sim \mu_n}[f(r) = 0]$ up to an additive error of $\epsilon/4$. If the estimate, denoted $\tilde{p}$, is below $\epsilon/2$, then the algorithm halts with output 1 (i.e., it accepts).

   Assuming the algorithm did not halt in Step 1, we may assume that $p_0 > \epsilon/4$.

2. Let X_n be the distribution μ_n conditioned on f evaluating to 0; that is, $\Pr_{x \sim X_n}[x = v] = \Pr_{x \sim \mu_n}[x = v | f(x) = 0]$. The algorithm invokes algorithm A_{vv} with parameter $\delta = \epsilon/(4\tilde{p})$ providing it with $s_0 \overset{\text{def}}{=} \tilde{O}(1/\delta^2) \cdot n/\log n$ samples of X_n, and obtaining a description of a distribution Y_n.

   Samples of X_n are obtained from the s labeled samples provided to the main algorithm; specifically, the main algorithm forwards the first $\tilde{O}(1/\delta^2) \cdot n/\log n$ samples that are labeled 0 to A_{vv}. With very high probability, the number of samples labeled 0 is at least $p_0 \cdot s/2 \geq \tilde{p}^2 \cdot s/4$, which equals s_0 (since we may set the parameters such that $s_0 = \epsilon^2 s/64\delta^2$).

3. The algorithm accepts if and only if Y_n is δ-close to a distribution that has support size smaller than $n/2$.

We now turn to the analysis of the foregoing algorithm. Consider first the case that $f \in \Pi_n$. If $p_0 \leq \epsilon/4$, then (by an additive Chernoff bound) with high constant probability $\tilde{p} < \epsilon/2$, and the algorithm accepts. Otherwise (by a multiplicative Chernoff bound) with high constant probability, $\tilde{p} \leq 2p_0$. Assuming the algorithm does not accept due to $\tilde{p}$ being smaller than $\epsilon/2$ (so that it continues to its second step), with high probability the distribution Y_n (output by A_{vv}) is δ-close to a relabeling of X_n, which in turn has support size smaller than $n/2$. Hence, in either cases, the algorithm accepts with high probability.

We next consider the case that that f is ϵ-far from Π_n with respect to the distribution μ_n. In this case $p_0 > \epsilon$, and with high probability it holds that $\tilde{p} > p_0/2 \geq \epsilon/2$, which means that the algorithm proceeds to Step 2. Furthermore, we claim that X_n is ϵ/p_0-far from having support size smaller than $n/2$. To verify this, assume, contrary to the claim, that X_n is ϵ/p_0-close to having support size smaller than $n/2$. Let the support size of X_n be $n/2 - 1 + t$. By the definition of X_n (and recalling that $p_0 = \mu_n(f^{-1}(0))$, this means that there is a subset $T \subset f^{-1}(0)$ such that $|T| = t$ and $\mu_n(T)/p_0 \leq \epsilon/p_0$. But in such a case if we define f' to be the same as f except that $f'(x) = 1$ for every $x \in T$, then $f' \in \Pi_n$ and f is ϵ-close to f' with respect to μ_n, contradicting our assumption on f.

Recalling that $\delta = \epsilon/4\tilde{p}$ (and $\tilde{p} > p_0/2$, which implies that $\epsilon/p_0 > \epsilon/2\tilde{p} = 2\delta$), it follows that (w.v.h.p.) Y_n is $(2\delta - \delta)$-far from any distribution having support smaller than $n/2$, which implies that our algorithm rejects. ∎

Theorem 3.2 (Item 2 of Theorem 1.3) follows. ∎

Acknowledgements

We wish to thank a few anonymous readers for their useful comments.

4. REFERENCES

[1] N. Alon and M. Krivelevich. Testing k-colorability. *SIAM Journal on Discrete Math*, 15(2):211–227, 2002.

[2] M. Balcan, E. Blais, A. Blum, and L. Yang. Active property testing. In *Proceedings of the Fifty-Third Annual Symposium on Foundations of Computer Science (FOCS)*, pages 21–30, 2012.

[3] T. Batu, L. Fortnow, R. Rubinfeld, W. Smith, and P. White. Testing that distributions are close. In *Proceedings of the Forty-First Annual Symposium on Foundations of Computer Science (FOCS)*, pages 259–269, 2000.

[4] M. Blum, M. Luby, and R. Rubinfeld. Self-testing/correcting with applications to numerical problems. *Journal of the ACM*, 47:549–595, 1993.

[5] E. Fischer, Y. Goldhirsh, , and O. Lachish. Partial tests, universal tests and decomposability. In *Proceedings of the Fifth Innovations in Computer Science conference (ITCS)*, pages 474–483, 2014.

[6] O. Goldreich. Introduction to testing graph properties. In [7].

[7] O. Goldreich, editor. *Property Testing: Current Research and Surveys*. Springer, 2010. LNCS 6390.

[8] O. Goldreich, S. Goldwasser, E. Lehman, D. Ron, and A. Samorodnitsky. Testing monotonicity. *Combinatorica*, 20(3):301–337, 2000.

[9] O. Goldreich, S. Goldwasser, and D. Ron. Property testing and its connection to learning and approximation. *Journal of the ACM*, 45(4):653–750, 1998.

[10] O. Goldreich and T. Kaufman. Proximity oblivious testing and the role of invariances. In *Proceedings of the Fifteenth International Workshop on Randomization and Computation (RANDOM)*, pages 579–592, 2011.

[11] O. Goldreich and D. Ron. Property testing in bounded degree graphs. *Algorithmica*, 32(2):302–343, 2002.

[12] O. Goldreich and D. Ron. On proximity oblivious testing. *SIAM Journal on Computing*, 40(2):534–566, 2011.

[13] O. Goldreich and D. Ron. On sample-based testers. Technical Report TR13-109, Electronic Colloquium on Computational Complexity (ECCC), 2013.

[14] O. Goldreich and I. Shinkar. Two-sided error proximity oblivious testing. In *Proceedings of the Sixteenth International Workshop on Randomization and Computation (RANDOM)*, pages 565–578, 2012.

[15] O. Goldreich and L. Trevisan. Three theorems regarding testing graph properties. *Random Structures and Algorithms*, 23(1):23–57, 2003.

[16] J. Katz and L. Trevisan. On the efficiency of local decoding procedures for error-correcting codes. In *Proceedings of the Thirty-Second Annual ACM*

Symposium on the Theory of Computing (STOC), pages 80–86, 2000.

[17] T. Kaufman and M. Sudan. Algebraic property testing: The role of invariances. In *Proceedings of the Fourtieth Annual ACM Symposium on the Theory of Computing (STOC),* pages 403–412, 2008.

[18] M. Kearns and D. Ron. Testing problems with sub-learning sample complexity. *Journal of Computer and System Sciences,* 61(3):428–456, 2000.

[19] M. Kearns and U. Vazirani. *An introduction to Computational Learning Theory.* MIT Press, 1994.

[20] D. Ron. Property testing: A learning theory perspective. *Foundations and Trends in Machine Learning,* 1(3):307–402, 2008.

[21] D. Ron. Algorithmic and analysis techniques in property testing. *Foundations and Trends in Theoretical Computer Science,* 5:73–205, 2010.

[22] R. Rubinfeld and M. Sudan. Robust characterization of polynomials with applications to program testing. *SIAM Journal on Computing,* 25(2):252–271, 1996.

[23] M. Sudan. Invariance in property testing. In [7], pages 211-227.

[24] G. Valiant and P. Valiant. Estimating the unseen: an $n/\log(n)$-sample estimator for entropy and support size, shown optimal via new CLTs. In *Proceedings of the Fourty-Third Annual ACM Symposium on the Theory of Computing (STOC),* pages 685–694, 2011. See *ECCC* TR10-180 for the algorithm, and TR10-179 for the lower bound.

[25] L. G. Valiant. A theory of the learnable. *CACM,* 27(11):1134–1142, Nov. 1984.

APPENDIX

A. FORMAL DEFINITIONS

Property testing is a relaxation of decision problems and it focuses on algorithms that can only read parts of the input. Thus, the input is represented as a function (to which the tester has oracle access) and the tester is required to accept functions that have some predetermined property (i.e., reside in some predetermined set) and reject any function that is "far" from the set of functions having the property. Distances between functions are defined as the fraction of the domain on which the functions disagree, and the threshold determining what is considered far is presented as a proximity parameter, which is explicitly given to the tester.

An asymptotic analysis is enabled by considering an infinite sequence of domains, functions, and properties. The domains and properties (in the infinite sequence) are described by a finite sequence of parameters, which include the size of the domain, denoted n. For simplicity, we shall present our results for sequences that are determined by this size parameter. That is, for any n, we consider functions from D_n to R_n, where $|D_n| = n$. (Often, one just assumes that $D_n = [n] \stackrel{\text{def}}{=} \{1, 2, \ldots, n\}$.) Thus, in addition to the input oracle, representing a function $f : D_n \to R_n$, the tester is explicitly given two parameters: a size parameter, denoted n, and a proximity parameter, denoted ϵ.

A.1 The standard definitions of query-based testers

In this section we recall the standard definition of property testing as well as the definition of proximity oblivious testers. Both definitions refer to oracle machines that are given oracle access to a function $f : D_n \to R_n$ (as well as free access to some relevant parameters such as n). We denote by $M^f(p)$ the output of oracle machine M on input parameter p when given oracle access to f.

DEFINITION A.1. (property tester, following [22, 9]): *Let* $\Pi = \bigcup_{n \in \mathbb{N}} \Pi_n$, *where* Π_n *contains functions defined over the domain* D_n *and ranging over* R_n. *A* tester for a property Π *is a probabilistic oracle machine* T *that satisfies the following two conditions:*

1. *The tester accepts each* $f \in \Pi$ *with probability at least* 2/3; *that is, for every* $n \in \mathbb{N}$ *and* $f \in \Pi_n$ *(and every* $\epsilon > 0$*), it holds that* $\Pr[T^f(n, \epsilon) = 1] \geq 2/3$.

2. *Given proximity parameter* $\epsilon > 0$ *and oracle access to any* f *that is* ϵ-far *from* Π, *the tester rejects with probability at least* 2/3; *that is, for every* $n \in \mathbb{N}$ *and* $\epsilon > 0$, *if* $f : D_n \to R_n$ *is* ϵ-far *from* Π_n, *then* $\Pr[T^f(n, \epsilon) = 0] \geq 2/3$, *where* f *is* ϵ-far *from* Π_n *if, for every* $g \in \Pi_n$, *it holds that* $\delta(f, g) \stackrel{\text{def}}{=} |\{e \in D_n : f(e) \neq g(e)\}|/n > \epsilon$. *Indeed, the* distance of f from Π, *denoted* $\delta_\Pi(f)$, *equals* $\min_{g \in \Pi_n} \{\delta(f, g)\}$.

If the tester accepts every function in Π *with probability 1, then we say that it has* one-sided error; *that is,* T *has one-sided error if for every* $f \in \Pi_n$ *and every* $\epsilon > 0$, *it holds that* $\Pr[T^f(n, \epsilon) = 1] = 1$. *A tester is called* non-adaptive *if it determines all its queries based solely on its internal coin tosses* (and the parameters n and ϵ); *otherwise it is called* adaptive.

Definition A.1 does not specify the query complexity of the tester, and indeed an oracle machine that queries the entire domain of the function qualifies as a tester (with zero error probability...). Needless to say, we are interested in testers that have significantly lower query complexity.

Some testers (e.g., the celebrated linearity tester of [4]) operate by repeating some basic tests for a number of times that depends on the proximity parameter, whereas the basic test is oblivious of the proximity parameter. Such basic tests are captured by the following definition.

DEFINITION A.2. (Proximity Oblivious Tester (POT), following [12, 14]): *Let* Π *be as in Definition A.1 and let* $\varrho : (0, 1] \to (0, 1]$ *be monotone. A* POT with detection probability ϱ for Π *is a probabilistic oracle machine* T *that makes a constant number of queries and satisfies the following two conditions with respect to some constant* $c \in (0, 1]$:

1. *For every* $n \in \mathbb{N}$ *and* $f \in \Pi_n$, *it holds that* $\Pr[T^f(n) = 1] \geq c$.

2. *For every* $n \in \mathbb{N}$ *and* $f : D_n \to R_n$ *not in* Π_n, *it holds that* $\Pr[T^f(n) = 1] \leq c - \varrho(\delta_\Pi(f))$,

The constant c *is called the* threshold probability. *A POT is said to have* one-sided error *if* $c = 1$.

We stress that, in contrast to a standard tester, a POT only gets one explicit parameter (i.e., the size parameter, n). Standard testers are obtained by invoking the POT for an adequate number of times. Specifically, for one-sided error POTs, we invoke the POT for $O(1/\varrho(\epsilon))$ times and accept if and only if all invocations returned 1. For general POTs with threshold probability c, we invoke the POT for $O(1/\varrho(\epsilon)^2)$ times and accept if and only if at least $c-(\varrho(\epsilon)/2)$ of the invocations returned 1.

A.2   Sample-based testers

A sample-based tester can be defined in two equivalent ways. The first definition views such a tester as one whose queries are distributed uniformly in the domain, independently of one another. That is, each query of such a tester is distributed uniformly in D_n, independently of all prior queries (and of the answers provided to these queries). The second definition views a sample-based tester as obtaining a sequence of "labeled samples" (i.e., the samples are independently and uniformly distributed in D_n and they are coupled with the corresponding values of the function), where the length of this sequence is predetermined based on n and ϵ:

DEFINITION A.3. (sample-based tester, following [9]): *Let Π be as in Definition A.1 and $s : \mathbb{N} \times (0,1] \to \mathbb{N}$. A* (sample-based) tester of sample complexity s for a property Π *is a probabilistic algorithm T that satisfies the following two conditions for every $n \in \mathbb{N}$:*

1. *For every $f \in \Pi_n$ (and every $\epsilon > 0$), it holds that*

$$\Pr_{r_1,\dots,r_s \in D_n}[T(n,\epsilon,(r_1,f(r_1)),\dots,(r_s,f(r_s)))=1] \geq \frac{2}{3},$$

   where $s = s(n,\epsilon)$ and $(r_1,\dots,r_s)$ is uniformly distributed in D_n^s.

2. *For every $\epsilon > 0$, and every $f : D_n \to R_n$ that is ϵ-far from Π,*

$$\Pr_{r_1,\dots,r_s \in D_n}[T(n,\epsilon,(r_1,f(r_1)),\dots,(r_s,f(r_s)))=0] \geq \frac{2}{3},$$

   where again $s = s(n,\epsilon)$ and $(r_1,\dots,r_s)$ is uniformly distributed in D_n^s.

The sequence $(r_1,f(r_1)),\dots,(r_s,f(r_s)))$ is called a sample labeled by f. *As in Definition A.1, if the tester accepts every function in Π with probability 1, then we say that it has* one-sided error.

The equivalence of this definition to the first one (or rather one of the directions of this equivalence) is based on our disregard of the computational complexity of the tester (i.e., the complexity of generating queries). This is clarified in the proof of the following proposition.

PROPOSITION A.4. (equivalence of the two formulations): *A property Π has a tester of query complexity q that uses queries that are uniformly and independently distributed in the domain if and only if it has a sample-based tester of sample complexity q.*

PROOF. Given a sample-based tester T', we easily obtain a corresponding querying tester T by letting the latter emulate T' in a straightforward manner. That is, on input n and ϵ, the tester T selects uniformly and independently an adequate number of queries, and feeds T' with the corresponding sequence of query and answer pairs, where T obtains the answers by querying its oracle.

The other direction is a bit more tricky. The issue is that the final decision of the tester may depend on the coins that it has used to produce the queries, and so merely replacing the queries with uniformly distributed samples will not do. We should augment these samples with a sequence of random coins that would have led the original tester to make these queries. Details follow.

We are given a (possibly adaptive) tester T with a guarantee on the distribution of its queries, and wish to construct a sample-based tester T'. The sample-based tester T' is given a sequence of pairs $(r_1,v_1),\dots,(r_s,v_s)$, where $v_i = f(r_i)$ for each $i \in [s]$, and it operates by selecting at random coins ω such that using coins ω and having oracle access to f, the oracle machine T makes the queries $r_1,\dots,r_s$. By the hypothesis, the set of such ω's constitutes an n^{-s} fraction of the set of all possible coin tosses. Furthermore, T' can reconstruct the former set without making any queries to f (by emulating the execution of T using coins ω and using v_i as the answer to the ith query, regardless of the identity of this query). ∎

On the operation of sample-based one-sided error testers.

The operation of any sample-based one-sided error tester is totally determined by its sample: Being sample-based, this tester has no control over its access to the function, and having one-sided error it has no real control on its decision; that is, without loss of generality, the tester accepts if and only if the labeled sample that it has obtained is consistent with some function that has the property. This is the case because in case of consistency it must accept, whereas in case of inconsistency it better reject (since this may only improve its performance).

ℓ_p Testing and Learning of Discrete Distributions

Bo Waggoner
Harvard
bwaggoner@fas.harvard.edu

ABSTRACT

The classic problems of testing uniformity of and learning a discrete distribution, given access to independent samples from it, are examined under general ℓ_p metrics. The intuitions and results often contrast with the classic ℓ_1 case. For $p > 1$, we can learn and test with a number of samples that is independent of the support size of the distribution: For $1 < p \leq 2$, with a ℓ_p distance parameter ϵ, $O(\sqrt{1/\epsilon^q})$ samples suffice for testing uniformity and $O(1/\epsilon^q)$ samples suffice for learning, where $q = p/(p-1)$ is the conjugate of p. These bounds are tight precisely when the support size n of the distribution exceeds $1/\epsilon^q$, which seems to act as an upper bound on the "apparent" support size.

For some ℓ_p metrics, uniformity testing becomes easier over larger supports: a 6-sided die requires fewer trials to test for fairness than a 2-sided coin, and a card-shuffler requires fewer trials than the die. In fact, this inverse dependence on support size holds if and only if $p > \frac{4}{3}$. The uniformity testing algorithm simply thresholds the number of "collisions" or "coincidences" and has an optimal sample complexity up to constant factors for all $1 \leq p \leq 2$. Another algorithm gives order-optimal sample complexity for ℓ_∞ uniformity testing. Meanwhile, the most natural learning algorithm is shown to have order-optimal sample complexity for all ℓ_p metrics.

The author thanks Clément Canonne for discussions and contributions to this work.

Categories and Subject Descriptors

F.2.0 [**Analysis of Algorithms and Problem Complexity**]: general; G.3 [**Probability and Statistics**]: probabilistic algorithms

General Terms

Algorithms, Theory

Keywords

uniformity testing; property testing; learning; discrete distributions; lp norms

1. INTRODUCTION

Given independent samples from a distribution, what we can say about it? This question underlies a broad line of work in statistics and computer science. Specifically, we would like algorithms that, given a small number of samples, can test whether some property of the distribution holds or can learn some attribute of the distribution.

This paper considers two natural and classic examples. *Uniformity testing* asks us to decide, based on the samples we have drawn, whether the distribution is uniform over a domain of size n, or whether it is "ϵ-far" from uniform according to some metric. *Distribution learning* asks that, given our samples, we output a sketch or estimate that is within a distance ϵ of the true distribution. For both problems, we would like to be correct except with some constant probability of failure (*e.g.* $\frac{1}{3}$). The question studied is the number of independent samples required to solve these problems.

In practical applications we might imagine, such as a web company wishing to quickly test or estimate the distribution of search keywords in a given day, the motivating goal is to formally guarantee good results while requiring as few samples as possible. Under the standard ℓ_1 distance metric (which is essentially equivalent to total variation distance – we will use the term ℓ_1 only in this paper), the question of uniformity testing over large domains was considered by Paninski [13], showing that $\Theta\left(\frac{\sqrt{n}}{\epsilon^2}\right)$ samples are necessary and sufficient for testing uniformity on support size n, and it is known by "folklore" that $\Theta\left(\frac{n}{\epsilon^2}\right)$ samples are necessary and sufficient for learning. Thus, these questions are mostly[1] settled (up to constant factors) if we are only interested in ℓ_1 distance.

However, in testing and learning applications, we may be interested in other choices of metric than ℓ_1. And more theoretically, we might wonder whether the known ℓ_1 bounds capture all of the important intuitions about the uniformity testing and distribution learning problems. Finally, we might like to understand our approaches for the ℓ_1 metric in a broader context or seek new techniques. This paper addresses these goals via ℓ_p metrics.

---

[1] [13] focused on the regime where support size is very large, so order-optimal ℓ_1 uniformity testing for the case of smaller n may have been technically open prior to this work.

1.1 Motivations for ℓ_p Metrics

In the survey "Taming Big Probability Distributions" [14], Rubinfeld notes that even sublinear bounds such as the above $\Theta\left(\frac{\sqrt{n}}{\epsilon^2}\right)$ may still depend unacceptably on n, the support size. If we do not have enough samples, Rubinfeld suggests possible avenues such as assuming that the distribution in question has some very nice property, e.g. monotonicity, or assuming that the algorithm has the power to make other types of queries.

However, it is still possible to ask what can be done without such assumptions. One answer is to consider what we can say about our data under other measures of distance than the ℓ_1 distance. Do fewer samples suffice to draw conclusions? A primary implication of this paper's results is that this approach does succeed under general ℓ_p metrics. The ℓ_p distance between two probability distributions $A, B \in \mathbb{R}^n$ for any $p \geq 1$, where A_i is the probability of drawing coordinate i from distribution A, is the ℓ_p norm of the vector of differences in probabilities:

$$\|A - B\|_p = \left(\sum_{i=1}^n |A_i - B_i|^p\right)^{1/p}.$$

The ℓ_∞ distance is the largest difference of any coordinate, i.e. $\|A - B\|_\infty = \max_i |A_i - B_i|$.

Unlike the ℓ_1 case, it will turn out that for $p > 1$, we can draw conclusions about our data with a number of samples that is *independent of n* and depends only on the desired error tolerance ϵ. We also find smaller dependences on the support size n; in fact, for uniformity testing we find sometimes (perhaps counterintuitively) that there is an *inverse* dependence on n. The upshot is that, if we have few samples, we may not be able to confidently solve an ℓ_1 testing or learning problem, but we may have enough data to draw conclusions about, say, $\ell_{1.5}$ distance. This may also be useful in saying something about the ℓ_1 case: If the true distribution A has small $\ell_{1.5}$ distance from our estimate $\hat{A}$, yet actually does have large ℓ_1 distance from $\hat{A}$, then it must have a certain shape (e.g. large support with many "light hitters").[2]

Thus, this is the first and primary motivation for the study of ℓ_p metrics: to be able to draw conclusions with few samples but without making assumptions.

A second motivation is to understand learning and testing under other ℓ_p metrics for their own sake. In particular, the ℓ_2 and ℓ_∞ cases might be considered important or fundamental. However, even these are not always well understood. For instance, common knowledge and conventional wisdom says that $\Theta\left(\frac{1}{\epsilon^2}\right)$ samples are required to determine if one side of a coin is ϵ-more likely to come up than it should be; one might naively think that the same number of trials are required to test if any card is ϵ-more likely to be top in a shuffle of a sorted deck. But the latter can be quadratically less, as small as $\Theta\left(\frac{1}{\epsilon}\right)$ (depending on the relationship of ϵ to the support size), so a large improvement is possible.

Other ℓ_p norms can also be of interest when different features of the distribution are of interest. These norms trade off between measuring the *tail* of the distribution ($p = 1$ measures the total deviation even if it consists of many tiny pieces) and measuring the *heavy* portion of the distribution ($p = \infty$ measures only the single largest difference and ig-

nores the others). Thus, an application that needs to strike a balance may find that it is best to test or estimate the distribution under the particular p that optimizes some tradeoff.

General ℓ_p norms, and especially ℓ_2 and ℓ_∞, also can have immediate applications toward testing and learning other properties. For instance, [1] developed and used an ℓ_2 tester as a black box in order to test the ℓ_1 distance between two distributions. Utilizing a better ℓ_2 tester (for instance, one immediately derived from the learner in this paper) leads to an immediate improvement in the samples required by their algorithm for the ℓ_1 problem.[3]

A third motivation for ℓ_p testing and learning, beyond drawing conclusions from less data and independent interest/use, is to develop a deeper understanding of ℓ_p spaces and norms in relation to testing and learning problems. Perhaps techniques or ideas developed for addressing these problems can lead to more simple, general, and/or sharp approaches in the special ℓ_1 case. More broadly, learning or sketching general ℓ_p vectors have many important applications in settings such as machine learning (e.g. [11]), are of independent interest in settings such as streaming and sketching (e.g. [10]), and are a useful tool for estimating other quantities (e.g. [5]). Improved understandings of ℓ_p questions have been used in the past to shed new light on well-studied ℓ_1 problems [12]. Thus, studying ℓ_p norms in the context of learning and testing distributions may provide the opportunity to apply, refine, or develop techniques relevant to these areas.

1.2 Organization

The next section summarizes the results and describes some of the key intuitions/conceptual takeaways from this work. Then, we will describe the results and techniques for the uniformity testing problem, and then the learning problem. We then conclude by discussing the broader context, prior work, and future work.

Most proofs are omitted in the body of the paper (though sketches are usually provided). The full version of the paper contains an appendix with all proofs.

2. SUMMARY AND KEY THEMES

At a technical level, this paper proves upper and lower bounds for number of samples required for testing uniformity and learning for ℓ_p metrics. These problems are formally defined as follows. For each problem, we are given i.i.d. samples from a distribution A. The algorithm must specify the number of samples m to draw and satisfy the stated guarantees.

Uniformity testing: If $A = U_n$, the uniform distribution on support size n, then output "uniform". If $\|A - U_n\|_p \geq \epsilon$, then output "not uniform". In each case, the output must be correct except with some constant failure probability δ (e.g. $\delta = \frac{1}{3}$).

Learning: Output a distribution $\hat{A}$ satisfying that $\|A - \hat{A}\|_p \leq \epsilon$. This condition must be satisfied except with some constant failure probability δ (e.g. $\delta = \frac{1}{3}$).

In both cases, the algorithm is given p, n, ϵ, δ.

SUMMARY THEOREM 1. *For the problems of testing uniformity of and learning a distribution, the number of samples necessary and sufficient satisfy, up to constant factors depending on p and δ, the bounds in Table 1.*

---

[2]I thank the anonymous reviewers for suggestions and comments regarding this motivation, including the $\ell_{1.5}$ example.

[3]Further improvement for this problem is achieved in [4].

In particular, for each fixed ℓ_p metric and failure probability δ, the upper and lower bounds match up to a constant factor for distribution learning for all parameters and for uniformity testing when $1 \leq p \leq 2$, when $p = \infty$, and when $p > 2$ and n is "large" ($n \geq \frac{1}{\epsilon^2}$).

Table 1 is intended as a reference and summary; the reader can safely skip it and read on for a description and explanation of the key themes and results, after which (it is hoped) Table 1 will be more comprehensible.

Later in the paper, we give more specific theorems containing (small) explicit constant factors for our algorithms.

Some of these bounds are new and employ new techniques, while others are either already known or can be deduced quickly from known bounds; discussion focuses on the novel aspects of these results and Section 6 describes the relationship to prior work. Regardless, all bounds have a self-contained proof in (the full version of) this paper.

The remainder of this section is devoted to highlighting the most important themes and conceptually important or surprising results (in the author's opinion). The following sections detail the techniques and results for the uniformity testing and learning problems respectively.

2.1 Fixed bounds for large n regimes

A primary theme of the results is the intuition behind ℓ_p testing and learning in the case where the support size n is large. In ℓ_p spaces for $p > 1$, we can achieve upper bounds for testing and learning that are independent of n. For for $p \geq 2$, for both problems $\Theta\left(\frac{1}{\epsilon^2}\right)$ samples are always sufficient (although for uniformity testing we can often do even better). For $1 < p \leq 2$, we observe the following behavior.

SUMMARY THEOREM 2. *For a fixed $1 < p \leq 2$, let q be the Hölder conjugate[4] of p with $\frac{1}{p} + \frac{1}{q} = 1$. Then $O\left(\sqrt{\frac{1}{\epsilon^q}}\right)$ samples are sufficient for testing uniformity and $O\left(\frac{1}{\epsilon^q}\right)$ are sufficient for learning. Furthermore, these bounds are tight precisely when the support size $n \geq \frac{1}{\epsilon^q}$.*

This implies that, for $1 < p \leq 2$, we can separate into "large n" and "small n" regimes[5], where the divider is $n^* = \frac{1}{\epsilon^q}$. In the small n regime, tight bounds depend on n, but in the large n regime where $n \geq n^*$, the number of samples is $\Theta(n^*)$ for learning and $\Theta(\sqrt{n^*})$ for uniformity testing. This suggests the intuition that, in ℓ_p space with tolerance ϵ, distributions' "apparent" support sizes are bounded by $n^* = \frac{1}{\epsilon^q}$. We next make two observations that align with this perspective. They are not used to prove any of our results, but develop intuitions for the setting. Recall that we view a distribution A on support size n as a vector in $\mathbb{R}^n$ with probability A_i on coordinate i.

OBSERVATION 2.1. *Let $1 < p$ and $q = \frac{p}{p-1}$. If the distribution A is "thin" in that $\max_i A_i \leq \epsilon^q$, then $\|A\|_p \leq \epsilon$. In particular, if both distributions A and B are thin, then even if they are completely disjoint,*

$$\|A - B\|_p \leq \|A\|_p + \|B\|_p \leq 2\epsilon.$$

---

[4]Note that 1 and ∞ are considered conjugates. This paper will also use math with infinity, so for instance, when $q = \infty$, $n^{1/q} = 1$ and it is never the case that $n \leq \frac{1}{\epsilon^q}$.

[5]For $p \geq 2$, this separation still makes sense in certain ways (see Observations 2.1 and 2.2 below) but does not appear in the sample complexity bounds in this paper.

- Learning for $1 \leq p \leq 2$:

regime	$n \leq \frac{1}{\epsilon^q}$	$n \geq \frac{1}{\epsilon^q}$
necessary and sufficient	$\frac{n}{(n^{1/q}\epsilon)^2}$	$\frac{1}{\epsilon^q}$

- Uniformity testing for $1 \leq p \leq 2$:

regime	$n \leq \frac{1}{\epsilon^q}$	$n \geq \frac{1}{\epsilon^q}$
necessary and sufficient	$\frac{\sqrt{n}}{(n^{1/q}\epsilon)^2}$	$\sqrt{\frac{1}{\epsilon^q}}$

- Learning for $2 \leq p \leq \infty$: $\frac{1}{\epsilon^2}$ (necessary and sufficient, all regimes).

- Uniformity testing for $p = \infty$:

regime	$\Theta\left(\frac{n}{\ln(n)}\right) \leq \frac{1}{\epsilon}$	$\frac{1}{\epsilon} \leq \Theta\left(\frac{n}{\ln(n)}\right)$
necessary and sufficient	$\frac{\ln(n)}{n\epsilon^2}$	$\frac{1}{\epsilon}$

- Uniformity testing for $2 < p < \infty$:

regime	$\Theta\left(\frac{n}{\ln(n)}\right) \leq \frac{1}{\epsilon}$	$\frac{1}{\epsilon} \leq \Theta\left(\frac{n}{\ln(n)}\right)$, $n \leq \frac{1}{\epsilon^2}$	$n \geq \frac{1}{\epsilon^2}$
necessary	$\frac{\ln(n)}{n\epsilon^2}$	$\frac{1}{\epsilon}$	$\frac{1}{\epsilon}$
sufficient	$\frac{1}{\sqrt{n}\epsilon^2}$	$\frac{1}{\sqrt{n}\epsilon^2}$	$\frac{1}{\epsilon}$

Table 1: **Results summary.** In each problem, we are given independent samples from a distribution on support size n. Each entry in the tables is the number of samples drawn necessary and/or sufficient, up to constant factors depending only on p and the fixed probability of failure. Throughout the paper, q is the Hölder conjugagte of p, with $q = \frac{p}{p-1}$ (and $q = \infty$ for $p = 1$).

In *uniformity testing*, we must decide whether the distribution is U_n, the uniform distribution on support size n, or is ℓ_p distance at least ϵ from U_n. [13] gave the optimal upper and lower bound in the case $p = 1$ (with unknown constants) for large n; other results are new to my knowledge.

In *learning*, we must output a distribution at ℓ_p distance at most ϵ from the given distribution, which has support size at most n. Optimal upper and lower bounds for learning in the cases $p = 1, 2$, and ∞ seem to the author to be all previously known as folklore (certainly for ℓ_1 and ℓ_∞); others are new to my knowledge.

PROOF. The claim holds immediately for $p = \infty$. For $1 < p < \infty$, by convexity, since $\sum_i A_i = 1$ and $\max_i A_i \leq \epsilon^q$, we have that $\|A\|_p^p = \sum_i A_i^p$ is maximized with as few nonzero entries as possible, each at its maximum value ϵ^q. This extreme example is simply the uniform distribution on $n = \frac{1}{\epsilon^q}$, when $\|A\|_p^p = n\left(\frac{1}{n}\right)^p = \frac{1}{n^{p-1}} = \epsilon$. The rest is the triangle inequality. $\square$

One takeaway from Observation 2.1 is that if we are interested in an ℓ_p error tolerance of $\Theta(\epsilon)$, then any sufficiently "thin" distribution may almost as well be the uniform distribution on support size $\frac{1}{\epsilon^q}$. This perspective is reinforced by Observation 2.2, which says that under the same circumstances, any distribution may almost as well be "discretized" into $\frac{1}{\epsilon^q}$ chunks of weight ϵ^q each.

OBSERVATION 2.2. *Fixing $1 < p$, for any distribution A, there is a distribution B whose probabilities are integer multiples of $\frac{1}{\epsilon^q}$ such that $\|A - B\|_p \leq 2\epsilon$. In particular, B's support size is at most $\frac{1}{\epsilon^q}$.*

PROOF. We can always choose B such that, on each coordinate i, $|A_i - B_i| \leq \frac{1}{\epsilon^q}$. (To see this, obtain the vector B' by rounding each coordinate of A up to the nearest integer multiple of ϵ^q, and obtain B'' by rounding each coordinate down. $\|B'\|_1 \geq 1 \geq \|B''\|_1$, so we can obtain a true probability distribution by taking some coordinates from B' and some from B''.) But this just says that the vector $A - B$ is "thin" in the sense of Observation 2.1. The same argument goes through here (even though $A - B$ is not a probability distribution): Since $\max_i |A_i - B_i| \leq \epsilon^q$ and $\sum_i |A_i - B_i| \leq 2$, by convexity $\|A - B\|_p$ is maximized when it has dimension $\frac{2}{\epsilon^q}$ and each entry $|A_i - B_i| = \epsilon^q$, so we get $\|A - B\|_p \leq 2\epsilon$. $\square$

2.2 Testing uniformity: biased coins and die

Given a coin, is it fair or ϵ-far from fair? It is well-known that $\Omega\left(\frac{1}{\epsilon^2}\right)$ independent flips of the coin are necessary to make a determination with confidence. One might naturally assume that deciding if a 6-sided die is fair or ϵ-far from fair would only be more difficult, requiring more rolls, and one would be correct — if the measure of "ϵ-far" is ℓ_1 distance. Indeed, it is known [13] that $\Theta\left(\frac{\sqrt{n}}{\epsilon^2}\right)$ rolls of an n-sided die are necessary if the auditor's distance measure is ℓ_1.

But what about other measures, say, if the auditor wishes to test whether any one side of the die is ϵ more likely to come up than it should be? For this ℓ_∞ question, it turns out that *fewer* rolls of the die are required than flips of the coin; specifically, we show that $\Theta\left(\frac{\ln n}{n\epsilon^2}\right)$ are necessary and sufficient, in a small n regime (specifically, $\Theta\left(\frac{n}{\ln(n)}\right) \leq \frac{1}{\epsilon}$). Once n becomes large enough, only $\Theta\left(\frac{1}{\epsilon}\right)$ samples are necessary and sufficient.

Briefly, the intuition behind this result in the ℓ_∞ case is as follows. When flipping a 2-sided coin, both a fair coin and one that is ϵ-biased will have many samples that are heads and many that are tails, making ϵ difficult to detect ($\frac{1}{\epsilon^2}$ flips are needed to overcome the variance of the process). On the other hand, imagine that we roll a die with $n =$ one million faces, for which one particular face is $\epsilon = 0.01$ more likely to come up than it should be. Then after only $\Theta\left(\frac{1}{\epsilon}\right) = $ a few hundred rolls of the die, we expect to see this face come up multiple times. These multiple-occurrences or "collisions" are vastly less likely if the die is fair, so we can distinguish the biased and uniform cases.

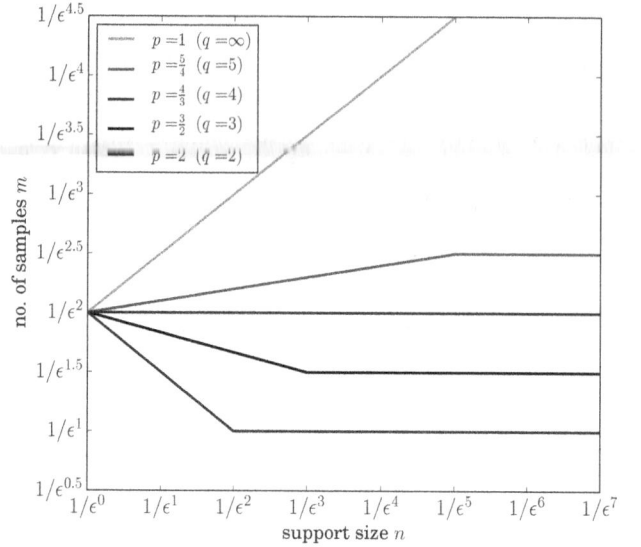

Figure 1: Samples (necessary and sufficient, up to constant factors) for testing uniformity with a fixed ℓ_p tolerance ϵ. On the horizontal axis is the support size n of the uniform distribution, and on the vertical axis is the corresponding number of samples required to test uniformity. The function plotted is $\frac{\sqrt{n}}{(n^{1/q}\epsilon)^2}$ for $n \leq \frac{1}{\epsilon^q}$ and $\sqrt{\frac{1}{\epsilon^q}}$ for $n \geq \frac{1}{\epsilon^q}$, for various choices of p and corresponding $q = \frac{p}{p-1}$. There is a phase transition at $p = \frac{4}{3}$: For $p < \frac{4}{3}$, the bound is initially increasing in n; for $p > \frac{4}{3}$, the bound is initially decreasing in n. For all p except $p = 1$, the number of necessary samples is constant for $n \geq 1/\epsilon^q$. Note the log-log scale.

So when the support is small, the variance of the uniform distribution can mask bias; but this fails to happen when the support size is large, making it easier to test uniformity over larger supports. These intuitions extend smoothly to the ℓ_p metrics below $p = \infty$: First, to be ϵ-far from uniform on a large set, it must be the case that the distribution has "heavy" elements; and second, these heavy elements cause many more collisions than the uniform distribution, making them easier to detect than when the support is small. However, this intuition only extends "down" to certain values of p.

SUMMARY THEOREM 3. *For $1 \leq p \leq 2$, for $n \leq n^* = \frac{1}{\epsilon^q}$, the sample complexity of testing uniformity is $\Theta\left(\frac{\sqrt{n}}{(n^{1/q}\epsilon)^2}\right)$. For $1 \leq p < \frac{4}{3}$, this is increasing in the support size n, and for $\frac{4}{3} < p \leq 2$, this is decreasing in n. For $p = \frac{4}{3}$, the sample complexity is $\Theta\left(\frac{1}{\epsilon^2}\right)$ for every value of n.*

Figure 1 illustrates these bounds for different values of p, including the phase transition at $p = \frac{4}{3}$.

3. UNIFORMITY TESTING FOR $1 \leq p \leq 2$

Recall the definition of uniformity testing: given i.i.d. samples from a distribution A, we must satisfy the following. If $A = U_n$, the uniform distribution on support size n, then output "uniform". If $\|A - U_n\|_p \geq \epsilon$, then output "not uniform". In each case, the output must be correct except with probability at most δ.

Algorithm 1 Uniformity Tester

On input p, n, ϵ, and failure probability δ:
Choose m to be "sufficient" for p, n, ϵ, δ according to proven bounds.
Draw m samples.
Let C be the number of collisions:
$\quad C = \sum_{1 \leq j < k \leq m} \mathbb{1}[j\text{th sample} = k\text{th sample}]$.
Let T be the threshold: $T = \binom{m}{2}\frac{1}{n} + \sqrt{\frac{1}{\delta}\binom{m}{2}\frac{1}{n}}$.
If $C \leq T$, output "uniform".
If $C > T$, output "not uniform".

The upper bounds for $1 \leq p \leq 2$ rely on a very simple algorithm, Algorithm 1, and straightforward (if slightly delicate) argument. We count the number of *collisions*: Pairs of samples drawn that are of the same coordinate. (Thus, if m samples are drawn, there are up to $\binom{m}{2}$ possible collisions.) The number of collisions C has the following properties.[6]

LEMMA 3.1. *On distribution A, the number of collisions C satisfies:*

1. *The expectation is*
$\mu_A = \binom{m}{2}\|A\|_2^2 = \binom{m}{2}\left(\frac{1}{n} + \|A - U\|_2^2\right)$.

2. *The variance is*
$Var(C) = \binom{m}{2}\left(\|A\|_2^2 - \|A\|_2^4\right) + 6\binom{m}{3}\left(\|A\|_3^3 - \|A\|_2^4\right)$.

Thus, the ℓ_2 distance to uniform, $\|A - U\|_2$, intuitively controls the number of collisions we expect to see, with a minimum when $A = U$. This is why Algorithm 1 simply declares the distribution nonuniform if the number of collisions exceeds a threshold.

THEOREM 3.1. *For uniformity testing with $1 \leq p \leq 2$, it suffices to run Algorithm 1 while drawing the following number of samples:*

$$m = \frac{9}{\delta}\begin{cases} \frac{\sqrt{n}}{(\epsilon n^{1/q})^2} & n \leq \frac{1}{\epsilon^q} \\ \frac{1}{2}\sqrt{\left(\frac{2}{\epsilon}\right)^q} & n \geq \frac{1}{\epsilon^q}. \end{cases}$$

The proof of Theorem 3.1 uses Chebyshev's inequality to bound the probability that C is far from its expectation in terms of $Var(C)$, for both the case where $A = U_n$ and $\|A - U_n\|_p \geq \epsilon$. It focuses on a careful analysis of the variance of the number of collisions, to show that, for m sufficiently large, the variance is small. For $1 \leq p \leq 2$, the dominant term eventually falls into one of two cases, which correspond directly to the two regimes for n considered in this paper: "large" ($n \geq \frac{1}{\epsilon^q}$) and "small" ($n \leq \frac{1}{\epsilon^q}$), where $q = \frac{p}{p-1}$.

[6] A possibly interesting generalization: The expected number of k-way collisions, for any $k = 2, 3, \ldots$, is equal to $\binom{m}{k}\|A\|_k^k$. To prove it, consider the probability that each k-sized subset is such a collision (*i.e.* all k are of the same coordinate), and use linearity of expectation over the $\binom{m}{k}$ subsets.

Collisions, also called "coincidences", have been implicitly, but not explicitly, used to test uniformity for the ℓ_1 case by Paninski [13]. Rather than directly testing the number of collisions, that paper tested "K_1", the number of coordinates that were sampled exactly once. That tester is designed for the regime where n is large, in which case K_1 is implicitly inversely related to C. I do not know of a prior case where C is directly tested in order to test uniformity, although the idea of using collisions as a tool in testing is common.

Algorithm 1 is optimal for all $1 \leq p \leq 2$, n, and ϵ, up to a constant factor depending on p and the failure probability δ.

THEOREM 3.2. *For uniformity testing with $1 \leq p \leq 2$, it is necessary to draw the following number of samples:*

$$m = \begin{cases} \sqrt{\ln\left(1 + (1 - 2\delta)^2\right)}\frac{\sqrt{n}}{(\epsilon n^{1/q})^2} & n \leq \frac{1}{\epsilon^q} \\ \sqrt{2(1 - 2\delta)}\sqrt{\frac{1}{(2\epsilon)^q}} & n \geq \frac{1}{\epsilon^q}. \end{cases}$$

In the large-n regime, the lower bound can be proven simply. We pick randomly from a set of nonuniform distributions A where, if not enough samples are drawn, then the probability of *any* collision is very low. But without collisions, the input is equally likely to come from U_n or from one of the nonuniform As, so no algorithm can distinguish these cases.

In the small-n regime, the order-optimal lower bound follows from the ℓ_1 lower bound of Paninski [13], which does not give constants. We give a rewriting of this proof with two changes: We make small adaptations to fit general ℓ_p metrics, and we obtain the constant factor. The idea behind the proof of [13] is to again pick randomly from a family of distributions that are close to uniform. A key lemma says that, if the distribution of the final set of samples obtained is close in ℓ_1 distance to the distribution of the sample set obtained from U_n, then no algorithm can be correct with good probability. It then remains to bound this ℓ_1 distance, completing the proof.

4. UNIFORMITY TESTING FOR $p > 2$

This paper fails to characterize the sample complexity of uniformity testing in the $p > 2$ regime, except for the case $p = \infty$ in which the bounds are tight. However, the remaining gap between the bounds we do prove is relatively small.

First, we note that Algorithm 1 can be slightly adapted for use for all $p > 2$, giving an upper bound on the number of samples required. The reason is that, by an ℓ_p-norm inequality, whenever $\|A - U\|_p \geq \epsilon$, we also have $\|A - U\|_2 \geq \epsilon$. So an ℓ_2 tester is also an ℓ_p tester for $p \geq 2$. This observation proves the following theorem.

THEOREM 4.1. *For uniformity testing with any $p > 2$, it suffices to run Algorithm 1 while drawing the number of samples for $p = 2$, namely*

$$m = \frac{9}{\delta}\begin{cases} \frac{1}{\sqrt{n}\epsilon^2} & n \leq \frac{1}{\epsilon^2} \\ \frac{1}{\epsilon} & n \geq \frac{1}{\epsilon^2}. \end{cases}$$

PROOF. If $A = U$, then by the guarantee of Algorithm 1, with probability $1 - \delta$ it outputs "uniform". If $\|A - U\|_p \geq \epsilon$, then $\|A - U\|_2 \geq \epsilon$: It is a property of ℓ_p norms that $\|V\|_2 \geq \|V\|_p$ for all vectors V when $p \geq 2$. Then, by the guarantee of Algorithm 1, with probability $1 - \delta$ it outputs "not uniform". $\square$

The same reasoning, but in the opposite direction, says that a lower bound for the ℓ_∞ case gives a lower bound for all $p < \infty$. Thus, by proving a lower bound for ℓ_∞ distance, we obtain the following theorem.

THEOREM 4.2. *For uniformity testing with any p, it is necessary to draw the following number of samples:*

$$m = \begin{cases} \frac{1}{2}\frac{\ln\left(1+n(1-2\delta)^2\right)}{n\epsilon^2} & \text{for all } n \\ \frac{1-2\delta}{2}\frac{1}{\epsilon} & n \geq \frac{1}{\epsilon}. \end{cases}$$

We find that the first bound is larger (better) for $\Theta\left(\frac{n}{\ln(n)}\right) \leq \frac{1}{\epsilon}$, *and the second is better for all larger n.*

PROOF. In the full version of the paper, it is proven that this is a lower-bound on the number of samples for the case $p = \infty$. By the p-norm inequality mentioned above, for any $p \leq \infty$ and any vector V, $\|V\|_p \geq \|V\|_\infty$. In particular, suppose we had an ℓ_p testing algorithm. When the sampling distribution $A = U_n$, then by the guarantee of the ℓ_p tester it is correct with probability at least $1-\delta$; when $\|A - U_n\|_\infty \geq \epsilon$, we must have $\|A - U_n\|_p \geq \epsilon$ and so again by the guarantee of the ℓ_p tester it is correct with probability $1 - \delta$. Thus the lower bound for ℓ_∞ holds for any ℓ_p algorithm as well. □

The lower bound for ℓ_∞ distance is proven by again splitting into the large and small n cases. In the large n case, we can simply consider the distribution

$$A^* = \left(\frac{1}{n} + \epsilon, \frac{1}{n} - \frac{\epsilon}{n-1}, \ldots, \frac{1}{n} - \frac{\epsilon}{n-1}\right).$$

If m is too small, then the algorithm probably does not draw any sample of the first coordinate; but conditioned on this, A^* is indistinguishable from uniform (since it is uniform on the remaining coordinates).

In the small n case, we adapt the general approach of [13] that was used to prove tight lower bounds for the case $p \leq 2$. We consider choosing a random permutation of A^* and then drawing m i.i.d. samples from this distribution. A correct algorithm should output "not uniform" with probability at least $1 - \delta$. The key lemma mentioned previously says that success probability of any algorithm can be bounded in terms of the ℓ_1 distance of the resulting distribution of these samples from uniform, so analyzing this distance completes the proof.

Comparing Theorems 4.1 and 4.2, we see a relatively small gap for the small n regime for $2 < p < \infty$, which is left open. A natural conjecture is that the sample complexity will be $\frac{1}{\epsilon}$ for the regime $n \geq \frac{1}{\epsilon^q}$. For the small n regime, it is not clear what to expect; perhaps $\frac{1}{n^{1/q}\epsilon^2}$, or $\frac{\ln(n)}{n^{1/q}\epsilon^2}$. New techniques seem to be required, since neither the analysis of collisions as in the case $p \leq 2$, nor the analysis of the single most different coordinate, as we will see for the $p = \infty$ case below, seems appropriate or tight for the case $2 < p < \infty$.

A better ℓ_∞ tester. For the ℓ_∞ case, the ℓ_2 tester is optimal in the regime where $n \geq \frac{1}{\epsilon^2}$, as proven in Theorem 4.1. For smaller n, a natural algorithm (albeit with some tricky specifics), Algorithm 2, gives an upper bound that matches the lower bound up to constant factors. We first state this upper bound, then give an explanation.

THEOREM 4.3. *For uniformity testing with ℓ_p distance, it suffices to run Algorithm 2 with the following number of samples:*

$$m = \begin{cases} 23\frac{\ln\left(\frac{2n}{\delta}\right)}{n\epsilon^2} & \epsilon \leq 2\alpha(n) \\ 35\frac{\ln\left(\frac{1}{\delta}\right)}{\epsilon} & \epsilon > 2\alpha(n) \end{cases}$$

where $\alpha(n) = \frac{1}{n}\left(1 + \frac{\ln(2n)}{\ln(1/\delta)}\right)$. *In particular, for a fixed failure probability δ, we have*

$$\alpha(n) = \Theta\left(\frac{\ln(n)}{n}\right).$$

To understand Algorithm 2, consider separately the two regimes: $\Theta\left(\frac{n}{\ln(n)}\right) \leq \frac{1}{\epsilon}$ and otherwise. For details of the analysis, rather than phrasing the threshold in this way, we phrase it as $\epsilon \leq 2\alpha(n)$ where $\alpha(n) = \Theta\left(\frac{\ln(n)}{n}\right)$, but the actual form of α is more complicated because it depends on δ.

In the first, smaller-n regime, our approach will essentially be a Chernoff plus union bound. We will draw $m = \Theta\left(\frac{\ln(n)}{n\epsilon^2}\right)$ samples. Then Algorithm 2 simply checks for any coordinate with an "outlier" number of samples (either too many or too few). The proof of correctness is that, if the distribution is uniform, then by a Chernoff bound on each coordinate and union-bound over the coordinates, with high probability no coordinate has an "outlier" number of samples; on the other hand, if the distribution is non-uniform, then there is an "outlier" coordinate in terms of its probability and by a Chernoff bound this coordinate likely has an "outlier" number of samples.

In the second, larger-n regime (where $\epsilon > 2\alpha(n)$), we will use the same approach, but first we will "bucket" the distribution into $\hat{n}$ groups of total probability at most $\frac{1}{\hat{n}}$ each (if the distribution is uniform), where $\epsilon = 2\alpha(\hat{n})$. In other words, no matter how large n is, we choose $\hat{n}$ so that $\epsilon = \Theta\left(\frac{\ln(\hat{n})}{\hat{n}}\right)$.

In this larger-n regime, a key point is that $\epsilon > \frac{1}{n}$, so in order for $\|A - U\|_\infty \geq \epsilon$, there must exist a coordinate i with $X_i \geq \frac{1}{n} + \epsilon$. Thus, to test uniformity we just need to draw enough samples so that this heavy coordinate is likely to be an outlier with lots of samples (by a Chernoff bound). (More accurately, the group containing this coordinate must be an outlier.) We also need, by a Chernoff plus union bound, that under the uniform distribution, probably no group is an outlier. Our choice of $\hat{n}$ turns out to exactly balance this probability bound.

5. DISTRIBUTION LEARNING

Recall the definition of the learning problem: Given i.i.d. samples from a distribution A, we must output a distribution $\hat{A}$ satisfying that $\|A - \hat{A}\|_p \leq \epsilon$. This condition must be satisfied except with probability at most δ.

5.1 Upper Bounds

Here, Algorithm 3 is the natural/naive one: Let the probability of each coordinate be the frequency with which it is sampled.

The proofs of the upper bounds rely on an elegant proof approach which is apparently "folklore" or known for the

Algorithm 2 Uniformity Tester for ℓ_∞

On input n, ϵ, and failure probability δ:
Choose m to be "sufficient" for n, ϵ, δ according to proven bounds.
Draw m samples.
Let $\alpha(x) = \frac{1}{x}\left(1 + \frac{\ln(2x)}{\ln(1/\delta)}\right) = \Theta\left(\frac{\ln(x)}{x}\right)$.
if $\epsilon \le 2\alpha(n)$ **then**
    Let $t = \sqrt{\frac{6m}{n}\ln\left(\frac{2n}{\delta}\right)}$.
    If, for all coordinates i, the number of samples $X_i \in \frac{m}{n} \pm t$, output "uniform".
    Otherwise, output "not uniform".
else
    Let $\hat{n}$ satisfy $\epsilon = 2\alpha(\hat{n})$.
    Partition the coordinates into at most $\lceil \hat{n} \rceil$ groups, each of size at most $\lfloor \frac{n}{\hat{n}} \rfloor$.
    For each group j, let X_j be the total number of samples of coordinates in that group.
    Let $t = \sqrt{6m\epsilon \ln\left(\frac{1}{\delta}\right)}$.
    If there exists a group j with $X_j \ge m\epsilon - t$, output "not uniform".
    Otherwise, output "uniform".
end if

Algorithm 3 Learner

On input p, n, ϵ:
Choose m to be "sufficient" for p, n, ϵ according to proven bounds.
Draw m samples.
Let X_i be the number of samples drawn of each coordinate $i \in \{1, \dots, n\}$.
Let each $\hat{A}_i = \frac{X_i}{m}$.
Output $\hat{A}$.

ℓ_2 setting, and was introduced to the author by Clément Canonne[3] who contributed it to this paper. The author and Canonne in collaboration extended the proof to general ℓ_p metrics in order to prove the bounds in this paper. Here, we give the theorem and proof for perhaps the most interesting and novel case, that for $1 < p \le 2$, $O\left(\frac{1}{\epsilon^q}\right)$ samples are sufficient independent of n. The other cases have a similar proof structure.

THEOREM 5.1. *For $1 < p \le 2$, to learn up to ℓ_p distance ϵ with failure probability δ, it suffices to run Algorithm 3 while drawing the following number of samples:*

$$m = \left(\frac{3}{\delta}\right)^{\frac{1}{p-1}} \frac{1}{\epsilon^q}.$$

PROOF. Let X_i be the number of samples of coordinate i and $\hat{A}_i = \frac{X_i}{m}$. Note that X_i is distributed Binomially with m independent trials of probability A_i each. We have that

$$\mathbb{E}\left\|\hat{A} - A\right\|_p^p = \frac{1}{m^p}\sum_{i=1}^{n} \mathbb{E}\left|X_i - \mathbb{E}\,X_i\right|^p.$$

We will show that, for each i, $\mathbb{E}\left|X_i - \mathbb{E}\,X_i\right|^p \le 3\,\mathbb{E}\,X_i$. This will complete the proof, as then

$$\mathbb{E}\left\|\hat{A} - A\right\|_p^p \le \frac{1}{m^p}\sum_{i=1}^{n} 3\,\mathbb{E}\,X_i$$
$$= \frac{1}{m^p}\sum_{i=1}^{n} 3m A_i$$
$$= \frac{3}{m^{p-1}};$$

and by Markov's Inequality,

$$\Pr[\|\hat{A} - A\|_p^p \ge \epsilon^p] \le \frac{3}{m^{p-1}\epsilon^p},$$

which for $m = \left(\frac{3}{\delta}\right)^{\frac{1}{p-1}}\frac{1}{\epsilon^q}$ is equal to δ.

To show that $\mathbb{E}\left|X_i - \mathbb{E}\,X_i\right|^p \le 3\,\mathbb{E}\,X_i$, fix any i and consider a possible realization x of X_i. If $|x - \mathbb{E}\,X_i| \ge 1$, then $|x - \mathbb{E}\,X_i|^p \le |x - \mathbb{E}\,X_i|^2$. We can thus bound the contribution of all such terms by $\mathbb{E}\left|X_i - \mathbb{E}\,X_i\right|^2 = Var\,X_i$.

If, on the other hand, $|x - \mathbb{E}\,X_i| < 1$, then $|X_i - \mathbb{E}\,X_i|^p \le |X_i - \mathbb{E}\,X_i|$; furthermore, at most two terms satisfy this condition, namely (letting $\beta := \lfloor \mathbb{E}\,X_i \rfloor$) $x = \beta$ and $x = \beta + 1$. These terms contribute a total of at most

$$\Pr[X_i = \beta]|\mathbb{E}\,X_i - \beta| + \Pr[X_i = \beta + 1]|\beta + 1 - \mathbb{E}\,X_i|$$
$$\le \mathbb{E}\,X_i + \Pr[X_i = \beta + 1].$$

Consider two cases. If $\mathbb{E}\,X_i \ge 1$, then the contribution is at most $\mathbb{E}\,X_i + 1 \le 2\,\mathbb{E}\,X_i$. If $\mathbb{E}\,X_i < 1$, then $\beta + 1 = 1$, and by Markov's Inequality, $\Pr[X_i \ge 1] \le \mathbb{E}\,X_i$, so the total contribution is again bounded by $2\,\mathbb{E}\,X_i$.

Thus, we have

$$\mathbb{E}\left|X_i - \mathbb{E}\,X_i\right|^p \le Var\,X_i + 2\,\mathbb{E}\,X_i$$
$$\le 3\,\mathbb{E}\,X_i$$

because $Var\,X_i = (1 - A_i)\,\mathbb{E}\,X_i$. $\square$

A slightly tighter analysis can be obtained by reducing to the ℓ_2 algorithm, in which the above proof technique is "tightest". It produces the following theorem:

THEOREM 5.2. *For learning a discrete distribution with* $1 \leq p \leq 2$, *it suffices to run Algorithm 3 with the following number of samples:*

$$m = \frac{1}{\delta} \begin{cases} \frac{n}{\left(n^{1/q}\epsilon\right)^2} & n \leq \left(\frac{2}{\epsilon}\right)^q \\ \frac{1}{4}\left(\frac{2}{\epsilon}\right)^q & n \geq \left(\frac{2}{\epsilon}\right)^q \end{cases}.$$

For $p \geq 2$, we can observe that an ℓ_2 learner also suffices to learn for ℓ_p distance due to the relation of ℓ_p norms. This observation proves the following theorem.

THEOREM 5.3. *For learning a discrete distribution with* $2 \leq p$, *it suffices to run Algorithm 3 with the sufficient number of samples for ℓ_2 learning, namely*

$$m = \frac{1}{\delta}\frac{1}{\epsilon^2}.$$

PROOF. By the guarantee of Algorithm 3 on $p = 2$, with probability $1 - \delta$, $\|\hat{A} - A\|_2 \leq \epsilon$. But by the inequality of p norms, whenever this occurs, we also have $\|\hat{A} - A\|_p \leq \|\hat{A} - A\|_2 \leq \epsilon$ for all $p \geq 2$. □

5.2 Lower bounds

To prove the lower bounds, we define the following game and give the associated lemma:

Distribution identification game: The game is parameterized by maximum support size n, the choice of distance metric ρ, and the tolerance ϵ. First, a finite set S of distributions is chosen, where for all pairs $A, B \in S$, $\rho(A, B) > 2\epsilon$. Every distribution in S is supported on at most $\hat{n} \leq n$ coordinates (it will be useful in our bounds to choose $\hat{n} \neq n$). The algorithm is given this set S. Second, a distribution A is chosen from S uniformly at random (but the algorithm is not told which). Third, the algorithm is given m i.i.d. samples from A. Fourth, the algorithm outputs a distribution from S. The algorithm wins if its output is A, the chosen oracle, and the algorithm loses otherwise.

LEMMA 5.1. *Any algorithm for learning to within distance ϵ using $m(n, p, \epsilon)$ samples with failure probability δ can be converted into an algorithm for distribution identification using $m(n, p, \epsilon)$ samples, with losing probability at most δ.*

PROOF. Suppose the true oracle is $A \in S$. Run the learning algorithm, obtaining $\hat{A}$, and output the member B of S that minimizes $\rho(\hat{A}, B)$ (where ρ is the distance metric of the game; for us, it will be ℓ_p distance). With probability at least $1 - \delta$, by the guarantee of the learning algorithm, $\|\hat{A} - A\|_p \leq \epsilon$. When this occurs, we always output the correct answer, A: For any $B \neq A$ in S, by the triangle inequality $\|\hat{A} - B\|_p \geq \|B - A\| - \|\hat{A} - A\| > 2\epsilon - \epsilon = \epsilon$. □

The proofs of the lower bounds then proceed in the following fashion, at a high level:

1. Show that the probability of winning the game is bounded by $\approx \frac{1}{|S|}\left(\sqrt{\frac{m}{\hat{n}}}\right)^{\hat{n}}$. This uses some details of the multinomial distribution (the set of input samples is distributed as a multinomial with n categories and m repetitions). One intuition for this fact is that the entropy of the input set of samples turns out to be about $\hat{n}\log\left(\sqrt{\frac{m}{\hat{n}}}\right)$, whereas the entropy of our choice of distribution is $\log|S|$, so the ratio captures the ratio between information we get and the information we need.

2. Construct a large set S of distributions. For instance, for $1 \leq p \leq 2$, we have $|S| \approx \left(\frac{1}{(\hat{n})^{1/q}\epsilon}\right)^{\hat{n}}$. The main idea is to use a sphere-packing argument as with *e.g.* the Gilbert-Varshamov bound in error-correcting codes. (In particular, the "construction" is not constructive; we merely prove that such a set exists.)

3. Combine these steps. For instance, for $1 \leq p \leq 2$, we get that the probability of winning is approximately

$$\left(\hat{n}^{1/q}\epsilon\sqrt{\frac{m}{\hat{n}}}\right)^{\hat{n}}$$

implying that, for a constant probability of winning, we must pick $m \approx \frac{\hat{n}}{((\hat{n})^{1/q}\epsilon)^2}$.

4. Choose $\hat{n} \leq n$. For $1 \leq p \leq 2$, in the small n regime where $n \leq \frac{1}{\epsilon^q}$, the best choice turns out to be $\hat{n} = n$; in the large n regime, the choice $\hat{n} = \frac{1}{\epsilon^q}$ turns out to be optimal and gives a lower bound $\tilde{\Theta}(\hat{n})$ that is independent of n for that range (since for any large enough n, we make the same choice of $\hat{n}$).

This approach yields the following bounds.

THEOREM 5.4. *To win the distribution identification game (and thus, by Lemma 5.1, to learn), the number of samples required for all p is at least*

$$m = \Omega\left(\frac{1}{\epsilon^2}\right).$$

For $p < \infty$, the number of samples required is at least

$$m = \begin{cases} \Omega\left(\frac{n}{\left(n^{1/q}\epsilon\right)^2}\right) & n \leq \frac{1}{\epsilon^q} + 1. \\ \Omega\left(\frac{1}{\epsilon^q}\right) & n \geq \frac{1}{\epsilon^q} + 1. \end{cases}$$

By checking the cases, we can observe that the first bound of $\Omega\left(\frac{1}{\epsilon^2}\right)$ is best for $p \geq 2$. In the proof, this corresponds to the fact that choosing $\hat{n} = 2$ is the optimal or "most difficult to learn" choice for all $p \geq 2$.

6. PRIOR AND FUTURE WORK

6.1 Discussion of Prior Work

The study of problems under ℓ_p metrics crops up in many areas of theoretical computer science and probability, as mentioned in the introduction. Close to this paper's setting and similar in spirit is Berman et al 2014 [2], which examined testing properties of real-valued functions such as monotonicity, Lipschitz constant, and convexity, all under various ℓ_p distances. Another case in which "exotic" metrics have been studied in connection with testing and learning is in Do et al 2011 [7], which studied the distance between and equality of two distributions under Earth Mover Distance.

For the problem of testing uniformity, Paninski 2008 [13] examines the ℓ_1 metric in the case of large-support distributions. The lower bound technique, which is slightly extended and utilized in this paper, establishes that $\Omega\left(\frac{\sqrt{n}}{\epsilon^2}\right)$ samples are necessary to test uniformity under the ℓ_1 metric (with constants unknown). This lower bound holds for all support sizes n. The algorithm that gives the upper bound in that paper, a matching $m = O\left(\frac{\sqrt{n}}{\epsilon^2}\right)$, holds for the case of very large support size n, namely $n > m$. This translates to $n = \Omega\left(\frac{1}{\epsilon^4}\right)$. The reason is that the algorithm counts the number of coordinates that are sampled exactly once; when $n > m$, this indirectly counts the number of collisions (more or less).

[13] justifies a focus on $n > m$ because, for small n, one could prefer to just learn the distribution, which tells one whether it is uniform or not. However, depending on ϵ, this paper shows that the savings can still be substantial: the number of samples required is on the order of $\frac{n}{\epsilon^2}$ to learn versus $\frac{\sqrt{n}}{\epsilon^2}$ to test uniformity using Algorithm 1. For example, if we had $\epsilon = 0.01$ and $n = 1000000$, learning requires on the order of 10^{10} samples, while uniformity testing requires only on the order of 10^7. If there has been no previous uniformity tester for small n (the author is not aware of any), then Algorithm 1 might be the first order-optimal uniformity tester for the ℓ_1 case in this regime.

More broadly, the idea of using collisions is common and also arises for related problems, e.g. by [9] in a different context, and by Batu et al 2013 [1] for testing closeness of two given distributions in ℓ_1 distance. This latter problem was resolved more tightly by Chan et al 2014 [4] who established a $\Theta\left(\max\left\{\frac{n^{2/3}}{\epsilon^{4/3}}, \frac{\sqrt{n}}{\epsilon^2}\right\}\right)$ sample complexity. This problem may be a good candidate for future ℓ_p testing questions. It may be that the collision-based analysis can easily be adapted for general ℓ_p norms.

The case of learning a discrete distribution seems to the author to be mostly folklore. It is known that $\Theta\left(\frac{n}{\epsilon^2}\right)$ samples are necessary and sufficient in ℓ_1 distance (as mentioned for instance in [6]). It is also known via the "DKW inequality" [8] that $\Theta\left(\frac{1}{\epsilon^2}\right)$ samples are sufficient in ℓ_∞ distance, with a matching lower bound coming from the biased coin setting (since learning must be at least as hard as distinguishing a 2-sided coin from uniform). It is not clear to the author exactly what bounds would be considered "known" or "folklore" for the learning problem in ℓ_2; perhaps the upper bound that $O\left(\frac{1}{\epsilon^2}\right)$ samples are sufficient in ℓ_2 distance is known. This work does provide a resolution to these questions, giving tight upper and lower bounds, as part of the general ℓ_p approach. But it should be noted that the results in at least these cases were already known and indeed the general upper-bound technique, introduced to the author by Clément Canonne [3], is not original here (possibly appearing in print for the first time).

6.2 Bounds and Algorithms via Conversions

As mentioned at times throughout the paper, conversions between ℓ_p norms can be used to convert algorithms from one case to another. In some cases this can give easy and tight bounds on the number of samples necessary and sufficient. The primary such inequality is Lemma 6.1.

LEMMA 6.1. *For $1 \le p \le s \le \infty$, for all vectors $V \in \mathbb{R}^n$,*

$$\frac{\|V\|_p}{n^{\frac{1}{p}-\frac{1}{s}}} \le \|V\|_s \le \|V\|_p.$$

For instance, suppose we have an ℓ_2 learning algorithm so that, when it succeeds, we have $\|\hat{A} - A\|_2 \le \alpha$. Then for $p > 2$, $\|\hat{A} - A\|_p \le \|\hat{A} - A\|_2 \le \alpha$, so we have an ℓ_p learner with the same guarantee. This also says that any lower bound for an ℓ_p learner, $p > 2$, immediately implies the same lower bound for ℓ_2.

Meanwhile, for $p < 2$, $\|\hat{A} - A\|_p \le \|\hat{A} - A\|_2 n^{\frac{1}{p}-\frac{1}{2}} \le \alpha n^{\frac{1}{p}-\frac{1}{2}}$. This implies that, to get an ℓ_p learner for distance ϵ, it suffices to use an ℓ_2 learner for distance $\alpha = \epsilon n^{\frac{1}{2}-\frac{1}{p}} = \epsilon n^{1/q}/\sqrt{n}$. This can also be used to convert a lower bound for ℓ_p, $p < 2$, into a lower bound for ℓ_2 learners.

While these conversions can be useful especially for obtaining the tightest possible bounds, the techniques in this paper primarily focus on using a general technique that applies to all ℓ_p norms separately. However, it should be noted that applying these conversions to prior work can obtain some of the bounds in this paper (primarily for learning).

6.3 Future Work

An immediate direction from this paper is to close the gap on uniformity testing with $2 < p < \infty$, where n is smaller than $1/\epsilon^2$. Although this case may be somewhat obscure or considered unimportant and although the gap is not large, it might require interesting new approaches.

A possibly-interesting problem is to solve the questions considered in this paper, uniformity testing and learning, when one is not given n, the support size. For uniformity testing, the question would be whether the distribution is ϵ far from every uniform distribution U_n, or whether it is equal to U_n for some n. For each $p > 1$, these problems should be solvable without knowing n by using the algorithms in this paper for the worst-case n (note that, unlike the $p = 1$ case, there is an n-independent maximum sample complexity). However, it seems possible to do better by attempting to learn or estimate the support size while samples are drawn and terminating when one is confident of one's answer.

A more general program in which this paper fits is to consider learning and testing problems under more "exotic" metrics than ℓ_1, such as ℓ_p, Earth Mover's distance [7], or others. Such work would benefit from finding motivating applications for such metrics. An immediate problem along these lines is testing whether two distributions are equal or ϵ-far from each other in ℓ_p distance.

One direction suggested by the themes of this work is the testing and learning of "thin" distributions: those with small ℓ_∞ norm (each coordinate has small probability). For $p > 4/3$, we have seen that uniformity testing becomes easier over thinner distributions, where n is larger. It also seems that we ought to be able to more quickly learn a thin distribution. At the extreme case, for $1 < p$, if $\max_i A_i \le \epsilon^q$, then by Observation 2.1, we can learn A to within distance 2ϵ with zero samples by always outputting the uniform distribution on support size $\frac{1}{\epsilon^q}$. Thus, it may be interesting to consider learning (and perhaps other problems as well) as parameterized by the thinness of the distribution.

Acknowledgements

The author thanks Clément Canonne for discussions and contributions to this work. Thanks to cstheory.stackexchange.com, via which the author first became interested in this problem. Thanks to Leslie Valiant and Scott Linderman, teaching staff of Harvard CS 228, in which some of these results were obtained as a class project. Finally, thanks to the organizers and speakers at the Workshop on Efficient Distribution Estimation at STOC 2014 for an interesting and informative introduction to and survey of the field.

7. REFERENCES

[1] T. Batu, L. Fortnow, R. Rubinfeld, W. D. Smith, and P. White. Testing closeness of discrete distributions. *Journal of the ACM (JACM)*, 60(1):4, 2013.

[2] P. Berman, S. Raskhodnikova, and G. Yaroslavtsev. Testing with respect to ℓ_p distances. In *Proceedings, ACM Symp. on Theory of Computing (STOC)*, volume 6, 2014.

[3] C. Canonne. Private communication, 2014. In collaboration with the author.

[4] S.-O. Chan, I. Diakonikolas, P. Valiant, and G. Valiant. Optimal algorithms for testing closeness of discrete distributions. In *SODA*, pages 1193–1203. SIAM, 2014.

[5] G. Cormode, M. Datar, P. Indyk, and S. Muthukrishnan. Comparing data streams using hamming norms (how to zero in). *Knowledge and Data Engineering, IEEE Transactions on*, 15(3):529–540, May 2003.

[6] C. Daskalakis, I. Diakonikolas, R. ODonnell, R. A. Servedio, and L.-Y. Tan. Learning sums of independent integer random variables. In *Foundations of Computer Science (FOCS), 2013 IEEE 54th Annual Symposium on*, pages 217–226. IEEE, 2013.

[7] K. Do Ba, H. L. Nguyen, H. N. Nguyen, and R. Rubinfeld. Sublinear time algorithms for earth moverâĂŹs distance. *Theory of Computing Systems*, 48(2):428–442, 2011.

[8] A. Dvoretzky, J. Kiefer, and J. Wolfowitz. Asymptotic minimax character of the sample distribution function and of the classical multinomial estimator. *The Annals of Mathematical Statistics*, pages 642–669, 1956.

[9] O. Goldreich and D. Ron. On testing expansion in bounded-degree graphs. In *Electronic Colloquium on Computational Complexity*. 2000.

[10] P. Indyk. Stable distributions, pseudorandom generators, embeddings, and data stream computation. *J. ACM*, 53(3):307–323, May 2006.

[11] M. Kloft, U. Brefeld, S. Sonnenburg, and A. Zien. lp-norm multiple kernel learning. *J. Mach. Learn. Res.*, 12:953–997, July 2011.

[12] J. R. Lee and A. Naor. Embedding the diamond graph in l_p and dimension reduction in l_1. *Geometric & Functional Analysis GAFA*, 14(4):745–747, 2004.

[13] L. Paninski. A coincidence-based test for uniformity given very sparsely sampled discrete data. *Information Theory, IEEE Transactions on*, 54(10):4750–4755, 2008.

[14] R. Rubinfeld. Taming big probability distributions. *XRDS*, 19(1):24–28, Sept. 2012.

Sunflowers and Testing Triangle-Freeness of Functions*

Ishay Haviv
School of Computer Science
The Academic College of Tel Aviv-Yaffo
Tel Aviv 61083, Israel

Ning Xie[†]
School of Computer and Information Sciences
Florida International University
Miami, FL 33199
nxie@cs.fiu.edu

ABSTRACT

A function $f : \mathbb{F}_2^n \to \{0, 1\}$ is *triangle-free* if there are no $x_1, x_2, x_3 \in \mathbb{F}_2^n$ satisfying $x_1 + x_2 + x_3 = 0$ and $f(x_1) = f(x_2) = f(x_3) = 1$. In testing triangle-freeness, the goal is to distinguish with high probability triangle-free functions from those that are ε-far from being triangle-free. It was shown by Green that the query complexity of the canonical tester for the problem is upper bounded by a function that depends only on ε (GAFA, 2005), however the best known upper bound is a tower type function of $1/\varepsilon$. The best known lower bound on the query complexity of the canonical tester is $1/\varepsilon^{13.239}$ (Fu and Kleinberg, RANDOM, 2014).

In this work we introduce a new approach to proving lower bounds on the query complexity of triangle-freeness. We relate the problem to combinatorial questions on collections of vectors in $\mathbb{Z}_D^n$ and to *sunflower conjectures* studied by Alon, Shpilka, and Umans (Comput. Complex., 2013). The relations yield that a refutation of the Weak Sunflower Conjecture over $\mathbb{Z}_4$ implies a super-polynomial lower bound on the query complexity of the canonical tester for triangle-freeness. Our results are extended to testing k-cycle-freeness of functions with domain $\mathbb{F}_p^n$ for every $k \geq 3$ and a prime p. In addition, we generalize the lower bound of Fu and Kleinberg to k-cycle-freeness for $k \geq 4$ by generalizing the construction of uniquely solvable puzzles due to Coppersmith and Winograd (J. Symbolic Comput., 1990).

Categories and Subject Descriptors

F.2 [**Design and analysis of algorithms**]: Streaming, sublinear and near linear time algorithms—*Lower bounds and information complexity*

General Terms

Theory

---

*A full version of this paper is available at http://arxiv.org/abs/1411.4692

[†]Research supported in part by NSF grant 1423034.

Keywords

Property Testing, Triangles, Sunflowers, Query Lower Bounds

1. INTRODUCTION

The research on *property testing*, initiated by Rubinfeld and Sudan [31] and by Goldreich, Goldwasser, and Ron [21], is concerned with very efficient algorithms that distinguish with high probability objects which satisfy a given property from those that are far from satisfying it. Typically, one can think of an input object as a function from a domain D to a range R, and of a property $\mathcal{P}$ as a subset of the function set $D \to R$. For a distance parameter ε, the goal of the randomized algorithm, called a *tester*, is to accept the functions of $\mathcal{P}$ and to reject functions which are ε-far from $\mathcal{P}$, that is, disagree with any function in $\mathcal{P}$ on at least ε-fraction of the inputs. In case that the functions of $\mathcal{P}$ are always accepted, we say that the tester has *one-sided* error. The main objective in property testing is to minimize the number of queries that the tester makes to the input object. If the number of queries depends solely on the distance parameter ε, we say that the property is *strongly testable*.

Since the invention of the property testing model, many natural properties were shown to be strongly testable. A considerable amount of attention was given to testing *graph* properties, and the strongly testable dense graph properties were fully characterized [3, 11]. An important graph property testing problem is that of deciding if a given undirected graph is H-free, i.e., contains no subgraph isomorphic to H, or is ε-far from H-freeness, where H is a fixed graph. Whereas H-freeness is known to be strongly testable for every graph H, it turns out that the graph H significantly affects the dependence of the query complexity on ε. Alon proved in [1] that for every bipartite graph H, the one-sided error query complexity of testing H-freeness is polynomial in $1/\varepsilon$, and that for every non-bipartite graph H, it is super-polynomial in $1/\varepsilon$, namely, at least $(1/\varepsilon)^{\Omega(\log(1/\varepsilon))}$. Interestingly, the lower bound for the non-bipartite case relies on a construction of Behrend [7] of dense sets of integers with no 3-term arithmetic progressions (see also [32, 16]) and on an extension of this construction given in [1].

Kaufman and Sudan initiated in [24] a systematic study of testing *algebraic* properties of functions with domain $\mathbb{F}^n$ for a field $\mathbb{F}$. They considered the class of *linear invariant* properties, those which are closed under all linear transformations of the domain, and asked for necessary and sufficient conditions for their strong testability (see [35, 8] for relevant surveys). This class includes the properties that can be described as freeness of solutions to (possibly infinite) systems of linear equations, which were shown to be strongly testable in [33] and in [27] (see also [9]). As opposed to the H-freeness property of graphs, it is not known which of these properties have query complexity polynomial in $1/\varepsilon$. The k-cycle-freeness properties, whose query complexity is the focus of the current work, fall into this category and are described next.

1.1 Testing k-Cycle-Freeness of Boolean Functions

Let n and $k \geq 3$ be integers, and let $\mathbb{F}_p$ be the finite field of prime order p. A k-cycle of a function $f : \mathbb{F}_p^n \to \{0,1\}$ is defined as k vectors $x_1, \ldots, x_k \in \mathbb{F}_p^n$ satisfying $x_1 + \cdots + x_k = 0$ and $f(x_i) = 1$ for every $1 \leq i \leq k$. In case that f has no k-cycles, we say that it is k-cycle-free. In the property testing problem of k-cycle-freeness over $\mathbb{F}_p$, the input is a function $f : \mathbb{F}_p^n \to \{0,1\}$, and the goal is to distinguish with high probability k-cycle-free functions from those that are ε-far from every k-cycle-free function.

In the *multiple-function variant* of the k-cycle-freeness problem, the input is a k-tuple of functions $f_1, \ldots, f_k : \mathbb{F}_p^n \to \{0,1\}$, and a k-cycle is defined as k vectors $x_1, \ldots, x_k \in \mathbb{F}_p^n$ satisfying $x_1 + \cdots + x_k = 0$ and $f_i(x_i) = 1$ for every $1 \leq i \leq k$. The goal here is to distinguish k-cycle-free k-tuples of functions from those that are ε-far from k-cycle-freeness, that is, at least $\varepsilon \cdot p^n$ values returned by the functions $f_1, \ldots, f_k$ should be changed in order to make the k-tuple free of k-cycles. Clearly, the query complexity of the multiple-function variant of k-cycle-freeness is at least as large as that of the one-function variant. We observe, though, that whenever p does not divide k, the two variants of testing k-cycle-freeness are essentially equivalent. On the other hand, in case that p does divide k, the one-function variant of the problem seems to be easier, and has query complexity $O(1/\varepsilon)$ (see Section 2.1 for details). Therefore, in order to understand the query complexity of testing k-cycle-freeness in the one-function case, it suffices to understand it for the multiple-function case. The latter is more convenient to deal with while studying lower bounds, so from now on, unless otherwise specified, we refer to the multiple-function variant as the k-cycle-freeness problem.

A natural tester for k-cycle-freeness over $\mathbb{F}_p$, known as the *canonical tester* of the problem, repeatedly picks independently and uniformly at random $k-1$ vectors $x_1, \ldots, x_{k-1} \in \mathbb{F}_p^n$ and checks if they form, together with $-x_1 - \cdots - x_{k-1}$, a k-cycle of the functions $f_1, \ldots, f_k$. If no k-cycle is found the tester accepts and otherwise it rejects. Despite the simplicity of this one-sided error tester, Green proved in [22] that for every k it has a constant probability of success for query complexity that depends only on ε, hence the k-cycle-freeness property is strongly testable. However, the query complexity achieved by Green has a huge dependence on ε, namely, it is a tower of twos whose height is polynomial in $1/\varepsilon$. An improved upper bound on the tower's height follows from results of [19] and [26] (see [19, Section 5] and [23]).

The study of lower bounds on the query complexity of testing k-cycle-freeness was initiated by Bhattacharyya and Xie in [10], where the case of triangles over $\mathbb{F}_2$ was considered. They provided the first non-trivial lower bound of $1/\varepsilon^{4.847}$ on the query complexity of the canonical tester for triangle-freeness over $\mathbb{F}_2$. They also studied connections between the query complexity of the canonical tester for k-cycle-freeness over $\mathbb{F}_2$ to that of more general testers for the problem.

The proof technique of the above lower bound involved the notion, introduced in [10], of *perfect-matching-free* families of vectors (PMFs). Roughly speaking, a PMF (for triangles over $\mathbb{F}_2$) is a collection $\{(a_i, b_i, c_i)\}_{i \in [m]}$ of m triples of vectors in $\mathbb{F}_2^n$ satisfying that $a_{i_1} + b_{i_2} + c_{i_3} = 0$ if and only if $i_1 = i_2 = i_3$. This means that the functions $f_1, f_2, f_3 : \mathbb{F}_2^n \to \{0,1\}$ defined as the characteristic functions of the a_i's, b_i's, and c_i's respectively, have m triangles which are pairwise disjoint. The distance of these functions from triangle-freeness is relatively large compared to the number of their triangles. Hence, they can be used to obtain lower bounds on the query complexity of the canonical tester for triangle-freeness over $\mathbb{F}_2$. The authors of [10] used a computer search to construct a PMF of vectors in $\mathbb{F}_2^n$ of size (roughly) 1.67^n, and this allowed them to get their $1/\varepsilon^{4.847}$ lower bound. Further, they showed that a PMF of size $(2 - o(1))^n$ implies a super-polynomial lower bound on the query complexity of the canonical tester for triangle-freeness over $\mathbb{F}_2$, and conjectured that such a PMF exists.

Very recently, Fu and Kleinberg [20] discovered an interesting connection between PMFs and the combinatorial objects known as *uniquely solvable puzzles* (USPs). The latter were introduced in the context of matrix multiplication algorithms and were explicitly defined by Cohn et al. in [12]. Coppersmith and Winograd [13] implicitly gave a probabilistic construction of n-dimensional USPs of size $(3/2^{2/3} - o(1))^n \approx 1.89^n$ that played a central role in their famous $O(n^{2.376})$-time algorithm for multiplication of n by n matrices, whose running time was improved only two decades later [34, 37]. It was shown in [20] that every USP implies a PMF of the same cardinality, and this led to an improved lower bound of $1/\varepsilon^{13.239}$ on the query complexity of the canonical tester for triangle-freeness over $\mathbb{F}_2$. However, it was observed in [12] that the USP construction of [13] is essentially optimal, hence it seems that the USP-based approach to proving lower bounds on testing triangle-freeness has been pushed to its limit, and, in particular, cannot yield super-polynomial lower bounds. Yet, a strengthened notion of USP, known as *strong* USP, was studied by Cohn et al. [12], who proved that if strong USPs of optimal size exist then the exponent of matrix multiplication is 2. A fascinating challenge, which was left open in [20], is to show that strong USPs might imply super-polynomial lower bounds on the query complexity of related testing problems.

In the current work we show that lower bounds on testing k-cycle-freeness might follow from the existence of certain collections of vectors in $\mathbb{Z}_D^n$. These collections are related to famous sunflower conjectures, which we turn to describe in the next section.

1.2 Sunflower Conjectures

A k-*sunflower* is a collection of k sets that have the same pairwise intersections. This notion was introduced in 1960 by Erdős and Rado [17], and besides being of great interest in combinatorics, it found applications in several areas of computer science, e.g., circuit complexity [30, 2], hardness of approximation [14], and property testing [4]. The main question regarding k-sunflowers is how large a collection of sets containing no k-sunflowers can be. It was shown in [17] that the size of any collection of subsets of size s of some universe U with no k-sunflowers is at most $s! \cdot (k-1)^s$. The classical sunflower conjecture of Erdős and Rado asserts the following.

CONJECTURE 1.1 (CLASSICAL SUNFLOWER CONJ. [17]).
For every $k > 0$ there exists a constant c_k, such that every collection of at least c_k^s subsets of size s of some universe U contains a k-sunflower.

The above conjecture is still open even for the special case of $k = 3$. For this case, Kostochka showed an improved upper bound of $c \cdot s! \cdot \left(\frac{30 \ln \ln \ln s}{\ln \ln s} \right)^s$ for some constant $c > 0$ [25]. Erdös and Szemerédi [18] presented in 1978 the following conjecture on 3-sunflowers inside $[n]$, and proved that Conjecture 1.1, even restricted to $k = 3$, implies it.

CONJECTURE 1.2 (SUNFLOWER CONJ. IN $\{0,1\}^n$ [18]).
There exists an $\varepsilon > 0$, such that every collection $\mathcal{F}$ of subsets of $[n]$ ($n \geq 2$) of size $|\mathcal{F}| \geq 2^{(1-\varepsilon)n}$ contains a 3-sunflower.

In a recent paper, Alon, Shpilka, and Umans [5] have studied a new notion of sunflowers over $\mathbb{Z}_D = \{1, \ldots, D\}$ and several related sunflower conjectures. Following their definition, we say that k vectors $v_1, \ldots, v_k$ in $\mathbb{Z}_D^n$ form a k-*sunflower* if for every $i \in [n]$ it holds that the ith entries $(v_1)_i, \ldots, (v_k)_i$ of the vectors are either all equal or all distinct. It was shown in [5] that Conjecture 1.2 can be *equivalently* formulated in terms of sunflowers of vectors as follows.

CONJECTURE 1.3 (SUNFLOWER CONJ. IN $\mathbb{Z}_D^n$ [5]). *There exist $\varepsilon > 0$, D_0 and n_0, such that for every $D \geq D_0$ and $n \geq n_0$, every collection $\mathcal{F}$ of vectors in $\mathbb{Z}_D^n$ of size $|\mathcal{F}| \geq D^{(1-\varepsilon)n}$ contains a 3-sunflower.*

The above conjecture, just like Conjecture 1.2, is widely believed to be true. Still, one might wonder if its assertion holds for small values of D. It is stated below for a specific integer D.

CONJECTURE 1.4 (WEAK SUNFLOWER CONJ. OVER $\mathbb{Z}_D$).
There exist $\varepsilon > 0$ and n_0, such that for every $n \geq n_0$, every collection $\mathcal{F}$ of vectors in $\mathbb{Z}_D^n$ of size $|\mathcal{F}| \geq D^{(1-\varepsilon)n}$ contains a 3-sunflower.

Of special importance is the Weak Sunflower Conjecture over $\mathbb{Z}_3$, which refers to the maximum possible size of a collection of vectors in the group $\mathbb{Z}_3^n$ with no 3-term arithmetic progressions (or, equivalently, non-trivial triples of vectors with zero sum modulo 3). The largest known construction of such collections has cardinality c^n for $c \approx 2.217$ [15]. An upper bound of $2 \cdot 3^n / n$ was shown by Meshulam in [29] (see [28] for a generalization of his result), and this was recently improved by Bateman and Katz to $O(3^n / n^{1+\varepsilon})$ for some constant $\varepsilon > 0$ [6].

Given the similarity between Conjecture 1.3 and the Weak Sunflower Conjecture over $\mathbb{Z}_D$, one might guess that the latter is true for small values of D. In fact, it was observed in [5] that for *every* $D \geq 3$, the assertion of the Weak Sunflower Conjecture over $\mathbb{Z}_D$ implies Conjecture 1.3. Nevertheless, Conjecture 1.3 seems to be much more likely to hold than Conjecture 1.4 for small values of D. For example, as explained in [5], the case of $D = 3$ can be viewed as a variant of the assertion that collections of $D^{(1-\varepsilon)n}$ vectors in $\mathbb{Z}_D^n$ must contain a 3-term arithmetic progression modulo D. However, a result of Salem and Spencer [32] implies that the latter is false for large values of D, namely, for $D > 2^{2/\varepsilon}$.

1.3 Our Contribution

In this work we introduce a new approach to proving lower bounds on the query complexity of testing k-cycle-freeness over $\mathbb{F}_p$ for general $k \geq 3$ and primes p. To do so, we show that certain collections of vectors in $\mathbb{Z}_D^n$, which are related to some of the sunflower conjectures described above, can be used to obtain perfect-matching-free vector families. For example, for the special case of triangle-freeness over $\mathbb{F}_2$, it is shown that a large collection of vectors in $\mathbb{Z}_4^n$ containing no 3-sunflowers implies a large perfect-matching-free family over $\mathbb{F}_2$, thus implying a lower bound on testing triangle-freeness over $\mathbb{F}_2$. In case that the size of the collection is $(4 - o(1))^n$, it yields a super-polynomial lower bound, as stated below.

THEOREM 1.5. *If the Weak Sunflower Conjecture (Conjecture 1.4) over $\mathbb{Z}_4$ is false, then the query complexity of the canonical tester for triangle-freeness over $\mathbb{F}_2$ for distance ε is super-polynomial in $1/\varepsilon$.*

As alluded to before, a refutation of the Weak Sunflower Conjecture over $\mathbb{Z}_D$ for small values of D would not be overly surprising, thus a super-polynomial lower bound on testing triangle-freeness over $\mathbb{F}_2$ might stem from the above theorem. Yet, even if the Weak Sunflower Conjecture over $\mathbb{Z}_4$ is true, large collections of vectors in $\mathbb{Z}_4^n$ containing no 3-sunflowers might provide improvements on the known lower bounds. Specifically, our results imply that any such collection of size $(c - o(1))^n$ for $c > 9/2^{4/3} \approx 3.57$ beats the best known lower bound of [20], but for $c < 4$ the obtained lower bound is only polynomial in $1/\varepsilon$ (see Theorem 3.4).

We then generalize Theorem 1.5 in a couple of ways. First, we obtain the following extension to triangle-freeness over $\mathbb{F}_p$, where p is an arbitrary prime.

THEOREM 1.6. *For every prime p, if the Weak Sunflower Conjecture (Conjecture 1.4) over $\mathbb{Z}_{p^2}$ is false, then the query complexity of the canonical tester for triangle-freeness over $\mathbb{F}_p$ for distance ε is super-polynomial in $1/\varepsilon$.*

Theorem 1.6 implies that for every prime p, a refutation of a certain Weak Sunflower Conjecture over $\mathbb{Z}_D$ (for $D = p^2$) implies a super-polynomial lower bound on the query complexity of the canonical tester for triangle-freeness over $\mathbb{F}_p$. Therefore, the unlikely event that for *some* prime p the query complexity is polynomial, implies Conjecture 1.3. On the other hand, it was shown in [5] that a conjecture of Coppersmith and Winograd, which was shown in [13] to imply that the matrix multiplication exponent is 2, implies that Conjecture 1.3 is false. Hence, the conjecture of [13] implies, if true, a super-polynomial lower bound on the number of queries made by the canonical tester for testing triangle-freeness over $\mathbb{F}_p$ for every prime p.

We note that for $p = 3$ one can show a stronger statement than that of Theorem 1.6. Indeed, in this case a super-polynomial lower bound follows quite easily from a refutation of the Weak Sunflower Conjecture over $\mathbb{Z}_3$ (which can be only weaker than its refutation over $\mathbb{Z}_9$; see Section 3). Interestingly, Alon et al. [5] studied a variant of this conjecture, called the *Multicolored* Sunflower Conjecture over $\mathbb{Z}_3$, and related it to the notion of *strong* uniquely solvable puzzles. It turns out that this multicolored conjecture coincides with our question on perfect-matching-free families over $\mathbb{F}_3$, and that their results imply an (unconditional) lower bound of $1/\varepsilon^{7.298}$ on the query complexity of the canonical tester for triangle-freeness over $\mathbb{F}_3$. Moreover, we use a result of [5] and the connection observed here to obtain that if the conjecture of [12] that strong USPs of optimal size exist is true, then the query complexity of the canonical tester for triangle-freeness over $\mathbb{F}_3$ is super-polynomial. This gives, in a sense, an affirmative answer to a question posed in [20].

The above results are also extended to testing k-cycle-freeness for every $k \geq 3$. We show how lower bounds on the query complexity of the canonical tester for k-cycle-freeness over $\mathbb{F}_p$ follow from the existence of certain collections of vectors in $\mathbb{Z}_D^n$ for an appropriate choice of D. Namely, we are interested in collections of vectors in $\mathbb{Z}_D^n$ for $D = p^{k-1}$, satisfying that for every k vectors in the collection (not all equal) there is some $i \in [n]$ for which the k vectors have exactly *two* distinct symbols in their ith entries. Notice that for $k = 3$ this simply means that the collection contains no 3-sunflowers. As before, for vector collections of optimal size $(D - o(1))^n$, the obtained lower bound on the query complexity turns out to be super-polynomial (see Section 3).

Finally, we show that the lower bound of Fu and Kleinberg [20] on testing triangle-freeness over $\mathbb{F}_2$ can be generalized to testing k-cycle-freeness over $\mathbb{F}_p$.

THEOREM 1.7. *For every $k \geq 3$ and a prime p, the query complexity of the canonical tester for k-cycle-freeness over $\mathbb{F}_p$ for distance ε is $\Omega(1/\varepsilon^{g(k)-o(1)})$ for*

$$g(k) = \frac{k - 1 - H(1/k)/\log_2 p}{1 - H(1/k)/\log_2 p},$$

where H stands for the binary entropy function.

The proof of Theorem 1.7 relies on a delicate extension of the construction of Coppersmith and Winograd [13] of uniquely solvable puzzles, which is based on a construction of Behrend [7], which found great interest in additive combinatorics. Interestingly, our construction requires an extension of Behrend's result, given in [1], that was used there for proving lower bounds on testing H-freeness of graphs.

1.4 Outline

The rest of the paper is organized as follows. In Section 2 we provide a background on the k-cycle-freeness problem, relate its one-function and multiple-function variants, present the notion of perfect-matching-free families of vectors (PMFs), and show how they imply lower bounds on the query complexity of the problem. In Section 3 we prove that PMFs can be constructed using certain collections of vectors in $\mathbb{Z}_D^n$ and derive relations to sunflower conjectures, including Theorem 1.6. Finally, in Section 4 we prove Theorem 1.7.

2. TESTING K-CYCLE-FREENESS

Let n and $k \geq 3$ be integers, and let $\mathbb{F}_p$ be the finite field of prime order p. A k-*cycle* of k functions $f_1, \ldots, f_k : \mathbb{F}_p^n \to \{0, 1\}$ is defined as k vectors $x_1, \ldots, x_k \in \mathbb{F}_p^n$ satisfying $x_1 + \cdots + x_k = 0$ and $f_i(x_i) = 1$ for every $1 \leq i \leq k$. If a k-tuple of functions $(f_1, \ldots, f_k)$ has no k-cycles, we say that it is k-*cycle-free*. Its *distance* from k-cycle-freeness is defined as $\min_{(g_1, \ldots, g_k)} \sum_{i=1}^{k} \text{dist}(f_i, g_i)$, where the minimum is over all the k-cycle-free k-tuples of functions $(g_1, \ldots, g_k)$, and $\text{dist}(f, g)$ denotes the fraction of points at which the functions f and g disagree. We say that a k-tuple of functions is ε-*far* from k-cycle-freeness if its distance from k-cycle-freeness is at least ε.

In the property testing problem of k-cycle-freeness over $\mathbb{F}_p$, the input is a k-tuple of functions $f_1, \ldots, f_k : \mathbb{F}_p^n \to \{0, 1\}$, and the goal is to accept k-cycle-free k-tuples of functions with probability at least $2/3$ and to reject k-tuple of functions which are ε-far from k-cycle-freeness with probability at least $2/3$. The *canonical tester* for k-cycle-freeness over $\mathbb{F}_p$ repeatedly picks uniformly and independently k vectors with zero sum and checks if they form a k-cycle of the input functions. If no k-cycle is found the tester accepts and otherwise it rejects.

2.1 Multiple-function vs. One-function

As mentioned before, one might consider the one-function variant of the k-cycle-freeness testing problem. A k-*cycle* of a function $f : \mathbb{F}_p^n \to \{0, 1\}$ is defined as k vectors that sum to the zero vector and are all mapped by f to 1. The input of the one-function variant is a single function $f : \mathbb{F}_p^n \to \{0, 1\}$, and the goal is to decide if f is k-cycle-free or ε-far from every k-cycle-free function. The canonical tester for k-cycle-freeness is naturally extended to the one-function case.

We observe that whenever p does not divide k, every k-tuple of functions can be transformed to a single function with the same number of k-cycles, a similar domain size, and a similar distance from k-cycle freeness. This implies that, in this case, the canonical testers for the multiple-function and the one-function variants of the problem have essentially the same query complexity.

LEMMA 2.1. *Let n be a positive integer, let $k \geq 3$ and p be fixed integers such that p is a prime that does not divide k, and let $\alpha > 0$ be a real number. Suppose that the k-tuple of functions $f_1, \ldots, f_k : \mathbb{F}_p^n \to \{0, 1\}$ is ε_1-far from k-cycle-freeness and that the canonical tester for k-cycle-freeness needs to make $q = \Omega(1/\varepsilon_1^{\alpha})$ queries to $(f_1, \ldots, f_k)$. Then, there exists a function $f : \mathbb{F}_p^{n+k-1} \to \{0, 1\}$, such that f is ε_2-far from k-cycle-freeness for $\varepsilon_2 = \varepsilon_1/p^{k-1}$, and the canonical tester needs to make $\Omega(1/\varepsilon_2^{\alpha})$ queries to f.*

Proof: For the functions $(f_1, \ldots, f_k)$, define $f : \mathbb{F}_p^{n+k-1} \to \{0, 1\}$ as follows. For all $y \in \mathbb{F}_p^n$ and $z \in \mathbb{F}_p^{k-1}$, let

$$f(y, z) = \begin{cases} f_i(y), & \text{if } z = e_i \text{ for } 1 \leq i \leq k-1, \\ f_k(y), & \text{if } z = -e_1 - \cdots - e_{k-1}, \\ 0, & \text{otherwise}, \end{cases}$$

where e_i denotes the vector whose entries are all 0 except the ith which is 1. First, observe that the only way to choose k vectors (repetitions are allowed) from the set $\{e_1, \ldots, e_{k-1}, -e_1 - \cdots - e_{k-1}\}$, so that their sum is the zero vector over $\mathbb{F}_p$, is to choose each of the vectors exactly once (because p does not divide k). This implies that all the k-cycles of f have exactly one point in each of the subfunctions $f_1, \ldots, f_k$. Hence there exists a bijection between the k-cycles of $f_1, \ldots, f_k$ and those of f. Since $(f_1, \ldots, f_k)$ is ε_1-far from k-cycle-freeness, it follows that f is ε_2-far from k-cycle-freeness for $\varepsilon_2 = \varepsilon_1/p^{k-1}$.

Let N_{cycles} be the number of k-cycles of $(f_1, \ldots, f_k)$ and of f. Since the query complexity of the canonical tester on a k-tuple of functions (resp. function) is proportional to the inverse of the number of k-cycles of the input k-tuple (resp. function), the query complexity on f is $\Omega(q')$ for

$$q' = p^{(n+k-1)(k-1)}/N_{\text{cycles}} = \Theta(p^{n(k-1)}/N_{\text{cycles}})$$
$$= \Theta(q) = \Omega(1/\varepsilon_1^{\alpha}) = \Omega(1/\varepsilon_2^{\alpha}). \qquad \blacksquare$$

In case that the prime p divides k, the one-function variant of k-cycle-freeness over $\mathbb{F}_p$ is quite easy. The reason is that in this case every vector in the support of a function $f : \mathbb{F}_p^n \to \{0,1\}$, taken with multiplicity k, forms a k-cycle of f. Thus, the problem reduces to deciding if the input function is the zero constant function or is ε-far from it. The tester that given a function f picks uniformly and independently $O(1/\varepsilon)$ random vectors in $\mathbb{F}_p^n$ and accepts if and only if they are all mapped by f to 0 implies the following.

CLAIM 2.2. *Let $k \geq 3$ be an integer divisible by a prime p. Then, for every $\varepsilon > 0$, there is a one-sided error tester for the one-function variant of k-cycle-freeness over $\mathbb{F}_p$ for distance ε with query complexity $O(1/\varepsilon)$.*

One may ask if a similar result can be shown once we consider only *non-trivial* cycles of f, that is, k vectors, not all equal, that sum to zero and are all mapped by f to 1. It turns out that if p divides k, $O(1/\varepsilon)$ queries are still sufficient to decide if a given function $f : \mathbb{F}_p^n \to \{0,1\}$ is free of non-trivial k-cycles or ε-far from this property. The reason is that the density of such functions turns out to be very small, as follows from the following (special case of a) theorem of Liu and Spencer [28].

THEOREM 2.3 ([28]). *For every n and a prime $p \geq 3$, if $A \subseteq \mathbb{F}_p^n$ contains no p vectors, not all equal, whose sum is the zero vector, then $|A| = o(p^n)$.*

Using the above theorem, it can be easily observed that if p divides k and $f : \mathbb{F}_p^n \to \{0,1\}$ is free of non-trivial k-cycles, then it is $o(1)$-close to the zero constant function. Thus, by the same tester that was used for Claim 2.2, we get query complexity $O(1/\varepsilon)$ and an "almost" one-sided error, that is, functions that are free of non-trivial k-cycles are accepted with probability that tends to 1 where n tends to infinity.

2.2 Perfect-Matching-Free Families

We now define the notion of *local perfect-matching-free* vector families, which can be used to obtain lower bounds on the query complexity of the canonical tester for k-cycle-freeness over $\mathbb{F}_p$.

DEFINITION 2.4. *An (n, m) local perfect-matching-free family (PMF) for k-cycles over $\mathbb{F}_p$ is a collection*

$$\{(x_i^{(1)}, x_i^{(2)}, \ldots, x_i^{(k)})\}_{i \in [m]},$$

such that for every $i \in [m]$, $x_i^{(1)}, x_i^{(2)}, \ldots, x_i^{(k)}$ are k vectors in $\mathbb{F}_p^n$ whose sum is zero, and for every $i_1, i_2, \ldots, i_k \in [m]$, if the sum of the vectors $x_{i_1}^{(1)}, x_{i_2}^{(2)}, \ldots, x_{i_k}^{(k)}$ is zero then $i_1 = i_2 = \cdots = i_k$. The local PMF capacity for k-cycles over $\mathbb{F}_p$ is the largest constant c for which there exist $(n, (c - o(1))^n)$ local PMFs for k-cycles over $\mathbb{F}_p$ for infinitely many values of n.

Two remarks are in order.

REMARK 2.5. *If the local PMF capacity for k-cycles over $\mathbb{F}_p$ is c, then there exist $(n, (c - o(1))^n)$ local PMFs for k-cycles over $\mathbb{F}_p$ for every sufficiently large value of n (and not only for infinitely many of them). To see this, for every n, denote by m_n the largest integer for which there exists an (n, m_n) local PMF for k-cycles over $\mathbb{F}_p$. Since $m_{n+n'} \geq m_n \cdot m_{n'}$, we may apply Fekete's lemma (see, e.g., [36, Lemma 11.6]) to show that the limit of $m_n^{1/n}$, as n tends to infinity, exists and equals the capacity c.*

REMARK 2.6. *Our definition of local PMFs is slightly different from the definition of PMFs given in [10]. Namely, the requirement in the definition of PMFs in [10] is that for every k permutations $\pi_1, \ldots, \pi_k$ of $[m]$, either $\pi_1 = \cdots = \pi_k$, or there exists an $i \in [m]$ for which the sum $x_{\pi_1(i)}^{(1)} + \cdots + x_{\pi_k(i)}^{(k)}$ is nonzero. Clearly, every local PMF is a PMF. Whereas the other direction does not hold, it is easy to see that the local PMF capacity for k-cycles over $\mathbb{F}_p$ equals the PMF capacity for k-cycles over $\mathbb{F}_p$. For completeness, we include a short proof (which resembles that of [12, Proposition 6.3]), and throughout the paper we prefer to consider the notion of local PMFs, mainly for simplicity of presentation.*

CLAIM 2.7. *The local PMF capacity for k-cycles over $\mathbb{F}_p$ equals the PMF capacity for k-cycles over $\mathbb{F}_p$.*

Proof: Clearly, the PMF capacity for k-cycles over $\mathbb{F}_p$ is at least as large as the local PMF capacity for k-cycles over $\mathbb{F}_p$. For the other direction, let $\mathcal{F}$ be an (n, m) PMF for k-cycles over $\mathbb{F}_p$ for $m = (c - o(1))^n$. For every permutation π of $[m]$ consider the k-tuple of vectors of length nm, obtained by concatenating the m k-tuples of vectors in $\mathcal{F}$ ordered according to π. Let $\mathcal{G}$ be the collection of all the k-tuples obtained this way. Observe that $\mathcal{G}$ is an $(nm, m!)$ local PMF for k-cycles over $\mathbb{F}_p$ and that

$$m! = m^{(1-o(1))m} = (c - o(1))^{(1-o(1))nm} = (c - o(1))^{nm}.$$

Thus, the local PMF capacity for k-cycles over $\mathbb{F}_p$ is at least c, and we are done. ∎

The following lemma and corollary show how local PMFs imply lower bounds for testing k-cycle-freeness. Similar statements were shown in [10], and we include here the proofs for completeness.

LEMMA 2.8. *Let $k \geq 3$ be an integer, and let p be a prime. Suppose that there exists an (n, m) local PMF for k-cycles over $\mathbb{F}_p$. Then, the query complexity of the canonical tester for k-cycle-freeness over $\mathbb{F}_p$ for distance ε on n variable functions is $\Omega(1/\varepsilon^\alpha)$ for $\varepsilon = m/p^n$ and $\alpha = \frac{k-1-(\log_p m)/n}{1-(\log_p m)/n}$.*

Proof: Let $\mathcal{F} = \{(x_i^{(1)}, x_i^{(2)}, \ldots, x_i^{(k)})\}_{i \in [m]}$ be an (n, m) local PMF for k-cycles over $\mathbb{F}_p$. For every $1 \leq j \leq k$, let $f_j : \mathbb{F}_p^n \to \{0,1\}$ be the characteristic function of the set $\{x_i^{(j)}\}_{i \in [m]}$. By definition of local PMFs, the number of k-cycles of the k-tuple of functions $(f_1, \ldots, f_k)$ is m, and these cycles are pairwise disjoint. Hence, in order to remove all the m cycles, one has to change at least m values of the functions, so this k-tuple is ε-far from k-cycle-freeness for $\varepsilon = \frac{m}{p^n}$. On the other hand, the probability that one iteration of the canonical tester, applied to $(f_1, \ldots, f_k)$, finds a k-cycle is $\frac{m}{p^{(k-1)n}}$, so its query complexity is $\Omega(q)$, for

$$q = \frac{p^{(k-1)n}}{m} = p^{(k-1)n - \log_p m} = (1/\varepsilon)^{\frac{k-1-(\log_p m)/n}{1-(\log_p m)/n}}.$$

∎

COROLLARY 2.9. *Let $k \geq 3$ and p be fixed integers, such that p is prime. If the local PMF capacity for k-cycles over $\mathbb{F}_p$ is c, then for every $d < c$, the query complexity of the canonical tester for k-cycle-freeness over $\mathbb{F}_p$ for distance ε*

is $\Omega(1/\varepsilon^\alpha)$ where $\alpha = \frac{k-1-\log_p d}{1-\log_p d}$. *Furthermore, for every sufficiently small ε there exists an $n_0 = n_0(\varepsilon)$ such that for every $n \geq n_0$ the lower bound holds for k-tuples of n variable functions that depend on all of their input variables. In particular, if the local PMF capacity for k-cycles over $\mathbb{F}_p$ is p, then the query complexity of the canonical tester for k-cycle-freeness over $\mathbb{F}_p$ for distance ε is super-polynomial in $1/\varepsilon$.*

Proof: Let c denote the local PMF capacity for k-cycles over $\mathbb{F}_p$, and take an arbitrary $d < c$. Using Remark 2.5, for every sufficiently large n there exists an $(n, \lceil d^n \rceil)$ local PMF for k-cycles over $\mathbb{F}_p$. Now, for a given sufficiently small ε, let $n_0 = n_0(\varepsilon)$ be the largest integer satisfying $\varepsilon \leq \frac{\lceil d^{n_0} \rceil}{p^{n_0}}$. For this n_0 there exists an $(n_0, \lceil d^{n_0} \rceil)$ local PMF for k-cycle-freeness over $\mathbb{F}_p$. By Lemma 2.8, the corresponding k-tuple of functions $f_1, \ldots, f_k : \mathbb{F}_p^{n_0} \to \{0,1\}$ is ε-far from k-cycle-freeness and requires $\Omega(1/\varepsilon^\alpha)$ queries of the canonical tester for α as in the statement of the corollary.

It remains to show that the above lower bound can be extended to k-tuples of functions with domain $\mathbb{F}_p^n$ for every $n \geq n_0$. For every $1 \leq j \leq k$ define the function $g_j : \mathbb{F}_p^n \to \{0,1\}$ such that $g_j(y) = 1$ if and only if $y = (x, z)$ for $x \in \mathbb{F}_p^{n_0}$ and $z \in \mathbb{F}_p^{n-n_0}$ satisfying $f_j(x) = 1$ and $\sum_{i=1}^{n-n_0} z_i = 0$.[1] The k-tuple of functions $(g_1, \ldots, g_k)$ has at least $\varepsilon \cdot p^{n_0} \cdot (p^{n-n_0-1})^{k-1}$ k-cycles, and every vector of these cycles belongs to $(p^{n-n_0-1})^{k-2}$ of the cycles. Therefore, $(g_1, \ldots, g_k)$ is ε'-far from k-cycle-freeness for $\varepsilon' = \varepsilon/p = \Theta(\varepsilon)$ and requires query complexity $\Omega(1/\varepsilon^\alpha)$, thus the required lower bound holds for every sufficiently small distance parameter. In addition, it is easy to verify that the k-tuple $(g_1, \ldots, g_k)$ depends on all of its input variables, as required.

Finally, observe that if the local PMF capacity for k-cycles over $\mathbb{F}_p$ is p, then for every $\alpha > 0$, the query complexity of the canonical tester for k-cycle-freeness over $\mathbb{F}_p$ for some distance ε is $\Omega(1/\varepsilon^\alpha)$, thus it is super-polynomial in $1/\varepsilon$. ∎

We turn to define (strong) uniquely solvable puzzles (USPs). Then we state a theorem of Alon et al. [5] that says that strong USPs imply local PMFs for triangles over $\mathbb{F}_3$ (in their language, collections of ordered 3-sunflowers in $\mathbb{Z}_3^n \times \mathbb{Z}_3^n \times \mathbb{Z}_3^n$ containing no *multicolored* sunflowers).

DEFINITION 2.10. *An n-dimensional uniquely solvable puzzle (USP) is a collection of vectors $\{x_i\}_{i \in [m]}$ in $\mathbb{Z}_3^n$ satisfying that for every three permutations π_1, π_2, π_3 of $[m]$, either $\pi_1 = \pi_2 = \pi_3$, or there exist $i \in [m]$ and $j \in [n]$ for which at least two of $(x_{\pi_1(i)})_j = 1$, $(x_{\pi_2(i)})_j = 2$, and $(x_{\pi_3(i)})_j = 3$ hold. A strong USP is defined similarly replacing the "at least two" by "exactly two". The (strong) USP capacity is the largest constant c for which there exist n-dimensional (strong) USPs of size $(c - o(1))^n$ for infinitely many values of n.*

THEOREM 2.11 ([5]). *If the strong USP capacity is at least c, then the local PMF capacity for triangles over $\mathbb{F}_3$ is at least $2^{2/3} \cdot c$.*

It is known that the strong USP capacity is at least $2^{2/3}$ [12, Proposition 3.8]. Hence, by Theorem 2.11, the local PMF

---

[1]This is a slight generalization of a construction due to Jakob Nordström (Private communication, 2010).

capacity for triangles over $\mathbb{F}_3$ is at least $2^{4/3}$. By Corollary 2.9, it follows that the query complexity of the canonical tester for triangle-freeness over $\mathbb{F}_3$ for distance ε is at least $1/\varepsilon^{7.298}$. Cohn, Kleinberg, Szegedy, and Umans conjectured that the strong USP capacity is $3/2^{2/3}$ and proved in [12] that their conjecture implies that the exponent of matrix multiplication is 2. By Theorem 2.11, if their conjecture is true then the local PMF capacity for triangles over $\mathbb{F}_3$ is 3, and the latter yields, by Corollary 2.9, a super-polynomial lower bound on the query complexity of the canonical tester for triangle-freeness over $\mathbb{F}_3$.

3. SUNFLOWER CONJECTURES VS. LOCAL PMFS

In this section we prove that local PMFs for k-cycles over $\mathbb{F}_p$ can be constructed from certain collections of vectors in $\mathbb{Z}_D^n$, some of which are related to sunflower conjectures of Alon et al. [5]. The idea behind the construction is quite simple: every vector of these collections is mapped to a k-tuple of vectors, in a way that every symbol of $\mathbb{Z}_D$ is replaced by certain k vectors over $\mathbb{F}_p$.

We need the following lemma and the corollary that follows it. We use here the notation $A^{(\ell)}$ to denote the ℓth column of a matrix A.

LEMMA 3.1. *For every prime p and a positive integer k, there exists a collection of p^k matrices $A_1, A_2, \ldots, A_{p^k}$ in $\mathbb{F}_p^{k \times k}$ such that for every $1 \leq i \neq j \leq p^k$ and every non-empty set $I \subseteq [k]$ it holds that*

$$\sum_{\ell \in I} A_i^{(\ell)} \neq \sum_{\ell \in I} A_j^{(\ell)}.$$

Proof: Denote $q = p^k$, and let $\alpha_1, \ldots, \alpha_q$ be the q elements of the field $\mathbb{F}_q$. Let $enc : \mathbb{F}_q \to \mathbb{F}_p^k$ be the natural encoding of the elements of $\mathbb{F}_q$ as distinct vectors in $\mathbb{F}_p^k$. This encoding is linear, that is, $enc(0) = (0, \ldots, 0)$ and $enc(x + y) = enc(x) + enc(y)$ for every $x, y \in \mathbb{F}_q$. Let β be a generator of the multiplicative group $\mathbb{F}_q^*$, and notice that the set $\{1, \beta, \beta^2, \ldots, \beta^{k-1}\}$ is linearly independent over $\mathbb{F}_p$.

Now, for every $1 \leq i \leq q$, define the k by k matrix A_i as the matrix whose columns are

$$enc(\alpha_i), enc(\alpha_i \cdot \beta), enc(\alpha_i \cdot \beta^2), \ldots, enc(\alpha_i \cdot \beta^{k-1}).$$

To prove that the collection $A_1, A_2, \ldots, A_q$ satisfies the requirement, take $1 \leq i \neq j \leq q$ and a non-empty set $I \subseteq [k]$. Assume, for the sake of contradiction, that the matrices A_i and A_j have the same sum of columns that correspond to indices in I. Viewing these sums as elements of $\mathbb{F}_q$, it follows that

$$\alpha_i \cdot \sum_{\ell \in I} \beta^{\ell-1} = \alpha_j \cdot \sum_{\ell \in I} \beta^{\ell-1}.$$

By linear independence, it follows that $\sum_{\ell \in I} \beta^{\ell-1}$ is nonzero, thus $\alpha_i = \alpha_j$, a contradiction. ∎

COROLLARY 3.2. *For every prime p and a positive integer k, there exists a collection of p^k matrices $B_1, B_2, \ldots, B_{p^k}$ in $\mathbb{F}_p^{k \times (k+1)}$ such that*

1. *for every $1 \leq i \leq p^k$, the sum of the columns of B_i is the zero vector, and*

2. for every $1 \leq i \neq j \leq p^k$ and every non-empty set $I \subset [k+1]$, the sum

$$\sum_{\ell \in I} B_i^{(\ell)} + \sum_{\ell \in [k+1] \setminus I} B_j^{(\ell)}$$

is nonzero.

Proof: By Lemma 3.1, there exists a collection of p^k matrices $A_1, A_2, \ldots, A_{p^k}$ in $\mathbb{F}_p^{k \times k}$ such that for every $1 \leq i \neq j \leq p^k$ and every non-empty set $I \subseteq [k]$ it holds that

$$\sum_{\ell \in I} A_i^{(\ell)} \neq \sum_{\ell \in I} A_j^{(\ell)}.$$

For every $1 \leq i \leq p^k$ define the k by $k+1$ matrix B_i as the matrix whose columns are

$$A_i^{(1)}, A_i^{(2)}, \ldots, A_i^{(k)}, -\sum_{\ell=1}^{k} A_i^{(\ell)}.$$

The collection $B_1, B_2, \ldots, B_{p^k}$ trivially satisfies Item 1. To prove that Item 2 is also satisfied, take $1 \leq i \neq j \leq p^k$ and a non-empty set $I \subset [k+1]$, and assume by contradiction that the sum of the columns of B_i corresponding to indices in I and the columns of B_j corresponding to indices in $[k+1] \setminus I$ is the zero vector. Assume without loss of generality that $k+1 \notin I$, and use Item 1 to observe that

$$\sum_{\ell \in I} A_i^{(\ell)} = \sum_{\ell \in I} B_i^{(\ell)} = -\sum_{\ell \in [k+1] \setminus I} B_j^{(\ell)} = \sum_{\ell \in I} B_j^{(\ell)} = \sum_{\ell \in I} A_j^{(\ell)},$$

in contradiction to the property of the collection $A_1, A_2, \ldots, A_{p^k}$. ∎

Now, equipped with Corollary 3.2, we are ready to show how certain collections of vectors in $\mathbb{Z}_D^n$ can be transformed to local PMFs over $\mathbb{F}_p$. An important property of the transformation is that it preserves optimal capacity, namely, vector collections of optimal size $(D - o(1))^n$ are transformed to local PMFs of optimal capacity p.

THEOREM 3.3. *Let $k \geq 3$ be an integer, and let p be a prime. Assume that for infinitely many values of n there exists a collection $\mathcal{F}$ of $(c - o(1))^n$ vectors in $\mathbb{Z}_{p^{k-1}}^n$ such that for every k vectors $v_1, \ldots, v_k \in \mathcal{F}$, not all equal, there exists an $i \in [n]$ for which $|\{(v_1)_i, \ldots, (v_k)_i\}| = 2$. Then, the local PMF capacity for k-cycles over $\mathbb{F}_p$ is at least $c^{1/(k-1)}$.*

Proof: Let $\mathcal{F} \subseteq \mathbb{Z}_{p^{k-1}}^n$ be a collection of $(c - o(1))^n$ vectors satisfying the condition given in the theorem. By Corollary 3.2, applied with $k-1$, there exists a collection of p^{k-1} matrices $B_1, B_2, \ldots, B_{p^{k-1}}$ in $\mathbb{F}_p^{(k-1) \times k}$ satisfying that (1) for every $1 \leq i \leq p^{k-1}$, the sum of the columns of B_i is the zero vector, and (2) for every $1 \leq i \neq j \leq p^{k-1}$ and every non-empty set $I \subset [k]$, the sum $\sum_{\ell \in I} B_i^{(\ell)} + \sum_{\ell \in [k] \setminus I} B_j^{(\ell)}$ is nonzero.

Consider the function $f : \mathbb{Z}_{p^{k-1}}^n \to \mathbb{F}_p^{n(k-1) \times k}$ that maps every vector $v \in \mathbb{Z}_{p^{k-1}}^n$ to the concatenation of the n matrices $B_{v_1}, B_{v_2}, \ldots, B_{v_n}$. We claim that the set $\mathcal{G} = \{f(v) \mid v \in \mathcal{F}\}$ is an $(n(k-1), (c - o(1))^n)$ local PMF for k-cycles over $\mathbb{F}_p$, thus the PMF capacity for k-cycles over $\mathbb{F}_p$ is at least $c^{1/(k-1)}$.

To see this, first observe that property (1) of the matrices $B_1, B_2, \ldots, B_{p^{k-1}}$ implies that the sum of the k columns of every $f(v)$ is the zero vector. Second, let $f(v_1), \ldots, f(v_k)$ be

k elements, not all equal, of $\mathcal{G}$. Our goal is to prove that the sum of the vectors $f(v_1)^{(1)}, \ldots, f(v_k)^{(k)}$ is nonzero. Since f is injective, the vectors $v_1, \ldots, v_k$ are not all equal, so there is an $i \in [n]$ for which $|\{(v_1)_i, \ldots, (v_k)_i\}| = 2$. Hence, the ith blocks (of length $k-1$) of the matrices $f(v_1), \ldots, f(v_k)$ contain exactly two distinct matrices B_j and $B_{j'}$. By property (2), the sum of the ith blocks of the vectors $f(v_1)^{(1)}, \ldots, f(v_k)^{(k)}$ is nonzero, hence the sum of these vectors is also nonzero, and we are done. ∎

Theorem 3.3 gives us a method to derive lower bounds on the query complexity of the canonical tester for k-cycle-freeness over $\mathbb{F}_p$ from certain collections of vectors in $\mathbb{Z}_{p^{k-1}}^n$. In the special case of $k = 3$, the vectors are in $\mathbb{Z}_{p^2}^n$, and for every three vectors, not all equal, there is a coordinate in which the three symbols are not all equal and are not all distinct. This exactly means that the three vectors do not form a 3-sunflower (see Section 1.2), yielding the following result.

THEOREM 3.4. *Let p be a prime, and assume that for infinitely many values of n there exists a collection of $(c - o(1))^n$ vectors in $\mathbb{Z}_{p^2}^n$ containing no 3-sunflowers. Then, for every $d < \sqrt{c}$, the query complexity of the canonical tester for triangle-freeness over $\mathbb{F}_p$ for distance ε is $\Omega(1/\varepsilon^\alpha)$ where $\alpha = \frac{2 - \log_p d}{1 - \log_p d}$.*

Proof: By Theorem 3.3, the assumption implies that the local PMF capacity for triangles over $\mathbb{F}_p$ is at least $\sqrt{c}$. Corollary 2.9 completes the proof. ∎

Observe that if the Weak Sunflower Conjecture over $\mathbb{Z}_D$ (Conjecture 1.4) is false for $D = p^2$, it follows from the above theorem that the query complexity of the canonical tester for triangle-freeness over $\mathbb{F}_p$ for distance ε is super-polynomial in $1/\varepsilon$, confirming Theorem 1.6.

For the special case of $p = 3$, it is easy to get a local PMF for triangles from a collection of vectors in $\mathbb{Z}_3^n$ containing no 3-sunflowers. Indeed, for such a collection $\mathcal{F}$, the set $\{(x, x, x)\}_{x \in \mathcal{F}}$ forms a local PMF for triangles over $\mathbb{F}_3$ of the same size. Thus, in case that the Weak Sunflower Conjecture over $\mathbb{Z}_3$ is false, a super-polynomial lower bound on the query complexity of the canonical tester follows. Note that this assumption can be only weaker than the assumption that the Weak Sunflower Conjecture over $\mathbb{Z}_9$ is false. The reason is that given a collection of $(9 - o(1))^n$ vectors in $\mathbb{Z}_9^n$ containing no 3-sunflowers one can replace every symbol of $\mathbb{Z}_9$ in the vectors by its base-3 representation to obtain a collection of $(3 - o(1))^{2n}$ vectors in $\mathbb{Z}_3^{2n}$ containing no 3-sunflowers.

We note that for $k \geq 4$ the property required in Theorem 3.3 from the collection $\mathcal{F} \subseteq \mathbb{Z}_D^n$ does not coincide with freeness of k-sunflowers. Indeed, the collection should satisfy that for every k vectors $v_1, \ldots, v_k \in \mathcal{F}$, not all equal, there exists a coordinate in which they contain exactly 2 distinct symbols. On the other hand, freeness of k-sunflowers means that for every such k vectors, there exists a coordinate in which the number of distinct symbols is in the range from 2 to $k - 1$.

It is natural to ask if one can relate local PMFs for k-cycles to collections of vectors with no k-sunflowers for $k \geq 4$. It seems, though, that the proof technique of Theorem 3.3 cannot achieve this in a way that preserves optimal capacity. To see this, observe that such an extension requires a mapping from $\mathbb{Z}_D$ to D matrices in $\mathbb{F}_p^{\ell \times k}$ for $D = p^\ell$ (because the transformation increases the length of the vectors by a factor of ℓ, and capacity D should be mapped to capacity p). The matrices returned by this mapping have to satisfy the following two properties: (1) the sum of the columns of each of the matrices should be zero, and (2) for every k of these matrices $B_1, \ldots, B_k$, not all equal and not all distinct, the sum of the vectors $B_1^{(1)}, \ldots, B_k^{(k)}$ should be nonzero. However, it is not difficult to show that such a collection of matrices does not exist for $k \geq 4$. First observe that the p^ℓ matrices should contain all the p^ℓ distinct vectors of $\mathbb{F}_p^\ell$ in each of their k columns, since otherwise two of the matrices contradict property (2). Now, take two arbitrary distinct matrices B_i and B_j, and consider the sum, say, of the first $k-2$ columns of B_i and the $(k-1)$th column of B_j. The unique vector that completes this sum to zero is the kth column of one of the p^ℓ matrices, so we again contradict property (2).

4. A LOWER BOUND ON TESTING K-CYCLE FREENESS

As mentioned before, the best known lower bound on the query complexity of the canonical tester for testing triangle-freeness over $\mathbb{F}_2$ for distance ε is $1/\varepsilon^{13.239}$, as was shown by Fu and Kleinberg [20]. Their proof is crucially based on a construction of uniquely solvable puzzles of Coppersmith and Winogard [13], which employs a construction of Behrend [7] of dense sets of integers with no 3-term arithmetic progressions. In this section we generalize the lower bound of [20] to testing k-cycle-freeness over $\mathbb{F}_p$ for every $k \geq 3$ and a prime p.

We need here a few notations. For a vector $v \in \mathbb{Z}_k^n$ we denote by $v|_j = \{i \in [n] \mid v_i = j\}$ the set of coordinates at which v has symbol $j \in \mathbb{Z}_k$. Note that for every vector $v \in \mathbb{Z}_k^n$, the sets $v|_1, \ldots, v|_k$ form a partition of $[n]$. In case that the sets $v|_1, \ldots, v|_k$ have the same size we say that the vector v is *balanced*. Finally, let H stand for the binary entropy function, defined by $H(p) = -p \log_2 p - (1-p) \log_2 (1-p)$ for $0 \leq p \leq 1$.

Let us start with a generalization of the construction of [13], stated below. Note that the case of $k = 3$ gives the construction of [13], which implies a uniquely solvable puzzle as was defined for the purpose of fast matrix multiplication (see Definition 2.10).

THEOREM 4.1. *For every fixed integer $k \geq 3$ and a sufficiently large n, there exists a collection $\mathcal{F}$ of $(2^{H(1/k)} - o(1))^{nk}$ balanced vectors in $\mathbb{Z}_k^{nk}$ such that for every k vectors $v_1, \ldots, v_k \in \mathcal{F}$, the sets $v_1|_1, \ldots, v_k|_k$ form a partition of $[n \cdot k]$ if and only if $v_1 = \cdots = v_k$.*

REMARK 4.2. *The cardinality of $\mathcal{F}$ in Theorem 4.1 is optimal up to the $o(1)$ term. Indeed, the requirement on $\mathcal{F}$ implies that the, say, $v|_1$'s for $v \in \mathcal{F}$ are distinct subsets of size n of $[n \cdot k]$, so $|\mathcal{F}| \leq \binom{nk}{n} \approx 2^{H(1/k)nk}$.*

In the proof of Theorem 4.1 we use the following extension of Behrend's result [7].

LEMMA 4.3 (LEMMA 3.1 IN [1]). *For every fixed integer $r \geq 2$ and every positive integer m, there exists a set*

$B \subseteq [m]$ *of size* $|B| \geq \frac{m}{e^{10\sqrt{\log m \log r}}}$ *with no non-trivial[2] solutions to the equation* $x_1 + x_2 + \cdots + x_r = r \cdot x_{r+1}$.

Proof of Theorem 4.1: For a sufficiently large n denote $N = n \cdot k$, and let M be the smallest prime which satisfies

$$M > c(k) \cdot \binom{n(k-1)}{n, \ldots, n}^{1/(k-2)}, \quad (1)$$

where $c = c(k)$ is a constant that depends solely on k and will be determined later. As is well known, M is at most twice its lower bound in (1). By Lemma 4.3, applied with $m = \lfloor M/(k-1) \rfloor$, there exists a set $B = \{b_1, \ldots, b_{|B|}\} \subseteq [m]$ of size $|B| = m^{1-o(1)} = M^{1-o(1)}$ with no non-trivial solutions to the equation

$$x_1 + x_2 + \cdots + x_{k-1} = (k-1) \cdot x_k. \quad (2)$$

Since B is contained in $[m]$, it contains no non-trivial solutions to Equation (2) taken modulo M as well.

Consider the set $\mathcal{I}$ of all the subsets of $[N]$ of size n, and identify the sets in $\mathcal{I}$ with their characteristic vectors in $\{0,1\}^N$. Let $w_1, \ldots, w_N$ and $c_1, \ldots, c_k$ be integers chosen at random uniformly and independently from $\mathbb{F}_M$, and denote $w = (w_1, \ldots, w_N)$. For these numbers we define k mappings $\beta_1, \ldots, \beta_k : \mathcal{I} \to \mathbb{F}_M$ as follows. For $1 \leq j \leq k-1$, β_j is defined by $\beta_j(I) = \langle w, I \rangle + c_j \mod M$, and β_k is defined by

$$\beta_k(I) = \left(\langle w, [N] \setminus I \rangle + \sum_{j=1}^{k-1} c_j \right) / (k-1) \mod M$$

The construction involves two steps. First, for every $1 \leq i \leq |B|$, let L_i denote the set of all k-tuples of sets $(I_1, \ldots, I_k) \in \mathcal{I}^k$ satisfying $I_1 \cup \cdots \cup I_k = [N]$ and $\beta_j(I_j) = b_i$ for every $1 \leq j \leq k$. Second, remove from every L_i all the k-tuples $(I_1, \ldots, I_k) \in L_i$ that share some set I_j with other k-tuples in L_i, that is, satisfy $I_j = J_j$ for some j and $(J_1, \ldots, J_k) \in L_i$. We denote by $L_i' \subseteq L_i$ the obtained set.

Every partition $(I_1, \ldots, I_k) \in \mathcal{I}^k$ of $[N]$ can be naturally encoded by a balanced vector v in $\mathbb{Z}_k^N$ defined by $v|_j = I_j$ for every $1 \leq j \leq k$. Define $\mathcal{F} \subset \mathbb{Z}_k^N$ to be the set of partitions in the union $\cup_{1 \leq i \leq |B|} L_i'$ encoded as vectors in $\mathbb{Z}_k^N$. We first show that $\mathcal{F}$ satisfies the property required in Theorem 4.1, and then analyze its expected size.

CLAIM 4.4. *For every k vectors $v_1, \ldots, v_k \in \mathcal{F}$, the sets $v_1|_1, \ldots, v_k|_k$ form a partition of $[N]$ if and only if $v_1 = \cdots = v_k$.*

Proof: It is clear that if $v_1 = \cdots = v_k$ then $v_1|_1, \ldots, v_k|_k$ form a partition of $[N]$. For the other direction, consider k vectors $v_1, \ldots, v_k \in \mathcal{F}$, and denote $I_j = v_j|_j$ for every $1 \leq j \leq k$. Assume by contradiction that the vectors are not all equal and that $(I_1, \ldots, I_k) \in \mathcal{I}^k$ is a partition of $[N]$. For every $1 \leq j \leq k$ denote $b_j = \beta_j(I_j)$, and observe that

$$\sum_{j=1}^{k-1} b_j = \sum_{j=1}^{k-1} \beta_j(I_j) = \sum_{j=1}^{k-1} \langle w, I_j \rangle + \sum_{j=1}^{k-1} c_j$$

$$= \langle w, [N] \setminus I_k \rangle + \sum_{j=1}^{k-1} c_j = (k-1) \cdot \beta_k(I_k)$$

$$= (k-1) \cdot b_k,$$

---

[2] A *trivial* solution is a solution that satisfies $x_1 = \cdots = x_{r+1}$.

where all the equalities hold modulo M. This implies that the numbers $b_1, \ldots, b_k \in B$ satisfy Equation (2) modulo M, hence by our choice of B, they must be all equal. Therefore, the vectors $v_1, \ldots, v_k$ correspond to k partitions in the same set L_i'. This implies that the partition $(I_1, \ldots, I_k)$ belongs to L_i and shares a subset of $\mathcal{I}$ with each of the partitions that correspond to the vectors $v_1, \ldots, v_k$. However, this implies that all these partitions were not added to L_i' in the second step of the construction. Hence all the v_i's are equal, in contradiction. ∎

We turn to analyze the expected size of the collection $\mathcal{F}$. We start with the size of the sets L_i (before performing the second step of the construction).

CLAIM 4.5. *For every* $1 \leq i \leq |B|$, *the expected size of the set* L_i *is* $\binom{nk}{n, \ldots, n} \cdot M^{-(k-1)}$.

Proof: Fix $1 \leq i \leq |B|$, and let $(I_1, \ldots, I_k) \in \mathcal{I}^k$ be a partition of $[N]$. Recall that $(I_1, \ldots, I_k)$ is added to L_i if $\beta_j(I_j) = b_i$ for every $1 \leq j \leq k$. We claim that this happens with probability $M^{-(k-1)}$. Indeed, the $k-1$ events $\beta_j(I_j) = b_i$, $1 \leq j \leq k-1$, are independent, each of them occurs with probability M^{-1}, and once they all occur, it follows that $\beta_k(I_k) = b_i$ as well. The number of partitions of $[N]$ in $\mathcal{I}^k$ is $\binom{nk}{n, \ldots, n}$, so by linearity of expectation the claim follows. ∎

We now turn to estimate the expected number of partitions that are removed from every L_i in the second step of the construction. To do so, we have to consider the probability of two distinct partitions in $\mathcal{I}^k$ that share some subset to belong to L_i. However, this probability depends on the specific pair of partitions. Indeed, sharing more than one subset of the partitions, or even a certain union of the subsets, might increase this probability. Hence, we need the following definition.

DEFINITION 4.6. *Let* $t_1 \leq \ldots \leq t_\ell$ *be* ℓ *positive integers satisfying* $\sum_{r=1}^{\ell} t_r = k$. *We say that two partitions* $(I_1, \ldots, I_k)$ *and* $(J_1, \ldots, J_k)$ *of* $[N]$ *in* $\mathcal{I}^k$ *are* $(t_1, \ldots, t_\ell)$-*similar if there exists a partition of* $[k]$ *into* ℓ *sets* $T_1, \ldots, T_\ell$ *of sizes* $t_1, \ldots, t_\ell$ *respectively, such that for some permutation* $\pi : [k] \to [k]$,

$$\cup_{i \in T_r} I_i = \cup_{i \in T_r} J_{\pi(i)} \qquad (3)$$

for every $1 \leq r \leq \ell$, *and, in addition, no refinement of the partition* $T_1, \ldots, T_\ell$ *satisfies (3) for any permutation* π.

CLAIM 4.7. *Let* $(I_1, \ldots, I_k)$ *and* $(J_1, \ldots, J_k)$ *be distinct* $(t_1, \ldots, t_\ell)$-*similar partitions of* $[N]$ *in* $\mathcal{I}^k$ *for some* ℓ *positive integers* $t_1 \leq \ldots \leq t_\ell$ *satisfying* $\sum_{r=1}^{\ell} t_r = k$. *Then, for every* $1 \leq i \leq |B|$, *the following holds.*

1. *For* $1 \leq \ell \leq k-1$, *the probability that the two partitions are in* L_i *is at most* $M^{-(k-1)} \cdot M^{-(k-\ell)}$.

2. *For* $\ell = k$, *the probability that the two partitions are in* L_i *is at most* $M^{-(k-1)} \cdot M^{-1}$.

Proof: Let $(I_1, \ldots, I_k)$ and $(J_1, \ldots, J_k)$ be distinct $(t_1, \ldots, t_\ell)$-similar partitions of $[N]$ in $\mathcal{I}^k$, and let $T_1, \ldots, T_\ell$ and π be the corresponding partition and permutation of $[k]$ as in Definition 4.6.

For Item 1, we fix the values of $c_1, \ldots, c_k$ and analyze the probability that the two partitions $(I_1, \ldots, I_k)$ and $(J_1, \ldots, J_k)$ are in L_i over the random choice of $w_1, \ldots, w_N$. First, notice that the $k-1$ events $\beta_j(I_j) = b_i$ for $1 \leq j \leq k-1$ are independent, occur with probability M^{-1} each, and imply the event $\beta_k(I_k) = b_i$. So the probability that $(I_1, \ldots, I_k) \in L_i$ is $M^{-(k-1)}$. For $1 \leq r \leq \ell$, let A_r denote the event that the equalities $\beta_{\pi(j)}(J_{\pi(j)}) = b_i$ hold for every $j \in T_r$. It can be shown that for every $1 \leq r \leq \ell$, the probability that A_r occurs conditioned on the event $(I_1, \ldots, I_k) \in L_i$ and on $A_1, \ldots, A_{r-1}$ is $M^{-(t_r-1)}$. Indeed, since no refinement of the partition $T_1, \ldots, T_\ell$ satisfies the condition of Definition 4.6, it follows that $t_r - 1$ of the equalities of A_r are independent, occur with probability M^{-1} each, and might imply the last one. This can be verified by observing that every vector J_j that corresponds to such an equality is linearly independent of the vectors that correspond to the previously considered equalities. Hence, the probability that the two k-tuples are in L_i is at most

$$M^{-(k-1)} \cdot M^{-\sum_{r=1}^{\ell} (t_r-1)} = M^{-(k-1)} \cdot M^{-(k-\ell)}.$$

For Item 2, take $\ell = k$ and notice that in this case, $(J_1, \ldots, J_k)$ is a permutation of $(I_1, \ldots, I_k)$, so we have $t_1 = \cdots = t_\ell = 1$. The probability that $(I_1, \ldots, I_k) \in L_i$ is again $M^{-(k-1)}$. Since the two partitions are distinct, there are distinct j, j' for which $I_j = J_{j'}$. Assume, without loss of generality, that $j' < k$. By the randomness of the choice of $c_{j'}$, the probability that $\beta_{j'}(J_{j'}) = b_i$, conditioned on $(I_1, \ldots, I_k) \in L_i$, is M^{-1}. Therefore, the probability that both the partitions are in L_i is at most $M^{-(k-1)} \cdot M^{-1}$. ∎

The proof of the following claim can be found in the full version of the paper.

CLAIM 4.8. *For every* $1 \leq i \leq |B|$, *the expected size of the set* L_i' *is at least* $\frac{1}{2} \cdot \binom{nk}{n, \ldots, n} \cdot M^{-(k-1)}$.

Finally, using Claim 4.8, we conclude that there exists a choice of $w_1, \ldots, w_N$ and $c_1, \ldots, c_k$ for which

$$|\mathcal{F}| = \sum_{i=1}^{|B|} |L_i'| \geq \frac{1}{2} \cdot \binom{nk}{n, \ldots, n} \cdot M^{-(k-1)} \cdot |B|$$

$$\geq \binom{nk}{n, \ldots, n} \cdot M^{-(k-2)-o(1)} \geq \binom{nk}{n}^{1-o(1)}.$$

By standard estimations of Binomial coefficients, this completes the proof of Theorem 4.1. ∎

COROLLARY 4.9. *For every* $k \geq 3$ *and a prime* p, *the local PMF capacity for* k-*cycles over* $\mathbb{F}_p$ *is at least* $2^{H(1/k)}$.

Proof: By Theorem 4.1, for every sufficiently large n, there exists a collection $\mathcal{F}$ of $(2^{H(1/k)} - o(1))^{nk}$ balanced vectors in $\mathbb{Z}_k^{nk}$ such that for every k vectors $v_1, \ldots, v_k \in \mathcal{F}$, the sets $v_1|_1, \ldots, v_k|_k$ form a partition of $[n \cdot k]$ if and only if $v_1 = \cdots = v_k$. For every vector $v \in \mathcal{F}$ consider the k-tuple of vectors, whose first $k-1$ vectors are the characteristic vectors of $v|_1, v|_2, \ldots, v|_{k-1}$, and the last one is the characteristic vector of $[n] \setminus v|_k$ multiplied by -1 (modulo p). Observe that the collection of all k-tuples obtained in this way from the vectors of $\mathcal{F}$ is an $(nk, |\mathcal{F}|)$ local PMF for k-cycles over $\mathbb{F}_p$. Hence, the local PMF capacity for k-cycles over $\mathbb{F}_p$ is at least $2^{H(1/k)}$, as required. ∎

The above corollary, combined with Lemma 2.8, completes the proof of Theorem 1.7.

5. REFERENCES

[1] N. Alon. Testing subgraphs in large graphs. *Random Struct. Algorithms*, 21(3-4):359–370, 2002. Preliminary version in FOCS'01.

[2] N. Alon and R. B. Boppana. The monotone circuit complexity of boolean functions. *Combinatorica*, 7(1):1–22, 1987.

[3] N. Alon, E. Fischer, I. Newman, and A. Shapira. A combinatorial characterization of the testable graph properties: It's all about regularity. *SIAM J. Comput.*, 39(1):143–167, 2009. Preliminary version in STOC'06.

[4] N. Alon, R. Hod, and A. Weinstein. On active and passive testing. *CoRR*, abs/1307.7364, 2013.

[5] N. Alon, A. Shpilka, and C. Umans. On sunflowers and matrix multiplication. *Computational Complexity*, 22(2):219–243, 2013. Preliminary version in CCC'12.

[6] M. Bateman and N. H. Katz. New bounds on cap sets. *J. Amer. Math. Soc.*, 25(2):585–613, 2012.

[7] F. A. Behrend. On sets of integers which contain no three terms in arithmetical progression. *Proc. National Academy of Sciences USA*, 32(12):331Ű–332, 1946.

[8] A. Bhattacharyya. Guest column: On testing affine-invariant properties over finite fields. *SIGACT News*, 44(4):53–72, 2013.

[9] A. Bhattacharyya, E. Grigorescu, and A. Shapira. A unified framework for testing linear-invariant properties. In *FOCS*, pages 478–487, 2010.

[10] A. Bhattacharyya and N. Xie. Lower bounds for testing triangle-freeness in boolean functions. In *SODA*, pages 87–98, 2010.

[11] C. Borgs, J. T. Chayes, L. Lovász, V. T. Sós, B. Szegedy, and K. Vesztergombi. Graph limits and parameter testing. In *STOC*, pages 261–270, 2006.

[12] H. Cohn, R. D. Kleinberg, B. Szegedy, and C. Umans. Group-theoretic algorithms for matrix multiplication. In *FOCS*, pages 379–388, 2005.

[13] D. Coppersmith and S. Winograd. Matrix multiplication via arithmetic progressions. *J. Symb. Comput.*, 9(3):251–280, 1990. Preliminary version in STOC'87.

[14] I. Dinur and S. Safra. On the hardness of approximating minimum vertex cover. *Annals of Mathematics*, 162(1):439–485, 2005. Preliminary version in STOC'02.

[15] Y. Edel. Extensions of generalized product caps. *Des. Codes Cryptography*, 31(1):5–14, 2004.

[16] M. Elkin. An improved construction of progression-free sets. *Israel J. of Math.*, 184(1):93–128, 2011. Preliminary version in SODA'10.

[17] P. Erdős and R. Rado. Intersection theorems for systems of sets. *J. London Math. Soc.*, 35:85–90, 1960.

[18] P. Erdős and E. Szemerédi. Combinatorial properties of systems of sets. *J. Comb. Theory, Ser. A*, 24(3):308–313, 1978.

[19] J. Fox. A new proof of the graph removal lemma. *Annals of Mathematics*, 174(1):561–579, 2011.

[20] H. Fu and R. Kleinberg. Improved lower bounds for testing triangle-freeness in boolean functions via fast matrix multiplication. In *RANDOM*, pages 669–676, 2014.

[21] O. Goldreich, S. Goldwasser, and D. Ron. Property testing and its connection to learning and approximation. *J. ACM*, 45(4):653–750, 1998. Preliminary version in FOCS'96.

[22] B. Green. A Szemerédi type regularity lemma in Abelian groups. *Geom. and Funct. Anal.*, 15(2):340Ű–376, 2005.

[23] P. Hatami, S. Sachdeva, and M. Tulsiani. An arithmetic analogue of Fox's triangle removal argument. *CoRR*, abs/1304.4921, 2013.

[24] T. Kaufman and M. Sudan. Algebraic property testing: the role of invariance. In *STOC*, pages 403–412, 2008.

[25] A. V. Kostochka. A bound of the cardinality of families not containing Δ-systems. In *The Mathematics of Paul Erdős II, Algorithms and Combinatorics*, volume 14, pages 229–235. Springer, Berlin, 1997.

[26] D. Král', O. Serra, and L. Vena. A combinatorial proof of the removal lemma for groups. *J. Comb. Theory, Ser. A*, 116(4):971–978, 2009.

[27] D. Král', O. Serra, and L. Vena. A removal lemma for systems of linear equations over finite fields. *Israel J. of Math.*, 187(1):193–207, 2012.

[28] Y.-R. Liu and C. V. Spencer. A generalization of Meshulam's theorem on subsets of finite Abelian groups with no 3-term arithmetic progression. *Des. Codes Cryptography*, 52(1):83–91, 2009.

[29] R. Meshulam. On subsets of finite Abelian groups with no 3-term arithmetic progressions. *J. Comb. Theory, Ser. A*, 71(1):168–172, 1995.

[30] A. A. Razborov. Lower bounds for the monotone complexity of some boolean functions. *Soviet Mathematics Doklady*, 31(2):354–357, 1985.

[31] R. Rubinfeld and M. Sudan. Robust characterizations of polynomials with applications to program testing. *SIAM J. Comput.*, 25(2):252–271, 1996. Preliminary version in SODA'92.

[32] R. Salem and D. C. Spencer. On sets of integers which contain no three terms in arithmetical progression. In *Proc. National Academy of Sciences USA*, volume 28(12), pages 561Ű–563, 1942.

[33] A. Shapira. A proof of Green's conjecture regarding the removal properties of sets of linear equations. *J. London Math. Soc.*, 81(2):355–373, 2010. Preliminary version in STOC'09.

[34] A. J. Stothers. *On the complexity of matrix multiplication*. PhD thesis, The University of Edinburgh, 2010.

[35] M. Sudan. Guest column: Testing linear properties: some general theme. *SIGACT News*, 42(1):59–80, 2011.

[36] J. H. van Lint and R. M. Wilson. *A course in combinatorics*. Cambridge University Press, second edition, 2001.

[37] V. V. Williams. Multiplying matrices faster than Coppersmith-Winograd. In *STOC*, pages 887–898, 2012.

Sketching Cuts in Graphs and Hypergraphs

Dmitry Kogan
Weizmann Institute of Science
Rehovot, Israel
dimakogan@gmail.com

Robert Krauthgamer
Weizmann Institute of Science
Rehovot, Israel
robert.krauthgamer@weizmann.ac.il

ABSTRACT

Sketching and streaming algorithms are in the forefront of current research directions for cut problems in graphs. In the streaming model, we show that $(1-\varepsilon)$-approximation for MAX-CUT must use $n^{1-O(\varepsilon)}$ space; moreover, beating 4/5-approximation requires polynomial space. For the sketching model, we show that every r-uniform hypergraph admits a $(1+\varepsilon)$-cut-sparsifier (i.e., a weighted subhypergraph that approximately preserves *all* the cuts) with $O(\varepsilon^{-2}n(r+\log n))$ edges. We also make first steps towards sketching general CSPs (Constraint Satisfaction Problems).

Categories and Subject Descriptors

E.1 [**Data**]: Data Structures; F.2 [**Theory**]: Analysis of Algorithms and Problem Complexity

General Terms

Theory, Algorithms

Keywords

Sketching, Sparsifiers, Streaming, Hypergraphs, Max-Cut

1. INTRODUCTION

The emergence of massive datasets has turned many algorithms impractical, because the standard assumption of having (fast) random access to the input is no longer valid. One example is when data is too large to fit in the main memory (or even on disk) of one machine; another is when the input can be accessed only as a stream, e.g., because its creation rate is so high, that it cannot even be stored in full for further processing. Luckily, the nature of the problems has evolved too, and we may often settle on approximate, rather than exact, solutions.

These situations have led to the rise of new computational paradigms. In the *streaming model* (aka *data-stream*), the input can be accessed only as a stream (i.e., a single pass

ITCS'15, January 11–13, 2015, Rehovot, Israel.
Copyright is held by the owner/author(s). Publication rights licensed to ACM.
ACM 978-1-4503-3333-7/15/01 ...$15.00.
http://dx.doi.org/10.1145/2688073.2688093.

of sequential access), and the algorithm's space complexity (storage requirement) must be small relative to the stream size. In the *sketching model*, the input is summarized (compressed) into a so-called sketch, which is short yet suffices for further processing without access to the original input. The two models are related – sketches are often useful in the design of streaming algorithms, and vice versa. In particular, lower bounds for sketch-size often imply lower bounds on the space complexity of streaming algorithms.

Graph problems.

Recently, the streaming model has seen many exciting developments on *graph problems*, where an input graph $G = (V, E)$ is represented by a stream of edges. The algorithm reads the stream and should then report a solution to a predetermined problem on G, such as graph connectivity or maximum matching; see e.g. the surveys [37, 27]. Throughout it will be convenient to denote $n = |V|$, and to assume edges have weights, given by $w : E \to \mathbb{R}_+$. While initial efforts focused on polylogarithmic-space algorithms, various intractability results have shifted the attention to what is called the *semi-streaming* model, where the algorithm's space complexity is $\tilde{O}(n)$.[1] In general, this storage is not sufficient to record the entire edge-set.

Cuts in graphs is a classical topic that has been studied extensively for more than half a century, and the last two decades have seen a surge of attention turning to the question of their succinct representation. The pioneering work of Benczúr and Karger [5] introduced the notion of *cut sparsifiers*: given an undirected graph $G = (V, E, w)$, a $(1 + \varepsilon)$-sparsifier is a (sparse) weighted subgraph $G' = (V, E', w')$ that preserves the value of every cut up to a multiplicative factor $1 + \varepsilon$. Formally, this is written as

$$\forall S \subset V, \qquad 1 \le \frac{w'(S, \bar{S})}{w(S, \bar{S})} \le 1 + \varepsilon; \qquad (1)$$

where $w(S, \bar{S}) = \sum_{e \in E : |e \cap S| = 1} w_e$ is used to denote the value of the cut. It is sometimes convenient to replace the left-hand side of (1) with $1 - \varepsilon$ or $\frac{1}{1+\varepsilon}$, which affects $\varepsilon \le \frac{1}{2}$ by only a constant factor. In addition to their role in saving storage, sparsifiers are important because they can speed-up graph algorithms whose running time depends on the number of edges. Observe that sparsifiers are a particularly strong form of graph-sketches since on top of retaining the value of all cuts, they hold the additional property of being subgraphs, rather than arbitrary data structures.

---

[1] We use $\tilde{O}(f)$ to denote $O(f \operatorname{polylog} f)$, which suppresses logarithmic terms.

Ahn and Guha [1] built upon the machinery of cut sparsifiers to present an $\tilde{O}(n/\varepsilon^2)$-space streaming algorithm that can produce a $(1 + \varepsilon)$-approximation to all cuts in a graph. Further improvements handle also edge deletions [2, 3, 10], or the stronger notion of spectral sparsification (see [16] and references therein). These results are nearly optimal, due to a space lower bound of $\Omega(n/\varepsilon^2)$ bits for sketching all cuts in a graph [4] (which improves an earlier bound of [1]).

Recent Directions.

These advances on sketching and streaming of graph cuts inspired new questions. One direction is to seek space-efficient streaming algorithms for *specific cut problems*, such as approximating MAX-CUT, rather than *all* cuts. A second direction concerns *hypergraphs*, asking whether cut sparsification, sketching and streaming can be generalized to hypergraphs. Finally, viewing cuts in graphs and hypergraphs as special cases of *constraint satisfaction problems* (CSPs), we ask whether also other CSPs admit sketches. Currently, there is a growing interest in generalizing graph cut problems to broader settings, such as sparsifying general *set systems* using small weighted samples [30], *high-dimensional expander theory* [20], sparsest-cuts in hypergraphs [26, 25], and applications of hypergraph cuts in *networking* [33].

1.1 Our Results

We first address a natural question raised in [14, Question 10], whether the well-known MAX-CUT problem admits approximation strictly better than factor $1/2$ by streaming algorithms that use space sublinear in n. Here, MAX-CUT denotes the problem of computing the *value* of a maximum cut in the input graph G (and not the cut itself), since *reporting* a cut requires space $\Omega(n)$ (see Section 2.2 for a short proof). We prove that for every fixed $\varepsilon \in (0, \frac{1}{5})$, streaming algorithms achieving $(1 - \varepsilon)$-approximation for MAX-CUT must use $n^{1-O(\varepsilon)}$ space. In fact, even beating $4/5$-approximation requires polynomial space. Our result is actually stronger and holds also in a certain sketching model. Previously, it was known that streaming computation of MAX-CUT *exactly* requires $\Omega(n^2)$ bits [36]. Our proof is by reduction from the BOOLEAN HIDDEN HYPERMATCHING problem, and captures the difficulty of distinguishing, under limited communication, whether the graph is a vertex-disjoint union of even-length cycles (in which case the graph is bipartite) or of odd-length cycles (in which case we can bound the maximum cut value). See Section 2 for details.

Second, we study sparsification of cuts in *hypergraphs*, and prove that every r-uniform hypergraph admits a sparsifier (weighted subhypergraph) of size $\tilde{O}(rn/\varepsilon^2)$ that approximates all cuts within factor $1 \pm \varepsilon$. This result immediately implies sketching and streaming algorithms (following [1]). Here, the weight of cut $(S, \bar{S})$ in a hypergraph $H = (V, E, w)$ is the total weight of all hyperedges $e \in E$ that intersect both S and $\bar{S}$.[2] This question was raised by de Carli Silva, Harvey and Sato [7, Corollary 8], who show that every r-uniform hypergraph has a sparsifier of size $O(n)$ that approximates all cuts within factor $\Theta(r^2)$. Along the way, we establish interesting, if not surprising, bounds on the number of ap-

proximately minimum cuts in hypergraphs. Technically, this is our most substantial contribution, see Section 3 for details.

Finally, as a step towards understanding the sketching complexity of a wider range of CSPs, we show that every k-SAT instance on n variables admits a sketch of size $\tilde{O}(kn/\varepsilon^2)$ that can be used to $(1+\varepsilon)$-approximate the value of all truth assignments. We prove this result in Section 3.3 by reducing it to hypergraph sparsification. We remark that sketching of CNF formulae was studied in a different setting, where some computational-complexity assumptions were used in [8] to preclude a significant size-reduction that *preserves the satisfiability* of the formula. Our sparsification result differs in that it *approximately preserves the value* of every assignment.

1.2 Related Work

Independently of our work, Kapralov, Khanna and Sudan [15] study the same problem of approximating MAX-CUT in the streaming model. They first prove that for every fixed $\varepsilon > 0$, streaming algorithms achieving $(1 - \varepsilon)$-approximation for MAX-CUT must use $n^{1-O(\varepsilon)}$ space. (This is similar to our Theorem 2.1.) They then make significant further progress, and show that achieving an approximation ratio strictly better than (the trivial) $1/2$ requires $\tilde{\Omega}(\sqrt{n})$ space. In fact, this result holds even if the edges of the graph are presented in a random (rather than adversarial) order.

Hypergraph sparsifiers of size $O(n^2/\varepsilon^2)$ are implied by a result of Newman and Rabinovich [30] for the following problem of approximating measures on *set systems*. Let $\mathcal{F}$ be a set system over a finite set X, let μ be a measure on X (which naturally extends to a measure on $\mathcal{F}$) and let $\varepsilon \in (0, 1)$. The goal is to construct a measure μ^*, supported on a *small* subset of X, such that the extensions of μ and of μ^* to $\mathcal{F}$ approximate each other, i.e., $\forall S \in \mathcal{F}$, $\mu^*(S) \in (1 \pm \varepsilon)\mu(S)$. They show a construction in which the support size of μ^* can be bounded by a structural parameter of $\mathcal{F}$ called *triangular rank* and denoted $\text{trk}(\mathcal{F})$. Specifically, in their construction $|\text{supp}(\mu^*)| = O(\text{trk}(\mathcal{F}) \cdot \log |\mathcal{F}|/\varepsilon^2)$. They also define *splitting set systems* – a special class of set systems in which $X, \mathcal{F} \subset 2^V$ are two families of subsets of some underlying set V. For splitting systems they prove [30, Claim 4.1] that $\text{trk}(\mathcal{F}) \leq |V| - 1$. The archetype of splitting set systems is in fact graph and hypergraph cuts, where V is the set of vertices, X is the set of hyperedges, and $\mathcal{F}$ is the set of cuts. Therefore their construction implies hypergraph sparsifiers of size $O(n^2/\varepsilon^2)$.[3]

More broadly, the general theme of *graph compression* – succinctly representing a graph while preserving some of its combinatorial properties – is studied extensively in the literature, with many examples of various flavors. A classical example is a *Gomory-Hu tree* [12] which is a weighted tree that represents the minimum $s - t$ cut values for all pairs of vertices in an input graph. Another notable example is the notion of *graph spanners* (defined by Peleg and Schäffer [31])

---

[2]Another possible definition, see [7, Corollary 7], is $\sum_{e \in E} w_e \cdot |e \cap S| \cdot |e \cap \bar{S}|$. The latter definition seems technically easier for sparsification, although both generalize the case of ordinary graphs ($r = 2$).

[3]Their argument does not imply a bound stronger than $O(n^2/\varepsilon^2)$ even for r-uniform hypergraphs. They show that $\text{trk}(\mathcal{F}) \geq \text{VCdim}(\mathcal{F})$ where $\text{VCdim}(\mathcal{F})$ is the Vapnik-Chervonenkis dimension of the set system. Even when $\mathcal{F}$ is the family of cuts of a (2-uniform) graph, it holds $\text{VCdim}(\mathcal{F}) \geq n - 1$, which follows, for example, from considering a path on n vertices, and observing that the set of $n - 1$ edges is shattered by the set of cuts.

– spar subgraphs that approximately preserve the shortest path distances between all pairs of vertices in the graph. The related notion of *distance oracles* (introduced by Thorup and Zwick [32]) deals with arbitrary data structures, rather than subgraphs, that can approximate the distances between all pairs of vertices, with emphasis on achieving low space and very fast query time. Other models aim to preserve the combinatorial property of interest only with respect to some predetermined (small) subset of the vertices, called *terminals*. For example, Moitra [28] introduced the notion of *vertex sparsifiers* – graphs (not necessarily subgraphs) that approximately preserve the values of minimum cuts separating any partition of the terminals. In a subsequent work, Leighton and Moitra [23] extended this definition and introduced *flow sparsifiers* – graphs that approximately preserve the congestion of every multicommodity flow with endpoints supported on the set of terminals.

2. SKETCHING MAX-CUT

The classical MAX-CUT problem is perhaps the simplest MAX-CSP problem. Thus, it has been studied extensively, leading to fundamental results both in approximation algorithms [11] and in hardness of approximation [21]. It is thus natural to study MAX-CUT also in the streaming model. As mentioned above, preserving the values of *all* cuts in a graph requires linear space even if only approximate values are required [1, 4], which raises the question whether smaller space suffices to approximate only the MAX-CUT value (as mentioned above, it is natural to require the algorithm to report only the value of the cut as opposed to the cut itself, see Section 2.2).

Sketching all cuts in a graph clearly preserves also the maximum-cut value, and thus an $\tilde{O}\left(\frac{n}{\varepsilon^2}\right)$ space streaming algorithm for $(1 - \varepsilon)$-approximation of MAX-CUT follows immediately from [1]. Yet since the maximum cut value is always $\Omega(m)$, where m is the total number (or weight) of all edges, a similar result can be obtained more easily by uniform sampling (achieving εm additive approximation for all cuts) [35, Theorem 21]. The latter approach has the additional advantage that it immediately extends to hypergraphs.

It turns out that this relatively straightforward approach is not far from optimal, as we prove that streaming algorithms for $(1 - \varepsilon)$-approximation of MAX-CUT require $n^{1-O(\varepsilon)}$ space.

THEOREM 2.1. *Fix a constant $\varepsilon \in (0, \frac{1}{5})$. Then every (randomized) streaming algorithm that computes a $(1 - \varepsilon)$-approximation of the MAX-CUT value in n-vertex graphs requires space $\Omega(n^{1-1/t})$ for $t = \lfloor \frac{1}{2\varepsilon} - \frac{1}{2} \rfloor$, which in particular means space $n^{1-O(\varepsilon)}$.*

To prove this result, we consider the somewhat stronger *one-way two-party communication model*, where instead of arriving as a stream, the set of edges of a graph is split between two parties, who engage in a communication protocol to compute (approximately) the graph's maximum-cut value. Since a lower bound in this model immediately translates to the original streaming model, the theorem above follows immediately from Theorem 2.3 below.

2.1 Proving Theorem 2.1

DEFINITION 2.2 (MAX-CUT$^\varepsilon$). *Let $G = (V, E_A \cup E_B)$ be an input graph on $|V| = n$ vertices with maximum cut value[4] c^*, and $\varepsilon > 0$ some small constant. MAX-CUT$^\varepsilon$ is a two-player communication game where Alice and Bob receive the edges E_A and E_B respectively and need to output a value c' such that with high probability $(1 - \varepsilon)c^* \leq c' \leq c^*$.*

THEOREM 2.3. *Fix a constant $\varepsilon \in (0, \frac{1}{5})$. Then the randomized one-way communication complexity of MAX-CUT$^\varepsilon$ is $\Omega(n^{1-1/t})$ for $t = \lfloor \frac{1}{2\varepsilon} - \frac{1}{2} \rfloor$.*

The proof is by a reduction from the following communication problem studied in [34].

DEFINITION 2.4 (BHH$_n^t$). *The BOOLEAN HIDDEN HYPERMATCHING problem is a communication complexity problem where*

- *Alice gets a boolean vector $x \in \{0, 1\}^n$ where $n = 2kt$ for some integer k,*
- *Bob gets a perfect hypermatching M on n vertices where each edge has t vertices and a boolean vector w of length n/t.*

Let Mx denote the length-n/t boolean vector

$$\left(\bigoplus_{1 \leq i \leq t} x_{M_{1,i}}, \ldots, \bigoplus_{1 \leq i \leq t} x_{M_{n/t,i}} \right)$$

where $(M_{1,1}, \ldots, M_{1,t}), \ldots, (M_{n/t,1}, \ldots, M_{n/t,t})$ are the edges of M. It is promised that either $Mx \oplus w = 1^{n/t}$ or $Mx \oplus w = 0^{n/t}$. The problem is to return 1 in the former case, and to return 0 in the latter.

LEMMA 2.5 ([34, THEOREM 2.1]). *The randomized one-way communication complexity of BHH$_n^t$ where $n = 2kt$ for some integer $k \geq 1$ is $\Omega(n^{1-1/t})$.*

PROOF OF THEOREM 2.3. We show a reduction from BHH$_n^t$ to MAX-CUT$^\varepsilon$. Consider an instance (x, M, w) of the BHH$_n^t$ problem: Alice gets $x \in \{0, 1\}^n$, and Bob gets a perfect hypermatching M and a vector $w \in \{0, 1\}^{n/t}$. We construct a graph G for the MAX-CUT$^\varepsilon$ problem as follows (see Figure 2.1 for an example):

- The vertices of G are $V = \{v_i\}_{i=1}^{2n} \cup \{u_i\}_{i=1}^{2n} \cup \{w_i\}_{i=1}^{2n/t}$.
- The edges E_A given to Alice are: for every $i \in [n]$, if $x_i = 0$, Alice is given two "parallel" edges (u_{2i-1}, v_{2i-1}), (u_{2i}, v_{2i}); if $x_i = 1$, Alice is given two "cross" edges $(u_{2i-1}, v_{2i}), (u_{2i}, v_{2i-1})$.
- The edges E_B given to Bob are: for each hyperedge $M_j = (i_1, i_2, \ldots, i_t) \in M$ (where the order is fixed arbitrarily):
  - For $k = 1, 2, \ldots, t - 1$, Bob is given $(u_{2i_k-1}, v_{2i_{k+1}-1})$ and $(u_{2i_k}, v_{2i_{k+1}})$
  - For $k = t$, Bob is given (u_{2i_t}, w_{2j}) and (v_{2i_t-1}, w_{2j-1});
  - If $w_j = 0$ Bob is given two "parallel" edges (w_{2j}, v_{2i_1}) and (w_{2j-1}, v_{2i_1-1}); if $w_j = 1$ Bob is given two "cross" edges (w_{2j}, v_{2i_1-1}) and (w_{2j-1}, v_{2i_1})

---

[4]For the proof of the lower bound it suffices to restrict our attention to unweighted graphs, with all edges having unit weight.

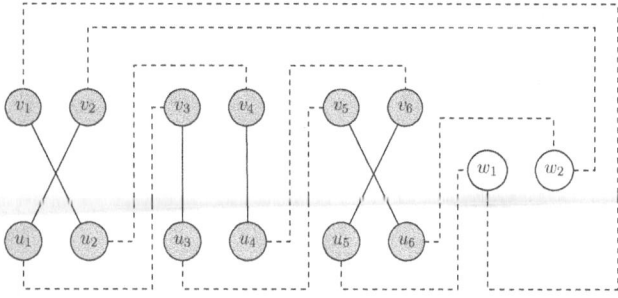

Figure 1: An example of a gadget constructed in the proof of Theorem 2.3 for $t = 3$, a matching M that contains the hyperedge $M_1 = (1, 2, 3)$, $x_1 = 1$, $x_2 = 0$, $x_3 = 1$ and $w_1 = 0$. The result is two paths of length 7. Alice's and Bob's edges are shown as solid and dashed lines respectively.

By definition, for each $j \in [n/t]$, if $M_j = (i_1, i_2, \ldots, i_t) \in M$ and $(Mx)_j \oplus w_j = 0$ we have $\sum_{k=1}^{t} x_{i_k} \oplus w_j = 0$. Since the number of 1 bits in the latter sum is even, when we start traversing from u_{2i_1} we go through an even number of "cross" edges and complete a cycle of length $2t + 1$. Similarly when starting our traversal at $u_{2i_1 - 1}$ we complete a different cycle of the same length. Therefore if (x, M, w) is a 0-instance the graph consists of $\frac{2n}{t}$ paths of (odd) length $2t + 1$ each. Therefore the maximum cut value is $c_0^* = 2t \cdot \frac{2n}{t} = 4n$.

On the other hand if $(Mx)_j \oplus w_j = 1$, starting our traversal at $u_{2i_1 - 1}$, we pass an odd number of cross edges and end up at u_{2i_1}, from where we once again pass an odd number of cross edges, to complete a cycle of total length $2 \cdot (2t + 1) = 4t + 2$ that ends back in $u_{2i_1 - 1}$. Therefore, if (x, M, w) is a 1-instance the graph consists of n/t paths of (even) length $4t + 2$ each. The maximum cut value in this case is $c_1^* = 4n + 2\frac{n}{t}$.

Observing that $c_0^*/c_1^* = \frac{4n}{4n + 2n/t} = \frac{2t}{2t+1} < 1 - \varepsilon$, we conclude that a randomized one-way protocol for MAX-CUT$^\varepsilon$ (on input size $n' = 4n + n/t = O(n)$) gives a randomized one-way protocol for BHH$_n^t$. By Lemma 2.5 the Theorem follows. □

PROOF OF THEOREM 2.3. Any streaming algorithm for MAX-CUT$^\varepsilon$ leads to a one-way communication protocol in the two party setting. Moreover the communication complexity of this protocol is exactly the space complexity of the streaming algorithm. Hence by Theorem 2.3 the streaming space complexity is at least as high as the one way randomized communication complexity. □

2.2 Reporting a Vertex-Bipartition (rather than a value)

We show a simple $\Omega(n)$ space lower bound for reporting a vertex-bipartition that gives an approximate maximum cut.

PROPOSITION 2.6. *Let $\varepsilon \in (0, \frac{1}{2})$ be some small constant. Suppose* sk *is a polynomial time sketching algorithm that outputs at most $s = s(n, \varepsilon)$ bits, and* est *is an estimation algorithm, such that together, for every n-vertex graph G, (with high probability) they output a vertex-bipartition that gives an approximately maximum cut; i.e.,* est(sk(G)) = S

such that $w(S, \bar{S}) \geq (1 - \varepsilon)\tilde{w}$ where $\tilde{w}$ is the maximum cut in G. Then $s \geq \Omega_\varepsilon(n)$.

PROOF. Let $\mathcal{C} \subset \{0, 1\}^n$ be a binary error-correcting code of size $|\mathcal{C}| = 2^{\Omega(n)}$ with relative distance ε. We may assume w.l.o.g. that for every $x \in \mathcal{C}$ the hamming weight $|x|$ is exactly $n/2$ (for instance by taking $\mathcal{C}' = \{x\bar{x} : x \in \mathcal{C}\}$ where $\bar{x}$ denotes the bitwise negation of x), and that there are no $x, y \in \mathcal{C}$ such that $|x - \bar{y}| \leq \frac{\varepsilon}{2}n$ (since for every $x \in \mathcal{C}$ there could be at most one "bad" y, and we can discard one codeword out of every such pair).

Fix a codeword $x \in \{0, 1\}^n$ and consider the complete bipartite graph $G_x = (V, E)$ where $V = [n]$ and $E = \{(i, j) : x_i = 0 \wedge x_j = 1\}$. The maximum cut value in G_x is obviously $\tilde{w} = n^2/4$. Let $y \in \{0, 1\}^n$ such that $\frac{1}{2}\varepsilon n \leq |x - y| \leq \frac{n}{2}$. Identifying x, y with subsets $S_x, S_y \subseteq [n]$, and using the fact that $|S_x \triangle S_y| = |x - y| \geq \frac{1}{2}\varepsilon n$, the value of the cut $(S_y, \bar{S}_y)$ in G_x is

$$|E(S_y, \bar{S}_y)| = \frac{n^2}{4} - |S_x \setminus S_y| \left(\frac{n}{2} - |S_y \setminus S_x|\right) - |S_y \setminus S_x| \left(\frac{n}{2} - |S_x \setminus S_y|\right) < (1 - \Omega(\varepsilon))\frac{n^2}{4}.$$

Let sk(G_x) be the sketch of G_x, and let est(sk(G_x)) = S be the output of the estimation algorithm on the sketch of G_x. Therefore if the sketch succeeds (which by our assumption happens with high probability) and the cut $(S, \bar{S})$ has value at least $(1 - \Omega(\varepsilon))\tilde{w}$, then by the preceding argument the corresponding vector x_S is of relative hamming distance smaller than $\frac{\varepsilon}{2}$ from x and then one can decode x from S.[5] By standard arguments from information theory, the size s of a sketch that succeeds with high probability must be at least $\Omega(\log |\mathcal{C}|) = \Omega_\varepsilon(n)$. □

2.3 2/3-Approximation of Max-Cut in the Two Party Model

While [15] have recently shown that a polynomial number of bits is necessary for any non-trivial (i.e., strictly better than 1/2) approximation of MAX-CUT *in the streaming model*, we remark that a 2/3-approximation communication protocol that uses only a logarithmic number of bits exists *in the one-way two-party model*. In the latter model, the problem of giving a $(1 - \varepsilon)$-approximation of the maximum cut exhibits an exponential gap in the communication complexity between the case of $\varepsilon = 1/5$, where we have shown that a polynomial number of bits is necessary, and the case $\varepsilon = 1/3$, for which logarithmically many bits suffice, as follows from the following simple protocol.

PROPOSITION 2.7. *Let $G = (V, E_A \cup E_B)$ be an input graph on $|V| = n$ vertices. Let w_A and w_B be the maximum cut values in $G_A = (V, E_A)$ and $G_B = (V, E_B)$ respectively. Then the maximum cut value w in G satisfies*

$$\frac{2}{3}(w_A + w_B) \leq w \leq w_A + w_B.$$

PROOF. Consider cuts $C_A, C_B : V \to \{0, 1\}$ such that $w(C_A) = w_A$ and $w(C_B) = w_B$. Let $C : V \to \{0, 1\}$ be a cut chosen uniformly at random from $\{C_A, C_B, C_A \oplus C_B\}$ where we define $(C_A \oplus C_B)(v) = C_A(v) + C_B(v) \pmod{2}$ for every $v \in V$. For an edge $e = (u, v) \in C_A$, either $C_B(u) \oplus C_B(v) = 1$ or $(C_A \oplus C_B)(u) + (C_A \oplus C_B)(v) =$

---

[5]Since the cuts $(\bar{S}, S)$ has the same value as $(S, \bar{S})$, the vector x_S can actually be ε-close to $\bar{x}$, but by taking our code to have no codeword being close to the negation of another codeword we can always try decoding both x_S and $\bar{x}_S$.

$(C_A(u) + C_A(v)) + (C_B(u) + C_B(v)) = 1 + 0 = 1$. Either way $\Pr_{C \in_R \{C_A, C_B, C_A \oplus C_B\}}[e \in C] = \frac{2}{3}$. Similarly the same holds for an edge $e \in C_B$. Therefore by linearity of expectation a random cut in $\{C_A, C_B, C_A \oplus C_B\}$ has value at least $\frac{2}{3}(w_A + w_B)$. The second inequality is trivial. $\square$

COROLLARY 2.8. *The one-way communication complexity of* MAX-CUT$^{1/3}$ *is* $O(\log n)$.

PROOF. Alice uses her input to compute the value w_A and sends it to Bob. Bob uses his input to compute the value w_B and outputs $\frac{2}{3}(w_A + w_B)$. $\square$

3. SKETCHING CUTS IN HYPERGRAPHS

In their celebrated work, Benczúr and Karger [5] (with further improvements and simplifications in [18, 19, 6]) showed an effective method to sketch the values of *all* the cuts of an undirected (weighted) graph $G = (V, E, w)$ by constructing a *cut-sparsifier*, which is a subgraph with different edge weights, that contains only $\tilde{O}\left(n/\varepsilon^2\right)$ edges, and approximates the weight of every cut in G up to multiplicative factor $1 \pm \varepsilon$. We generalize the ideas of Benczúr and Karger to obtain cut-sparsifiers of hypergraphs, as stated below. Such sparsifiers (and sketches) can be computed by streaming algorithms that use $\tilde{O}(rn)$ space for r-uniform hypergraphs using known techniques (of [1] and subsequent work). Throughout this work we allow r-uniform hypergraphs to contain also hyperedges with less than r endpoints (for instance by allowing duplicate vertices in the same hyperedge).

THEOREM 3.1. *For every r-uniform hypergraph $H = (V, E, w)$ and an error parameter $\varepsilon \in (0, 1)$, there is a subhypergraph H_ε (with different edge weights) such that:*

- *H_ε has $O\left(n(r + \log n)/\varepsilon^2\right)$ hyperedges.*
- *The weight of every cut in H_ε is within $1 \pm \varepsilon$ times the weight of the corresponding cut in H.*

Furthermore, H can be constructed in $O(mn^2)$ time where $m = |E|$ is the number of hyperedges in the original hypergraph.

A key combinatorial property exploited in the Benczúr-Karger analysis is an upper bound on the number of cuts of near-minimum weight [17]. It asserts that the number of minimum-weight cuts in an n-vertex graph is at most n^2 (which had been previously shown by [24] and [9]), and more generally, there are at most $n^{2\alpha}$ cuts whose weight is at most $\alpha \geq 1$ times the minimum (more refined bounds for $\alpha = 4/3$ and $\alpha = 3/2$ appear in [29] and [13] respectively). These bounds are known to be tight (e.g., for an n-cycle). Correctly generalizing this property to r-uniform hypergraphs appears to be a nontrivial question. A fairly simple analysis generalizes the latter bound to $n^{r\alpha}$, but using new ideas, we manage to obtain the following tighter bound.

THEOREM 3.2. *Let $H = (V, E, w)$ be a weighted r-uniform hypergraph with n vertices and minimum cut value $\hat{w}$. Then for every half-integer $\alpha \geq 1$, the number of cuts in H of weight at most $\alpha\hat{w}$ is at most $O(2^{\alpha r} n^{2\alpha})$.*

We prove this "cut-counting" bound in Section 3.1. With this bound at hand, we prove Theorem 3.1 similarly to the original proof of [5] for graphs, as outlined in Section 3.2.

Cuts in hypergraphs are perhaps one of the simplest examples of CSPs, which we now formally define.

DEFINITION 3.3. *A Constraint Satisfaction Problem is a quintuple (Σ, X, P, C, w) where:*

- *Σ is a finite alphabet,*
- *$X = \{x_1, \dots, x_n\}$ is a set of variables taking their values from Σ,*
- *$P = \{P_1, \dots, P_k\}$ is set of r-ary predicates,*
- *$C = \{C_1, \dots, C_m\}$ is a set of constraints, where each constraint C_i consists of one of the predicates P_j and a sequence of variables $(x_{ij})_{j=1}^r$ from X,*
- *$w : C \to \mathbb{R}_+$ is a weight function on the set of constraints.*

For example, in the case of cuts in hypergraphs, the vertices are variables over the binary alphabet, and the hyperedges are constraints defined by the predicate NOT-ALL-EQUAL. A natural question is whether general CSPs admit sketches as well, where a sketch should provide an approximation to the value of every assignment to the CSP (as usual, the value of an assignment is the total weight of constraints it satisfies). Specifically we think of both Σ and P as being of constant size, and are interested in the dependence on n and r. Although we are still far from answering this question in full generality, we prove that for the well-known SAT problem, sketching is indeed possible.

THEOREM 3.4. *For every error parameter $\varepsilon \in (0, 1)$, there is a polynomial time sketching algorithm that produces from an r-CNF formula Φ on n variables a sketch of size $\tilde{O}(rn/\varepsilon^2)$, that can be used to $(1 \pm \varepsilon)$-approximate the value of every assignment to Φ.*

3.1 Counting Near-Minimum Cuts in Hypergraphs

In this subsection we prove our upper bound on the number of near-minimum cuts (Theorem 3.2). We generalize Karger's min-cut algorithm [17] to hypergraphs, and then show that its probability to output any individual cut is not small (Theorem 3.6), which immediately yields a bound on the number of distinct cuts. Finally, we show that the exponential dependence on r in Theorem 3.2 is necessary (Section 3.1.3).

3.1.1 A Randomized Contraction Algorithm

Consider the following generalization of Karger's contraction algorithm [17] to hypergraphs.

Algorithm 3.5 CONTRACTHYPERGRAPH

Input: an r-uniform weighted hypergraph $H = (V, E, w)$
        a parameter $\alpha > 1$
Output: a cut $C = (S, V \setminus S)$
1: $H' \leftarrow H$
2: **while** $|V(H')| > \alpha r$ **do**
3:     $e \leftarrow$ random hyperedge in H' with probability proportional to its weight
4:     contract e by merging all its endpoints and removing self-loops[6]
5: $C' \leftarrow$ random cut in H' (bipartition of $V(H')$)
6: **return** the cut C in H induced[7] by the cut C'

---

[6] Self-loops refers to hyperedges that contain only a single vertex. Note also that the cardinality of an edge can only decrease as a result of contractions.

[7] Since after the sequence of contractions, each vertex in $V(H)$ corresponds to exactly one vertex in $V(H')$, a vertex

THEOREM 3.6. *Let $H = (V, E, w)$ be a weighted r-uniform hypergraph with minimum cut value $\hat{w}$, let $n = |V|$, and let $\alpha \geq 1$ be some half-integer. Fix $C = (S, V \setminus S)$ to be some cut in H of weight at most $\alpha\hat{w}$. Then Algorithm 3.5 outputs the cut C with probability at least $\frac{Q_{n,r,\alpha}}{2^{\alpha r - 1} - 1}$ for*

$$Q_{n,r,\alpha} = \frac{2\alpha + 1}{(r+1)}\binom{n - \alpha(r-2)}{2\alpha}^{-1}$$

if $\alpha r < n$ and $Q_{n,r,\alpha} = 1$ otherwise.

Since Theorem 3.6 gives a lower bound on the probability to output a specific cut (of certain weight), and different cuts correspond to disjoint events, the theorem implies that the number of cuts of weight at most $\alpha\hat{w}$ is at most

$$\frac{2^{\alpha r - 1} - 1}{Q_{n,r,\alpha}} \leq \frac{(2^{\alpha r - 1} - 1)(r+1)}{2\alpha + 1}\binom{n}{2\alpha} = O\left(2^{\alpha r} n^{2\alpha}\right),$$

proving Theorem 3.2.

PROOF. Fix $C = (S, V \setminus S)$ to be some cut of weight $\alpha\hat{w}$ in H. For $t \in [n]$, denote by I_t the iteration of the algorithm where H' contains t vertices. Since a contraction of a hyperedge may reduce the number of vertices by anywhere between 1 and $r - 1$, in a specific execution of the algorithm, not necessarily all the $\{I_t\}_{t=1}^n$ occur. Similarly, let the random variable E_t be the edge contracted in iteration t.

We say that an iteration I_t is *bad* if $E_t \in C$ (i.e., the hyperedge contains vertices from both S and $V \setminus S$). Otherwise, we say it is *good* (including iterations that do not occur in the specific execution such as $I_1, \ldots, I_{\alpha r}$). For any fixed $e_n, \ldots, e_{t+1} \in E$ define

$$q_t(e_n, \ldots, e_{t+1}) =$$
$$\Pr\left[I_t, \ldots, I_1 \text{ are good} | E_n = e_n, \ldots, E_{t+1} = e_{t+1}\right]$$

Note that q_n is simply the probability that all iterations of the algorithm are good i.e., no edge of the cut C is contracted. When that happens, in step 5 of the algorithm, there exists a cut C' in H' that corresponds to the cut C in H. Since at that stage, there are at most αr vertices in H', the probability of choosing C' is at least $\frac{1}{2^{\alpha r - 1} - 1}$. Hence the overall probability of outputting cut C is at least $q_n \cdot \frac{1}{2^{\alpha r - 1} - 1}$. We thus need to give a lower bound on q_n. To this end we prove below the following lemma.

LEMMA 3.7. *$q_t(e_n, \ldots, e_{t+1}) \geq Q_{t,r,\alpha}$ for every $t \in [n]$, and every $e_n, \ldots, e_{t+1} \in E \setminus C$.*

Using the lemma for $t = n$ bounds the overall probability of outputting cut C and proves Theorem 3.6. □

3.1.2 Proof of Lemma 3.7

We prove the lemma by (complete) induction on t. For the base case, note that $q_t(e_n, \ldots, e_{t+1}) = 1$ for $1 \leq t \leq \alpha r$ since no contractions take place in those iterations.

For the general case, fix an iteration I_t and from now on, condition on some set of values $E_n = e_n, \ldots, E_{t+1} = e_{t+1}$. All probabilities henceforth are thus conditioned, and for brevity we omit it from our notation. Observe that depending on the cardinality of E_t, the next iteration (*after* iteration I_t) may be one of $I_{t-1}, \ldots, I_{t-r+1}$. Let $p_i = \Pr[|E_t| = i]$

bipartition in H' naturally induces a vertex bipartition in H.

and let $y_i = \Pr[|E_t| = i \wedge E_t \in C]$.[8],[9] We can now write a recurrence relation:

$$q_t(e_n, \ldots, e_{t+1}) =$$
$$= \Pr\left[I_t, \ldots, I_1 \text{ are good} \mid E_n = e_n, \ldots, E_{t+1} = e_{t+1}\right]$$
$$= \sum_{i=2}^{r} \Pr\left[|E_t| = i \wedge E_t \notin C\right]$$
$$\qquad \cdot \Pr\left[I_{t-i+1}, \ldots, I_1 \text{ are good} \mid |E_t| = i, E_t \notin C\right]$$
$$= \sum_{i=2}^{r}(p_i - y_i)\mathbb{E}_{E_t}\left[q_{t-i+1}(e_n, \ldots, e_{t+1}, E_t) \mid |E_t| = i, E_t \notin C\right]$$
$$\geq \sum_{i=2}^{r}(p_i - y_i)Q_{t-i+1,r,\alpha}.$$

For $i = 2, \ldots, r$ let $W_i = \sum_{e' \in H' : |e'| = i} w(e')$ be the total weight of hyperedges in H' of cardinality i (at iteration t) and let $W = \sum_{i=2}^{r} W_i$ be the total weight in H'.

Observe that $p_i = \frac{W_i}{W}$ since E_t is chosen with probability proportional to the hyperedge's weight, and $\sum_{v \in V'} deg(v) = \sum_{i=2}^{r} i \cdot W_i$ since a hyperedge of cardinality i is counted i times on the left-hand side. By averaging, there exists a vertex $v \in V(H')$ such that $deg(v) \leq \frac{1}{t}\sum_{i=2}^{r} i \cdot W_i$, and since it induces a cut in H whose weight is exactly $deg(v)$, we obtain that $\hat{w} \leq deg(v) \leq \frac{1}{t}\sum_{i=2}^{r} i \cdot W_i$.

Next note that

$$\sum_{i=2}^{r} y_i = \Pr[E_t \in C] \leq \frac{\alpha\hat{w}}{W} \leq \frac{\alpha}{t}\sum_{i=2}^{r} i \cdot \frac{W_i}{W} = \frac{\alpha}{t}\sum_{i=2}^{r} i \cdot p_i,$$

where the first inequality uses the conditioning on all previous iterations being good, which means that all hyperedges in C have survived in H', and thus $w_H(C) = w_{H'}(C)$.

Altogether, to prove the lemma it suffices to show that the value of the following linear program is at least $Q_{t,r,\alpha}$. From now on we omit the subscripts r and α, denoting $Q_t = Q_{t,r,\alpha}$.

$$\text{minimize } \sum_{i=2}^{r}(p_i - y_i)Q_{t-i+1}$$
$$\text{subject to } 0 \leq y_i \leq p_i \qquad \forall i = 2, \ldots, r$$
$$\sum_{i=2}^{r} p_i = 1$$
$$\sum_{i=2}^{r} y_i \leq \frac{\alpha}{t}\sum_{i=2}^{r} i \cdot p_i.$$

First observe that the last constraint implies

$$\sum_{i=2}^{r} y_i \leq \frac{\alpha}{t}\sum_{i=2}^{r} i \cdot p_i \leq \frac{\alpha}{t}\sum_{i=2}^{r} r \cdot p_i = \frac{\alpha r}{t}\sum_{i=2}^{r} p_i < \sum_{i=2}^{r} p_i, \quad (2)$$

which means that in every *feasible* solution there is always some $y_i < p_i$. This implies that in every *optimal* solution, the last constraint is tight, since otherwise increasing such a

---

[8]Since not all iterations occur in all executions, it might be the case that *no* edge is contracted in iteration t. In that case iteration t is good, and hence by the induction hypothesis the claim holds.

[9]Note that $|e|$ refers to the edge's cardinality, whereas $w(e_i)$ refers to its weight.

y_i will decrease the value of the solution, without violating any of the other constraints.

It is easy to see that this linear program is both feasible and bounded, and therefore has an optimal solution that is basic (i.e., a vertex of the polytope). The dimension of the linear program (i.e., the number of variables) is $2r - 2$, and thus in a basic feasible solution (at least) $2r - 2$ of the $2r$ constrains must be tight. Therefore there are at most 2 loose (i.e., not tight) constraints among the $2r-2$ constraints $0 \leq y_i \leq p_i$, meaning there are at most 2 indices i, j such that $p_i \neq 0$. We proceed by analyzing the four possible cases:

- $0 < y_i = p_i$ and $0 < y_j = p_j$. This case is not possible, since that would have implied $\sum_{i=2}^{r} y_i = \sum_{i=2}^{r} p_i$, contradicting (2).

- $0 = y_i < p_i$ and $0 = y_j < p_j$. This case is also not possible since that would have implied $\sum_{i=2}^{r} y_i = 0$, contradicting the tightness of the last constraint in an optimal solution.

- $0 = y_i < p_i$ and $0 < y_j = p_j$. Since all other $p_\ell = 0$, the other LP constraints become

$$p_i + p_j = 1$$
$$0 + p_j = y_i + y_j = \frac{\alpha}{t}(ip_i + jp_j).$$

Solving the two equations we obtain:

$$\text{LP} = \left(1 - \frac{\alpha i}{t + \alpha i - \alpha j}\right) Q_{t-i+1}$$
$$\geq \left(1 - \frac{\alpha i}{t + \alpha i - \alpha r}\right) Q_{t-i+1} = \frac{t - \alpha r}{t + \alpha i - \alpha r} Q_{t-i+1}. \quad (3)$$

To use the induction hypothesis, we distinguish between two cases:

1. $t - i + 1 \geq \alpha r$, in which case it is thus sufficient to prove the following claim.

   CLAIM 3.8. *For every half-integer $\alpha \geq 1$ and integers $r \geq i \geq 2$ and $t \geq \alpha r + i - 1$, it holds $\frac{Q_{t-i+1,r,\alpha}}{Q_{t,r,\alpha}} \geq \frac{t+\alpha i-\alpha r}{t-\alpha r}$.*

   PROOF. Recall that $Q_t = \frac{2\alpha+1}{(r+1)}\binom{t-\alpha(r-2)}{2\alpha}^{-1}$ and denote $t' = t - \alpha r$. Then

$$\frac{Q_{t-i+1,r,\alpha}}{Q_{t,r,\alpha}} = \frac{\frac{2\alpha+1}{(r+1)}\binom{t'+2\alpha}{2\alpha}}{\frac{2\alpha+1}{(r+1)}\binom{t'-i+2\alpha+1}{2\alpha}}$$
$$= \frac{(t'+2\alpha)\cdots(t'+1)}{(t'+2\alpha-i+1)\cdots(t'+1-i+1)}$$
$$= \frac{(t'+2\alpha)\cdots(t'+2\alpha-i+2)}{t'\cdots(t'-i+2)}$$
$$= \left(1 + \frac{2\alpha}{t'}\right)\cdots\left(1 + \frac{2\alpha}{t'-i+2}\right)$$
$$\geq \left(1 + \frac{2\alpha}{t'}\right)^{i-1}$$
$$\geq 1 + \frac{2\alpha(i-1)}{t'}$$
$$\geq 1 + \frac{\alpha i}{t'} = \frac{t+\alpha i-\alpha r}{t-\alpha r}. \quad \square$$

2. $t - i + 1 < \alpha r$, in which case $Q_{t-i+1} = 1$. Here we get

$$\text{LP} \geq 1 - \frac{\alpha i}{t-\alpha r+\alpha i} \geq 1 - \frac{\alpha i}{\alpha i+1} = \frac{1}{\alpha i+1} \geq \frac{1}{\alpha r+1}$$
$$\geq \frac{2\alpha+1}{(r+1)\binom{t-\alpha(r-2)}{2\alpha}} = Q_t,$$

where the last inequality follows from the fact that $t - \alpha(r-2) \geq \alpha r + 1 - \alpha(r-2) \geq 2\alpha + 1$.

- $0 < y_i < p_i$ and $0 = y_j = p_j$. In this case $p_i = 1$, $y_i = \frac{\alpha i}{t}$, and therefore

$$\text{LP} = \left(1 - \frac{\alpha i}{t}\right) Q_{t-i+1} \geq \left(1 - \frac{\alpha i}{t-\alpha(r-i)}\right) Q_{t-i+1},$$

which is exactly as in (3) in the previous case.

Having bounded the value of the linear program, this completes the proof of Lemma 3.7.

3.1.3 Lower Bound

For completeness, we remark that at least for $\alpha > 1$, the exponential dependence on r in Theorem 3.2 is indeed necessary. Consider a "sunflower" hypergraph on $n = rm - m + 1$ vertices that consists of m hyperedges of size r, intersecting at a single vertex, supplemented with m two-uniform cliques of size r each – one for each of the hyperedges. Each of the cardinality-r hyperedges is given weight 1 and each of the cardinality-two edges is given weight $\frac{\alpha-1}{2r}$. The minimum cut value in this graph is 1, since every cut contains at least one of the r-hyperedges. However, all $\Omega(m \cdot 2^r)$ cuts given by the 2^r bipartitions of a single r-hyperedge, are of weight at most α.

3.2 Proof Of Theorem 3.1

We prove Theorem 3.1 by closely following the proof in the original setting of graphs in [5], and thus we refrain from repeating the full details. Instead, we present an outline of the proof (following the presentation in [6]) while emphasizing the reasons it translates to the hypergraph setting and handling the differences that require a separate treatment.

The main tool used by Benczúr and Karger is random sampling: each edge e is included in the sparsifier with probability p_e, and given weight w_e/p_e if it is included. It is immediate that every cut in the sparsifier preserves its weight in expectation. The main task is thus to carefully select the sampling probabilities p_e in order to both obtain the required number of edges in the sparsifier, and guarantee the required concentration bounds.

As a rough sketch, to guarantee concentration, one needs to apply a Chernoff bound to estimate the probability that the weight of a specific cut (which is a sum of the independent samples of the edges it contains) deviates from its expectation. Subsequently, a union bound over all cuts is used to show the concentration of *all* cuts. A priori it is unclear whether the Chernoff bound is strong enough to handle the exponentially many different cuts in the union bound. The remedy comes from Theorem 3.2 that counts the number of cuts of each weight. It is still unclear how should the random sampling be tuned to handle both the small and large cuts simultaneously. If we are to chose the sampling probability to be small enough to handle the exponentially many large cuts, we run into trouble of small cuts having large variance. On the other hand, increasing the sampling probability imposes a risk of ending up with too many edges in the sparsifier.

Following Benczúr and Karger, we now show that when no edge carries a large portion of the weight in any of the cuts, the cut-counting theorem is sufficient to obtain concentration.

THEOREM 3.9. *Let $H = (V, E, w)$ be a r-uniform hypergraph on n vertices, let $\varepsilon > 0$ be an error parameter, and fix $d \geq 1$. If $H' = (V, E', w')$ is a random subhypergraph of H where the weights w' are independent random variables distributed arbitrarily (and not necessarily identically) in the interval $[0, 1]$, and the expected weight of every cut in H' exceeds $\rho_\varepsilon = \frac{3}{\varepsilon^2}(r + (d+2)\ln n)$, then with probability at least $1 - n^{-d}$, every cut in H' has weight within $1 \pm \varepsilon$ of its expectation.*

One can verify that the proof of the analogous theorem for graphs, as appears in [19], easily extends to the hypergraph setting. Indeed, for the sake of this proof, a cut is merely a sum of independently sampled edges/hyperedges. The lower bound on the weight of the minimum expected cut $\hat{w}$ allows one to show that probability of a cut of weight $\alpha\hat{w}$ to deviate from its expectation is at most $n^{-\alpha(d+2)} \cdot e^{-\alpha r}$ which trades-off nicely with the bound on the number of cuts given by Theorem 3.2.

Informally, Theorem 3.9 implies that in order to obtain the desired concentration bound in the general case, the sampling probability of an edge must be inversely proportional to the size of the largest cut that contains that edge. This motivates the following definitions, and the theorem that follows them.

DEFINITION 3.10. *A hypergraph H is k-connected if the weight of each cut in H is at least k.*

DEFINITION 3.11. *A k-strong component of H is a maximal k-connected vertex-induced subhypergraph of H.*

DEFINITION 3.12. *The strong connectivity of hyperedge e, denoted k_e, is the maximum value of k such that a k-strong component contains (all endpoints of) e.*

Note that one can compute the strong connectivities of all hyperedges in a hypergraph in polynomial time as follows. Compute the global minimum cut, and then proceed recursively into each of the two subhypergraphs induced by the minimum cut. The strong connectivity of an edge would then be the maximum among the minimum cuts of all the subhypergraphs it has been a part of throughout the recursion. The minimum cut in a hypergraph was shown by [22] to be computable in $O(n^2 \log n + mn)$ time. Note that since the total number of subhypergraphs considered throughout the recursion is at most n, there are at most n different strong-connectivity values in any hypergraph.

THEOREM 3.13. *Let H be an r-uniform hypergraph, and let $\varepsilon > 0$ be an error parameter. Consider the hypergraph H_ε obtained by sampling each hyperedge e in H independently with probability $p_e = \frac{3(r+(d+2)\ln n)}{k_e \varepsilon^2}$, giving it weight w_e/p_e if it is included. Then with probability at least $1 - O(n^{-d})$*

1. *The hypergraph H_ε has $O\left(\frac{n}{\varepsilon^2}(r + \log n)\right)$ edges.*

2. *Every cut in H_ε has weight between $(1 - \varepsilon)$ and $(1 + \varepsilon)$ times its weight in H.*

The proof of the theorem is again identical to the proof of [6, Theorem 2.6] for the graph setting. This includes a bound on the total number of edges in H_ε that follows from the property that $\sum_{e \in E} w_e/k_e \leq n - 1$ (see [6, Lemma 2.7]). The only thing that needs verifying is that strong-connectivity induces a recursive partitioning of the vertices of the hypergraph, just as it does when dealing with graphs. This is in fact the case, mainly because the components considered in the definitions are vertex-induced, and therefore the cardinality of the hyperedges plays no part. One can then decompose the hyperedges of the hypergraph to "layers", based on their strong-connectivity, and apply Theorem 3.9 to each layer separately.

As to the running time, it is dominated by the time required to compute the strong connectivities of all the edges in the hypergraph, which as mentioned above, can be done by running the $O(n^2 \log n + mn)$ min-cut algorithm at most n times. Therefore, the total running time required to compute H_ε is $O(n^3 \log n + mn^2)$. Since we may assume that $m = \Omega(n \log n)$ (as there is no point to construct the sparsifier otherwise), the second term dominates and thus the running time is simply $O(mn^2)$.

To complete our discussion we bring the reader's attention to a couple of places where the cardinality of the hyperedges has played part:

- The modified parameter $p_e = \frac{3(r+(d+3)\ln n)}{k_e \varepsilon^2}$ counters the number of cuts from Theorem 3.2 (at most $O(2^{\alpha r} n^{2\alpha})$ cuts of weight $\alpha\hat{w}$) and the number of distinct edge-connectivity values, which is at most n.[10]

- The number of edges in the sparsifier is (with high probability) $O\left(\frac{n}{\varepsilon^2}(r + \log n)\right)$ since the sampling probability is also linear in r.

3.3 SAT Sparsification

LEMMA 3.14. *For every r-CNF formula Φ with n variables and m clauses, there exists an $(r+1)$-uniform hypergraph H with $2n + 1$ vertices, and a mapping $\Pi : \{0,1\}^n \to \{0,1\}^{2n+1}$ (from assignments to Φ, to cuts in H), such that for every assignment φ, it holds that $val_\Phi(\varphi) = val_H(\Pi(\varphi))$.*

PROOF. Consider an r-CNF formula Φ with variables $\{x_i\}_{i \in [n]}$. We construct the weighted hypergraph H whose vertices are $\{x_i, \neg x_i\}_{i \in [n]}$ and a special vertex F. For each clause $\ell_{i_1} \vee \ell_{i_2} \vee \cdots \vee \ell_{i_r}$, we add a hyperedge $\{\ell_{i_1}, \ldots, \ell_{i_r}, F\}$. Moreover, let Π be the mapping that maps an assignment to Φ to the cut in H obtained by placing all vertices corresponding to true literals on one side, and the F vertex together with all vertices corresponding to false literals on the other side.

For an assignment φ to Φ, it is clear that a hyperedge is contained in the cut $\Pi(\varphi)$ if and only if at least one of the vertices it contains is on the opposite side of F. Therefore the weight of $\Phi(\varphi)$ is exactly the value of φ. □

Theorem 3.4 follows from Lemma 3.14 and Theorem 3.1. The running time for constructing the sketch of the CNF formula is dominated by the running time of constructing the hypergraph sparsifier, which is $O(mn^2)$, where m is the number of clauses in the original CNF formula.

---

[10]In their analysis [6] take a union bound over n^2 distinct edge-connectivity values. For hypergraphs using the stronger linear bound (instead of the trivial n^r) is crucial.

4. FUTURE DIRECTIONS

Our results raise several questions that deserve further work.

Sketching Max-Cut.

Our results and the results of [15] make progress on the *streaming* complexity of approximating MAX-CUT, showing polynomial space lower bounds. To fully resolve this problem, one still needs to determine whether $\Omega(n)$ space is necessary for any non-trivial approximation (i.e., strictly better than $1/2$), or whether there is a sublinear-space streaming algorithm that beats the $1/2$-approximation barrier.

Also of interest is the *communication complexity* of approximating MAX-CUT in the *multi-round two-party* model, and even a multi-round analogue of BOOLEAN HIDDEN HYPERMATCHING.

Sketching Cuts in Hypergraphs.

Can one improve over the linear dependence on r in hypergraph sparsification (Theorem 3.1)? Or perhaps prove a matching lower bound? Such a refinement could be especially significant when the hyperedge cardinality is unbounded, in which case the known upper bound is $O(n^2/\varepsilon^2)$.

General CSPs.

Do all CSPs admit sketches of size (in bits or in machine words) $o(n^r)$, or even $\tilde{O}(n)$, that preserve the values of all assignments? From the direction of lower bounds, we may even restrict ourselves to sketches that are *sub-instances*, and ask whether there exist CSPs where such sketches require size $\Omega(nr)$ or even $n^{\Omega(r)}$?

5. ACKNOWLEDGEMENTS

We thank Alexandr Andoni and David Woodruff for useful discussions at early stages of this work. Work supported in part by a US-Israel BSF grant #2010418, Israel Science Foundation grant #897/13, and by the Citi Foundation.

6. REFERENCES

[1] K. J. Ahn and S. Guha. Graph sparsification in the semi-streaming model. In *36th International Colloquium on Automata, Languages and Programming: Part II*, ICALP '09, pages 328–338. Springer-Verlag, 2009. arXiv:0902.0140, doi:10.1007/978-3-642-02930-1_27.

[2] K. J. Ahn, S. Guha, and A. McGregor. Analyzing graph structure via linear measurements. In *Proceedings of the 23rd Annual ACM-SIAM Symposium on Discrete Algorithms*, SODA '12, pages 459–467. SIAM, 2012. doi:10.1137/1.9781611973099.40.

[3] K. J. Ahn, S. Guha, and A. McGregor. Graph sketches: Sparsification, spanners, and subgraphs. In *Proceedings of the 31st Symposium on Principles of Database Systems*, PODS '12, pages 5–14. ACM, 2012. doi:10.1145/2213556.2213560.

[4] A. Andoni, R. Krauthgamer, and D. P. Woodruff. The sketching complexity of graph cuts. *CoRR*, abs/1403.7058, 2014. arXiv:1403.7058.

[5] A. A. Benczúr and D. R. Karger. Approximating s-t minimum cuts in $\tilde{O}(n^2)$ time. In *Proceedings of the 28th Annual ACM Symposium on Theory of Computing*, STOC '96, pages 47–55, New York, NY, USA, 1996. ACM. doi:10.1145/237814.237827.

[6] A. A. Benczúr and D. R. Karger. Randomized approximation schemes for cuts and flows in capacitated graphs. *CoRR*, cs.DS/0207078, 2002. arXiv:cs/0207078.

[7] M. K. de Carli Silva, N. J. A. Harvey, and C. M. Sato. Sparse sums of positive semidefinite matrices. *CoRR*, abs/1107.0088, 2011. arXiv:1107.0088.

[8] H. Dell and D. van Melkebeek. Satisfiability allows no nontrivial sparsification unless the polynomial-time hierarchy collapses. In *Proceedings of the 42nd ACM Symposium on Theory of Computing*, STOC '10, pages 251–260. ACM, 2010. doi:10.1145/1806689.1806725.

[9] E. A. Dinitz, A. V. Karzanov, and M. V. Lomonosov. On the structure of the system of minimum edge cuts in a graph. *Issledovaniya po Diskretnoi Optimizatsii*, pages 290–306, 1976. URL: http://alexander-karzanov.net/ScannedOld/76_cactus_transl.pdf.

[10] A. Goel, M. Kapralov, and I. Post. Single pass sparsification in the streaming model with edge deletions. *CoRR*, abs/1203.4900, 2012. arXiv:1203.4900.

[11] M. X. Goemans and D. P. Williamson. Improved approximation algorithms for maximum cut and satisfiability problems using semidefinite programming. *J. ACM*, 42(6):1115–1145, Nov. 1995. doi:10.1145/227683.227684.

[12] R. E. Gomory and T. C. Hu. Multi-terminal network flows. *Journal of the Society for Industrial and Applied Mathematics*, 9:551–570, 1961. doi:10.1137/0109047.

[13] M. Henzinger and D. P. Williamson. On the number of small cuts in a graph. *Information Processing Letters*, 59(1):41 – 44, 1996. doi:10.1016/0020-0190(96)00079-8.

[14] P. Indyk, A. McGregor, I. Newman, and K. Onak. Open questions in data streams, property testing, and related topics. http://people.cs.umass.edu/~mcgregor/papers/11-openproblems.pdf, 2011. See also http://sublinear.info/45.

[15] M. Kapralov, S. Khanna, and M. Sudan. Streaming lower bounds for approximating MAX-CUT. In *Proceedings of the 25th Annual ACM-SIAM Symposium on Discrete Algorithms*, 2015. To Appear. arXiv:1409.2138.

[16] M. Kapralov, Y. T. Lee, C. Musco, C. Musco, and A. Sidford. Single pass spectral sparsification in dynamic streams. In *Proceedings of the 55th Annual IEEE Symposium on Foundations of Computer Science*, 2014. arXiv:1407.1289.

[17] D. R. Karger. Global min-cuts in $\mathcal{RNC}$, and other ramifications of a simple min-cut algorithm. In *Proceedings of the 4th Annual ACM-SIAM Symposium on Discrete Algorithms*, SODA '93, pages 21–30, Philadelphia, PA, USA, 1993. Society for Industrial and Applied Mathematics. URL: http://dl.acm.org/citation.cfm?id=313559.313605.

[18] D. R. Karger. Better random sampling algorithms for flows in undirected graphs. In *Proceedings of the Ninth Annual ACM-SIAM Symposium on Discrete Algorithms*, SODA '98, pages 490–499. SIAM, 1998.

URL:
http://dl.acm.org/citation.cfm?id=314613.314833.

[19] D. R. Karger. Random sampling in cut, flow, and network design problems. *Mathematics of Operations Research*, 24(2):383–413, 1999. doi:10.1287/moor.24.2.383.

[20] T. Kaufman, D. Kazhdan, and A. Lubotzky. Ramanujan complexes and bounded degree topological expanders. In *Proceedings of the 55th Annual IEEE Symposium on Foundations of Computer Science*, 2014. arXiv:1409.1397.

[21] S. Khot, G. Kindler, E. Mossel, and R. O'Donnell. Optimal inapproximability results for MAX-CUT and other 2-variable CSPs? *SIAM Journal on Computing*, 37(1):319–357, 2007. doi:10.1137/S0097539705447372.

[22] R. Klimmek and F. Wagner. A simple hypergraph min cut algorithm. Technical Report B 96-02, Freie Universität Berlin, Fachbereich Mathematik, 1996. URL: http://edocs.fu-berlin.de/docs/servlets/MCRFileNodeServlet/FUDOCS_derivate_000000000297/1996_02.pdf.

[23] F. T. Leighton and A. Moitra. Extensions and limits to vertex sparsification. In *42nd ACM symposium on Theory of computing*, STOC, pages 47–56. ACM, 2010. doi:10.1145/1806689.1806698.

[24] M. V. Lomonosov and V. Polesskii. Lower bound of network reliability. *Problemy Peredachi Informatsii*, 8(2):47–53, 1972. URL: http://www.mathnet.ru/links/36bd620cb75111781cef454d72f0d773/ppi824.pdf.

[25] A. Louis. Hypergraph Markov operators, eigenvalues and approximation algorithms. *CoRR*, abs/1408.2425, 2014. arXiv:1408.2425.

[26] A. Louis and Y. Makarychev. Approximation algorithms for hypergraph small set expansion and small set vertex expansion. In *Approximation, Randomization, and Combinatorial Optimization. Algorithms and Techniques (APPROX/RANDOM 2014)*, volume 28, pages 339–355, 2014. doi:10.4230/LIPIcs.APPROX-RANDOM.2014.339.

[27] A. McGregor. Graph stream algorithms: A survey. *SIGMOD Rec.*, 43(1):9–20, May 2014. doi:10.1145/2627692.2627694.

[28] A. Moitra. Approximation algorithms for multicommodity-type problems with guarantees

independent of the graph size. In *50th Annual Symposium on Foundations of Computer Science*, FOCS, pages 3–12. IEEE, 2009. doi:10.1109/FOCS.2009.28.

[29] H. Nagamochi, K. Nishimura, and T. Ibaraki. Computing all small cuts in an undirected network. *SIAM Journal on Discrete Mathematics*, 10(3):469–481, 1997. doi:10.1137/S0895480194271323.

[30] I. Newman and Y. Rabinovich. On multiplicative λ-approximations and some geometric applications. *SIAM Journal on Computing*, 42(3):855–883, 2013. doi:10.1137/100801809.

[31] D. Peleg and A. A. Schäffer. Graph spanners. *J. Graph Theory*, 13(1):99–116, 1989. doi:10.1002/jgt.3190130114.

[32] M. Thorup and U. Zwick. Approximate distance oracles. *J. ACM*, 52(1):1–24, 2005. doi:10.1145/1044731.1044732.

[33] Y. Yamaguchi, A. Ogawa, A. Takeda, and S. Iwata. Cyber security analysis of power networks by hypergraph cut algorithms. In *Proceedings of the Fifth Annual IEEE International Conference on Smart Grid Communications*, 2014. To appear. URL: http://www.keisu.t.u-tokyo.ac.jp/research/techrep/data/2014/METR14-12.pdf.

[34] W. Yu and E. Verbin. The streaming complexity of cycle counting, sorting by reversals, and other problems. In *Proceedings of the 22nd Annual ACM-SIAM Symposium on Discrete Algorithms*, pages 11–25, 2011. doi:10.1137/1.9781611973082.2.

[35] M. Zelke. *Algorithms for Streaming Graphs*. PhD thesis, Mathematisch-Naturwissenschaftliche Fakultät II, Humboldt-Universität zu Berlin, 2009. Published at Südwestdeutscher Verlag für Hochschulschriften. URL: http://www.tks.informatik.uni-frankfurt.de/data/doc/diss.pdf.

[36] M. Zelke. Intractability of min- and max-cut in streaming graphs. *Inf. Process. Lett.*, 111(3):145–150, Jan. 2011. doi:10.1016/j.ipl.2010.10.017.

[37] J. Zhang. A survey on streaming algorithms for massive graphs. In C. C. Aggarwal and H. Wang, editors, *Managing and Mining Graph Data*, volume 40 of *Advances in Database Systems*, pages 393–420. Springer, 2010. doi:10.1007/978-1-4419-6045-0_13.

Very Sparse Additive Spanners and Emulators

Greg Bodwin
Department of Computer Science
Stanford University
Stanford, CA
gbodwin@cs.stanford.edu

Virginia Vassilevska Williams
Department of Computer Science
Stanford University
Stanford, CA
virgi@cs.stanford.edu

ABSTRACT

We obtain new upper bounds on the additive distortion for graph emulators and spanners on relatively few edges. We introduce a new subroutine called "strip creation," and we combine this subroutine with several other ideas to obtain the following results:

1. Every graph has a spanner on $O(n^{1+\epsilon})$ edges with $\tilde{O}(n^{1/2-\epsilon/2})$ additive distortion.

2. Every graph has an emulator on $\tilde{O}(n^{1+\epsilon})$ edges with $\tilde{O}(n^{1/3-2\epsilon/3})$ additive distortion whenever $\epsilon \in [0, \frac{1}{5}]$.

3. Every graph has a spanner on $\tilde{O}(n^{1+\epsilon})$ edges with $\tilde{O}(n^{2/3-5\epsilon/3})$ additive distortion whenever $\epsilon \in [0, \frac{1}{4}]$.

Our first spanner has the new best known asymptotic edge-error tradeoff for additive spanners whenever $\epsilon \in [0, \frac{1}{7}]$. Our second spanner has the new best tradeoff whenever $\epsilon \in [\frac{1}{7}, \frac{3}{17}]$. Our emulator has the new best asymptotic edge-error tradeoff whenever $\epsilon \in [0, \frac{1}{5}]$.

1. INTRODUCTION

A spanner of a graph G is a sparser subgraph of G over the same vertex set that approximately preserves all pairwise distances between nodes. An emulator of a graph G is a possibly weighted graph H on the same vertex set as G such that the pairwise distances in H approximate the pairwise distances in G. Researchers try to improve the tradeoff between the sparsity of the spanner/emulator and the accuracy with which it preserves the distances of the original graph. Spanners were first introduced in the 1980s, where they were used to speed up protocols run over unsynchronized networks [3, 20]. Emulators were introduced by Dor, Halperin and Zwick [13]. Spanners and emulators have since found a wide variety of applications, including compact routing schemes [10, 11, 21, 23, 24], almost-shortest path algorithms [16, 14, 15, 13], distance oracles [25, 7, 4, 23], broadcasting [18], and many others.

Much of the initial theoretical work on spanners studied *multiplicative* stretch spanners, that is, all pairwise distances are preserved up to a small multiplicative factor. Althofer et al. [2] discovered that there exist spanners on $O(n^{1+1/k})$ edges with multiplicative stretch $2k-1$ for all integers $k \geq 1$. This upper bound is tight for multiplicative spanners assuming an unproven conjecture of Erdös [17]. Recent work has focused more on mixed and additive spanners. An additive spanner preserves the distances within a small additive error, and mixed spanners allow both a multiplicative and an additive error.

There are three known constructions that produce spanners of constant additive error. Aingworth et al. [1] gave a construction for spanners on $O(n^{3/2})$ edges with additive error of 2, Chechik [9] showed how to construct spanners on $\tilde{O}(n^{7/5})$[1] edges with additive distortion of 4, and Baswana et al. [6, 5] gave a construction for spanners on $\tilde{O}(n^{4/3})$ edges with additive distortion of 6 (the runtime of this construction was improved by Woodruff [27]). Knudsen [19] later simplified the constructions of +2 and +6 spanners while obtaining the same edge bounds. Dor, Halperin and Zwick [13] obtain an additive emulator on $\tilde{O}(n^{4/3})$ edges and +4 distortion. It remains a major open problem whether or not all graphs admit spanners *or* emulators of constant additive distortion with $\tilde{O}(n^{4/3-\epsilon})$ edges for any $\epsilon > 0$. Notably, Woodruff [26] has proven the existence of a graph family for which any spanner of $2k - 1$ additive distortion has at least $O(k^{-1}n^{1+1/k})$ edges, so we cannot hope for $\tilde{O}(n)$ edge spanners with constant additive distortion.

In light of this, some attempts have been made to produce relatively efficient spanners below the $n^{4/3}$ threshold. Bollobás et al. [8] showed a construction for spanners on $O(2^{1/\epsilon}n^{1+\epsilon})$ edges and $n^{1-2\epsilon}$ additive distortion; the distortion was later improved to $O(n^{1-3\epsilon})$ by Baswana et al [6]. Pettie [22] achieved $n^{9/16-7\epsilon/8}$ distortion, and Chechik [9] achieved $n^{1/2-3\epsilon/2}$ distortion whenever $\epsilon \in [\frac{3}{17}, \frac{1}{3}]$. Jointly, these last two spanners form the current state of the art. The construction of Baswana et al [6] can be generalized in a straightforward way to produce emulators with $n^{1/2-3\epsilon/2}$ additive distortion for any $\epsilon \in [0, \frac{1}{3}]$ (they do not discuss this explicitly in their paper), but no other results for emulators are known.

Our Work.

We introduce a new subroutine that is useful for spanner/emulator construction called "strip creation," and we

---

[1]The notation $\tilde{O}(f(n))$ suppresses poly $\log n$ factors.

apply this subroutine to obtain some significantly improved upper bounds on the accuracy/sparsity tradeoff available for spanners and emulators below the $n^{4/3}$ edge threshold. In Section 3, we use this subroutine in a straightforward way to produce a spanner on $O(n^{1+\epsilon})$ edges with $\tilde{O}(n^{1/2-\epsilon/2})$ additive distortion. In Section 4, we merge this idea with some others to achieve an emulator construction with $\tilde{O}(n^{1/3-2\epsilon/3})$ additive distortion, so long as $\epsilon \in [0, \frac{1}{5}]$, and a spanner of additive distortion $\tilde{O}(n^{2/3-5\epsilon/3})$, so long as $\epsilon \in [0, \frac{1}{4}]$.

Our emulator has the best tradeoff whenever $\epsilon \in [0, \frac{1}{5}]$ (it ties the generalization of Baswana et al [6], or Chechik's spanner [9], at $\epsilon = \frac{1}{5}$). The state-of-the-art asymptotics for purely additive spanners are summarized in the following table:[2]

Author	Distortion	Best When
Before this paper		
Pettie [22]	$\tilde{O}(n^{9/16-7\epsilon/8})$	$\epsilon \in [0, \frac{3}{17}]$
Chechik [9]	$\tilde{O}(n^{1/2-3\epsilon/2})$	$\epsilon \in [\frac{3}{17}, \frac{1}{3}]$
After this paper		
New; Section 3	$\tilde{O}(n^{1/2-\epsilon/2})$	$\epsilon \in [0, \frac{1}{7}]$
New; Section 4	$\tilde{O}(n^{2/3-5\epsilon/3})$	$\epsilon \in [\frac{1}{7}, \frac{3}{17}]$
Chechik [9]	$\tilde{O}(n^{1/2-3\epsilon/2})$	$\epsilon \in [\frac{3}{17}, \frac{1}{3}]$

Preliminaries.

All graphs in this paper are undirected and unweighted. The number of nodes in all of our graphs is n, unless otherwise stated. For a graph $G = (V, E)$ and $u, v \in V$, we denote by $\delta_G(u, v)$ the length of the shortest path in G from u to v.

We will often refer to *the* shortest path between two nodes in a graph, when in fact there may be many equally short paths. Any shortest path may be chosen for each pair of nodes, as long as (1) the choice is consistent, and (2) the paths are as nested as possible - that is, any two shortest paths intersect on at most one subpath. We will use this second property in our constructions. We will use the notation $\rho_G(u, v)$ to refer to the chosen shortest path between u and v in G.

Given a graph G, spanners and emulators are sparser versions of G that approximately preserve shortest path distance between every pair of nodes. More formally:

DEFINITION 1. *A weighted, undirected graph $H = (V, E', w)$ is an (α, β)-emulator of another graph $G = (V, E)$ (on the same vertex set) if, for all nodes $u, v \in V$, we have*

$$\delta_G(u, v) \le \delta_H(u, v) \le \alpha \delta_G(u, v) + \beta.$$

DEFINITION 2. *An unweighted (α, β)-emulator of a graph G is called an (α, β)-spanner of G if it is a subgraph of G.*

When $\alpha = 1$, we say that the spanner/emulator is *additive* with *distortion* β, and when $\beta = 0$, we say that the spanner/emulator is *multiplicative* with *stretch* α. If neither of these is the case, then the spanner/emulator is *mixed*.

---

[2]Some authors consider spanners whose error is a function of d, the original distance between the nodes, rather than n; these results are not included in our table.

2. STRIP CREATION

In this section, we will describe our main subroutine, called "strip creation."

Graph Clustering.

This is an important auxiliary subroutine. A very similar subroutine to this one has been used in many different spanner and emulator constructions (see [13, 9] for example). The input is a graph $G = (V, E)$ and an integer e, and the output is a partial partitioning of V into "clusters." The algorithm works as follows:

Algorithm 1: cluster(G, e)

Data: A graph $G = (V, E)$ and an integer e

1 Initialize $\mathcal{C} = \emptyset$;
2 Unmark all nodes;
3 **while** *there is an unmarked node u with at least $e - 1$ unmarked neighbors* **do**
4   Initialize C to be the set u plus any $e - 1$ of its unmarked neighbors;
5   Mark all nodes in C;
6   Add C to $\mathcal{C}$;
7 **end**
8 **return** $\mathcal{C}$;

Intuitively, we think each $C \in \mathcal{C}$ as a "cluster" of nodes. Each cluster contains a node at distance one from all other nodes; this is called the "cluster center." The subroutine of generating these clusters will be called **cluster**(G, e). The subroutine of picking out the center of a given cluster will be called **center**(C). A node is *clustered* if it belongs to some $C \in \mathcal{C}$ and *unclustered* otherwise.

Our version of graph clustering differs slightly from the typical clustering algorithm used in other spanner constructions. We produce clusters that necessarily have at least e nodes each (this property will be important later). The other important feature is that there are at most ne edges in the graph between unclustered nodes:

CLAIM 1. *Let $\mathcal{C}$ be the output of **cluster**(G, e). There are at most ne edges in G with both endpoints unclustered in $\mathcal{C}$.*

PROOF. First, note that at termination of the **cluster** subroutine, no node can have at least $e - 1$ unmarked neighbors: if it did, then we could turn it into a new cluster and add it to $\mathcal{C}$. Therefore, we have at most $e - 1$ edges with both endpoints unclustered incident on any given unclustered node. We have at most n unclustered nodes in total, and the claim follows. $\square$

Strip Creation.

This is our main subroutine. We will add a carefully-chosen set of shortest paths to the spanner that collectively have some convenient coverage properties. The subroutine works as follows:

Algorithm 2: createStrips($G, \mathcal{C}, d, m$)

> **Data**: A graph $G = (V, E)$, a clustering $\mathcal{C}$ of G, and integers d, m.
>
> **1** Initialize a set $\mathcal{S} = \emptyset$;
> **2 while** *there exist $u, v \in V$ such that the following properties all hold:*
>
> > *1. $\delta_G(u, v) \leq d$*
> >
> > *2. $\rho_G(u, v)$ intersects at most m different paths in $\mathcal{S}$*
> >
> > *3. $\rho_G(u, v)$ intersects exactly m clusters that are disjoint from all paths in $\mathcal{S}$*
>
> **3 do**
> **4** | Add $\rho_G(u, v)$ to $\mathcal{S}$;
> **5 end**
> **6 return** $\mathcal{S}$;

The paths in $\mathcal{S}$ are the *strips* of the graph. This subroutine will be called **createStrips**$(G, \mathcal{C}, d, m)$.

One property that makes this subroutine useful is that it is very cheap to add the edges in $\mathcal{S}$ to our spanner. This is our first lemma.

LEMMA 1. *The set $\mathcal{S}$ contains only $O(n)$ edges that are incident on a clustered node.*

PROOF. When we add a new path $\rho_G(u, v)$ to $\mathcal{S}$, we sort its edges (a, b) into the following cases:

1. The nodes a and b are both unclustered: this edge is not incident on a clustered node, so we can ignore it.

2. There is no edge already in $\mathcal{S}$ that touches a (or the same condition holds for b): there are $O(n)$ of this type of edge in total.

3. There is an edge in $\mathcal{S}$ that touches a and another edge in $\mathcal{S}$ that touches b, but no edge (a, b): this type of edge must go between two strips that are already in $\mathcal{S}$. Since two shortest paths intersect on at most one subpath, there can be at most two of these edges per path in $\mathcal{S}$ that intersects $\rho_G(u, v)$. Therefore, the number of this type of edge in $\rho_G(u, v)$ is at most $2m$. There are at most $\frac{n}{m}$ paths added to $\mathcal{S}$ in total (since each one must be the first to touch m new clusters), so the total number of this type of edge in the graph is $O(n)$.

4. The edge (a, b) is already in $\mathcal{S}$: this does not add a new edge to $\mathcal{S}$, so we can ignore it.

□

Adding the edges of a strip set to our graph gives it some convenient connectivity properties. This is the subject of our next two lemmas.

DEFINITION 3. *A cluster is* clean *if it does not share a node with any strip $S \in \mathcal{S}$.*

LEMMA 2. *Let H be a subgraph of G over the same vertex set, and suppose H contains exactly the edges of* **multspan**(G) *and* **createStrips**$(G, \mathcal{C}, d, m)$. *Let u, v be nodes in G with the property that $\rho_G(u, v)$ intersects at most k strips and at most k clean clusters. Then $\rho_H(u, v) \leq \rho_G(u, v) + \tilde{O}(k)$.*

PROOF. Construct a new path P as follows:

1. Start at u.

2. Repeat until you reach v:

   (a) Walk down $\rho_G(u, v)$ until you encounter a node x that belongs to a non-clean cluster C. Let S be a strip that intersects C. Let $s \in S \cap C$.

   (b) Travel the shortest path from x to s.

   (c) Walk along S until the last cluster C' intersected by both S and $\rho_G(u, v)$. Let $s' \in S \cap C'$. Let $x' \in \rho_G(u, v) \cap C'$.

   (d) Travel the shortest path from s' to x'.

   (e) Walk along $\rho_G(u, v)$ until you exit C'.

First, we will argue that P is only $O(k)$ longer than $\rho_G(u, v)$. Each time P departs from $\rho_G(u, v)$, we travel distance at most two (from x to s, which belong to the same cluster), and when P rejoins $\rho_G(u, v)$ we again travel distance at most two (from s' to x', which again belong to the same cluster). Let $a \in \rho_G(u, v)$ be a node immediately before one of these departures, and let $b \in \rho_G(u, v)$ be a node immediately after one of these departures. It follows from the triangle equality that $|P[a \leftrightarrow b]| \leq \delta_G(a, b) + 8$. Since we assume there are at most k departures in total, this implies that $|P| \leq \delta_G(a, b) + 8k$.

Second, we will argue that only $O(k)$ edges in P are missing from H. To see this, each edge $(a, b) \in P$ falls into one of the following cases:

1. The nodes a and b are both unclustered: this edge is present in H.

2. At least one of the nodes belongs to a clean cluster: this edge might not be present in H. We have assumed that $\rho_G(u, v)$ intersects at most k clean clusters, and therefore P intersects at most k clean clusters as well. We can verify that P intersects a clean cluster on at most four edges. Therefore, there are at most $4k$ of this type of edge in total in P.

3. At least one of the nodes belongs to a non-clean cluster, but (a, b) is not contained in any strip: this must be one of the edges immediately preceding or immediately following a departure of P from $\rho_G(u, v)$. As discussed above, there are at most four of these edges per departure. There are at most k departures, so there are at most $4k$ of this type of edge in total in P.

4. The edge (a, b) is contained in a strip: this edge is present in H.

Therefore, at most $8k$ edges in P are missing from H. For each missing edge (a, b), we know from edges added in the **multspan** subroutine that $\rho_H(a, b) = \tilde{O}(1)$. From this, we can conclude $|P| \leq \rho_G(u, v) + O(k)$, so $\rho_H(u, v) \leq \rho_G(u, v) + \tilde{O}(k)$. □

LEMMA 3. *Let H be a subgraph of G over the same vertex set, and suppose H contains exactly the edges of* **multspan**(G) *and* **createStrips**$(G, \mathcal{C}, d, m)$. *Let u, v be nodes in G with the property that $\rho_G(u, v)$ intersects exactly k clean clusters and fewer than $\frac{k}{2}$ strips. Then $\delta_G(u, v) \geq \Omega(\frac{kd}{m})$.*

PROOF. Partition $\rho_G(u,v)$ into $\frac{k}{m}$ sections, where each section contains exactly m clean clusters (the last section might contain fewer). For each of these sections, we evidently chose not to add this subpath P of $\rho_G(u,v)$ as a new strip. That means that either (1) P intersects at least m clusters, or (2) P has length at least d. The former can only be the case at most half the time, otherwise $\rho_G(u,v)$ intersects at least $\frac{k}{2}$ strips. Therefore, at least half of these sections have length at least d, so the total length of $\rho_G(u,v)$ is at least $\frac{kd}{2m}$. $\quad\square$

3. FIRST SPANNER CONSTRUCTION

Here we will prove the following theorem:

THEOREM 1. *For any parameter $\epsilon \in [0,1]$, there exists a spanner on $O(n^{1+\epsilon})$ edges with additive distortion $\tilde{O}(n^{1/2-\epsilon/2})$.*

Before we begin our construction, we require one new subroutine.

Very Sparse Multiplicative Spanners.

In [2], the authors describe an efficient algorithm that generates spanners on $O(n^{1+1/k})$ edges with multiplicative stretch $2k-1$. We will employ this algorithm as a subroutine several times throughout this paper; for simplicity, we will always set $k = \log n$. This gives us a spanner on $O(n)$ edges with $\tilde{O}(1)$ multiplicative stretch.

The subroutine of generating such a spanner will be called **multspan**(G).

Main Construction.

Our first spanner construction is as follows:

Algorithm 3: $\tilde{O}(n^{1/2-\epsilon/2})$ additive distortion spanners on $O(n^{1+\epsilon})$ edges

Data: An unweighted, undirected graph $G = (V,E)$ and a number ϵ

1 Initialize $H = \textbf{multspan}(G)$;
2 Initialize $\mathcal{C} = \textbf{cluster}(G, n^{\epsilon})$;
3 Initialize $\mathcal{S} \leftarrow \textbf{createStrips}(G, \mathcal{C}, \infty, n^{1/2-\epsilon/2})$
  $\quad // \ (G, \mathcal{C}, d, m)$
4 Add all edges in $\mathcal{S}$ to H;
5 Add all edges to H whose endpoints are both unclustered in $\mathcal{C}$;
6 **return** H;

Our edge bound for this construction is very straightforward. The **multspan** subroutine adds $O(n)$ edges, the **createStrips** subroutine adds $O(n)$ edges, and since every unclustered node has at most n^{ϵ} unclustered neighbors (otherwise we could have turned these into a new cluster), there are at most $n^{1+\epsilon}$ edges with both endpoints unclustered.

We will now prove our error bound.

CLAIM 2. *Any shortest path $\rho_G(u,v)$ intersects at most $n^{1/2-\epsilon/2}$ clean clusters.*

PROOF. If $\rho_G(u,v)$ intersected more than $n^{1/2-\epsilon/2}$ clean clusters, then we would add one of its subpaths as a new strip before terminating the **createStrips** subroutine. $\quad\square$

CLAIM 3. *The graph H returned by Algorithm 3 spans G with additive distortion of $\tilde{O}(n^{1/2-\epsilon/2})$.*

PROOF. First, note that there are at most $n^{1/2-\epsilon/2}$ strips in $\mathcal{S}$, since each strip intersects $n^{1/2-\epsilon/2}$ previously clean clusters, and there are at most $n^{1-\epsilon}$ clusters in total. The error bound is now immediate from Lemma 2. $\quad\square$

4. SECOND SPANNER CONSTRUCTION

We will prove the following results:

THEOREM 2. *Every graph has a spanner on $\tilde{O}(n^{1+\epsilon})$ edges with $\tilde{O}(n^{2/3-5\epsilon/3})$ additive distortion, whenever $\epsilon \in [0, \frac{1}{4}]$.*

THEOREM 3. *Every graph has an emulator on $\tilde{O}(n^{1+\epsilon})$ edges with $\tilde{O}(n^{1/3-2\epsilon/3})$ additive distortion, whenever $\epsilon \in [0, \frac{1}{5}]$.*

Hitting Sets.

We will need one last subroutine before we proceed with the construction. Let $V = \{1, \ldots, n\}$ be a set of nodes, and let $\mathcal{R}$ be a set of subsets of V. We say that $H \subset V$ is a *hitting set* of $\mathcal{R}$ if for every $R \in \mathcal{R}$, there is a node $h \in H \cap R$. The following result is well known:

LEMMA 4. *Let m be the minimum size of any element $R \in \mathcal{R}$. Then $\mathcal{R}$ has a (polynomial-time constructible) hitting set H with $|H| = O(\frac{n}{m}\log(|\mathcal{R}|))$.*

It can be shown that the greedy algorithm, which repeatedly selects the node h that hits the most un-hit sets in $\mathcal{R}$, will suffice to implement this lemma. It can also be shown that a sufficiently large random sample of nodes will implement this lemma with high probability. We will not prove this here; instead, we will simply use the notation **hittingSet**$(\mathcal{R})$ as a subroutine that constructs a hitting set of $\mathcal{R}$ of the asymptotic size bound given in the above lemma.

Main Construction.

This time, we will have two parameters in our construction: Δ and μ. For the emulator construction, we set $\mu = \frac{1}{6} - \frac{5}{6}\epsilon$ and $\Delta = \frac{1}{3} - \frac{2}{3}\epsilon$. For the spanner construction, we set $\mu = \frac{1}{3} - \frac{4}{3}\epsilon$ and $\Delta = \frac{2}{3} - \frac{5}{3}\epsilon$. Note that we have the constraint $\mu \geq 0$. This gives rise to the restrictions $\epsilon \in [0, \frac{1}{5}]$ for the emulator and $\epsilon \in [0, \frac{1}{4}]$ for the spanner.

Algorithm 4: Algorithm that implements Theorems 3 and 2

Data: A graph $G = (V, E)$ and a number ϵ

1 Initialize $H \leftarrow \mathbf{multspan}(G)$;
2 Initialize $\mathcal{C} \leftarrow \mathbf{cluster}(G, n^\epsilon)$;
3 Initialize $\mathcal{S} \leftarrow \mathbf{createStrips}(G, \mathcal{C}, n^\Delta, n^\mu)$
    // $(G, \mathcal{C}, d, m)$
4 Add all edges in $\mathcal{S}$ to H;
5 Add all edges between unclustered nodes to H;
6 Initialize $\mathcal{Q} \leftarrow \emptyset$;
7 **for** *every ordered pair of nodes u, v such that $\rho_G(u, v)$ intersects at least $\frac{n^\Delta}{2}$ strips or at least n^Δ clean clusters* **do**
8   Let x be the first node on $\rho_G(u, v)$ such that $\rho_G(u, x)$ intersects at least $\frac{n^\Delta}{2}$ strips or at least n^Δ clean clusters;
9   **if** *$\rho_G(u, x)$ intersects at least $\frac{n^\Delta}{2}$ strips* **then**
10   Initialize Q to be the set of all nodes within distance two of any of these strips;
11   Add Q to $\mathcal{Q}$;
12   **else**
13   Initialize Q to be the set of nodes in $\rho_G(u, x)$;
14   Add Q to $\mathcal{Q}$;
15   **end**
16 **end**
17 Initialize $\mathcal{T} \leftarrow \mathbf{hittingSet}(\mathcal{Q})$;

Algorithm 4: Spanner Continuation (Theorem 2)
---
18 Add to H all edges in $\mathbf{subsetspan}(G, \mathcal{T})$;
19 **return** H;

Algorithm 4: Emulator Continuation (Theorem 3)
---
18 **for** *every pair $t_1, t_2 \in \mathcal{T}$* **do**
19   Add an edge to H between t_1 and t_2 of weight $\delta_G(t_1, t_2)$;
20 **end**
21 **return** H;

The main **for** loop in this algorithm omits pairs u, v with the property that $\rho_G(u, v)$ intersects less than $\frac{n^\Delta}{2}$ strips and less than n^Δ clean clusters. We can ignore these paths because we already have enough edges in place to span these paths with $\tilde{O}(n^\Delta)$ (this is immediate from Lemma 2).

We will now prove our certificates for this construction.

CLAIM 4 (EDGE BOUND). *In either case, the returned graph H has $\tilde{O}(n^{1+\epsilon})$ edges.*

PROOF. Our first goal is to place a lower bound on the minimum size of any element $Q \in \mathcal{Q}$. We create these elements Q in lines 10 and 13. In the first case, we are adding the nodes within distance two of $\Omega(n^\Delta)$ different strips. Each of these strips was the first to intersect n^μ distinct clusters, each of which contains at least n^ϵ nodes. Therefore, the size of each of these elements is $\Omega(n^{\Delta+\mu+\epsilon})$. In line

13, we add all of $\delta_G(u, x)$ to Q. We know that this path intersects at least n^Δ clean clusters and at most $\frac{n^\Delta}{2}$ strips. By Lemma 3, we conclude that this path has length at least $\Omega(n^{2\Delta-\mu})$.

By Lemma 4, the size of $\mathcal{T}$ is at most $\tilde{O}(n^{\max(1-\Delta-\mu-\epsilon, 1-2\Delta+\mu)})$. For the emulator parameter settings, this gives $|\mathcal{T}| = \tilde{O}(n^{1/2+\epsilon/2})$, so we add $|\mathcal{T}|^2 = \tilde{O}(n^{1+\epsilon})$ edges to H in the emulator continuation. For the spanner parameter settings, this gives $|\mathcal{T}| = \tilde{O}(n^{2\epsilon})$. Then $\mathbf{subspan}(G, \mathcal{T})$ has $n|\mathcal{T}|^{1/2} = \tilde{O}(n^{1+\epsilon})$ edges. $\square$

CLAIM 5 (ERROR BOUND). *The returned graph H spans/emulates G with $\tilde{O}(n^\Delta)$ additive distortion.*

PROOF. Let u, v be arbitrary nodes in V. First, suppose that $\rho_G(u, v)$ intersects fewer than $\frac{n^\Delta}{2}$ strips and fewer than n^Δ clean clusters. Then by Lemma 2, we already have $\rho_H(u, v) \leq \rho_G(u, v) + \tilde{O}(n^\Delta)$.

Otherwise, let x_u be the first node on $\rho_G(u, v)$ such that $\rho_G(u, x_u)$ does *not* have this property, and let x_v be the same for $\rho_G(v, u)$. First, suppose $\rho_G(u, x_u)$ intersects at least $\frac{n^\Delta}{2}$ strips. Then there is some node $t_u \in \mathcal{T}$ on one of these strips (Line 10). Otherwise, there is some node $t_u \in \mathcal{T}$ that sits directly on the path $\rho_G(u, x_u)$ (Line 13). Let w_u be the closest node on $\rho_G(u, x_u)$ to t_u. Define t_v, w_v similarly with respect to v.

We now proceed by the triangle inequality. We have

$$\delta_G(t_u, t_v) \leq \delta_G(t_u, w_u) + \delta_G(w_u, w_v) + \delta_G(w_v, t_v)$$

We know that $\delta_G(t_u, w_u)$ and $\delta_G(w_v, t_v)$ are both $O(n^\Delta)$, since t_u (t_v) is within distance two of a strip that intersects $\rho_G(u, x_u)$ ($\rho_G(x_v, v)$). We can then write

$$\delta_G(w_u, t_u) + \delta_G(t_u, t_v) + \delta_G(t_v, w_v) \leq \delta_G(w_u, w_v) + O(n^\Delta)$$

Some algebra yields

$$\delta_G(u, w_u) + \delta_G(w_u, t_u) + \delta_G(t_u, t_v) + \delta_G(t_v, w_v) + \delta_G(w_v, v)$$
$$\leq \delta_G(u, w_u) + \delta_G(w_u, w_v) + \delta_G(w_v, v) + \tilde{O}(n^\Delta)$$

Since $w_u, w_v \in \rho_G(u, v)$, the right-hand side simplifies.

$$\delta_G(u, w_u) + \delta_G(w_u, t_u) + \delta_G(t_u, t_v) + \delta_G(t_v, w_v) + \delta_G(w_v, v)$$
$$\leq \delta_G(u, v) + \tilde{O}(n^\Delta)$$

It follows from Lemma 2 that $\delta_H(u, w_u) \leq \delta_G(u, w_u) + \tilde{O}(n^\Delta)$ and $\delta_H(w_v, v) \leq \delta_G(w_v, v) + \tilde{O}(n^\Delta)$. We also know that $\delta_G(w_u, t_u) \leq n^\Delta$ and $\delta_G(t_v, w_v) \leq n^\Delta$. Additionally, we know that $\delta_H(t_u, t_v) \leq \delta_G(t_u, t_v) + 2$, because we have added a subset spanner (or a direct emulator edge) that enforces this property on every pair of nodes in $\mathcal{T}$. This gives us

$$\delta_H(u, w_u) + \delta_H(w_u, t_u) + \delta_H(t_u, t_v) + \delta_H(t_v, w_v) + \delta_H(w_v, v)$$
$$\leq \delta_G(u, v) + \tilde{O}(n^\Delta)$$

We finish by applying the triangle inequality to the left-hand side.

$$\delta_H(u, v) \leq \delta_G(u, v) + \tilde{O}(n^\Delta)$$

$\square$

It is worth noting that better spanners would follow quickly from better subset spanners. It is not yet known how to generalize the subset spanner result in [12] to fewer edges and a non-constant error bound; for our purposes, any error of up to n^Δ would be acceptable. This seems to be an attainable and relevant problem, which we leave open.

5. CONCLUSION

We have improved the additive distortion bounds for spanners and emulators for many values of ϵ below the $n^{4/3}$ edge threshold. The main open question of spanner research still remains: do there exist spanners or emulators on $O(n^{4/3-\delta})$ edges with additive distortion $n^{o(1)}$ for some constant $\delta > 0$?

Our work also suggests that further improvements in spanner construction may follow from generalizations of the recent work in subset spanners. More formally: can we construct a subset spanner on an asymptotically smaller number of edges, given a subset size of $|S|$ and a budget of n^Δ additive distortion?

6. REFERENCES

[1] D. Aingworth, C. Chekuri, P. Indyk, and R. Motwani. Fast estimation of diameter and shortest paths (without matrix multiplication). *SIAM J. Comput.*, 28:1167–1181, 1999.

[2] I. Althöfer, G. Das, D. Dobkin, D. Joseph, and J. Soares. On sparse spanners of weighted graphs. *Discrete & Computational Geometry*, 9:81–100, 1993.

[3] B. Awerbuch. Complexity of network synchronization. *Journal of the ACM*, pages 32, 804–823, 1985.

[4] S. Baswana and T. Kavitha. Faster algorithms for approximate distance oracles and all-pairs small stretch paths. *Proc. 47th IEEE Symposium on Foundations of Computer Science (FOCS)*, pages 591–602, 2006.

[5] S. Baswana, T. Kavitha, K. Mehlhorn, and S. Pettie. Additive spanners and (α, β)-spanners. *ACM Trans. Algo.*, 7:A.5, 2005.

[6] S. Baswana, T. Kavitha, K. Mehlhorn, and S. Pettie. New constructions of (α, β)-spanners and purely additive spanners. *Proc. 16th SODA*, pages 672–681, 2005.

[7] S. Baswana and S. Sen. A simple and linear time randomized algorithm for computing sparse spanners in weighted graphs. *Journal of Random Structures and Algorithms 30*, pages 4, 532–563, 2007.

[8] B. Bollobás, D. Coppersmith, and M. Elkin. Sparse distance preservers and additive spanners. *Proc. 14th ACM-SIAM Symp. on Discrete Algorithms (SODA)*, pages 414–423, 2003.

[9] Shiri Chechik. New additive spanners. *SODA*, pages 498–512, 2013.

[10] L. J. Cowen. Compact routing with minimum stretch. *Journal of Algorithms*, pages 28, 170–183, 2001.

[11] L. J. Cowen and C. G. Wagner. Compact roundtrip routing in directed networks. *Journal of Algorithms*, pages 50, 1, 79–95, 2004.

[12] M. Cygan, F. Grandoni, and T. Kavitha. On pairwise spanners. *Symposium on Theoretical Aspects of Computer Science (STACS)*, 2013.

[13] Dorit Dor, Shay Halperin, and Uri Zwick. All pairs almost shortest paths. *Proc. 37th Annual Symp. on Foundations of Computer Science (FOCS)*, pages 452–461, 1996.

[14] M. Elkin. Computing almost shortest paths. *ACM Trans. Algorithms*, pages 1(2):283–323, 2005.

[15] M. Elkin. A near-optimal distributed fully dynamic algorithm for maintaining sparse spanners. *Proc. 26th ACM Symposium on Principles of Distributed Computing (PODC)*, pages 185–194, 2007.

[16] M. Elkin and J. Zhang. Efficient algorithms for constructing $(1 + \epsilon, \beta)$-spanners in the distributed and streaming models. *Distributed Compting 18*, pages 5, 375–385, 2006.

[17] P. Erdös. Extremal problems in graph theory. *Theory of graphs and its applications*, pages 29–36, 1964.

[18] A. M. Farley, A. Proskurowski, D. Zappala, and K. Windisch. Spanners and message distribution in networks. *Discrete Applied Mathematics*, pages 137(2):159–171, 2004.

[19] Mathias Bæk Tejs Knudsen. Additive spanners: A simple construction. *Symposium and Workshop on Algorithm Theory (SWAT)*, pages 277–281, 2014.

[20] D. Peleg and J. D. Ullman. An optimal synchronizer for the hypercube. *SIAM Journal of Computing*, pages 18, 740–747, 1989.

[21] D. Peleg and E. Upfal. A trade-off between space and efficiency for routing tables. *Journal of the ACM*, pages 36(3):510–530, 1989.

[22] Seth Pettie. Low distortion spanners. *34th International Colloquium on Automata, Languages, and Programming (ICALP)*, pages 78–89, 2007.

[23] L. Roditty, M. Thorup, and U. Zwick. Roundtrip spanners and roundtrip routing in directed graphs. *ACM Trans. Algorithms*, page 3(4): Article 29, 2008.

[24] M. Thorup and U. Zwick. Compact routing schemes. *Proc. 13th ACM Symposium on Parallel Algorithms and Architectures (SPAA)*, pages 1–10, 2001.

[25] M. Thorup and U. Zwick. Approximate distance oracles. *Journal of the ACM 52*, pages 1, 1–24, 2005.

[26] D. P. Woodruff. Lower bounds for additive spanners, emulators, and more. *Proc. 47th IEEE Symp. on Foundations of Computer Science (FOCS)*, pages 389–398, 2006.

[27] D. P. Woodruff. Additive spanners in nearly quadratic time. *37th International Colloquium on Automata, Languages, and Programming (ICALP)*, pages 463–474, 2010.

Monotone Properties of k-Uniform Hypergraphs are Weakly Evasive

Timothy Black
University of Chicago
timblack@math.uchicago.edu

ABSTRACT

A boolean function in n variables is *weakly evasive* if its decision-tree complexity is $\Omega(n)$. By k-graphs we mean k-uniform hypergraphs. A *k-graph property* on v vertices is a boolean function on $n = \binom{v}{k}$ variables corresponding to the k-subsets of a v-set that is invariant under the $v!$ permutations of the v-set (isomorphisms of k-graphs).

Rivest and Vuillemin (1976) proved that all non-constant monotone graph properties ($k = 2$) are weakly evasive, confirming a conjecture of Aanderaa and Rosenberg (1973). Kulkarni, Qiao, and Sun (2013) proved the analogous result for 3-graphs. We extend these results to k-graphs for every fixed k. From this, we show that monotone boolean functions invariant under the action of a large primitive group are weakly evasive.

While KQS (2013) employ the powerful topological approach of Kahn, Saks, and Sturtevant (1984) combined with heavy number theory, our argument is elementary and self-contained (modulo some basic group theory). Inspired by the outline of the KQS approach, we formalize the general framework of "orbit augmentation sequences" of sets with group actions. We show that a parameter of such sequences, called the "spacing," is a lower bound on the decision-tree complexity for any nontrivial monotone property that is Γ-invariant for all groups Γ involved in the orbit augmentation sequence, assuming all those groups are p-groups. We develop operations on such sequences such as composition and direct product which will provide helpful machinery for our applications. We apply this general technique to k-graphs via certain liftings of k-graphs with wreath product action of p-groups.

Categories and Subject Descriptors

F.2.2 [**Analysis of Algorithms and Problem Complexity**]: Nonnumerical Algorithms and Problems—*Computations on discrete structures*; G.2.2 [**Discrete Mathematics**]: Graph Theory—*Hypergraphs*; F.1.3 [**Computation by Abstract Devices**]: Complexity Measures and Classes

ITCS'15, January 11–13, 2015, Rehovot, Israel.
Copyright is held by the owner/author(s). Publication rights licensed to ACM.
ACM 978-1-4503-3333-7/15/01 ...$15.00.
http://dx.doi.org/10.1145/2688073.2688085.

General Terms

Theory

Keywords

Decision-tree complexity; Evasiveness Conjecture; monotone hypergraph properties.

1. INTRODUCTION

Suppose we are given a property of subsets of a finite set X, and we are trying to determine whether a particular subset S of X which is hidden from us has the property by asking membership queries (questions of the form "$x \in S$?"). The maximum number of queries we need to ask over all choices of S, assuming we are using a strategy that minimizes this maximum, is called the *decision-tree complexity* of the property. A property over X is said to be *evasive* if its decision-tree complexity is $|X|$. A collection of properties is said to be *weakly evasive* if each property has decision-tree complexity within a constant factor of the size of its underlying set.

Particular attention has been given to properties that have an amount of symmetry. Kahn, Saks, and Sturtevant conjectured (see [6]) that nontrivial monotone properties that are invariant under a transitive group action are evasive. This conjecture was a modification of a 1973 conjecture of Rivest and Vuillemin (see [10]) that KSS disproved. The conjecture remains open, although there has been progress on weakened versions of it.

In this paper, we prove that the conjecture holds for large primitive groups, if evasiveness is replaced by weak evasiveness (see Section 2 for the definition of primitive group).

THEOREM 1.1. *For each fixed $\varepsilon > 0$, nontrivial monotone properties over $[n]$ that are invariant under the action of a primitive group of order at least $\exp(n^\varepsilon)$ are weakly evasive.*

Typical examples of large primitive groups are the induced action of the symmetric group $\mathrm{Sym}(V)$ on $\binom{V}{k}$, the set of k-element subsets of V. Symmetry under this action defines k-uniform hypergraph (k-graph) properties.

COROLLARY 1.2. *For every fixed k, nontrivial monotone k-graph properties are weakly evasive.*

Our estimate for the constant hidden in the definition of weak evasiveness is $\exp(-O(k^2))$ (see Theorem 6.3 for a more specific statement).

Recently, Kulkarni, Qiao, and Sun [8] proved Corollary 1.2 for 3-graphs ($k = 3$). Their work motivated the present paper. The KQS result extends work of Rivest and Vuillemin [10] who proved the result for $k = 2$, confirming a conjecture of Aanderaa and Rosenberg (see [6]).

Karp conjectured (see [6]) that nontrivial monotone graph properties are not just weakly evasive, but evasive. Kahn, Saks, and Sturtevant [6] confirmed this when the number of vertices is a prime-power, but the general case remains open.

Yao [14], using the KSS method, proved that nontrivial monotone bipartite graph properties are evasive. KQS [8] generalized this to k-partite k-graphs, weakening the conclusion to weak evasiveness. We further generalize this to partwise-uniform hypergraphs.

Definition 1. For positive integers k, t, $k_1, \ldots, k_t$ such that $k_1 + \ldots + k_t = k$, we say that a k-graph is *t-partite and $(k_1, \ldots, k_t)$-uniform* if its vertices are partitioned into t parts, and each edge has k_i vertices in part i. When $k_1, \ldots, k_t$ are clear from context, we speak of *partwise-uniform k-graphs*.

We shall show that the following result is a consequence of Corollary 1.2.

COROLLARY 1.3. *For bounded k and t, and a partition $k = k_1 + \cdots + k_t$, nontrivial monotone properties of t-partite $(k_1, \ldots, k_t)$-uniform k-graphs are weakly evasive.*

KQS proved this for the case $k_1 = \cdots = k_t = 1$. Corollary 1.3 is used in the proof of Theorem 1.1.

1.1 Structure of the Paper

Our main technical result is Corollary 1.2, which we prove in Sections 3–6. In Section 7 we derive Corollary 1.3 from Corollary 1.2 and use Corollary 1.3 along with a result of Cameron [2] on large primitive groups to prove Theorem 1.1.

We explain the structure of the paper in greater detail in Section 1.3.

1.2 Previous methods

A *p-group* is a group of order a power of the prime p. The connection of the evasiveness problem to p-groups was discovered by Rivest and Vuillemin in their 1976 paper [10] that proved the Aanderaa—Rosenberg Conjecture. They showed that if a property $\mathscr{P}$ over a set X is invariant under a transitive p-group action and $\mathscr{P}$ holds for exactly one of $\emptyset$ and X, then $\mathscr{P}$ is evasive (see Theorem 3.1 below). They used this result via *subproperties* to obtain weak evasiveness of properties where the size of the underlying set was not a prime power. (A "subproperty" is obtained from a property over the set X by fixing the membership status of some elements of the underlying set; this corresponds to the notion of *restriction* of boolean functions.)

This basic pattern has been maintained in virtually all subsequent work on the subject, including the seminal 1984 paper by Kahn, Saks, and Sturtevant [6] where it is used through a lemma from [7].

KSS discovered that if a monotone property, viewed as a simplicial complex, is not contractible then the property is evasive. To use this criterion, KSS and all subsequent work relied on powerful results by Oliver [9] on the fixed-point complexes of groups acting on the complex. Oliver's results apply to a very special class of groups, called "Oliver groups."

Definition 2. A finite group Γ is an **Oliver group** if it has subgroups Γ_1 and Γ_2 with $\Gamma_1 \trianglelefteq \Gamma_2 \trianglelefteq \Gamma$ such that $|\Gamma/\Gamma_2|$ is a power of a prime, Γ_2/Γ_1 is cyclic, and $|\Gamma_1|$ is a power of a (possibly different) prime.

Note in particular that *all Oliver groups are solvable*. As KSS point out, Oliver's results define the limits of their approach. Indeed it is the very strict constraints on the structure of Oliver groups that makes it unlikely that the method used by Kulkarni, Qiao, and Sun [8] to prove weak evasiveness of nontrivial monotone 3-graph properties could be extended to k-graph properties for $k \geq 4$.

A permutation group is *transitive* if all elements of the permutation domain are equivalent under the group action. A permutation group is *t-transitive* if the action is transitive on the set of ordered t-tuples of distinct elements of the permutation domain.

The KQS approach requires the construction of doubly transitive (2-transitive) Oliver groups acting on a large and well-controlled number of points. Such groups do exist on domains of size a prime power (the groups of affine transformations $x \mapsto ax + b$ over a finite field) and have already been used by KSS to prove that nontrivial monotone graph properties for a prime-power number of vertices are evasive. For proper control of the numbers on which such groups act, KQS invoke a uniform version of Vinogradov's celebrated 3-Primes Theorem [13] (that every sufficiently large odd integer is a sum of three primes that are nearly equal). However, an extension of the KQS approach to k-graphs would require $(k-1)$-transitive Oliver groups; but it is known that there is only a finite number of very small 3-transitive solvable groups; only S_4 is 4-transitive and solvable; and there are no 5-transitive solvable groups. (The last statement is an immediate consequence of the fact that the symmetric group S_5 is not solvable.)

Another concern regarding the use of the topological approach via Oliver's results is that Oliver groups don't combine well. While virtually any reasonable operation on groups (direct product, semidirect product, wreath product, group extension, etc.), when applied to p-groups (for the same prime p) yields a p-group, even a direct product of two Oliver groups is not an Oliver group in general. Of course every p-group is an Oliver group, but to the extent that the class of Oliver groups is richer than just the p-groups, we find this added variety more an obstacle than help in proving weak evasiveness.

Since the KSS paper, virtually all articles in this area have used the topological approach via Oliver's results. The papers [14, 12, 4, 3, 1, 8] are but a small sample. In the light of the concerns mentioned, it seems appropriate that we break this three-decades-old tradition.

1.3 Our methods

Rather than using the topological approach, we devise a combination of combinatorial and group theoretic techniques to carry out what on a high level might be called the Rivest—Vuillemin plan: use p-groups through carefully designed subproperties.

Inspired by the outline of the KQS approach, we define a general framework which we call "orbit augmentation sequences" (OA sequences) of sets with group actions. Such a sequence is defined as a sequence of pairs (B_i, A_i) of disjoint subsets of the underlying set X with a sequence Γ_i of subgroups of group Γ that acts on X such that Γ_i fixes the sets B_i and A_i (setwise) and acts transitively on A_i (so A_i is an orbit of Γ_i) and $B_{i-1} \cup A_{i-1} \supseteq B_i$, hence the name "orbit augmentation sequence." (See Definition 18.) The minimum size of the A_i is the *spacing* of the sequence. We consider orbit augmentation sequences that start with $B_1 = \emptyset$ and end with $B_m \cup A_m = X$; we call these "full OA sequences."

Our basic observation is that *the spacing of a full OA sequence is a lower bound on the decision-tree complexity of any nontrivial monotone Γ-invariant property* (Proposition 3.2), assuming each subgroup involved is a p-group (or more generally, an Oliver group, but we only use p-groups). We develop the theory of orbit augmentation sequences in Section 3 where we introduce operations such as composition and direct product that will give us a helpful machinery for our applications. As indicated, Oliver groups are an obstacle to direct product operations; but the machinery works very well when we limit the groups involved to p-groups.

The bulk of the paper (Sections 4–6) shows how to implement OA sequences for k-graph properties. One of our combinatorial tools will be a lifting of k-graphs (a special case of their lexicographic product) with wreath product action of the groups involved; these concepts are discussed in Section 4.

Section 5 implements such sequences in the context of k-graphs with a prime-power number of vertices. Like KQS, we partition the vertices into equally-sized sets, and classify edges by how many vertices they have in each set. We then build a sequence by adding each class of edges one at a time. KQS added each class in a single step of the sequence, which required more complicated groups, and thus limited the types of edges that could be added. We add each class through an OA sequence. We add the edges that have all vertices in a single set of the partition by inducting on the number of vertices, building up to the next level by taking a lifting of a smaller complete graph. Each other class of edges can be thought of as a product of complete k_i-graphs with $k_i < k$; we add such a class using induction on k and our direct product lemma. Our composition lemma allows us to do each of these additions of classes consecutively in order to build up a full OA sequence for our original k-graph.

In Section 6 we extend the result of Section 5, constructing orbit augmentation sequences on an arbitrary number of vertices. We build off of the sequences from Section 5, once again constructing them inductively using direct products and composition.

The final section, Section 7, uses the result of Section 6 to prove the main theorem, that nontrivial monotone properties invariant under the action of a large primitive group are weakly evasive. A result of Cameron says that all large permutation groups have a subgroup that looks like the group of symmetries of a hypergraph, raised to some power. We apply the result of Section 6, along with our direct product lemma, to this subgroup.

2. PRELIMINARIES

2.1 Groups

Definition 3. For X a finite set and $k \geq 0$, let $\binom{X}{k}$ denote the set of k-element subsets of X. Let $\mathcal{P}(X)$ denote the power-set of X, the set of all subsets of X.

Our general reference to basic group theory is [11].

Definition 4. Write $\Delta \leq \Gamma$ to denote that Δ is a subgroup of Γ. For prime p, a **p-group** is a group whose order is a power of p.

Definition 5. Let Γ be a group and X a set; let $\mathrm{Sym}(X)$ denote the group of all permutations of X (the symmetric group acting on X). An **action** of Γ on X is a homomorphism $\Gamma \to \mathrm{Sym}(X)$. We denote the image of $x \in X$ under the permutation corresponding to $\gamma \in \Gamma$ by x^γ. The action is **transitive** if $(\forall x, y \in X)(\exists \gamma \in \Gamma)(x^\gamma = y)$. For $S \subseteq X$ and $\gamma \in \Gamma$ we write $S^\gamma = \{s^\gamma \mid s \in S\}$. Thus, an action of Γ on X **induces** an action of Γ on $\binom{X}{k}$, where k is a nonnegative integer, and on $\mathcal{P}(X)$.

Definition 6. A **permutation group** is a subgroup $\Gamma \leq \mathrm{Sym}(X)$. When $\Gamma \to \mathrm{Sym}(X)$ is injective, we will sometimes find it convenient to identify Γ with its image.

Definition 7. Let $\Gamma \leq \mathrm{Sym}(V)$ and $\Delta \leq \mathrm{Sym}(W)$ be permutation groups. The **wreath product** $\Gamma \wr \Delta$ is defined as a subgroup of $\mathrm{Sym}(V \times W)$ as follows: we think of the domain $V \times W$ as the union of $|W|$ copies of V; the group $\Gamma \times \cdots \times \Gamma$ acts on this set by independently permuting each copy of V by elements of Γ; one element of Δ permutes the copies. Formally, the elements of $\Gamma \wr \Delta$ correspond to the Cartesian product $\Gamma^W \times \Delta$; and the element $(\gamma_w : w \in W, \delta) \in \Gamma \wr \Delta$ (where $(\forall w \in W)(\gamma_w \in \Gamma)$ and $\delta \in \Delta$) takes $(v, w) \in V \times W$ to (v^{γ_w}, δ_w). This action of $\Gamma \wr \Delta$ is called the **imprimitive action**. The group $\Gamma \wr \Delta$ also acts on V^W; identify each $(v_w : w \in W) \in V^W$ with the $|W|$-element set $\{(v_w, w) \mid w \in W\}$, then the imprimitive action induces an action on these sets. This is the **product action**.

Note that $|\Gamma \wr \Delta| = |\Gamma|^{|W|} |\Delta|$. So in particular if both Γ and Δ are p-groups (for the same prime p) then their wreath product $\Gamma \wr \Delta$ is also a p-group.

We will introduce one more action of $\Gamma \wr \Delta$ in Section 4.

Definition 8. Let V be a set with $|V| \geq 2$ and $\Gamma \leq \mathrm{Sym}(V)$ a group that acts transitively on V. A **system of imprimitivity** for Γ is a partition of V that is invariant under the action of Γ. If no such system exists other than $\{V\}$ and the discrete partition (consisting of singletons), say Γ is **primitive**.

2.2 Properties and Evasiveness

Definition 9. For n a nonnegative integer, a **boolean function on n variables** is a function $f : \{0,1\}^n \to \{0,1\}$.

Definition 10. For X a finite set, $\mathscr{P}$ is a **property over X** if $\mathscr{P} \subseteq \mathcal{P}(X)$.

Properties $\mathscr{P}$ over $[n] = \{1, \ldots, n\}$ can be identified with boolean functions $f : \{0,1\}^n \to \{0,1\}$ by setting $f(x_1, \ldots, x_n) = 1 \Leftrightarrow \{i \mid x_i = 1\} \in \mathscr{P}$. Here, we find it more convenient to work with properties over $[n]$.

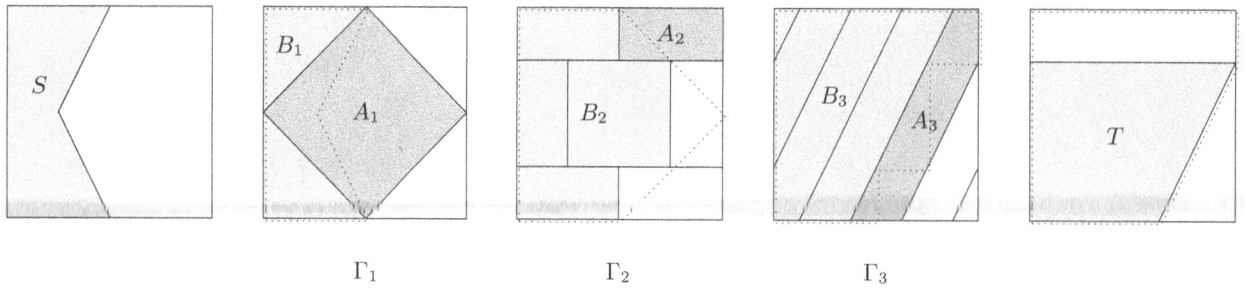

Figure 1: A pictorial interpretation of an (S,T) OA sequence. The entire square is the set X, and each region is an orbit of Γ_i. A dotted line outlines $B_{i-1} \cup A_{i-1}$.

Definition 11. A property $\mathscr{P}$ over X is **nontrivial** if $\mathscr{P} \neq \emptyset$ and $\mathscr{P} \neq \mathcal{P}(X)$.

Definition 12. Property $\mathscr{P}$ is **monotone** if for all $T \in \mathscr{P}$ and $S \subseteq T$, we have $S \in \mathscr{P}$.

Definition 13. Let $\mathscr{P}$ be a property over X and let B, A be disjoint subsets of X. The **subproperty** of $\mathscr{P}$ defined by the pair (B, A) is the set $\mathscr{Q} = \{S \subseteq A \mid B \cup S \in \mathscr{P}\}$. Note that $\mathscr{Q}$ is a property over A.

Remark 1. In the language of boolean functions, a subproperty corresponds to a restriction of a function.

Definition 14. If Γ is a group acting on X and $\mathscr{P}$ is a property over X, say that $\mathscr{P}$ is **invariant under the action of** Γ, or Γ-**invariant**, if for all $\gamma \in \Gamma$ and $S \in \mathscr{P}$, we have $S^\gamma \in \mathscr{P}$.

Remark 2. A boolean function $f : \{0,1\}^n \to \{0,1\}$ is Γ-invariant if for all $\gamma \in \Gamma$ and $(x_1, \ldots, x_n) \in \{0,1\}^n$, we have $f(x_1, \ldots, x_n) = f(x_{1\gamma}, \ldots, x_{n\gamma})$.

Definition 15. A decision tree is a binary tree in which each non-leaf node is labeled with an element of a finite set X, and each leaf is labeled with either "true" or "false". Given a decision tree and a subset S of X, traverse the tree starting at the root node by moving to the left child whenever the label on the node is in S (and to right child otherwise) until reaching a leaf. The decision tree is said to compute $\mathscr{P} \subseteq \mathcal{P}(X)$ if for all $S \subseteq X$, this traversal process ends with "true" exactly when $S \in \mathscr{P}$. For a property $\mathscr{P}$ over X, the **decision-tree complexity** of $\mathscr{P}$, denoted $D(\mathscr{P})$, is the least depth of any decision tree computing $\mathscr{P}$.

Note that $D(\mathscr{P}) \leq |X|$.

Definition 16. A property $\mathscr{P}$ over X is **evasive** if $D(\mathscr{P}) = |X|$.

Definition 17. For some infinite index set I, let $\{X_i \mid i \in I\}$ be a collection of sets and let $\mathscr{P}_i$ be a property of X_i. Say that the collection $\{\mathscr{P}_i \mid i \in I\}$ is **weakly evasive** if $D(\mathscr{P}_i) \geq \Omega(|X_i|)$.

3. ORBIT AUGMENTATION SEQUENCES

Our main tool for proving weak evasiveness of nontrivial monotone k-graph properties, orbit augmentation sequences, relies on this result of Rivest and Villemin.

THEOREM 3.1 (RIVEST AND VUILLEMIN [10]). *Let X be a finite set with $|X|$ a power of a prime, Γ a group acting transitively on X, and $\mathscr{P}$ a property over X that is Γ-invariant with exactly one of $\emptyset, X$ in $\mathscr{P}$. Then $\mathscr{P}$ is evasive.*

To show that a property has a large decision-tree complexity, Rivest and Vuillemin and others, including Kulkarni, Qiao, and Sun, looked at subproperties to which they could apply Theorem 3.1 (or a related theorem of Kahn, Saks, and Sturtevant). They used the fact that properties pass on some of their symmetry to subproperties, and that the decision-tree complexity of a subproperty bounds the decision-tree complexity of the property from which it is induced, as stated in the next two observations.

Observation 1. If the property $\mathscr{P}$ from Definition 13 is Γ-invariant, and Γ fixes each of B and A, then the subproperty $\mathscr{Q}$ is also Γ-invariant.

PROOF. For all $\gamma \in \Gamma$ and $S \in \mathscr{Q}$ we have $S^\gamma \subseteq A$ and $B \cup S^\gamma = (B \cup S)^\gamma \in \mathscr{P}$, so $S^\gamma \in \mathscr{Q}$. $\square$

Observation 2. If $\mathscr{Q}$ is a subproperty of $\mathscr{P}$, then $D(\mathscr{P}) \geq D(\mathscr{Q})$. $\square$

We now introduce the central concept of our work: "orbit augmentation sequences". These will enable us to build up ever larger sets with the property, eventually getting that the whole set has the property and so the property is trivial. Along the way, we use transitive p-group actions on subproperties via the Rivest-Vuillemin Theorem (Theorem 3.1).

Definition 18.

- Let X be a finite set, $S, T \subseteq X$, $m \geq 0$;
- for $1 \leq i \leq m$, let B_i, A_i be disjoint subsets of X;
- for each i, let Γ_i be a group acting on X;
- for each i, assume Γ_i fixes B_i and A_i (setwise);
- for each i, assume the Γ_i-action on A_i is transitive;
- for each $i > 1$, assume $B_{i-1} \cup A_{i-1} \supseteq B_i$; and
- assume $S \supseteq B_1$ and $B_m \cup A_m \supseteq T$.

Then we will say that $((B_1, A_1, \Gamma_1), \ldots, (B_m, A_m, \Gamma_m))$ is an (S, T) **orbit augmentation sequence (OA sequence)** for X using the groups $\Gamma_1 \ldots, \Gamma_m$. A **full OA sequence** for X is an $(\emptyset, X)$ OA sequence for X.

The **spacing** of the OA sequence is defined to be $\min_{1 \leq i \leq m} |A_i|$ if $m \geq 1$, and ∞ if $m = 0$.

The next result connects decision-tree complexity with orbit augmentation sequences and thus provides our main technical tool.

PROPOSITION 3.2 (SPACING LOWER BOUND). *Let $\mathscr{P}$ be a nontrivial monotone Γ-invariant property over X and suppose there is a full OA sequence for X with spacing d using subgroups of Γ, with the order of each subgroup a power of a prime. Then the decision-tree complexity of $\mathscr{P}$ is $D(\mathscr{P}) \geq d$.*

Remark 3. It follows from the KSS arguments [6] that we don't need to require the groups Γ_i to have prime-power orders; it would suffice if they are Oliver groups.

PROOF OF PROPOSITION 3.2. Suppose for the sake of contradiction that $D(\mathscr{P}) < d$. Say $((B_1, A_1, \Gamma_1), \ldots, (B_m, A_m, \Gamma_m))$ is a full OA sequence for X. Since $\mathscr{P}$ is nontrivial and monotone, $B_m \cup A_m = X \notin \mathscr{P}$. Let i be minimal subject to $B_i \cup A_i \notin \mathscr{P}$. If $i = 1$, then $B_1 = \emptyset \in \mathscr{P}$, and if $i > 1$, $B_i \subseteq B_{i-1} \cup A_{i-1} \in \mathscr{P}$, so $B_i \in \mathscr{P}$. Let $\mathscr{Q}$ be a property over A_i, defined as the subproperty of $\mathscr{P}$ given by $\mathscr{Q} = \{S \subseteq A_i \mid B_i \cup S \in \mathscr{P}\}$. We have that $\mathscr{Q}$ is monotone and Γ_i-invariant, Γ_i acts transitively on A_i and $|\Gamma_i|$ is a power of a prime (and therefore $|A_i|$ is a power of a prime), thus by Theorem 3.1, $\mathscr{Q}$ is trivial or evasive. But if $\mathscr{Q}$ were evasive, $D(\mathscr{P}) \geq D(\mathscr{Q}) = |A_i|$ by Observation 2, which we assumed was not the case. So, $\mathscr{Q}$ is trivial. We have $B_i \in \mathscr{P}$, so $\emptyset \in \mathscr{Q}$, so $A_i \in \mathscr{Q}$, so $B_i \cup A_i \in \mathscr{P}$. This contradicts the choice of i. $\square$

Next we derive some properties of orbit augmentation sequences.

Observation 3. If $T \supseteq S'$, then the concatenation of an (S, T) OA sequence for X with an (S', T') OA sequence for X is an (S, T') OA sequence for X. If these OA sequences have spacing d and d' respectively, the concatenation has spacing $\min\{d, d'\}$.

Observation 4. Suppose there is an (S, T) OA sequence for X and that the action of each group used in the OA sequence fixes $U \subseteq X$. Then there is a $(U \cup S, U \cup T)$ OA sequence with the same spacing as the original OA sequence and using the same groups.

Remark 4. This observation also holds with intersection in place of union.

PROOF. Let $((B_1, A_1, \Gamma_1), \ldots, (B_m, A_m, \Gamma_m))$ be an (S, T) OA sequence for X. Then

$$(((U \setminus A_1) \cup B_1, A_1, \Gamma_1), \ldots, ((U \setminus A_m) \cup B_m, A_m, \Gamma_m))$$

is a $(U \cup S, U \cup T)$ OA sequence for X. $\square$

COROLLARY 3.3. *Suppose there is an $(\emptyset, T)$ OA sequence for X with spacing d and an $(\emptyset, T')$ OA sequence for X with spacing d' using subgroups of Γ'. Suppose the action of Γ' fixes T. Then there is an $(\emptyset, T \cup T')$ OA sequence for X with spacing $\min\{d, d'\}$ using the groups used in the two original OA sequences.*

PROOF. By Observation 4 with $U = T$, there is a $(T, T \cup T')$ OA sequence for X with spacing d' using the same groups used in the $(\emptyset, T')$ OA sequence. Concatenate the $(\emptyset, T)$ OA sequence with the $(T, T \cup T')$ OA sequence. $\square$

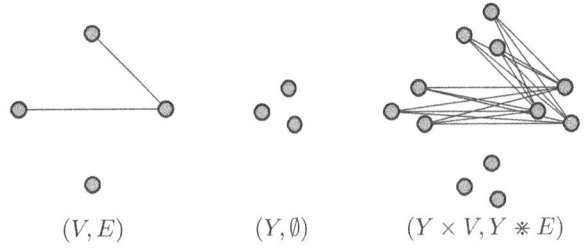

Figure 2: An example of a Y-lifting $Y \ast E$

COROLLARY 3.4 (COMPOSITION LEMMA). *Suppose that for each i with $1 \leq i \leq s$, there is an $(\emptyset, T^{(i)})$ OA sequence for X with spacing $d^{(i)}$. Suppose that for $2 \leq i \leq s$, the $(\emptyset, T^{(i)})$ OA sequence uses subgroups of Γ. Suppose that for $1 \leq i \leq s - 1$, the action of Γ fixes $T^{(i)}$. Then there is an $(\emptyset, T^{(1)} \cup \cdots \cup T^{(s)})$ OA sequence for X with spacing $\min_{1 \leq i \leq s} d^{(i)}$ using the groups used in the s original OA sequences.*

PROOF. By induction on s. The base case $s = 2$ is Corollary 3.3. $\square$

Observation 5. Let $A \subseteq X$ and let Γ be a group acting transitively on A. Suppose there is a full OA sequence for X' with spacing d' using groups $\Gamma'_1, \ldots \Gamma'_{m'}$. Then there is an $(\emptyset, A \times X')$ OA sequence for $X \times X'$ with spacing $|A|d'$ using the groups $\Gamma \times \Gamma'_i$, $1 \leq i \leq m'$.

PROOF. Let $((B'_1, A'_1, \Gamma'_1), \ldots, (B'_{m'}, A'_{m'}, \Gamma'_{m'}))$ be a full OA sequence for X'. Then

$$((A \times B'_1, A \times A'_1, \Gamma \times \Gamma'_1), \ldots, (A \times B'_{m'}, A \times A'_{m'}, \Gamma_1 \times \Gamma'_{m'}))$$

is an $(\emptyset, A \times T')$ OA sequence for $X \times X'$. $\square$

LEMMA 3.5 (DIRECT PRODUCT). *Suppose there is a full OA sequence for X with spacing d using groups $\Gamma_1, \ldots \Gamma_m$, and there is a full OA sequence for X' with spacing d' using groups $\Gamma'_1, \ldots \Gamma'_{m'}$. Then there is a full OA sequence for $X \times X'$ with spacing dd' using the groups $\Gamma_i \times \Gamma'_j$, $1 \leq i \leq m$, $1 \leq j \leq m'$.*

PROOF. For each $1 \leq i \leq m$, apply Observation 5 to produce an $(\emptyset, A_i \times X')$ OA sequence for $X \times X'$ with spacing $|A_i|d'$ using the groups $\Gamma_i \times \Gamma'_j$, $1 \leq j \leq m'$. Apply Observation 4 to the above with $U = B_i \times X'$ to give a $(B_i \times X', (B_i \cup A_i) \times X')$ OA sequence for $X \times X'$ with spacing $|A_i|d'$ using the same groups.

The concatenation of these OA sequences for $1 \leq i \leq m$ is a full OA sequence for $X \times X'$ with spacing dd'. $\square$

4. LIFTINGS OF HYPERGRAPHS AND WREATH PRODUCT ACTION

Definition 19. Let V be a finite set, and k a positive integer. Let $\mathrm{Sym}(V)$ denote the symmetric group on V. A **property of k-uniform hypergraphs with vertex set V**, or **k-graph property**, is a property over $\binom{V}{k}$ that is $\mathrm{Sym}(V)$-invariant (under the induced action, where $\sigma \in \mathrm{Sym}(V)$ sends $e \in \binom{V}{k}$ to $e^\sigma = \{v^\sigma \mid v \in e\}$).

Next we introduce a technical tool: Y-liftings of a k-graph, where Y is a set.

Definition 20. Let V and Y be finite sets, $k \geq 1$, and $E \subseteq \binom{V}{k}$. Let the Y-**lifting of** E, $Y * E$, be $\{\{(y_1, v_1), \ldots (y_k, v_k)\} \in \binom{Y \times V}{k} \mid y_1, \ldots, y_k \in Y, \{v_1, \ldots, v_k\} \in E\}$ (in particular, $v_1, \ldots, v_k$ are distinct). Thinking of E as the edge set of a k-graph, $Y * E$ is the edge set of the k-graph obtained by replacing each vertex with a copy of Y.

If $\Gamma \leq \text{Sym}(Y)$ and $\Delta \leq \text{Sym}(V)$, then the imprimitive action of $\Gamma \wr \Delta$ on $Y \times V$ induces an action (the **lifting action**) on $Y * \binom{V}{k}$.

Remark 5. In hypergraph terminology, the k-graph with vertex set $Y \times V$ and edge set $Y * E$ is the anti-lexicographic product of the empty k-graph on vertex set Y and the k-graph (V, E) (cf. [5]).

Observation 6. Suppose there is an (S, T) OA sequence for $X \subseteq \binom{V}{k}$ with spacing d using subgroups $\Gamma_1, \ldots, \Gamma_m$ of $\text{Sym}(V)$. Let Y be a finite set, and let $\Gamma' \leq \text{Sym}(Y)$ act transitively. Then there is a $(Y * S, Y * T)$ OA sequence for $Y * X$ with spacing $d|Y|^k$ using the groups $\Gamma' \wr \Gamma_i$, $1 \leq i \leq m$, with the lifting action.

PROOF. Let $((B_1, A_1, \Gamma_1), \ldots, (B_m, A_m, \Gamma_m))$ be an (S, T) OA sequence for X. Then

$$((Y * B_1, Y * A_1, \Gamma' \wr \Gamma_1), \ldots, (Y * B_m, Y * A_m, \Gamma' \wr \Gamma_m))$$

is an $(Y * S, Y * T)$ OA sequence for $Y * X$. $\square$

We find it convenient to deal with Y-liftings in the language of multisets.

Definition 21. A **multiset** with underlying set I is a function $f : I \to \mathbb{Z}_{\geq 0}$. The **cardinality** of f is $|f| = \sum_{i \in I} f(i)$. The **support** of f is $\text{supp}(f) = \{i \in I \mid f(i) \neq 0\}$. To mirror the notation for sets, we may depict a multiset f as $\{\!\{i_1, i_2, \ldots, i_{|f|}\}\!\}$, where $i_1, \ldots, i_{|f|} \in I$, and each $i \in I$ appears with multiplicity $f(i)$. For a positive integer k, we will write $f < k$ to denote that for all i, $f(i) < k$. Let $\binom{\!\binom{I}{k}\!}{}$ denote the set of multisets with underlying set I and cardinality k.

5. HYPERGRAPHS WITH A PRIME-POWER NUMBER OF VERTICES

We can now make our key construction of an OA sequence with large spacing for hypergraphs with a prime-power number of vertices.

LEMMA 5.1. *Let $r_k = \frac{1}{2}k^2 + \frac{1}{2}k - 1$. Then for all $k \geq 2$ and all multisets f with $|f| = k$, $f < k$, we have $k + \sum_{i \in \text{supp}(f)} r_{f(i)} \leq r_k$.*

PROOF. We have

$$\sum r_{f(i)} = \sum \frac{1}{2}(f(i) + 2)(f(i) - 1)$$
$$\leq \sum \frac{1}{2}(k+1)(f(i) - 1)$$
$$= \frac{1}{2}(k+1)(k - |\text{supp}(f)|)$$
$$\leq \frac{1}{2}(k+1)(k-2),$$

where the sums are taken over i in the support of f. So $k + \sum r_{f(i)} \leq k + \frac{1}{2}(k+1)(k-2) = r_k$. Equality holds if and only if $f(i) = k - 1$ for some i. $\square$

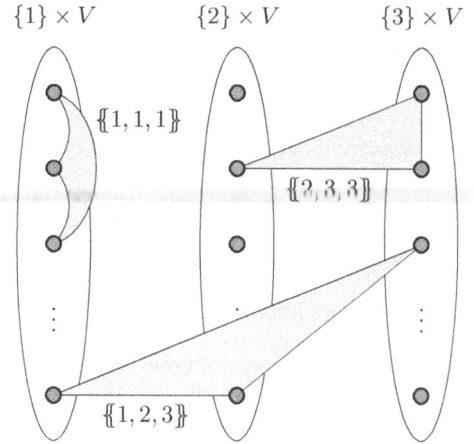

Figure 4: **Each hyperedge in the figure is labeled with its "type", its image under π. All the hyperedges with the same type are added to the OA sequence in the same batch.**

PROPOSITION 5.2. *For each positive integer k, there is a real number r_k such that for any prime p and nonnegative integer ℓ, there is a full OA sequence for $\binom{[p^\ell]}{k}$ with spacing at least $p^{\ell k - r_k}$ using p-groups that are subgroups of $\text{Sym}([p^\ell])$.*

Note that now our main technical result, Corollary 1.2, is immediate in the case when the number of vertices is a power of a prime. We state this as a corollary.

COROLLARY 5.3. *For any fixed prime p and fixed positive integer k, nontrivial monotone properties of k-uniform hypergraphs with a power of p vertices are weakly evasive.*

PROOF OF PROPOSITION 5.2. Let r_k be as in Lemma 5.1. Proceed by induction on k.

As a base case, take $k = 1$ with the OA sequence $((\emptyset, \binom{[p^\ell]}{1}), \mathbb{Z}/p^\ell\mathbb{Z}))$.

For the inductive step, consider $k > 1$. Let ℓ_0 be the smallest ℓ such that $p^\ell \geq k$. Proceed by induction on ℓ.

As a base case, for any $\ell < \ell_0$, $\binom{V}{k} = \emptyset$, and an OA sequence of zero length suffices.

For the inductive step, consider $\ell \geq \ell_0$. Let V be a set with $|V| = p^{\ell-1}$. Since $|[p] \times V| = p^\ell$, it suffices to construct a full OA sequence for $\binom{[p] \times V}{k}$ using subgroups of $\text{Sym}([p] \times V)$.

Let $\pi : \binom{[p] \times V}{k} \to \binom{\!\binom{[p]}{k}\!}{}$ be defined by $\{(i_1, v_1), \ldots, (i_k, v_k)\} \mapsto \{\!\{i_1, \ldots, i_k\}\!\}$. The image of a hyperedge under π is the hyperedge's "type". We will construct an OA sequence in batches, and all hyperedges of the same type will be in the same batch.

Adding edges of the type $\{\!\{i, i, \ldots i\}\!\}$, $i \in [p]$: By the induction hypothesis for ℓ, there is a full OA sequence for $\binom{V}{k}$ with spacing at least $p^{\ell k - k - r_k}$ using p-groups that are subgroups of $\text{Sym}(V)$. By Observation 6, there is a full OA sequence for $[p] * \binom{V}{k} \subseteq \binom{[p] \times V}{k}$ with spacing $p^{\ell k - r_k}$ using p-groups that are subgroups of $\mathbb{Z}/p\mathbb{Z} \wr \text{Sym}(V)$. Since $\bigcup_{i \in [p]} \pi^{-1}(\{\!\{i, i, \ldots, i\}\!\}) = \bigcup_{i \in [p]} \binom{\{i\} \times V}{k} \subseteq [p] * \binom{V}{k}$, this sequence is an $\left(\emptyset, \bigcup_{i \in [p]} \binom{\{i\} \times V}{k}\right)$ OA sequence for $\binom{[p] \times V}{k}$.

Adding hyperedges of other types: Consider any $f \in \binom{\!\binom{[p]}{k}\!}{}$ with $f < k$. For each $i \in \text{supp}(f)$, by the induction hypothe-

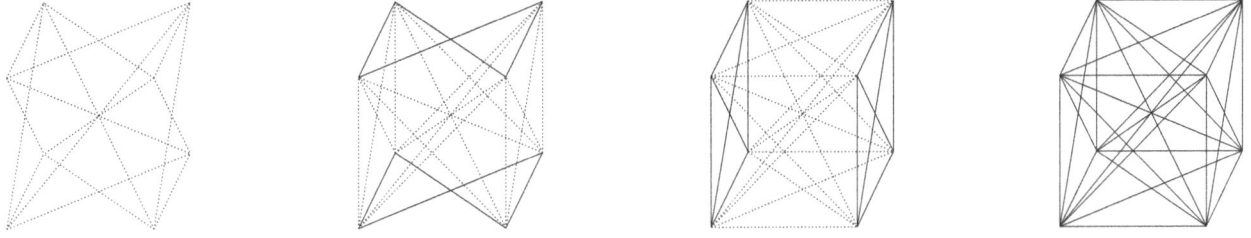

$S = B_1 = \emptyset$

$A_1 = [2] * ([2] * \binom{[2]}{2})$

$\Gamma_1 = \mathbb{Z}/2\mathbb{Z}^{\text{a}} \wr (\mathbb{Z}/2\mathbb{Z}^{\text{b}} \wr 1^{\text{c}})$

$B_2 = [2] * (\binom{\{1\}\times[2]}{2} \cup \binom{\{2\}\times[2]}{2})$

$A_2 = [2] * (\binom{\{1\}\times[2]}{1} \times \binom{\{2\}\times[2]}{1})$

$\Gamma_2 = \mathbb{Z}/2\mathbb{Z}^{\text{d}} \wr (\mathbb{Z}/2\mathbb{Z}^{\text{e}} \times \mathbb{Z}/2\mathbb{Z}^{\text{f}})$

$B_3 = \binom{\{1\}\times[2]^2}{2} \cup \binom{\{2\}\times[2]^2}{2}$

$A_3 = \binom{\{1\}\times[2]^2}{1} \times \binom{\{2\}\times[2]^2}{1}$

$\Gamma_3 = \mathbb{Z}/2^2\mathbb{Z}^{\text{g}} \times \mathbb{Z}/2^2\mathbb{Z}^{\text{h}}$

$T = \binom{[2]^3}{2}$

[a] swaps left and right
[b] swaps top and bottom
[c] fixes front and back

[d] swaps left and right
[e] swaps bottom front and bot. back
[f] swaps top front and top back

[g] cycles left four vertices
[h] cycles right four vertices

Figure 3: The full OA sequence for $\binom{[2]^3}{2}$ constructed in the proof of Proposition 5.2. The sets B_i are shown with solid edges, and the sets A_i are shown with dotted edges.

sis for k, there is a full OA sequence for $\binom{\{i\}\times V}{f(i)}$ with spacing at least $p^{(\ell-1)f(i)-r_{f(i)}}$ using p-groups that are subgroups of $\mathrm{Sym}(\{i\} \times V)$. Let $T_f = \prod_{i\in\mathrm{supp}(i)} \binom{\{i\}\times V}{f(i)}$. By the Direct Product Lemma (Lemma 3.5), there is a full OA sequence for T_f with spacing at least $\prod_{i\in\mathrm{supp}(f)} p^{\ell f(i)-f(i)-r_{f(i)}}$ using p-groups that are subgroups of $\prod_{i\in\mathrm{supp}(f)} \mathrm{Sym}(\{i\} \times V)$. By Lemma 5.1, this spacing is at least $p^{\ell k-r_k}$. This group can be identified with a subgroup of $\mathrm{Sym}([p] \times V)$, and T_f can be identified with $\pi^{-1}(f)$ by $(e_1, e_2, \ldots, e_{|\mathrm{supp}(f)|}) \mapsto e_1 \cup e_2 \cup \ldots \cup e_{|\mathrm{supp}(f)|}$. These identifications preserve the group action. So, there is a full OA sequence for $\pi^{-1}(f)$ with spacing at least $p^{\ell k-r_k}$ using p-groups that are subgroups of $\prod_{i\in[p]} \mathrm{Sym}(\{i\} \times V)$.

Combining the batches: Apply the Composition Lemma (Corollary 3.4) with the above $\left(\emptyset, \bigcup_{i\in[p]} \binom{\{i\}\times V}{k}\right)$ OA sequence as the first OA sequence, and the above $(\emptyset, \pi^{-1}(f))$ OA sequences, $f \in \left(\!\binom{[p]}{k}\!\right)$, $f < k$, as the other OA sequences. Since

$$\left(\bigcup_{i\in[p]} \binom{\{i\}\times V}{k}\right) \cup \bigcup_{f\in\left(\!\binom{[p]}{k}\!\right), f<k} \pi^{-1}(f) = \binom{[p]\times V}{k},$$

this produces a full OA sequence for $\binom{[p]\times V}{k}$ using p-groups that are subgroups of $\mathrm{Sym}([p] \times V)$.

This completes the inductive step for ℓ, and also for k. □

6. AN ARBITRARY NUMBER OF VERTICES

We can now construct OA sequences with large spacing for hypergraphs with any number of vertices.

LEMMA 6.1. *Let $q_k = k^2 + 2k - 2$. Then for all $k \geq 2$ and all multisets f with $|f| = k$, $f < k$, we have $k \leq q_k$, $2k + \sum_{i\in\mathrm{supp}(f)} q_{f(i)} \leq q_k$, and $2k + r_k \leq q_k$, where r_k is as in Lemma 5.1.*

PROOF. We have

$$\sum q_{f(i)} = \sum((f(i)+3)(f(i)-1)+1)$$
$$\leq \sum((k+2)(f(i)-1)+1)$$
$$= (k+2)(k-|\mathrm{supp}(f)|)+|\mathrm{supp}(f)|$$
$$\leq (k+2)(k-2)+2,$$

where the sums are taken over $i \in \mathrm{supp}(f)$. So $2k+\sum q_{f(i)} \leq 2k+(k+2)(k-2)+2 = q_k$. Equality holds if and only if $f(i) = k-1$ for some i.

And, $q_k - (2k+r_k) = \frac{1}{2}(k-2)(k+1) \geq 0$ since $k \geq 2$. □

THEOREM 6.2. *Let p be a prime. For each positive integer k, there is a real number q_k such that for any nonnegative integer v, V a set with $|V| = v$, there is a full OA sequence for $\binom{V}{k}$ with spacing at least $p^{-q_k} v^k$ using p-groups that are subgroups of $\mathrm{Sym}(V)$.*

Our main technical result, Corollary 1.2 is now immediate. □

PROOF OF THEOREM 6.2. Let r_k and q_k be as in Lemmas 5.1 and 6.1. We proceed by induction on k.

As a base case, consider $k = 1$. If $v = 0$, an OA sequence of length zero suffices. Consider any positive integer v. Let ℓ be the largest integer with $p^\ell \leq v$. There are $V_1, \ldots, V_p \subseteq V$, not necessarily disjoint, with $|V_1| = \cdots = |V_p| = p^\ell$, $V_1 \cup \cdots \cup V_p = V$. Let $\Gamma_1, \ldots \Gamma_p$ be subgroups of $\mathrm{Sym}(V_1), \ldots, \mathrm{Sym}(V_p)$, respectively, each generated by a cycle of length p^ℓ. Then the sequence of length p whose i entry is $\left(\binom{(V_1\cup\cdots\cup V_{i-1})\setminus V_i}{1}, \binom{V_i}{1}, \Gamma_i\right)$ is a full OA sequence for $\binom{V}{1}$ of length p using p-groups that are subgroups of $\mathrm{Sym}(V)$.

For the inductive step, consider $k > 1$. If $v < k$, an OA sequence of length zero suffices. If $k \leq v < p$, an OA sequence of length $\binom{v}{k}$ using the trivial group suffices, with spacing $1 = p^{-k}p^k \geq p^{-q_k}v^k$. Consider any $v \geq p$. Let ℓ be the largest integer with $p^{\ell+1} \leq v$. Note $p^\ell > p^{-2}v$. Let s be the largest integer such that $sp^\ell \leq v$, and let $V_1, V_2, \ldots, V_s$ be a partition of V with $|V_1| = \cdots = |V_{s-1}| = p^\ell$ and $p^\ell \leq |V_s| < 2 \cdot p^\ell$. Let $V' \supseteq V_s$ with $|V'| = p^{\ell+1}$. By Proposition 5.2, there is an $(\emptyset, \binom{V}{k})$ OA sequence for $\binom{V}{k}$

389

with spacing $p^{(\ell+1)k-r_k} \geq p^{-k-r_k}v^k$ using p-groups that are subgroups of $\mathrm{Sym}(V')$. This OA sequence is an $(\emptyset, \binom{V_s}{k})$ OA sequence. By Proposition 5.2, for each i with $1 \leq i \leq s-1$, there is an $(\emptyset, \binom{V_i}{k})$ OA sequence for $\binom{V}{k}$ with spacing $p^{\ell k-r_k} \geq p^{-2k-r_k}v^k$ using p-groups that are subgroups of $\mathrm{Sym}(V_i)$. By Lemma 6.1, the spacing of each of these OA sequences is at least $p^{-q_k}v^k$.

Let $\pi : \binom{V}{k} \to \binom{\binom{[s]}{k}}{k}$ be defined by $\pi(e)(i) = |e \cap V_i|$.

As in the proof of Proposition 5.2, consider any $f \in \binom{\binom{[s]}{k}}{k}$ with $f < k$. For each $i \in \mathrm{supp}(f)$, by the induction hypothesis for induction on k, there is a full OA sequence for $\binom{V_i}{f(i)}$ with spacing at least $p^{-q_{f(i)}}|V_i|^{f(i)} \geq p^{\ell f(i)-q_{f(i)}}$ using p-groups that are subgroups of $\mathrm{Sym}(V_i)$. Let $T_f = \prod_{i \in \mathrm{supp}(f)} \binom{V_i}{f(i)}$. By the Direct Product Lemma (Lemma 3.5), there is a full OA sequence for T_f with spacing at least $\prod_{i \in \mathrm{supp}(f)} p^{\ell f(i)-q_{f(i)}}$ using p-groups that are subgroups of $\prod_{i \in \mathrm{supp}(f)} \mathrm{Sym}(V_i)$. By Lemma 6.1, using $p^\ell \geq p^{-2}v$, this spacing is at least $p^{-q_k}v^k$. This group can be identified with a subgroup of $\mathrm{Sym}(V)$, and T_f can be identified with $\pi^{-1}(f)$ by $(e_1, e_2, \ldots, e_{|\mathrm{supp}(f)|}) \mapsto e_1 \cup e_2 \cup \ldots \cup e_{|\mathrm{supp}(f)|}$. These identifications preserve the group action. So, there is an $(\emptyset, \pi^{-1}(f))$ OA sequence for $\pi^{-1}(f)$ with spacing at least $p^{-q_k}v^k$ using p-groups that are subgroups of $\prod_{i \in [s]} \mathrm{Sym}(V_i)$.

Apply the Composition Lemma (Corollary 3.4) with the above $(\emptyset, \binom{V_s}{k})$ OA sequence as the first OA sequence, the above $(\emptyset, \binom{V_i}{k})$ OA sequences, $1 \leq i \leq s-1$, as the next OA sequences, and the above $(\emptyset, \pi^{-1}(f))$ OA sequences, $f \in \binom{\binom{[s]}{k}}{k}$, $f < k$, as the other OA sequences. Since

$$\binom{V_s}{k} \cup \bigcup_{1 \leq i \leq s-1} \binom{V_i}{k} \cup \bigcup_{f \in \binom{\binom{[s]}{k}}{k}, f < k} \pi^{-1}(f) = \binom{V}{k},$$

this produces a full OA sequence for $\binom{V}{k}$ using p-groups that are subgroups of $\mathrm{Sym}(V)$.

This completes the inductive step. $\square$

Combining Lemma 6.1 and Theorem 6.2 with the Spacing Lower Bound (Proposition 3.2) we obtain our main technical result:

THEOREM 6.3. *The decision-tree complexity of a nontrivial monotone property of k-graphs with v vertices is at least*

$$2^{-(k+1)^2+3}v^k.$$

7. MONOTONE PROPERTIES INVARIANT UNDER LARGE PRIMITIVE GROUPS

Our main result, that nontrivial monotone properties invariant under large primitive groups are weakly evasive, relies on a theorem of Cameron that such groups have subgroups that look like the group of symmetries that describe a product of hypergraphs.

Definition 22. Let S_v denote $\mathrm{Sym}([v])$, let $A_v \leq S_v$ denote the alternating group, consisting of the even permutations on $[v]$, let $S_v^{(k)} \leq \mathrm{Sym}(\binom{[v]}{k})$ be the image of S_v under the induced action on $\binom{[v]}{k}$, and define $A_v^{(k)} \leq \mathrm{Sym}(\binom{[v]}{k})$ analogously. Note that $S_v^{(k)} \times \cdots \times S_v^{(k)}$ (t copies) can be

identified with the subgroup of $S_v^{(k)} \wr S_t$ corresponding to the identity element in S_t.

THEOREM 7.1 (CAMERON 1981 [2]). *For all $\varepsilon > 0$, there are positive integers k and t such that for sufficiently large n, any primitive permutation group $\Gamma \leq S_n$ with order at least $\exp(n^\varepsilon)$ is isomorphic to a group Γ' with*

$$A_v^{(k)} \times \cdots \times A_v^{(k)} \leq \Gamma' \leq S_v^{(k)} \wr S_t,$$

where $S_v^{(k)} \wr S_t$ acts by the product action, and $kt = O(\frac{1}{\varepsilon})$.

The results of the previous sections allow us to put a bound on the decision-tree complexity of nontrivial monotone $(A_v^{(k)} \times \cdots \times A_v^{(k)})$-invariant properties.

THEOREM 7.2. *Let t be a positive integer, let $v_1, \ldots v_t$, $k_1, \ldots, k_t$ be positive integers, and let $X = \binom{[v_1]}{k_1} \times \cdots \times \binom{[v_t]}{k_t}$. Note $\Gamma = A_{v_1}^{(k_1)} \times \cdots \times A_{v_t}^{(k_t)}$ acts on X. Any nontrivial monotone Γ-invariant property over X has decision-tree complexity at least $3^{-q_{k_1}-q_{k_2}-\cdots-q_{k_t}}v_1^{k_1} \cdots v_t^{k_t}$.*

In particular, nontrivial monotone properties of t-partite partwise-uniform k-graphs are weakly evasive for bounded k, t.

Remark 6. When $k = 1$ and $t = 2$, we have bipartite hypergraphs, which Yao [14] showed to be evasive (not just weakly evasive). When $t = 1$ we have k-graphs.

PROOF OF THEOREM 7.2. Since every element of S_{v_i} of odd order is in A_{v_i}, by Theorem 6.2 with $p = 3$, there is a full OA sequence for $\binom{[v_i]}{k_i}$ with spacing $3^{-q_{k_i}}v_i^{k_i}$ using subgroups of $A_{v_i}^{(k_i)}$. By the Direct Product Lemma (Lemma 3.5), there is a full OA sequence for X with spacing $\prod_{i=1}^t 3^{-q_{k_i}}v_i^{k_i}$ using subgroups of Γ. $\square$

As a corollary of these two results, we have our main result:

THEOREM 7.3. *For each fixed $\varepsilon > 0$, nontrivial monotone properties over $[n]$ that are invariant under the action of a primitive group of order at least $\exp(n^\varepsilon)$ are weakly evasive.*

8. ACKNOWLEDGEMENTS

I wish to thank my advisor Laci Babai for suggesting that I work on this problem and for helpful discussions. I also wish to thank Sasha Razborov for his encouragement.

9. REFERENCES

[1] L. Babai, A. Banerjee, R. Kulkarni, and V. Naik. Evasiveness and the distribution of prime numbers. In *STACS 2010: 27th International Symposium on Theoretical Aspects of Computer Science*, volume 5 of *LIPIcs. Leibniz Int. Proc. Inform.*, pages 71–82. Schloss Dagstuhl. Leibniz-Zent. Inform., Wadern, 2010.

[2] P. J. Cameron. Finite permutation groups and finite simple groups. *Bull. London Math. Soc.*, 13(1):1–22, 1981.

[3] A. Chakrabarti, S. Khot, and Y. Shi. Evasiveness of subgraph containment and related properties. *SIAM J. Comput.*, 31(3):866–875, Mar. 2002.

[4] S. Gao and G. Lin. Decision tree complexity of graph properties with dimension at most 5. *J. Comput. Sci. Tech.*, 15(5):416–422, 2000.

[5] M. Hellmuth, L. Ostermeier, and P. F. Stadler. A survey on hypergraph products. *Math. Comput. Sci.*, 6(1):1–32, 2012. `http://www.bioinf.uni-leipzig.de/Publications/PREPRINTS/12-027.pdf`.

[6] J. Kahn, M. Saks, and D. Sturtevant. A topological approach to evasiveness. *Combinatorica*, 4(4):297–306, 1984.

[7] D. J. Kleitman and D. J. Kwiatkowski. Further results on the Aanderaa-Rosenberg conjecture. *J. Combin. Theory Ser. B*, 28(1):85–95, 1980.

[8] R. Kulkarni, Y. Qiao, and X. Sun. Any monotone property of 3-uniform hypergraphs is weakly evasive. In T.-H. Chan, L. Lau, and L. Trevisan, editors, *Theory and Applications of Models of Computation*, volume 7876 of *Lecture Notes in Computer Science*, pages 224–235. Springer Berlin Heidelberg, 2013.

[9] R. Oliver. Fixed-point sets of group actions on finite acyclic complexes. *Comment. Math. Helv.*, 50:155–177, 1975.

[10] R. L. Rivest and J. Vuillemin. On recognizing graph properties from adjacency matrices. *Theoret. Comput. Sci.*, 3(3):371–384, 1976/77.

[11] J. J. Rotman. *An Introduction to the Theory of Groups*. Springer-Verlag, New York, 1995.

[12] E. Triesch. On the recognition complexity of some graph properties. *Combinatorica*, 16(2):259–268, 1996.

[13] I. M. Vinogradov. *The Method of Trigonometrical Sums in the Theory of Numbers (Russian). Trav. Inst. Math. Stekloff*, 10, 1937.

[14] A. C.-C. Yao. Monotone bipartite graph properties are evasive. *SIAM J. Comput.*, 17(3):517–520, June 1988.

Author Index

www.ingramcontent.com/pod-product-compliance
Lightning Source LLC
Chambersburg PA
CBHW080658220326
41598CB00033B/5252